McDougal Littell

# THE LANGUAGE OF
# LITERATURE

EMILY DICKINSON

AMY TAN

WALT WHITMAN

EDNA ST. VINCENT MILLAY

MAYA ANGELOU

ROBERT FROST

KURT VONNEGUT, JR.

O. HENRY

LEO TOLSTOY

GABRIELA MISTRAL

SIR THOMAS MALORY

ALICE WALKER

CORETTA SCOTT KING

AGATHA CHRISTIE

LANGSTON HUGHES

STEPHEN CRANE

SANDRA CISNEROS

ISABEL ALLENDE

CHINUA ACHEBE

MARK TWAIN

GUY DE MAUPASSANT

CARL SANDBURG

NIKKI GIOVANNI

TIM O'BRIEN

RAY BRADBURY

EDGAR ALLAN POE

ANTON CHEKHOV

PABLO NERUDA

WILLIAM SHAKESPEARE

JOHN STEINBECK

DORIS LESSING

McDougal Littell

# THE LANGUAGE OF
# LITERATURE

Arthur N. Applebee

Andrea B. Bermúdez

Sheridan Blau

Rebekah Caplan

Peter Elbow

Susan Hynds

Judith A. Langer

James Marshall

McDougal Littell

A DIVISION OF HOUGHTON MIFFLIN COMPANY

# Acknowledgments

**Unit One**

   **Delacorte Press/Seymour Lawrence:** "Harrison Bergeron," from *Welcome to the Monkey House* by Kurt Vonnegut, Jr. Copyright © 1961 by Kurt Vonnegut, Jr. Used by permission of Delacorte Press/Seymour Lawrence, a division of Bantam Doubleday Dell Publishing Group, Inc.

   **Brandt & Brandt Literary Agents:** "Searching for Summer," from *The Green Flash* by Joan Aiken. Copyright © 1969 by Joan Aiken. Reprinted by permission of Brandt & Brandt Literary Agents, Inc.

   "By the Waters of Babylon" by Stephen Vincent Benét, from *Selected Works of Stephen Vincent Benét,* published by Holt, Rinehart & Winston, Inc. Copyright © 1937 by Stephen Vincent Benét. Copyright renewed © 1955 by Rosemary Carr Benét. Reprinted by permission of Brandt & Brandt Literary Agents, Inc.

   **Beacon Press:** "The Sun," from *New and Selected Poems* by Mary Oliver. Copyright © 1992 by Mary Oliver. Reprinted by permission of Beacon Press, Boston.

   **Simon & Schuster:** "There Will Come Soft Rains" by Sara Teasdale, from *Collected Poems of Sara Teasdale.* Copyright © 1937 by Macmillan Publishing Company. Reprinted with the permission of Simon & Schuster.

   **Viking Penguin and Penguin Books Canada:** "The Thrill of the Grass," from *The Thrill of the Grass* by W. P. Kinsella. Copyright © 1984 by W. P. Kinsella. Used by permission of Viking Penguin, a division of Penguin Putnam Inc., and Penguin Books Canada Limited.

*Continued on page 1306*

ISBN-13: 978-0-618-60138-7    ISBN-10: 0-618-60138-4

# Senior Consultants

The senior consultants guided the conceptual development for *The Language of Literature* series. They participated actively in shaping prototype materials for major components, and they reviewed completed prototypes and/or completed units to ensure consistency with current research and the philosophy of the series.

**Arthur N. Applebee** Professor of Education, State University of New York at Albany; Director, Center for the Learning and Teaching of Literature; Senior Fellow, Center for Writing and Literacy

**Andrea B. Bermúdez** Professor of Studies in Language and Culture; Director, Research Center for Language and Culture; Chair, Foundations and Professional Studies, University of Houston-Clear Lake

**Sheridan Blau** Senior Lecturer in English and Education and former Director of Composition, University of California at Santa Barbara; Director, South Coast Writing Project; Director, Literature Institute for Teachers; Former President, National Council of Teachers of English

**Rebekah Caplan** Senior Associate for Language Arts for middle school and high school literacy, National Center on Education and the Economy, Washington, D.C.; served on the California State English Assessment Development Team for Language Arts; former co-director of the Bay Area Writing Project, University of California at Berkeley

**Peter Elbow** Emeritus Professor of English, University of Massachusetts at Amherst; Fellow, Bard Center for Writing and Thinking

**Susan Hynds** Professor and Director of English Education, Syracuse University, Syracuse, New York

**Judith A. Langer** Professor of Education, State University of New York at Albany; Co-director, Center for the Learning and Teaching of Literature; Senior Fellow, Center for Writing and Literacy

**James Marshall** Professor of English and English Education; Chair, Division of Curriculum and Instruction, University of Iowa, Iowa City

# Contributing Consultants

**Linda Diamond** Executive Vice President, Consortium on Reading Excellence (CORE); co-author of *Building a Powerful Reading Program*

**Lucila A. Garza** ESL Consultant, Austin, Texas

**Jeffrey N. Golub** Assistant Professor of English Education, University of South Florida, Tampa

**William L. McBride, Ph.D.** Reading and Curriculum Specialist; former middle and high school English instructor

**Sharon Sicinski-Skeans, Ph.D.** Assistant Professor of Reading, University of Houston-Clear Lake; primary consultant on *The InterActive Reader*

# Multicultural Advisory Board

The multicultural advisors reviewed literature selections for appropriate content and made suggestions for teaching lessons in a multicultural classroom.

*Julie A. Anderson,* English Department Chairperson, Dayton High School, Dayton, Oregon

*Vikki Pepper Ascuena,* Meridian High School, Meridian, Idaho

*Dr. Joyce M. Bell,* Chairperson, English Department, Townview Magnet Center, Dallas, Texas

*Linda F. Bellmore,* Livermore High School, Livermore, California

*Dr. Eugenia W. Collier,* Author; lecturer; Chairperson, Department of English and Language Arts; Teacher of Creative Writing and American Literature, Morgan State University, Maryland

*Dr. Bill Compagnone,* English Department Chairperson, Lawrence High School, Lawrence, Massachusetts

*Kathleen S. Fowler,* President, Palm Beach County Council of Teachers of English, Boca Raton Middle School, Boca Raton, Florida

*Jan Graham,* Cobb Middle School, Tallahassee, Florida

*Barbara J. Kuhns,* Camino Real Middle School, Las Cruces, New Mexico

*Patricia J. Richards,* Prior Lake, Minnesota

*Janna Rigby,* Clovis High School, Clovis, California

*Continued on page* 1317

# Teacher Review Panels

The following educators provided ongoing review during the development of the tables of contents, lesson design, and key components of the program.

### CALIFORNIA

*Steve Bass,* 8th Grade Team Leader, Meadowbrook Middle School, Ponway Unified School District

*Cynthia Brickey,* 8th Grade Academic Block Teacher, Kastner Intermediate School, Clovis Unified School District

*Continued on page* 1318

# Manuscript Reviewers

The following educators reviewed prototype lessons and tables of contents during the development of *The Language of Literature* program.

*David Adcox,* Trinity High School, Euless, Texas

*Carol Alves,* English Department Chairperson, Apopka High School, Apopka, Florida

*Jacqueline Anderson,* James A. Foshay Learning Center, Los Angeles, California

*Continued on page* 1319

## Student Board

The student board members read and evaluated selections to assess their appeal for 10th-grade students.

*Marcus Allen,* Southeast High School, North Carolina

*Jayme Charak,* Niles North High School, Illinois

*Alisia Darby,* McCallum High School, Texas

*RonAmber Deloney,* Roosevelt High School, Texas

*Amy Doblestein,* Shades Valley Resource Learning Center, Alabama

*Quoleshna Z. Elbert,* Lincoln College Preparatory Academy, Missouri

*Katrina Gorski,* Loudon County High School, Virginia

*Rafael Gutierrez,* Garner High School, North Carolina

*Geoffrey L. Harvey,* Phineas Banning High School, California

*Karina Hernandez,* Waltrip High School, Texas

*Ellen Hooper,* Casa Roble High School, California

*Sunita Juneja,* Strongsville High School, Ohio

*Scott McGregor,* Broadneck High School, Maryland

*Katherine McGuire,* Lyons Township High School, Illinois

*Tim Mosher,* Clarkston North High School, New York

*Emily Myers,* Union High School, Grand Rapids, Michigan

*Eulizer Nazario,* Mission Bay High School, California

*Jacob Parks,* Newton High School, Kansas

*Ronnie G. Pigao,* Phineas Banning High School, California

*Wendy Pomales,* Boston High School, Massachusetts

*Josh Raub,* Lakeview High School, Minnesota

*Jessica Reynolds,* Eastern Hills High School, Texas

*Kevin Schatzman,* Miami Killian Sr. High School, Florida

*Stephanie Stone,* John Marshall High School, Texas

*Sabrina Van Damme,* Choctawhatchee High School, Florida

*Cynthia Villicana,* Phineas Banning High School, California

*Adriana M. Zuniga,* San Marcos High School, Texas

# The Language of Literature
# Overview

## Student Resource Bank

Reading Handbook
Writing Handbook
Communication Handbook
Grammar Handbook
Academic Reading Handbook
Glossary of Literary Terms
Glossary of Words to Know in English and Spanish

## Literature Connections

Each of the books in the *Literature Connections* series combines a novel or play with related readings—poems, stories, plays, personal essays, articles—that add new perspectives on the theme or subject matter of the longer work.

Listed below are some of the most popular choices to accompany the Grade 10 anthology:

**Great Expectations** by Charles Dickens

**The Chosen** by Chaim Potok

**Fahrenheit 451** by Ray Bradbury

**Farewell to Manzanar** by Jeanne Wakatsuki Houston and James D. Houston

**Kaffir Boy** by Mark Mathabane

**A Midsummer Night's Dream** by William Shakespeare

**A Place Where the Sea Remembers** by Sandra Benítez

**A Tale of Two Cities** by Charles Dickens

**A Separate Peace** by John Knowles

**The Underdogs** by Mariano Azuela

**West with the Night** by Beryl Markham

**When Rain Clouds Gather** by Bessie Head

## THE LANGUAGE OF LITERATURE

# *Reading Strategies*

## UNIT ONE

# The *Challenge* of *Change*    14

# UNIT TWO

## In the *Name* of *Love*

# UNIT THREE

# The *Search* for *Identity*  380

# UNIT FOUR

## *Lessons* of *History*

# UNIT FIVE

# *Discovering* the *Truth*

Detail of *The Arming & Departure of the Knights of the Round Table on the Quest for the Holy Grail* (1895–1896), Sir Edward Coley Burne-Jones. From the *Holy Grail Tapestry Series*. Birmingham City Council Museums and Art Gallery, England.

# UNIT SIX

# The *Making* of *Heroes*

958

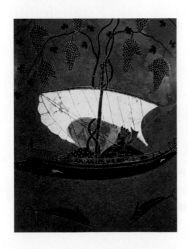

# Student *Resource Bank*

# *Selections* by Genre

## Fiction

## Romance

## Nonfiction

## Drama

## Electronic Library

The *Electronic Library* is a CD-ROM that contains additional fiction, nonfiction, poetry, and drama for each unit in *The Language of Literature*. Here is a sampling from the titles included in Grade 10.

**The Stolen Bacillus**
H. G. Wells

**Half a Day**
Naguib Mahfouz

**The Spring Returns**
Petrarch

**Leaving Crete**
Sappho

**The Story of Pyramus and Thisbe**
Ovid

**Intimate**
Gabriela Mistral

**Verotchka**
Anton Chekhov

**A Doll's House**
Henrik Ibsen

**To Imagination**
Emily Brontë

**The Stamp Collection**
Karel Čapek

**To Posterity**
Bertolt Brecht

**The Silver Mine**
Selma Lagerlöf

**A Hunger Artist**
Franz Kafka

**Tartuffe**
Molière

**The Birthmark**
Nathaniel Hawthorne

**The Myth of Sisyphus**
Albert Camus

*from* **The Apology**
Plato

**The Lady of Moge**
Ursula K. Le Guin

**Eldorado**
Edgar Allan Poe

**Prometheus**
Johann Wolfgang von Goethe

# *Special Features* in This Book

# Writing Workshops

# Communication Workshops

# Building Vocabulary

# Assessment Pages

# Realms of the Imagination

*Look at the words on the poster at the right. "Imagine a world where dreams come true . . . and magic is real." Which of us hasn't imagined a world like that, or a world where space travel is an everyday occurrence, or where scientists can re-create the age of the dinosaurs?*

*We all love to visit the world of the imagination. This is the reason we watch movies and television shows. It is also the reason we read literature. With writers such as Ray Bradbury and Kurt Vonnegut, Jr., we can travel to the future, while Shakespeare and Malory can transport us to the past. Other writers, such as Alice Walker, Tim O'Brien, and Sandra Cisneros, introduce us to worlds closer to home. As you will see, good literature feeds the imagination.*

A scene from *Star Trek: Voyager,* a television show.

**"I think that science fiction and fantasy offer the liveliest, freshest approaches to many of our problems today, and I always hope to write in this vivid and vigorous form. . . ."**

**—Ray Bradbury**
**Contemporary writer**

2

# MERLIN

IMAGINE A WORLD
WHERE DREAMS
COME TRUE...
AND MAGIC IS REAL.

A poster for the television movie *Merlin*.

Young Arthur pulls Excalibur from the stone.

"When I was nine, I took siege with King Arthur's fellowship of knights. . . . The magic happened. . . . Perhaps a passionate love for the English language opened to me from this one book [Malory's *Morte d'Arthur*]"

—*John Steinbeck*
*Nobel Prize–winning writer*

- **Why do some stories capture the imagination of generations of readers?**
- **What kinds of stories most appeal to you?**
- **How can you find excitement and relevance in literature you read?**

*The answers lie on the next few pages.*

# THE *Language* OF LITERATURE

# Get Involved with the Literature

*Think about an activity that you do well, whether it's playing the piano or throwing a baseball. How did you learn to master and appreciate that activity? While you no doubt learned from others, you probably learned the most by doing the activity yourself. Just about any activity is richer and more interesting when you are actively involved. The same is true with literature. Good readers don't simply absorb the words; they become actively engaged with what they read.*

## Your Reader's Notebook

Almost any kind of notebook can be used to help you interact with literature. Use your Reader's Notebook to keep track of what's going on inside your mind as you read. Here are three ways to interact.

### ❶ Record Your Thoughts

In your 📖 **READER'S NOTEBOOK** , jot down ideas, responses, connections, and questions before, while, and after you read a selection. (See "Strategies for Reading," page 7.) Summarize important passages, and include sketches and charts, too, if they will help. If you wish, compare your ideas with those of a classmate.

> "The Interlopers"
> by Saki
>
> (page 8) What kind of enemy is this man worried about?
> Important Idea
> These two enemies are finally going to settle the score.
> In a way, it's hard to tell them apart—they're so filled
> with hate.

grown into a personal one since Ulrich had come to be head of his family; if there was a man in the world whom he detested and wished ill to it was Georg Znaeym, the inheritor of the quarrel and the tireless game-snatcher and raider of the disputed border-forest. The feud might, perhaps, have died down or been compromised if the personal ill-will of the two men had not stood in the way; as boys they had thirsted for one another's blood, as men each prayed that misfortune might fall on the other, and this wind-scourged winter night Ulrich had banded together his foresters to watch the dark forest, not in quest of four-footed quarry, but to keep a lookout for the prowling thieves whom he suspected of being afoot from across the land boundary. The roebuck, which usually kept in the sheltered hollows during a storm wind, were running like driven things tonight, and there was movement and unrest among the creatures that were wont to sleep through the dark hours. Assuredly there was a disturbing element in the forest, and Ulrich could guess the quarter from whence it came.

He strayed away by himself from the watchers whom he had placed in ambush on the crest of the hill, and wandered far down the steep slopes amid the wild tangle of undergrowth, peering through the tree trunks and listening through the whistling and skirling of the wind and the restless beating of the branches for sight or sound of the marauders. If only on this wild night, in this dark, lone spot, he might come across Georg Znaeym, man to man, with none to witness—that was the wish that was uppermost in his thoughts. And as he stepped around the trunk of a huge beech, he came face to face with the man he sought.

The two enemies stood glaring at one another for a long silent moment.

Each had a rifle in his hand, each had hate in his heart and murder uppermost in his mind. The chance had come to give full play to the passions of a lifetime. But a man who has been brought up under the code of a restraining civilization cannot easily nerve himself to shoot down his neighbor in cold blood and without word spoken, except for an offense against his hearth and honor. And before the moment of hesitation had given way to action a deed of Nature's own violence overwhelmed them both. A fierce shriek of the storm had been answered by a splitting crash over their heads, and ere they could leap aside a mass of falling beech tree had thundered down on them. Ulrich von Gradwitz found himself stretched on the ground, one arm numb beneath him and the other held almost as helplessly in a tight tangle of forked branches, while both legs were pinned beneath the fallen

*Thuy: I picture Ulrich and Georg as having rocky childhoods. These two guys hated each other and were very competitive.*
**EVALUATING**

*Thuy: Ulrich is hunting not for animals but for people who are trespassing. That's the game for him*
**CLARIFYING**

*Robert: This is a very dense forest; the vegetation is so thick that walking must be difficult.*
**VISUALIZING**

*Thuy: He's got vengeance in his eyes; he wants to murder Georg. He's bloodthirsty!*
**CLARIFYING**

*Robert: It's ironic that Ulrich found Georg just as he had hoped. Seems unrealistic. I'm reminded that so many wars are just about land. Murder seems too harsh a penalty for a land dispute.*
**EVALUATING / CONNECTING**

*Thuy: I'm beginning to think I know where the story is going. I think they'll be caught and then both might die. Or, they might not hate each other in the end and have to work together to save their lives.*
**PREDICTING**

THE INTERLOPERS **9**

*"The Interlopers"*
*by Saki*

*Writing Ideas*
* *I could take this plot and adapt it to a contemporary situation.*
* *It might be interesting to write about two enemies in school who finally make peace.*

## Your Working Portfolio

Artists and writers keep portfolios in which they store works in progress or the works they are most proud of. Your portfolio can be a folder, a box, or a notebook—the form doesn't matter. Just make sure to keep adding to it—with drafts of your writing experiments, summaries of your projects, and your own goals and accomplishments as a reader and writer. Later in this book, on the Reflect and Assess pages, you will choose your best or favorite work to place in a *Presentation Portfolio*.

# Become an Active Reader

*The strategies you need to become an active reader are already within your grasp. In fact, you use them every day to make sense of the images and the events in your world. Whether watching a movie or interpreting a photograph, you already know how to employ such strategies.*

Take a look at this puzzling photograph. Read the comments alongside it, made by one student. As you will see, this student used four different strategies—Question, Clarify, Predict, and Connect—to understand and interpret the situation shown in the photograph. These and the other reading strategies listed on the next page can help you interact with literature as well.

**Question** *Who are these people? Where are they? What could have caused such massive destruction?*

**Clarify** *The man is holding her gown so it doesn't drag. They're trying not to spoil their wedding clothes.*

**Predict** *I wonder what kind of wedding ceremony will take place.*

**Connect** *This reminds me of photos from European cities after bombing in World War II.*

# Strategies for Reading

Following are specific reading strategies that are introduced and applied throughout this book. Use them when you read and interact with the various literature selections. Occasionally **monitor** how well the strategies are working for you and, if desired, modify them to suit your needs.

**PREDICT** Try to figure out what will happen next and how the selection might end. Then read on to see how accurate your guesses were.

**VISUALIZE** Visualize characters, events, and setting to help you understand what's happening. When you read nonfiction, pay attention to the images that form in your mind as you read.

**CONNECT** Connect personally with what you're reading. Think of similarities between the descriptions in the selection and what you have personally experienced, heard about, and read about.

**QUESTION** Question what happens while you read. Searching for reasons behind events and characters' feelings can help you feel closer to what you are reading.

**CLARIFY** Stop occasionally to review what you understand, and expect to have your understanding change and develop as you read on. Reread and use resources to help you clarify your understanding. Also watch for answers to questions you had earlier.

**EVALUATE** Form opinions about what you read, both while you're reading and after you've finished. Develop your own ideas about characters and events.

**On the next page, you will see how two readers applied these strategies to the story "The Interlopers."**

**Go Beyond the Text** If you really become an active reader, your involvement doesn't stop with the last line of the text. Decide what else you'd like to know. Discuss your ideas with others, do some research, or jump on the Internet.

 **More Online**
www.mcdougallittell.com

"How the whole region would stare and gabble if we rode into the market square together. No one living can remember seeing a Znaeym and a von Gradwitz talking to one another in friendship. And what peace there would be among the forester folk if we ended our feud tonight. And if we choose to make peace among our people, there is none other to interfere, no interlopers from outside. . . . You would come and keep the Sylvester night beneath my roof, and I would come and feast on some high day at your castle. . . . I would never fire a shot on your land, save when you invited me as a guest; and you should come and shoot with me down in the marshes where the wildfowl are. In all the countryside there are none that could hinder if we willed to make peace. I never thought to have wanted to do other than hate you all my life, but I think I have changed my mind about things too, this last half-hour. And you offered me your wine flask. . . . Ulrich von Gradwitz, I will be your friend."

For a space both men were silent, turning over in their minds the wonderful changes that this dramatic reconciliation would bring about. In the cold, gloomy forest, with the wind tearing in fitful gusts through the naked branches and whistling around the tree trunks, they lay and waited for the help that would now bring release and succor to both parties. And each prayed a private prayer that his men might be the first to arrive, so that he might be the first to show honorable attention to the enemy that had become a friend.

Presently, as the wind dropped for a moment, Ulrich broke silence.

"Let's shout for help," he said; "in this lull our voices may carry a little way."

"They won't carry far through the trees and undergrowth," said Georg, "but we can try. Together, then."

The two raised their voices in a prolonged hunting call.

"Together again," said Ulrich a few minutes later, after listening in vain for an answer halloo.

"I heard something that time, I think," said Ulrich.

"I heard nothing but the pestilential wind," said Georg hoarsely.

There was silence again for some minutes, and then Ulrich gave a joyful cry.

"I can see figures coming through the wood. They are following in the way I came down the hillside."

Both men raised their voices in as loud a shout as they could muster.

*Border Patrol* (1951), Andrew Wyeth. Private collection.

"They hear us! They've stopped. Now they see us. They're running down the hill towards us," cried Ulrich.

"How many of them are there?" asked Georg.

"I can't see distinctly," said Ulrich; "nine or ten."

"Then they are yours," said Georg; "I had only seven out with me."

"They are making all the speed they can, brave lads," said Ulrich gladly.

"Are they your men?" asked Georg. "Are they your men?"

"No," said Ulrich with a laugh, the idiotic chattering laugh of a man unstrung with hideous fear.

"Who are they?" asked Georg quickly, straining his eyes to see what the other would gladly not have seen.

"*Wolves.*" ❖

*Thuy:* Why "hideous fear"? If men are coming, it doesn't matter who they are.
**QUESTIONING**

*Thuy:* Now I see. Now they're going to die together. I like the ending.
**CLARIFYING / EVALUATING**

# THE CHALLENGE OF CHANGE

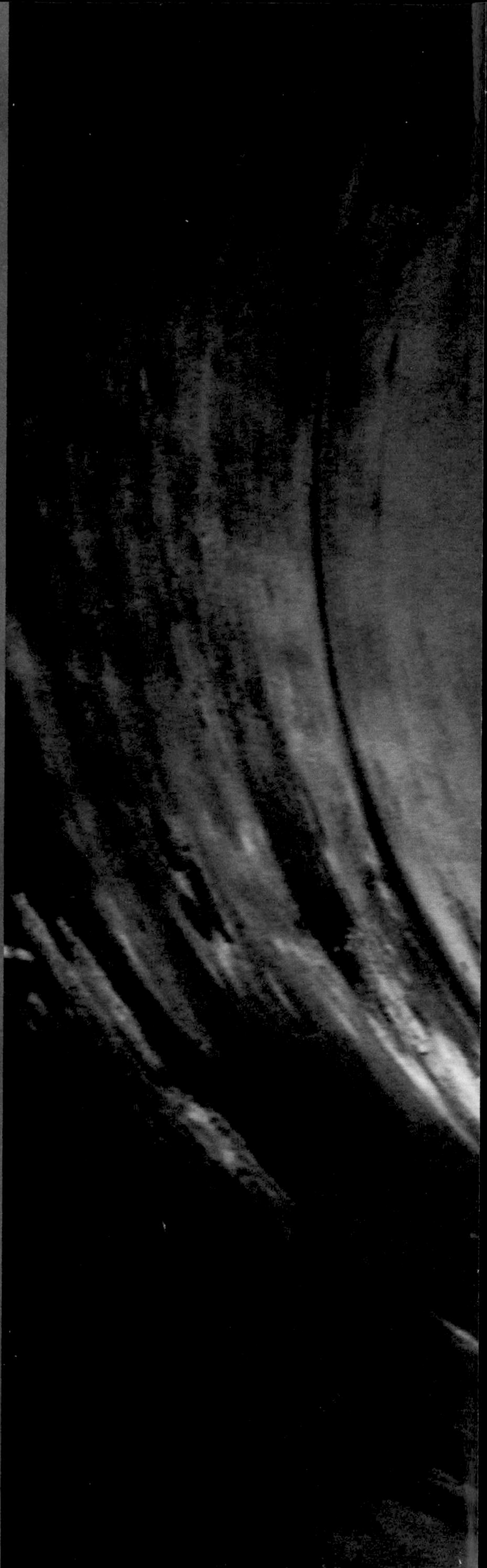

There is

nothing permanent

except

change.

HERACLITUS

How do you view progress? Do you believe that we are moving inevitably toward a better life, aided by electronic wizardry, or are you worried about what might be lost along the way as our world changes rapidly? This part of Unit One features stories of people who must contend with forces of change. In various ways the selections challenge you to determine the price of progress.

**ACTIVITY**

Create two illustrations—one suggesting progress and the other suggesting the opposite of progress. Then compare your illustrations with those of other classmates and discuss what the images reveal about your views of progress.

# LEARNING *the Language of* *Literature*

$\mathcal{F}$**iction** is narrative writing that springs from a writer's imagination, though it may be based on actual events and real people. Although one purpose of fiction is to entertain, it can also provide important insights into human nature. The two major types of fiction are **short stories,** brief works that can usually be read in a sitting, and **novels,** longer and generally more complex narratives. Both short stories and novels share the elements of **plot, character, setting, theme,** and **point of view.** Use the following passages from Saki's "The Interlopers" to learn more about the elements of fiction.

## Plot

The word *plot* refers to the chain of related events that take place in a story. In most plots, events are set in motion by **conflicts**—struggles between or within characters. Most plots include the following stages:

| Element | Definition |
|---|---|
| exposition | provides needed background information |
| rising action | the part of the plot in which the conflict intensifies |
| climax | the turning point of the action, when the reader's interest is at its highest point |
| falling action or dénouement | the action after the climax, in which the conflict is often resolved |

**YOUR TURN** What conflict is introduced in the passage at the right?

### PLOT

A famous lawsuit, in the days of his grandfather, had wrested it [a woodland] from the illegal possession of a neighboring family of petty landowners; the dispossessed party had never acquiesced in the judgment of the Courts, and a long series of poaching affrays and similar scandals had embittered the relationships between the families for three generations.

## Character

**Characters** are the individuals, real or imaginary, who take part in the action of stories. The characters who are at the center of a story's action are called **main characters;** less important ones are **minor characters.** Characters that grow or change as the plot unfolds are called **dynamic characters,** while **static characters** remain unchanged. The development of characters in fiction is known as **characterization.** There are four basic methods of characterization: physical description; a character's own speech, thoughts, feelings, and actions; the speech, thoughts, feelings, and actions of other characters; and a narrator's comments.

**YOUR TURN** In this passage, what techniques of characterization has Saki used?

### CHARACTER

Each had a rifle in his hand, each had hate in his heart and murder uppermost in his mind. The chance had come to give full play to the passions of a lifetime. But a man who has been brought up under the code of a restraining civilization cannot easily nerve himself to shoot down his neighbor in cold blood.

# Setting

The **setting** of a story is the time and place in which the events occur. The place can be real or imaginary, and the time can be a particular time of day, a season, a period of history, or even the future. Setting plays an important part in some stories, having a major effect on what happens to the characters. In other stories, the settings are only backdrops. In "The Interlopers," the setting serves as the scene of a key conflict between man and nature.

# Theme

A **theme** is a central idea or message in a work of literature. It is not the work's subject but a perception about life or human nature that the writer wants to communicate. Themes are seldom stated directly; usually they must be inferred. A theme can be revealed by the ways characters change during a story and the conflicts they experience, statements in which the narrator or a character says something important about life, or by a work's title.

**YOUR TURN** From the passage at the right, what can you infer about a possible theme of the story?

> **THEME**
>
> "We have quarreled like devils all our lives over this stupid strip of forest, where the trees can't even stand upright in a breath of wind. Lying here tonight, thinking, I've come to think we've been rather fools; there are better things in life than getting the better of a boundary dispute."

# Point of View

The term **point of view** refers to the relationship between a narrator and the events he or she describes. When a story's narrator is a character participating in the story's action, the story is said to be written from a **first-person point of view.** In a story told from a **third-person point of view,** on the other hand, a narrator outside the action describes the events and characters. This point of view can be subdivided into **third-person omniscient,** in which the narrator is "all-knowing," able to see into the minds of all the characters, and **third-person limited,** in which the narrator perceives events only as an observer or only through the eyes of one character. A narrator whose viewpoint is limited to that of a single character will describe only that character's feelings and only the events that the character witnesses.

> **POINT OF VIEW**
>
> Ulrich was silent for a few minutes and lay listening to the weary screeching of the wind. An idea was slowly forming and growing in his brain, an idea that gained strength every time that he looked across at the man who was fighting so grimly against pain and exhaustion.

**YOUR TURN** What clues in this passage can help you identify the point of view from which the story is told?

F iction has the capacity to entertain and the power to illuminate through compelling plots, strong characterization, detailed descriptions of setting, and universal themes. Though each story is unique, the reading strategies outlined here can help you get the most from any work of fiction you read.

# Reading Fiction

## Strategies for Using Your 📖 READER'S NOTEBOOK

As you read, take notes to
- **connect** your personal experiences to the feelings, motives, and actions of the characters you are reading about
- record any phrases, passages, images, or ideas that you find interesting
- write down any **questions** you have about plot, character, setting, theme, or point of view

**1 Strategies for Understanding Plot**
- Note the cause-and-effect links between events.
- Identify the main conflict, but also take note of the minor difficulties and problems that characters encounter.

**2 Strategies for Analyzing Characters**
- In a chart like this one, record examples of the methods of characterization that the writer uses. Note which characters are dynamic and which are static.
- Look for clues to each character's motives and actions. **Evaluate** the character's personality, and **predict** what he or she will do next.
- Watch for signs of internal conflict—that is, emotional or psychological conflict within characters.

| "The Interlopers" | |
|---|---|
| Character | Ulrich |
| Words & actions | "I've come to think we've been rather fools." |
| Thoughts | |
| Appearance | |
| What others think | |

**3 Strategies for Visualizing Setting**
- Look for specific adjectives and details that convey the place and time of the story.
- Use the writer's descriptions to help you **visualize,** or "see," the characters in that setting.
- **Evaluate** the effects the setting may have on the characters and on the plot of the story.

**4 Strategies for Recognizing Themes**
- Note any sentences or ideas that you find especially interesting. They might be clues to a theme.
- Observe how characters change and what lessons they learn during the story.
- **Question** whether a title offers any clues to a theme.

**5 Strategies for Determining Point of View**
- Observe the pronouns the narrator uses. *I, me,* and *us* signal a first-person point of view; *he, she,* and *they,* a third-person point of view.
- If the story is told from a third-person point of view, **question** whether an omniscient narrator is supplying information that no single observer could know, or if the information is limited to what an outside observer or a single character might see and hear.

## Need More Help?

Remember that active readers use the essential reading strategies explained on page 7: **visualize, predict, clarify, question, connect, evaluate, monitor.**

# Harrison Bergeron

*Short Story by* KURT VONNEGUT, JR.

## Connect to Your Life

**Equal Is as Equal Does** Can you think of a time when you've had to hide your skills for someone else's sake? Maybe you gave a wrong answer in class, just to avoid looking too smart in front of friends. Or perhaps you let a friend beat you at a video game. Discuss the advantages and disadvantages of covering up your strengths to pretend as though you are "equal" to someone else. Use examples to support your opinion.

## Build Background

**What's Your Handicap?** If you've played golf or run a footrace, you might know the term "handicap." It's a way to even up the game so that good, average, and poor players can compete as equals. In a footrace, for example, faster runners might handicap themselves by giving slower runners a head start. In golf, where players win by completing the course with the fewest number of strokes, better golfers sometimes start the game with a handicap of extra strokes. In "Harrison Bergeron," people are given handicaps in daily life, so that no one will be any stronger, smarter, or better-looking than anyone else.

WORDS TO KNOW
**Vocabulary Preview**

| | |
|---|---|
| calibrated | symmetry |
| consternation | synchronizing |
| cower | vague |
| hindrance | vigilance |
| luminous | wince |

## Focus Your Reading

**LITERARY ANALYSIS** **THEME** Stories often have a central idea or message, also known as the **theme.** Theme gives meaning to the story by providing some insight into life or human nature. The first lines of "Harrison Bergeron" give you a clue to the story's theme:

*The year was 2081, and everybody was finally equal. They weren't only equal before God and the law. They were equal every which way.*

As you read, think about how the issue of equality relates to the theme of the story.

**ACTIVE READING** **MAKING INFERENCES** Inferences are logical guesses based on clues in the text and on common sense. Read the following sentence from "Harrison Bergeron":

*It wasn't clear at first as to what the bulletin was about, since the announcer, like all announcers, had a serious speech impediment.*

In that society, all news announcers have speech impediments, which would make them unfit for the job by today's standards. From this clue, you can infer that people in that society are not hired according to their strengths.

**READER'S NOTEBOOK** As you read this story, jot down at least five inferences you can make about the main characters and the society. Fill in a chart like the one shown.

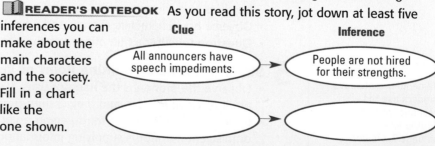

| Clue | | Inference |
|---|---|---|
| All announcers have speech impediments. | → | People are not hired for their strengths. |
| | → | |

# Harrison Bergeron

## Kurt Vonnegut, Jr.

THE YEAR WAS 2081, and everybody was finally equal. They weren't only equal before God and the law. They were equal every which way. Nobody was smarter than anybody else. Nobody was better looking than anybody else. Nobody was stronger or quicker than anybody else. All this equality was due to the 211th, 212th, and 213th Amendments to the Constitution, and to the unceasing vigilance of agents of the United States Handicapper General.

Some things about living still weren't quite right, though. April, for instance, still drove people crazy by not being springtime. And it was in that clammy month that the H-G men took George and Hazel Bergeron's fourteen-year-old son, Harrison, away.

It was tragic, all right, but George and Hazel couldn't think about it very hard. Hazel had a perfectly average intelligence, which meant she couldn't think about anything except in short bursts. And George, while his intelligence was way above normal, had a little mental handicap radio in his ear. He was required by law to wear it at all times. It was tuned to a government transmitter.[1] Every twenty seconds or so, the transmitter would send out some sharp noise to keep people like George from taking unfair advantage of their brains.

Detail of *The Spirit of Our Time* (about 1920), Raoul Hausmann. Assemblage with wigmaker's dummy head, 12 ¾″ high. Collections Musée National d'Art Moderne, Centre Georges Pompidou, Paris.

---

1. **transmitter:** an electronic device for broadcasting radio signals.

WORDS TO KNOW

**vigilance** (vĭj′ə-ləns) *n.* alert attention; watchfulness

George and Hazel were watching television. There were tears on Hazel's cheeks, but she'd forgotten for the moment what they were about.

On the television screen were ballerinas.

A buzzer sounded in George's head. His thoughts fled in panic, like bandits from a burglar alarm.

"That was a real pretty dance, that dance they just did," said Hazel.

"Huh?" said George.

"That dance—it was nice," said Hazel.

"Yup," said George. He tried to think a little about the ballerinas. They weren't really very good—no better than anybody else would have been, anyway. They were burdened with sashweights[2] and bags of birdshot,[3] and their faces were masked, so that no one, seeing a free and graceful gesture or a pretty face, would feel like something the cat drug in. George was toying with the vague notion that maybe dancers shouldn't be handicapped. But he didn't get very far with it before another noise in his ear radio scattered his thoughts.

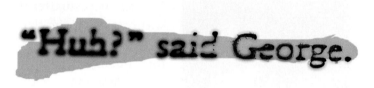
"Huh?" said George.

George winced. So did two out of the eight ballerinas.

Hazel saw him wince. Having no mental handicap herself, she had to ask George what the latest sound had been.

"Sounded like somebody hitting a milk bottle with a ball peen hammer,[4]" said George.

"I'd think it would be real interesting, hearing all the different sounds," said Hazel, a little envious. "All the things they think up."

"Um," said George.

"Only, if I was Handicapper General, you know what I would do?" said Hazel. Hazel, as a matter of fact, bore a strong resemblance to the Handicapper General, a woman named Diana Moon Glampers. "If I was Diana Moon Glampers," said Hazel, "I'd have chimes on Sunday—just chimes. Kind of in honor of religion."

"I could think, if it was just chimes," said George.

"Well—maybe make 'em real loud," said Hazel. "I think I'd make a good Handicapper General."

"Good as anybody else," said George.

"Who knows better'n I do what normal is?" said Hazel.

"Right," said George. He began to think glimmeringly about his abnormal son who was now in jail, about Harrison, but a twenty-one-gun salute in his head stopped that.

"Boy!" said Hazel, "that was a doozy, wasn't it?"

It was such a doozy that George was white and trembling, and tears stood on the rims of his red eyes. Two of the eight ballerinas had collapsed to the studio floor and were holding their temples.

"All of a sudden you look so tired," said Hazel. "Why don't you stretch out on the sofa, so's you can rest your handicap bag on the pillows, honeybunch." She was referring to the

---

2. **sashweights:** lead weights used in some kinds of windows to keep them from falling shut when raised.

3. **birdshot:** tiny lead pellets made to be loaded in shotgun shells.

4. **ball peen hammer:** a hammer with a head having one flat side and one rounded side.

---

**ACTIVE READING**

**VISUALIZE** Imagine the dancers with their masks and handicaps. What do you think their dance looks like?

**ACTIVE READING**

**MAKE INFERENCES** What inference can you make about the ballerinas from this description?

---

WORDS TO KNOW

**vague** (vāg) *adj.* unclear; hazy
**wince** (wĭns) *v.* to shrink or flinch involuntarily, especially in pain

forty-seven pounds of birdshot in a canvas bag, which was padlocked around George's neck. "Go on and rest the bag for a little while," she said. "I don't care if you're not equal to me for a while."

George weighed the bag with his hands. "I don't mind it," he said. "I don't notice it any more. It's just a part of me."

"You been so tired lately—kind of wore out," said Hazel. "If there was just some way we could make a little hole in the bottom of the bag, and just take out a few of them lead balls. Just a few."

"Two years in prison and two thousand dollars fine for every ball I took out," said George. "I don't call that a bargain."

"If you could just take a few out when you came home from work," said Hazel. "I mean—you don't compete with anybody around here. You just set around."

"If I tried to get away with it," said George, "then other people'd get away with it—and pretty soon we'd be right back to the dark ages again, with everybody competing against everybody else. You wouldn't like that, would you?"

"I'd hate it," said Hazel.

"There you are," said George. "The minute people start cheating on laws, what do you think happens to society?"

If Hazel hadn't been able to come up with an answer to this question, George couldn't have supplied one. A siren was going off in his head.

"Reckon it'd fall all apart," said Hazel.

"What would?" said George blankly.

*The Spirit of Our Time* (about 1921), Raoul Hausmann. Assemblage with wigmaker's dummy head, 12¾″ high. Collections Musée National d'Art Moderne, Centre Georges Pompidou, Paris.

"Society," said Hazel uncertainly. "Wasn't that what you just said?"

"Who knows?" said George.

The television program was suddenly interrupted for a news bulletin. It wasn't clear at first as to what the bulletin was about, since the announcer, like all announcers, had a serious speech impediment.[5] For about half a minute, and in a state of high excitement, the announcer tried to say, "Ladies and gentlemen—" He finally gave up, handed the bulletin to a ballerina to read.

"That's all right—" Hazel said of the announcer, "he tried. That's the big thing. He tried to do the best he could with what God gave him. He should get a nice raise for trying so hard."

"Ladies and gentlemen—" said the ballerina, reading the bulletin. She must have been extraordinarily beautiful, because the mask she wore was hideous. And it was easy to see that she was the strongest and most graceful of all the dancers, for her handicap bags were as big as those worn by two-hundred-pound men.

And she had to apologize at once for her voice, which was a very unfair voice for a woman to use. Her voice was a warm, <u>luminous</u>, timeless

---

5. **speech impediment** (ĭm-pĕd′ə-mənt): a physical defect that prevents a person from speaking normally.

melody. "Excuse me—" she said, and she began again, making her voice absolutely uncompetitive.

"Harrison Bergeron, age fourteen," she said in a grackle[6] squawk, "has just escaped from jail, where he was held on suspicion of plotting to overthrow the government. He is a genius and an athlete, is under-handicapped, and should be regarded as extremely dangerous."

**ACTIVE READING**

**PREDICT** What do you think will happen now that Harrison has escaped?

A police photograph of Harrison Bergeron was flashed on the screen—upside down, then sideways, upside down again, then right side up. The picture showed the full length of Harrison against a background <u>calibrated</u> in feet and inches. He was exactly seven feet tall.

The rest of Harrison's appearance was Halloween and hardware. Nobody had ever born heavier handicaps. He had outgrown <u>hindrances</u> faster than the H-G men could think them up. Instead of a little ear radio for a mental handicap, he wore a tremendous pair of earphones, and spectacles with thick wavy lenses. The spectacles were intended to make him not only half blind, but to give him whanging headaches besides.

Scrap metal was hung all over him. Ordinarily, there was a certain <u>symmetry</u>, a military neatness to the handicaps issued to strong people, but Harrison looked like a walking junkyard. In the race of life, Harrison carried three hundred pounds.

And to offset his good looks, the H-G men required that he wear at all times a red rubber ball for a nose, keep his eyebrows shaved off, and cover his even white teeth with black caps at snaggle-tooth random.

"If you see this boy," said the ballerina, "do not—I repeat, do not—try to reason with him."

There was the shriek of a door being torn from its hinges.

Screams and barking cries of <u>consternation</u> came from the television set. The photograph of Harrison Bergeron on the screen jumped again and again, as though dancing to the tune of an earthquake.

George Bergeron correctly identified the earthquake, and well he might have—for many was the time his own home had danced to the same crashing tune. . . . "That must be Harrison!" said George.

The realization was blasted from his mind instantly by the sound of an automobile collision in his head.

When George could open his eyes again, the photograph of Harrison was gone. A living, breathing Harrison filled the screen.

Clanking, clownish, and huge, Harrison stood in the center of the studio. The knob of the uprooted studio door was still in his hand. Ballerinas, technicians, musicians, and announcers <u>cowered</u> on their knees before him, expecting to die.

"I am the Emperor!" cried Harrison. "Do you hear? I am the Emperor! Everybody must do what I say at once!" He stamped his foot and the studio shook.

---

6. **grackle:** a blackbird with a harsh, unpleasant call.

WORDS
TO
KNOW

**calibrated** (kăl′ə-brā′tĭd) *adj.* marked with measurements **calibrate** *v.*
**hindrance** (hĭn′drəns) *n.* something that interferes with an activity; obstacle
**symmetry** (sĭm′ĭ-trē) *n.* a similarity between the two sides of something; balance
**consternation** (kŏn′stər-nā′shən) *n.* a confused amazement or fear
**cower** (kou′ər) *v.* to draw back in fear; cringe

*The Mad Painter [Il pittore matto]* (1981–1982), Enzo Cucchi. Oil on canvas, 119½″ × 83¾″. Solomon R. Guggenheim Museum, New York. Exxon Corporation Purchase Award with additional funds contributed by the Junior Associates, 1982. Photo by David Heald copyright © The Solomon R. Guggenheim Foundation, New York (FN 82.2927).

guaranteed to support five thousand pounds.

Harrison's scrap-iron handicaps crashed to the floor.

Harrison thrust his thumbs under the bar of the padlock that secured his head harness. The bar snapped like celery. Harrison smashed his headphones and spectacles against the wall.

He flung away his rubber-ball nose, revealed a man that would have awed Thor, the god of thunder.

"I shall now select my Empress!" he said, looking down on the cowering people. "Let the first woman who dares rise to her feet claim her mate and her throne!"

A moment passed, and then a ballerina arose, swaying like a willow.

Harrison plucked the mental handicap from her ear, snapped off her physical handicaps with marvelous delicacy. Last of all, he removed her mask.

She was blindingly beautiful. "Now—" said Harrison, taking her hand, "shall we show the people the meaning of the word dance? Music!" he commanded.

The musicians scrambled back into their chairs, and Harrison stripped them of their handicaps, too. "Play your best," he told them, "and I'll make you barons and dukes and earls."

The music began. It was normal at first—cheap, silly, false. But Harrison snatched two musicians from their chairs, waved them like batons as he sang the music as he wanted it

"Even as I stand here—" he bellowed, "crippled, hobbled, sickened—I am a greater ruler than any man who ever lived! Now watch me become what I *can* become!"

Harrison tore the straps of his handicap harness like wet tissue paper, tore straps

played. He slammed them back into their chairs.

The music began again and was much improved.

Harrison and his Empress merely listened to the music for a while—listened gravely, as though <u>synchronizing</u> their heartbeats with it.

They shifted their weights to their toes.

Harrison placed his big hands on the girl's tiny waist, letting her sense the weightlessness that would soon be hers.

And then, in an explosion of joy and grace, into the air they sprang!

Not only were the laws of the land abandoned, but the law of gravity and the laws of motion as well.

They reeled, whirled, swiveled, flounced, capered, gamboled,[7] and spun.

They leaped like deer on the moon.

The studio ceiling was thirty feet high, but each leap brought the dancers nearer to it.

It became their obvious intention to kiss the ceiling.

They kissed it.

And then, neutralizing gravity with love and pure will, they remained suspended in air inches below the ceiling, and they kissed each other for a long, long time.

It was then that Diana Moon Glampers, the Handicapper General, came into the studio with a double-barreled ten-gauge shotgun. She fired twice, and the Emperor and the Empress were dead before they hit the floor.

Diana Moon Glampers loaded the gun again.

They leaped
like deer
on
the moon.

She aimed it at the musicians and told them they had ten seconds to get their handicaps back on.

It was then that the Bergerons' television tube burned out.

Hazel turned to comment about the blackout to George. But George had gone out into the kitchen for a can of beer.

George came back in with the beer, paused while a handicap signal shook him up. And then he sat down again. "You been crying?" he said to Hazel.

"Yup," she said.

"What about?" he said.

"I forget," she said. "Something real sad on television."

"What was it?" he said.

"It's all kind of mixed up in my mind," said Hazel.

"Forget sad things," said George.

"I always do," said Hazel.

"That's my girl," said George. He winced. There was the sound of a riveting[8] gun in his head.

"Gee—I could tell that one was a doozy," said Hazel.

"You can say that again," said George.

"Gee—" said Hazel, "I could tell that one was a doozy." ❖

---

7. **flounced, capered, gamboled** (găm′bəld): bounced, leaped, frolicked.

8. **riveting** (rĭv′ĭ-tĭng) **gun:** a power tool used to hammer the bolts (called rivets) used in construction work to fasten metal beams or plates together.

26

# *Thinking* through the LITERATURE

## Connect to the Literature

1. **What Do You Think?** What is your response to the story's ending? Discuss it with your classmates.

> **Comprehension Check**
> - Why does Harrison's father, George, have difficulty thinking about anything for very long?
> - What is the purpose of all the gear Harrison wears?
> - What does Diana Moon Glampers do to Harrison? Why?

## Think Critically

2. What do you think Harrison's rebellion reveals about his **character** and his values? Support your opinion with references to the text.

3. Do you feel sorry for George and Hazel Bergeron, or do you find fault with the way they respond to events? Explain your answer.

   **THINK ABOUT**
   - George's handicap
   - Hazel's "perfectly average intelligence"
   - their comments about their son

4. **ACTIVE READING   MAKING INFERENCES**   Based on the chart you made in your  **READER'S NOTEBOOK**, what conclusions can you draw about the society in which the characters live?

5. What do you think Vonnegut might be trying to say about today's society and the role a government can play in achieving equality among people? Use examples from the story to support your opinion.

## Extend Interpretations

6. **What If?** Imagine that Diana Moon Glampers had missed and that Harrison and the ballerina escaped. How might the story's **plot** have changed? Write your response in your **READER'S NOTEBOOK**.

7. **Connect to Life** The United States has often been called the land of opportunity. This suggests that individuals are free to pursue their dreams to the best of their abilities, which may differ greatly. At the same time, our Declaration of Independence states that all people are created equal. In what ways is there a tension between equality and opportunity in our nation today?

## Literary Analysis

**THEME**   The **theme** of a story is its central message. It expresses an attitude or insight into life or human nature. To identify the theme of a story, you must draw inferences from clues. One way to uncover the theme is to consider what happens to the main characters. For example, Harrison's death and the subsequent responses of his parents suggest that Vonnegut is criticizing both the society, the government, and the parents.

**Activity** Look back through the story. List phrases, sentences, or events that provide clues to the theme. Pay attention to the relationship between the phrases Vonnegut uses and the events he writes about. You may find that his use of humor is not entirely lighthearted. Then write a sentence stating the theme in your own words. Compare your theme statement with those of your classmates.

**SCIENCE FICTION**   Stories that tell about the future by blending scientific data and theory with the author's creative imagination are called **science fiction.** Most science fiction comments in some way on present-day society. In "Harrison Bergeron," the author imagines a future society in which competition and inequality have been eliminated.

**Paired Activity** Work with a partner and look for elements of science fiction in the story. Keep track of these elements, and when you are done, discuss your results with a larger group.

# Choices & CHALLENGES

## Writing Options

**1. Glampers's Report** In order to satisfy her superiors, Diana Moon Glampers must make a complete report of events that led her to shoot Harrison. Write the official report. Explain events from her point of view. Include her rationale for her extreme action.

**2. Warden's Address** Alarmed by Harrison's escape, the head of the prison delivers a speech to the heads of state, urging them to clamp down on inequality. Write the speech, detailing the warden's concerns and suggestions. Place the report in your **Working Portfolio.**

## Activities & Explorations

**1. News at Six** With three or four classmates, create a TV news report on Harrison Bergeron's escape and death. Divide up the roles of news reporter, Diana Moon Glampers, and various eyewitnesses. Present your telecast before your class.
~ **SPEAKING AND LISTENING**

**2. Video Viewing** View the video excerpt of *Harrison Bergeron* provided with this program. In a small group, discuss how the filmmakers changed the setting and content of the story. Decide whether you think the changes are in keeping with the theme of the story. ~ **VIEWING AND REPRESENTING**

 **V I D E O   Literature in Performance**

## Inquiry & Research

**Public Opinion** Should sports teams hold tryouts so that only the best are chosen or should the coaches let anyone play? Should the choir make people audition? In other words, where should schools draw the line between recognizing excellence and achieving equality? With your classmates, conduct a survey of public opinion about no-cut policies for school teams or clubs. Prepare a questionnaire and then interview other students in your school. Discuss your findings. What can you infer from the results?

## Vocabulary in Action

**EXERCISE A: CONTEXT CLUES** Write the Word to Know that best completes the meaning of each sentence.

1. In Vonnegut's vision of the future, intelligent people hear loud noises in fitted radios that hurt their ears and make them _____.

2. The ballerina is very strong and beautiful. She seems _____, or glowing with an inner light.

3. As Harrison and the ballerina dance, they begin _____ their movements.

4. Harrison Bergeron does not let the handicaps he is fitted with be a _____ to him.

5. If Diana Moon Glampers approached you with a shotgun, would you _____ and tremble in fear?

**EXERCISE B: SYNONYMS** On your paper, write the Word to Know that belongs in each group of synonyms.

1. dismay, terror, _____
2. equilibrium, _____, proportion
3. _____, gradated, measured
4. acuity, _____, diligence
5. indistinct, unclear, _____

**Building Vocabulary**
For an in-depth study of context clues, see page 56.

| WORDS TO KNOW | calibrated | cower | luminous | synchronizing | vigilance |
|---|---|---|---|---|---|
| | consternation | hindrance | symmetry | vague | wince |

# Grammar in Context: Proper Nouns

In the short story "Harrison Bergeron," Kurt Vonnegut invents proper nouns that help create satire.

> "Harrison Bergeron, age fourteen," she said in a grackle squawk, "has just escaped from jail, where he was held on suspicion of plotting to overthrow the government."

A **proper noun** names a specific person, place, or thing. In the example, Vonnegut has created a proper noun that alludes to a quality of the character it names. The name *Bergeron* contains the French word *berger,* which means "shepherd." Harrison is a sort of shepherd who tries to lead people away from the evil influence of the handicapper general.

**Apply to Your Writing** In fiction writing, using carefully chosen proper nouns can help you suggest character traits and convey a satirical or realistic tone.

**WRITING EXERCISE** Replace the underlined words with proper nouns of your own creation. Try to convey a particular tone or attitude with each proper noun. Remember to capitalize each name.

**Example: *Original*** The dance company danced the same routine every night.
***Rewritten*** The Lead-Footed Leapers danced the same routine every night.

1. The Bergerons' house is neat, small, and exactly like every other house on the street.
2. The television set, manufactured by a national company, produces a wavy picture and static-filled sound.
3. The announcer garbles half of every sentence.
4. The jail looms gray and forbidding.
5. When the orchestra plays the song, Harrison and the ballerina spring into the air.

**Grammar Handbook**
Nouns, p. 1182.

# Kurt Vonnegut, Jr.
1922–

**Other Works**
*The Sirens of Titan*
*Mother Night*
*Cat's Cradle*
*God Bless You, Mr. Rosewater*
*Jailbird*
*Slaughterhouse Five*

**Serious Humor** Kurt Vonnegut began writing short stories in the late 1940s, and he achieved quick success. Because so many of his stories deal with science and social criticism, he has been dubbed a science fiction writer, although he has never liked that designation. For Vonnegut, no subject is off-limits. He writes about the brutality in human nature and our fears of technology, war, and politics. Although he deals with devastatingly serious topics, his writing is easy to read. He often attacks his subjects with dark humor and wild absurdities.

**Real Life into Fiction** Vonnegut's life has not always been easy. His mother died while he was home on leave from the army during World War II. He was a prisoner of war in Dresden, Germany, when that city was leveled by bombing; he witnessed great destruction during the war and immediately afterward. In 1958, his sister died of cancer. Many of these wrenching experiences have found their way into Vonnegut's fiction.

**Critical Arrival** Although Vonnegut has always been popular, he has not always been critically praised. In the 1970s that changed. He is now regarded as one of the most important writers of the late 20th century. "Harrison Bergeron" was published in a 1968 collection of Vonnegut stories called *Welcome to the Monkey House.*

## Author Activity

Look for book reviews of Vonnegut's work from the early part of his career (before 1970) and the later part (after 1970). How did critics' reactions change over time? Bring copies of at least two contrasting reviews to class and discuss them with your classmates.

# Searching for Summer

*Short Story by* JOAN AIKEN

## ( Connect to Your Life )

**Aftermath of a Disaster** Every year, people all over the world experience natural and technological disasters, such as tornadoes or oil spills. Sometimes communities can recover from them fairly quickly. Others have effects that last for years. Think of a disaster that you have experienced or heard about. How lasting were the effects? What adjustments did the community or nation have to make as a result? Discuss your reply with a partner.

## Build Background

**Nuclear Anxiety** Joan Aiken wrote "Searching for Summer" in the 1950s, setting the story in a future "eighties," perhaps the 1980s or the 2080s. At the time of publication, the memory of the 1945 atomic bombing of Hiroshima and Nagasaki in Japan remained fresh in the minds of many. People lived with the lurking threat of nuclear war. As a result of nuclear weapons testing, radioactive matter, also known as fallout, would rain down from the sky, polluting the environment. The weapons themselves were growing more advanced and powerful all the time, and no one knew exactly what would happen to the earth in the event of a nuclear war. Many writers, artists, and filmmakers explored this issue in their work, imagining the possible outcomes of a nuclear disaster.

> WORDS TO KNOW
> **Vocabulary Preview**
> indomitable    voluble
> omen          withered
> unavailing

## Focus Your Reading

**LITERARY ANALYSIS** **CHARACTER** **Characters** are the people who participate in the action of a story or other literary work. In many stories, characters undergo some sort of change as the **plot** unfolds. Such characters are called **dynamic characters,** as opposed to **static characters,** who remain the same. As you read the following story, think about whether the characters change, and if so, how they change. How is this change or lack of change significant to the story?

**ACTIVE READING** **IDENTIFYING CHARACTERS' MOTIVES** A character's **motive** is the intention or desire that causes him or her to act in a particular way. Understanding why characters act as they do can help you to understand the events of a story.

**READER'S NOTEBOOK** As you read this story, complete a graphic like the one shown with your ideas about the motives of Mr. Noakes, Lily, Tom, and Mrs. Hatching.

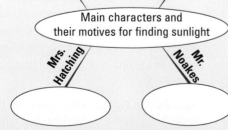

Main characters and their motives for finding sunlight

# Searching for
# Summer

*Joan Aiken*

*The Mysterious Bird* (1917), Charles Burchfield. Watercolor and pencil on paper, 20¾″ × 17¾″,
Delaware Art Museum, Wilmington, bequest of John L. Sexton, 1955.

tawny[16] and hot
and sweet; the
clock's tick was like
a bird chirping;
every now and then
a log settled in the
grate; Lily looked
sleepily around the
little room, so rich
and peaceful, and
thought, I wish we
were staying here. I
wish we needn't go
back to that horri-
ble pub. . . . She
leaned against Tom's
comforting arm.

"Look at the
sky," she whispered
to him. "Out there
between the gera-
niums. Blue!"

*Embrace II* (1981), George Tooker.  Egg tempera on gesso panel, 18″ × 24″, private collection.

"And ee'll come up and see my spare bedroom, won't ee now?" Mrs. Hatching said,
breaking off the thread of her questions—which
indeed was not a thread, but merely a savoring[17]
of her pleasure and astonishment at this
unlooked-for visit—"Bide here, why don't ee?
Mid as well. The lil un's fair wore out. Us'll do
for ee better 'n rangy old Noakes; proper old
scoundrel 'e be. Won't us, William?"

"Ah," William said appreciatively. "I'll sing
ee some o' my songs."

A sight of the spare room settled any doubts.
The great white bed, huge as a prairie, built up
with layer upon solid layer of mattress, blanket,
and quilt, almost filled the little shadowy room
in which it stood. Brass rails shone in the green
dimness. "Isn't it quiet," Lily whispered. Mrs.
Hatching, silent for the moment, stood looking
at them proudly, her bright eyes slowly moving
from face to face. Once her hand fondled, as if
it might have been a baby's downy head, the
yellow brass knob.

And so, almost without any words, the
matter was decided.

## Three days later they remembered

that they must go to the village and collect the
scooter which must, surely, be mended by now.

They had been helping old William pick a
basketful of beans. Tom had taken his shirt off,
and the sun gleamed on his brown back; Lily
was wearing an old cotton print which Mrs.
Hatching, with much chuckling, had shortened
to fit her.

It was amazing how deftly, in spite of his
blindness, William moved among the beans,
feeling through the rough, rustling leaves for
the stiffness of concealed pods. He found twice
as many as Tom and Lily, but then they, even

16. **tawny:** tan in color.
17. **savoring:** full appreciation or enjoyment.

on the third day, were still stopping every other minute to exclaim over the blueness of the sky. At night they sat on the back doorstep while Mrs. Hatching clucked inside as she dished the supper, "Starstruck ee'll be! Come along in, do-ee, before soup's cold; stars niver run away yet as I do know."

"Can we get anything for you in the village?" Lily asked, but Mrs. Hatching shook her head.

"Baker's bread and suchlike's no use but to cripple thee's innardses wi' colic.[18] I been living here these eighty year wi'out troubling doctors, and I'm not faring to begin now." She waved to them and stood watching as they walked into the wood, thin and frail beyond belief, but wiry, <u>indomitable</u>, her black eyes full of zest. Then she turned to scream menacingly at a couple of pullets[19] who had strayed and were scratching among the potatoes.

Almost at once they noticed, as they followed the path, that the sky was clouded over.

"It *is* only there on that one spot," Lily said in wonder. "All the time. And they've never even noticed that the sun doesn't shine in other places."

"That's how it must have been all over the world, once," Tom said.

At the garage they found their scooter ready and waiting. They were about to start back when they ran into Mr. Noakes.

"Well, well, well, well, *well!*" he shouted, glaring at them with ferocious good humor. "How many wells make a river, eh? And where did you slip off to? Here's me and the missus was just going to tell the police to have the rivers dragged. But hullo, hul*lo*, what's this? Brown, eh? Suntan? Scrumptious," he said, looking meltingly at Lily and giving her another tremendous pinch. "Where'd you get it, eh? That wasn't all got in half an hour, *I* know. Come on, this means money to you and me; tell us the big secret. Remember what I said; land around these parts is dirt cheap."

Tom and Lily looked at each other in horror. They thought of the cottage, the bees humming among the runner beans, the sunlight glinting in the red-and-gold teacups. At night, when they had lain in the huge sagging bed, stars had shone through the window, and the whole wood was as quiet as the inside of a shell.

"Oh, we've been miles from here," Tom lied hurriedly. "We ran into a friend, and he took us right away beyond Brinsley." And as Mr. Noakes still looked suspicious and unsatisfied, he did the only thing possible. "We're going back there now," he said. "The sunbathing's grand." And opening the throttle, he let the scooter go. They waved at Mr. Noakes and chugged off toward the gray hills that lay to the north.

"My wedding dress," Lily said sadly. "It's on our bed."

They wondered how long Mrs. Hatching would keep tea hot for them, who would eat all the pasties.[20]

"Never mind, you won't need it again," Tom comforted her.

At least, he thought, they had left the golden place undisturbed. Mr. Noakes never went into the wood. And they had done what they intended; they had found the sun. Now they, too, would be able to tell their grandchildren, when beginning a story, "Long, long ago, when we were young, in the days when the sky was blue . . ." ❖

---

18. **cripple . . . colic** (kŏl′ĭk): give yourself a bad case of indigestion.

19. **pullets:** young hens.

20. **pasties** (păs′tēz): a British term for meat pies.

# The Sun

*Mary Oliver*

Have you ever seen
anything
in your life
more wonderful

5  than the way the sun,
every evening,
relaxed and easy,
floats toward the horizon

and into the clouds or the hills,
10  or the rumpled sea,
and is gone—
and how it slides again

out of the blackness,
every morning,
15  on the other side of the world,
like a red flower

streaming upward on its heavenly oils,
say, on a morning in early summer,
at its perfect imperial distance—
20  and have you ever felt for anything

such wild love—
do you think there is anywhere, in any language,
a word billowing enough
for the pleasure

25  that fills you,
as the sun
reaches out,
as it warms you

as you stand there,
30  empty-handed—
or have you too
turned from this world—

or have you too
gone crazy
35  for power,
for things?

**19 imperial:** of great size; majestic.

# *Thinking* through the LITERATURE

## Connect to the Literature

**1. What Do You Think?**
Write a sentence that expresses your feelings about the outcome of the story.

**Comprehension Check**
- What is the setting of this story?
- Why are Tom and Lily driving around the country on their scooter?
- What is Mr. Noakes like?
- What do Tom and Lily find when they return Mrs. Hatching's handbag?

## Think Critically

**2.** What words and phrases would you use to describe the **setting** of the story?

**3.** **ACTIVE READING** **UNDERSTANDING CHARACTERS' MOTIVES**
Look at the characters' motives you recorded in your  **READER'S NOTEBOOK.** Compare Lily and Tom's motives for finding a bit of sunlight with those of Mr. Noakes.

**4.** Why do you think the sun shines only over the Hatchings's cottage?

**5.** Do you think Tom and Lily do the right thing in not going back to the cottage? Explain your opinion.

**6.** What **themes,** or messages, do you see in this story?

> **THINK ABOUT**
> - the disastrous events alluded to at the beginning of the story
> - why sunshine is important to Tom and Lily
> - which **characters** are presented positively and which negatively

## Extend Interpretations

**7. Critic's Corner** Student reviewer Jayme Charak remarked, "The story went to the heart. It was a sweet story and makes you think about the future." How does this reaction compare with your own?

**8. Comparing Texts** In the poem "The Sun," how does Mary Oliver's depiction of the sun differ from the sun as described in Joan Aiken's story? How is it similar?

**9. Connect to Life** Think of situations in your own community or elsewhere in which there has been a conflict between some people's desire to protect places of natural beauty and other people's desire to develop those places for economic gain. How should such conflicts be resolved?

## Literary Analysis

**CHARACTER** The **characters** of a literary work are the individuals that participate in the action. In many stories, one or more characters undergo a change. These are called **dynamic characters,** whereas those who do not change are called **static characters.** Dynamic characters generally change by learning a major lesson or altering a **character trait,** or consistent part of their personality.

**Activity** Fill out a chart like the one started below, in which you identify each of the story's four main characters as dynamic or static. Explain your answer for each character.

| Character | Dynamic or static? | Why? |
|-----------|--------------------|------|
| Lily      |                    |      |
| Tom       |                    |      |
|           |                    |      |

**FANTASY** **Fantasy** is a type of fiction that contains events, places, or other details that could not exist in the real world. The characters in a fantasy are often realistic, but they have experiences that overstep the bounds of reality. The purpose of fantasy may be to delight and amuse or it might make a serious comment on reality. **Science fiction** is also a form of fantasy, as they both include strong imaginary components.

**Cooperative Learning Activity** In a small group, make a list of examples from the story that show how this story illustrates the definition of fantasy. Share your list with another group and discuss your responses.

## Writing Options

**1. Evening Dialogue** Write a dialogue Tom and Lily might have in the evening after leaving Molesworth, discussing whether they will ever return to the Hatchings's cottage.

**2. Story Outline** Write an outline for a story like "Searching for Summer," but one in which the sun burns constantly and clouds are rare. Use the outline below as a model.

**Writing Handbook**
See pages 1155–1156: Narrative Writing.

> I. Scene 1: early morning
>
>    A. The sun rises.
>
>    B. Birds sit weakly in
>       the trees.
>
>    C. Mr. Jones fills the bathtub
>       with ice.
>
> II. Scene 2: classroom
>
>    A. Children rush from the car
>       to an air-conditioned school.
>
>    B. Teacher closes the
>       classroom blinds.

## Activities & Explorations

**1. Story Illustrations** Prepare a set of illustrations for "Searching for Summer." Include pictures of the main characters, various landscapes, and a caption for each of the pictures. Then show your illustrations to the class and read the captions. ~ **ART**

**2. Radio Advertisement** Imagine that Mr. Noakes has discovered the sunshine over the Hatchings's home. With a partner, create and present to the class a radio commercial that Mr. Noakes might put together to advertise the area as a tourist attraction. ~ **SPEAKING AND LISTENING**

## Inquiry & Research

**Nuclear Fallout** Atomic and nuclear explosions have created terrible environmental damage, both at the time of explosion and through fallout, or the descent of radioactive particles after such an explosion. Research the effects of fallout as experienced in Japan after World War II, in the Ukraine with the 1986 accident at Chernobyl, or at various nuclear testing sites. How much does Aiken's world resemble a real-life nuclear aftermath? How is it different? Write a short research paper about your findings.

 **More Online: Research Starter**
www.mcdougallittell.com

Ruined nuclear reactor at Chernobyl.

## Vocabulary in Action

**EXERCISE: IDIOMS** Write the vocabulary word that is suggested by each set of idioms below.

1. run off at the mouth, have the gift of gab, be a chatterbox, talk till the cows come home

2. a black cat crossing your path, gathering clouds, a feeling in one's bones, seeing the handwriting on the wall

3. be a lion, have an iron will, never say die, not be a pushover

4. waste away, curl up and die, dry up and blow away, be a shadow of a former self

5. cry over spilt milk, close the barn door after the horse is stolen, carry water in a sieve

**Building Vocabulary**
Several Words to Know in this lesson contain prefixes and suffixes. For an in-depth lesson on word parts, see page 856.

| WORDS TO KNOW | | |
|---|---|---|
| indomitable | voluble | |
| omen | withered | |
| unavailing | | |

# Grammar in Context: Adjectives

In "Searching for Summer," Joan Aiken uses adjectives to help convey the impact of an unexpected patch of sunlight in the midst of a gray, desolate world.

> Then it was true, it was not their imagination, that a great dusty golden square of sunshine lay on the fireplace wall, where the brass pendulum of the clock at every swing blinked into sudden brilliance?

You may recall that an **adjective** is a word that modifies a noun or pronoun. Joan Aiken has carefully chosen adjectives that help a reader imagine how extraordinary sunlight is in the world of her story.

**Apply to Your Writing** Choosing adjectives carefully can help you

- create a specific mood or tone
- create vivid images in your readers' minds
- add information about a place or character

*Punctuation Tip:* When you use more than one adjective, you may need to use commas or hyphens.

**WRITING EXERCISE** The sentences below describe the Hatchings's beautiful world. Supply your own adjectives to complete the sentences.

**Example:** _____ ivy curls around a tree behind the house.
Green-and-white-striped ivy curls around a tree behind the house.

1. Sunlight gives a _____ gleam to the clock on the mantle.
2. Tom and Lily take one look at the _____ spare room and decide to stay.
3. The young couple revel in the _____ days and _____ nights.
4. Despite their age and physical problems, Mrs. Hatching and William are _____ people.

**Grammar Handbook**
Adjectives, p. 1188

# Joan Aiken
1924–

**Other Works**
*The Windscreen Weepers and Other
    Tales of Horror and Suspense*
*The Haunting of Lamb House*
*Morningquest*

**In Her Fathers' Footsteps** The daughter of the American poet Conrad Aiken, Joan Aiken grew up in England, where her parents settled before she was born. After her parents divorced, her mother married another writer, Martin Armstrong. "I knew I was going to be a writer," Joan explains, "like Conrad, like Martin, whose books were to be seen around the house."

**A Career Begun** In 1945, Aiken met and married Ronald Brown and also began having her poems and stories published in magazines. Her first book of fiction for young adults, *All You've Ever Wanted and Other Stories,* appeared in 1953. Widowed about two years

later and needing to support her two children, she became an editor for *Argosy* magazine but continued to write in her spare time.

**Literature of the Imagination** Joan Aiken has devoted much of her career to writing richly imaginative literature for children and young adults. These stories create worlds of fantasy, mystery, and humor—"what I would have liked to read as a child," she says. In the 1960s she won critical acclaim for a series of books that present alternative histories of England. *The Wolves of Willoughby Chase* (1962), the first in the series, explores what England might have been like if a different royal family had come to power in the 1700s. The series also includes *Black Hearts in Battersea* (1964) and *Night Birds on Nantucket* (1966). Themes of fantasy, mystery, and history also carry through into Aiken's books for adults. Her novel *Mansfield Revisited* was written as a sequel to Jane Austen's *Mansfield Park*.

# By the Waters of Babylon

*Short Story by* STEPHEN VINCENT BENÉT

**( Connect to Your Life )**

**Through These Doors** Think about events that mark the passage from childhood to adulthood in your own life. Are you considered an adult upon graduating from high school? Are there cultural or religious rituals that mark this important transition? Discuss any rites of passage that you have experienced. How did you change as a result, and what knowledge did you gain?

## Build Background

**Rites of Passage** Most cultures have rites of passage to mark the journey from childhood to adulthood or from one role in life to another. Commonly, the participants in a rite of passage stop their normal activities, separate from their community in some way, and concentrate on gaining new knowledge or insights to prepare for their new roles. When the process is completed, the participants return to society and take up their new role in the community. In the selection you are about to read, John, the main character, goes on a journey that becomes a rite of passage and gives him new knowledge.

**By the Waters of Babylon** The title of this selection is based upon a passage from Psalm 137: "By the waters of Babylon we sat down and wept, when we remembered thee, O Zion." This psalm was composed when Jewish people were enslaved by the Babylonians around 600 B.C. The psalm expresses the Jews' longing for their homeland. Babylon was the largest city of the ancient world, a center of culture, learning, and world trade.

## Focus Your Reading

**LITERARY ANALYSIS** **PLOT** The **plot** is the chain of related events that take place in a story. Usually, the events of a plot progress because of a **conflict**, or struggle between opposing forces. In the following selection, the main character decides to take a journey, though, as this passage indicates, such a journey is against the ancient laws of his people:

> *It is forbidden to cross the great river and look upon the place that was the Place of the Gods. . . . We do not even say its name.*

As you read, pay attention to the conflicts that John must face on his journey and what he learns from them.

**ACTIVE READING** **SEQUENCE** When you read, it helps to pay close attention to the sequence of events. In this story, the main events follow chronological order; that is, the events are arranged in the order of their occurrence. As you read the story, look for signal words and phrases, such as *after a time, then,* and *when,* that mark the order of events.

**READER'S NOTEBOOK** Create a chart like the one started, and as you read keep track of important events in the story. In each box, describe an event and tell what the narrator learns from it.

**Narrator's journey**

| Event: | Event: |
|---|---|
| Narrator learns: | Narrator learns: |

# BY THE WATERS OF BABYLON

## STEPHEN VINCENT BENÉT

*Starburst*, Colin Hay.

The north and the west and the south are good hunting ground, but it is forbidden to go east. It is forbidden to go to any of the Dead Places except to search for metal, and then he who touches the metal must be a priest or the son of a priest. Afterwards, both the man and the metal must be purified. These are the rules and the laws; they are well made. It is forbidden to cross the great river and look upon the place that was the Place of the Gods—this is most strictly forbidden. We do not even say its name, though we know its name. It is there that spirits live, and demons—it is there that there are the ashes of the Great Burning. These things are forbidden—

*Hills* (1914), Man Ray. Oil on canvas, 10⅛″ × 12″, Munson-Williams-Proctor Institute, Museum of Art, Utica, New York, museum purchase.

After that, they gave me the good piece of meat and the warm corner by the fire. My father watched over me—he was glad that I should be a priest. But when I boasted or wept without a reason, he punished me more strictly than my brothers. That was right.

After a time, I myself was allowed to go into the dead houses and search for metal. So I learned the ways of those houses—and if I saw bones, I was no longer afraid. The bones are light and old—sometimes they will fall into dust if you touch them. But that is a great sin.

they have been forbidden since the beginning of time.

My father is a priest; I am the son of a priest. I have been in the Dead Places near us, with my father—at first, I was afraid. When my father went into the house to search for the metal, I stood by the door, and my heart felt small and weak. It was a dead man's house, a spirit house. It did not have the smell of man, though there were old bones in a corner. But it is not fitting that a priest's son should show fear. I looked at the bones in the shadow and kept my voice still.

Then my father came out with the metal—a good, strong piece. He looked at me with both eyes, but I had not run away. He gave me the metal to hold—I took it and did not die. So he knew that I was truly his son and would be a priest in my time. That was when I was very young—nevertheless, my brothers would not have done it, though they are good hunters.

I was taught the chants and the spells—I was taught how to stop the running of blood from a wound and many secrets. A priest must know many secrets—that was what my father said. If the hunters think we do all things by chants and spells, they may believe so—it does not hurt them. I was taught how to read in the old books and how to make the old writings—that was hard and took a long time. My knowledge made me happy—it was like a fire in my heart. Most of all, I liked to hear of the Old Days and the stories of the gods. I asked myself many questions that I could not answer, but it was good to ask them. At night, I would lie awake and listen to the wind—it seemed to me that it was the voice of the gods as they flew through the air.

We are not ignorant like the Forest People—our women spin wool on the wheel; our priests wear a white robe. We do not eat grubs from the tree; we have not forgotten the old writings, although they are hard to understand. Nevertheless, my knowledge and my lack of knowledge burned in me—I wished to know more. When I was a man at last, I came to my father and said, "It is time for me to go on my journey. Give me your leave."

He looked at me for a long time, stroking his beard; then he said at last, "Yes. It is time." That night, in the house of the priesthood, I asked for and received purification. My body hurt, but my spirit was a cool stone. It was my father himself who questioned me about my dreams.

He bade me look into the smoke of the fire and see—I saw and told what I saw. It was what I have always seen—a river, and, beyond it, a great Dead Place and in it the gods walking. I have always thought about that. His eyes were stern when I told him—he was no longer my father but a priest. He said, "This is a strong dream."

"It is mine," I said, while the smoke waved and my head felt light. They were singing the star song in the outer chamber, and it was like the buzzing of bees in my head.

He asked me how the gods were dressed, and I told him how they were dressed. We know how they were dressed from the book, but I saw them as if they were before me. When I had finished, he threw the sticks three times and studied them as they fell.

"This is a very strong dream," he said. "It may eat you up."

"I am not afraid," I said and looked at him with both eyes. My voice sounded thin in my ears, but that was because of the smoke.

He touched me on the breast and the forehead. He gave me the bow and the three arrows.

"Take them," he said. "It is forbidden to travel east. It is forbidden to cross the river. It is forbidden to go to the Place of the Gods. All these things are forbidden."

"All these things are forbidden," I said, but it was my voice that spoke and not my spirit. He looked at me again.

"My son," he said. "Once I had young dreams. If your dreams do not eat you up, you may be a great priest. If they eat you, you are still my son. Now go on your journey."

I went fasting, as is the law. My body hurt but not my heart. When the dawn came, I was out of sight of the village. I prayed and purified myself, waiting for a sign. The sign was an eagle. It flew east.

Sometimes signs are sent by bad spirits. I waited again on the flat rock, fasting, taking no food. I was very still—I could feel the sky above me and the earth beneath. I waited till the sun was beginning to sink. Then three deer passed in the valley, going east—they did not wind me or see me. There was a white fawn with them—a very great sign.

I followed them, at a distance, waiting for what would happen. My heart was troubled about going east, yet I knew that I must go. My head hummed with my fasting—I did not even see the panther spring upon the white fawn. But, before I knew it, the bow was in my hand. I shouted, and the panther lifted his head from the fawn. It is not easy to kill a panther with one arrow, but the arrow went through his eye and into his brain. He died as he tried to spring—he rolled over, tearing at the ground. Then I knew I was meant to go east—I knew that was my journey. When the night came, I made my fire and roasted meat.

"THIS IS A VERY STRONG DREAM," HE SAID. "IT MAY EAT YOU UP."

It is eight suns' journey to the east, and a man passes by many Dead Places. The Forest People are afraid of them, but I am not. Once I made my fire on the edge of a Dead Place at night, and next morning, in the dead house, I found a good knife, little rusted. That was small to what came afterward, but it made my heart feel big. Always when I looked for game, it was in front of my arrow, and twice I passed hunting parties of the Forest People without their knowing. So I knew my magic was strong and my journey clean, in spite of the law.

Toward the setting of the eighth sun, I came to the banks of the great river. It was half a day's journey after I had left the god road—we do not use the god roads now, for they are falling apart into great blocks of stone, and the forest is safer going. A long way off, I had seen the water through trees, but the trees were thick. At last, I came out upon an open place at the top of a cliff. There was the great river below, like a giant in the sun. It is very long, very wide. It could eat all the streams we know and still be thirsty. Its name is Ou-dis-sun, the Sacred, the Long. No man of my tribe had seen it, not even my father, the priest. It was magic, and I prayed.

Then I raised my eyes and looked south. It was there, the Place of the Gods.

How can I tell what it was like—you do not know. It was there, in the red light, and they were too big to be houses. It was there with the red light upon it, mighty and ruined. I knew that in another moment the gods would see me. I covered my eyes with my hands and crept back into the forest.

Surely, that was enough to do, and live. Surely it was enough to spend the night upon the cliff. The Forest People themselves do not come near. Yet, all through the night, I knew that I should have to cross the river and walk in the places of the gods, although the gods ate me up. My magic did not help me at all, and yet there was a fire in my bowels, a fire in my mind. When the sun rose, I thought, "My journey has been clean. Now I will go home from my journey." But, even as I thought so, I knew I could not. If I went to the Place of the Gods, I would surely die, but, if I did not go, I could never be at peace with my spirit again. It is better to lose one's life than one's spirit, if one is a priest and the son of a priest.

Nevertheless, as I made the raft, the tears ran out of my eyes. The Forest People could have killed me without fight, if they had come upon me then, but they did not come. When the raft was made, I said the sayings for the dead and painted myself for death. My heart was cold as a frog and my knees like water, but the burning in my mind would not let me have peace. As I pushed the raft from the shore, I began my death song—I had the right. It was a fine song.

*"I am John, son of John," I sang. "My people are the Hill People.*
*They are the men.*
*I go into the Dead Places, but I am not slain. I take the metal from the Dead Places, but I am not blasted.*
*I travel upon the god roads and am not afraid. E-yah! I have killed the panther; I have killed the fawn!*
*E-yah! I have come to the great river. No man has come there before.*
*It is forbidden to go east, but I have gone, forbidden to go on the great river, but I am there.*
*Open your hearts, you spirits, and hear my song.*
*Now I go to the Place of the Gods; I shall not return.*
*My body is painted for death and my limbs weak, but my heart is big as I go to the Place of the Gods!"*

All the same, when I came to the Place of the Gods, I was afraid, afraid. The current of the great river is very strong—it gripped my raft with its hands. That was magic, for the river itself is wide and calm. I could feel evil spirits about me, in the bright morning; I could feel their breath on my neck as I was swept down the stream. Never have I been so much alone—I tried to think of my knowledge, but it was a squirrel's heap of winter nuts. There was no strength in my knowledge anymore, and I felt small and naked as a new-hatched bird—alone upon the great river, the servant of the gods.

Yet, after a while, my eyes were opened, and I saw. I saw both banks of the river—I saw that once there had been god roads across it, though now they were broken and fallen like broken vines. Very great they were, and wonderful and broken—broken in the time of the Great Burning when the fire fell out of the sky. And always the current took me nearer to the Place of the Gods, and the huge ruins rose before my eyes.

I do not know the customs of rivers—we are the People of the Hills. I tried to guide my raft with the pole, but it spun around. I thought the river meant to take me past the Place of the Gods and out into the Bitter Water of the legends. I grew angry then—my heart felt strong. I said aloud, "I am a priest and the son of a priest!" The gods heard me—they showed me how to paddle with the pole on one side of the raft. The current changed itself—I drew near to the Place of the Gods.

When I was very near, my raft struck and turned over. I can swim in our lakes—I swam to the shore. There was a great spike of rusted metal sticking out into the river—I hauled myself up upon it and sat there, panting. I had saved my bow and two arrows and the knife I found in the Dead Place, but that was all. My raft went whirling downstream toward the Bitter Water. I looked after it, and thought if it

had trod me under, at least I would be safely dead. Nevertheless, when I had dried my bowstring and restrung it, I walked forward to the Place of the Gods.

It felt like ground underfoot; it did not burn me. It is not true what some of the tales say, that the ground there burns forever, for I have been there. Here and there were the marks and stains of the Great Burning, on the ruins, that is true. But they were old marks and old stains. It is not true either, what some of our priests say, that it is an island covered with fogs and enchantments. It is not. It is a great Dead Place—greater than any Dead Place we know. Everywhere in it there are god roads, though most are cracked and broken. Everywhere there are the ruins of the high towers of the gods.

How shall I tell what I saw? I went carefully, my strung bow in my hand, my skin ready for danger. There should have been the wailings of spirits and the shrieks of demons, but there were not. It was very silent and sunny where I had landed—the wind and the rain and the birds that drop seeds had done their work—the grass grew in the cracks of the broken stone. It is a fair island—no wonder the gods built there. If I had come there, a god, I also would have built.

How shall I tell what I saw? The towers are not all broken—here and there one still stands, like a great tree in a forest, and the birds nest high. But the towers themselves look blind, for the gods are gone. I saw a fish hawk, catching fish in the river. I saw a little dance of white butterflies over a great heap of broken stones and columns. I went there and looked about me—there was a carved stone with cut letters,

IT IS NOT TRUE WHAT SOME OF THE TALES SAY . . .

*Toto* (1988), Jimmy Lee Sudduth. Paint with mud on wood, 31¾″ × 24″, from *American Self-Taught*, by Frank Maresca and Roger Ricco, published by Knopf, 1993.

or, perhaps, they used them for sacrifices. There are wild cats that roam the god roads, green-eyed, unafraid of man. At night they wail like demons, but they are not demons. The wild dogs are more dangerous, for they hunt in a pack, but them I did not meet till later. Everywhere there are the carved stones, carved with magical numbers or words.

I went north—I did not try to hide myself. When a god or a demon saw me, then I would die, but meanwhile I was no longer afraid. My hunger for knowledge burned in me—there was so much that I could not understand. After a while, I knew that my belly was hungry. I could have hunted for my meat, but I did not hunt. It is known that the gods did not hunt as we do—they got their food from enchanted boxes and jars. Sometimes these are still found in the Dead Places—once, when I was a child and foolish, I opened such a jar and tasted it and found the food sweet. But my father found out and punished me for it strictly, for, often, that food is death.

broken in half. I can read letters, but I could not understand these. They said UBTREAS. There was also the shattered image of a man or a god. It had been made of white stone, and he wore his hair tied back like a woman's. His name was ASHING, as I read on the cracked half of a stone. I thought it wise to pray to ASHING, though I do not know that god.

How shall I tell what I saw? There was no smell of man left, on stone or metal. Nor were there many trees in that wilderness of stone. There are many pigeons, nesting and dropping in the towers—the gods must have loved them,

Now, though, I had long gone past what was forbidden, and I entered the likeliest towers, looking for the food of the gods.

I found it at last in the ruins of a great temple in the mid-city. A mighty temple it must have been, for the roof was painted like the sky at night with its stars—that much I could see, though the colors were faint and dim. It went down into great caves and tunnels—perhaps they kept their slaves there. But when I started to climb down, I heard the squeaking of rats, so I did not go—rats are unclean, and there must have been many tribes of them, from the squeaking. But near there, I found food, in the heart of a ruin, behind a door that still opened. I ate only the fruits from the jars—they had a very sweet taste. There was drink, too, in bottles of glass—the drink of the gods was strong and made my head swim. After I had eaten and drunk, I slept on the top of a stone, my bow at my side.

When I woke, the sun was low. Looking down from where I lay, I saw a dog sitting on his haunches. His tongue was hanging out of his mouth; he looked as if he were laughing. He was a big dog, with a gray-brown coat, as big as a wolf. I sprang up and shouted at him, but he did not move—he just sat there as if he were laughing. I did not like that. When I reached for a stone to throw, he moved swiftly out of the way of the stone. He was not afraid of me; he looked at me as if I were meat. No doubt I could have killed him with an arrow, but I did not know if there were others. Moreover, night was falling.

I looked about me—not far away there was a great, broken god road, leading north. The towers were high enough, but not so high, and while many of the dead houses were wrecked, there were some that stood. I went toward this god road, keeping to the heights of the ruins, while the dog followed. When I had reached the god road, I saw that there were others behind him. If I had slept later, they would have come upon me asleep and torn out my throat. As it was, they were sure enough of me; they did not hurry. When I went into the dead house, they kept watch at the entrance—doubtless they thought they would have a fine hunt. But a dog cannot open a door, and I knew, from the books, that the gods did not like to live on the ground but on high.

I had just found a door I could open when the dogs decided to rush. Ha! They were surprised when I shut the door in their faces—it was a good door, of strong metal. I could hear their foolish baying beyond it, but I did not stop to answer them. I was in darkness—I found stairs and climbed. There were many stairs, turning around till my head was dizzy. At the top was another door—I found the knob and opened it. I was in a long small chamber—on one side of it was a bronze door that could not be opened, for it had no handle. Perhaps there was a magic word to open it, but I did not have the word. I turned to the door in the opposite side of the wall. The lock of it was broken, and I opened it and went in.

Within, there was a place of great riches. The god who lived there must have been a powerful god. The first room was a small anteroom—I waited there for some time, telling the spirits of the place that I came in peace and not as a robber. When it seemed to me that they had had time to hear me, I went on. Ah, what riches! Few, even, of the windows had been broken—it was all as it had been. The great windows that looked over the city had not been broken at all, though they were dusty and streaked with many years. There were coverings on the floors, the colors not greatly faded, and the chairs were soft and deep. There were pictures upon the walls, very strange, very wonderful—I remember one of a bunch of flowers in a jar—if you came close to it, you could see nothing but bits of color, but if you stood away from it, the flowers might have been picked yesterday. It made my heart feel strange to look at this picture—and to look at the figure of a bird, in some hard clay, on a table and see it so like our birds. Everywhere

prayed and was purified. He touched my lips and my breast; he said, "You went away a boy. You come back a man and a priest." I said, "Father, they were men! I have been in the Place of the Gods and seen it! Now slay me, if it is the law—but still I know they were men."

He looked at me out of both eyes. He said, "The law is not always the same shape—you have done what you have done. I could not have done it my time, but you come after me. Tell!"

I told, and he listened. After that, I wished to tell all the people, but he showed me otherwise. He said, "Truth is a hard deer to hunt. If you eat too much truth at once, you may die of the truth. It was not idly that our fathers forbade the Dead Places." He was right—it is better the truth should come little by little. I have learned that, being a priest. Perhaps, in the old days, they ate knowledge too fast.

Nevertheless, we make a beginning. It is not for the metal alone we go to the Dead Places now—there are the books and the writings. They are hard to learn. And the magic tools are broken—but we can look at them and wonder. At least, we make a beginning. And, when I am chief priest, we shall go beyond the great river. We shall go to the Place of the Gods—the place newyork—not one man but a company. We shall look for the images of the gods and find the god ASHING and the others—the gods Lincoln and Biltmore[1] and Moses.[2] But they were men who built the city, not gods or demons. They were men. I remember the dead man's face. They were men who were here before us. We must build again. ❖

---

1. **Biltmore:** the name of a famous hotel in New York City.

2. **Moses:** Robert Moses (1888–1981), a New York City public official whose name appears on many bridges and other structures built during his administration.

## THERE WILL COME SOFT RAINS
### SARA TEASDALE

There will come soft rains and the
  smell of the ground,
And swallows circling with their
  shimmering sound;

And frogs in the pools singing at
  night,
And wild plum-trees in tremulous
  white;

5   Robins will wear their feathery fire
Whistling their whims on a low
  fence-wire;

And not one will know of the war,
  not one
Will care at last when it is done.

Not one would mind, neither bird
  nor tree
10   If mankind perished utterly;

And Spring herself, when she woke
  at dawn,
Would scarcely know that we were
  gone.

## Connect to the Literature

**1. What Do You Think?** At what point in the story did you begin to figure out what the Place of the Gods was? Explain how you reached your conclusion.

---

**Comprehension Check**
- When and where does the story take place?
- Why does John travel to the Place of the Gods?
- What does John discover when he arrives at his destination?

---

## Think Critically

**2.** **ACTIVE READING** **RECOGNIZING SEQUENCE** Review the chart that you made in your **READER'S NOTEBOOK**, which identified events and what the narrator learned from them. Which events do you think contribute the most to the narrator's coming of age? Explain your reasoning.

**3.** Why do you think it is forbidden for anyone but a priest to visit the Dead Places? Explain your opinion.

**4.** How would you describe John as a **character?**

**THINK ABOUT**
- the way that he uses language
- his determination to finish his journey and complete his rite of passage
- the importance he gives to knowledge
- what he means by "It is better to lose one's life than one's spirit" (page 46)
- his statement "We must build again"

**5.** How does the **title** of this selection add to your understanding of Benét's story?

**6.** What do you think is the **theme,** or message, of the story? Support your ideas with evidence from the story.

## Extend Interpretations

**7. Comparing Texts** How does the world described in the poem "There Will Come Soft Rains" on page 52 compare with the world described in "By the Waters of Babylon"?

**8. Connect to Life** Do you think it is dangerous for a person or a society to have too much knowledge? Support your opinion.

---

## Literary Analysis

**PLOT** The **plot** of a story is the writer's blueprint for what happens, when it happens, and to whom it happens. Typically, most include the following stages:

---

**Exposition** This stage provides groundwork for the plot. Characters are introduced, the setting is described, and conflicts are identified.

**Rising Action** As the story progresses, complications usually arise, causing difficulties for the main characters.

**Climax** This is the turning point of the story, the moment when interest and intensity reach their peak. Usually, an important discovery or decision is made.

**Falling Action** This stage consists of events that occur after the climax. Often, the conflict is resolved.

---

**Paired Activity** With a partner, review the sequence of events that you listed in your **READER'S NOTEBOOK.** Classify the events according to the plot stages described above. Then compare your results with those of your classmates.

---

**POINT OF VIEW** The term **point of view** refers to the kind of narrator used in a literary work. In the **first-person point of view,** the narrator is a character in the story who tells everything in his own words. "By the Waters of Babylon" is told in the first person.

**Activity** Rewrite a key passage from the story using a different point of view. For example, what if the narrator had been John's father or someone outside of the action?

## Writing Options

**1. Journals of the Dead** Compose a series of journal entries that the dead man sitting at the window might have left in his safe, to be found by someone like John.

**2. Debate Dialogue** Imagine that a powerful priest of the Hill People is against John's making public the insights he gained on his journey. Write a dialogue of the debate between John and the priest about whether the people should learn the truth about the gods. Begin by listing the reasons that you think John and the priest would give.

## Activities & Explorations

**1. Journey Map** With a group of classmates, develop a map that shows the territory in which John lives and travels. Be sure to show the sites of important events in John's journey. Add other details to make your map complete.
~ **GEOGRAPHY**

**2. Artifact Collection** Put together a collection of artifacts that John might have brought back from his visit to the Place of the Gods. Present your collection to the class as John might have presented it to the people of his village.
~ **SPEAKING AND LISTENING**

## Inquiry & Research

**1. News Reel** Benét published "By the Waters of Babylon" in 1937. Find out about world events and the general public mood of that time to learn what might have prompted him to write such a story.

Present your findings to the class as a script for a movie newsreel or as a series of news headlines or articles.

**2. Film Study** View the film *The Gods Must Be Crazy,* in which people from a primitive culture make unexpected contact with modern society. Compare and contrast the film and the Benét story.

## Art Connection

Does the painting *Starburst* on page 43 reflect your own image of the Place of the Gods? Explain your answer.

*Starburst,*
Colin Hay.

## Grammar in Context: Pronouns

In the excerpt below, Benét uses pronouns to establish the narrative point of view. A **pronoun** is a word used in place of a noun or another pronoun.

> **He** asked **me** how the gods were dressed, and **I** told **him** how they were dressed. **We** know how they were dressed from the book. . . .

Benét's use of first-person pronouns (*me, I, we*) shows that the story is being told from the point of view of one of the characters. The reader experiences events only through that character's eyes and mind. The use of the pronouns *him* and *they* in place of "my father" and "the gods" makes the writing smoother and more concise. How would the story be different if it were told from a third-person point of view (*"His father* asked *him, . . .* and *he* told *his father . . ."*)?

**WRITING EXERCISE** Rewrite the sentences below, changing first-person pronouns to third-person pronouns. Where appropriate, replace repeated nouns with pronouns.

**Example: *Original*** I go with my father to get metal and hold a piece of the metal.
***Rewritten*** <u>He</u> goes with <u>his</u> father to get metal and holds a piece of <u>it</u>.

1. I dream about walking in the Dead Places and about returning to tell my people all about the Dead Places.
2. I tell my father that I have decided to leave.
3. My father gives me a blessing and wishes me well.
4. I wonder about the buildings—who made the buildings and how the buildings were destroyed.

**Grammar Handbook**
Pronouns, p. 1183

## Stephen Vincent Benét
### 1898–1943

**Other Works**
*The Devil and Daniel Webster*
*Ballads and Poems*
*Selected Works of*
  *Stephen Vincent Benét*

**Born to Books** Stephen Vincent Benét was the most famous member of a writing family that also included his brother William and his sister Laura. Benét was born in Bethlehem, Pennsylvania, and grew up on various army bases in California and in other parts of the country. As a boy he was studious, and his main companions were the books in the family library. A love of poetry came naturally to him because his father often read poetry aloud and would discuss its form and content with his children. Benét studied literature at Yale University and at the Sorbonne in Paris, France. There he met Rosemary Carr, who worked for the Paris edition of the *Chicago Tribune*. Benét and Carr eventually married, and they collaborated on various literary pieces.

**A Proud American** Benét was deeply patriotic, and much of his writing is based on American history and folklore. With his wife, he wrote *A Book of Americans* (1933), a collection of historical sketches for younger readers. He was best known for his poetry and short stories, but he also wrote many other kinds of works, including novels and scripts for radio and film. He even wrote an operetta. Based on Washington Irving's classic tale "The Legend of Sleepy Hollow," it was nationally broadcast on the radio in 1937.

**Versatile Writer** Among Benét's best-known works are the humorous short story "The Devil and Daniel Webster" (1937), for which he received an O. Henry Memorial Prize, and *John Brown's Body* (1928), a long narrative poem about the Civil War, based on information that Benét culled from military records in his father's library. The poem won Benét the first of his two Pulitzer Prizes. The second came for *Western Star* (1943), another long poem about the history of America, which was to have been the first volume in a series. The series remained unfinished at the time of Benét's death.

## Author Activity

A noted historian, Henry Steele Commager, said that Benét "loved his country passionately, gave his life to singing her beauty and glory." Find passages from Benét's *America*, his *We Stand United*, or another work that illustrates how Benét viewed the United States, its people, and its history.

## Meaning Through Context

Do you pause when you come across an unfamiliar word or phrase, or do you continue reading? Doing both might be a good idea—first pausing and thinking about a possible meaning, then reading for clues in the following sentences. Try using this method to figure out the meaning of the highlighted words in the excerpt at the right.

In Vonnegut's vision of the future, smart people must wear radios that interrupt their thoughts, serving as an "equalizing" handicap. This is made clear by the **context** in which *mental handicap radio* occurs—especially by the last sentence of the excerpt, which describes how the handicap works.

> And George, while his intelligence was way above normal, had a little mental handicap radio in his ear.
> . . . It was tuned to a government transmitter. Every twenty seconds or so, the transmitter would send out some sharp noise to keep people like George from taking unfair advantage of their brains.
>
> —Kurt Vonnegut, "Harrison Bergeron"

## Strategies for Building Vocabulary

In the example above, a type of context clue known as a description clue helped you understand an unfamiliar expression. Here are some other types of context clues.

❶ **Comparison and Contrast Clues** Sometimes the idea expressed by an unfamiliar word may be compared or contrasted with the idea expressed by a word that you know. A comparison clue can take the form of a simile (a comparison containing *like* or *as*), as in the sentence "Those summer days stayed in his memory indelibly, like pictures carved in stone." Here, the simile comparing the memories to stone carvings can help you see that *indelibly* means "in a way impossible to erase."

A contrast clue illuminates the meaning of an unfamiliar word by contrasting it with the idea expressed by another word. Words that signal contrasts include *although, but, however, in spite of, yet,* and *in contrast.* How does the contrast with *moved on* clarify the meaning of *mesmerized* in the sentence "He stood momentarily mesmerized by the Dead Place, but the barking dog broke the spell and he moved on"?

❷ **Cause-and-Effect Clues** When the cause of an action is stated by means of an unfamiliar word, a clue to its meaning may be found in the effect. Some words that signal cause-and-effect relationships are *because, since, consequently,* *therefore, when,* and *as a result.* Notice how the words that follow *as a result* clarify the meaning of *boycott* in this sentence: "People began a boycott of the city bus system, and as a result, the buses traveled empty while many people walked to work."

❸ **Inference Clues** Sometimes you can infer the meaning of a word by considering the main idea of the passage in which it occurs. How does the main idea of the following passage allow you to infer the meaning of *consternation:* "There was the shriek of a door being torn from its hinges. Screams and barking cries of consternation came from the television set. The photograph of Harrison Bergeron on the screen jumped again and again, as though dancing to the tune of an earthquake."

**EXERCISE** Define the underlined words in these sentences. In each case, tell what kind of context clue helped you understand the word's meaning.

1. William moved <u>deftly</u> in spite of his blindness.
2. The prisoners <u>cowered</u> before the emperor, expecting to die. He studied them grimly while his soldiers gripped their swords.
3. The pie was as <u>delectable</u> as the mouthwatering creations his mother used to make.
4. Scoring the winning goal filled her with <u>jubilation</u>.
5. The path to the Dead Place was <u>tortuous</u>. It wound through forests and zigzagged through narrow valleys.

# The Thrill of the Grass

## W. P. Kinsella

Like other sports, the game of baseball has changed over the years. A major change occurred in 1965 when the city of Houston built its Astrodome, the first indoor baseball stadium. This stadium featured a nylon, grasslike carpet called AstroTurf® that served as a substitute for natural grass. Over the next few decades, variations of this artificial turf, which is padded and covers an asphalt surface, came to be used in other stadiums. People who support the use of artificial turf note that it holds up well in any weather and requires little maintenance. Critics, however, point out that its hard surface causes injuries and makes the ball bounce in unusual ways. They also regret the loss of natural grass, which they associate with pleasant memories of baseball in years past.

"The Thrill of the Grass" deals with the issue of artificial turf and the strong feelings that it elicits from fans. The story is set during the baseball strike of 1981, when, for 49 days, major-league players refused to play while they awaited a new contract.

AstroTurf® is a registered trademark of Southwest Recreational Industries, Inc.

*Busch Stadium* (1982), Jim Dow. Three-panel panorama from 8″ × 10″ color negatives.

# 1981: the summer the baseball players went on strike. The dull weeks drag by, the summer deepens, the strike is nearly a month old. Outside the city the corn rustles and ripens in the sun.

Summer without baseball: a disruption to the psyche.[1] An unexplainable aimlessness engulfs me. I stay later and later each evening in the small office at the rear of my shop. Now, driving home after work, the worst of the rush hour traffic over, it is the time of the evening I would normally be heading for the stadium.

I enjoy arriving an hour early, parking in a far corner of the lot, walking slowly toward the stadium, rays of sun dropping softly over my shoulders like tangerine ropes, my shadow gliding with me, black as an umbrella. I like to watch young families beside their campers, the mothers in shorts, grilling hamburgers, their men drinking beer. I enjoy seeing little boys dressed in the home team uniform, barely toddling, clutching hotdogs in upraised hands.

I am a failed shortstop. As a young man, I saw myself diving to my left, graceful as a toppling tree, fielding high grounders like a cat leaping for butterflies, bracing my right foot and tossing to first, the throw true as if a steel ribbon connected my hand and the first baseman's glove. I dreamed of leading the American League in hitting—being inducted into the Hall of Fame. I batted .217 in my senior year of high school and averaged 1.3 errors per nine innings.

I know the stadium will be deserted; nevertheless I wheel my car down off the freeway, park, and walk across the silent lot, my footsteps rasping and mournful. Strangle-grass and creeping charlie are already inching up through

---

1. **psyche** (sī'kē): the human spirit or soul.

the gravel, surreptitious, surprised at their own ease. Faded bottle caps, rusted bits of chrome, an occasional paper clip, recede into the earth. I circle a ticket booth, sun-faded, empty, the door closed by an oversized padlock. I walk beside the tall, machinery-green, board fence. A half mile away a few cars hiss along the freeway; overhead a single-engine plane fizzes lazily. The whole place is silent as an empty classroom, like a house suddenly without children.

It is then that I spot the door-shape. I have to check twice to be sure it is there: a door cut in the deep green boards of the fence, more the promise of a door than the real thing, the kind of door, as children, we cut in the sides of cardboard boxes with our mother's paring knives. As I move closer, a golden circle of lock, like an acrimonious[2] eye, establishes its certainty.

I stand, my nose so close to the door I can smell the faint odour of paint, the golden eye of a lock inches from my own eyes. My desire to be inside the ballpark is so great that for the first time in my life I commit a criminal act. I have been a locksmith for over forty years. I take the small tools from the pocket of my jacket, and in less time than it would take a speedy runner to circle the bases I am inside the stadium. Though the ballpark is open-air, it smells of abandonment; the walkways and seating areas are cold as basements. I breathe the odours of rancid popcorn and wilted cardboard.

The maintenance staff were laid off when the strike began. Synthetic grass does not need to be cut or watered. I stare down at the ball

diamond, where just to the right of the pitcher's mound, a single weed, perhaps two inches high, stands defiant in the rain-pocked dirt.

The field sits breathless in the orangy glow of the evening sun. I stare at the potato-coloured earth of the infield, that wide, dun[3] arc, surrounded by plastic grass. As I contemplate the prickly turf, which scorches the thighs and buttocks of a sliding player as if he were being seared by hot steel, it stares back in its uniform ugliness. The seams that send routinely hit ground balls veering at tortuous angles, are vivid, grey as scars.

I remember the ballfields of my childhood, the outfields full of soft hummocks[4] and brown-eyed gopher holes.

I stride down from the stands and walk out to the middle of the field. I touch the stubble that is called grass, take off my shoes, but find it is like walking on a row of toothbrushes. It was an evil day when they stripped the sod from this ballpark, cut it into yard-wide swathes,[5] rolled it, memories and all, into great green-and-black cinnamon-roll shapes, trucked it away. Nature temporarily defeated. But Nature is patient.

Over the next few days an idea forms within me, ripening, swelling, pushing everything else into a corner. It is like knowing a new,

"Baseball is meant to be played on summer evenings and Sunday afternoons, on grass just cut by a horse-drawn mower."

---

2. **acrimonious** (ăk′rə-mō′nē-əs): harsh; bitter.
3. **dun:** brownish gray.
4. **hummocks:** low, rounded hills.
5. **swathes** (swŏths): strips as wide as the blade of a mowing machine.

wonderful joke and not being able to share. I need an accomplice.

I go to see a man I don't know personally, though I have seen his face peering at me from the financial pages of the local newspaper, and the *Wall Street Journal,* and I have been watching his profile at the baseball stadium, two boxes to the right of me, for several years. He is a fan. Really a fan. When the weather is intemperate, or the game not close, the people around us disappear like flowers closing at sunset, but we are always there until the last pitch. I know he is a man who attends because of the beauty and mystery of the game, a man who can sit during the last of the ninth with the game decided innings ago, and draw joy from watching the first baseman adjust the angle of his glove as the pitcher goes into his windup.

He, like me, is a first-base-side fan. I've always watched baseball from behind first base. The positions fans choose at sporting events are like politics, religion, or philosophy: a view of the world, a way of seeing the universe. They make no sense to anyone, have no basis in anything but stubbornness.

I brought up my daughters to watch baseball from the first-base side. One lives in Japan and sends me box scores from Japanese newspapers, and Japanese baseball magazines with pictures of superstars politely bowing to one another. She has a season ticket in Yokohama;[6] on the first-base side.

**"T**ell him a baseball fan is here to see him," is all I will say to his secretary. His office is in a skyscraper, from which he can look out over the city to where the prairie rolls green as mountain water to the limits of the eye. I wait all afternoon in the artificially cool, glassy reception area with its yellow and mauve chairs, chrome and glass coffee tables. Finally, in the late afternoon, my message is passed along.

"I've seen you at the baseball stadium," I say, not introducing myself.

"Yes," he says. "I recognize you. Three rows back, about eight seats to my left. You have a red scorebook and you often bring your daughter . . . "

"Granddaughter. Yes, she goes to sleep in my lap in the late innings, but she knows how to calculate an ERA[7] and she's only in Grade 2."

"One of my greatest regrets," says this tall man, whose moustache and carefully styled hair are polar-bear white, "is that my grandchildren all live over a thousand miles away. You're very lucky. Now, what can I do for you?"

"I have an idea," I say. "One that's been creeping toward me like a first baseman when the bunt sign is on.[8] What do you think about artificial turf?"

"Hmmmf," he snorts, "that's what the strike should be about. Baseball is meant to be played on summer evenings and Sunday afternoons, on grass just cut by a horse-drawn mower," and we smile as our eyes meet.

"I've discovered the ballpark is open, to me anyway," I go on. "There's no one there while the strike is on. The wind blows through the high top of the grandstand, whining until the pigeons in the rafters flutter. It's lonely as a ghost town."

"And what is it you do there, alone with the pigeons?"

"I dream."

"And where do I come in?"

"You've always struck me as a man who dreams. I think we have things in common. I

---

6. **Yokohama** (yō´kə-hä´mə): a large city in Japan.

7. **ERA:** earned run average for a baseball pitcher; that is, the average number of earned runs—runs scored without the aid of an error—a pitcher allows every nine innings.

8. **when the bunt sign is on:** when the coach has signaled the batter to tap at the pitched ball instead of swinging at it.

think you might like to come with me. I could show you what I dream, paint you pictures, suggest what might happen . . . "

He studies me carefully for a moment, like a pitcher trying to decide if he can trust the sign his catcher has just given him.

"Tonight?" he says. "Would tonight be too soon?"

"Park in the northwest corner of the lot about 1:00 A.M. There is a door about fifty yards to the right of the main gate. I'll open it when I hear you."

He nods.

I turn and leave.

The night is clear and cotton warm when he arrives. "Oh, my," he says, staring at the stadium turned chrome-blue by a full moon. "Oh, my," he says again, breathing in the faint odours of baseball, the reminder of fans and players not long gone.

"Let's go down to the field," I say. I am carrying a cardboard pizza box, holding it on the upturned palms of my hands, like an offering.

When we reach the field, he first stands on the mound, makes an awkward attempt at a windup, then does a little sprint from first to about half-way to second. "I think I know what you've brought," he says, gesturing toward the box, "but let me see anyway."

I open the box, in which rests a square foot of sod, the grass smooth and pure, cool as a swatch of satin, fragile as baby's hair.

"Ohhh," the man says, reaching out a finger to test the moistness of it. "Oh, I see."

We walk across the field, the harsh, prickly turf making the bottoms of my feet tingle, to the left-field corner where, in the angle formed by the foul line and the warning track, I lay down the square foot of sod. "That's beautiful," my friend says, kneeling beside me, placing his hand, fingers spread wide, on the verdant[9] square, leaving a print faint as a veronica.[10]

I take from my belt a sickle-shaped blade, the kind used for cutting carpet. I measure along the edge of the sod, dig the point in and pull carefully toward me. There is a ripping sound, like tearing an old bed sheet. I hold up the square of artificial turf like something freshly killed, while all the time digging the sharp point into the packed earth I have exposed. I replace the sod lovingly, covering the newly bared surface.

"A protest," I say.

"But it could be more," the man replies.

"I hoped you'd say that. It could be. If you'd like to come back . . . "

"Tomorrow night?"

"Tomorrow night would be fine. But there will be an admission charge . . . "

"A square of sod?"

"A square of sod two inches thick . . . "

"Of the same grass?"

"Of the same grass. But there's more."

"I suspected as much."

"You must have a friend . . . "

"Who would join us?"

"Yes."

"I have two. Would that be all right?"

"I trust your judgment."

"My father. He's over eighty," my friend says. "You might have seen him with me once or twice. He lives over fifty miles from here, but if I call him, he'll come. And my friend . . . "

"If they pay their admission, they'll be welcome . . . "

"And *they* may have friends . . . "

"Indeed they may. But what will we do with this?" I say, holding up the sticky-backed square of turf, which smells of glue and fabric.

---

9. **verdant** (vŭr′dnt): covered with green growth.

10. **a print faint as a veronica** (və-rŏn′ĭ-kə): a simile referring to the image of Jesus' face supposedly left on the handkerchief offered to him by Saint Veronica for wiping away his blood on the way to the crucifixion.

*Stretching at First* (about 1976), John Dobbs. Oil on canvas, 36″ × 40″, collection of Gilbert Kinney, Washington, D.C.

"We could mail them anonymously to base-ball executives, politicians, clergymen."

"Gentle reminders not to tamper with Nature."

We dance toward the exit, rampant with excitement.

"You will come back? You'll bring others?"

"Count on it," says my friend.

They do come, those trusted friends, and friends of friends, each making a live, green deposit. At first, a tiny row of sod squares begins to inch along toward left-centre field. The next night even more people arrive, the following night more again, and the night after there is positively a crowd. Those who come once seem always to return accompanied by friends, occasionally a son or young brother, but mostly men my age or older, for we are the ones who remember the grass.

Night after night the pilgrimage continues. The first night I stand inside the deep green door, listening. I hear a vehicle stop; hear a car door close with a snug thud. I open the door when the sound of soft-soled shoes on gravel tells me it is time. The door swings silent as a snake. We nod curt greetings to each other. Two men pass me, each carrying a grasshopper-legged sprinkler. Later, each sprinkler will sizzle like frying onions as it wheels, a silver sparkler in the moonlight.

During the nights that follow, I stand sentinel-like at the top of the grandstand, watching as my cohorts arrive. Old men walking across a parking lot in a row, in the dark, carrying coiled hoses, looking like the many wheels of a loco-motive, old men who have slipped away from their homes, skulked down their sturdy side-walks, breathing the cool, grassy, after-midnight air. They have left behind their sleeping, grey-haired women, their immaculate bungalows, their manicured lawns. They continue to walk across the parking lot, while occasionally a soft wheeze, a nibbling, breathy sound like an old horse might make, divulges their humanity.

They move methodically toward the baseball stadium which hulks against the moon-blue sky like a small mountain. Beneath the tint of starlight, the tall light standards which rise above the fences and grandstand glow purple, necks bent forward, like sunflowers heavy with seed.

It is like my compatriots and I are involved in a ritual for true believers only.

My other daughter lives in this city, is married to a fan, but one who watches baseball from behind third base. And like marrying outside the faith, she has been converted to the third-base side. They have their own season tickets, twelve rows up just to the outfield side of third base. I love her, but I don't trust her enough to let her in on my secret.

I could trust my granddaughter, but she is too young. At her age she shouldn't have to face such responsibility. I remember my own daughter, the one who lives in Japan, remember her at nine, all knees, elbows and missing teeth—remember peering in her room, seeing her asleep, a shower of well-thumbed baseball cards scattered over her chest and pillow.

I haven't been able to tell my wife—it is like my compatriots and I are involved in a ritual for true believers only. Maggie, who knew me when I still dreamed of playing professionally myself—

Maggie, after over half a lifetime together, comes and sits in my lap in the comfortable easy chair which has adjusted through the years to my thickening shape, just as she has. I love to hold the lightness of her, her tongue exploring my mouth, gently as a baby's finger

"Where do you go?" she asks sleepily when I crawl into bed at dawn.

I mumble a reply. I know she doesn't sleep well when I'm gone. I can feel her body rhythms change as I slip out of bed after midnight.

"Aren't you too old to be having a change of life," she says, placing her toast-warm hand on my cold thigh.

I am not the only one with this problem.

"I'm developing a reputation," whispers an affable man at the ballpark. "I imagine any number of private investigators following any number of cars across the city. I imagine them creeping about the parking lot, shining pen-lights on licence plates, trying to guess what we're up to. Think of the reports they must prepare. I wonder if our wives are disappointed that we're not out discoing with frizzy-haired teenagers?"

Night after night, virtually no words are spoken. Each man seems to know his assignment. Not all bring sod. Some carry rakes, some hoes, some hoses, which, when joined together, snake across the infield and outfield, dispensing the blessing of water. Others cradle in their arms bags of earth for building up the infield to meet the thick, living sod.

I often remain high in the stadium, looking down on the men moving over the earth, dark as ants, each sodding, cutting, watering, shaping. Occasionally the moon finds a knife blade as it trims the sod or slices away a chunk of artificial turf, and tosses the reflection skyward like a bright ball. My body tingles. There should be symphony music playing. Everyone should be humming "America the Beautiful."

Toward dawn, I watch the men walking away in groups, like small patrols of soldiers, carrying instead of arms, the tools and utensils which breathe life back into the arid ballfield.

Row by row, night by night, we lay the little squares of sod, moist as chocolate cake with green icing. Where did all the sod come from? I picture many men, in many parts of the city, surreptitiously cutting chunks out of their own lawns in the leafy midnight darkness, listening to the uncomprehending protests of their wives the next day—pretending to know nothing of it—pretending to have called the police to investigate.

When the strike is over, I know we will all be here to watch the workouts, to hear the recalcitrant[11] joints crackling like twigs after the forced inactivity. We will sit in our regular seats, scattered like popcorn throughout the stadium, and we'll nod as we pass on the way to the exits, exchange secret smiles, proud as new fathers.

For me, the best part of all will be the surprise. I feel like a magician who has gestured hypnotically and produced an elephant from thin air. I know that I am not alone in my wonder. I know that rockets shoot off in half-a-hundred chests—the excitement of birthday mornings, Christmas eves, and hometown doubleheaders, boils within each of my

---

11. **recalcitrant** (rĭ-kăl′sĭ-trənt): showing stubborn resistance.

conspirators. Our secret rites[12] have been performed with love, like delivering a valentine to a sweetheart's door in that blue-steel span of morning just before dawn.

Players and management are meeting around the clock. A settlement is imminent. I have watched the stadium covered square foot by square foot until it looks like green graph paper. I have stood and felt the cool odours of the grass rise up and touch my face. I have studied the lines between each small square, watched those lines fade until they were visible to my eyes alone, then not even to them.

What will the players think, as they straggle into the stadium and find the miracle we have created? The old-timers will raise their heads like ponies, as far away as the parking lot, when the thrill of the grass reaches their nostrils. And,

as they dress, they'll recall sprawling in the lush fields of childhood, the grass as cool as a mother's hand on a forehead.

"Goodbye, goodbye," we say at the gate, the smell of water, of sod, of sweat, small perfumes in the air. Our secrets are safe with each other. We go our separate ways.

Alone in the stadium in the last chill darkness before dawn, I drop to my hands and knees in the centre of the outfield. My palms are sodden. Water touches the skin between my spread fingers. I lower my face to the silvered grass, which, wonder of wonders, already has the ephemeral[13] odours of baseball about it. ❖

---

12. **rites:** ceremonies.
13. **ephemeral** (ĭ-fĕm′ər-əl): short-lived; passing quickly.

## W. P. Kinsella
### 1935–

**Other Works**
*The Dixon Cornbelt League and
  Other Baseball Stories*
*Box Socials*
*Shoeless Joe*
*The Alligator Report*
*The Iowa Baseball Confederacy*
*The Further Adventures of Slugger
  McBatt*

**Slow Beginnings** Success did not come easily to William Patrick Kinsella. Born in Edmonton, Alberta, Canada, Kinsella says that he always thought of himself as a writer, though he wrote more than 50 stories before getting published. He also worked at various odd jobs, such as running his own pizza restaurant, managing a credit agency, and driving a taxicab. Kinsella did not begin college until he was in his 30s.

**A True Fan** Kinsella grew up loving the game of baseball, though he was a poor player himself. He penned his first baseball story, a murder mystery called "Diamond Doom," when he was in the eighth grade. Kinsella published his first collection of baseball stories, *Shoeless Joe Jackson Comes to Iowa,* in 1980. He expanded the title story into his award-winning novel *Shoeless Joe* (1982), which garnered much attention when it was adapted and produced as the 1989 Hollywood movie *Field of Dreams.*

## Author Activity

**Hollywood's Take** View the film *Field of Dreams,* based on Kinsella's novel *Shoeless Joe.* Then present an oral movie review similar to those provided by television movie critics. In your review, include comparisons with "The Thrill of the Grass."

# Author Study
# Ray Bradbury

*"Here's a teller of tales . . . who wanted to celebrate things . . . even the dark things because they have meaning."*

—*Ray Bradbury, suggesting his own epitaph*

HIS LIFE
HIS TIMES

1920–

## Social Critic for the Future

*A major writer of fantasy and science fiction, Ray Bradbury explores the future, outer space—and the human heart. He has lived to see much science fiction become science fact. Yet Bradbury's work presents very human themes. His most chilling stories comment on the human consequences of progress and often reflect on the ironies of life. Explore the life, work, and passions of a remarkable figure who has been called the world's greatest living science fiction writer.*

SHAPED BY THE FUTURE Ray Bradbury was born in 1920 in Waukegan, Illinois, a town north of Chicago. From an early age, his spongelike mind was directed toward fantasy by the popular culture of his day. He was a fan of movies, radio, comics, museums, traveling circuses, and science fiction magazines. At the age of 12, the Century of Progress exhibit in Chicago captured his interest. However, a more realistic setting—the public library—would also leave permanent impressions on his imagination. Bradbury

| 1920 | 1923 | | 1932 | 1934 |
|---|---|---|---|---|
| **Is born Aug. 22 in Waukegan, Illinois** | **Is "profoundly affected" by film** *Hunchback of Notre Dame* | | **Attempts first lengthy writing** | **Moves with family to Los Angeles** |

**1920**      **1925**      **1930**

| 1920 | 1926 | 1930 |
|---|---|---|
| *New York Times* editorial predicts multistage rockets will never reach the moon. | First liquid-fuel rocket is flown. | The planet Pluto is discovered. |

constantly checked out what he called "all those gorgeous books," many by early science fiction writers such as H. G. Wells and Jules Verne. These writers inspired him to begin writing outer-space adventure stories of his own.

**EDUCATED IN A LIBRARY** In 1934, Bradbury moved with his family to Los Angeles. By age 15, he was sending stories for publication to national magazines, though with no success at first. At this time, most science fiction was viewed as popular but lightweight entertainment.

After finishing high school in 1938, Bradbury sold newspapers on Los Angeles street corners, continuing to write in his spare time. That same year, his first short story was published in a little-known, local magazine. Unpaid but encouraged, he submitted his stories to the well-established *Weird Tales* magazine. He sharpened his storytelling craft, though he had no formal schooling after high school. About his background, Bradbury once said, "I never went to college, so I raised and educated myself in a library."

Reading the fiction of serious writers like John Steinbeck and Ernest Hemingway influenced Bradbury's maturing style. After

selling his first story, "The Pendulum," in 1941, he was ready to take more definite steps toward a profession. At age 22, he quit selling newspapers and began living entirely off his income from writing.

## A SOARING CAREER

From 1942 to 1945, Bradbury sold a story each month to *Weird Tales*. His work was also reaching a wider, more literary audience in such national magazines as *The Saturday Evening Post* and *The New Yorker*. In 1947, he published his first book, *Dark Carnival*, a collection of horror tales. In 1950, *The Martian Chronicles*, his book about Earth colonists on Mars, received critical acclaim. The work reflects what Bradbury has expressed as a basic theme of his writing: "Science ran too far ahead of us too quickly, and the people

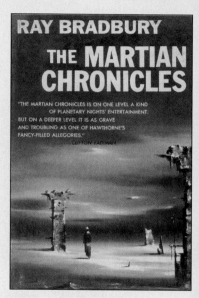

RAY BRADBURY
THE MARTIAN CHRONICLES

"THE MARTIAN CHRONICLES IS ON ONE LEVEL A KIND OF PLANETARY NIGHTS' ENTERTAINMENT. BUT ON A DEEPER LEVEL IT IS AS GRAVE AND TROUBLING AS ONE OF HAWTHORNE'S FANCY-FILLED ALLEGORIES."
—CLIFTON FADIMAN

Bradbury's 1950 book became the basis for a popular 1980 TV miniseries.

---

| 1938 | 1942 | | 1947 | 1950 | 1953 |
|------|------|--|------|------|------|
| Has first story published in amateur magazine | Begins selling stories to *Weird Tales* | | Wins first writing award; has first book published | *The Martian Chronicles* published | Has *Fahrenheit 451* published |

| **1940** | **1945** | **1950** | **1955** |
|------|------|------|------|

| | 1942 | 1945 | 1946 | 1952 | 1957 |
|--|------|------|------|------|------|
| | First fission chain reaction leads to atomic-bomb creation. | U.S. drops atomic bombs on Japan. | First automatic digital electronic computer is developed. | U.S. explodes first hydrogen bomb. | Soviet launch of the satellite *Sputnik* starts space race. |

Sputnik

got lost in a mechanical wilderness." Many readers, themselves surrounded by rapid technological change, agreed with this view.

In 1953, Bradbury published *Fahrenheit 451*, which many consider his most important book. It depicts a future government that controls its people by eliminating mental stimulation. Some critics have compared *Fahrenheit 451* with George Orwell's *1984* and Aldous Huxley's *Brave New World*, novels that warn of controlling trends in society.

Most of the themes of Bradbury's work come out of his childhood. Because of that, he is considered the most autobiographical science fiction writer. He claims to possess an extraordinary memory of the events of his life, including every book he's read and every film he's seen. His attachment to the memory of Waukegan is legendary. Features of his hometown are reworked into the fictional Green Town found in several of his stories.

**"FUN WITH IDEAS"** Ray Bradbury's distinguished career includes other types of writing. His plays, many of them adaptations of his stories, have been staged since 1960. He has written screenplays and television scripts, including 42 he produced for a cable network's *Ray Bradbury Television Theatre* from 1985 to 1990. In addition, he helped design Spaceship Earth for Epcot Center in Disney World and contributed to the design of public spaces in Los Angeles and San Diego.

However, it is writing that remains most important to Bradbury. Since his childhood,

## LITERARY
### *Contributions*

Ray Bradbury's work has been recognized for bringing the literary craft to the field of science fiction. Here are some of Bradbury's more than 500 works.

**Novels**
*Fahrenheit 451* (1953)
*Something Wicked This Way Comes* (1962)
*A Graveyard for Lunatics* (1990)
*Green Shadows, White Whale* (1992)

**Short-Story Collections**
*Dark Carnival* (1947)
*The Martian Chronicles* (1950)
*The Illustrated Man* (1951)
*The Golden Apples of the Sun* (1953)
*The October Country* (1955)
*Dandelion Wine* (1957)
*A Medicine for Melancholy* (1960)
*I Sing the Body Electric* (1969)
*Long After Midnight* (1976)
*The Toynbee Convector* (1988)
*Quicker Than the Eye* (1996)
*Driving Blind* (1997)

**Plays**
*The Wonderful Ice-Cream Suit* (1972)
*Pillar of Fire* (1975)

1963
Is nominated for Academy Award for documentary film script

1965
Has a story in *Fifty Best American Short Stories: 1916–1965*

1971
Moon crater named Dandelion in honor of *Dandelion Wine*

**1960**      **1965**      **1970**      **1975**

1961
Soviet cosmonaut becomes first human in outer space.

1969
Three-stage rocket lands astronauts on the moon; the *Times* retracts its 1920 editorial.

1971
Microchip is invented.

# Author Study: Ray Bradbury

he has written for hours almost daily. Although a leading figure in science fiction writing, Bradbury himself has never driven an automobile and did not fly in an airplane until after he was 70 years old. Yet, he believes that humankind has a "manifest destiny in space"; he is a strong advocate for space flight. (In 1971 the *Apollo 15* crew named a moon crater Dandelion Crater in honor of Bradbury's book *Dandelion Wine*.)

While much of his writing reveals someone wrestling with problems that affect human existence, Bradbury tries not to weigh down his work. "I write for fun," he has said. "You can't get too serious. I don't pontificate [express opinions] in my work. I have fun with ideas."

**More Online: Author Link**
www.mcdougallittell.com

## Bradbury on Screen

Ray Bradbury's first connection to Hollywood came in 1952, when he wrote the screenplay for his short story "The Fog Horn." This resulted in the 1953 monster film *The Beast from 20,000 Fathoms*. Soon after, Bradbury developed the concept for a film that came to be known as *It Came from Outer Space*. To experience the three-dimensional special effects of the film, viewers wore specially tinted glasses like those shown here. In 1966, French filmmaker François Truffaut filmed Bradbury's novel *Fahrenheit 451*.

**Poster for movie version of *Fahrenheit 451*, 1966**

***It Came from Outer Space*, 1953**

**3-D glasses enabled 1950s moviegoers to experience "realistic" special effects.**

---

**1977**
Receives Life Achievement Award at World Fantasy Convention

**1989**
Receives Grand Master Award from Science Fiction Writers of America

Bradbury in Waukegan

**1996**
Returns to Waukegan Public Library to publicize latest book

## 1980      1985      1990      1995

**1976**
Two U.S. *Viking* spacecraft land on Mars to search for life.

**1981**
First manned space shuttle orbits Earth for 54 hours.

**1983**
*Pioneer 10* becomes first spacecraft to leave the solar system.

**1990**
Hubble Space Telescope is launched.

**1997**
Martian probe *Sojourner* transmits startling images to Earth.

**1998**
The Hubble finds a planet outside our solar system.

# PREPARING to *Read*

# A Sound of Thunder

*Short Story by* RAY BRADBURY

## Connect to Your Life

**Time Travel** If traveling through time were possible, what era would you most like to visit? Would you want to travel back to the past or ahead into the future? Would you want to travel just a few dozen years, or would you travel hundreds, a thousand, or even more years? Share your thoughts in a class discussion.

## Build Background

**The Fourth Dimension** Time travel has been a popular idea in science fiction ever since the British author H. G. Wells wrote his short novel *The Time Machine* in 1895. In his novel, Wells suggested that in addition to the three dimensions of length, height, and width, there was a fourth dimension of duration, or time. Wells speculated that if a machine could be invented to move along the fourth dimension, travel backward and forward in time would be possible.

Science fiction writers since Wells's time have continued to use time travel as a basis for many adventures. Films such as *Back to the Future* popularized the notion of time travel. The story that follows is set in the future, yet the characters travel back into the distant past.

WORDS TO KNOW
**Vocabulary Preview**

| | |
|---|---|
| annihilate | revoke |
| expendable | sheathed |
| infinitesimally | subliminal |
| primeval | taint |
| resilient | undulate |

## Focus Your Reading

**LITERARY ANALYSIS**  **FORESHADOWING**  Bradbury uses **foreshadowing** to prepare a reader for events and plot twists that will occur later in a story. This technique creates **suspense**—excitement or tension—and prepares the reader for what is to come. Often, a reader can pick up on foreshadowing just by knowing how stories work. Sometimes foreshadowing is apparent when a character makes an unusual statement or issues a strong warning. For example, in Bradbury's story a man named Travis, a guide on a dinosaur hunt, has this exchange with another character:

> *"So be careful. Stay on the Path. Never step off!"*
> *"I see," said Eckels.*

Watch for other examples of foreshadowing as you read Bradbury's story.

**ACTIVE READING**  **PREDICTING**  **Prediction** involves using text clues to make a reasonable guess about what will happen in a story. Sometimes your predictions will miss the mark. Other times, you'll recognize foreshadowing or other clues in a story and be able to make accurate predictions. Reread the exchange in the Literary Analysis section. What clue could help you predict what will happen later?

📖 **READER'S NOTEBOOK** As you read, create a chart like this one to record your predictions together with the clues on which you based them.

| What Will Happen Next? | |
|---|---|
| Text Clues | Predictions |
| | |

# A Sound of Thunder

### RAY BRADBURY

The sign on the wall seemed to quaver under a film of sliding warm water. Eckels felt his eyelids blink over his stare, and the sign burned in this momentary darkness:

> TIME SAFARI, INC.
>
> SAFARIS TO ANY YEAR IN THE PAST.
>
> YOU NAME THE ANIMAL.
>
> WE TAKE YOU THERE.
>
> YOU SHOOT IT.

A warm phlegm gathered in Eckels's throat; he swallowed and pushed it down. The muscles around his mouth formed a smile as he put his hand slowly out upon the air, and in that hand waved a check for ten thousand dollars to the man behind the desk.

"Does this safari guarantee I come back alive?"

"We guarantee nothing," said the official, "except the dinosaurs." He turned. "This is Mr. Travis, your Safari Guide in the Past. He'll tell you what and where to shoot. If he says no shooting, no shooting. If you disobey instructions, there's a stiff penalty of another ten thousand dollars, plus possible government action, on your return."

Eckels glanced across the vast office at a mass and tangle, a snaking and humming of wires and steel boxes, at an aurora[1] that flickered now orange, now silver, now blue. There was a sound like a gigantic bonfire burning all of Time, all the years and all the parchment calendars, all the hours piled high and set aflame.

A touch of the hand and this burning would, on the instant, beautifully reverse itself. Eckels remembered the wording in the advertisements to the letter. Out of chars and ashes, out of dust and coals, like golden salamanders, the old years, the green years, might leap; roses sweeten the air, white hair turn Irish-black, wrinkles vanish; all, everything fly back to seed, flee death, rush down to their beginnings, suns rise in western skies and set in glorious easts, moons eat themselves opposite to the custom, all and everything cupping one in another like Chinese boxes,[2] rabbits into hats, all and everything returning to the fresh death, the seed death, the green death, to the time before the beginning. A

---

1. **aurora:** a light that changes colors.
2. **Chinese boxes:** a series of boxes, each of which fits neatly inside the next larger one.

touch of a hand might do it, the merest touch of a hand.

"Unbelievable." Eckels breathed, the light of the Machine on his thin face. "A real Time Machine." He shook his head. "Makes you think. If the election had gone badly yesterday, I might be here now running away from the results. Thank God Keith won. He'll make a fine President of the United States."

"Yes," said the man behind the desk. "We're lucky. If Deutscher had gotten in, we'd have the worst kind of dictatorship. There's an anti-everything man for you, a militarist, anti-Christ, anti-human, anti-intellectual. People called us up, you know, joking but not joking. Said if Deutscher became President they wanted to go live in 1492. Of course it's not our business to conduct Escapes, but to form Safaris. Anyway, Keith's President now. All you got to worry about is—"

"Shooting my dinosaur," Eckels finished it for him.

"A *Tyrannosaurus rex*. The Tyrant Lizard, the most incredible monster in history. Sign this release. Anything happens to you, we're not responsible. Those dinosaurs are hungry."

Eckels flushed angrily. "Trying to scare me!"

"Frankly, yes. We don't want anyone going who'll panic at the first shot. Six Safari leaders were killed last year, and a dozen hunters. We're here to give you the severest thrill a *real* hunter ever asked for. Traveling you back sixty million years to bag the biggest game in all of Time. Your personal check's still there. Tear it up."

Mr. Eckels looked at the check. His fingers twitched.

"Good luck," said the man behind the desk. "Mr. Travis, he's all yours."

They moved silently across the room, taking their guns with them, toward the Machine, toward the silver metal and the roaring light.

First a day and then a night and then a day and then a night, then it was day-night-day-night-day. A week, a month, a year, a decade! A.D. 2055. A.D. 2019. 1999! 1957! Gone! The Machine roared.

They put on their oxygen helmets and tested the intercoms.

Eckels swayed on the padded seat, his face pale, his jaw stiff. He felt the trembling in his arms, and he looked down and found his hands tight on the new rifle. There were four other men in the Machine. Travis, the Safari Leader; his assistant, Lesperance; and two other hunters, Billings and Kramer. They sat looking at each other, and the years blazed around them.

"Can these guns get a dinosaur cold?" Eckels felt his mouth saying.

"If you hit them right," said Travis on the helmet radio. "Some dinosaurs have two brains, one in the head, another far down the spinal column. We stay away from those. That's stretching luck. Put your first two shots into the eyes, if you can, blind them, and go back into the brain."

The Machine howled. Time was a film run backward. Suns fled, and ten million moons fled after them. "Think," said Eckels. "Every hunter that ever lived would envy us today. This makes Africa seem like Illinois."

The Machine slowed; its scream fell to a murmur. The Machine stopped.

The sun stopped in the sky.

The fog that had enveloped the Machine blew away, and they were in an old time, a very old time indeed, three hunters and two Safari Heads with their blue metal guns across their knees.

"Christ isn't born yet," said Travis. "Moses has not gone to the mountain to talk with God. The Pyramids are still in the earth, waiting to be cut out and put up. *Remember* that. Alexander, Caesar, Napoleon, Hitler—none of them exists."

The man nodded.

"That"—Mr. Travis pointed—"is the jungle of sixty million two thousand and fifty-five years before President Keith."

He indicated a metal path that struck off into green wilderness, over streaming swamp, among giant ferns and palms.

"And that," he said, "is the Path, laid by Time Safari for your use. It floats six inches above the earth. Doesn't touch so much as one grass blade, flower, or tree. It's an antigravity metal. Its purpose is to keep you from touching this world of the past in any way. Stay on the Path. Don't go off it. I repeat. *Don't go off.* For *any* reason! If you fall off, there's a penalty. And don't shoot any animal we don't okay."

"Why?" asked Eckels.

*"Unbelievable." Eckels breathed, the light of the Machine on his thin face. "A real Time Machine."*

They sat in the ancient wilderness. Far birds' cries blew on a wind, and the smell of tar and an old salt sea, moist grasses, and flowers the color of blood.

"We don't want to change the Future. We don't belong here in the Past. The government doesn't *like* us here. We have to pay big graft to keep our franchise.[3] A Time Machine is finicky business. Not knowing it, we might kill an important animal, a small bird, a roach, a flower even, thus destroying an important link in a growing species."

"That's not clear," said Eckels.

"All right," Travis continued, "say we accidentally kill one mouse here. That means all the future families of this one particular mouse are destroyed, right?"

"Right."

"And all the families of the families of the families of that one mouse! With a stamp of your foot, you <u>annihilate</u> first one, then a dozen, then a thousand, a million, a *billion* possible mice!"

"So they're dead," said Eckels. "So what?"

"So what?" Travis snorted quietly. "Well, what about the foxes that'll need those mice to survive? For want of ten mice, a fox dies. For want of ten foxes, a lion starves. For want of a lion, all manner of insects, vultures, infinite billions of life forms are thrown into chaos and destruction. Eventually it all boils down to this: fifty-nine million years later, a caveman, one of a dozen on the *entire world,* goes hunting wild boar or saber-toothed tiger for food. But you, friend, have *stepped* on all the tigers in that region. By stepping on *one* single mouse. So the caveman starves. And the caveman, please note, is not just *any* <u>expendable</u> man, no! He is an *entire future nation.* From his loins would have sprung ten sons. From *their* loins one hundred sons, and thus onward to a civilization. Destroy this one man, and you destroy a race, a people, an entire history of life. It is comparable to slaying some of Adam's grandchildren. The

---

3. **graft to keep our franchise:** money paid as a bribe to officials in return for their approval of the business.

stomp of your foot, on one mouse, could start an earthquake, the effects of which could shake our earth and destinies down through Time, to their very foundations. With the death of that one caveman, a billion others yet unborn are throttled in the womb. Perhaps Rome never rises on its seven hills. Perhaps Europe is forever a dark forest, and only Asia waxes healthy and teeming. Step on a mouse, and you crush the Pyramids. Step on a mouse, and you leave your print, like a Grand Canyon, across Eternity. Queen Elizabeth might never be born; Washington might not cross the Delaware; there might never be a United States at all. So be careful. Stay on the Path. *Never* step off!"

"I see," said Eckels. "Then it wouldn't pay for us even to touch the *grass?*"

"Correct. Crushing certain plants could add up <u>infinitesimally</u>. A little error here would multiply in sixty million years, all out of proportion. Of course maybe our theory is wrong. Maybe Time *can't* be changed by us. Or maybe it can be changed only in little subtle ways. A dead mouse here makes an insect imbalance there, a population disproportion later, a bad harvest further on, a depression, mass starvation, and, finally, a change in *social* temperament in far-flung countries. Something much more subtle, like that. Perhaps only a soft breath, a whisper, a hair, pollen on the air, such a slight, slight change that unless you looked close you wouldn't see it. Who knows? Who really can say he knows? We don't know. We're guessing. But until we do know for certain whether our messing around in Time *can* make a big roar or a little rustle in history, we're being careful. This Machine, this Path, your clothing and bodies, were sterilized, as you know, before the journey. We wear these oxygen helmets so we can't introduce our bacteria into an ancient atmosphere."

"How do we know which animals to shoot?"

"They're marked with red paint," said Travis. "Today, before our journey, we sent Lesperance here back with the Machine. He came to this particular era and followed certain animals."

"Studying them?"

"Right," said Lesperance. "I track them through their entire existence, noting which of them lives longest. Very few. How many times they mate. Not often. Life's short. When I find one that's going to die when a tree falls on him, or one that drowns in a tar pit, I note the exact hour, minute, and second. I shoot a paint bomb. It leaves a red patch on his side. We can't miss it. Then I correlate our arrival in the Past so that we meet the Monster not more than two minutes before he would have died anyway. This way, we kill only animals with no future, that are never going to mate again. You see how *careful* we are?"

"But if you came back this morning in Time," said Eckels eagerly, "you must've bumped into *us,* our Safari! How did it turn out? Was it successful? Did all of us get through—alive?"

Travis and Lesperance gave each other a look.

"That'd be a paradox," said the latter. "Time doesn't permit that sort of mess—a man meeting himself. When such occasions threaten, Time steps aside. Like an airplane hitting an air pocket. You felt the Machine jump just before we stopped? That was us passing ourselves on the way back to the Future. We saw nothing. There's no way of telling *if* this expedition was a success, *if we* got our monster, or whether all of us—meaning *you,* Mr. Eckels—got out alive."

Eckels smiled palely.

"Cut that," said Travis sharply. "Everyone on his feet!"

They were ready to leave the Machine.

The jungle was high and the jungle was broad

---

WORDS TO KNOW    **infinitesimally** (ĭn′fĭn-ĭ-tĕs′ə-mə-lē) *adv.* in steps so small as to be immeasurable or incalculable

and the jungle was the entire world forever and forever. Sounds like music and sounds like flying tents filled the sky, and those were pterodactyls[4] soaring with cavernous gray wings, gigantic bats of delirium and night fever.[5] Eckels, balanced on the narrow Path, aimed his rifle playfully.

"Stop that!" said Travis. "Don't even aim for fun, blast you! If your guns should go off—"

Eckels flushed. "Where's our *Tyrannosaurus?*"

Lesperance checked his wristwatch. "Up ahead. We'll bisect his trail in sixty seconds. Look for the red paint! Don't shoot till we give the word. Stay on the Path. *Stay on the Path!*"

They moved forward in the wind of morning.

"Strange," murmured Eckels. "Up ahead, sixty million years, Election Day over. Keith made President. Everyone celebrating. And here we are, a million years lost, and they don't exist. The things we worried about for months, a lifetime, not even born or thought of yet."

"Safety catches off, everyone!" ordered Travis. "You, first shot, Eckels. Second, Billings. Third, Kramer."

"I've hunted tiger, wild boar, buffalo, elephant, but now, this is *it*," said Eckels. "I'm shaking like a kid."

"Ah," said Travis.

Everyone stopped.

Travis raised his hand. "Ahead," he whispered. "In the mist. There he is. There's His Royal Majesty now."

The jungle was wide and full of twitterings,

Illustration copyright © Douglas Henderson. From *The Complete T-Rex* by John Horner and Don Lessem, published by Simon & Schuster.

rustlings, murmurs, and sighs.

Suddenly it all ceased, as if someone had shut a door.

Silence.

A sound of thunder.

Out of the mist, one hundred yards away, came *Tyrannosaurus rex*.

---

4. **pterodactyls** (tĕr´ə-dăk´təlz): extinct flying reptiles having a wingspan of up to 40 feet.

5. **bats . . . fever:** the sort of bats that appear in nightmares and visions caused by drugs or illness.

a terrible warrior. Each thigh was a ton of meat, ivory, and steel mesh. And from the great breathing cage of the upper body those two delicate arms dangled out front, arms with hands which might pick up and examine men like toys, while the snake neck coiled. And the head itself, a ton of sculptured stone, lifted easily upon the sky. Its mouth gaped, exposing a fence of teeth like daggers. Its eyes rolled, ostrich eggs, empty of all expression save hunger. It closed its mouth in a death grin. It ran, its pelvic bones crushing aside trees and bushes, its taloned feet clawing damp earth, leaving prints six inches deep wherever it settled its weight. It ran with a gliding ballet step, far too poised and balanced for its ten tons. It moved into a sunlit arena warily, its beautifully reptilian hands feeling the air.

"Why, why," Eckels twitched his mouth. "It could reach up and grab the moon."

"Sh!" Travis jerked angrily. "He hasn't seen us yet."

"It," whispered Eckels. "It . . ."

"Sh!"

It came on great oiled, <u>resilient</u>, striding legs. It towered thirty feet above half of the trees, a great evil god, folding its delicate watchmaker's claws close to its oily reptilian chest. Each lower leg was a piston, a thousand pounds of white bone, sunk in thick ropes of muscle, <u>sheathed</u> over in a gleam of pebbled skin like the mail of

"It can't be killed." Eckels pronounced this verdict quietly, as if there could be no argument. He had weighed the evidence, and this was his considered opinion. The rifle in his hands seemed a cap gun. "We were fools to come. This is impossible."

"Shut up!" hissed Travis.

"Nightmare."

"Turn around," commanded Travis. "Walk

WORDS   **resilient** (rĭ-zĭl′yənt) *adj.* capable of bouncing or springing back to an original
TO      shape after being stretched, bent, or compressed
KNOW    **sheathed** (shē*th*d) *adj.* enclosed in a protective covering  **sheathe** *v.*

quietly to the Machine. We'll remit one-half your fee."

"I didn't realize it would be this *big*," said Eckels. "I miscalculated, that's all. And now I want out."

"It *sees* us!"

"There's the red paint on its chest!"

The Tyrant Lizard raised itself. Its armored flesh glittered like a thousand green coins. The coins, crusted with slime, steamed. In the slime, tiny insects wriggled, so that the entire body seemed to twitch and <u>undulate</u>, even while the monster itself did not move. It exhaled. The stink of raw flesh blew down the wilderness.

"Get me out of here," said Eckels. "It was never like this before. I was always sure I'd come through alive. I had good guides, good safaris, and safety. This time, I figured wrong. I've met my match and admit it. This is too much for me to get hold of."

"Don't run," said Lesperance. "Turn around. Hide in the Machine."

"Yes." Eckels seemed to be numb. He looked at his feet as if trying to make them move. He gave a grunt of helplessness.

"Eckels!"

He took a few steps, blinking, shuffling.

"Not *that* way!"

The Monster, at the first motion, lunged forward with a terrible scream. It covered one hundred yards in six seconds. The rifles jerked up and blazed fire. A windstorm from the beast's mouth engulfed them in the stench of slime and old blood. The Monster roared, teeth glittering with sun.

Copyright © 1996 Glenn Dean.

Eckels, not looking back, walked blindly to the edge of the Path, his gun limp in his arms, stepped off the Path, and walked, not knowing it, in the jungle. His feet sank into green moss. His legs moved him, and he felt alone and remote from the events behind.

The rifles cracked again. Their sound was lost in shriek and lizard thunder. The great level of the reptile's tail swung up, lashed sideways. Trees exploded in clouds of leaf and branch. The Monster twitched its jeweler's hands down to fondle at the men, to twist them in half, to crush them like berries, to cram them into its teeth and its screaming throat. Its boulder-stone eyes leveled with the men. They saw themselves mirrored. They fired at the metallic eyelids and the blazing black iris.

Like a stone idol, like a mountain avalanche, *Tyrannosaurus* fell. Thundering, it clutched trees, pulled them with it. It wrenched and tore the metal Path. The men flung themselves back and away. The body hit, ten tons of cold flesh and stone. The guns fired. The Monster lashed its armored tail, twitched its snake jaws, and lay still. A fount of blood spurted from its throat. Somewhere inside, a sac of fluids burst. Sickening gushes drenched the hunters. They stood, red and glistening.

The thunder faded.

The jungle was silent. After the avalanche, a green peace. After the nightmare, morning.

Billings and Kramer sat on the pathway and threw up. Travis and Lesperance stood with smoking rifles, cursing steadily.

In the Time Machine, on his face, Eckels lay shivering. He had found his way back to the Path, climbed into the Machine.

Travis came walking, glanced at Eckels, took cotton gauze from a metal box, and returned to the others, who were sitting on the Path.

"Clean up."

They wiped the blood from their helmets. They began to curse too. The Monster lay, a hill of solid flesh. Within, you could hear the sighs and murmurs as the furthest chambers of it died, the organs malfunctioning, liquids running a final instant from pocket to sac to spleen, everything shutting off, closing up forever. It was like standing by a wrecked locomotive or a steam shovel at quitting time, all valves being released or levered tight. Bones cracked; the tonnage of its own flesh, off balance, dead weight, snapped the delicate

forearms, caught underneath. The meat settled, quivering.

Another cracking sound. Overhead, a gigantic tree branch broke from its heavy mooring, fell. It crashed upon the dead beast with finality.

"There." Lesperance checked his watch. "Right on time. That's the giant tree that was scheduled to fall and kill this animal originally." He glanced at the two hunters. "You want the trophy picture?"

"What?"

## In the Time Machine, on his face, Eckels lay shivering.

"We can't take a trophy back to the Future. The body has to stay right here where it would have died originally, so the insects, birds, and bacteria can get at it, as they were intended to. Everything in balance. The body stays. But we *can* take a picture of you standing near it."

The two men tried to think, but gave up, shaking their heads.

They let themselves be led along the metal Path. They sank wearily into the Machine cushions. They gazed back at the ruined Monster, the stagnating mound, where already strange reptilian birds and golden insects were busy at the steaming armor.

A sound on the floor of the Time Machine stiffened them. Eckels sat there, shivering.

"I'm sorry," he said at last.

"Get up!" cried Travis.

Eckels got up.

"Go out on that Path alone," said Travis. He had his rifle pointed. "You're not coming back in the Machine. We're leaving you here!"

Lesperance seized Travis's arm. "Wait—"

"Stay out of this!" Travis shook his hand away. "This fool nearly killed us. But it isn't *that* so much, no. It's his *shoe*s! Look at them! He ran off the Path. That *ruins* us! We'll forfeit! Thousands of dollars of insurance! We guarantee no one leaves the Path. He left it. Oh, the fool! I'll have to report to the government. They might <u>revoke</u> our license to travel. Who knows *what* he's done to Time, to History!"

"Take it easy; all he did was kick up some dirt."

"How do we *know?*" cried Travis. "We don't know anything! It's all a mystery! Get out there, Eckels!"

Eckels fumbled his shirt. "I'll pay anything. A hundred thousand dollars!"

Travis glared at Eckels's checkbook and spat. "Go out there. The Monster's next to the Path. Stick your arms up to your elbows in his mouth. Then you can come back with us."

"That's unreasonable!"

"The Monster's dead, you idiot. The bullets! The bullets can't be left behind. They don't belong in the Past; they might change anything. Here's my knife. Dig them out!"

The jungle was alive again, full of the old tremorings and bird cries. Eckels turned slowly to regard the <u>primeval</u> garbage dump, that hill of nightmares and terror. After a long time, like a sleepwalker he shuffled out along the Path.

He returned, shuddering, five minutes later, his arms soaked and red to the elbows. He held out his hands. Each held a number of steel bullets. Then he fell. He lay where he fell, not moving.

"You didn't have to make him do that," said Lesperance.

"Didn't I? It's too early to tell." Travis nudged the still body. "He'll live. Next time he won't go hunting game like this. Okay." He jerked his thumb wearily at Lesperance. "Switch on. Let's go home."

1492. 1776. 1812.

They cleaned their hands and faces. They changed their caking shirts and pants. Eckels was up and around again, not speaking. Travis glared at him for a full ten minutes.

"Don't look at me," cried Eckels. "I haven't done anything."

"Who can tell?"

"Just ran off the Path, that's all, a little mud on my shoes—what do you want me to do—get down and pray?"

"We might need it. I'm warning you, Eckels, I might kill you yet. I've got my gun ready."

"I'm innocent. I've done nothing!"

1999. 2000. 2055.

The Machine stopped.

"Get out," said Travis.

The room was there as they had left it. But not the same as they had left it. The same man sat behind the same desk. But the same man did not quite sit behind the same desk.

Travis looked around swiftly. "Everything okay here?" he snapped.

"Fine. Welcome home!"

Travis did not relax. He seemed to be looking at the very atoms of the air itself, at the way the sun poured through the one high window.

"Okay, Eckels, get out. Don't ever come back."

Eckels could not move.

"You heard me," said Travis. "What're you *staring* at?"

Eckels stood smelling of the air, and there was a thing to the air, a chemical <u>taint</u> so subtle, so slight, that only a faint cry of his

WORDS TO KNOW
**revoke** (rĭ-vōk′) *v.* to cancel or withdraw
**primeval** (prī-mē′vəl) *adj.* belonging to the earliest times or ages
**taint** (tānt) *n.* a trace of something that harms, spoils, or corrupts

subliminal senses warned him it was there. The colors, white, gray, blue, orange, in the wall, in the furniture, in the sky beyond the window, were . . . were . . . And there was a *feel*. His flesh twitched. His hands twitched. He stood drinking the oddness with the pores of his body. Somewhere, someone must have been screaming one of those whistles that only a dog can hear. His body screamed silence in return. Beyond this room, beyond this wall, beyond this man who was not quite the same man seated at this desk that was not quite the same desk . . . lay an entire world of streets and people. What sort of world it was now, there was no telling. He could feel them moving there, beyond the walls, almost, like so many chess pieces blown in a dry wind. . . .

But the immediate thing was the sign painted on the office wall, the same sign he had read earlier today on first entering.

Somehow, the sign had changed:

TYME SEFARI INC.
SEFARIS TU ANY YEER EN THE PAST.
YU NAIM THE ANIMALL.
WEE TAEKYUTHAIR.
YU SHOOT ITT.

Eckels felt himself fall into a chair. He fumbled crazily at the thick slime on his boots. He held up a clod of dirt, trembling, "No, it *can't* be. Not a *little* thing like that. No!"

Embedded in the mud, glistening green and gold and black, was a butterfly, very beautiful and very dead.

"Not a little thing like *that!* Not a butterfly!" cried Eckels.

It fell to the floor, an exquisite thing, a small thing that could upset balances and knock down a line of small dominoes and then big dominoes and then gigantic dominoes, all down the years across Time. Eckels's mind whirled. It *couldn't* change things. Killing one butterfly

couldn't be *that* important! Could it?

His face was cold. His mouth trembled, asking: "Who—who won the presidential election yesterday?"

The man behind the desk laughed. "You joking? You know very well. Deutscher, of course! Who else? Not that fool weakling Keith. We got an iron man now, a man with guts!" The official stopped. "What's wrong?"

Eckels moaned. He dropped to his knees. He scrabbled at the golden butterfly with shaking fingers. "Can't we," he pleaded to the world, to himself, to the officials, to the Machine, "can't we take it *back*; can't we *make* it alive again? Can't we start over? Can't we—"

He did not move. Eyes shut, he waited, shivering. He heard Travis breathe loud in the room; he heard Travis shift his rifle, click the safety catch, and raise the weapon.

There was a sound of thunder. ❖

WORDS TO KNOW    **subliminal** (sŭb-lĭm′ə-nəl) *adj.* below the threshold of conscious perception; subconscious

## Connect to the Literature

**1. What Do You Think?** What was your reaction to the "sound of thunder" at the end of the story?

> **Comprehension Check**
> • What kind of business does Time Safari, Inc. operate?
> • What does Eckels do that has such far-reaching consequences?
> • What is different when Eckels returns to his own time?

## Think Critically

**2.** How would you describe Eckels?

> **THINK ABOUT**
> • his reasons for going on a safari
> • his response to the tyrannosaurus
> • his attitude about stepping off the path

**3.** How would you characterize the business practices of Time Safari, Inc.?

**4.** **ACTIVE READING** **PREDICTING** How accurate were the **predictions** you made in your **READER'S NOTEBOOK**? Discuss with classmates the details that either helped or misled you.

**5.** In your opinion, what **theme,** or message, is Bradbury conveying through the story?

> **THINK ABOUT**
> • the society Eckels returns to as compared with the society depicted at the beginning of the story
> • the significance of the butterfly

## Extend Interpretations

**6. Critic's Corner** In a review of *Dinosaur Tales,* the collection of Bradbury stories that contains "A Sound of Thunder," the critic Andrew Andrews remarks that Bradbury "gets to you—in simple ways he shows you how to marvel over these awesome, startling creatures." What was your reaction to Bradbury's portrayal of the dinosaurs in the story?

**7. Connect to Life** Recall the ideas you discussed about time travel before you read the story. Why do you think time travel has become such a popular topic of stories and movies?

## Literary Analysis

**FORESHADOWING** **Fore-shadowing** is a device a writer uses to prepare a reader for an event that happens later in the story. The use of foreshadowing also adds suspense. Foreshadowing takes the form of hints—bits of information that suggest to the reader what is coming. Writers provide foreshadowing by creating a **mood** that prepares a reader emotionally for what is to come, by including facts and details that provide clues, by revealing **character traits** that determine future action, or by describing events that suggest what might happen later.

**Paired Activity** Now that you know the outcome of the story, review it with a partner to find additional foreshadowing that you may have missed. Make a chart like the one below to record your results. When you have listed three or four hints and outcomes, discuss the story's title. How might it work as an example of foreshadowing?

| Hint | Outcome |
| --- | --- |
| "If you disobey instructions . . ." | Eckels disobeys instructions. |

**REVIEW** **SCIENCE FICTION**
**Science fiction** is prose writing in which the writer explores possibilities of the future, using known scientific information as well as his or her imagination. When considering the difference between fantasy and science fiction, Bradbury once explained that science fiction "could happen." Why do you think "A Sound of Thunder" qualifies as science fiction?

# Choices & CHALLENGES

## Writing Options

**1. Adventure Advertisement** Write persuasive copy for a poster or magazine advertisement inviting hunters to venture across time to hunt prehistoric creatures. Try to convince readers that this adventure is worth the high price and that it is important for them to responsibly follow every rule.

**2. Incident Report** Writing as Travis, compose a two-paragraph report to your superiors in which you describe the main incident from the story, what you presume are its consequences, and how you propose to make sure nothing like this happens again.

## Activities & Explorations

**1. Butterfly Drawing** Create a fanciful picture of a butterfly in which you visually convey the notion—presented in the story through prose—that the butterfly contains within it the seeds of history. For example, you might include pictures on the wings. ~ **ART**

**2. Video Adaptation** As you view the clip from the film of "A Sound of Thunder," compare the way the dinosaur appears with the way you imagined it as you read. What did you find scarier, the tyrannosaurus you imagined or the one you viewed? Discuss your responses with other students. ~ **VIEWING AND REPRESENTING**

 **Literature in Performance**

## Inquiry & Research

**Science** Have you ever heard of the "butterfly effect"—the notion that the flapping of a butterfly's wings can change the weather? With a partner, research the connections between the butterfly effect and chaos theory, which offers a scientific explanation of apparently random or irregular behavior of systems in nature. Then, in an oral report for your classmates, explain how the story reflects these scientific theories.

**Astronomy** With a partner, research the nature of time in outer space, and how space travel is travel through time as well.

**More Online: Research Starter** www.mcdougallittell.com

---

# Vocabulary in Action

**EXERCISE: ASSESSMENT PRACTICE** On your paper, write the letter of the word that is the best synonym for each boldfaced word.

1. **infinitesimally:** (a) lastingly, (b) microscopically, (c) happily
2. **undulate:** (a) hover, (b) ripple, (c) surrender
3. **revoke:** (a) repeat, (b) modify, (c) repeal
4. **primeval:** (a) wicked, (b) ancient, (c) best
5. **resilient:** (a) elastic, (b) shiny, (c) weak
6. **expendable:** (a) difficult, (b) costly, (c) nonessential
7. **annihilate:** (a) demolish, (b) confuse, (c) restore
8. **taint:** (a) purity, (b) rotation, (c) contamination
9. **subliminal:** (a) instinctive, (b) underground, (c) inhuman
10. **sheathed:** (a) exposed, (b) surrounded, (c) beautified

### Building Vocabulary

For an in-depth lesson on the denotation and connotation of words, see page 494.

# Interview with Ray Bradbury

## Preparing to Read

### Build Background

With the authority acquired from more than 60 years of constant story production, Bradbury often speaks frankly to young writers and students about the art of writing. Because of this, he is usually a good source for colorful quotes on the subject of writing and the way he approaches it. In this interview, the writer promotes "the old-fashioned virtues of hard, constant labor."

### Focus Your Reading

**PRIMARY SOURCES** **INTERVIEW**

An **interview** is a recorded conversation of questions and answers with a person having firsthand or expert knowledge on some subject. A good interviewer will be prepared with background knowledge on the interviewee. In addition, a good interviewer is armed with two essentials:

- a list of questions, most of which require thoughtful responses
- the flexibility to let the conversation stray if the interviewee goes off in an unexpected, interesting direction

## Interview by FRANK FILOSA

**Do you write every day?**
Every day of my life except weekends, which are for the family: my wife and my four lovely daughters.

**Could you describe a typical day, your process of writing?**
I do a first draft as passionately and as quickly as I can. I believe a story is only valid when it is immediate and passionate; when it dances out of your subconscious.[1] If you interfere in any way, you destroy it. There's no difference between a short story and life. Surprise is where creativity comes. Allow your subconscious[1] to come out into the light and say what it has to say. Let your characters have their way. Let your secret life be lived. Then at your leisure, in the succeeding weeks, months or years, you let the story cool off, and then, instead of rewriting, you relive it. If you try to rewrite, which is a cold exercise, you'll wind up with all kinds of Band-aids on your story, which people can see. It's very important that a story have a skin around it just as we have a skin. A story must have the same sort of life we have though it is shorter. It has this fantastic entity[2] to itself, a need to run to its end, and you just have to let it go.

---

1. **subconscious:** the part of the mind below the level of conscious awareness.
2. **entity:** unique existence.

**You wrote, "Success is a continuing process. Failure is a stoppage. The man who keeps moving and working does not fail."**
The average young person you meet today seems to have the motto, "If at first you don't succeed, stop right there." They want to start at the top of their profession and not to learn their art on the way up. That way they miss all the fun. If you write a hundred short stories and they're all bad, that doesn't mean you've failed. You fail only if you stop writing. I've written about 2,000 short stories; I've only published about 300, and I feel I'm still learning. Any man who keeps working is not a failure. He may not be a great writer, but if he applies the old-fashioned virtues of hard, constant labor, he'll eventually make some kind of career for himself as a writer.

**Isn't this hard to do for most people? The rent has to be paid. You have to do mundane³ things like eat. In your teens you sold newspapers, and between editions you wrote, but didn't you have to give up most of the things people feel they have to have?**
Depends on what you have to have.

You can get along on a very small amount of money. You can give up clothes. You can give up movies and theater. You can eat Kraft Dinner every day of your life. I'm a student of Kraft Dinner. I'm a specialist in Campbell's Tomato Soup. You can go to the market today, and for a few cents you can have a banquet. I still love Campbell's Tomato Soup. This is a free plug for them, and I hope they send me a free can of soup. I'm the cheapest freeloader in the history of mankind. My idea of a real meal is to sit down with a can of tomato soup, a couple glasses of milk, and a half a pound of crackers. I went through a record of expenses I kept during my first year of marriage. At that time I

was making about $30 a week writing, and my wife was making $35 at a job to support us so I could get my writing done. We'd go down to Ocean Park at night and have a couple of hot dogs and a Coke. We'd go through the penny arcade, and for 32 cents we'd have a magnificent evening. If you have someone who cares about you, it's very easy to give up things. If you're alone, you buy things to compensate for⁴ your loneliness.

Money is not important. The material things are not important. Getting the work done beautifully and proudly is important. If you do that, strangely enough, the money will come as a just reward for work beautifully done. A tape recorder, an automobile, they don't really belong to you. What really belongs to you? Yourself, you. That's all you'll ever have. I am ruthless with anyone around me who doesn't think or create always at the top of his form.

---

3. **mundane:** ordinary; day-to-day.
4. **compensate for:** make up for.

# There Will Come Soft Rains

*Short Story by* RAY BRADBURY

## Connect to Your Life

**Progress or Danger?** One reason cellular phones have become popular is that they enable people to make business calls while commuting; unfortunately, that practice has led to a sharp increase in automobile accidents. Millions of people find helpful information on the Internet; however, some people fear that criminals will have access to their personal financial information. Overall, do you think that technology provides more benefits or poses more hazards? Discuss your ideas with a classmate.

## Build Background

**Technology: No Guarantee** At first, electrically powered machines assisted people only in their workplaces. Around the turn of the 20th century, however, with the spread of electricity, machines started to appear in people's homes. For example, the electric washing machine was invented in 1901, the electric vacuum cleaner in 1907, and the electric toaster in 1909.

Science fiction writers of this time began writing of ideal situations in which people were freed from time-consuming everyday tasks by various appliances. Writers imagined self-sufficient machine beings, acting as servants; in 1921, a writer coined the word *robot.* On the surface, the idea of being freed from daily chores had great appeal. However, as writers probed the idea more deeply, it became apparent that technological advancement did not necessarily guarantee social progress.

## Focus Your Reading

**LITERARY ANALYSIS** **SETTING** Every story has a **setting**—a time and place for its action. For science fiction writers, setting has no boundaries. Ray Bradbury is known for bringing together the fantastic and the ordinary, as he does in this early sentence from "There Will Come Soft Rains": "'Today is August 4, 2026,' said a second voice from the kitchen ceiling, 'in the city of Allendale, California.'"

The story takes place in the future, on what begins as an ordinary day. As you read, look for signs suggesting how this place differs from today's world. Also, pay close attention to the progression of time.

**ACTIVE READING** **VISUALIZING** When you **visualize,** you use your imagination to form pictures in your mind. The more precise the **details** a writer supplies, the better a reader is able to visualize a story's **setting, characters,** and **events.**

**READER'S NOTEBOOK** As you read the story, fill in a chart like this one. Record each time of day. Jot down any words or phrases that help you "see" both ordinary and unusual happenings.

| Time of Day | What Seems Ordinary? | What Seems Unusual? |
|---|---|---|
|  |  |  |
|  |  |  |
|  |  |  |

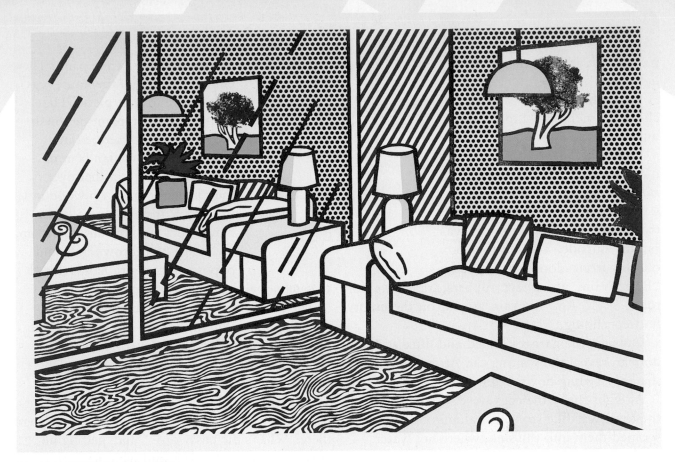

*Blue Floor* (1990), Roy Lichtenstein.
12-color lithograph/woodblock/screen-print, 57¾″ × 83½″. Copyright 1990
© Estate of Roy Lichtenstein/Gemini
G.E.L., Los Angeles, California.

# THERE WILL COME SOFT RAINS

## RAY BRADBURY

In the living room the voice-clock sang, *Tick-tock, seven o'clock, time to get up, time to get up, seven o'clock!* as if it were afraid that nobody would. The morning house lay empty. The clock ticked on, repeating and repeating its sounds into the emptiness. *Seven-nine, breakfast time, seven-nine!*

In the kitchen the breakfast stove gave a hissing sigh and ejected from its warm interior eight pieces of perfectly browned toast, eight eggs sunnyside up, sixteen slices of bacon, two coffees, and two cool glasses of milk.

"Today is August 4, 2026," said a second voice from the kitchen ceiling, "in the city of Allendale, California." It repeated the date three times for memory's sake. "Today is Mr. Featherstone's birthday. Today is the anniversary of Tilita's marriage. Insurance is payable, as are the water, gas, and light bills."

Somewhere in the walls, relays[1] clicked, memory tapes glided under electric eyes.

*Eight-one, tick-tock, eight-one o'clock, off to school, off to work, run, run, eight-one!* But no doors slammed, no carpets took the soft tread of rubber heels. It was raining outside. The weather box on the front door sang quietly: "Rain, rain, go away; rubbers, raincoats for today . . ." And the rain tapped on the empty house, echoing.

Outside, the garage chimed and lifted its door to reveal the waiting car. After a long wait the door swung down again.

At eight-thirty the eggs were shriveled and the toast was like stone. An aluminum wedge scraped them into the sink, where hot water whirled them down a metal throat which digested and flushed them away to the distant sea. The dirty dishes were dropped into a hot washer and emerged twinkling dry.

*Nine-fifteen,* sang the clock, *time to clean.*

Out of warrens[2] in the wall, tiny robot mice darted. The rooms were acrawl with the small cleaning animals, all rubber and metal. They thudded against chairs, whirling their mustached runners, kneading the rug nap, sucking gently at hidden dust. Then, like mysterious invaders, they popped into their burrows. Their pink electric eyes faded. The house was clean.

*Ten o'clock.* The sun came out from behind the rain. The house stood alone in a city of rubble and ashes. This was the one house left standing. At night the ruined city gave off a radioactive glow which could be seen for miles.

*Ten-fifteen.* The garden sprinklers whirled up in golden founts, filling the soft morning air with scatterings of brightness. The water pelted windowpanes, running down the charred west side where the house had been burned

> Until this day, how well the house had kept its peace.

evenly free of its white paint. The entire west face of the house was black, save for five places. Here the silhouette[3] in paint of a man mowing a lawn. Here, as in a photograph, a woman bent to pick flowers. Still farther over, their images burned on wood in one titanic instant, a small boy, hands flung into the air; higher up, the image of a thrown ball, and opposite him a girl, hands raised to catch a ball which never came down.

The five spots of paint—the man, the woman, the children, the ball—remained. The rest was a thin charcoaled layer.

The gentle sprinkler rain filled the garden with falling light.

Until this day, how well the house had kept its peace. How carefully it had inquired, "Who goes there? What's the password?" and, getting no answer from lonely foxes and whining cats, it had shut up its windows and drawn shades in an old-maidenly preoccupation with self-protection which bordered on a mechanical paranoia.[4]

It quivered at each sound, the house did. If a sparrow brushed a window, the shade snapped up. The bird, startled, flew off! No, not even a bird must touch the house!

The house was an altar with ten thousand attendants, big, small, servicing, attending, in choirs. But the gods had gone away, and the ritual of the religion continued senselessly, uselessly.

*Twelve noon.*

A dog whined, shivering, on the front porch.

The front door recognized the dog voice and opened. The dog, once huge and fleshy, but now

---

1. **relays:** devices that automatically turn switches in electric circuits on and off.

2. **warrens:** passageways or burrows.

3. **silhouette** (sĭl′ōō-ĕt′): a shadowlike image of the outline of a person's shape.

4. **paranoia** (păr′ə-noi′ə): an irrational fear of danger or misfortune.

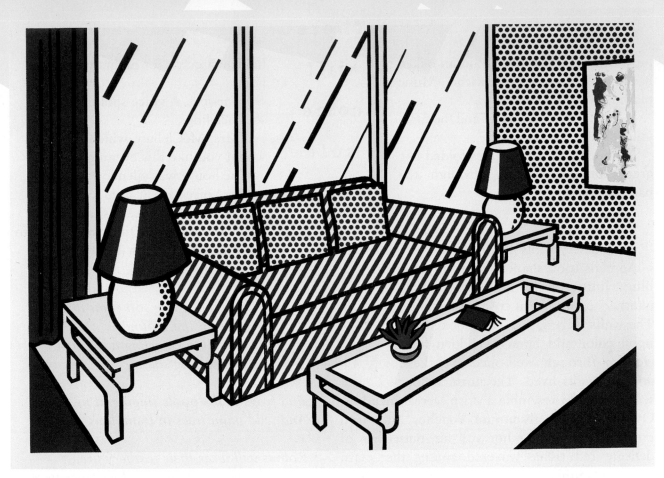

*Red Lamps* (1990), Roy Lichtenstein. 11-color lithograph/woodblock/screenprint, 57 ¼″ × 78 ¾″.
Copyright © 1990 Estate of Roy Lichtenstein/Gemini G.E.L., Los Angeles, California.

gone to bone and covered with sores, moved in and through the house, tracking mud. Behind it whirred angry mice, angry at having to pick up mud, angry at inconvenience.

For not a leaf fragment blew under the door but what the wall panels flipped open and the copper scrap rats flashed swiftly out. The offending dust, hair, or paper, seized in miniature steel jaws, was raced back to the burrows. There, down tubes which fed into the cellar, it was dropped into the sighing vent of an incinerator which sat like evil Baal[5] in a dark corner.

The dog ran upstairs, hysterically yelping to each door, at last realizing, as the house realized, that only silence was here.

It sniffed the air and scratched the kitchen door. Behind the door, the stove was making pancakes which filled the house with a rich baked odor and the scent of maple syrup.

The dog frothed at the mouth, lying at the door, sniffing, its eyes turned to fire. It ran wildly in circles, biting at its tail, spun in a frenzy, and died. It lay in the parlor for an hour.

*Two o'clock,* sang a voice.

Delicately sensing decay at last, the regiments of mice hummed out as softly as blown gray leaves in an electrical wind.

*Two-fifteen.*

The dog was gone.

In the cellar, the incinerator glowed suddenly and a whirl of sparks leaped up the chimney.

*Two thirty-five.*

Bridge tables sprouted from patio walls. Playing cards fluttered onto pads in a shower of

---

5. **Baal** (bā′əl): an idol worshiped by certain ancient peoples of the Middle East.

pips. Martinis manifested[6] on an oaken bench with egg-salad sandwiches. Music played.

But the tables were silent and the cards untouched.

At four o'clock the tables folded like great butterflies back through the paneled walls.

*Four-thirty.*

The nursery walls glowed.

Animals took shape: yellow giraffes, blue lions, pink antelopes, lilac panthers cavorting in crystal substance. The walls were glass. They looked out upon color and fantasy. Hidden films clocked through well-oiled sprockets, and the walls lived. The nursery floor was woven to resemble a crisp, cereal meadow. Over this ran aluminum roaches and iron crickets, and in the hot still air butterflies of delicate red tissue wavered among the sharp aroma of animal spoors! There was the sound like a great matted yellow hive of bees within a dark bellows, the lazy bumble of a purring lion. And there was the patter of okapi[7] feet and the murmur of a fresh jungle rain, like other hoofs, falling upon the summer-starched grass. Now the walls dissolved into distances of parched weed, mile on mile, and warm endless sky. The animals drew away into thorn brakes and water holes.

It was the children's hour.

*Five o'clock.* The bath filled with clear hot water.

*Six, seven, eight o'clock.* The dinner dishes manipulated like magic tricks, and in the study a *click*. In the metal stand opposite the hearth where a fire now blazed up warmly, a cigar popped out, half an inch of soft gray ash on it, smoking, waiting.

*Nine o'clock.* The beds warmed their

**There will come soft rains and the smell of the ground**

hidden circuits, for nights were cool here.

*Nine-five.* A voice spoke from the study ceiling:

"Mrs. McClellan, which poem would you like this evening?"

The house was silent.

The voice said at last, "Since you express no preference, I shall select a poem at random." Quiet music rose to back the voice. "Sara Teasdale. As I recall, your favorite. . . ."

*"There will come soft rains and the
  smell of the ground,
And swallows circling with their
  shimmering sound;*

*And frogs in the pools singing at night,
And wild plum trees in tremulous[8] white;*

*Robins will wear their feathery fire,
Whistling their whims on a low fence-wire;*

*And not one will know of the war, not one
Will care at last when it is done.*

*Not one would mind, neither bird nor tree,
If mankind perished utterly;*

*And Spring herself, when she woke at dawn
Would scarcely know that we were gone."*

The fire burned on the stone hearth and the cigar fell away into a mound of quiet ash on its tray. The empty chairs faced each other between the silent walls, and the music played.

---

6. **manifested:** appeared.
7. **okapi** (ō-kä′pē): an antelope-like hoofed mammal of the African jungle.
8. **tremulous** (trĕm′yə-ləs): trembling.

*Yellow Vase* (1990), Roy Lichtenstein. 11-color lithograph/woodblock/screenprint, 55½″ × 84½″.
Copyright © 1990 Estate of Roy Lichtenstein/Gemini G.E.L., Los Angeles, California.

At ten o'clock the house began to die.

The wind blew. A falling tree bough crashed through the kitchen window. Cleaning solvent, bottled, shattered over the stove. The room was ablaze in an instant!

"Fire!" screamed a voice. The house lights flashed, water pumps shot water from the ceilings. But the solvent spread on the linoleum, licking, eating, under the kitchen door, while the voices took it up in chorus: "Fire, fire, fire!"

The house tried to save itself. Doors sprang tightly shut, but the windows were broken by the heat and the wind blew and sucked upon the fire.

The house gave ground as the fire in ten billion angry sparks moved with flaming ease from room to room and then up the stairs. While scurrying water rats squeaked from the walls, pistoled their water, and ran for more. And the wall sprays let down showers of mechanical rain.

But too late. Somewhere, sighing, a pump shrugged to a stop. The quenching rain ceased.

The reserve water supply which had filled baths and washed dishes for many quiet days was gone.

The fire crackled up the stairs. It fed upon Picassos and Matisses[9] in the upper halls, like delicacies, baking off the oily flesh, tenderly crisping the canvases into black shavings.

Now the fire lay in beds, stood in windows, changed the colors of drapes!

And then, reinforcements.

From attic trapdoors, blind robot faces peered down with faucet mouths gushing green chemical.

The fire backed off, as even an elephant must at the sight of a dead snake. Now there were twenty snakes whipping over the floor, killing the fire with a clear cold venom of green froth.

But the fire was clever. It had sent flame outside the house, up through the attic to the

---

9. **Picassos and Matisses:** paintings by the famous 20th-century artists Pablo Picasso (päb′lō pĭ-kä′sō) and Henri Matisse (än-rē′ mə-tēs′).

pumps there. An explosion! The attic brain which directed the pumps was shattered into bronze shrapnel on the beams.

The fire rushed back into every closet and felt of the clothes hung there.

The house shuddered, oak bone on bone, its bared skeleton cringing from the heat, its wire, its nerves revealed as if a surgeon had torn the skin off to let the red veins and capillaries quiver in the scalded air. Help, help! Fire! Run, run! Heat snapped mirrors like the first brittle winter ice. And the voices wailed Fire, fire, run, run, like a tragic nursery rhyme, a dozen voices, high, low, like children dying in a forest, alone, alone. And the voices fading as the wires popped their sheathings like hot chestnuts. One, two, three, four, five voices died.

In the nursery the jungle burned. Blue lions roared, purple giraffes bounded off. The panthers ran in circles, changing color, and ten million animals, running before the fire, vanished off toward a distant steaming river. . . .

Ten more voices died. In the last instant under the fire avalanche, other choruses, oblivious,[10] could be heard announcing the time, playing music, cutting the lawn by remote-control mower, or setting an umbrella frantically out and in the slamming and opening front door, a thousand things happening, like a clock shop when each clock strikes the hour insanely before or after the other, a scene of maniac confusion, yet unity; singing, screaming, a few last cleaning mice darting bravely out to carry the horrid ashes away! And one voice,

*Girl with Tear III* (1977), Roy Lichtenstein. Oil and magna on canvas, 46″ × 40″. Copyright © Estate of Roy Lichtenstein/Leo Castelli Gallery, New York.

with sublime[11] disregard for the situation, read poetry aloud in the fiery study, until all the film spools burned, until all the wires withered and the circuits cracked.

The fire burst the house and let it slam flat down, puffing out skirts of spark and smoke.

In the kitchen, an instant before the rain of fire and timber, the stove could be seen making breakfasts at a psychopathic[12] rate, ten dozen eggs, six loaves of toast, twenty dozen bacon strips, which, eaten by fire, started the stove working again, hysterically hissing!

The crash. The attic smashing into kitchen and parlor. The parlor into cellar, cellar into sub-cellar. Deep freeze, armchair, film tapes, circuits, beds, and all like skeletons thrown in a cluttered mound deep under.

Smoke and silence. A great quantity of smoke.

Dawn showed faintly in the east. Among the ruins, one wall stood alone. Within the wall, a last voice said, over and over again and again, even as the sun rose to shine upon the heaped rubble and steam:

"Today is August 5, 2026, today is August 5, 2026, today is . . ." ❖

---

10. **oblivious** (ə-blĭv′ē-əs): paying no attention; heedless.
11. **sublime:** splendid.
12. **psychopathic** (sī′kə-păth′ĭk): insane.

## Connect to the Literature

**1. What Do You Think?** If you were to think back to this story in the days and weeks to come, what image do you think would most likely come to your mind?

**Comprehension Check**
- What unusual qualities and appliances does the house have?
- What has happened outside the house?
- What finally destroys the house?

## Think Critically

**2.** Only as the story progresses do you learn something of what has happened outside the McClellan home. What effect do you think this delay creates?

**3.** What do you think has happened to the former inhabitants of the house?

- the announcements that the voice in the kitchen ceiling makes
- the duties the house performs
- the silhouettes on the side of the house

**4.** **ACTIVE READING** **VISUALIZING** Review the information you recorded in your ▯**READER'S NOTEBOOK.** What description led you to think that something very out of the ordinary had happened outside the home?

**5.** What effect does Bradbury create by including the Teasdale poem in his story?

- the message, or **theme,** of each selection
- the **settings** of the poem and story

## Extend Interpretations

**6. What If?** Suppose the mechanical house were programmed to detect early signs of nuclear fallout. What warning do you think it might have issued, or what defensive action might it have taken?

**7. Connect to Life** Think about the discussion you had for Connect to Your Life, on page 86, about the benefits and dangers of technology. Has the story changed your opinion? Why or why not?

## Literary Analysis

**SETTING** **Setting** is the time and place of the action of a story. Setting may also include details of a story's social and cultural environment. In "There Will Come Soft Rains," you quickly learn the basic time and place of the story. From the voice from the kitchen ceiling, you also get hints that the story is set in a routine, middle-class environment:

*"Today is Mr. Featherstone's birthday. Today is the anniversary of Tilita's marriage. Insurance is payable, as are the water, gas, and light bills."*

These details suggest that the day should have been an ordinary one for the McClellan family. It is against this typical American social setting that Bradbury contrasts the annihilation of atomic war. This contrast gives the story its power.

**Activity** Review "There Will Come Soft Rains," paying special attention to the passage of time. Note the details about setting provided in the passages that follow each time announcement. How does this add to your understanding of the events that took place before the story began?

**POINT OF VIEW** The perspective from which a story is told is called **point of view. Third-person** point of view occurs when a narrator outside the action describes events and characters. How does the third-person narrator of "There Will Come Soft Rains" maintain interest in a story where there are no human characters? Explain.

# *Choices* & CHALLENGES

## Writing Options

**1. House Monologue** Imagine that the attic "brain" has developed human understanding. The house now realizes what has happened to its inhabitants. Replace the house's "spoken" monologue in the story with a new one that reflects the house's knowledge of its critical situation.

**2. Appliance Argument** Write a persuasive essay expressing your views on whether the technological devices in "There Will Come Soft Rains" could improve people's lives. Cite evidence to support your arguments. Put your persuasive essay in your **Working Portfolio.**

**Writing Handbook**
See pages 1161–1162: Persuasive Writing.

## Activities & Explorations

**1. Future Set Design** Design a diorama of the McClellan home. Create cutaway sections to show the hidden devices. ~ **ART**

**2. Readers Theater** In a Readers Theater presentation, performers read aloud, using a work of literature as a script. Divide Bradbury's story into time periods, and assign a reader to each section. Before performing, decide what tones of voice are appropriate to the narration and automated machines of the story. ~ **PERFORMING**

## Inquiry & Research

**1. Political Climate** Bradbury's story was written in 1950–51 and reflects some common fears of the time. What was making Americans nervous? Find out about the international political climate of the period and how that might have contributed to the development of this story. Report what you find to the class.

**2. Poetry Connection** Find out about Sara Teasdale and the circumstances behind her writing the poem "There Will Come Soft Rains." Compare and contrast Bradbury's and Teasdale's basic themes.

## Grammar in Context: Action Verbs

In "There Will Come Soft Rains," Ray Bradbury's use of action verbs allows the reader to form a clear image of what happens to eggs and toast that go uneaten in an empty house in the year 2026.

> An aluminum wedge scraped them into the sink, where hot water whirled them down a metal throat which digested and flushed them away to the distant sea.

Bradbury's strong verbs convey the cold efficiency of the robot-operated house. The verb *digested* makes it sound as if the house were a living organism. Think about how much less lively the writing would be if Bradbury had used *moved* instead of *scraped*, *washed* instead of *whirled*, *received* instead of *digested*, and *sent* instead of *flushed*.

**Apply to Your Writing** Using strong action verbs can help you

- make your writing more vivid and lively

- describe events more effectively
- give the reader clues to characters' qualities and appearances

**WRITING EXERCISE** Substitute an action verb for the underlined verb in each sentence.

**Example: *Original*** The cleaning mice <u>went</u> across the carpet and into the kitchen.

***Rewritten*** The cleaning mice <u>whirred</u> across the carpet and into the kitchen.

1. The sprinklers <u>put</u> water on the garden.
2. A radioactive glow <u>came</u> from the ruined city.
3. The dog <u>fell</u> on the floor and died.
4. A falling tree limb <u>broke</u> the kitchen window.
5. Fire <u>moved</u> through the rooms of the house.

**Connect to the Literature** Write down four action verbs that appear on page 92. What sort of mood do these verbs create? Why might Bradbury have chosen them?

# The Pedestrian

*Short Story by* RAY BRADBURY

**( Connect to Your Life )**

**Walking Habits** In the story you are about to read, Leonard Mead is the pedestrian, out walking one night "for air, and to see, and just to walk." As he walks he passes a number of homes, wondering what TV programs the people inside are watching. When you yourself take a walk, is it merely to get somewhere? Or do you ever walk just to "get away from it all"? Jot down a description of the kind of walking you do.

## Build Background

**It's a TV World** By the mid-1990s, 99 percent of households in the United States had a television, and 38 percent had more than one. There were 776 televisions for every 1,000 Americans, the world's highest ratio. It was determined that each American TV was on for an average of 51 to 52 hours per week, or more than 7 hours per day. Ray Bradbury anticipated such statistics as far back as 1951, when he wrote this story—except that he imagined that TV viewing would not reach such a high level until well into the 21st century!

## Focus Your Reading

**LITERARY ANALYSIS** **DESCRIPTION** Bradbury brings "The Pedestrian" to life through **description**—writing that helps a reader picture the **scenes, events,** and **characters** in a story. Description often involves the use of precise language and the composing of vivid and original phrases. These are found in this sample passage:

> *There was a good crystal frost in the air; it cut the nose and made the lungs blaze like a Christmas tree inside.*

Think about the effects created by the descriptive details you encounter in the story.

**ACTIVE READING** **RECOGNIZING SENSORY DETAILS** **Sensory details** are references to sight, smell, hearing, taste, and touch. In appealing to the five senses, they help readers to more fully experience what is happening. Notice the senses Bradbury calls to mind in this passage from the story:

> *During the day it was a thunderous surge of cars, . . . as the scarab-beetles, a faint incense puttering from their exhausts, skimmed homeward to the far directions.*

**READER'S NOTEBOOK** As you read this story, record some sensory details that help you experience Leonard Mead's night in the city. Here's an example:

| Sensory Details | |
|---|---|
| **Phrase or Sentence** | **Sense(s) Appealed to** |
| "patterns of frosty air . . . like the smoke of a cigar" | sight |

# The Pedestrian

Ray Bradbury

**To enter out** into that silence that was the city at eight o'clock of a misty evening in November, to put your feet upon that buckling concrete walk, to step over grassy seams and make your way, hands in pockets, through the silences, that was what Mr. Leonard Mead most dearly loved to do. He would stand upon the corner of an intersection and peer down long moonlit avenues of sidewalk in four directions, deciding which way to go, but it really made no difference; he was alone in this world of A.D. 2053, or as good as alone, and with a final decision made, a path selected, he would stride off, sending patterns of frosty air before him like the smoke of a cigar.

Sometimes he would walk for hours and miles and return only at midnight to his house. And on his way he would see the cottages and homes with their dark windows, and it was not unlike walking through a graveyard where only the faintest glimmers of firefly light appeared in flickers behind the windows. Sudden gray phantoms seemed to manifest upon inner room walls where a curtain was still undrawn against the night, or there were whisperings and murmurs where a window in a tomblike building was still open.

Mr. Leonard Mead would pause, cock his head, listen, look, and march on, his feet

*Night Shadows* (1921), Edward Hopper. Etching, 6⅞″ × 8¼″. Sheldon Memorial Art Gallery, University of Nebraska-Lincoln, F. M. Hall Collection (1951.H-333).

making no noise on the lumpy walk. For long ago he had wisely changed to sneakers when strolling at night, because the dogs in intermittent[1] squads would parallel his journey with barkings if he wore hard heels, and lights might click on and faces appear and an entire street be startled by the passing of a lone figure, himself, in the early November evening.

On this particular evening he began his journey in a westerly direction, toward the hidden sea. There was a good crystal frost in the air; it cut the nose and made the lungs blaze like a Christmas tree inside; you could feel the cold light going on and off, all the branches filled with invisible snow. He listened to the faint push of his soft shoes through autumn leaves with satisfaction, and whistled a cold quiet whistle between his teeth, occasionally picking up a leaf as he passed, examining its skeletal pattern in the infrequent lamplights as he went on, smelling its rusty smell.

"Hello, in there," he whispered to every house on every side as he moved. "What's up tonight on Channel 4, Channel 7, Channel 9? Where are the cowboys rushing, and do I see

---

1. **intermittent:** appearing from time to time.

the United States Cavalry over the next hill to the rescue?"

The street was silent and long and empty, with only his shadow moving like the shadow of a hawk in midcountry. If he closed his eyes and stood very still, frozen, he could imagine himself upon the center of a plain, a wintry, windless Arizona desert with no house in a thousand miles, and only dry river beds, the streets, for company.

"What is it now?" he asked the houses, noticing his wrist watch. "Eight-thirty P.M.? Time for a dozen assorted murders? A quiz? A revue? A comedian falling off the stage?"

Was that a murmur of laughter from within a moon-white house? He hesitated, but went on when nothing more happened. He stumbled over a particularly uneven section of sidewalk. The cement was vanishing under flowers and grass. In ten years of walking by night or day, for thousands of miles, he had never met another person walking, not one in all that time.

**He** came to a cloverleaf intersection which stood silent where two main highways crossed the town. During the day it was a thunderous surge of cars, the gas stations open, a great insect rustling and a ceaseless jockeying for position as the scarab-beetles, a faint incense puttering from their exhausts, skimmed homeward to the far directions. But now these highways, too, were like streams in a dry season, all stone and bed and moon radiance.

He turned back on a side street, circling around toward his home. He was within a block of his destination when the lone car turned a corner quite suddenly and flashed a fierce white cone of light upon him. He stood entranced, not unlike a night moth, stunned by the illumination, and then drawn toward it.

A metallic voice called to him:

"Stand still. Stay where you are! Don't move!"

He halted.

"Put up your hands!"

"But—" he said.

"Your hands up! Or we'll shoot!"

The police, of course, but what a rare, incredible thing; in a city of three million, there was only one police car left, wasn't that correct? Ever since a year ago, 2052, the election year, the force had been cut down from three cars to one. Crime was ebbing; there was no need now for the police, save for this one lone car wandering and wandering the empty streets.

"Your name?" said the police car in a metallic whisper. He couldn't see the men in it for the bright light in his eyes.

"Leonard Mead," he said.

"Speak up!"

"Leonard Mead!"

"Business or profession?"

"I guess you'd call me a writer."

"No profession," said the police car, as if talking to itself. The light held him fixed, like a museum specimen, needle thrust through chest.

"You might say that," said Mr. Mead. He hadn't written in years. Magazines and books didn't sell any more. Everything went on in the tomblike houses at night now, he thought, continuing his fancy. The tombs, ill-lit by television light, where the people sat like the dead, the grey or multicolored lights touching their faces, but never really touching *them*.

"No profession," said the phonograph voice, hissing. "What are you doing out?"

"Walking," said Leonard Mead.

"Walking!"

"Just walking," he said simply, but his face felt cold.

"Walking, just walking, walking?"

"Yes, sir."

*Flying Man with Briefcase No. 2816932* (1983),
Jonathan Borofsky. Painted Gatorfoam, 94½″ ×
24½″ × 1″. Copyright © 1983 Jonathan
Borofsky/Gemini G.E.L., Los Angeles, California.

"Walking where? For what?"

"Walking for air. Walking to see."

"Your address!"

"Eleven South Saint James Street."

"And there is air in your house, you have an air *conditioner,* Mr. Mead?"

"Yes."

"And you have a viewing screen in your house to see with?"

"No."

"No?" There was a crackling quiet that in itself was an accusation.

"Are you married, Mr. Mead?"

"No."

"Not married," said the police voice behind the fiery beam. The moon was high and clear among the stars and the houses were gray and silent.

"Nobody wanted me," said Leonard Mead with a smile.

"Don't speak unless you're spoken to!"

Leonard Mead waited in the cold night.

"Just *walking,* Mr. Mead?"

"Yes."

"But you haven't explained for what purpose."

"I explained; for air, and to see, and just to walk."

"Have you done this often?"

"Every night for years."

The police car sat in the center of the street with its radio throat faintly humming.

"Well, Mr. Mead," it said.

"Is that all?" he asked politely.

"Yes," said the voice. "Here." There was a sigh, a pop. The back door of the police car sprang wide. "Get in."

"Wait a minute, I haven't done anything!"

"Get in."

"I protest!"

"Mr. Mead."

**"Just *walking,* Mr. Mead?"**

He walked like a man suddenly drunk. As he passed the front window of the car he looked in. As he had expected, there was no one in the front seat, no one in the car at all.

"Get in."

He put his hand to the door and peered into the back seat, which was a little cell, a little black jail with bars. It smelled of riveted steel. It smelled of harsh antiseptic;[2] it smelled too clean and hard and metallic. There was nothing soft there.

"Now if you had a wife to give you an alibi," said the iron voice. "But—"

"Where are you taking me?"

The car hesitated, or rather gave a faint whirring click, as if information, somewhere, was dripping card by punch-slotted card under electric eyes. "To the Psychiatric Center for Research on Regressive Tendencies.[3]"

He got in. The door shut with a soft thud.

The police car rolled through the night avenues, flashing its dim lights ahead.

They passed one house on one street a moment later, one house in an entire city of houses that were dark, but this one particular house had all of its electric lights brightly lit, every window a loud yellow illumination, square and warm in the cool darkness.

"That's *my* house," said Leonard Mead.

No one answered him.

The car moved down the empty river-bed streets and off away, leaving the empty streets with the empty sidewalks, and no sound and no motion all the rest of the chill November night. ❖

---

2. **antiseptic:** a substance used to kill germs.

3. **Regressive Tendencies:** habits of acting in ways that belong to a more primitive stage of development.

# Connect to the Literature

1. **What Do You Think?**
Do you think Leonard Mead will ever again walk his city's streets? Explain.

**Comprehension Check**
- What interrupts Leonard's walk one November night?
- What makes him appear suspicious to the police?
- Where is he taken at the end of the story?

# Think Critically

2. **ACTIVE READING** **RECOGNIZING SENSORY DETAILS** Review the examples of sensory details that you recorded in your **READER'S NOTEBOOK**. Which passage do you think best conveys Leonard Mead's separation from others?

3. What are your impressions of Leonard's world of 2053?

**THINK ABOUT**
- what Leonard hasn't seen in ten years of nightly walks
- what passes for "normal" night behavior in the city
- the condition of the city's sidewalks

4. Of Leonard's several responses to the police car, which do you think gets him into the most trouble? Why?

5. Would you call Leonard a rebel? Why or why not?

6. What kind of statement about TV do you think Bradbury tries to make?

# Extend Interpretations

7. **Critic's Corner** According to Bradbury's biographer David Mogan, "The Pedestrian" is science fiction that comments on present-day irritations with society and technology by portraying a future in which the problems are exaggerated. On the basis of the selections you've read in this Author Study, what would you say are some of Bradbury's specific concerns about the modern world? Defend your views with evidence from the selections.

8. **Connect to Life** Bradbury's science fiction stories have been termed "warning fictions." Which of the three stories in this Author Study do you feel holds the most powerful warning for readers of your generation? Explain the reasons for your choice.

# Literary Analysis

**DESCRIPTION** **Description** is the process by which a writer creates a word picture of a scene, event, or character. Good descriptive writing appeals to the senses, helping the reader to see, hear, smell, taste, or feel the subject being described. It relies on vivid and precise language.

In the following passage, Bradbury reveals the impersonal, insensitive way that Leonard Mead is being observed:

*And on his way he would see the cottages and homes with their dark windows, and it was not unequal to walking through a graveyard where only the faintest glimmers of firefly light appeared in flickers behind the windows.*

**Paired Activity** With a partner, choose three or four more examples of description that you found particularly well crafted. Discuss how each example contributes to the mood of the story.

**REVIEW** **CHARACTER** The individuals who participate in the action of a literary work are called **characters.** The most important characters are main characters, and the less prominent ones are minor characters. "The Pedestrian" has an unusual cast of characters. Briefly review the story. How much do you feel you know about the story's main character? Explain. The robot voices in the police car can be considered minor characters. What human traits do you feel they imitate, if any?

# THE AUTHOR'S STYLE
## Bradbury's Compelling Compositions

A piece of literature's **style** is the particular way in which it is written. Style is not so much *what* is said as *how* it is said. It is the writer's uniquely individual way of communicating ideas. Critics have noted that Bradbury's style conveys urgency, excitement, "a sense of breathless wonder," and a hint of sadness. The qualities that make up his style come from a variety of techniques.

### Key Aspects of Bradbury's Style

- short phrases that form one long sentence and lend a flowing, almost poetic quality to his lines
- use of sensory details and frequent use of **similes**—comparisons that use the word *like* or *as* ("teeth like daggers")—and more direct comparisons called **metaphors** ("watchmaker's claws")
- use of rhythm and repetition
- intriguing beginnings that capture readers' interest

## Analysis of Style

At the right are excerpts from each of the Bradbury stories you have read. Study the list above, and then read each excerpt carefully. Complete the following activities:

- Find examples of each stylistic device in the three paragraphs.
- Find examples of other devices you see at work in each excerpt.
- The term *poetic* is sometimes used to describe Bradbury's prose. Which lines do you consider most poetic? Support your answer.

## Applications

1. **Speaking and Listening** Alone or with a group, read aloud each excerpt at the right in an attempt to reveal the characteristics that the critics have noted. As a class, discuss the differences in mood and intensity you hear among these oral interpretations.

2. **Imitating Style** Choose one of the stories and add to it somewhere another paragraph that you have created using Bradbury's style. Share your work by reading it to the class.

3. **Changing Style** Rewrite one of the excerpts in a simpler way. Be sure to keep the same idea. Then read your versions and the originals aloud and compare them. Discuss the differences in effect with your classmates.

*from* **A Sound of Thunder**

Out of chars and ashes, out of dust and coals, like golden salamanders, the old years, the green years, might leap; roses sweeten the air, white hair turn Irish-black, wrinkles vanish; all, everything fly back to seed, flee death, rush down to their beginnings, suns rise in western skies and set in glorious easts, moons eat themselves opposite to the custom, all and everything cupping one in another like Chinese boxes, rabbits into hats, all and everything returning to the fresh death, the seed death, the green death, to the time before the beginning.

*from* **There Will Come Soft Rains**

In the last instant under the fire avalanche, other choruses, oblivious, could be heard announcing the time, playing music, cutting the lawn by remote-control mower, or setting an umbrella frantically out and in the slamming and opening front door, a thousand things happening, like a clock shop when each clock strikes the hour insanely before or after the other, a scene of maniac confusion, yet unity; singing, screaming, a few last cleaning mice darting bravely out to carry the horrid ashes away!

*from* **The Pedestrian**

To enter out into that silence that was the city at eight o'clock of a misty evening in November, to put your feet upon that buckling concrete walk, to step over grassy seams and make your way, hands in pockets, through the silences, that was what Mr. Leonard Mead most dearly loved to do.

# *Choices* & CHALLENGES

## Writing Options

**1. Citizen Profile** Create a short profile of an "average" citizen of Leonard Mead's world of 2053. You might review the story for details of the characteristics, listing them in a graphic like the one below.

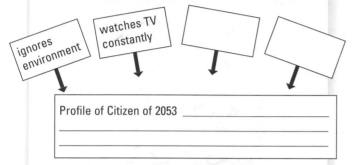

ignores environment

watches TV constantly

Profile of Citizen of 2053 _____
_____
_____

**2. Critical Review** Write a review of "The Pedestrian." Address the importance of science in the story. Also offer your opinion of how closely the world of Leonard Mead matches your view of the not-so-distant future. Put your review in your **Working Portfolio.**

## Activities & Explorations

**1. Panel Discussion** In the mid-1960s, Bradbury adapted "The Pedestrian" for the stage. With a small group, hold a panel discussion in which you examine the following questions: What are the differences between a one-character story and a play? What are the different ways that character is revealed in the two genres? Which genre do you think you prefer?
**~ SPEAKING AND LISTENING**

**2. Comic-Book Version** Working in teams, depict scenes from "The Pedestrian" in comic-book form. Display your drawings in a single class book. **~ ART**

## Inquiry & Research

**TV of the Past** In small groups, investigate typical programming in TV's early days and compare it to typical programming today.

Netscape: Welcome to Netscape

Ray Bradbury

**Author Study Project**

MOVIE-TRAILER STORYBOARD

Create and present to your class a story-board for a **trailer**—a short filmed movie advertisement—to be used as a preview for a film of a story by Ray Bradbury. A **storyboard** is a series of rough, cartoonlike drawings, often on posterboards, that depicts scenes of a film, trailer, television show, or the like. The storyboard represents a number of decisions that ultimately provide the guide for the finished product on film.

**Launching the Project** Choose teams to take the project to the stage of actual storyboard creation. After a group has selected one of Bradbury's stories, it can select scenes for consideration for the trailer.

**Organizing the Trailer** A trailer should be a teaser, creating interest in the film by revealing some essential information about the setting and costuming and some fragmented information about plot.

**Preparing the Storyboard** Divide your group into new teams for the actual creation of the storyboard. Sketches can be created by the group's better illustrators; however, if equipment is available, you may use computer software to create images from the Bradbury tale you've selected. Eventually, transfer all the scenes of your storyboard to chart paper or large posterboard sheets. Also, remember that your trailer can run no more than two minutes. Estimate the running time for each of your sketched scenes.

 **More Online: Research Starter**
www.mcdougallittell.com

# LEARNING the Language of *Literature*

## *N*onfiction is prose writing about real people, places, and events.
Unlike fiction, nonfiction is mainly written to convey factual information, although writers of nonfiction shape information in accordance with their own purposes and attitudes. Nonfiction includes a diverse range of writing: newspaper articles, cookbooks, letters, movie reviews, speeches, true-life adventure stories, advertising, and more. Nonfiction can be a good source of information, but readers frequently have to examine it more carefully than fiction in order to detect biases, notice gaps in the information, and identify errors in logic. Use the following passages to learn about some of the major types of nonfiction.

## Autobiography

An **autobiography** is a writer's account of his or her own life and is, in almost every case, told from the first-person point of view. Generally, an autobiography focuses on the most significant events and people in the writer's life over a period of time and on the ways in which those events and people affected the writer. Shorter autobiographical narratives include such private writings as **journals, diaries,** and **letters.** An **autobiographical essay,** another type of short autobiographical work, focuses on a single person or event in the writer's life.

**YOUR TURN** From the excerpt at the right—part of an autobiographical essay—what do you learn about the writer's feelings about her heritage?

> ### AUTOBIOGRAPHY
>
> When I found out that my parents had invited the minister's family over for Christmas Eve dinner, I cried. What would Robert think of our shabby *Chinese* Christmas? What would he think of our noisy *Chinese* relatives who lacked proper American manners?
>
> —Amy Tan, "Fish Cheeks"

## Biography

A **biography** is an account of a person's life written by another person. The writer of a biography usually researches his or her subject in order to present accurate information. The best biographers strive for honesty and balance in their accounts of their subjects' lives, highlighting weaknesses as well as strengths, failures as well as achievements. Remember, though, that every writer has attitudes and feelings that can influence the way he or she writes about a subject.

**YOUR TURN** In this excerpt from a biographical essay, what words and phrases reveal the writer's attitude toward Nelson Mandela?

> ### BIOGRAPHY
>
> After more than two decades in prison, confident that on some crucial issues a leader must make decisions on his own, Mandela decided on a new approach. And after painstaking preliminaries, the most famous prisoner in the world was escorted, in the greatest secrecy, to the State President's office to start negotiating not only his own release but also the nation's transition from apartheid to democracy.
>
> —Andre Brink, "Nelson Mandela"

# Memoir

A **memoir** is a form of autobiographical writing in which a writer focuses on his or her involvement with noted people, significant events, or both. Memoirs are usually anecdotal or intimate in tone, giving the reader insight into the impact of historical events on people's lives. The focus of a memoir is usually on newsworthy people and events that the writer has known at first hand.

**YOUR TURN** The excerpt at the right tells of events on the day after Rosa Parks was arrested for refusing to surrender her seat on a bus to a white person. E. D. Nixon and Ralph Abernathy were civil rights leaders. As you read the excerpt, look for characteristics of a memoir.

### MEMOIR

The first we knew about it [the Montgomery bus boycott] was when Mr. Nixon called my husband early in the morning of Friday, December 2. He had already talked to Ralph Abernathy. After describing the incident, Mr. Nixon said, "We have taken this type of thing too long. I feel the time has come to boycott the buses."

—Coretta Scott King, "Montgomery Boycott"

# Essay

An **essay** is a brief work of nonfiction that deals with a single subject. Some essays are **formal;** in these, writers systematically develop their ideas in an impersonal manner. Others are **informal,** perhaps including anecdotes and humor. Two common types of essay are the persuasive essay and the expository essay. In a **persuasive essay** a writer tries to convince you to share a belief, to agree with a position, or to take some action. The primary purpose of an **expository essay** is to convey or explain information.

**YOUR TURN** Read this excerpt from an expository essay. What explanation is the writer offering?

### ESSAY

Clockwise is the turning direction of the hands of a clock, and counterclockwise is the opposite of that. Since throughout the day we often stare at clocks (dial clocks that is), we have no trouble in following directions or descriptions that include those words.

But if dial clocks disappear, so will the meaning of those words for anyone who never has stared at anything but digitals.

—Isaac Asimov, "Dial Versus Digital"

# Personal Essay

A **personal essay** is an essay that expresses a writer's thoughts, feelings, and opinions on a subject. This type of essay allows a writer to explore the meaning of events and issues in his or her own life. Personal essays tend to be written in an informal, conversational style.

**YOUR TURN** As you read this excerpt, look for clues as to the essay's subject and the author's attitude toward the subject.

### PERSONAL ESSAY

One summer, along about 1904, my father rented a camp on a lake in Maine and took us all there for the month of August. We all got ringworm from some kittens . . . and my father rolled over in a canoe with all his clothes on; but outside of that the vacation was a success and from then on none of us ever thought there was any place in the world like that lake in Maine.

—E. B. White, "Once More to the Lake"

Nonfiction writing is our primary form of written communication. Many of the strategies you use in reading fiction can also be used in reading narrative nonfiction. In addition, the reading strategies explained here can help.

# Reading Nonfiction

## 1 Strategies for Analyzing an Autobiography or a Biography

- Keep track of the sequence of events, perhaps using a chart like this one. **Evaluate** events' effects on the subject of the work.

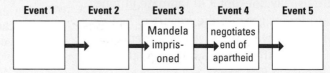

| Event 1 | Event 2 | Event 3 | Event 4 | Event 5 |
|---------|---------|---------|---------|---------|
|         |         | Mandela imprisoned | negotiates end of apartheid |         |

- Form judgments about the work's subject. **Clarify** what qualities contributed to his or her success (or failure).
- When reading an autobiography, **question** what the events included—and the writer's attitude toward them—reveal about the writer.
- When reading a biography, analyze the writer's attitude toward the subject. Notice whether the account is favorable, negative, or balanced.

## 2 Strategies for Understanding a Memoir

- **Connect** to the memoir by using your prior knowledge. What insights into events or time periods that you already know about does the writer give?
- **Visualize** the people and events described in the memoir.
- Be alert for evidence of a bias in the writing.
- Consider the writer's motives: Is he or she primarily sharing personal experiences or interpreting historical events?

## 3 Strategies for Evaluating an Essay

- Distinguish between facts and opinions on a chart like this one. A fact can be proved or disproved. An opinion expresses a belief that cannot be proved or disproved. Opinions supported by facts are still opinions.
- **Clarify** your understanding by summarizing main ideas as you read.

| Fact | The cabin is located 50 feet from the lake. |
|------|---------------------------------------------|
| Opinion | The cabin is comfortable. |
| Opinion Supported by Facts | With its modern plumbing, the cabin is very comfortable. |

- Try to determine the writer's purpose for writing the essay.
- When reading a persuasive essay, **evaluate** the writer's ideas and reasoning.

## 4 Strategies for Appreciating a Personal Essay

- Set purposes to guide your reading. Try to **predict** what information the work will provide.
- **Connect** the writer's comments to your own experiences.

**Need More Help?**

Remember that active readers use the essential reading strategies explained on page 7: **visualize, predict, clarify, question, connect, evaluate, monitor.**

# Dial Versus Digital

*Essay by* ISAAC ASIMOV

**(Connect to Your Life)**

**Fast Forward!** Computers, video games, software, telephones, fax machines, televisions—what will they be like 10 or 20 years from now? Will the technological wonders of today be collecting dust in a closet? Think about some of the changes in technology that you have witnessed in your own lifetime. How have they affected you? Do you think progress in technology always improves the quality of life? Discuss your opinions with other classmates.

## Build Background

**The Great Explainer** Isaac Asimov earned the nickname "The Great Explainer" for his remarkable ability to explain even the most difficult scientific concepts in a way that almost everyone can understand. In his hundreds of books and essays, Asimov delves into every aspect of science and technology, from the solar system to algebra to nuclear fusion. He also expresses his personal opinion on these subjects, especially when they cause him to worry about the effect that progress will have on the future. In "Dial Versus Digital," he worries that digital clocks will change more than just how we tell time.

## Focus Your Reading

**LITERARY ANALYSIS   EXPOSITORY ESSAY**   An **expository essay** explains a particular subject with the purpose of helping the reader understand the subject more thoroughly. Like other types of essays, it gives information and often reveals the opinions of the writer, as the following passage from this essay shows:

> *And yet there will be a loss in the conversion of dial to digital, and few people seem to be worrying about it.*

As you read this essay, look for explanations of how the disappearance of dial clocks could affect our future.

**ACTIVE READING   ANALYZING TEXT STRUCTURE**   Writers always choose a **structure**, or pattern of organization, to present their information. Nonfiction writers can choose from a variety of structures and usually pick the one that best fits their purpose for writing. In "Dial Versus Digital," for example, Asimov uses the **cause-and-effect** structure. He begins by discussing a cause—the loss of the dial clock—and proceeds by examining the effects that are likely to occur.

**READER'S NOTEBOOK**   Create a chart like the one shown to help you identify each effect that the author predicts.

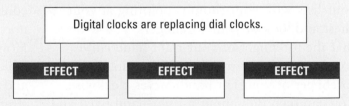

| Digital clocks are replacing dial clocks. | | |
|:---:|:---:|:---:|
| **EFFECT** | **EFFECT** | **EFFECT** |
|  |  |  |

# DIAL VERSUS DIGITAL

## Isaac Asimov

There seems no question but that the clock dial, which has existed in its present form since the Seventeenth Century and in earlier forms since ancient times, is on the way out. More common today are digital clocks, which mark off the hours, minutes, and seconds in changing numbers.

This certainly seems an advance in technology. People no longer will have to interpret the meaning of "the big hand on the 11 and the little hand on the 5"; digital clocks will indicate at once that it is 4:55.

And yet there will be a loss in the conversion of dial to digital, and few people seem to be worrying about it.

When something turns, it can turn in just one of two ways, either clockwise or counterclockwise, and we all know which is which. Clockwise is the turning direction of the hands of a clock, and counterclockwise is the opposite of that. Since throughout the day we often stare at clocks (dial clocks that is), we have no trouble in following directions or descriptions that include those words.

But if dial clocks disappear, so will the meaning of those words for anyone who never has stared at anything but digitals. There are no good substitutes for *clockwise* or *counterclockwise*. The nearest you can come is by a consideration of your hands. If you clench your fists with your thumbs pointing at your chest and look at your forefingers, you will see that the forefinger of your right hand curves counterclockwise from knuckle to tip, while the forefinger of your left hand curves clockwise. You can then talk about a right-hand twist and a left-hand twist. But people don't stare at their hands the way they stare at clocks, and this will never be an adequate substitute.

Nor is this a minor matter. Astronomers define the north pole and south pole of any rotating body in such terms. If you are hovering above a pole of rotation and the body is rotating counterclockwise, it is the north pole; if it is rotating clockwise, it is the south pole. Astronomers also speak of direct motion and retrograde motion, by which they mean counterclockwise and clockwise, respectively.

Here is another example. Suppose you are looking through a microscope at some object on a slide, or through a telescope at some view in the sky. In either case you may wish to point out something to a colleague. "Notice that object at 11 o'clock," you may say—or 5 o'clock, or 2 o'clock, or whatever.

Everyone knows the location of any number from 1 to 12 on the clock dial and easily can use such a reference to find an object.

Once the dial is gone, location by *o'clock* also will be gone, and there is no good substitute. Of course, you can use directions instead: northeast, southwest by south, and so on. However, this would assume you always know which direction is north. Or, if you are arbitrary[1] and decide to let north be straight ahead or straight up regardless of its real location, it still remains true that very few people are as familiar

**ACTIVE READING**

**RECOGNIZE CAUSE AND EFFECT** Asimov has just finished discussing the first effect of the switch from dial to digital. Look ahead. How does Asimov signal the next effects?

ACTIVE READING

CONNECT In what other situations might you use a clock face to point out the location of something?

with a compass as they are with a clock face.

Here's still another point. When children are learning to count, once they master the first few numbers, they quickly get the whole idea. You go from 0 to 9 and 0 to 9 over and over again. In other words, you go from 0 to 9, then from 10 to 19, then from 20 to 29, and so on until you reach 90 to 99, and then you pass on to 100, when the whole thing starts again. It is very systematic, and once you learn it you never forget.

Time is different. Since the early Sumerians[2] couldn't handle fractions very well, they chose 60 as their base because it can be divided evenly in a number of ways. Ever since, we have continued to use 60 in certain applications, the chief of which is in the measurement of time. Thus, there are 60 minutes to an hour.

If you are using a dial, that doesn't matter. You simply note the position of the hands, and they automatically become a measure of time: "half past 5," "a quarter past 3," "a quarter to 10," and so on. You see time as space and not as numbers.

In a digital clock, however, time is measured only as numbers, so you go from 1:01 to 1:59 and then move directly to 2:00. It introduces an irregularity in the number system that is going to insert an unnecessary stumbling block into education. Just think: 5.50 is halfway between 5 and 6 if we measure length or weight or money or anything but time. In time, 5:50 is nearly 6; it is 5:30 that is halfway between 5 and 6.

What shall we do about all this? I can think of nothing. There is an odd conservatism[3] among people that will make them fight to the death against making time decimal and having 100 minutes to the hour.

But even so, what can be done about the lost meaning of *clockwise, counterclockwise,* and *o'clock* as points of reference? It will be a pretty problem for our descendants. ❖

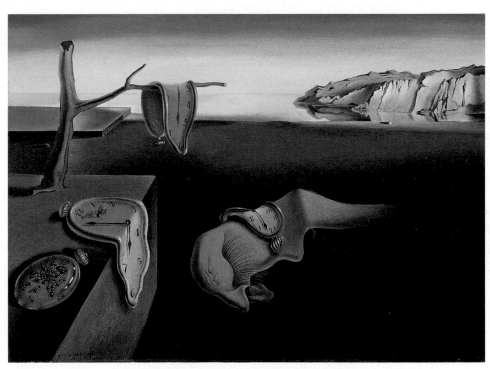

*The Persistence of Memory [Persistence de la mémoire]* (1931), Salvador Dali. Oil on canvas, 9½″ × 13″. The Museum of Modern Art, New York. Given anonymously. Photograph © 1998 The Museum of Modern Art, New York.

---

1. **arbitrary** (är′bĭ-trĕr′ē): making a choice on the basis of what is convenient rather than what is reasonable or natural.
2. **Sumerians** (sōō-mîr′ē-ənz): the people of one of the earliest human civilizations, which flourished from 5,000 to 4,000 years ago in the Middle East.
3. **conservatism** (kən-sûr′və-tĭz′əm): unwillingness to change.

# Connect to the Literature

**1. What Do You Think?** Did you find Asimov's examples convincing? Explain your response.

**Comprehension Check**
- What is the technological change that worries the author?
- How might this change affect the way we give directions?
- How could it affect the way children learn to tell time?

# Think Critically

**2.** Do you agree that "there are no good substitutes" for the words *clockwise* and *counterclockwise?* Why or why not?

**3.** Do you think the author is arguing against the use of digital clocks? Explain your judgment.

> THINK ABOUT
> - his opinion of digital clocks
> - the **tone** he uses in his conclusion

**4.** **ACTIVE READING** | **ANALYZING TEXT STRUCTURE** | Study the **cause-effect** chart that you created in your  **READER'S NOTEBOOK**. Notice how Asimov organizes information about the effects, beginning with the most immediate and obvious ones. How does this structure affect your understanding or interest?

**5.** What do you think is the **theme,** or most important message, of the essay?

# Extend Interpretations

**6. Critic's Corner** One critic has said that Asimov is "thankfully, a teacher first and a scientist second." How would you explain this quotation? Find details from the essay that support this statement.

**7. Connect to Life** What do you think is gained or lost when progress in modern technology changes the way we live? List examples of recent changes and their effects to support your opinion.

## Literary Analysis

**EXPOSITORY ESSAY** In an **expository essay,** a writer wants to explain something or give information about a topic. In this essay, for example, Asimov gives information about two different types of clocks.
**Activity** Review the selection to look for ways that Asimov involves the reader. For example, in key places he uses the pronoun *you,* as if the reader were actually performing actions. Find other examples of the techniques Asimov uses to involve the reader.

**ACTIVE READING** | **FACT AND OPINION** A **fact** is a statement about something that has happened or something that can be observed. A fact can be proven to be correct; for example, Asimov writes:

*When something turns, it can turn in just one of two ways, either clockwise or counterclockwise.*

On the other hand, **opinions, judgments,** feelings, or beliefs can be expressed by using words and phrases such as *I think, it seems, always, never, probably, most, all,* or *none.* For example, Asimov expresses this opinion:

*And yet there will be a loss in the conversion of dial to digital, and few people seem to be worrying about it.*

With a partner, go back through the essay and make a list of both facts and opinions that Asimov has used to help you understand his concerns about clocks. When you are done, compare your list with other classmates'.

# Choices & CHALLENGES

## Writing Options

**1. Tech Paragraph** Basing your answer on recent advances in technology, do you agree or disagree that the effects of progress are usually positive? Write your opinion in an expository paragraph and place it in your **Working Portfolio.**

**Writing Handbook**
See page 1158: Cause and Effect.

**2. Invented Terms** Develop two new words that you think would be adequate substitutes for *clockwise* and *counterclockwise.* Then write a set of directions in which you use your new words.

## Activities & Explorations

**1. Personal Interviews** Interview six or seven older adults on the impact that modern technology has had on them. What difference has it made in your life? Share your findings with classmates. ~ **SPEAKING AND LISTENING**

**2. Progress Presentation** In an oral report, tell how specific inventions have changed our lives. Use visual aids to help your classmates understand your information. ~ **SPEAKING AND LISTENING**

## Inquiry & Research

Find out more about the history of timepieces and what kinds of instruments were used to tell time before the dial clock. Draw simple sketches to illustrate some of these instruments. Then share your findings with other classmates and discuss the following question: What kind of timepiece might eventually replace the digital clock?

## Art Connection

Take another look at Dali's painting *The Persistence of Memory* on page 109. What do you think is the connection between the painting and "Dial versus Digital"?

---

## Isaac Asimov
### 1920–1992

**Other Works**
*The Robots of Dawn*
*Robot Dreams*
*Frontiers*
*The Subatomic Monster*
*The Disappearing Man and Other Mysteries*
*Computer Crimes and Capers*

**A Working Youth** Isaac Asimov was born in Russia, and came with his parents to the United States when he was just three. His parents owned a candy store, where Asimov worked from ages 9 to 22. He and his family always worked long hours and kept the store open seven days a week. Asimov had no time for extracurricular activities, but his years in the candy store gave him two qualities that would affect his whole life—a strong work ethic and a fascination for science fiction. Asimov once said that he always kept "candy-store hours."

**Prolific Writer** In his lifetime, the "Great Explainer" wrote over 470 books in addition to countless essays and magazine articles. He did all his own research and typing and wrote constantly, 7 days a week, 12 hours a day. He even taught himself to type 90 words a minute so that he could keep up with his busy work schedule.

**Leader in Science Fiction** According to many critics, Asimov wrote some of the best science-fiction stories ever published. He first discovered this genre in magazines that were for sale in his family's store. His father thought magazines were unsuitable reading material, but he allowed his son to read a science-fiction magazine only because it had the word *science* in the title. At age 17, Asimov wrote his own science-fiction story, and eventually he originated many of the classic ideas used by other science-fiction writers, including concepts involving robots and robotics.

# Once More to the Lake

*Essay by* E. B. WHITE

## Connect to Your Life

**Childhood Revisited** Think of a special place from childhood that you would like to revisit. Jot down specific details that this place brings to mind and describe what you would hope to find if you returned there.

## Build Background

**Essayist for the Ages** Although well-known for his classic children's books, such as *Stuart Little* and *Charlotte's Web,* E. B. White may be best known for his essays, which appeared for many years in *The New Yorker* magazine. He once described the essayist as a writer "sustained by the childish belief that everything he thinks about, everything that happens to him, is of general interest." Few writers have been able to capture the wonders of everyday life as well as White has. In the following essay, a simple visit to a lake becomes a moving experience as White recalls his own childhood.

WORDS TO KNOW
**Vocabulary Preview**

| | |
|---|---|
| haunt | petulant |
| indelible | tentatively |
| languidly | |

## Focus Your Reading

**LITERARY ANALYSIS** **PERSONAL ESSAY** A **personal essay** is a brief nonfiction work that expresses the writer's thoughts, feelings, and opinions on events and issues in his or her own life. As you read this essay, look for details about White's own views and recollections. What do you learn about him as a person?

**ACTIVE READING** **IDENTIFYING COMPARISON AND CONTRAST**

**Comparison and contrast** is a device used by a writer to identify similarities and differences between two things. In the essay you are about to read, White compares his childhood vacations in Maine with a vacation in the present with his own son. When comparing two different times, writers use certain words or phrases to signal comparison and contrast.

**Compare:** *same, just as, still, always*
**Contrast:** *since, difference, now, nowadays, in those days, more, not so much*

**READER'S NOTEBOOK** As you read this story, jot down characteristics of the lake during White's childhood and the lake as it is in the present. Then make a Venn diagram like the one here to show the differences and similarities.

Then — Both — Now

Boats had quiet inboard motors.

People took boats on the lake.

Boats have noisy outboard motors.

# Once More to the Lake

## E. B. White

Illustration by Gary Head.

From the Potomac River Series, 1991, Diana Suttenfield. Mary Bell Galleries, Chicago.

kept remembering everything, lying in bed in the mornings—the small steamboat that had a long rounded stern like the lip of a Ubangi,[5] and how quietly she ran on the moonlight sails, when the older boys played their mandolins and the girls sang and we ate doughnuts dipped in sugar, and how sweet the music was on the water in the shining night, and what it had felt like to think about girls then. After breakfast we would go up to the store and the things were in the same place—the minnows in a bottle, the plugs and spinners disarranged and pawed over by the youngsters from the boys' camp, the Fig Newtons and the Beeman's gum. Outside, the road was tarred and cars stood in front of the store. Inside, all was just as it had always been, except there was more Coca-Cola and not so much Moxie and root beer and birch beer and sarsaparilla. We would walk out with the bottle of pop apiece and sometimes the pop would backfire up our noses and hurt. We explored the streams, quietly, where the turtles slid off the sunny logs and dug their way into the soft bottom; and we lay on the town wharf and fed worms to the tame bass. Everywhere we went I had trouble making out which was I, the one walking at my side, the one walking in my pants.

**ACTIVE READING**

CLARIFY How does White's son remind him of himself?

One afternoon while we were there at that lake a thunderstorm came up. It was like the revival of an old melodrama that I had seen long ago with childish awe. The second-act climax of the drama of the electrical disturbance over a lake in America had not changed in any important respect. This was the big scene, still the big scene. The whole thing was so familiar, the first feeling of oppression and heat and a general air around camp of not wanting to go very far away. In midafternoon (it was all the same) a curious darkening of the sky, and a lull in everything that had made life tick; and then the way the boats suddenly swung the other way at their moorings with the coming of a breeze out of the new quarter, and the premonitory rumble. Then the kettledrum, then the snare, then the bass drum and cymbals, then crackling light against the dark, and the gods grinning and licking their chops in the hills. Afterward the calm, the rain steadily rustling in the calm lake, the return of light and hope and spirits, and the campers running out in joy and relief to go swimming in the rain, their bright cries perpetuating the deathless joke about how they were getting simply drenched, and the children screaming with delight at the new sensation of bathing in the rain, and the joke about getting drenched linking the generations in a strong indestructible chain. And the comedian who waded in carrying an umbrella.

When the others went swimming, my son said he was going in, too. He pulled his dripping trunks from the line where they had hung all through the shower and wrung them out. Languidly, and with no thought of going in, I watched him, his hard little body, skinny and bare, saw him wince slightly as he pulled up around his vitals the small, soggy, icy garment. As he buckled the swollen belt, suddenly my groin felt the chill of death. ❖

---

5. **Ubangi** (yōō-băng′gē): a woman of a people living near the Ubangi River in Africa, with pierced lips enlarged by saucerlike disks.

# A Letter from E. B. White

**I**'m not an expert on what goes on under my hood, but I'll try to answer your questions.

When I wrote "Once More to the Lake," I was living year round in this place on the coast of Maine and contributing a monthly department to Harper's.[1] I had spent many summers as a boy on Great Pond—one of the Belgrade Lakes. It's only about 75 miles from here and one day I felt an urge to revisit the lake and have a week of freshwater life, which is very different from saltwater. So I went over with my small son and we did some fishing. I simply started with a desire to see again and experience again what I had seen and experienced as a boy. During our stay over there, the "idea of time" naturally insinuated itself into my thoughts, because my son was the age I had been in the previous life at the lake, and so I felt a sort of mixed-up identity. I don't recall whether I had the title from the start. Probably not. I don't believe the title had anything to do with the composing process. The "process" is probably every bit as mysterious to me

as it is to some of your students—if that will make them feel any better.

Sorry I can't be more explicit.[2] Writing, for me, is simply a matter of trying to find out and report what's going on in my head and get it down on paper. I haven't any devices, shortcuts, or tricks.

---

1. **contributing . . . Harper's:** writing a regular feature for the magazine *Harper's Bazaar.*
2. **explicit:** clear and detailed.

## Connect to the Literature

1. **What Do You Think?** What scene from the essay stands out most in your mind? Why?

   ### Comprehension Check
   - Why does White take a vacation at this particular lake?
   - Which change at the lake bothers White the most?
   - When does White feel a "chill of death"?

## Think Critically

2. Why do you think this return trip to the lake is so important to White?

    **THINK ABOUT**
   - what he remembers about this childhood place
   - the fact that he brings his son with him
   - details in the first paragraph

3. What insights does White seem to gain from this experience?

    **THINK ABOUT**
   - his identification with his son
   - his identification with his father
   - what has changed and what has stayed the same over time

4. What do you make of White's phrase "the chill of death" in the last sentence of the essay? Explain your response.

5. **ACTIVE READING** **IDENTIFYING COMPARISON AND CONTRAST**
   In this essay, White talks about the similarities as well as the differences between the lake of his childhood and the lake now. Which do you think are more important to White, the similarities or the differences? Refer to your Venn diagram as well as the text in explaining your opinion.

6. What insights about "Once More to the Lake" do you gain from reading "A Letter from E. B. White"?

## Extend Interpretations

7. **Critic's Corner** White's friend and *New Yorker* colleague James Thurber once praised him for "those silver and crystal sentences which have a ring like nobody else's sentences in the world." In your opinion, which sentences in the essay might be described this way?

8. **Connect to Life** In this essay, written more than half a century ago, White suggests that there is a "strong indestructible chain" linking the generations. Do you believe such a chain exists today? Explain your opinion.

## Literary Analysis

**PERSONAL ESSAY** A brief piece of nonfiction that expresses the writer's thoughts, feelings, and opinions on events and issues from his or her own life is called a **personal essay.** For E. B. White, the personal essay was a favorite form of writing. Personal essays sometimes include elements of **autobiography,** a form of writing in which a person tells the story of his or her own life. Some personal essays, however, focus more on reflections or ideas than on a narrative of events. Many deal with both.

**Cooperative Learning Activity** With a small group, look at the essay and examine how much White uses personal reflection as compared to the narration of events. Construct a pie chart like the one below, showing the approximate proportion of reflection to narration. Discuss how this proportion contributes to the essay's total effect and how the piece might be different if White had used less personal reflection.

actual events depicted

personal reflection

## Writing Options

**1. Vacation Essay** Draft an essay that White's son might have written in school when asked to describe his summer vacation. Make sure to include the son's observations of his father.

**2. Slide Show Script** Prepare the script that White might have used to give a slide presentation to his neighbors after his return home.

**3. Newspaper Editorial** Suppose developers are planning to clear away the cottages and build high-rise condominiums around this lake. Write an editorial for the local newspaper, opposing or approving of the plan. Place the entry in your **Working Portfolio.**

**Writing Handbook**
See pages 1161–1162: Persuasive Writing.

## Activities & Explorations

**1. Travel Advertisement** Create an illustrated travel brochure advertising the place described in this essay. Scan the essay for details about the lake in Maine and its surroundings in the present day. Draw pictures of the lake, including captions and text to convince travelers to choose your spot for their next vacation. ~ **ART**

**2. Cross-Generational Presentation** Think of some activity or tradition that has been repeated for more than one generation in your family or community. How has this activity remained the same? How has it changed? Make a presentation in which you describe to your class the history of this event.
~ **SPEAKING AND LISTENING**

## Inquiry & Research

**Vacation Spots** With increased technology and the development of rural areas, family vacations in America have changed over the past 100 years; people drive more cars, use more motorboats, and in some regions must travel farther to find quiet, secluded areas. Research tourism in the United States at the beginning of the century and now. Write a short report about the changes that have occurred as well as the things that have remained constant.

# Vocabulary in Action

**EXERCISE A: WORD MEANING** For each phrase in the first column, write the letter of the synonymous phrase in the second column.

1. languidly loiter
2. tentatively tell
3. Harold's haunt
4. petulant person
5. indelible ink

a. permanent pigment
b. cross character
c. listlessly linger
d. Harry's hangout
e. doubtfully disclose

**EXERCISE B** With a partner, try creating music that helps to convey the meanings of three of the Words to Know. You could clap out a rhythm, hum a tune, or use a musical instrument.

**Building Vocabulary**
For an in-depth study of synonyms, see page 1000.

| WORDS TO KNOW | haunt indelible languidly | petulant tentatively |
| --- | --- | --- |

# Grammar in Context: Active and Passive Voice

E. B. White uses both the active and the passive voice in this sentence from "Once More to the Lake."

> Some of the cottages were owned by nearby farmers, and you would live at the shore and eat your meals at the farmhouse.

Verbs in the **active voice,** like those shown in blue type, emphasize the people or things performing actions (you *would live, eat*). They create lively, energetic images, like those in a movie. Verbs in the **passive voice,** like the one shown in red type, emphasize the people or things that are acted upon (cottages *were owned*). The images they create are more like photographs or still lifes. Experienced writers make use of both voices to convey precise shades of meaning in their writing.

*Usage Tip:* You can use passive voice when the subject of the sentence is not known, or when you want to shift emphasis to another word.

**WRITING EXERCISE** Rewrite each sentence, changing the voice of the verb from active to passive or vice versa. Briefly explain how your revision changed the focus of the sentence.

**Example: *Original*** The shoreline is dotted with cottages. (passive)
***Rewritten*** Cottages dot the shoreline. (active, shifts emphasis to the cottages)

1. Some of the farmers serve hot meals.
2. The camp is already rented out.
3. Cars have worn away the middle track of the road.
4. The whir of outboard motors breaks the silence.
5. The ocean is stirred up by strong winds.

**Connect to the Literature** Skim White's essay for sentences in which he uses the passive voice. How does the use of this voice help create a sense of time's standing still?

**Grammar Handbook** Active and Passive Voice, p. 1187

## E. B. White
1899–1985

**Other Works**
*One Man's Meat*
*The Points of My Compass*
*The Elements of Style*
*Charlotte's Web*
*Poems and Sketches of E. B. White*

**Rise to Success** In addition to being regarded as one of the 20th century's finest essayists, E. B. White has been acclaimed as a poet, humorist, and children's author. Born in Mount Vernon, New York, Elwyn Brooks White attended Cornell University, where he edited the college newspaper. In 1922, after serving in World War I and then completing his education at Cornell, he briefly worked as a reporter for the *Seattle Times* and served as mess boy on a ship to Alaska. On returning to the New York area, White began submitting his writing to the then-new magazine *The New Yorker.* He soon joined the *New Yorker* staff and remained associated with the magazine for the rest of his writing career.

**A Man for All Seasons** The subject matter of White's essays is extremely varied—everything "from the tremor of a leaf in the afternoon sun to the malaise of modern man," as one critic observed. Often he wrote about rural Maine, where he vacationed as a child and as an adult.

**Celebrated Accomplishments** White is well-known for the 1959 edition of *The Elements of Style,* a writing manual that he coauthored with his former college professor William Strunk, Jr. He also collaborated with his wife, Katherine, in editing the 1941 anthology *A Subtreasury of American Humor.* His many literary awards include a Pulitzer Prize special citation.

## Author Activity

**White Retrospective** At the library, look up some of White's essays from his years at *The New Yorker.* Choose one and, in your own words, summarize the essay and explain how it fits the definition of a personal essay on page 105.

# Montgomery Boycott

*Memoir by* CORETTA SCOTT KING

## Connect to Your Life

**Liberty and Justice for All** What do you know about the civil rights movement and two of its key participants, Rosa Parks and Martin Luther King, Jr.? Share your knowledge with your classmates in a class discussion.

## Build Background

**Times of Protest** In the 1890s and early decades of the 20th century, many states, especially in the South, passed laws to ensure segregation, the complete separation of the races in public places. These so-called Jim Crow laws—named after a character in an old song—discriminated against African Americans. After World War II, opponents of these laws challenged their legality. In 1954 the Supreme Court, reversing an earlier decision, declared that it was unconstitutional to force whites and blacks to attend separate schools. Soon afterward, African Americans in Montgomery, Alabama, began the bus boycott that is the subject of the following selection.

A pivotal event in the civil rights movement, the Montgomery boycott first brought to national attention the Reverend Martin Luther King, Jr., the writer's husband. King's eye-opening efforts of nonviolent protest helped inspire many others in the struggle for civil rights. In 1960, for example, African-American students in Greensboro, North Carolina, initiated a new protest strategy, the sit-in, when they risked arrest for insisting on being served at a local segregated lunch counter.

| WORDS TO KNOW<br>**Vocabulary Preview** | |
| --- | --- |
| coercion | exposé |
| coherently | militant |
| degrading | oppression |
| devoid | perpetuation |
| exaltation | radiant |

## Focus Your Reading

**LITERARY ANALYSIS** **MEMOIR** A **memoir** is a work of nonfiction that is based on a writer's memory of key events and people in his or her life. In this selection, Coretta Scott King shares her memory of her husband's involvement in a history-making event, as illustrated by this passage:

> *Our greatest concern was how we were going to reach the fifty thousand people of Montgomery, no matter how hard we worked.*

As you read, notice how Mrs. King blends historical reporting with her own private memories.

**ACTIVE READING** **CAUSE AND EFFECT** Events in real life are often related by **cause and effect,** which means that one event is the reason that another event happens. The first event is the **cause;** the events produced by the cause are the **effects.** "Montgomery Boycott" reports a now-famous incident from the civil rights movement in which Mrs. Rosa Parks refused to give up her seat on a bus. Her one act produced many important effects.

**READER'S NOTEBOOK** As you read the selection, look for evidence of the different effects caused by Mrs. Parks's decision. Notice how different people and groups in Montgomery responded to her action. Jot down your findings on a diagram like this one.

Cause: Rosa Parks keeps bus seat → Effects

# MONTGOMERY BOYCOTT

## CORETTA SCOTT KING

NOTICE
IT IS REQUIRED BY LAW UNDER
PENALTY OF FINE OF $5.00 TO $25.00
THAT WHITE AND NEGRO PASSENGERS MUST
OCCUPY THE RESPECTIVE SPACE OR SEATS
INDICATED BY SIGNS IN THIS VEHICLE

TEXAS PENAL CODE ARTICLE 1659 SEC 4
DALLAS CITY ORDINANCE NO 2904

COLORED.

At one time, signs ordering the segregation of black and white passengers were posted on buses and trains in the South. This photograph was taken the day the Supreme Court banned segregation on public transportation. UPI/Bettmann Newsphotos.

Of all the facets of segregation in Montgomery, the most degrading were the rules of the Montgomery City Bus Lines. This northern-owned corporation outdid the South itself. Although seventy percent of its passengers were black, it treated them like cattle—worse than that, for nobody insults a cow. The first seats on all buses were reserved for whites. Even if they were unoccupied and the rear seats crowded, blacks would have to stand at the back in case some whites might get aboard; and if the front seats happened to be occupied and more white people boarded the bus, black people seated in the rear were forced to get up and give them their seats. Furthermore—and I don't think northerners ever realized this—blacks had to pay their fares at the front of the bus, get off, and walk to the rear door to board again. Sometimes the bus would drive off without them after they had paid their fare. This would happen to elderly people or pregnant women, in bad weather or good, and was considered a joke by the drivers. Frequently the white bus drivers abused their passengers, calling them . . . black cows, or black apes. Imagine what it was like, for example, for a black man to get on a bus with his son and be subjected to such treatment.

There had been one incident in March 1955, when fifteen-year-old Claudette Colvin refused to give up her seat to a white passenger. The high school girl was handcuffed and carted off to the police station. At that time Martin served on a committee to protest to the city and bus-company officials. The committee was received politely—and nothing was done.

The fuel that finally made that slow-burning fire blaze up was an almost routine incident. On December 1, 1955, Mrs. Rosa Parks, a forty-two-year-old seamstress whom my husband aptly described as "a charming person with a radiant personality," boarded a bus to go home after a long day working and shopping. The bus was crowded, and Mrs. Parks found a seat at the beginning of the black section. At the next stop more whites got on. The driver ordered Mrs. Parks to give her seat to a white man who boarded; this meant that she would have to stand all the way home. Rosa Parks was not in a revolutionary frame of mind. She had not planned to do what she did. Her cup had run over. As she said later, "I was just plain tired, and my feet hurt." So she sat there, refusing to get up. The driver called a policeman, who arrested her and took her to the courthouse. From there Mrs. Parks called E. D. Nixon, who came down and signed a bail bond for her.

Mr. Nixon was a fiery Alabamian. He was a Pullman porter[1] who had been active in A. Philip Randolph's Brotherhood of Sleeping Car Porters, and in civil rights activities. Suddenly he also had had enough; suddenly, it seemed, almost every African American in Montgomery had had enough. It was spontaneous combustion.[2] Phones began ringing all over the black section of the city. The Women's Political Council suggested a one-day boycott of the buses as a protest. E. D. Nixon courageously agreed to organize it.

The first we knew about it was when Mr. Nixon called my husband early in the morning of Friday, December 2. He had already talked to Ralph Abernathy.[3] After describing the incident, Mr. Nixon said, "We have taken this type

---

1. **Pullman porter:** a railroad employee who serves people in a Pullman car; that is, a passenger car with seats that can be converted into beds.

2. **spontaneous combustion** (spŏn-tā′nē-əs kəm-bŭs′chən): literally, the situation that occurs when something bursts into flames on its own, without the addition of heat from an outside source.

3. **Ralph Abernathy** (1926–1990): a minister who became a close colleague of Martin Luther King, Jr., and an important civil rights leader.

# NOTICE

## . . . blacks had to pay their fares at the front of the bus, get off, and walk to the rear door to board again.

of thing too long. I feel the time has come to boycott the buses. It's the only way to make the white folks see that we will not take this sort of thing any longer."

Martin agreed with him and offered the Dexter Avenue Church as a meeting place. After much telephoning, a meeting of black ministers and civic leaders was arranged for that evening. Martin said later that as he approached his church Friday evening, he was nervously wondering how many leaders would really turn up. To his delight, Martin found over forty people, representing every segment of African-American life, crowded into the large meeting room at Dexter. There were doctors, lawyers, businessmen, federal-government employees, union leaders, and a great many ministers. The latter were particularly welcome, not only because of their influence, but because it meant that they were beginning to accept Martin's view that "religion deals with both heaven and earth. . . . Any religion that professes to be concerned with the souls of men and is not concerned with the slums that doom them, the economic conditions that strangle them, and the social conditions that cripple them, is dry-as-dust religion." From that very first step, the Christian ministry provided the leadership of our struggle, as Christian ideals were its source.

Martin told me after he got home that the meeting was almost wrecked because questions or suggestions from the floor were cut off. However, after a stormy session, one thing was clear: however much they differed on details,

everyone was unanimously for a boycott. It was set for Monday, December 5. Committees were organized; all the ministers present promised to urge their congregations to take part. Several thousand leaflets were printed on the church mimeograph machine, describing the reasons for the boycott and urging all blacks not to ride buses "to work, to town, to school, or anyplace on Monday, December 5." Everyone was asked to come to a mass meeting at the Holt Street Baptist Church on Monday evening for further instructions. The Reverend A. W. Wilson had offered his church because it was larger than Dexter and more convenient, being in the center of the black district.

Saturday was a busy day for Martin and the other members of the committee. They hustled around town talking with other leaders, arranging with the black-owned taxi companies for special bulk fares and with the owners of private automobiles to get the people to and from work. I could do little to help because Yoki[4] was only two weeks old, and my physician, Dr. W. D. Pettus, who was very careful, advised me to stay in for a month. However, I was kept busy answering the telephone, which rang continuously, and coordinating from that central point the many messages and arrangements.

Our greatest concern was how we were going to reach the fifty thousand black people of Montgomery, no matter how hard we worked. The white press, in an outraged exposé, spread

---

4. **Yoki:** nickname of the Kings' daughter Yolanda.

| WORDS TO KNOW | **exposé** (ĕk'spō-zā') *n.* an account that reveals something negative to the public |
| --- | --- |

Martin and Ralph went together to the meeting. When they got within four blocks of the Holt Street Baptist Church, there was an enormous traffic jam. Five thousand people stood outside the church listening to loudspeakers and singing hymns. Inside it was so crowded, Martin told me, the people had to lift Ralph and him above the crowd and pass them from hand to hand over their heads to the platform. The crowd and the singing inspired Martin, and God answered his prayer. Later Martin said, "That night I understood what the older preach-

Dr. Martin Luther King, Jr. (*left*), and Coretta Scott King in their early days as civil rights activists. Culver Pictures.

# "... we are tired. Tired of being segregated and humiliated; tired of being kicked about by the brutal feet of oppression."

ers meant when they said, 'Open your mouth and God will speak for you.' "

First the people sang "Onward, Christian Soldiers" in a tremendous wave of five thousand voices. This was followed by a prayer and a reading of the Scriptures. Martin was introduced. People applauded; television lights beat upon him. Without any notes at all he began to speak. Once again he told the story of Mrs. Parks, and rehearsed some of the wrongs black people were suffering. Then he said,

> But there comes a time when people get tired. We are here this evening to say to those who have mistreated us so long, that we are tired. Tired of being segregated and humiliated; tired of being kicked about by the brutal feet of oppression.

The audience cheered wildly, and Martin said,

> We have no alternative but to protest. We have been amazingly patient . . . but we come here tonight to be saved from that patience that makes us patient with anything less than freedom and justice.

Taking up the challenging newspaper comparison with the White Citizens Councils and the Klan,[8] Martin said,

> They are protesting for the perpetuation of injustice in the community; we're

protesting for the birth of justice . . . their methods lead to violence and lawlessness. But in our protest there will be no cross-burnings, no white person will be taken from his home by a hooded Negro mob and brutally murdered . . . We will be guided by the highest principles of law and order.

Having roused the audience for militant action, Martin now set limits upon it. His study of nonviolence and his love of Christ informed his words. He said,

> No one must be intimidated to keep them from riding the buses. Our method must be persuasion, not coercion. We will only say to the people, "Let your conscience be your guide." . . . Our actions must be guided by the deepest principles of the Christian faith. . . . Once again we must hear the words of Jesus, "Love your enemies. Bless them that curse you. Pray for them that despitefully use you." If we fail to do this, our protest will end up as a meaningless drama on the stage of history and its memory will be shrouded in the

---

8. **Klan:** the Ku Klux Klan, a secret society trying to establish white power and authority by unlawful and violent methods directed against African Americans and other minority groups.

| WORDS TO KNOW | **oppression** (ə-prĕsh′ən) *n.* unjust or cruel exercise of power or authority |
| --- | --- |
| | **perpetuation** (pər-pĕch′ōō-ā′shən) *n.* a long-lasting continuation |
| | **coercion** (kō-ûr′zhən) *n.* the use of power or threats to force someone to do something |

131

ugly garments of shame. . . . We must not become bitter and end up by hating our white brothers. As Booker T. Washington[9] said, "Let no man pull you so low as to make you hate him."

Finally, Martin said,

*If you will protest courageously, and yet with dignity and Christian love, future historians will say, "There lived a great people—a black people—who injected new meaning and dignity into the veins of civilization." This is our challenge and our overwhelming responsibility.*

As Martin finished speaking, the audience rose cheering in <u>exaltation</u>. And in that speech my husband set the keynote and the tempo of the Movement he was to lead, from Montgomery onward. ❖

---

9. **Booker T. Washington** (1856–1915): African-American educator and writer.

# SIT-INS

## Margaret Walker

*Greensboro, North Carolina, in the Spring of 1960*

You were our first brave ones to defy their
   dissonance of hate
With your silence
With your willingness to suffer
Without violence
5  Those first bright young to fling names across pages
Of new southern history
With courage and faith, convictions, and intelligence
The first to blaze a flaming path for justice
And awaken consciences
10  Of these stony ones.

*Come, Lord Jesus, Bold Young Galilean[1]*
*Sit Beside this Counter, Lord, with Me!*

---

1. **Galilean** (găl′ə-lē′ən): a term used as a synonym for Jesus, because Galilee was the center of Jesus' ministry.

## Connect to the Literature

1. **What Do You Think?** What went through your mind while reading the selection? Describe your thoughts.

> **Comprehension Check**
> • What did the African-American leaders in Montgomery do to protest Mrs. Parks's arrest?
> • Why was the first day of the boycott a success?
> • What method of protest did Dr. King recommend?

## Think Critically

2. **ACTIVE READING** | **CAUSE AND EFFECT** Review the cause-and-effect diagram that you made in your **READER'S NOTEBOOK** as you read the selection. What do you think were the most important effects of Rosa Parks's decision not to give up her bus seat?

3. Do you think the phrase "spontaneous combustion" is a good description of the events leading up to the boycott?

**THINK ABOUT**
> • Rosa Parks's motivation for challenging the system
> • how segregation had affected the African-American community

4. What does the selection suggest about the character, goals, and principles of Martin Luther King, Jr.?

5. What is your opinion of Rosa Parks and her accomplishments? Explain your opinion.

6. Based on your understanding of "Montgomery Boycott," what qualities do you think were valued by the early participants in the civil rights movement?

## Extend Interpretations

7. **Comparing Texts** Compare and contrast the ways in which "Montgomery Boycott" and the poem "Sit-Ins" depict the actions and motivations of civil rights protesters. Cite evidence from the poem, as well as from the memoir.

8. **Connect to Life** Do you think a boycott is an effective and fair means of protest? Use examples to explain your reasoning.

## Literary Analysis

**MEMOIR** A **memoir** is a type of nonfiction that focuses on a person's life. In some cases, *memoir* is simply another word for **autobiography,** a work that tells about the personal experiences of the author. In other cases, however, a memoir can be a **biography** or a **biographical sketch.** For example, people can write memoirs about famous friends or family members. A biographical memoir usually blends the writer's knowledge of the subject with other sources of information about the subject. Mrs. King's memoir combines elements of biography and autobiography.

**Cooperative Learning Activity** In a small group, review "Montgomery Boycott" to decide where Mrs. King is likely to have gathered her information. For example, a statement such as "Martin came home late Sunday night," probably came from her own memory. But other statements probably required outside sources of information, such as interviews or newspaper accounts. Create a chart, like the one shown, to record information. For each statement recorded, decide whether it is likely to have come from Mrs. King's memory or from other sources.

| Sources of Information | | |
|---|---|---|
| Statement/Information | Memory | Other Sources |
| "Martin came home late Sunday night." | ✓ | |
| | | |
| | | |

# *Choices&* CHALLENGES

## Writing Options

**1. Historic Diary** Write the diary entry Rosa Parks might have written just after her famous bus ride and arrest. Expand on ideas touched upon in the selection and in your discussions.

**2. Newspaper Editorial** Write an editorial on the Montgomery boycott that might have appeared the day after it began. In your editorial, consider the reasons both for and against the boycott. Then recommend a course of action. Use a diagram like the one below to jot down notes for writing. Place the editorial in your **Working Portfolio.**

| Reasons for | Reasons against |
|---|---|

## Activities & Explorations

**1. Storytelling** Retell the story of the boycott as if you were presenting it to an audience of young children celebrating Martin Luther King Day. If possible, make arrangements to tell your story to an appropriate audience. **~ SPEAKING AND LISTENING**

**2. Historical Exhibit** Find and photocopy news stories and magazine articles that reported the Montgomery boycott when it happened. Use them in a "Moments in History" bulletin-board display or exhibit. **~ VIEWING AND REPRESENTING**

**3. Speech for the Ages** Bring to class and play a recording of a speech by Martin Luther King, Jr. Explain when and where he made the speech and why it is significant. **~ SPEAKING AND LISTENING**

## Inquiry & Research

**1. A Dark Day in History** Martin Luther King, Jr., was assassinated on April 4, 1968. Find out how another national leader reacted to King's death and was able to offer words of comfort to others.

 **Real World Link** To begin your research, read Robert Kennedy's speech about King on pages 136–137.

**2. We Shall Overcome** Research and prepare a time line that identifies and briefly describes events in the civil rights movement. You might begin with the Montgomery boycott or with the 1954 Supreme Court decision in *Brown* v. *Board of Education of Topeka, Kansas.*

Martin Luther King, Jr. leads protest march from Selma to Montgomery, 1965.

## Vocabulary in Action

**EXERCISE: ASSESSMENT PRACTICE** On your paper, indicate whether the following pairs of words are synonyms or antonyms.

1. degrading—humiliating
2. radiant—dim
3. exposé—tribute
4. oppression—injustice
5. coherently—sensibly
6. militant—meek
7. devoid—full
8. perpetuation—halt
9. coercion—intimidation
10. exaltation—glorification

### Building Vocabulary

For an in-depth lesson on word origins, see page 356.

# Grammar in Context: Adverbs

In the excerpt from "Montgomery Boycott," Coretta Scott King frequently uses adverbs to add detail. An **adverb,** as you may recall, is a word that modifies a verb, an adjective, or another adverb.

> time
> [E. D. Nixon] had **already** talked to Ralph Abernathy.
>
> degree    degree
> **However much** they differed on details,
>
>                          manner
> everyone was **unanimously** for a boycott.

As the labels above the sentences show, adverbs can supply information about when, to what degree, or in what manner things are done. They can also tell where and how often events occur.

*Usage Tip:* Be sure not to use an adjective when an adverb is called for. Example: He ran quickly (not quick).

**WRITING EXERCISE** Supply an adverb to complete each sentence.

> **Example:** Dr. King _____ decided to attend the meeting. (When?)
> Dr. King <u>later</u> decided to attend the meeting.

1. White bus drivers _____ treated black riders with contempt. (How often?)
2. Dr. King waited _____ for the other leaders, wondering if they would show up. (In what manner?)
3. People who could not get into the church waited _____. (Where?)
4. Dr. King said that blacks had been _____ patient about trying to change unjust laws. (To what degree?)
5. Now he recommended that people protest _____. (In what manner?)

**Grammar Handbook**
Adverbs, p. 1188

## Coretta Scott King
1927–

**Other Works**
*The Words of Martin Luther King, Jr.*

**Struggle for Equality** As a child in Heiberger, Alabama, Coretta Scott had to walk five miles a day to a one-room schoolhouse while white children rode past her on a school bus. That experience and others made her determined to struggle for racial equality. Recognizing education as the key to winning that struggle, she studied hard and eventually won a scholarship to Antioch College in Ohio, where her sister Edythe had been the first African-American student on campus.

**Fateful Encounter** After graduation, Coretta Scott moved to Boston to study music and there met Martin Luther King, Jr., then a graduate student at Boston University, whose dreams of fighting for racial equality coincided with her own. The two were married in 1953.

**Civil-Rights Champion** Over the years, Coretta Scott King has shown great determination and courage in her fight for civil rights. In 1956 her home was bombed; in 1968 her husband was assassinated in Memphis, Tennessee. Nevertheless, on the day before her husband's funeral, she led a march of striking Memphis garbage collectors, and the next year she published *My Life with Martin Luther King, Jr.,* the book from which "Montgomery Boycott" is taken. Since then, she has remained a tireless champion in the struggle for racial justice, most notably as founder and chief executive officer of the Martin Luther King, Jr., Center for Nonviolent Social Change in Atlanta, Georgia.

## Author Activity

With a partner, investigate recent efforts to reopen the case of Martin Luther King's assassination. Find out what Mrs. King and her children have to say about the murder of Dr. King and the handling of the original investigation.

# A EULOGY TO DR. MARTIN LUTHER KING, JR.

### BY ROBERT F. KENNEDY

*On April 4, 1968, hundreds of African Americans gathered for what they thought would be an exciting political event. A presidential candidate, Robert Kennedy, was coming to speak to them. Before he was to deliver his speech, however, Kennedy was informed that Martin Luther King, Jr., had been assassinated earlier that day. He nevertheless went to the rally, where he found the people upbeat in anticipation of his appearance. Realizing that they were unaware of the tragic event, he began his speech with the following words.*

I have bad news for you, for all of our fellow citizens, and people who love peace all over the world, and that is that Martin Luther King was shot and killed tonight.

Martin Luther King dedicated his life to love and to justice for his fellow human beings, and he died because of that effort.

In this difficult day, in this difficult time for the United States, it is perhaps well to ask what kind of a nation we are and what direction we want to move in. For those of you who are black—considering the evidence there evidently is that there were white people who were responsible—you can be filled with bitterness, with hatred, and a desire for revenge. We can move in that direction as a country, in great polarization—black people amongst black, white people amongst white, filled with hatred toward one another.

Or we can make an effort, as Martin Luther King did, to understand and to comprehend, and to replace

**❶**

## Reading for Information

Has a teacher, a coach, a politician, or a community leader ever given a speech that inspired you? If so, he or she may have used some of the **rhetorical techniques**—ways of using language persuasively—that Kennedy used in this address.

### PERSUASIVE RHETORIC

Kennedy sensed that there might be an intense reaction to the news of the assassination. In his speech, he used certain rhetorical techniques to persuade the crowd to remain calm.

**YOUR TURN** Use the questions and activities below to help you explore Kennedy's persuasive techniques.

❶ The **ethical appeal** is a persuasive technique in which the speaker appeals to the audience's sense of right, justice, and virtue. For example, Kennedy says:

> "We can move in that direction as a country, in great polarization—black people amongst black, white people amongst white, filled with hatred . . . Or we can make an effort . . . to understand and to comprehend, and to replace that violence, that stain of bloodshed . . . with an effort to understand with compassion and love."

Kennedy is appealing to the audience's sense of ethics in order to persuade them to his point of view. What does Kennedy say in the next paragraph that may reveal how he identifies with the situation?

**❶** that violence, that stain of bloodshed that has spread across our land, with an effort to understand with compassion and love.

For those of you who are black and are tempted to be filled with hatred and distrust at the injustice of such an act, against all white people, I can only say that I feel in my own heart the same kind of feeling. I had a member of my family killed, but he was killed by a white man. But we have to make an effort in the United States, we have to make an effort to understand, to go beyond these rather difficult times.

My favorite poet was Aeschylus. He wrote, "In our sleep, pain which cannot forget falls drop by drop upon the heart until, in our own despair, against our will, comes wisdom through the awful grace of God."

**❷** What we need in the United States is not division; what we need in the United States is not hatred; what we need in the United States is not violence or lawlessness but love and wisdom, and compassion toward one another, and a feeling of justice towards those who still suffer within our country, whether they be white or they be black.

So I shall ask you tonight to return home, to say a prayer for the family of Martin Luther King, that's true, but more importantly to say a prayer for our own country, which all of us love—a prayer for understanding and that compassion of which I spoke.

**❸** We can do well in this country. We will have difficult times. We've had difficult times in the past. We will have difficult times in the future. It is not the end of violence; it is not the end of lawlessness; it is not the end of disorder.

But the vast majority of white people and the vast majority of black people in this country want to live together, want to improve the quality of our life, and want justice for all human beings who abide in our land.

Let us dedicate ourselves to what the Greeks wrote so many years ago: to tame the savageness of man and to make gentle the life of this world.

Let us dedicate ourselves to that, and say a prayer for our country and for our people.

**❷** **Repetition** of words or phrases is a rhetorical device used to emphasize concepts or ideas. An example is Kennedy's repetition of the phrase "what we need in the United States is not." How effective do you think this device is? Identify at least two additional examples of repetition in the speech.

**❸** **Parallelism** is a form of repetition in which similar grammatical structures are used to emphasize ideas or concepts. For example, Kennedy's "We can do well in this country. . . We will . . . We've had . . . We will . . ." shows the use of parallelism. Parallel sentence structures also create a rhythm that helps to call attention to the point being made. Find two additional examples of parallelism in the speech, and explain how they emphasized Kennedy's ideas.

## Inquiry & Research

**Activity Link: "Montgomery Boycott," p. 124**

With a partner, go back through Kennedy's speech, and point out passages that you find particularly moving. How do you think Kennedy's audience might have reacted to these passages?

# *Writing* Workshop

**Opinion Statement**

## Expressing your opinion . . .

**From Reading to Writing** The opinions of Kurt Vonnegut and W. P. Kinsella come through clearly in their stories. Mary Oliver expresses her views throughout her poem "The Sun." All writers express their opinions directly or indirectly. Some writers, however, create an **opinion statement**, an essay or article specifically designed to express an opinion or persuade. Opinion pieces often appear in newspapers and magazines.

**For Your Portfolio**

**WRITING PROMPT** Write an opinion statement on a topic you feel strongly about.

> **Purpose:** To persuade, to share an opinion
> **Audience:** Readers of your school or local newspaper, your classmates

### Basics in a Box

**Opinion Statement at a Glance**

Presents the issue and states your opinion — Introduction

WHY I BELIEVE IT

Supporting evidence | Supporting evidence | Supporting evidence — Body

Summary of opinion — Conclusion

**RUBRIC  Standards for Writing**

**A successful opinion statement should**

- state the issue and your opinion on it clearly
- support your opinion with convincing examples, facts, and/or statistics
- show an awareness of your audience in word choice and tone
- exhibit clear reasoning
- summarize your opinion in a strong conclusion

**138**  UNIT ONE   PART 1: THE PRICE OF PROGRESS

# Analyzing a Student Model

Aina Calabrese
Southwest High School

### Buckle Up!

On a warm June evening nearly a year ago, my 21-year-old neighbor got into his sports car and took off for his girlfriend's house. He never got there. When she saw him later that evening, he was in the intensive care unit of the local hospital, barely clinging to life after a car accident. His doctors say that he has permanent brain damage and probably will never be able to return to work or live on his own. The doctors also say that his injuries would have been much less severe if he had been wearing a safety belt.

Our state is not one of those that have a law requiring motorists to wear safety belts. I strongly believe that the state legislature should pass such a law as soon as possible. I also believe that people should make it their personal rule to buckle up as soon as they get into a car.

Statistics show that fewer than 20 percent of American motorists use safety belts regularly. If everyone wore a safety belt, as many as 16,000 lives would be saved a year and severe injuries would be greatly reduced. According to the National Highway Traffic Safety Administration (NHTSA), wearing safety belts reduces the likelihood of serious or fatal injuries by 40 to 55 percent. NHTSA surveys also show that more people wear safety belts in areas that have safety-belt laws.

Wearing safety belts would not only save lives and reduce injuries, but it would also save society a great deal of money. Traffic accidents cost approximately $8.5 billion per year. By reducing accidents, the use of safety belts would lower this amount. The medical benefits paid by insurance companies would decrease, resulting in lower vehicle insurance premiums. Companies would also lose less money due to employee absences.

Although no one can argue with these statistics, not everyone agrees with me. Opponents of safety-belt laws say that the laws violate the individual's freedom of choice. They say it is not the role of government to protect people from themselves and the consequences of their actions.

An individual's actions often affect other people as well, however. My neighbor's choice not to wear a safety belt, for example, not only ruined his life, but also devastated his family.

The individual's freedom of choice is not an absolute freedom, though. People do not live in isolation. We are part of an interconnected society

**❶** This writer begins with a powerful anecdote illustrating the issue.
**Other Options:**
• State your opinion directly.
• Ask a question.

**❷** States her opinion clearly and succinctly

**❸** Uses facts and statistics to support her opinions
**Other Options:**
• Cite expert opinions.
• Give examples.

**❹** Addresses opposing arguments

that will function well only if we all consider other people's needs as well as our own. In deciding to do as we please, we have to think about other individuals' right to do the same. Our lives are not ours to take reckless chances with when our deaths will bring terrible pain to our families and friends. Putting on a safety belt is such a simple thing to do. Using a device that has been proven to save lives does not restrict people's freedom, but just shows their good sense.

An individual's choice not to wear a safety belt can affect not just his or her family and friends, but also society as a whole. I already mentioned increased costs to insurance companies and businesses. Injured motorists who require long-term care can also become a financial burden on society. My neighbor is a good example. His medical costs have been so high that his benefits will soon run out. Since he is unable to take care of himself and his family cannot afford to pay for private nursing care, he will have to go into a state-supported nursing home.

<u>In addition</u> to paying these monetary costs, society also loses the productivity and unique contributions of each person who is killed or severely injured in an automobile accident. Society cannot tell people how to develop their individual talents. <u>On the other hand</u>, people have a responsibility to use those talents to make a contribution to society. Throwing away our lives because we don't want to insert a metal buckle into a holder is turning our backs on our social responsibility.

The evidence showing that safety belts reduce traffic deaths and the severity of injuries could not be clearer. It is also clear that people wear safety belts if there are laws requiring their use. There is no question that the benefits to society from the use of safety belts far outweigh the individual's freedom of choice in this matter. So speak out to support laws requiring the use of safety belts. And until those laws are passed—and afterwards, too—be safe, be responsible, and buckle up.

❺ Continues her arguments

❻ Uses transitions to keep the arguments clear and logical

❼ Ends with a summary and strong statement of opinion

# Writing Your Opinion Statement

## ❶ Prewriting

As you begin to think about your opinion statement, **list** a few issues you have strong feelings about. What are your views about school policies, social problems, sports, or modern art and music? **Recall** the last time you were really pleased by an event or learned about something that made you angry or disappointed. See the **Idea Bank** in the margin for more suggestions. After you select an issue to write about, follow the steps below.

### Planning Your Opinion Statement

▶ **1. Think about your opinion on the issue.** What aspects of the issue particularly concern you? How can you best state your opinion about it?

▶ **2. Evaluate why you hold your belief.** What reasons convinced you to form your opinion? What reasons will be convincing to your audience? How can you answer opposing beliefs?

▶ **3. Research the issue.** Where can you find examples, facts, and statistics that support your opinion? Which evidence is strongest?

▶ **4. Consider the tone of your writing.** Do you want to present a serious, scholarly essay? Would you influence your audience more by adopting a humorous or satirical tone?

## ❷ Drafting

> *Don't recite other people's opinions. . . . Tell me what you know.*
> **Ralph Waldo Emerson**

As you start putting your opinion in writing, just follow your thoughts where they take you. Remember, part of drafting is clarifying and refining your ideas. You can organize and fine-tune your work later in the writing process. As you draft, keep in mind that you eventually will have to **state your opinion** clearly and succinctly and **present examples, facts, and statistics** that support it. You might consider using an especially strong or striking example or fact to introduce your writing.

As you draft your arguments, be sure you have used valid reasoning. Especially watch out for these illogical arguments:

**Circular reasoning**—simply restating a point without providing evidence (*This is the best plan because it is better than the others.*)

**Over-generalization**—making a statement that is too broad to prove (*No one would vote for that candidate.*)

For more on faulty reasoning see **Communication Handbook,** pp. 1175–1176.

**IDEA Bank**

**1. Your Working Portfolio**
Look for ideas in the **Writing Options** you completed earlier in this unit:

• **Warden's Address,** p. 28

• **Tech Paragraph,** p. 111

• **Newspaper Editorial,** p. 122

• **Newspaper Editorial,** p. 134

**2. Debugging**
With a small group of classmates, talk about issues that bug you.

**3. Media Quest**
Look through newspapers or weekly newsmagazines for articles or columns on issues that you feel strongly about.

**Have a question?**

See the **Writing Handbook**
Persuasive Writing, pp. 1161–1162

### Ask Your Peer Reader

• How would you restate the issue I'm writing about?

• How would you summarize my opinion?

• What are my most convincing reasons?

• What other facts support my position?

• What information, if any, is unclear or unneeded?

**Need revising help?**

Review the **Rubric,**
p. 138

Consider **peer reader**
comments

Check **Revision
Guidelines,** p. 1145

## ❸ Revising

**TARGET SKILL ▶ REFINING TOPIC SENTENCES** Your opinions will be
most convincing to readers if your writing is well organized. One way to stay on
track is to make sure each paragraph includes a good topic sentence and that
all the details in the paragraph relate to its topic sentence.

> *not only*                               *but it would also save society*
> *a great deal of money.*
> Wearing safety belts would save lives and reduce injuries.
>
> Traffic accidents cost approximately $8.5 billion per year.
>
> By reducing accidents, the use of safety belts would lower
>
> this amount. The medical benefits paid by insurance com-
>
> panies would decrease, resulting in lower vehicle insurance
>                                        *due to employee absences*
> premiums. Companies would also lose less money.

## ❹ Editing and Proofreading

**TARGET SKILL ▶ PRONOUN-ANTECEDENT AGREEMENT** When you
focus on stating your opinion and supporting it clearly, you might overlook issues
such as making pronouns and their antecedents agree. Errors in pronoun agreement baffle readers and weaken your arguments, though. Make sure that
pronouns agree with their antecedents in number, gender, and person.

**Perplexed by
pronouns?**

See the **Grammar
Handbook,**
pp. 1183–1184

> *their*
> Society cannot tell people how to develop its individual
>
> talents. On the other hand, people have a responsibility to
>
> use those talents to make a contribution to society.
>
> Throwing away our lives because we don't want to insert
>                                        *our*
> a metal buckle into a holder is like turning their backs on
>
> our social responsibility.

**Publishing
IDEAS**

• Invite students to
hear you read your
opinion statement.
Perhaps put up an
announcement with
the time and place on
the school bulletin
board. Ask for
discussion about the
issue.

• Send your opinion
statement to a
newspaper as a letter
to the editor.

**More Online:
Publishing Options**
www.mcdougallittell.com

## ❺ Reflecting

**FOR YOUR WORKING PORTFOLIO** What did you learn about the issue you wrote
about? How did your opinion on it change or become stronger? Save your
opinion statement in your **Working Portfolio.**

Read this paragraph from the first draft of an opinion statement. The underlined sections may include the following kinds of errors:

- **double negatives**
- **incorrect possessive forms**
- **lack of pronoun-antecedent agreement**
- **sentence fragments**

For each underlined section, choose the revision that most improves the writing.

---

<u>What does one get when you buy an organic tomato?</u> Was it grown using
(1)
chemical fertilizers? Was the <u>tomatos' DNA</u> genetically altered to make it less
(2)
perishable? <u>Under current consumer laws. You can't find out the answers to</u>
(3)
<u>these questions for sure.</u> Yet people have the right to know what's in <u>their food.</u>
(4)
<u>The organic food industry doesn't seem to agree. Since it doesn't regulate</u>
(5)
<u>labeling.</u> Government guidelines for the organic food industry are a good idea.

Without them, consumers <u>cannot hardly know</u> what they are getting when they
(6)
buy "organic" food.

---

1. **A.** What does one get when they buy an organic tomato?
   **B.** What does one get when we buy an organic tomato?
   **C.** What do you get when you buy an organic tomato?
   **D.** Correct as is

2. **A.** tomato's DNA
   **B.** tomatos's DNA
   **C.** tomatos dna
   **D.** Correct as is

3. **A.** Under current consumer laws; you can't find out the answers to these questions for sure.
   **B.** Under current consumer laws, you can't find out the answers to these questions for sure.
   **C.** You can't find out the answers to these questions for sure. Especially under current consumer laws.
   **D.** Correct as is

4. **A.** your food
   **B.** our food
   **C.** his or her food
   **D.** Correct as is

5. **A.** The organic food industry doesn't seem to agree: since it doesn't regulate labeling.
   **B.** The organic food industry doesn't seem to agree, since it doesn't regulate labeling.
   **C.** Since it doesn't regulate labeling. The organic food industry doesn't seem to agree.
   **D.** Correct as is

6. **A.** can know
   **B.** can't not know
   **C.** cannot know
   **D.** Correct as is

**Need extra help?**

See the **Grammar Handbook**

**Possessive Nouns**, p. 1182

**Pronoun Agreement**, p. 1183

**Correcting Sentence Fragments**, p. 1199

# Theme Expressed Through Plot

Since the characters' actions drive the plot, the decisions that they make, including the outcomes of those decisions, often express a theme, or insight about life. Tom and Lily's lie to Mr. Noakes about where they've been is intended to keep the cottage a secret. Their decision suggests that places where the sun shines are natural treasures that need to be protected from humans, not exploited for profit. Only a few people, like Tom and Lily and the Hatchings, can be trusted, since humans had caused the problem in the first place. The story ends very much as it begins, with a reference to future generations.

**YOUR TURN** Add together what you know about the setting (the effects of the lack of sun), character (how Tom and Lily choose to act), and plot (the unfolding of events). Then, write a sentence stating your interpretation of the story's theme. Try stating the theme as a moral to the story or a warning for the future.

> **PLOT CLUES**
>
> At least, [Tom] thought, they had left the golden place undisturbed. Mr. Noakes never went into the wood. And they had done what they intended; they had found the sun. Now they, too, would be able to tell their grandchildren, when beginning a story, "Long, long ago, when we were young, in the days when the sky was blue . . ."
>
> —Joan Aiken, "Searching for Summer"

# Theme in Nonfiction

In narrative forms of nonfiction, such as autobiography and biography, theme is very similar to what it is in fiction, a perception about life that must be inferred from the events and the development of a person's life. In nonnarrative forms of nonfiction, such as news reports, articles, and essays, the theme is the main idea or opinion that a writer wants a reader to understand.

The theme of an essay is often called a **thesis** and is more directly stated than the theme of a story. For example, in his essay "Dial Versus Digital" (page 107), Isaac Asimov states his theme in the third paragraph: "And yet there will be a loss in the conversion of dial to digital, and few people seem to be worrying about it." Asimov sees a problem, and he wants people to be worried about it. The rest of his essay consists of alarming examples to prove his thesis, or theme.

**YOUR TURN** How does the example in the passage at the right support Asimov's theme? Discuss your response with a classmate.

> **NONFICTION CLUES**
>
> When something turns, it can turn in just one of two ways, either clockwise or counterclockwise, and we all know which is which. . . . But if dial clocks disappear, so will the meaning of those words for anyone who never has stared at anything but digitals. There are no good substitutes for *clockwise* or *counterclockwise*.
>
> —Isaac Asimov, "Dial Versus Digital"

Whether you read about real or imaginary people and events, recognizing themes can give you valuable insights into human nature. Use the strategies here to help you draw conclusions about themes in the works you read.

## Drawing Conclusions

When you draw a conclusion, you combine text information with prior knowledge. After you have looked at all the events and details in a selection, you're ready to make a logical conclusion about the meaning of these details—just like a judge weighing evidence. Use the following strategies to help you draw conclusions about the theme of a selection.

### 1 Strategies for Drawing Conclusions about Theme

- Use a graphic like the one below to gather clues about setting, character, and plot that hint at a deeper meaning.

| Setting | Effects of no sunshine: drab, gray landscape |
|---|---|
| Character | Tom and Lily learn how precious the sun is. |
| Plot | They decide to protect the cottage from Mr. Noakes. |
| Theme | |

- **Connect** the experiences discussed in the piece of writing to your own experiences.
- Most themes in literature are implied. **Draw conclusions** from the details to make general statements about characters, events, and setting.

### 2 Using Setting to Determine Theme

- Think about why the writer chose a particular setting. Ask yourself if the same events could have happened elsewhere or at another time.
- **Draw conclusions** about how the setting affects the characters, the plot, or the overall atmosphere of the story.

### 3 Using Character to Determine Theme

- Pay close attention to the characters, roles, actions, and motives.
- Determine what ideas about life or human nature a character's personality and values reveal.
- Apply your own **generalizations** about human nature as you read.

### 4 Using Plot to Determine Theme

- Identify the **conflict.** A writer's choice of conflict and the way the conflict is resolved may be clues to a theme.
- **Draw conclusions** from a character's actions, the results of these actions, and the things a character learns from the actions.

### 5 Strategies for Recognizing Theme in Nonfiction

- In autobiographies and other forms of narrative nonfiction, look at important events and **draw conclusions** about a person's values.
- In news reports, articles, and essays, look for a strong statement at the beginning or the end that expresses the main idea or thesis.

**Need More Help?**

Remember that active readers use the essential reading strategies explained on page 7: **visualize, predict, clarify, question, connect, evaluate, monitor.**

# No Witchcraft for Sale

*Short Story by* DORIS LESSING

## Connect to Your Life

**Clash of Cultures** Think of an incident in which people from different cultures or races have misjudged or misunderstood one another. Perhaps you have personally experienced such a misunderstanding, or perhaps you have read about one. In a small group, describe the incident, offering your explanation of what happened.

## Build Background

**Colonial Africa** Africa has long been a setting for misunderstanding and confrontation between cultures and races. In the 1800s and early 1900s, most African countries became colonies of European powers. Although many of the African countries had been strong kingdoms with well-developed economies and cultures, they came to be dominated politically, economically, and culturally by their European rulers.

In the 1890s, the region that would become Southern Rhodesia (and eventually Zimbabwe) fell under British control. A land of great beauty and mineral wealth, Southern Rhodesia had a large population of British settlers that for decades dominated the country, both as a British colony and, after 1965, as an independent nation. Following a sometimes violent struggle, the black majority gained control of the country—in 1980 renaming it Zimbabwe, after the ancient African capital city of the region. "No Witchcraft for Sale" takes place in Southern Rhodesia during the time of white rule.

WORDS TO KNOW
**Vocabulary Preview**
anecdote      efficacy
annul         indifferently
distasteful

## Focus Your Reading

**LITERARY ANALYSIS** | **THEME AND CHARACTER** A **theme** is an important idea or message conveyed by a work of fiction. One way to discover the theme is to study the **characters** in the story. By examining conflicts between characters and the changes that main characters undergo, you can often detect a central idea. As you read this story, look for details about the characters and their relationships that will help you to understand Lessing's message.

**ACTIVE READING** | **DRAWING CONCLUSIONS** To **draw conclusions,** you need to put together various pieces of information—from your reading and what you already know—to make logical statements. To draw a conclusion about a **character,** for example, you put together evidence about what that character says or does. In this story, Gideon, an African, is a servant to the Farquars, white colonists in Southern Rhodesia. Consider what the passage below reveals about Gideon's view of his world.

> *Gideon, who was watching, shook his head wonderingly, and said: "Ah, missus, these are both children, and one will grow up to be a baas [master], and one will be a servant."*

**READER'S NOTEBOOK** As you read, keep track of how Gideon and Mrs. Farquar interact. In a chart similar to the one below, note what each character does or says.

| Character | Action | Speech |
|-----------|--------|--------|
| Gideon | | |
| Mrs. Farquar | | |

*Conjur Woman* (1975),
Romare Bearden. Collage on
board, 46″ × 36″, private
collection, courtesy of Sheldon
Ross Gallery, Birmingham,
Michigan. Copyright © Romare
Bearden Foundation/Licensed by
VAGA, New York.

# No Witchcraft for Sale

**Doris Lessing**

The Farquars had been childless for years when little Teddy was born; and they were touched by the pleasure of their servants, who brought presents of fowls and eggs and flowers to the homestead when they came to rejoice over the baby, exclaiming with delight over his downy golden head and his blue eyes. They congratulated Mrs. Farquar as if she had achieved a very great thing, and she felt that she had—her smile for the lingering, admiring natives was warm and grateful.

Later, when Teddy had his first haircut, Gideon the cook picked up the soft gold tufts from the ground and held them reverently in his hand. Then he smiled at the little boy and said: "Little Yellow Head." That became the native name for the child. Gideon and Teddy were great friends from the first. When Gideon had finished his work, he would lift Teddy on his shoulders to the shade of a big tree, and play with him there, forming curious little toys from twigs and leaves and grass, or shaping animals from wetted soil. When Teddy learned to walk, it was often Gideon who crouched before him, clucking encouragement, finally catching him when he fell, tossing him up in the air till they both became breathless with laughter. Mrs. Farquar was fond of the old cook because of his love for her child.

There was no second baby; and one day Gideon said: "Ah, missus, missus, the Lord above sent this one; Little Yellow Head is the most good thing we have in our house." Because of that "we" Mrs. Farquar felt a warm impulse towards her cook; and at the end of the month she raised his wages. He had been with her now for several years; he was one of the few natives who had his wife and children in the compound and never wanted to go home to his kraal,[1] which was some hundreds of miles away. Sometimes a small piccanin[2] who had been born the same time as Teddy, could be seen peering from the edge of the bush, staring in awe at the little white boy with his miraculous fair hair and Northern blue eyes. The two little children would gaze at each other with a wide, interested gaze, and once Teddy put out his hand curiously to touch the black child's cheeks and hair.

Gideon, who was watching, shook his head wonderingly, and said: "Ah, missus, these are both children, and one will grow up to be a baas,[3] and one will be a servant"; and Mrs. Farquar smiled and said sadly, "Yes, Gideon, I was thinking the same." She sighed. "It is God's will," said Gideon, who was a mission boy.[4]

> "Gideon, look at me!"
> And Gideon would
> laugh and say: "Very clever,
> Little Yellow Head."

The Farquars were very religious people; and this shared feeling about God bound servant and masters even closer together.

Teddy was about six years old when he was given a scooter, and discovered the intoxications of speed. All day he would fly around the homestead, in and out of flowerbeds, scattering squawking chickens and irritated dogs, finishing with a wide dizzying arc into the kitchen door. There he would cry: "Gideon, look at me!" And Gideon would laugh and say: "Very clever, Little Yellow Head." Gideon's youngest son, who was now a herdsboy, came especially up from the compound to see the scooter. He was afraid to come near it, but Teddy showed off in

---

1. **kraal** (krôl): a native village in southern Africa.
2. **piccanin** (pĭk′ə-nĭn′): a native child (the term *piccanin* is usually considered offensive).
3. **baas**: boss.
4. **mission boy**: a boy educated at a school run by Christian missionaries.

front of him. "Piccanin," shouted Teddy, "get out of my way!" And he raced in circles around the black child until he was frightened and fled back to the bush.

"Why did you frighten him?" asked Gideon, gravely reproachful.

Teddy said defiantly: "He's only a black boy," and laughed.

Then, when Gideon turned away from him without speaking, his face fell. Very soon he slipped into the house and found an orange and brought it to Gideon, saying: "This is for you." He could not bring himself to say he was sorry; but he could not bear to lose Gideon's affection either. Gideon took the orange unwillingly and sighed. "Soon you will be going away to school, Little Yellow Head," he said wonderingly, "and then you will be grown up." He shook his head gently and said, "And that is how our lives go." He seemed to be putting a distance between himself and Teddy, not because of resentment, but in the way a person accepts something inevitable. The baby had lain in his arms and smiled up into his face: the tiny boy had swung from his shoulders and played with him by the hour. Now Gideon would not let his flesh touch the flesh of the white child. He was kind, but there was a grave formality in his voice that made Teddy pout and sulk away. Also, it made him into a man: with Gideon he was polite, and carried himself formally, and if he came into the kitchen to ask for something, it was in the way a white man uses towards a servant, expecting to be obeyed.

But on the day that Teddy came staggering into the kitchen with his fists to his eyes, shrieking with pain, Gideon dropped the pot full of hot soup that he was holding, rushed

ACTIVE READING

EVALUATE How does Teddy view Gideon?

to the child, and forced aside his fingers. "A snake!" he exclaimed. Teddy had been on his scooter and had come to a rest with his foot on the side of a big tub of plants. A tree snake, hanging by its tail from the roof, had spat full into his eyes. Mrs. Farquar came running when she heard the commotion. "He'll go blind," she sobbed, holding Teddy close against her. "Gideon, he'll go blind!" Already the eyes, with perhaps half an hour's sight left in them, were swollen up to the size of fists: Teddy's small white face was distorted by great purple oozing protuberances.[5] Gideon said: "Wait a minute, missus, I'll get some medicine." He ran off into the bush.

Mrs. Farquar lifted the child into the house and bathed his eyes with permanganate.[6] She had scarcely heard Gideon's words; but when she saw that her remedies had no effect at all, and remembered how she had seen natives with no sight in their eyes because of the spitting of a snake, she began to look for the return of her cook, remembering what she heard of the efficacy of native herbs. She stood by the window, holding the terrified, sobbing little boy in her arms, and peered helplessly into the bush. It was not more than a few minutes before she saw Gideon come bounding back, and in his hand he held a plant.

"Do not be afraid, missus," said Gideon, "this will cure Little Yellow Head's eyes." He stripped the leaves from the plant, leaving a small white fleshy root. Without even washing it, he put the root in his mouth, chewed it vigorously, and then held the spittle there while he took the child forcibly from Mrs. Farquar.

---

5. **protuberances** (prō-tōō′bər-ən-səz): bulges or swellings.

6. **permanganate** (pər-măng′gə-nāt′): a solution of the chemical potassium permanganate, formerly used as an antidote to snake poison.

WORDS TO KNOW   **efficacy** (ĕf′ĭ-kə-sē) *n.* the power to produce a desired effect; effectiveness

*The Ukimwi Road* (1994), John Harris.

He gripped Teddy down between his knees, and pressed the balls of his thumbs into the swollen eyes, so that the child screamed and Mrs. Farquar cried out in protest: "Gideon, Gideon!" But Gideon took no notice. He knelt over the writhing child, pushing back the puffy lids till chinks of eyeball showed, and then he spat hard, again and again, into first one eye, and then the other. He finally lifted Teddy gently into his mother's arms, and said: "His eyes will get better." But Mrs. Farquar was weeping with terror, and she could hardly thank him: it was impossible to believe that Teddy could keep his sight. In a couple of hours the swellings were gone: the eyes were inflamed and tender but Teddy could see. Mr. and Mrs. Farquar went to Gideon in the kitchen and thanked him over and over again. They felt helpless because of their gratitude: it seemed they could do nothing to express it. They gave Gideon presents for his wife and children, and a big increase in wages, but these things could not pay for Teddy's now completely cured eyes. Mrs. Farquar said: "Gideon, God chose you as an instrument for His goodness," and Gideon said: "Yes, missus, God is very good."

Now, when such a thing happens on a farm, it cannot be long before everyone hears of it. Mr. and Mrs. Farquar told their neighbors and the story was discussed from one end of the district to the other. The bush is full of secrets. No one can live in Africa, or at least on the veld,[7] without learning very soon that there is an ancient wisdom of leaf and soil and season— and, too, perhaps most important of all, of the darker tracts of the human mind—which is the

_____

7. **veld** (vĕlt): an open, grass-covered plain of southern Africa.

black man's heritage. Up and down the district people were telling <u>anecdotes</u>, reminding each other of things that had happened to them.

"But I saw it myself, I tell you. It was a puff-adder bite. The kaffir's[8] arm was swollen to the elbow, like a great shiny black bladder. He was

> **The scientist explained how humanity might benefit if this new drug could be offered for sale.**

groggy after a half a minute. He was dying. Then suddenly a kaffir walked out of the bush with his hands full of green stuff. He smeared something on the place, and next day my boy was back at work, and all you could see was two small punctures in the skin."

This was the kind of tale they told. And, as always, with a certain amount of exasperation, because while all of them knew that in the bush of Africa are waiting valuable drugs locked in bark, in simple-looking leaves, in roots, it was impossible to ever get the truth about them from the natives themselves.

The story eventually reached town; and perhaps it was at a sundowner party, or some such function, that a doctor, who happened to be there, challenged it. "Nonsense," he said. "These things get exaggerated in the telling. We are always checking up on this kind of story, and we draw a blank every time."

Anyway, one morning there arrived a strange car at the homestead, and out stepped one of the workers from the laboratory in town, with cases full of test-tubes and chemicals.

Mr. and Mrs. Farquar were flustered and pleased and flattered. They asked the scientist to lunch, and they told the story all over again, for the hundredth time. Little Teddy was there too, his blue eyes sparkling with health, to prove the truth of it. The scientist explained how humanity might benefit if this new drug could be offered for sale; and the Farquars were even more pleased: they were kind, simple people, who liked to think of something good coming about because of them. But when the scientist began talking of the money that might result, their manner showed discomfort. Their feelings over the miracle (that was how they thought of it) were so strong and deep and religious, that it was <u>distasteful</u> to them to think of money. The scientist, seeing their faces, went back to his first point, which was the advancement of humanity. He was perhaps a trifle perfunctory: it was not the first time he had come salting the tail of[9] a fabulous bush-secret.

Eventually, when the meal was over, the Farquars called Gideon into their living-room and explained to him that this baas, here, was a big Doctor from the Big City, and he had come all that way to see Gideon. At this Gideon seemed afraid; he did not understand; and Mrs. Farquar explained quickly that it was because of the wonderful thing he had done with Teddy's eyes that the Big Baas had come.

Gideon looked from Mrs. Farquar to Mr. Farquar, and then at the little boy, who was showing great importance because of the occasion. At last he said grudgingly: "The Big Baas want to know what medicine I used?" He spoke incredulously, as if he could not believe

---

8. **kaffir's** (kăf′ərz): belonging to a black African (usually considered offensive).

9. **salting the tail of:** trying to capture (from the childhood belief that birds can be caught by putting salt on their tail).

---

WORDS
TO
KNOW

**anecdote** (ăn′ĭk-dōt′) *n.* a short account of an interesting or humorous incident
**distasteful** (dĭs-tāst′fəl) *adj.* unpleasant; disagreeable

ACTIVE READING

**DRAW CONCLUSIONS**

What can you conclude about the relationship between Gideon and the Farquars?

his old friends could so betray him. Mr. Farquar began explaining how a useful medicine could be made out of the root, and how it could be put on sale, and how thousands of people, black and white, up and down the continent of Africa, could be saved by the medicine when that spitting snake filled their eyes with poison. Gideon listened, his eyes bent on the ground, the skin of his forehead puckering in discomfort. When Mr. Farquar had finished he did not reply. The scientist, who all this time had been leaning back in a big chair, sipping his coffee and smiling with skeptical good-humor, chipped in and explained all over again, in different words, about the making of drugs and the progress of science. Also, he offered Gideon a present.

There was silence after this further explanation, and then Gideon remarked <u>indifferently</u> that he could not remember the root. His face was sullen and hostile, even when he looked at the Farquars, whom he usually treated like old friends. They were beginning to feel annoyed; and this feeling <u>annulled</u> the guilt that had been sprung into life by Gideon's accusing manner. They were beginning to feel that he was unreasonable. But it was at that moment that they all realized he would never give in. The magical drug would remain where it was, unknown and useless except for the tiny scattering of Africans who had the knowledge, natives who might be digging a ditch for the municipality in a ragged shirt and a pair of patched shorts, but who were still born to healing, hereditary healers, being the nephews or sons of the old witch doctors whose ugly masks and bits of bone and all the uncouth properties of magic were the outward signs of real power and wisdom.

The Farquars might tread on that plant fifty times a day as they passed from house to garden, from cow kraal[10] to mealie[11] field, but they would never know it.

But they went on persuading and arguing, with all the force of their exasperation; and Gideon continued to say that he could not remember, or that there was no such root, or that it was the wrong season of the year, or that it wasn't the root itself, but the spit from his mouth that had cured Teddy's eyes. He said all these things one after another, and seemed not to care they were contradictory. He was rude and stubborn. The Farquars could hardly recognize their gentle, lovable old servant in

> **But they went on persuading and arguing, with all the force of their exasperation.**

this ignorant, perversely obstinate[12] African, standing there in front of them with lowered eyes, his hands twitching his cook's apron, repeating over and over whichever one of the stupid refusals that first entered his head.

And suddenly he appeared to give in. He lifted his head, gave a long, blank angry look at the circle of whites, who seemed to him like a circle of yelping dogs pressing around him, and said: "I will show you the root."

They walked single file away from the homestead down a kaffir path. It was a blazing

---

10. **cow kraal:** a livestock enclosure or corral.

11. **mealie:** corn.

12. **perversely obstinate:** stubbornly and wrongly insistent on having one's own way.

December afternoon, with the sky full of hot rain-clouds. Everything was hot: the sun was like a bronze tray whirling overhead, there was a heat shimmer over the fields, the soil was scorching underfoot, the dusty wind blew gritty and thick and warm in their faces. It was a terrible day, fit only for reclining on a verandah[13] with iced drinks, which is where they would normally have been at that hour.

From time to time, remembering that on the day of the snake it had taken ten minutes to find the root, someone asked: "Is it much further, Gideon?" And Gideon would answer over his shoulder, with angry politeness: "I'm looking for the root, baas." And indeed, he would frequently bend sideways and trail his hand among the grasses with a gesture that was insulting in its perfunc-toriness. He walked them through the bush along unknown paths for two hours, in that melting destroying heat, so that the sweat trickled coldly down them and their heads ached. They were all quite silent: the Farquars because they were angry, the scientist because he was being proved right again; there was no such plant. His was a tactful silence.

**ACTIVE READING**

**PREDICT** Do you think Gideon will find the root?

At last, six miles from the house, Gideon suddenly decided they had had enough; or perhaps his anger evaporated at that moment. He picked up, without an attempt at looking anything but casual, a handful of blue flowers from the grass, flowers that had been growing plentifully all down the paths they had come.

He handed them to the scientist without looking at him, and marched off by himself on the way home, leaving them to follow him if they chose.

When they got back to the house, the scientist went to the kitchen to thank Gideon: he was very very polite, even though there was an amused look in his eyes. Gideon was not

there. Throwing the flowers casually into the back of his car, the eminent visitor departed on his way back to his laboratory.

Gideon was back in his kitchen in time to prepare dinner, but he was sulking. He spoke to Mr. Farquar like an unwilling servant. It was days before they liked each other again.

The Farquars made inquiries about the root from their laborers. Sometimes they were answered with distrustful stares. Sometimes the natives said: "We do not know. We have never heard of the root." One, the cattle boy, who had been with them a long time, and had grown to trust them a little, said: "Ask your boy in the kitchen. Now, there's a doctor for you. He's the son of a famous medicine man who used to be in these parts, and there's nothing he cannot cure." Then he added politely: "Of course, he's not as good as the white man's doctor, we know that, but he's good for us."

After some time, when the soreness had gone from between the Farquars and Gideon, they began to joke: "When are you going to show us the snake-root, Gideon?" And he would laugh and shake his head, saying, a little uncomfortably: "But I did show you, missus, have you forgotten?"

Much later, Teddy, as a schoolboy, would come into the kitchen and say: "You old rascal, Gideon! Do you remember that time you tricked us all by making us walk miles all over the veld for nothing? It was so far my father had to carry me!"

And Gideon would double up with polite laughter. After much laughing, he would suddenly straighten himself up, wipe his old eyes, and look sadly at Teddy, who was grinning mischievously at him across the kitchen: "Ah, Little Yellow Head, how you have grown! Soon you will be grown up with a farm of your own . . ." ❖

_____

13. **verandah** (və-răn′də): a long porch.

# *Thinking through the* LITERATURE

## Connect to the Literature

1. **What Do You Think?** Which part of this story evoked the strongest response in you? Describe your reaction to that part of the story and compare it to your classmates' responses.

**Comprehension Check**
- What happens to Teddy's eyes?
- How is Teddy saved from blindness?
- What does Gideon give the scientist?

## Think Critically

2. **ACTIVE READING  DRAWING CONCLUSIONS**  Look at the details about Gideon and Mrs. Farquar that you entered in your **READER'S NOTEBOOK**. What conclusions can you draw about each **character**? How do those conclusions help you to understand the **conflict** between them?

3. Do you think Gideon was justified in his refusal to share his knowledge of the medicinal plant? Why or why not?

   **THINK ABOUT**
   - the relationship between the whites and the blacks
   - the **title** of the story
   - the plant's effectiveness against snake poison
   - what you think motivates Gideon's actions

4. The Farquars believe themselves to be people of good will. Do you agree with them? Support your opinion.

5. Do you think the cultural and racial misunderstandings in this story could have been avoided? Use examples from the story to support your opinion.

## Extend Interpretations

6. **What If?**  Imagine that Gideon had cooperated with the white scientist by revealing his people's secret herbal treatments. How would that have changed your judgment of his **character?**

7. **Connect to Life**  In this story, Gideon stands up for his own dignity and the dignity of his culture. Think of other instances you know of in which an individual has taken a stand to protect his or her rights or culture. How successful do you think such actions can be in influencing people's attitudes?

## Literary Analysis

**THEME AND CHARACTER**  Writers of fiction use their stories to convey messages and insights about life and human nature. The message, or **theme,** of any story can often be understood by reflecting upon what happens to the central **characters**. For example, in this story, the author examines the reasons for the distrust and misunderstandings between races and cultures by focusing on the interaction between Gideon and Mrs. Farquar. Gideon's transformation from a dutiful servant to a quietly defiant healer helps the reader understand Lessing's message.

**Paired Activity**  With a partner, study the action and speech of Teddy and the scientist. Use two diagrams, each like the one shown, to record significant details and your own conclusions about each character. In what ways do you think these two characters contribute to the cultural clashes in this story? Share your ideas with your classmates. Then expand your discussion to consider how all of Lessing's characters and their interaction help you understand the author's theme.

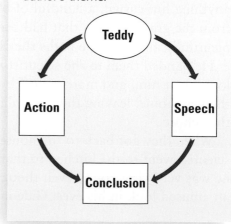

# Choices&CHALLENGES

## Writing Options

**1. Letter from the Author** Assume the identity of Doris Lessing and write a letter to her publisher in which she explains the story's theme. Also explain which characters reflect values that she supports.

**2. Medicine Man Dialogue** Write a dialogue between Gideon and his son in which Gideon explains why he did not give the scientist the healing root.

## Activities & Explorations

**1. Oral Tale** Prepare an oral tale that Gideon might tell his neighbors about his "helping" the scientist, and tell it to your classmates. ~ **SPEAKING AND LISTENING**

**2. Bar Graph** Create a bar graph in which you rate each character's power in society, with the longest bar representing the most powerful character. Then explain your ratings to the class. ~ **VIEWING AND REPRESENTING**

High

Low

Mrs. Farquar   Gideon   Teddy   Scientist

**3. Editorial Page** In a small group, work to develop a newspaper editorial page focusing on the events in this story. Include an editorial presenting the paper's position on whether Gideon was right to keep his secret. Express other points of view about

Gideon's decision in letters to the editor from doctors, snakebite victims, and traditional healers.
~ **JOURNALISM**

## Inquiry & Research

**Alternative Medicine** With a partner, research the medicinal properties of plants native to your part of the country. Present your findings by displaying a sample or picture of each plant along with an explanation of its medicinal use.

**More Online:**
**Research Starter**
www.mcdougallittell.com

## Vocabulary in Action

**EXERCISE: MEANING CLUES** Answer the following questions.

1. Is a **distasteful** activity one that is popular, one that is difficult, or one that is unappealing?

2. Are you most likely to react **indifferently** to a remark that angers you, that bores you, or that surprises you?

3. Is an **anecdote** a story that is amusing, that is boring, or that is instructional?

### Building Vocabulary

Several Words to Know in this lesson contain prefixes and suffixes. For an in-depth lesson on word parts, see page 856.

4. Would a medicine known for its **efficacy** have a reputation for working well, for being expensive, or for having side effects?

5. In an effort to **annul** the effects of an insulting remark you made, would you repeat it, add to it, or say you were kidding?

## Grammar in Context: Using Adverbs to Clarify Actions

Notice how in "No Witchcraft for Sale" Doris Lessing uses adverbs to provide information about Gideon.

> At last he said grudgingly: "The Big Baas want to know what medicine I used?"
>
> He would frequently bend sideways and trail his hand among the grasses. . . . Gideon suddenly decided they had had enough.

In these sentences, adverbs reveal important characteristics of Gideon. The reader can feel his emotions, see him in action, and imagine his thoughts. **Usage note**: The placement of an adverb can change the meaning of a sentence. Position it carefully.

**WRITING EXERCISE** Supply an adverb to clarify the verb in each sentence. Use an adverb of the type named in parentheses.

**Example:** Gideon _____ lifts Teddy on his shoulders and carries him around the yard. (time) Gideon often lifts Teddy on his shoulders and carries him around the yard.

1. While learning to walk, Teddy would _____ fall, but Gideon was there to catch him. (manner)
2. One day, Gideon sees Teddy riding his scooter _____ around Gideon's youngest son. (manner)
3. _____ Teddy stops his scooter near a tree snake, which spits poison into his eyes. (time)

**Grammar Handbook**
Adverbs, p. 1188

# Doris Lessing
## 1919–

**Other Works**
*Going Home*
*African Stories*
*This Was the Old Chief's Country*
*The Golden Notebook*
*Under My Skin*
*Volume One of My Autobiography, to 1949*

**A Different Childhood** Born to British parents in Persia, Doris Lessing grew up in Southern Rhodesia, where her family went to farm when she was about five. Her childhood was fairly solitary, and she spent most of her time reading or walking outdoors. "The storms, the winds, the silences of the bush; the sunlit or rain-whipped mountains; fields of maize miles long; sunflowers that turned their heads after the sun; cotton plants with their butterfly-like pink and white flowers—these, and the neighbors, were my education," she said.

**African Themes** Lessing left school at 14 and worked as a nursemaid and telephone operator in Salisbury, Southern Rhodesia, until she married at the age of 19. In 1949, after two failed marriages, she moved to England, which remains her place of residence. Not long afterward, Lessing published her first novel, *The Grass Is Singing* (1950), and the story collection *This Was the Old Chief's Country* (1951). These stories were based on her intimate knowledge of Southern Rhodesia, especially the problems between blacks and whites. Because of her outspoken criticism of racism and her radical political sympathies, Lessing was banned from her homeland and South Africa. Nonetheless, her works have been praised for their honest portrayal of colonial Africa and its mysterious, often harsh, natural beauty.

**Contemporary Masterpiece** Another major theme in Lessing's writing is the role of women in modern society. *The Golden Notebook* (1962), an experimental novel about a woman coming to terms with her personal relationships and her role in the world, is widely regarded as her masterpiece.

# Author Activity

**Another Dimension** Some of Lessing's best-known works are her science fiction novels. Find out the subject matter and title of her five-novel science fiction series.

# PREPARING to *Read*

# The Son from America

*Short Story by* ISAAC BASHEVIS SINGER

## Connect to Your Life

**Strangers in a Strange Land** What kinds of changes do you think people go through when they immigrate to the United States and adapt to a new way of life? How might their departure from their native lands affect the family and friends they leave behind? Use a chart like the one shown to explore the answers to these questions. Share personal experiences of immigration, if possible, in a small group.

| Effects on Immigrants | Effects on Those Left Behind |
|---|---|
| Need to find a job | |

## Build Background

**Jewish Immigrants** Millions of eastern European Jews immigrated to the United States near the beginning of the 20th century, often fleeing religious persecution or seeking a better way of life. Life in America at the time bore little resemblance to the life these immigrants had left behind. In the "old country"—particularly in rural villages—change occurred slowly, if at all, and people lived simply, as their ancestors before them had lived. In the United States, however, change was occurring at a rapid pace as economic and urban development transformed the nation and its people.

To meet the challenge of living in a new country, immigrants learned English, found jobs, and often became assimilated, or absorbed, into mainstream American culture. In order to fit in, some abandoned the cultural and religious traditions that had formerly shaped their lives. However, as they adapted to their newfound freedom and relative prosperity, most tried to maintain the feeling of community they had left behind. Typically, they settled among other Jews from the same towns or regions in eastern Europe. They also formed social groups, or societies, that raised money to help support those still living in their native villages.

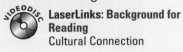

**LaserLinks: Background for Reading**
Cultural Connection

### WORDS TO KNOW
**Vocabulary Preview**

abdicate
benediction
contour
flax
heretic

hinterland
illegible
raspingly
recite
thatched

## Focus Your Reading

**LITERARY ANALYSIS**   **PLOT AND THEME**

**Plot** refers to the chain of related events that take place in a story. In many stories, the outcome of the plot—the way in which the central **conflict** or misunderstanding is resolved—helps to reveal the writer's **theme,** or message. As you read this story, consider how the twists and turns of the plot contribute to the story's theme.

**ACTIVE READING**   **MAKING PREDICTIONS**

A **prediction** is a reasonable guess about what will happen next. To make predictions about the outcome of this story, consider the following as you read:

• the description of the **setting**
• specific details about the **characters**
• important statements made by the characters
• the **title** of the selection

**READER'S NOTEBOOK** Before you begin reading, reflect upon the story's title and predict what you think will happen. As you read, jot down new predictions, based upon what you learn about the characters and their setting.

# The Son from America

## Isaac Bashevis Singer

The village of Lentshin was tiny—a sandy marketplace where the peasants of the area met once a week. It was surrounded by little huts with <u>thatched</u> roofs or shingles green with moss. The chimneys looked like pots. Between the huts there were fields, where the owners planted vegetables or pastured their goats.

In the smallest of these huts lived old Berl, a man in his eighties, and his wife, who was called Berlcha (wife of Berl). Old Berl was one of the Jews who had been driven from their villages in Russia and had settled in Poland. In Lentshin, they mocked the mistakes he made while praying aloud. He spoke with a sharp "r." He was short, broad-shouldered, and had a small white beard, and summer and winter he wore a sheepskin hat, a padded cotton jacket, and stout boots. He walked slowly, shuffling his feet. He had a half acre of field, a cow, a goat, and chickens.

The couple had a son, Samuel, who had gone to America forty years ago. It was said in Lentshin that he became a millionaire there. Every month, the Lentshin letter carrier brought old Berl a money order and a letter that no one could read because many of the words were English. How much money Samuel sent his parents remained a secret. Three times a year, Berl and his wife went on foot to Zakroczym[1] and cashed the money orders there. But they never seemed to use the money. What for? The garden, the

---

1. **Zakroczym** (zä-krô′chəm).

*The Grey House* (1917), Marc Chagall. Thyssen-Bornemisza Museum, Madrid, Spain, Nimatallah/Art Resource, New York. Copyright © 1996 Artists Rights Society (ARS), New York/ADAGP, Paris.

cow, and the goat provided most of their needs. Besides, Berlcha sold chickens and eggs, and from these there was enough to buy flour for bread.

No one cared to know where Berl kept the money that his son sent him. There were no thieves in Lentshin. The hut consisted of one room, which contained all their belongings: the table, the shelf for meat, the shelf for milk foods, the two beds, and the clay oven. Sometimes the chickens roosted in the woodshed and sometimes, when it was cold, in a coop near the oven. The goat, too, found shelter inside when the weather was bad. The more prosperous villagers had kerosene lamps, but Berl and his wife did not believe in newfangled gadgets. What was wrong with a wick in a dish of oil? Only for the Sabbath[2] would Berlcha buy three tallow candles at the store. In summer, the couple got up at sunrise and retired with the chickens. In the long winter evenings, Berlcha spun <u>flax</u> at her spinning wheel, and Berl sat beside her in the silence of those who enjoy their rest.

Once in a while when Berl came home from the synagogue after evening prayers, he brought news to his wife. In Warsaw there were strikers who demanded that the czar <u>abdicate</u>. A <u>heretic</u> by the name of Dr. Herzl[3] had come up with the idea that Jews should settle again in Palestine. Berlcha listened and shook her bonneted head. Her face was yellowish and wrinkled like a cabbage leaf. There were bluish sacks under her eyes. She was half deaf. Berl had to repeat each word he said to her. She would say, "The things that happen in the big cities!"

Here in Lentshin nothing happened except usual events: a cow gave birth to a calf, a young couple had a circumcision party,[4] or a girl was born and there was no party. Occasionally, someone died. Lentshin had no cemetery, and the corpse had to be taken to Zakroczym. Actually, Lentshin had become a village with few young people. The young men left for Zakroczym, for Nowy Dwor, for Warsaw, and sometimes for the United States. Like Samuel's, their letters were <u>illegible</u>, the Yiddish[5] mixed with the languages of the countries where they were now living. They sent photographs in which the men wore top hats and the women fancy dresses like squiresses.[6]

Berl and Berlcha also received such photographs. But their eyes were failing, and neither he nor she had glasses. They could barely make out the pictures. Samuel had sons and daughters with Gentile[7] names—and grandchildren who had married and had their own offspring. Their names were so strange that Berl and Berlcha could never remember them. But what difference do names make? America was far, far away on the other side of the ocean, at the edge of the world. A Talmud[8] teacher who came to Lentshin had said that Americans walked with their heads down and their feet up. Berl and Berlcha could not grasp this. How was it possible? But since the teacher said so, it must be true. Berlcha pondered for some time, and then she said,

---

2. **the Sabbath:** a weekly day of rest and worship for Jews, beginning at sundown Friday and ending at sundown Saturday.

3. **Dr. Herzl** (hĕrt′səl): Theodor Herzl, an Austrian writer and journalist who, in response to anti-Jewish feeling in Europe in the late 1800s, called for the establishment of a Jewish state.

4. **circumcision party:** a party following the Jewish ceremony called *brith milah* (brĭt′ mē-lä′), in which a baby boy is circumcised and given a Hebrew name on the eighth day after birth.

5. **Yiddish:** a language—containing elements of German, Hebrew, and several other languages—spoken by Jews in central and eastern Europe and by their descendants in other countries.

6. **squiresses:** wives of country gentlemen (squires).

7. **Gentile** (jĕn′tīl′): not Jewish (usually applied to people and things Christian).

8. **Talmud** (täl′mŏŏd): the writings that are the basis of Jewish civil and religious law.

---

<table>
<tr><td>WORDS<br>TO<br>KNOW</td><td>flax (flăks) n. a plant that is the source of the fibers used to make linen<br>abdicate (ăb′dĭ-kāt′) v. to give up an office or position<br>heretic (hĕr′ĭ-tĭk) n. a person who disagrees with accepted beliefs, particularly those of a religious group<br>illegible (ĭ-lĕj′ə-bəl) adj. unreadable</td></tr>
</table>

"One can get accustomed to everything."

And so it remained. From too much thinking—God forbid—one may lose one's wits.

One Friday morning, when Berlcha was kneading the dough for the Sabbath loaves, the door opened and a nobleman entered. He was so tall that he had to bend down to get through the door. He wore a beaver hat and a cloak bordered with fur. He was followed by Chazkel, the coachman from Zakroczym, who carried two leather valises with brass locks. In astonishment Berlcha raised her eyes.

The nobleman looked around and said to the coachman in Yiddish, "Here it is." He took out a silver ruble and paid him. The coachman tried to hand him change, but he said, "You can go now."

When the coachman closed the door, the nobleman said, "Mother, it's me, your son Samuel—Sam."

Berlcha heard the words and her legs grew numb. Her hands, to which pieces of dough were sticking, lost their power. The nobleman hugged her, kissed her forehead, both her cheeks. Berlcha began to cackle like a hen, "My son!" At that moment Berl came in from the woodshed, his arms piled with logs. The goat followed him. When he saw a nobleman kissing his wife, Berl dropped the wood and exclaimed, "What is this?"

The nobleman let go of Berlcha and embraced Berl. "Father!"

For a long time Berl was unable to utter a sound. He wanted to recite holy words that he had read in the Yiddish Bible, but he could remember nothing. Then he asked, "Are you Samuel?"

"Yes, Father, I am Samuel."

"Well, peace be with you." Berl grasped his son's hand. He was still not sure that he was not being fooled. Samuel wasn't as tall and heavy as this man, but then Berl reminded himself that Samuel was only fifteen years old when he had left home. He must have grown in that faraway country. Berl asked, "Why didn't you let us know that you were coming?"

"Didn't you receive my cable?" Samuel asked.

Berl did not know what a cable was.

Berlcha had scraped the dough from her hands and enfolded her son. He kissed her again and asked, "Mother, didn't you receive a cable?"

"What? If I lived to see this, I am happy to die," Berlcha said, amazed by her own words. Berl, too, was amazed. These were just the words he would have said earlier if he had been able to remember. After a while Berl came to himself and said, "Pescha, you will have to make a double Sabbath pudding in addition to the stew."

It was years since Berl had called Berlcha by her given name. When he wanted to address her, he would say, "Listen," or "Say." It is the young or those from the big cities who call a wife by her name. Only now did Berlcha begin to cry. Yellow tears ran from her eyes, and everything became dim. Then she called out, "It's Friday—I have to prepare for the Sabbath." Yes, she had to knead the dough and braid the loaves. With such a guest, she had to make a larger Sabbath stew. The winter day is short, and she must hurry.

Her son understood what was worrying her, because he said, "Mother, I will help you."

Berlcha wanted to laugh, but a choked sob came out. "What are you saying? God forbid."

*Le juif en vert* [Jew in green] (1914), Marc Chagall. Oil on cardboard 38⅜″ × 30¾″, private collection, Geneva, Switzerland. Copyright © 1996 Artists Rights Society (ARS), New York/ADAGP, Paris.

goat sat down near the oven; she gazed with surprise at this strange man—his height and his bizarre clothes.

The neighbors had heard the good news that Berl's son had arrived from America, and they came to greet him. The women began to help Berlcha prepare for the Sabbath. Some laughed; some cried. The room was full of people, as at a wedding. They asked Berl's son, "What is new in America?"

And Berl's son answered, "America is all right."

"Do Jews make a living?"

"One eats white bread there on weekdays."

"Do they remain Jews?"

"I am not a Gentile."

After Berlcha blessed the candles, father and son went to the little synagogue across the street. A new snow had fallen. The son took large steps, but Berl warned him, "Slow down."

In the synagogue the Jews recited "Let Us Exult" and "Come, My Groom." All the time, the snow outside kept falling. After prayers, when Berl and Samuel left the Holy Place, the village was unrecognizable. Everything was covered in snow. One could see only the <u>contours</u> of the roofs and the candles in the windows. Samuel said, "Nothing has changed here."

Berlcha had prepared gefilte fish,[10] chicken

The nobleman took off his cloak and jacket and remained in his vest, on which hung a solid-gold watch chain. He rolled up his sleeves and came to the trough. "Mother, I was a baker for many years in New York," he said, and he began to knead the dough.

"What! You are my darling son who will say Kaddish[9] for me." She wept <u>raspingly</u>. Her strength left her, and she slumped onto the bed.

Berl said, "Women will always be women." And he went to the shed to get more wood. The

---

9. **Kaddish** (kä′dĭsh): a Jewish prayer recited by mourners after the death of a close relative.

10. **gefilte** (gə-fĭl′tə) **fish:** a traditional Jewish food made from finely chopped fish.

soup with rice, meat, carrot stew. Berl <u>recited</u> the <u>benediction</u> over a glass of ritual wine. The family ate and drank, and when it grew quiet for a while, one could hear the chirping of the house cricket. The son talked a lot, but Berl and Berlcha understood little. His Yiddish was different and contained foreign words.

After the final blessing Samuel asked, "Father, what did you do with all the money I sent you?"

Berl raised his white brows. "It's here."

"Didn't you put it in a bank?"

"There is no bank in Lentshin."

"Where do you keep it?"

Berl hesitated. "One is not allowed to touch money on the Sabbath, but I will show you." He crouched beside the bed and began to shove something heavy. A boot appeared. Its top was stuffed with straw. Berl removed the straw, and the son saw that the boot was full of gold coins. He lifted it.

"Father, this is a treasure!" he called out.

"Well."

"Why didn't you spend it?"

"On what? Thank God, we have everything."

"Why didn't you travel somewhere?"

"Where to? This is our home."

The son asked one question after the other, but Berl's answer was always the same: they wanted for nothing. The garden, the cow, the goat, the chickens provided them with all they needed. The son said, "If thieves knew about this, your lives wouldn't be safe."

"There are no thieves here."

"What will happen to the money?"

"You take it."

Slowly, Berl and Berlcha grew accustomed to their son and his American Yiddish. Berlcha could hear him better now. She even recognized his voice. He was saying, "Perhaps we should build a larger synagogue."

"The synagogue is big enough," Berl replied.

"Perhaps a home for old people."

"No one sleeps in the street."

The next day after the Sabbath meal was eaten, a Gentile from Zakroczym brought a paper—it was the cable. Berl and Berlcha lay down for a nap. They soon began to snore. The goat, too, dozed off. The son put on his cloak and his hat and went for a walk. He strode with his long legs across the marketplace. He stretched out a hand and touched a roof. He wanted to smoke a cigar, but he remembered it was forbidden on the Sabbath. He had a desire to talk to someone, but it seemed that the whole of Lentshin was asleep. He entered the synagogue. An old man was sitting there, reciting psalms. Samuel asked, "Are you praying?"

"What else is there to do when one gets old?"

"Do you make a living?"

The old man did not understand the meaning of these words. He smiled, showing his empty gums, and then he said, "If God gives health, one keeps on living."

Samuel returned home. Dusk had fallen. Berl went to the synagogue for the evening prayers, and the son remained with his mother. The room was filled with shadows.

Berlcha began to recite in a solemn singsong, "God of Abraham, Isaac, and Jacob, defend the poor people of Israel and Thy name. The Holy Sabbath is departing; the welcome week is coming to us. Let it be one of health, wealth, and good deeds."

"Mother, you don't need to pray for wealth,"

Samuel said. "You are wealthy already."

Berlcha did not hear—or pretended not to. Her face had turned into a cluster of shadows.

In the twilight Samuel put his hand into his jacket pocket and touched his passport, his checkbook, his letters of credit. He had come here with big plans. He had a valise filled with presents for his parents. He wanted to bestow gifts on the village. He brought not only his own money but funds from the Lentshin Society in New York, which had organized a ball for the benefit of the village. But this village in the hinterland needed nothing. From the synagogue one could hear hoarse chanting. The cricket, silent all day, started again its chirping. Berlcha began to sway and utter holy rhymes inherited from mothers and grandmothers:

> *Thy holy sheep*
> *In mercy keep,*
> *In Torah and good deeds;*
> *Provide for all their needs,*
> *Shoes, clothes, and bread*
> *And the Messiah's tread.* ❖

*Translated by the author and Dorothea Straus*

# GRUDNOW
## LINDA PASTAN

When he spoke of where he
   came from,
my grandfather could have been
clearing his throat
of that name, that town
5   sometimes Poland, sometimes Russia,
the borders penciled in
with a hand as shaky as his.
He left, I heard him say,
because there was nothing there.

10   I understood what he meant
when I saw the photograph
of his people standing
against a landscape emptied
of crops and trees, scraped raw
15   by winter. Everything
was in sepia, as if the brown earth
had stained the faces,
stained even the air.

20   I would have died there, I think
in childhood maybe
of some fever,
my face pressed for warmth
against a cow with flanks
like those of the great-aunts
25   in the picture. Or later
I would have died of history
like the others, who dug
their stubborn heels into that earth,
heels as hard as the heels
30   of the bread my grandfather tore
from the loaf at supper. He always
sipped his tea through a cube of sugar
clenched in his teeth, the way
he sipped his life here, noisily,
35   through all he remembered
that might have been sweet in
   Grudnow.

# *Thinking* through the LITERATURE

## Connect to the Literature

**1. What Do You Think?**
How did you react to the outcome of the story? Jot down some of your first thoughts.

> **Comprehension Check**
> • How do Berl and Berlcha live?
> • Why didn't Berl spend the money Samuel had sent him?
> • What plan did Samuel have for Lentshin?

## Think Critically

**2.** **ACTIVE READING** **PREDICTING** Compare the predictions you made in your **READER'S NOTEBOOK** about the outcome of the **plot.** Were your predictions correct? At what points in the story were you able to make predictions?

**3.** What are your impressions of Berl and Berlcha?

THINK ABOUT
- the description of their home and community
- their understanding of the world
- their reasons for not spending the money their son has sent
- the role of tradition and religion in their life

**4.** What are your impressions of their son, Samuel?

THINK ABOUT
- why he returns to Lentshin
- how he has adapted to life in his new country
- how he reacts to his parents' life

**5.** How would you explain what Samuel has realized by the end of the story?

## Extend Interpretations

**6. Comparing Texts** Would you say that the grandfather in the poem "Grudnow" has more in common with Samuel or with Samuel's parents? Why?

**7. Critic's Corner** In awarding Singer its prize for literature, the Nobel Prize committee praised his "impassioned narrative art which, with roots in a Polish-Jewish cultural tradition, brings universal human conditions to life." Would you say that "The Son from America" deals with universal human conditions? Explain your answer.

**8. Connect to Life** Do aspects of life in Lentshin exist anywhere in the United States today? Cite details from the story as you share your opinion with classmates.

## Literary Analysis

**PLOT AND THEME** The **theme** or message of a story is often developed through the **plot,** which is the writer's blueprint for what happens, when it happens, and to whom it happens. Through the action of the story and the resolution of **conflict,** a writer may reveal a truth about human behavior or an observation about the human condition. In this story, the plot takes a number of unexpected turns, which suggest a great deal about what Singer values in life.

**Paired Activity** With a partner, create a chart similar to the one below. List important events from the story's plot. Then consider the outcomes of these events. What theme, or themes, do these outcomes suggest?

| Event | Outcome |
|---|---|
| 1. Son moves to America. | 1. Son makes money as a baker. |
| 2. | 2. |
| 3. | 3. |
| **Theme:** | |

THE SON FROM AMERICA    **167**

# *Choices & CHALLENGES*

## Writing Options

**1. Lentshin Newsletter** Imagine that you are Samuel. Write a newsletter article for the Lentshin Society magazine, describing your trip to Lentshin, Poland. Be sure to explain why you have returned to New York with the money that the society has raised for the village.

**2. Literary Review** Write a review of this story, telling what you liked or didn't like about Singer's storytelling techniques.

**3. Old World Sketches** Write character sketches of Berl and Berlcha. Use quotations from the story to help you describe the characters' appearance, their home, and how they live and relate to each other. Place the entry in your **Working Portfolio.**

**Writing Handbook**
See page 1153: Description.

## Activities & Explorations

**1. A Son's Portrait** Draw or paint a portrait of Samuel as seen through his parents' eyes. ~ **ART**

**2. A Son's Scrapbook** Work with two classmates to create a scrapbook of Samuel's trip to Lentshin. Use old photos, art reproductions, bits of writing or clippings, and drawings of your own to depict the most important aspects of his visit. Include captions explaining how the images reflect Samuel's encounters and realizations.
~ **VIEWING AND REPRESENTING**

**3. Personal Interview** Conduct an interview with someone you know who has immigrated to America. Then summarize what you have learned about this person's experiences. ~ **SPEAKING AND LISTENING**

## Inquiry & Research

**World Religions** Research the Jewish celebration of the Sabbath. Look for information on the symbolism of candles, bread, and wine and on the traditional laws governing behavior on the Sabbath, some of which are mentioned in the story. Present your findings to your classmates in an oral report.

## Vocabulary in Action

**EXERCISE A: RELATED WORDS** On your paper, write the letter of the word in each group that does not belong with the other words.

1. (a) matted, (b) detonated, (c) thatched, (d) shingled
2. (a) appoint, (b) abdicate, (c), gesticulate, (d) rule
3. (a) contour, (b) size, (c) shade, (d) consternation
4. (a) preach, (b) lecture, (c) percussively, (d) recite
5. (a) club moss, (b) flax, (c) quartz, (d) elm

**EXERCISE B: ASSESSMENT PRACTICE** Write the letter of the antonym of each boldfaced word below.

1. **illegible:** (a) knowledgeable, (b) advisable, (c) discernible
2. **heretic:** (a) cynic, (b) valet, (c) adherent
3. **raspingly:** (a) melodically, (b) repeatedly, (c) marginally
4. **hinterland:** (a) allowance, (b) metropolis, (c) villain
5. **benediction:** (a) benefit, (b) slander, (c) diction

**Building Vocabulary**
For an in-depth study on context clues, involving antonyms and synonyms, see page 1000.

| WORDS TO KNOW | | | | |
|---|---|---|---|---|
| abdicate | contour | heretic | illegible | recite |
| benediction | flax | hinterland | raspingly | thatched |

# Grammar in Context: Using Nouns to Establish Tone and Mood

Notice the simple nouns Singer uses to describe Berl and Berlcha's home in "The Son from America."

> The hut consisted of one room, which contained all their belongings: the table, the shelf for meat, the shelf for milk foods, the two beds, and the clay oven.

You may recall that a **noun** is a word that refers to a person, place, or thing. The nouns in this sentence help to convey the simple outlook and lifestyle of Berl and Berlcha. How would the tone of the sentence be different if *hut* were replaced with *house* or if *meat* were replaced with *steaks?*

**WRITING EXERCISE** Change the underlined nouns in these sentences so that they refer to life in a wealthy modern city instead of life in a rural town.

**Example: *Original*** Their furniture includes two stools and a table covered with oilcloth.
***Rewritten*** Their furniture includes two armchairs and a sofa covered with velvet.

1. In the marketplace, peasants buy flour and eggs.
2. His father has a goat, some chickens, and a cow.
3. Berl wears boots and a jacket made of cotton.
4. At night, Berlcha takes out her spinning wheel and makes thread out of flax.

**Grammar Handbook**
Nouns, p. 1182

## Isaac Bashevis Singer
### 1904–1991

**Other Works**
*Gimpel the Fool and Other Stories*
*In My Father's Court*
*Yentl the Yeshiva Boy*
*Shosha*
*The Collected Stories of Isaac Bashevis Singer*

**Early Years** One of the world's foremost Yiddish-language authors, Isaac Bashevis Singer was born in a tiny village in rural Poland and spent most of his youth in Warsaw, the country's capital. His father and both of his grandfathers were rabbis, so he received a traditional religious education. Singer was very close with his older brother, I. J. Singer, a writer who rejected some traditional beliefs and supported the modernization of Judaism. "I was fascinated both with my brother's rationalism and with my parents' mysticism," he once remarked, and both interests are evident in his writings. He also said that he preferred "to write about the world which I knew, which I know best." As a result, much of his fiction is set in the Polish-Jewish communities of his boyhood, which no longer exist.

**A Writer's Journey** In the 1920s, while working in Warsaw as a proofreader for a Yiddish literary journal edited by his brother, Singer began writing and publishing his own stories and book reviews. In 1932 he became coeditor of *Globus,* a literary magazine in which he published portions of what would become his first novel, *Satan in Goray.* The complete novel appeared in 1935, the same year that Singer left for America to join his brother, who had emigrated the year before. He settled in New York City and began writing articles, book reviews, and short stories for the *Daily Forward,* a Yiddish newspaper.

**World Renown** Over the course of his career, Singer won a great number of honors and awards for his writing, including the 1978 Nobel Prize in literature. He always wrote in Yiddish, his native tongue, even though he learned English and even collaborated on English translations of his works. Singer once said, "When I was a boy, they called me a liar . . . for telling stories. Now they call me a writer. It's more advanced, but it's the same thing." He also believed that "every experience becomes important when it's told, not before."

## Author Activity

**Storyteller Singer** Read at least two other stories by Singer, paying close attention to his style. Based on your readings, what generalizations can you make about Singer's style and subject matter?

# Through the One-Way Mirror

*Essay by* MARGARET ATWOOD

# The Border: A Glare of Truth

*Essay by* PAT MORA

## Connect to Your Life

**Borderline Views** Think about life in your community or neighborhood. What are the boundaries that define different neighborhoods? How often do you cross these boundaries to go into the next town or another neighborhood? With a partner, jot down what you have noticed about the borders that separate the two communities or neighborhoods and what life is like on the other side.

## Build Background

**Long Borders** Our nation shares borders with two major countries, Canada to the north and Mexico to the south. Those who live along the border are part of a border culture, often characterized by a blending of two traditions and two languages. Our border with Canada has long been a peaceful one, although after the Civil War many Canadians feared that the United States would expand its borders. With the exception of French-speaking Quebec, the United States and Canada share English as an official language as well as historic ties with Great Britain, Ireland, France, and Scandinavia. This historic legacy helps explain the cultural similarities between the two countries.

In contrast, our southern border's geographic location has often been contested by Mexico, whose people were among the original settlers of the Southwest. In fact, Texas was part of Mexico until 1836; it became part of the United States in 1845. Fighting along the border continued until the United States declared war on Mexico to settle the dispute. In 1848, Mexico signed a treaty giving up land that became California, Nevada, and Utah, and parts of Arizona, Colorado, New Mexico, and Wyoming. These historic events help explain why the Spanish language and many Mexican traditions and customs play a significant role along the Mexican border.

## Focus Your Reading

**LITERARY ANALYSIS** **THEME IN NONFICTION** Sometimes the **theme,** or message, of a nonfiction selection is directly stated. Other times it is implied, or stated indirectly. As a reader of nonfiction, you can gain insight into the theme of a work by looking for passages that reveal or hint at the writer's opinion. As you read the following two selections, look for details or passages that offer clues to the theme of the selections.

**ACTIVE READING** **COMPARISON AND CONTRAST** In both of the following essays, the authors rely on **comparison and contrast** to organize their material and create a text structure. In a comparison, the similarities of two or more objects, persons, events, stories, or, in this case, cultures are examined. Similarities are often indicated by words such as *all, each, both, likewise, also, just,* and *as.* When two or more things are contrasted, the differences are examined. Differences are often indicated by these words: *on the other hand, however, different, whereas,* and *even though.*

**READER'S NOTEBOOK** Create charts like the ones shown to record the similarities and differences each author uses to develop and organize her essay.

| Life in U. S. | Life in Canada |
|---|---|
|  |  |

| Life in El Paso | Life in Ohio |
|---|---|
|  |  |

# THROUGH THE ONE-WAY

**THE NOSES** of a great many Canadians resemble Porky Pig's. This comes from spending so much time pressing them against the longest undefended one-way mirror in the world. The Canadians looking through this mirror behave the way people on the hidden side of such mirrors usually do: they observe, analyze, ponder, snoop and wonder what all the activity on the other side means in decipherable human terms.

The Americans, bless their innocent little hearts, are rarely aware that they are even being watched, much less by the Canadians. They just go on doing body language, playing in the sandbox of the world, bashing one another on the head and planning how to blow things up, same as always. If they think about Canada at all, it's only when things get a bit snowy or the water goes off or the Canadians start fussing over some piddly detail, such as fish.[1] Then they regard them as unpatriotic; for Americans don't really see Canadians as foreigners, not like the

---

1. **some piddly . . . fish:** a reference to the occasional clashes between U.S. and Canadian fishers over the boundaries of their fishing territories.

# MIRROR
## Margaret Atwood

WORDS
TO
KNOW

**analyze** (ăn′ə-līz′) *v.* to study carefully by separating into parts

**171**

Mexicans, unless they do something weird like speak French or beat the New York Yankees at baseball. Really, think the Americans, the Canadians are just like us, or would be if they could.

Or we could switch metaphors and call the border the longest undefended backyard fence in the world. The Canadians are the folks in the neat little bungalow, with the tidy little garden and the duck pond. The Americans are the other folks, the ones in the sprawly mansion with the bad-taste statues on the lawn. There's a perpetual party, or something, going on there—loud music, raucous laughter, smoke billowing from the barbecue. Beer bottles and Coke cans land among the peonies. The Canadians have their own beer bottles and barbecue smoke, but they tend to overlook it. Your own mess is always more forgivable than the mess someone else makes on your patio.

The Canadians can't exactly call the police—they suspect that the Americans are the police—and part of their distress, which seems permanent, comes from their uncertainty as to whether or not they've been invited. Sometimes they do drop by next door, and find it exciting but scary. Sometimes the Americans drop by their house and find it clean. This worries the Canadians. They worry a lot. Maybe those Americans want to buy up their duck pond, with all the money they seem to have, and turn it into a cesspool or a water-skiing emporium.

It also worries them that the Americans don't seem to know who the Canadians are, or even where, exactly, they are. Sometimes the Americans call Canada their backyard, sometimes their front yard, both of which imply ownership. Sometimes they say they are the Mounties and the Canadians are Rose Marie.[2] (All these things have, in fact, been said by American politicians.) Then they accuse the Canadians of being paranoid and having an identity crisis. Heck, there is no call for the Canadians to fret about their identity, because everyone knows they're Americans, really. If the Canadians disagree with that, they're told not to be so insecure.

One of the problems is that Canadians and Americans are educated backward from one another. The Canadians—except for the Québecois,[3] one keeps saying—are taught about the rest of the world first and Canada second. The Americans are taught about the United States first, and maybe later about other places, if they're of strategic importance. The Vietnam War draft dodgers got more culture shock in Canada than they did in Sweden. It's not the clothing that is different, it's those mental noises.

Of course, none of this holds true when you get close enough, where concepts like "Americans" and "Canadians" dissolve and people are just people, or anyway some of them are, the ones you happen to approve of. I, for instance, have never met any Americans I didn't like, but I only get to meet the nice ones. That's what the businessmen think too, though they have other individuals in mind. But big-scale national mythologies have a way of showing up in things like foreign policy, and at events like international writers' congresses, where the Canadians often find they have more to talk about with the Australians, the West Indians, the New Zealanders[4] and even the once-loathed snooty Brits, now declining into humanity with the dissolution of empire, than they do with the impenetrable and mysterious Yanks.

But only sometimes. Because surely the Canadians understand the Yanks. Shoot, don't they see Yank movies, read Yank mags, bobble

---

2. **Mounties . . . Rose Marie:** a reference to the 1926 operetta *Rose Marie* (later the basis of a popular film starring Nelson Eddy and Jeanette MacDonald), in which the main characters are a Royal Canadian Mounted Policeman and the woman he loves.

3. **Québecois** (kā´bĕ-kwä´): the French-speaking residents of the Canadian province of Quebec.

4. **Australians . . . New Zealanders:** peoples whose countries were, like Canada, once part of the British Empire.

---

WORDS TO KNOW

**raucous** (rô´kəs) *adj.* loud and disorderly; boisterous
**impenetrable** (ĭm-pĕn´ĭ-trə-bəl) *adj.* impossible to understand; incapable of being pierced

around to Yank music and watch Yank telly, as well as their own, when there is any?

Sometimes the Canadians think it's their job to interpret the Yanks to the rest of the world; explain them, sort of. This is an illusion: they don't understand the Yanks as much as they think they do, and it isn't their job.

But, as we say up here among God's frozen people, when Washington catches a cold, Ottawa sneezes. Some Canadians even refer to their capital city as Washington North and wonder why we're paying those guys in Ottawa when a telephone order service would be cheaper. Canadians make jokes about the relationship with Washington which the Americans, in their thin-skinned, bunion-toed way, construe as anti-American (they tend to see any nonworshipful comment coming from that gray, protoplasmic fuzz outside their borders as anti-American). They are no more anti-American than the jokes Canadians make about the weather: it's there, it's big, it's hard to influence, and it affects your life.

Of course, in any conflict with the Dreaded Menace, whatever it might be, the Canadians would line up with the Yanks, probably, if they thought it was a real menace, or if the Yanks twisted their arms or other bodily parts enough or threatened a "scorched-earth policy" (another real quote). Note the qualifiers. The Canadian idea of a menace is not the same as the U.S. one. Canada, for instance, never broke off diplomatic relations with Cuba, and it was quick to recognize China. Contemplating the U.S.-Soviet growling match, Canadians are apt to recall a line from Blake[5]: "They became what they beheld." Certainly both superpowers suffer from the imperial diseases once so noteworthy among the Romans, the British and the French: arrogance and myopia. But the bodily-parts threat is real enough, and accounts for the observable wimpiness and flunkiness of some Ottawa politicians. Nobody, except at welcoming-committee time, pretends this is an equal relationship.

Americans don't have Porky Pig noses. Instead they have Mr. Magoo eyes, with which they see the rest of the world. That would not be a problem if the United States were not so powerful. But it is, so it is. ❖

_____
5. **Blake:** the British poet and artist William Blake.

## Thinking Through the Literature

1. **Comprehension Check**  What is the "one-way mirror"?

2. **ACTIVE READING** **COMPARE AND CONTRAST**  Examine the list of details about life in the United States and life in Canada that you compiled in your **READER'S NOTEBOOK.** What do you think are the most important similarities and differences?

3. Why do you think Atwood uses Mr. Magoo to describe the Americans and Porky Pig to describe the Canadians?

4. What does Atwood really think about Americans and Canadians? Cite evidence from her essay to support your opinion.

| WORDS TO KNOW | **construe** (kən-strōō′) v. to interpret <br> **myopia** (mī-ō′pē-ə) n. nearsightedness |
|---|---|

# The Border

## A Glare of Truth

Pat Mora

**I moved away** for the first time from the U.S.-Mexican border in the fall of 1989. Friends were sure I'd miss the visible evidence of Mexico's proximity found in cities such as my native El Paso. Friends smiled that I'd soon be back for good Mexican food, for the delicate taste and smell of cilantro,[1] for soft tortillas freshly made. There were jokes about care packages flying to the Midwest.

Although most of my adult home and work life had been spent speaking English, I was prepared to miss the sound of Spanish weaving in and out of my days like the warm aroma from a familiar bakery. I knew I'd miss the pleasure of moving back and forth between two languages—a pleasure that can deepen human understanding and increase our versatility conceptually as well as linguistically.

And indeed, when I hear a phrase in Spanish in a Cincinnati restaurant, my head turns quickly. I listen, silently wishing to be part of that other conversation, if only for a few moments, to feel Spanish in my mouth. I'm reading more poetry in Spanish, sometimes reading the lines aloud to myself, enjoying sounds I don't otherwise hear. Recently I heard a voice on National Public Radio say that learning another language is renaming the world. What an interesting perception. Because language shapes as well as reflects our reality, exploring it allows us to see and to explore our world anew, much as experiencing the world with a young child causes us to pause, savor.

I smile when my children, who were too busy when they were younger, now inform me that when they visit they hope we'll be speaking Spanish. They have discovered as I did that languages are channels, sometimes to other people, sometimes to other views of the world, sometimes to other aspects of ourselves. So we struggle with irregular verbs, laughing together.

Is it my family—children, parents, siblings, niece, nephews—that I miss in this land of leaves so unlike my bare desert? Of course, but

---

1. **cilantro** (sē-län′trô) *Spanish:* coriander—an herb whose leaves are used as a seasoning.

175

my family, although miles away, is with me daily. The huge telephone bills and the steady stream of letters and cards are a long-distance version of the web of caring we once created around kitchen tables. Our family web just happens to stretch across these United States, a sturdy, elastic web steadily maintained by each in his or her own way.

Oh, I miss the meals seasoned with that family phrase, "Remember the time when . . . ?" But I've learned through the years to cherish our gatherings when I'm in the thick of them, to sink into the faces and voices, to store the memories and stories like the industrious Ohio squirrel outside my window stores her treasures.

I've enjoyed this furry, scurrying companion as I've enjoyed the silence of bare tree limbs against an evening sky, updrafts of snow outside our third-floor window, the ivory light of cherry blossoms. I feel fortunate to be experiencing the geographical center of this country, which astutely calls itself the Heartland. If I'm hearing the "heart," its steady, predictable rhythms, what am I missing from this country's southern border, its margin?

Is it other rhythms? I remember my mixed feelings as a young girl whenever my father selected a Mexican station on the radio, feelings my children now experience about me. I wanted so to *be an American*, which in my mind, and perhaps in the minds of many on the border, meant (and means) shunning anything from Mexico.

But as I grew I learned to like dancing to those rhythms. I learned to value not only the rhythms but all that they symbolized. As an adult, such music became associated with celebrations and friends, with warmth and the sharing of emotions. I revel in a certain Mexican passion not for life or about life, but *in* life—a certain intensity in the daily living of it, a certain abandon in such music, in the hugs, sometimes in the anger. I miss the *chispas*, "sparks," that spring from the willingness, the habit, of allowing the inner self to burst through polite restraints. Sparks can be dangerous but, like risks, are necessary.

I brought cassettes of Mexican and Latin American music with us when we drove to Ohio. I'd roll the car window down and turn the volume up, taking a certain delight in sending such sounds like mischievous imps across fields and into trees. Broadcasting my culture, if you will.

### Foreign Spooks

*Released full blast into the autumn air*
*from trumpets, drums, flutes,*
*the sounds burst from my car like confetti*
*riding the first strong current.*
*The invisible imps from Peru, Spain,*
*Mexico grin as they spring from guitars,*
*harps, hand claps, and violins,*
*they stream across the flat fields of Ohio,*
*hide in the drafts of abandoned gray barns,*
*and the shutters of stern, white houses,*
*burrow into cold cow's ears and the crackle*
*of dry corn, in squirrel fur, pond ripple,*
  *tree gnarl,*
*owl hollow, until the wind sighs*

*and they open their wide, impudent*
*mouths, and together con gusto*[2]
*startle sleeping farm wives,*
*sashaying raccoons, and even*
*the old harvest moon.*

---

2. **con gusto** (kôn gōōs'tô) *Spanish:* with pleasure.

On my first return visit to Texas, I stopped to hear a group of *mariachis* playing their instruments with proud gusto. I was surprised and probably embarrassed when my eyes filled with tears not only at the music, but at the sight of wonderful Mexican faces. The musicians were playing for some senior citizens. The sight of brown, knowing eyes that quickly accepted me with a smile, the stories in those eyes and in the wrinkled faces were more delicious than any *fajitas* or *flan*[3].

When I lived on the border, I had the privilege accorded to a small percentage of our citizens: I daily saw the native land of my grandparents. I grew up in the Chihuahua desert, as did they, only we grew up on different sides of the Rio Grande. That desert—its firmness, resilience, and fierceness, its whispered chants and tempestuous dance, its wisdom and majesty—shaped us as geography always shapes its inhabitants. The desert persists in me, both inspiring and compelling me to sing about her and her people, their roots and blooms and thorns.

The desert is harsh, hard as life, no carpet of leaves cushions a walk, no forest conceals the shacks on the other side of the sad river. Although a Midwest winter is hard, it ends, melts into rich soil yielding the yellow trumpeting of daffodils. But the desert in any season can be relentless as poverty and hunger, realities prevalent as scorpions in that stark terrain. Anthropologist Renato Rosaldo, in his provocative challenge to his colleagues, *Culture and Truth,* states that we live in a world "saturated with inequality, power, and domination."

The culture of the border illustrates this truth daily, glaringly. Children go to sleep hungry and stare at stores filled with toys they'll never touch, with books they'll never read. Oddly, I miss that clear view of the difference between my comfortable life and the lives of so many who also speak Spanish, value family, music, celebration. In a broader sense, I miss the visible reminder of the difference between my insulated, economically privileged life and the life of most of my fellow humans. What I miss about the sights and sounds of the border is, I've finally concluded, its stern honesty. The fierce light of that grand, wide Southwest sky not only filled me with energy, it revealed the glare of truth. ❖

---

3. **fajitas** (fä-hē′täs) . . . **flan** (flän) *Spanish:* two popular Mexican foods—the first a dish of grilled meat wrapped in tortillas, the second a custard dessert.

## Connect to the Literature

**1. What Do You Think?**
What impressions of the author did you form as a result of reading this essay?

> **Comprehension Check**
> - Describe three things that Mora remembers affectionately about her life in El Paso.
> - How does the desert link Mora to the native land of her grandparents?

## Think Critically

**2.** **ACTIVE READING** **COMPARISON AND CONTRAST** Compare the chart you created in your  **READER'S NOTEBOOK** with a classmate's chart. Discuss what you think are the most important similarities and differences between life in El Paso and life in Ohio.

**3.** How does Mora's heritage enrich her life?

> **THINK ABOUT**
> - her views about language
> - what she values about Mexican and Latin American music
> - what she means by the "Mexican passion not for life or about life but *in* life"

**4.** Do you think that Mora could have come to the same conclusions about her heritage if she had not moved away from El Paso? Explain your opinion.

**5.** What do you think Mora means by the title "The Border: A Glare of Truth"?

> **THINK ABOUT**
> - her view of the desert and its influence on culture
> - what she means by the "stern honesty" of the border
> - the diversity represented by the "culture of the border"

## Literary Analysis

**THEME IN NONFICTION** The **theme** is the message of a nonfiction selection. It is not the same as the subject, although in nonfiction, it often has something to do with the subject. Rather, the theme reveals the writer's understanding of life, or human nature. For example, in "The Border," Pat Mora's subject is culture, and her theme reveals what she thinks about cultural differences.

**Paired Activity** With a partner, review Atwood's essay, identifying clues that suggest her perceptions of Canadian and American cultural differences. Then write a sentence that states Atwood's theme. Compare it with those of your classmates. Next, review Mora's selection by studying examples of what she misses from her border culture. Use this list to help you write a sentence that states her theme.

| Atwood's Perceptions | What Mora Misses |
|---|---|
| • Canadians are in "the neat little bungalow"; Americans are in "the sprawly mansion." | • Speaking and hearing Spanish |

## Extend Interpretations

**6. Comparing Texts** Study how each author has organized the information in her essay. Though both Atwood and Mora rely on **comparison and contrast,** they do so in different ways. Do you think one way is more helpful to the reader than another? Explain your opinion.

**7. Connect to Life** In what ways do you think it would be difficult to live next to the United States? Explain your opinion.

# *Choices* & CHALLENGES

## Writing Options

**1. Border Interview** Imagine that a television news station has decided to interview Mora and Atwood together. Write the interview between the newscaster and the two guests. In your interview, have the authors address the advantages and disadvantages of life on the border. If possible, include direct quotations from both essays.

**2. Image Analysis** In describing Americans, Atwood wrote, "Americans don't have Porky Pig noses. Instead, they have Mr. Magoo eyes, with which they see the rest of the world." Write an analysis of what you think she means by this image.

**Writing Handbook**
See page 1159: Analysis.

**3. Heritage Essay** Write a personal essay in which you describe a significant cultural tradition in your life that makes you reflect on the importance of ethnic ties. Place the entry in your **Working Portfolio.**

## Activities & Explorations

**1. Visual Essay** Both selections have many images that appeal to the sense of sight. Working with a partner or a small group, choose one of the essays and create illustrations that tell the essay's story in pictures or cartoons.
**~ VIEWING AND REPRESENTING**

**2. Illustrated Map** Choose either of our geographic neighbors and design a map that shows its border with the United States. Be sure to include major border cities.
**~ GEOGRAPHY**

## Inquiry and Research

Over the course of the 20th century, millions of people have immigrated to the United States. Find out more facts about our nation's recent immigrants and their countries of origin.

**Real World Link**
Begin your research by reading the magazine article on page 181.

**More Online: Research Starter**
www.mcdougallittell.com

## Vocabulary in Action

**EXERCISE A: CONTEXT CLUES** Find the word that is used incorrectly in each sentence below. Rewrite the sentence, replacing the incorrect word with a Word to Know.

1. Atwood's article is about how the people of two neighboring countries can misunderstand one another as they try to cower one another's attitudes.

2. Canadians see Americans as loud, delicate, and tasteless.

3. Relations between the United States and the former Soviet Union included an element of influenza, according to Atwood.

4. She says that Americans prevail any criticism as anti-American.

5. Even though Americans and Canadians are so similar, they remain an unavailable mystery to one another.

**EXERCISE B: MEANING CLUES** Choose the Word to Know that is the best solution for each riddle.

1. I happen often in many places.
2. I have many talents.
3. I describe a clever way of doing things.
4. I am extremely rude.
5. I am nearer than you think.

**Building Vocabulary**

For an in-depth discussion on how to expand your vocabulary, see page 1102.

| WORDS TO KNOW | | | | |
|---|---|---|---|---|
| | analyze | construe | impudent | prevalent | raucous |
| | astutely | impenetrable | myopia | proximity | versatility |

# *Choices & CHALLENGES*

## Grammar in Context: Abstract and Concrete Nouns

Pat Mora uses abstract and concrete nouns to describe living on the U.S.-Mexican border.

> **The culture of the border illustrates this truth daily, glaringly. Children go to sleep hungry and stare at stores filled with toys they'll never touch, with books they'll never read.**

**Abstract nouns,** like those shown in blue type, name things that cannot be perceived with the senses. **Concrete nouns,** like those shown in red type, name objects that can be seen, heard, smelled, touched, or tasted. Often writers follow abstract nouns that express general concepts (like *culture* and *truth)* with concrete nouns that illustrate or clarify those concepts.

**WRITING EXERCISE** In each sentence, supply a group of words containing concrete nouns that illustrate the concept named by the underlined abstract noun.

**Example:** An intense <u>longing</u> _____ envelops her now that she is away from home.

An intense longing <u>for her scratched-up desk, battered green stapler, and bright blue pencil holder</u> envelops her now that she is away from home.

1. At the border there is <u>evidence</u> of the nearness of Mexico, such as _____.
2. When Pat Mora moved to Cincinnati, she missed her <u>family</u>—all the _____.
3. Mora and her family engage in long-distance <u>communication</u> through _____.

# Margaret Atwood
### 1939–

**Other Works**
*The Circle Game*
*Lady Oracle*
*Surfacing*
*The Handmaid's Tale*
*Cat's Eye*

**Canada's Treasure**  Margaret Atwood, a poet, novelist, essayist, critic, and short-story writer, has been called "a national heroine of the arts." Her novels, which have won worldwide critical acclaim, typically focus on female characters who search for identity in a confusing and often threatening world. A number of her books have become best-sellers, earning her a loyal audience. As reporter Judy Klemesrud notes, "People follow her on the streets and in stores." A frequent guest on Canadian television and radio, she is one of her country's most visible writers.

**Wilderness Roots**  Born in the city of Ottawa in Ontario, Canada, Atwood spent much of her childhood in wilderness regions, where she accompanied her scientist father on long field trips. Atwood grew up in a highly educated family that encouraged her to think for herself. She began writing poetry at age 5; when she was 16, she realized that writing was all she wanted to do.

# Pat Mora
### 1942–

**Other Works**
*Chants*
*Borders*
*Communion*
*Agua Santa/Holy Water*

**On the Border**  In her poetry, short stories, and essays, Pat Mora portrays the cultural diversity and visual beauty of the Southwest and the harmony that can exist between nature and human beings. Mora has spent most of her life in El Paso, where she was born. (Her four grandparents had migrated from Mexico to El Paso to escape a revolution.) She has said that when she was young, she spoke Spanish at home with her grandmother and aunt, but she did not always want her school friends to know that she spoke Spanish. After receiving a master's degree from the University of Texas at El Paso, Mora pursued a career in teaching.

**The Value of Heritage**  In 1986, Mora received a Kellogg National Fellowship to study ways of preserving cultures. She explains, "I am interested in how we save languages and traditions. What we have inside of our homes and our families is a treasure chest that we don't pay attention to."

# *from* To Make a Nation:
## How Immigrants Are Changing America

BY PENNY LOEB, DORIAN FRIEDMAN, MARY C. LORD,
DAN McGRAW AND KUKULA GLASTRIS

**1** More than 8.6 million immigrants entered the United States during the 1980s, an influx which has impacted the United States. economically, politically, and socially.

Communities across America are grappling with what many politicians, pundits, and talk-show hosts refer to simply as the "immigrant problem." In the 1980s, the nation absorbed more than 8.6 million newcomers, mostly from Asia, Latin America, and the Caribbean. . . .

**2** To better understand who the new immigrants are and what impact they have on the nation, *U.S. News* conducted a computer analysis of 12.5 million recently released census records. Reporters also interviewed dozens of immigrants and local government officials in eight communities across the nation. The results reveal a somewhat surprising picture of the newest Americans—those who arrived between 1980 and 1990. Principal findings of the *U.S. News* study:

**3**
- Far from being uneducated huddled masses, a majority of recent immigrants have high-school educations; the exceptions are Mexicans and Indochinese refugees. More than half those from nations such as the Philippines have bachelor's degrees.

- Contrary to popular opinion, immigrants do not rob citizens of jobs but either expand employment niches or take jobs few Americans want.

- Most newcomers do not rely on welfare. Though public assistance increased much faster for a few immigrant groups than for citizens, overall only about 4 percent of new immigrants received welfare aid.

- While only 20 percent of recent immigrants boast incomes higher than the average U.S. citizen, they catch up. After a decade in this country, immigrants, on average, took home salaries comparable to those of nonimmigrant Americans.

- There is no significant difference in political opinions between immigrants and American-born citizens. While immigrants are more apt to register as independents, both immigrants and native-born citizens hold nearly identical beliefs on issues such as crime and welfare, a comparison of polling data from the University of Chicago shows.

## Reading for Information

When you read a magazine article, are you able to sort facts from opinions? How do you know whether the facts you're reading are accurate?

**DISTINGUISHING FACT AND OPINION**
A **fact** is a statement that can be proved to be correct or incorrect. Because statements of fact can sometimes be incorrect, it is important for readers to consider the source of the information and judge its **reliability,** or dependability. A reliable source for statistics on population growth would be the U.S. Census Bureau, for example.

An **opinion** is a statement of someone's beliefs, judgments, or feelings—things that are not factual. An opinion cannot be proved or disproved, and for this reason it is sometimes referred to as a **nonfact.** Words like *terrible, wonderful, always, never, probably, most, all,* and *none* often signal opinions; so do phrases such as *I think, I believe,* and *it seems.*

**YOUR TURN** To help you distinguish facts and opinions in this magazine article, use the activities below.

**1** Is there a sentence in the first paragraph that expresses an opinion? Explain how you know.

**2** **Judging Reliability** How accurate do you think the "findings" of the *U.S. News* study are? Explain your opinion.

**3** Write an opinion of your own, based on the facts contained in this excerpt.

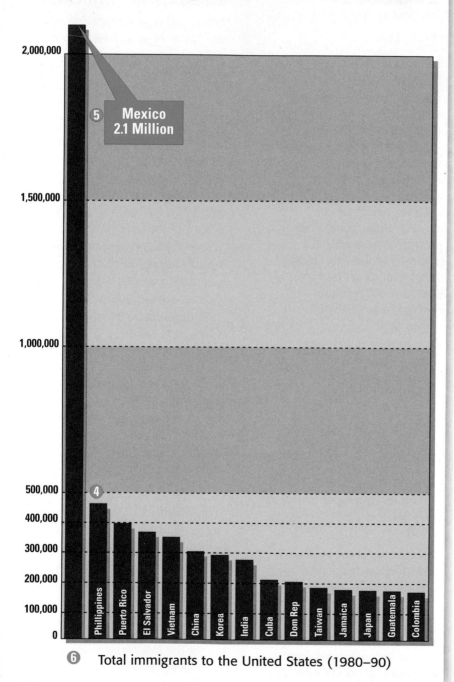

# 1990 U.S. Immigration Census Profile

**5** Mexico 2.1 Million

2,000,000

1,500,000

1,000,000

500,000

400,000

300,000

200,000

100,000

0

**4**

Phillippines · Puerto Rico · El Salvador · Vietnam · China · Korea · India · Cuba · Dom Rep · Taiwan · Jamaica · Japan · Guatemala · Colombia

**6** Total immigrants to the United States (1980–90)

## Interpreting Graphs

The bar graph at the left shows how the top 15 countries of origin contributed to the total of 8.6 million immigrants to the United States in 1980–1990.

**YOUR TURN** Use the questions below to help you interpret the graph.

**4** What does each bar represent?

**5** Which country was the source of the greatest number of immigrants?

**6** Although Mexico's bar looks huge in the graph, what percentage of the 8.6 million total immigrants actually came from that country?

**Spotting Trends** If the bar graph were expanded to include the top 30 countries of origin, would you expect the 30th country to have been the source of more than 100,000 or less than 100,000 immigrants?

## Inquiry & Research

**Activity Link: "The Border: A Glare of Truth," p. 170**

Update this bar graph with the most recent immigration statistics. Use the Internet, or a recently published encyclopedia or almanac. Compare the statistics you find with the 1980–1990 figures. Have there been any major shifts in the rankings of countries of origin?

## Word Parts and Meaning

Have you ever opened up a word to see how it works? A word may be composed of several parts that serve specific functions in shaping the word's meaning. Consider the words in blue type on the right.

*Bluntly* is made up of two parts: the base word *blunt*, meaning "frank" or "abrupt," and *-ly*, a suffix that makes an adverb of manner. *Cosmopolitan* is made up of three parts: the Greek roots *cosm* ("world") and *polit* ("citizen") and *-an*, a suffix that makes an adjective. Together, the parts of

This was said so seriously and so bluntly that Nene could not find speech immediately. In the cosmopolitan atmosphere of the city it had always seemed to her something of a joke that a person's tribe could determine whom he married.
—Chinua Achebe, "Marriage Is a Private Affair"

*cosmopolitan* form a word that means "sophisticated" or "worldly." Recognizing the parts of a word can often help you determine the word's meaning.

## Strategies for Building Vocabulary

When you encounter an unfamiliar word, see if it has recognizable parts. A **base word,** such as *blunt,* can stand alone. A **root,** such as *cosm,* cannot stand alone—other roots or affixes need to be added to it. An **affix,** like *-ly* in *bluntly,* is attached to a base word or a root to change its meaning or function. An **affix** at the beginning of a word is called a **prefix;** one at the end is called a **suffix.**

**❶ Roots and Affixes** An understanding of word parts can help you decipher unfamiliar words. See if you can use the following information to determine the meaning of *dissuasion:*

| Prefix | Root | Suffix |
|--------|------|--------|
| dis- | suas | -ion |
| "away" | "urge" | "a process of" |

The root *suas* comes from the Latin *suadere,* meaning "to urge." The prefix *dis-* means "away"; the suffix *-ion* means "a process of." Therefore, the word *dissuasion* refers to a process of urging someone away from doing something.

**❷ Word Families** Words containing the same root are usually related in meaning. Knowing the root can help you understand other words in the same word family. For example, the word *efficacy* contains the Latin root *fic,* which means "do" or "make." The idea of doing can be seen in the definition of *efficacy*—"the power to produce a desired effect"—and the same idea is involved in the meanings of other words in the *fic* family, such as *efficient, proficient,* and *sufficient.*

**❸ Learning the Roots** Use these charts to help you learn several Greek and Latin roots.

| Greek Root | Meaning | Example |
|------------|---------|---------|
| derm | skin | dermatology, dermatitis |
| gen | birth, race | generation, genetics |
| gram | something written | diagram, grammatical |
| hydr | water | hydrogen, hydroelectric |
| pan | all, entire | panorama, pandemic |
| psych | mind, soul | psychology, psychic |

| Latin Root | Meaning | Example |
|------------|---------|---------|
| centr | center | central, concentric |
| cred, credit | believe | credit, credible |
| fer | bear, carry | transfer, infer |
| fug, fugit | flee | fugitive, refuge |
| pos, posit | place, put | position, impose |
| sign | sign, mark | insignificant, signify |

**EXERCISE** Identify the roots in these words, as well as the meanings of the roots and of the words. Then use each word correctly in a sentence.

1. composition
2. ungrammatical
3. centrifugal
4. proficient
5. epidermis

The Chinese-American experience is the focus of Amy Tan's writing, both in fiction and nonfiction. Born in California, the daughter of Chinese immigrants, she often tells about the difficulty of growing up with roots in one culture while living in another. Her writing describes the embarrassing moments, painful misunderstandings, and mixed feelings that are a result of dual loyalty. In this selection, Tan remembers an awkward Christmas Eve dinner.

# Fish Cheeks

## Amy Tan

**I fell in love** with the minister's son the winter I turned fourteen. He was not Chinese, but as white as Mary in the manger. For Christmas I prayed for this blond-haired boy, Robert, and a slim new American nose.

When I found out that my parents had invited the minister's family over for Christmas Eve dinner, I cried. What would Robert think of our shabby *Chinese* Christmas? What would he think of our noisy *Chinese* relatives who lacked proper American manners? What terrible disappointment would he feel upon seeing not a roasted turkey and sweet potatoes but *Chinese* food?

On Christmas Eve I saw that my mother had outdone herself in creating a strange menu. She was pulling black veins out of the backs of fleshy prawns. The kitchen was littered with appalling mounds of raw food: A slimy rock cod with bulging fish eyes that pleaded not to be thrown into a pan of hot oil. Tofu, which looked like stacked wedges of rubbery white sponges. A bowl soaking dried fungus back to life. A plate of squid, their backs crisscrossed with knife markings so they resembled bicycle tires.

*Um den Fisch* [Around the fish] (1926), Paul Klee. Oil on canvas, 18⅛″ × 25⅛″, The Museum of Modern Art, New York, Abby Aldrich Rockefeller Fund, photo copyright © 1995 The Museum of Modern Art, New York.

And then they arrived—the minister's family and all my relatives in a clamor of doorbells and rumpled Christmas packages. Robert grunted hello, and I pretended he was not worthy of existence.

Dinner threw me deeper into despair. My relatives licked the ends of their chopsticks and reached across the table, dipping them into the dozen or so plates of food. Robert and his family waited patiently for platters to be passed to them. My relatives murmured with pleasure when my mother brought out the whole steamed fish. Robert grimaced. Then my father poked his chopsticks just below the fish eye and plucked out the soft meat. "Amy, your favorite," he said, offering me the tender fish cheek. I wanted to disappear.

At the end of the meal my father leaned back and belched loudly, thanking my mother for her fine cooking. "It's a polite Chinese custom to show you are satisfied," explained my father to our astonished guests. Robert was looking down at his plate with a reddened face. The minister managed to muster up a quiet burp. I was stunned into silence for the rest of the night.

After everyone had gone, my mother said to me, "You want to be the same as American girls on the outside." She handed me an early gift. It was a miniskirt in beige tweed. "But inside you must always be Chinese. You must be proud you are different. Your only shame is to have shame."

And even though I didn't agree with her then, I knew that she understood how much I had suffered during the evening's dinner. It wasn't until many years later—long after I had gotten over my crush on Robert—that I was able to fully appreciate her lesson and the true purpose behind our particular menu. For Christmas Eve that year, she had chosen all my favorite foods. ◉⫿⫿⊂

## Amy Tan
### 1952–

**Other Works**
*The Joy Luck Club*
*The Kitchen God's Wife*

**Cultural Struggles**  Amy Tan was not always the proud Chinese American that she is now. She recalls dreaming, when she was young, of making her features look more Western by having plastic surgery. It was not until she made her first trip to China in 1987 that Tan could truly accept both the Chinese and American cultures as her own.

**Changing Directions**  Though Tan won a writing contest at the age of eight, her identity as a writer was also slow in coming. In fact, she did not plan on a literary career. After two years of postgraduate study at the University of California in Berkeley, Tan worked for several years as a consultant to programs for children with disabilities. She then became a reporter for a medical publication and eventually a freelance technical writer. Later, Tan turned to playing jazz piano and writing fiction.

**From Book to Film**  After getting some of her stories published in magazines, Tan combined the stories with others to form a novel called *The Joy Luck Club*. The book became a bestseller and was made into a movie. It portrays the cultural and generational gaps between four young Chinese-American women and their mothers.

## Author Activity

**Read On**  Tan's famous novel *The Joy Luck Club* (1989) has enjoyed wide success. Read additional stories about Chinese-American life from this collection.

## Comparing Literature

# Love and Marriage Across Cultures

| Marriage Is a Private Affair | Love Must Not Be Forgotten |
|---|---|
| *Short Story by* CHINUA ACHEBE | *Short Story by* ZHANG JIE |

## What's the Connection?

**Love at the Crossroads** Every society in some way seeks to set standards for love and marriage. Often, tension exists between what a society or culture expects and what the individual wants. In choosing a spouse, an individual may face pressures from family, friends, community members, or public opinion.

In the following two selections, you will read about characters who are torn between their personal desires and the traditions and expectations of society. While both stories focus on individuals, they also reflect the conflicts and tensions of the societies portrayed.

A Chinese bride and groom in traditional wedding attire.

## Points of Comparison

**Analyzing Similar Problems in Different Cultures** In this unit, you have read about conflicts that arise when two cultures meet, or when one culture changes. In the pages that follow, you will analyze and compare the problems of characters who challenge cultural traditions and social expectations in an attempt to find love and fulfillment.

### Critical Thinking: Analyze and Compare

The first step in analysis is to define the parts of the whole. To analyze the problems of characters who seek love in a changing world, it will help you to develop a kind of graphic called an **analysis frame.** This frame will help you break each problem into parts. To begin, think about the ways in which the standards of our own society might present obstacles for a person in search of an ideal mate. Continue to identify other potential obstacles to love and marriage. The analysis frame shown has been started for you.

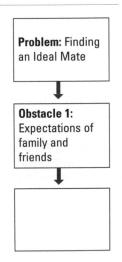

**READER'S NOTEBOOK** As you read the following stories, note the various obstacles faced by the main characters, which contribute to their problems. At each Points of Comparison, you will be asked to create a separate analysis frame for the story you have read.

# Marriage Is a Private Affair

*Short Story by* CHINUA ACHEBE

## Connect to Your Life

**Marry Who?** Marriage customs vary greatly throughout the world. In some cultures, people's marriages are traditionally arranged by their parents; in others, the partners make up their own minds. Discuss what you know about arranged marriages. What purpose do they serve? What advantages and disadvantages might they have?

## Build Background

**Nigerian Crossroads** This story takes place in the West African country of Nigeria, a land of great cultural diversity. Centuries-old traditions continue to govern life in Nigerian villages, where parents often play a decisive role in choosing mates for their children. In the cities, however, modern practices have displaced many of the village traditions, including the role of parent as matchmaker. The tension between old and new ways of living sometimes creates conflict within families, especially between generations.

The following story focuses on a conflict between a father and son about the choice of the son's marriage partner. Both men are Ibo (ē'bō), members of one of Nigeria's largest ethnic groups. The son, like many of his contemporaries, has moved away from the village of his birth and lives in a city—in this case, Lagos (lā'gŏs), the economic and commercial center of the nation, with a population of 1.4 million. In the villages of Nigeria, the Ibo live apart from other peoples, maintaining their traditional way of life. In Lagos, ethnic groups, cultures, and religions mingle freely.

| WORDS TO KNOW **Vocabulary Preview** | | | |
|---|---|---|---|
| commiserate | dissuasion | perfunctorily | remorse |
| cosmopolitan | forsaken | persevere | theological |
| deference | homily | | |

## Focus Your Reading

**LITERARY ANALYSIS** **CULTURAL CONFLICT** The plot of every story is constructed around **conflict,** or the struggle between opposing forces. In some stories, struggles occur as a result of cultural differences; these **cultural conflicts** arise from differences in values, beliefs, or customs.

As you read the following story, look for examples of conflicts arising from cultural friction.

**ACTIVE READING** **IDENTIFYING CULTURAL CHARACTERISTICS** In order to understand the conflict in this story, you will need to pay close attention to the cultural context. The following passage, for example, shows a tension between city ways and tribal ways of life.

*In the cosmopolitan atmosphere of the city it had always seemed to her something of a joke that a person's tribe could determine whom be married.*

**READER'S NOTEBOOK** As you read, take notes on the cultural characteristics of the village and the city. Use a chart like the one shown.

| Culture of the City | Culture of the Village |
|---|---|
| People can marry across cultural and ethnic lines. | |

# MARRIAGE Is a Private Affair

## Chinua Achebe

"Have you written to your dad yet?" asked Nene[1] one afternoon as she sat with Nnaemeka[2] in her room at 16 Kasanga Street, Lagos.

"No. I've been thinking about it. I think it's better to tell him when I get home on leave!"

"But why? Your leave is such a long way off yet—six whole weeks. He should be let into our happiness now."

Nnaemeka was silent for a while and then began very slowly as if he groped for his words: "I wish I were sure it would be happiness to him."

"Of course it must," replied Nene, a little surprised. "Why shouldn't it?"

"You have lived in Lagos all your life, and you know very little about people in remote parts of the country."

"That's what you always say. But I don't believe anybody will be so unlike other people that they will be unhappy when their sons are engaged to marry."

"Yes. They are most unhappy if the engagement is not arranged by them. In our case it's worse—you are not even an Ibo."

This was said so seriously and so bluntly that Nene could not find speech immediately. In the <u>cosmopolitan</u> atmosphere of the city it had always seemed to her something of a joke that a person's tribe could determine whom he married.

At last she said, "You don't really mean that he will object to your marrying me simply on that account? I had always thought you Ibos were kindly disposed to other people."

"So we are. But when it comes to marriage, well, it's not quite so simple. And this," he added, "is not peculiar to the Ibos. If your father were alive and lived in the heart of Ibibioland, he would be exactly like my father."

"I don't know. But anyway, as your father is

---

1. **Nene** (nā′nā).
2. **Nnaemeka** (ən-nä′ā-mā′kä).

so fond of you, I'm sure he will forgive you soon enough. Come on then, be a good boy and send him a nice lovely letter . . ."

"It would not be wise to break the news to him by writing. A letter will bring it upon him with a shock. I'm quite sure about that."

"All right, honey, suit yourself. You know your father."

As Nnaemeka walked home that evening, he turned over in his mind different ways of overcoming his father's opposition, especially now that he had gone and found a girl for him. He had thought of showing his letter to Nene but decided on second thoughts not to, at least for the moment. He read it again when he got home and couldn't help smiling to himself. He remembered Ugoye[3] quite well, an Amazon[4] of a girl who used to beat up all the boys, himself included, on the way to the stream, a complete dunce at school.

*I have found a girl who will suit you admirably—Ugoye Nweke, the eldest daughter of our neighbor, Jacob Nweke. She has a proper Christian upbringing. When she stopped schooling some years ago, her father (a man of sound judgment) sent her to live in the house of a pastor where she has received all the training a wife could need. Her Sunday school teacher has told me that she reads her Bible very fluently. I hope we shall begin negotiations when you come home in December.*

On the second evening of his return from Lagos Nnaemeka sat with his father under a cassia tree. This was the old man's retreat where he went to read his Bible when the parching December sun had set and a fresh, reviving wind blew on the leaves.

"Father," began Nnaemeka suddenly, "I have come to ask for forgiveness."

"Forgiveness? For what, my son?" he asked in amazement.

"It's about this marriage question."

"Which marriage question?"

"I can't—we must—I mean it is impossible for me to marry Nweke's daughter."

"Impossible? Why?" asked his father.

"I don't love her."

"Nobody said you did. Why should you?" he asked.

"Marriage today is different . . ."

"Look here, my son," interrupted his father, "nothing is different. What one looks for in a wife are a good character and a Christian background."

Nnaemeka saw there was no hope along the present line of argument.

"Moreover," he said, "I am engaged to marry another girl who has all of Ugoye's good qualities, and who . . ."

His father did not believe his ears. "What did you say?" he asked slowly and disconcertingly.

"She is a good Christian," his son went on, "and a teacher in a girls' school in Lagos."

"Teacher, did you say? If you consider that a qualification for a good wife, I should like to point out to you, Emeka, that no Christian woman should teach. St. Paul in his letter to the Corinthians says that women should keep silence." He rose slowly from his seat and paced forwards and backwards. This was his pet subject, and he condemned vehemently those church leaders who encouraged women to teach in their schools. After he had spent his emotion on a long

---

3. **Ugoye** (o͞o-gō′yā).

4. **Amazon:** an exceptionally tall, strong woman.

*Wooing* (1984), Varnette Honeywood. Collage. Copyright © 1984 Varnette P. Honeywood.

homily, he at last came back to his son's engagement, in a seemingly milder tone.

"Whose daughter is she, anyway?"

"She is Nene Atang."

"What!" All the mildness was gone again. "Did you say Neneataga; what does that mean?"

"Nene Atang from Calabar.⁵ She is the only girl I can marry." This was a very rash reply, and Nnaemeka expected the storm to burst. But it did not. His father merely walked away into

his room. This was most unexpected and perplexed Nnaemeka. His father's silence was infinitely more menacing than a flood of threatening speech. That night the old man did not eat.

When he sent for Nnaemeka a day later, he applied all possible ways of dissuasion. But the young man's heart was hardened, and his father eventually gave him up as lost.

"I owe it to you, my son, as a duty to show you what is right and what is wrong. Whoever put this idea into your head might as well have cut your throat. It is Satan's work." He waved his son away.

"You will change your mind, Father, when you know Nene."

"I shall never see her" was the reply. From that night the father scarcely spoke to his son. He did not, however, cease hoping that he would realize how serious was the danger he was heading for. Day and night he put him in his prayers.

Nnaemeka, for his own part, was very deeply affected by his father's grief. But he kept hoping that it would pass away. If it had occurred to him that never in the history of his people had a man married a woman who spoke a different tongue, he might have been less optimistic. "It has never been heard," was the verdict of an old man speaking a few weeks later. In that

---

5. **Calabar:** a seaport in southeastern Nigeria.

short sentence he spoke for all of his people. This man had come with others to <u>commiserate</u> with Okeke[6] when news went round about his son's behavior. By that time the son had gone back to Lagos.

"It has never been heard," said the old man again with a sad shake of his head.

"What did Our Lord say?" asked another gentleman. "Sons shall rise against their fathers; it is there in the Holy Book."

"It is the beginning of the end," said another.

The discussion thus tending to become <u>theological</u>, Madubogwu, a highly practical man, brought it down once more to the ordinary level.

"Have you thought of consulting a native doctor about your son?" he asked Nnaemeka's father.

"He isn't sick" was the reply.

"What is he then? The boy's mind is diseased, and only a good herbalist[7] can bring him back to his right senses. The medicine he requires is *Amalile*, the same that women apply with success to recapture their husbands' straying affection."

"Madubogwu is right," said another gentleman. "This thing calls for medicine."

"I shall not call in a native doctor." Nnaemeka's father was known to be obstinately ahead of his more superstitious neighbors in these matters. "I will not be another Mrs. Ochuba. If my son wants to kill himself, let him do it with his own hands. It is not for me to help him."

"But it was her fault," said Madubogwu. "She ought to have gone to an honest herbalist. She was a clever woman, nevertheless."

"She was a wicked murderess," said Jonathan, who rarely argued with his neighbors because, he often said, they were incapable of reasoning.

"The medicine was prepared for her husband, it was his name they called in its preparation, and I am sure it would have been perfectly beneficial to him. It was wicked to put it into the herbalist's food and say you were only trying it out."

Six months later, Nnaemeka was showing his young wife a short letter from his father:

*It amazes me that you could be so unfeeling as to send me your wedding picture. I would have sent it back. But on further thought I decided just to cut off your wife and send it back to you because I have nothing to do with her. How I wish that I had nothing to do with you either.*

When Nene read through this letter and looked at the mutilated picture, her eyes filled with tears, and she began to sob.

"Don't cry, my darling," said her husband. "He is essentially good-natured and will one day look more kindly on our marriage." But years passed, and that one day did not come.

For eight years, Okeke would have nothing to do with his son, Nnaemeka. Only three times (when Nnaemeka asked to come home and spend his leave) did he write to him.

"I can't have you in my house," he replied on one occasion. "It can be of no interest to me where or how you spend your leave—or your life, for that matter."

The prejudice against Nnaemeka's marriage was not confined to his little village. In Lagos, especially among his people who worked there,

---

6. **Okeke** (ō-kā′kā).

7. **herbalist** (ûr′bə-lĭst): a person who is expert in the use of medicinal herbs.

WORDS TO KNOW    **commiserate** (kə-mĭz′ə-rāt′) *v.* to express sorrow or pity for another's trouble
**theological** (thē′ə-lŏj′ĭ-kəl) *adj.* having to do with the study of God and religion

192

it showed itself in a different way. Their women, when they met at their village meeting, were not hostile to Nene. Rather, they paid her such excessive <u>deference</u> as to make her feel she was not one of them. But as time went on, Nene gradually broke through some of this prejudice and even began to make friends among them. Slowly and grudgingly they began to admit that she kept her home much better than most of them.

The story eventually got to the little village in the heart of the Ibo country that Nnaemeka and his young wife were a most happy couple. But his father was one of the few people in the village who knew nothing about this. He always displayed so much temper whenever his son's name was mentioned that everyone avoided it in his presence. By a tremendous effort of will he had succeeded in pushing his son to the back of his mind. The strain had nearly killed him, but he had <u>persevered</u> and won.

Then one day he received a letter from Nene, and in spite of himself he began to glance through it <u>perfunctorily</u> until all of a sudden the expression on his face changed and he began to read more carefully.

> *. . . Our two sons, from the day they learnt that they have a grandfather, have insisted on being taken to him. I find it impossible to tell them that you will not see them. I implore you to allow Nnaemeka to bring them home for a short time during his leave next month. I shall remain here in Lagos . . .*

The old man at once felt the resolution he had built up over so many years falling in. He was telling himself that he must not give in. He tried to steel his heart against all emotional appeals. It was a reenactment of that other struggle. He leaned against a window and looked out. The sky was overcast with heavy black clouds, and a high wind began to blow, filling the air with dust and dry leaves. It was one of those rare occasions when even Nature takes a hand in a human fight. Very soon it began to rain, the first rain in the year. It came down in large sharp drops and was accompanied by the lightning and thunder which mark a change of season. Okeke was trying hard not to think of his two grandsons. But he knew he was now fighting a losing battle. He tried to hum a favorite hymn, but the pattering of large raindrops on the roof broke up the tune. His mind immediately returned to the children. How could he shut his door against them? By a curious mental process he imagined them standing, sad and <u>forsaken</u>, under the harsh angry weather—shut out from his house.

That night he hardly slept, from <u>remorse</u>—and a vague fear that he might die without making it up to them. ❖

---

WORDS
TO
KNOW

**deference** (dĕf′ər-əns) *n.* courteous regard or respect
**persevere** (pûr′sə-vîr′) *v.* to persist in the face of difficulties
**perfunctorily** (pər-fŭngk′tə-rĭ-lē) *adv.* in a careless, uninterested way
**forsaken** (fôr-sā′kən) *adj.* abandoned  **forsake** *v.*
**remorse** (rĭ-môrs′) *n.* a deep sense of guilt over a wrong one has done

# Thinking *through the* LITERATURE

## Connect to the Literature

**1. What Do You Think?**
Which character do you think is the most sympathetically portrayed? Explain your reaction.

**Comprehension Check**
- What does Nnaemeka's father try to do for him in the village while Nnaemeka works in Lagos?
- Why does Okeke oppose Nnaemeka's choice of a wife?
- What happens at the end of the story?

## Think Critically

**2.** How would you explain Okeke's reaction to his son's marriage, and his change of attitude at the end of the story?

**THINK ABOUT**
- the cultural traditions that influence Okeke
- how he feels about his son's actions
- how he is affected by Nene's letter

**3.** How well do you think Nnaemeka handles his father's opposition to his marriage?

**4.** What is your opinion of Nene's personality and judgment?

**5.** **ACTIVE READING** **IDENTIFYING CULTURAL CHARACTERISTICS** Look over the chart of cultural characteristics you created for your **READER'S NOTEBOOK**. In your opinion, what is the most important difference between Nnaemeka's city life and Okeke's village life? Explain.

**6.** How do you think the story's **title** relates to its **theme?**

## Extend Interpretations

**7. Critic's Corner** The critic G. D. Killam has said about Achebe's work, "Through it all the spirit of man and the belief in the possibility of triumph endures." Do you think this comment applies in any way to "Marriage Is a Private Affair"? Explain your response.

**8. Connect to Life** What do you think is gained and lost when a society changes from traditional ways of life to modern ways?

**9.** **Points of Comparison** Review the analysis frame graphic that you created to identify different kinds of obstacles to finding an ideal mate. Now make a second frame analyzing the obstacles in this story. How do the obstacles you identified compare with the various obstacles revealed in this story?

## Literary Analysis

**CULTURAL CONFLICT** When customs or socially influenced beliefs push people in different directions, cultural conflict often occurs. The conflict may happen when two different cultures come in contact, or it may occur when a culture changes. In this story, conflict arises around changing marriage customs as well as the contact between urban and rural cultures in Nigeria. For example, Nene faces prejudice among the Ibo women in Lagos:

*Their women, when they met at their village meeting, were not hostile to Nene. Rather, they paid her such excessive deference as to make her feel she was not one of them.*

**Paired Activity** Review the story once more with a partner, and identify each place in which cultural conflict occurs. List the incident and think about the beliefs motivating the people on each side of the conflict. Compare your results with those of other students.

## Writing Options

**Okeke's Letter** Write a letter that Okeke might send in response to Nene's letter. Your letter should reflect the father's personality and feelings.

## Inquiry & Research

**Marrying for Love** When did romantic love become a basis for marriage? What countries are associated with the origins of romantic love as we know it? Do library research to learn the answers to these or other questions about the origins of modern Western marriage customs. Give an oral report on your findings.

## Vocabulary in Action

**EXERCISE A: ASSESSMENT PRACTICE** For each group of words below, write the letter of the word that is an antonym of the boldfaced word.

1. **perservere:** _____
   (a) praise, (b) quit,  (c) accept

2. **dissuasion:** _____
   (a) improvement, (b) silence, (c) encouragement

3. **remorse:** _____
   (a) attraction, (b) improvement, (c) satisfaction

4. **cosmopolitan:** _____
   (a) provincial, (b) widespread, (c) elegant

5. **perfunctorily:** _____
   (a) thoroughly, (b) naturally,  (c) wisely

**EXERCISE B: MEANING CLUES** Read each title below and write the vocabulary word, not used in Exercise A, that you might expect to find in a magazine article with that title.

1. "Sermons to Live By"
2. "The Tragedy of America's Cast-Off Pets"
3. "How to Help When a Loved One Hurts"
4. "Prayer in the Schools: The Debate Goes On"
5. "The Wisdom of Age: Honoring Our Elderly"

| WORDS TO KNOW | commiserate | forsaken | remorse |
|---|---|---|---|
| | cosmopolitan | homily | theological |
| | deference | perfunctorily | |
| | dissuasion | persevere | |

## Chinua Achebe
### 1930–

**Other Works**
*Arrow of God*
*A Man of the People*
*Beware, Soul Brother, and*
*   Other Poems*
*Anthills of the Savannah*
*Things Fall Apart*

**The Stories of His People** Chinua Achebe is one of contemporary Africa's most famous authors. A member of the Ibo people of eastern Nigeria, Achebe was born in the village of Ogidi, where his father taught at a Christian mission school. As a child, Achebe learned both the Ibo and the English languages. He first considered a writing career while a student at Nigeria's University of Ibadan. "I read some appalling European novels about Africa," he explains, "... and realized that our story could not be told for us by anyone else."

**Political Years** During the Nigerian civil war of 1967–1970, Achebe supported the independence effort of Biafra, a predominately Ibo region in eastern Nigeria. He served on diplomatic missions representing Biafra. After the fall of Biafra, Achebe took a university position in Nigeria. He has devoted his life to teaching and writing ever since.

**Literary Legacy** Although fluent in Ibo, Achebe usually writes in English. He is generally regarded as the most accomplished of the African novelists who write in English. In addition to novels and short stories, Achebe has written children's books and collections of essays and poetry. "Marriage Is a Private Affair" is from *Girls at War and Other Stories*, published in 1973.

# Love Must Not Be Forgotten

*Short Story by* ZHANG JIE

( **Connect to Your Life** )

**What Makes a Marriage?** Think about married couples that you know. Based on your observations, what qualities are essential to a good marriage? Discuss your ideas with a group of classmates.

## Build Background

**Chinese Cultural Revolution** In the 1960s and 1970s, when this selection takes place, many institutions of Chinese life, including marriage, were subjected to intense questioning. Since 1949, Mao Zedong (sometimes spelled Mao Tse-tung) and his Communist forces had been in control of China. By the mid 1960s Mao felt that new blood was needed to keep the ideals of Communism alive, so he implemented the Cultural Revolution in 1966. For the next three years, groups of young students and other radicals removed and replaced older Communist Party leaders. Many leaders were executed; others were sent to prison or to the countryside to be "re-educated" in communist thought.

Despite sweeping political changes, many Chinese customs were slow to change. For example, centuries-old traditions dictated that marriages be arranged by the couple's families when the prospective spouses were still young children. Although new laws enacted by the Communists allowed individuals to choose their own marriage partners, marrying for love was still frowned upon because communist teachings encouraged individuals to suppress personal desires for the greater social good.

WORDS TO KNOW
**Vocabulary Preview**

| | |
|---|---|
| ardent | heretic |
| atonement | naiveté |
| aversion | parry |
| censure | renounce |
| coyness | wistful |

## Focus Your Reading

LITERARY ANALYSIS   CULTURAL SETTING   The time and place of a short story's action is called the **setting.** Setting can also include the social and cultural environment in which the action of a story takes place. In the story you are about to read, the author provides many clues about the story's **cultural setting,** such as the following passage:

> *It was clear from the tear-stained pages of Mother's diary that he had been harshly denounced; but the steadfast old man never knuckled under to the authorities.*

As you read this story, look for other examples of the story's cultural setting.

ACTIVE READING   IDENTIFYING CULTURAL CHARACTERISTICS   The culture of China during the time of this story strongly influences the plot and the characters' attitudes and motivations. To understand the characters and events, you need to pay attention to what the story reveals about the traditions, political institutions, and beliefs and values of Chinese culture.

📖 **READER'S NOTEBOOK** As you read, take notes on the cultural characteristics of China that are revealed in the story.

*Cultural Characteristics*

*1. Communist government*

*2.*

*Red Peonies* (1929), Ch'i Pai-Shih.
Arthur M. Sackler Museum,
Harvard University.

# Love Must Not Be Forgotten

## Zhang Jie

I am thirty, the same age as our People's Republic.
For a republic thirty is still young. But a girl of thirty
is virtually on the shelf.

Actually, I have a bona fide[1] suitor. Have you seen
the Greek sculptor Myron's Discobolus? Qiao Lin[2] is
the image of that discus thrower. Even the padded
clothes he wears in winter fail to hide his fine
physique. Bronzed, with clear-cut features, a broad
forehead and large eyes, his appearance alone attracts
most girls to him.

But I can't make up my mind to marry him. I'm
not clear what attracts me to him, or him to me.

---

1. **bona fide** (bō′nə fīd): authentic; genuine.
2. **Qiao Lin** (chou′lĭn′).

I know people are gossiping behind my back, "Who does she think she is, to be so choosy?"

To them, I'm a nobody playing hard to get. They take offense at such preposterous behavior.

Of course, I shouldn't be captious.[3] In a society where commercial production still exists, marriage like most other transactions is still a form of barter.

I have known Qiao Lin for nearly two years, yet still cannot fathom whether he keeps so quiet from <u>aversion</u> to talking or from having nothing to say. When, by way of a small intelligence test, I demand his opinion of this or that, he says "good" or "bad" like a child in kindergarten.

Once I asked, "Qiao Lin, why do you love me?" He thought the question over seriously for what seemed an age. I could see from his normally smooth but now wrinkled forehead that the little grey cells in his handsome head were hard at work cogitating.[4] I felt ashamed to have put him on the spot.

Finally he raised his clear childlike eyes to tell me, "Because you're good!"

Loneliness flooded my heart. "Thank you, Qiao Lin!" I couldn't help wondering, if we were to marry, whether we could discharge our duties to each other as husband and wife. Maybe, because law and morality would have bound us together. But how tragic simply to comply with law and morality! Was there no stronger bond to link us?

When such thoughts cross my mind, I have the strange sensation that instead of being a girl

> *How tragic simply to comply with law and morality! Was there no stronger bond to link us?*

contemplating marriage I am an elderly social scientist.

Perhaps I worry too much. We can live like most married couples, bringing up children together, strictly true to each other according to the law. . . . Although living in the seventies of the twentieth century, people still consider marriage the way they did millennia ago, as a means of continuing the race, a form of barter or a business transaction in which love and marriage can be separated. As this is the common practice, why shouldn't we follow suit?

But I still can't make up my mind. As a child, I remember, I often cried all night for no rhyme or reason, unable to sleep and disturbing the whole household. My old nurse, a shrewd though uneducated woman, said an ill wind had blown through my ear. I think this judgment showed prescience,[5] because I still have that old weakness. I upset myself over things which really present no problem, upsetting other people at the same time. One's nature is hard to change.

I think of my mother too. If she were alive, what would she say about my attitude to Qiao Lin and my uncertainty about marrying him?

My thoughts constantly turn to her, not because she was such a strict mother that her ghost is still watching over me since her death. No, she was not just my mother but my closest

---

3. **captious** (kăp′shəs): quick to find fault; quibbling.
4. **cogitating** (kŏj′ĭ-tā′tĭng): thinking carefully; pondering.
5. **prescience** (prē′shē-əns): knowledge of things before they happen; foresight.

friend. I loved her so much that the thought of her leaving me makes my heart ache.

She never lectured me, just told me quietly in her deep, unwomanly voice about her successes and failures, so that I could learn from her experience. She had evidently not had many successes—her life was full of failures.

During her last days she followed me with her fine, expressive eyes, as if wondering how I would manage on my own and as if she had some important advice for me but hesitated to give it. She must have been worried by my naiveté and sloppy ways. She suddenly blurted out, "Shanshan,[6] if you aren't sure what you want, don't rush into marriage—better live on your own!"

Other people might think this strange advice from a mother to her daughter, but to me it embodied her bitter experience. I don't think she underestimated me or my knowledge of life. She loved me and didn't want me to be unhappy.

"I don't want to marry, mum!" I said, not out of bashfulness or a show of coyness. I can't think why a girl should pretend to be coy. She had long since taught me about things not generally mentioned to girls.

"If you meet the right man, then marry him. Only if he's right for you!"

"I'm afraid no such man exists!"

"That's not true. But it's hard. The world is so vast, I'm afraid you may never meet him." Whether I married or not was not what concerned her, but the quality of the marriage.

"Haven't you managed fine without a husband?"

"Who says so?"

"I think you've done fine."

"I had no choice. . . ." She broke off, lost in thought, her face wistful. Her wistful lined face reminded me of a withered flower I had pressed in a book.

"Why did you have no choice?"

"You ask too many questions," she parried, not ashamed to confide in me but afraid that I might reach the wrong conclusion. Besides, everyone treasures a secret to carry to the grave. Feeling a bit put out, I demanded bluntly, "Didn't you love my dad?"

"No, I never loved him."

"Did he love you?"

"No, he didn't."

"Then why get married?"

She paused, searching for the right words to explain this mystery, then answered bitterly, "When you're young, you don't always know what you're looking for, what you need, and people may talk you into getting married. As you grow older and more experienced, you find out your true needs. By then, though, you've done many foolish things for which you could kick yourself. You'd give anything to be able to make a fresh start and live more wisely. Those content with their lot will always be happy, they say, but I shall never enjoy that happiness." She added, self-mockingly, "A wretched idealist, that's all I am."

Did I take after her? Did we both have genes which attracted ill winds?

"Why don't you marry again?"

"I'm afraid I'm still not sure what I really want." She was obviously unwilling to tell me the truth.

I cannot remember my father. He and Mother split up when I was very small. I just recall her telling me sheepishly that he was a fine handsome fellow. I could see she was ashamed of having judged by appearances and made a futile choice. She told me, "When I can't sleep at night, I force myself to sober up by recalling all those

---

6. **Shanshan** (shän′shän′).

stupid blunders I made. Of course it's so distasteful that I often hide my face in the sheet for shame, as if there were eyes watching me in the dark. But distasteful as it is, I take some pleasure in this form of <u>atonement</u>."

I was really sorry that she hadn't remarried. She was such a fascinating character, if she'd married a man she loved, what a happy household ours would surely have been. Though not beautiful, she had the simple charm of an ink landscape. She was a fine writer too. Another author who knew her well used to say teasingly, "Just reading your works is enough to make anyone love you!"

**ACTIVE READING**

**CLARIFY** Why does the narrator think that her mother should have remarried?

She would retort, "If he knew that the object of his affection was a white-haired old crone, that would frighten him away."

At her age, she must have known what she really wanted, so this was obviously an evasion. I say this because she had quirks which puzzled me.

For instance, whenever she left Beijing on a trip, she always took with her one of the twenty-seven volumes of Chekhov's[7] stories published between 1950 and 1955. She also warned me, "Don't touch these books. If you want to read Chekhov, read that set I bought you." There was no need to caution me. Having a set of my own why should I touch hers? Besides, she'd told me this over and over again. Still she was on her guard. She seemed bewitched by those books.

So we had two sets of Chekhov's stories at home. Not just because we loved Chekhov, but to parry other people like me who loved Chekhov. Whenever anyone asked to borrow a volume, she would lend one of mine. Once, in her absence, a close friend took a volume from her set. When she found out, she was frantic and at once took a volume of mine to exchange for it.

Ever since I can remember, those books were on her bookcase. Although I admire Chekhov as a great writer, I was puzzled by the way she never tired of reading him. Why, for over twenty years, had she had to read him every single day?

Sometimes, when tired of writing, she poured herself a cup of strong tea and sat down in front of the bookcase, staring raptly at that set of books. If I went into her room then, it flustered her, and she either spilt her tea or blushed like a girl discovered with her lover.

I wondered: Has she fallen in love with Chekhov? She might have if he'd still been alive.

When her mind was wandering just before her death, her last words to me were: "That set. . . ." She hadn't the strength to give it its complete title. But I knew what she meant. "And my diary . . . 'Love Must Not Be Forgotten'. . . . Cremate them with me."

I carried out her last instruction regarding the works of Chekhov, but couldn't bring myself to destroy her diary. I thought, if it could be published, it would surely prove the most moving thing she had written. But naturally publication was out of the question.

At first I imagined the entries were raw material she had jotted down. They read neither like stories, essays, a diary or letters. But after reading the whole I formed a hazy impression, helped out by my imperfect memory. Thinking it over, I finally realized that this was no lifeless manuscript I was holding, but an anguished, loving heart. For over twenty years one man had occupied her heart, but he was not for her. She used these diaries as a substitute for him, a means of pouring out her feelings to him, day after day, year after year.

---

7. **Chekhov's** (chĕk′ôfs): Anton Chekhov (1860–1904; also spelled Chekov), a Russian author, whose short stories were first published in Chinese in the 1950s.

WORDS
TO
KNOW

**atonement** (ə-tōn′mənt) *n.* the act of making up for a serious error, sin, or wrong

No wonder she had never considered any eligible proposals, had turned a deaf ear to idle talk whether well-meant or malicious. Her heart was already full, to the exclusion of anybody else. "No lake can compare with the ocean, no cloud with those on Mount Wu."[8] Remembering those lines I often reflected sadly that few people in real life could love like this. No one would love me like this.

I learned that towards the end of the thirties, when this man was doing underground work for the Party[9] in Shanghai, an old worker had given his life to cover him, leaving behind a helpless wife and daughter. Out of a sense of duty, of gratitude to the dead and deep class feeling, he had unhesitatingly married the girl. When he saw the endless troubles caused by "love" of couples who had married for "love," he may have thought, "Thank Heaven, though I didn't marry for love, we get on well, able to help each other." For years, as man and wife they lived through hard times.

**ACTIVE READING**

**IDENTIFY CULTURAL CHARACTERISTICS** What do these events reveal about the values of Chinese culture?

He must have been my mother's colleague. Had I ever met him? He couldn't have visited our home. Who was he?

In the spring of 1962, Mother took me to a concert. We went on foot, the theatre being quite near.

A black limousine pulled up silently by the pavement. Out stepped an elderly man with white hair in a black serge tunicsuit. What a striking shock of white hair! Strict, scrupulous, distinguished, transparently honest—that was my impression of him. The cold glint of his flashing eyes reminded me of lightning or swordplay. Only <u>ardent</u> love for a woman really deserving his love could fill cold eyes like those with tenderness.

He walked up to Mother and said, "How are

*Forbidden Fruit*, Simon Ng. Reprinted with the permission of Simon & Schuster Books for Young Readers, an imprint of Simon & Schuster Children's Publishing Division. From *Tales from Gold Mountain: Stories of the Chinese in the New World*, a Groundwood Book/Douglas & McIntyre. Text Copyright © 1989 by Paul Yee, illustrations Copyright © 1989 by Simon Ng.

you, Comrade Zhong Yu?[10] It's been a long time."

"How are you!" Mother's hand holding mine suddenly turned icy cold and trembled a little.

They stood face to face without looking at each other, each appearing upset, even stern. Mother fixed her eyes on the trees by the roadside, not yet in leaf. He looked at me. "Such a

---

8. **Mount Wu:** a high mountain in southern China.

9. **the Party:** the Communist Party.

10. **Zhong Yu** (jŏng′yo͞o′).

big girl already. Good, fine—you take after your mother."

Instead of shaking hands with Mother he shook hands with me. His hand was as icy as hers and trembling a little. As if transmitting an electric current, I felt a sudden shock. Snatching my hand away I cried, "There's nothing good about that!"

"Why not?" he asked with the surprised expression grown-ups always have when children speak out frankly.

I glanced at Mother's face. I did take after her, to my disappointment. "Because she's not beautiful!"

He laughed, then said teasingly, "Too bad that there should be a child who doesn't find her own mother beautiful. Do you remember in '53, when your mum was transferred to Beijing, she came to our ministry to report for duty? She left you outside on the verandah,[11] but like a monkey you climbed all the stairs, peeped through the cracks in doors, and caught your finger in the door of my office. You sobbed so bitterly that I carried you off to find her."

"I don't remember that." I was annoyed at his harking back to a time when I was still in open-seat pants.[12]

"Ah, we old people have better memories." He turned abruptly and remarked to Mother, "I've read that last story of yours. Frankly speaking, there's something not quite right about it. You shouldn't have condemned the heroine. . . . There's nothing wrong with falling in love, as long as you don't spoil someone else's life. . . . In fact, the hero might have loved her too. Only for the sake of a third person's happiness, they had to <u>renounce</u> their love. . . ."

A policeman came over to where the car was parked and ordered the driver to move on. When the driver made some excuse, the old man looked around. After a hasty "Goodbye" he strode to the car and told the policeman, "Sorry. It's not his fault, it's mine. . . ."

I found it amusing watching this old cadre[13] listening respectfully to the policeman's strictures.[14] When I turned to Mother with a mischievous smile, she looked as upset as a first-form[15] primary schoolchild standing forlornly in front of the stern headmistress. Anyone would have thought she was the one being lectured by the policeman.

The car drove off, leaving a puff of smoke. Very soon even this smoke vanished with the wind, as if nothing at all had happened. But the incident stuck in my mind.

Analyzing it now, he must have been the man whose strength of character won Mother's heart. That strength came from his firm political convictions, his narrow escapes from death in the revolution, his active brain, his drive at work, his well-cultivated mind. Besides, strange to say, he and Mother both liked the oboe. Yes, she must have worshipped him. She once told me that unless she worshipped a man, she couldn't love him even for one day.

But I could not tell whether he loved her or not. If not, why was there this entry in her diary?

*"This is far too fine a present. But how did you know that Chekhov's my favorite writer?"*

---

11. **verandah** (və-răn′də): a partly enclosed porch.
12. **open-seat pants:** pants with a slit down the back, worn by young children.
13. **cadre** (kăd′rē): a member of a tightly knit revolutionary party or military group.
14. **strictures** (strĭk′chərz): rules or remarks setting limits or making restrictions.
15. **first-form:** first-grade.

WORDS TO KNOW  **renounce** (rĭ-nouns) *v.* to give up, especially as a matter of principle

"You said so."

"I don't remember that."

"I remember. I heard you mention it when you were chatting with someone."

So he was the one who had given her the *Selected Stories of Chekhov*. For her that was tantamount[16] to a love letter.

Maybe this man, who didn't believe in love, realized by the time his hair was white that in his heart was something which could be called love. By the time he no longer had the right to love, he made the tragic discovery of this love for which he would have given his life. Or did it go deeper than that?

This is all I remember about him.

How wretched Mother must have been, deprived of the man to whom she was devoted! To catch a glimpse of his car or the back of his head through its rear window, she carefully figured out which roads he would take to work and back. Whenever he made a speech, she sat at the back of the hall watching his face rendered hazy by cigarette smoke and poor lighting. Her eyes would brim with tears, but she swallowed them back. If a fit of coughing made him break off, she wondered anxiously why no one persuaded him to give up smoking. She was afraid he would get bronchitis again. Why was he so near yet so far?

He, to catch a glimpse of her, looked out of the car window every day, straining his eyes to watch the streams of cyclists, afraid that she might have an accident. On the rare evenings on which he had no meetings, he would walk by a roundabout way to our neighborhood, to pass our compound gate. However busy, he would always make time to look in papers and journals for her work.

*We agreed to forget each other. But I deceived you, I have never forgotten.*

His duty had always been clear to him, even in the most difficult times. But now confronted by this love he became a weakling, quite helpless. At his age it was laughable. Why should life play this trick on him?

Yet when they happened to meet at work, each tried to avoid the other, hurrying off with a nod. Even so, this would make Mother blind and deaf to everything around her. If she met a colleague named Wang, she would call him Guo[17] and mutter something unintelligible.

It was a cruel ordeal for her. She wrote:

*We agreed to forget each other. But I deceived you, I have never forgotten. I don't think you've forgotten either. We're just deceiving each other, hiding our misery. I haven't deceived you deliberately, though; I did my best to carry out our agreement. I often stay far away from Beijing, hoping time and distance will help me to forget you. But on my return, as the train pulls into the station, my head reels. I stand on the platform looking around intently, as if someone were waiting for me. Of course there is no one. I realize then that I have forgotten nothing. Everything is unchanged. My love is like a tree the roots of which strike deeper year after year—I have no way to uproot it.*

*At the end of every day, I feel as if I've forgotten something important. I may*

16. **tantamount** (tăn′tə-mount′): equal in effect or value.

17. **Guo** (gwō): The Chinese characters for this family name are similar to those for the name *Wang*.

*wake with a start from my dreams wondering what has happened. But nothing has happened. Nothing. Then it comes home to me that you are missing! So everything seems lacking, incomplete, and there is nothing to fill up the blank. We are nearing the ends of our lives, why should we be carried away by emotion like children? Why should life submit people to such ordeals, then unfold before you your lifelong dream? Because I started off blindly, I took the wrong turning, and now there are insuperable[18] obstacles between me and my dream.*

Yes, Mother never let me go to the station to meet her when she came back from a trip, preferring to stand alone on the platform and imagine that he had met her. Poor mother with her greying hair was as infatuated as a girl.

**ACTIVE READING**

**CLARIFY** Why was the mother unable to fulfill her dream?

Not much space in the diary was devoted to their romance. Most entries dealt with trivia: Why one of her articles had not come off; her fear that she had no real talent; the excellent play she missed by mistaking the time on the ticket; the drenching she got by going out for a stroll without her umbrella. In spirit they were together day and night, like a devoted married couple. In fact, they spent no more than twenty-four hours together in all. Yet in that time they experienced deeper happiness than some people in a whole lifetime. Shakespeare makes Juliet say, "I cannot sum up half my sum of wealth." And probably that is how Mother felt.

He must have been killed in the "cultural revolution." Perhaps because of the conditions then, that section of the diary is ambiguous and obscure. Mother had been so fiercely attacked for her writing, it amazed me that she went on keeping a diary. From some veiled allusions I gathered that he had queried the theories advanced by that "theoretician" then at the height of favor, and had told someone, "This is sheer Rightist[19] talk." It was clear from the tear-stained pages of Mother's diary that he had been harshly denounced; but the steadfast old man never knuckled under to the authorities. His last words were, "When I go to meet Marx,[20] I shall go on fighting my case!"

That must have been in the winter of 1969, because that was when Mother's hair turned white overnight, though she was not yet fifty. And she put on a black arm band. Her position then was extremely difficult. She was criticized for wearing this old-style mourning, and ordered to say for whom she was in mourning.

"For whom are you wearing that, mum?" I asked anxiously.

"For my lover." Not to frighten me she explained, "Someone you never knew."

"Shall I put one on too?" She patted my cheeks, as she had when I was a child. It was years since she had shown me such affection. I often felt that as she aged, especially during these last years of persecution, all tenderness had left her, or was concealed in her heart, so that she seemed like a man.

She smiled sadly and said, "No, you needn't wear one."

Her eyes were as dry as if she had no more tears to shed. I longed to comfort her or do something to please her. But she said, "Off you go."

I felt an inexplicable dread, as if dear Mother had already half left me. I blurted out, "Mum!"

Quick to sense my desolation, she said gently, "Don't be afraid. Off you go. Leave me alone for a little."

---

18. **insuperable** (ĭn-sōō′pər-ə-bəl): impossible to overcome; insurmountable.

19. **Rightist:** belonging to a conservative or reactionary politics.

20. **Marx:** Karl Marx (1818–1883), a German economic philosopher revered by communists.

A painting in the class-education exhibition, Niutung People's Commune No. 4 (about 1970),
Niutung People's Commune Spare-Time Art Group.

I was right. She wrote:

*You have gone. Half my soul seems to have taken flight with you.*

*I had no means of knowing what had become of you, much less of seeing you for the last time. I had no right to ask either, not being your wife or friend. . . . So we are torn apart. If only I could have borne that inhuman treatment for you, so that you could have lived on! You should have lived to see your name cleared and take up your work again, for the sake of those who loved you. I knew you could not be a counter-revolutionary. You were one of the finest men killed. That's why I love you—I am not afraid now to avow it.*

*Snow is whirling down. . . . This whiteness covers up your blood and the scandal of your murder.*

*I have never set store by my life. But now I keep wondering whether anything I say or do would make you contract your shaggy eyebrows in a frown. I must live a worthwhile life like you and do some honest work for our country. Things can't go on like this—those criminals will get what's coming to them.*

*I used to walk alone along that small asphalt road, the only place where we once walked together, hearing my footsteps in the silent night. . . . I always paced to and fro and lingered there, but never as wretchedly as now. Then, though you were not beside me, I knew you were still in this world and felt that you were keeping me company. Now I can hardly believe that*

> ## I must live a worthwhile life like you and do some honest work for our country.

*you have gone.*

*At the end of the road I would retrace my steps, then walk along it again. Rounding the fence I always looked back, as if you were still standing there waving goodbye. We smiled faintly, like casual acquaintances, to conceal our undying love. That ordinary evening in early spring, a chilly wind was blowing as we walked silently away from each other. You were wheezing a little because of your chronic bronchitis. That upset me. I wanted to beg you to slow down, but somehow I couldn't. We both walked very fast, as if some important business were waiting for us. How we prized that single stroll we had together, but we were afraid we might lose control of ourselves and burst out with "I love you"—those three words which had tormented us for years. Probably no one else could believe that we never once even clasped hands!*

No, Mother, I believe it. I am the only one able to see into your locked heart.

Ah, that little asphalt road, so haunted by bitter memories. We shouldn't overlook the most insignificant spots on earth. For who knows how much secret grief and joy they may hide.

No wonder that when tired of writing, she would pace slowly along that little road behind our window. Sometimes at dawn after a sleepless night, sometimes on a moonless, windy evening. Even in winter during howling gales which hurled sand and pebbles against the windowpane. . . . I thought this was one of her eccentricities, not knowing that she had gone to meet him in spirit.

She liked to stand by the window too, staring at the small asphalt road. Once I thought from her expression that one of our closest friends must be coming to call. I hurried to the window. It was a late autumn evening. The cold wind was stripping dead leaves from the trees and blowing them down the small empty road.

She went on pouring out her heart to him in her diary as she had when he was alive. Right up to the day when the pen slipped from her fingers. Her last message was:

*I am a materialist,*[21] *yet I wish there were a Heaven. For then, I know, I would find you there waiting for me. I am going there to join you, to be together for eternity. We need never be parted again or keep at a distance for fear of spoiling someone else's life. Wait for me, dearest, I am coming—*

I do not know how Mother, on her death bed, could still love so ardently with all her heart. To

ACTIVE READING

EVALUATE What is your opinion of the mother's devotion to her loved one?

me it seemed not love but a form of madness, a passion stronger than death. If undying love really exists, she reached its extreme. She obviously died happy, because she had known true love. She had no regrets.

Now these old people's ashes have mingled with the elements. But I know that, no matter what form they may take, they still love each other. Though not bound together by earthly laws or morality, though they never once clasped hands, each possessed the other completely. Nothing could part them. Centuries to come, if one white cloud trails another, two grasses grow side by side, one wave splashes

another, a breeze follows another . . . believe me, that will be them.

Each time I read that diary "Love Must Not Be Forgotten" I cannot hold back my tears. I often weep bitterly, as if I myself experienced their ill-fated love. If not a tragedy it was too laughable. No matter how beautiful or moving I find it, I have no wish to follow suit!

Thomas Hardy[22] wrote that "the call seldom produces the comer, the man to love rarely coincides with the hour for loving." I cannot <u>censure</u> them from conventional moral standards. What I deplore is that they did not wait for a "missing counterpart" to call them.

If everyone could wait, instead of rushing into marriage, how many tragedies could be averted!

When we reach communism,[23] will there still be cases of marriage without love? Maybe, because since the world is so vast, two kindred spirits may be unable to answer each other's call. But how tragic! However, by that time, there may be ways to escape such tragedies.

Why should I split hairs?

Perhaps after all we are responsible for these tragedies. Who knows? Maybe we should take the responsibility for the old ideas handed down from the past. Because if someone never marries, that is a challenge to these ideas. You will be called neurotic, accused of having guilty secrets or having made political mistakes. You may be regarded as an eccentric who looks down on ordinary people, not respecting age-old customs—a <u>heretic</u>. In short they will trump up endless vulgar and futile charges to ruin

---

21. **materialist** (mə-tîr′ē-ə-lĭst): here, a person who believes that the physical world is the only reality.

22. **Thomas Hardy** (1840–1928): a British author.

23. **When we reach communism:** When we reach the ideal state by following communist principles.

WORDS TO KNOW

**censure** (sĕn′shər) *v.* to criticize severely; to blame
**heretic** (hĕr′ĭ-tĭk) *n.* a person who holds controversial opinions that do not conform to the prevailing opinions of a society, religion, or group

*New Look of a Village* (about 1970), Niutung People's Commune Spare-Time Art Group.

your reputation. Then you have to knuckle under to those ideas and marry willy-nilly. But once you put the chains of a loveless marriage around your neck, you will suffer for it for the rest of your life.

I long to shout: "Mind your own business! Let us wait patiently for our counterparts. Even waiting in vain is better than willy-nilly marriage. To live single is not such a fearful disaster. I believe it may be a sign of a step forward in culture, education and the quality of life." ❖

*Translated by Gladys Yang*

# Connect to the Literature

**1. What Do You Think?**
What is your response to the mother's life story?

```
Comprehension Check
• What decision does the narrator face?
• What advice does her mother give her?
• What prevented the mother and her lover from marrying?
```

# Think Critically

**2.** How do you think the **narrator** is affected by her mother's advice and experiences?

THINK ABOUT

- the narrator's feelings about her relationship with Qiao Lin
- the narrator's views on love and marriage
- how the narrator says she is viewed by society

**3.** Do you think the mother and the man she loved made the right choices about their relationship? Explain your opinion.

**4.** **ACTIVE READING** | **IDENTIFYING CULTURAL CHARACTERISTICS**
Look over the notes on cultural characteristics that you created for your 📖 **READER'S NOTEBOOK**. In your opinion, to what extent were the lives of the narrator and her mother affected by their culture? Give evidence from your notes and from the story to support your response.

**5.** Do you agree or disagree with the mother that it is better to live on one's own than to rush into marriage? Use examples from the story to support your opinion.

**6.** Predict the narrator's future. Will she marry, and if so, will she be happy? Explain why or why not.

# Extend Interpretations

**7. Comparing Texts** What advice do you think the mother in this story would have given Okeke in "Marriage Is a Private Affair" when he rejected his son's decision to marry Nene?

**8. Connect to Life** Do you think that our society puts pressures on people to get married? Discuss your views with your classmates.

**9.** **Points of Comparison** Look at the analysis frames that you developed on pages 187 and 194. Make a third frame for this story, identifying the obstacles to love. How do these obstacles in this story compare with the various obstacles to love identified on your previous charts?

# Literary Analysis

**CULTURAL SETTING** The **setting** is the time and place of the action of a story. However, a setting does not only consist in the physical location. It also includes the cultural environment in which the events unfold. In some stories, setting is not very important; the events could happen almost anywhere at almost anytime. In other stories, such as this one, the events are greatly influenced by the cultural setting.

**Cooperative Learning Activity**
Working with a group, review the selection. Identify each major event in the story and discuss to what extent the event is influenced by the cultural setting. Consider whether the event could have occurred at some other place or time. Record your findings on a table like the one shown below.

| Major event | Influenced by cultural setting? Why or why not? |
|---|---|
| Mother's loved one marries another woman. | Yes—he did it out of duty, gratitude to the dead, and class feeling. |

# Choices & CHALLENGES

## Writing Options

**1. Mother's Monologue** Write a monologue in which the mother describes her feelings toward her daughter.

**2. Character Profile** Write a character evaluation of any prominent figure in the selection. First, provide an objective description of the character, and then state your opinion of that character. Base your statements on details in the selection.

## Inquiry & Research

**Cultural Revolution** China's Cultural Revolution had wide-ranging effects on the country. Use current books as well as magazine and newspaper articles from the period to investigate ways in which the Cultural Revolution affected common people. Present your findings in an oral report.

## Art Connection

The painting on page 208 shows workers at a political meeting in China. What does this painting tell you about the power of the Communist government over the lives of the characters in this selection?

## Vocabulary in Action

**EXERCISE: ASSESSMENT PRACTICE** Determine the relationship between each pair of boldfaced words below. On your paper, write the letter of the choice that shows the most similar relationship.

1. **renounce** : **accept** :: (a) agree : approve (b) despise: disapprove (c) abandon : join

2. **wistful** : **sad** :: (a) warm : hot (b) bashful : shy (c) cheerful : gloomy

3. **atonement** : **sin** :: (a) question : answer (b) fact : opinion (c) apology : insult

4. **naiveté** : **worldliness** :: (a) beauty : youth (b) simplicity : complexity (c) love : marriage

5. **parry** : **question** :: (a) dodge : bullet (b) donate : gift (c) suffer : injury

6. **coyness** : **modesty** :: (a) intelligence : foolishness (b) bravado : courage (c) cowardice : fear

7. **censure** : **opponent** :: (a) advise : counselor (b) ridicule : mockery (c) praise : hero

8. **ardent** : **fond** :: (a) hilarious : funny (b) cool : icy (c) wicked : evil

9. **heretic** : **society** :: (a) criminal : prison (b) outlaw : community (c) voter : democracy

10. **aversion** : **dislike** :: (a) passion : fondness (b) innocence : guilt (c) elm : tree

### Building Vocabulary

For an in-depth study of analogies, see page 263.

## Zhang Jie
### 1937–

**Other Works**
*As Long as Nothing Happens, Nothing Will*
*Heavy Wings*

**Pursuing a Dream** Zhang Jie has been one of China's most highly acclaimed and, at times, controversial authors. Brought up in poverty and forced by the government to pursue college studies in economics instead of in literature as she had dreamed, Zhang Jie developed a strong sensitivity to injustices within the Communist system. After college Zhang Jie was directed to become a statistician, and during the Cultural Revolution, she, like many other college graduates, was sent to southern China to work in a factory. Finally, in 1976, Zhang Jie was able to move to Beijing and begin a writing career. Her first story, published in 1978, won her the first of many writing awards. By the early 1980s, Zhang Jie was a best-selling writer in her homeland. With "Love Must Not Be Forgotten," she became the first Chinese author in years to write about romantic love, marriage, and the role of women.

# Comparing Literature: Assessment Practice

In writing
assessments, you
will often be asked
to analyze and
compare two
literary works with
similar themes like
"Marriage Is a
Private Affair" and
"Love Must Not Be
Forgotten." You are
now going to
practice writing an
essay with this
kind of focus.

## PART 1   Reading the Prompt

You will often be asked to write in response to a prompt like the one below. In such situations, you first need to read the prompt carefully. Then you should read it again, searching for key words that help you identify the purpose of the essay and decide how to approach it.

**Writing Prompt**

"Marriage Is a Private Affair" and "Love Must Not Be Forgotten" both explore the problems of individuals seeking love and fulfillment in a changing culture. In an essay, analyze the **❶** problem faced by a main character in each story. Compare the way in which each main **❷** character challenges the traditions and expectations of his or her society. To what degree does each succeed? Include evidence from the **❸** selection to support your analysis.

**STRATEGIES**
IN ACTION

**❶** I need to write an essay that will **analyze**—or break down—the problems faced by the main characters.

**❷** I have to **compare** how the main characters challenge their society.

**❸** I need to include **examples** or **quotations** from the stories.

## PART 2   Planning an Analysis Essay

- Devise a graphic like the one shown to help organize your analysis.

- For each main character, break down the problem that he or she faces by listing the various obstacles to love and marriage. (Refer to the charts you developed on pages 187, 194, and 209.)

- Look for similarities and differences among the problems, the obstacles, and the characters' responses to the obstacles.

| Marriage Is a Private Affair | Love Must Not Be Forgotten |
|---|---|
| Problem: | Problem: |
| Obstacles: | Obstacles: |
| Character's Response: | Character's Response: |

## PART 3   Drafting Your Essay

**Introduction** Identify the main problem of each character. Describe how each character responds to the problem.

**Organization** For each character, you will need to break the problem down, discussing one obstacle at a time. You probably will find it helpful to discuss one story in its entirety, then the other.

Make sure that you draw comparisons between the characters and their situations. Include examples.

**Conclusion**
End your essay with a clear statement that compares and contrasts the problems faced by the two characters and their responses.

# *Writing* Workshop

## Creating a vivid description . . .

**From Reading to Writing** In Isaac Bashevis Singer's story "The Son from America," the main characters' simple lives are shown through singular details: a goat who lives in their one-room hut, an oil dish that serves as their lamp. Through **focused description,** authors like Singer can create vivid settings and help readers grasp some aspects of the characters' inner lives. Similarly, lawyers, police officers, doctors, and reporters also rely on focused descriptions in their work to communicate experiences or problems to others.

### For Your Portfolio

**WRITING PROMPT** Write a focused description of a scene or situation.

**Purpose:** To convey a vivid picture that helps the reader share your experience

**Audience:** Classmates, friends, or people who know about the scene or situation you are describing

---

## Basics in a Box

### Focused Description at a Glance

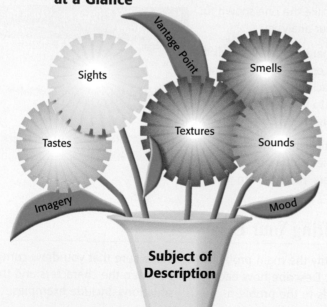

Vantage Point · Sights · Smells · Textures · Tastes · Sounds · Imagery · Mood · **Subject of Description**

### RUBRIC Standards for Writing

**A successful description should**

- focus on a person, place, or object
- convey a clear sense of purpose
- use sensory details and precise words to create a vivid picture, establish a mood, or express emotion
- include figurative language or dialogue when appropriate
- use a consistent method of organization such as spatial order, order of importance, or order of impression

---

# Analyzing a Student Model

**Katie Eskra**
**Evanston Township High School**

## Miles of Aisles in Wisconsin

We were driving along Highway 42, coming home from Aspen Bay. My parents were talking in the front seat, probably about what they had to do the next day. I wanted to have an argument with my sister, but I looked over and she was reading a book. I think it was about people pretending to kill other people on Halloween or something, but I'm not sure. It was one of those books you can read in about half an hour and then can't remember the plot the next day. I had decided just to look out the window at the snow and trees and occasional silo when my mom remembered we had forgotten to go to the store that morning. We were out of milk and a few other things, and we wanted to get some cake mix for that night. We're always making cakes for no particular reason when we're in Wisconsin. A huge grocery store appeared down the road, so we pulled into the lot. Suddenly a wave of sadness and depression washed over me.

The store looked normal enough at first glance, and yet there seemed to be a forlorn and forgotten aura surrounding it. The building was in the middle of nowhere, but it looked ready to accommodate great hordes of people if they ever decided to show up. I think it got lost on the way to a big city and ended up where it was by accident. The parking lot was an enormous expanse of asphalt, neatly plowed and divided precisely by thick yellow lines into countless spaces. There were only four or five cars in the lot, all dilapidated and rusting and about twenty years old. One of the license plates read ILUVWI, though it was hard to read because of the big scratches in the metal. We parked next to one of the scrap heaps and all decided to go inside.

The automatic doors opened promptly, and we stepped into an area with numerous shopping carts standing in perfect lines against the wall. Most of them had bits of paper or wrappers in them, but we chose one that didn't. A second set of doors opened, and we pushed our cart through into a colossal, artificially lit room. The fluorescent lights on

**RUBRIC**
IN ACTION

❶ The writer opens with details that describe her mood and situation.

**Other Options:**
· Open with dialogue.
· Bring the reader directly into the main setting you want to describe.

❷ Introduces the store as the focus. The writer also names the mood the store evokes.

❸ Includes specific details to show the parking lot

❹ Uses spatial order of organization—from outside to inside the store

the ceiling far above our heads seemed pathetic in the immensity of the store. The walkways were long and foreboding, and we decided to get what we needed as fast as possible and leave.

We bravely attacked every aisle in search of what we needed, but there were no signs indicating what kind of food was in each row so it took us quite a while. The cement floor was cracked and dirty, and every time the cart hit a bump it let out a clatter that echoed faintly in our ears. The food all seemed to come in gigantic bulk packages and was organized neatly and efficiently. Many of the cans were dented or rusty, however, and everything in the store was covered with a thin layer of dust that came off on our hands when we touched anything. We came across one other shopper who was stooped over, searching furtively through her handbag in the cereal aisle. We didn't stop to ask what she was doing.

❺ Uses sensory details to describe sight and sound

Finally we found what we needed and quickly made our way to the front of the store. The checkout lady peered at us suspiciously over her thick reading glasses and put down her magazine with a sigh when she saw we actually wanted to buy something. She checked our purchases through slowly, then bagged them all herself. There were six other women sitting at the other registers, doing their nails or reading cheap magazines. None of them looked up as we paid for our groceries and prepared to leave the store.

❻ Describes the women with details that support the writer's sadness

"Have a nice day," the lady mumbled, not expecting us to hear, as we walked out the door.

"You too," I replied over the lump in my throat.

My mood lifted as we crossed the parking lot and climbed back into our car. Soon we were on the highway, heading away from that strange, sad place—so big and so empty.

# Writing Your Focused Description

## ❶ Prewriting

*You can observe a lot by watching.*
**Yogi Berra, baseball player and manager**

To find a subject for your description, you might try **recalling** a time when you found something so interesting you couldn't wait to describe it to your friends. Make a **list** of places—both strange and familiar—that you find fascinating. Or think of interesting or unusual people you know. See the **Idea Bank** in the margin for more suggestions. After you select a subject to describe, follow the steps below.

### Planning Your Focused Description

▶ **1. Decide your purpose.** Why are you describing this particular thing? Do you want to write to someone you care about to show why something is important to you? to make a person vivid and memorable? to create a particular mood? to recreate a scary event?

▶ **2. Gather information through your senses.** Because careful observation is the key to powerful descriptive writing, you need to gather as many sensory details as possible. Close your eyes and imagine the smells, sounds, or textures you associate with the person, place, object, or event. What colors or shapes help describe your subject?

▶ **3. Identify your audience.** What do your readers know about your subject? What part of your description might need some background information? What additional information do your readers need?

## ❷ Drafting

Begin writing even if you have not refined your purpose or chosen a specific focus. Keep going. Your focus will become clearer as you develop and refine your ideas.

Start by stating the most important aspect of your subject and providing details that support the subject and contribute to the overall effect. Use **sensory language** to convey a mood clearly. Words like *dilapidated, rusty, cracked, dirty, clatter,* and *searching furtively* all contribute to the forlorn feel of the store in the student model. **Show** what you are describing. If you include people, use **actions** or **dialogue** to let them reveal themselves.

You may choose an **organization** before you begin your draft, or you may order and rearrange your details in a later draft. At some point, however, you must

### IDEA Bank

**1. Your Working Portfolio**
Look for ideas in the **Writing Options** you completed earlier in this unit.
• **Old World Sketches,** p. 168
• **Heritage Essay,** p. 179

**2. Time Out**
Sit quietly for 5 to 10 minutes in a park or on a busy street corner. Look for a writing topic by jotting down details of what you see, hear, and smell.

**3. Post Cards**
Recall interesting or unusual places you have seen or heard about. Try to picture these places as they might appear on a post card. Write about the place for which you have the most vivid mental picture.

**Have a question?**
See the **Writing Handbook**
**Descriptive Writing,** pp. 1153–1154

### Ask Your Peer Reader

• What do you think my purpose is for describing this subject?
• Which details help you imagine my subject most clearly?
• What else would you like to know about my subject?

choose a method of organization in order to create a clear, well-ordered description. There are three common methods for organizing a description:

- **Spatial order**
Arrange details from bottom to top, left to right, inside to outside, and so on.

- **Order of importance**
Present the most significant detail first. Other, less important details follow. Or begin with the least important details and work up to the most important ones.

- **Order of impression**
Arrange details according to what first catches your attention. Then descibe details you notice later. This type of organization can give a "you are there" quality to your description.

# ❸ Revising

**Need revising help?**

Review the **Rubric,** p. 212

Consider **peer reader** comments

Check **Revision Guidelines,** p. 1145

**TARGET SKILL ▶ WORD CHOICE** Apt word choices add punch to your descriptions. Vague or abstract words can leave the image fuzzy for the reader. Try adding concrete words to leave a stronger impression.

> There were ~~not many~~ cars ~~around,~~ all ~~ugly~~ and about
> *only four or five* *in the lot* *dilapidated and rusting*
> twenty years old. One of the license plates was hard to read
> *read |LUVWI, though it*
> because of the big scratches in the metal.

# ❹ Editing and Proofreading

**Stumped by subject-verb agreement?**

See the **Grammar Handbook,** pp. 1200–1202

**TARGET SKILL ▶ SUBJECT-VERB AGREEMENT** During revision, if you change the number of your subject, don't forget to match your verb to the subject. Below, the writer changed the singular subject, then matched the verb and details.

> We came across ~~other shoppers who were~~ stooped over,
> *one shopper who was*
> searching furtively through ~~handbags~~ in the cereal aisle ~~and~~
> *her handbag*
> ~~peeking into the frozen foods.~~

**Publishing IDEAS**

- Submit your description to the school literary magazine or newspaper.

- Send your description to an e-mail buddy.

**More Online: Publishing Options** www.mcdougallittell.com

# ❺ Reflecting

**FOR YOUR WORKING PORTFOLIO** How did writing a focused description help you see something in a new way? What lessons do you have for yourself about writing based on what you did here? Attach your answer to your finished work. Save your focused description in your **Working Portfolio.**

Read this paragraph from the first draft of a focused description. The underlined sections may include the following kinds of errors:

- **vague word choice**
- **inconsistent verb tenses**
- **lack of subject-verb agreement**
- **run-on sentences**

For each underlined section, choose the revision that most improves the writing.

> Standing alone on stage behind the curtain, I feel <u>funny</u>. I can hear the
> (1)
> audience settling down and growing quiet. The stage manager and the lighting
> operator <u>sits</u> in the darkened electronics booth. The actors are ready.  My
> (2)
> senses have become <u>sharper I can smell</u> the sticky greasepaint on my face. My
> (3)
> neck <u>burned</u> with the heat from the stage lights. <u>The house lights dim the</u>
> (4)                                                              (5)
> <u>curtain begins to rise</u>. It catches slightly on the way up; so does my pulse.
> Suddenly <u>the curtain is up, and the show has begun</u>.
>          (6)

1. **A.** nervous and excited.
   **B.** indifferent and tired.
   **C.** some emotion inside.
   **D.** something strange.

2. **A.** sat
   **B.** sit
   **C.** sitting
   **D.** Correct as is

3. **A.** sharper. I can smell
   **B.** sharper I can smell,
   **C.** sharper, I can smell
   **D.** Correct as is

4. **A.** burn
   **B.** has burnt
   **C.** burns
   **D.** Correct as is

5. **A.** The house lights dim, the curtain begins to rise.
   **B.** The house lights dim, curtain begins to rise.
   **C.** The house lights dim, and the curtain begins to rise.
   **D.** Correct as is

6. **A.** the curtain is up. And the show has begun.
   **B.** the curtain is up, the show had begun.
   **C.** the curtain is up the show has begun.
   **D.** Correct as is

**Need extra help?**

See the **Grammar Handbook**

**Verb Tense**, p. 1186

**Correcting Run-on Sentences**, p. 1199

**Subject-Verb Agreement**, pp. 1200–1202

# The Challenge of Change

The selections in this unit show many dimensions of change, from changes that mark an individual's life to ones that affect an entire culture. How has your own understanding of change been affected by the selections? Explore this question by completing one or more of the options in each section.

Chicago Tribune photo by Heather Stone.
Copyright © 1998 Chicago Tribune. World rights reserved.

## Reflecting on Theme

OPTION 1

**Charting Responses to Change**  Look at the illustrations you made in the activity from page 16, showing your ideas about progress. With these in mind, would you say you are a person who welcomes change, or do you tend to regard it with caution? Make a two-column chart, with one column labeled "Welcome Changes" and the other labeled "Unwelcome Changes." Fill in the chart by listing, in the appropriate columns, some changes that are presented in this unit's selections, as well as ones that you have faced in your own life. Underline the entries that you have the strongest feelings about. Then write an evaluation of your own attitude toward change.

OPTION 2

**Graphing the Causes of Change**  Work with a partner to create a pie chart showing what you believe to be the major causes of cultural change affecting individuals and societies. To identify the causes, consider the changes presented in this unit's selections and reflect on your own experiences with cultural change. Consider also the news stories you found for the activity on page 144. Remember that the largest section of your chart should represent the most important or most common cause of change. Compare your pie chart with those of your classmates, and discuss their similarities and differences.

OPTION 3

**Evaluating a Quotation**  Consider the quotation from the philosopher Heraclitus at the beginning of this unit: "There is nothing permanent except change." Which of the characters and authors in this unit might agree with this statement? Which might disagree? Make two lists of characters and authors—one list showing those who would agree, the other showing those who would disagree. Include yourself in one of the lists.

**Self ASSESSMENT**

📖 **READER'S NOTEBOOK**
Which of the selections in this unit might have the greatest influence on you in the future—those dealing with the price of progress (Part 1) or those examining cultural issues (Part 2)? Create a list of the selection titles, arranging them in their order of impact.

# Reviewing Literary Concepts

### OPTION 1

**Interpreting Theme**  Review at least four selections from this unit and for each one, write down a sentence stating the theme in your own words. Then consider what each selection suggests about the author's attitude toward change. Record your comments in a chart like the one shown. Discuss your responses with your classmates.

| Selection | Theme | Author's Attitude Toward Change |
|---|---|---|
| The Thrill of the Grass | By working together in small ways, people can resist change. | Some things, like baseball, should not be changed. |

### OPTION 2

**Analyzing Nonfiction**  All of the nonfiction selections in this unit deal in one way or another with the concept of technological or cultural change. Choose three nonfiction pieces from the unit that you find most interesting. What does each have to say about change? Then review the definitions of fiction on pages 17–18 and of nonfiction on pages 104–105. What is it about each piece that makes it nonfiction rather than fiction? Use details from the selections to support your response. Compare your responses with those of your classmates.

# Building Your Portfolio

- **Writing Options**  Imagine that you are applying for a job and your prospective employer has asked to see a writing sample. Review your Writing Options for this unit, paying particular attention to any that reflect the world of work, such as an advertisement, a newsletter article, or an editorial. Choose the one that you feel would most impress an employer. Write a note explaining your choice. Then add the piece and the note to your **Presentation Portfolio.**

- **Writing Workshops**  In this unit you wrote an Opinion Piece on a topic you feel strongly about. You also wrote a Focused Description of a scene or situation. Reread these pieces and decide which is a stronger example of your writing. Explain your choice in a note attached to the preferred piece. Place the piece in your **Presentation Portfolio.**

- **Additional Activities**  Think back to any of the assignments you completed under **Activities & Explorations** and **Inquiry & Research.** Which activity or piece of writing would you most like to expand into a larger project? Write a note explaining your choice, and add it, along with your record of the original work, to your portfolio.

## Self ASSESSMENT

**READER'S NOTEBOOK**
Imagine that a rich, eccentric patron of your school is offering a $5,000 prize to students who show mastery of the following terms. There is a catch, however—you have only 15 minutes to review the terms. To help you use your time efficiently, divide the terms into three categories: those you don't need to review, those you need to review only briefly, and those for which you require extensive review. Then spend 15 minutes reviewing the necessary terms (and hope that you find that rich patron!).

| | |
|---|---|
| theme | expository essay |
| science fiction | personal essay |
| character | memoir |
| fantasy | autobiography |
| plot | biography |
| point of view | theme |
| foreshadowing | nonfiction |
| setting | cultural conflict |
| description | cultural setting |

## Self ASSESSMENT

**Presentation Portfolio.**
Review the pieces that you have chosen to include. Do they have anything in common? What do they suggest about your strengths and interests as a writer?

### Setting GOALS

As you worked through the activities in this unit, you probably became more aware of your strengths and weaknesses in reading and writing skills. After reviewing the work that you did for this unit, create a list of skills that you would like to work on in the next unit.

LITERATURE CONNECTIONS

## Fahrenheit 451

RAY BRADBURY

This classic science fiction novel, first published in 1953, depicts a terrifying future in which reading is banned and the job of firemen is to burn books. The novel follows the progress of Guy Montag, a fireman who becomes curious about the books he is destroying. A searing attack on censorship, the book is also fiercely critical of the dehumanizing effects of mass media, commercialism, and modern technology.

**These thematically related readings are provided along with *Fahrenheit 451*:**

**Afterword to the Novel**
RAY BRADBURY

**The Portable Phonograph**
WALTER VAN TILBURG CLARK

**"You Have Insulted Me"**
KURT VONNEGUT, JR.

**Burning a Book**
WILLIAM STAFFORD

**A Summer's Reading**
BERNARD MALAMUD

**The Paterson Public Library**
JUDITH ORTIZ COFER

**The Phoenix**
SYLVIA TOWNSEND WARNER

## And Even *More . . .*

### Things Fall Apart

CHINUA ACHEBE

Set in an Ibo village in Nigeria in the late 1800s, the story of Okonkwo unfolds like a Greek tragedy as traditional Ibo customs are challenged by new European ways. Achebe's first novel, *Things Fall Apart* was published in England in 1958. Critics both within and outside of Africa consider it a classic. The book is also part of the *Literature Connections* series published by McDougal Littell.

### Books

**Brave New World**
ALDOUS HUXLEY
In this nightmarish future world, the government controls all aspects of human life, aided by science and technology. The book is also part of the *Literature Connections* series published by McDougal Littell.

**The Time Machine**
H.G. WELLS
The inventor of a time machine travels to a distant future, where he discovers two races of people, the childlike Eloi and the hideous Morlocks.

# Picture Bride

YOSHIKO UCHIDA

Yoshiko Uchida tells the story of Hana Omiya, a Japanese woman who comes to the United States as a "picture bride"—a woman whose marriage is arranged by family members through an exchange of photographs. The novel follows Hana's experiences, beginning with her arrival in San Francisco in 1917 and continuing through her family's relocation to a Japanese internment camp in Utah in 1943. Her expectations of life in the United States change constantly, causing her to adapt to America on her own terms.

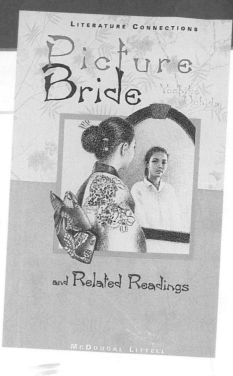

**These thematically related readings are provided along with *Picture Bride*:**

*from* **City in the Sun**
PAUL BAILEY

*from* **Farewell to Manzanar**
JEANNE WAKATSUKI HOUSTON
AND JAMES D. HOUSTON

**No Speak English**
SANDRA CISNEROS

**A Migration Created by a Burden of Suspicion**
DIRK JOHNSON

**Breaking Silence for My Father**
JANICE MIRIKITANI

**Clothes**
CHITRA BANERJEE DIVAKARUNI

**The Heart of a Woman**
GEORGIA DOUGLAS JOHNSON

---

**Having Our Say: The Delany Sisters' First 100 Years**
SARAH LOUISE DELANY AND ANNIE ELIZABETH DELANY
Two African-American sisters share stories about their remarkable lives, each of which spanned over 100 years.

**An Island Like You: Stories from the Barrio**
JUDITH ORTIZ COFER
Stories about Puerto Rican teenagers who are often caught between the traditions of their heritage and the new ways of life in the United States.

**Other Media**
**Isaac Bashevis Singer: Isaac in America**
Documentary on the life and works of Nobel prize-winning storyteller Isaac Bashevis Singer. In the words of the subject: "It's a masterpiece. I'm in it, but it's still a masterpiece." Monterey Home Video.
(VIDEOCASSETTE)

**Eyes on the Prize**
An award-winning series on the civil rights movement in the United States. News footage and eyewitness accounts help to chronicle the struggle for equality from 1954 to 1965. PBS Video.
(VIDEOCASSETTE)

**A Necklace of Raindrops and Other Stories by Joan Aiken**
Caedmon.
(AUDIOCASSETTE)

**Chinua Achebe Reads**
American Audio Prose Library
(AUDIOCASSETTE)

*The Lovers (Somali Friends)* (1950), Lois Mailou Jones. Casein on canvas, The Evans-Tibbs Collection, Washington, D.C.

# In the Name of *Love*

Great literature,

past or present, is the

expression of great

knowledge of the

human heart.

*Edith Hamilton*
*German-born educator,*
*writer, and classical scholar*
*1867–1963*

# PART 1 | Ties that Bind

The writers who created the original Star Trek series for television imagined an entire race of people—the Vulcans—defined by their logic and absence of emotion. For the Vulcans, love's passions posed a threat to reason. In this part of Unit Two, you will read selections that would certainly puzzle the Vulcans. Here, you will encounter a variety of ties created by love.

**ACTIVITY**

Think about a loving relationship in your own life. List various feelings that you experience in that relationship. Then create a bar graph that shows the relative frequencies of these feelings. For example, the longest bar might be used to represent contentment, while the shortest bar might be used to represent anger. As you read, compare your experience of love with those described in the selections.

# LEARNING the Language of *Literature*

$\mathcal{P}$oetry is something that most people recognize when they see it, even if they cannot define the term *poetry* precisely. In poetry, unlike prose, the look and sound of the words are inseparable from a poem's meaning. The word *poet* comes from the Greek word *poiētēs*, meaning "one who makes or fashions," and writing a poem involves a careful choice and crafting of language. Reading a poem, too, is different from reading prose; it is an experience that involves all the senses. As the French poet Paul Valéry said, "Prose [is] walking, poetry dancing."

## Form

The **form** of a poem is the physical arrangement of the words on the page. This includes the length and placement of the lines and the way they are grouped into **stanzas.** Some poetry is written in strict formal patterns. Other poetry, known as **free verse,** is not. Poets choose forms that help them convey their ideas.

**YOUR TURN** Look at the two excerpts at the right. Which is an example of free verse? Explain your answer.

## Sound Devices

Poets use a variety of techniques to produce special qualities of sound. **Alliteration, assonance, consonance,** and **rhyme** involve repetition of sounds.

- **Alliteration** is a repetition of initial consonant sounds in nearby words (as in "to **j**iggle and **j**ump for **j**oy").
- **Assonance** is a repetition of vowel sounds within words (as in "a gr**ee**d as d**ee**p as the s**ea**").
- **Consonance** is a repetition of consonant sounds within or at the end of words (as in "of flee**t** foo**t** and sou**nd** mi**nd**").
- **Rhyme** is a repetition of final sounds in two or more words (as in "a s**tray** g**ray tray**"). The **rhyme scheme** of a poem is the pattern formed by the rhymes at the end of the lines.

**Onomatopoeia** is the use of words—like *snort, clank,* and *whir*—that sound like what they refer to.

**YOUR TURN** Find and identify examples of sound devices in the excerpt at the right.

---

### FORM

Love can not fill the thickened lung with breath,
Nor clean the blood, nor set the fractured bone;
Yet many a man is making friends with death
Even as I speak, for lack of love alone.

—Edna St. Vincent Millay, "Sonnet 30"

she spun herself into a web
and    looking for a place to rest
turned to him
but he stood straight
declining to be her corner

—Nikki Giovanni, "Woman"

---

### SOUND DEVICES

There will come soft rains and the
   smell of the ground,
And swallows circling with their
   shimmering sound;

And frogs in the pools singing at night,
And wild plum-trees in tremulous white;

Robins will wear their feathery fire
Whistling their whims on a low fence-wire;

—Sara Teasdale, "There Will Come Soft Rains"

**Rhythm** is the pattern, or beat, of stressed and unstressed syllables in a line of poetry. When a rhythm is repeated throughout a poem, it is known as the poem's **meter**. Poets use rhythm to highlight the musical quality of language and to emphasize ideas and feelings. In the following line from Shakespeare's "Sonnet 18," the stressed syllables are marked (´) and the unstressed syllables are marked (˘):

**Shăll Í cŏmpáre thĕe tŏ ă súmmĕr's dáy?**

**YOUR TURN** Tap out the pattern of stressed and unstressed syllables in the excerpt from Millay's "Sonnet 30" at the right. How does the poem's meter help you read the lines?

## Figurative Language

Most poets try to create word pictures in their poems that help readers see, hear, feel, smell, and even taste the experiences they present. Such word pictures are called **imagery**. One technique poets use to create strong imagery is **figurative language,** which conveys meanings beyond the literal meanings of the words. Similes and metaphors are kinds of figurative language involving comparisons between things that have something in common.

- In a **simile** (such as "My life is like an open book"), a word such as *like* or *as* signals the comparison.
- A **metaphor** (such as "Jealousy is a green-eyed monster") is a direct comparison, with no signal word.

**YOUR TURN** How does the simile in this excerpt help you understand the relationship between the speaker and the person addressed?

**Personification** is a type of figurative language in which animals, inanimate objects, or ideas are given human qualities (as in "The teakettle ordered us back to the kitchen").

**YOUR TURN** What does the personification in the excerpt at the right tell you about the speaker's frame of mind?

---

**RHYTHM**

Love is not all: it is not meat nor drink
Nor slumber nor a roof against the rain;
Nor yet a floating spar to men that sink
And rise and sink and rise and sink again;

—Edna St. Vincent Millay, "Sonnet 30"

---

**SIMILE**

What did we say to each other
that now we are as the deer
who walk in single file

—N. Scott Momaday, "Simile"

---

**PERSONIFICATION**

I'd wake and hear the cold splintering, breaking.
When the rooms were warm, he'd call,
and slowly I would rise and dress,
fearing the chronic angers of that house,

—Robert Hayden, "Those Winter Sundays"

A poet doesn't create a poem just by writing an essay and dividing it into short lines. A poem therefore shouldn't be read in the same way an essay is read. Reading poetry requires paying attention not only to the meanings of the words but also to what their sound and arrangement on the page conveys. The strategies on this page will help you learn to read and enjoy poetry.

# Reading Poetry

## Strategies for Using Your 📖 READER'S NOTEBOOK

As you read, take notes to
- record striking or memorable images or uses of language
- analyze the poem's meter and rhyme
- explore your reactions to the poem's message

### 1 Strategies for Examining Form
- Look at the poem before you read it. **Question** whether the lines and stanzas form a regular pattern on the page.
- As you read the poem, first aloud and then to yourself, listen for rhythmic patterns. Ask yourself if you hear a regular beat.
- Pause in your reading where punctuation marks appear, not necessarily at the ends of lines. In poetry, the end of a line does not always indicate the end of a thought.

### 2 Strategies for Appreciating Sound
- Read the poem aloud several times.
- Identify the sound devices—alliteration, assonance, consonance, rhyme, and onomatopoeia—that the poet uses.
- Determine whether the poem has a rhyme scheme.
- **Monitor** your reactions to hearing the poem. Do the sounds calm you, make you sad, or cause you to feel other emotions?

*Sound Devices*
*Alliteration:*
*Assonance:*
*Consonance:*
*Rhyme:*
*Onomatopoeia:*

### 3 Strategies for Understanding Figurative Language
- Identify the types of figurative language that the poet uses.
  - **Visualize** the objects, ideas, or people compared in similes and metaphors. Try using a Venn diagram like the one at the right to chart the similarities and differences.
  - Analyze how the similes, metaphors, and personifications you encounter change or **clarify** your understanding of the poem.

**"Simile"**
The speaker and the person addressed are compared with deer.

deer following each other | silent solitary | people not getting along

### 4 Strategies for Determining Meaning
- **Question** whether the title offers any clues about the poem's message.
- **Connect** your personal memories and feelings with what you read. They may provide you with insights into the poem's meaning.
- Summarize the idea or feeling the poem leaves you with.

## Need More Help?

Remember that active readers use the essential reading strategies explained on page 7: **visualize, predict, clarify, question, connect, evaluate, monitor.**

# Piano
*Poetry by* D. H. LAWRENCE

# Those Winter Sundays
*Poetry by* ROBERT HAYDEN

## Connect to Your Life

**Childhood Memories** Recall a routine household activity from your childhood that now evokes strong feelings in you. Perhaps your mother read to you at night, your father patiently helped you with homework, or your grandmother baked a weekly pie. Create a simple chart, like the one shown here, to record sensations that you associate with that memory. Fill in all applicable boxes.

| Sense | Sensation Associated with Memory |
|---|---|
| Sight | |
| Hearing | |
| Touch | |
| Smell | |
| Taste | |

## Build Background

**Early Years** The two poems that you are about to read draw upon the poets' memories of their own childhood. D. H. Lawrence, the son of a coal miner and his cultured wife, grew up in the late 19th century near Nottingham, England. Robert Hayden, born in 1913, was raised by poor, hard-working foster parents in Detroit, Michigan. Each poet, coincidentally, examines a parent's legacy by recalling activities of long-ago winter Sundays.

## Focus Your Reading

**LITERARY ANALYSIS** **IMAGERY** When writers use words and phrases to re-create vivid sensory experiences for the reader, they are making use of **imagery.** Although most imagery appeals to the visual sense, imagery may also appeal to the senses of smell, hearing, taste, or touch. In this passage from "Those Winter Sundays," the experience of bitter cold is made vivid by imagery:

> *Sundays too my father got up early*
> *and put his clothes on in the blueblack cold,*

As you read the following poems, pay attention to how each poet's use of imagery affects you as a reader.

**ACTIVE READING** **VISUALIZING** **Visualizing,** the act of mentally picturing something you read, can help you understand and appreciate the imagery in poetry. Certain questions can help you to visualize what you read:

- Where and when does the poem take place?
- Are there people portrayed? If so, who are they and what do they look like?
- What details in the **setting** of the poem trigger your own mental pictures?

**READER'S NOTEBOOK** As you read these two poems, develop your own mental pictures of the characters and the scenes that are described. Make a list of the images that you can most easily visualize.

# Piano

D. H. LAWRENCE

Softly, in the dusk, a woman is singing to me;
Taking me back down the vista of years, till I see
A child sitting under the piano, in the boom of the
    tingling strings
And pressing the small, poised feet of a mother who
    smiles as she sings.

5  In spite of myself, the insidious mastery of song
Betrays me back, till the heart of me weeps to belong
To the old Sunday evenings at home, with winter outside
And hymns in the cozy parlour, the tinkling piano
    our guide.

So now it is vain for the singer to burst into clamour
10 With the great black piano appassionato. The glamour
Of childish days is upon me, my manhood is cast
Down in the flood of remembrance, I weep like a child
    for the past.

**Guide for Reading**

**2 vista** (vĭs′tə): a passage affording a distant view.

What mental picture do you form when reading this stanza?

**5 insidious** (ĭn-sĭd′ē-əs): working subtly and gradually; treacherous.

**9 vain:** useless.

**10 appassionato** (ə-pä′sē-ə-nä′tō): an Italian word meaning "with deep emotion," used as a musical direction.

## Thinking Through the Literature

1. **Comprehension Check** What is being recalled in this poem?

2. **ACTIVE READING** **VISUALIZING** Look back at the list of **images** from "Piano" in your **READER'S NOTEBOOK**. Compare the mental pictures that you formed with those formed by your classmates. What details in the poem contributed to those mental pictures?

3. Why does the **speaker**—the voice that talks to the reader—"weep like a child for the past"?

   **THINK ABOUT**
   - what he means by "the glamour of childish days"
   - what he values about "the old Sunday evenings at home"

4. Why does the speaker say that "now it is vain for the singer to burst into clamour"?

   **THINK ABOUT**
   - why the woman might be singing to him
   - the difference between his situations now and in the past

*Sunday Morning Breakfast* (1943), Horace Pippin. Private collection, courtesy of Galerie St. Etienne, New York.

# Those Winter Sundays

### ROBERT HAYDEN

Sundays too my father got up early
and put his clothes on in the blueblack cold,
then with cracked hands that ached
from labor in the weekday weather made
5  banked fires blaze. No one ever thanked him.

I'd wake and hear the cold splintering, breaking.
When the rooms were warm, he'd call,
and slowly I would rise and dress,
fearing the chronic angers of that house,

10  Speaking indifferently to him,
who had driven out the cold
and polished my good shoes as well.
What did I know, what did I know
of love's austere and lonely offices?

**Guide for Reading**

What do you think the "blueblack cold" feels like?

**9 chronic** (krŏn′ĭk): lasting or recurring for a long time.

**14 austere** (ô-stîr′): stern; severe; offices: duties; ceremonies.

# *Thinking* through the LITERATURE

## Connect to the Literature

**1. What Do You Think?** Jot down three words or phrases describing the sensations you experienced while reading "Those Winter Sundays."

**Comprehension Check**
- What time is recalled in this poem?
- What does the father do for his son?
- How does the child react to his father?

## Think Critically

**2.** **ACTIVE READING** **VISUALIZING** Look back to the list of **images** from "Those Winter Sundays" in your **READER'S NOTEBOOK.** Read aloud the words and phrases from the poem that helped you to form mental pictures. What image is the strongest one for you?

**3.** What is your opinion of the **speaker**?

- the speaker's observations in lines 5 and 10
- the question that ends the poem
- the possible reason that the speaker recalls this memory

**4.** What lessons might be learned from this poem? Explain your answer.

## Extend Interpretations

**5. Comparing Texts** Compare and contrast the speakers' attitudes toward their childhood in "Piano" and "Those Winter Sundays."

**6. Connect to Life** What feelings or memories from your own life did these poems awaken?

## Literary Analysis

**IMAGERY** The use of words and phrases to create sensory experiences for readers is called **imagery.** Images can appeal to one or more of the five senses: sight, hearing, taste, smell, and touch. For example, "A child sitting under the piano" appeals to the sense of sight; "the boom of the tingling strings" appeals to the senses of hearing and touch; and "pressing the small, poised feet" appeals to the senses of sight and touch.

**Paired Activity** With a partner, list three more images from "Piano" and three from "Those Winter Sundays," naming the sense or senses to which each image appeals. Then discuss which poem, in your opinion, uses imagery more effectively.

**SPEAKER** The **speaker** is the voice in a poem that "talks" to the reader, similar to the narrator in fiction. The speaker is not necessarily the same as the poet, although in some cases it may be. Sometimes, a poet will create a speaker with a distinct identity in order to achieve a certain effect.

**Activity** Identify the speakers in "Piano" and "Those Winter Sundays." Consider what the poems say explicitly about them as children and what is implied about them as adults. What can you infer about the speakers and their present perspective? For each poem, fill out a graphic like the one shown to help you organize your ideas.

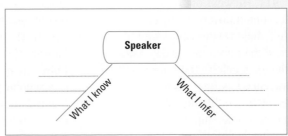

## Writing Options

**1. Childhood Poem** Use the chart you created for Connect to Your Life on page 228 as the starting point for a poem about your childhood memory. Include vivid imagery that appeals to different senses. Place the poem in your **Working Portfolio.**

**2. Image Dictionary** Create a dictionary of sensory images. Under the headings "Sight," "Hearing," "Touch," "Taste," and "Smell," record words and phrases from your reading, including those encountered in "Piano" and "Those Winter Sundays."

## Activities & Explorations

**Choral Reading** With a small group, prepare a choral reading of one of these poems. Discuss what emotions should be expressed, where pauses should fall, and which words or phrases should be given emphasis. Then practice your reading aloud. **~ SPEAKING AND LISTENING**

---

# D. H. Lawrence
### 1885–1930

**Other Works**
*The Complete Short Stories of
   D. H. Lawrence*
*The Complete Poems of
   D. H. Lawrence*

**Coal Miner's Son** David Herbert Lawrence grew up in poverty in the coal-mining district of Nottinghamshire, England. His father was a hard-working, hard-drinking coal miner; his mother, to whom he was deeply attached, was a former schoolteacher who instilled in her son a love of learning and culture. A sickly but intellectually gifted child, Lawrence attended school on scholarships and after graduation became a schoolteacher himself, writing fiction and poetry in his spare time.

**His Path to Fame** Lawrence's first poems were published when a girlfriend submitted them to a magazine whose editor was impressed with Lawrence's efforts. With the editor's help, Lawrence was able to publish his first novel, *The White Peacock,* in 1911. He went on to produce a string of critically acclaimed novels, many of which focus on male-female relationships with a frankness that shocked the public of his day. Aside from being one of the most celebrated novelists of the 20th century, Lawrence has long been recognized as a first-rate poet. "Piano," a famous example of his poetic craftsmanship, was written in 1918, seven years after his mother died.

# Robert Hayden
### 1913–1980

**Other Works**
*Angle of Ascent: New and
   Selected Poems*
*Collected Prose*
*Robert Hayden: Collected Poems*

**The Making of a Poet** Robert Hayden grew up in Detroit, Michigan, where he was raised by foster parents who made great sacrifices to insure his education. Their efforts were also encouraged by Hayden's natural mother, who occasionally sent him books to read. Hayden began writing poems in elementary school, although for years he doubted that he could make a career of it. In 1936 he was employed by the Federal Writers' Project to research African-American history and folklore. Soon afterward, he began working part-time for an African-American weekly paper whose editor helped him publish his first book of poetry, *Heart-Shape in the Dust* (1940).

**An Academic Life** In 1941, Hayden enrolled in graduate school at the University of Michigan, where one of his most inspiring professors was the British poet W. H. Auden. Eventually becoming a professor himself, Hayden taught for over 20 years at Fisk University in Nashville, Tennessee. As his reputation as a scholar grew, so did his fame as a poet. "Those Winter Sundays," one of his best-known shorter poems, was first collected in the volume *A Ballad of Remembrance,* published in 1962.

# Sonnet 18

*Poetry by*
WILLIAM SHAKESPEARE

# Sonnet 30

*Poetry by*
EDNA ST. VINCENT MILLAY

## Connect to Your Life

**What Is Love?** Poets, like songwriters, often make use of comparisons when describing love. Love may be compared to an illness or a fire or even a balloon drifting in the air. With a partner, come up with different comparisons to describe love or a beloved person. You may use lyrics from popular music or any other phrases that come to mind. Share your best responses with your classmates. Then discuss what the comparisons reveal about people's attitudes towards love.

## Build Background

**Sonnet Origins** Poets have often explored the topic of love in **sonnets,** which are 14-line poems that have been a popular form of expression for many centuries. The sonnet originated in Italy; in fact, the word sonnet comes from the Italian for "little song." The form was first popularized by the Italian poet Petrarch (1304–1374), who wrote a famous sonnet sequence, or series, expressing his love for a woman named Laura. From Italy, the form spread to France, Spain, and England, where many poets, including William Shakespeare, experimented with the form. Shakespeare's 154 sonnets are widely regarded as the finest in English. Like Petrarch's, Shakespeare's sonnets often focus on romantic love; they also address the love between friends. Since Shakespeare's day, many English-language poets have tried their hand at writing sonnets. Among them is the 20th-century American poet Edna St. Vincent Millay.

## Focus Your Reading

**LITERARY ANALYSIS** | **SONNET STRUCTURE** | The **structure** of the **sonnet** is reflected by the **rhyme scheme,** or the pattern of rhyme in a poem. Poets use rhyme not only to please the ear but also to mark units of thought.

To identify a poem's rhyme scheme, you assign a letter of the alphabet to each rhymed sound at the end of the line. The example below, from another Shakespeare sonnet, illustrates an *abab* rhyme scheme. Note that *fled* rhymes with *dead* and that *bell* rhymes with *dwell.*

| | |
|---|---|
| *No longer mourn for me when I am <u>dead</u>* | **a** |
| *Than you shall hear the ruly sullen <u>bell</u>* | **b** |
| *Give warning to the world that I am <u>fled</u>* | **a** |
| *From this vile world, with vilest worms to <u>dwell</u>.* | **b** |

The **English,** or **Shakespearean, sonnet** is characterized by the fixed rhyme scheme *abab cdcd efef gg.* This type of sonnet is divided into three **quatrains,** or groups of four rhymed lines, and one **couplet,** or rhymed pair of lines. Each group of lines usually corresponds to a unit of thought in the poem. The **couplet** provides commentary on the subject developed in the preceding three quatrains.

**ACTIVE READING** | **STRATEGIES FOR READING SONNETS** | The following strategies can help you to understand a **sonnet** and to recognize how the **structure** contributes to its meaning:

1. Identify the **rhyme scheme** and the major units of thought.
2. In your own words, describe the situation, problem, or question that is introduced at the beginning of the poem.
3. Identify the **turning point,** if there is one.
4. Find out how the situation is clarified, the problem resolved, or the question answered.
5. Summarize the message of the poem in your own words.

**READER'S NOTEBOOK** As you read the following sonnets, apply the five strategies described above. Record the results of each task.

# Sonnet 18
### William Shakespeare

Shall I compare thee to a summer's day?
Thou art more lovely and more temperate:
Rough winds do shake the darling buds of May,
And summer's lease hath all too short a date:
5   Sometime too hot the eye of heaven shines,
And often is his gold complexion dimmed;
And every fair from fair sometime declines,
By chance or nature's changing course untrimmed;
But thy eternal summer shall not fade,
10   Nor lose possession of that fair thou owest;
Nor shall Death brag thou wander'st in his shade,
When in eternal lines to time thou growest:
    So long as men can breathe, or eyes can see,
    So long lives this, and this gives life to thee.

**2 temperate** (tĕm'pər-ĭt): moderate; mild.

**8 untrimmed:** stripped of beauty.

**10 thou owest** (ō'əst): you own; you possess.

## Thinking Through the Literature

1. **Comprehension Check** What basic comparison is made in this poem?

2. What words would you use to describe how the **speaker** feels about the person being addressed? Support your opinion with details from the poem.

3. **ACTIVE READING** | **STRATEGIES FOR READING SONNETS**   Refer to what you recorded in your **READER'S NOTEBOOK.**
How did your analysis of this sonnet's **structure** help you to understand the poem?

**THINK ABOUT**
- the question raised in the first line
- the **rhyme scheme**
- the main point of each **quatrain** and **couplet**

*Lovers III* (1990),
Eng Tay. Edition 175,
intaglio. Published
by Tapir Editions,
New York.

# Sonnet 30

*Edna St. Vincent Millay*

Love is not all: it is not meat nor drink
Nor slumber nor a roof against the rain;
Nor yet a floating spar to men that sink
And rise and sink and rise and sink again;
<sub>5</sub> Love can not fill the thickened lung with breath,
Nor clean the blood, nor set the fractured bone;
Yet many a man is making friends with death
Even as I speak, for lack of love alone.
It well may be that in a difficult hour,
<sub>10</sub> Pinned down by pain and moaning for release,
Or nagged by want past resolution's power,
I might be driven to sell your love for peace,
Or trade the memory of this night for food.
It well may be. I do not think I would.

**3 spar:** a pole used to support a ship's sails.

**11 want:** need.

## Connect to the Literature

1. **What Do You Think?** Which lines of Millay's "Sonnet 30" did you find most memorable? Describe your response to those lines.

   **Comprehension Check**
   - What does Millay say that love is *not?*
   - How would you paraphrase what she says in lines 7 and 8?

## Think Critically

2. Consider all the details that the speaker uses to explain why "Love is not all." In your opinion, what do these details have in common?

3. **ACTIVE READING** **STRATEGIES FOR READING SONNETS**

   Refer to your  **READER'S NOTEBOOK**. How did your analysis of this **sonnet's structure** help you to understand the poem?

   **THINK ABOUT**
   - the statement in the poem's first line
   - the **rhyme scheme**
   - the main point of each **quatrain** and **couplet**

4. What seems to be the speaker's overall opinion of love?

## Extend Interpretations

5. **Comparing Texts** Do you think Shakespeare's "Sonnet 18" and Millay's "Sonnet 30" follow the same structure? Explain, using your knowledge of sonnet structure and details from the poems.

6. **Connect to Life** Do you think these poems convey attitudes about love that are still common today? Draw upon the discussion from Connect to Your Life on page 233 to support your opinion.

## Literary Analysis

**SONNET STRUCTURE** In addition to the **rhyme scheme, sonnet structure** is also determined by the sound pattern. **Sonnets** usually follow a regular **rhythm** called **meter.** The meter of a poem is like the beat of a song. Each unit of meter is known as a **foot.** In English, the most commonly used type of metrical foot is an **iamb,** which is an unstressed syllable followed by a stressed syllable (ˇ ´).

Two terms are used to identify the meter of a line of poetry. The first word describes the main type of metrical foot in the line. The second word describes the number of feet in the line: **trimeter** (three feet), **tetrameter** (four feet), **pentameter** (five feet), and so on. Thus, the meter of a poem might be **iambic trimeter** or **iambic pentameter.** The following example from Millay's sonnet illustrates iambic pentameter, the most common pattern. Note the iambic pattern of unstressed, followed by stressed, syllables. Also note that each line consists of five iambs (pentameter).

*Nŏr yét ă flóatĭng spár tŏ mén*
   *thăt sínk*

*Aňd risé aňd sínk aňd rísе aňd*
   *sínk ăgaín;*

**Cooperative Learning Activity** Work in a small group to identify the metrical pattern of Shakespeare's and Millay's sonnets.

# *Choices* & CHALLENGES

## Writing Options

**1. Speaker Profile** Create a personality profile of one of the speakers in the two poems. Use details from the poem to support your opinion of the speaker's personality.

Shakespeare's speaker | Millay's speaker

**2. Not-love Poem** Write a sonnet or another poem in which, like Millay, you express your own view of love by defining what it is not. Place the entry in your **Working Portfolio.**

## Activities & Explorations

**1. Comparative Description** Prepare a "weather report" that is not about the weather at all but about the qualities of a person whom you know well. In your report, try to imitate some of the techniques used by Shakespeare to make comparisons. Present your report to the class, using any visual materials that will enhance your presentation.
~ **SPEAKING AND LISTENING**

**2. Rock Sonnet** Turn either sonnet into a song and perform it before the class. ~ **MUSIC**

## Inquiry & Research

**Earlier English** Shakespeare wrote almost 500 years ago. Study his sonnet for words or expressions that are no longer commonly used. Then create a list of those terms and try to come up with a modern substitute for each one, looking up in the dictionary words that are unfamiliar to you. Compare your results with those of your classmates.

## Grammar in Context: Rhetorical Questions

Consider this line from Shakespeare's "Sonnet 18." Do you think the speaker expects an answer to his question?

> **"Shall I compare thee to a summer's day?"**

This question is actually a rhetorical question. It is asked not to get an answer but to create an effect. A writer who uses a rhetorical question usually does so because the question is more striking and dramatic than a statement would be.

| Statement | Rhetorical Question |
|---|---|
| • Never was such nonsense written. | • Was ever such nonsense written? |
| • There will never be an end to this. | • Will there ever be an end to this? |
| • I shall compare thee to a summer's day. | • Shall I compare thee to a summer's day? |

***Usage Tip:*** You can often turn a statement into a rhetorical question by switching the positions of the subject and a helping verb or by replacing the subject with an interrogative pronoun, such as *who* or *what.*

**WRITING EXERCISE** Rewrite each statement as a rhetorical question.

> **Example: *Original*** No one has evoked more poignantly than Shakespeare the quickness of beauty's fading.
>
> ***Rewritten*** Who has evoked more poignantly than Shakespeare the quickness of beauty's fading?

1. It has never been easy to express powerful feelings.
2. We stumble and stutter every time we try.
3. I don't know who could express such feelings better than a poet.
4. There aren't any sonnets that surpass Shakespeare's.

**Connect to the Literature** Try changing a line of "Sonnet 18" (other than the first) into a rhetorical question. Do you think your change improves the poem, or do you like the line better as a statement? Explain your answer.

## William Shakespeare
### 1564–1616

**Other Works**
*Romeo and Juliet*
*Julius Caesar*
*Macbeth*
*As You Like It*
*Twelfth Night*

## Edna St. Vincent Millay
### 1892–1950

**Other Works**
*A Few Figs from Thistles*
*The Harp-Weaver and Other Poems*
*Conversation at Midnight*

**The Bard of Avon** The son of a merchant, William Shakespeare grew up in the market town of Stratford-upon-Avon, England, where he attended the local grammar school. In 1582 he married Anne Hathaway, who later gave birth to three children. Shakespeare probably moved to London in the 1580s and began a career as an actor with the Lord Chamberlain's Men, London's leading theater company. In the 1590s he began writing plays for the group. Great acclaim followed, under both Queen Elizabeth I and her successor, King James I, who became the theater company's patron. From then on known as the King's Players, the group performed mainly at London's Globe Theatre, where Shakespeare was a part owner.

**The Bard's Legacy** When he died, Shakespeare was able to leave his heirs a large inheritance. Of course, Shakespeare's greatest legacy was his writing—over 150 sonnets and over 35 dramas that are generally regarded as the world's finest. These include tragedies such as *Hamlet* and *King Lear* and comedies such as *The Taming of the Shrew* and *A Midsummer Night's Dream*.

**Vassar Girl Makes Good** Edna St. Vincent Millay was still a student when she burst on the literary scene in 1912 with her poem "Renascence." After graduating from Vassar College, she settled in Greenwich Village, a New York City neighborhood then enjoying its heyday as a center for poets and artists. Millay quickly became one of Greenwich Village's social lions, admired as much for her offbeat, romantic lifestyle as for her skill with the pen. Though Millay lived the life of a nonconformist, her well-crafted verse usually conformed to poetic traditions of the past. She was one of the few poets of her day who did not abandon rhyme and meter, and her sonnets are still considered masterpieces.

**In Times of Change** In 1923, Millay became the first woman to win the Pulitzer Prize in poetry. Her work reflected many of the social changes that swept through the United States during that era and won her international acclaim. "Love is not all," which appears as Sonnet 30 in her *Collected Sonnets* (1941), was first published in her sonnet sequence *Fatal Interview* (1931).

## Author Activity

**Shall I Compare Thee to Another Sonnet?** Find a collection of Shakespeare's sonnets and choose one that you like. Then compare it with Sonnet 18. With a group, share your chosen sonnets and discuss what they all have in common.

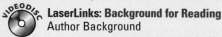
**LaserLinks: Background for Reading**
Author Background

## Author Activity

**Rhyme and Rhythm** Look for poems other than sonnets by Millay and read them with an ear for the rhyme and meter. Choose a few and read them aloud. How much variety do you find in the form of the poems? Compare your findings with those of your classmates.

# Sweet Potato Pie

*Short Story by* EUGENIA COLLIER

## Connect to Your Life

**All in the Family** Think about the relationship between the oldest and youngest siblings in a family. What qualities are typical of that relationship? In your opinion, who has it easier, the oldest or the youngest? Why? Discuss your ideas on the matter with your classmates.

## Build Background

**One Family, Two Worlds** In "Sweet Potato Pie," the narrator recalls two very different settings: the sharecropper's shanty where he grew up with his family and his eldest brother's home in Harlem. Sharecropping, or tenant farming, is a system in which a person or family works someone else's farm in exchange for a share of the profits. Traditionally, sharecroppers have been very poor. In the United States, sharecropping arose after the Civil War and declined as modern, mechanized farming was introduced. Sharecropping is still a way of life in other parts of the world.

From the late 19th century through World War II, millions of African Americans left farms and small towns in the South to seek economic opportunity in Northern big cities. The first wave of this movement, ending in the 1920s, was known as the Great Migration. Cities such as Chicago, Detroit, and New York grew considerably in size. In the 1920s Harlem, a part of New York City, became the world's largest urban black community. Though crowded and generally poor, Harlem became a focus of African-American culture, music, and art.

> **WORDS TO KNOW**
> **Vocabulary Preview**
>
> boisterous    nuance
> edifice       panorama
> entity        reminiscence
> gaunt         reverently
> impersonal    sultry

## Focus Your Reading

**LITERARY ANALYSIS** **CHARACTERIZATION** **Characterization** refers to the techniques used by a writer to develop characters. Writers portray characters through a combination of physical description; the speech, thoughts, feelings, or actions of the characters; and direct commentary by the narrator. In this passage from the story you are about to read, the author characterizes the narrator's brother Charley by his speech:

> *"Lucky for you, you got a mind. And that's something ain't everybody got."*

As you read the following story, pay special attention to the main characters and the author's methods of characterization.

**ACTIVE READING** **SEQUENCE OF EVENTS** Many fiction writers make use of **flashback,** or an account of something that took place before the beginning of a story. Often, a flashback interrupts a story's **sequence of events** to provide information about the past. To help the reader keep track of the time order of events, writers use tense changes as well as signal words and phrases, especially at the beginning of paragraphs. Such phrases from this story include the following: *one day, years later, the war came along,* and *when we were young.*

**READER'S NOTEBOOK** As you read, keep track of the chronological order of events by constructing a timeline similar to the one shown.

| Buddy graduates from high school. | | | Bea serves sweet potato pie. |
|---|---|---|---|

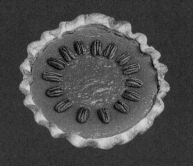

# Sweet

## Eugenia Collier

**From up here** on the fourteenth floor, my brother Charley looks like an insect scurrying among other insects. A deep feeling of love surges through me. Despite the distance, he seems to feel it, for he turns and scans the upper windows, but failing to find me, continues on his way. I watch him moving quickly—gingerly, it seems to me—down Fifth Avenue and around the corner to his shabby taxicab. In a moment he will be heading back uptown.

# Potato Pie

*Looking Along Broadway Towards Grace Church* (1981), Red Grooms. Mixed media, 71″ × 63 ¾″ × 28 ¾″. Courtesy Marlborough Gallery, New York. Copyright © 2000 Red Grooms/Artists Rights Society (ARS), New York.

students to know your brother wasn't nothing but a cab driver. You *somebody.*"

"You're a nut," I said gently. "You should've told that kid the truth." I wanted to say, I'm proud of you, you've got more on the ball than most people I know, I wouldn't have been anything at all except for you. But he would have been embarrassed.

Bea brought in the dessert—homemade sweet potato pie! "Buddy, I must of knew you were coming! I just had a mind I wanted to make sweet potato pie."

There's nothing in this world I like better than Bea's sweet potato pie! "Lord, girl, how you expect me to eat all that?"

The slice she put before me was outrageously big—and moist and covered with a light, golden crust—I ate it all.

"Bea, I'm gonna have to eat and run," I said at last.

Charley guffawed. "Much as you et, I don't see how you gonna *walk,* let alone *run.*" He went out to get his cab from the garage several blocks away.

Bea was washing the tiny girl's face. "Wait a minute, Buddy, I'm gon give you the rest of that pie to take with you."

"Great!" I'd eaten all I could hold, but my *spirit* was still hungry for sweet potato pie.

Bea got out some waxed paper and wrapped up the rest of the pie. "That'll do you for a snack tonight." She slipped it into a brown paper bag.

I gave her a long goodbye hug. "Bea, I love you for a lot of things. Your cooking is one of them!" We had a last comfortable laugh together. I kissed the little girls and went outside to wait for Charley, holding the bag of pie reverently.

In a minute Charley's ancient cab limped to the curb. I plopped into the seat next to him, and we headed downtown. Soon we were assailed[16] by the garish lights of New York on a sultry spring night. We chatted as Charley skillfully managed the heavy traffic. I looked at his long hands on the wheel and wondered what they could have done with artists' brushes.

We stopped a bit down the street from my hotel. I invited him in, but he said he had to get on with his evening run. But as I opened the door to get out, he commanded in the old familiar voice, "Buddy, you wait!"

For a moment I thought my coat was torn or something. "What's wrong?"

"What's that you got there?"

I was bewildered. "That? You mean this bag? That's a piece of sweet potato pie Bea fixed for me."

"You ain't going through the lobby of no big hotel carrying no brown paper bag."

"Man, you *crazy!* Of course I'm going— Look, Bea fixed it for me—*That's my pie—*"

Charley's eyes were miserable. "Folks in that hotel don't go through the lobby carrying no

brown paper bags. That's *country*. And you can't neither. You *somebody*, Buddy. You got to be *right*. Now gimme that bag."

"I want that pie, Charley. I've got nothing to prove to anybody—"

I couldn't believe it. But there was no point in arguing. Foolish as it seemed to me, it was important to him.

"You got to look *right*, Buddy. Can't nobody look dignified carrying a brown paper bag."

So finally, thinking how tasty it would have been and how seldom I got a chance to eat anything that good, I handed over my bag of sweet potato pie. If it was that important to him—

I tried not to show my irritation. "Okay, man—take care now." I slammed the door harder than I had intended, walked rapidly to the hotel, and entered the brilliant, crowded lobby.

"That Charley!" I thought. Walking slower now, I crossed the carpeted lobby toward the elevator, still thinking of my lost snack. I had to admit that of all the herd of people who jostled each other in the lobby, not one was carrying a brown paper bag. Or anything but expensive attaché cases or slick packages from exclusive shops. I suppose we all operate according to the symbols that are meaningful to us, and to Charley a brown paper bag symbolizes the humble life he thought I had left. I was *somebody*.

I don't know what made me glance back, but I did. And suddenly the tears of laughter, toil, and love of a lifetime burst around me like fireworks in a night sky.

For there, following a few steps behind, came Charley, proudly carrying a brown paper bag full of sweet potato pie. ❖

---

16. **assailed:** attacked.

# Salvador Late or Early

### Sandra Cisneros

Salvador with eyes the color of caterpillar, Salvador of the crooked hair and crooked teeth, Salvador whose name the teacher cannot remember, is a boy who is no one's friend, runs along somewhere in that vague direction where homes are the color of bad weather, lives behind a raw wood doorway, shakes the sleepy brothers awake, ties their shoes, combs their hair with water, feeds them milk and corn flakes from a tin cup in the dim dark of the morning.

Salvador, late or early, sooner or later arrives with the string of younger brothers ready. Helps his mama, who is busy with the business of the baby. Tugs the arms of Cecilio, Arturito, makes them hurry, because today, like yesterday, Arturito has dropped the cigar box of crayons, has let go the hundred little fingers of red, green, yellow, blue, and nub of black sticks that tumble and spill over and beyond the asphalt puddles until the crossing-guard lady holds back the blur of traffic for Salvador to collect them again.

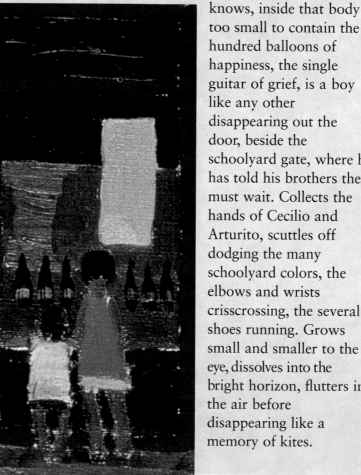

Salvador inside that wrinkled shirt, inside the throat that must clear itself and apologize each time it speaks, inside that forty-pound body of boy with its geography of scars, its history of hurt, limbs stuffed with feathers and rags, in what part of the eyes, in what part of the heart, in that cage of the chest where something throbs with both fists and knows only what Salvador knows, inside that body too small to contain the hundred balloons of happiness, the single guitar of grief, is a boy like any other disappearing out the door, beside the schoolyard gate, where he has told his brothers they must wait. Collects the hands of Cecilio and Arturito, scuttles off dodging the many schoolyard colors, the elbows and wrists crisscrossing, the several shoes running. Grows small and smaller to the eye, dissolves into the bright horizon, flutters in the air before disappearing like a memory of kites.

*Street Corner Shop*, Colin Middleton. Christie's Images.

# Choices & CHALLENGES

## Grammar in Context: Compound Verbs

In "Sweet Potato Pie," Eugenia Collier uses a compound verb to describe the actions of the narrator, Buddy, when he was a child.

> With glee I outread, outfigured, and outspelled the country boys who mocked my poverty.

A **compound verb** consists of two or more verbs that have the same subject and are joined by a conjunction. Think about the choices Collier made in writing the sentence above and about the effects of those choices.

| Choice | Effect |
|---|---|
| • Use of three verbs rather than one<br>• Use of verbs containing the same prefix *(out-)* | • Emphasizes that Buddy did better than his classmates in every subject<br>• Creates rhythm and emphasis |

**Apply to Your Writing** You can use compound verbs to combine ideas and to create rhythms in your own writing. Compound verbs can also help you convey sequences of events.

**WRITING EXERCISE** Combine each pair of sentences to form a single sentence containing a compound verb.

**Punctuation Tip:** In a series containing three or more elements, use a comma after each element except the last one.

**Example:** *Original* Charley protects his youngest brother, Buddy. Charley also guides and encourages him.

*Rewritten* Charley <u>protects, guides, and encourages</u> his youngest brother, Buddy.

1. On payday Mama gathers the money on the table. Then she counts it and divides it.
2. Lil punishes the younger children. But she also comforts them.
3. After Pa studies Buddy's face, he ponders. Then he decides.
4. On graduation night, Charley nags Buddy. Charley criticizes him; he also fusses at him.
5. While Buddy makes his graduation speech, his family members beam. They also sit proudly and look respectful.

**Grammar Handbook**
Punctuation, p. 1203

---

# Eugenia Collier
### 1928–

**Other Works**
*Breeder and Other Stories*
*Spread My Wings*

**Upbringing and Education** Eugenia Collier was born in Baltimore, Maryland, which is still her home. The daughter of a physician and a teacher, she graduated with honors from Howard University in 1948 and earned her master of arts from Columbia University in 1950. She went on to become a professor of English.

**Stepping Stones** Collier wrote that when she discovered "the richness, the diversity, the beauty of my black heritage," it helped her determine her personal and professional goals. After five years as a caseworker in the Baltimore Department of Public Welfare, Collier turned to teaching college. Later, she started writing, and in 1969, she received the Gwendolyn Brooks Award for Fiction from *Negro Digest* for her story "Marigolds."

**Publication** Soon after she received the award, anthologies and magazines began to carry Collier's work. Her stories attempt to convey something about the lives of a segment of society that Collier felt was not well represented in contemporary fiction. Along with her poems and articles, her stories have appeared in *Negro Digest*, *TV Guide*, *Black World*, the *New York Times*, and other journals.

# PREPARING to *Read*

## Simile
Poetry by
### N. SCOTT MOMADAY

## Moon Rondeau
Poetry by
### CARL SANDBURG

## Woman
Poetry by
### NIKKI GIOVANNI

*Mondrian Dancing* (1984–1985), Susan Rothenberg. Oil on canvas, 78¼″ × 91″. St. Louis (Missouri) Art Museum. Purchase: Funds given by the Shoenberg Foundation, Inc.

**Connect to Your Life**

**The Nature of Love** Poets often rely on nature to communicate their ideas about love. In Shakespeare's "Sonnet 18," for example, the speaker's beloved is compared to a summer's day. If a poet were to write about you, what aspect of nature might you be compared to? Write an impromptu poem that draws a comparison between you and an object or event in nature. Let your imagination run free.

## Build Background

**Nature's Gifts** The poet William Blake once expressed his desire "to see a World in a Grain of Sand / And a heaven in a Wild Flower." In the hands of poets, the objects of the natural world—plant, mineral, and animal—can take on a significance limited only by one's imagination. To a poet, a blade of grass, the smell of leaf mold, or the movement of deer may evoke original thought. Each of the following three poems makes use of objects in the natural world to explore the mysteries of romantic relationships.

## Focus Your Reading

**LITERARY ANALYSIS** **FIGURATIVE LANGUAGE** Words or phrases known as **figurative language** communicate ideas beyond the ordinary, literal meanings of the words. These lines from the poem "Woman" provide an example:

*she wanted to be a robin singing*
*through the leaves*

In all likelihood, the woman does not really want to be transformed into a bird, but this passage does tell you about her personality and her desires. As you read the poems that follow, look carefully at the use of figurative language.

**ACTIVE READING** **UNDERSTANDING COMPARISONS** Poets often make **comparisons** in order to convey meaning or emotion in fresh and interesting ways. In the poem "Moon Rondeau," the poet compares love with a door. Like a door, love can open the way to new experiences and new vistas.

**READER'S NOTEBOOK** As you read the following poems, look for comparisons. For each poem, create a chart like the one shown to track the comparisons that you find. First identify the two things being compared. Then jot down a few words or a phrase that describes the meaning or emotions that the comparison evokes.

| Item 1 | Item 2 | Suggested Meaning |
|--------|--------|-------------------|
| love | door | Love can open the way to new experiences. |

# Simile

## N. Scott Momaday

What did we say to each other
that now we are as the deer
who walk in single file
with heads high
5   with ears forward
with eyes watchful
with hooves always placed on
    firm ground
in whose limbs there is latent flight

**8 latent** (lāt'nt): present but not active; potential.

## Thinking Through the Literature

1. How would you describe the **mood,** or feeling, of this poem?

2. **ACTIVE READING** **UNDERSTANDING COMPARISONS** Review the chart that you completed in your  **READER'S NOTEBOOK** for this poem. What human emotions and experiences are evoked by comparing the two people to deer?

   **THINK ABOUT**
   - the relationship between the speaker and the person being addressed
   - the physical description of the deer
   - what is suggested by the first line of the poem

3. How do you think the **speaker** feels about the future of the relationship he is describing? Explain your opinion.

4. Is it possible for two people to remain close without sometimes quarreling? Share your opinions with classmates.

*Corn Maiden* (1982), David Dawangyumptewa. Photo Copyright © 1987 by Jerry Jacka.

*Mondrian Dancing* (1984–1985),
Susan Rothenberg. Oil on canvas,
78 ¼″ × 91″. St. Louis (Missouri)
Art Museum. Purchase: Funds given
by the Shoenberg Foundation, Inc.

# Moon
Rondeau

Carl
Sandburg

"Love is a door we shall open together."
So they told each other under the moon
One evening when the smell of leaf mould
And the beginnings of roses and potatoes
5    Came on a wind.

Late in the hours of that evening
They looked long at the moon and called it
A silver button, a copper coin, a bronze wafer,
A plaque of gold, a vanished diadem,
10   A brass hat dripping from deep waters.

        "People like us,
            us two,
        We own the moon."

**3 leaf mould:** a mixture of
decomposed leaves and other
organic material.

**9 diadem** (dī′ə-dĕm′): a crown.

## Thinking Through the Literature

1. **Comprehension Check** What happens in this poem?

2. **ACTIVE READING** **UNDERSTANDING COMPARISONS** Refer to the
chart you made for this poem in your **READER'S NOTEBOOK**.
In this poem, the two people in love compare the moon to six
different objects. What do these comparisons suggest about the
couple and their relationship?

3. How do you interpret the poem's last three lines, and how do
those lines help you to understand the rest of the poem?

# WOMAN

## Nikki Giovanni

she wanted to be a blade
of grass amid the fields
but he wouldn't agree
to be the dandelion

5 she wanted to be a robin singing
through the leaves
but he refused to be
her tree

she spun herself into a web
10 and      looking for a place to rest
turned to him
but he stood straight
declining to be her corner

she tried to be a book
15 but he wouldn't read

she turned herself into a bulb
but he wouldn't let her grow

she decided to become
a woman
20 and though he still refused
to be a man
she decided it was all
right

*White Breeze* (1995),
Jonathan Green.
Oil on canvas, 48″ × 60″.
Collection of Gilbert
and Elizabeth Ney.
Photograph by
Tim Stamm.

## Connect to the Literature

**1. What Do You Think?** What do you think of the woman in this poem?

> **Comprehension Check**
> • What happens each time the woman tries to forge a relationship with the man?
> • What does she decide in the end?

## Think Critically

**2.** **ACTIVE READING** **UNDERSTANDING COMPARISONS** After reviewing the chart that you completed in your 📖 **READER'S NOTEBOOK** for this poem, discuss what each of the comparisons suggests about the woman and her relationship with the man. Which comparison do you think is the most revealing?

**THINK ABOUT**

- what the woman ("she") wants from the man ("he")
- what the poem suggests about the man's personality
- what the woman learns from her experience
- the meaning of the poem's last **stanza**

**3.** Do you think this poem is mainly about love or about independence? Support your answer with evidence from the poem.

**4.** How do you think the woman now feels about her relationship with the man? Explain.

## Extend Interpretations

**5. Comparing Texts** In terms of **mood,** which of the two preceding poems, "Moon Rondeau" and "Simile," is most like "Woman"? Give details from the poems to support your answer.

**6. Comparing Texts** Which of the three poems makes the most effective use of **figurative language** drawn from nature? Support your answer with examples from the poems.

**7. Connect to Life** Of the three poems, which most nearly reflects your own attitude about love relationships? Explain your answer.

## Literary Analysis

**FIGURATIVE LANGUAGE** Poets use **figurative language** to convey ideas beyond the literal meanings of the words. When the couple in Sandburg's poem describes the moon as a "vanished diadem," the poet is not telling the reader that there is an actual crown in the sky, but suggesting that the moon is in its waning crescent stage. His use of this image lends the moon an elegance that it would not have, had he described it literally. Figurative language also includes specific **figures of speech,** such as **simile** and **metaphor.** A simile is a stated comparison using the words *like* or *as:* "now we are as the deer." A metaphor is an exaggerated comparison that does not use the words *like* or *as:* "Love is a door we shall open together."

**Activity** Identify other examples of similes and metaphors or other figurative language in the poems. Then choose one poem and think of new comparisons for an extension of that poem. Try to retain the spirit of the original poem.

**FREE VERSE** Poetry that does not contain regular patterns of **rhyme** and **meter** is known as **free verse.** The lines in free verse often flow more naturally than rhymed, metrical lines do. Therefore, they achieve a rhythm more like everyday human speech.

**Paired Activity** With a partner, take turns reading the three poems aloud. In what ways does each poem resemble everyday speech? Discuss your responses.

# Choices & CHALLENGES

## Writing Options

**1. His Poem** "Woman" is told from "her" point of view. How might "he" see the relationship? Write a poem modeled on "Woman," from the man's perspective. Place the entry in your **Working Portfolio.**

**2. Love Letter** Choose one of the three poems and write a letter from one character in the poem to the other. Think of what the poem tells you about the couple's relationship and use it as a basis for your letter.

## Activities & Explorations

**1. Poetic Pictures** Choose one poem and create an illustration or series of illustrations to convey an idea or emotion suggested by the poem. ~ **ART**

**2. Multimedia Presentation** Using a computer with appropriate software, create a multimedia presentation to accompany one of the poems. Use graphics, sound effects, and music to capture the mood and meaning of the poem.
~ **VIEWING AND REPRESENTING**

## Inquiry & Research

**Dictionary Explorations** Look up the **etymology,** or word origins, of *metaphor* and *simile.* How do the origins of these terms help you to understand and remember their meaning? Then look up the word *rondeau.* What do the different meanings suggest about the relationship between poetry and song?

## Art Connection

**She Wanted to Be** What connection do you see between the woman and the sky in this painting? In light of this connection, what similarity do you see between the painting and the poem "Woman"?

## N. Scott Momaday
1934–

**Other Works**
*The Way to Rainy Mountain
Angle of Geese and Other Poems
The Names: A Memoir*

**Inspired by Heritage** N. Scott Momaday's poetry and prose reflect his deeply felt love for his Kiowa Indian ancestry. His father, a member of the Kiowa tribe, was one of the finest Native American artists of his day; his mother was a writer and a teacher. When asked how his heritage affected his work, Momaday told an interviewer, "When I was growing up on the reservations of the Southwest, I saw people who were deeply involved in their traditional life, in the memories of their blood. They had, as far as I could see, a certain strength and beauty that I find missing in the modern world at large. I like to celebrate that involvement in my writing."

**Literary Achievement** Momaday has received a number of honors and awards for his writing, including the Pulitzer Prize for fiction in 1969 for his novel *House Made of Dawn.* Momaday has since published several books of poetry and fiction, as well as essays and articles on preserving the environment. Momaday says, "I sometimes think [writing] is a very lonely sort of work. But when you get into it, it can be exhilarating, tremendously fulfilling and stimulating."

## Author Activity

**Kiowa Values** How does Momaday's experiences growing up as a Kiowa resonate in his writing? Read some additional pieces of his writing and look for evidence of his Kiowa upbringing. Share your findings in class.

## Carl Sandburg
### 1878–1967

**Other Works**
*Selected Poems of Carl Sandburg*
*Honey and Salt*
*The American Songbag*
*Good Morning, America*
*Abraham Lincoln*

## Nikki Giovanni
### 1943–

**Other Works**
*Black Feeling, Black Talk/Black*
   *Judgement*
*Cotton Candy on a Rainy Day*
*Those Who Ride the Night Winds*
*Conversations with Nikki Giovanni*
*Truth Is on Its Way*

**Jack of All Trades** Sandburg was born in Galesburg, Illinois, to Swedish parents. He finished grammar school at age 13 and started driving a milk wagon. Over the coming years, he held a long series of jobs, among them harvesting ice, washing dishes, and working for a tinsmith. After serving in the Spanish-American War (April–August 1898), Sandburg attended Lombard College in Galesburg, where he captained the basketball team and edited the college newspaper. After college, he continued from job to job, with stints as a salesman, fireman, pamphleteer, and newspaperman.

**Rise to Fame** In 1914, Sandburg published a group of poems in *Poetry* magazine, and two years later, his first book of poems, *Chicago Poems*. With those two publications, Sandburg embarked on his path to widespread fame. Over the next 50 years, he wrote poetry, history, biography, and fiction; his biography of Abraham Lincoln is considered one of the great works of the 20th century. Sandburg had a deep, rich voice and traveled widely to read his poetry, sometimes accompanying himself on the guitar.

**The Good Life** Despite his fame, Sandburg continued to lead a modest life, wanting most "to be out of jail, . . . to eat regular, . . . to get what I write printed, . . . a little love at home, . . . [and] to sing every day." Sandburg won two Pulitzer Prizes, one in poetry and one in history.

## Author Activity

**What's Poetry?** In his book *Good Morning, America,* Sandburg provides 38 definitions of poetry. Look them up and discuss them with your class. How do they fit the poems you have read?

**Young Militant** Nikki Giovanni's maternal grandmother was one of the great inspirations of her life. She was outspoken and proud of her race, and Giovanni grew up to be like her grandmother. In college, she became an activist in the black political movements of the 1960s, and her first volumes of poems combine militant rage with skillful wordplay. These volumes established Giovanni as a leading voice among contemporary African-American poets. In the early 1970s, after the birth of her son Tommy, her work became more introspective, turning from the political to the personal. She began to concentrate and sharpen her powers as a poet, writing of themes such as family love, loneliness, and frustration. Black pride, however, continues to echo throughout her poetry.

**Storyteller** Another important aspect of Giovanni's poetry is its sound and rhythm. "I come from a long line of storytellers," she once said. Her grandfather was a Latin scholar and her mother a lover of literature; both loved telling stories. "I appreciated the quality and the rhythm of the telling of the stories," Giovanni said. It was important to her to use language in ways that could be spoken aloud. She has made numerous recordings of her poetry.

## Author Activity

**Spoken Verse** Locate a recording of Giovanni reading her own poetry. Listen to the rhythm and accents she gives her poems. Then select one poem and rehearse your own performance of it.

## The Importance of Comparison

Comparison is an important aspect of thinking. When you see how an object can be compared to other objects, your understanding of the object is enriched. Literature provides many examples of comparisons, or analogies; two are shown on the right.

Shakespeare could simply have said that his beloved was beautiful, and Sandburg could have described the moon as shiny and round. By using comparisons, however, they were able to make their descriptions more insightful and vivid.

> Shall I compare **thee** to a summer's day?
> Thou art more lovely and more temperate:
> —William Shakespeare, "Sonnet 18"
>
> Late in the hours of that evening
> They looked long at the **moon** and called it
> A silver button, a copper coin, a bronze wafer,
> A plaque of gold, a vanished diadem,
> A brass hat dripping from deep waters.
> —Carl Sandburg, "Moon Rondeau"

## Strategies for Building Vocabulary

Literature is not the only place where analogies can be found. They are also found in tests, in problems that ask you to identify similarities in the relationships expressed by pairs of words. Analogy problems are often stated like this:

CHRONIC : RECURRING :: (A) gymnast : agile, (B) irritation : fury, (C) gratitude : appreciation, (D) sporadic : ongoing

This problem may be restated as "*Chronic* is to *recurring* as \_\_\_?\_\_\_ is to \_\_\_?\_\_\_." To solve such a problem, use the following strategies.

❶ **Find the Relationship** Figure out the relationship expressed by the first two words before thinking about the analogy as a whole. In the example above, the capitalized words are synonyms, or words with like meanings. Therefore, you need to find a pair of synonyms among the choices. The correct answer is C—*gratitude* and *appreciation* are synonyms. The other pairs of words express different kinds of relationships.

Sometimes analogy problems are set up so that you need determine only the last word in each analogy, as in the following example:

MUSICIAN : HORN :: carpenter : _____
(A) house, (B) hammer, (C) carpentry, (D) music

❷ **Kinds of Analogies** The pairs of words in analogies can express a variety of kinds of relationships. The chart below shows several of the most common.

**EXERCISE** Complete each analogy by choosing a word from the following list. Identify the kind of relationship on which the analogy is based.

| | | |
|---|---|---|
| convalescence | medicine | diligence |
| irresistible | amateur | fruit |
| adamant | inevitability | diminished |

1. CONVICTION : BELIEF :: dedication : _____

2. PLACID : AGITATED :: professional : _____

3. TRANSCEND : TRANSCENDENCE :: convalesce : _____

4. OCCASIONAL : INTERMINABLE :: attractive : _____

5. RETRIEVER : DOG :: apple : _____

| Types of Relationships in Analogies | | |
|---|---|---|
| **Type** | **Example** | **Relationship** |
| Part to whole | BRANCH : TREE | is a part of |
| Synonyms | PLAUSIBLE : BELIEVABLE | means the same as |
| Antonyms | INDIFFERENCE : CONCERN | means the opposite of |
| Cause to effect | STARVATION : EMACIATION | results in or leads to |
| Object to purpose | LADDER : CLIMBING | is used for |
| Degree of intensity | TROTTING : GALLOPING | is less (or more) intense than |
| Grammar | INDIGNANT : INDIGNATION | is grammatically related to |
| Item to category | MARS : PLANET | is a type or example of |

# A Case of Cruelty

James Herriot felt very strong ties to animals of all kinds. For years he worked as a veterinarian, treating both pets and farm animals in a rural part of the English county of Yorkshire. Recognizing that his experiences might make for good reading, he eventually began to put them down on paper. Herriot won fame with a series of books about the veterinary practice he shared with his partner, Siegfried, in a village called Darrowby. "A Case of Cruelty," from that series, recounts an experience involving the "small animal" side of their practice.

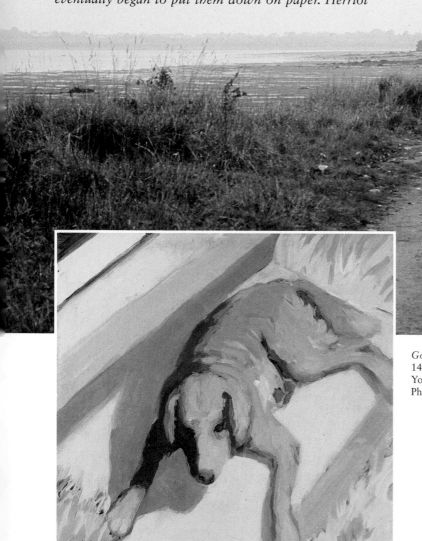

*Golden Retriever* (1972), Fairfield Porter. Oil on wood panel, 14⅛″ × 15⅛″, The Parrish Art Museum, Southampton, New York, gift of the Estate of Fairfield Porter (1980.10.124). Photo by Jim Strong, Inc.

# James Herriot

The silvery haired old gentleman with the pleasant face didn't look the type to be easily upset, but his eyes glared at me angrily, and his lips quivered with <u>indignation</u>.

"Mr. Herriot," he said. "I have come to make a complaint. I strongly object to your <u>callousness</u> in subjecting my dog to unnecessary suffering."

"Suffering? What suffering?" I was mystified.

"I think you know, Mr. Herriot. I brought my dog in a few days ago. He was very lame, and I am referring to your treatment on that occasion."

I nodded. "Yes, I remember it well . . . but where does the suffering come in?"

"Well, the poor animal is going around with his leg dangling, and I have it on good authority that the bone is fractured and should have been put in plaster immediately." The old gentleman stuck his chin out fiercely.

"All right, you can stop worrying," I said. "Your dog has a radial paralysis[1] caused by a blow on the ribs, and if you are patient and follow my treatment he'll gradually improve. In fact I think he'll recover completely."

"But he trails his leg when he walks."

"I know—that's typical, and to the layman it does give the appearance of a broken leg. But he shows no sign of pain, does he?"

---

1. **radial paralysis:** loss of movement in the lower part of the leg.

WORDS TO KNOW

**indignation** (ĭn′dĭg-nā′shən) *n.* anger aroused by something unjust, mean, or unworthy
**callousness** (kăl′əs-nĭs) *n.* emotional hardness; lack of feeling

"No, he seems quite happy, but this lady seemed to be absolutely sure of her facts. She was <u>adamant</u>."

"Lady?"

"Yes," said the old gentleman. "She is very clever with animals, and she came around to see if she could help in my dog's <u>convalescence</u>. She brought some excellent condition powders[2] with her."

"Ah!" A blinding shaft pierced the fog in my mind. All was suddenly clear. "It was Mrs. Donovan, wasn't it?"

"Well . . . er, yes. That was her name."

Old Mrs. Donovan was a woman who really got around. No matter what was going on in Darrowby—weddings, funerals, house-sales— you'd find the dumpy little figure and walnut face among the spectators, the darting, black-button eyes taking everything in. And always, on the end of its lead, her terrier dog.

When I say "old," I'm only guessing, because she appeared ageless; she seemed to have been around a long time, but she could have been anything between fifty-five and seventy-five. She certainly had the vitality of a young woman because she must have walked vast distances in her dedicated quest to keep abreast of events. Many people took an uncharitable view of her acute curiosity, but whatever the motivation, her activities took her into almost every channel of life in the town. One of these channels was our veterinary practice.

Because Mrs. Donovan, among her other widely ranging interests, was an animal doctor. In fact I think it would be safe to say that this facet of her life <u>transcended</u> all the others.

She could talk at length on the ailments of small animals, and she had a whole armory of medicines and remedies at her command, her two specialities being her miracle-working con-

## She could talk at length on the ailments of small animals.

dition powders and a dog shampoo of unprecedented value for improving the coat. She had an uncanny ability to sniff out a sick animal, and it was not uncommon when I was on my rounds to find Mrs. Donovan's dark, gypsy face poised intently over what I had thought was my patient, while she administered calf's foot jelly[3] or one of her own patent nostrums.[4]

I suffered more than Siegfried because I took a more active part in the small animal side of our practice. I was anxious to develop this aspect and to improve my image in this field, and Mrs. Donovan didn't help at all. "Young Mr. Herriot," she would confide to my clients, "is all right with cattle and such like, but he don't know nothing about dogs and cats."

And of course they believed her and had implicit faith in her. She had the irresistible <u>mystic</u> appeal of the amateur, and on top of that there was her habit, particularly endearing in Darrowby, of never charging for her advice, her medicines, her long periods of diligent nursing.

Older folk in the town told how her husband, an Irish farm worker, had died many years ago and

---

2. **condition powders:** medicines for keeping an animal in good condition.

3. **calf's foot jelly:** meat gelatin made by boiling calves' feet; an old-fashioned, nutritious remedy.

4. **patent nostrums** (păt′nt nŏs′trəmz): nonprescription medicines whose effectiveness has not been proven scientifically; quack remedies.

---

WORDS
TO
KNOW

**adamant** (ăd′ə-mənt) *adj.* remaining firm despite the pleas or reasoning of others; stubbornly unyielding
**convalescence** (kŏn′və-lĕs′əns) *n.* the gradual return to health and strength after an illness or an injury
**transcend** (trăn-sĕnd′) *v.* to move above and beyond; to be greater than
**mystic** (mĭs′tĭk) *adj.* showing supernatural powers; spiritual; inspiring mystery or wonder

how he must have had a "bit put away" because Mrs. Donovan had apparently been able to indulge all her interests over the years without financial strain. Since she inhabited the streets of Darrowby all day and every day, I often encountered her, and she always smiled up at me sweetly and told me how she had been sitting up all night with Mrs. So-and-so's dog that I'd been treating. She felt sure she'd be able to pull it through.

There was no smile on her face, however, on the day when she rushed into the surgery[5] while Siegfried and I were having tea.

"Mr. Herriot!" she gasped. "Can you come? My little dog's been run over!"

I jumped up and ran out to the car with her. She sat in the passenger seat with her head bowed, her hands clasped tightly on her knees.

"He slipped his collar and ran in front of a car," she murmured. "He's lying in front of the school half way up Cliffend Road. Please hurry."

I was there within three minutes, but as I bent over the dusty little body stretched on the pavement, I knew there was nothing I could do. The fast-glazing eyes, the faint, gasping respirations, the ghastly pallor of the mucous membranes[6] all told the same story.

"I'll take him back to the surgery and get some saline[7] into him, Mrs. Donovan," I said. "But I'm afraid he's had a massive internal hemorrhage.[8] Did you see what happened exactly?"

She gulped. "Yes, the wheel went right over him."

Ruptured liver, for sure. I passed my hands under the little animal and began to lift him gently, but as I did so, the breathing stopped, and the eyes stared fixedly ahead.

Mrs. Donovan sank to her knees, and for a few moments she gently stroked the rough hair of the head and chest. "He's dead, isn't he?" she whispered at last.

"I'm afraid he is," I said.

She got slowly to her feet and stood bewilderedly among the little group of bystanders on the pavement. Her lips moved, but she seemed unable to say any more.

I took her arm, led her over to the car and opened the door. "Get in and sit down," I said. "I'll run you home. Leave everything to me."

I wrapped the dog in my calving overall[9] and laid him in the boot[10] before driving away. It wasn't until we drew up outside Mrs. Donovan's house that she began to weep silently. I sat there without speaking till she finished. Then she wiped her eyes and turned to me.

"Do you think he suffered at all?"

"I'm certain he didn't. It was all so quick—he wouldn't know a thing about it."

She tried to smile. "Poor little Rex, I don't know what I'm going to do without him. We've traveled a few miles together, you know."

"Yes, you have. He had a wonderful life, Mrs. Donovan. And let me give you a bit of advice—you must get another dog. You'd be lost without one."

She shook her head. "No, I couldn't. That little dog meant too much to me. I couldn't let another take his place."

"Well I know that's how you feel just now, but I wish you'd think about it. I don't want to seem callous—I tell everybody this when they lose an animal, and I know it's good advice."

"Mr. Herriot, I'll never have another one." She shook her head again, very decisively. "Rex was my faithful friend for many years, and I just want to remember him. He's the last dog I'll ever have."

---

5. **surgery:** in Britain, a general term for a physician's or veterinarian's office.

6. **mucous membranes:** thin layers of tissue lining the nose, mouth, and other body passages.

7. **saline** (sā'lēn'): a salt solution used to stem the effects of blood loss.

8. **internal hemorrhage** (hĕm'ər-ĭj): excessive bleeding inside the body.

9. **calving overall:** a special heavy overall worn by the veterinarian assisting in the birth of a calf.

10. **boot:** British term for the trunk of a car.

I often saw Mrs. Donovan around the town after this, and I was glad to see she was still as active as ever, though she looked strangely incomplete without the little dog on its lead. But it must have been over a month before I had the chance to speak to her.

It was on the afternoon that Inspector Halliday of the R.S.P.C.A.[11] rang me.

"Mr. Herriot," he said. "I'd like you to come and see an animal with me. A cruelty case."

"Right, what is it?"

"A dog, and it's pretty grim. A dreadful case of neglect." He gave me the name of a row of old brick cottages down by the river and said he'd meet me there.

Halliday was waiting for me, smart and business-like in his dark uniform, as I pulled up in the back lane behind the houses. He was a big, blond man with cheerful blue eyes, but he didn't smile as he came over to the car.

"He's in here," he said and led the way towards one of the doors in the long, crumbling wall. A few curious people were hanging around, and with a feeling of inevitability I recognized a gnome-like brown face. Trust Mrs. Donovan, I thought, to be among those present at a time like this.

We went through the door into the long garden. I had found that even the lowliest dwellings in Darrowby had long strips of land at the back as though the builders had taken it for granted that the country people who were going to live in them would want to occupy themselves with the pursuits of the soil; with vegetable and fruit growing, even stock keeping[12] in a small way. You usually found a pig there, a few hens, often pretty beds of flowers.

But this garden was a wilderness. A chilling air of desolation hung over the few gnarled apple and plum trees standing among a tangle of <u>rank</u> grass as though the place had been forsaken by all living creatures.

Halliday went over to a ramshackle wooden shed with peeling paint and a rusted corrugated iron roof. He produced a key, unlocked the padlock and dragged the door partly open. There was no window, and it wasn't easy to identify the jumble inside; broken gardening tools, an ancient mangle, rows of flower pots and partly used paint tins.[13] And right at the back, a dog sitting quietly.

I didn't notice him immediately because of the gloom and because the smell in the shed started me coughing, but as I drew closer, I saw that he was a big animal, sitting very upright, his collar secured by a chain to a ring in the wall. I had seen some thin dogs, but this advanced emaciation reminded me of my textbooks on anatomy; nowhere else did the bones of pelvis, face and rib cage stand out with such horrifying clarity. A deep, smoothed out hollow in the earth floor showed where he had lain, moved about, in fact lived, for a very long time.

The sight of the animal had a stupefying effect on me; I only half took in the rest of the scene— the filthy shreds of sacking scattered nearby, the bowl of scummy water.

"Look at his back end," Halliday muttered.

I carefully raised the dog from his sitting position and realized that the stench in the place was not entirely due to the piles of excrement. The hindquarters were a welter of pressure sores which had turned gangrenous,[14] and strips of sloughing tissue[15] hung down from them. There were similar sores along the sternum[16] and ribs. The coat, which seemed to be a dull yellow, was matted and caked with dirt.

---

11. **R.S.P.C.A.:** the Royal Society for the Prevention of Cruelty to Animals.

12. **stock keeping:** keeping farm animals.

13. **tins:** British term for cans.

14. **gangrenous** (găng′grə-nəs): infected with gangrene, which is the death or decay of body tissue due to loss of blood supply.

15. **sloughing** (slŭf′ĭng) **tissue:** dead body tissue separating from the surrounding living tissue.

16. **sternum:** the breastbone, from which the ribs branch off.

*Old Farmhouse* (1872), Edward Henry Fahey, RI. Watercolor and bodycolor, heightened with gum arabic, 13¾″ × 9¾″, Anthony Reed Gallery, London.

Just an occasional whimper perhaps as he sat interminably in the empty blackness which had been his world and at times wondered what it was all about.

"Well, Inspector, I hope you're going to throw the book at whoever's responsible," I said. Halliday grunted. "Oh, there won't be much done. It's a case of diminished responsibility. The owner's definitely simple. Lives with an aged mother who hardly knows what's going on either. I've seen the fellow, and it seems he threw in a bit of food when he felt like it, and that's about all he did. They'll fine him and stop him keeping an animal in the future but nothing more than that."

"I see." I reached out and stroked the dog's head, and he immediately responded by resting a paw on my wrist. There was a pathetic dignity about the way he held himself erect, the calm eyes regarding me, friendly and unafraid. "Well, you'll let me know if you want me in court."

"Of course, and thank you for coming along." Halliday hesitated for a moment. "And now I expect you'll want to put this poor thing out of his misery right away."

I continued to run my hand over the head and ears while I thought for a moment. "Yes . . . yes, I suppose so. We'd never find a home for him in this state. It's the kindest thing to do. Anyway, push the door wide open will you so that I can get a proper look at him."

In the improved light I examined him more thoroughly. Perfect teeth, well-proportioned limbs with a fringe of yellow hair. I put my stethoscope on his chest, and as I listened to the slow, strong thudding of the heart, the dog again put his paw on my hand.

I turned to Halliday, "You know, Inspector,

The inspector spoke again. "I don't think he's ever been out of here. He's only a young dog—about a year old—but I understand he's been in this shed since he was an eight-week-old pup. Somebody out in the lane heard a whimper, or he'd never have been found."

I felt a tightening of the throat and a sudden nausea which wasn't due to the smell. It was the thought of this patient animal sitting starved and forgotten in the darkness and filth for a year. I looked again at the dog and saw in his eyes only a calm trust. Some dogs would have barked their heads off and soon been discovered, some would have become terrified and vicious, but this was one of the totally undemanding kind, the kind which had complete faith in people and accepted all their actions without complaint.

inside this bag of bones there's a lovely healthy golden retriever. I wish there was some way of letting him out."

As I spoke, I noticed there was more than one figure in the door opening. A pair of black pebble eyes were peering intently at the big dog from behind the inspector's broad back. The other spectators had remained in the lane, but Mrs. Donovan's curiosity had been too much for her. I continued conversationally as though I hadn't seen her.

"You know, what this dog needs first of all is a good shampoo to clean up his matted coat."

"Huh?" said Halliday.

"Yes. And then he wants a long course of some really strong condition powders."

"What's that?" The inspector looked startled.

"There's no doubt about it," I said. "It's the only hope for him, but where are you going to find such things? Really powerful enough, I mean." I sighed and straightened up. "Ah well, I suppose there's nothing else for it. I'd better put him to sleep right away. I'll get the things from my car."

When I got back to the shed, Mrs. Donovan was already inside examining the dog despite the feeble remonstrances[17] of the big man.

"Look!" she said excitedly, pointing to a name roughly scratched on the collar. "His name's Roy." She smiled up at me. "It's a bit like Rex, isn't it, that name?"

"You know, Mrs. Donovan, now you mention it, it is. It's very like Rex, the way it comes off your tongue." I nodded seriously.

She stood silent for a few moments, obviously in the grip of a deep emotion, then she burst out.

"Can I have 'im? I can make him better, I know I can. Please, please let me have 'im!"

"Well I don't know," I said. "It's really up to the inspector. You'll have to get his permission."

Halliday looked at her in bewilderment, then he said: "Excuse me, Madam," and drew me to one side. We walked a few yards through the long grass and stopped under a tree.

"Mr. Herriot," he whispered, "I don't know what's going on here, but I can't just pass over an animal in this condition to anybody who has a casual whim. The poor beggar's had one bad break already—I think it's enough. This woman doesn't look a suitable person . . ."

I held up a hand. "Believe me, Inspector, you've nothing to worry about. She's a funny old stick, but she's been sent from heaven today. If anybody in Darrowby can give this dog a new life it's her."

Halliday still looked very doubtful. "But I still don't get it. What was all that stuff about him needing shampoos and condition powders?"

"Oh never mind about that. I'll tell you some other time. What he needs is lots of good grub, care and affection, and that's just what he'll get. You can take my word for it."

"All right, you seem very sure." Halliday looked at me for a second or two then turned and walked over to the eager little figure by the shed.

I had never before been deliberately on the lookout for Mrs. Donovan: she had just cropped up wherever I happened to be, but now I scanned the streets of Darrowby anxiously day by day without sighting her. I didn't like it when Gobber Newhouse got drunk and drove his bicycle determinedly through a barrier into a ten-foot hole where they were laying the new sewer and Mrs. Donovan was not in evidence among the happy crowd who watched the council workmen[18] and two policemen trying to get him out; and when she was nowhere to be seen when they had to fetch the fire engine to

---

17. **remonstrances** (rĭ-môn′strəns-ĭz): protests; complaints; objections.

18. **council workmen:** construction workers for the local government, here putting in the new sewer.

the fish and chip shop the night the fat burst into flames, I became seriously worried.

Maybe I should have called round to see how she was getting on with that dog. Certainly I had trimmed off the necrotic tissue[19] and dressed the sores before she took him away, but perhaps he needed something more than that. And yet at the time I had felt a strong conviction that the main thing was to get him out of there and clean him and feed him, and nature would do the rest. And I had a lot of faith in Mrs. Donovan—far more than she had in me—when it came to animal doctoring; it was hard to believe I'd been completely wrong.

It must have been nearly three weeks, and I was on the point of calling at her home, when I noticed her stumping briskly along the far side of the market place, peering closely into every shop window exactly as before. The only difference was that she had a big yellow dog on the end of the lead.

I turned the wheel and sent my car bumping over the cobbles till I was abreast of her. When she saw me getting out, she stopped and smiled impishly, but she didn't speak as I bent over Roy and examined him. He was still a skinny dog, but he looked bright and happy, his wounds were healthy and granulating[20] and there was not a speck of dirt in his coat or on his skin. I knew then what Mrs. Donovan had been doing all this time; she had been washing and combing and teasing at that filthy tangle till she had finally conquered it.

As I straightened up, she seized my wrist in a grip of surprising strength and looked up into my eyes.

"Now, Mr. Herriot," she said. "Haven't I made a difference to this dog!"

"You've done wonders, Mrs. Donovan," I said. "And you've been at him with that marvelous shampoo of yours, haven't you?"

She giggled and walked away, and from that

# I had a lot of faith in Mrs. Donovan—far more than she had in me.

~

day I saw the two of them frequently but at a distance, and something like two months went by before I had a chance to talk to her again. She was passing by the surgery as I was coming down the steps, and again she grabbed my wrist.

"Mr. Herriot," she said, just as she had done before. "Haven't I made a difference to this dog!"

I looked down at Roy with something akin to awe. He had grown and filled out, and his coat, no longer yellow but a rich gold, lay in luxuriant shining swathes over the well-fleshed ribs and back. A new, brightly studded collar glittered on his neck, and his tail, beautifully fringed, fanned the air gently. He was now a golden retriever in full magnificence. As I stared at him, he reared up, plunked his forepaws on my chest and looked into my face, and in his eyes I read plainly the same calm affection and trust I had seen in that black, noisome[21] shed.

"Mrs. Donovan," I said softly, "he's the most beautiful dog in Yorkshire." Then, because I knew she was waiting for it. "It's those wonderful condition powders. Whatever do you put in them?"

"Ah, wouldn't you like to know!" She bridled[22] and smiled up at me <u>coquettishly</u> and indeed she was nearer being kissed at that moment than for many years.

---

19. **necrotic tissue:** tissue in which the cells have died through injury or disease.
20. **granulating:** healing by forming fleshy new growth and tiny new blood vessels.
21. **noisome** (noi′səm): foul; disgusting.
22. **bridled:** lifted the head and drew in the chin, like a horse restrained by its bridle.

*Portrait of Fridel Battenberg* (1920), Max Beckmann. Oil on canvas, 97 cm × 48.5 cm, Kunstmuseum Hannover (Germany) mit Sammlung Sprengel. Copyright © 1996 Artists Rights Society (ARS), New York/VG Bild-Kunst, Bonn, Germany.

I suppose you could say that that was the start of Roy's second life. And as the years passed, I often pondered on the beneficent providence which had decreed that an animal which had spent his first twelve months abandoned and unwanted, staring uncomprehendingly into that unchanging, stinking darkness, should be whisked in a moment into an existence of light and movement and love. Because I don't think any dog had it quite so good as Roy from then on.

His diet changed dramatically from odd bread crusts to best stewing steak and biscuit, meaty bones and a bowl of warm milk every evening. And he never missed a thing. Garden fêtes,[23] school sports, evictions, gymkhanas[24]—he'd be there. I was pleased to note that as time went on, Mrs. Donovan seemed to be clocking up an even greater daily mileage. Her expenditure on shoe leather must have been phenomenal, but of course it was absolute pie[25] for Roy—a busy round in the morning, home for a meal then straight out again; it was all go.

Mrs. Donovan didn't confine her activities to the town center; there was a big stretch of common land down by the river where there were seats, and people used to take their dogs for a gallop, and she liked to get down there fairly regularly to check on the latest developments on the domestic scene. I often saw Roy loping majestically over the grass among a pack of assorted canines, and when he wasn't doing that, he was submitting to being stroked or patted or generally fussed over. He was handsome, and he just liked people; it made him irresistible.

It was common knowledge that his mistress had bought a whole selection of brushes and combs of various sizes with which she labored over his coat.

---

23. **fêtes** (fāts): outdoor parties; festivals.
24. **gymkhanas** (jĭm-kä′nəz): sporting events in which gymnastics, horse-jumping, or other contests are held.
25. **pie:** slang for something highly desirable; a treat.

Some people said she had a little brush for his teeth, too, and it might have been true, but he certainly wouldn't need his nails clipped—his life on the roads would keep them down.

Mrs. Donovan, too, had her reward; she had a faithful companion by her side every hour of the day and night. But there was more to it than that; she had always had the compulsion to help and heal animals, and the salvation of Roy was the high point of her life—a blazing triumph which never dimmed.

I know the memory of it was always fresh because many years later I was sitting on the sidelines at a cricket match, and I saw the two of them; the old lady glancing keenly around her, Roy gazing <u>placidly</u> out at the field of play,

apparently enjoying every ball. At the end of the match I watched them move away with the dispersing crowd; Roy would be about twelve then, and heaven only knows how old Mrs. Donovan must have been, but the big golden animal was trotting along effortlessly, and his mistress, a little more bent perhaps and her head rather nearer the ground, was going very well.

When she saw me, she came over, and I felt the familiar tight grip on my wrist.

"Mr. Herriot," she said, and in the dark probing eyes the pride was still as warm, the triumph still as bursting new as if it had all happened yesterday.

"Mr. Herriot, haven't I made a difference to this dog!" ❖

# James Herriot
## 1916–1995

**Other Works**
*All Things Wise and Wonderful*
*The Lord God Made Them All*
*Every Living Thing*

**First Career** James Herriot, whose real name was James Alfred Wight, was only 13 when he decided to become a vet. After training in Scotland, he settled in England and in 1938 began working in Yorkshire. "The life of a country vet was dirty, uncomfortable, sometimes dangerous," he once told an interviewer. "It was terribly hard work and I loved it."

**Rising to the Challenge** For over 25 years Herriot kept coming home from work and telling his wife about interesting on-the-job experiences, always promising to write a book about them. One day she finally challenged him, observing that vets of 50 do not write first books. "Well, that did it," Herriot later explained. "I stormed out and bought some paper and taught myself to type." The result

was *If Only They Could Talk,* published in England in 1970 and followed two years later by *It Shouldn't Happen to a Vet.* For his first American edition Herriot joined the two books together under the title *All Creatures Great and Small* (1972), and the new version became a bestseller. Three similar books followed.

## Author Activity

**Quite a Character** Herriot's books are filled with colorful characters such as Mrs. Donovan. Find one of his books and read a chapter or two. Then write a short description of the characters you encounter and share it with your class.

## Inquiry & Research

Research reported cases of cruelty to animals.

**Real World Link**
Begin your research by reading the magazine article on page 276.

**WORDS TO KNOW**  **placidly** (plăs′ĭd-lē) *adv.* in an undisturbed manner; quietly; calmly

# Eight Puppies

GABRIELA MISTRAL

Between the thirteenth and the
    fifteenth day
the puppies opened their eyes.
Suddenly they saw the world,
anxious with terror and joy.
5  They saw the belly of their mother,
saw the door of their house,
saw a deluge of light,
saw flowering azaleas.

They saw more, they saw all,
10  the red, the black, the ash.
Scrambling up, pawing and clawing
more lively than squirrels,
they saw the eyes of their mother,
heard my rasping cry and my laugh.

15  And I wished I were born with them.
Could it not be so another time?
To leap from a clump of banana
    plants
one morning of wonders—
a dog, a coyote, a deer;
20  to gaze with wide pupils,
to run, to stop, to run, to fall,
to whimper and whine and jump with
    joy,
riddled with sun and with barking,
a hallowed child of God, his secret,
    divine servant.

*Translated by Doris Dana*

# Ocho Perritos

GABRIELA MISTRAL

Los perrillos abrieron sus ojos
del treceavo al quinceavo día.
De golpe vieron el mundo,
con ansia, susto y alegría.
5  Vieron el vientre de la madre,
la puerta suya que es la mía,
el diluvio de la luz,
las azaleas floridas.

Vieron más: se vieron todos,
10  el rojo, el negro, el ceniza,
gateando y aupándose,
más vivos que las ardillas;
vieron los ojos de la madre
y mi grito rasgado, y mi risa.

15  Y yo querría nacer con ellos.
¿Por qué otra vez no sería?
Saltar de unos bananales
una mañana de maravilla,
en can, en coyota, en venada;
20  mirar con grandes pupilas,
correr, parar, correr, tumbarme
y gemir y saltar de alegría,
acribillada de sol y ladridos
hija de Dios, sierva oscura y divina.

*Still Life with Three Puppies* (1888), Paul Gauguin. Oil on wood, 36⅛″ × 24⅝″,
The Museum of Modern Art, New York, Mrs. Simon Guggenheim Fund.
Photo Copyright © 1995 The Museum of Modern Art, New York.

# AN ANGRY PUBLIC BACKS CHAMP

**❶** Every dog has his day, and Champ finally is going to have a nice one. As a result, thousands of dog lovers can breathe a bit easier; the 18-month-old German shepherd mix won't be going home to Kevin Deschene, the owner who beat him and stomped him.

**❷** Champ's plight became known after Jim Molloy, 31, Deschene's next-door neighbor in Lowell, Mass., took a series of photographs in November of Deschene savagely abusing the dog. The pictures helped convict Deschene, 19, of animal cruelty, for which he was sentenced to six months in jail and fined $500.

But Deschene's family, insisting that Kevin had done no wrong, promised a court battle to regain custody of the dog from the Lowell Humane Society. Outraged animal lovers, all with a higher opinion of the dog than of Kevin, rebelled, deluging the Humane Society with 3,700 letters and submitting petitions bearing 21,000 signatures demanding that Champ be protected. Hundreds of the letter writers—some of them offering to pay long-distance shipping charges—wanted to adopt Champ themselves.

Allan Davidson, executive director of the Lowell Humane Society, showed up for a May 4 hearing in Lowell District Court with the letters and petitions—but without Champ. "I put the dog in a safe house, sort of a witness protection program," Davidson said. "I would have faced contempt charges rather than turn the dog over."

As it turned out, Davidson's precautions were unnecessary. At the last minute, the Deschenes decided not to contest custody of Champ. The family, it seemed, had more pressing legal matters to attend to. On the day of the hearing, Barbara Deschene, Kevin's mother, was arrested for alleged welfare fraud, and his sister Kim, 22, was charged with intimidating witness Molloy by shouting obscenities and throwing eggs at his home.

In the meantime, Davidson has picked out a new home for Champ, about 30 miles from Lowell. Since the dog still harbors ill will toward men, Davidson says he will be living in "a female-only household, where there are four cats, some horses, another dog, and 18 acres of land."

Kevin, now serving his time in a less hospitable environment—a House of Correction—will not be as fortunate.

How would you react if you witnessed an unjust action taking place, such as someone abusing an animal? In this feature article, a witness decides to take action to save an animal—and goes above and beyond the expected response.

**READING A FEATURE ARTICLE**
Feature articles usually involve the direct presentation of facts with limited analysis or interpretation. In addition to informing readers, features should also be engaging.

**YOUR TURN** Use the questions and activities below to help you read the feature article.

**❶ Summarizing Main Ideas**
Feature articles often begin by summarizing the main idea. What key information does the first paragraph contain?

**❷** An effective news article usually deals with the "five W's"—*who, what, where, when,* and *why* (and sometimes *how*). Additionally, facts, descriptions, quotations, and other details draw readers into the human side of events. For example, the detail that the event occurred in Lowell, Massachusetts, is the *where* of the account. Identify the other W's throughout the article.

## Inquiry & Research
**Activity Link: "A Case of Cruelty," p. 273**

How does your community deal with abused animals? How does it treat animal abusers? Discuss these questions with your classmates, and compare the information you gather with that given in the article.

# *Writing* Workshop

## Expressing your ideas and feelings in verse . . .

**From Reading to Writing** People have many mistaken ideas about what **poetry** should look and sound like. A poem is not just a jingle or a simple rhyme. It can take any form and may be written on any subject. Some poems, like D. H. Lawrence's "Piano," capture an experience and tell a brief story. Others make surprise observations. Poems often present small scenes that take place in memory or imagination or in the world. In writing a poem, poets condense an experience into well-chosen sensory words that embody the meaning of the experience and make it come alive for readers.

### For Your Portfolio

**WRITING PROMPT** Write a poem that describes an experience, an idea, a place, a person, or a feeling.

**Purpose:** To express yourself
**Audience:** Your classmates, friends, or family

---

## Basics in a Box

### Poetry at a Glance

rhythm

sensory words

rhyme

mood

figurative language

sound devices

free verse

stanzas

### RUBRIC Standards for Writing

**A successful poem should**

• focus on a single experience, idea, or feeling

• use precise, sensory words in a fresh, interesting way

• incorporate figurative language such as similes and metaphors

• include sound devices as appropriate, such as alliteration, assonance, and rhyme to support the affect and meaning of the poem

# Analyzing Student Models

## Sheila Schmitt
## Litchfield High School

### Through Whispers in the Wind

Out the door
with the wind whispering
in my ear,
for the first time
in love

**RUBRIC**
IN ACTION

❶ Uses alliteration to help re-create the sound of the wind

❷ Offers a fresh, vivid image of love as a door opening

## Nathan Fellman
## Kent School

### Perspective

It was our place in the springtime
behind the old auction house.
We'd sit on the back steps
leading to the French doors
and rest ourselves against the wall.
Chipped paint, blue-gray with age,
broken glass from little boys' games,
and the broken gutters hanging uselessly.
We used to climb those gutters
to watch the tall grass field.
The wind made it crawl
like a caterpillar going nowhere.
Tracks in the distance
created a border for the field,
but no train would ever
disturb the peace in that place.
Hours we'd sit
amused by the waves of the field
that rolled off over the tracks.
When we sat too long,
a rooster reminded us of our intrusion,
but no one else bothered to care.
The air was too sweet to leave.

❶ This writer creates a sense of unity by not dividing his poem into stanzas.
**Other Options:**
• Create separate stanzas.
• Use a rhyme scheme.

❷ Uses an unexpected, concrete simile to express the sense of wind in the grass

**Mara Noëlle Scanlon**
**Greensburg Central Catholic High School**

### In the Steel City

Pap-pap had the greenest thumb
in all the North Hills
of Pittsburgh, though
anything green was admired
there. A gray man
in a gray city, he once
spit melon seeds
from his kitchen window
and grew three juicy
beauties. Tiny roses
climbed around the patio
and a patch of gold and fuchsia
waved wildly on the lawn.
A plumber at fourteen,
he knew the city's slimy depths
and said the world was full
of jackasses, but he coddled
his mums like newborn lambs
and knelt to breathe
the wet black earth.

When the city steps became
impossible, Pap-pap
packed up Grandma
and their green brocade sofa,
settling with his battered pipe
and history books in his
brown corduroy armchair. He'd left
his heart buried in the strawberry bed,
waiting for spring in strangers'
young hands. There was
no plot of begonias
in the russet-hued apartment,
packed with modern conveniences;
he wilted, sick and finally old.

Father's Day brought
pots of purple daisies
and a balcony window box
where tomatoes formed
on splintered wooden rods.
Listless hands grew dirty again;
Pap-pap thrived
in the warm summer rain.

**❶** Draws the reader into the poem by using simple, direct language

**❷** Uses repetition and assonance to create a contrast

**❸** Breaks lines within sentences for emphasis

**❹** Creates a vivid image with a striking simile

**❺** Includes precise, sensory words

**❻** Uses a well-chosen metaphor

**❼** Chooses words carefully *(wilted)* to draw a parallel between Pap-pap and his plants

**1. Your Working Portfolio**
Look for ideas in the **Writing Options** you completed earlier in this unit:

• **Childhood Poem**, p. 232

• **Not-love Poem**, p. 237

• **Family Poem**, p. 253

• **His Poem**, p. 261

**2. And Then She Said . . .**
Listen carefully to people's conversations at school, at home, and in the streets. Choose a line of dialogue as the basis for your poem.

**3. Borrowed Beginning**
Choose a line from a poem, book, or movie that you like. Use it as the first line of your own poem

# Writing Your Poem

## ❶ Prewriting

*Anything is good material for poetry. Anything.*
**William Carlos Williams, American poet**

Poems often grow out of a word or phrase that captures the writer's imagination because of its sound, rhythm, or meaning. Try just sitting quietly and letting feelings, memories, and words run through your mind. **Jot down** words and ideas that interest you, specifically those that describe sounds, sights, tastes, smells, and feelings. See the **Idea Bank** in the margin for more suggestions. After you choose a topic for your poem, follow the steps below.

### Planning Your Poem

▶ **1. Freewrite about your topic.** Read over the notes you made in searching for a topic. Circle interesting words, images, and details. Make a web to explore your associations with those details, or begin a new freewrite. Which details do you want to include in your poem?

▶ **2. Identify the mood you want to express.** Examine your feelings about the topic: Do you feel happy, sad, thoughtful, amused, angry? Focus on creating additional images and details that reinforce that mood.

▶ **3. Choose a starting point.** Which word, line, or image draws you most strongly? Which seems to lead to other interesting images and ideas? Look for one powerful line that can be the focus of your poem.

## ❷ Drafting

Play with ideas and words that come to mind as you think about your topic. Let your language flow freely. Read your writing aloud and listen to the sounds and rhythms of your words. Explore sound devices such as **alliteration** (life-long), **assonance** (greedy schemer), and **rhyme** (stay away). Also try using **figurative language—simile, metaphor, and personification**—comparisons that help readers see your subject in a new way.

Also consider the overall **mood** of your poem. Choose words whose positive or negative **connotations** emphasize that mood. For example, you might use the word *cabin* to create one kind of mood and the word *shack* to create another. Experiment with different structures, too. Rhythm, rhyme, and stanza breaks can give your poem a more formal feel.

Read your draft aloud to yourself and listen to the words you have written. Think about how you might begin to shape the poem by changing words, line breaks, and punctuation.

### Ask Your Peer Reader

• What is the overall mood of my poem?

• Which images appeal to you the most? Why?

## ❸ Revising

**TARGET SKILL ▶ ADDING DETAIL**  The success of a poem depends largely on the clarity and concreteness of the picture it paints. Add precise, concrete details to make your poem an experience for all the senses.

> *blue-gray with age,*
> Chipped paint, broken glass
>                       ^
>
> from little boys' games,
>
> and the gutters hanging uselessly.
>
> We used to climb those gutters
>           *tall grass*
> to watch the field.
>           ^        *crawl*
> The wind made it ~~look as~~
> *like a caterpillar going nowhere*
> ~~though it were crawling.~~
> ^

**Need revising help?**

Review the **Rubric**, p. 277

Consider **peer reader** comments

Check **Revision Guidelines**, p. 1145

## ❹ Editing and Proofreading

**TARGET SKILL ▶ USING PUNCTUATION**  In a poem, a sentence may end in the middle of a line or may extend for several lines. Use the standard rules for punctuating sentences to make sure your lines are not misread.

> Pap-pap had the greenest thumb
>
> in all the North Hills
>
> of Pittsburgh though
>                    ^
> anything green was admired
>
> there a gray man
>      ⊙̲=
> in a gray city he once
>              ^
> spit melon seeds
>
> from his kitchen window . . .

**Puzzled by punctuating poetry?**

See the **Grammar Handbook**, pp. 1203–1204

**Publishing IDEAS**

- Publish your poem in your school literary magazine.
- Read your poem aloud at a class poetry circle. Record the readings on videotape or audiotape.

**More Online: Publishing Options** www.mcdougallittell.com

## ❺ Reflecting

**FOR YOUR WORKING PORTFOLIO**  What did you discover about your feelings or your topic while writing your poem? What techniques would you like to try in your next poem? Attach your answer to your poem. Save your poem in your **Working Portfolio.**

Read this opening from the first draft of a student essay. The underlined sections may include the following kinds of errors:

- **sentence fragments**
- **comma errors**
- **lack of parallel structure**
- **lack of subject-verb agreement**

For each underlined section, choose the revision that most improves the writing.

> My friend Charles and I <u>publish</u> a monthly literary magazine. <u>Our magazine, called Fresh Words showcases</u> student poetry and prose. Running a magazine <u>take</u> a lot of work. As editors, we <u>read submissions, choose the pieces we will publish, and are inputting the student work.</u> Charles is a good sketch artist and designer. <u>He adds illustrations. Decides how each page should look.</u> <u>We truly enjoy creating the magazine and, students seem to enjoy reading it.</u>
>
> (1)   (2)   (3)   (4)   (5)   (6)

1. **A.** publishing
   **B.** to publish
   **C.** publishers
   **D.** Correct as is

2. **A.** Our magazine called Fresh Words, showcases
   **B.** Our magazine, called Fresh Words, showcases
   **C.** Our magazine called, Fresh Words, showcases
   **D.** Correct as is

3. **A.** takes
   **B.** took
   **C.** taken
   **D.** Correct as is

4. **A.** reading submissions, choosing the pieces we will publish, and inputting the student work.
   **B.** read submissions, choose the pieces we will publish, and input the student work.
   **C.** are reading submissions, choose the pieces we will publish, and inputting the student work.
   **D.** Correct as is

5. **A.** He adds illustrations, decides how each page should look.
   **B.** He adds illustrations and how each page should look.
   **C.** He adds illustrations and decides how each page should look.
   **D.** Correct as is

6. **A.** We truly enjoy creating the magazine, and students seem to enjoy reading it.
   **B.** We truly enjoy creating, the magazine, and students seem to enjoy reading it.
   **C.** We truly enjoy creating the magazine, and, students seem to enjoy reading it.
   **D.** Correct as is

**Need extra help?**

See the **Grammar Handbook**
**Punctuation Chart**, pp. 1203–1204
**Subject-Verb Agreement**, pp. 1200–1201
**Writing Complete Sentences**, p. 1199

# PART 2 Mysteries of the Heart

Consider the Roman god of love, Cupid. Young, beautiful, mischievous—even cruel—he shoots his arrows of love, and the results are almost always unpredictable. His characteristics reflect love's mysterious powers. As you will see in this part of Unit Two, love can have a profound impact, for better or worse, on people's lives.

**ACTIVITY**

With a group of classmates, create a brief glossary of expressions that convey the strange, wonderful, and even frightful effects of love. You may want to include phrases such as *love-crazed* and *head over heels in love,* as well as expressions that you have heard at home or through the media. Define each expression, and give an example of its use. After reading these selections, you may have ideas for additions to the glossary.

# LEARNING *the Language of Literature*

**D**rama is broadly defined as any story told in dialogue form that is performed by actors for an audience. In fact, the word *drama* comes from the Greek word *dran*, meaning "to do" or "to act." Today, drama includes movies, TV shows, live stage productions, and radio plays. Dramatic works can be poetry or prose, comedy or tragedy, fiction or fact, a one-person show or a cast of thousands. You can also enjoy these works as literature, visualizing the action and characters as you read. Dramas share the common elements of character, dialogue, stage directions, and plot. Use the following passages from *The Bear* by Anton Chekhov to learn more about these dramatic elements.

## Character

In drama, as in fiction, the story revolves around **main characters,** with **minor characters** contributing to the action. **Round** (or **dynamic**) characters change during the course of the story, while **flat** (or **static**) characters remain the same. Audiences usually identify with the central character, or **protagonist.** Opposing the protagonist is the **antagonist.** The struggle between them creates the conflict in the story. Characters known as **foils** have qualities that offer a striking contrast to the traits of other characters.

**YOUR TURN** Read the excerpt at the right. Compare the traits of the two main characters. Would you choose Mrs. Popov or Smirnov to be the protagonist? the antagonist?

## Dialogue

**Dialogue,** or conversation between characters, conveys everything in drama, from plot details to character revelations. In addition to dialogue between two or more characters, drama uses other types of speech: the **monologue,** a long, uninterrupted speech by one character that reveals his or her thoughts and feelings; the **soliloquy,** in which the character is alone and speaks his or her private thoughts aloud as if the audience were not there; and the **aside,** a short speech delivered directly to the audience as if the other characters could not hear it.

**YOUR TURN** What does this soliloquy reveal about Mrs. Popov's feelings, motives, and possible future actions?

### CHARACTER

**Smirnov.** . . . Tell me frankly, did you ever see a sincere, faithful, true woman? You know you didn't. . . . You'll never find a constant woman, not in a month of Sundays, you won't, not once in a blue moon!

**Mrs. Popov.** Well, I like that! Then who is true and faithful in love to your way of thinking? Not men by any chance?

**Smirnov.** Yes, madam. Men.

**Mrs. Popov.** *Men!* (*gives a bitter laugh*) Men true and faithful in love! That's rich, I must say. (*vehemently*) . . . If it comes to that, the best man I've ever known was my late husband. . . . I loved him passionately. . . . And—what do you think? This best of men was shamelessly deceiving me all along the line!

### DIALOGUE

**Mrs. Popov** (*looking at the snapshot* [*of her deceased husband*]). Now you shall see how I can love and forgive, Nicholas. My love will only fade when I fade away myself, when this poor heart stops beating. (*laughs, through tears*) Well, aren't you ashamed of yourself? I'm your good, faithful little wifie; I've locked myself up, and I'll be faithful to the grave, while you—aren't you ashamed, you naughty boy? You deceived me, and you used to make scenes and leave me alone for weeks on end.

# Stage Directions

**Stage directions,** usually printed in italics and set off in parentheses, are the playwright's instructions for how the play should be staged and performed. They often provide background information on characters, historical periods, and actions occurring before the play begins. They are also used to describe **scenery,** or **setting**—the physical environment that suggests a specific time or place. In addition, they tell the actors how to play their parts and specify lighting, costumes, music, sound effects, and **props**—or objects, like furniture, used in a performance. In television or films, directions include camera angles and shots.

**YOUR TURN** In this passage, what information do the stage directions give about costumes, props, and the actors' performances?

---

**STAGE DIRECTIONS**

**Mrs. Popov** (*with a vicious laugh*). He likes me! He dares to say he likes me! (*points to the door*) I won't detain you.

**Smirnov** (*puts down the revolver without speaking, picks up his peaked cap and moves off; near the door he stops, and for about half a minute the two look at each other without speaking; then he speaks, going up to her hesitantly*). Listen. Are you still angry? I'm absolutely furious myself, but you must see—how can I put it? The fact is that, er, it's this way, actually— (*shouts*) Anyway, can I help it if I like you? (*clutches the back of a chair, which cracks and breaks*)

---

# Plot

The **plot** in a drama is a series of related events that usually begin with a problem or conflict that intensifies, reaches a peak, and is eventually resolved. Conflict can be **external,** pitting one character against another person or an outside force, or **internal,** involving a struggle within a character. The elements of plot—**exposition, rising action, climax, falling action,** and **resolution**—are discussed on pages 17–18. Dramatic plots are often divided into **scenes,** each scene establishing a different place or time. Longer plays are divided into **acts,** with an act comprising a number of related scenes. *The Bear* is a one-act play composed of 11 scenes.

**YOUR TURN** Read the passage at the right. Does the conflict appear to be internal, external, or both? Explain your choice.

David Suchet (Smirnov) and Pauline Collins (Mrs. Popov) in *The Bear*; Royal Court Theater, 1978.

---

**PLOT**

**Smirnov.** . . . I've gone all sloppy, soft, and sentimental. Kneeling like an imbecile, offering my hand! Disgraceful! Scandalous! I haven't been in love for five years, I swore not to, and here I am crashing head over heels, hook, line, and sinker! I offer you my hand. Take it or leave it. (*gets up and hurries to the door*).

**Mrs. Popov.** Just a moment.

**Smirnov** (*stops*). What is it?

**Mrs. Popov.** Oh, never mind, just go away. But wait. No, go, go away. . . . Oh, if you knew how furious I am!

Drama, as literature, can be as exciting as any novel. Memorable characters, exotic settings, and surprising plots match the best in prose fiction. To get the most from any play you read, try the reading strategies explained here.

# Reading Drama

## Strategies for Using Your 📖 READER'S NOTEBOOK

As you read, take notes to
• record stage directions that are key to understanding plot or character
• note any dialogue you think is particularly revealing or interesting
• **connect** your personal experiences to the events in the drama
• write down any questions you have about setting, plot, or characters

## 1 Strategies for Exploring Characters

• **Visualize** the characters as you read the stage directions, which often describe a character's appearance and reactions.
• **Evaluate** the characters' actions and words, and **question** what motivates them.
• Create a simple graphic like this one to compare and contrast the two main characters.
• Notice changes in characters.

| Character 1 | Shared Traits | Character 2 |
|---|---|---|
|  |  |  |
|  |  |  |
|  |  |  |
|  |  |  |

## 2 Strategies for Understanding Dialogue

• Analyze the writer's use of monologues and asides to reveal a character's motives, feelings, and conflicts.
• Note how the stage directions help you understand the action and the characters' thoughts and feelings.
• Read the play aloud, alone or with others.

## 3 Strategies for Visualizing Drama

• Read the stage directions, and sketch the sets and scenery described.
• Identify the time period and location of the play.
• **Evaluate** how setting influences the play's mood and tone.

## 4 Strategies for Examining Plot

• Read the opening stage directions for any background to the action.
• Identify the main conflict. Diagram the **external** and **internal conflicts** of the characters, as in the chart at right.
• Note at what points the conflict intensifies, reaches a peak, and resolves.
• **Evaluate** whether the ending is a satisfactory resolution to the conflict.

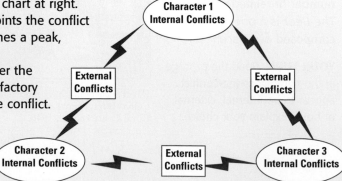

**Need More Help?**

Remember that active readers use the essential reading strategies explained on page 7: **visualize, predict, clarify, question, connect, evaluate, monitor.**

# The Bear

*Drama by* ANTON CHEKHOV (chĕk'ôf)

## Connect to Your Life

**Battle Lines** What does the phrase "battle of the sexes" mean to you? In a class discussion, share your definition of the term and your opinions about it. Also describe examples of the battle of the sexes from books, movies, plays, or television shows.

## Build Background

**The Russian Gentry** In the following one-act comedy, the battle of the sexes takes place on a country estate in 19th-century Russia. The two combatants are both members of what was then Russia's privileged land-owning class. One is a woman who would describe herself as a genteel widow with delicate sensibilities, while the other is an outspoken gentleman farmer whose hot temper makes him seem like a bear, or a crude, insensitive person. Like others of his class, he is educated enough to know French—considered a language of refinement by upper-class Russians of the day—but he pokes fun at those who insist on speaking it. Far more at home with the "manly" pursuits of his class, such as riding, dueling, and managing his farm, he seems out of place in the widow's elegant drawing room, the formal room for receiving guests that is the setting of the play's "battle."

WORDS TO KNOW
**Vocabulary Preview**

| | |
|---|---|
| emancipation | liberty |
| futile | sniveling |
| languish | |

## Focus Your Reading

**LITERARY ANALYSIS** **FARCE** A **farce** is a humorous play that typically involves ridiculous situations and physical comedy. Characters are often **stereotypes;** that is, they conform to a fixed pattern or lack complexity as characters. They frequently display exaggerated behavior or language, as the character Smirnov does in these lines from *The Bear:*

> *Oh, I'm so furious! I could pulverize the whole world, I'm in such a rage. I feel quite ill.*

As you read, be aware of the elements of farce in Chekhov's play.

**ACTIVE READING** **VISUALIZING** A work of drama is primarily written to be performed—it must be interpreted by a director, actors, set designers and others. When you read a drama, you do not have access to this collaboration of talents. Instead, you must **visualize** the setting and the action. While reading, picture the events described and form an image of each major character. Try to "hear" the words as each character speaks. As well as visualizing what is revealed through **dialogue,** pay attention to the **stage directions,** which describe the scenery and props. The stage directions also provide hints to the performers—and the readers—on how the characters look, move, and speak.

**READER'S NOTEBOOK** As you read, make notes describing the image you have formed of each of the major characters and of the play's setting.

Mrs. Popov:

Luke:

Smirnov:

Setting:

# The Bear
## A Farce in One Act

*by Anton Chekhov*

### Cast of Characters

**Mrs. Helen Popov**, a young widow with dimpled cheeks, a landowner

**Gregory Smirnov**, a landowner in early middle age

**Luke**, Mrs. Popov's old manservant

*The action takes place in the drawing room of Mrs. Popov's country house.*

## Scene 1

(Mrs. Popov, *in deep mourning, with her eye fixed on a snapshot, and* Luke)

**Luke.** This won't do, madam; you're just making your life a misery. Cook's out with the maid picking fruit, every living creature's happy, and even our cat knows how to enjoy herself—she's parading round the yard trying to pick up a bird or two. But here you are cooped up inside all day like you was in a convent cell[1]—you never have a good time. Yes, it's true. Nigh on twelve months it is since you last set foot outdoors.

**Mrs. Popov.** And I'm never going out again; why should I? My life's finished. He lies in his grave; I've buried myself inside these four walls—we're both dead.

**Luke.** There you go again! I don't like to hear such talk, I don't. Your husband died and that was that—God's will be done, and may he rest in peace. You've shed a few tears and that'll

---

1. **convent cell:** a small room occupied by an individual nun in a convent, a community of nuns living under strict religious vows.

*Portrait of the Pianist, Conductor, and Composer A. G. Rubinstein* (1881), Ilya Efimovich Repin.
Oil on canvas, 80 cm × 62.3 cm, The State Tretyakov Gallery, Moscow, acquired by
P. M. Tretyakov from the artist.

do; it's time to call it a day—you can't spend your whole life a-moaning and a-groaning. The same thing happened to me once, when my old woman died, but what did I do? I grieved a bit, shed a tear or two for a month or so, and that's all she's getting. Catch me wearing sackcloth and ashes[2] for the rest of my days; it'd be more than the old girl was worth! (*sighs*) You've neglected all the neighbors—won't go and see them or have them in the house. We never get out and about, lurking here like dirty great spiders, saving your presence. The mice have been at my livery[3] too. And it's not for any lack of nice people either—the county's full of 'em, see. There's the regiment stationed at Ryblovo, and them officers are a fair treat; a proper sight for sore eyes they are. They have a dance in camp of a Friday, and the brass band plays most days. This ain't right, missus. You're young, and pretty as a picture with that peaches-and-cream look, so make the most of it. Them looks won't last forever, you know. If you wait another ten years to come out of your shell and lead them officers a dance, you'll find it's too late.

**Mrs. Popov** (*decisively*). Never talk to me like that again, please. When Nicholas died, my life lost all meaning, as you know. You may think I'm alive, but I'm not really. I swore to wear this mourning and shun society till my dying day, do you hear? Let his departed spirit see how I love him! Yes, I realize you know what went on—that he was often mean to me, cruel and, er, unfaithful even; but I'll be true to the grave and show him how much I can love. And he'll find me in the next world just as I was before he died.

**Luke.** Don't talk like that—walk round the garden instead. Or else have Toby or Giant harnessed and go and see the neighbors.

**Mrs. Popov.** Oh dear! (*weeps*)

**Luke.** Missus! Madam! What's the matter? For heaven's sake!

**Mrs. Popov.** He was so fond of Toby—always drove him when he went over to the Korchagins' place and the Vlasovs'. He drove so well too! And he looked so graceful when he pulled hard on the reins, remember? Oh Toby, Toby! See he gets an extra bag of oats today.

**Luke.** Very good, madam.

(*A loud ring.*)

**ACTIVE READING**

**VISUALIZE** What picture have you formed in your mind of Mrs. Popov and Luke?

**Mrs. Popov** (*shudders*). Who is it? Tell them I'm not at home.

**Luke.** Very well, madam. (*goes out*)

## Scene 2

(Mrs. Popov, *alone*)

**Mrs. Popov** (*looking at the snapshot*). Now you shall see how I can love and forgive, Nicholas. My love will only fade when I fade away myself, when this poor heart stops beating. (*laughs, through tears*) Well, aren't you ashamed of yourself? I'm your good, faithful little wifie; I've locked myself up, and I'll be faithful to the grave, while you—aren't you ashamed, you naughty boy? You deceived me, and you used to make scenes and leave me alone for weeks on end.

## Scene 3

(Mrs. Popov *and* Luke)

**Luke** (*comes in, agitatedly*). Someone's asking for you, madam. Wants to see you—

---

2. **sackcloth and ashes:** rough, scratchy clothing and ashes worn as symbols of mourning.

3. **livery:** a servant's uniform.

**Mrs. Popov.** Then I hope you told them I haven't received visitors since the day my husband died.

**Luke.** I did, but he wouldn't listen—his business is very urgent, he says.

**Mrs. Popov.** *I am not at home!*

**Luke.** So I told him, but he just swears and barges straight in, drat him. He's waiting in the dining room.

**Mrs. Popov** (*irritatedly*). All right, ask him in here then. Aren't people rude?

(Luke *goes out.*)

**Mrs. Popov.** Oh, aren't they all a bore? What do they want with me; why must they disturb my peace? (*sighs*) Yes, I see I really shall have to get me to a nunnery.[4] (*reflects*) I'll take the veil;[5] that's it.

## Scene 4

(Mrs. Popov, Luke *and* Smirnov)

**Smirnov** (*coming in, to* Luke). You're a fool, my talkative friend. . . . (*seeing* Mrs. Popov, *with dignity*) May I introduce myself, madam? Gregory Smirnov, landed gentleman[6] and lieutenant of artillery retired. I'm obliged to trouble you on most urgent business.

**Mrs. Popov** (*not holding out her hand*). What do you require?

**Smirnov.** I had the honor to know your late husband. He died owing me twelve hundred roubles[7]—I have his two IOUs. Now I've some interest due to the land bank tomorrow, madam, so may I trouble you to let me have the money today?

**Mrs. Popov.** Twelve hundred roubles—How did my husband come to owe you that?

**Smirnov.** He used to buy his oats from me.

**Mrs. Popov** (*sighing, to* Luke). Oh yes—Luke, don't forget to see Toby has his extra bag of oats. (Luke *goes out.* To Smirnov.) Of course I'll pay if Nicholas owed you something, but I've nothing on me today, sorry. My manager will be back from town the day after tomorrow, and I'll get him to pay you whatever it is then, but for the time being I can't oblige. Besides, it's precisely seven months today since my husband died, and I am in no fit state to discuss money.

**Smirnov.** Well, I'll be in a fit state to go bust with a capital B if I can't pay that interest tomorrow. They'll have the bailiffs[8] in on me.

**Mrs. Popov.** You'll get your money the day after tomorrow.

**Smirnov.** I don't want it the day after tomorrow; I want it now.

**Mrs. Popov.** I can't pay you now, sorry.

**Smirnov.** And I can't wait till the day after tomorrow.

**Mrs. Popov.** Can I help it if I've no money today?

**Smirnov.** So you can't pay then?

**Mrs. Popov.** Exactly.

**Smirnov.** I see. And that's your last word, is it?

**Mrs. Popov.** It is.

**Smirnov.** Your last word? You really mean it?

**Mrs. Popov.** I do.

**Smirnov** (*sarcastic*). Then I'm greatly obliged to you; I'll put it in my diary! (*shrugs*) And people expect me to be cool and collected! I met the local excise man[9] on my way here just now. "My dear Smirnov," says he, "why are you always losing your temper?" But how can I

---

4. **get me to a nunnery:** go and live in a convent. This is probably a reference to a line from Shakespeare's *Hamlet* in which Hamlet angrily tells his girlfriend, "Get thee to a nunnery."

5. **veil:** the outer covering of a nun's headdress and, by extension, the life of a nun.

6. **landed gentleman:** a land owner. In Russia before the Russian Revolution, only a few people owned land.

7. **roubles:** units of Russian money; often spelled *rubles.*

8. **bailiffs:** assistants or deputies to the police chief.

9. **excise man:** tax man.

help it, I ask you? I'm in desperate need of money! Yesterday morning I left home at crack of dawn. I call on everyone who owes me money, but not a soul forks out. I'm dog tired. I spend the night in some . . . awful place. Then I fetch up here, fifty miles from home, hoping to see the color of my money, only to be fobbed off[10] with this "no fit state" stuff! How *can* I keep my temper?

**Mrs. Popov.** I thought I'd made myself clear. You can have your money when my manager gets back from town.

**Smirnov.** It's not your manager I'm after; it's you. What the blazes, pardon my language, do I want with your manager?

**Mrs. Popov.** I'm sorry, my dear man, but I'm not accustomed to these peculiar expressions and to this tone. I have closed my ears. (*hurries out*)

## Scene 5

(Smirnov, *alone*)

**Smirnov.** Well, what price that! "In no fit state!" Her husband died seven months ago, if you please! Now have I got my interest to pay or not? I want a straight answer—yes or no? All right, your husband's dead, you're in no fit state and so on and so forth, and your blasted manager's hopped it. But what am I supposed to do? Fly away from my creditors by balloon, I take it! Or go and bash the old brain-box against a brick wall? I call on Gruzdev—not at home. Yaroshevich is in hiding. I have a real old slanging match[11] with Kuritsyn and almost chuck him out of the window. Mazutov has the bellyache, and this creature's "in no fit state." Not one of the swine will pay. This is what comes of being too nice to them and behaving like some <u>sniveling</u> no-hoper or old woman. It doesn't pay to wear kid gloves with

this lot! All right, just you wait—I'll give you something to remember me by! You don't make a monkey out of me, blast you! I'm staying here—going to stick around till she coughs up. Pah! I feel well and truly riled today. I'm shaking like a leaf, I'm so furious—choking I am. Phew, . . . I really think I'm going to pass out! (*shouts*) Hey, you there!

## Scene 6

(Smirnov *and* Luke)

**Luke** (*comes in*). What is it?

**Smirnov.** Bring me some kvass[12] or water, will you?

(Luke *goes out*)

**Smirnov.** What a mentality, though! You need money so bad you could shoot yourself, but she won't pay, being "in no fit state to discuss money," if you please! There's female logic for you and no mistake! That's why I don't like talking to women. Never have. Talk to a woman—why, I'd rather sit on top of a powder magazine![13] Pah! It makes my flesh creep, I'm so fed up with her, her and that great trailing dress! Poetic creatures they call 'em! Why, the very sight of one gives me cramp in both legs, I get so aggravated.

## Scene 7

(Smirnov *and* Luke)

**Luke** (*comes in and serves some water*). Madam's unwell and won't see anyone.

---

10. **fobbed off:** put off with a trick or an excuse.
11. **slanging match:** the exchange of angry, abusive language.
12. **kvass** (kväs): Russian beer.
13. **powder magazine:** a room in which gun powder and other explosives are stored in a fort or on a ship.

---

*A Room in the Brasovo Estate* (1916), Stanislav Iulianovich Zhukovskii. Oil on canvas, 80 cm × 107 cm, The State Tretyakov Gallery, Moscow, accessioned from the People's Commissariate of Foreign Affairs, 1941.

**Smirnov.** You clear out!

(Luke *goes out*)

**Smirnov.** "Unwell and won't see anyone." All right then, don't! I'm staying put, chum, and I don't budge one inch till you unbelt.[14] Be ill for a week, and I'll stay a week; make it a year, and a year I'll stay. I'll have my rights, lady! As for your black dress and dimples, you don't catch me that way—we know all about those dimples! (*shouts through the window*) Unhitch, Simon; we're here for some time—I'm staying put. Tell the stable people to give my horses oats. And you've got that animal tangled in the reins again, you great oaf! (*imitates him*) "I don't care." I'll give you don't care! (*moves away from the window*) How ghastly—it's unbearably hot, no one will pay up, I had a bad night, and now here's this female with her long black dress and her states. I've got a headache. How about a glass of vodka? That might be an idea. (*shouts*) Hey, you there!

**Luke** (*comes in*). What is it?

**Smirnov.** Bring me a glass of vodka.

(Luke *goes out*)

**Smirnov.** Phew! (*sits down and looks himself over*) A fine specimen I am, I must say—dust all over me, my boots dirty, unwashed, hair unbrushed, straw on my waistcoat. I bet the little woman took me for a burglar. (*yawns*) It's not exactly polite to turn up in a drawing room in this rig! Well, anyway, I'm not a guest here; I'm collecting money. And there's no such thing as correct wear for the well-dressed creditor.

**ACTIVE READING**

**VISUALIZE** What impression do you have of Smirnov's appearance, voice, and mannerisms?

---

14. **unbelt:** take off a belt designed to hold money; in this case, to pay what is due.

**Luke.** Kind sir! (*kneels*) Grant me a favor; pity an old man and leave this place. First you frighten us out of our wits; now you want to fight a duel.

**Smirnov** (*not listening*). A duel! There's true women's emancipation for you! That evens up the sexes with a vengeance! I'll knock her off as a matter of principle. But what a woman! (*mimics her*) ". . . I'll put a bullet through that thick skull." Not bad, eh? Flushed all over, flashing eyes, accepts my challenge! You know, I've never seen such a woman in my life.

**Luke.** Go away, sir, and I'll say prayers for you till the day I die.

**Smirnov.** There's a regular woman for you, something I do appreciate! A proper woman—not some namby-pamby, wishy-washy female, but a really red-hot bit of stuff, a regular pistol-packing little spitfire. A pity to kill her, really.

**Luke** (*weeps*). Kind sir—do leave. Please!

**Smirnov.** I definitely like her. Definitely! Never mind her dimples; I like her. I wouldn't mind letting her off what she owes me, actually. And I don't feel angry anymore. Wonderful woman!

## Scene 10

(*The above and* Mrs. Popov)

**Mrs. Popov** (*comes in with the pistols*). Here are the pistols. But before we start would you mind showing me how to fire them? I've never had a pistol in my hands before.

**ACTIVE READING**

**PREDICT** What do you think will be the outcome of the duel?

**Luke.** Lord help us! Mercy on us! I'll go and find the gardener and coachman. What have we done to deserve this? (*goes out*)

**Smirnov** (*examining the pistols*). Now, there are several types of pistol. There are Mortimer's special dueling pistols with percussion caps.[25]

Now, yours here are Smith and Wessons, triple action with extractor,[26] center-fired. They're fine weapons, worth a cool ninety roubles the pair. Now, you hold a revolver like this. (*aside*) What eyes, what eyes! She's hot stuff all right!

**Mrs. Popov.** Like this?

**Smirnov.** Yes, that's right. Then you raise the hammer and take aim like this. Hold your head back a bit; stretch your arm out properly. Right. And then with this finger you press this little gadget; and that's it. But the great thing is—don't get excited, and do take your time about aiming. Try and see your hand doesn't shake.

**Mrs. Popov.** All right. We can't very well shoot indoors; let's go in the garden.

**Smirnov.** Very well. But I warn you, I'm firing in the air.

**Mrs. Popov.** Oh, this is the limit! Why?

**Smirnov.** Because, because—That's my business.

**Mrs. Popov.** Got cold feet, eh? I see. Now don't shilly-shally, sir. Kindly follow me. I shan't rest till I've put a bullet through your brains. . . . Got the wind up, have you?

**Smirnov.** Yes.

**Mrs. Popov.** That's a lie. Why won't you fight?

**Smirnov.** Because, er, because you, er, I like you.

**Mrs. Popov** (*with a vicious laugh*). He likes me! He dares to say he likes me! (*points to the door*) I won't detain you.

**Smirnov** (*puts down the revolver without speaking, picks up his peaked cap and moves off; near the door he stops, and for about half a minute the two look at each other without speaking; then he speaks, going up to her hesitantly*). Listen. Are you still angry? I'm

---

25. **percussion caps:** small powder caps used to set off some older guns.

26. **extractor:** the part of a gun that pulls the shell case out of the chamber so that it may be ejected after firing.

absolutely furious myself, but you must see—how can I put it? The fact is that, er, it's this way, actually—(*shouts*) Anyway, can I help it if I like you? (*clutches the back of a chair, which cracks and breaks*) . . . fragile stuff, furniture! I like you! Do you understand? I, er, I'm almost in love.

**Mrs. Popov.** Keep away from me; I loathe you.

**Smirnov.** God, what a woman! Never saw the like of it in all my born days. I'm sunk! Without trace! Trapped like a mouse!

**Mrs. Popov.** Get back or I shoot.

**Smirnov.** Shoot away. I'd die happily with those marvelous eyes looking at me; that's what you can't see—die by that dear little velvet hand. Oh, I'm crazy! Think it over and make your mind up now, because once I leave this place we shan't see each other again. So make your mind up. I'm a gentleman and a man of honor, I've ten thousand a year, I can put a bullet through a coin in midair and I keep a good stable. Be my wife.

**Mrs. Popov** (*indignantly brandishes the revolver*). A duel! We'll shoot it out!

**Smirnov.** I'm out of my mind! Nothing makes any sense. (*shouts*) Hey, you there—water!

**Mrs. Popov** (*shouts*). We'll shoot it out!

**Smirnov.** I've lost my head, fallen for her like some damfool boy! (*Clutches her hand. She shrieks with pain.*) I love you! (*kneels*) I love you as I never loved any of my twenty-one other women—twelve times it was me broke it off; the other nine got in first. But I never loved anyone as much as you. I've gone all sloppy, soft and sentimental. Kneeling like an imbecile, offering my hand! Disgraceful! Scandalous! I haven't been in love for five years, I swore not to, and here I am crashing head over heels, hook, line and sinker! I offer you my hand. Take it or leave it. (*gets up and hurries to the door*)

**Mrs. Popov.** Just a moment.

**Smirnov** (*stops*). What is it?

**Mrs. Popov.** Oh, never mind, just go away. But wait. No, go, go away. I hate you. Or no—don't go away. Oh, if you knew how furious I am! (*throws the revolver on the table*) My fingers are numb from holding this beastly thing. (*tears a handkerchief in her anger*) Why are you hanging about? Clear out!

**Smirnov.** Good-bye.

**Mrs. Popov.** Yes, yes, go away! (*shouts*) Where are you going? Stop. Oh, go away then. I'm so furious! Don't you come near me, I tell you.

**Smirnov.** (*going up to her*). I'm so fed up with myself! Falling in love like a schoolboy! Kneeling down! It's enough to give you the willies! (*rudely*) I love you! Oh, it's just what the doctor ordered, this is! There's my interest due in tomorrow, hay making's upon us—and *you* have to come along! (*takes her by the waist*) I'll never forgive myself.

**Mrs. Popov.** Go away! You take your hands off me! I, er, hate you! We'll sh-shoot it out!

(*A prolonged kiss*)

## Scene 11

(*The above,* Luke *with an axe, the gardener with a rake, the coachman with a pitchfork and some workmen with sundry sticks and staves*)

**Luke** (*seeing the couple kissing*). Mercy on us! (*pause*)

**Mrs. Popov** (*lowering her eyes*). Luke, tell them in the stables—Toby gets no oats today.

*Curtain*

*Translated by Ronald Hingley*

# Gold Is Found
## and a Nation Goes Wild

In the process of building Sutter's Mill, pictured above, James Marshall discovered gold there in 1848.

**❶** John August Sutter was a short, fat, kindly man whom everyone in California knew for his hospitality. He had come to America from Switzerland in 1834, and catching the western fever, had traveled across the plains to Oregon. In time he arrived in the Sacramento Valley, where the Mexican governor welcomed his plan to develop the country and granted him some land. Sutter built a fort, and gathering Indians, Hawaiians, and white settlers around him, established a colony called New Helvetia, which he ruled like a feudal baron.[1]

**❷** Early in 1848, he began building a sawmill on his property, along the south fork of the American River. On the morning of January 24, a mechanic from New Jersey named James Marshall saw something glint in the water. Stepping down into the ditch, he picked up a shiny nugget, and all day he and the camp housekeeper at the mill boiled the bit of metal in a kettle of lye. When it failed to tarnish, Marshall gathered

---

1. **feudal** (fyōōd′ l) **baron:** a nobleman and landholder in medieval Europe.

## Reading for Information

Do you sometimes find reading about historical events confusing? Some descriptions of eventful periods are so involved that a reader can become overwhelmed with details. To begin to make sense of historical writing, readers often need to establish the correct order, or chronology, of events.

### CHRONOLOGICAL ORDER

Writers make choices about how they organize the information they present. One way of structuring a historical account is to present events in **chronological order**—the order in which they occurred.

**YOUR TURN** To help you recognize the chronological order in this historical article, use the questions and activities below.

**❶ Constructing a Time Line** A time line is a graphic device that can help you establish chronological order. It can also help you analyze the relationships between historical events during a particular era. Make a time line of the events described in this article, beginning with the year of Sutter's arrival in the United States. Refer to the dates and other references to time in the article as you complete the time line.

Sutter comes to
America from
Switzerland.

1834

more of the glistening flakes and specks, wrapped them in a rag, and on January 28 took them to the fort. Sutter examined them. "Yes, it looks like gold," he agreed. "Come, let us test it."

Gold it was indeed, and the two men were unable to keep their secret. Laborers at the fort heard the rumor first and deserted their work; then the report spread to nearby settlements and on to the coast. By summer whole towns were emptied by a fevered rush to Sutter's land. Men abandoned their families, left homes and trades, jumped ships in the harbors. In Monterey, wrote the alcalde,[2] "A whole platoon of soldiers from the fort left only their colors behind," and he added that some people were going even on crutches, and one had been carried to the mines on a litter.

Six months later a report to Congress by President Polk confirmed the news to the world, and the greatest gold rush in history was on. From the East an army of Americans stampeded for California, crossing the plains in wagons, on mules, and afoot, following every route that the pioneers had blazed. Others went around Cape Horn by ship or hurried across the continent at Panama or Mexico. At the diggings they were joined by Australians, Peruvians, pigtailed Chinese, and men from every land that had heard the news. By the end of 1849, California's population had jumped from 20,000 to nearly 100,000, and the biggest waves of newcomers were still to arrive.

The discovery that made fortunes for many ruined Sutter. There was neither law nor force to restrain the prospectors. They overran his land, butchered his cattle, and destroyed everything that he had labored to build. By 1852 he was bankrupt. Afterward he pleaded for redress, and California granted him a pension of $250 a month. But it ended in 1878, and the man who had once been known for his open-armed hospitality died two years later in a little town in Pennsylvania, still petitioning Congress for the return of his lost acres. James Marshall, who had discovered the gold, fared even worse. He died in poverty, selling his autograph to support himself.

---

2. **alcalde** (ăl-käl′ dē): mayor or chief official.

**❷** A time line can be used to gauge the intervals of time separating events. Determine how much time passed between the discovery of gold in California and President Polk's report to Congress. What might the length of the interval indicate about communication and transportation in the 1800s?

**❸** A time line may also provide clues to possible cause-and-effect relationships between events. Between January 1848 and the end of 1849, California's population swelled dramatically. Examine your time line. What event probably caused that population explosion?

**Examining Your Time Line** Review the entries in your time line. To be sure you've covered the important events, check the entries against the information in the article. You may want to illustrate your time-line entries with simple sketches.

## Inquiry & Research

**Activity Link: "The Californian's Tale," p. 312**
As "The Californian's Tale" and this article illustrate, fortune seekers were just as likely to find misfortune as to become rich in the Gold Rush. Review your research about John Sutter or James Marshall. Share your favorite story about one of these men with your classmates.

# Brigid

*Short Story by* MARY LAVIN

*Fire and Water* (1927),
Winifred Nicholson.
Copyright © artist's family.

## Connect to Your Life

**Home Care** What should people do when a family member is too old or disabled to take care of himself or herself? Some feel that the elderly and disabled should remain with their families, whatever the cost. Others believe that the needs of such people are better met in special homes where they will be cared for by professionals. What do you think? With a small group of classmates, discuss the pros and cons of each option.

## Build Background

**Rural Ireland** This story is set in Ireland, a rainy, largely agricultural land. Irish farms are small by American standards, and most farm families struggle to support themselves. "Brigid" takes place in the 1930s or 1940s, when farmers were typically poor. Farms like the one in the story often lacked electricity, indoor plumbing, and many of the other conveniences we associate with modern life.

Despite the poverty—or perhaps because of it—Irish farming families remained close-knit, with children expected to care for aging parents and for other relatives unable to care for themselves. As author Joe McCarthy noted in the 1960s, "The bonds of an Irish family are deep between brothers and sisters and their uncles, aunts, and grandparents. . . . It is a disgrace for a family to let old relatives live alone, and a scandalous shame to put a grand-uncle or an aged aunt among strangers in a nursing home or public institution."

## Focus Your Reading

**LITERARY ANALYSIS** **CONFLICT**

"Brigid" opens with an argument between a married couple:

> *"What harm is a sup of rain?" he said.*
> *"That's you all over again," she said. "What harm is anything, as long as it doesn't affect yourself?"*

This kind of **conflict,** in which characters struggle against each other, is an example of **external conflict.** However, conflict may also be **internal,** occurring within a character. As you read "Brigid," look for examples of conflict and consider whether each conflict is external or internal.

**ACTIVE READING** **ANALYZING MOTIVATION** Understanding a character's **motivation**—the driving force behind his or her thoughts, feelings, and actions—is often the key to understanding an entire story.

**READER'S NOTEBOOK** As you read "Brigid," use two diagrams like the one shown below to record the motivation of Owen and his wife for the things they say and do. Identify the moment at which the motivation and behavior of Owen's wife radically changes.

| Character: Owen | |
|---|---|
| **Action/Statement** | **Motivation** |
| • Owen goes to check on Brigid | |
| • | |
| • | |
| • | |

# Brigid

## MARY LAVIN

The rain came
sifting through the air
and settled like a bloom on
the fields. But under the trees
it fell in single heavy drops,
noisily, like cabbage water
running through the
holes of a colander.[1]

---

1. **colander** (kŭl′ən-dər): a bowl-shaped, perforated kitchen
   utensil for draining off liquid and rinsing food.

The house was in the middle of the trees.

"Listen to that rain!" said the woman to her husband. "Will it never stop?"

"What harm is a sup[2] of rain?" he said.

"That's you all over again," she said. "What harm is anything, as long as it doesn't affect yourself?"

"How do you mean, when it doesn't affect me? Look at my feet. They're sopping. And look at my hat. It's soused."[3] He took the hat off and shook the rain from it onto the spitting bars of the grate.

"Quit that," said the woman. "Can't you see you're raising ashes?"

"What harm is ashes?"

"I'll show you what harm," she said, taking down a plate of cabbage and potato from the shelf over the fire. "There's your dinner destroyed with them." The yellow cabbage was lightly sprayed with ash.

"Ashes is healthy, I often heard said. Put it here!" He sat down at the table, taking up his knife and fork, and indicating where the plate was to be put by tapping the table with the handle of the knife. "Is there no bit of meat?" he asked, prodding the potato critically.

"There's plenty in the town, I suppose."

"In the town? And why didn't somebody go to the town, might I ask?"

"Who was there to go? You know as well as I do there's no one here to be traipsing in and out every time there's something wanted from the town."

"I suppose one of our fine daughters would think it the end of the world if she was asked to go for a bit of a message? Let me tell you they'd get husbands for themselves quicker if they were seen doing a bit of work once in a while."

"Who said anything about getting husbands for them?" said the woman. "They're time enough getting married."

"Is that so? Mind you now, anyone would think that you were anxious to get them off your hands with the way every penny that comes into the house goes out again on bits of silks and ribbons for them."

"I'm not going to let them be without their bit of fun just because you have other uses for your money than spending it on your own children!"

"What other uses have I? Do I smoke? Do I drink? Do I play cards?"

"You know what I mean."

"I suppose I do." The man was silent. He left down his fork. "I suppose you're hinting at poor Brigid again?" he said. "But I told you forty times, if she was put into a home[4] she'd be just as much of an expense to us as she is in the little house above there." He pointed out of the window with his fork.

"I see there's no use in talking about it," said the woman. "All I can say is God help the girls, with you, their own father, putting a drag on them so that no man will have anything to do with them after hearing about Brigid."

"What do you mean by that? This is something new. I thought it was only the bit of bread and tea she got that you grudged the poor thing. This is something new. What is this?"

"You oughtn't to need to be told, a man like you that saw the world, a man that traveled like you did, a man that was in England and London."

"I don't know what you're talking about." He took up his hat and felt it to see if the side he had placed near the fire was dry. He turned the other side toward the fire. "What are you trying to say?" he said. "Speak plain!"

---

2. **sup:** a small quantity of liquid.

3. **soused** (soust): soaking wet; drenched.

4. **home:** here, a residential institution where people are cared for.

*Rebecca* (about 1947), Raphael Soyer. Oil on canvas, 26″ × 20″, courtesy of Forum Gallery, New York.

# Lalla

**Rosamunde Pilcher**

There was a Before and After. Before was before our father died, when we lived in London, in a tall narrow house with a little garden at the back. When we went on family skiing holidays every winter and attended suitable—and probably very expensive—day schools.

*Portrait of Amber* (1991), Charles Warren Mundy. Oil on canvas, 8″ × 10″, private collection.

Our father was a big man, outgoing and immensely active. We thought he was immortal, but then most children think that about their father. The worst thing was that Mother thought he was immortal too, and when he died, keeling over on the pavement between the insurance offices where he worked, and the company car into which he was just about to climb, there followed a period of ghastly limbo. <u>Bereft</u>, uncertain, lost, none of us knew what to do next. But after the funeral and a little talk with the family lawyer, Mother quietly pulled herself together and told us.

At first we were horrified. "Leave London? Leave school?" Lalla could not believe it. "But I'm starting 'O' levels[1] next year."

"There are other schools," Mother told her.

"And what about Jane's music lessons?"

"We'll find another teacher."

"I don't mind about leaving school," said Barney. "I don't much like my school anyway."

Mother gave him a smile, but Lalla persisted in her inquisition.[2] "But where are we going to *live?*"

"We're going to Cornwall."

And so it was After. Mother sold the lease of the London house and a removals firm[3] came and packed up all the furniture and we traveled, each silently thoughtful, by car to Cornwall. It was spring, and because Mother had not realized how long the journey would take, it was dark by the time we found the village and, finally, the house. It stood just inside a pair of large gates, backed by tall trees. When we got out of the car, stiff and tired, we could smell the sea and feel the cold wind.

"There's a light in the window," observed Lalla.

> We were living in the country and there were no boundaries to our new territory.

"That'll be Mrs. Bristow," said Mother, and I knew she was making a big effort to keep her voice cheerful. She went up the little path and knocked at the door, and then, perhaps realizing it was <u>ludicrous</u> to be knocking at her own door, opened it. We saw someone coming down the narrow hallway towards us—a fat and bustling lady with grey hair and a hectically flowered pinafore.[4]

"Well, my dear life," she said, "what a journey you must have had. I'm all ready for you. There's a kettle on the hob[5] and a pie in the oven."

The house was tiny compared to the one we had left in London, but we all had rooms to ourselves, as well as an attic for the dolls' house, the books, bricks,[6] model cars and paint-boxes we had refused to abandon, and a ramshackle shed alongside the garage where we could keep our bicycles. The garden was even smaller than the London garden, but this didn't matter because now we were living in the country and there were no boundaries to our new territory.

---

1. **'O' levels:** in Britain, a series of secondary-school examinations given before students can advance to higher studies.
2. **inquisition** (ĭn′kwĭ-zĭsh′ən): a lengthy series of questions.
3. **removals firm:** chiefly British term for a moving company.
4. **pinafore** (pĭn′ə-fôr): an apron.
5. **hob:** a warming shelf, especially on the back or side of a fireplace.
6. **bricks:** chiefly British term for building blocks.

WORDS TO KNOW **bereft** (bĭ-rĕft′) *adj.* suffering the death of a loved one; deprived of someone or something important
**ludicrous** (lŏo′dĭ-krəs) *adj.* laughably absurd; ridiculous

We explored, finding a wooded lane which led down to a huge inland estuary[7] where it was possible to fish for flounder from the old sea wall.[8] In the other direction, a sandy right-of-way[9] led past the church and over the golf links[10] and the dunes to another beach—a wide and empty shore where the ebb tide[11] took the ocean out half a mile or more.

The Roystons, father, mother and two sons, lived in the big house and were our landlords. We hadn't seen them yet, though Mother had walked, in some trepidation, up the drive to make the acquaintance of Mrs. Royston, and to thank her for letting us have the house. But Mrs. Royston hadn't been in, and poor Mother had had to walk all the way down the drive again with nothing accomplished.

"How old are the Royston boys?" Barney asked Mrs. Bristow.

"I suppose David's thirteen and Paul's about eleven." She looked at us. "I don't know how old you lot are."

"I'm seven," said Barney, "and Jane's twelve and Lalla's fourteen."

"Well," said Mrs. Bristow. "That's nice. Fit in nicely, you would."

"They're far too young for me," said Lalla. "Anyway, I've seen them. I was hanging out the washing for Mother, and they came down the drive and out of the gate on their bicycles. They didn't even look my way."

"Come now," said Mrs. Bristow, "they're probably shy as you are."

"We don't particularly want to know them," said Lalla.

"But . . ." I started and then stopped. I wasn't like Lalla. I wanted to make friends. It would be nice to know the Royston boys. They had a tennis court; I had caught a glimpse of it through the trees. I wouldn't mind being asked to play tennis.

But for Lalla, of course, it was different. Fourteen was a funny age, neither one thing nor the other. And as for the way that Lalla looked! Sometimes I thought that if I didn't love her, and she wasn't my sister, I should hate her for her long, cloudy brown hair, the tilt of her nose, the amazing blue of her eyes, the curve of her pale mouth. During the last six months she seemed to have grown six inches.

 was short and square and my hair was too curly and horribly tangly. The awful bit was, I couldn't remember Lalla ever looking the way I looked, which made it fairly unlikely that I should end up looking like her.

A few days later Mother came back from shopping in the village to say that she had met Mrs. Royston in the grocer's and we had all been asked for tea.

Lalla said, "I don't want to go."

"Why not?" asked Mother.

"They're just little boys. Let Jane and Barney go."

"It's just for tea," pleaded Mother.

She looked so anxious that Lalla gave in. She shrugged and sighed, her face closed in resignation.

We went, and it was a failure. The boys didn't want to meet us any more than Lalla wanted to meet them. Lalla was at her coolest, her most

---

7. **estuary** (ĕs′chōo-ĕr′ē): the wide part of a river where its currents meet the tides of an ocean or sea.

8. **sea wall:** a wall or embankment built to shelter the coast from storms or erosion.

9. **right-of-way:** a path or road on which the public is allowed to cross private property.

10. **golf links:** a golf course.

11. **ebb tide:** the outgoing tide.

WORDS TO KNOW
**trepidation** (trĕp′ĭ-dā′shən) *n.* a state of alarm or dread; apprehension; anxiety
**resignation** (rĕz′ĭg-nā′shən) *n.* the act of giving up; submission

remote. I knocked over my teacup, and Barney, who usually chatted to everybody, was silenced by the superiority of his hosts. When tea was over, Lalla stayed with the grown-ups, but Barney and I were sent off with the boys.

"Show Jane and Barney your tree house," Mrs. Royston told them as we trailed out of the door.

They took us out into the garden and showed us the tree house. It was a marvelous piece of construction, strong and roomy. Barney's face was filled with longing. "Who built it?" he asked.

"Our cousin Godfrey. He's eighteen. He can build anything. It's our club, and you're not members."

They whispered together and went off, leaving us standing beneath the forbidden tree house.

When the summer holidays came, Mother appeared to have forgotten about our social debt to the Royston boys, and we were careful not to remind her. So their names were never raised, and we never saw them except at a distance, cycling off to the village or down to the beach. Sometimes on Sunday afternoons they had guests and played tennis on their court. I longed to be included, but Lalla, deep in a book, behaved as though the Roystons didn't exist. Barney had taken up gardening, and, with his usual singlemindedness, was concentrating on digging himself a vegetable patch. He said he was going to sell lettuces, and Mother said that maybe he was the one who was going to make our fortune.

It was a hot summer, made for swimming. Lalla had grown out of her old swimsuit, so Mother made her a cotton bikini out of scraps. It was pale blue, just right for her tan and her long, pale hair. She looked beautiful in it, and I longed to look just like her. We went to the beach most days and often saw the Royston boys there. But the beach was so vast that there was no necessity for social contact, and we all avoided each other.

Until one Sunday. The tide came in during the afternoon that day, and Mother packed us a picnic so we could set off after lunch. When we got to the beach, Lalla said she was going to swim right away, but Barney and I decided we would wait. We took our spades and went down to where the outgoing tide had left shallow pools in the sand. There we started the construction of a large and complicated harbor. Absorbed in our task, we lost track of time, and never noticed the stranger approaching. Suddenly a long shadow fell across the sparkling water.

I looked up, shading my eyes against the sun. He said "Hello" and squatted down to our level.

"Who are you?" I asked.

"I'm Godfrey Howard, the Roystons' cousin. I'm staying with them."

Illustration by
Robbin Gourley

Barney suddenly found his tongue. "Did you build the tree house?"

"That's right."

"How *did* you do it?"

odfrey began to tell him. I listened and wondered how any person apparently so nice could have anything to do with those hateful Royston boys. It wasn't that he was particularly good-looking. His hair was mousey, his nose too big and he wore spectacles. He wasn't even very tall. But there was something warm and friendly about his deep voice and his smile.

"Did you go up and look at it?"

Barney went back to his digging. Godfrey looked at me. I said, "They wouldn't let us. They said it was a club. They didn't like us."

"They think you don't like them. They think you come from London and that you're very grand."

This was astonishing. "Grand? *Us?*" I said indignantly. "We never even pretended to be grand." And then I remembered Lalla's coolness, her pale, unsmiling lips. "I mean—Lalla's older—it's different for her." His silence at this was encouraging. "I wanted to make friends," I admitted.

He was sympathetic. "It's difficult sometimes. People are shy." All at once he stopped, and looked over my shoulder. I turned to see what had caught his attention and saw Lalla coming towards us across the sand. Her hair lay like wet silk over her shoulders, and she had knotted her red towel around her hips like a sarong.[12] As she approached, Godfrey stood up. I said, introducing them the way Mother introduced people, "This is Lalla."

"Hello, Lalla," said Godfrey.

"He's the Roystons' cousin," I went on quickly. "He's staying with them."

"Hello," said Lalla.

Godfrey said, "David and Paul are wanting to play cricket. It's not much good playing cricket with just three people and I wondered if you'd come and join us?"

"Lalla won't want to play cricket," I told myself. "She'll snub him and then we'll never be asked again."

But she didn't snub him. She said, uncertainly, "I don't think I'm much good at cricket."

"But you could always try?"

"Yes." She began to smile, "I suppose I could always try."

And so we all finally got together. We played a strange form of beach cricket invented by Godfrey, which involved much lashing out at the ball and hysterical running. When we were too hot to play any longer, we swam. The Roystons had a couple of wooden surfboards, and they let us have turns, riding in on our stomachs on the long, warm breakers of the flood tide.[13] By five o'clock we were ready for tea, and we collected our various baskets and haversacks[14] and sat around in a circle on the sand. Other people's picnics are always much nicer than one's own, so we ate the Royston sandwiches and chocolate biscuits, and they ate Mother's scones with loganberry jam in the middle.

We had a last swim before the tide turned, and then gathered up our belongings and walked slowly home together. Barney and the two Roystons led the way, planning the next day's activities, and I walked with Godfrey and Lalla. But gradually, in the natural manner of events, they fell behind me. Plodding up and over the springy turf of the golf course, I listened to their voices.

"Do you like living here?"

---

12. **sarong:** a skirtlike garment formed by wrapping cloth around the waist.

13. **flood tide:** the incoming tide.

14. **haversacks** (hăvʹər-săksʹ): supply bags carried over one shoulder, popular with hikers.

*First Sail* (1993), Charles Warren Mundy. Oil on canvas, 30″ × 40″, private collection.

"It's different from London."

"That's where you lived before?"

"Yes, but my father died, and we couldn't afford to live there any more."

"I'm sorry, I didn't know. Of course, I envy your living here. I'd rather be at Carwheal than anywhere else in the world."

"Where do you live?"

"In Bristol."

"Are you at school there?"

"I've finished with school. I'm starting college in September. I'm going to be a vet."

"A vet?" Lalla considered this. "I've never met a vet before."

He laughed. "You haven't actually met one yet."

I smiled to myself in satisfaction. They sounded like two grown-ups talking. Perhaps a grown-up friend of her own was all that Lalla had needed. I had a feeling that we had crossed another watershed.[15] After today, things would be different.

---

15. **watershed:** a critical point that marks a division or a change of course; a turning point.

The Roystons were now our friends. Our relieved mothers—for Mrs. Royston, faced with our unrelenting <u>enmity</u>, had been just as concerned and conscience-stricken as Mother—took advantage of the truce, and after that Sunday we were never out of each other's houses. Through the good offices[16] of the Roystons, our social life widened, and Mother found herself driving us all over the county to attend various beach picnics, barbecues, sailing parties and teenage dances. By the end of the summer we had been accepted. We had dug ourselves in. Carwheal was home. And Lalla grew up.

She and Godfrey wrote to each other. I knew this because I would see his letters to her lying on the table in the hall. She would take them upstairs to read them in secret in her room, and we were all too great respecters of privacy ever to mention them. When he came to Carwheal, which he did every holiday, to stay with the Roystons, he was always around first thing in the morning on the first day. He said it was to see us all, but we knew it was Lalla he had come to see.

He now owned a battered second-hand car. A lesser man might have scooped Lalla up and taken her off on her own, but Godfrey was far too kind, and he would drive for miles, to distant coves and hilltops, with the whole lot of us packed into his long-suffering car, and the boot[17] filled with food and towels and snorkels and other assorted clobber.[18]

But he was only human, and often they would drift off on their own and walk away from us. We would watch their progress and let them go, knowing that in an hour or two they would be back—Lalla with a bunch of wild flowers or some shells in her hand, Godfrey sunburned and tousled—both of them smiling and content in a way that we found reassuring and yet did not wholly understand.

Lalla had always been such a certain person, so positive, so unveering from a chosen course, that we were all taken by surprise by her <u>vacillating</u> indecision as to what she was going to do with her life. She was nearly eighteen, with her final exams over and her future spread before her like a new country observed from the peak of some painfully climbed hill.

Mother wanted her to go to university.

"Isn't it rather a waste of time if I don't know what I'm going to do at the end of it? How can I decide now what I'm going to do with the rest of my life? It's inhuman. Impossible."

"But darling, what do you want to do?"

"I don't know. Travel, I suppose. Of course, I could be really original and take a typing course."

"It might at least give you time to think things over."

This conversation took place at breakfast. It might have continued forever, reaching no satisfactory conclusion, but the post arrived as we sat there over our empty coffee cups. There was the usual dull bundle of envelopes, but, as well, a large square envelope for Lalla. She opened it idly, read the card inside and made a face. "Goodness, how grand, a proper invitation to a proper dance."

"How nice," said Mother, trying to <u>decipher</u> the butcher's bill. "Who from?"

"Mrs. Menheniot," said Lalla.

We were all instantly agog, grabbing at the invitation in order to gloat over it. We had once been to lunch with Mrs. Menheniot, who lived with Mr. Menheniot and a tribe of junior Menheniots in a beautiful house on the Fal.[19] For

---

16. **offices:** kind acts performed to help someone else.
17. **boot:** British term for the trunk of a car.
18. **clobber:** British slang for clothing or equipment.
19. **Fal:** a river in western Cornwall.

some unspecified reason they were very rich, and their house was vast and white with a pillared portico[20] and green lawns which sloped down to the tidal inlets of the river.

"Are you going to go?" I asked.

Lalla shrugged. "I don't know."

"It's in August. Perhaps Godfrey will be here and you can go with him."

"He's not coming down this summer. He has to earn money to pay his way through college."

She would not make up her mind whether or not she would go to Mrs. Menheniot's party and probably never would have come to any decision if it had not been for the fact that, before very long, I had been invited too. I was really too young, as Mrs. Menheniot's booming voice pointed out over the telephone when she rang Mother, but they were short of girls and it would be a blessing if I could be there to swell the numbers. When Lalla knew that I had been asked as well, she said of course we would go. She had passed her driving test, and we would borrow Mother's car.

We were then faced with the problem of what we should wear, as Mother could not begin to afford to buy us the sort of evening dresses we wanted. In the end she sent away to Liberty's[21] for yards of material, and she made them for us, beautifully, on her sewing machine. Lalla's was pale blue lawn and in it she looked like a goddess—Diana the Huntress

perhaps. Mine was a sort of tawny-gold, and I looked quite presentable in it, but of course not a patch on[22] Lalla.

When the night of the dance came, we put on our dresses and set off together in Mother's Mini,[23] giggling slightly with nerves. But when we reached the Menheniots' house, we stopped giggling because the whole affair was so grand as to be awesome. There were floodlights and car parks[24] and hundreds of sophisticated-looking people all making their way towards the front door.

Indoors, we stood at the foot of the crowded staircase, and I was filled with panic. We knew nobody. There was not a single familiar face. Lalla whisked a couple of glasses of champagne from a passing tray and gave me one. I took a sip, and at that very moment a voice rang out above the hubbub. "Lalla!" A girl was coming down the stairs, a dark girl in a strapless satin dress that had very obviously not been made on her mother's sewing machine.

---

20. **pillared portico** (pĭl'ərd pôr'tĭ-kō'): a porch with a roof supported by columns.

21. **Liberty's:** a London store especially famous for the fabric it sells.

22. **not a patch on:** not nearly as good as.

23. **Mini** (mĭn'ē): a small, fairly inexpensive, popular British car.

24. **car parks:** British term for parking lots.

Illustration by Robbin Gourley

Lalla looked up. "Rosemary!"

She was Rosemary Sutton from London. She and Lalla had been at school together in the old days. They fell into each other's arms and embraced as though this was all either of them had been waiting for. "What are you doing? I never thought I'd see you here. How marvelous. Come and meet Allan. You remember my brother Allan, don't you? Oh, this is exciting."

Allan was so good-looking as to be almost unreal. Fair as his sister was dark, impeccably turned out. Lalla was tall, but he was taller. He looked down at her, and his rather wooden features were filled with both surprise and obvious pleasure. He said, "But of course I remember." He smiled and laid down his glass. "How could I forget? Come and dance."

I scarcely saw her again all evening. He took her away from me, and I was bereft, as though I had lost my sister forever. At one point I was rescued by Mrs. Menheniot herself, who dragooned[25] some young man into taking me to supper, but after supper even he melted away. I found an empty sofa in a deserted sitting-out room,[26] and collapsed into it. It was half-past-twelve, and I longed for my bed. I wondered what people would think if I put up my feet and had a little snooze.

Somebody came into the room and then withdrew again. I looked up and saw his retreating back view. I said, "Godfrey." He turned back. I got up off the sofa, back on to my aching feet.

"What are you doing here? Lalla said you were working."

> I couldn't say any more. I couldn't tell Godfrey to go and claim her for himself.

"I am, but I wanted to come. I drove down from Bristol. That's why I'm so late." I knew why he had wanted to come. To see Lalla. "I didn't expect to see you."

"They were short of girls, so I got included."

We gazed glumly at each other, and my heart felt very heavy. Godfrey's dinner jacket looked as though he had borrowed it from some larger person, and his bow tie was crooked. I said, "I think Lalla's dancing."

"Why don't you come and dance with me, and we'll see."

I thought this a rotten idea but didn't like to say so. Together we made our way towards the ballroom. The ceiling lights had been turned off, and the disco lights now flashed red and green and blue across the smoky darkness. Music thumped and rocked an assault on our ears, and the floor seemed to be filled with an unidentifiable confusion of people, of flying hair and arms and legs. Godfrey and I joined in at the edge, but I could tell that his heart wasn't in it. I wished that he had never come. I prayed that he would not find Lalla.

But of course, he saw her, because it was impossible not to. It was impossible to miss Allan Sutton as well. They were both so tall, so beautiful. Godfrey's face seemed to close up.

"Who's she with?" he asked.

"Allan Sutton. He and his sister have come down from London. Lalla used to know them."

I couldn't say any more. I couldn't tell Godfrey

---

25. **dragooned** (drə-gōōnd′): compelled by threats or force. The term is used humorously here.

26. **sitting-out room:** a room used by those not dancing.

WORDS
TO    **impeccably** (ĭm-pĕk′ə-blē) *adv.* flawlessly; perfectly
KNOW

to go and claim her for himself. I wasn't even certain by then what sort of a reception she would have given him. And anyway, as we watched them, Allan stopped dancing and put his arm around Lalla, drawing her towards him, whispering something into her ear. She slipped her hand into his, and they moved away towards the open French window.[27] The next moment they were lost to view, swallowed into the darkness of the garden beyond.

At four o'clock in the morning Lalla and I drove home in silence. We were not giggling now. I wondered sadly if we would ever giggle together again. I ached with exhaustion, and I was out of sympathy with her. Godfrey had never even spoken to her. Soon after our dance he had said goodbye and disappeared, presumably to make the long, lonely journey back to Bristol.

She, on the other hand, had an aura of happiness about her that was almost tangible. I glanced at her and saw her peaceful, smiling profile. It was hard to think of anything to say.

It was Lalla who finally broke the silence. "I know what I'm going to do. I mean, I know what I'm going to do with my life. I'm going back to London. Rosemary says I can live with her. I'll take a secretarial course or something, then get a job."

"Mother will be disappointed."

"She'll understand. It's what I've always wanted. We're buried down here. And there's another thing; I'm tired of being poor. I'm tired of homemade dresses and never having a new car. We've always talked about making our fortunes, and as I'm the eldest, I might as well make a start. If I don't do it now, I never will."

I said, "Godfrey was there this evening."

"Godfrey?"

"He drove down from Bristol."

She did not say anything, and I was angry. I wanted to hurt her and make her feel as bad as I felt. "He came because he wanted to see you. But you didn't even notice him."

"You can scarcely blame me," said Lalla, "for that."

And so she went back to London, lived with Rosemary, and took a secretarial course, just as she said she would. Later, she got a job on the editorial staff of a fashionable magazine, but it was not long before one of the photographers spied her potential, seduced her from her typewriter, and started taking pictures of her. Soon her lovely face smiled at us from the cover of the magazine.

"How does it feel to have a famous daughter?" people asked Mother, but she never quite accepted Lalla's success, just as she never quite accepted Allan Sutton. Allan's devotion to Lalla had proved unswerving and he was her constant companion.

"Let's hope he doesn't marry her," said Barney, but of course eventually, inevitably, they decided to do just that. "We're engaged!" Lalla rang up from London to tell us. Her voice sounded, <u>unnervingly</u>, as though she was calling from the next room.

"Darling!" said Mother, faintly.

"Oh, do be pleased. Please be pleased. I'm so happy and I couldn't bear it if you weren't happy, too."

So of course Mother said that she was pleased, but the truth was that none of us really liked Allan very much. He was—well—spoilt. He was conceited. He was too rich. I said as much to Mother, but Mother was loyal to Lalla.

---

27. **French window:** a type of window that extends to the floor.

She said, "*Things* mean a lot to Lalla. I think they always have. I mean, possessions and security. And perhaps someone who truly loves her."

I said, "Godfrey truly loved her."

"But that was when they were young. And perhaps Godfrey couldn't give her love."

"He could make her laugh. Allan never makes her laugh."

"Perhaps," said Mother sadly, "she's grown out of laughter."

And then it was Easter. We hadn't heard from Lalla for a bit and didn't expect her to come to Carwheal for the spring holiday. But she rang up, out of the blue, and said that she hadn't been well and was taking a couple of weeks off. Mother was delighted, of course, but concerned about her health.

By now we were all more or less grown-up. David was studying to be a doctor, and Paul had a job on the local newspaper. I had achieved a place at the Guildhall School of Music, and Barney was no longer a little boy but a gangling teenager with an insatiable appetite. Still, however, we gathered for the holidays, and that Easter Godfrey abandoned his sick dogs and ailing cows to the ministrations[28] of his partner and joined us.

It was lovely weather, almost as warm as summer. The sort of weather that makes one feel young again—a child. There was scented thyme on the golf links, and the cliff walks were starred with primroses and wild violets. In the Roystons' garden the daffodils blew in the long grass beneath the tree house, and Mrs. Royston put up the tennis net and swept the cobwebs out of the summer house.

It was during one of these sessions that Godfrey and I talked about Lalla. We were in the summer house together, sitting out while the others played a set.

"Tell me about Lalla."

"She's engaged."

"I know. I saw it in the paper." I could think of nothing to say. "Do you like him—Allan Sutton, I mean?"

I said "Yes," but I was never much good at lying.

Godfrey turned his head and looked at me. He was wearing old jeans and a white shirt, and I thought that he had grown older in a subtle way. He was more sure of himself and somehow more attractive.

He said, "That night of the Menheniots' dance, I was going to ask her to marry me."

"Oh, Godfrey."

"I hadn't even finished my training, but I thought perhaps we'd manage. And when I saw her, I knew that I had lost her. I'd left it too late."

On the day that Lalla was due to arrive, I took Mother's old car into the neighboring town to do some shopping. When the time came to return home, the engine refused to start. After struggling for a bit, I walked to the nearest garage and persuaded a kindly, oily man to come and help me. But he told me it was hopeless.

We walked back to the garage, and I telephoned home. But it wasn't Mother who answered the call, it was Godfrey.

I explained what had happened. "Lalla's train is due at the junction in about half an hour and we said someone would meet her."

There was a momentary hesitation, then Godfrey said, "I'll go. I'll take my car."

When I finally reached home, exhausted from carrying the laden grocery bags from the bus stop, Godfrey's car was nowhere to be seen.

---

28. **ministrations** (mĭn´ĭ-strā´shəns): services performed to aid someone or something.

*The Cove* (1964), Fairfield Porter. Oil on canvas, 37″ × 53½″, The Metropolitan Museum of Art, New York, bequest of Arthur M. Bullowa, 1993 (1993.406.7). Copyright © 1995 The Metropolitan Museum of Art.

A short time later the telephone rang. But it wasn't Lalla, explaining where they were, it was a call from London and it was Allan Sutton.

"I have to speak to Lalla."

His voice sounded frantic. I said cautiously, "Is anything wrong?"

"She's broken off our engagement. I got back from the office and found a letter from her and my ring. She said she was coming home. She doesn't want to get married."

I found it in my heart to be very sorry for him. "But Allan, you must have had *some* idea."

"None. Absolutely none. It's just a bolt from the blue. I know she's been a bit off-color lately, but I thought she was just tired."

"She must have her reasons, Allan," I told him, as gently as I could.

"Talk to her, Jane. Try to make her see sense."

He rang off at last. I put the receiver back on the hook and stood for a moment, gathering my wits about me and assessing this new and startling turn of events. I found myself caught up in a tangle of conflicting emotions. Enormous sympathy for Allan; a reluctant admiration for Lalla, who had had the courage to take this shattering decision; but, as well, a sort of rising excitement.

Godfrey. Godfrey and Lalla. Where were they? I knew then that I could not face Mother and Barney before I had found out what was going on. Quietly, I opened the door and went out of the house, through the gates, down the lane. As soon as I turned the corner at the end of the lane, I saw Godfrey's car parked on the patch of grass outside the church.

It was a marvelously warm, <u>benign</u> sort of evening. I took the path that led past the church and towards the beach. Before I had gone very far, I saw them, walking up over the golf links towards me. The wind blew Lalla's hair over her face. She was wearing her London high-heeled boots so was taller than Godfrey. They should have appeared ill-assorted, but there was something about them that was totally right. They were a couple, holding hands, walking up from the beach as they had walked innumerable times, together.

I stopped, suddenly reluctant to disturb their intimacy. But Lalla had seen me. She waved and then let go of Godfrey's hand and began to run towards me, her arms flailing like windmills.

"Jane!" I had never seen her so exuberant.

"Oh, Jane." I ran to meet her. We hugged each other, and for some stupid reason my eyes were full of tears.

"Oh, darling Jane . . ."

"I had to come and find you."

"Did you wonder where we were? We went for a walk. I had to talk to Godfrey. He was the one person I could talk to."

"Lalla, Allan's been on the phone."

"I had to do it. It was all a ghastly mistake."

"But you found out in time. That's all that matters."

"I thought I was going after what I wanted. I thought I had what I wanted, and then I found out that I didn't want it at all. Oh, I've missed you all so much. There wasn't anybody I could talk to."

Over her shoulder I saw Godfrey coming, tranquilly, to join us. I let go of Lalla and went to give him a kiss. I didn't know what they had been discussing as they paced the lonely beach, and I knew that I never would. But still, I had the feeling that the outcome could be nothing but good for all of us.

I said, "We must go back. Mother and Barney don't know about anything. They'll be thinking that I've dissolved into thin air, as well as the pair of you."

"In that case," said Godfrey, and he took Lalla's hand in his own once more, "perhaps we'd better go and tell them."

And so we walked home, the three of us. In the warm evening, in the sunshine, in the fresh wind. ❖

# *Thinking through the* LITERATURE

## Connect to the Literature

**1. What Do You Think?** What was your reaction to the story? Discuss your reaction with a classmate.

> **Comprehension Check**
> - Why does Lalla's family move to Cornwall?
> - As teenagers, how do Lalla and Godfrey feel about each other?
> - Who is Allan Sutton?
> - Why does Lalla move to London?

## Think Critically

**2.** Do you think Lalla makes a wise choice in the end? Why or why not?

**3.** **ACTIVE READING** | **PREDICTING** | Review the **predictions** that you made in your  **READER'S NOTEBOOK.** How close were your predictions to what actually happens? To what extent do you think the story's **exposition** provides clues about Lalla's future behavior? Explain your answer.

**4.** In what ways, if any, do you think Lalla's **character** and values change as she gets older? Use examples from the story to support your opinion.

> **THINK ABOUT**
> - her reaction to moving to Cornwall
> - her relationships with Godfrey and Allan
> - her comments to Jane after the Menheniots' dance
> - her final decision

**5.** How does Jane's view of her older sister affect what you think of Lalla?

## Extend Interpretations

**6. Critic's Corner** A magazine editor once noted, "When Rosamunde Pilcher writes about people, in crisis or at peace, falling in or out of love, discovering new life or accepting death, readers see themselves . . . or their children . . . or their parents." Do you agree? Explain.

**7. Connect to Life** What values do you think are most important for people to consider when they choose a mate?

## Literary Analysis

> **POINT OF VIEW**   Point of view refers to the type of **narrator** used in a story. The short story "Lalla" uses a **first-person point of view,** in which the narrator is a character in the story who tells everything in her own words. This narrator, Lalla's sister Jane, describes characters and relates events as she sees and understands them.

**Cooperative Learning Activity** Working in a small group, review the story and take notes about Jane's judgment of the following characters and settings: Lalla, Godfrey, Allan, Jane herself, Cornwall, London. Then consider how Jane's point of view influences your own judgment of the characters, events, and places in the story. What do you learn about Jane's values as a result of your reading?

*Lalla: Sometimes aloof ("Lalla was at her coolest, her most remote," Page 332)*

*Godfrey:*

# *Choices & CHALLENGES*

## Writing Options

**1. Movie Title** Imagine that this story is being turned into a television movie. Write a proposal for a new title that will attract viewers. Be sure to explain your reasoning.

**2. Lalla's List** Create the two lists of pros and cons Lalla might have made before she decided to return to Cornwall. On one list, show the benefits and problems of staying with Allan. On the other, analyze the advantages and disadvantages of returning to Godfrey.

**3. Telephone Talk** Write a script for a telephone conversation between Lalla and Allan in which she explains why she is leaving him and moving back to Cornwall.

## Activities & Explorations

**1. Values Poster** Create a poster. One side should include images that represent Allan's values; the other side should represent Godfrey's values. ~ **ART**

**2. Future Conversation** With three or four other classmates, act out an imaginary conversation that takes place 10 years after the story. Choose among the roles of Lalla, Godfrey, Jane, Mother, and Allan, and reminisce about "the old days." In the role of your character, talk about what happened and why you made the decisions you did. ~ **SPEAKING AND LISTENING**

## Inquiry & Research

**Exploring England** Find out more information about London and Cornwall. Then, in the light of your findings, discuss which of these two locations you would prefer to live in.

 **More Online: Research Starter** www.mcdougallittell.com

## Vocabulary in Action

**EXERCISE A: CONTEXT CLUES** Write the word that is closest in meaning to the italicized word or phrase in each sentence.

1. Allan spoke with *grudging acceptance* of Lalla's engagement to Godfrey.

2. Jane knew she would feel *very lonely* after Lalla got married.

3. Mother was exasperated with Lalla for *changing her mind* so often about the wedding plans.

4. For Lalla's sake, Godfrey and Allan put aside their *intense dislike* for each other.

5. On the wedding day the weather turned sunny and *mild.*

6. Before the ceremony, Uncle Peter spoke *distressingly* to Godfrey about the responsibilities of married life.

7. Remembering Uncle Peter's advice, Godfrey felt some *anxiety* about getting married.

8. Aunt Fran arrived wearing a *very silly* green feathered hat.

9. Allan missed the wedding because he could not *figure out* the map Barney sent him.

10. The ceremony went exactly as planned, and the organist played the wedding music *without a single mistake.*

**EXERCISE B** With a partner, take turns using facial expressions and/or body gestures to act out the meaning of three Words to Know each and guessing what word is being shown.

**Building Vocabulary**
For an in-depth lesson on context clues, see page 56.

| WORDS TO KNOW | | | | |
|---|---|---|---|---|
| benign | decipher | impeccably | resignation | unnervingly |
| bereft | enmity | ludicrous | trepidation | vacillating |

# Grammar in Context: Complex Sentences

In "Lalla," Rosamunde Pilcher uses complex sentences to show how events are related in time.

> **When the night of the dance came,** we put on our dresses and set off together in Mother's Mini.
>
> **As soon as I turned the corner at the end of the lane,** I saw Godfrey's car parked on the patch of grass outside the church.

A **complex sentence** consists of one independent clause and one or more subordinate clauses. An independent clause can stand alone as a sentence; a subordinate clause cannot. In the sentences above, the independent clauses are shown in blue, and the subordinate clauses are shown in red.

In a complex sentence, the independent clause expresses the main idea of the sentence. The subordinate clause or clauses express ideas that are less important than, but related to, the main idea. In the examples above, the subordinate clauses indicate the times at which the events related in the independent clauses took place. Subordinate clauses can also be used to express relationships of cause, condition, manner, place, and purpose.

**Usage Tip:** Subordinate clauses begin with subordinating conjunctions. These include *although, as soon as, because, than, that, when,* and *where.*

**WRITING EXERCISE** Rewrite each pair of sentences as a single complex sentence by turning the first sentence into a subordinate clause beginning with the conjunction shown in parentheses. Use a comma to separate the two clauses.

**Example:** ***Original*** The father dies. The family moves to Cornwall. *(after)*

***Rewritten*** <u>After the father dies</u>, the family moves to Cornwall.

1. Mother goes to the Roystons' house to introduce herself. Mrs. Royston isn't home. *(when)*
2. Mrs. Royston learns that Mother has come to visit. She invites the family over for tea. *(as soon as)*
3. Mrs. Royston chats with Mother. The children go to see the tree house. *(while)*
4. Lalla meets Allan Sutton at the dance. She has been close friends with Godfrey Royston. *(until)*
5. Lalla breaks her engagement with Allan. She starts spending time with Godfrey again. *(after)*

**Grammar Handbook**
The Structure of Sentences, p. 1198

## Rosamunde Pilcher
### 1924–

**Other Works**
*The Shell Seekers*
*The Blue Bedroom and Other Stories*
*September*
*Flowers in the Rain and Other Stories*

**Writer from Cornwall** Although she now lives in Scotland, Rosamunde Pilcher grew up in Cornwall, the setting of her story "Lalla." She joined the Women's Royal Naval Service during World War II and became a writer soon after the war ended. From 1949 to 1987 she published more than 20 romantic novels. Though her work was largely ignored by British critics, some of it was well received in America. Praise from the *New York*

*Times* for her novel *Sleeping Tiger* (1967) brought Rosamunde Pilcher to the attention of *Good Housekeeping* magazine, which has since published many of her stories. Nevertheless, it was not until *The Shell Seekers* appeared in 1987 that she found herself treated as a serious novelist.

**Fighting for Respect** Pilcher accepts being called a writer of "light fiction," but she dislikes the label "romantic fiction" and the contempt that often goes with it. After winning respect with *The Shell Seekers,* she commented, "All my life I've had people coming up and saying, 'Sat under the hair dryer and read one of your little stories, dear. So clever of you. Wish I had the time to do it myself.' . . . And now I'm hoping that nobody will ever, ever say that again."

# Love Without Love

**Poetry by LUIS LLORÉNS TORRES**
(lōō-ēs′ yô-rĕns′ tô′rĕs)

# The Taxi

**Poetry by AMY LOWELL**

## Connect to Your Life

**Images of Love** In a small group, identify images that suggest romantic love in our culture. For example, you might think of a movie scene with two people on a moonlit walk or a television commercial that portrays a man and a woman nestled before a fireplace. Then discuss what these images reveal about our views of romantic love. Use a chart like the one shown to keep track of your images and what they reveal. Share your findings with your classmates.

| Romantic Love in Our Culture | |
|---|---|
| **Image**<br>a man and a woman on a moonlit walk | **What It Reveals**<br>• peacefulness of love<br>• love removed from the harsh realities of ordinary life |

## Build Background

**Love Poetry** The following two poems use vivid, unexpected images to convey the poets' ideas about romantic love. The first poem is by Luis Lloréns Torres, a famous Puerto Rican poet who began publishing his verse in 1899 and was noted for his love poems and his patriotic verse. The second poem is by Amy Lowell, an American poet who won fame just a few years after Lloréns Torres. This poem reflects Lowell's interest in **imagism,** a literary movement that stressed the importance of using clear, precise images in poetry.

## Focus Your Reading

**LITERARY ANALYSIS   METAPHOR AND SIMILE**   A **simile** is a direct comparison, using the words *like* or *as,* between two unlike things that have something in common. A **metaphor** is a similar form of comparison, but without the use of *like* or *as.* In "Love Without Love," for example, the speaker refers to "the dog of my heart," which is a metaphor. As you read the two poems, note the poets' use of these forms of figurative language. Ask yourself how each poet's use of metaphor and simile contributes to the main ideas of each poem.

**ACTIVE READING   PARAPHRASING**   One strategy that can help you understand a poem more fully is to **paraphrase** it—that is, to restate parts or all of the poem in your own words. When you paraphrase, you will often need to use more words than the poet, as shown by the example below. Your paraphrase should attempt to convey the meaning of the events, emotions, and attitudes suggested by the poem.

**READER'S NOTEBOOK** As you read these poems, identify lines that seem particularly significant to the poem or whose meaning is not completely clear to you. Paraphrase these lines, using a chart like the one shown to the right.

| Poem: "Love Without Love" | |
|---|---|
| **Line:**<br>Suddenly I've felt you flying through my soul . . . | **Paraphrase:**<br>Unexpectedly I have your presence, as if you were moving through me. |

# Love Without Love

### Luis Lloréns Torres

I love you, because in my thousand and one nights of dreams,
I never once dreamed of you.
I looked down paths that traveled from afar,
but it was never you I expected.
5  Suddenly I've felt you flying through my soul
in quick, lofty flight,
and how beautiful you seem way up there, far
from my always idiot heart!
Love me that way, flying over everything.
10  And, like the bird on its branch, land in my arms
only to rest,
then fly off again.
Be not like the romantic ones who,
    in love, set me on fire.
When you climb up my mansion,
15  enter so lightly, that as you enter
the dog of my heart will not bark.

*Translated by Julio Marzán*

## Thinking Through the Literature

1. Think about the **image** from this poem that stands out the most to you. What does this image make you think of?

2. What does the **speaker's** choice of images say to you about his attitude toward his relationship with his loved one?

   **THINK ABOUT**
   - the image of the bird flying through his soul in lines 5–6
   - the speaker's reference to his "idiot heart" in line 8
   - the contrast between his beloved and "the romantic ones" in line 13
   - the speaker's request in lines 15–16

3. What does the **title** of the poem mean to you?

4. Compare and contrast your ideas about love with those of the speaker.

# THE TAXI

## AMY LOWELL

When I go away from you
The world beats dead
Like a slackened drum.
I call out for you against the jutted stars
5  And shout into the ridges of the wind.
Streets coming fast,
One after the other,
Wedge you away from me,
And the lamps of the city prick my eyes
10  So that I can no longer see your face.
Why should I leave you,
To wound myself upon the sharp edges of the night?

*Times Square, New York City No. 2* (1990), Robert Gniewek. Oil on linen, 38″ × 60″,
courtesy of Louis K. Meisel Gallery, New York. Photo by Steve Lopez.

# Connect to the Literature

1. **What Do You Think?** What questions would you like to ask the speaker in "The Taxi"?

# Think Critically

2. Based on the **images** used in this poem, how would you describe the speaker's feelings about love?

THINK
ABOUT

- the sound a slackened drum would make, as described in lines 2–3
- her sense of the streets wedging her loved one away from her in line 8
- the last two lines, where she compares leaving her loved one to being wounded

3. Do you think "The Taxi" is a good **title** for this poem? Explain your reasoning.

4. **ACTIVE READING** **PARAPHRASING** Look back at the lines you paraphrased in your **READER'S NOTEBOOK.** Compare your **paraphrases** with those of your classmates. What lines were the most difficult to paraphrase? Did you find it easier to paraphrase one of the poems, or did both present a similar level of difficulty?

# Extend Interpretations

5. **Comparing Texts** Compare and contrast the **speakers'** attitudes toward love in "Love Without Love" and "The Taxi."

6. **Connect to Life** Which speaker's view of love appeals more to you? Explain your choice.

## Literary Analysis

**METAPHOR AND SIMILE**

**Metaphors** and **similes** are forms of **figurative language** that make comparisons between things that are basically unlike but have something in common. For example, Lowell compares the wind with a solid, physical obstacle in the metaphor "the ridges of the wind." Unlike a metaphor, a simile states the comparison between two things directly by using the word *like* or *as.* Identify one simile and at least one metaphor in each poem. What ideas are being communicated in each of these examples of figurative language?

**Paired Activity** Explain the metaphor in lines 5–9 of "Love Without Love." How does the image of love expressed in this metaphor compare with some of the images you identified and discussed for Connect to Your Life on page 346?

| METAPHOR | SIMILE |
| --- | --- |
| is | like *or* as |

# TONIGHT
## *I Can Write . . .*

PABLO NERUDA

Tonight I can write the saddest lines.

Write, for example, 'The night is shattered
and the blue stars shiver in the distance.'

The night wind revolves in the sky and sings.

5    Tonight I can write the saddest lines.
I loved her, and sometimes she loved me too.

Through nights like this one I held her in my arms.
I kissed her again and again under the endless sky.

She loved me, sometimes I loved her too.
10   How could one not have loved her great still eyes.

Tonight I can write the saddest lines.
To think that I do not have her. To feel that I have lost her.

To hear the immense night, still more immense without her.
And the verse falls to the soul like dew to the pasture.

15   What does it matter that my love could not keep her.
The night is shattered and she is not with me.

This is all. In the distance someone is singing. In the distance.
My soul is not satisfied that it has lost her.

My sight searches for her as though to go to her.
20   My heart looks for her, and she is not with me.

The same night whitening the same trees.
We, of that time, are no longer the same.

I no longer love her, that's certain, but how I loved her.
My voice tried to find the wind to touch her hearing.

25   Another's. She will be another's. Like my kisses before.
Her voice. Her bright body. Her infinite eyes.

I no longer love her, that's certain, but maybe I love her.
Love is so short, forgetting is so long.

Because through nights like this one I held her in my arms
30   my soul is not satisfied that it has lost her.

Though this be the last pain that she makes me suffer
and these the last verses that I write for her.

*Translated by W. S. Merwin*

# PUEDO
## *Escribir Los Versos . . .*
### PABLO NERUDA

Puedo escribir los versos más tristes esta noche.

Escribir, por ejemplo: 'La noche está estrellada,
y tiritan, azules, los astros, a lo lejos.'

El viento de la noche gira en el cielo y canta.

5 Puedo escribir los versos más tristes esta noche.
Yo la quise, y a veces ella también me quiso.

En las noches como ésta la tuve entre mis brazos.
La besé tantas veces bajo el cielo infinito.

Ella me quiso, a veces yo también la quería.
10 Cómo no haber amado sus grandes ojos fijos.

Puedo escribir los versos más tristes esta noche.
Pensar que no la tengo. Sentir que la he perdido.

Oir la noche inmensa, más inmensa sin ella.
Y el verso cae al alma como al pasto el rocío.

15 Qué importa que mi amor no pudiera guardarla.
La noche está estrellada y ella no está conmigo.

Eso es todo. A lo lejos alguien canta. A lo lejos.
Mi alma no se contenta con haberla perdido.

Como para acercarla mi mirada la busca.
20 Mi corazón la busca, y ella no está conmigo.

La misma noche que hace blanquear los mismos arboles.
Nosotros, los de entonces, ya no somos los mismos.

Ya no la quiero, es cierto, pero cuánto la quise.
Mi voz buscaba el viento para tocar su oído.

25 De otro. Será de otro. Como antes de mis besos.
Su voz, su cuerpo claro. Sus ojos infinitos.

Ya no la quiero, es cierto, pero tal vez la quiero.
Es tan corto el amor, y es tan largo el olvido.

Porque en noches como ésta la tuve entre mis brazos,
30 mi alma no se contenta con haberla perdido.

Aunque éste sea el último dolor que ella me causa,
y éstos sean los últimos versos que yo le escribo.

## Connect to the Literature

**1. What Do You Think?**
Which lines of "Tonight I Can Write . . ." are the most memorable for you? Why?

**Comprehension Check**
- Why is the speaker's soul "not satisfied"?
- What aspects of nature are most prominent in the poem?

## Think Critically

**2.** [ACTIVE READING] [INTERPRETING COMPARISONS] Review the chart that you created in your [📖] **READER'S NOTEBOOK.** What do the **images** from nature reveal about the speaker's emotions and experience?

**THINK ABOUT**
- why the speaker says "The night is shattered and the blue stars shiver"
- what you learn about the speaker's relationship with the woman
- why the night feels "still more immense without her"
- what this night reminds him of

**3.** Do you think the **speaker** still loves the woman? Support your opinion.

**4.** Reread the last two lines of the poem. What is your opinion of the speaker's conclusion?

**5.** How do you think "Tonight I Can Write . . . " relates to the **theme** of this part of the unit, "Mysteries of the Heart"? Explain.

## Extend Interpretations

**6. Comparing Texts** Do you think this poem has more in common with Amy Lowell's "Taxi" (page 348) or with N. Scott Momaday's "Simile" (page 256)? Cite details to support your evaluation.

**7. Connect to Life** Why do you think so many poems and songs are about love and its loss? Discuss this question with your classmates, using examples of songs or other poems about lost love that you find particularly memorable.

## Literary Analysis

[REPETITION] **Repetition** is a literary technique in which sounds, words, phrases, or lines are repeated for emphasis or unity. In "Tonight I Can Write . . ." Neruda repeats the first line three times to emphasize the speaker's sorrow and to help unify the poem.

**Paired Activity** With a partner, make a list of other repeated words, phrases, or lines. Then discuss how each instance of repetition affects your understanding of the speaker's feelings. Why do you think Neruda sometimes repeats part of a line and then adds new information?

[REVIEW] [FIGURATIVE LANGUAGE]
Review the poem and identify each **metaphor, simile,** or **personification.** Then create one metaphor, one simile, and one personification of your own to compare your feelings to objects in nature.

## Writing Options

**1. Lovelorn Paragraph** Draft a paragraph that explains the speaker's situation. Include details or quotations from the poem. Then share your writing with a classmate and compare your explanations.

**2. Personal Poem** Express your own ideas about love and loss in a poem. Try to include images from nature as well as repetition and figurative language to help emphasize and unify your ideas.

## Activities & Explorations

**Dramatic Monologue** In a dramatic monologue, give the other side of the story for the poem. In other words, assume the identity of the loved one in the poem and express your feelings and ideas about the relationship described by the speaker. ~ **PERFORMING**

## Inquiry & Research

**Mood Music** Find a contemporary song that reveals some of the same emotions conveyed by "Tonight I Can Write . . ." Share the song with your classmates and discuss how it relates to the poem.

## Pablo Neruda
### 1904–1973

**Other Works**
*Residence on Earth*
*Elemental Odes*
*The Heights of Macchu Picchu*
*Extravagaria*

**Early Success** Pablo Neruda, the pen name of Ricardo Eliezer Neftalí Reyes y Basoalto, was drawn to poetry at an early age, even though his working-class family scoffed at his literary ambitions. He began publishing poems at the age of 15. When just 20, he won celebrity throughout his native Chile with *Twenty Love Poems and a Song of Despair* in which "Tonight I Can Write . . ." first appeared.

**Political Poetry** After Neruda served in his nation's diplomatic corps—an honor then commonly granted to talented Latin American writers—he shifted the focus of his poetry to political and social criticism. In the early 1970s, Neruda supported Chile's socialist leader Salvador Allende and served as his nation's ambassador to France. When the poet received the 1971 Nobel Prize in literature, the event was celebrated as a national holiday in his homeland. Neruda produced more than 40 volumes of poetry, translations, and verse drama during his literary career.

## Author Activity

**With Hindsight** In later life, Neruda renounced much of his earlier work. Find out why and report your findings back to the class. Then discuss what you think about Neruda's verdict.

## Ancient Roots

The English language is like a city with a long history—if you dig below the modern surface, you find remains of former civilizations. In English, some of the most important remains are Greek and Latin; these two languages underlie many of the words we use every day. Take a look, for example, at the excerpt on the right. The highlighted words would look familiar to citizens of ancient Rome.

The word *delicious* is a descendant of the Latin word *dēliciōsus*. *Populous* and *solitude* come from the

> It was a lovely region, woodsy, balmy, delicious, and had once been populous, long years before, but now the people had vanished and the charming paradise was a solitude.
>
> —Mark Twain, "The Californian's Tale"

Latin words *populōsus* and *sōlitūdō*. In each case, the meanings of the modern English word and the ancient Latin word are just about the same.

## Strategies for Building Vocabulary

The words *delicious*, *populous*, and *solitude* are modeled closely on their ancient Latin sources. Familiarizing yourself with word origins can help you determine and remember the meanings of unfamiliar words.

❶ **Word Families** The core of the word *solitude* is the Latin root *sol*, meaning "alone"—a root that also appears in a number of other English words, such as *soliloquy* and *solitary*. Because these words contain the same root, they are related in meaning. You can often figure out the meanings of words in such a "word family" if you know the meaning of the root they share. The chart below shows several members of the *sol* family. Note the shared element in their meanings.

| English Words Containing the Latin Root *Sol* | |
| --- | --- |
| **Word** | **Meaning** |
| *desolation* | a state of being abandoned; loneliness |
| *sole* | only |
| *soliloquy* | a speech by a character alone on stage |
| *solitaire* | a card game played by one person |
| *solitary* | living or going without others |
| *solitude* | a state of being alone |
| *solo* | a performance by single individual |

❷ **Spelling** Recognizing roots and word families can also help you spell words correctly. For example, *pictograph*, *phonograph*, and *geography* all contain the Greek root *graph*. Knowing how to

spell the root makes it easier to figure out how to spell the words that contain it.

❸ **Word Histories** If a word has an interesting history, or etymology, knowing that history can help you remember the word's meaning. Consider the word *dragoon*, meaning "to compel by threats or force." This word comes from the French word *dragon* and was originally a noun denoting a kind of firearm (one that "breathed fire" like a dragon). Later, it was used to refer to a soldier armed with that type of gun. Then, in the 17th and 18th centuries, when European monarchs frequently used these soldiers to keep their subjects in line, the word came to be used as a verb in the way it is today. If you remember *dragoon*'s history, you will have no trouble remembering its meaning.

**EXERCISE** Identify the root of each word and tell what the root means. Then write the word's meaning, a sentence containing the word, and at least one related word. Use a dictionary if you need help.

1. predecessor
2. significant
3. implore
4. seismograph
5. creditable

Bill Cosby's talent lies in his ability to share, in a humorous way, experiences that we all know or understand. From childhood tales like "Tonsils" and "Cool Covers" on his early comedy albums to later routines about his growing family to his portrayal of Dr. Huxtable on *The Cosby Show*, his best comedy has always flowed out of real-life situations. His is the art of drawing people closer together by showing us how much we have in common.

In this excerpt from *Love and Marriage*, Cosby relates a story that, despite its humorous treatment, still rings true—how hurt pride and disappointment can make us do crazy things.

# from Love and Marriage

## Bill Cosby

During my last year of high school, I fell in love so hard with a girl that it made my love for Sarah McKinney seem like a stupid infatuation with a teacher. Charlene Gibson was the Real Thing and she would be Mrs. Charlene Cosby, serving me hot dogs and watching me drive to the hoop and giving me the full-court press for the rest of my life.

In tribute to our great love, I was moved to give Charlene something to wear. A Temple[1] T-shirt didn't seem quite right and neither did my Truman button.[2] What Charlene needed was a piece of jewelry; and I was able to find the perfect one, an elegant pin, in my mother's dresser drawer.

---

1. **Temple:** Temple University in Philadelphia, Pennsylvania, which Cosby attended.

2. **Truman button:** a button supporting the candidacy of Harry Truman (1884–1972) who became president after the death of Franklin Roosevelt in 1945 and ran for the office on his own in 1948.

Putting my face close to Artemis's face, I broke into laughter, as if she had just said something hilarious.

But he was wrong: I had *lost* my head in beauty, so the Friday party became a blend of revenge and desire for me. A few minutes after Artemis and I had arrived, while I was busy parading her like a poodle going for Best in Show, Charlene came in—and suddenly, my future and past were together in one room. Charlene saw me with Artemis, of course, and I was delighted that her suffering had begun. Putting my face close to Artemis's face, I broke into laughter, as if she had just said something hilarious.

"You feelin' okay?" she said.

"Never better," I told her, still laughing.

"You been hittin' that high bar a lot?"

"I love it when you talk like that."

A few seconds later, seeing Charlene move to the punch bowl, I said to Artemis, "Will you excuse me for a moment?"

"For as long as you want," she replied.

I turned and walked over to Charlene, casually saying, "Why, Charlene Gibson, I *thought* it was you. What're *you* doing here?"

"Making a big mistake," she said. "Artemis and *you?* Since when did she start doing social work with thieves?"

"Glad you're having fun, Charlene."

"What're you gonna steal for *her?* Your mother's *watch?*"

"Have some pink and white mints. They'll really clear your head."

"I know you, Bill Cosby. You're just rentin' that girl to make me feel bad. I thought you wanted to be friends."

"Well, I did," I said, suddenly wishing that I had chosen a more gracious revenge.

"I thought you wanted me to be able to ask you questions."

"Well . . . yeah."

"Okay, here's one: Are you ever gonna grow up?"

It was a simple true-false question, the kind on which I usually guessed, and so I took a guess now: "I certainly am."

Often through the years, I have thought of Charlene's question; and I now know the answer is that no man ever grows up in the eyes of a woman—or ever grows familiar with the rules for dealing with her. Sigmund Freud[8] once said, "What do women want?" The only thing I have learned in fifty-two years is that women want men to stop asking dumb questions like that. ❖

---

8. **Sigmund Freud** (sĭg′mənd froid): an Austrian doctor who developed the theory and practice of psychoanalysis.

## Bill Cosby
1937–

**Other Works**
*Fatherhood*

**Versatility with a Smile** Actor, author, comic, educator—Bill Cosby is very funny, but he is also multifaceted. In the early 1960s, Cosby toured the country and made albums as a comic. His first acting job was playing a secret agent in the espionage series *I Spy,* which ran from 1965 to 1968. He was the first African American to have a starring dramatic role on network television, and his fine work earned him three Emmy Awards. His animated program *Fat Albert and the Cosby Kids* won him a new generation of viewers, and the role of Dr. Heathcliff Huxtable on *The Cosby Show* broadened his popularity further. In 1984, Cosby was inducted into the Television Hall of Fame.

**Values Education** Cosby is justifiably proud of his education, which is why the credits for *The Cosby Show* list him as William H. Cosby, Jr., Ed.D. Cosby left high school without earning his diploma, but passed his equivalency exam while in the U.S. Navy. Once out of the military, Cosby won an athletic scholarship to Temple University in Philadelphia, but he left during his sophomore year to pursue his comedy career. He later resumed his studies at the University of Massachusetts and was awarded a doctorate degree in education in 1977. Cosby and his wife, Camile, are active in promoting education among African Americans. In 1988 they donated $20 million to Spelman College in Atlanta.

## Author Activity

**Art Imitates Life** Select a segment from one of Cosby's works that typifies his humor. Share your choice with your classmates, either by reading aloud or by playing an audio or video recording. Discuss the basis of Cosby's appeal.

# Writing Workshop

## Recommending a course of action. . .

**From Reading to Writing** The story "Lalla" is about a young woman who solves a problem: Which man should she marry, and what kind of life should she lead? Fiction dealing with problems compels interest because life also has many problems and conflicts. One way to deal with these difficulties is to analyze the problem and explore possible solutions. **Problem-solution** writing can be found in places ranging from newspaper editiorials to personal letters.

**For Your Portfolio**

**WRITING PROMPT** Write a problem-solution essay that examines a problem that deeply interests you.

**Purpose:** To inform, to persuade
**Audience:** Anyone interested in the problem you are addressing

---

## Basics in a Box

### Problem-Solution Essay at a Glance

**Introduction**
present and analyze the problem

**Body**
present and explain possible solutions

**Conclusion**
restate the problem and the benefits of the solution

---

**RUBRIC** **Standards for Writing**

**A successful problem-solution essay should**

- clearly state a problem and explain its significance
- explore all aspects of the problem, including its causes and effects
- offer one or more reasonable solutions and explain how to put them into effect
- use anecdotes, examples, facts, or statistics to support the proposed solutions
- use logical reasoning to persuade the audience

---

# Analyzing a Student Model

**Raleigh Postiglione**
**Whitney Young High School**

### High School Cliques in Today's Society

Today, high school is not only a steppingstone to higher education but it is a time for teenagers to create themselves, meet new people, and begin discovering and nurturing their talents. However, such obstacles as cliques can hamper this progress. A clique is a small group of people who socialize mainly among themselves and exclude others. Whether these cliques are based on appearance, wealth, or race, they can harm both their own members and those excluded from them. Cliques thrive on ignorance and prejudice and restrict academic performance and social interaction. They can have permanent psychological effects.

On an academic level, cliques inhibit such activities as group work and class discussion. In the classroom, it is extremely important to have an environment where students can feel comfortable and safe. Otherwise, it will be difficult for them to reach their full potential. A teacher's job is to promote interaction among all students in order to expose them to new ideas. When only a few students dominate the group and ridicule or reject others, there can be no open exchange of ideas in the classroom.

Cliques also create social obstacles. From as early as kindergarten, cliques gradually begin to form, and they can grow tighter and more selective as the years pass. This is why it is so important for parents to instill open-mindedness in their children from an early age. Kids who view the world through biased eyes are often the cause of cliques. Young children have great potential to be independent thinkers and caring souls, but they can also be very fragile. For example, at a magnet school where students come from all over the city and from many different backgrounds, some children may judge and reject others on the basis of physical appearance, fashion, or other trivial matters. This kind of rejection can snowball and continue for years.

Though it is hard to believe that rejection from a few teenagers could permanently scar an individual, it happens. A high school student looks on this rejection not as mere dislike from a bunch of kids but as cruel rejection by his or her peers, those who should provide support and understanding. If a person is sensitive and vulnerable, this reaction from fellow classmates can be traumatic and make it difficult to reach one's full academic and personal potential. Growing up is tough, but there is often

## RUBRIC
### IN ACTION

**❶** Defines the problem and explains why it is significant

**❷** Explores one aspect of the problem

**❸** Identifies a possible cause of another aspect of the problem

**❹** Uses transitional words to clarify the connections between ideas

comfort in knowing that others can relate to your problems and that everyone is basically in the same boat. Cliques isolate some students and leave them to fend for themselves. High school is a jungle. The fittest survive, and those who cannot conform and fit in somewhere are left in the dust.

Even those who do "fit in" may feel the negative effects of being in a clique later in life. Being in a select group of friends from whom you never fear rejection and humiliation leaves you with little experience in coping with the real world. Cliques are present not only in high school but in the workplace and the social world as well. Just because you may have been accepted among one group does not necessarily mean you will receive as warm a welcome in a different setting.

Although many students would like to eliminate cliques, it may not be possible for students alone to bring their different social circles together. A push from teachers is necessary. Teachers cannot control whom their students associate with at lunch and on weekends, but they can promote positive interaction in their classrooms. It is a teacher's duty not just to lecture to a nameless group of students but to some extent to guide students' social interaction. For instance, in my sophomore English Literature class, my teacher puts us in groups of four several times a week. To complete the work, we must cooperate and listen to everyone's comments. Whether students are reluctant or not, the teacher should consciously pair a "bookworm" with a "jock" and a "prep" with a "rebel." This shows people that though they may dress differently and like different things, deep down they all want to have friends and be respected and liked.

Outside the classroom, teachers, students, and counselors could sponsor assemblies at which student leaders tell of personal experiences with cliques and encourage everyone to reach out to others. Many schools have sponsored anti-clique programs in which students make a real attempt to befriend a large variety of people.

In a world where everyone must strive to overcome prejudice and bias of some sort, there is no place for cliques. Good friendships are one thing, but elite, discriminating kids are another. To achieve a more open-minded society, it must be instilled in children early to be respectful and understanding of all people and never to prejudge. At the time, a high school clique may not appear to be a big deal, but its effects can last late into life. Students should avoid cliques, give everyone a chance, and perceive the world as it is: an ever-changing society made up of unique individuals who must be appreciated and respected for who and what they are.

**❺** Offers one solution to the problem and supports it with a specific example

**❻** This writer gives a second possible solution and tells how to put it into effect.

**Other Options:**
- Elaborate on the first solution with facts or statistics.
- Discuss the merits and drawbacks of the first solution.

**❼** Concludes by using valid reasoning to persuade the audience to adopt the proposed solutions

# Writing Your Problem-Solution Essay

## ❶ Prewriting

*Man is a problem-solving animal. . .*

**Joyce Carol Oates, American writer**

Begin by thinking of a meaningful problem. **Brainstorm** problems that you have discussed with your friends lately. **Recall** current school, community, national, and international problems. See the **Idea Bank** in the margin for more suggestions. After you have selected a problem in need of a solution, follow the steps below.

### Planning Your Problem-Solution Essay

▶ **1. Think about the problem.** Why do you think it is a serious problem? What are its causes and effects?

▶ **2. Brainstorm possible solutions.** How might the problem be solved? Consider drawing a cluster map to display possible solutions.

▶ **3. Consider each solution and eliminate impractical ones.** Does one solution stand out as the best solution? Will people support it? Will it draw political and economic backing?

▶ **4. Identify your audience.** Who will read your essay? What do they already know and feel about the problem? How can you address their concerns?

▶ **5. Research necessary supporting facts.** What kinds of data will help support the solution to the problem? Do you need to do research, consult experts, or examine your own thoughts?

## ❷ Drafting

As you begin drafting, don't be too concerned about form or completeness. You can perfect your writing later. You may want to try the following organization:

- **Identify** the problem and explain why it is significant.

- **Explain** the causes and effects of the problem, giving facts, statistics, examples, or quotations to support your points.

- **Explain and support** the proposed solutions. Address any concerns or objections your audience may have.

- **Conclude** by describing how to achieve the solutions.

### Ask Your Peer Reader

- How would you define the problem I describe?

- Which information did you find most and least convincing?

- What information is missing or unclear?

### IDEABank

**1. Your Working Portfolio**
Build on one of the **Writing Options** you completed earlier in this unit :

**Alternative Solutions**, p. 313

**Problem-Solution Essay**, p. 327

**2. Issues and Answers**
Read the letters to the editor in a local newspaper. What issues are people concerned about? What reasonable solutions can you offer?

**3. Problem Interview**
Ask several people to name a personal, local, national, and international problem that concerns them. Chart their answers and choose one problem to write about.

**Need revising help?**

Review the **Rubric,**
p. 364

Consider **peer reader**
comments

Check **Revision
Guidelines,** p. 1145

# ❸ Revising

**TARGET SKILL** ▶ **SENTENCE COMBINING** Using too many short sentences makes your writing choppy and often doesn't show the logical relationship between ideas. In a problem-solution essay, you may want to join sentences with words such as *because, therefore, although,* and *but.*

> *Although*
> ∧Many students would like to eliminate cliques. It may
>
> not be possible for students alone to bring their different
>
> social circles together. A push from teachers is necessary.
>
> Teachers cannot control whom their students associate
>
> *but*
> with at lunch and on weekends. They can promote positive
>
> interaction in their classroom.

**Rattled by run-ons
and fragments?**

See the **Grammar
Handbook,** p. 1199

# ❹ Editing and Proofreading

**TARGET SKILL** ▶ **RUN-ONS** Run-on sentences—two or more sentences written as though they were one—can confuse your readers. Correct run-ons by rewriting long sentences as two separate sentences, by joining them with a semicolon or coordinating conjunction, or by making one of the sentences into a subordinate clause.

> *but*
> Growing up is tough,∧there is often comfort in knowing that
>
> others can relate to your problems and that everyone is
>
> basically in the same boat. Cliques isolate some students
>
> and leave them to fend for themselves. High school is a
>
> jungle, the fittest survive and those who cannot conform and
>
> fit in somewhere are left in the dust.

**Publishing
IDEAS**

• Send your essay as
a letter to the editor
of a school or local
newspaper.

• E-mail your essay to
a friend. If it deals
with a larger
problem, E-mail it to
a list of people with
interest in the issue.

**More Online:
Publishing Options**
www.mcdougallittell.com

# ❺ Reflecting

**FOR YOUR WORKING PORTFOLIO** How did writing your essay help you find a solution to the problem? Attach your answer to your finished work. Save your problem-solution essay in your **Working Portfolio.** 📁

Read this paragraph from the first draft of a problem-and-solution essay. The underlined sections may include the following kinds of errors:

- **correctly written sentences that should be combined**
- **lack of pronoun-antecedent agreement**
- **run-on sentences**
- **spelling errors**

For each underlined section, choose the revision that most improves the writing.

---

<u>Some teenagers feel shy. This isn't unusual</u>. Some shy teenagers are afraid of
<u>(1)</u>
appearing <u>aukward</u> in front of their peers. Others worry that <u>they</u> don't have
<u>(2)</u> <u>(3)</u>
anything interesting to say. "For me, being in a room full of strangers is scary,"
explains one high school student. "<u>What if people don't like me what if nobody</u>
<u>(4)</u>
<u>says anything to me?</u>" Most teenagers will <u>probly</u> overcome their shyness as they
<u>(5)</u>
get older. However, there are techniques teens can use to help <u>themselves</u>, such as
<u>(6)</u>
striking up a conversation with a new student.

---

1. **A.** Some teenagers feel shy, this isn't unusual.
   **B.** Some teenagers feel shy this isn't unusual.
   **C.** It isn't unusual for teenagers to feel shy.
   **D.** Correct as is

2. **A.** awkward
   **B.** akward
   **C.** alkward
   **D.** Correct as is

3. **A.** we
   **B.** them
   **C.** us
   **D.** Correct as is

4. **A.** "What if people don't like me, what if nobody says anything to me?"
   **B.** "What if people don't like me? What if nobody says anything to me?"
   **C.** "What if people don't like me. what if nobody says anything to me?"
   **D.** Correct as is

5. **A.** probably
   **B.** probabley
   **C.** probley
   **D.** Correct as is

6. **A.** himself
   **B.** ourselves
   **C.** theirselves
   **D.** Correct as is

**Need extra help?**

See the **Grammar Handbook**
**Correcting Run-on Sentences**, p. 1199
**Pronoun Agreement**, p. 1183

# The Search for IDENTITY

"Who
in the
world
am I?
Ah,
that's
the great
puzzle!"

LEWIS CARROLL

*Allées Piétonnières* (1995),
Jean-Pierre Stora.
The Grand Design, Leeds,
England/Superstock.

# INITIATION

## SYLVIA PLATH

The basement room was dark and warm, like the inside of a sealed jar, Millicent thought, her eyes getting used to the strange dimness. The silence was soft with cobwebs, and from the small, rectangular window set high in the stone wall there sifted a faint bluish light that must have been coming from the full October moon. She could see now that what she was sitting on was a woodpile next to the furnace.

Millicent brushed back a strand of hair. It was stiff and sticky from the egg that they had broken on her head as she knelt blindfolded at the sorority altar a short while before. There had been a silence, a slight crunching sound, and then she had felt the cold, slimy egg-white flattening and spreading on her head and sliding down her neck. She had heard someone smothering a laugh. It was all part of the ceremony.

Then the girls had led her here, blindfolded still, through the corridors of Betsy Johnson's house and shut her in the cellar. It would be an hour before they came to get her, but then Rat Court would be all over and she would say what she had to say and go home.

For tonight was the grand finale, the trial by fire. There really was no doubt now that she would get in. She could not think of anyone who had ever been invited into the high school sorority and

There really was no doubt now that she would get in.

failed to get through initiation time. But even so, her case would be quite different. She would see to that. She could not exactly say what had decided her revolt, but it definitely had something to do with Tracy and something to do with the heather birds.

What girl at Lansing High would not want to be in her place now? Millicent thought, amused. What girl would not want to be one of the elect,[1] no matter if it did mean five days of initiation before and after school, ending in the climax of Rat Court on Friday night when they made the new girls members? Even Tracy had been wistful when she heard that Millicent had been one of the five girls to receive an invitation.

"It won't be any different with us, Tracy," Millicent had told her. "We'll still go around together like we always have, and next year you'll surely get in."

"I know, but even so," Tracy had said quietly, "you'll change, whether you think you will or not. Nothing ever stays the same."

And nothing does, Millicent had thought. How horrible it would be if one never changed . . . if she were condemned to be the plain, shy Millicent of a few years back for the rest of her life. Fortunately there was always the changing, the growing, the going on.

It would come to Tracy, too. She would tell Tracy the silly things the girls had said, and Tracy would change also, entering eventually into the magic circle. She would grow to know the special ritual as Millicent had started to last week.

"First of all," Betsy Johnson, the vivacious blonde secretary of the sorority, had told the five new candidates over sandwiches in the school cafeteria last Monday, "first of all, each of you has a big sister. She's the one who bosses you around, and you just do what she tells you."

"Remember the part about talking back and smiling," Louise Fullerton had put in, laughing.

She was another celebrity in high school, pretty and dark and Vice-President of the Student Council. "You can't say anything unless your big sister asks you something or tells you to talk to someone. And you can't smile, no matter how you're dying to." The girls had laughed a little nervously, and then the bell had rung for the beginning of afternoon classes.

It would be rather fun for a change, Millicent mused, getting her books out of her locker in the hall, rather exciting to be part of a closely knit group, the exclusive set at Lansing High. Of course, it wasn't a school organization. In fact, the principal, Mr. Cranton, wanted to do away with initiation week altogether, because he thought it was undemocratic and disturbed the routine of school work. But there wasn't really anything he could do about it. Sure, the girls had to come to school for five days without any lipstick on and without curling their hair, and of course everybody noticed them, but what could the teachers do?

Millicent sat down at her desk in the big study hall. Tomorrow she would come to school, proudly, laughingly, without lipstick, with her brown hair straight and shoulder length, and then everybody would know, even the boys would know, that she was one of the elect. Teachers would smile helplessly, thinking perhaps: So now they've picked Millicent Arnold. I never would have guessed it.

A year or two ago, not many people would have guessed it. Millicent had waited a long time for acceptance, longer than most. It was as if she had been sitting for years in a pavilion[2] outside a dance floor, looking in through the windows at the golden interior, with the lights clear and the air like honey, wistfully watching the gay couples

---

1. **elect:** elite group; "in" crowd.
2. **pavilion** (pə-vĭl′yən): a small roofed structure in a garden or park.

waltzing to the never-ending music, laughing in pairs and groups together, no one alone.

But now at last, amid a week of <u>fanfare</u> and merriment, she would answer her invitation to enter the ballroom through the main entrance marked "Initiation." She would gather up her velvet skirts, her silken train, or whatever the <u>disinherited</u> princesses wore in the story books, and come into her rightful kingdom. . . . The bell rang to end study hall.

"Millicent, wait up!" It was Louise Fullerton behind her, Louise who had always before been very nice, very polite, friendlier than the rest, even long ago, before the invitation had come.

"Listen," Louise walked down the hall with her to Latin, their next class, "are you busy right after school today? Because I'd like to talk to you about tomorrow."

"Sure. I've got lots of time."

"Well, meet me in the hall after home room then, and we'll go down to the drugstore or something."

Walking beside Louise on the way to the drugstore, Millicent felt a surge of pride. For all anyone could see, she and Louise were the best of friends.

"You know, I was so glad when they voted you in," Louise said.

Millicent smiled. "I was really thrilled to get the invitation," she said frankly, "but kind of sorry that Tracy didn't get in, too."

Tracy, she thought. If there is such a thing as a best friend, Tracy has been just that this last year.

*Bauhaus Stairway* (1932), Oskar Schlemmer. Oil on canvas, 63⅞" × 45". The Museum of Modern Art, New York. Gift of Philip Johnson. Photograph copyright © 1998 The Museum of Modern Art.

"Yes, Tracy," Louise was saying, "she's a nice girl, and they put her up on the slate, but . . . well, she had three blackballs against her."

"Blackballs? What are they?"

"Well, we're not supposed to tell anybody outside the club, but seeing as you'll be in at the end of the week I don't suppose it hurts." They were at the drugstore now.

"You see," Louise began explaining in a low voice after they were seated in the privacy of the booth, "once a year the sorority puts up all the likely girls that are suggested for membership . . ."

Millicent sipped her cold, sweet drink slowly, saving the ice cream to spoon up last. She listened carefully to Louise, who was going on, ". . . and then there's a big meeting, and all the girls' names are read off and each girl is discussed."

"Oh?" Millicent asked mechanically, her voice sounding strange.

"Oh, I know what you're thinking," Louise laughed. "But it's really not as bad as all that. They keep it down to a minimum of catting.[3] They just talk over each girl and why or why not they think she'd be good for the club. And then they vote. Three blackballs eliminate a girl."

"Do you mind if I ask you what happened to Tracy?" Millicent said.

Louise laughed a little uneasily. "Well, you know how girls are. They notice little things. I mean, some of them thought Tracy was just a bit *too* different. Maybe you could suggest a few things to her."

"Like what?"

"Oh, like maybe not wearing knee socks to school, or carrying that old bookbag. I know it doesn't sound like much, but well, it's things like that which set someone apart. I mean, you know that no girl at Lansing would be seen dead wearing knee socks, no matter how cold it gets, and it's kiddish and kind of green to carry a bookbag."

"I guess so," Millicent said.

"About tomorrow," Louise went on. "You've drawn Beverly Mitchell for a big sister. I wanted to warn you that she's the toughest, but if you get through all right it'll be all the more credit for you."

"Thanks, Lou," Millicent said gratefully, thinking, this is beginning to sound serious. Worse than a loyalty test, this grilling over the coals. What's it supposed to prove anyway? That I can take orders without flinching? Or does it just make them feel good to see us run around at their beck and call?

"All you have to do really," Louise said, spooning up the last of her sundae, "is be very meek and obedient when you're with Bev and do just what she tells you. Don't laugh or talk back or try to be funny, or she'll just make it harder for you, and believe me, she's a great one for doing that. Be at her house at seven-thirty."

And she was. She rang the bell and sat down on the steps to wait for Bev. After a few minutes the front door opened and Bev was standing there, her face serious.

"Get up, gopher," Bev ordered.

There was something about her tone that annoyed Millicent. It was almost malicious.[4] And there was an unpleasant anonymity[5] about the label "gopher," even if that was what they

---

3. **catting:** petty, nasty gossip.
4. **malicious** (mə-lĭsh′əs): spiteful; cruel.
5. **anonymity** (ăn′ə-nĭm′ĭ-tē): lack of recognition as an individual.

"Well, you know how girls are. They notice little things. I mean,

always called the girls being initiated. It was degrading, like being given a number. It was a denial of individuality.

Rebellion flooded through her.

"I said get up. Are you deaf?"

Millicent got up, standing there.

"Into the house, gopher. There's a bed to be made and a room to be cleaned at the top of the stairs."

Millicent went up the stairs mutely. She found Bev's room and started making the bed. Smiling to herself, she was thinking: How absurdly funny, me taking orders from this girl like a servant.

Bev was suddenly there in the doorway. "Wipe that smile off your face," she commanded.

There seemed something about this relationship that was not all fun. In Bev's eyes, Millicent was sure of it, there was a hard, bright spark of exultation.[6]

On the way to school, Millicent had to walk behind Bev at a distance of ten paces, carrying her books. They came up to the drugstore, where there already was a crowd of boys and girls from Lansing High waiting for the show.

The other girls being initiated were there, so Millicent felt relieved. It would not be so bad now, being part of the group.

"What'll we have them do?" Betsy Johnson asked Bev. That morning Betsy had made her "gopher" carry an old colored parasol through the square and sing "I'm Always Chasing Rainbows."

"I know," Herb Dalton, the good-looking basketball captain, said.

A remarkable change came over Bev. She was all at once very soft and coquettish.[7]

"You can't tell them what to do," Bev said sweetly. "Men have nothing to say about this little deal."

"All right, all right," Herb laughed, stepping back and pretending to fend off a blow.

"It's getting late." Louise had come up. "Almost eight-thirty. We'd better get them marching on to school."

The "gophers" had to do a Charleston step[8] all the way to school, and each one had her own song to sing, trying to drown out the other four. During school, of course, you couldn't fool around, but even then, there was a rule that you mustn't talk to boys outside of class or at lunch time . . . or any time at all after school. So the sorority girls would get the most popular boys to go up to the "gophers" and ask them out, or try to start them talking, and sometimes a "gopher" was taken by surprise and began to say something before she could catch herself. And then the boy reported her and she got a black mark.

Herb Dalton approached Millicent as she was getting an ice cream at the lunch counter that noon. She saw him coming before he spoke to her, and looked down quickly, thinking: He is too princely, too dark and smiling. And I am

---

6. **exultation** (ĕk´səl-tā´shən): triumphant joy.

7. **coquettish** (kō-kĕt´ĭsh): flirtatious.

8. **Charleston step:** a step used in a dance popular in the 1920s.

# some of them thought Tracy was just a bit *too* different . . ."

much too vulnerable.[9] Why must he be the one I have to be careful of?

I won't say anything, she thought, I'll just smile very sweetly.

She smiled up at Herb very sweetly and mutely. His return grin was rather miraculous. It was surely more than was called for in the line of duty.

"I know you can't talk to me," he said, very low. "But you're doing fine, the girls say. I even like your hair straight and all."

Bev was coming toward them, then, her red mouth set in a bright, <u>calculating</u> smile. She ignored Millicent and sailed up to Herb.

"Why waste your time with gophers?" she caroled gaily. "Their tongues are tied, but completely."

Herb managed a parting shot. "But that one keeps *such* an attractive silence."

Millicent smiled as she ate her sundae at the counter with Tracy. Generally, the girls who were outsiders now, as Millicent had been, scoffed at the initiation antics as childish and absurd to hide their secret envy. But Tracy was understanding, as ever.

"Tonight's the worst, I guess, Tracy," Millicent told her. "I hear that the girls are taking us on a bus over to Lewiston and going to have us performing in the square."

"Just keep a poker face outside," Tracy advised. "But keep laughing like mad inside."

Millicent and Bev took a bus ahead of the rest of the girls; they had to stand up on the way to Lewiston Square. Bev seemed very cross about something. Finally she said, "You were talking with Herb Dalton at lunch today."

"No," said Millicent honestly.

"Well, I *saw* you smile at him. That's practically as bad as talking. Remember not to do it again."

Millicent kept silent.

"It's fifteen minutes before the bus gets into town," Bev was saying then. "I want you to go up and down the bus asking people what they eat for breakfast. Remember, you can't tell them you're being initiated."

Millicent looked down the aisle of the crowded bus and felt suddenly quite sick. She thought: How will I ever do it, going up to all those stony-faced people who are staring coldly out of the window . . .

"You heard me, gopher."

"Excuse me, madam," Millicent said politely to the lady in the first seat of the bus, "but I'm taking a survey. Could you please tell me what you eat for breakfast?"

"Why . . . er . . . just orange juice, toast and coffee," she said.

"Thank you very much." Millicent went on to the next person, a young businessman. He ate eggs sunny side up, toast and coffee.

By the time Millicent got to the back of the bus, most of the people were smiling at her. They obviously know, she thought, that I'm being initiated into something.

Finally, there was only one man left in the corner of the back seat. He was small and jolly, with a ruddy, wrinkled face that spread into a beaming smile as Millicent approached. In his brown suit with the forest-green tie he looked something like a <u>gnome</u> or a cheerful leprechaun.

"Excuse me, sir," Millicent smiled, "but I'm taking a survey. What do you eat for breakfast?"

"Heather birds' eyebrows on toast," the little man rattled off.

---

9. **vulnerable:** defenseless.

> ## So many people were shut up tight inside themselves like boxes, yet they would open up, unfolding quite wonderfully, if only you were interested in them.

"*What?*" Millicent exclaimed.

"Heather birds' eyebrows," the little man explained. "Heather birds live on the mythological moors and fly about all day long, singing wild and sweet in the sun. They're bright purple and have *very* tasty eyebrows."

Millicent broke out into <u>spontaneous</u> laughter. Why, this was wonderful, the way she felt a sudden <u>comradeship</u> with a stranger.

"Are you mythological, too?"

"Not exactly," he replied, "but I certainly hope to be some day. Being mythological does wonders for one's ego."

The bus was swinging into the station now; Millicent hated to leave the little man. She wanted to ask him more about the birds.

And from that time on, initiations didn't bother Millicent at all. She went gaily about Lewiston Square from store to store asking for broken crackers and mangoes, and she just laughed inside when people stared and then brightened, answering her crazy questions as if she were quite serious and really a person of consequence.[10] So many people were shut up tight inside themselves like boxes, yet they would open up, unfolding quite wonderfully, if only you were interested in them. And really, you didn't have to belong to a club to feel related to other human beings.

One afternoon Millicent had started talking with Liane Morris, another of the girls being initiated, about what it would be like when they were finally in the sorority.

"Oh, I know pretty much what it'll be like," Liane had said. "My sister belonged before she graduated from high school two years ago."

"Well, just what *do* they do as a club?" Millicent wanted to know.

"Why, they have a meeting once a week . . . each girl takes turns entertaining at her house . . ."

"You mean it's just a sort of exclusive social group . . ."

"I guess so . . . though that's a funny way of putting it. But it sure gives a girl <u>prestige</u> value. My sister started going steady with the captain of the football team after she got in. Not bad, I say."

No, it wasn't bad, Millicent had thought, lying in bed on the morning of Rat Court and listening to the sparrows chirping in the gutters. She thought of Herb. Would he ever have been so friendly if she were without the sorority label? Would he ask her out (if he ever did) just for herself, no strings attached?

---

10. **consequence:** importance.

WORDS TO KNOW

**spontaneous** (spŏn-tā′nē-əs) *adj.* occurring or acting without a plan; impulsive
**comradeship** (kŏm′răd-shĭp′) *n.* companionship
**prestige** (prĕ-stēzh′) *n.* high status; esteem

Then there was another thing that bothered her. Leaving Tracy on the outskirts. Because that is the way it would be; Millicent had seen it happen before.

Outside, the sparrows were still chirping, and as she lay in bed Millicent visualized them, pale gray-brown birds in a flock, one like the other, all exactly alike.

And then, for some reason, Millicent thought of the heather birds. Swooping carefree over the moors, they would go singing and crying out across the great spaces of air, dipping and darting, strong and proud in their freedom and their sometime loneliness. It was then that she made her decision.

Seated now on the woodpile in Betsy Johnson's cellar, Millicent knew that she had come triumphant through the trial of fire, the searing period of the ego which could end in two kinds of victory for her. The easiest of which would be her coronation[11] as a princess, labeling her <u>conclusively</u> as one of the select flock.

The other victory would be much harder, but she knew that it was what she wanted. It was not that she was being noble or anything. It was just that she had learned there were other ways of getting into the great hall, blazing with lights, of people and of life.

It would be hard to explain to the girls tonight, of course, but she could tell Louise later just how it was. How she had proved something to herself by going through everything, even Rat Court, and then deciding not to join the sorority after all. And how she could still be friends with everybody. Sisters with everybody. Tracy, too.

The door behind her opened and a ray of light sliced across the soft gloom of the basement room.

"Hey, Millicent, come on out now. This is it." There were some of the girls outside.

"I'm coming," she said, getting up and moving out of the soft darkness into the glare of light, thinking: This is it, all right. The worst part, the hardest part, the part of initiation that I figured out myself.

But just then, from somewhere far off, Millicent was sure of it, there came a melodic fluting, quite wild and sweet, and she knew that it must be the song of the heather birds as they went wheeling and gliding against wide blue horizons through vast spaces of air, their wings flashing quick and purple in the bright sun.

Within Millicent another melody soared, strong and exuberant,[12] a triumphant answer to the music of the darting heather birds that sang so clear and lilting over the far lands. And she knew that her own private initiation had just begun. ❖

---

11. **coronation:** crowning.
12. **exuberant** (ĭg-zōō′bər-ənt): full of unrestrained joy.

WORDS TO KNOW

**conclusively** (kən-klōō′sĭv-lē) *adv.* unquestionably; decisively

## Connect to the Literature

1. **What Do You Think?** What do you think of Millicent at the end of the story? Support your opinion.

> **Comprehension Check**
> - What tasks did Millicent have to perform as part of the hazing process?
> - Why wasn't Millicent's friend Tracy asked to join the sorority?
> - What happens on the bus that helps Millicent make her decision?

## Think Critically

2. What is Millicent's **motivation** for not joining the sorority?

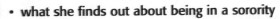

**THINK ABOUT**
- her relationships with Tracy and Bev
- the tasks required of her during initiation week
- what she finds out about being in a sorority
- the effect of her conversation with the older man on the bus

3. Do you think Herb will have any interest in Millicent when she is not in the sorority? Why or why not?

4. How do you explain the meaning of the last sentence in the story?

5. **ACTIVE READING**  **SEQUENCE OF EVENTS**  With a partner, review the events that you recorded in your **READER'S NOTEBOOK**. How do you think your understanding of these events is influenced by the author's use of a **flashback?**

## Extend Interpretations

6. **What If?** Imagine that Millicent had joined the sorority with the belief that she could persuade the others to invite Tracy to join. What would this have suggested about Millicent's **character?**

7. **Connect to Life** "Initiation" takes place in the early 1950s. Do you think this story is dated, or does its **theme,** or message, still apply today? Explain your reasoning.

## Literary Analysis

**INTERNAL CONFLICT**  **Conflict,** the struggle between opposing forces, is the basis of **plot** in most narrative literature. **Internal conflict** occurs when the struggle takes place within a character. In this story, Millicent experiences internal conflict in the process of deciding whether to join the sorority.

**Paired Activity** Working with a partner, return to the chart in your **READER'S NOTEBOOK.** What do you think were the most significant events that influenced Millicent's internal conflict and her decision to reject membership in the sorority? Cite evidence from the story to support your opinion.

**SYMBOL**  A **symbol** is a person, place, or thing that stands for something beyond itself. In literature, objects and images are often used to symbolize abstract ideas. What do you think the heather birds symbolize for Millicent in the story?

**REVIEW**  **CLIMAX AND PLOT** Where do you think the **climax** of the **plot** occurs in this story? How can you tell?

# Choices & CHALLENGES

## Writing Options

**1. Rat Court Script** Imagine what Millicent does and says at Rat Court. Write a script to portray the scene.

**2. Sorority Sister Analysis** Write an analysis of Millicent's character in which you compare and contrast her to the girls in the sorority. In what ways is she similar to the sorority girls? In what ways is she different? Use a Venn diagram like the one shown to organize your thoughts.
**Writing Handbook**
See page 1157: Compare and Contrast.

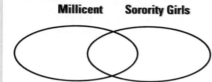

## Activities & Explorations

**1. TV Talk Show** In a group of four, stage a talk show in which Louise and Bev argue in favor of sororities in high school and Millicent argues against them. One member can play the role of the host. The rest of the class can play the part of the audience.
**~ SPEAKING AND LISTENING**

**2. Fashion Update** Imagine Millicent, Tracy, Louise, and Bev in a contemporary high school. Design an outfit for each of them that conveys each girl's personality and social standing.
**~ART**

## Inquiry and Research

**Initiation in Publishing** At the age of 20, Sylvia Plath submitted this story to *Seventeen* magazine. It was published in 1953. Find out more about Sylvia Plath's early successes in publishing.

 **Real World Link** Before conducting your research, read the letter on page 410 to learn more about Plath's experience in getting this story published.

## Art Connection

Notice the rounded, robot-like figures in the painting on page 401. What feelings are conveyed by the artist's rendering of the students at the Bauhaus school? How well do you think the painting evokes the setting of Millicent's school?

---

# Vocabulary in Action

**EXERCISE A: CONTEXT CLUES** Note each boldfaced word. On your paper, write the letter of the phrase that best completes the sentence.

1. Students with **prestige** among their classmates are (a) held in high regard, (b) not respected, (c) totally ignored.

2. Millicent broke into **spontaneous** laughter at the man's strange story because (a) she knew what he was going to say, (b) she was not expecting such an odd response, (c) she had been in a silly mood all day.

3. An **exclusive** sorority might (a) welcome large numbers of new members, (b) open membership to male students, (c) try to restrict membership.

4. If the girls voted **conclusively** to accept Millicent, the sorority would (a) reject her immediately, (b) have to take another vote, (c) not need to vote again on the issue.

5. Girls who joined the sorority for **comradeship** hoped to (a) be left alone, (b) antagonize others, (c) make friends.

**EXERCISE B: MEANING CLUES** On your paper, write the Word to Know that best completes each title.

1. How to Be a Spirited and _____ Hostess
2. The Dashed Hopes of the _____ Heir
3. Parades, Celebrations, and Other Forms of _____
4. The Devious and _____ Plots of Caesar Carrington
5. The _____: A Creature of Folklore

| WORDS TO KNOW | calculating | conclusively | exclusive | gnome | spontaneous |
|---|---|---|---|---|---|
| | comradeship | disinherited | fanfare | prestige | vivacious |

# Grammar in Context: Verb Tenses

In the following sentence from "Initiation," Sylvia Plath uses several verb tenses as Tracy makes a prediction about her friend Millicent.

> present                          past perfect
> **"I know, but even so,"** **Tracy** had said **quietly,**
>                  future        present future
> **"you'll change, whether you** think **you** will **or**
> **not."**

By changing the tense of a verb, you can indicate whether something is happening now, has happened in the past, or will happen in the future. In the example above, Sylvia Plath uses a tense known as the **past perfect tense.** This tense is used to indicate that an action occurred before some other action in the past.

**WRITING EXERCISE** Rewrite each sentence, following the directions in parentheses to change the tenses of the verbs.

**Example: *Original*** She will decide what to do when the clock strikes midnight. (Change two verbs to past tense.)

***Rewritten*** She <u>decided</u> what to do when the clock <u>struck</u> midnight.

1. Millicent is planning what to say when the other girls welcome her into the sorority. (Change two verbs to past tense.)
2. She is invited to join the club because she has changed. (Change one verb to past tense and another to past perfect tense.)
3. "Bev is your big sister," Betsy said, "and you have to obey her every command." (Change two verbs to future tense.)

# Sylvia Plath
## 1932–1963

**Other Works**
*Ariel*
*Winter Trees*
*The Bell Jar*
*Collected Poems*

**Pressures of Achievement** Few modern writers can match the early successes of Sylvia Plath. By the age of eight, Plath had experienced two extraordinary events—the publication of her first poem and her father's unexpected death—both of which would have long-lasting effects. Even before she entered college, Plath had drawings, stories, and poems published in national publications. She attended Smith College on a scholarship, where she continued to publish steadily and win honors for her work. By age 21, she was named a guest editor at *Mademoiselle* magazine after winning the magazine's College Fiction Contest.

**Creative Dedication** The glittering triumphs of early success, however, proved difficult to sustain. While still in college, Plath suffered a serious mental breakdown. After treatment, she returned to Smith, graduated with top honors, and was awarded the prestigious Fulbright scholarship which allowed her to study in England at Cambridge University. In England, Plath met the poet Ted Hughes, whom she later married. He observed that her drive to express herself and to define herself through her poetry picked up momentum over the years, until it reached almost a frenzied state.

**Triumph for Poetry** Plath's poems are intensely personal and complex; through her poetry she explored the painful dilemmas of her own life as poet, wife, mother, and daughter. Her only novel, *The Bell Jar* (1963), was based upon her personal experience of mental breakdown. In 1963, after battling years of depression, she took her own life. As a critic observed, her final poems are a "triumph for poetry at the moment that they are a defeat for their author." Even after her premature death, her reputation continued to grow, and in 1982 her work *Collected Poems* was awarded the Pulitzer Prize.

### from *Letters Home*
On Getting "Initiation" Published, by Sylvia Plath

October 6, 1952

Dear Mummy,

**❶**     Wow! Speak of appropriate psychological moments for getting unexpected good news, this was one. I wandered lazily downstairs just before lunch today and glanced casually in my mailbox. Two letters from you. I opened the little one first, looked at it, puzzled for a few minutes before it suddenly dawned on me what the contents were. I never even cherished the smallest hope of getting one of the third prizes [from *Seventeen* for "Initiation"] this year—as you know, I figured out the relative deadline for their decision by my other story and had long since given up thinking about it.

Sylvia Plath, her mother, and her brother, pictured above in 1949.

    This news makes me feel that I am maybe not destined to deteriorate, after all. . . .

**❷**     Your last big morale-building letter was most appreciated. You are the most wonderful mummy that a girl ever had, and I only hope I can continue to lay more laurels at your feet. Warren and I both love you and admire you more than anybody in the world for all you have done for us all our lives. For it is you who has given us the heredity and the incentive to be mentally ambitious. Thank you a million times!

*Your very own Sivvy*

## Reading for Information

*Letters Home* is a collection of letters Sylvia Plath wrote to her mother from 1950 to 1963. The letter reprinted here was written after she had won second prize ($200) for "Initiation" in *Seventeen's* short story contest. It provides details that shed light on the writer's personal life and its relationship to her writing.

### ANALYZING A LETTER

A letter is a **primary source** because it offers firsthand information about a topic. From the personal details in letters, you can often gain insight into an individual's thoughts and emotions. You may also get a detailed account of an event.

**YOUR TURN** Use the activities below to analyze the letter.

**❶** How does Plath react to the news that her story has won a prize? What clues suggest Plath's feelings about her writing?

**❷** From this passage, how would you describe Plath's relationship with her mother?

## Inquiry & Research
**Activity Link: "Initiation" p. 408**
Beginning with the publication of "Initiation," create a time line of Plath's published works. Refer to the Internet, encyclopedia articles, published letters, and critical reviews for information.

 **More Online: Research Starter**
www.mcdougallittel.com

# Getting a Job

## *from* I Know Why the Caged Bird Sings

### *Autobiography by* MAYA ANGELOU

"... in the struggle lies the glory."

## Connect to Your Life

**On the Job** Think about a part-time or summer job that you have had in the past or one that you hope to have in the future. How would you feel if you were denied the job because of your race, religion, ethnic background, or something else that had nothing to do with your qualifications? How would you respond to such a situation?

## Build Background

**Job Discrimination** "Getting a Job" takes place in San Francisco in the 1940s during a period when more and more jobs were opening up to American women because so many men were overseas fighting in World War II. However, despite these new opportunities for women, racial prejudice still limited the types of employment open to African Americans.

The following selection is an excerpt from *I Know Why the Caged Bird Sings*, the first in a series of autobiographical works written by Maya Angelou. Angelou, born Marguerite Johnson, was raised by her grandmother in Arkansas, but at the age of 12 she moved to San Francisco to live with her mother.

WORDS TO KNOW
**Vocabulary Preview**

| | |
|---|---|
| ascend | haphazardly |
| charade | haughty |
| comprehend | hypocrisy |
| dexterous | ostensibly |
| diametrically | terse |

## Focus Your Reading

LITERARY ANALYSIS   NARRATIVE NONFICTION   An autobiography can be classified as a work of **narrative nonfiction**, which tells a true story about real people, places, and events. As such, it has many of the same elements that a fictional narrative has. Angelou, for example, creates a vivid **setting**, as illustrated by this description of her room:

*My room had all the cheeriness of a dungeon and the appeal of a tomb.*

As you read this selection, look for evidence of other fictional elements, such as **plot** and **conflict**, that Angelou uses to bring events to life.

ACTIVE READING   IDENTIFYING CAUSE AND EFFECT IN NONFICTION   When reading narrative nonfiction, you often get a better understanding of events if you pause to consider their **cause-and-effect** relationships. The following sentence illustrates such a relationship:

*Women had replaced men on the streetcars as conductors and motormen* [cause], *and the thought of sailing up and down the hills of San Francisco in a dark-blue uniform . . . caught my fancy* [effect].

The first condition—women working as streetcar conductors—caused the effect: Angelou imagined herself doing such work.

READER'S NOTEBOOK   As you read this selection, jot down at least three causes that led Marguerite to seek the job of streetcar conductor. Then list at least three effects that this experience had on her life.

*In "The Opportunity," a young woman is given an unexpected chance to fulfill her dream of becoming an actress. As you will see, her opportunity leads to a surprising turn of events.*

# THE OPPORTUNITY

## John Cheever

Mrs. Wilson sometimes thought that her daughter Elise was dumb. Elise was her only daughter, her only child, but Mrs. Wilson was not so blinded by love that the idea that Elise might be stupid did not occasionally cross her mind. The girl's father had died when she was eight, Mrs. Wilson had never remarried, and the girl and her mother lived affectionately and closely. When Elise was a child, she had been responsive and lively, but as she grew into adolescence, as her body matured, her disposition changed, and some of the wonderful clarity of her spirit was lost. At sixteen she seemed indolent,[1] and to have developed a stubborn indifference to the hazards and rewards of life. She was a beautiful girl with dark hair and a discreet and striking grace, but Mrs. Wilson sometimes thought sadly that there was a discrepancy[2] between Elise's handsome brow and what went on behind it. Her face and her grace were almost never matched by anything she had to say. She would sit for an hour on the edge of her bed, staring at nothing. "What are you thinking

---

1. **indolent** (ĭn′də-lənt): lazy.
2. **discrepancy** (dĭ-skrĕp′ən-sē): inconsistency.

*Johanna IV* (1985), Franz Gertsch. Mixed media on board, 29½″ × 29½″. Courtesy Louis K. Meisel Gallery, New York.

brat out of here. I've got sensibilities just the same as she has. Telephone Hollywood. Get Dolores Random. Get anybody. Get her out of here."

Elise stood. They were all watching. "I'm sorry it turned out this way," she said. "It was very good of you to offer me the chance." She opened the door and went out. Gloria followed and stopped her in the hall. "Is this really what you mean, darling?" she asked. "Are you really turning down this job because you think it isn't any good?"

"Yes," Elise said.

"You little punk," Gloria said. Elise started down the stairs. Gloria shouted after her, "You brat, you baby-sitter, you . . . fool."

Elise telephoned Mrs. Cogswell from a drugstore and asked if she could come back to work. Mrs. Cogswell was delighted. An hour later, Elise was absentmindedly pushing a baby carriage down First Avenue, eating a strawberry ice-cream cone, and smiling at the delivery boys from the grocery store.

Either through forgetfulness or disappointment, Elise never mentioned her experience in the theater again. But Mrs. Wilson couldn't put the experience out of her mind as easily as her daughter, and she began to read eagerly the theater page of the morning paper in order to follow the fortunes of the play.

The beginning of rehearsals was announced. Elise's part was taken by someone from Hollywood. When the company went to Wilmington for the opening, Mrs. Wilson thought of the train ride that she and Elise might have taken, their hotel suite there, and the excitement of an opening. A week later, when the company went to Philadelphia, she made the trip vicariously.[14] She had never been to Philadelphia, but her vision of that city was clear. A week after the opening in Philadelphia, she went to

---

14. **vicariously** (vī-kâr′ē-əs-lē): in imagination, by picturing the experiences of those actually taking part.

Detail of *Johanna IV* (1985), Franz Gertsch.
Mixed media on board, 29½″ × 29½″.
Courtesy Louis K. Meisel Gallery, New York.

Times Square and bought a trade paper to read a review of the play. It was late and the sidewalk was crowded, but she opened the paper, standing in the middle of the sidewalk, and read the review in the light from the newsstand.

Scorn, ridicule, abuse, and disgust were heaped on the playwright and his associates, but this vituperation[15] was, in a sense, wasted, for at the bottom of the notice Mrs. Wilson read that the play had closed in Philadelphia after five performances. Mr. Belber was returning to his grandfather's abrasive business, and Mr. Traveler and Mr. Leary had gone to their farms. She read the review twice to make sure, and then threw the paper into an ashcan and took a subway home. Elise was sitting in her room, surrounded by her pictures. A text on double-entry bookkeeping was open in front of her, but she wasn't studying, she was staring at nothing. Mrs. Wilson looked at her daughter with profound love, for she knew that there was some connection between the beauty of the girl's face and the beauty of her judgments. ❖

---

15. **vituperation** (vī-tōō′pə-rā′shən): harsh condemnation; abusive words.

# John Cheever
## 1912–1982

### Other Works
*The Enormous Radio and Other Stories*
*The Housebreaker of Shady Hill and Other Stories*
*The Wapshot Chronicle*
*The Stories of John Cheever*

**Unexpected Opportunity** Ironically, the origins of John Cheever's literary career can be traced to his expulsion from prep school. At age 17, Cheever wrote a short story titled "Expelled" based upon his dismissal from Thayer Academy, a prestigious school in his home state of Massachusetts. The story was published by the *New Republic,* and a literary career was born. In his early years of writing, Cheever lived in poverty in New York City. After years of honing his storytelling skills, he became a regular contributor to the *New Yorker,* a magazine famous for the quality of its fiction. His first collection of short stories, *The Way Some People Live,* was published in 1942.

**A Brilliant Observer** In the 1950s Cheever's reputation continued to grow as he published three more volumes of short stories and his first novel, *The Wapshot Chronicle,* which garnered a National Book Award. His fiction typically examines the life and morals of suburban America, using humor and irony to portray the disappointments and tragedies hidden beneath the appearance of success. Because of his ability to use seemingly insignificant events as a means of unmasking truths about his characters, he was praised as the "Chekhov of the suburbs."

**Recognized Master** Cheever continued to publish steadily in the 1960s and 1970s and came to be regarded as a master of the short story. *The Stories of John Cheever,* published in 1978, became one of the few short-story anthologies ever to make the *New York Times* bestseller list; that same collection earned the Pulitzer Prize and the National Book Critics Circle Award. Two of his earlier stories, "The Country Husband" (1956) and "The Embarkment for Cythera," (1964) won the O. Henry Award. According to one admiring critic, Cheever "won fame as a chronicler of mid-century manners, but his deeper subject was life and death."

# Author Activity

Read two more stories by Cheever; then, in an oral report, compare and contrast the setting of those stories with that of "The Opportunity." If Cheever were writing today, where do you think his stories would be set?

# LEARNING *the Language of Literature*

$\mathcal{A}$uthor's Perspective is a unique combination of ideas, attitudes, feelings, values, and beliefs that make up the way a writer looks at the world. According to E. B. White, "Every writer, by the way he uses language, reveals something of his spirit, his habits, his capacities, his bias." Of course, we each have a perspective, too, complete with our own biases—personal preferences and prejudices—that color that perspective.

## Author's Perspective in Nonfiction

An author's perspective is easier to detect in nonfiction than in fiction. For example, Isaac Asimov's essay "Dial Versus Digital" (page 107) is basically a one-sided argument in favor of dial clocks. Such a stand against digital clocks may sound strange coming from a science fiction writer, but therein lies a lesson for the reader. Don't make assumptions about an author's perspective. Base your judgment on what a writer says or implies in his or her work.

## The Interpretation of Experience

In autobiographical nonfiction, writers' interpretations of events in their lives offer a key to their perspectives. For example, in "Getting a Job" (page 411), Maya Angelou explores two different interpretations of her experience with the receptionist at the Market Street Railway Company.

**YOUR TURN** Read the two passages at the right. Which passage best reveals Angelou's adult beliefs and values—in other words, her perspective? Why do you think she included both her interpretations of the event?

> ### THE INTERPRETATION OF EXPERIENCE
>
> 1 The miserable little encounter had nothing to do with me, the me of me, any more than it had to do with that silly clerk. The incident was a recurring dream, concocted years before by stupid whites and it eternally came back to haunt us all. . . .
>
> I went further than forgiving the clerk, I accepted her as a fellow victim of the same puppeteer.
>
> 2 All lies, all comfortable lies. The receptionist was not innocent and neither was I. The whole charade we had played out in that crummy waiting room had directly to do with me, Black, and her, white.
>
> —Maya Angelou, "Getting a Job"

## Tone

The attitude that a writer takes toward a particular subject is called **tone**. The tone of a literary work can vary greatly, ranging from a serious tone to a humorous tone, as in the excerpt from Bill Cosby's *Love and Marriage* (page 357). Tone reveals a writer's values and feelings in a very personal way. Imagine how different Bill Cosby's tone would be if he had written about his failure with Charlene right after it happened, instead of years later. Humor is often just a matter of perspective.

# Cultural Context

The behavior, beliefs, institutions, art, and values of a community or time period make up a culture. For some writers, culture plays an important part in defining their perspective. For instance, Margaret Atwood tries to be fair, if not objective, in her essay, "Through the One-Way Mirror" (page 170): she criticizes both Canadians and Americans. But something in her tone reveals strong feelings about Americans that stem, at least in part, from her perspective as a Canadian.

**YOUR TURN**  Read the passage at the right from Atwood's essay. How is Atwood's perspective influenced by her culture? What is her tone in the passage? Point out words that reveal her tone.

# Portrayal of Individuals

The way various individuals are presented in most nonfiction is also an important clue to the author's perspective. In "A Celebration of Grandfathers" (page 455), Rudolfo Anaya celebrates all grandfathers by praising his own grandfather.

**YOUR TURN**  In the passage at the right, what can you infer about Anaya's own values? Point out words that reveal those values.

# Author's Perspective in Fiction

Most writers keep their personal opinions out of their fiction. Their perspectives are given directly only in interviews, in nonfiction they write themselves, or in articles about them written by someone else. Still, readers can sometimes infer an author's perspective from elements in a story—such as plot, character, and theme—and from the tone and cultural context of a story.

**YOUR TURN**  Read Mark Twain's description of Tuttletown from "The Californian's Tale" (page 303). What does it suggest about Twain's perspective on the California Gold Rush?

## TONE AND CULTURAL CONTEXT

The Americans, bless their innocent little hearts, are rarely aware that they are even being watched, much less by the Canadians. . . If they think about Canada at all, it's only when things get a bit snowy or the water goes off or the Canadians start fussing over some piddly detail, such as fish. Then they regard them as unpatriotic; for Americans don't really see Canadians as foreigners, . . . Really, think the Americans, the Canadians are just like us, or would be if they could.

—Margaret Atwood, "Through the One-Way Mirror"

## PORTRAYAL OF INDIVIDUALS

I grew up speaking Spanish, and oh! how difficult it was to learn English. Sometimes I would give up and cry out that I couldn't learn. Then he would say *"Ten paciencia."* Have patience. *Paciencia*, a word with the strength of centuries . . . "You have to learn the language of the Americanos," he said. "Me, I will live my last days in my valley. You will live in a new time."

—Rudolfo A. Anaya, "A Celebration of Grandfathers"

## FICTION

In some few cases these cabins were still occupied; and when this was so, you could depend upon it that the occupant was the very pioneer who had built the cabin; that he was there because he had once had his opportunity to go home to the States rich, and had not done it; had rather lost his wealth, and had then in his humiliation resolved to sever all communication with his home relatives and friends, and be to them thenceforth as one dead.

—Mark Twain, "The Californian's Tale"

Why do you think Mark Twain wrote "The Californian's Tale"? Did he have more than one reason? These questions are at the heart of an author's purpose. The strategies here can help you better understand such purposes as you read.

## Purposes for Writing

### 1 Determining Author's Purpose

**Author's purpose** refers to the reasons an author has for writing something. Usually, an author has one of these four basic purposes in mind: to entertain; to inform or explain; to persuade or influence; to express emotions, thoughts, or ideas.

Most writing, however, is complex enough to have more than one purpose. For example, Twain probably wrote "The Californian's Tale" to entertain, but he also may have wanted to inform readers about the bleaker side of the California Gold Rush.

- **Understanding the Author's Message** Don't assume that there is only one level of interpretation of a story. A humorous story, for example, may actually have a serious message beneath its surface.
- **Understanding the "How"** Awareness of an author's purpose sometimes suggests *how* to read. If you realize that an author is trying to inform you, you will pay close attention to the details he or she provides.

---

**Strategies for Determining Purpose**

Look for direct statements of purpose in the introduction. (In nonfiction, the purpose is often part of the **thesis statement.**) Or, you may have to **infer** the purpose from the theme, from what you already know about the genre or the author, or from your own response to the writing.

**Monitor** your own reaction to a piece of writing. Are you entertained? Are you learning something? Are you being persuaded to believe something or to take action?

**Analyze** any facts in the piece. How are they used—to explain, to support an argument, to add realism to a story?

---

### 2 Evaluating What You Read

**Evaluating** how well the author achieves his or her purpose is the next step. Ask yourself the following questions, and be prepared to support your opinion with evidence:

- If the purpose was to entertain, did I enjoy the selection? Was the language appropriate to the purpose, and were effective literary techniques used?
- If the purpose was to explain, did I understand the subject? Was the information presented thoroughly and logically?
- If the author was trying to persuade, was I convinced? Did I feel that the opinion was supported with sound reasons and sufficient evidence?
- If the purpose was to create a certain mood or share personal experiences, beliefs, or feelings, did I understand why the author felt as he or she did?

**Need More Help?**

Remember that active readers use the essential reading strategies explained on page 7: **visualize, predict, clarify, question, connect, evaluate, monitor.**

# A Celebration of Grandfathers

*Memoir by* RUDOLFO A. ANAYA

## ( Connect to Your Life )

**Generation to Generation** Think about the elderly people in your life—perhaps relatives, neighbors, or friends of your family. How would you describe their values and view of the world? In what ways are these different from the values and worldview of your own generation? Discuss your thoughts with a small group of classmates, giving examples of the different attitudes and values of the two generations.

## Build Background

**Pride of Place** Rudolfo Anaya's Mexican-American heritage and the landscape of New Mexico, the state in which he was born and still resides, are important elements in most of the author's writing. This southwestern state is a place of geographical contrasts. Central New Mexico is part of the Rocky Mountains, and Taos—the Native American pueblo settlement in northern New Mexico that Anaya believes was home to his ancestors—is near the highest mountain in the state, Wheeler Peak. In sharp contrast, the eastern portion of the state is an extension of the Great Plains. It was on this flat terrain, along the Pecos River, that Anaya's grandfather settled and worked the land. Until the late 1940s, the life described in Anaya's story was still quite common, but after World War II, as more people moved to New Mexico, many of the small agricultural villages were deserted.

## Focus Your Reading

**LITERARY CONCEPT** **AUTHOR'S PERSPECTIVE AND TONE** The language and details a writer chooses help to create **tone,** the attitude a writer displays toward a subject. The tone of a work can help you recognize and understand an **author's perspective**—what the author thinks and believes. As you read this memoir, think about how Anaya's attitude toward his grandfather reflects his own beliefs and ideas.

**ACTIVE READING** **IDENTIFYING AUTHOR'S PURPOSE** The author's purpose refers to a writer's main reason for writing. Generally, a writer of nonfiction writes for one or more of the following purposes: to inform; to express ideas, opinions, and feelings; to analyze; to persuade; or to entertain. To help you determine Anaya's purpose(s) in writing this memoir, look for the following as you read:

- facts about places or people (inform)
- comments the author makes about the facts he has reported (express ideas, opinions, and feelings)
- statements that explain how a subject is defined or how it works (analyze)
- statements that seem to be trying to convince you of something (persuade)
- passages that you find particularly enjoyable (entertain)

**READER'S NOTEBOOK** As you read the selection, jot down any statements that appear to indicate the author's purpose(s).

# A Celebration

# of Grandfathers

Rudolfo A. Anaya

## "*Buenos días le de Dios, abuelo.*"

God give you a good day, grandfather. This is how I was taught as a child to greet my grandfather, or any grown person. It was a greeting of respect, a cultural value to be passed on from generation to generation, this respect for the old ones.

The old people I remember from my childhood were strong in their beliefs, and as we lived daily with them, we learned a wise path of life to follow. They had something important to share with the young, and when they spoke, the young listened. These old *abuelos* and *abuelitas*[1] had worked the earth all their lives, and so they knew the value of nurturing, they knew the sensitivity of the earth. . . . They knew the rhythms and cycles of time, from the preparation of the earth in the spring to the digging of the *acequias*[2] that brought the water to the dance of harvest in the fall. They shared good times and hard times. They helped each other through the epidemics and the personal tragedies, and they shared what little they had when the hot winds burned the land and no rain came. They learned that to survive one had to share in the process of life. . . .

My grandfather was a plain man, a farmer from the valley called Puerto de Luna on the Pecos River. He was probably a descendant of those people who spilled over the mountain from Taos, following the Pecos River in search of farmland. There in that river valley he settled and raised a large family.

*Campesino* [Farmer] (1976), Daniel Desiga. Oil on canvas, 50 ½" × 58 ½". Collection of Alfredo Aragón. Courtesy UCLA at the Armand Hammer Museum of Art and Cultural Center, Los Angeles.

DESIGA 76

---

1. *abuelos* (ä-bwĕ′lôs) . . . *abuelitas* (ä-bwĕ-lē′täs) *Spanish:* grandfathers . . . grannies.
2. *acequias* (ä-sĕ′kyäs) *Spanish:* irrigation ditches.

# The Study of History

*Short Story by* FRANK O'CONNOR

## Connect to Your Life

**Quirks of Fate** What would your life have been like if your ancestors had made different decisions before you were born? For example, what if your family had decided to settle in a different country? What if your mother had chosen a different mate, so that you had a different father? Imagine a different set of circumstances in your family background. Then freewrite for five minutes about who you might be or what your life might be like.

## Build Background

**Fiction and Reality** The boy who would come to be known as Frank O'Connor often daydreamed about who he might have been if his family background had been different. Born Michael Francis O'Donovan in 1903, O'Connor grew up in Barrackton, a slum on the outskirts of Cork in southwestern Ireland. He shared a close bond with his mother, and he adopted her maiden name when he decided to write under a pseudonym.

Not only did O'Connor write two autobiographies; he also wrote autobiographical fiction about a boy named Laurence ("Larry") Delaney. Larry appears in a number of O'Connor's short stories, and like the author himself, he is an only child who is sometimes frustrated by the sharp contrasts between the rich and the poor in Cork. Naive and full of insecurities, he is often embarrassed by the commonness of his parents. Larry Delaney is the main character in the story you are about to read.

WORDS TO KNOW
**Vocabulary Preview**

| | | |
|---|---|---|
| biased | exasperated | saucy |
| brooding | impertinent | uncanny |
| complacently | incredulously | |
| contemptuously | ordained | |

## Focus Your Reading

**LITERARY ANALYSIS** **CHARACTERIZATION** O'Connor brings the **characters** in "The Study of History" to life through his methods of **characterization.** This includes the following techniques: physical description; the speech, thoughts, feelings, and actions of a character; the responses of other characters to a character; the narrator's direct comments about a character.

Because the story is told from a **first-person point of view,** the narrator, Larry, is the only character whose thoughts and feelings are revealed to us directly, as in this example:

*. . . I felt wretched and guilty and I didn't know why.*

As you read, be aware of how the author develops characters. In particular, notice how the thoughts and feelings of the first-person narrator help reveal Larry's personality.

**ACTIVE READING** **MAKING INFERENCES ABOUT CHARACTERS**
To build a rounded picture of a **character,** readers must **make inferences,** or logical guesses, on the basis of **details** revealed about that character. For example, Larry's reluctance to talk to Mrs. O'Brien, whom he wishes to see, might indicate his shyness. As you read "The Study of History," pay attention to the details that O'Connor uses in describing his characters. What do these details tell you about the characters' personalities, attitudes, and family backgrounds?

**READER'S NOTEBOOK** Note details about each character in a cluster diagram like the one shown below.

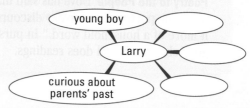

# THE STUDY OF HISTORY

## Frank O'Connor

The discovery of where babies came

from filled my life with excitement

and interest. Not in the way it's

generally supposed to, of course.

Oh, no! I never seem to have done any-

thing like a natural child in a standard

textbook. I merely discovered

the fascination of history.

# The Teacher Who Changed My Life

*Essay by* NICHOLAS GAGE

### Connect to Your Life

**Life Changers** Think of the various people who have influenced the course of your life. When you look back, 10 or 20 years from now, which of these people do you think will have made a lasting impression on you? Jot down your thoughts about one of these people.

## Build Background

**War Refugee** Nicholas Gage was born in 1939 in Lia, a mountain village in northwestern Greece. Nicholas lived his early years with his mother, Eleni, and four older sisters. His father, Christos, had left his impoverished village to find work in the United States, eventually settling in Worcester, Massachusetts. Before World War II began, his father had been able to return home for extended visits, but the war and the German occupation of Greece made such travel impossible.

After World War II, Eleni and her five children found themselves caught in Greece's bitter civil war between the Communists and the royalists, those who supported rule by the king. In 1947 the Communists took control of Lia, blocking all exit opportunities. In the spring of 1948, the Communists began retreating into nearby Albania, taking the village children with them. Eleni made secret arrangements for the family to flee, but her plan was only partially successful. Though Nicholas and three sisters escaped, one daughter and the mother were left behind. Eventually, Nicholas and his three sisters were able to join their father in the United States.

WORDS TO KNOW
**Vocabulary Preview**

| | |
|---|---|
| authoritarian | mentor |
| catalyst | mortify |
| emphatically | muse |
| formidable | tact |
| hone | void |

## Focus Your Reading

**LITERARY ANALYSIS** **AUDIENCE** The **audience** for a piece of writing is the person or persons intended to read it. "The Teacher Who Changed My Life" was first published in a newspaper magazine supplement intended for a general American readership. As you read, consider how Gage's sense of the audience he is writing for helps determines the **content, style,** and **purpose** of his essay.

**ACTIVE READING** **DISTINGUISHING FACT FROM NONFACT** Gage's essay contains verifiable **facts**— statements that can be proved—both about the civil war he fled in Greece and about his experiences in the United States. However, a personal essay includes more than just basic facts. The strength of Gage's essay arises from his recollection of his **feelings** and **opinions** about events and people in his life. Such elements in a personal essay can be described as **nonfact;** although they are true, they cannot be objectively verified in the way that facts can. As you read "The Teacher Who Changed My Life," be aware of the relationship between verifiable facts and the author's account of his personal reactions to his experiences.

**READER'S NOTEBOOK** Record examples of **fact and nonfact** in Gage's essay, using a chart like the one shown.

| Fact | Nonfact |
|---|---|
| Gage arrived in the United States in 1949. | He felt "very lucky" to have come to the United States. |

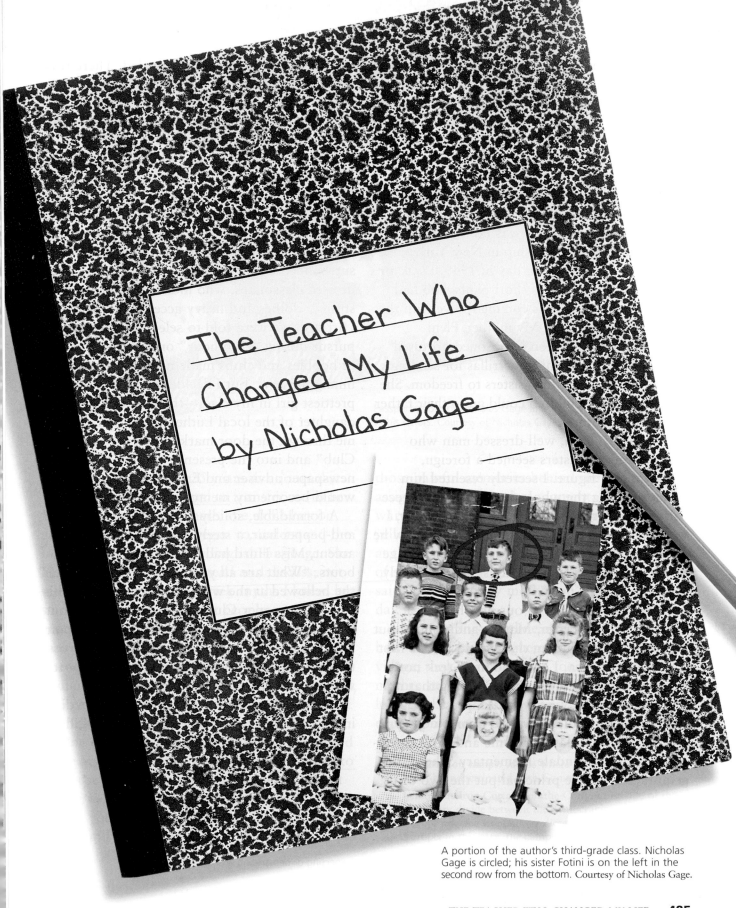

The Teacher Who
Changed My Life
by Nicholas Gage

A portion of the author's third-grade class. Nicholas Gage is circled; his sister Fotini is on the left in the second row from the bottom. Courtesy of Nicholas Gage.

## LITERARY *Contributions*

**Poetry** Alice Walker first made her name as a poet, and her reputation has grown with the following works:

*Once: Poems* (1968)

*Revolutionary Petunias and Other Poems* (1973)

*Horses Make a Landscape Look More Beautiful* (1984)

*Her Blue Body Everything We Know: Earthling Poems 1965–1990* (1991)

**Fiction** Walker is probably best known for her novels and short stories:

*The Third Life of Grange Copeland* (1970)

*In Love and Trouble: Stories of Black Women* (1973)

*The Color Purple* (1982)

*The Temple of My Familiar* (1989)

*Possessing the Secret of Joy* (1992)

**Nonfiction** Walker has written about her life and her vision in nonfiction:

*In Search of Our Mothers' Gardens: Womanist Prose* (1983)

*The Same River Twice: Honoring the Difficult* (1996)

*Anything We Love Can Be Saved: A Writer's Activism* (1997)

Within this setting, the greatest influence in Walker's life was her mother, Minnie Tallulah Grant Walker. From her mother, Walker became aware of the inner strength of African-American women, who, despite their lack of choices, maintained their independence and fought for a better future for their children. Walker has claimed that her own assurance and strength come from her mother and her aunts: "It is because of them, I know women can do anything."

**PERSONAL STRUGGLE AND GROWTH** When Walker was eight years old, one of her brothers accidentally shot her in the eye with a BB gun. She lost sight in one eye and had a disfiguring scar, which made her intensely self-conscious. "For six years I do not stare at anyone, because I do not raise my head," she explained later. It was at this time that she started to write poems and to notice the importance of relationships in her life. When she was 14, a simple operation removed the physical scar, but the effects of being an outcast remained.

Thanks to money raised by her community and a scholarship from the state of Georgia, Walker enrolled at Spelman College in Atlanta in 1961. At Spelman, the oldest college for African-American women in the United States, Walker embraced the civil rights movement that was sweeping through the South. She described herself and her fellow protesters as "young and bursting with fear and determination to change our world."

**1961**
Enters Spelman College in Atlanta

**1964**
Travels to Uganda as exchange student

**1965**
Graduates from Sarah Lawrence College

**1967**
Marries Melvyn Leventhal

**1969**
Daughter, Rebecca, is born

**1960**

**1965**

**1970**

**1955**
Black riders boycott buses in Montgomery, Alabama, to protest segregated seating.

**1961**
Freedom Riders try to desegregate public transportation in the South.

**1963**
Martin Luther King, Jr., leads March on Washington; publication of Betty Friedan's *The Feminine Mystique* launches the modern feminist movement in the United States.

**1968**
Martin Luther King, Jr., is assassinated in Memphis.

**1970**
Maya Angelou publishes *I Know Why the Caged Bird Sings.*

Rosa Parks

After two years at Spelman, Walker transferred to Sarah Lawrence College in New York. There Walker discovered feminism and realized that sexism was as great a barrier for African-American women as racism. During her senior year, Walker experienced a period of loneliness and despair. Supported emotionally by her college friends and thoughts of her family and community back home, Walker gradually emerged from her depression and feverishly began to write a series of poems. These poems were eventually published, starting Walker on the road to health and a career in writing.

## A LIFE OF ACTIVISM AND WRITING

Shortly after college graduation, Walker returned to the South to work in voter-registration drives. Here she met and eventually married Melvyn Leventhal, a civil rights lawyer, in 1967. Her first book, *Once: Poems*, was published in 1968, and the birth of her daughter, Rebecca, followed in 1969. Her first novel, *The Third Life of Grange Copeland*, came out in 1970. Throughout the 1970s, Walker regularly published stories and poems and taught at various colleges and universities.

In 1976, Walker divorced her husband and eventually moved to San Francisco with her daughter. It was during this time that she began writing *The Color Purple*, the novel that would make her famous. By 1985, with the release of the film version of *The Color Purple* directed by Steven Spielberg, Alice Walker had become a household name.

With fame, however, came controversy. Walker was one of the first African-American women to publicly take up the cause of feminism. Some civil rights activists felt that Walker's attack on sexism in the black community amounted to a betrayal of the fight against racism. Then, after the popular movie version of *The Color Purple* came out, Walker was criticized in the media for her negative portrayals of male characters and for

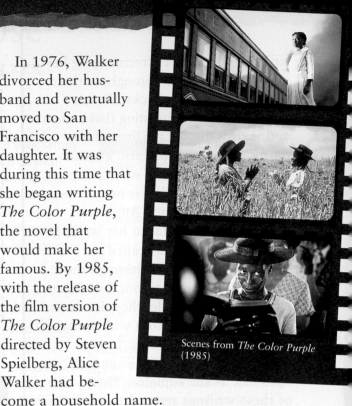

Scenes from *The Color Purple* (1985)

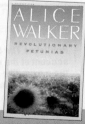

| 1973 | 1979 | 1983 | 1985 |
|------|------|------|------|
| Receives National Book Award nomination for *Revolutionary Petunias and Other Poems* | Moves to San Francisco | *The Color Purple* wins the Pulitzer Prize. | Film version of *The Color Purple* is released. |

**1975** **1980** **1985**

| 1977 | 1981 | 1982 | 1984 |
|------|------|------|------|
| Record numbers of viewers watch TV adaptation of Alex Haley's *Roots*. | Sandra Day O'Connor becomes first female Supreme Court Justice. | Equal Rights Amendment fails to win ratification. | President Ronald Reagan is reelected. |

# Women & Poem at Thirty-Nine

*Poetry by* ALICE WALKER

## Connect to Your Life

**Parents** You may not often think about your relationship with your parents or guardians. But take a moment now to reflect on this important relationship. Think about two or three good things that a parent or guardian has taught you. What other ways have they helped shape who you are?

## Build Background

**Life in the South** Alice Walker's parents lived in the South at a time when African Americans had very little freedom. Educational opportunities were minimal, and the sharecropping system trapped many black people in a cycle of grueling work and poverty. Qualifying restrictions kept most blacks from voting, while segregation laws kept them separated from whites. In spite of these injustices, Southern blacks developed strong communities and deep family commitments that led them to envision a better life for their children. In these two poems, Alice Walker pays tribute to her parents and to this larger black tradition of which they were a part.

## Focus Your Reading

**LITERARY ANALYSIS** **DICTION** **Diction** is a writer's choice of words. In analyzing diction, focus on two things:
- **vocabulary,** or the individual words
- **syntax,** or the arrangement or order of the words

Alice Walker has received critical praise for the clarity and effectiveness of her diction. While reading her poems, pay special attention to the words she has chosen and their arrangement to make your own judgment about her diction.

**ACTIVE READING** **DENOTATION / CONNOTATION** **Denotation** is the literal meaning of a word, the definition you'd find in the dictionary. **Connotation** is the emotional response and mental association evoked by a word. For example, what feelings and associations do you have with the word *hand*? You may have positive feelings and think of holding something, reaching out, or giving help. Now what about the word *fist*? This word may evoke feelings of struggle, as in a fight or in beating down a door.

**READER'S NOTEBOOK** As you read these poems, notice the connotations as well as the denotations of important words. Write down words that you think have powerful connotations. You might create a chart similar to the one shown.

| Word | Denotation | Connotation |
|------|------------|-------------|
|  |  |  |
|  |  |  |

# Women

**Alice Walker**

They were women then
My mama's generation
Husky of voice—Stout of
Step
5   With fists as well as
Hands
How they battered down
Doors
And ironed
10  Starched white
Shirts
How they led
Armies
Headragged Generals
15  Across mined
Fields
Booby-trapped
Kitchens
To discover books
20  Desks
A place for us
How they knew what we
*Must* know
Without knowing a page
25  Of it
Themselves.

*Three Sisters* (1985), Jonathan Green. Oil on masonite, 11″ × 14″. Collection of Ted Carlsen. Photograph by Tim Stamm.

## Thinking Through the Literature

1. What **images** from this poem stand out in your mind?

2. What do you think Walker admires most about her mother's generation? Cite evidence from the poem to support your opinion.

3. Why do you think the mothers are described as "Headragged Generals" crossing "mined fields" and "booby-trapped kitchens"?

   **THINK ABOUT** { • what the mothers are fighting for
   • what obstacles they had to overcome

4. Point out words in the poem that you think have strong **connotations** or most effectively express Walker's meaning. Explain your choices.

# UNIT FOUR

# LESSONS OF
# HISTORY

Fellow citizens,

we cannot

escape

history.

ABRAHAM LINCOLN

*Roman Forum, Rome, Italy.*
Copyright © Michael Yamashita.

# The Pit and the

## EDGAR ALLAN POE

Impia tortorum longos hic turba furores

Sanguinis innocui, non satiata, aluit.

Sospite nunc patria, fracto nunc funeris antro,

Mors ubi dira fuit vita salusque patent.[1]

[Quatrain composed for the gates of
a market to be erected upon the site
of the Jacobin[2] Club House at Paris.]

1. Impia . . . patent *Latin:* Here the wicked crowd of tormentors, unsated, fed their long-time lusts for innocent blood.
   Now that our homeland is safe, now that the tomb is broken, life and health appear where once was dread death.
2. Jacobin (jăk′ə-bĭn): belonging to a radical French political
   group famous for its terrorist policies during the French
   Revolution.

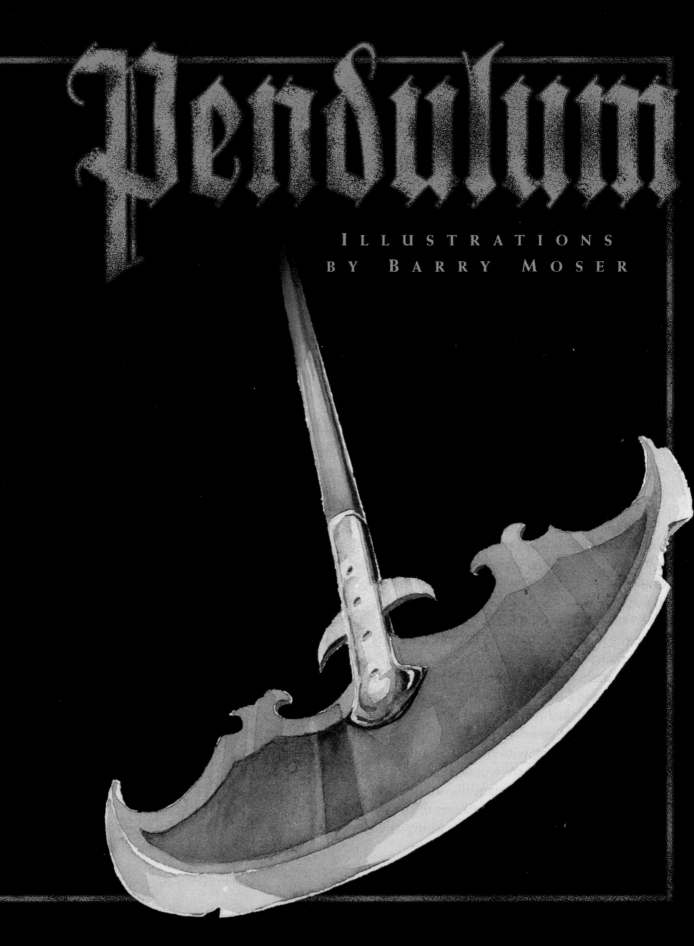

Yet not for a moment did I suppose myself actually dead. Such a supposition, notwithstanding what we read in fiction, is altogether inconsistent with real existence;—but where and in what state was I? The condemned to death, I knew, perished usually at the *auto-da-fé*,[11] and one of these had been held on the very night of the day of my trial. Had I been remanded to my dungeon, to await the next sacrifice, which would not take place for many months? This I at once saw could not be. Victims had been in immediate demand. Moreover, my dungeon, as well as all the condemned cells at Toledo, had stone floors, and light was not altogether excluded.

A fearful idea now suddenly drove the blood in torrents upon my heart, and for a brief period, I once more relapsed into insensibility. Upon recovering, I at once started to my feet, trembling convulsively in every fiber. I thrust my arms wildly above and around me in all directions. I felt nothing; yet dreaded to move a step, lest I should be impeded by the walls of the *tomb*. Perspiration burst from every pore and stood in cold big beads on my forehead. The agony of suspense grew at length intolerable, and I cautiously moved forward, with my arms extended, and my eyes straining from their sockets, in the hope of catching some faint ray of light. I proceeded for many paces; but still all was blackness and vacancy. I breathed more freely. It seemed evident that mine was not, at least, the most hideous of fates.

And now, as I still continued to step cautiously onward, there came thronging[12] upon my recollection a thousand vague rumors of the horrors of Toledo. Of the dungeons there had been strange things narrated—fables I had always deemed them—but yet strange, and too ghastly to repeat, save in a whisper. Was I left to perish of starvation in the subterranean world of darkness; or what fate, perhaps even more fearful, awaited me? That the result would be death, and a death of more than customary bitterness, I knew too well the character of my judges to doubt. The mode and the hour were all that occupied or distracted me.

My outstretched hands at length encountered some solid obstruction. It was a wall, seemingly of stone masonry—very smooth, slimy, and cold. I followed it up! stepping with all the careful distrust with which certain antique narratives had inspired me. This process, however, afforded me no means of ascertaining the dimensions of my dungeon; as I might make its circuit, and return to the point whence I set out, without being aware of the fact; so perfectly uniform seemed the wall. I therefore sought the knife which had been in my pocket, when led into the inquisitorial chamber; but it was gone; my clothes had been exchanged for a wrapper of coarse serge.[13] I had thought of forcing the blade in some minute crevice of the masonry, so as to identify my point of departure. The difficulty, nevertheless, was but trivial; although, in the disorder of my fancy, it seemed at first insuperable. I tore a part of the hem from the robe and placed the fragment at full length, and at right angles to the wall. In groping my way around the prison I could not fail to encounter this rag upon completing the circuit. So, at least I thought: but I had not

> **ACTIVE READING**
>
> **VISUALIZE** What do you think the narrator would see if there were light in the dungeon?

---

11. *auto-da-fé* (ou′tō-də-fā′) *Portuguese:* act of faith—a public execution of people tried by the Inquisition, carried out by the civil authorities.
12. **thronging:** crowding.
13. **serge** (sûrj): a woolen cloth.

---

WORDS
TO
KNOW

**supposition** (sŭp′ə-zĭsh′ən) *n.* an opinion or assumption
**relapse** (rĭ-lăps′) *v.* to fall back into a former state
**insuperable** (ĭn-sōō′pər-ə-bəl) *adj.* impossible to overcome

dared not go farther than this reflection. I dwelt upon it with a <u>pertinacity</u> of attention—as if, in so dwelling, I could arrest *here* the descent of the steel. I forced myself to ponder upon the sound of the crescent as it should pass across the garment—upon the peculiar thrilling

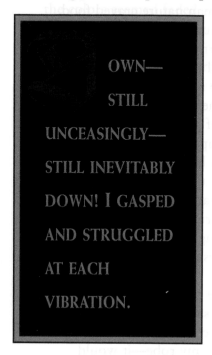

OWN— STILL UNCEASINGLY— STILL INEVITABLY DOWN! I GASPED AND STRUGGLED AT EACH VIBRATION.

sensation which the friction of cloth produces on the nerves. I pondered upon all this frivolity until my teeth were on edge.

Down—steadily down it crept. I took a frenzied pleasure in contrasting its downward with its lateral velocity. To the right—to the left—far and wide— with the shriek of a . . . spirit; to my heart with the stealthy pace of the tiger! I alternately laughed and howled as the one or the other idea grew predominant.

Down—certainly, relentlessly down! It vibrated within three inches of my bosom! I struggled violently, furiously, to free my left arm. This was free only from the elbow to the hand. I could reach the latter, from the platter beside me, to my mouth, with great effort, but no farther. Could I have broken the fastenings above the elbow, I would have seized and attempted to arrest the pendulum. I might as well have attempted to arrest an avalanche!

Down—still unceasingly—still inevitably down! I gasped and struggled at each vibration. I shrunk convulsively at its every sweep. My eyes followed its outward or upward whirls with the eagerness of the most unmeaning despair; they closed themselves spasmodically at the descent, although death would have been a relief, oh! how unspeakable! Still I quivered in every nerve to think how slight a sinking of the machinery would precipitate that keen, glistening axe upon my bosom. It was *hope* that prompted the nerve to quiver—the frame to shrink. It was *hope*—the hope that triumphs on the rack[29]—that whispers to the death-condemned even in the dungeons of the Inquisition.

I saw that some ten or twelve vibrations would bring the steel in actual contact with my robe, and with this observation there suddenly came over my spirit all the keen, collected calmness of despair. For the first time during many hours—or perhaps days— I *thought*. It now occurred to me that the bandage, or surcingle, which enveloped me, was *unique*. I was tied by no separate cord. The first stroke of the razor-like crescent athwart[30] any portion of the band, would so detach it that it might be unwound from my person by means of my left hand. But how fearful, in that case, the proximity of the steel! The result of the slightest struggle how deadly! Was it likely, moreover, that the minions[31] of the torturer had not foreseen and provided for this possibility! Was it probable that the bandage crossed my bosom in the track of the pendulum? Dreading to find my faint, and, as it seemed, my last hope frustrated, I so far elevated my head as to obtain a distinct view of my breast. The surcingle enveloped my limbs and body close in all directions—*save in the path of the destroying crescent.*

---

29. **rack:** a device for torturing people by gradually stretching their bodies.

30. **athwart:** across.

31. **minions** (mĭn′yənz): followers; servants.

WORDS TO KNOW  **pertinacity** (pûr′tn-ăs′ĭ-tē) *n.* a persistent stubbornness

**ACTIVE READING**

**PREDICT** What do you think the narrator is planning?

Scarcely had I dropped my head back into its original position, when there flashed upon my mind what I cannot better describe than as the unformed half of that idea of deliverance to which I have previously alluded, and of which a moiety[32] only floated indeterminately through my brain when I raised food to my burning lips. The whole thought was now present—feeble, scarcely sane, scarcely definite,—but still entire. I proceeded at once, with the nervous energy of despair, to attempt its execution.

For many hours the immediate vicinity of the low framework upon which I lay, had been literally swarming with rats. They were wild, bold, ravenous; their red eyes glaring upon me as if they waited but for motionlessness on my part to make me their prey. "To what food," I thought, "have they been accustomed in the well?"

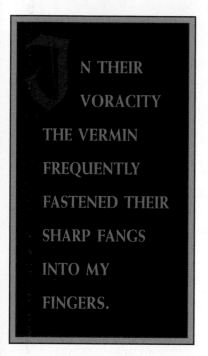

IN THEIR VORACITY THE VERMIN FREQUENTLY FASTENED THEIR SHARP FANGS INTO MY FINGERS.

They had devoured, in spite of all my efforts to prevent them, all but a small remnant of the contents of the dish. I had fallen into an habitual see-saw, or wave of the hand about the platter, and, at length, the unconscious uniformity of the movement deprived it of effect. In their <u>voracity</u> the vermin frequently fastened their sharp fangs into my fingers. With the particles of the oily and spicy viand[33] which now remained, I thoroughly rubbed the bandage wherever I could reach it; then, raising my hand from the floor, I lay breathlessly still.

At first the ravenous animals were startled and terrified at the change—at the cessation of movement. They shrank alarmedly back; many sought the well. But this was only for a moment. I had not counted in vain upon their voracity. Observing that I remained without motion, one or two of the boldest leaped upon the framework, and smelt at the surcingle. This seemed the signal for a general rush. Forth from the well they hurried in fresh troops. They clung to the wood—they overran it, and leaped in hundreds upon my person. The measured movement of the pendulum disturbed them not at all. Avoiding its strokes they busied themselves with the anointed bandage. They pressed—they swarmed upon me in ever accumulating heaps. They writhed upon my throat; their cold lips sought my own; I was half stifled by their thronging pressure; disgust, for which the world has no name, swelled my bosom, and chilled, with a heavy clamminess, my heart. Yet one minute, and I felt that the struggle would be over. Plainly I perceived the loosening of the bandage. I knew that in more than one place it must be already severed. With a more than human resolution I lay *still*.

Nor had I erred in my calculations—nor had I endured in vain. I at length felt that I was *free*. The surcingle hung in ribands[34] from my body. But the stroke of the pendulum already pressed upon my bosom. It had divided the serge of the robe. It had cut through the linen beneath.

---

32. **moiety** (moi′ĭ-tē): half.
33. **viand** (vī′ənd): food.
34. **ribands** (rĭb′əndz): ribbons.

WORDS TO KNOW
**voracity** (vô-răs′ĭ-tē) *n.* greed for food; ravenousness

Twice again it swung, and a sharp sense of pain shot through every nerve. But the moment of escape had arrived. At a wave of my hand my deliverers hurried tumultuously away. With a steady movement—cautious, sidelong, shrinking, and slow—I slid from the embrace of the bandage and beyond the reach of the scimitar. For the moment, at least, *I was free.*

Free!—and in the grasp of the Inquisition! I had scarcely stepped from my wooden bed of horror upon the stone floor of the prison, when the motion of the hellish machine ceased and I beheld it drawn up, by some invisible force, through the ceiling. This was a lesson which I took desperately to heart. My every motion was undoubtedly watched. Free!—I had but escaped death in one form of agony, to be delivered unto worse than death in some other. With that thought I rolled my eyes nervously around the barriers of iron that hemmed me in. Something unusual—some change which at first I could not appreciate distinctly—it was obvious, had taken place in the apartment. For many minutes in a dreamy and trembling abstraction, I busied myself in vain, unconnected conjecture.[35] During this period, I became aware, for the first time, of the origin of the sulphurous light which illuminated the cell. It proceeded from a fissure, about half an inch in width, extending entirely around the prison at the base of the walls, which thus appeared, and were, completely separated from the floor. I endeavored, but of course in vain, to look through the aperture.[36]

As I arose from the attempt, the mystery of the alteration in the chamber broke at once upon my understanding. I have observed that, although the outlines of the figures upon the walls were sufficiently distinct, yet the colors seemed blurred and indefinite. These colors had now assumed, and were momentarily assuming, a startling and most intense brilliancy, that gave to the spectral and fiendish portraitures an aspect that might have thrilled even firmer nerves than my own. Demon eyes, of a wild and ghastly vivacity,[37] glared upon me in a thousand directions, where none had been visible before, and gleamed with the lurid luster of a fire that I could not force my imagination to regard as unreal.

*Unreal!*—Even while I breathed there came to my nostrils the breath of the vapor of heated iron! A suffocating odor pervaded the prison! A deeper glow settled each moment in the eyes that glared at my agonies! A richer tint of crimson diffused itself over the pictured horrors of blood. I panted! I gasped for breath! There could be no doubt of the design of my tormentors—oh! most unrelenting! oh! most demoniac of men! I shrank from the glowing metal to the center of the cell. Amid the thought of the fiery destruction that impended, the idea of the coolness of the well came over my soul like balm.[38] I rushed to its deadly brink. I threw my straining vision below. The glare from the enkindled roof illumined its inmost recesses. Yet, for a wild moment, did my spirit refuse to comprehend the meaning of what I saw. At length it forced—it wrestled its way into my soul—it burned itself in upon my shuddering reason.—Oh! for a voice to speak!—oh! horror!—oh! any horror but this! With a shriek, I rushed from the margin, and buried my face in my hands—weeping bitterly.

The heat rapidly increased, and once again I looked up, shuddering as with a fit of the

---

35. **conjecture:** guesswork; speculation.

36. **aperture** (ăp′ər-chər): opening.

37. **vivacity** (vĭ-văs′ĭ-tē): liveliness.

38. **balm** (bäm): a soothing ointment.

ague.[39] There had been a second change in the cell—and now the change was obviously in the *form*. As before, it was in vain that I, at first, endeavored to appreciate or understand what was taking place. But not long was I left in doubt. The Inquisitorial vengeance had been hurried by my two-fold escape, and there was to be no more dallying with the King of Terrors. The room had been square. I saw that two of its iron angles were now acute—two, consequently, obtuse. The fearful difference quickly increased with a low rumbling or moaning sound. In an instant the apartment had shifted its form into that of a lozenge. But the alteration stopped not here—I neither hoped nor desired it to stop. I could have clasped the red walls to my bosom as a garment of eternal peace. "Death," I said, "any death but that of the pit!" Fool! might I have not known that *into the pit* it was the object of the burning iron to urge me? Could I resist its glow? or, if even that, could I withstand its pressure? And now, flatter and flatter grew the

"EATH," I SAID, "ANY DEATH BUT THAT OF THE PIT!"

lozenge, with a rapidity that left me no time for contemplation. Its center, and of course, its greatest width, came just over the yawning gulf. I shrank back—but the closing walls pressed me resistlessly onward. At length for my seared and writhing body there was no longer an inch of foothold on the firm floor of the prison. I struggled no more, but the agony of my soul found vent in one loud, long, and final scream of despair. I felt that I tottered upon the brink—I averted my eyes—

There was a <u>discordant</u> hum of human voices! There was a loud blast of many trumpets! There was a harsh grating as of a thousand thunders! The fiery walls rushed back! An outstretched arm caught my own as I fell, fainting, into the abyss. It was that of General Lasalle. The French army had entered Toledo. The Inquisition was in the hands of its enemies. ❖

---

39. **the ague** (ā′gyo͞o): a feverish illness.

## Connect to the Literature

**1. What Do You Think?** What part of the story did you find most suspenseful? Explain your judgment.

### Comprehension Check

- Where is the narrator?
- What are the first two dangers that he faces?
- How does he manage to break free from his bonds?
- Who or what seems to save him at the end?

## Think Critically

**2.** What do you think really happens to the **narrator** at the end of the story?

**3.** Who do you think shows the greater ingenuity in this story, the narrator or his torturers?

**THINK ABOUT**

- the methods of torture used
- how the torturers exploit human fears
- how the narrator saves himself from each torture

**4.** Which aspect of the narrator's torture—physical or psychological—do you find more horrible? Why?

**5.** **ACTIVE READING** **VISUALIZING** Think about the visual details you recorded in your **READER'S NOTEBOOK.** How did visualizing help you appreciate this story? What, in particular, did it help you to understand better?

## Extend Interpretations

**6. What If?** How might your reaction to the tale have been different if the dungeon had not been invaded by General Lasalle at the end?

**7. Critic's Corner** Critic Diane Johnson noted that Poe's "imagination is visual and three-dimensional. . . . If he had been alive today he probably would be a filmmaker." How do you think this story would succeed as a film? Consider what one would have to change in order to translate the story for the screen.

**8. Connect to Life** How do you think this story differs from contemporary tales of horror, whether in fiction or on film? Explain your answer.

## Literary Analysis

**SUSPENSE** **Suspense** is the excitement or tension that readers feel as they become involved in a story and eager to know the outcome. In "The Pit and the Pendulum," Poe builds suspense by using an ominous **setting,** bizarre complications of **plot,** and a **first-person narrator** who gives a vivid description of his mental state at each turn of events. Each time the narrator finds a way to cope with the danger immediately facing him, the reader experiences a temporary release of tension. Each release, however, is followed by a new threat.

**Activity** Imagine you are creating a soundtrack for a film version of this story. First, identify the moments of greatest suspense, where the music should be the most dramatic. Then create a line graph showing the story events and their level of suspense. An example has been started for you.

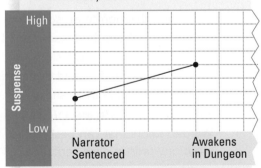

**REVIEW** **FIRST-PERSON POINT OF VIEW**

When a character who participates in the action of a story describes it in his or her own words, this is known as **first-person point of view.** Discuss the effects of Poe's use of a first-person **narrator** in "The Pit and the Pendulum." How does it help to build suspense?

## Writing Options

**1. Critical Review** Write a review of Poe's story in which you evaluate its effectiveness as a horror story. Before you begin to write, decide on criteria that you will use to judge the story's effectiveness. To do so, you might create a series of statements beginning, "A horror story should . . ."

**2. Poe Parody** Write a parody, or comic imitation, of Poe based upon this story. For example, you might create a narrator who is "tortured" by the process of waking up on a school day. Try to imitate Poe's style.

**3. Inquisition Exposé** Imagine that you are a reporter who has followed General Lasalle and his army into Toledo. Write a newspaper story in which you describe the rescue of the narrator and the secret horrors in the dungeons of the Inquisition. Include quotations from Poe's narrator.

## Activities & Explorations

**1. Illustrated Scene** Choose one scene from the story and carefully

read it again, noting the visual details. Then create your own illustration of that scene. ~ **ART**

**2. Radio Soundtrack** Make a tape of background music and sound effects that you might use for a radio adaptation of "The Pit and the Pendulum." ~ **MUSIC**

## Inquiry & Research

**Inquisition Report** Find out more about the Spanish Inquisition and its victims. Present your findings in an oral report.

An artist's rendering of an *auto-da-fé,* a ritual of the Spanish Inquisition.

## Vocabulary in Action

**EXERCISE A: MEANING CLUES** On your paper, write the Word to Know suggested by each phrase.

1. a firm decision to do something
2. a guess about the reason for a friend's absence
3. a well-worded expression
4. an easy-to-understand explanation
5. an unshakable listlessness

**EXERCISE B: SYNONYMS** On your paper, write the Word to Know that can best replace the italicized word or words in each sentence.

1. For several centuries the Inquisition was a *very strong* political force in Spain.
2. The prisoner is left alone in a *hazardous* cell.
3. High walls *encircle* the prisoner on all sides.

4. He moves *in a furtive way* around his cell, measuring its dimensions.
5. The movement of the pendulum is almost *invisible* as it descends.
6. The sound of the metal swinging in the air becomes more *jarring* as the pendulum drops.
7. Rats devour his food with *grasping greed.*
8. Several times, the prisoner starts to *sink back* into a deep sleep.
9. For a time, his *persistence* in trying to devise a way of escape keeps him going.
10. Sometimes, his predicament seems *hopeless.*

### Building Vocabulary

For an in-depth lesson on using synonyms as context clues, see page 1000.

| WORDS TO KNOW | | | | | |
|---|---|---|---|---|---|
| discordant | imperceptible | lucid | relapse | supposition |
| eloquent | insuperable | pertinacity | resolution | treacherous |
| encompass | lethargy | potent | stealthily | voracity |

# Grammar in Context: Appositive Phrases

In these excerpts, appositive phrases clarify the narrator's meaning and help to convey a sense of horror.

> The sentence—the dread sentence of death—was the last of distinct accentuation which reached my ears.

> Something unusual—some change which at first I could not appreciate distinctly—it was obvious, had taken place in the apartment.

An **appositive phrase** consists of a noun and its modifiers; it serves to explain or add information about another noun or pronoun. In the examples above, the appositive phrases indicate that "the sentence" refers to a death sentence and that the "something unusual" is a subtle (and perhaps ominous) change in the surroundings.

*Punctuation Tip:* If an appositive phrase is not essential to the meaning of a sentence, set it off with commas or dashes.

**WRITING EXERCISE** Combine each pair of sentences by changing the second sentence into an appositive phrase. Underline the appositive phrase.

**Example:** *Original* I have no doubt of the design of my tormentors. They are unrelenting and demonic men!

*Rewritten* I have no doubt of the design of my tormentors—those unrelenting and demonic men!

1. Poe's story "The Pit and the Pendulum" is set during the time of the Inquisition. It was a period of religious persecution.
2. He describes the horrors in great detail. There is the pit, the pendulum, thirst, rats, and slime.
3. The figures on the walls seem to mock the narrator. They are fiends with skeletal forms and menacing faces.
4. On the ceiling is a painted image of Time. This figure is usually depicted with a scythe in his hand.

**Grammar Handbook** Phrases, p. 1195

# Edgar Allan Poe
1809–1849

**Other Works**
"Annabel Lee"
"The Bells"
"The Black Cat"
"The Fall of the House of Usher"
"The Murders in the Rue Morgue"
"The Telltale Heart"

**A Troubled Youth** The son of traveling actors, Edgar Poe was orphaned at an early age and taken in by John and Frances Allan, a wealthy couple from Richmond, Virginia. A moody adolescent, Poe quarreled with John Allan, who scorned his literary ambitions and wanted him to join the family business. He left the University of Virginia without graduating and was expelled from the U.S. Military Academy at West Point in 1831. He then moved in with his aunt and his cousin Virginia, whom he wed in 1836, when she was just 13 years old.

**An Erratic Career** Having already published three slim volumes of poetry, Poe began writing reviews and stories for magazines. In 1839 he collected the stories in *Tales of the Grotesque and Arabesque.* Fame came when his mystery tale "The Gold Bug" won first prize in an 1843 contest and especially with the publication, two years later, of his eerie poem "The Raven." By then Virginia was in the throes of the tuberculosis that soon claimed her life. Poe antagonized the literary community by attacking popular writers. He grew ill himself and died on a Baltimore street at age 40.

**A Valuable Legacy** Although he led an unhappy life shortened by illness, Poe helped to define the modern short story and pioneered the detective mystery. His haunting, sometimes terrifying poems are praised for their brilliant musical sound effects, and his horror tales established him as a master of psychological terror.

# the sonnet-ballad
*Poetry by*
GWENDOLYN BROOKS

# Do not weep, maiden, for war is kind
*Poetry by* STEPHEN CRANE

## Connect to Your Life

**The Costs of War** Throughout history, humans have waged and endured one war after another; it is a constantly recurring part of the human experience. Do you know anyone who has been involved in a war, either as a participant or a bystander? With your class, discuss the effects of war as you have heard them described or as you imagine them.

## Build Background

**War Experiences** Stephen Crane's "Do not weep, maiden, for war is kind" appeared in a collection of poetry called *War Is Kind* in 1899. Crane never fought in a war, but he served as a special news correspondent in 1898 during Cuba's war for independence from Spain and also covered a war between Greece and Turkey in 1897.

Gwendolyn Brooks belonged to a later generation. She was born during World War I and came of age during World War II. Her poem "the sonnet-ballad" appeared in *Annie Allen,* a collection of poems that was published in 1949.

## Focus Your Reading

**LITERARY ANALYSIS** **VERBAL IRONY** **Verbal irony** occurs when someone says one thing but means another. The first line of Crane's poem provides an example of such irony:

> *Do not weep, maiden, for war is kind.*

War, by definition, cannot be considered kind. Clearly, the speaker—and poet—mean something quite different than "war is kind." Look for other examples of verbal irony as you read the following poems.

**ACTIVE READING** **DRAWING CONCLUSIONS** The process of **drawing conclusions** involves combining information from a text with your own prior knowledge to make logical statements about characters, events, or ideas. In the poems that follow, the poets expect that you already know something about war and what happens to many soldiers who participate. The more you understand about the wartime context for these poems, the more you will appreciate their impact, especially their use of verbal irony.

**READER'S NOTEBOOK** Read the poems once. Then go back and read them a second time, jotting down words or phrases that serve as clues to figuring out each speaker's attitude toward war. Combine this evidence from the poems with your own prior knowledge to draw conclusions about the speakers and their attitudes toward war.

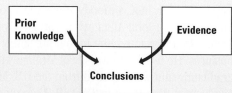

# the sonnet-ballad

## Gwendolyn Brooks

**O**h mother, mother, where is happiness?
They took my lover's tallness off to war,
Left me lamenting. Now I cannot guess
What I can use an empty heart-cup for.
5　He won't be coming back here any more.
Some day the war will end, but, oh, I knew
When he went walking grandly out that door
That my sweet love would have to be untrue.
Would have to be untrue. Would have to court
10　Coquettish death, whose impudent and strange
Possessive arms and beauty (of a sort)
Can make a hard man hesitate—and change.
And he will be the one to stammer, "Yes."
Oh mother, mother, where is happiness?

**10 coquettish** (kō-kĕt′ĭsh): behaving like a flirt; **impudent** (ĭm′pyə-dənt): shamelessly bold.

## Thinking Through the Literature

1. **Comprehension Check**  Where has the speaker's lover gone?

2. **ACTIVE READING   DRAWING CONCLUSIONS**  Look at the notes you made in your  **READER'S NOTEBOOK**. What can you conclude about the speaker and her attitude toward war?

   THINK ABOUT
   - the question she asks her mother
   - her fear that her lover will be untrue
   - her description of death
   - how she expects her lover to respond to death

3. The speaker describes death as a rival, calling it "coquettish" and "beautiful." What do you think she means?

4. What kind of answer do you think the mother might give to the question, "where is happiness?"

# Do not weep, maiden, for war is kind

**Stephen Crane**

Do not weep, maiden, for war is kind.
Because your lover threw wild hands toward the sky
And the affrighted steed ran on alone,
Do not weep.
5  War is kind.

Hoarse, booming drums of the regiment,
Little souls who thirst for fight,
These men were born to drill and die.
The unexplained glory flies above them,
10  Great is the Battle-God, great, and his Kingdom—
A field where a thousand corpses lie.

Do not weep, babe, for war is kind.
Because your father tumbled in the yellow trenches,
Raged at his breast, gulped and died,
15  Do not weep.
War is kind.

Swift blazing flag of the regiment,
Eagle with crest of red and gold,
These men were born to drill and die.
20  Point for them the virtue of slaughter,
Make plain to them the excellence of killing
And a field where a thousand corpses lie.

Mother whose heart hung humble as a button
On the bright splendid shroud of your son,
25  Do not weep.
War is kind.

*We Regret to Inform You*
(1982), Cleveland R. Wright.
Oil on canvas, 36″ × 24″.
Courtesy of the artist.

## Connect to the Literature

**1. What Do You Think?**
What **image** from the poem made the strongest impression on you?

> **Comprehension Check**
> • Whom does the **speaker** address in this poem?
> • What is lying on the battlefield?
> • What has happened to the father of the babe addressed in the third **stanza**?

## Think Critically

**2.** | ACTIVE READING | DRAWING CONCLUSIONS | Refer to the notes you made in your READER'S NOTEBOOK. What can you conclude about the speaker's attitude toward war? On what do you base your conclusion?

 **THINK ABOUT**
- the repetition of the phrase "war is kind"
- the people to whom the poem is addressed
- the poet's use of battle **imagery**

**3.** Why do you think Crane indents the second and fourth **stanzas**? What sets these stanzas apart from the other three?

## Extend Interpretations

**4. Comparing Texts** Compare and contrast the language—including **figures of speech** and **imagery**—that is used to describe war in the two poems.

**5. Comparing Texts** Which poem makes the strongest statement against war? Give evidence from the poems to support your opinion.

**6. Connect to Life** Do you think there are occasions or events that make war appropriate or necessary? Explain your answer.

## Literary Analysis

| VERBAL IRONY | **Irony** is a contrast between what is expected and what actually happens or exists. **Verbal irony** occurs when someone says one thing but means another. In "Do not weep, maiden, for war is kind," Crane uses verbal irony when he says that "war is kind" and when he alludes to the "virtue of slaughter." These statements, taken literally, would be surprising to anyone who knows about the cruelty of war. However, Crane places these statements beside vivid descriptions of war's horrors, such as the "thousand corpses" and the father who "tumbled in the yellow trenches, / Raged at his breast, gulped, and died." This stark contrast highlights the irony and makes it clearer that he is not speaking literally.

Brooks also uses verbal irony in "the sonnet-ballad," as in her description of death as "coquettish" and as a "beauty." In characterizing death as irresistible, Brooks makes the point that death is something many soldiers cannot avoid, no matter how they try.

**Cooperative Learning Activity** With a group, discuss the use of verbal irony by Crane and Brooks. Why do you think they use this device? Do you think it is fitting to use irony with the topic of war? Why or why not?

| REVIEW | SONNET STRUCTURE | Review the information about **sonnet structure** on pages 233 and 236. What features of the sonnet can you find in "the sonnet-ballad"?

## Writing Options

**1. Mother's Poem** Write a poem from the point of view of the mother in "the sonnet-ballad," written in response to her daughter's question.

**2. Speaker Comparison** In a paragraph, compare and contrast the speakers' attitudes toward war in "Do not weep, maiden, for war is kind" and "the sonnet-ballad." You might want to create a Venn diagram to help clarify your thoughts before writing.

**Speakers**

Do not weep, maiden, for war is kind | the sonnet-ballad

**Writing Handbook**
See page 1157: Compare and Contrast.

**3. Letter to the Author** Write a letter to Stephen Crane or Gwendolyn Brooks, giving your opinion of his or her poem and asking any questions you might have about it.

## Activities & Explorations

**1. War Collage** Find illustrations and photographs in newspapers, magazines, or books, or via the Internet, that reflect your attitude toward war. Assemble these images in a collage. ~ **VIEWING AND REPRESENTING**

**2. Art from the Home Front** Create a sculpture, painting, or drawing that expresses the experience or feelings of someone who has watched a loved one go off to war. ~ **ART**

**3. Interpretive Dance** Working with one of the two poems, choose appropriate music and choreograph a dance that tells the same story or expresses the same ideas and feelings as the poem. Work with a partner if you wish. Perform your dance before the class.
~ **MUSIC AND DANCE**

## Inquiry & Research

**1. War Through Time** Crane wrote about wars from the Civil War to the end of the 19th century. Brooks wrote about wars of the 20th century, primarily World War II. How were the methods of warfare of these two periods alike and different? Research one war from each period and write a summary of your findings.

**2. War Journals and Letters** Do research in your library to locate letters and journals written by soldiers during wartime. Prepare an oral report about the soldiers' perspectives on war, using excerpts from the journals and letters to illustrate what you have learned.

 **More Online: Research Starter**
www.mcdougallittell.com

Soldiers relax in the trenches in World War I.

## Stephen Crane
### 1871–1900

**Other Works**
*The Black Riders, and Other Lines*
*The Red Badge of Courage: An
    Episode of the American Civil War*
*The Open Boat, and Other Tales
    of Adventure*
*War Is Kind*

**The Classroom of the Streets** Stephen Crane was born in Newark, New Jersey. An unremarkable student at Syracuse University, he was known better for his prowess on the baseball field than for anything else. While in school, he supported himself by reporting and writing for his brother's news agency. He had trouble finishing his coursework and finally left school to become a writer. Crane was most interested in writing about the lives of the poor and moved to the Bowery, a rough part of New York, where he could live among the people he wished to write about. When his Civil War novella *The Red Badge of Courage,* published in 1895, achieved enormous critical and popular acclaim, he felt slightly embarrassed to receive so much attention for writing on a topic with which he had so little experience. However, he obliged his readers' demand for more war stories. Around the same time, he began to write poetry, after reading the verse of Emily Dickinson.

**War Correspondence** Shortly thereafter, Crane began to work as a foreign correspondent, covering wars in Cuba and Greece. He began to learn firsthand about war and its accompanying experiences. Crane was once shipwrecked on his way to Cuba and spent 30 hours at sea in a lifeboat. This experience inspired his famous short story "The Open Boat." He eventually moved to England, where he wrote in the company of such famous British writers as Joseph Conrad. However, Crane suffered from poor health throughout this time until his death of tuberculosis at age 29. Despite his limited years, Crane produced a prodigious number of poems, short stories, and novels. Many have become classics.

## Gwendolyn Brooks
### 1917–2000

**Other Works**
*Annie Allen*
*The Bean Eaters*
*Family Pictures*
*Black Love*
*Children Coming Home*

**Chicago Childhood** Gwendolyn Brooks lived most of her life in Chicago. She grew up on the city's south side and remained strongly attached to her hometown and to the city's African-American community. Brooks began to write poetry as a child, with the encouragement of her parents. A shy teenager, Brooks continued to write and read poetry, some of which she showed to the poet Langston Hughes, who encouraged her as well. In 1950, she won the Pulitzer Prize for poetry for *Annie Allen,* the poetry collection in which "the sonnet-ballad" appeared. She was the first African American to win the award.

**Poetic Development** In her early poetry, Brooks was strongly influenced by traditional literary forms. As her work evolved, she relied more on free verse, seeking to write poems that would reach out to the African-American people she wrote about. "I've written hundreds . . . of sonnets, and I'll probably never write another one, because I don't feel that this is a sonnet time," she once said of this change. "It seems to me it's a wild, raw, ragged free verse time."

**Community Activism** Brooks became a spokesperson on racial issues in addition to working as a poet. One critic observed that Brooks, "more than any other nationally acclaimed writer, has remained in touch with the community she writes about. She lives in the core of Chicago's black community. . . . She is her work." A dedicated educator, Brooks taught poetry at numerous universities and received more than 50 honorary doctorates in recognition of her outstanding achievements.

# Understanding Foreign Words

Have you ever made a *faux pas* ("blunder") because you used a foreign phrase that was *malapropos* ("not appropriate")? What do you do when you come across a foreign expression in your reading? What is your *modus operandi* ("method of operating")? For example, how would you find the meaning of *auto-da-fé* in the sentence on the right?

If you look in a standard English dictionary, you will find something close to this definition of *auto-da-fé*: "the public announcement and execution of sentences on persons tried and found guilty by the Inquisition." Many foreign terms, however, are not

> The condemned to death, I knew, perished usually at the *auto-da-fé,* and one of these had been held on the very night of the day of my trial.
> —Edgar Allan Poe, "The Pit and the Pendulum"

included in English dictionaries, so you may need to consult other reference aids when you encounter expressions you don't know.

## Strategies for Building Vocabulary

Words move from language to language in a word migration that has been going on for centuries. Some foreign words and phrases have been adopted into the English language, especially when there are no English words to convey certain ideas. At one time the Latin words *capsule* and *habitual*, the Greek word *catastrophe*, and the French word *detail* would have sounded strange to English speakers. Today, however, these words are considered a part of the English vocabulary.

Foreign words are frequently used in literature, and you will likely encounter some that are unfamiliar to you. Learning how to find their meanings in reference aids will help your comprehension.

❶ **Use a Dictionary** When you need to translate a foreign phrase, you will often find it in an English dictionary by looking for it as one word. For example, even though the French phrase *en route* (meaning "on the way") consists of two words, it is listed in the dictionary among the *enro*-words, right after the verb *enroot*.

❷ **Use Other Reference Tools** When you can't find a term in an English dictionary, try a foreign-language dictionary; most libraries have such dictionaries. You can also use the Internet to find a translation of a word. Type the name of the foreign language you need and the word "dictionary" in the search engine box (example: French language

dictionary). A list of available dictionaries or translation sites will appear. When you go to one of these sites, type the foreign word or phrase, and the English translation will appear.

❸ **Learn Foreign Words and Phrases** The following list includes some commonly used foreign words and phrases.

| Word or Phrase | Meaning |
|---|---|
| en route (French) | on the way |
| laissez faire (French) | noninterference |
| mea culpa (Latin) | my fault |
| per (Latin) | for, according to |
| status quo (Latin) | the way things are |
| aloha (Hawaiian) | hello or goodbye |
| dolce vita (Italian) | the sweet life |
| pièce de résistance (French) | an outstanding accomplishment |

**EXERCISE** Use a reference tool to translate the following commonly used foreign words and phrases.

1. en masse
2. coup d'état
3. Zeitgeist
4. alfresco
5. carte blanche

*This story takes place during the Korean War, a conflict that often pitted friend against friend and even brother against brother. In 1948, shortly after World War II, the nation of Korea, which occupies a peninsula on the eastern shore of Asia, became officially divided. Two separate governments were established: a Communist government in the north and a non-Communist government in the south. In 1950, North Korea invaded South Korea, beginning a civil war in which other nations, including the United States and China, soon became involved. A truce was signed in 1953, but tension between the two Koreas has continued for decades.*

*Much of the war took place near the 38th parallel of north latitude, the dividing line between the two countries. This area was the scene of hotly contested battles in which thousands died and the control of villages often shifted back and forth between the North Koreans and the South Koreans. One of these villages is the setting of "Cranes."*

# CRANES

## HWANG SUNWŎN

The northern village lay snug beneath the high, bright autumn sky, near the border at the Thirty-eighth Parallel.

White gourds lay one against the other on the dirt floor of an empty farmhouse. Any village elders who passed by extinguished their bamboo pipes first, and the children, too, turned back some distance off. Their faces were marked with fear.

As a whole, the village showed little damage from the war, but it still did not seem like the same village Sŏngsam[1] had known as a boy.

At the foot of a chestnut grove on the hill behind the village he stopped and climbed a chestnut tree. Somewhere far back in his mind he heard the old man with a wen[2] shout, "You bad boy, climbing up my chestnut tree again!"

The old man must have passed away, for he was not among the few village elders Sŏngsam had met. Holding on to the trunk of the tree, Sŏngsam gazed up at the blue sky for a time. Some chestnuts fell to the ground as the dry clusters opened of their own accord.

A young man stood, his hands bound, before a farmhouse that had been converted into a Public Peace Police office. He seemed to be a stranger, so Sŏngsam went up for a closer look.

---

1. **Sŏngsam** (sǝng′säm′).
2. **wen:** a harmless skin tumor.

He was stunned: this young man was none other than his boyhood playmate, Tŏkchae.[3]

Sŏngsam asked the police officer who had come with him from Ch'ŏnt'ae[4] for an explanation. The prisoner was the vice-chairman of the Farmers' Communist League and had just been flushed[5] out of hiding in his own house, Sŏngsam learned.

Sŏngsam sat down on the dirt floor and lit a cigaret.

Tŏkchae was to be escorted to Ch'ŏngdan[6] by one of the peace police.

After a time, Sŏngsam lit a new cigaret from the first and stood up.

"I'll take him with me."

Tŏkchae averted his face and refused to look at Sŏngsam. The two left the village.

Sŏngsam went on smoking, but the tobacco had no flavor. He just kept drawing the smoke in and blowing it out. Then suddenly he thought that Tŏkchae, too, must want a puff. He thought of the days when they had shared dried gourd leaves behind sheltering walls, hidden from the adults' view. But today, how could he offer a cigaret to a fellow like this?

Once, when they were small, he went with Tŏkchae to steal some chestnuts from the old man with the wen. It was Sŏngsam's turn to climb the tree. Suddenly the old man began shouting. Sŏngsam slipped and fell to the ground. He got chestnut burrs all over his bottom, but he kept on running. Only when the two had reached a safe place where the old man could not overtake them did Sŏngsam turn his bottom to Tŏkchae. The burrs hurt so much as they were plucked out that Sŏngsam could not keep tears from welling up in his eyes. Tŏkchae produced a fistful of chestnuts from his pocket and thrust them into Sŏngsam's . . . Sŏngsam threw away the cigaret he had just lit, and then made up his mind not to light another while he was escorting Tŏkchae.

They reached the pass at the hill where he and Tŏkchae had cut fodder[7] for the cows until Sŏngsam had to move to a spot near Ch'ŏnt'ae, south of the Thirty-eighth Parallel, two years before the liberation.

Sŏngsam felt a sudden surge of anger in spite of himself and shouted, "So how many have you killed?"

For the first time, Tŏkchae cast a quick glance at him and then looked away.

"You! How many have you killed?" he asked again.

Tŏkchae looked at him again and glared. The glare grew intense, and his mouth twitched.

"So you managed to kill quite a few, eh?" Sŏngsam felt his mind becoming clear of itself, as if some obstruction had been removed. "If you were vice-chairman of the Communist League, why didn't you run? You must have been lying low with a secret mission."

Tŏkchae did not reply.

"Speak up. What was your mission?"

Tŏkchae kept walking. Tŏkchae was hiding something, Sŏngsam thought. He wanted to take a good look at him, but Tŏkchae kept his face averted.

Fingering the revolver at his side, Sŏngsam went on: "There's no need to make excuses. You're going to be shot anyway. Why don't you tell the truth here and now?"

"I'm not going to make any excuses. They made me vice-chairman of the League because I was a hardworking farmer and one of the poorest. If that's a capital offense,[8] so be it. I'm still what I used to be—the only thing I'm good at is

---

3. **Tŏkchae** (tək'jă').
4. **Ch'ŏnt'ae** (chən'tă').
5. **flushed:** driven from hiding.
6. **Ch'ŏngdan** (chəng'dän').
7. **fodder:** coarsely chopped hay or straw used as food for farm animals.
8. **capital offense:** a crime calling for the death penalty.

tilling the soil." After a short pause, he added, "My old man is bedridden at home. He's been ill almost half a year." Tŏkchae's father was a widower, a poor, hardworking farmer who lived only for his son. Seven years before his back had given out, and he had contracted a skin disease.

"Are you married?"

"Yes," Tŏkchae replied after a time.

"To whom?"

"Shorty."

"To Shorty?" How interesting! A woman so small and plump that she knew the earth's vastness, but not the sky's height. Such a cold fish! He and Tŏkchae had teased her and made her cry. And Tŏkchae had married her!

"How many kids?"

"The first is arriving this fall, she says."

Sŏngsam had difficulty swallowing a laugh that he was about to let burst forth in spite of himself. Although he had asked how many children Tŏkchae had, he could not help wanting to break out laughing at the thought of the wife sitting there with her huge stomach, one span around. But he realized that this was no time for joking.

"Anyway, it's strange you didn't run away."

"I tried to escape. They said that once the South invaded, not a man would be spared. So all of us between seventeen and forty were taken to the North. I thought of evacuating, even if I had to carry my father on my back. But Father said no. How could we farmers leave the land behind when the crops were ready for harvesting? He grew old on that farm depending on me as the prop and the mainstay of the family. I wanted to be with him in his last moments so I could close his eyes with my own hand. Besides, where can farmers like us go, when all we know how to do is live on the land?"

Sŏngsam had had to flee the previous June. At night he had broken the news privately to his father. But his father had said the same thing: Where could a farmer go, leaving all the chores behind? So Sŏngsam had left alone. Roaming about the strange streets and villages in the South, Sŏngsam had been haunted by thoughts of his old parents and the young children, who had been left with all the chores. Fortunately, his family had been safe then, as it was now.

They had crossed over a hill. This time Sŏngsam walked with his face averted. The autumn sun was hot on his forehead. This was an ideal day for the harvest, he thought.

When they reached the foot of the hill, Sŏngsam gradually came to a halt. In the middle of a field he espied a group of cranes that resembled men in white, all bent over. This had been the demilitarized zone[9] along the Thirty-eighth Parallel. The cranes were still living here, as before, though the people were all gone.

Once, when Sŏngsam and Tŏkchae were about twelve, they had set a trap here, unbeknown to the adults, and caught a crane, a Tanjŏng crane.[10] They had tied the crane up, even binding its wings, and paid it daily visits, patting its neck and riding on its back. Then one day they overheard the neighbors whispering: someone had come from Seoul[11] with a permit from the governor-general's office to catch cranes as some kind of specimens. Then and there the two boys had dashed off to the field. That they would be found out and punished had no longer mattered; all they cared about was the fate of their crane. Without a moment's delay, still out of breath from running, they untied the crane's feet and wings, but the bird could hardly walk. It must have been weak from having been bound.

The two held the crane up. Then, suddenly, they heard a gunshot. The crane fluttered its wings once or twice and then sank back to the ground.

---

9. **demilitarized zone:** an area—generally one separating two hostile nations or armies—from which military forces are prohibited.

10. **Tanjŏng** (tän′jəng′) **crane:** a type of crane found in Asia.

11. **Seoul** (sōl): the capital and largest city of South Korea.

Yi Dynasty rank badge (about 1600–1700). Colored silk and gold paper, thread on figured silk, Victoria & Albert Museum, London / Art Resource, New York.

The boys thought their crane had been shot. But the next moment, as another crane from a nearby bush fluttered its wings, the boys' crane stretched its long neck, gave out a whoop, and disappeared into the sky. For a long while the two boys could not tear their eyes away from the blue sky up into which their crane had soared.

"Hey, why don't we stop here for a crane hunt?" Sŏngsam said suddenly.

Tŏkchae was dumbfounded.

"I'll make a trap with this rope; you flush a crane over here."

Sŏngsam had untied Tŏkchae's hands and was already crawling through the weeds.

Tŏkchae's face whitened. "You're sure to be shot anyway"—these words flashed through his mind. Any instant a bullet would come flying from Sŏngsam's direction, Tŏkchae thought.

Some paces away, Sŏngsam quickly turned toward him.

"Hey, how come you're standing there like a dummy? Go flush a crane!"

Only then did Tŏkchae understand. He began crawling through the weeds.

A pair of Tanjŏng cranes soared high into the clear blue autumn sky, flapping their huge wings. ❖

*Translated by Peter H. Lee*

# Hwang Sunwŏn
## 1915 –

**Other Works**
*Trees on the Cliff*
*The Book of Masks*
*Shadows of a Sound*

**Enemy Tongues** For Korea's Hwang Sunwŏn, becoming a published writer in his native tongue was no easy matter. For the first three decades of Hwang's life, Korea was ruled by Japan. The Japanese tried to stamp out Korean nationalism by setting up Japanese-language schools, arresting Korean scholars, and at one point even forcing Koreans to adopt Japanese names. Hwang had to travel to Japan to receive his higher education. However, his years at Waseda University proved stimulating, and he returned to his homeland to publish his first story collection in 1940.

**The Interference of War** Two years later, his career plans were temporarily blocked when, at the height of World War II, the Japanese banned all Korean-language publications. After the Japanese departed at the war's end, Hwang and his family still faced hardships in the Communist-dominated north where they lived. Luckily, they were able to flee to the south, but invasion by the North Korean forces at the start of the Korean War soon made them refugees once again. Only after the signing of the truce in 1953 was Hwang able to return full-time to his writing. Over the years, Hwang has produced 7 novels and over 100 short stories, which have won him several prestigious awards in his homeland. "Cranes," written in 1953, was the title story of a 1956 collection.

# Inquiry & Research

The Korean War lasted just over three years, but almost as many Americans died there as in 10 years in Vietnam. Learn more about the Korean War through personal accounts of soldiers who fought there.

 **Real World Link**
Begin your research by reading the magazine article on page 590.

## THE REMEMBERED WAR:
## A Korean War Vet Offers a History Lesson

by Angus Deming

*In the United States, the Korean War sometimes is referred to as the "forgotten war." As the writer reminds us, this war was both devastating and momentous, and the soldiers who fought in it were just as dedicated and brave as those who fought in World War II and the Vietnam War.*

**❶** The weather was almost as perverse[1] as anything we'd known in Korea. Thousands of us—Korean War veterans from all over the country and even overseas—filled the Washington Mall last week. We had come to take part in the dedication of the Korean War Veterans Memorial, honoring those who served in the first of the cold war's hot wars. South Korea's President Kim Young Sam thanked us for helping to save his country from the communist invaders from the North. Bill Clinton praised our "never surpassed" courage in the face of extreme hardship. Mercifully, both spoke briefly; we were beginning to keel over in the sweltering heat. A thunderstorm washed out the evening's entertainment. But the weather didn't bother us. This was a long overdue celebration. The Korean War—our war—was no longer lost somewhere between World War II and Vietnam. It was no longer the "forgotten war."

The Korean Memorial occupies a grove beneath the Lincoln Memorial, across the reflecting pool from the Vietnam Wall. It's dominated by 19 large, steel statues of infantry-men—a silent patrol moving warily up a slope. They look weary, as though they've been on too many patrols and climbed too many hills. That was us in Korea, the way we were, too. Off to the side there's a granite wall with hundreds of faces etched on it, faces taken from actual photographs of men and women who served in Korea as support troops: truckdrivers, engineers, flight crewmen, nurses, chaplains, sailors. These ghostly faces seem to say, "Don't forget us."

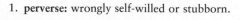

---

1. **perverse:** wrongly self-willed or stubborn.

Korean War
Veterans Memorial,
Washington, D.C.

## Reading for Information

Have you ever built a house of cards with your friends? If so, you know that it doesn't take much to knock it over. Think of a weak argument as a house of cards—easy to knock down. But think of a strong argument as a battleship—virtually indestructible. In this article, the writer constructs an argument about the significance of the Korean War, and the reader must evaluate its strengths and weaknesses.

### EVALUATING AN ARGUMENT

An effective argument shows an honest concern about a problem, a grasp of the issues involved, and a respectful attitude toward the audience. In addition, to win over an audience, a writer must establish and maintain credibility, or believability.

**YOUR TURN** Use the questions and activities below to help you evaluate the writer's argument.

**❶ Identifying the Main Idea** To communicate an argument effectively, a writer generally has to engage both the minds and the emotions of readers. What is Deming's main point in his article? What emotions do you think Deming wants you to feel?

We never understood how the Korean War could have been "forgotten" in the first place. It caused such incredible devastation: more than 2 million people dead and more than 2.5 million wounded or injured in just three years. About 54,000 Americans died there, almost as many as in Vietnam in 10 years. More than 8,000 Americans are still listed as missing in action in Korea. Losses on the Communist side were staggering: more than 400,000 Chinese soldiers dead, almost 215,000 North Koreans killed in action. Korea itself—North and South alike—was left in total ruins.

The war ushered in the era of jet fighters and was the first in which helicopters were used in combat. It also was the first (and perhaps last) in which a multinational force fought effectively under the United Nations flag. We did not wear blue helmets, of course; we were in Korea as war makers, not peacekeepers. But Korea was, most of all, a ground war, and "gravel crunchers"— infantry grunts—had a miserable time. The terrain was as much an enemy as the one that was shooting at us. There was always another hill to climb, and the weather seemed to be of two kinds: unbearable heat or unbearable cold. . . .

The war lasted three years, one month, and two days. The Marines alone suffered more than 2,000 casualties in the final two months, even as peace talks neared the end. On July 25, 1953, two Chinese battalions attacked a remote Marine outpost on the western front. Sgt. Ambrosio Guillen won a posthumous[2] Congressional Medal of Honor helping repel the assault. The next day the Chinese hit the outpost again, and another Marine sergeant won a posthumous Navy Cross. The following morning the armistice was signed at Panmunjom.

In the tight little world of a frontline rifle company, we seldom saw the big picture. We didn't realize then that, as Clinton told us, we had helped South Korea become a free and prosperous nation. Mostly we fought for each other, or to uphold the honor of the Corps—that was what mattered. Most of us escaped the kind of trauma suffered by so many Vietnam vets. It was a different war at a different time, to be sure. But our mindset was also different: we were closer to the World War II generation, and we answered the call simply because our country needed us. Our only anger, really, was that so much bravery, so much uncomplaining devotion to duty, went unrecognized for so long. Now that lingering bitterness has been laid to rest at last.

---

2. **posthumous** (pŏs′ chə-məs): occurring or continuing after one's death.

**2** **Providing Evidence** To show that the argument is well thought out, a writer must provide evidence. Statistical information and facts can strengthen a writer's argument. What facts or statistics does Deming provide to support his main idea? Which of these facts did you find most surprising?

**3** Writers also use details to support their general statements and opinions. What details that illustrate the intensity of the fight does the writer provide?

**4** **Determining Credibility** In your opinion, does Deming's argument have **credibility?** What do you think is his **motivation** for putting forth this argument? Do you think the fact that he served in Korea strengthens or weakens his argument?

**Evaluating the Argument** Does the writer provide enough convincing information to support his main idea? On the basis of what you've read, has Deming made a sound, convincing argument? Explain.

## Inquiry & Research

**Activity Link: "Cranes," p. 589**
What added insight about the Korean War did you get from reading this article? Have the facts in the article about the human toll of the war shed new light on Sŏngsam's inner conflict about his duties as a soldier? Discuss your thoughts with a partner.

# Learning from History

| *from* **Night** | *from* **Nobel Prize Acceptance Speech** | *from* **Farewell to Manzanar** |
|---|---|---|
| *Memoir by* ELIE WIESEL | *Speech by* ELIE WIESEL | *Memoir by* JEANNE WAKATSUKI HOUSTON AND JAMES HOUSTON |

## What's the Connection?

**Victims of Injustice** You are about to read the true stories of people who were victims of terrible injustices. Elie Wiesel, a Jew born in Romania, lived in a concentration camp in Germany as a teenager and lost members of his family to the Holocaust. When Jeanne Wakatsuki was a young girl in the United States, her family was forced to leave their home and live for three years in a California detention camp—all because of fears that Japanese Americans would be disloyal in World War II.

As you will see, human beings find ways of dealing with adversity, even in the worst of circumstances. By reading about what others have lived through, we can at least begin to understand these events. By keeping alive their stories, we can perhaps avoid repeating the injustices of the past.

Japanese Americans being transported to detention camps in World War II.

## Points of Comparison

**Drawing Lessons from History** In this unit so far, you have encountered various characters trapped by the forces of history. The next selections deal with real people who are similarly trapped by forces beyond their control. In the pages that follow, you will be asked to synthesize—a task that involves combining ideas or information to form new ideas—so that you can draw lessons from the experience of these authors.

**Critical Thinking: From Analysis to Synthesis**
To form a synthesis from two or more works of literature, you first need to analyze the information in each selection. The chart on the right will help you focus on important aspects of each work. Create a separate chart for the two major selections.

**READER'S NOTEBOOK** You will be asked to fill in your chart at the Points of Comparison in the following selections. Add other categories to your chart as necessary.

**Cause of Situation:**
↓
**How the Author and Other Victims Are Treated:**
↓
**Psychological Effects on Victims:**
↓
**How People Try to Cope:**
↓
**Author's Purpose in Telling About Events:**

# PREPARING to *Read*

## *from* **Night**

*Memoir by* ELIE WIESEL (ĕl'ē vē-sĕl')

---

### Connect to Your Life

**Jewish Holocaust** With a small group of classmates, share what you know about the Holocaust—the slaughter of millions of Jews in Europe during World War II. Where did you learn what you know? How did you react when you first learned about it?

---

## Build Background

**Holocaust Origins** In the 1920s and 1930s, Germany was in the midst of a major economic depression; millions were unemployed. When Adolf Hitler became chancellor in 1933, he promised people jobs while providing them with a scapegoat for the nation's problems: the Jews. Hitler's Nazi party began its campaign against the Jews by revoking their citizenship, boycotting their businesses, and banning them from certain professions.

Germany's invasion of Poland in 1939 marked the beginning of World War II. Hitler's goal was to expand his empire across Europe and to eliminate the Jews at the same time. In Germany and from each nation Germany occupied, Jews— as well as gypsies, homosexuals, and intellectuals and artists who opposed Hitler—were transported to the concentration camps. Everyone entering the camps was tattooed with a number on the left forearm; the number served to replace one's name. Most of the 6 million Jews who were killed during World War II died in concentration camps. They were put to death in gas chambers, were shot by firing squads, or succumbed to starvation, torture, and disease. This selection is from the memoir of a survivor who was imprisoned when he was only 15.

WORDS TO KNOW
**Vocabulary Preview**

din            notorious
emaciated      stature
interminable

## Focus Your Reading

**LITERARY ANALYSIS** **STYLE** **Style** is the particular way a piece of literature is written—not *what* is said but *how* it is said. Every writer struggles to find an appropriate style to convey his or her message. Choice of words, length of sentences, and tone all contribute to the style of a writer's work, as illustrated by the following passage from *Night*:

> *There were only Tibi and Yossi in front of me. They passed. I had time to notice that Mengele had not written their numbers down. Someone pushed me. It was my turn. I ran without looking back.*

As you read this excerpt by Elie Wiesel, pay attention to the manner in which he relates his experiences. Think about why he might have chosen to tell his story in such a simple and straightforward style.

**ACTIVE READING** **CONNECTING** When you read anything, you are bound to compare it with what you have previously read, heard about, or experienced yourself. In this way, you are **connecting** with what you are reading. You might also imagine yourself in a situation similar to that of a character or person that you read about. Literature with especially powerful content may provoke strong feelings or reflections about yourself or the world you know.

**READER'S NOTEBOOK** As you read this excerpt, keep notes of your mental and emotional reactions to the events and conversations related by Wiesel. After you have finished reading, spend a few minutes writing your reflections on the piece itself and on the Holocaust in general.

**Survivors of a Nazi concentration camp, 1945.** The Bettmann Archive.

# FROM
# NIGHT

## Elie Wiesel

The SS[1] gave us a fine New Year's gift.

We had just come back from work. As soon as we had passed
through the door of the camp, we sensed something different in the
air. Roll call did not take so long as usual. The evening soup was
given out with great speed and swallowed down at once in anguish.

---

1. SS: an elite military unit of the Nazi party that served as Hitler's personal guard and as a
   special security force.

I was no longer in the same block as my father. I had been transferred to another unit, the building one, where, twelve hours a day, I had to drag heavy blocks of stone about. The head of my new block was a German Jew, small of <u>stature</u>, with piercing eyes. He told us that evening that no one would be allowed to go out after the evening soup. And soon a terrible word was circulating—selection.

We knew what that meant. An SS man would examine us. Whenever he found a weak one, a *musulman* as we called them, he would write his number down: good for the crematory.

After soup, we gathered together between the beds. The veterans said:

"You're lucky to have been brought here so late. This camp is paradise today, compared with what it was like two years ago. Buna[2] was a real hell then. There was no water, no blankets, less soup and bread. At night we slept almost naked, and it was below thirty degrees. The corpses were collected in hundreds every day. The work was hard. Today, this is a little paradise. The Kapos[3] had orders to kill a certain number of prisoners every day. And every week—selection. A merciless selection. . . . Yes, you're lucky."

"Stop it! Be quiet!" I begged. "You can tell your stories tomorrow or on some other day."

They burst out laughing. They were not veterans for nothing.

"Are you scared? So were we scared. And there was plenty to be scared of in those days."

The old men stayed in their corner, dumb, motionless, haunted. Some were praying.

An hour's delay. In an hour, we should know the verdict—death or a reprieve.

And my father? Suddenly I remembered him. How would he pass the selection? He had aged so much. . . .

The head of our block had never been outside concentration camps since 1933. He had already been through all the slaughterhouses, all the factories of death. At about nine o'clock, he took up his position in our midst:

"Achtung!"[4]

There was instant silence.

"Listen carefully to what I am going to say." (For the first time, I heard his voice quiver.) "In a few moments the selection will begin. You must get completely undressed. Then one by one you go before the SS doctors. I hope you will all succeed in getting through. But you must help your own chances. Before you go into the next room, move about in some way so that you give yourselves a little color. Don't walk slowly, run! Run as if the devil were after you! Don't look at the SS. Run, straight in front of you!"

He broke off for a moment, then added:

"And, the essential thing, don't be afraid!"

Here was a piece of advice we should have liked very much to be able to follow.

I got undressed, leaving my clothes on the bed. There was no danger of anyone stealing them this evening.

Tibi and Yossi, who had changed their unit at the same time as I had, came up to me and said:

"Let's keep together. We shall be stronger."

Yossi was murmuring something between his teeth. He must have been praying. I had never realized that Yossi was a believer. I had even always thought the reverse. Tibi was silent, very pale. All the prisoners in the block stood naked

---

2. **Buna** (bo͞o′nə): a forced-labor camp in Poland, near the Auschwitz concentration camp.

3. **Kapos** (kä′pōz): the prisoners who served as foremen, or heads, of each building or cell block.

4. **Achtung!** (äКН-to͝ong′) *German:* Attention!

WORDS
TO
KNOW

**stature** (stăch′ər) *n.* a person's height

between the beds. This must be how one stands at the last judgment.

"They're coming!"

There were three SS officers standing around the <u>notorious</u> Dr. Mengele,[5] who had received us at Birkenau.[6] The head of the block, with an attempt at a smile, asked us:

"Ready?"

Yes, we were ready. So were the SS doctors. Dr. Mengele was holding a list in his hand: our numbers. He made a sign to the head of the block: "We can begin!" As if this were a game!

The first to go by were the "officials" of the block: *Stubenaelteste*,[7] Kapos, foremen, all in perfect physical condition of course! Then came the ordinary prisoners' turn. Dr. Mengele took stock of them from head to foot. Every now and then, he wrote a number down. One single thought filled my mind: not to let my number be taken; not to show my left arm.

There were only Tibi and Yossi in front of me. They passed. I had time to notice that Mengele had not written their numbers down. Someone pushed me. It was my turn. I ran without looking back. My head was spinning: you're too thin, you're too weak, you're too thin, you're good for the furnace. . . . The race seemed <u>interminable</u>. I thought I had been running for years. . . . You're too thin, you're too weak. . . . At last I had arrived exhausted. When I regained my breath, I questioned Yossi and Tibi:

"Was I written down?"

"No," said Yossi. He added, smiling: "In any case, he couldn't have written you down, you were running too fast. . . ."

I began to laugh. I was glad. I would have liked to kiss him. At that moment, what did the others matter! I hadn't been written down.

Those whose numbers had been noted stood apart, abandoned by the whole world. Some were weeping in silence.

The SS officers went away. The head of the block appeared, his face reflecting the general weariness.

"Everything went off all right. Don't worry. Nothing is going to happen to anyone. To anyone."

Again he tried to smile. A poor, <u>emaciated</u>, dried-up Jew questioned him avidly in a trembling voice:

"But . . . but, *Blockaelteste*,[8] they did write me down!"

The head of the block let his anger break out. What! Did someone refuse to believe him!

"What's the matter now? Am I telling lies then? I tell you once and for all, nothing's going to happen to you! To anyone! You're wallowing in your own despair, you fool!"

The bell rang, a signal that the selection had been completed throughout the camp.

With all my might I began to run to Block 36. I met my father on the way. He came up to me:

"Well? So you passed?"

"Yes. And you?"

"Me too."

How we breathed again, now! My father had brought me a present—half a ration of bread obtained in exchange for a piece of rubber, found

---

5. **Dr. Mengele** (mĕng′ə-lə): Josef Mengele, a German doctor who personally selected nearly half a million prisoners to die in gas chambers at Auschwitz. He also became infamous for his medical experiments on inmates.

6. **Birkenau** (bĭr′kə-nou): a large section of the Auschwitz concentration camp.

7. *Stubenaelteste* (shtoō′bən-ĕl′tə-stə): a rank of Kapos; literally "elders of the rooms."

8. *Blockaelteste* (blôk′ĕl′tə-stə): a rank of Kapos; literally "elders of the building."

at the warehouse, which would do to sole a shoe.

The bell. Already we must separate, go to bed. Everything was regulated by the bell. It gave me orders, and I automatically obeyed them. I hated it. Whenever I dreamed of a better world, I could only imagine a universe with no bells.

Several days had elapsed. We no longer thought about the selection. We went to work as usual, loading heavy stones into railway wagons. Rations had become more meager: this was the only change.

We had risen before dawn, as on every day. We had received the black coffee, the ration of bread. We were about to set out for the yard as usual. The head of the block arrived, running.

"Silence for a moment. I have a list of numbers here. I'm going to read them to you. Those whose numbers I call won't be going to work this morning; they'll stay behind in the camp."

And, in a soft voice, he read out about ten numbers. We had understood. These were numbers chosen at the selection. Dr. Mengele had not forgotten.

The head of the block went toward his room. Ten prisoners surrounded him, hanging onto his clothes:

"Save us! You promised . . . ! We want to go to the yard. We're strong enough to work. We're good workers. We can . . . we will . . . ."

He tried to calm them to reassure them about their fate, to explain to them that the fact that they were staying behind in the camp did not mean much, had no tragic significance.

"After all, I stay here myself every day," he added.

It was a somewhat feeble argument. He realized it, and without another word went and shut himself up in his room.

The bell had just rung.

"Form up!"

It scarcely mattered now that the work was hard. The essential thing was to be as far away as possible from the block, from the crucible of death, from the center of hell.

I saw my father running toward me. I became frightened all of a sudden.

"What's the matter?"

**"THOSE WHOSE NUMBERS I CALL WON'T BE GOING TO WORK THIS MORNING; THEY'LL STAY BEHIND IN THE CAMP."**

Out of breath, he could hardly open his mouth.

"Me, too . . . me, too . . . ! They told me to stay behind in the camp."

They had written down his number without his being aware of it.

"What will happen?" I asked in anguish.

But it was he who tried to reassure me.

"It isn't certain yet. There's still a chance of escape. They're going to do another selection today . . . a decisive selection."

I was silent.

He felt that his time was short. He spoke quickly. He would have liked to say so many things. His speech grew confused; his voice choked. He knew that I would have to go in a few moments. He would have to stay behind alone, so very alone.

"Look, take this knife," he said to me. "I don't need it any longer. It might be useful to you. And take this spoon as well. Don't sell them. Quickly!

Go on. Take what I'm giving you!"

The inheritance.

"Don't talk like that, Father." (I felt that I would break into sobs.) "I don't want you to say that. Keep the spoon and knife. You need them as much as I do. We shall see each other again this evening, after work."

He looked at me with his tired eyes, veiled

## WERE THERE STILL MIRACLES ON THIS EARTH?

with despair. He went on:

"I'm asking this of you. . . . Take them. Do as I ask, my son. We have no time. . . . Do as your father asks."

Our Kapo yelled that we should start.

The unit set out toward the camp gate. Left, right! I bit my lips. My father had stayed by the block, leaning against the wall. Then he began to run, to catch up with us. Perhaps he had forgotten something he wanted to say to me. . . .

But we were marching too quickly . . . Left, right!

We were already at the gate. They counted us, to the din of military music. We were outside.

The whole day, I wandered about as if sleepwalking. Now and then Tibi and Yossi would throw me a brotherly word. The Kapo, too, tried to reassure me. He had given me easier work today. I felt sick at heart. How well they were treating me! Like an orphan! I thought: even now, my father is still helping me.

I did not know myself what I wanted—for the day to pass quickly or not. I was afraid of finding myself alone that night. How good it would be to die here!

At last we began the return journey. How I longed for orders to run!

The military march. The gate. The camp.

I ran to Block 36.

Were there still miracles on this earth? He was alive. He had escaped the second selection. He had been able to prove that he was still useful. . . . I gave him back his knife and spoon. ❖

WORDS
TO
KNOW

**din** (dĭn) *n.* a jumble of loud noises

# *from* Nobel Prize Acceptance Speech

## Elie Wiesel

It is with a profound sense of humility that I accept the honor you have chosen to bestow upon me. I know: your choice transcends me. This both frightens and pleases me.

It frightens me because I wonder: do I have the right to represent the multitudes who have perished? Do I have the right to accept this great honor on their behalf? I do not. That would be presumptuous. No one may speak for the dead, no one may interpret their mutilated dreams and visions.

It pleases me because I may say that this honor belongs to all the survivors and their children, and through us, to the Jewish people with whose destiny I have always identified.

I remember: it happened yesterday or eternities ago. A young Jewish boy discovered the kingdom of night. I remember his bewilderment, I remember his anguish. It all happened so fast. The ghetto. The deportation. The sealed cattle car. The fiery altar upon which the history of our people and the future of mankind were meant to be sacrificed.

I remember: he asked his father: "Can this be true? This is the 20th century, not the Middle Ages. Who would allow such crimes to be committed? How could the world remain silent?"

And now the boy is turning to me: "Tell me," he asks. "What have you done with my future? What have you done with your life?"

And I tell him that I have tried. That I have tried to keep memory alive, that I have tried to fight those who would forget. Because if we forget, we are guilty, we are accomplices.

And then I explained to him how naive we were, that the world did know and remain silent. And that is why I swore never to be silent whenever and wherever human beings endure suffering and humiliation. We must always take sides. Neutrality helps the oppressor, never the victim. Silence encourages the tormentor, never the tormented.

## Connect to the Literature

1. **What Do You Think?** What mental image did you form of the **narrator** while reading? Explain your thinking.

**Comprehension Check**
- What occurs at the "selection"?
- Why do the men in the block try to run as fast as they can in front of the SS doctors?
- What does Wiesel learn about his father at the end of the selection?

## Think Critically

2. **ACTIVE READING   CONNECTING** Refer to the notes you made in your 📖 **READER'S NOTEBOOK.** How would you describe this selection's effect on you?

3. What are your impressions of the people portrayed in this excerpt?

4. How would you describe Wiesel's **tone**?

**THINK ABOUT**
- his comment that the SS "gave us a fine New Year's gift"
- his reference to the knife and spoon as his "inheritance"

5. Why do you think Wiesel called his book *Night?*

**THINK ABOUT**
- the circumstances he recounts
- what the word *night* might symbolize
- Wiesel's remarks on accepting the Nobel Peace Prize

## Extend Interpretations

6. **Comparing Texts** What does the excerpt from Wiesel's Nobel Prize acceptance speech tell you about his motivation for writing *Night?*

7. **Points of Comparison** Fill in the chart that you began on page 592. What do you consider the worst circumstance in this portion of Wiesel's concentration camp experiences? Explain.

8. **Connect to Life** Do you agree with Wiesel's statement from his Nobel Prize acceptance speech that "neutrality helps the oppressor, never the victim"? Support your opinion.

## Literary Analysis

**STYLE**   **Style** is the way in which a literary work is written. Style refers not to what is said but to how it is said. Elements that contribute to a writer's personal style include the following: word choice, or **diction;** sentence length, structure, and variety; **tone, imagery,** and **dialogue.** In the following passage, for example, Wiesel relies on short sentences, simple words, and minimal description:

*"Look, take this knife," he said to me. "I don't need it any longer. It might be useful to you. And take this spoon as well. Don't sell them. Quickly! Go on. Take what I'm giving you!"*

*The inheritance.*

This simple and direct style heightens the drama of the event.

**Paired Activity** Choose a passage of five or six paragraphs from this excerpt and analyze it in terms of the elements of style mentioned above. Use a chart like the one started below. When you have finished, discuss how Wiesel's style affects your response to the events described. Why do you think Wiesel chose to tell about his experience in this manner?

| Passage beginning | "I was no longer in the same block as my father." |
|---|---|
| Word choice | simple words; not many adjectives |
| Sentence length, structure, and variety | Short, simple sentences |
| Tone | |
| Imagery | |
| Dialogue | |

## Writing Options

**1. Holocaust Essay** In recent years, some extremists have argued that the Holocaust never happened. Write a persuasive essay in which you argue against that position, using the excerpts from *Night* and Wiesel's speech as part of your evidence. Add additional factual support as needed. Place the essay in your **Working Portfolio.**

**2. Interview Questions** Make a list of questions you would ask Wiesel if you had the chance.

## Inquiry & Research

**1. Night Report** Read all of *Night* to find out more about Wiesel's experiences during the Holocaust. Present an oral book report.

**2. Film Review** Obtain and view a video recording of *Schindler's List,* the 1993 film about a man who enabled more than a thousand Jews to escape the Holocaust. Then locate a review of the movie and compare your response to that of the reviewer. Share your ideas about the movie and its impact in a brief presentation.

## Vocabulary in Action

**EXERCISE: CONTEXT CLUES** On your paper, indicate which of the Words to Know could best replace the italicized word or phrase in each sentence below.

1. To those in concentration camps, the war seemed *as if it would never end.*
2. Auschwitz was *famous in a negative way* for torture and mass murder.
3. Those not killed immediately were fed little and soon grew *incredibly skinny.*
4. Backbreaking labor bent once-tall prisoners to half their *size.*
5. The *clashing background sound* of German patriotic music tore at the prisoners' ears.

| WORDS TO KNOW | din | interminable | stature |
|---|---|---|---|
| | emaciated | notorious | |

**Building Vocabulary**
For a lesson on affixes, see page 856.

## Elie Wiesel
### 1928–

**Other Works**
*Dawn*
*The Accident*
*A Beggar in Jerusalem*
*Legends of Our Time*
*A Jew Today*

**Victim of War** Elie Wiesel was born in the town of Sighet (sē′gĕt), Transylvania, an area of Romania that the Germans made part of Hungary when they overran both nations in 1940, during World War II. Cut off by the war from most communication, the 15,000 Jews of Sighet had no idea where they were going when, in the spring of 1944, the Nazis ordered their deportation and shipped them on a cattle train to Auschwitz in Poland. Wiesel's mother and one of his three sisters were murdered there. In 1945, Wiesel and his father were sent to Buchenwald concentration camp in Germany; sadly, Wiesel's father died of starvation and dysentery less than three months before the camp was liberated by the Allies.

**Holocaust Survivor** After the war, Wiesel settled in France. He studied at the Sorbonne and worked as a writer and journalist, but he made a vow to write nothing about his concentration camp experience for ten years. "I didn't want to use the wrong words," he later explained. Wiesel's 900-page autobiographical account was first written in Yiddish, the language of his childhood, and published in 1956. He condensed the work to just over 100 pages and published it in French as *La Nuit* in 1958. Two years later, the book was published in English as *Night.* A U.S. citizen since 1963, Wiesel has worked tirelessly to call attention to human rights violations in countries around the world, including South Africa, Cambodia, Bangladesh, and Bosnia. He was awarded the Nobel Peace Prize in 1986.

## Author Activity

**Advocate for Peace** Read about Wiesel as a human rights advocate. What were the activities that caused him to be awarded the Nobel Peace Prize? With your classmates, discuss your findings.

# *from* Farewell to Manzanar

*Memoir by* JEANNE WAKATSUKI HOUSTON AND JAMES D. HOUSTON

## Connect to Your Life

**Civil Rights** What do you know about the relocation of Japanese Americans in the United States during World War II? Share your knowledge with your classmates. Why do you think many Japanese Americans were forced to move, while German Americans and Italian Americans did not generally suffer the same consequences?

## Build Background

**Japanese Internment** When Japan's attack on Pearl Harbor drew the United States into World War II in December 1941, people on the West Coast of the United States began to fear that those of Japanese descent living in their communities might secretly aid Japan's war effort. Despite the fact that there was no evidence of Japanese-American espionage or sabotage, and that most of the Japanese had become U.S. citizens or legal residents, racist suspicion fueled public policy.

In February 1942, President Franklin D. Roosevelt signed an order that cleared the way for the removal of Japanese people from their homes. Virtually the entire Japanese-American population of the West Coast—almost 120,000 people—was bused to ten inland "relocation" centers in the western states and Arkansas, where they were interned, or confined, for the duration of the war. With sometimes only 24 hours' notice, they were forced to abandon their homes, farms, and businesses and most of their possessions, most of which they were never able to reclaim.

Jeanne Wakatsuki was seven years old and living in Ocean Park, California, when the United States entered the war. The selection is an excerpt from the memoir that Jeanne Wakatsuki Houston wrote with her husband three decades after the war. At the opening of this selection, her family is living in Los Angeles, after having been forced to move twice by the government.

## Focus Your Reading

**LITERARY ANALYSIS** **MEMOIR** A **memoir** is a form of nonfiction in which the writer recalls significant events and people in his or her life. This passage comes from the memoir you are about to read:

> *I remember my brothers sitting around the table talking very intently about what we were going to do, how we would keep the family together. They had seen how quickly Papa was removed, and they knew now that he would not be back for quite a while.*

As you read the following selection, consider what you learn about the writer's personal perspective of events.

**ACTIVE READING** **CONNECTING** Just as you did with the excerpt from *Night,* pay attention to your own reactions to this selection. Note what comes to your mind as you are reading, and consider how you would respond if you were in a similar situation. The fact that these events occurred here in the United States may cause you to think differently about them than if they had occurred on another continent.

**READER'S NOTEBOOK** As you read, keep notes of your reactions to this piece, and spend a few minutes afterward writing your general reflections.

## from

# FAREWELL TO MANZANAR

JEANNE

WAKATSUKI

HOUSTON

AND

JAMES D.

HOUSTON

The American Friends Service[1] helped us find a small house in Boyle Heights, another minority ghetto, in downtown Los Angeles, now inhabited briefly by a few hundred Terminal Island refugees. Executive Order 9066 had been signed by President Roosevelt, giving the War Department authority to define military areas in the western states and to exclude from them anyone who might threaten the war effort. There was a lot of talk about internment, or moving inland, or something like that in store for all Japanese Americans. I remember my brothers sitting around the table talking very intently about what we were going to do, how we would keep the family together. They had seen how quickly Papa was removed, and they knew now that he would not be back for quite a while. Just before leaving Terminal Island, Mama had received her first letter, from Bismarck, North Dakota. He had been imprisoned at Fort Lincoln, in an all-male camp for enemy aliens.

Papa had been the patriarch.[2] He had always decided everything in the family. With him gone, my brothers, like councilors in the absence of a chief, worried about what should be done. The ironic thing is, there wasn't much left to decide. These were mainly days of quiet, desperate waiting for what seemed at the time to be inevitable. There is a phrase the Japanese use in such situations, when something difficult must be endured.

You would hear the older heads, the Issei,[3] telling others very quietly, *"Shikata ga nai"* (It cannot be helped). *"Shikata ga nai"* (It must be done).

Mama and Woody went to work packing celery for a Japanese produce dealer. Kiyo and

my sister May and I enrolled in the local school, and what sticks in my memory from those few weeks is the teacher—not her looks, her remoteness. In Ocean Park my teacher had been a kind, grandmotherly woman who used to sail with us in Papa's boat from time to time and who wept the day we had to leave. In Boyle Heights the teacher felt cold and distant. I was confused by all the moving and was having trouble with the classwork, but she would never help me out. She would have nothing to do with me.

This was the first time I had felt outright hostility from a Caucasian. Looking back, it is easy enough to explain. Public attitudes toward the Japanese in California were shifting rapidly. In the first few months of the Pacific war, America was on the run. Tolerance had turned to distrust and irrational fear. The hundred-year-old tradition of anti-Orientalism on the west coast soon resurfaced, more vicious than ever. Its result became clear about a month later, when we were told to make our third and final move.

The name Manzanar meant nothing to us when we left Boyle Heights. We didn't know where it was or what it was. We went because the government ordered us to. And, in the case of my older brothers and sisters, we went with a certain amount of relief. They had all heard stories of Japanese homes being attacked, of

## Tolerance had turned to distrust and irrational fear.

---

1. **American Friends Service:** a Quaker charity often aiding political and religious refugees and other displaced persons.
2. **patriarch** (pā′trē-ärk′): the man who heads his family or clan.
3. **Issei** (ēs′sā′): people born in Japan who immigrate to the United States.

beatings in the streets of California towns. They were as frightened of the Caucasians as Caucasians were of us. Moving, under what appeared to be government protection, to an area less directly threatened by the war seemed not such a bad idea at all. For some it actually sounded like a fine adventure.

Our pickup point was a Buddhist church in Los Angeles. It was very early, and misty, when we got there with our luggage. Mama had bought heavy coats for all of us. She grew up in eastern Washington and knew that anywhere inland in early April would be cold. I was proud of my new coat, and I remember sitting on a duffel bag trying to be friendly with the Greyhound driver. I smiled at him. He didn't smile back. He was befriending no one. Someone tied a numbered tag to my collar and to the duffel bag (each family was given a number, and that became our official designation until the camps were closed), someone else passed out box lunches for the trip, and we climbed aboard.

I had never been outside Los Angeles County, never traveled more than ten miles from the coast, had never even ridden on a bus. I was full of excitement, the way any kid would be, and wanted to look out the window. But for the first few hours the shades were drawn. Around me other people played cards, read magazines, dozed, waiting. I settled back, waiting too, and finally fell asleep. The bus felt very secure to me. Almost half its

passengers were immediate relatives. Mama and my older brothers had succeeded in keeping most of us together, on the same bus, headed for the same camp. I didn't realize until much later what a job that was. The strategy had been, first, to have everyone living in the same district when the evacuation began, and then to get all of us included under the same family number, even though names had been changed

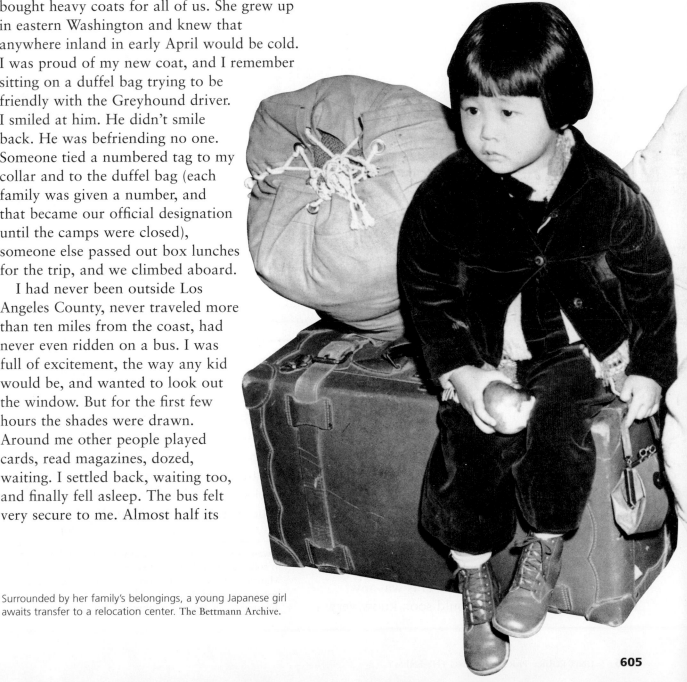

Surrounded by her family's belongings, a young Japanese girl awaits transfer to a relocation center. The Bettmann Archive.

The 550-acre Manzanar internment camp was located 200 miles northeast of Los Angeles at the foot of the Sierra Nevada. When the war ended in 1945, the camp's staff buildings and barracks were quickly disassembled and auctioned off. AP/Wide World Photos.

by marriage. Many families weren't as lucky as ours and suffered months of anguish while trying to arrange transfers from one camp to another.

We rode all day. By the time we reached our destination, the shades were up. It was late afternoon. The first thing I saw was a yellow swirl across a blurred, reddish setting sun. The bus was being pelted by what sounded like splattering rain. It wasn't rain. This was my first look at something I would soon know very

well, a billowing flurry of dust and sand churned up by the wind through Owens Valley.[4]

We drove past a barbed-wire fence, through a gate, and into an open space where trunks and sacks and packages had been dumped from the baggage trucks that drove out ahead

4. **Owens Valley:** referring to the valley of the Owens River in south central California west of Death Valley, where Manzanar was built. The once lush and green valley had become dry and deserted in the 1930s after water was diverted to an aquaduct supplying Los Angeles.

ominously silent. I didn't understand this. Hadn't we finally arrived, our whole family intact? I opened a window, leaned out, and yelled happily. "Hey! This whole bus is full of Wakatsukis!"

Outside, the greeters smiled. Inside there was an explosion of laughter, hysterical, tension-breaking laughter that left my brothers choking and whacking each other across the shoulders.

We had pulled up just in time for dinner. The mess halls weren't completed yet. An outdoor chow line snaked around a half-finished building that broke a good part of the wind. They issued us army mess kits, the round metal kind that fold over, and plopped in scoops of canned Vienna sausage, canned string beans, steamed rice that had been cooked too long, and on top of the rice a serving of canned apricots. The Caucasian servers were thinking that the fruit poured over rice would make a good dessert. Among the Japanese, of course, rice is never eaten with sweet foods, only with salty or savory foods. Few of us could eat such a mixture. But at this point no one dared protest. It would have been impolite. I was horrified when I saw the apricot syrup seeping through my little mound of rice. I opened my mouth to complain. My mother jabbed me in the back to keep quiet. We moved on through the line and joined the others squatting in the lee[5] of half-raised walls, dabbing courteously at what was, for almost everyone there, an inedible concoction.

After dinner we were taken to Block 16, a cluster of fifteen barracks that had just been finished a day or so earlier—although finished was hardly the word for it. The shacks were built of one thickness of pine planking covered with tarpaper. They sat on concrete footings, with

of us. I could see a few tents set up, the first rows of black barracks, and beyond them, blurred by sand, rows of barracks that seemed to spread for miles across this plain. People were sitting on cartons or milling around, with their backs to the wind, waiting to see which friends or relatives might be on this bus. As we approached, they turned or stood up, and some moved toward us expectantly. But inside the bus no one stirred. No one waved or spoke. They just stared out the windows,

---

5. **lee:** the side sheltered from the wind.

about two feet of open space between the floorboards and the ground. Gaps showed between the planks, and as the weeks passed and the green wood dried out, the gaps widened. Knotholes gaped in the uncovered floor.

Each barracks was divided into six units, sixteen by twenty feet, about the size of a living room, with one bare bulb hanging from the ceiling and an oil stove for heat. We were assigned two of these for the twelve people in our family group; and our official family "number" was enlarged by three digits—16 plus the number of this barracks. We were issued steel army cots, two brown army blankets each, and some mattress covers, which my brothers stuffed with straw.

The first task was to divide up what space we had for sleeping. Bill and Woody contributed a blanket each and partitioned off the first room: one side for Bill and Tomi, one side for Woody and Chizu and their baby girl. Woody also got the stove, for heating formulas.

The people who had it hardest during the first few months were young couples like these, many of whom had married just before the evacuation began, in order not to be separated and sent to different camps. Our two rooms were crowded, but at least it was all in the family. My oldest sister and her husband were shoved into one of those sixteen-by-twenty-foot compartments with six people they had never seen before—two other couples, one recently married like themselves, the other with two teenage boys. Partitioning off a room like that wasn't easy. It was bitter cold when we arrived, and the wind did not abate. All they had to use for room dividers were those army blankets, two of which were barely enough to keep one person warm. They argued over whose blanket should be sacrificed and later argued about noise at night—the parents wanted their boys asleep by 9:00 p.m.—and they continued arguing over matters like that for six months,

until my sister and her husband left to harvest sugar beets in Idaho. It was grueling work up there, and wages were pitiful, but when the call came through camp for workers to alleviate the wartime labor shortage, it sounded better than their life at Manzanar. They knew they'd have, if nothing else, a room, perhaps a cabin of their own.

That first night in Block 16, the rest of us squeezed into the second room—Granny; Lillian, age fourteen; Ray, thirteen; May, eleven; Kiyo, ten; Mama; and me. I didn't mind this at all at the time. Being youngest meant I got to sleep with Mama. And before we went to bed I had a great time jumping up and down on the mattress. The boys had stuffed so much straw into hers, we had to flatten it some so we wouldn't slide off. I slept with her every night after that until Papa came back.

We woke early, shivering and coated with dust that had blown up through the knotholes and in through the slits around the doorway. During the night Mama had unpacked all our clothes and heaped them on our beds for warmth. Now our cubicle looked as if a great laundry bag had exploded and then been sprayed with fine dust. A skin of sand covered the floor. I looked over Mama's shoulder at Kiyo, on top of his fat mattress, buried under jeans and overcoats and sweaters. His eyebrows were gray, and he was starting to giggle. He was looking at me, at my gray eyebrows and coated hair, and pretty soon we were both giggling. I looked at Mama's face to see if she thought Kiyo was funny. She lay very still next to me on our mattress, her eyes scanning everything—bare rafters, walls, dusty kids—scanning slowly, and I think the mask of her face would have cracked had not Woody's voice just then come at us through the wall. He was rapping on the planks as if testing to see if they were hollow.

"Hey!" he yelled. "You guys fall into the same flour barrel as us?"

"No," Kiyo yelled back. "Ours is full of Japs." All of us laughed at this.

"Well, tell 'em it's time to get up," Woody said. "If we're gonna live in this place, we better get to work."

He gave us ten minutes to dress, then he came in carrying a broom, a hammer, and a sack full of tin can lids he had scrounged somewhere. Woody would be our leader for a while now, short, stocky, grinning behind his mustache. He had just turned twenty-four. In later years he would tour the country with Mr. Moto, the Japanese tag-team wrestler, as his sinister assistant Suki—karate chops through the ropes from outside the ring, a chunky leg reaching from under his kimono to trip up Mr. Moto's foe. In the ring Woody's smile looked sly and crafty; he hammed it up. Offstage it was whimsical, as if some joke were bursting to be told.

"Hey, brother Ray, Kiyo," he said. "You see these tin can lids?"

"Yeah, yeah," the boys said drowsily, as if going back to sleep. They were both young versions of Woody.

"You see all them knotholes in the floor and in the walls?"

They looked around. You could see about a dozen.

Woody said, "You get those covered up before breakfast time. Any more sand comes in here through one of them knotholes, you have to eat it off the floor with ketchup."

"What about sand that comes in through the cracks?" Kiyo said.

Woody stood up very straight, which in itself was funny, since he was only about five-foot-six.

"Don't worry about the cracks," he said. "Different kind of sand comes in through the cracks."

He put his hands on his hips and gave Kiyo a sternly comic look, squinting at him through one eye the way Papa would when he was asserting his authority. Woody mimicked Papa's voice: "And I can tell the difference. So be careful."

The boys laughed and went to work nailing down lids. May started sweeping out the sand. I was helping Mama fold the clothes we'd used for cover, when Woody came over and put his arms around her shoulder. He was short; she was even shorter, under five feet.

He said softly, "You okay, Mama?"

She didn't look at him, she just kept folding clothes and said, "Can we get the cracks covered too, Woody?"

Outside the sky was clear, but icy gusts of wind were buffeting our barracks every few minutes, sending fresh dust puffs up through the floorboards. May's broom could barely keep up with it, and our oil heater could scarcely hold its own against the drafts.

"We'll get this whole place as tight as a barrel, Mama. I already met a guy who told me where they pile all the scrap lumber."

"Scrap?"

"That's all they got. I mean, they're still building the camp, you know. Sixteen blocks left to go. After that, they say maybe we'll get some stuff to fix the insides a little bit."

> **During the night Mama had unpacked all our clothes and heaped them on our beds for warmth.**

Her eyes blazed then, her voice quietly furious. "Woody, we can't live like this. Animals live like this."

It was hard to get Woody down. He'd keep smiling when everybody else was ready to explode. Grief flickered in his eyes. He blinked it away and hugged her tighter. "We'll make it better, Mama. You watch."

We could hear voices in other cubicles now. Beyond the wall Woody's baby girl started to cry.

"I have to go over to the kitchen," he said, "see if those guys got a pot for heating bottles. That oil stove takes too long—something wrong with the fuel line. I'll find out what they're giving us for breakfast."

"Probably hotcakes with soy sauce," Kiyo said, on his hands and knees between the bunks.

"No." Woody grinned, heading out the door. "Rice. With Log Cabin syrup and melted butter."

I don't remember what we ate that first morning. I know we stood for half an hour in cutting wind waiting to get our food. Then we took it back to the cubicle and ate huddled around the stove. Inside, it was warmer than when we left, because Woody was already making good his promise to Mama, tacking up some ends of lath[6] he'd found, stuffing rolled paper around the door frame.

Trouble was, he had almost nothing to work with. Beyond this temporary weather stripping, there was little else he could do. Months went by, in fact, before our "home" changed much at all from what it was the day we moved in—bare floors, blanket partitions, one bulb in each compartment dangling from a roof beam, and open ceilings overhead so that mischievous boys like Ray and Kiyo could climb up into the rafters and peek into anyone's life.

The simple truth is the camp was no more ready for us when we got there than we were ready for it. We had only the dimmest ideas of what to expect. Most of the families, like us, had moved out from southern California with as much luggage as each person could carry. Some old men left Los Angeles wearing Hawaiian shirts and Panama hats and stepped off the bus at an altitude of 4000 feet, with nothing available but sagebrush and tarpaper to stop the April winds pouring down off the back side of the Sierras.[7]

The War Department was in charge of all the camps at this point. They began to issue military surplus from the First World War—olive-drab knit caps, earmuffs, peacoats, canvas leggings. Later on, sewing machines were shipped in, and one barracks was turned into a clothing factory. An old seamstress took a peacoat of mine, tore the lining out, opened and flattened the sleeves, added a collar, put arm holes in and handed me back a beautiful cape. By fall, dozens of seamstresses were working full-time transforming thousands of these old army clothes into capes, slacks, and stylish coats. But until that factory got going and packages from friends outside began to fill out our wardrobes, warmth was more important than style. I couldn't help laughing at Mama walking around in army earmuffs and a pair of wide-cuffed, khaki-colored wool trousers several sizes too big for her. Japanese are generally smaller than Caucasians, and almost all these clothes were oversize. They flopped, they dangled, they hung.

It seems comical, looking back; we were a band of Charlie Chaplins[8] marooned in the

---

6. **lath** (lăth): a thin strip of wood.

7. **Sierras** (sē-ĕr′əz): referring to the Sierra Nevada mountain range in eastern California.

8. **Charlie Chaplins:** referring to actor and director Charlie Chaplin, who portrayed a tramp in baggy clothing in several comedy films of the 1920s and 1930s.

California desert. But at the time, it was pure chaos. That's the only way to describe it. The evacuation had been so hurriedly planned, the camps so hastily thrown together, nothing was completed when we got there, and almost nothing worked.

I was sick continually, with stomach cramps and diarrhea. At first it was from the shots they gave us for typhoid, in very heavy doses and in assembly-line fashion: swab, jab, swab, *Move along now,* swab, jab, swab, *Keep it moving.* That knocked all of us younger kids down at once, with fevers and vomiting. Later, it was the food that made us sick, young and old alike. The kitchens were too small and badly ventilated. Food would spoil from being left out too long. That summer, when the heat got fierce, it would spoil faster. The refrigeration kept breaking down. The cooks, in many cases, had never cooked before. Each block had to provide its own volunteers. Some were lucky and had a professional or two in their midst. But the first chef in our block had been a gardener all his life and suddenly found himself preparing three meals a day for 250 people.

"The Manzanar runs" became a condition of life, and you only hoped that when you rushed to the latrine, one would be in working order.

That first morning, on our way to the chow line, Mama and I tried to use the women's latrine in our block. The smell of it spoiled what little appetite we had. Outside, men were working in an open trench, up to their knees in muck—a common sight in the months to come. Inside, the floor was covered with excrement,

> ### The simple truth is the camp was no more ready for us when we got there than we were ready for it.

and all twelve bowls were erupting like a row of tiny volcanoes.

Mama stopped a kimono-wrapped woman stepping past us with her sleeve pushed up against her nose and asked, "What do you do?"

"Try Block Twelve," the woman said, grimacing. "They have just finished repairing the pipes."

It was about two city blocks away. We followed her over there and found a line of women waiting in the wind outside the latrine. We had no choice but to join the line and wait with them.

Inside it was like all the other latrines. Each block was built to the same design just as each of the ten camps, from California to Arkansas, was built to a common master plan. It was an open room, over a concrete slab. The sink was a long metal trough against one wall, with a row of spigots for hot and cold water. Down the center of the room twelve toilet bowls were arranged in six pairs, back to back, with no partitions. My mother was a very modest person, and this was going to be agony for her, sitting down in public, among strangers.

One old woman had already solved the problem for herself by dragging in a large cardboard carton. She set it up around one of the bowls, like a three-sided screen. OXYDOL was printed in large black letters down the front. I remember this well, because that was the soap we were issued for laundry; later on, the smell of it would permeate these rooms. The upended carton was about four feet high. The old woman behind it wasn't much taller. When she stood, only her head showed over the top.

She was about Granny's age. With great effort she was trying to fold the sides of the screen together. Mama happened to be at the head of the line now. As she approached the vacant bowl, she and the old woman bowed to each other from the waist. Mama then moved to help her with the carton, and the old woman said very graciously, in Japanese, "Would you like to use it?"

Happily, gratefully, Mama bowed again and said, *"Arigato"* (Thank you). *"Arigato gozaimas"* (Thank you very much). "I will return it to your barracks."

"Oh, no. It is not necessary. I will be glad to wait."

The old woman unfolded one side of the cardboard, while Mama opened the other; then she bowed again and scurried out the door.

Those big cartons were a common sight in the spring of 1942. Eventually sturdier partitions appeared, one or two at a time. The first were built of scrap lumber. Word would get around that Block such and such had partitions now, and Mama and my older sisters would walk halfway across the camp to use them. Even after every latrine in camp was screened, this quest for privacy continued. Many would wait in line at night. Ironically, because of this, midnight was often the most crowded time of all.

Like so many of the women there, Mama never did get used to the latrines. It was a humiliation she just learned to endure: *shikata ga nai,* this cannot be helped. She would quickly subordinate her own desires to those of the family or the community, because she knew cooperation was the only way to survive. At the same time, she placed a high premium on personal privacy, respected it in others and insisted upon it for herself. Almost everyone at Manzanar had inherited this pair of traits from the generations before them who had learned to live in a small, crowded country like Japan. Because of the first, they were able to take a desolate stretch of wasteland and gradually make it livable. But the entire situation there, especially in the beginning—the packed sleeping quarters, the communal mess halls, the open toilets—all this was an open insult to that other, private self, a slap in the face you were powerless to challenge. ❖

## Connect to the Literature

**1. What Do You Think?**
What is your impression of the Wakatsuki family?

**Comprehension Check**
- How did the Wakatsukis get to Manzanar?
- What kind of housing were they given?
- Why did Mama have to borrow the cardboard box?

## Think Critically

**2.** **ACTIVE READING** **CONNECTING** Look at the notes you made in your **READER'S NOTEBOOK.** How would you characterize your response to the piece? How do you think you would have reacted if you had been brought to Manzanar?

**3.** What do you learn about the family from their reactions upon waking up in the dust-covered barracks?

**THINK ABOUT**
- Mama's reaction
- Woody's reaction
- the family's solution to the problem

**4.** What do you think was the most difficult aspect of the camp experience for the people there? Cite evidence from the selection when giving your answer.

**5.** How would you describe the author's **tone** in this excerpt? Cite passages that illustrate that tone. What effect does the tone have on your perception of the family's experience at Manzanar?

**6.** In the foreword to *Farewell to Manzanar,* Jeanne Wakatsuki Houston says, "It has taken me 25 years to reach the point where I could talk openly about Manzanar." Why do you think it took so long for her to be able to talk about her experience?

## Extend Interpretations

**7. Connect to Life** Do you think that a forced internment, like that experienced by the Wakatsuki family, could happen in America today? Why or why not?

**8.** **Points of Comparison** Fill in the chart you created on page 592 with details from this selection. Then compare this chart with the one you created for *Night.* For each category, jot down notes about the similarities and differences between the two selections and the experiences of the authors.

## Literary Analysis

**MEMOIR** A **memoir** is a form of nonfiction in which a person recalls significant events or people in his or her life. In some cases, *memoir* is simply another word for **autobiography,** a work that tells about the personal experiences of the author. Most memoirs share the following characteristics:

- They are usually structured as first-person narratives in the writer's own voice.
- Though some names may be changed to protect privacy, memoirs are generally true accounts of actual events.
- Despite their personal nature, memoirs may deal with newsworthy events with a significance beyond the writers' own lives.
- Unlike strictly historical accounts, memoirs often include the writers' feelings and opinions about historical events, giving insight into the impact of history on people's lives.

**Paired Activity** With a partner, review the selection. One of you should write down statements that convey information that might be found in a history book about Japanese relocation. The other should record notes that convey information about the author's personal experience of events. Record your information. Then discuss the following questions: What does a memoir offer that cannot usually be found in a history text? How reliable is a memoir in recording information about events in history?

# *Choices* & CHALLENGES

## Writing Options

**1. Political Letter** Imagine that you are at Manzanar at the same time as the Wakatsukis. Write a persuasive letter to your senator or representative, explaining the circumstances of your relocation and telling him or her what you think should be done about the situation. Place the letter in your **Working Portfolio.**

**2. Manzanar Dialogue** The book *Farewell to Manzanar* was adapted for film. Choose a scene from the selection that you think would translate well into the visual medium of film. Then write a dialogue based upon details from the selection.

## Inquiry & Research

**1. Photo Exhibit** Photographer Dorothea Lange took a series of photographs at Manzanar during its operation. Look for her photos and others, both from Manzanar and from other Japanese relocation centers. Photocopy the pictures from books or download them from the Internet and create your own exhibit.

**2. Reparations Bill** In 1988 Congress passed the Civil Liberties Act, which contained an apology to Japanese Americans who had been interned and agreed to pay them $20,000 apiece. Find out more about this bill, the events that led up to it, and the consequent response from Japanese Americans.

**3. Video Viewing** Watch the excerpt from *Mitsuye and Nellie*, a documentary about the experience of Asian immigrants during World War II, which is supplied by McDougal Littell. How does the video add to your understanding of what Jeanne Wakatsuki Houston and her family endured at Manzanar?

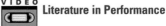 **Literature in Performance**

## Jeanne Wakatsuki Houston
### 1934–

**Other Works**
*Don't Cry, It's Only Thunder* (with Paul G. Hensler)
*Beyond Manzanar and Other Views of Asian-American Womanhood*

## James D. Houston
### 1933–

**Other Works**
*Between Battles*
*Gig*
*Californians: Searching for the Golden State*

**Coming to Terms** The daughter of a Japanese father and a Japanese-American mother, Jeanne Wakatsuki Houston and her mother, brothers, and sisters were among the first to be interned at Manzanar and among the last to be released. In the foreword to her book *Farewell to Manzanar*, Houston says that it took her 25 years to be able to talk about what happened to her and her family in the internment camp. Writing the book, she says, was "a way of coming to terms with the impact these years have had on my entire life." The book, coauthored with her writer husband, James D. Houston, won instant attention and critical praise when it was published in 1973;

three years later, the Houstons collaborated on an award-winning screenplay based on the book.

**A Writerly Pair** The Houstons have spent most of their lives on the West Coast and have written mainly about their home state of California. James Houston served in the U.S. Air Force from 1957 to 1960 and went on to become an award-winning writer of novels and short stories as well as nonfiction.

## Author Activity

Read two or three chapters from *Farewell to Manzanar* to find out more about what happened to the Wakatsuki family. Give a brief oral report.

# Comparing Literature: Assessment Practice

In writing assessments, you will often be asked to develop your own ideas by synthesizing what you have learned from literary works like *Night* and *Farewell to Manzanar*. You are now going to practice writing an essay with this kind of focus.

## PART 1  Reading the Prompt

When you are asked to write in response to a prompt, you should read the entire prompt carefully. Then you should read through it again, looking for key words.

### Writing Prompt

In *Night*, Elie Wiesel brought to light the terrible experience of life in a concentration camp. *Farewell to Manzanar* exposed a long-neglected episode from the same time period—the forced internment of Japanese Americans. In an essay that synthesizes what you have learned ❶ from your readings, discuss what lessons can ❷ be drawn from the injustices exposed by these two works. Why is it important, as Wiesel himself said, "to keep memory alive"? Support ❸ your ideas by using examples from both works. ❹

### STRATEGIES IN ACTION

❶ I will need to **synthesize**, or pull together, what I know, based on my readings.

❷ My answer needs to do two things. First, I must **draw lessons** from these works.

❸ Second, I need to **connect** the Wiesel quote to the lessons that I draw.

❹ I need **examples** or **quotations** from the works to support my opinion.

## PART 2  Planning a Synthesis Essay

- Analyze the two selections, paying attention to what they have in common and what sets them apart. (Refer to the charts you completed on pages 600 and 613. You may combine them as shown.)

- Make generalizations based upon what you learned from both works. Come up with your own ideas or insights.

- Clearly show the relationship between your ideas and the selections. Use evidence from the selections as support.

|  | Night | Farewell to Manzanar |
|---|---|---|
| **Cause:** |  |  |
| **How Victims Are Treated:** |  |  |
| **Psychological Effects:** |  |  |
| **How People Cope:** |  |  |
| **Author's Purpose:** |  |  |
| **Lessons Learned:** |  |  |

## PART 3  Drafting Your Essay

**Introduction** Begin by introducing your topic and summarizing the lessons to be learned. You may use Wiesel's quote here or later in the paper.

**Organization** Analyze one work at a time to show how it illustrates the lessons that you have identified, or discuss one lesson at a time and explain how both works illustrate it. Use signal words, such as *similarly, also, like, but, unlike,* and *while,* to call attention to similarities and differences between the two selections. Use examples from the works.

**Conclusion** Wrap up your essay by summing up the lessons you've drawn and emphasizing their importance.

# Writing Workshop

## Presenting a convincing argument . . .

**From Reading to Writing** The authors of "Night" and "Farewell to Manzanar" describe terrible injustices that they experienced. You, too, may want to take a stand against injustice or express an unpopular opinion that you believe in strongly. One way to convince others that you are right is to write a **persuasive essay** in which you present and defend your position. Many editorials, proposals, petitions, and advertisements also use persuasive techniques to convince their readers.

### For Your Portfolio

**WRITING PROMPT** Write a persuasive essay on an issue you feel strongly about.

**Purpose:** To persuade
**Audience:** Classmates, friends, family, or community members

---

## Basics in a Box

### Persuasive Essay at a Glance

Introduction

Presents the issue and states your opinion

**WHY YOU SHOULD BELIEVE IT**

Body

| Supporting evidence | Supporting evidence | Supporting evidence |

Conclusion

Summary of opinion
What readers should do

### RUBRIC Standards for Writing

**A successful persuasive essay should**

- state the issue and your position on it clearly in the introduction
- be geared to the audience you're trying to convince
- support your position with facts, statistics, and reasons
- answer possible objections to your position
- show clear reasoning
- conclude with a summary of your position or a call to action

---

# Analyzing a Student Model

**Jessica Marie Johnson**
**Whitney Young High School**

## Support School Uniforms

Clothes consciousness is out. School uniforms are in. And, though I know most other students don't agree, I think uniforms are the best thing that could happen to our nation's youth and to the educational system as a whole.

Walking through the halls of some schools used to be like attending a fashion show. <u>Baggy jeans, splashy cropped tops, khaki trousers, and patterned sweaters created a whirlwind of color and styles</u>. Not anymore. School uniforms and uniform dress codes have taken over in many schools and are being considered in many others. A great number of students are rebelling, claiming that wearing a uniform violates their freedom of expression. <u>One student called it "like being in jail," and another complained that "if you wear decent clothes, you shouldn't have to wear uniforms."</u> Some students show their discontent by deliberately dressing sloppily or wearing unapproved colors. I don't think these students have thought the issue through clearly.

I agree that an important goal of education is to foster individuality and creativity, but I don't agree that uniforms limit these qualities. Most schools have a four-day uniform policy that allows students to wear modified uniforms or outfits of their choice on one day—often Friday, as in the business world. In addition, many public schools have adopted a dress code rather than a strict uniform policy. The dress code sets up guidelines for students' clothing choices.

In fact, I think that wearing uniforms actually contributes to the development of creativity and individuality. By removing the focus from externals such as clothes, uniforms allow each student to express his or her personality in more important and meaningful ways. Students naturally form cliques in an effort to belong, and students with the same look instinctively seek each other out. With the clothing barrier out of the way, students begin to respond to one another as individuals and to form friendships based on similar outlooks and interests. They begin to get along better.

**RUBRIC**
IN ACTION

❶ States the issue and her position in the introduction

❷ Gives details and quotations to support her statements

❸ Counters objections with facts

❹ Develops her arguments with clear reasoning

As a result, discrimination, jealousy, and even violence and gang activity decrease. According to *Education Week*, in Long Beach, California, the first school district in the nation to establish a uniform code, there was a 34-percent decrease in assault and battery cases, a 51 percent decrease in physical fights, and a 32-percent decrease in suspensions in grades K–8 after the code was established.

Uniforms will have other beneficial effects on education and on the school as a whole. Wearing the same clothes will encourage students to focus on the reason they are in school in the first place. And that is to learn. When they can no longer compete in the fashion arena, they will begin to concentrate less on their appearance and more on academics.

Uniforms also tend to instill in students a sense of community and pride in their school. A parent at one school said, "When a student wears a uniform, it's her job to be the best student she can possibly be." Wearing neat and businesslike clothing will carry over into students' schoolwork. Uniforms help keep students in line.

<u>In addition</u> to improving the atmosphere at school, uniforms could also have a positive effect at home. Parents often complain about how much money and time their teens spend buying clothes. School uniforms are much less expensive than regular clothes, and they are quick and easy to buy. Most major chain stores now carry uniforms, some even made by brand-name clothing manufacturers. Some schools even make uniforms available to students very cheaply—from $15 to $30 for a pair of pants and a shirt—far less than a typical outfit.

School uniforms promote personal and social growth and contribute to a healthy learning atmosphere. And they're economical as well. Schools across the nation should implement uniform policies, over students' protests if necessary.

**❺** This writer uses statistics to support her argument.
**Other Options:**
• Use quotations.
• Present an anecdote.

**❻** Uses transitions to maintain a flow of connected ideas

**❼** Concludes with a summary of her arguments and a call to action

# Writing Your Persuasive Essay

## ❶ Prewriting

*Good writers are those who keep the language efficient. That is to say, keep it accurate, keep it clear.*

**Ezra Pound, poet**

Think about issues that are important to you and about which people disagree. Freewrite about events that have affected you strongly. Leafing through newspaper and magazine articles and letters to the editor, and watching news coverage on television, might provide ideas. See the **Idea Bank** in the margin for more suggestions. After you select an issue that you feel strongly about, follow the steps below.

> ### Planning Your Persuasive Essay
>
> ▶ **1. Clearly state your position.** What do you believe about the issue? What are your reasons for believing that way?
>
> ▶ **2. Consider your audience.** What do your readers know about the issue? What are their opinions on it?
>
> ▶ **3. Gather support for your arguments.** Where will you find the information you need? What facts, statistics, examples, anecdotes, and quotations support your position? Which evidence is strongest? What support might people who object to your position present? How can you answer those objections?

## ❷ Drafting

Drafting is the time to continue exploring and developing your ideas. It's perfectly all right to revise your opinion as you write. Eventually, you will need to state your opinion clearly and support it with convincing evidence, such as facts, statistics, examples, quotations, and anecdotes. You should present a strong case, but beware of using unfair language and faulty reasoning. Avoid these illogical arguments and faulty and deceptive uses of language:

- **circular reasoning**—restating something in other words without offering proof (That's the worst idea I ever heard because it's really stupid.)

- **over-generalization**—making a statement that's too broad to prove (Nobody could possibly believe any other way.)

- **either-or fallacy**—inappropriately stating that there are only two possible alternatives (Either I get an A on the test or my life will be over.)

- **cause-and-effect fallacy**—assuming that because event B followed event A, A caused B (I got chosen for the team because I wore my lucky charm.)

## IDEA Bank

**1. Your Working Portfolio** 🗁
Look for ideas in the **Writing Options** you completed earlier in this unit:
- **Holocaust Essay**, p. 601
- **Political Letter**, p. 614

**2. Change the World**
Ask a group of friends or classmates to complete this sentence: "If I could do one thing to change the world, I would. . . ." Develop one of the ideas into a persuasive essay.

**3. In This Corner . . .**
Think about issues you argue about with your friends and family. Choose one for your topic.

**Have a question?**

See the **Writing Handbook**
**Persuasive Writing** pp. 1161-1162

> ### Ask Your Peer Reader
>
> - How would you express my position on this issue?
> - What is unclear about the issue or my position?
> - What are my most and least convincing arguments?

**Need revising help?**

Review the **Rubric**, p. 616

Consider **peer reader** comments

Check **Revision Guidelines**, p. 1145

# ❸ Revising

**TARGET SKILL** ▶ **WRITING EFFECTIVE INTRODUCTIONS** Your persuasive essay will be most effective if you capture your readers' attention immediately. Try using a bold statement, an unusual fact, an interesting anecdote, a lively description, a question, or a quotation.

> *Clothes consciousness*
> *is out* School uniforms are ~~an issue that I care a lot about.~~ *in.* And, though I know most other students don't agree, I think uniforms are ~~a really good idea.~~ *the best thing that could happen to our nation's youth and to the educational system as a whole.*

**Befuddled by fragments?**

See the **Grammar Handbook**

**Correcting Fragments**, p. 1199

# ❹ Editing and Proofreading

**TARGET SKILL** ▶ **CORRECTING FRAGMENTS** Sentence fragments do not express complete thoughts. For that reason, they make your writing difficult to understand and weaken your arguments. Correct fragments by adding whatever is missing from the sentence—subject, verb, or independent clause.

> In fact, I think that wearing uniforms. /Actually contribute**s** to the development of creativity and individuality. By removing the focus from externals such as clothes. /*uniforms* Allow each student to express *his or her* ~~their~~ personality. /In more important and meaningful ways.

**Publishing IDEAS**

• Submit your essay as a letter to the editor of your school or local newspaper.

• Present your essay as a speech and have it videotaped.

**More Online: Publishing Options** www.mcdougallittell.com

# ❺ Reflecting

**FOR YOUR WORKING PORTFOLIO** What did you learn about your issue in writing your persuasive essay? What persuasive techniques were most convincing to your audience? Attach your reflections to your finished work. Save your persuasive essay in your **Working Portfolio.**

# Assessment Practice Revising & Editing

Read this paragraph from the first draft of a persuasive essay. The underlined sections may include the following kinds of errors:

- **spelling errors**
- **sentence fragments**
- **lack of parallel structure**
- **comma errors**

For each underlined section, choose the revision that most improves the writing.

A model United Nations program offers students a chance to be diplomats. They play the roles of <u>ambassedors</u> to the United Nations. They meet in an
(1)
assembly <u>hall just like the real diplomats and debate</u> current issues. This
(2)
simulation can help students develop <u>negotiation skills and mediate</u>. Debates
(3)
focus on complex global <u>issues, such as the environment, human rights, and</u>
(4)
<u>disarmament.</u> <u>Involving students from our entire county. The program could</u>
(5)
also strengthen inter-school ties. A model United Nations can <u>invigorate, and</u>
(6)
<u>educate both the participants and spectators.</u>

1. **A.** ambassadors
   **B.** ambasadors
   **C.** ambassaders
   **D.** Correct as is

2. **A.** hall, just like the real diplomats and debate
   **B.** hall just like the real diplomats, and debate
   **C.** hall, just like the, real, diplomats and debate
   **D.** Correct as is

3. **A.** mediation skills and negotiate
   **B.** negotiation skills and mediation
   **C.** negotiation and mediation skills
   **D.** Correct as is

4. **A.** issues: such as the environment, human rights, and disarmament.
   **B.** issues such as the environment, human rights, and, disarmament.

   **C.** issues such as, the environment, human rights, and disarmament.
   **D.** Correct as is

5. **A.** By involving students from our entire county, the program could also strengthen inter-school ties.
   **B.** Involving students from our entire county. The program could also strengthen inter-school ties.
   **C.** The program could also strengthen inter-school ties. Involving students from the entire country.
   **D.** Correct as is

6. **A.** invigorate and educate, both the participants and spectators.
   **B.** invigorate and educate both the participants and spectators.
   **C.** invigorate, and educate both the participants, and spectators.
   **D.** Correct as is

**Need extra help?**

See the **Grammar Handbook**
**Correcting Fragments**, p. 1199
**Punctuation Chart**, pp. 1203–1204

# PART 2  Tests of Conviction

What are some of your most deeply-held values and beliefs? What would you do to defend them? Tests of conviction come in all forms. Sometimes historical circumstances force people to decide where they stand and whether to fight or flee. In other cases, the struggle may be more personal, born in the depths of the human heart. In this part of Unit Four, you will explore different situations in which people's convictions are put to the test.

## ACTIVITY

Working with a partner, think of two or three people— perhaps historical figures, contemporary leaders, or others whose actions have gained attention—who have stood up for their convictions in some way. What do they have in common? Were they successful in achieving their goals? How are they different from one another? Tell the class about these people in a brief oral presentation, and compare your examples with those of other pairs of classmates.

# LEARNING the Language of *Literature*

$\mathcal{P}$oint of view refers to the vantage point from which a story is told. Think of it as the lens that a writer chooses for the reader to look through. Point of view determines much about a story—from its overall tone to our opinion of its characters and how much we learn about them. The following passages demonstrate three points of view that writers use most: first-person point of view, third-person omniscient point of view, and third-person limited point of view.

## First-Person Point of View

In **first-person point of view,** the narrator is a character in the story, narrating the action as he or she perceives it. A first-person narrator—who may or may not be a major character in the story—speaks directly to the reader, using the pronoun *I* to refer to himself or herself. First-person point of view allows the reader to understand a great deal about the narrator's thoughts and feelings. However, the reader knows only what the narrator is able to know.

Sometimes, a first-person narrator is biased and tells a one-sided story. This kind of narrator is called an **unreliable narrator.** In other cases, the narrator does not fully comprehend what he or she relates. Such a narrator is called a **naive narrator.**

**YOUR TURN** Read the excerpt at the right. How does this narrative point of view affect your feeling of suspense?

### FIRST-PERSON POINT OF VIEW

A fearful idea now suddenly drove the blood in torrents upon my heart, and for a brief period, I once more relapsed into insensibility. Upon recovering, I at once started to my feet, trembling convulsively in every fiber. I thrust my arms wildly above and around me in all directions. I felt nothing; yet dreaded to move a step, lest I should be impeded by the walls of a *tomb*. Perspiration burst from every pore, and stood in cold big beads upon my forehead. The agony of suspense grew at length intolerable, and I cautiously moved forward, with my arms extended, and my eyes straining from their sockets, in the hope of catching some faint ray of light.

—Edgar Allan Poe, "The Pit and the Pendulum"

| | | |
|---|---|---|
| **First Person** | ADVANTAGE | • Allows narrator to speak directly to reader, creating a greater sense of intimacy<br>• Allows writer to add depth to story by use of unreliable or naive narrator |
| | DISADVANTAGE | • Provides only limited knowledge of other characters and events—readers know only what the narrator knows |
| **Third Person Omniscient** | ADVANTAGE | • Provides readers with insight into several characters<br>• Allows the writer to develop a more complicated plot or to examine broader issues |
| | DISADVANTAGE | • May leave readers detached from the story—no obvious character on whom to focus and no character speaking directly to them |
| **Third Person Limited** | ADVANTAGE | • Provides readers with a character they can get to know intimately<br>• Allows readers some emotional distance<br>• Allows a writer to withhold information to create suspense or mystery |
| | DISADVANTAGE | • Limits reader's knowledge of other characters |

# On the Rainy River

*Short Story by* TIM O'BRIEN

**( Connect to Your Life )**

**Life on the Line** In this story, a young man must decide whether to fight in a war he opposes. Under what conditions would you be willing to fight in a war? Under what conditions would you be unwilling to fight? Discuss your thoughts with a small group of classmates.

## Build Background

**Country at War** The Vietnam War (1957–1975) was one of the most controversial military conflicts in the history of the United States. The United States entered the war in 1964 in hopes of preventing the spread of communism throughout Southeast Asia. During the course of the war, nearly 3 million Americans were sent overseas to defend the South Vietnamese government against a takeover by Communist North Vietnam and the Viet Cong, a South Vietnamese Communist rebel force.

During the war, nearly 2 million men were drafted into the military. Those who were drafted but who opposed the war faced a difficult decision: whether to risk their lives in a foreign war they couldn't justify or risk imprisonment at home by refusing to serve. Some burned their draft cards as a form of protest; others fled the country, most often by crossing the border into Canada.

**WORDS TO KNOW**
**Vocabulary Preview**

| | |
|---|---|
| acquiescence | platitude |
| consensus | preoccupied |
| fathom | pretense |
| impassive | reticence |
| imperative | vigil |

## Focus Your Reading

**LITERARY ANALYSIS** **FIRST-PERSON POINT OF VIEW** "On the Rainy River" is told from the **first-person point of view.** The **narrator** is a **character** in the story and so participates in the events he recounts. Readers see everything through the narrator's eyes. His comments and descriptions convey the difficulty of the momentous decision he faces:

> *I was bitter, sure. But it was so much more than that. The emotions went from outrage to terror to bewilderment to guilt to sorrow and then back again to outrage.*

In this story, the author blurs the line between fact and fiction by calling his narrator "Tim O'Brien." The story, however, is still a work of fiction. As you read, notice how O'Brien's use of the first-person point of view affects your feelings about the narrator.

**ACTIVE READING** **MAKING JUDGMENTS** A reader is always processing information. Good readers not only receive information, but they also **make judgments** about it. As you read this story, you will receive considerable information about the narrator and the decision he faces. To make a judgment about a character's decision, you need to think about standards, or criteria for judging. For example, you might consider whether the character has acted honorably or considered the consequences of his decision.

**READER'S NOTEBOOK** In a chart like the one shown, note the reasons the narrator puts forward in support of each option facing him. What is your judgment of his options and of his ultimate decision? Give reasons to support your judgment.

| Going to Vietnam | Going to Canada |
|---|---|
| Narrator's Views: | Narrator's Views: |
| My Judgment and Reasons: | My Judgment and Reasons: |

# On the Rainy River

## Tim O'Brien

*Portrait of Donald Schrader* (1962), Fairfield Porter. The Metropolitan Museum of Art, bequest of Arthur M. Bullowa, 1993 (1993.406.12). Copyright © 1995 The Metropolitan Museum of Art.

This is one story I've never told before. Not to anyone. Not to my parents, not to my brother or sister, not even to my wife. To go into it, I've always thought, would only cause embarrassment for all of us, a sudden need to be elsewhere, which is the natural response to a confession. Even now, I'll admit, the story makes me squirm. For more than twenty years I've had to live with it, feeling the shame, trying to push it away, and so by this act of remembrance, by putting the facts down on paper, I'm hoping to relieve at least some of the pressure on my dreams.

Still, it's a hard story to tell. All of us, I suppose, like to believe that in a moral emergency we will behave like the heroes of our youth, bravely and forthrightly, without thought of personal loss or discredit. Certainly that was my conviction back in the summer of 1968. Tim O'Brien: a secret hero. The Lone Ranger. If the stakes ever became high enough—if the evil were evil enough, if the good were good enough—I would simply tap a secret reservoir of courage that had been accumulating inside me over the years. Courage, I seemed to think, comes to us in finite quantities, like an inheritance, and by being frugal and stashing it away, and letting it earn interest, we steadily increase our moral capital in preparation for that day when the account must be drawn down. It was a comforting theory. It dispensed with all those bothersome little acts of daily courage; it offered hope and grace to the repetitive coward; it justified the past while amortizing the future.

In June of 1968, a month after graduating from Macalester College, I was drafted to fight a war I hated. I was twenty-one years old. Young, yes, and politically naive, but even so the American war in Vietnam seemed to me wrong. Certain blood was being shed for uncertain reasons. I saw no unity of purpose, no consensus on matters of philosophy or history or law. The very facts were shrouded in uncertainty: Was it a civil war? A war of national liberation or simple aggression? Who started it, and when, and why? What really happened to the U.S.S. *Maddox* on that dark night in the Gulf of Tonkin?[1] Was Ho Chi Minh[2] a Communist stooge, or a nationalist savior, or both, or neither? What about the Geneva Accords?[3] What about SEATO[4] and the Cold War?[5] What about dominoes?[6] America was

divided on these and a thousand other issues, and the debate had spilled out across the floor of the United States Senate and into the streets, and smart men in pinstripes could not agree on

> ## I was too *good* for this war. Too smart, too compassionate, too everything.

even the most fundamental matters of public policy. The only certainty that summer was moral confusion. It was my view then, and still is, that you don't make war without knowing why. Knowledge, of course, is always imperfect, but it seemed to me that when a nation goes to war it must have reasonable confidence in the justice and imperative of its cause. You can't fix your mistakes. Once people are dead, you can't make them undead.

In any case those were my convictions, and back in college I had taken a modest stand against the war. Nothing radical, no hothead stuff, just ringing a few doorbells for Gene

---

1. **U.S.S. *Maddox* . . . Gulf of Tonkin:** an alleged attack on the U.S. destroyer *Maddox* in the Gulf of Tonkin, off the coast of North Vietnam, in 1964, which provided a basis for expanding U.S. involvement in the Vietnam conflict.

2. **Ho Chi Minh** (hō′ chē′ mǐn′): a political leader who waged a successful fight against French colonial rule and established a Communist government in North Vietnam.

3. **Geneva Accords:** a 1954 peace agreement providing for the temporary division of Vietnam into North and South Vietnam and calling for national elections.

4. **SEATO:** the Southeast Asia Treaty Organization, an alliance of seven nations, including the United States, formed to halt Communist expansion in Southeast Asia after Communist forces defeated France in Indochina.

5. **Cold War:** a term for the post–World War II struggle for influence between Communist and democratic nations.

6. **dominoes:** refers to the domino theory, which holds that if a nation becomes a Communist state, neighboring nations will also become Communist.

WORDS TO KNOW

**consensus** (kən-sĕn′səs) *n.* general agreement by a group
**imperative** (ĭm-pĕr′ə-tĭv) *n.* urgent necessity or duty

McCarthy,[7] composing a few tedious, uninspired editorials for the campus newspaper. Oddly, though, it was almost entirely an intellectual activity. I brought some energy to it, of course, but it was the energy that accompanies almost any abstract endeavor; I felt no personal danger; I felt no sense of an impending crisis in my life. Stupidly, with a kind of smug removal that I can't begin to <u>fathom</u>, I assumed that the problems of killing and dying did not fall within my special province.

The draft notice arrived on June 17, 1968. It was a humid afternoon, I remember, cloudy and very quiet, and I'd just come in from a round of golf. My mother and father were having lunch out in the kitchen. I remember opening up the letter, scanning the first few lines, feeling the blood go thick behind my eyes. I remember a sound in my head. It wasn't thinking, it was just a silent howl. A million things all at once—I was too *good* for this war. Too smart, too compassionate, too everything. It couldn't happen. I was above it. I had the world—Phi Beta Kappa and summa cum laude and president of the student body and a full-ride scholarship for grad studies at Harvard. A mistake, maybe—a foul-up in the paperwork. I was no soldier. I hated Boy Scouts. I hated camping out. I hated dirt and tents and mosquitoes. The sight of blood made me queasy, and I couldn't tolerate authority, and I didn't know a rifle from a slingshot. I was a *liberal:* If they needed fresh bodies, why not draft some back-to-the-stone-age hawk? Or some dumb jingo[8] in his hardhat and Bomb Hanoi button? Or one of LBJ's[9] pretty daughters? Or Westmoreland's[10] whole family—nephews and nieces and baby grandson? There should be a law, I thought. If you support a war, if you think it's worth the price, that's fine, but you have to put your own life on the line. You have to head for the front and hook up with an infantry unit and help spill

ACTIVE READING

**MAKE JUDGMENTS** How reasonable do you find the kind of law the narrator suggests?

the blood. And you have to bring along your wife, or your kids, or your lover. A *law,* I thought.

I remember the rage in my stomach. Later it burned down to a smoldering self-pity, then to numbness. At dinner that night my father asked what my plans were.

"Nothing," I said. "Wait."

spent the summer of 1968 working in an Armour meat-packing plant in my hometown of Worthington, Minnesota. The plant specialized in pork products, and for eight hours a day I stood on a quarter-mile assembly line—more properly, a disassembly line—removing blood clots from the necks of dead pigs. My job title, I believe, was Declotter. After slaughter, the hogs were decapitated, split down the length of the belly, pried open, eviscerated, and strung up by the hind hocks on a high conveyer belt. Then gravity took over. By the time a carcass reached my spot on the line, the fluids had mostly drained out, everything except for thick clots of blood in the neck and upper chest cavity. To remove the stuff, I used a kind of water gun. The machine was heavy, maybe eighty pounds, and was suspended from the ceiling by a heavy rubber cord. There was some bounce to it, an

---

7. **Gene McCarthy:** Eugene McCarthy, U.S. senator from Minnesota and Vietnam War critic who unsuccessfully sought the 1968 Democratic presidential nomination.

8. **jingo** (jĭng′gō): one who aggressively supports his or her country and favors war as a means of settling political disputes.

9. **LBJ:** Lyndon B. Johnson, U.S. president from 1963 to 1969.

10. **Westmoreland's:** referring to William Westmoreland, American general and the senior commander of U.S. forces in Vietnam from 1964 to 1968.

WORDS TO KNOW **fathom** (făth′əm) *v.* to penetrate the meaning or understand the nature of

elastic up-and-down give, and the trick was to maneuver the gun with your whole body, not lifting with the arms, just letting the rubber cord do the work for you. At one end was a trigger; at the muzzle end was a small nozzle and a steel roller brush. As a carcass passed by, you'd lean forward and swing the gun up against the clots and squeeze the trigger, all in one motion, and the brush would whirl and water would come shooting out and you'd hear a quick splattering sound as the clots dissolved into a fine red mist. It was not pleasant work. Goggles were a necessity, and a rubber apron, but even so it was like standing for eight hours a day under a lukewarm blood-shower. At night I'd go home smelling of pig. I couldn't wash it out. Even after a hot bath, scrubbing hard, the stink was always there—like old bacon, or sausage, a dense greasy pig-stink that soaked deep into my skin and hair. Among other things, I remember, it was tough getting dates that summer. I felt isolated; I spent a lot of time alone. And there was also that draft notice tucked away in my wallet.

In the evenings I'd sometimes borrow my father's car and drive aimlessly around town, feeling sorry for myself, thinking about the war and the pig factory and how my life seemed to be collapsing toward slaughter. I felt paralyzed. All around me the options seemed to be narrowing, as if I were hurtling down a huge black funnel, the whole world squeezing in tight. There was no happy way out. The government had ended most graduate school deferments; the waiting lists for the National Guard and Reserves[11] were impossibly long; my health was solid; I didn't qualify for CO[12] status—no religious grounds, no history as a pacifist.[13] Moreover, I could not claim to be opposed to war as a matter of general principle. There were occasions, I believed, when a nation was justified in using military force to achieve its ends, to stop a Hitler or some comparable evil, and I told myself that in such circumstances I would've willingly marched off to the battle. The problem, though, was that a draft board did not let you choose your war.

Beyond all this, or at the very center, was the raw fact of terror. I did not want to die. Not ever. But certainly not then, not there, not in a wrong war. Driving up Main Street, past the courthouse and the Ben Franklin store, I sometimes felt the fear spreading inside me like weeds. I imagined myself dead. I imagined myself doing things I could not do—charging an enemy position, taking aim at another human being.

At some point in mid-July I began thinking seriously about Canada. The border lay a few hundred miles north, an eight-hour drive. Both my conscience and my instincts were telling me to make a break for it, just take off and run like hell and never stop. In the beginning the idea seemed purely abstract, the word Canada printing itself out in my head; but after a time I could see particular shapes and images, the sorry details of my own future—a hotel room in Winnipeg, a battered old suitcase, my father's eyes as I tried to explain myself over the telephone. I could almost hear his voice, and my mother's. Run, I'd think. Then I'd think, Impossible. Then a second later I'd think, *Run*.

---

11. **National Guard and Reserves:** military reserve units run by each state in the United States. Some men joined these units to avoid service in Vietnam.

12. **CO:** conscientious objector, a person exempted from military service because of strongly held moral or religious beliefs that do not permit participation in war.

13. **pacifist** (păs′ə-fĭst): one who opposes war or other violence as a means of settling disputes.

It was a kind of schizophrenia.[14] A moral split. I couldn't make up my mind. I feared the war, yes, but I also feared exile. I was afraid of walking away from my own life, my friends and my family, my whole history, everything that mattered to me. I feared losing the respect of my parents. I feared the law. I feared ridicule and censure.[15] My hometown was a conservative little spot on the prairie, a place where tradition counted, and it was easy to imagine people sitting around a table at the old Gobbler Café on Main Street, coffee cups poised, the conversation slowly zeroing in on the young O'Brien kid, how the damned sissy had taken off for Canada. At night, when I couldn't sleep, I'd sometimes carry on fierce arguments with those people. I'd be screaming at them, telling them how much I detested their blind, thoughtless, automatic acquiescence to it all, their simple-minded patriotism, their prideful ignorance, their love-it-or-leave-it platitudes, how they were sending me off to fight a war they didn't understand and didn't want to understand. I held them responsible. By God, yes I *did*. All of them—I held them personally and individually responsible— the polyestered Kiwanis boys, the merchants and farmers, the pious churchgoers, the chatty housewives, the PTA and the Lions club and the Veterans of Foreign Wars and the fine upstanding gentry out at the country club. They didn't know Bao Dai[16] from the man in the moon. They didn't know history. They didn't know the first thing about Diem's[17] tyranny, or the nature of Vietnamese nationalism, or the long colonialism of the French—this was all too damned complicated, it required some reading—but no matter, it was a war to stop the Communists, plain and simple, which was how they liked things, and you were treasonous if you had second thoughts about killing or dying for plain and simple reasons.

I was bitter, sure. But it was so much more than that. The emotions went from outrage to terror to bewilderment to guilt to sorrow and then back again to outrage. I felt a sickness inside me. Real disease.

Most of this I've told before, or at least hinted at, but what I have never told is the full truth. How I cracked. How at work one morning, standing on the pig line, I felt something break open in my chest. I don't know what it was. I'll never know. But it was real. I know that much, it was a physical rupture—a cracking-leaking-popping feeling. I remember dropping my water gun. Quickly, almost without thought, I took off my apron and walked out of the plant and drove home. It was midmorning, I remember, and the house was empty. Down in my chest there was still that leaking sensation, something very warm and precious spilling out, and I was covered with blood and hog-stink, and for a long while I just concentrated on holding myself together. I remember taking a hot shower. I remember packing a suitcase and carrying it out to the kitchen, standing very still for a few minutes, looking carefully at the familiar objects all around me. The old chrome toaster, the telephone, the pink and white Formica on the kitchen counters. The room was full of bright sunshine.

SUPPORT OUR BOYS IN VIETNAM

---

14. **schizophrenia** (skĭt′sə-frē′nē-ə): a mental disorder. Here, the narrator refers to a split personality.

15. **censure** (sĕn′shər): an expression of strong disapproval or harsh criticism.

16. **Bao Dai** (bou′dī′): the last emperor of Vietnam (1926–1945) and chief of state from 1949 to 1955.

17. **Diem:** Ngo Dinh Diem (nō′ dĭn′ dē-ĕm′), the first president of South Vietnam, who led his country like a brutal dictator. He was murdered by his own generals in 1963.

---

WORDS TO KNOW   **acquiescence** (ăk′wē-ĕs′əns) *n.* passive agreement; agreement without protest
**platitude** (plăt′ĭ-tōōd′) *n.* a trite or unoriginal statement, especially one expressed as if it were original or significant; a cliché

Everything sparkled. My house, I thought. My life. I'm not sure how long I stood there, but later I scribbled out a short note to my parents.

What it said exactly, I don't recall now. Something vague. Taking off, will call, love Tim.

I drove north.

It's a blur now, as it was then, and all I remember is a sense of high velocity and the feel of the steering wheel in my hands. I was riding on adrenaline.[18] A giddy feeling, in a way, except there was the dreamy edge of impossibility to it—like running a dead-end maze—no way out—it couldn't come to a happy conclusion and yet I was doing it anyway because it was all I could think to do. It was pure flight, fast and mindless. I had no plan. Just hit the border at high speed and crash through and keep on running. Near dusk I passed through Bemidji, then turned northeast toward International Falls. I spent the night in the car behind a closed-down gas station a half mile from the border. In the morning, after gassing up, I headed straight west along the Rainy River, which separates Minnesota from Canada, and which for me separated one life from another. The land was mostly wilderness. Here and there I passed a motel or bait shop, but otherwise the country unfolded in great sweeps of pine and birch and sumac. Though it was still August, the air already had the smell of October, football season, piles of yellow-red leaves, everything crisp and clean. I remember a huge blue sky. Off to my right was the Rainy River, wide as a lake in places, and beyond the Rainy River was Canada.

For a while I just drove, not aiming at anything, then in the late morning I began looking for a place to lie low for a day or two. I was exhausted, and scared sick, and around noon I pulled into an old fishing resort called the Tip Top Lodge. Actually, it was not a lodge at all,

just eight or nine tiny yellow cabins clustered on a peninsula that jutted northward into the Rainy River. The place was in sorry shape. There was a dangerous wooden dock, an old minnow tank, a flimsy tar paper boathouse along the shore. The main building, which stood in a

> **It was pure flight, fast and mindless. I had no plan. Just hit the border at high speed . . . and keep on running.**

cluster of pines on high ground, seemed to lean heavily to one side, like a cripple, the roof sagging toward Canada. Briefly, I thought about turning around, just giving up, but then I got out of the car and walked up to the front porch.

The man who opened the door that day is the hero of my life. How do I say this without sounding sappy? Blurt it out—the man saved me. He offered exactly what I needed, without questions, without any words at all. He took me in. He was there at the critical time—a silent, watchful presence. Six days later, when it ended, I was unable to find a proper way to thank him, and I never have, and so, if nothing else, this story represents a small gesture of gratitude twenty years overdue.

Even after two decades I can close my eyes and return to that porch at the Tip Top Lodge. I can see the old guy staring at me. Elroy Berdahl: eighty-one years old, skinny and shrunken and mostly bald. He wore a flannel shirt and brown work pants. In one hand, I remember, he carried a green apple, a small paring knife in the other. His eyes had the bluish gray color of a razor

---

18. **adrenaline** (ə-drĕn′ə-lĭn): a hormone that is released into the bloodstream in response to physical or mental stress, such as fear, and that initiates or heightens several physical responses, including an increase in heart rate.

blade, the same polished shine, and as he peered up at me I felt a strange sharpness, almost painful, a cutting sensation, as if his gaze were somehow slicing me open. In part, no doubt, it was my own sense of guilt, but even so I'm absolutely certain that the old man took one look and went right to the heart of things—a kid in trouble. When I asked for a room, Elroy made a little clicking sound with his tongue. He nodded, led me out to one of the cabins, and dropped a key in my hand. I remember smiling at him. I also remember wishing I hadn't. The old man shook his head as if to tell me it wasn't worth the bother.

"Dinner at five-thirty," he said. "You eat fish?"

"Anything," I said.

Elroy grunted and said, "I'll bet."

We spent six days together at the Tip Top Lodge. Just the two of us. Tourist season was over, and there were no boats on the river, and the wilderness seemed to withdraw into a great permanent stillness. Over those six days Elroy Berdahl and I took most of our meals together. In the mornings we sometimes went out on long hikes into the woods, and at night we played Scrabble or listened to records or sat reading in front of his big stone fireplace. At times I felt the awkwardness of an intruder, but Elroy accepted me into his quiet routine without fuss or ceremony. He took my presence for granted, the same way he might've sheltered a stray cat—no wasted sighs or pity—and there was never any talk about it. Just the opposite. What I remember more than anything is the man's willful, almost ferocious silence. In all that time together, all those hours, he never asked the obvious questions: Why was I there? Why alone? Why so preoccupied? If Elroy was curious about any of this, he was careful never to put it into words.

My hunch, though, is that he already knew. At least the basics. After all, it was 1968, and guys were burning draft cards, and Canada was just a boat ride away. Elroy Berdahl was no hick. His bedroom, I remember, was cluttered with books and newspapers. He killed me at the Scrabble board, barely concentrating, and on those occasions when speech was necessary, he had a way of compressing large thoughts into small, cryptic[19] packets of language. One evening, just at sunset, he pointed up at an owl circling over the violet-lighted forest to the west.

"Hey, O'Brien," he said. "There's Jesus."

The man was sharp—he didn't miss much. Those razor eyes. Now and then he'd catch me staring out at the river, at the far shore, and I could almost hear the tumblers clicking in his head. Maybe I'm wrong, but I doubt it.

One thing for certain, he knew I was in desperate trouble. And he knew I couldn't talk about it. The wrong word—or even the right word—and I would've disappeared. I was wired and jittery. My skin felt too tight. After supper one evening I vomited and went back to my cabin and lay down for a few moments and then vomited again; another time, in the middle of the afternoon, I began sweating and couldn't shut it off. I went through whole days feeling dizzy with sorrow. I couldn't sleep; I couldn't lie still. At night I'd toss around in bed, half awake, half dreaming, imagining how I'd sneak down to the beach and quietly push one of the old man's boats out into the river and start paddling

**ACTIVE READING**

**QUESTION** What do you think this incident reveals about Elroy?

---

19. **cryptic** (krĭp′tĭk): having a hidden or mysterious meaning; mystifying.

my way toward Canada. There were times when I thought I'd gone off the psychic edge. I couldn't tell up from down, I was just falling, and late in the night I'd lie there watching weird pictures spin through my head. Getting chased by the Border Patrol—helicopters and searchlights and barking dogs—I'd be crashing through the woods, I'd be down on my hands and knees—people shouting out my name—the law closing in on all sides—my hometown draft board and the FBI and the Royal Canadian Mounted Police. It all seemed crazy and impossible. Twenty-one years old, an ordinary kid with all the ordinary dreams and ambitions, and all I wanted was to live the life I was born to—a mainstream life—I loved baseball and hamburgers and cherry Cokes—and now I was off on the margins of exile, leaving my country forever, and it seemed so impossible and terrible and sad.

I'm not sure how I made it through those six days. Most of it I can't remember. On two or three afternoons, to pass some time, I helped Elroy get the place ready for winter, sweeping down the cabins and hauling in the boats, little chores that kept my body moving. The days were cool and bright. The nights were very dark. One morning the old man showed me how to split and stack firewood, and for several hours we just worked in silence out behind his house. At one point, I remember, Elroy put down his maul[20] and looked at me for a long time, his lips drawn as if framing a difficult question, but then he shook his head and went back to work. The man's self-control was amazing. He never pried. He never put me in a position that required lies or denials. To an extent, I supposed, his <u>reticence</u> was typical of that part of Minnesota, where privacy still held value, and even if I'd been walking around with some horrible deformity—four arms and three heads—I'm sure the old man would've talked about everything except those

extra arms and heads. Simple politeness was part of it. But even more than that, I think, the man understood that words were insufficient. The problem had gone beyond discussion. During that long summer I'd been over and over the various arguments, all the pros and cons, and it was no longer a question that could be decided by an act of pure reason. Intellect had come up against emotion. My conscience told me to run, but some irrational and powerful force was resisting, like a weight pushing me toward the war. What it came down to, stupidly, was a sense of shame. Hot, stupid shame. I did not want people to think badly of me. Not my parents, not my brother and sister, not even the folks down at the Gobbler Café. I was ashamed to be there at the Tip Top Lodge. I was ashamed of my conscience, ashamed to be doing the right thing.

Some of this Elroy must've understood. Not the details, of course, but the plain fact of crisis.

Although the old man never confronted me about it, there was one occasion when he came close to forcing the whole thing out into the open. It was early evening, and we'd just finished supper, and over coffee and dessert I asked him about my bill, how much I owed so far. For a long while the old man squinted down at the tablecloth.

"Well, the basic rate," he said, "is fifty bucks a night. Not counting meals. This makes four nights, right?"

I nodded. I had three hundred and twelve dollars in my wallet.

Elroy kept his eyes on the tablecloth. "Now that's an on-season price. To be fair, I suppose we should knock it down a peg or two." He leaned back in his chair. "What's a reasonable number, you figure?"

"I don't know," I said. "Forty?"

---

20. **maul** (môl): heavy, long-handled hammer.

WORDS TO KNOW

**reticence** (rĕt′ĭ-səns) *n.* the state or quality of being reserved and keeping one's thoughts to oneself

*Sea Air* (1987), Douglas Brega. Dry brush on paper, 14″ × 21″, courtesy of the artist.

"Forty's good. Forty a night. Then we tack on food—say another hundred? Two hundred sixty total?"

"I guess."

He raised his eyebrows. "Too much?"

"No, that's fair. It's fine. Tomorrow, though . . . I think I'd better take off tomorrow."

Elroy shrugged and began clearing the table. For a time he fussed with the dishes, whistling to himself as if the subject had been settled. After a second he slapped his hands together.

"You know what we forgot?" he said. "We forgot wages. Those odd jobs you done. What we have to do, we have to figure out what your time's worth. Your last job—how much did you pull in an hour?"

"Not enough," I said.

"A bad one?"

"Yes. Pretty bad."

Slowly then, without intending any long sermon, I told him about my days at the pig plant. It began as a straight recitation of the facts, but before I could stop myself I was talking about the blood clots and the water gun and how the smell had soaked into my skin and how I couldn't wash it away. I went on for a long time. I told him about wild hogs squealing in my dreams, the sounds of butchery, slaughterhouse sounds, and how I'd sometimes wake up with that greasy pig-stink in my throat.

When I was finished, Elroy nodded at me.

"Well, to be honest," he said, "when you first showed up here, I wondered about that. The aroma, I mean. Smelled like you was awful damned fond of pork chops." The old man almost smiled. He made a snuffling sound, then sat down with a pencil and a piece of paper. "So what'd this crud job pay? Ten bucks an hour? Fifteen?"

"Less."

Elroy shook his head. "Let's make it fifteen. You put in twenty-five hours here, easy. That's three hundred seventy-five bucks total wages. We subtract the two hundred sixty for food and lodging. I still owe you a hundred and fifteen."

He took four fifties out of his shirt pocket and laid them on the table.

"Call it even," he said.

"No."

"Pick it up. Get yourself a haircut."

The money lay on the table for the rest of the evening. It was still there when I went back to my cabin. In the morning though, I found an envelope tacked to my door. Inside were the four fifties and a two-word note that said EMERGENCY FUND.

The man knew.

Looking back after twenty years, I sometimes wonder if the events of that summer didn't happen in some other dimension, a place where your life exists before you've lived it, and where it goes afterward. None of it ever seemed real. During my time at the Tip Top Lodge I had the feeling that I'd slipped out of my own skin, hovering a few feet away while some poor yo-yo with my name and face tried to make his way toward a future he didn't understand and didn't want. Even now I can see myself as I was then. It's like watching an old home movie: I'm young and tan and fit. I've got hair—lots of it. I don't smoke or drink. I'm wearing faded blue jeans and a white polo shirt. I can see myself sitting on Elroy Berdahl's dock near dusk one evening, the sky a bright shimmering pink, and I'm finishing up a letter to my parents that tells what I'm about to do and why I'm doing it and how sorry I am that I've never found the courage to talk to them about it. I ask them not to

be angry. I try to explain some of my feelings, but there aren't enough words, and so I just say that it's a thing that has to be done. At the end of the letter I talk about the vacations we used to take up in this north country, at a place called Whitefish Lake, and how the scenery here reminds me of those good times. I tell them I'm fine. I tell them I'll write again from Winnipeg or Montreal or wherever I end up.

On my last full day, the sixth day, the old man took me out fishing on the Rainy River. The afternoon was sunny and cold. A stiff breeze came in from the north, and I remember how the little fourteen-foot boat made sharp rocking motions as we pushed off from the dock. The current was fast. All around us, I remember, there was a vastness to the world, an unpeopled rawness, just the trees and the sky and the water reaching out toward nowhere. The air had the brittle scent of October.

For ten or fifteen minutes Elroy held a course upstream, the river choppy and silver-gray, then he turned straight north and put the engine on full throttle. I felt the bow lift beneath me. I remember the wind in my ears, the sound of the old outboard Evinrude. For a time I didn't pay attention to anything, just feeling the cold spray against my face, but then it occurred to me that at some point we must've passed into Canadian waters, across that dotted line between two different worlds, and I remember a sudden tightness in my chest as I looked up and watched the far shore come at me. This wasn't a daydream. It was tangible and real. As we came in toward land, Elroy cut the engine, letting the boat fishtail lightly about twenty yards off shore. The old man didn't look at me or speak. Bending

ACTIVE READING

**PREDICT** What do you think will happen on the fishing trip?

down, he opened up his tackle box and busied himself with a bobber and a piece of wire leader, humming to himself, his eyes down.

It struck me then that he must've planned it. I'll never be certain, of course, but I think he meant to bring me up against the realities, to guide me across the river and to take me to the edge and to stand a kind of vigil as I chose a life for myself.

I remember staring at the old man, then at my hands, then at Canada. The shoreline was dense with brush and timber. I could see tiny red berries on the bushes. I could see a squirrel up in one of the birch trees, a big crow looking at me from a boulder along the river. That close—twenty yards—and I could see the delicate latticework of the leaves, the texture of the soil, the browned needles beneath the pines, the configurations of geology and human history. Twenty yards. I could've done it. I could've jumped and started swimming for my life. Inside me, in my chest, I felt a terrible squeezing pressure. Even now, as I write this, I can still feel that tightness. And I want you to feel it—the wind coming off the river, the waves, the silence, the wooded frontier. You're at the bow of a boat on the Rainy River. You're twenty-one years old, you're scared, and there's a hard squeezing pressure in your chest.

What would you do?

Would you jump? Would you feel pity for yourself? Would you think about the family and your childhood and your dreams and all you're leaving behind? Would it hurt? Would it feel like dying? Would you cry, as I did?

I tried to swallow it back. I tried to smile, except I was crying.

Now, perhaps, you can understand why I've never told this story before. It's not just the embarrassment of tears. That's part of it, no doubt, but what embarrasses me much more, and always will, is the paralysis that took my heart. A moral freeze: I couldn't decide, I couldn't act, I couldn't comport myself with even a pretense of modest human dignity.

All I could do was cry. Quietly, not bawling, just the chest-chokes.

At the rear of the boat Elroy Berdahl pretended not to notice. He held a fishing rod in his hands,

> I think he meant to bring me up against the realities . . . to stand a kind of vigil as I chose a life for myself.

his head bowed to hide his eyes. He kept humming a soft, monotonous little tune. Everywhere, it seemed, in the trees and water and sky, a great worldwide sadness came pressing down on me, a crushing sorrow, sorrow like I had never known before. And what was so sad, I realized, was that Canada had become a pitiful fantasy. Silly and hopeless. It was no longer a possibility. Right then, with the shore so close, I understood that I would not do what I should do. I would not swim away from my hometown and my country and my life. I would not be brave. That old image of myself as a hero, as a man of conscience and courage, all that was just a threadbare pipe dream.[21] Bobbing there on the Rainy River, looking back at the Minnesota shore, I felt a sudden swell of helplessness come over me, a drowning sensation, as if I had toppled overboard and was being swept away by the sil-

---

21. **pipe dream:** daydream or fantasy that will never happen; vain hope.

*Atascadero Dusk* (about 1990), Robert Reynolds. Watercolor, 22″ × 15″. *From Painting Nature's Beautiful Places,* published by North Light Books.

ver waves. Chunks of my own history flashed by. I saw a seven-year-old boy in a white cowboy hat and a Lone Ranger mask and a pair of holstered six-shooters; I saw a twelve-year-old Little League shortstop pivoting to turn a double play; I saw a sixteen-year-old kid decked out for his first prom, looking spiffy in a white tux and a black bow tie, his hair cut short and flat, his shoes freshly polished. My whole life seemed to spill out into the river, swirling away from me, everything I had ever been or ever wanted to be. I couldn't get my breath; I couldn't stay afloat; I couldn't tell which way to swim. A hallucination, I suppose, but it was as real as anything I would ever feel. I saw my parents calling to me from the far shoreline. I saw my brother and sister, all the townsfolk, the mayor and the entire Chamber of Commerce and all my old teachers and girlfriends and high school buddies. Like some weird sporting event: everybody screaming from the sidelines, rooting me on—a loud stadium roar. Hotdogs and popcorn—stadium smells, stadium heat. A squad of cheerleaders did cartwheels along the banks of the Rainy River; they had megaphones and pompoms and smooth brown thighs. The crowd swayed left and right. A marching band played fight songs. All my aunts and uncles were there, and Abraham Lincoln and Saint George,[22] and a nine-year-old girl named Linda who had died of a brain tumor back in fifth grade, and several members of the United States Senate, and a blind poet scribbling notes, and LBJ, and Huck Finn, and Abbie Hoffman,[23] and all the dead soldiers back from the grave, and the many thousands who were later to die—villagers with terrible burns, little kids without arms or legs—yes, and the Joint Chiefs of Staff[24] were there, and a couple of popes, and a first lieutenant named Jimmy Cross, and the last surviving veteran of the American Civil War, and Jane Fonda dressed up as Barbarella,[25] and an old man sprawled beside a pigpen, and my grandfather, and Gary Cooper,[26]

and a kind-faced woman carrying an umbrella and a copy of Plato's *Republic*,[27] and a million ferocious citizens waving flags of all shapes and colors—people in hardhats, people in headbands—they were all whooping and chanting and urging me toward one shore or the other. I saw faces from my distant past and distant future. My wife was there. My unborn daughter waved at me, and my two sons hopped up and down, and a drill sergeant named Blyton sneered and shot up a finger and shook his head. There was a choir in bright purple robes. There was a cabbie from the Bronx. There was a slim young man I would one day kill with a hand grenade along a red clay trail outside the village of My Khe.[28]

The little aluminum boat rocked softly beneath me. There was the wind and the sky.

I tried to will myself overboard.

I gripped the edge of the boat and leaned forward and thought, *Now*.

I did try. It just wasn't possible.

All those eyes on me—the town, the whole universe—and I couldn't risk the embarrassment. It was as if there were an audience to my life, that swirl of faces along the river, and in my

---

22. **Saint George:** Christian martyr (killed about A.D. 303) and patron saint of England who, according to legend, slew a frightening dragon.

23. **Abbie Hoffman:** social organizer and radical anti–Vietnam War activist known for his humor and politically inspired pranks.

24. **Joint Chiefs of Staff:** the principal military advisors of the U.S. president, including the chiefs of the army, navy, and air force and the commandant of the marines.

25. **Jane Fonda dressed up as Barbarella:** anti–Vietnam War activist and actress Jane Fonda (1937– ), dressed as Barbarella, the title character she played in a 1968 science fiction film.

26. **Gary Cooper:** American actor famous for playing strong, quiet heroes.

27. **Plato's *Republic*:** a famous work in which the ancient Greek philosopher Plato describes the ideal state or society.

28. **My Khe** (mē′ kē′).

## Connect to the Literature

**1. What Do You Think?**
What is your reaction to the narrator's final decision?

**Comprehension Check**
- Why does the narrator drive up near the Canadian border?
- What does Elroy Berdahl do to help the narrator make up his mind?

## Think Critically

**2.** The **narrator** feels he was a coward for fighting in the Vietnam War. Do you share his opinion? Why or why not?

**3.** What do you think the narrator means when he says that Elroy Berdahl "saved" him?

THINK ABOUT
- the effect of Elroy's silence
- his offer of money to the narrator
- why he takes the narrator fishing

**4.** The narrator gives a detailed **description** of his summer job in a meat-packing plant. Why do you think this description is included?

**5.** ACTIVE READING | MAKING JUDGMENTS | Review the chart in your READER'S NOTEBOOK. What judgment did you make about the narrator's final decision? If you had been in his position, would you have chosen to fight in the war or to flee to Canada? Explain your answer.

**6.** "Tests of Conviction" is the title given to this part of Unit Four. What conviction do you think is being tested in this story? In your opinion, does the narrator "pass" the test? Why or why not?

## Extend Interpretations

**7. What If?** What do you think would have happened if the narrator had decided to do the "brave" thing and flee to Canada? How might Elroy have reacted? Would the narrator have regretted his decision? Give reasons to support your answers.

**8. Connect to Life** Should a government be able to compel citizens to fight in wars? Why or why not?

## Literary Analysis

**POINT OF VIEW** In the **first-person point of view,** the **narrator** is a **character** in the story who tells everything in his or her own words. A first-person narrator tends to involve the reader in the story and to communicate a sense of immediacy and personal concern. In the opening of this story, for example, the narrator talks directly to the reader, as if the reader were a close friend or confidant:

*This is one story I've never told before. Not to anyone. Not to my parents, not to my brother or sister, not even to my wife.*

The first-person point of view can also sometimes make a fictional story seem more true to life.

**Cooperative Learning Activity** In a small group, choose three or four passages in the story that you think are crucial for understanding the narrator's decision. Take turns reading the passages aloud in a way that communicates the narrator's emotions and state of mind. Based on your readings, discuss how O'Brien's use of first-person point of view affects your feelings about the narrator and your judgment of his action.

# *Choices & CHALLENGES*

## Writing Options

**1. Elroy's Letter** Assume the identity of Elroy in "On the Rainy River" and write a letter to a relative, telling about your unusual week with the boy from Minnesota.

**2. Definition of Courage** Draft an essay that develops your own definition of courage, showing how your personal definition is similar to or different from the narrator's.

**3. New Ending** Imagine that when the narrator feels the impulse to jump from the boat and swim toward Canada, he actually does so. Write an alternative ending to the story from this point on.

**Writing Handbook**
See page 1155: Narrative Writing.

## Activities & Explorations

**1. Point/Counterpoint Discussion** With your entire class, conduct a point/counterpoint discussion that explores both sides of the narrator's conscience. One side of the class should argue in favor of military service; the other side should argue in favor of fleeing to Canada. Use evidence from the story to support your views.
**~ SPEAKING AND LISTENING**

**2. Rainy River Collage** Create a collage based on the vision the narrator has while he's on the Rainy River (pages 637–640). You may include photos, clippings from newspapers and magazines, and your own drawings of the images that the narrator thinks he sees. **~ ART**

**3. Protest Songs** Bring in recordings of folk and rock protest songs from the Vietnam War era and play them for your class. Discuss how these songs express moral and political objections to the conflict. **~ MUSIC**

## Inquiry & Research

**Living History** Tape-record or videotape interviews with people who lived through the Vietnam War era. Have them describe their feelings about the war and their experiences with the draft, the fighting itself, and the rallies or protests on the home front. Then write a feature story for the school newspaper.

## Art Connection

What do you think is the connection between the painting *Portrait of Donald Schrader* on page 627 and the first part of the story?

## Vocabulary in Action

**EXERCISE: CONTEXT CLUES** Choose the word that best completes each of the following sentences.

1. Grandma says that long before Dad was drafted, he was so _____ with the Vietnam War that he couldn't focus on his schoolwork.

2. Dad believed in the _____ of defending one's country, but he didn't understand how the Vietnam War connected to freedom at home.

3. He found the tangled web of Vietnamese politics difficult to _____.

4. In the United States, there was no _____ about the war; hawks said one thing, and doves said another.

5. My grandfather understood Dad's reluctance to fight in that war; he used to say "War is hell," but that was only a _____.

6. After receiving his draft notice, Dad stayed up all night holding a lonely _____.

7. Since Dad was usually so cheerful and talkative in the morning, his _____ at breakfast the next day made my grandfather feel sad.

8. To Grandma he seemed calm, but that was merely _____, for he was troubled.

9. He kept his face _____ so that Grandma could not observe his feelings.

10. When Grandma asked if he would soon be going overseas to fight, he nodded in _____.

| WORDS TO KNOW | acquiescence | fathom | imperative | preoccupied | reticence |
| --- | --- | --- | --- | --- | --- |
| | consensus | impassive | platitude | pretense | vigil |

**Building Vocabulary**
For an in-depth study on context clues, see page 56.

## Grammar in Context: Gerund Phrases

In this excerpt from "On the Rainy River," the narrator recalls the morning he left home and headed north.

> I remember packing a suitcase and carrying it out to the kitchen, standing very still for a few minutes, looking carefully at the familiar objects all around me.

A **gerund phrase** consists of a gerund (a verb form that ends in *-ing* and functions as a noun) along with its modifiers and complements. In the sentence above, the gerund phrases help to convey the vividness, even after 20 years, of the narrator's memory. If the gerunds *packing, carrying, standing,* and *looking* were replaced with verbs in the past tense, the events would seem more distant.

**Usage Tip:** Gerund phrases can be used as subjects or objects of verbs or as objects of prepositions.

**WRITING EXERCISE** Rewrite these sentences, changing parts of them into gerund phrases. Underline each gerund phrase.

**Example:** *Original* When I tell the story, it makes me squirm.

*Rewritten* Telling the story makes me squirm.

1. I asked a lot of questions about the war, but it didn't help me find answers.
2. I worked in the factory; it couldn't silence the howls of war in my head.
3. My modest antiwar activities included support for the campaign of Eugene McCarthy.

**Grammar Handbook** Verbals, p. 1196

## Tim O'Brien
1946–

**Other Works**
*Going After Cacciato*
*Northern Lights*
*In the Lake of the Woods*

**Fact and Fiction** Though the events depicted in "On the Rainy River" are fictional, many details in the story match the writer's own experiences. Like the narrator, the real Tim O'Brien grew up in Minnesota and was an exceptional student at Macalester College. He also was drafted into the U.S. Army immediately after graduation. O'Brien, like the narrator, debated fleeing the country but ultimately he decided to serve. "I did not want to be a soldier, not even an observer to war," he later wrote. "But neither did I want to upset a peculiar balance between the order I knew, the people I knew, and my own private world."

**"Story Truth"** During the Vietnam War, O'Brien was promoted to the rank of sergeant; he also was wounded in combat and awarded the Purple Heart. His first book, *If I Die in a Combat Zone,*

*Box Me Up and Ship Me Home* (1973), is a nonfiction memoir of his tour of duty. O'Brien's novel about Vietnam, *Going After Cacciato,* won two O. Henry Memorial Awards and the 1978 National Book Award. "On the Rainy River" appeared in *The Things They Carried* (1990), a collection of interrelated stories about the Vietnam War and its victims. Despite the presence of a narrator named Tim O'Brien, the stories in the collection are fictional. For O'Brien, whether a story is literally true is less important than the truths it conveys. "I want you to feel what I felt," he once explained. "I want you to know why story truth is truer sometimes than happening truth."

## Author Activity

**The "Real" Tim O'Brien** In a nonfiction article entitled "The Vietnam in Me," published in the *New York Times Magazine* on October 2, 1994, O'Brien writes of his own decision to fight: "I was a coward. I went to Vietnam." Read the article to learn about O'Brien's experience.

# The Artilleryman's Vision
*Poetry by* WALT WHITMAN

# look at this)
*Poetry by* E. E. CUMMINGS

## Connect to Your Life

**It's War!** People react to war in very different ways. Some are fascinated by the decisions of politicians and generals. Others take interest in the latest weaponry. Still others focus on how the war affects ordinary citizens, perhaps taking pity on its innocent victims or protesting against those who initiate war. Think of a war that has occurred during your lifetime or one that you have learned about. What images of the conflict stick in your mind? What are your thoughts and feelings about that war and its effects?

## Build Background

**Wartime Poets** Both Walt Whitman and E. E. Cummings were strongly affected by the experience of war. During the Civil War, Whitman traveled to the war front in Virginia after learning that his younger brother had been wounded. He remained in Washington, D.C., to work as a volunteer nurse, caring for the war's sick and wounded. Drawing on these experiences, he wrote Civil War poems such as "Come Up From the Fields Father," "Memories of President Lincoln," and "The Artilleryman's Vision."

E. E. Cummings volunteered for duty in another war. He served in the Ambulance Corps in France during World War I, joining a volunteer American corps before the United States entered the war. His prose book *The Enormous Room* is considered to be an outstanding literary account of World War I.

## Focus Your Reading

**LITERARY ANALYSIS** **TONE AND DICTION** The **tone** of a work—the attitude a writer takes toward his or her subject—may be bitter, serious, angry, or detached, among other possibilities. One element that contributes to a work's tone is **diction,** or word choice. Diction consists of **vocabulary** and **syntax,** or the arrangement and order of the words. Cummings's vocabulary and syntax are highly unusual, an effect heightened by the poet's unique use of punctuation and capitalization, as illustrated by the poem's opening:

> *look at this)*
> *a 75 done*
> *this . . .*

By contrast, Whitman's diction helps to portray a battle in vivid detail:

> *The crashing and smoking, the pride of the men in their pieces . . .*

As you read, notice how each poet's use of diction contributes to the work's tone.

**ACTIVE READING** **COMPARING AND CONTRASTING SPEAKERS** In poetry, the **speaker** is the voice that "talks" to the reader. The speakers in the following two poems have something in common: both have experienced warfare. In "The Artilleryman's Vision," the speaker recalls the chaos of battle when "the wars are long over." The speaker in "look at this)" reacts to the loss of life in war in a more immediate context, commenting on the recent death of a "buddy." As you read the two poems, continue to **compare** and **contrast** the two speakers and their experiences of war.

**READER'S NOTEBOOK** While reading each poem, think about the kind of person the speaker seems to be and the attitude he has toward war. Jot down notes to keep track of your observations.

# The Artilleryman's Vision

### Walt Whitman

While my wife at my side lies slumbering, and the wars are over
    long,
And my head on the pillow rests at home, and the vacant midnight
    passes,
And through the stillness, through the dark, I hear, just hear, the
    breath of my infant,
There in the room as I wake from sleep this vision presses upon me;

5 The engagement opens there and then in fantasy unreal,
The skirmishers begin, they crawl cautiously ahead, I hear the
    irregular snap! snap!
I hear the sounds of the different missiles, the short *t-h-t! t-h-t!* of
    the rifle balls,
I see the shells exploding leaving small white clouds, I hear the great
    shells shrieking as they pass,
The grape like the hum and whirr of wind through the trees,
    (tumultuous now the contest rages,)

10 All the scenes at the batteries rise in detail before me again,
The crashing and smoking, the pride of the men in their pieces,
The chief-gunner ranges and sights his piece and selects a fuse of the
    right time,
After firing I see him lean aside and look eagerly off to note the
    effect;
Elsewhere I hear the cry of a regiment charging, (the young colonel
    leads himself this time with brandish'd sword,)

15 I see the gaps cut by the enemy's volleys, (quickly fill'd up, no
    delay,)
I breathe the suffocating smoke, then the flat clouds hover low
    concealing all;
Now a strange lull for a few seconds, not a shot fired on either side,
Then resumed the chaos louder than ever, with eager calls and
    orders of officers,
While from some distant part of the field the wind wafts to my ears
    a shout of applause, (some special success,)

**5 engagement:** battle.

**6 skirmishers:** soldiers sent out in advance of a main attack.

**9 grape:** grapeshot—small iron balls shot in a bunch from a cannon.

**10 batteries:** groups of cannons.

**14 brandish'd:** raised and waving.

**15 volleys:** groups of cannonballs fired at the same time.

Union soldiers drill in preparation for battle during the Civil War.

20 And ever the sound of the cannon far or near, (rousing even in
    dreams a devilish exultation and all the old mad joy in the depths
    of my soul,)
And ever the hastening of infantry shifting positions, batteries,
    cavalry, moving hither and thither,
(The falling, dying, I heed not, the wounded dripping and red I heed
    not, some to the rear are hobbling,)
Grime, heat, rush, aide-de-camps galloping by or on a full run,
With the patter of small arms, the warning *s-s-t* of the rifles, (these
    in my vision I hear or see,)
25 And bombs bursting in air, and at night the vari-color'd rockets.

**20 rousing:**
awakening.

**23 aide-de-camps**
(ād'dĭ-kămps'):
assistants to military
commanders.

## Thinking Through the Literature

1. **Comprehension Check** Where is the artilleryman when he
experiences his "vision," and what time is it?

2. How do you think the **speaker** feels about the incidents he
describes? Do you think his feelings have changed since his days as
a soldier? Use evidence from the poem to support your answer.

3. Why might the artilleryman have such a vision at this particular
moment?

4. Why do you think Whitman chose to end the poem as he did?

# look at this)

### E. E. Cummings

look at this)
a 75 done
this nobody would
have believed
5   would they no
kidding this was my particular

pal
funny aint
it we was
10   buddies
i used to

know
him lift the
poor cuss
15   tenderly this side up handle

with care
fragile
and send him home

to his old mother in
20   a new nice pine box

(collect

## Connect to the Literature

1. **What Do You Think?** How did you react to the speaker's remark about the pine box at the end of the poem?

> **Comprehension Check**
> • What is the situation described in the poem?
> • What happened to the speaker's friend?

## Think Critically

2. How do you think the **speaker** feels about what happened to his friend?

**THINK ABOUT**
> • the words he uses to describe their relationship
> • his instructions to the person he is addressing
> • the poem's final image

3. What elements of Cummings's **style** might be considered unusual? In what way do you think this style influences your response to the poem?

4. Which **detail** in each poem do you think you are most likely to remember? Why?

5. **ACTIVE READING** **COMPARING AND CONTRASTING SPEAKERS** What similarities and differences do you see between the speakers of "look at this)" and "The Artilleryman's Vision"? Base your response on the observations you wrote in your **📖 READER'S NOTEBOOK.**

6. Both of the poems deal with the human cost of warfare. Which poem do you think is more critical of war? Explain your response.

## Extend Interpretations

7. **Comparing Texts** How do you think the narrator of "On the Rainy River" would respond to these two poems? Which one comes closest to his own attitude toward war? Cite reasons to support your answer.

8. **Connect to Life** Do you think any of the thoughts expressed in these poems would be relevant to soldiers fighting in wars today? Explain your answer.

## Literary Analysis

**TONE AND DICTION** **Tone** is the attitude a writer takes toward a subject. To identify the tone of these poems, you might find it helpful to read them aloud, as if giving a dramatic reading before an audience. The emotions that you convey in reading should give you hints about the tone of the work.

One way in which writers create tone is through **diction,** or word choice, which includes both **vocabulary** and **syntax,** or word order. For example, in "look at this)," the use of terms such as "this side up" and "handle with care" contributes to a tone of bitterness about the loss of life in warfare.

**Paired Activity** With a partner, decide which of the following words best describes the tone of each poem. More than one word may apply.

- serious
- proud
- sad
- shocked
- playful
- bitter
- anxious

Review each poem and find examples of ways in which the poet's diction contributes to the tone you have identified.

## Writing Options

**1. Advice Column** In Whitman's poem, the artilleryman's wife is shown sleeping peacefully, but she may well be aware of her husband's visions. Imagine that you are an advice columnist who has received a letter from her. Write a response offering suggestions to help her understand and deal with her husband's visions. Place the response in your **Working Portfolio.**

**2. Comparison Essay** Write a brief essay comparing and contrasting the speakers of these poems. Consider their personalities, their attitudes toward war, and the effect that combat has had on them. Use the notes in your **READER'S NOTEBOOK** and your answer to question 5 as a starting point.

**Writing Handbook**
See page 1157: Compare-Contrast.

**3. Consoling Letter** Write a letter of condolence from the speaker in Cummings's poem to the parents of the dead soldier. Describe your relationship with the soldier and explain the circumstances of his death. Try to capture the personality of the speaker in your letter, although you will probably want to be more tactful than the speaker is in the poem.

## Activities & Explorations

**1. Illustrations of War** Draw a picture to illustrate one of the poems, trying to capture the speaker's attitude toward war. After you are finished, explain to your classmates which words or phrases inspired your artwork. **~ ART**

**2. Spoken Word** In a small group, perform a round-robin reading of "The Artilleryman's Vision." Before reading the poem aloud, decide which lines each student will read and go over the poem together to clarify difficult words and phrases. Think about how you can use the speed and pitch of your voice to suggest the speaker's emotions. **~ SPEAKING AND LISTENING**

**3. Martial Music** Select a piece of music to accompany one of the poems. As you consider possible music, think about the speaker's emotional reactions as well as the events he describes. After you play the music for the class, explain why you chose it. **~ MUSIC**

## Inquiry & Research

**1. Civil Warfare** In "The Artilleryman's Vision," Whitman offers a vivid description of a Civil War battle. Consult history books about the war for information on battlefield tactics and weaponry used by Union and Confederate soldiers. Write a brief report explaining some of the war imagery in Whitman's poem.

 **More Online: Research Starter**
www.mcdougallittell.com

**2. Invisible Wounds of War** Soldiers from all wars have experienced problems that lingered long after they returned home. Such problems have gone by several names over the years: shell shock, battle fatigue, and post-traumatic stress disorder. Find out more about such problems faced by veterans and report your findings to the class. You might contact a local veterans' organization for information.

An American soldier stares in disbelief after being freed from a Korean prison camp.

# Walt Whitman
## 1819–1892

**Other Works**
*Leaves of Grass*
"When Lilacs Last in the Dooryard
   Bloom'd"
*Specimen Days and Collect*

**End of Childhood**  Walt Whitman grew up in a hurry. He left school at age 11, and within a few years he was living on his own in New York City. He drifted from job to job, working as a printer, journalist, and carpenter. He loved to stroll around the city, taking in sights and sounds that he would later use in his poetry.

**Leaves of Grass**  In 1855, Whitman published 12 poems in a volume called *Leaves of Grass.* During the rest of his life, he continually added new poems and revised older ones, putting out nine editions of the book. On one occasion, he compared the finished book to a tree with its successive rings of growth. Upon receiving a copy of the first edition, the poet Ralph Waldo Emerson declared that it was "the most extraordinary piece of wit and wisdom that America has yet contributed"; he went on to say that Whitman was "at the beginning of a great career." However, other distinguished American writers shunned Whitman, who at first was better appreciated in Europe than at home. Most editions of *Leaves of Grass* were published by Whitman himself.

**Later Years**  In 1873, Whitman suffered a stroke that left him partially paralyzed. He spent the rest of his life in Camden, New Jersey. In the decades following his death, Whitman gained recognition as one of the greatest American poets, and today *Leaves of Grass* is regarded as one of the most influential books of American poetry.

## Author Activity

**Civil War Experiences**  As you know, Whitman devoted much of his time during the Civil War to caring for wounded and diseased soldiers. Read excerpts from *Specimen Days,* Whitman's prose account of his wartime experiences. Then discuss with classmates how his hospital work might have influenced his poetry.

# E. E. Cummings
## 1894–1962

**Other Works**
*Collected Poems*
*The Enormous Room*
*Him*

**A Question of Individuality**  Edward Estlin Cummings was raised in Cambridge, Massachusetts. He came from a cultured family that encouraged him to pursue artistic interests. His earliest poems were traditional sonnets, but while studying at Harvard University he fell under the influence of modernist poets such as Ezra Pound, and he began to write more experimental verse. In many of his poems, Cummings ignored rules of standard punctuation and capitalization, sometimes creating new words or spellings and running words together. He once remarked, "So far as I am concerned, poetry and every other art was and is and forever will be strictly and distinctly a question of individuality."

**Military Service**  Cummings went overseas in 1917 to serve in the Ambulance Corps in France. With his spontaneity and irreverence, it may have been inevitable that he came into conflict with his superiors. An army censor falsely accused him of treason, and he spent three months in a military prison. He wrote a prose account of this experience, *The Enormous Room,* which made him famous when it was published in 1922.

**Growing Popularity**  After the war ended, Cummings lived for several years in Paris before settling in New York City. He had difficulty getting his work published during the 1930s, but in the last two decades of his life he became increasingly popular. He is now regarded as one of the most important American poets of the 20th century. Besides writing poetry, Cummings was a prolific painter.

## Author Activity

**Poet at War**  Read excerpts from *The Enormous Room* and discuss how Cummings's experiences in World War I may have led to his writing poems such as "look at this)."

# The Prisoner Who Wore Glasses

*Short Story by* BESSIE HEAD

## Connect to Your Life

**Assert Yourself** In a class discussion, tell what you think it means to be assertive. Then discuss the possible advantages and disadvantages of acting assertively. Use examples from various social situations—at home, at school, in your community, and so on.

## Build Background

**Discrimination by Law** From the late 1940s to the early 1990s, black South Africans who tried to be assertive frequently became political prisoners. Some people were imprisoned, for example, simply for speaking out against the government or publicly protesting government policies. South Africa was then ruled by a white minority government whose official policy of apartheid (ə-pärt'hīt') kept the races separate and legally discriminated against the nation's black majority and other people of color. "The Prisoner Who Wore Glasses" is set on a South African prison farm in the years when apartheid was still the law of the land. The two main characters in the story are a black political prisoner and a white prison guard, or warder. The warder is an Afrikaner (ăf'rĭ-kä'nər), a white South African of Dutch descent, who speaks English with a heavy accent.

| WORDS TO KNOW |  |
|---|---|
| **Vocabulary Preview** | |
| acute | cower |
| bedlam | irrelevant |
| chaos | perpetrate |
| commodity | ruefully |
| conviction | tirade |

## Focus Your Reading

**LITERARY ANALYSIS**  **THIRD-PERSON POINT OF VIEW**  In this story, the author employs **third-person point of view,** the narrative method that occurs when a **narrator** outside the action describes **events** and **characters** without the use of first-person pronouns such as *I, me, we,* and *us.* As you read "The Prisoner Who Wore Glasses," pay attention to the author's use of the third-person point of view. Notice whose thoughts and feelings are revealed to the reader.

**ACTIVE READING**  **DRAWING CONCLUSIONS**  **Drawing conclusions** about a work of fiction involves combining your prior knowledge of the world with your reading of the text in order to make logical statements about elements in a story. As you read this story, combine your knowledge of the political system that existed in South Africa with the story's account of the conditions suffered by one political prisoner.

**READER'S NOTEBOOK**
As you read, record significant details in the story that will help you to draw conclusions about South African society at the time of the story.

*Detail*

Ten political prisoners in Span One

No "black warder" allowed to "be in charge of a political prisoner."

The prisoners "felt no guilt."

# The Prisoner Who Wore Glasses

**Bessie Head**

Scarcely a breath of wind disturbed the stillness of the day, and the long rows of cabbages were bright green in the sunlight. Large white clouds drifted slowly across the deep blue sky. Now and then they obscured the sun and caused a chill on the backs of the prisoners who had to work all day long in the cabbage field.

*Chain Gang* (1939–1940), William H. Johnson. National Museum of American Art, Washington, D.C./Art Resource, New York.

This trick the clouds were playing with the sun eventually caused one of the prisoners who wore glasses to stop work, straighten up and peer shortsightedly at them. He was a thin little fellow with a hollowed-out chest and comic knobbly knees. He also had a lot of fanciful ideas because he smiled at the clouds.

"Perhaps they want me to send a message to the children," he thought tenderly, noting that the clouds were drifting in the direction of his home some hundred miles away. But before he could frame the message, the warder in charge of his work span[1] shouted:

"Hey, what you tink you're doing, Brille?"[2]

The prisoner swung round, blinking rapidly, yet at the same time sizing up the enemy. He was a new warder, named Jacobus Stephanus Hannetjie.[3] His eyes were the color of the sky but they were frightening. A simple, primitive, brutal soul gazed out of them. The prisoner bent down quickly and a message was quietly passed down the line:

"We're in for trouble this time, comrades."

"Why?" rippled back up the line.

"Because he's not human," the reply rippled down, and yet only the crunching of the spades as they turned over the earth disturbed the stillness.

This particular work span was known as Span One. It was composed of ten men, and they were all political prisoners. They were grouped together for convenience, as it was one of the prison regulations that no black warder should be in charge of a political prisoner lest this prisoner convert him to his views. It never seemed to occur to the authorities that this very reasoning was the strength of Span One and a clue to the strange terror they aroused in the warders. As political prisoners they were unlike the other prisoners in the sense that they felt no guilt nor were they outcasts of society. All guilty men instinctively <u>cower</u>, which was why it was

the kind of prison where men got knocked out cold with a blow at the back of the head from an iron bar. Up until the arrival of Warder Hannetjie, no warder had dared beat any member of Span One and no warder had lasted more than a week with them. The battle was entirely psychological. Span One was assertive and it was beyond the scope of white warders to handle assertive black men. Thus, Span One had got out of control. They were the best thieves and liars in the camp. They lived all day on raw cabbages. They chatted and smoked tobacco. And since they moved, thought and acted as one, they had perfected every technique of group concealment.

Trouble began that very day between Span One and Warder Hannetjie. It was because of the shortsightedness of Brille. That was the nickname he was given in prison and is the Afrikaans[4] word for someone who wears glasses. Brille could never judge the approach of the prison gates, and on several previous occasions he had munched on cabbages and dropped them almost at the feet of the warder, and all previous warders had overlooked this. Not so Warder Hannetjie.

"Who dropped that cabbage?" he thundered.

Brille stepped out of line.

"I did," he said meekly.

"All right," said Hannetjie. "The whole span goes three meals off."

"But I told you I did it," Brille protested.

The blood rushed to Warder Hannetjie's face.

---

1. **work span:** a work group in the prison.
2. **Brille** (brĭl'ə).
3. **Jacobus Stephanus Hannetjie** (yä-kō'büs stä-fän'üs hä'nĕt-yē).
4. **Afrikaans** (ăf'rĭ-kans'): a language closely related to Dutch and spoken by South Africans of Dutch descent.

WORDS TO KNOW    **cower** (kou'ər) v. to cringe in fear

"Look 'ere," he said. "I don't take orders from a kaffir.[5] I don't know what kind of kaffir you tink you are. Why don't you say Baas.[6] I'm your Baas. Why don't you say Baas, hey?"

Brille blinked his eyes rapidly but by contrast his voice was strangely calm.

"I'm twenty years older than you," he said. It was the first thing that came to mind, but the comrades seemed to think it a huge joke. A titter swept up the line. The next thing Warder Hannetjie whipped out a knobkerrie[7] and gave Brille several blows about the head. What surprised his comrades was the speed with which Brille had removed his glasses or else they would have been smashed to pieces on the ground.

That evening in the cell Brille was very apologetic.

"I'm sorry, comrades," he said. "I've put you into a mess."

"Never mind, brother," they said. "What happens to one of us, happens to all."

"I'll try to make up for it, comrades," he said. "I'll steal something so that you don't go hungry."

Privately, Brille was very philosophical about his head wounds. It was the first time an act of violence had been perpetrated against him, but he had long been a witness of extreme, almost unbelievable human brutality. He had twelve children and his mind traveled back that evening through the sixteen years of bedlam in which he had lived. It had all happened in a small drab little three-bedroomed house in a small drab little street in the Eastern Cape,[8] and the children kept coming year after year because neither he nor Martha managed the contraceptives the right way and a teacher's salary never allowed moving to a bigger house and he was always taking exams to improve this salary only to have it all eaten up by hungry mouths. Everything was pretty horrible, especially the way the children fought. They'd get hold of each other's heads and give them a good bashing against the wall. Martha gave up somewhere along the line, so they worked out a thing between them. The bashings, biting and blood were to operate in full swing until he came home. He was to be the bogeyman,[9] and when it worked he never failed to have a sense of godhead[10] at the way in which his presence could change savages into fairly reasonable human beings.

Yet somehow it was this chaos and mismanagement at the center of his life that drove him into politics. It was really an ordered beautiful world with just a few basic slogans to learn along with the rights of mankind. At one stage, before things became very bad, there were conferences to attend, all very far away from home.

"Let's face it," he thought ruefully. "I'm only learning right now what it means to be a politician.

> ## "But I told you I did it,"
> ## Brille protested.
> ## The blood rushed to
> ## Warder Hannetjie's face.

5. **kaffir** (kăf′ər): in South Africa, an insulting term for a black.
6. **Baas** (bäs): Afrikaans for *master*. The word has the same Dutch origins as the English *boss*.
7. **knobkerrie** (nŏb′kĕr′ē): a short club with a knobbed end.
8. **the Eastern Cape:** the eastern part of the Cape Province in southern South Africa.
9. **bogeyman** (boŏg′ē-măn′): a terrifying figure of fear, dread, or harassment.
10. **godhead:** divinity; the quality or state of being a god.

| WORDS TO KNOW | **perpetrate** (pûr′pĭ-trāt′) *v.* to commit<br>**bedlam** (bĕd′ləm) *n.* a place or situation of great noise and confusion<br>**chaos** (kā′ŏs′) *n.* total disorder<br>**ruefully** (rōo′fə-lē) *adv.* with regret |
| --- | --- |

*Le nègre Scipion* [Black Scipio] (about 1866–1868), Paul Cézanne. Museu de Arte de São Paulo (Brazil) Assis Chateaubriand. Photo by Luiz Hossaka.

All this while I've been running away from Martha and the kids."

And the pain in his head brought a hard lump to his throat. That was what the children did to each other daily and Martha wasn't managing, and if Warder Hannetjie had not interrupted him that morning, he would have sent the following message:

"Be good comrades, my children. Cooperate, then life will run smoothly."

The next day Warder Hannetjie caught this old man with twelve children stealing grapes from the farm shed. They were an enormous quantity of grapes in a ten-gallon tin,[11] and for this misdeed the old man spent a week in the isolation cell. In fact, Span One as a whole was in constant trouble. Warder Hannetjie seemed

---

11. **tin:** the British word for a can, used in South Africa and many other former British colonies.

to have eyes at the back of his head. He uncovered the trick about the cabbages, how they were split in two with the spade and immediately covered with earth and then unearthed again and eaten with split-second timing. He found out how tobacco smoke was beaten into the ground, and he found out how conversations were whispered down the wind.

For about two weeks Span One lived in acute misery. The cabbages, tobacco and conversations had been the pivot of jail life to them. Then one evening they noticed that their good old comrade who wore the glasses was looking rather pleased with himself. He pulled out a four-ounce packet of tobacco by way of explanation, and the comrades fell upon it with great greed. Brille merely smiled. After all, he was the father of many children. But when the last shred had disappeared, it occurred to the comrades that they ought to be puzzled. Someone said:

"I say, brother. We're watched like hawks these days. Where did you get the tobacco?"

"Hannetjie gave it to me," said Brille.

There was a long silence. Into it dropped a quiet bombshell.

"I saw Hannetjie in the shed today," and the failing eyesight blinked rapidly. "I caught him in the act of stealing five bags of fertilizer, and he bribed me to keep my mouth shut."

There was another long silence.

"Prison is an evil life," Brille continued, apparently discussing some irrelevant matter. "It makes a man contemplate all kinds of evil deeds."

He held out his hand and closed it.

"You know, comrades," he said. "I've got Hannetjie. I'll betray him tomorrow."

Everyone began talking at once.

"Forget it, brother. You'll get shot."

Brille laughed.

"I won't," he said. "That is what I mean about evil. I am a father of children, and I saw today that Hannetjie is just a child and stupidly truthful. I'm going to punish him severely because we need a good warder."

The following day, with Brille as witness, Hannetjie confessed to the theft of the fertilizer and was fined a large sum of money. From then on Span One did very much as they pleased while Warder Hannetjie stood by and said nothing. But it was Brille who carried this to extremes. One day, at the close of work Warder Hannetjie said:

"Brille, pick up my jacket and carry it back to the camp."

"But nothing in the regulations says I'm your servant, Hannetjie," Brille replied coolly.

"I've told you not to call me Hannetjie. You must say Baas," but Warder Hannetjie's voice lacked conviction. In turn, Brille squinted up at him.

"I'll tell you something about this Baas business, Hannetjie," he said. "One of these days we are going to run the country. You are going to clean my car. Now, I have a fifteen-year-old son, and I'd die of shame if you had to tell him that I ever called you Baas."

Warder Hannetjie went red in the face and picked up his coat.

On another occasion Brille was seen to be walking about the prison yard, openly smoking tobacco. On being taken before the prison commander he claimed to have received the tobacco from Warder Hannetjie. All throughout the tirade from his chief, Warder Hannetjie failed to defend himself, but his nerve broke completely. He called Brille to one side.

"Brille," he said. "This thing between you and me must end. You may not know it, but I

| WORDS TO KNOW | **acute** (ə-kyōōt′) *adj.* very sharp or severe |
| | **irrelevant** (ĭ-rĕl′ə-vənt) *adj.* not related to the matter at hand |
| | **conviction** (kən-vĭk′shən) *n.* certainty; a strong belief |
| | **tirade** (tī′rād′) *n.* a long, angry speech |

have a wife and children, and you're driving me to suicide."

"Why don't you like your own medicine, Hannetjie?" Brille asked quietly.

"I can give you anything you want," Warder Hannetjie said in desperation.

"It's not only me but the whole of Span One," said Brille cunningly. "The whole of Span One wants something from you."

Warder Hannetjie brightened with relief.

"I tink I can manage if it's tobacco you want," he said.

Brille looked at him, for the first time struck with pity and guilt. He wondered if he had carried the whole business too far. The man was really a child.

"It's not tobacco we want, but you," he said. "We want you on our side. We want a good warder because without a good warder we won't be able to manage the long stretch ahead."

Warder Hannetjie interpreted this request in his own fashion, and his interpretation of what was good and human often left the prisoners of Span One speechless with surprise. He had a way of slipping off his revolver and picking up a spade and digging alongside Span One. He had a way of producing unheard-of luxuries like boiled eggs from his farm nearby and things like cigarettes, and Span One responded nobly and got the reputation of being the best work span in the camp. And it wasn't only taken from their side. They were awfully good at stealing <u>commodities</u> like fertilizer which were needed on the farm of Warder Hannetjie. ❖

> Brille looked at him, for the first time struck with pity and guilt.

WORDS
TO
KNOW

**commodity** (kə-mŏd′ĭ-tē) *n.* an item—especially a farming or mining product—that can be turned to commercial use or that can provide another advantage

658

# They Have Not Been Able

# No Han Podido

### Armando Valladares
(är-män'dô bä-yä-dä'rĕs)

They have not been able to take away
the rain's song
not yet
not even in this cell
5  but perhaps they'll do it tomorrow
that's why I want to enjoy it now,
to listen to the drops
drumming against
the boarded windows.
10  And suddenly it comes
through I don't know what crack
through I don't know what opening
that pungent odor
of wet earth
15  and I inhale deeply
filling myself to the brim
because perhaps they will also
prohibit that tomorrow.

*Translated by*
*Marguerite Guzman Bouvard*

*No han podido quitarme*
*todavía*
*en este encierro*
*el canto de la lluvia*
5  *pero quizás lo hagan mañana*
*por eso quiero ahora disfrutarlo*
*escuchar las gotas*
*más allá de mis ojos*
*y los esperos muros*
10  *golpear con insistencia*
*las ventanas tapiadas.*
*Y de pronto me llega*
*no sé por qué ranura*
*no sé por qué intersticio*
15  *ese olor agradable*
*de la tierra mojada*
*y la aspiro muy hondo*
*para llenarme bien*
*porque quizás también*
20  *lo prohiban mañana.*

*Hombre y su sombra* [Man and his shadow] (1971), Rufino Tamayo. Oil on canvas, 50 cm × 40 cm, collection of INBA-Museo de Arte Moderno, Mexico City.

## Connect to the Literature

**1. What Do You Think?**
How would you describe the relationship between Brille and Hannetjie?

.................................................
**Comprehension Check**
- Why is Brille in prison?
- Why does Hannetjie give Brille tobacco?
- What do the prisoners want from Hannetjie?
.................................................

## Think Critically

**2.** Why do you think Hannetjie becomes such a "good warder" at the end of the story?

**3.** How does Brille's relationship with his children compare with his relationship with Hannetjie?

**4.** In your opinion, what is this story's **theme,** or message, about assertiveness and cooperation?

> **THINK ABOUT**
> - how the different **characters** assert themselves
> - the effectiveness of assertive acts in the story
> - how the men cooperate at the end of the story

**5.** **ACTIVE READING** **DRAWING CONCLUSIONS** Look at the notes in your  **READER'S NOTEBOOK.** What conclusions can you draw about social and political issues in South Africa at the time of the story? Compare your conclusions with those of a classmate and discuss what elements of the story you think support your conclusions.

## Extend Interpretations

**6. Comparing Texts** Compare Brille's attitude with that of the speaker in the poem "They Have Not Been Able," on page 659.

**7. Comparing Texts** Compare Brille's means of challenging the system with that of the narrator in "The Thrill of the Grass" by W. P. Kinsella. Which character did you find more clever? Why?

**8. Connect to Life** Consider the hardships endured by Brille and the other prisoners of Span One. What do you think would be the most difficult aspect of life in prison?

## Literary Analysis

**THIRD-PERSON POINT OF VIEW**

**Point of view** refers to the narrative method used in a literary work. In **first-person point of view,** the narrator is a character in the story who describes the action in his or her own words. In **third-person point of view,** the narrator is not a character but instead stands outside the action, referring to all characters with third-person pronouns such as *he, she,* and *they.* "The Prisoner Who Wore Glasses" uses a third-person point of view. In a **third-person omniscient point of view,** the narrator is omniscient, or all-knowing, and can see into the minds of more than one character. In the **third-person limited point of view,** the narrator describes the thoughts of only one character.

**Activity** Look back over the story and decide whether the author uses a third-person limited point of view or a third-person omniscient point of view. Why do you think Head tells the story in this way? Why do you think she chose not to have Brille narrate the story?

**REVIEW** **SETTING** The **setting** of this story is South Africa at a time when apartheid was still in effect. Why do you think Head set the story in a prison instead of a factory, a slum, or some other place?

## Writing Options

**1. Letter to Brille's Children** Assume Brille's identity and write a letter to his children. In it, reveal what you have learned as a result of your experience in prison.

**2. Personal Response Essay** Draft a personal essay in which you compare Brille's response to his warder with your likely response to such a situation.

## Activities & Explorations

**1. Narrative Cartoon** Create a narrative cartoon based on this story. ~ **ART**

**2. Political Speech** Deliver a speech that Brille might have made to political supporters on the day of his release from prison. ~ **SPEAKING AND LISTENING**

## Inquiry & Research

**From Prisoner to National Leader** In some ways, Brille's situation mirrors the experiences of South Africa's most famous former prisoner, Nelson Mandela. Find out more about Mandela's life and his time as a political prisoner.

 **Real World Link** Begin your research by reading the article on pages 662–663.

## Vocabulary in Action

**EXERCISE: WORD KNOWLEDGE** For each Word to Know, complete a list like the one shown for the word *assertive*. Use a dictionary or thesaurus if you need help.

**Word:** assertive
**Definition:** inclined to bold expression or action
**Synonyms:** forceful, confident, outspoken, insistent, aggressive
**Sentence:** The prisoner was assertive when he defied the warder.

# Bessie Head
### 1937–1986

**Other Works**
*When Rain Clouds Gather*
*The Collector of Treasures*
*Serowe: Village of the Rain Wind*
*Tales of Tenderness and Power*

**Emigration to Botswana** Born in South Africa, Bessie Head experienced firsthand the effects of apartheid. Designated as a "colored" person (part black and part white) under apartheid's rigid classification system, she was denied the full privileges of citizenship in her homeland. Head never knew her parents; she was raised from birth by a child welfare agency and was later placed with foster parents. After training in a missionary school, she worked for several years as a teacher and journalist before emigrating to a small village in Botswana, a neighboring country that was then under British control. Head taught for a few more years, then led a quiet life of writing and farming.

**Thoughts of Home** Though Head left South Africa physically, its problems were rarely far from her thoughts. While some of her novels and stories explore village life in Botswana, many writings reveal the tragedies and injustices of the land where she was born. Her attitude toward South Africa blended realism and idealism. "It is to be hoped," she once said, "that great leaders will arise there who remember the suffering of racial hatred and out of it formulate a common language of human love for all people." Though she died of hepatitis before reaching her 50th birthday, she left behind an impressive body of work, remarkable for its attentiveness to the lives of ordinary people.

**Building Vocabulary**
For an in-depth study of connotation and denotation, see page 494.

| WORDS TO KNOW | | | | | |
|---|---|---|---|---|---|
| acute | chaos | conviction | irrelevant | ruefully | |
| bedlam | commodity | cower | perpetrate | tirade | |

# Nelson Mandela

## by André Brink

President Nelson Mandela and Deputy President F. W. de Klerk

*Despite spending nearly 35 years in prison, South Africa's first black president, Nelson Mandela, championed forgiveness and peace. In the following article, André Brink explores the roots of Mandela's moral courage and strength.*

**①** Rolihlahla Mandela was born deep in the black homeland of Transkei on July 18, 1918. His first name could be interpreted, prophetically, as "troublemaker." The Nelson was added later, by a primary school teacher. . . . Mandela's boyhood was peaceful enough, spent on cattle herding and other rural pursuits, until the death of his father landed him in the care of a powerful relative. . . . But it was only after he left the missionary College of Fort Hare, where he had become involved in student protests against the white colonial rule of the institution, that he set out on the long walk toward personal and national liberation.

Having run away from his guardian to avoid an arranged marriage, he joined a law firm in Johannesburg as an apprentice. Years of daily exposure to the inhumanities of apartheid, where being black reduced one to the status of a nonperson, kindled in him a kind of absurd courage to change the world. It meant that instead of the easy life in a rural setting he'd been brought up for, or even a modest measure of success as a lawyer, his only future certainties would be sacrifice and suffering. . . .

**②** In these circumstances Mandela opted for nonviolence as a strategy. He joined the Youth League of the African National Congress and became involved in programs of passive resistance against the laws that forced blacks to carry passes and kept them in a position of permanent servility.

Exasperated, the government mounted a massive treason trial against its main opponents, Mandela among them. It dragged on for five years, until 1961, ending in the acquittal of all 156 accused. But by that time the country had been convulsed by the massacre of peaceful black demonstrators at Sharpeville in March 1960, and the government was intent on crushing all opposition. Most liberation movements, including the A.N.C., were banned. . . .

---

## Reading for Information

A **biography** is an account of a person's life written by another person. The writer of a biography researches his or her subject to present accurate information that traces the major events in that subject's life.

### ORGANIZING INFORMATION CHRONOLOGICALLY

**Chronological order** is the order in which events occur. The writer uses time order to structure the work.

**YOUR TURN** To help you trace the momentous events in Nelson Mandela's life that are covered in the article, use these suggestions and activities.

**①** **Creating a Time Line** Begin with the date mentioned here, and create a time line of the significant events and achievements of Mandela's life. What new knowledge about Mandela did you gain from exploring the events chronologically?

**②** Brink states that before Mandela joined the African National Congress (A.N.C.), he "opted for nonviolence as a strategy." What steps did Mandela take to act on his philosophy of nonviolence?

Mandela went underground for more than a year and traveled abroad to enlist support for the A.N.C.

Soon after his return, he was arrested and sentenced to imprisonment on Robben Island for five years. . . . [But within months] Mandela was hauled from prison to face with [the leaders of the A.N.C.] an almost certain death sentence. His statement from the dock was destined to smolder in the homes and servant quarters, the shacks and shebeens and huts and hovels of the oppressed, and to burn in the conscience of the world: "During my lifetime I have dedicated myself to the struggle of the African people. I have fought against white domination, and I have fought against black domination. I have cherished the ideal of a democratic and free society in which all persons live together in harmony and with equal opportunities. It is an ideal which I hope to live for and to achieve. But, if needs be, it is an ideal for which I am prepared to die."

Without any attempt to find a legal way out, Mandela assumed his full responsibility. This conferred a new status of moral dignity on his leadership, which became evident from the moment he was returned to Robben Island.

Even on his first arrival, two years before, he had set an example by refusing to obey an order to jog from the harbor, where the ferry docked, to the prison gates. The warden in charge warned him bluntly that unless he started obeying, he might quite simply be killed. . . . Whereupon Mandela quietly retorted, "If you so much as lay a hand on me, I will take you to the highest court in the land, and when I finish with you, you will be as poor as a church mouse." Amazingly, the warden backed off. . . .

After more than two decades in prison, confident that on some crucial issues a leader must make decisions on his own, Mandela decided on a new approach. And after painstaking preliminaries, the most famous prisoner in the world was escorted, in the greatest secrecy, to the State President's office to start negotiating not only his own release but also the nation's transition from apartheid to democracy. On Feb. 2, 1990, President F. W. de Klerk lifted the ban on the A.N.C. and announced Mandela's imminent release.

Then began the real test. Every inch of the way, Mandela had to win the support of his own followers. More difficult still was the process of allaying[1] white fears. But the patience, the wisdom, the visionary quality Mandela brought to his struggle, and above all the moral integrity with which he set about to unify a divided people, resulted in the country's first democratic elections and his selection as President.

---

1. **allaying:** reducing the intensity of.

❸ Mandela's statement to the court shows his moral stand on the issue of freedom. Identify other events from the article that reveal Mandela's commitment to his cause.

❹ Of the events in Mandela's life that you entered on your time line, what do you think was Mandela's most difficult challenge? How did he meet that challenge?

## Inquiry & Research

**Activity Link: "The Prisoner Who Wore Glasses," p. 661**

Use a graphic organizer to compare and contrast the character Brille with Nelson Mandela. If you need more information, check reference sources or other materials.

# After the Ball

*Short Story by* LEO TOLSTOY

## Connect to Your Life

**Good vs. Evil** List the qualities and behaviors that you associate with a good person, and then list those that you associate with an evil person. Now think of several famous people you have heard of, and try to classify each as good or evil. Can you always tell whether a person is good or evil?

## Build Background

**Morality and Society** Leo Tolstoy was an important Russian writer, reformer, and moral thinker of the 19th century. For much of his life he was preoccupied with questions of good and evil, the meaning of life, and the structure of society. The major events in "After the Ball" take place in the 1840s. The characters belong to the polite society of the time, for whom lavish dances, or balls, were major social events.

WORDS TO KNOW
**Vocabulary Preview**

| | |
|---|---|
| chagrin | majestic |
| detestable | maliciously |
| ethereal | perspicacity |
| imposing | pummel |
| irate | unassuming |

## Focus Your Reading

**LITERARY ANALYSIS** **FLASHBACK** In this story, the elderly Ivan Vassilievich recounts a significant episode in his life, describing events that helped to shape his world view when he was a young man. Because of this, most of "After the Ball" is told in flashback, an account of events that happened before the beginning of a story.

As you read this story, identify where the flashback begins and ends, and consider what the use of this technique adds to Tolstoy's story.

**ACTIVE READING** **EVALUATING CHARACTERS** Ivan tells his tale in order to make a point about people's ability to tell good from evil. As you read Tolstoy's story, be aware of your own evaluation of each character, based on your own standards of right and wrong.

**READER'S NOTEBOOK** Use a chart like the one below to keep track of the personal qualities and behaviors of the **main characters**. Decide whether you think each quality or behavior is good or evil or a mixture of the two, and record your evaluation in the appropriate box.

| Qualities and Behaviors | | | |
|---|---|---|---|
| **Character** | **Good** | **Evil** | **Mixture** |
| Ivan Vassilievich | | | |
| Varenka | | | |
| Varenka's father, the Colonel | | | |

# After the Ball

## Leo Tolstoy

*"You say a man can't tell good from evil, that everything depends on circumstances, that circumstances determine everything. While I think everything depends on chance. I speak from my own experience."*

These were the much-respected Ivan Vassilievich's[1] introductory words following a discussion we had had about the necessity of changing living conditions before people could improve themselves. Strictly speaking, no one had said it was impossible to tell good from evil, but Ivan Vassilievich had a way of answering the thoughts a discussion provoked in his own mind, and then recounting episodes of his own life related to these thoughts. He was often so transported by his story, particularly since he told stories earnestly and honestly, that he completely forgot his reason for telling it. That is what happened this time, too.

"I speak from my own experience. My whole life took one direction instead of another, not because of circumstances, but something completely different."

---

1. **Ivan Vassilievich** (ĭ-vän′ və-syĭl′yə-vĭch′).

*The Reception* (about 1883–1885), James Tissot. Oil on canvas, 56″ × 40″,
Albright-Knox Art Gallery, Buffalo, New York, gift of William M. Chase, 1909.

"What was it then?" we asked.

"Well, that's a long story. To make you understand, I'd have to explain it at length."

"Well, tell us."

Ivan Vassilievich became thoughtful, nodded his head.

"Yes," he said. "My whole life was changed by one night, or rather by one morning."

"But what happened?"

"It happened that I was greatly in love. I had been in love many times, but this was my greatest love. It's past: she has married daughters by now. It was B——, yes, Varenka B—— (Ivan Vassilievich mentioned her surname). At the age of fifteen, she was already a remarkable beauty. As a young girl of eighteen, she was enchanting: tall, well-formed, graceful, majestic—most of all, majestic. She carried herself unusually erect as though she were unable to do otherwise, tipping her head slightly back. Despite her slenderness, even boniness, this posture gave her, with her beauty and her height, a sort of queenly aspect which would have frightened people away from her had it not been for her tenderness, the merry smile on her lips, her enchanting, sparkling eyes, and her whole sweet young self."

"How well Ivan Vassilievich describes her!"

"No matter how much I described her, I could never make you realize what she was like. But that's beside the point; what I wanted to tell about happened in the forties. I was then a student in a provincial university. Whether it was good or bad I don't know, but at that time we had no clubs or theories in our universities; and we were simply young men, living as young men do: studying and being merry. I was a very gay and venturesome boy, and rich as well. I had a fast trotter and used to take sleigh rides in the hills with the ladies (skates were not yet in fashion) and carouse with my comrades (at that time we drank nothing but champagne; if we had no money, we didn't drink, but we never drank vodka as we do now). Parties and balls were my greatest pleasures. I was a good dancer and not ugly."

"No need to be modest," interrupted one of the ladies. "After all, we've seen your daguerreotype.[2] You weren't just not ugly; you were handsome."

"Handsome or not, that's beside the point. The point is that at the time of my greatest love for her, I was at a ball given the last day of Shrovetide[3] by the provincial governor, an affable old man, rich, a generous host, and a nobleman. His wife received equally graciously in a puce velvet dress with her diamond coronet on her head, and her bare, old, plump, white shoulders and throat like the portrait of Elizabeth Petrovna.[4] The ball was marvelous: an excellent ballroom, singers, and musicians—the serfs of a music-loving landowner who were then famous, a magnificent buffet, and a sea of champagne.

> "At the age of fifteen, she was already a remarkable beauty. As a young girl of eighteen, she was enchanting: tall, well formed, graceful, majestic—most of all, majestic."

---

2. **daguerreotype** (də-gâr′ə-tīp′): an early type of photograph.

3. **the last day of Shrovetide:** Mardi Gras, a day of festivity preceding the fasting and penance of the Christian season of Lent.

4. **Elizabeth Petrovna** (pə-trôv′nə): empress of Russia from 1741 to 1762.

WORDS TO KNOW

**majestic** (mə-jĕs′tĭk) *adj.* showing lofty dignity or nobility; stately

# Choices & CHALLENGES

## Writing Options

**1. Gossip Column** Imagine that you are a gossip columnist for a Russian newspaper. Write a newspaper column about the ball. Include descriptions of Varenka, her father, and Ivan, as well as details about romance in the making.

**2. Father-Daughter Scene** Write a dramatic scene in which the colonel explains to his daughter the beating of the Tartar.

**3. Punishment Proposal** With a partner, devise an alternative to the gauntlet as a means of punishing deserters. Write a proposal to the czar in which you explain your idea.

## Activities & Explorations

**1. Modern Adaptation** Work with a small group to adapt the plot of "After the Ball" to a contemporary American setting. For example, you might have the events take place at a high school prom, or you might have Varenka's father be a police officer. Perform your adaptation as an improvisation for the class. ~ **PERFORMING**

**2. Musical Representation** Put together a series of musical recordings that represent the different parts of the story. For example, you might choose a waltz or mazurka to represent the ball; a darker, more serious piece of music might represent Ivan's witnessing the beating. Share your recordings with the class. ~ **MUSIC**

## Art Connection

How does the portrait on page 671 compare with your own mental image of the young Ivan?

## Vocabulary in Action

**EXERCISE A: ASSESSMENT PRACTICE** Determine the relationship between each pair of capitalized words below. On your paper, write the letter of the choice that shows the most similar relationship.

1. QUEEN : **MAJESTIC** :: (a) comedy : tragic
   (b) sky : dark    (c) recreation : sports
   (d) monster : gruesome
   (e) education : elementary

2. **CHAGRIN** : EMBARRASSMENT ::
   (a) ability : musical    (b) expense : tax
   (c) misery : joy    (d) sleep : death
   (e) worry : anxiety

3. BOXERS : **PUMMEL** :: (a) teachers : punish
   (b) lawyers : win    (c) detectives : investigate
   (d) scholars : cheat    (e) collectors : lose

4. HEAVEN : **ETHEREAL** :: (a) grass : dried
   (b) water : muddy    (c) baseball : athletic
   (d) desert : arid    (e) soup : cold

5. **PERSPICACITY** : SHARP ::
   (a) intelligence : clever    (b) fool : wise
   (c) courage : stupid    (d) shyness : sociable
   (e) sense : visual

**EXERCISE B: MEANING CLUES** Using your understanding of the boldfaced word, write on your paper the letter of the word or phrase that best completes each sentence below.

1. Tolstoy talked **maliciously** about his wife, Sonya, because he
   (a) admired her,
   (b) fought bitterly with her,
   (c) enjoyed her wit.

2. She became **irate** when he
   (a) showed her kindness,
   (b) wanted to give away their wealth,
   (c) managed their estate wisely.

3. The pilgrims who came to Tolstoy's estate found him **imposing** because of his
   (a) reputation,  (b) forgetfulness,  (c) unruly hair.

4. Sonya thought the visitors were **detestable** because they
   (a) lacked refinement,
   (b) enjoyed her company,
   (c) earned her respect.

5. In old age, Tolstoy was **unassuming** about his earlier works; he judged them
   (a) boldly original,  (b) perfect,  (c) flawed.

**Building Vocabulary**
For an in-depth lesson on analogies, see page 263.

# *Choices* & CHALLENGES

## Grammar in Context: Participial Phrases

In this excerpt, Leo Tolstoy uses participial phrases to impart a sense of ongoing action to the scene.

> **The colonel walked on, looking now at the victim, now at his own feet, drawing in his breath, blowing out his cheeks,** and **letting the air out slowly through his puckered mouth.**

A **participial phrase** consists of a participle (a verb form that functions as an adjective) along with its modifiers and complements. Besides using participial phrases to provide details, writers use them to create interesting rhythms and to vary their sentence structures. In the sentence above, Tolstoy's use of the participles *looking, drawing, blowing,* and *letting* emphasizes that these actions were ongoing as the colonel walked, not isolated actions that occurred one after the other.

**WRITING EXERCISE** Rewrite each group of sentences as a single sentence containing one or more participial phrases. Underline each participial phrase.

*Punctuation Tip:* In many cases, participial phrases should be set off with commas.

**Example: *Original*** The memory has been buried for years. It comes back when he hears her name.

***Rewritten*** The memory, buried for years, comes back when he hears her name.

1. Varenka carries herself unusually erect. She tips her head back in a regal way.
2. He dances every dance with her. He whirls her around. He feels giddy and light as air.
3. The colonel drops to one knee. He inspires the crowd's applause.
4. Near her house he stops. He hears strange, evil music.

**Grammar Handbook** Verbals, p. 1196

## Leo Tolstoy
### 1828–1910

**Other Works**
*Anna Karenina*
*War and Peace*
*The Death of Ivan Ilyich and Other Stories*
*Master and Man, and Other Stories*

**From the Army to Literary Fame** Nothing about Tolstoy's life, or death, was small. Born into a wealthy, aristocratic family, Tolstoy was orphaned by the age of nine and was raised by aunts. As a young man dissatisfied with his life, he volunteered for the Russian Army. His experience as a soldier in the Crimean War provided material for *Sevastopol Sketches* (1855), a collection of stories that won him literary fame. The next 25 years saw the publication of his two greatest novels, *War and Peace* (1869) and *Anna Karenina* (1877).

**Moral Crisis** At the height of his creativity, Tolstoy underwent a spiritual crisis that led him to reexamine his life and works. In the last 30 years of his life, he became a kind of prophet, preaching his own gospel for the world's salvation. Though Tolstoy continued literary work, he now believed that literature must teach moral truths. He wrote many books and essays about his beliefs, which included love for humanity, rejection of private property, and suspicion of all forms of government.

**Front-Page News** Tolstoy's efforts to give up his property led to quarrels with his wife, Sonya, the mother of his 13 children. He eventually decided to leave her, fleeing in the company of his youngest daughter and his doctor. Just days later, the 82-year-old Tolstoy died at a small railroad station, an event that became news around the world.

## Author Activity

**Philosophical Legacy** Research Tolstoy's philosophy of nonviolent resistance and its effects on Martin Luther King, Jr., and Mohandas K. Gandhi. Write a brief report on your findings.

## Multiple Personalities of Words

A single word can help readers understand an opinion, or it can cause them confusion. Read the passage on the right and think about how the words *removal* and *province* are used.

Both *removal* and *province* have more than one definition. *Removal* can mean "a psychological distancing," "relocation," or "dismissal." *Province* can mean "a territory," "an area of knowledge," or "the range of one's duties." Which meaning of each word do you think O'Brien intends?

> I felt no sense of an impending crisis in my life. Stupidly, with a kind of smug removal that I can't begin to fathom, I assumed that the problems of killing and dying did not fall within my special province.
> —Tim O'Brien, "On the Rainy River"

## Strategies for Building Vocabulary

In your writing, make sure readers understand the word meanings you intend. When a word has more than one meaning, make the intended meaning obvious from the context.

❶ **Convey Meaning Through Context** A word's meaning is often revealed through the sentence or paragraph in which the word appears—its context. Such is the case in the following example.

> "I've told you not to call me Hannetjie. You must say Baas," but Warder Hannetjie's voice lacked conviction.
> —Bessie Head, "The Prisoner Who Wore Glasses"

In this context, *conviction* clearly means "a fixed or strong belief," rather than its other meaning, "the act or process of finding or proving guilty."

❷ **Watch Out for Homonyms** Homonyms are words that have the same pronunciation and often the same spelling, but differ in meaning. Note the use of the homonym *sound* in the following sentence.

> Surely the only sound foundation for a civilisation is a sound state of mind.
> —E. M. Forster, "Tolerance"

If you were to look up *sound* in a dictionary, you might find four different entries, each showing a different derivation and different meanings, including "a noise," "having a firm basis," "a body of water," and "to measure depth." Which meaning do you think Forster intended?

❸ **Consider a Word's Meanings** Writers sometimes purposefully use words that have multiple meanings in order to enrich and extend a statement's meaning. Poets especially use this technique. For example, in "the sonnet-ballad," by Gwendolyn Brooks, the speaker describes the seductive powers death has on soldiers and laments that "Coquettish death . . . Can make a hard man hesitate—and change." In this poem, the word *hard* describes a man who is not only "rugged," but also "strong-minded," and perhaps even "calloused" to the grim realities of war.

**EXERCISE** Look up each underlined word below in a dictionary and choose the intended meaning or meanings.

1. My brother did not like society at all and did not go to balls. (Leo Tolstoy, "After the Ball")
2. But before he could frame the message, the warder in charge of his work span shouted . . . . (Bessie Head, "The Prisoner Who Wore Glasses")
3. When a nation goes to war it must have reasonable confidence in the justice and imperative of its cause. (Tim O'Brien, "On the Rainy River")
4. His legs were not sufficiently limber for all the elegant, rapid steps he tried to execute. (Leo Tolstoy, "After the Ball")
5. He was there at the critical time—a silent, watchful presence. (Tim O'Brien, "On the Rainy River")

## *from* TOLERANCE

### E. M. Forster

*Italian Landscape II: Europa* (1944), Ben Shahn. Copyright © 1995 Estate of Ben Shahn / Licensed by VAGA, New York.

*Great Britain's E. M. Forster ranked tolerance high among the qualities necessary for the world at large. The essay that follows is one of several that Forster broadcast over the radio during or just after World War II (1939–1945) and later collected in his volume* Two Cheers for Democracy *(1951). In these essays, Forster often explores the means by which citizens of democracies can counter the spread of the kind of thinking that leads to brutal dictatorships—dictatorships like that of Nazi Germany, Britain's foe during the war. With their claims of racial superiority, their attempts to conquer neighboring nations that they labeled as inferior, and their mass murder of ethnic groups that they branded as undesirable, the Nazis were the supreme example of intolerance.*

Surely the only sound foundation for a civilisation is a sound state of mind. Architects, contractors, international commissioners, marketing boards, broadcasting corporations will never, by themselves, build a new world. They must be inspired by the proper spirit, and there must be the proper spirit in the people for whom they are working. . . .

What though is the proper spirit? . . . There must be a sound state of mind before diplomacy or economics or trade conferences can function. But what state of mind is sound? Here we may differ. Most people, when asked what spiritual quality is needed to rebuild civilisation, will reply "Love." Men must love one another, they say; nations must do likewise, and then the series of cataclysms[1] which is threatening to destroy us will be checked.

Respectfully but firmly, I disagree. Love is a great force in private life; it is indeed the greatest of all things: but love in public affairs does not work. It has been tried again and again: by the Christian civilisations of the Middle Ages, and also by the French Revolution, a secular movement which reasserted the brotherhood of man.[2] And it has always failed. The idea that nations should love one another, or that business concerns or marketing boards should love one another, or that a man in Portugal should love a man in Peru of whom he has never heard—it is absurd, unreal, dangerous. It leads us into perilous and vague sentimentalism.[3] "Love is what is needed," we chant and then sit back, and the world goes on as before. The fact is we can only love what we know personally. And we cannot know much. In public affairs, in the rebuilding of civilisation, something much less dramatic and emotional is needed, namely,

> NO ONE HAS EVER WRITTEN AN ODE TO TOLERANCE OR RAISED A STATUE TO HER. YET THIS IS THE QUALITY WHICH WILL BE MOST NEEDED AFTER THE WAR.

tolerance. Tolerance is a very dull virtue. It is boring. Unlike love, it has always had a bad press. It is negative. It merely means putting up with people, being able to stand things. No one has ever written an ode[4] to tolerance or raised a statue to her. Yet this is the quality which will be most needed after the war. This is the sound state of mind which we are looking for. This is the only force which will enable different races and classes and interests to settle down together to the work of reconstruction.

The world is very full of people—appallingly full; it has never been so full before, and they are all tumbling over each other. Most of these people one doesn't know, and some of them one doesn't like; doesn't like the colour of their skins, say, or the shapes of their noses, or the way they blow them or don't blow them, or the way they talk, or their smell, or their clothes, or their fondness for jazz or their dislike of jazz, and so on. Well, what is one to do? There are two solutions. One of them is the Nazi solution. If you don't like people, kill them, banish them, segregate them, and then strut up and down proclaiming that you are the salt of the earth.[5] The other way is much less thrilling, but it is on the whole the way of the democracies, and I

---

1. **cataclysms** (kăt′ə-klĭz′əmz): violent upheavals causing great change and destruction.
2. **French Revolution . . . brotherhood of man:** the French Revolution, which lasted from 1789 to 1799, had the motto "Liberty! Equality! Brotherhood!"
3. **sentimentalism** (sĕn′tə-mĕn′tl-ĭz′əm): a tendency toward too much tender, often shallow emotion.
4. **ode** (ōd): a usually formal poem on a serious subject.
5. **salt of the earth:** the finest or noblest people. The expression derives from a statement in the New Testament of the Bible (Matthew 5:13).

prefer it. If you don't like people, put up with them as well as you can. Don't try to love them: you can't; you'll only strain yourself. But try to tolerate them. On the basis of that tolerance a civilised future may be built. Certainly I can see no other foundation for the postwar world.

For what it will most need is the negative virtues: not being huffy, touchy, irritable, revengeful. I have lost all faith in positive militant ideals; they can so seldom be carried out without thousands of human beings getting maimed or imprisoned. Phrases like "I will purge this nation," "I will clean up this city," terrify and disgust me. They might not have mattered when the world was emptier: they are horrifying now, when one nation is mixed up with another, when one city cannot be organically separated from its neighbours. . . .

I don't then regard tolerance as a great eternally established divine principle, though I might perhaps quote "In my Father's house are many mansions"[6] in support of such a view. It is just a makeshift, suitable for an overcrowded and overheated planet. It carries on when love gives out, and love generally gives out as soon as we move away from our home and our friends and stand among strangers in a queue[7] for potatoes. Tolerance is wanted in the queue; otherwise we think, "Why will people be so slow?"; it is wanted in the tube,[8] or "Why will people be so fat?"; it is wanted at the telephone, or "Why are they so deaf?" or conversely, "Why do they mumble?" It is wanted in the street, in the office, at the factory, and it is wanted above all between classes, races, and nations. It's dull. And yet it entails imagination. For you have all the time to be putting yourself in someone else's place. Which is a desirable spiritual exercise. ❖

---

6. **"In my Father's house are many mansions":** a quotation from the New Testament (John 14:2).

7. **queue** (kyo͞o): a chiefly British expression for a line of people.

8. **tube:** British term for the Underground, or London subway.

## E. M. Forster
### 1879–1970

**Other Works**
*A Room with a View*
*A Passage to India*
*Howards End*
*Abinger Harvest*
*Two Cheers for Democracy*

**Worst Years of His Life** Edward Morgan Forster, who was born in London, England, spent the early part of his life hating the private boys' school that he attended, where he was subjected to the taunts of classmates and the severity of teachers. He felt liberated by his subsequent years of study at Cambridge University, which enabled him to expand his intellectual horizons, make close friends, and dedicate himself to the literary life.

**Literary Triumph** Forster began publishing stories soon after graduation and published his first novel in 1905. There followed a number of acclaimed novels; the best known of these—*A Room with a View* (1908), *Howards End* (1910), and *A Passage to India* (1924)—have recently enjoyed a resurgence of popularity sparked by successful film adaptations.

**Farewell to Fiction** During the 1920s, Forster achieved prominence as a literary critic, but in the next two decades he turned increasingly to social criticism and virtually gave up writing fiction. Horrified by events in Germany and elsewhere, Forster reacted with lectures and radio broadcasts that stressed the value of goodwill and reason in combating totalitarian thinking.

## Author Activity

**Literary Virtues** Read excerpts from, or watch a film adaptation of, one of Forster's novels. What can you infer from your reading or viewing about the virtues that Forster believed mattered the most?

D o you like to have power? Or are you happy to leave it to others? Some people clearly like to be in charge of things, and will go to great lengths to serve their own ambitions, dreams, or ideals. The play you are about to read is one of literature's most famous explorations of power, ambition, and idealism. Add intrigue, deceit, and betrayal, and you have ingredients for a drama that has captivated audiences since the 16th century.

## ACTIVITY

With a small group, brainstorm a list of situations in which people can seize power. These situations can fall in the arena of school, family, or government, or any other arena you can think of. Discuss these situations with others in your group, and consider what kind of personal qualities might be found in a person who would seize power in each of the situations. Finally, discuss whether or not you find these qualities admirable.

# SHAKESPEARE'S WORLD

## SHAKESPEARE'S ENGLAND

Poet and playwright William Shakespeare is considered by many to be the world's greatest writer. Shakespeare lived in England during the Renaissance, the blossoming of European learning that followed the Middle Ages. During the Middle Ages, the European world view had focused on God and the afterlife, but with the Renaissance came a renewal of interest in individual human achievement and in life right here on earth. The new emphasis on personal achievement spurred human beings to expand their horizons in all sorts of ways—scientifically, geographically, commercially, philosophically, artistically. In 1564, when Shakespeare was born, England had already embraced the spirit of Renaissance creativity; in the decades to come, Shakespeare himself would help carry the Renaissance to even greater heights.

Six years before Shakespeare was born, Elizabeth I became queen of England, and the period of her reign, from 1558 to 1603, is known as the Elizabethan Age. Elizabeth I supported all the arts—literature, painting, sculpture, music, and theater. She was also a frugal and clever leader who, despite frequent political in-fighting and religious turmoil, managed to steer England down a middle road to stability and prosperity. In the first three decades of her reign, the greatest overseas threat to England's interests came from Spain, but in 1588 the English defeated an attempted invasion by the Spanish Armada, a powerful naval fleet. The victory, which was aided by the weather, underscored England's emergence as a major European power.

In this golden age of English achievement, London flourished as a great commercial center, not only the capital of the nation but the hub of

Elizabeth I

England's growing overseas empire. It was also the hub of the artistic efforts that Queen Elizabeth championed, drawing talented and ambitious individuals from all over the land. Because a true Renaissance figure was supposed to excel in many fields, Elizabeth's courtiers often dabbled in writing. In fact, some of them, like Sir Walter Raleigh, produced memorable poetry that is still being read today. Topping the list of the era's fine literature, however, was its **verse drama,** plays in which the dialogue consists mostly or entirely of poetry. Several outstanding dramatists appeared, none more notable than William Shakespeare, and by the end of the 16th century, London had more theaters than any other city in Europe.

## SHAKESPEARE'S THEATER

From the early 1590s, Shakespeare was affiliated with a theater company known as the Lord Chamberlain's Men, whose chief sponsors were a father and son who served consecutively as England's Lord Chamberlain, an influential

*Below,* photo of the interior of the New Globe Theatre. *At left,* a drawing of what experts believe the Old Globe Theatre looked like.

member of Elizabeth's court. Not only did Shakespeare write the company's plays; he was also a shareholder, or part owner, and at first even performed occasionally as an actor. In 1599, with the other company shareholders, he became part owner of the Globe Theatre, the new London home of the Lord Chamberlain's Men. Four years later, when Queen Elizabeth died, the company at the Globe acquired a new sponsor, the new King James I, and became known as the King's Men.

Located on the banks of the River Thames (tĕmz) in central London, the Globe Theatre was a three-story wooden building that held up to three thousand theatergoers. In the center was an open-air courtyard with a platform stage on which the plays were performed. Those paying the lowest admission charges, known as groundlings, stood in the pit, the part of the courtyard right near the stage. Wealthier theatergoers sat in the building's interior balconies, or galleries, which surrounded all sides of the courtyard except for the part of the building directly behind the stage.

Judging from the success of Shakespeare's company, both classes of theatergoers seem to have enjoyed his plays. That's probably because they included something for everyone—powerful speeches, fancy sword fights, humor, eerie supernatural events, and insightful observations about human nature. Such a mixture was important to Shakespeare. As a playwright, he wanted to explore human behavior, to understand how different people deal with universal problems. Yet he was also part of a commercial venture, writing for an audience that wanted, first and foremost, to be entertained. He made sure that his plays included enough action and excitement to keep just about anyone interested. Audience members in the pit were particularly loud in their appreciation, cheering the heroes, yelling insults at the villains, and laughing loudly at humorous characters and jokes. In fact, by the standards of today's

The Old Globe Theatre

theater, Elizabethan performances were rather rowdy events.

Since the Globe had no artificial lighting or heating, performances were given in daylight in warmer weather. The stage also had no scenery; usually, lines of dialogue told the audience where a scene was taking place. Despite the lack of scenery, productions were by no means drab; costumes could be quite ornate, and props such as swords, shields, and swirling banners added to the colorful display. From behind the stage came sound effects—the chiming of a clock, for instance, or the sound of a cannon. The stage had no curtain. Instead, performers usually walked on and off in full view of the audience.

## SHAKESPEARE'S LEGACY

Some of the most familiar lines in the English language come from the plays of Shakespeare: "Friends, Romans, countrymen, lend me your ears" *(Julius Caesar)*, "O Romeo, Romeo! wherefore art thou Romeo?" *(Romeo and Juliet)*, "To be or not to be" *(Hamlet)*. Why do readers and theatergoers continue to enjoy Shakespeare's plays four centuries after they were written? One answer is that Shakespeare thoroughly understood the theater and knew all the tricks of stagecraft: how to move an audience, create an exciting scene, sketch out a setting using only the spoken word. Another answer lies in Shakespeare's language—the beautiful lines and phrases that resound in the minds of all who experience his plays. No other writer, before or since, has developed the potential of the English language to such heights. Still another answer lies in Shakespeare's profound understanding of human psychology, revealed in the unforgettable characters he created. Today, as much as ever, to understand Shakespeare's plays is to understand what is most important about human beings and about life.

# $hakespearean Drama

generally falls into one of three classifications: **tragedy,** a play that traces the main character's downfall; **comedy,** a play that ends happily and that usually contains many humorous elements; and **history,** a play that chronicles the life of an English monarch. All of these types of plays share the following characteristics: most are written in blank verse and contain soliloquies and asides, rhetorical devices, and dramatic irony. Studying the excerpts from Julius Caesar presented here will help you learn more about these and other characteristics of Shakespearean drama.

## Tragedy and the Tragic Hero

Shakespeare's tragedies are often cited as his greatest plays. A **tragedy** is a work in which a series of actions leads to the downfall of the main character, or **tragic hero**. *Julius Caesar* is a tragedy.

| QUALITIES OF A TRAGIC HERO |
| --- |
| • Possesses importance or high rank |
| • Exhibits extraordinary talents |
| • Displays a tragic flaw—an error in judgment or defect in character—that leads to downfall |
| • Faces downfall with courage and dignity |

## Blank Verse

Shakespeare's plays are **verse dramas**, plays in which the dialogue consists almost entirely of poetry. Generally, Shakespeare wrote his verse dramas in **blank verse**, or unrhymed lines of **iambic pentameter**. Iambic pentameter is a fixed pattern of rhythm, or meter, in which most lines contain five unstressed syllables each followed by a stressed syllable.

**YOUR TURN** The stressed and unstressed syllables in the first two lines in the passage at the right have been marked. Copy the last two lines, and mark the syllables. Which lines seem to vary from perfect iambic pentameter? Why do you think Shakespeare chose to vary the meter?

> **BLANK VERSE**
>
> Let me have men about me that are fat,
> Sleek-headed men, and such as sleep o' nights.
>
> Yond Cassius has a lean and hungry look;
> He thinks too much, such men are dangerous.
>
> —Act One, Scene 2, Lines 192–195

# Soliloquy and Aside

Like all stage plays, Shakespearean drama uses certain devices that an audience is expected to accept even though they are not used in real life. These devices include the soliloquy and the aside.

- A **soliloquy** is a long speech given by a character while alone on stage to reveal his or her private thoughts or intentions.

- An **aside** is a character's quiet remark to the audience or another character that no one else on stage is supposed to hear. A stage direction (often in brackets) indicates an aside.

**YOUR TURN** What does this aside by Trebonius suggest about his true feelings for Caesar? What mood is created by the aside?

> **ASIDE TO AUDIENCE**
>
> Trebonius. Caesar, I will. [*Aside*] And so near will I be
> That your best friends shall wish I had been further.
>
> —Act Two, Scene 2, Lines 124–125

# Rhetorical Devices

Shakespeare's plays often contain speeches known for their masterful use of **rhetorical**, or persuasive, **devices**. These devices use language and sound to appeal to the audience's emotions and make the speech more convincing and memorable. Among these devices are the following:

- the **repetition** of words and sounds

- **parallelism**, or repeated grammatical structures

- **rhetorical questions**, or questions requiring no answer

**YOUR TURN** In the examples at the right, which device do you find most effective? Share your ideas with a classmate.

> **RHETORICAL DEVICES**
>
> **Repetition:**
> And do you now put on your best attire?
> And do you now cull out a holiday?
>
> —Act One, Scene 1, Lines 50–51
>
> **Parallelism:**
> Not that I loved Caesar less, but that I loved Rome more.
>
> —Act Three, Scene 2, Lines 22–23
>
> **Rhetorical question:**
> Why friends, you go to do you know not what.
> Wherein hath Caesar thus deserved your loves?
> Alas, you know not!
>
> —Act Three, Scene 2, Lines 238–240

# Dramatic Irony

Another powerful tool used by Shakespeare is irony. **Irony** exists when there is a contrast between appearance and reality. In **dramatic irony**, the audience or reader knows something that one or more characters do not know. Because of that knowledge, the audience has a bigger picture of the action.

**YOUR TURN** In Act Two, Caesar invites Brutus and the other conspirators into his home, even though—as the reader knows—they are plotting his murder. How does the repetition of the word *friends* in this passage emphasize the dramatic irony?

> **DRAMATIC IRONY**
>
> Caesar. Good friends, go in and taste some wine with me,
> And we (like friends) will straightway go together.
>
> —Act Two, Scene 2, Lines 126–127

Shakespeare's plays often present challenges to contemporary audiences. Unusual vocabulary, grammar, and word order can be difficult to understand. Even the stage directions and other dramatic conventions can be challenging. The reading strategies explained here can help you enjoy Shakespearean drama.

# Reading Shakespearean Drama

## Strategies for Using Your 📖 READER'S NOTEBOOK

As you read, take notes to
- keep track of the characters and their relationships
- record any dialogue, soliloquies, and asides that interest you
- write down any words or terms that you don't understand

## 1 Strategies for Reading Drama
- Familiarize yourself with the opening cast of characters.
- Try to **visualize** the setting from any details provided.
- Pay attention to the character labels and stage directions.
- To get a better idea of what the dialogue would sound like, read some of it out loud.
- **Evaluate** a character's speech and actions to help you determine his or her personality, thoughts, and motives.

## 2 Strategies for Understanding Shakespeare's Language
- Review in the chart shown here the examples from *Julius Caesar* of particular aspects of Shakespeare's use of language.
- Use the sidenotes, context clues, or a dictionary to learn the meaning of unfamiliar vocabulary. Paraphrase lines to **clarify** the meaning.
- Be aware that English spoken in Shakespeare's time contains grammatical forms and structures that are no longer used today.
- Untangle unusual word order so that it conforms to modern usage.
- **Evaluate** puns (jokes that suggest two or more meanings of a word) and allusions (references to well-known people, places, or things) to enrich your understanding of the play. Read sidenotes when they are available, since the wordplay may depend on meanings that are no longer used.

| Shakespeare's Language | |
|---|---|
| **Unfamiliar Vocabulary** | It was mere *foolery*; I did not mark it [*foolery* for *foolishness; mark* for *notice*] |
| **Grammatical Forms** | O judgment, *thou art* fled to brutish beasts! [instead of "you are"] |
| **Grammatical Structure** | *I denied you not* [instead of "did not deny you"] |
| **Unusual Word Order** | Did this *in Caesar seem ambitious*? [instead of "seem ambitious in Caesar"] |
| **Puns** | A trade, sir, that I hope I may use with a safe conscience, which is indeed, sir, a mender of bad *soles*. [pun on *souls* and *soles*] |
| **Allusions** | Why, man, he doth bestride the narrow world / Like a *Colossus*. [allusion to the giant statue] |

### Need More Help?

Remember that active readers use the essential reading strategies explained on page 7: **visualize, predict, clarify, question, connect, evaluate, monitor.**

# The Tragedy of Julius Caesar

*Drama by* WILLIAM SHAKESPEARE

## Connect to Your Life

**Ambition and Power** In *Julius Caesar,* Shakespeare tells a story about the hunger for power, a story based on real people and events from the days when Rome ruled much of the world. Think of stories—fictional or true—that you've read or seen about people who hunger for power. In a group, exchange at least two such stories. Where were they set? Who were the power-hungry individuals? What happened to them? If you're familiar with such stories, you know something about the main theme of *Julius Caesar.*

Like all of Shakespeare's plays, however, *Julius Caesar* deals with many other themes. One of these is friendship. You'll find some interesting views on friendship in the play you're about to read. For example, is it right to persuade a close friend to do something dangerous? This drama also deals with such universal themes as ambition, vanity, envy, and revenge.

## Build Background

**Roman Politics** Julius Caesar was a Roman general and politician who lived from about 100 to 44 B.C. One of the greatest military leaders in Roman history, Caesar conquered most of Gaul, a land that covered the areas now known as France and Belgium. He also brought Roman civilization to the island that eventually came to be Britain and later led his army in a takeover of Egypt.

Caesar gained so much military power that the Roman Senate feared he would try to control the government. To keep that from happening, the Senate ordered him to disband his army around 50 B.C. Caesar refused and led his army into Italy, the peninsula where Rome lay. There he fought a civil war against the armies of his former friend and ally Pompey. The battles spread as far as Spain and Egypt, ending with Caesar's victory in 46 B.C.

## Focus Your Reading

**LITERARY ANALYSIS** **BLANK VERSE** Blank verse consists of unrhymed lines of **iambic pentameter,** in which a line has five unstressed syllables each followed by a stressed syllable.

*You blŏcks, yŏu stónes, yŏu wórse thăn sénsĕlĕss thíngs!*

Many people consider iambic pentameter the most natural poetic pattern for English, a language that is based on stressed and unstressed syllables. As you read, decide for yourself by reciting some of Shakespeare's lines aloud. Be sure not to put too much emphasis on the accented syllables.

**ACTIVE READING** **UNDERSTANDING SHAKESPEARE'S PLAYS**
Because the English language has changed a great deal since Shakespeare lived, Shakespeare's way of saying things can be difficult for a modern reader to understand. For that reason, virtually every modern edition of a play by Shakespeare includes sidenotes or footnotes that explain unfamiliar language and allusions. In the upcoming text, the sidenotes include questions in blue that will help lead you through the more complex parts of the play.

**READER'S NOTEBOOK** You may also find the play easier to follow if you keep track of the **characters.** As you read, use a chart like the one shown to list the characters you encounter.

| Pro-Caesar | Anti-Caesar | Neutral |
|---|---|---|
| | | |

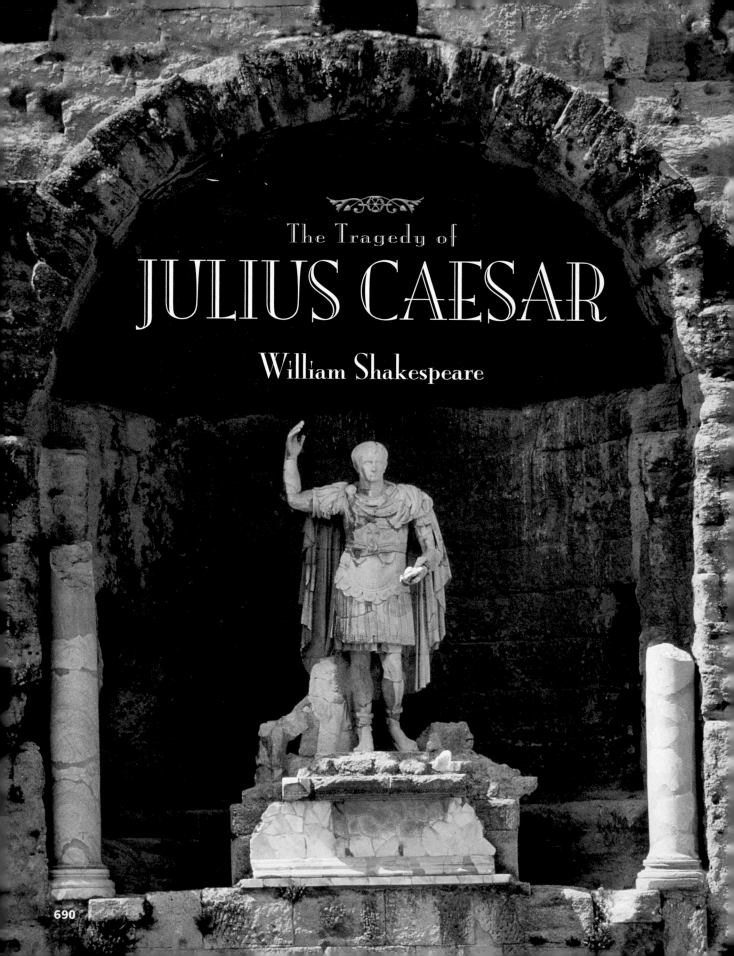

The Tragedy of
# JULIUS CAESAR

William Shakespeare

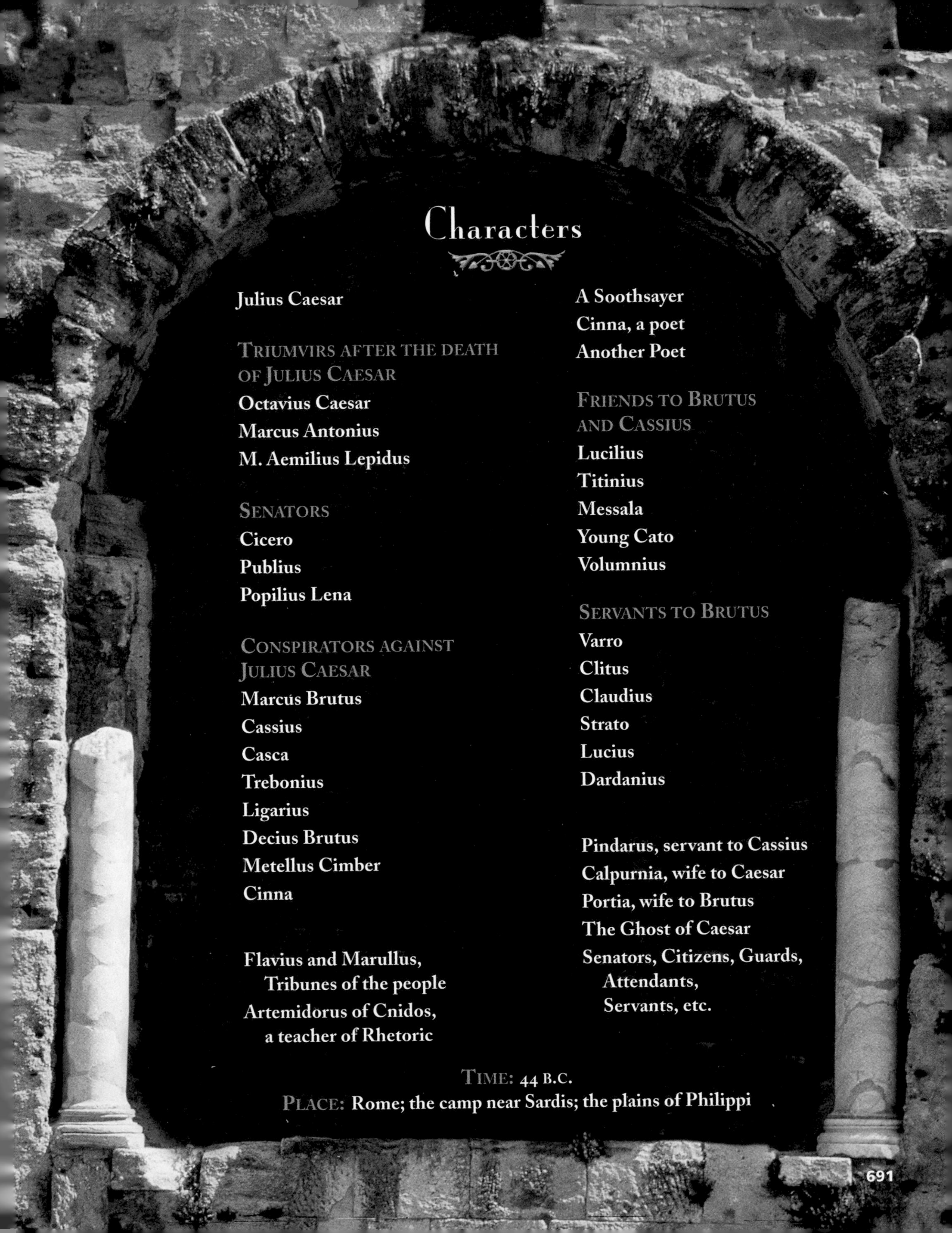

# Characters

**Julius Caesar**

**TRIUMVIRS AFTER THE DEATH OF JULIUS CAESAR**
Octavius Caesar
Marcus Antonius
M. Aemilius Lepidus

**SENATORS**
Cicero
Publius
Popilius Lena

**CONSPIRATORS AGAINST JULIUS CAESAR**
Marcus Brutus
Cassius
Casca
Trebonius
Ligarius
Decius Brutus
Metellus Cimber
Cinna

Flavius and Marullus,
    Tribunes of the people
Artemidorus of Cnidos,
    a teacher of Rhetoric

A Soothsayer
Cinna, a poet
Another Poet

**FRIENDS TO BRUTUS AND CASSIUS**
Lucilius
Titinius
Messala
Young Cato
Volumnius

**SERVANTS TO BRUTUS**
Varro
Clitus
Claudius
Strato
Lucius
Dardanius

Pindarus, servant to Cassius
Calpurnia, wife to Caesar
Portia, wife to Brutus
The Ghost of Caesar
Senators, Citizens, Guards,
    Attendants,
    Servants, etc.

**TIME:** 44 B.C.
**PLACE:** Rome; the camp near Sardis; the plains of Philippi

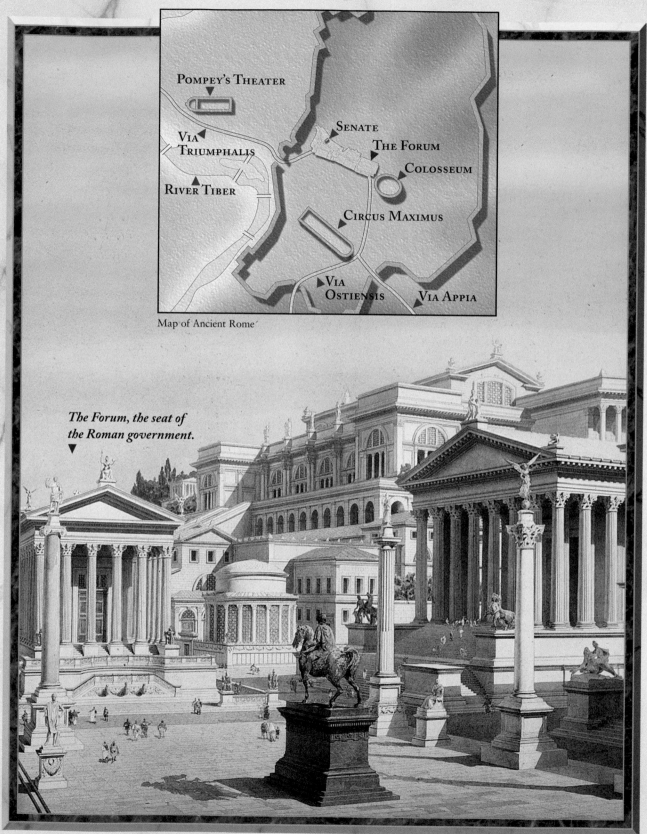

Pompey's Theater

Senate

The Forum

Colosseum

Via
Triumphalis

River Tiber

Circus Maximus

Via
Ostiensis

Via Appia

Map of Ancient Rome

*The Forum, the seat of
the Roman government.*
▼

# ACT ONE

## SCENE 1    A STREET IN ROME.

*The play begins on February 15, the religious feast of Lupercal. Today the people have a particular reason for celebrating. Julius Caesar has just returned to Rome after a long civil war in which he defeated the forces of Pompey, his rival for power. Caesar now has the opportunity to take full control of Rome.*

*In this opening scene, a group of workmen, in their best clothes, celebrate in the streets. They are joyful over Caesar's victory. The workers meet Flavius and Marullus, two tribunes—government officials—who supported Pompey. The tribunes express their anger at the celebration, and one worker responds with puns. Finally, the two tribunes scatter the crowd.*

**Flavius.** Hence! home, you idle creatures, get you
        home!
    Is this a holiday? What, know you not,
    Being mechanical, you ought not walk
    Upon a laboring day without the sign
5   Of your profession? Speak, what trade art thou?

**First Commoner.** Why, sir, a carpenter.

**Marullus.** Where is thy leather apron and thy rule?
    What dost thou with thy best apparel on?
    You, sir, what trade are you?

10  **Second Commoner.** Truly sir, in respect of a fine
    workman I am but, as you would say, a cobbler.

**Marullus.** But what trade art thou? Answer me
        directly.

**Second Commoner.** A trade, sir, that I hope I may
    use with a safe conscience, which is indeed, sir, a
15  mender of bad soles.

**Marullus.** What trade, thou knave? Thou naughty
        knave, what trade?

**GUIDE FOR READING**

**2–5  What, know . . . profession:**
Since you are workers
(**mechanical**), you should be
carrying the tools of your trade
(**sign / Of your profession**). What is
Flavius' attitude toward these
workers?

**10–27** In this conversation, the
**cobbler** (shoemaker) makes several
puns, which all go over the head
of Marullus. Imagine the workmen
laughing, as Marullus gets angrier
and angrier, wondering what's so
funny.

**16–18** Marullus accuses the
commoner of being a wicked, sly
person (**naughty knave**), but the
commoner begs Marullus not to
be angry with him (**be not out
with me**).

**Cassius.** Brutus, I do observe you now of late;
    I have not from your eyes that gentleness
    And show of love as I was wont to have.
35    You bear too stubborn and too strange a hand
    Over your friend that loves you.

**Brutus.**                    Cassius,
    Be not deceived. If I have veiled my look,
    I turn the trouble of my countenance
    Merely upon myself. Vexed I am
40    Of late with passions of some difference,
    Conceptions only proper to myself,
    Which give some soil, perhaps, to my behaviors;
    But let not therefore my good friends be grieved
    (Among which number, Cassius, be you one)
45    Nor construe any further my neglect
    Than that poor Brutus, with himself at war,
    forgets the shows of love to other men.

**Cassius.** Then, Brutus, I have much mistook your
      passion,
    By means whereof this breast of mine hath buried
50    Thoughts of great value, worthy cogitations.
    Tell me, good Brutus, can you see your face?

**Brutus.** No, Cassius, for the eye sees not itself
    But by reflection, by some other things.

**Cassius.** 'Tis just.
55    And it is very much lamented, Brutus,
    That you have no such mirrors as will turn
    Your hidden worthiness into your eye,
    That you might see your shadow. I have heard
    Where many of the best respect in Rome
60    (Except immortal Caesar), speaking of Brutus
    And groaning underneath this age's yoke,
    Have wished that noble Brutus had his eyes.

**Brutus.** Into what dangers would you lead me, Cassius,
    That you would have me seek into myself
65    For that which is not in me?

**Cassius.** Therefore, good Brutus, be prepared to hear;
    And since you know you cannot see yourself
    So well as by reflection, I, your glass,
    Will modestly discover to yourself
70    That of yourself which you yet know not of.
    And be not jealous on me, gentle Brutus.

**32–34 I do observe . . . to have:** Lately I haven't seen the friendliness in your face that I used to see **(was wont to have).** Can you sometimes look into a friend's eyes and tell how he or she is feeling?

**38–47 I turn . . . other men:** I have been frowning at myself, not at you. I have been troubled **(Vexed)** lately by mixed emotions **(passions of some difference).** They are personal matters that are, perhaps, marring my good manners. I hope my friends won't interpret **(construe)** my actions as anything more than my own private concerns. Do you ever avoid your friends when you have a lot on your mind?

**48–50 I have . . . cogitations:** I have misunderstood your feelings. As a result, I have kept certain thoughts to myself.

**55–62 it is . . . eyes:** It is too bad you don't have a mirror that would show you your inner qualities **(hidden worthiness).** In fact, many respected citizens suffering under Caesar's rule **(this age's yoke)** have wished that Brutus could see how much better he is than Caesar. What is Cassius trying to tell Brutus?

**66–70 Therefore . . . not of:** Listen, Brutus, since you cannot see yourself, I will be your mirror **(glass)** and show you what you truly are.

**71 jealous on me:** suspicious of me.

Were I a common laugher, or did use
To stale with ordinary oaths my love
To every new protester; if you know
75  That I do fawn on men and hug them hard,
And after scandal them; or if you know
That I profess myself in banqueting
To all the rout, then hold me dangerous.

[*Flourish and shout.*]

**Brutus.** What means this shouting? I do fear the people
80  Choose Caesar for their king.

**Cassius.**                                   Ay, do you fear it?
Then must I think you would not have it so.

**Brutus.** I would not, Cassius, yet I love him well.
But wherefore do you hold me here so long?
What is it that you would impart to me?
85  If it be aught toward the general good,
Set honor in one eye and death i' the other,
And I will look on both indifferently;
For let the gods so speed me as I love
The name of honor more than I fear death.

90  **Cassius.** I know that virtue to be in you, Brutus,
As well as I do know your outward favor.
Well, honor is the subject of my story.
I cannot tell what you and other men
Think of this life, but for my single self,
95  I had as lief not be as live to be
In awe of such a thing as I myself.
I was born free as Caesar, so were you;
We both have fed as well, and we can both
Endure the winter's cold as well as he.
100  For once, upon a raw and gusty day,
The troubled Tiber chafing with her shores,
Caesar said to me, "Dar'st thou, Cassius, now
Leap in with me into this angry flood
And swim to yonder point?" Upon the word,
105  Accoutered as I was, I plunged in
And bade him follow. So indeed he did.
The torrent roared, and we did buffet it
With lusty sinews, throwing it aside
And stemming it with hearts of controversy.
110  But ere we could arrive the point proposed,
Caesar cried, "Help me, Cassius, or I sink!"

**72–78 Were I . . . dangerous:** If you think I am a fool **(common laugher)** or someone who pretends to be the friend of everyone I meet, or if you believe that I show friendship and then talk evil about my friends **(scandal them)** behind their backs, or that I try to win the affections of the common people **(all the rout),** then consider me dangerous and don't trust me.

**80–81 do you . . . it so:** Imagine Cassius blurting out this line, maybe a little more eagerly than he had intended. He is trying to find a meaning in Brutus' words that may or may not be there.

**85–87 If it . . . indifferently:** If what you have in mind concerns the good of Rome **(the general good),** I would face either honor or death to do what must be done.

**91 outward favor:** physical appearance.

**95–96 I had . . . I myself:** I would rather not live, than to live in awe of someone no better than I am.

**101 troubled . . . shores:** The Tiber River was rising in the middle of a storm.

**105 Accoutered:** dressed.

**107–109 we did . . . controversy:** We fought the tide with strong muscles **(lusty sinews),** conquering it with our spirit of competition **(hearts of controversy).**

**110 ere:** before.

I, as Aeneas, our great ancestor,
Did from the flames of Troy upon his shoulder
The old Anchises bear, so from the waves of Tiber
115   Did I the tired Caesar. And this man
Is now become a god, and Cassius is
A wretched creature and must bend his body
If Caesar carelessly but nod on him.
He had a fever when he was in Spain,
120   And when the fit was on him, I did mark
How he did shake. 'Tis true, this god did shake.
His coward lips did from their color fly,
And that same eye whose bend doth awe the world
Did lose his luster. I did hear him groan.
125   Ay, and that tongue of his that bade the Romans
Mark him and write his speeches in their books,
Alas, it cried, "Give me some drink, Titinius,"
As a sick girl! Ye gods! it doth amaze me
A man of such a feeble temper should
130   So get the start of the majestic world
And bear the palm alone.

[*Shout. Flourish.*]

**Brutus.** Another general shout?
I do believe that these applauses are
For some new honors that are heaped on Caesar.

135   **Cassius.** Why, man, he doth bestride the narrow
      world
Like a Colossus, and we petty men
Walk under his huge legs and peep about
To find ourselves dishonorable graves.
Men at some time are masters of their fates.
140   The fault, dear Brutus, is not in our stars,
But in ourselves, that we are underlings.
"Brutus," and "Caesar." What should be in that
    "Caesar"?
Why should that name be sounded more than yours?
Write them together: yours is as fair a name.
145   Sound them, it doth become the mouth as well.
Weigh them, it is as heavy. Conjure with 'em:
"Brutus" will start a spirit as soon as "Caesar."
Now in the names of all the gods at once,
Upon what meat doth this our Caesar feed
150   That he is grown so great? Age, thou are shamed!
Rome, thou hast lost the breed of noble bloods!

**112–115 I, as Aeneas . . . Caesar:** Aeneas (ĭ-nē′ əs), the mythological founder of Rome, carried his father, Anchises (ăn-kī′ sēz), out of the burning city of Troy. Cassius says he did the same for Caesar when Caesar could no longer swim in the raging river.

**117 bend his body:** bow.

**122 His coward . . . fly:** His lips turned pale.

**123 bend:** glance.

**125–131 that tongue . . . alone:** The same tongue that has led Romans to memorize his speeches cried out in the tone of a sick girl. I'm amazed that such a weak man should get ahead of the rest of the world and appear as the victor (**bear the palm**) all by himself. (A palm leaf was a symbol of victory in war.)

**132–134 Another . . . on Caesar:** The shouts of the crowd are coming from offstage. Brutus is troubled by this cheering for Caesar, worried about where it might lead.

**135–136 he doth . . . Colossus:** Cassius compares Caesar to Colossus, the huge statue of the Greek god Apollo at Rhodes. The statue supposedly spanned the entrance to the harbor and was so high that ships could sail through the space between its legs. What is Cassius' tone in these lines?

**140–141 The fault . . . underlings:** It is not the stars that have determined our fate; we are inferiors through our own fault.

**146 Conjure:** call up spirits.

**150 Age . . . shamed:** It is a shameful time (**Age**) in which to be living.

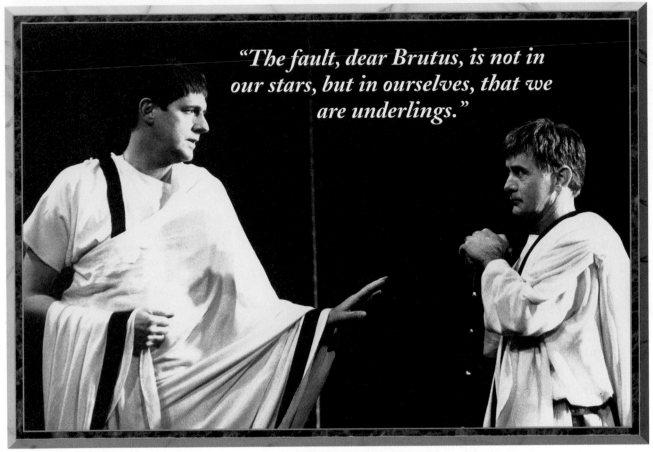

*"The fault, dear Brutus, is not in our stars, but in ourselves, that we are underlings."*

Edward Herrmann as Cassius and Martin Sheen as Brutus (New York Shakespeare Festival, 1988).
Photo copyright © George E. Joseph.

When went there by an age since the great Flood
But it was famed with more than with one man?
When could they say (till now) that talked of Rome
155   That her wide walls encompassed but one man?
Now is it Rome indeed, and room enough,
When there is in it but one only man!
O, you and I have heard our fathers say
There was a Brutus once that would have brooked
160   The eternal devil to keep his state in Rome
As easily as a king.

**Brutus.** That you do love me I am nothing jealous.
What you would work me to, I have some aim.
How I have thought of this, and of these times,
165   I shall recount hereafter. For this present,
I would not (so with love I might entreat you)
Be any further moved. What you have said
I will consider; what you have to say

**159–161 There was . . . a king:** Cassius is referring to an ancestor of Brutus who drove the last of the ancient kings from Rome.

**162 am nothing jealous:** am sure.

**163 have some aim:** can guess.

**164–167 How I have . . . moved:** I will tell you later (**recount hereafter**) my thoughts about this topic. For now, I ask you as a friend not to try to convince me further.

I will with patience hear, and find a time

170 Both meet to hear and answer such high things.
Till then, my noble friend, chew upon this:
Brutus had rather be a villager
Than to repute himself a son of Rome
Under these hard conditions as this time
175 Is like to lay upon us.

**Cassius.**                    I am glad
That my weak words have struck but thus much
    show
Of fire from Brutus.

[*Voices and Music are heard approaching.*]

**Brutus.** The games are done, and Caesar is returning.

**Cassius.** As they pass by, pluck Casca by the sleeve,
180 And he will (after his sour fashion) tell you
What hath proceeded worthy note today.

[*Reenter* Caesar *and his train of followers.*]

**Brutus.** I will do so. But look you, Cassius!
The angry spot doth glow on Caesar's brow,
And all the rest look like a chidden train.
185 Calpurnia's cheek is pale, and Cicero
Looks with such ferret and such fiery eyes
As we have seen him in the Capitol,
Being crossed in conference by some senators.

**Cassius.** Casca will tell us what the matter is.

[Caesar *looks at* Cassius *and turns to* Antony.]

190 **Caesar.** Antonius.

**Antony.** Caesar?

**Caesar.** Let me have men about me that are fat,
Sleek-headed men, and such as sleep o' nights.
Yond Cassius has a lean and hungry look;
195 He thinks too much, such men are dangerous.

**Antony.** Fear him not, Caesar, he's not dangerous.
He is a noble Roman, and well given.

**Caesar.** Would he were fatter! But I fear him not.
Yet if my name were liable to fear,
200 I do not know the man I should avoid
So soon as that spare Cassius. He reads much,
He is a great observer, and he looks
Quite through the deeds of men. He loves no plays
As thou dost, Antony; he hears no music.

**170 meet:** appropriate.

**173 repute himself:** present himself as.

**175** What do you think Brutus might be prepared to do?

**178** The private conversation is now over. Caesar and his admirers return, with the crowd following close behind.

**181 worthy note:** worth remembering.

**184 chidden train:** a group of followers who have been scolded.

**185–188 Cicero . . . senators:** Cicero was a highly respected senator. Brutus says he has the angry look of a **ferret** (a fierce little animal), the look he gets when other senators disagree with him at the Capitol.

**190–214** Brutus and Cassius take Casca aside. The conversation Caesar has with Antony is not heard by any of the other characters around them.

**197 well given:** Antony says that Cassius, despite his appearance, is a supporter of Caesar.

**200–203 I do not . . . of men:** Caesar labels Cassius dangerous and, at the same time, one who can see through people and understand their secrets. Caesar makes a boast about himself.

205 Seldom he smiles, and smiles in such a sort
As if he mocked himself and scorned his spirit
That could be moved to smile at anything.
Such men as he be never at heart's ease
Whiles they behold a greater than themselves,
210 And therefore are they very dangerous.
I rather tell thee what is to be feared
Than what I fear, for always I am Caesar.
Come on my right hand, for this ear is deaf,
And tell me truly what thou think'st of him.

[*Trumpets sound. Exeunt* Caesar *and all his train except*
Casca, *who stays behind.*]

215 **Casca.** You pulled me by the cloak. Would you speak
with me?

**Brutus.** Ay, Casca. Tell us what hath chanced today
That Caesar looks so sad.

**Casca.** Why, you were with him, were you not?

**Brutus.** I should not then ask Casca what had
chanced.

220 **Casca.** Why, there was a crown offered him; and
being offered him, he put it by with the back of his
hand, thus. And then the people fell a-shouting.

**Brutus.** What was the second noise for?

**Casca.** Why, for that too.

225 **Cassius.** They shouted thrice. What was the last cry
for?

**Casca.** Why, for that too.

**Brutus.** Was the crown offered him thrice?

**Casca.** Ay, marry, was't! and he put it by thrice, every
time gentler than other; and at every putting-by
230 mine honest neighbors shouted.

**Cassius.** Who offered him the crown?

**Casca.** Why, Antony.

**Brutus.** Tell us the manner of it, gentle Casca.

**Casca.** I can as well be hanged as tell the manner of it.
235 It was mere foolery; I did not mark it. I saw Mark
Antony offer him a crown—yet 'twas not a crown
neither, 'twas one of these coronets—and, as I told
you, he put it by once. But for all that, to my
thinking, he would fain have had it. Then he offered

210 What is Caesar's opinion of
Cassius? Why does he feel this
way?

213 What does Caesar reveal
about himself in this line?

215 Now only Brutus, Cassius, and
Casca remain on stage.

216 **hath chanced:** has happened.

221 **put it by:** pushed it aside.

228 **Ay, marry, was't:** Yes, indeed,
it was. *Marry* was a mild oath used
in Shakespeare's time (but not in
ancient Rome). The word means
"by the Virgin Mary."

237 **coronets:** small crowns made
out of laurel branches twisted
together. A coronet was less of an
honor than the kind of crown a
king would wear.

239 **fain:** gladly.

240　it to him again; then he put it by again; but to my
　　　thinking, he was very loath to lay his fingers off it.
　　　And then he offered it the third time. He put it the
　　　third time by; and still as he refused it, the rabblement
　　　hooted, and clapped their chapped hands, and
245　threw up their sweaty nightcaps, and uttered such a
　　　deal of stinking breath because Caesar refused the
　　　crown that it had, almost, choked Caesar; for he
　　　swounded and fell down at it. And for mine own
　　　part, I durst not laugh, for fear of opening my lips
250　and receiving the bad air.

　　　**Cassius.** But soft, I pray you. What, did Caesar
　　　　swound?

　　　**Casca.** He fell down in the market place and foamed
　　　　at mouth and was speechless.

　　　**Brutus.** 'Tis very like. He hath the falling sickness.

255　**Cassius.** No, Caesar hath not it; but you, and I,
　　　And honest Casca, we have the falling sickness.

　　　**Casca.** I know not what you mean by that, but I am
　　　　sure Caesar fell down. If the tag-rag people did not
　　　　clap him and hiss him, according as he pleased and
260　displeased them, as they use to do the players in
　　　the theater, I am no true man.

　　　**Brutus.** What said he when he came unto himself?

　　　**Casca.** Marry, before he fell down, when he perceived
　　　　the common herd was glad he refused the crown, he
265　plucked me ope his doublet and offered them his
　　　throat to cut. An I had been a man of any occupation,
　　　if I would not have taken him at a word I
　　　would I might go to hell among the rogues. And so
　　　he fell. When he came to himself again, he said, if
270　he had done or said anything amiss, he desired their
　　　worships to think it was his infirmity. Three or four
　　　wenches where I stood cried, "Alas, good soul!" and
　　　forgave him with all their hearts. But there's no heed
　　　to be taken of them. If Caesar had stabbed their
275　mothers, they would have done no less.

　　　**Brutus.** And after that, he came thus sad away?

　　　**Casca.** Ay.

　　　**Cassius.** Did Cicero say anything?

　　　**Casca.** Ay, he spoke Greek.

**241 loath:** reluctant.

**243 rabblement:** unruly crowd.

**248 swounded:** fainted.

**251 soft:** Wait a moment.

**252–254** There is some historical evidence that Caesar had epilepsy. In Shakespeare's time, this illness was known as the falling sickness (because someone having an epileptic seizure is likely to fall to the floor).

**256** Cassius sarcastically uses the phrase **falling sickness** to refer to the tendency to bow down before Caesar.

**265 ope his doublet:** open his jacket.

**266–268 An . . . rogues:** If (An) I had been a worker with a proper tool, may I go to hell with the sinners (rogues) if I would not have done as he asked (**taken him at a word**).

**270 amiss:** wrong.

**271 infirmity:** sickness.

**272 wenches:** common women.

**Cassius.** To what effect?

**Casca.** Nay, an I tell you that, I'll ne'er look you i' the face again. But those that understood him smiled at one another and shook their heads; but for mine own part, it was Greek to me. I could tell you more news, too. Marullus and Flavius, for pulling scarfs off Caesar's images, are put to silence. Fare you well. There was more foolery yet, if I could remember it.

**Cassius.** Will you sup with me tonight, Casca?

**Casca.** No, I am promised forth.

**Cassius.** Will you dine with me tomorrow?

**Casca.** Ay, if I be alive, and your mind hold, and your dinner worth eating.

**Cassius.** Good. I will expect you.

**Casca.** Do so. Farewell both.

[*Exit.*]

**Brutus.** What a blunt fellow is this grown to be!
He was quick mettle when he went to school.

**Cassius.** So is he now in execution
Of any bold or noble enterprise,
However he puts on this tardy form.
This rudeness is a sauce to his good wit,
Which gives men stomach to digest his words
With better appetite.

**Brutus.** And so it is. For this time I will leave you.
Tomorrow, if you please to speak with me,
I will come home to you; or if you will,
Come home to me, and I will wait for you.

**Cassius.** I will do so. Till then, think of the world.

[*Exit* Brutus.]

Well, Brutus, thou art noble; yet I see
Thy honorable mettle may be wrought
From that it is disposed. Therefore it is meet
That noble minds keep ever with their likes;
For who so firm that cannot be seduced?
Caesar doth bear me hard, but he loves Brutus.
If I were Brutus now and he were Cassius,
He should not humor me. I will this night,
In several hands, in at his windows throw,
As if they came from several citizens,
Writings, all tending to the great opinion

**286 put to silence:** This may mean that the two tribunes have been put to death or that they have been barred from public life.

**289 I am promised forth:** I have another appointment.

**296 quick mettle:** clever, intelligent.

**297–302 So is . . . appetite:** Cassius says that Casca can still be intelligent in carrying out an important project. He only pretends to be slow (**tardy**). His rude manner makes people more willing to accept (**digest**) the things he says.

**308–322** Now Cassius is alone on stage. The thoughts he expresses in this speech are thoughts he would not want Brutus to know about.

**309–310 Thy . . . disposed:** Your honorable nature can be manipulated (**wrought**) into something not quite so honorable.

**313 bear me hard:** hold a grudge against me.

**315 He should . . . me:** I wouldn't let him get away with fooling me.

**315–319 I will . . . his name:** Cassius plans to leave messages at Brutus' home that appear to be from several people.

That Rome holds of his name; wherein obscurely
320  Caesar's ambition shall be glanced at.
And after this let Caesar seat him sure,
For we will shake him, or worse days endure.

[*Exit.*]

**322 we will . . . endure:** We will remove Caesar from his high position or suffer the consequences.

# SCENE 3    A STREET IN ROME.

*It is the night of March 14. Amid violent thunder and lightning, a terrified Casca fears that the storm and other omens predict terrible events to come. Cassius interprets the storm as a sign that Caesar must be overthrown. Cassius and Casca agree that Caesar's rise to power must be stopped by any means. Cinna, another plotter, enters, and they discuss how to persuade Brutus to follow their plan.*

[*Thunder and lightning. Enter, from opposite sides,* Casca, *with his sword drawn, and* Cicero.]

**Cicero.** Good even, Casca. Brought you Caesar home?
Why are you breathless? and why stare you so?

**Casca.** Are not you moved when all the sway of earth
Shakes like a thing unfirm? O Cicero,
5    I have seen tempests when the scolding winds
Have rived the knotty oaks, and I have seen
The ambitious ocean swell and rage and foam
To be exalted with the threat'ning clouds;
But never till tonight, never till now,
10   Did I go through a tempest dropping fire.
Either there is a civil strife in heaven,
Or else the world, too saucy with the gods,
Incenses them to send destruction.

**Cicero.** Why, saw you anything more wonderful?

15   **Casca.** A common slave—you know him well by
sight—
Held up his left hand, which did flame and burn
Like twenty torches joined; and yet his hand,
Not sensible of fire, remained unscorched.
Besides—I ha' not since put up my sword—
20   Against the Capitol I met a lion,
Who glared upon me, and went surly by
Without annoying me. And there were drawn
Upon a heap a hundred ghastly women,

**3 sway of earth:** the natural order of things.

**5 tempests:** storms.

**6 rived:** torn.

**8 To be exalted with:** to raise themselves to the level of.

**11–13 Either . . . destruction:** Such a terrible storm could be caused by only two things—a civil war **(strife)** in heaven or angry gods destroying the world.

**14 saw . . . wonderful:** Did you see anything else that was strange?

**18 Not sensible of fire:** not feeling the fire.

**19–20 I ha' not . . . lion:** I haven't put my sword back into its scabbard since I saw a lion at the Capitol building.

**22–23 drawn / Upon:** huddled together.

Transformed with their fear, who swore they saw
25 Men, all in fire, walk up and down the streets.
And yesterday the bird of night did sit
Even at noonday upon the market place,
Hooting and shrieking. When these prodigies
Do so conjointly meet, let not men say,
30 "These are their reasons, they are natural,"
For I believe they are portentous things
Unto the climate that they point upon.

**Cicero.** Indeed it is a strange-disposed time.
But men may construe things after their fashion,
35 Clean from the purpose of the things themselves.
Comes Caesar to the Capitol tomorrow?

**Casca.** He doth, for he did bid Antonius
Send word to you he would be there tomorrow.

**Cicero.** Good night then, Casca. This disturbed sky
40 Is not to walk in.

**Casca.**                          Farewell, Cicero.

[*Exit* Cicero.]

[*Enter* Cassius.]

**Cassius.** Who's there?

**Casca.**                          A Roman.

**Cassius.**                                   Casca, by your voice.

**Casca.** Your ear is good. Cassius, what night is this!

**Cassius.** A very pleasing night to honest men.

**Casca.** Who ever knew the heavens menace so?

45 **Cassius.** Those that have known the earth so full of
      faults.
For my part, I have walked about the streets,
Submitting me unto the perilous night,
And, thus unbraced, Casca, as you see,
Have bared my bosom to the thunder-stone;
50 And when the cross blue lightning seemed to open
The breast of heaven, I did present myself
Even in the aim and very flash of it.

**Casca.** But wherefore did you so much tempt the
      heavens?
It is the part of men to fear and tremble
55 When the most mighty gods by tokens send
Such dreadful heralds to astonish us.

**26 bird of night:** the owl, usually seen only at night.

**28–32 When these . . . upon:** When strange events (**prodigies**) like these happen at the same time (**conjointly meet**), no one should say there are natural explanations for them. I believe they are bad omens (**portentous things**) for the place where they happen.

**33–35 Indeed . . . themselves:** Cicero does not accept Casca's superstitious explanation of events. He agrees that the times are strange. But he says people can interpret events the way they want to, no matter what actually causes the events.

**41 Who's there?:** Cassius probably has his sword out. Remember, with no light other than moonlight, it could be dangerous to come upon a stranger in the street.

**46–52 For my . . . flash of it:** Cassius brags that he offered himself to the dangerous night, with his coat open (**unbraced**), exposing his chest to the thunder and lightning. Why might he do this?

**54–56 It is . . . astonish us:** Men are supposed to tremble when the gods use signs (**tokens**) to send frightening messengers (**heralds**) to scare us.

"*this dreadful night that thunders, lightens, opens graves, and roars*"

Edward Herrmann as Cassius (New York Shakespeare Festival, 1988).
Photo copyright © George E. Joseph.

**Cassius.** You are dull, Casca, and those sparks of life
That should be in a Roman you do want,
Or else you use not. You look pale, and gaze,
60 And put on fear, and cast yourself in wonder,
To see the strange impatience of the heavens.
But if you would consider the true cause
Why all these fires, why all these gliding ghosts,
Why birds and beasts, from quality and kind;
65 Why old men fool and children calculate;
Why all these things change from their ordinance,
Their natures, and preformed faculties,
To monstrous quality, why, you shall find
That heaven hath infused them with these spirits
70 To make them instruments of fear and warning
Unto some monstrous state.
Now could I, Casca, name to thee a man
Most like this dreadful night
That thunders, lightens, opens graves, and roars
75 As doth the lion in the Capitol;
A man no mightier than thyself or me
In personal action, yet prodigious grown
And fearful, as these strange eruptions are.

**Casca.** 'Tis Caesar that you mean. Is it not, Cassius?

80 **Cassius.** Let it be who it is. For Romans now
Have thews and limbs like to their ancestors.
But woe the while! our fathers' minds are dead,
And we are governed with our mothers' spirits,
Our yoke and sufferance show us womanish.

85 **Casca.** Indeed, they say the senators tomorrow
Mean to establish Caesar as king,
And he shall wear his crown by sea and land
In every place save here in Italy.

**Cassius.** I know where I will wear this dagger then;
90 Cassius from bondage will deliver Cassius.
Therein, ye gods, you make the weak most strong;
Therein, ye gods, you tyrants do defeat.
Nor stony tower, nor walls of beaten brass,
Nor airless dungeon, nor strong links of iron,
95 Can be retentive to the strength of spirit;
But life, being weary of these worldly bars,
Never lacks power to dismiss itself.
If I know this, know all the world besides,

**58 want:** lack.

**62–71** Cassius insists that heaven has brought about such things as birds and animals that change their natures (**from quality and kind**) and children who predict the future (**calculate**)—all these beings that act unnaturally (**change from their ordinance / Their natures, and preformed faculties**). Heaven has done all this, he says, to warn the Romans of an evil condition that they should correct.

**77 prodigious grown:** become enormous and threatening. To whom does Cassius refer in lines 72–78?

**80–84 Romans . . . womanish:** Modern Romans have muscles (**thews**) and limbs like our ancestors, but we have the minds of our mothers, not our fathers. Our acceptance of a dictator (**yoke and sufferance**) shows us to be like women, not like men. (In Shakespeare's time—and in ancient Rome—women were considered weak creatures.)

**87–88 he shall . . . Italy:** The senators will make Caesar the king of all Roman territories except (**save**) Rome itself (**Italy**), since Romans would never let their own land be ruled by a king.

**89–90 I know . . . deliver Cassius:** I will free myself from slavery (**bondage**) by killing myself (**wear this dagger**).

**91–97** Cassius shouts these lines toward the sky, trying to be heard over the thunder. Only through suicide, he says angrily, do the gods make the weak strong and able to defeat tyrants. The strong spirit cannot be imprisoned by tower, metal walls, dungeons, or iron chains. The reason is that one can always commit suicide (**life . . . Never lacks power to dismiss itself**). Do you think Cassius would really kill himself?

# VIEW AND COMPARE

**What do these images all suggest about the character of Julius Caesar? What sets them apart? Study the posture, facial expressions, and costuming.**

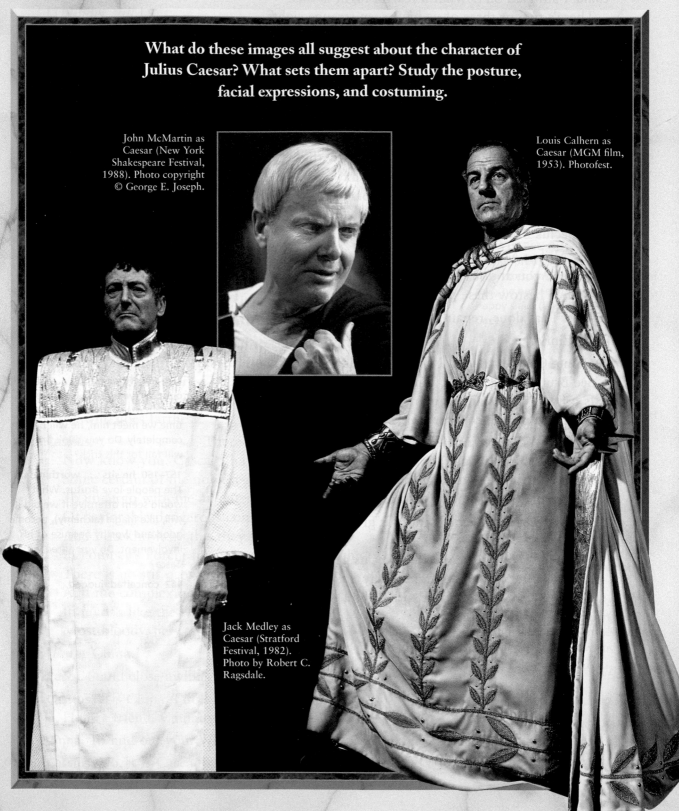

John McMartin as Caesar (New York Shakespeare Festival, 1988). Photo copyright © George E. Joseph.

Louis Calhern as Caesar (MGM film, 1953). Photofest.

Jack Medley as Caesar (Stratford Festival, 1982). Photo by Robert C. Ragsdale.

# Connect to the Literature

1. **What Do You Think?**
   Write one or two adjectives that describe each of these men: Cassius, Brutus, Casca, Antony, and Caesar.

   > **Comprehension Check**
   > - What warning does the Soothsayer give Caesar?
   > - What does Casca report happened when Mark Antony offered Caesar the crown?
   > - What does Cassius hope to convince Brutus to do?

# Think Critically

2. In Act One, Scene 1, what seems to be tribunes' and commoners' attitudes toward one another? Cite evidence from the scene to support your opinion.

3. What is your opinion of Caesar in this act?

   **THINK ABOUT**
   - his actions and appearance
   - his remarks about himself and others
   - other characters' remarks about him

4. Why do you think Cassius wants Brutus to join the conspiracy? Do you think Brutus will join? Explain.

5. Who do you think is the most important character in the play so far? Support your answer.

6. What **humor** did you find in Act One? Why do you think Shakespeare included it?

7. **ACTIVE READING** **UNDERSTANDING SHAKESPEARE'S PLAYS**
   Review the chart begun in your  **READER'S NOTEBOOK.** In which column did you put the **characters** who appear in Act One, Scene 1? Continue to add to and revise your chart as you read the rest of the play.

# Extend Interpretations

8. **Critic's Corner** The editors of the Folger Library edition of *Julius Caesar* point out that Elizabethans "did not have our modern distaste for dictators, . . . and they admired forceful and successful leaders like Caesar." Do you see evidence of this admiration in Act One of the play? Would you say that Shakespeare himself admires Julius Caesar? Cite details from Act One to support your opinions.

9. **Connect to Life** Based on the details in Act One, what do you think Shakespeare's opinion would be of democracy as practiced in America today?

# Literary Analysis

**BLANK VERSE** **Blank verse** is unrhymed lines of poetry written in **iambic pentameter,** meaning that the lines generally contain five unstressed syllables each followed by a stressed syllable. This makes 10 syllables in each line.

*Ŭpón whăt méat dŏth thís ŏur Cáesar feed*

Playwrights like Shakespeare who wrote their plays in verse chose blank verse because, more than other verse forms, it approximates the sound of spoken English. However, Shakespeare's plays are not completely written in blank verse. Sometimes he has characters speak in prose, and occasionally he uses rhymed lines of iambic pentameter to stress a point or to signal actors that a scene or act is about to end.

**Paired Activity** With a partner, choose and copy a blank-verse passage from Act One of *Julius Caesar,* marking its unstressed (˘) and stressed (′) syllables to show that it is written in blank verse. How well do you think the passage captures the sound of spoken English?

Now examine the use of prose in Act One, Scene 1. Why do you think Shakespeare had the commoners speak in prose?

# ACT TWO

## SCENE 1 BRUTUS' ORCHARD IN ROME.

*It is a few hours before dawn on March 15—the ides of March. Brutus, unable to sleep, walks in his garden. He faces a crucial decision: either to continue living under the tyranny of Caesar or to kill Caesar and thus end his rule. While considering the problem, Brutus receives an anonymous letter (from Cassius) suggesting that Brutus take action against Caesar. Shortly after, Cassius and the conspirators visit Brutus, and they all agree to assassinate Caesar that day.*

**Brutus.** What, Lucius, ho!
   I cannot by the progress of the stars
   Give guess how near to day. Lucius, I say!
   I would it were my fault to sleep so soundly.
5   When, Lucius, when? Awake, I say! What, Lucius!

[*Enter* Lucius *from the house.*]

**Lucius.** Called you, my lord?

**Brutus.** Get me a taper in my study, Lucius.
   When it is lighted, come and call me here.

**Lucius.** I will, my lord.

[*Exit.*]

[Brutus *returns to his brooding.*]

10   **Brutus.** It must be by his death; and for my part,
   I know no personal cause to spurn at him,
   But for the general. He would be crowned.
   How that might change his nature, there's the
      question.
   It is the bright day that brings forth the adder,
15   And that craves wary walking. Crown him that,
   And then I grant we put a sting in him
   That at his will he may do danger with.

**2–3 I cannot . . . day:** There are no stars in the sky to tell me how near it is to morning.

**4 I would . . . soundly:** I wish I could sleep so soundly.

**7 taper:** candle.

**10–34** Brutus, alone again, thinks out loud about the problem of Caesar. In general, Brutus fears that Caesar will become too powerful.

**10–12 It must . . . general:** It can only be solved by Caesar's death. I have no personal grudge against him; I'm thinking only of the general welfare.

**14–15 It is . . . walking:** Sunshine brings out the poisonous snake **(adder),** so walk carefully.

The abuse of greatness is when it disjoins
Remorse from power. And to speak truth of Caesar,
20   I have not known when his affections swayed
More than his reason. But 'tis a common proof
That lowliness is young ambition's ladder,
Whereto the climber-upward turns his face;
But when he once attains the upmost round,
25   He then unto the ladder turns his back,
Looks in the clouds, scorning the base degrees
By which he did ascend. So Caesar may.
Then lest he may, prevent. And since the quarrel
Will bear no color for the thing he is,
30   Fashion it thus: that what he is, augmented,
Would run to these and these extremities;
And therefore think him as a serpent's egg,
Which, hatched, would as his kind grow mischievous,
And kill him in the shell.

[*Reenter* Lucius *with a letter.*]

35   **Lucius.** The taper burneth in your closet, sir.
Searching the window for a flint, I found
This paper, thus sealed up, and I am sure
It did not lie there when I went to bed.

[*Gives him the letter.*]

**Brutus.** Get you to bed again; it is not day.
40   Is not tomorrow, boy, the ides of March?

**Lucius.** I know not, sir.

**Brutus.** Look in the calendar and bring me word.

**Lucius.** I will, sir.

[*Exit.*]

**Brutus.** The exhalations, whizzing in the air,
45   Give so much light that I may read by them.

[*Opens the letter and reads.*]

"Brutus, thou sleep'st. Awake, and see thyself!
Shall Rome, etc. Speak, strike, redress!"
"Brutus, thou sleep'st. Awake!"
Such instigations have been often dropped
50   Where I have took them up.
"Shall Rome, etc." Thus must I piece it out:
Shall Rome stand under one man's awe? What,
   Rome?
My ancestors did from the streets of Rome

---

**18–27 The abuse . . . may:**
Greatness is misused when it
separates pity (**disjoins / Remorse**)
from power. I have never known
Caesar to be ruled by his heart
rather than his head. What does
Brutus think Caesar will do if he
gets to the top of **ambition's
ladder**? What will Caesar's attitude
be toward those at the ladder's
lower rungs (**base degrees**)?

**28–34 lest . . . shell:** Rather than
let Caesar do that, I should take
steps to prevent it. Since our case
against Caesar is weak (**Will bear
no color**) at present, we must
shape (**Fashion**) our argument
against him in the following way:
We know what kind of person
Caesar is now. If his true nature
were allowed to develop
(**augmented**), it would reach
terrible extremes. So we must treat
him as a serpent's egg and kill him
before he hatches.

**35 closet:** private room.

**44 exhalations:** meteors.

**47 etc.:** and so forth; **redress:** right
a wrong. The letter is meant to
suggest certain things to Brutus,
without actually spelling them out.

**49 instigations:** suggestions.

**51 Thus . . . out:** I must guess the
rest of the sentence.

**52 Shall . . . awe:** Should Rome
have such fear and respect for just
one man?

*"Shall Rome stand under one man's awe?"*

Martin Sheen as Brutus (New York Shakespeare Festival, 1988). Photo copyright © George E. Joseph.

The Tarquin drive when he was called a king.
55  "Speak, strike, redress!" Am I entreated
To speak and strike? O Rome, I make thee promise,
If the redress will follow, thou receivest
Thy full petition at the hand of Brutus!

[*Reenter* Lucius.]

**Lucius.** Sir, March is wasted fifteen days.

[*Knocking within.*]

60  **Brutus.** 'Tis good. Go to the gate, somebody knocks.

[*Exit* Lucius.]

Since Cassius first did whet me against Caesar,
I have not slept.
Between the acting of a dreadful thing
And the first motion, all the interim is
65  Like a phantasma or a hideous dream.
The genius and the mortal instruments

**53–54 My ancestors . . . king:**
Brutus refers to his ancestor who drove out Rome's last king. After that, rule by the Senate was established.

**56–58 I make . . . Brutus:** I promise you, Rome, if a remedy for our troubles can follow from my action, you will get what you need from Brutus.

**61 whet me:** sharpen my appetite.

**63–69 Between . . . insurrection:**
The time between the earliest thought of a terrible act and the actual performance of it is a nightmare. The soul **(genius)** and body **(mortal instruments)** debate the subject, while the man himself feels like a kingdom undergoing a civil war. What is Brutus' internal conflict?

Are then in council, and the state of man,
Like to a little kingdom, suffers then
The nature of an insurrection.

[*Reenter* Lucius.]

70 **Lucius.** Sir, 'tis your brother Cassius at the door,
Who doth desire to see you.

**Brutus.**                    Is he alone?

**Lucius.** No, sir, there are more with him.

**Brutus.**                         Do you know them?

**Lucius.** No, sir. Their hats are plucked about their ears
And half their faces buried in their cloaks,
75 That by no means I may discover them
By any mark of favor.

**Brutus.**               Let 'em enter.

[*Exit* Lucius.]

They are the faction. O conspiracy,
Sham'st thou to show thy dang'rous brow by night,
When evils are most free? O, then by day
80 Where wilt thou find a cavern dark enough
To mask thy monstrous visage? Seek none,
   conspiracy,
Hide it in smiles and affability!
For if thou path, thy native semblance on,
No Erebus itself were dim enough
85 To hide thee from prevention.

[*Enter the conspirators,* Cassius, Casca, Decius, Cinna,
Metellus Cimber, *and* Trebonius.]

**Cassius.** I think we are too bold upon your rest.
Good morrow, Brutus. Do we trouble you?

**Brutus.** I have been up this hour, awake all night.
Know I these men that come along with you?

90 **Cassius.** Yes, every man of them; and no man here
But honors you; and every one doth wish
You had but that opinion of yourself
Which every noble Roman bears of you.
This is Trebonius.

**Brutus.**               He is welcome hither.

95 **Cassius.** This, Decius Brutus.

**Brutus.**                         He is welcome too.

**Cassius.** This, Casca; this, Cinna; and this, Metellus
Cimber.

**70 brother:** Cassius, the husband of Brutus' sister, is his brother-in-law.

**75–76 by no . . . favor:** There is no way I can tell who they are.

**77–85 O conspiracy . . . prevention:** If these plotters are afraid to be seen at night, how will they keep these terrible plans from showing on their faces during the day? They must smile and show friendliness **(affability)**. If they go out showing their true natures **(native semblance),** even the dark gateway to hell **(Erebus** ĕr′ ə bəs**)** couldn't hide them.

**86 I think . . . rest:** I think we may have come too early.

**Brutus.** They are all welcome.
What watchful cares do interpose themselves
Betwixt your eyes and night?

100 **Cassius.** Shall I entreat a word?

[*They whisper.*]

**Decius.** Here lies the east. Doth not the day break
here?

**Casca.** No.

**Cinna.** O, pardon, sir, it doth; and yon grey lines
That fret the clouds are messengers of day.

105 **Casca.** You shall confess that you are both deceived.
Here, as I point my sword, the sun arises,
Which is a great way growing on the south,
Weighing the youthful season of the year.
Some two months hence, up higher toward the north

110 He first presents his fire; and the high east
Stands as the Capitol, directly here.

[Brutus *and* Cassius *rejoin the others.*]

**Brutus.** Give me your hands all over, one by one.

**Cassius.** And let us swear our resolution.

**Brutus.** No, not on oath. If not the face of men,

115 The sufferance of our souls, the time's abuse—
If these be motives weak, break off betimes,
And every man hence to his idle bed.
So let high-sighted tyranny range on
Till each man drop by lottery. But if these

120 (As I am sure they do) bear fire enough
To kindle cowards and to steel with valor
The melting spirits of women, then, countrymen,
What need we any spur but our own cause
To prick us to redress? what other bond

125 Than secret Romans that have spoke the word
And will not palter? and what other oath
Than honesty to honesty engaged
That this shall be, or we will fall for it?
Swear priests and cowards and men cautelous,

130 Old feeble carrions and such suffering souls
That welcome wrongs; unto bad causes swear
Such creatures as men doubt; but do not stain
The even virtue of our enterprise,

**98–99 What watchful . . . night:** What troubles keep you awake at night?

**100 Shall I entreat a word?:** Cassius asks Brutus to step aside and talk privately with him. While they talk, the others chatter about the sky (lines 99–108), pretending to be not at all interested in what Cassius and Brutus are discussing.

**104 fret:** stripe.

**107–108 Which is . . . year:** from a southerly direction, since it is still early in the year.

**114–119 If not . . . lottery:** We do not need to swear our loyalty to one another. The sadness of people's faces, our own suffering, and the awful time we live in—if these aren't strong enough to hold us together, then let us all go back to bed. In that case, let tyranny live, while we die off, one at a time, by chance **(by lottery).**

**123–128** What does Brutus believe is even stronger than any oath the men could take together? Do you agree?

**126 palter:** go back on our word.

# VIEW AND COMPARE

Blocking—where characters stand in relation to each other and the set—is a crucial part of a director's job. Compare and contrast what these images suggest about the relationship between Brutus and the conspirators.

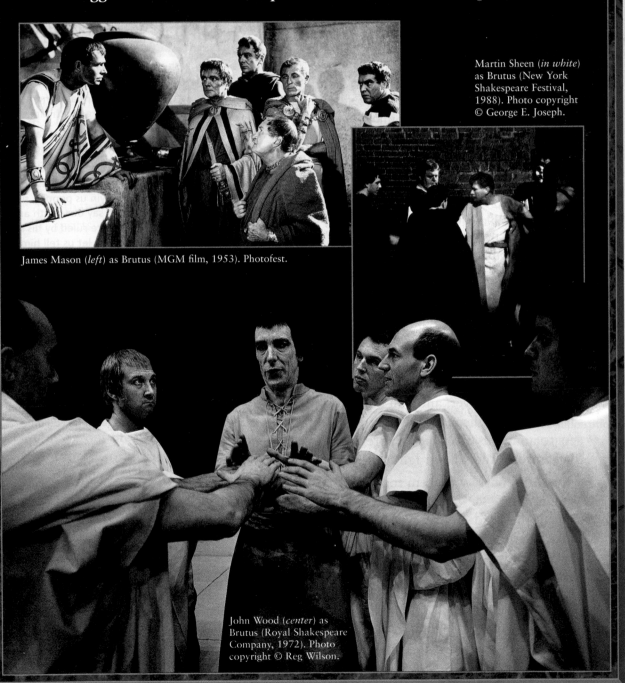

Martin Sheen (*in white*) as Brutus (New York Shakespeare Festival, 1988). Photo copyright © George E. Joseph.

James Mason (*left*) as Brutus (MGM film, 1953). Photofest.

John Wood (*center*) as Brutus (Royal Shakespeare Company, 1972). Photo copyright © Reg Wilson.

Let me work,
210 For I can give his humor the true bent,
And I will bring him to the Capitol.

**Cassius.** Nay, we will all of us be there to fetch him.

**Brutus.** By the eighth hour. Is that the uttermost?

**Cinna.** Be that the uttermost, and fail not then.

215 **Metellus.** Caius Ligarius doth bear Caesar hard,
Who rated him for speaking well of Pompey.
I wonder none of you have thought of him.

**Brutus.** Now, good Metellus, go along by him.
He loves me well, and I have given him reasons.
220 Send him but hither, and I'll fashion him.

**Cassius.** The morning comes upon's. We'll leave you,
Brutus.
And, friends, disperse yourselves; but all remember
What you have said and show yourselves true
Romans.

**Brutus.** Good gentlemen, look fresh and merrily.
225 Let not our looks put on our purposes,
But bear it as our Roman actors do,
With untired spirits and formal constancy.
And so good morrow to you every one.

[*Exeunt all but* Brutus.]

Boy! Lucius! Fast asleep? It is no matter.
230 Enjoy the honey-heavy dew of slumber.
Thou hast no figures nor no fantasies
Which busy care draws in the brains of men;
Therefore thou sleep'st so sound.

[*Enter* Portia, *Brutus' wife.*]

**Portia.**                              Brutus, my lord!

**Brutus.** Portia! What mean you? Wherefore rise you
now?
235 It is not for your health thus to commit
Your weak condition to the raw cold morning.

**Portia.** Nor for yours neither. Y'have ungently, Brutus,
Stole from my bed. And yesternight at supper
You suddenly arose and walked about,
240 Musing and sighing with your arms across;
And when I asked you what the matter was,
You stared upon me with ungentle looks.
I urged you further, then you scratched your head

**210 I can give . . . true bent:** I can get him into the right mood.

**213 By the . . . uttermost:** By eight o'clock. Do we all agree that eight is the latest we will be there?

**215–217 Caius . . . of him:** Caius Ligarius has a grudge against Caesar, who criticized him for supporting Pompey. I don't know why you haven't asked him to join our plot.

**220 fashion:** persuade.

**225 Let not . . . purposes:** Let's not let our appearances give away (**put on**) what we are planning to do.

**228** All the other conspirators leave, and Brutus is once again alone in his garden.

**233** As you read the conversation between Brutus and his wife, think about the kind of relationship they have.

And too impatiently stamped with your foot.
245 Yet I insisted, yet you answered not,
But with an angry wafture of your hand
Gave sign for me to leave you. So I did,
Fearing to strengthen that impatience
Which seemed too much enkindled, and withal
250 Hoping it was but an effect of humor,
Which sometime hath his hour with every man.
It will not let you eat nor talk nor sleep,
And could it work so much upon your shape
As it hath much prevailed on your condition,
255 I should not know you Brutus. Dear my lord,
Make me acquainted with your cause of grief.

**Brutus.** I am not well in health, and that is all.

**Portia.** Brutus is wise and, were he not in health,
He would embrace the means to come by it.

260 **Brutus.** Why, so I do. Good Portia, go to bed.

**Portia.** Is Brutus sick, and is it physical
To walk unbraced and suck up the humors
Of the dank morning? What, is Brutus sick,
And will he steal out of his wholesome bed
265 To dare the vile contagion of the night,
And tempt the rheumy and unpurgéd air,
To add unto his sickness? No, my Brutus.
You have some sick offense within your mind,
Which by the right and virtue of my place
270 I ought to know of; and upon my knees
I charm you, by my once commended beauty,
By all your vows of love, and that great vow
Which did incorporate and make us one,
That you unfold to me, yourself, your half,
275 Why you are heavy, and what men tonight
Have had resort to you; for here have been
Some six or seven, who did hide their faces
Even from darkness.

**Brutus.**                    Kneel not, gentle Portia.

**Portia.** I should not need if you were gentle Brutus.
280 Within the bond of marriage, tell me, Brutus,
Is it excepted I should know no secrets
That appertain to you? Am I yourself
But, as it were, in sort or limitation?
To keep with you at meals, comfort your bed,

245 **Yet:** still.
246 **wafture:** gesture.

249 **withal:** also.
250 **humor:** mood.

253–255 **And could . . . you Brutus:**
If a mood like that could change
your appearance **(shape)** the way
it changes your personality
**(condition),** I would not recognize
you.
257 Why do you think Brutus lies
to Portia?

261–267 **Is Brutus . . . sickness:**
Do you expect me to believe that
you're sick? Is it healthy to walk
without a coat **(unbraced)** and
breathe the air of a damp morning
or the unhealthy night air that is
not yet cleansed **(unpurged)** by
the sun?

268–270 **You have . . . know of:**
You have a sickness of the mind; as
your wife, I have a right to know
what it is.

275 **heavy:** sad.

282 **appertain:** relate.
283 **in sort or limitation:** only
in part.

*"Tell me your counsels;
I will not disclose 'em."*

Martin Sheen as Brutus and Joan MacIntosh as Portia (New York Shakespeare Festival, 1988).
Photo by Martha Swope, copyright © Time Inc.

285　　　And talk to you sometimes? Dwell I but in the
　　　　　　suburbs
　　　　　Of your good pleasure? If it be no more,
　　　　　Portia is Brutus' harlot, not his wife.

　　　**Brutus.** You are my true and honorable wife,
　　　　　As dear to me as are the ruddy drops
290　　　That visit my sad heart.

289–290 the ruddy . . . heart: my blood.

　　　**Portia.** If this were true, then should I know this
　　　　　　secret.
　　　　　I grant I am a woman, but withal
　　　　　A woman that Lord Brutus took to wife.
　　　　　I grant that I am a woman, but withal
295　　　A woman well reputed, Cato's daughter.
　　　　　Think you I am no stronger than my sex,
　　　　　Being so fathered and so husbanded?
　　　　　Tell me your counsels; I will not disclose 'em.
　　　　　I have made strong proof of my constancy,
300　　　Giving myself a voluntary wound
　　　　　Here, in the thigh. Can I bear that with patience,
　　　　　And not my husband's secrets?

296–302 Think you . . . secrets: How can you consider me merely a typical woman, when I am the daughter of Cato (a highly respected Roman) and the wife of Brutus? So tell me your secret. I have proven my strength by wounding myself here in the thigh. If I can put up with that pain, I can certainly deal with my husband's secrets. Should Brutus tell Portia his secret?

　　　**Brutus.**　　　　　　　　　　O ye gods,
　　　　　Render me worthy of this noble wife!
　　　[*Knocking within.*]
　　　　　Hark, hark! one knocks. Portia, go in awhile,
305　　　And by-and-by thy bosom shall partake
　　　　　The secrets of my heart.
　　　　　All my engagements I will construe to thee,
　　　　　All the charactery of my sad brows.
　　　　　Leave me with haste.
　　　[*Exit* Portia.]
　　　　　　　　　　　Lucius, who's that knocks?

307–308 All may . . . brows: I will explain all my dealings and the reason for my sad looks.

　　　[*Reenter* Lucius *with* Caius Ligarius.]

310　　　**Lucius.** Here is a sick man that would speak with you.

　　　**Brutus.** Caius Ligarius, that Metellus spake of.
　　　　　Boy, stand aside. Caius Ligarius, how?

　　　**Caius.** Vouchsafe good morrow from a feeble tongue.

313 Vouchsafe . . . tongue: Accept a good morning from a sick man.

　　　**Brutus.** O, what a time have you chose out, brave
　　　　　　Caius,
315　　　To wear a kerchief! Would you were not sick!

315 kerchief: a covering to protect the head during sickness.

　　　**Caius.** I am not sick if Brutus have in hand
　　　　　Any exploit worthy the name of honor.

**Brutus.** Such an exploit have I in hand, Ligarius,
    Had you a healthful ear to hear of it.

320 **Caius.** By all the gods that Romans bow before,
    I here discard my sickness! Soul of Rome!
    Brave son, derived from honorable loins!
    Thou like an exorcist has conjured up
    My mortified spirit. Now bid me run,
325    And I will strive with things impossible;
    Yea, get the better of them. What's to do?

**Brutus.** A piece of work that will make sick men
        whole.

**Caius.** But are not some whole that we must make
        sick?

**Brutus.** That must we also. What it is, my Caius,
330    I shall unfold to thee as we are going
    To whom it must be done.

**Caius.**                         Set on your foot,
    And with a heart new-fired I follow you,
    To do I know not what; but it sufficeth
    That Brutus leads me on.

[*Thunder.*]

**Brutus.**                         Follow me then.

[*Exeunt.*]

**318 exploit:** deed.

**321 I here discard my sickness!:** I declare myself cured.

**322 derived . . . loins:** descended from noble Romans.

**323 exorcist:** someone who can call up spirits.

**328** What does Caius mean?

**331 Set on your foot:** Lead the way.

**333 it sufficeth:** It is enough.

# SCENE 2     CAESAR'S HOUSE IN ROME.

*It is now past dawn on March 15. Like everyone else in Rome, Caesar and his wife have slept badly because of the storm. There is still some lightning and thunder. Caesar prepares to go to the Capitol, but because of the many threatening omens, his wife Calpurnia insists that he stay home. Caesar agrees, for Calpurnia's sake. He changes his mind when Decius, one of the conspirators, persuades him that he must not seem swayed by his wife's superstitions. Although Caesar doesn't know it, the other conspirators are on their way to his house to make sure he does not decide to stay at home.*

[*Enter* Caesar *in his nightgown.*]

**Caesar.** Nor heaven nor earth have been at peace
        tonight.
    Thrice hath Calpurnia in her sleep cried out

"Help, ho! They murder Caesar!" Who's within?

[*Enter a* Servant.]

**Servant.** My lord?

5   **Caesar.** Go bid the priests do present sacrifice,
    And bring me their opinions of success.

**Servant.** I will, my lord.

[*Exit.*]

[*Enter Caesar's wife,* Calpurnia, *alarmed.*]

**Calpurnia.** What mean you, Caesar? Think you to
    walk forth?
    You shall not stir out of your house today.

10  **Caesar.** Caesar shall forth. The things that threatened me
    Ne'er looked but on my back. When they shall see
    The face of Caesar, they are vanished.

**Calpurnia.** Caesar, I never stood on ceremonies,
    Yet now they fright me. There is one within,
15  Besides the things that we have heard and seen,
    Recounts most horrid sights seen by the watch.
    A lioness hath whelped in the streets,
    And graves have yawned and yielded up their dead.
    Fierce fiery warriors fought upon the clouds
20  In ranks and squadrons and right form of war,
    Which drizzled blood upon the Capitol.
    The noise of battle hurtled in the air,
    Horses did neigh, and dying men did groan,
    And ghosts did shriek and squeal about the streets.
25  O Caesar, these things are beyond all use,
    And I do fear them!

**Caesar.**                  What can be avoided
    Whose end is purposed by the mighty gods?
    Yet Caesar shall go forth, for these predictions
    Are to the world in general as to Caesar.

30  **Calpurnia.** When beggars die there are no comets seen;
    The heavens themselves blaze forth the death of
        princes.

**Caesar.** Cowards die many times before their deaths;
    The valiant never taste of death but once.
    Of all the wonders that I yet have heard,
35  It seems to me most strange that men should fear,
    Seeing that death, a necessary end,
    Will come when it will come.

**5–6 Go bid . . . success:** Roman priests would kill an animal as a sacrifice to the gods. Then they would cut the animal open and examine its internal organs for signs of future events.

**10–56** As you read this conversation, think about Caesar's view of himself. Remember the way he talked of himself to Antony in Act One. Look for new evidence of Caesar's view of his own importance and his power.

**10–12 The things . . . vanished:** When I turn to face the things that threaten me, they disappear.

**13–26 Caesar, I never . . . fear them:** Calpurnia tells Caesar that she has never before believed in omens **(stood on ceremonies),** but now she is frightened. She describes the terrible things she has heard of from the men who were on guard during the night.

**25 beyond all use:** unlike anything we are accustomed to.

**26–29** Caesar insists that, if these are omens and if the gods have destined that certain things will happen, no one can avoid them. He will go out, since the predictions, he believes, apply to the whole world, not only to Caesar.

[*Reenter* Servant.]

What say the augurers?

**Servant.** They would not have you to stir forth today.
Plucking the entrails of an offering forth,
40 They could not find a heart within the beast.

**Caesar.** The gods do this in shame of cowardice.
Caesar should be a beast without a heart
If he should stay at home today for fear.
No, Caesar shall not. Danger knows full well
45 That Caesar is more dangerous than he.
We are two lions littered in one day,
And I the elder and more terrible,
And Caesar shall go forth.

**Calpurnia.**                    Alas, my lord!
Your wisdom is consumed in confidence.
50 Do not go forth today. Call it my fear
That keeps you in the house and not your own.
We'll send Mark Antony to the Senate House,
And he shall say you are not well today.
Let me upon my knee prevail in this.

55 **Caesar.** Mark Antony shall say I am not well,
And for thy humor I will stay at home.
[*Enter* Decius.]
Here's Decius Brutus, he shall tell them so.

**Decius.** Caesar, all hail! Good morrow, worthy Caesar!
I come to fetch you to the Senate House.

60 **Caesar.** And you are come in very happy time
To bear my greetings to the senators
And tell them that I will not come today.
Cannot, is false; and that I dare not, falser.
I will not come today. Tell them so, Decius.

65 **Calpurnia.** Say he is sick.

**Caesar.**                    Shall Caesar send a lie?
Have I in conquest stretched mine arm so far
To be afeard to tell greybeards the truth?
Decius, go tell them Caesar will not come.

**Decius.** Most mighty Caesar, let me know some cause,
70 Lest I be laughed at when I tell them so.

**Caesar.** The cause is in my will: I will not come.
That is enough to satisfy the Senate;
But for your private satisfaction,

**46 littered in one day:** born at the same time.

**65–68 Shall . . . not come:** Caesar is appalled by his wife's suggestion that he lie to a bunch of old men (**greybeards**) about his reason for not going to the Senate. How might an actor say these lines?

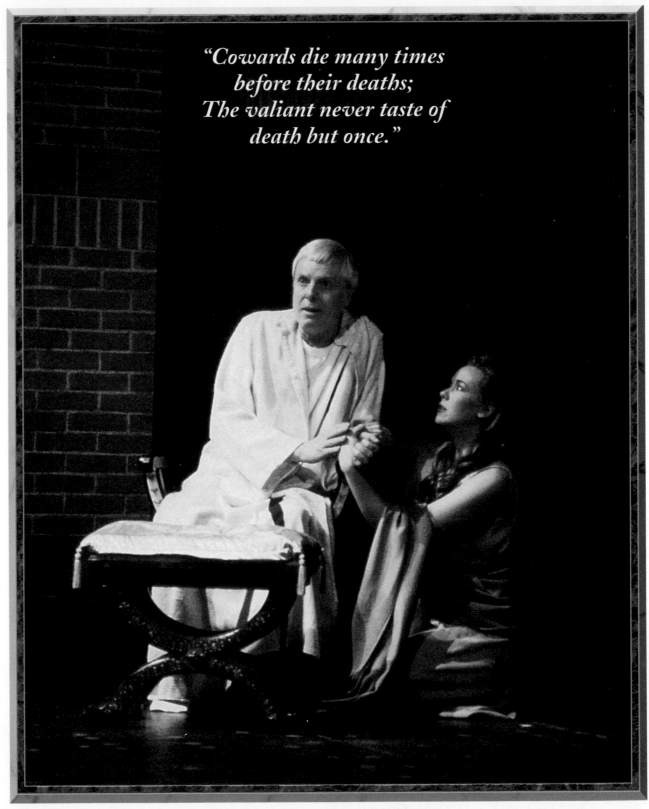

*"Cowards die many times before their deaths; The valiant never taste of death but once."*

John McMartin as Caesar and Harriet Harris as Calpurnia (New York Shakespeare Festival, 1988). Photo by Martha Swope, copyright © Time Inc.

Because I love you, I will let you know.
75 Calpurnia here, my wife, stays me at home.
She dreamt tonight she saw my statue,
Which, like a fountain with an hundred spouts,
Did run pure blood, and many lusty Romans
Came smiling and did bathe their hands in it.
80 And these does she apply for warnings and portents
And evils imminent, and on her knee
Hath begged that I will stay at home today.

**Decius.** This dream is all amiss interpreted;
It was a vision fair and fortunate.
85 Your statue spouting blood in many pipes,
In which so many smiling Romans bathed,
Signifies that from you great Rome shall suck
Reviving blood, and that great men shall press
For tinctures, stains, relics, and cognizance.
90 This by Calpurnia's dream is signified.

**Caesar.** And this way have you well expounded it.

**Decius.** I have, when you have heard what I can say:
And know it now, the Senate have concluded
To give this day a crown to mighty Caesar.
95 If you shall send them word you will not come,
Their minds may change. Besides, it were a mock
Apt to be rendered, for some one to say
"Break up the Senate till another time,
When Caesar's wife shall meet with better dreams."
100 If Caesar hide himself, shall they not whisper
"Lo, Caesar is afraid"?
Pardon me, Caesar, for my dear dear love
To your proceeding bids me tell you this,
And reason to my love is liable.

105 **Caesar.** How foolish do your fears seem now,
    Calpurnia!
I am ashamed I did yield to them.
Give me my robe, for I will go.

[*Enter* Brutus, Ligarius, Metellus, Casca, Trebonius, Cinna, *and* Publius.]

And look where Publius is come to fetch me.

**Publius.** Good morrow, Caesar.

**Caesar.**                               Welcome Publius.
110 What Brutus, are you stirred so early too?
Good morrow, Casca. Caius Ligarius,

**80 portents:** signs of evil to come.

**83–90** Decius has to think fast. He promised the others that he could flatter Caesar into believing anything. Now he must give Caesar a new interpretation of Calpurnia's dream, one that will get him out of the house.

**83 amiss:** wrongly.

**88–89 great men . . . cognizance:** Great men will come to you for honors and souvenirs to remember you by.

**96–97 it were . . . rendered:** It's likely that someone will make a sarcastic comment.

**102–104 my dear . . . liable:** My sincere interest in your career (**proceeding**) makes me tell you this. My feeling for you overtakes my intelligence (**reason**). What arguments does Decius use to change Caesar's mind?

Caesar was ne'er so much your enemy
As that same ague which hath made you lean.
What is't o'clock?

**113 ague:** sickness.

**Brutus.**                    Caesar, 'tis strucken eight.

115  **Caesar.** I thank you for your pains and courtesy.

[*Enter* Antony.]

See! Antony, that revels long o'nights,
Is notwithstanding up. Good morrow, Antony.

**116–117 Antony . . . up:** Even Antony, who parties (**revels**) late into the night, is up early today.

**Antony.** So to most noble Caesar.

**Caesar.**                              Bid them prepare within.
I am to blame to be thus waited for.
120  Now, Cinna, now, Metellus. What, Trebonius!
I have an hour's talk in store for you;
Remember that you call on me today;
Be near me, that I may remember you.

**Trebonius.** Caesar, I will. [*Aside.*] And so near will I be

**124 Aside:** privately, in a way that keeps the other characters from hearing what is said. Think of it as a whisper that the audience happens to overhear.

125  That your best friends shall wish I had been further.

**Caesar.** Good friends, go in and taste some wine with
    me,
And we (like friends) will straightway go together.

**Brutus.** [*Aside.*] That every like is not the same, O
    Caesar,
The heart of Brutus yearns to think upon.

**128–129 That every . . . upon:** The fact that we behave like friends doesn't mean we are friends. My heart grieves (**yearns**) to think of it. What is Brutus saying about his friendship with Caesar?

[*Exeunt.*]

# SCENE 3   A STREET IN ROME NEAR THE CAPITOL.

*In this brief scene, Caesar has still another chance to avoid the path that
leads to his death. Artemidorus, a supporter of Caesar, has learned
about the plot. He reads a letter he has written to warn Caesar. Then he
waits in the street for Caesar to pass by on his way to the Capitol.*

[*Enter* Artemidorus, *reading a paper.*]

**Artemidorus.** "Caesar, beware of Brutus; take heed of
    Cassius; come not near Casca; have an eye to Cinna;
    trust not Trebonius; mark well Metellus Cimber;
    Decius Brutus loves thee not; thou hast wronged Caius
5    Ligarius. There is but one mind in all these men,

and it is bent against Caesar. If thou beest not immortal, look about you. Security gives way to conspiracy. The mighty gods defend thee!

9 **Lover:** devoted friend.

"Thy Lover,
"ARTEMIDORUS."

10 Here will I stand till Caesar pass along
And as a suitor will I give him this.
My heart laments that virtue cannot live
Out of the teeth of emulation.

13–14 **My heart . . . emulation:** My heart is sad that Caesar's greatness cannot escape jealousy (**the teeth of emulation**).
16 **contrive:** plot.

15 If thou read this, O Caesar, thou mayst live;
If not, the Fates with traitors do contrive.

[*Exit.*]

# SCENE 4   IN FRONT OF BRUTUS' HOUSE.

*Shakespeare continues to build suspense with another short scene. This one involves Brutus' wife, Portia, who feels anxious about the conspiracy. Portia nervously orders the servant Lucius to go and see what is happening at the Capitol. She next meets the Soothsayer, who makes her even more anxious as he continues to predict danger for Caesar.*

[*Enter* Portia *and* Lucius.]

**Portia.** I prithee, boy, run to the Senate House.
    Stay not to answer me, but get thee gone!
    Why dost thou stay?

**Lucius.**             To know my errand, madam.

**Portia.** I would have had thee there and here again
5     Ere I can tell thee what thou shouldst do there.
    O constancy, be strong upon my side,
    Set a huge mountain 'tween my heart and tongue!
    I have a man's mind, but a woman's might.
    How hard it is for women to keep counsel!
10     Art thou here yet?

**Lucius.**            Madam, what should I do?
    Run to the Capitol and nothing else?
    And so return to you and nothing else?

**Portia.** Yes, bring me word, boy, if thy lord look well,
    For he went sickly forth; and take good note
15     What Caesar doth, what suitors press to him.
    Hark, boy! What noise is that?

4–5 **I would have . . . do there:** I would have had you travel there and back without telling you what I wanted you to do. (Portia is upset with herself for acting foolishly.)

9 **keep counsel:** keep a secret.
What do you think of Portia's (or Shakespeare's) statement that it is hard for a woman to keep a secret?

15 **what suitors press to him:** what people stand near him.

**Lucius.** I hear none, madam.

**Portia.**                    Prithee, listen well.
   I heard a bustling rumor like a fray,
   And the wind brings it from the Capitol.

20  **Lucius.** Sooth, madam, I hear nothing.

[*Enter the* Soothsayer.]

**Portia.** Come hither, fellow. Which way hast thou
      been?

**Soothsayer.** At mine own house, good lady.

**Portia.** What is't o'clock?

**Soothsayer.**                    About the ninth hour, lady.

**Portia.** Is Caesar yet gone to the Capitol?

25  **Soothsayer.** Madam, not yet. I go to take my stand,
   To see him pass on to the Capitol.

**Portia.** Thou hast some suit to Caesar, hast thou not?

**Soothsayer.** That I have, lady. If it will please Caesar
   To be so good to Caesar as to hear me,
30  I shall beseech him to befriend himself.

**Portia.** Why, know'st thou any harm's intended
      towards him?

**Soothsayer.** None that I know will be, much that I
      fear may chance.
   Good morrow to you. Here the street is narrow.
   The throng that follows Caesar at the heels,
35  Of senators, of praetors, common suitors,
   Will crowd a feeble man almost to death.
   I'll get me to a place more void and there
   Speak to great Caesar as he comes along.

[*Exit.*]

**Portia.** I must go in. Ay me, how weak a thing
40  The heart of woman is! O Brutus,
   The heavens speed thee in thine enterprise—
   Sure the boy heard me.—Brutus hath a suit
   That Caesar will not grant.—O, I grow faint.—
   Run, Lucius, and commend me to my Lord;
45  Say I am merry. Come to me again
   And bring me word what he doth say to thee.

[*Exeunt severally.*]

---

**18 I heard . . . fray:** Portia imagines that she has heard a noise like a battle (**fray**).

**20 Sooth:** truthfully.

**21** The Soothsayer is the same fortuneteller who warned Caesar to beware the ides of March. He is now on his way to the street near the Capitol building where he usually sits.

**27 Thou hast . . . Caesar:** Have you some favor to ask of Caesar?

**32 None . . . chance:** I'm not sure of any danger, but I fear that some may chance to happen.

**42–43 Brutus hath . . . not grant:** Brutus has a favor to ask that Caesar will not give him.

**44 commend . . . Lord:** Give my husband my good wishes.

**severally:** in different directions.

# VIEW AND COMPARE

**What do these photos suggest about Portia and her relationship to Brutus? Which one comes closest to your own understanding of their relationship?**

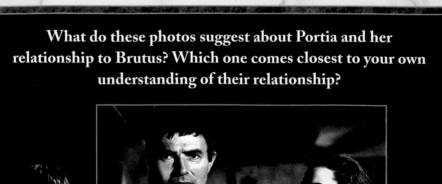

James Mason as Brutus and Deborah Kerr as Portia (MGM film, 1953). Hulton Getty/Liaison Agency.

Marti Maraden as Portia and Brian Bedford as Brutus (Stratford Festival, 1990). Photo by David Cooper.

Joan MacIntosh as Portia and Martin Sheen as Brutus (New York Shakespeare Festival, 1988). Photo copyright © George E. Joseph.

## Connect to the Literature

1. **What Do You Think?** Whom do you side with at this point, Caesar or the conspirators? Why?

**Comprehension Check**
- What does Brutus decide in the orchard?
- What does Brutus promise Portia?
- What omens does Calpurnia mention to Caesar in an effort to warn him?

## Think Critically

2. Think about Brutus' reasoning, set forth in Act Two, Scene 1, about why Caesar must die. Do you find his argument convincing? Explain your opinion.

3. Do the **details** in Act Two cause you to change your opinion of Caesar? Why or why not?

**THINK ABOUT**
- his actions and appearance
- his remarks about himself and others
- other **characters'** remarks about him

4. Who do you think would make a better replacement for Caesar as leader of Rome, Brutus or Cassius? Support your opinion.

5. Contrast the relationship between Caesar and Calpurnia with the relationship between Brutus and Portia. What do the differences suggest about the character of the two men?

6. How would you describe Portia's emotional state in Act Two, Scene 4? What effect might it be intended to have on the **audience**?

7. **ACTIVE READING** **READING SHAKESPEAREAN DRAMA**
Revisit your chart in your **READER'S NOTEBOOK**. What changes or additions did you make—or would you now like to make—based on your reading of Act Two?

## Extend Interpretations

8. **Critic's Corner** Try to visualize Act Two as it might be performed on stage. What special effects do you imagine? How do you think the audience would react to them?

9. **Connect to Life** Imagine that you are Portia. What advice would you have for Brutus?

## Literary Analysis

**SOLILOQUY/ASIDE** In real life, people don't usually make speeches when no one is listening or whisper loudly and expect not to be heard. On stage, however, an audience needs to accept certain conventions as realistic, even though they are not the way real people behave. A **soliloquy** is a long speech that a **character** makes while alone on stage or when no one on stage is supposed to be listening. An **aside** is a remark that a character says in an undertone to the audience or to another character but that everyone else on stage is not supposed to hear. Shakespeare uses both devices to reveal characters' thoughts to the audience.

**Activity** Identify the soliloquies and asides in Act Two. Also explain what each soliloquy or aside reveals about the character who speaks it. You might want to make use of a chart similar to the following to organize the information.

| Scene and Line Nos. | |
|---|---|
| Character Who Speaks It | |
| Soliloquy or Aside? | |
| What It Reveals About the Character | |

**REVIEW** **FIGURATIVE LANGUAGE**
In Act Two, Scene 2, Caesar says, "Cowards die many times before their deaths; / The valiant never taste of death but once." What do you think this remark means? Do you agree with it? Explain.

# ACT THREE

## SCENE 1 THE CAPITOL IN ROME.

*Outside the Capitol, Caesar refuses to look at Artemidorus' letter of warning. Caesar next moves into the Capitol. There, the conspirators surround him, pretending to plead a case. Suddenly, they stab him to death. Mark Antony flees, but Brutus persuades the conspirators to let him live. Brutus himself promises to explain the killing and its reasons to the Roman people. Antony returns and pretends to be an ally of the conspirators. Secretly, however, he plans to strike back with help from Octavius Caesar, who is now on his way to Rome.*

[*The Senate sits on a higher level, waiting for* Caesar *to appear.* Artemidorus *and the* Soothsayer *are among the crowd. A flourish of trumpets. Enter* Caesar, Brutus, Cassius, Casca, Decius, Metellus, Trebonius, Cinna, Antony, Lepidus, Popilius, *and others.* Caesar *stops in front of the* Soothsayer.]

**Caesar.** The ides of March are come.

**Soothsayer.** Ay, Caesar, but not gone.

[Artemidorus *steps up to* Caesar *with his warning.*]

**Artemidorus.** Hail, Caesar! Read this schedule.

[Decius *steps up quickly with another paper.*]

**Decius.** Trebonius doth desire you to o'erread
5     (At your best leisure) this his humble suit.

**Artemidorus.** O Caesar, read mine first, for mine's a suit
    That touches Caesar nearer. Read it, great Caesar!

**Caesar.** What touches us ourself shall be last served.

[Caesar *pushes the paper aside and turns away.*]

**Artemidorus.** Delay not, Caesar! Read it instantly!

10 **Caesar.** What, is the fellow mad?

**Publius.**                 Sirrah, give place.

**3 schedule:** document.
**4–13** Artemidorus is the man who has prepared a written warning for Caesar to read **(o'erread)** about the men plotting against him. The conspirators suspect this and do not want him to get to Caesar. Decius steps in front of Artemidorus and offers a written request from someone else. Then Publius (who is not a conspirator) and Cassius push Artemidorus aside.
**10 Sirrah:** a form of address used toward a servant or inferior, often to express anger or disrespect; **give place:** get out of the way.

[*Publius and the conspirators force* Artemidorus *away from* Caesar.]

**Cassius.** What, urge you your petitions in the street?
    Come to the Capitol.

[Caesar *goes into the Senate House, the rest following.*
Popilius *speaks to* Cassius *in a low voice.*]

**Popilius.** I wish your enterprise today may thrive.

**Cassius.** What enterprise, Popilius?

**Popilius.**                        Fare you well.

[*Advances to* Caesar.]

15  **Brutus.** What said Popilius Lena?

**Cassius.** He wished today our enterprise might thrive.
    I fear our purpose is discovered.

**Brutus.** Look how he makes to Caesar. Mark him.

**Cassius.** Casca, be sudden, for we fear prevention.
20     Brutus, what shall be done? If this be known,
    Cassius or Caesar never shall turn back,
    For I will slay myself.

**Brutus.**                 Cassius, be constant.
    Popilius Lena speaks not of our purposes,
    For look, he smiles, and Caesar doth not change.

25  **Cassius.** Trebonius knows his time, for look you, Brutus,
    He draws Mark Antony out of the way.

[*Exeunt* Antony *and* Trebonius.]

**Decius.** Where is Metellus Cimber? Let him go
    And presently prefer his suit to Caesar.

**Brutus.** He is addressed. Press near and second him.

30  **Cinna.** Casca, you are the first that rears your hand.

[Caesar *seats himself in his high Senate chair.*]

**Caesar.** Are we all ready? What is now amiss
    That Caesar and his Senate must redress?

**Metellus.** Most high, most mighty, and most puissant
      Caesar,
    Metellus Cimber throws before thy seat
35     An humble heart.

[*Kneeling.*]

**Caesar.**              I must prevent thee, Cimber.
    These couchings and these lowly courtesies
    Might fire the blood of ordinary men

**13 I wish . . . thrive:** I hope your
venture is successful.

**18–24 Look how . . . change:**
Brutus and Cassius watch Popilius
Lena talk privately with Caesar.
They fear he is telling Caesar of
their plot. Then, seeing Popilius
Lena smile, they know they were
mistaken.

**28 prefer . . . Caesar:** ask his favor
of Caesar.

**29 Press . . . him:** Get near him
(Metellus Cimber) and back up his
request.

**33 puissant:** powerful.

And turn preordinance and first decree
Into the law of children. Be not fond
40  To think that Caesar bears such rebel blood
That will be thawed from the true quality
With that which melteth fools—I mean, sweet words,
Low-crookèd curtsies, and base spaniel fawning.
Thy brother by decree is banished.
45  If thou dost bend and pray and fawn for him,
I spurn thee like a cur out of my way.
Know, Caesar doth not wrong, nor without cause
Will he be satisfied.

**Metellus.** Is there no voice more worthy than my own,
50  To sound more sweetly in great Caesar's ear
For the repealing of my banished brother?

**Brutus.** I kiss thy hand, but not in flattery, Caesar,
Desiring thee that Publius Cimber may
Have an immediate freedom of repeal.

55  **Caesar.** What, Brutus?

**Cassius.**                    Pardon, Caesar! Caesar, pardon!
As low as to thy foot doth Cassius fall
To beg enfranchisement for Publius Cimber.

**Caesar.** I could be well moved, if I were as you;
If I could pray to move, prayers would move me;
60  But I am constant as the Northern Star,
Of whose true-fixed and resting quality
There is no fellow in the firmament.
The skies are painted with unnumbered sparks,
They are all fire, and every one doth shine;
65  But there's but one in all doth hold his place.
So in the world: 'tis furnished well with men.
And men are flesh and blood, and apprehensive,
Yet in the number I do not know but one
That unassailable holds on his rank,
70  Unshaked of motion; and that I am he,
Let me a little show it, even in this,
That I was constant Cimber should be banished
And constant do remain to keep him so.

**Cinna.** O Caesar!

**Caesar.**                    Hence! Wilt thou lift up Olympus?

75  **Decius.** Great Caesar!

**Caesar.**                    Doth not Brutus bootless kneel?

**Casca.** Speak hands for me!

**35–48  I must prevent . . . satisfied:**
Caesar claims that, unlike ordinary men, he cannot be moved by bowing and scraping. He will not let such things change the laws of the country (**preordinance and first decree**). His heart cannot be melted by sweet words, bowing (**curtsies**), and behavior fit for a dog (**base spaniel fawning**). Metellus Cimber's brother, Caesar says, has been banished by law. Begging won't change that. Does Caesar evaluate his own personality correctly?

**54  freedom of repeal:** the right to return to Rome from exile.

**55–57** Caesar is surprised that Brutus would beg for freedom (**enfranchisement**) for Publius Cimber. Actually, Brutus, like the rest of the conspirators, is only looking for an excuse to carry out their plan.

**58–74  I could be . . . Olympus:**
Caesar says he is too strong to be moved by begging, even when it comes from these respected men. He compares himself to the North Star, which sailors use for direction because it always appears at the same place in the sky. Like that star, Caesar says, which has no equal in the sky (**fellow in the firmament**), he cannot be moved. They might as well try to lift Mount Olympus (the mountain where the Greek gods were believed to live). Is Caesar bragging?

**75  Doth not . . . kneel:** Can't you see that even Brutus' kneeling doesn't sway me? **Bootless** means "without any effect," like a kick from a foot that has no boot.

[*They stab* Caesar. Casca, *the others in turn, then* Brutus.]

**Caesar.** *Et tu, Brute?*—Then fall Caesar!

[*Dies.*]

77 *Et tu, Brute?*: Even you, Brutus?

**Cinna.** Liberty! Freedom! Tyranny is dead!
Run hence, proclaim, cry it about the streets!

80  **Cassius.** Some to the common pulpits and cry out
"Liberty, freedom, and enfranchisement!"

**Brutus.** People and Senators, be not affrighted.
Fly not; stand still. Ambition's debt is paid.

**Casca.** Go to the pulpit, Brutus.

**Decius.**                   And Cassius, too.

85  **Brutus.** Where's Publius?

**Cinna.** Here, quite confounded with this mutiny.

**Metellus.** Stand fast together, lest some friend of Caesar's
Should chance—

80 Some . . . pulpits: Some of you go to the speakers' platforms. The scene is now chaos—people yelling, screaming, and running in fear. Cassius and Brutus are trying to avoid a riot.

"*Liberty, freedom, and enfranchisement!*"

Edward Herrmann as Cassius (New York Shakespeare Festival, 1988).
Photo copyright © George E. Joseph.

**Brutus.** Talk not of standing! Publius, good cheer.
90  There is no harm intended to your person
Nor to no Roman else. So tell them, Publius.

**Cassius.** And leave us, Publius, lest that the people,
Rushing on us, should do your age some mischief.

**92–93 leave . . . mischief:** Cassius wants Publius, an old man, to leave before he gets hurt by the crowd.
**94 abide:** suffer for.

**Brutus.** Do so, and let no man abide this deed
95  But we the doers.

[*Reenter* Trebonius.]

**Cassius.**                  Where is Antony?

**Trebonius.** Fled to his house amazed.
Men, wives, and children stare, cry out, and run,
As it were doomsday.

**Brutus.**                  Fates, we will know your pleasures.
That we shall die, we know; 'tis but the time,
100  And drawing days out, that men stand upon.

**Cassius.** Why, he that cuts off twenty years of life
Cuts off so many years of fearing death.

**Brutus.** Grant that, and then is death a benefit.
So are we Caesar's friends, that have abridged
105  His time of fearing death. Stoop, Romans, stoop,
And let us bathe our hands in Caesar's blood
Up to the elbows and besmear our swords.
Then walk we forth, even to the market place,
And waving our red weapons o'er our heads,
110  Let's all cry, "Peace, freedom, and liberty!"

**105–110** Brutus leads the others in covering themselves with Caesar's blood. He wants the Romans to think of their act as a public one, an act they are not trying to hide.

**Cassius.** Stoop then and wash. How many ages hence
Shall this our lofty scene be acted over
In states unborn and accents yet unknown!

**Brutus.** How many times shall Caesar bleed in sport,
115  That now on Pompey's basis lies along
No worthier than the dust!

**111–114 How many . . . sport:** This scene will often be performed as a play in the future in countries and languages that don't even exist now. Why do you think Shakespeare added this line?

**115 Pompey's basis:** the foot of Pompey's statue.

**Cassius.**                  So oft as that shall be.
So often shall the knot of us be called
The men that gave their country liberty.

**Decius.** What, shall we forth?

**Cassius.**                  Ay, every man away.
120  Brutus shall lead, and we will grace his heels
With the most boldest and best hearts of Rome.

[*Enter a* Servant.]

**Brutus.** Soft! who comes here? A friend of Antony's.

**Servant.** Thus, Brutus, did my master bid me kneel;
Thus did Mark Antony bid me fall down;

125 And being prostrate, thus he bade me say:
Brutus is noble, wise, valiant, and honest;
Caesar was mighty, bold, royal, and loving.
Say I love Brutus and I honor him;
Say I feared Caesar, honored him, and loved him.

130 If Brutus will vouchsafe that Antony
May safely come to him and be resolved
How Caesar hath deserved to lie in death,
Mark Antony shall not love Caesar dead
So well as Brutus living, but will follow

135 The fortunes and affairs of noble Brutus
Through the hazards of this untrod state
With all true faith. So says my master Antony.

**Brutus.** Thy master is a wise and valiant Roman.
I never thought him worse.

140 Tell him, so please him come unto this place,
He shall be satisfied and, by my honor,
Depart untouched.

**Servant.**                    I'll fetch him presently.

[*Exit.*]

**Brutus.** I know that we shall have him well to friend.

**Cassius.** I wish we may. But yet have I a mind

145 That fears him much; and my misgiving still
Falls shrewdly to the purpose.

[*Reenter* Antony.]

**Brutus.** But here comes Antony. Welcome, Mark
Antony.

**Antony.** O mighty Caesar! Dost thou lie so low?
Are all thy conquests, glories, triumphs, spoils,

150 Shrunk to this little measure? Fare thee well.
I know not, gentlemen, what you intend,
Who else must be let blood, who else is rank.
If I myself, there is no hour so fit
As Caesar's death's hour; nor no instrument

155 Of half that worth as those your swords, made rich
With the most noble blood of all this world.
I do beseech ye, if you bear me hard,
Now, whilst your purpled hands do reek and smoke,
Fulfill your pleasure. Live a thousand years,

160 I shall not find myself so apt to die;

**123–136** Fearful for his own life, Antony sends a message with his servant. Lying face down on the floor **(being prostrate)**, the servant begs for assurance that Brutus will promise **(vouchsafe)** Antony's safety so that he may come and be given an explanation **(be resolved)** for Caesar's murder. Then Antony will agree to follow Brutus through the dangers of this new, untried government **(the hazards of this untrod state)**.

**140–142** What promise does Brutus tell the servant to relay to Antony?

**142 presently:** immediately.

**144–146 But yet . . . purpose:** Unlike Brutus, Cassius doesn't trust Antony. He adds that his doubts **(misgiving)** in matters like this are usually accurate. Who do you think is right, Cassius or Brutus?

**148–163** The sight of Caesar's body causes Antony to break down. Keep in mind that he truly loved Caesar, almost as a son loves his father.

**152–163 Who else . . . this age:** Who else is so diseased **(rank)** that he must be "cured" by the knives of the men who just killed Caesar? Antony says he would be honored to be killed at the same time, with the same weapons, and by the same blood-stained **(purpled)** hands that killed Caesar. He adds that the honor would come partly from being killed by such great men **(the choice and master spirits of this age)**. Do you believe that Antony is being honest here?

No place will please me so, no mean of death,
As here by Caesar, and by you cut off,
The choice and master spirits of this age.

**Brutus.** O Antony, beg not your death of us!
165     Though now we must appear bloody and cruel,
As by our hands and this our present act
You see we do, yet see you but our hands
And this the bleeding business they have done.
Our hearts you see not. They are pitiful;
170     And pity to the general wrong of Rome
(As fire drives out fire, so pity pity)
Hath done this deed on Caesar. For your part,
To you our swords have leaden points, Mark Antony.
Our arms in strength of malice, and our hearts
175     Of brothers' temper, do receive you in
With all kind of love, good thoughts, and reverence.

**Cassius.** Your voice shall be as strong as any man's
In the disposing of new dignities.

**Brutus.** Only be patient till we have appeased
180     The multitude, beside themselves with fear,
And then we will deliver you the cause
Why I, that did love Caesar when I struck him,
Have thus proceeded.

**Antony.**             I doubt not of your wisdom.
Let each man render me his bloody hand.
185     First, Marcus Brutus, will I shake with you;
Next, Caius Cassius, do I take your hand;
Now, Decius Brutus, yours; now yours, Metellus;
Yours, Cinna; and, my valiant Casca, yours.
Though last, not least in love, yours, good
     Trebonius.
190     Gentlemen all—Alas, what shall I say?
My credit now stands on such slippery ground
That one of two bad ways you must conceit me,
Either a coward or a flatterer.
That I did love thee, Caesar, O, 'tis true!
195     If then thy spirit look upon us now,
Shall it not grieve thee dearer than thy death
To see thy Antony making his peace,
Shaking the bloody fingers of thy foes,
Most noble! in the presence of thy corse?
200     Had I as many eyes as thou hast wounds,

**171 As fire . . . pity:** As one fire consumes another, our sorrow for Rome became greater than our sorrow for Caesar.

**173–178 To you . . . dignities:** As far as you're concerned, Antony, our swords are harmless (**have leaden points**). Our arms, even though they seem cruel (**in strength of malice**), and our hearts, full of brotherly feeling, welcome you. You will have as much to say as anyone in handing out honors from the new government.

**191 credit:** reputation.
**192 conceit:** think of.

**195–210** These lines are addressed to the corpse (**corse**) of Caesar. Antony is so upset that he temporarily forgets who is with him.

Weeping as fast as they stream forth thy blood,
It would become me better than to close
In terms of friendship with thine enemies.
Pardon me, Julius! Here wast thou bayed, brave hart;
205   Here didst thou fall; and here thy hunters stand,
Signed in thy spoil, and crimsoned in thy lethe.
O world, thou wast the forest to his hart;
And this indeed, O world, the heart of thee!
How like a deer, strucken by many princes,
210   Dost thou here lie!

**Cassius.** Mark Antony—

**Antony.**             Pardon me, Caius Cassius.
The enemies of Caesar shall say this;
Then, in a friend, it is cold modesty.

**Cassius.** I blame you not for praising Caesar so;
215   But what compact mean you have with us?
Will you be pricked in number of our friends,
Or shall we on, and not depend on you?

**Antony.** Therefore I took your hands; but was indeed
Swayed from the point by looking down on Caesar.
220   Friends am I with you all, and love you all,
Upon this hope, that you shall give me reasons
Why and wherein Caesar was dangerous.

**Brutus.** Or else were this a savage spectacle.
Our reasons are so full of good regard
225   That were you, Antony, the son of Caesar,
You should be satisfied.

**Antony.**             That's all I seek;
And am moreover suitor that I may
Produce his body to the market place
And in the pulpit, as becomes a friend,
230   Speak in the order of his funeral.

**Brutus.** You shall, Mark Antony.

**Cassius.**             Brutus, a word with you.

[*Aside to* Brutus.]

You know not what you do. Do not consent.
That Antony speak in his funeral.
Know you how much the people may be moved
235   By that which he will utter?

**Brutus.**             By your pardon,

[*Aside to* Cassius.]

**204 Here . . . hart:** This is the place where you were trapped (**bayed**) like a hunted deer (**hart**).

**206 Signed . . . lethe:** Marked with your blood (**spoil**) and red in your death. At this point, Antony is probably having difficulty speaking through his tears.

**211–213** With these lines, Antony regains control of himself. He points out that even Caesar's enemies will say such things as he has just said.

**215 compact:** agreement.

**216 pricked:** listed; marked by punching a hole in a wax tablet.

**218 Therefore . . . hands:** That is why I shook hands with all of you (because I intend to be counted as an ally of yours).

**223 Or else . . . spectacle:** If we could not give you reasons for what we have done, it would be nothing but an uncivilized show.

**226–235 That's all . . . utter:** Antony asks permission to carry Caesar's body outside and make a funeral speech in his honor. Brutus agrees, but Cassius fears that Antony's words might incite the people in Caesar's favor.

"*Thou art the ruins of the noblest man.*"

Al Pacino as Antony and John McMartin as Caesar (New York Shakespeare Festival, 1988).
Photo by Martha Swope, copyright © Time Inc.

I will myself into the pulpit first
And show the reason of our Caesar's death.
What Antony shall speak, I will protest
He speaks by leave and by permission,
240  And that we are contented Caesar shall
Have all true rites and lawful ceremonies.
It shall advantage more than do us wrong.

**Cassius.**

[*Aside to* Brutus.]

I know not what may fall. I like it not.

**Brutus.** Mark Antony, here, take you Caesar's body.
245  You shall not in your funeral speech blame us,
But speak all good you can devise of Caesar,
And say you do't by our permission.
Else shall you not have any hand at all
About his funeral. And you shall speak
250  In the same pulpit whereto I am going,
After my speech is ended.

**Antony.**                              Be it so.
I do desire no more.

**Brutus.** Prepare the body then, and follow us.

[*Exeunt all but* Antony, *who looks down at* Caesar's body.]

**Antony.** O, pardon me, thou bleeding piece of earth,
255  That I am meek and gentle with these butchers!
Thou art the ruins of the noblest man
That ever lived in the tide of times.
Woe to the hand that shed this costly blood!
Over thy wounds now do I prophesy
260  (Which, like dumb mouths, do ope their ruby lips
To beg the voice and utterance of my tongue),
A curse shall light upon the limbs of men;
Domestic fury and fierce civil strife
Shall cumber all the parts of Italy;
265  Blood and destruction shall be so in use
And dreadful objects so familiar
That mothers shall but smile when they behold
Their infants quartered with the hands of war,
All pity choked with custom of fell deeds;
270  And Caesar's spirit, ranging for revenge,
With Até by his side come hot from hell,
Shall in these confines with a monarch's voice
Cry "Havoc!" and let slip the dogs of war,

**238 protest:** explain.

**242 It shall . . . wrong:** His speech will do us more good **(advantage more)** than harm.

**254–275** Now that Antony is alone with Caesar's corpse, he speaks truthfully. His speech shows what he really thinks of the men who have just left and what he intends to do about the murder.

**257 in the tide of times:** in all of history.

**263–269 Domestic fury . . . deeds:** Rome **(Italy)** will be torn by civil war. People will become so accustomed to horrible sights that mothers will simply smile when they see their children cut into pieces **(quartered)**. Pity will disappear among so much cruelty.

**271 Até** (ā′ tē): the Greek goddess of revenge.
**273 "Havoc!":** a battle cry signaling mass killings.

That this foul deed shall smell above the earth
275     With carrion men, groaning for burial.

[*Enter* Octavius' Servant.]

    You serve Octavius Caesar, do you not?

**Servant.** I do, Mark Antony.

**Antony.** Caesar did write for him to come to Rome.

**Servant.** He did receive his letters and is coming,
280     And bid me say to you by word of mouth—
    O Caesar!

**Antony.** Thy heart is big. Get thee apart and weep.
    Passion, I see, is catching, for mine eyes,
    Seeing those beads of sorrow stand in thine,
285     Began to water. Is thy master coming?

**Servant.** He lies tonight within seven leagues of Rome.

**Antony.** Post back with speed and tell him what hath
      chanced.
    Here is a mourning Rome, a dangerous Rome,
    No Rome of safety for Octavius yet.
290     Hie hence and tell him so. Yet stay awhile.
    Thou shalt not back till I have borne this corse
    Into the market place. There shall I try
    In my oration how the people take
    The cruel issue of these bloody men,
295     According to the which thou shall discourse
    To young Octavius of the state of things.
    Lend me your hand.

[*Exeunt with* Caesar's *body*.]

**275 With carrion . . . burial:** like rotting corpses begging to be buried.
**276** Antony is interrupted by a servant of Octavius, an ally of Caesar. The servant begins to relay a message, then sees the bleeding corpse on the floor.

**286 He lies . . . Rome:** Octavius will set up camp tonight about twenty-one miles (**seven leagues**) outside Rome.

**287–297 Post back . . . your hand:** Antony tells the servant to hurry back and tell Octavius what has happened. Then he tells the servant to wait. He wants the servant to listen to his funeral speech and report to Octavius how the crowd responds to it. What do you think Antony's funeral speech will be like?

# SCENE 2    THE FORUM IN ROME.

*Brutus speaks before a group of "citizens," or common people of Rome. He explains why Caesar had to be slain for the good of Rome. Then, Brutus leaves and Antony speaks to the citizens. A far better judge of human nature than Brutus, Antony cleverly manages to turn the crowd against the conspirators by telling them of Caesar's good works and his concern for the people, as proven by the slain ruler's will. He has left all his wealth to the people. As Antony stirs the citizens to pursue the assassins and kill them, he learns that Octavius has arrived in Rome and that Brutus and Cassius have fled.*

[*Enter* Brutus *and* Cassius *and a throng of* Citizens, *disturbed by the death of Caesar.*]

**Citizens.** We will be satisfied! Let us be satisfied!

**Brutus.** Then follow me and give me audience, friends.
　　Cassius, go you into the other street
　　And part the numbers.
5 　　Those that will hear me speak, let 'em stay here;
　　Those that will follow Cassius, go with him;
　　And public reasons shall be rendered
　　Of Caesar's death.

**First Citizen.** 　　　　　I will hear Brutus speak.

**Second Citizen.** I will hear Cassius, and compare their
10 　　reasons when severally we hear them rendered.

[*Exit* Cassius, *with some of the* Citizens. Brutus *goes into the pulpit.*]

**Third Citizen.** The noble Brutus is ascended. Silence!

**Brutus.** Be patient till the last.
　　Romans, countrymen, and lovers, hear me for my
　　cause, and be silent, that you may hear. Believe me
15 　　for mine honor, and have respect to mine honor,
　　that you may believe. Censure me in your wisdom,
　　and awake your senses, that you may the better
　　judge. If there be any in this assembly, any dear
　　friend of Caesar's, to him I say that Brutus' love to
20 　　Caesar was no less than his. If then that friend
　　demand why Brutus rose against Caesar, this is my
　　answer: Not that I loved Caesar less, but that I loved
　　Rome more. Had you rather Caesar were living, and
　　die all slaves, than that Caesar were dead, to live all

**2–8 give me audience:** Listen to me. Brutus is shouting, trying to get the crowd to quiet down so he can speak. He asks Cassius to divide the crowd **(part the numbers)** and speak to another group. We will tell the people our reasons **(public reasons shall be rendered)** for killing Caesar, he says.

**13–41** As you read Brutus' speech, think about the kinds of arguments he uses to persuade the crowd. *Does he try to appeal to their emotions? Do you think he truly believes that the killing was justified?*

**13 lovers:** friends.

**16 Censure me:** Judge me.

"*Not that I loved Caesar less, but that I loved Rome more.*"

Martin Sheen as Brutus and Al Pacino as Antony (New York Shakespeare Festival, 1988). Photo by Martha Swope, copyright © Time Inc.

25 freemen? As Caesar loved me, I weep for him; as he was fortunate, I rejoice at it; as he was valiant, I honor him; but—as he was ambitious, I slew him. There is tears for his love; joy for his fortune; honor for his valor; and death for his ambition. Who is
30 here so base that would be a bondman? If any, speak, for him have I offended. Who is here so rude that would not be a Roman? If any, speak, for him have I offended. Who is here so vile that will not love his country? If any, speak, for him have I offended. I
35 pause for a reply.

**All.** None, Brutus, none!

**Brutus.** Then none have I offended. I have done no more to Caesar than you shall do to Brutus. The question of his death is enrolled in the Capitol; his
40 glory not extenuated, wherein he was worthy, nor his offenses enforced, for which he suffered death.

**29–30 Who is . . . bondman:** Which of you is so low that you would prefer to be a slave?

**31 rude:** uncivilized.

**38–41 The question . . . death:** The reasons for his death are on record in the Capitol. We have not belittled **(extenuated)** his accomplishments or overemphasized **(enforced)** the failings for which he was killed.

[*Enter* Antony *and others, with* Caesar's *body.*]

   Here comes his body, mourned by Mark Antony, who
   though he had no hand in his death, shall receive
   the benefit of his dying, a place in the commonwealth,
45   as which of you shall not? With this I depart,
   that, as I slew my best lover for the good of Rome, I
   have the same dagger for myself when it shall please
   my country to need my death.

**All.** Live, Brutus! live, live!

50   **First Citizen.** Bring him with triumph home unto his
        house.

**Second Citizen.** Give him a statue with his ancestors.

**Third Citizen.** Let him be Caesar.

**Fourth Citizen.**                       Caesar's better parts
        Shall be crowned in Brutus.

**First Citizen.** We'll bring him to his house with shouts
        and clamors.

55   **Brutus.** My countrymen—

**Second Citizen.**                       Peace! silence! Brutus speaks.

**First Citizen.** Peace ho!

**Brutus.** Good countrymen, let me depart alone,
        And, for my sake, stay here with Antony.
        Do grace to Caesar's corpse, and grace his speech
60      Tending to Caesar's glories which Mark Antony,
        By our permission, is allowed to make.
        I do entreat you, not a man depart,
        Save I alone, till Antony have spoke.

[*Exit*]

**First Citizen.** Stay, ho! and let us hear Mark Antony.

65   **Third Citizen.** Let him go up into the public chair.
        We'll hear him. Noble Antony, go up.

**Antony.** For Brutus' sake I am beholding to you.

[*Goes into the pulpit.*]

**Fourth Citizen.** What does he say of Brutus?

**Third Citizen.**                       He says for Brutus'
        Sake he finds himself beholding to us all.

70   **Fourth Citizen.** 'Twere best he speak no harm of Brutus
        here!

**First Citizen.** This Caesar was a tyrant.

**49–55** What is the mood of the crowd as Brutus finishes his speech?

**59 grace his speech:** Listen to him respectfully.

**63 Save:** except.

**64** Is Brutus wise to depart before Antony makes his speech?

**65 public chair:** speaker's platform.

**67 beholding:** indebted.

**68–72** Notice what the people are now saying about Caesar, only minutes after they were crying for him. Antony hears all this. How do you think he will respond?

**Third Citizen.**                           Nay, that's certain.
We are blest that Rome is rid of him.

**Second Citizen.** Peace! Let us hear what Antony can say.

**Antony.** You gentle Romans—

**All.**                      Peace, ho! Let us hear him.

75    **Antony.** Friends, Romans, countrymen, lend me your
         ears;
     I come to bury Caesar, not to praise him.
     The evil that men do lives after them;
     The good is oft interred with their bones.
     So let it be with Caesar. The noble Brutus
80      Hath told you Caesar was ambitious.
     If it were so, it was a grievous fault,
     And grievously hath Caesar answered it.
     Here, under leave of Brutus and the rest
     (For Brutus is an honorable man;
85      So are they all, all honorable men),
     Come I to speak in Caesar's funeral.
     He was my friend, faithful and just to me;
     But Brutus says he was ambitious,
     And Brutus is an honorable man.
90      He hath brought many captives home to Rome,
     Whose ransoms did the general coffers fill.
     Did this in Caesar seem ambitious?
     When that the poor have cried, Caesar hath wept;
     Ambition should be made of sterner stuff.
95      Yet Brutus says he was ambitious;
     And Brutus is an honorable man.
     You all did see that on the Lupercal
     I thrice presented him a kingly crown,
     Which he did thrice refuse. Was this ambition?
100     Yet Brutus says he was ambitious;
     And sure he is an honorable man.
     I speak not to disprove what Brutus spoke,
     But here I am to speak what I do know.
     You all did love him once, not without cause.
105     What cause withholds you then to mourn for him?
     O judgment, thou art fled to brutish beasts,
     And men have lost their reason! Bear with me,
     My heart is in the coffin there with Caesar,
     And I must pause till it come back to me.

110    **First Citizen.** Methinks there is much reason in his
         sayings.

**75–139** Antony's words at Caesar's funeral make up one of the most famous speeches in all of Shakespeare's plays. Remember that Antony wants to stir the people into a civil war. He must work on them gradually, since they are now supporters of Brutus. One gradual change is in his use of the word *honorable*. As the speech goes on, the word becomes more and more sarcastic.

**77–79 The evil . . . Caesar:** Let Caesar's good deeds die with him; let him be remembered by his faults.

**78 interred:** buried.

**81 grievous:** serious.

**83 under leave of:** with the permission of.

**91 general coffers:** the Roman government's treasury.

**98 thrice:** three times.

**107–109 Bear with . . . to me:** Antony stops speaking and turns to the corpse. He says he is overcome with grief (**My heart is in the coffin**) and needs to pause for a while. What other reasons might Antony have for pausing at this point in his speech?

**Second Citizen.** If thou consider rightly of the matter,
Caesar has had great wrong.

**Third Citizen.**                    Has he, masters?
I fear there will a worse come in his place.

**Fourth Citizen.** Marked ye his words? He would not take
the crown;
115    Therefore 'tis certain he was not ambitious.

**First Citizen.** If it be found so, some will dear abide it.

**Second Citizen.** Poor soul! his eyes are red as fire with
weeping.

**Third Citizen.** There's not a nobler man in Rome than
Antony.

**Fourth Citizen.** Now mark him. He begins again to
speak.

120  **Antony.** But yesterday the word of Caesar might
Have stood against the world. Now lies he there,
And none so poor to do him reverence.
O masters! If I were disposed to stir
Your hearts and minds to mutiny and rage,
125    I should do Brutus wrong, and Cassius wrong,
Who, you all know, are honorable men.
I will not do them wrong. I rather choose
To wrong the dead, to wrong myself and you,
Than I will wrong such honorable men.
130    But here's a parchment with the seal of Caesar.
I found it in his closet; 'tis his will.
Let but the commons hear this testament,
Which (pardon me) I do not mean to read,
And they would go and kiss dead Caesar's wounds
135    And dip their napkins in his sacred blood;
Yea, beg a hair of him for memory,
And dying, mention it within their wills,
Bequeathing it as a rich legacy
Unto their issue.

140  **Fourth Citizen.** We'll hear the will! Read it, Mark
Antony.

**All.** The will, the will! We will hear Caesar's will!

**Antony.** Have patience, gentle friends, I must not read it.
It is not meet you know how Caesar loved you.
You are not wood, you are not stones, but men;
145    And being men, hearing the will of Caesar,

**116 some will dear abide it:** Some will pay dearly for it.

**120 But:** only.

**126 honorable men:** By this point, Antony is using the term more as an insult than a compliment. He spits it out angrily, wanting the crowd to know that he doesn't believe for a second that it describes the assassins.

**130 parchment:** document.

**133 Which . . . read:** Mark Antony is manipulating the crowd here. He has every intention of reading the will, but wants the crowd to force him to do so.

**135 napkins:** handkerchiefs.

**138–139 Bequeathing . . . issue:** People would leave it (a hair from Caesar's head) in their wills for their children (**issue**).

**143 meet:** proper.

# VIEW AND COMPARE

**What do these images suggest about Antony's emotional response to Caesar's death? How is emotion conveyed by each image?**

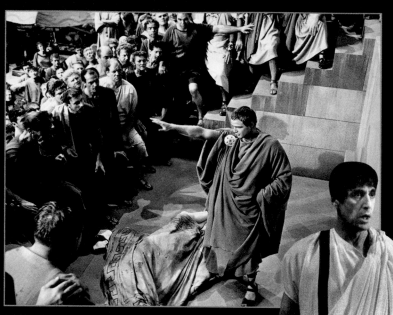

Marlon Brando as Antony (MGM film, 1953).
Photofest.

Al Pacino as Antony and John McMartin as
Caesar (New York Shakespeare Festival, 1988).
Photo copyright © George E. Joseph.

It will inflame you, it will make you mad.
'Tis good you know not that you are his heirs,
For if you should, O, what would come of it?

**Fourth Citizen.** Read the will! We'll hear it, Antony!
150     You shall read us the will, Caesar's will!

**Antony.** Will you be patient? Will you stay awhile?
I have o'ershot myself to tell you of it.
I fear I wrong the honorable men
Whose daggers have stabbed Caesar; I do fear it.

155 **Fourth Citizen.** They were traitors. Honorable men!

**All.** The will! the testament!

**Second Citizen.** They were villains, murderers! The will!
Read the will!

**Antony.** You will compel me then to read the will?
160     Then make a ring about the corpse of Caesar
And let me show you him that made the will.
Shall I descend? and will you give me leave?

**All.** Come down.

**Second Citizen.** Descend.

165 **Third Citizen.** You shall have leave.

[Antony *comes down.*]

**Fourth Citizen.** A ring! Stand round.

**First Citizen.** Stand from the hearse! Stand from the
body!

**Second Citizen.** Room for Antony, most noble Antony!

170 **Antony.** Nay, press not so upon me. Stand far off.

**All.** Stand back! Room! Bear back!

**Antony.** If you have tears, prepare to shed them now.
You all do know this mantle. I remember
The first time ever Caesar put it on.
175     'Twas on a summer's evening in his tent,
That day he overcame the Nervii.
Look, in this place ran Cassius' dagger through.
See what a rent the envious Casca made.
Through this the well-beloved Brutus stabbed;
180     And as he plucked his cursed steel away,
Mark how the blood of Caesar followed it,
As rushing out of doors to be resolved
If Brutus so unkindly knocked or no;
For Brutus, as you know, was Caesar's angel.

**152 I have . . . of it:** I have gone too far in even mentioning it to you.

**162 Shall I . . . leave:** Will you give me permission to come down? Antony pretends to be at the mercy of the crowd. Why do you think he does this?

**173 mantle:** Caesar's toga.

**176 the Nervii:** a Belgian tribe that Caesar defeated thirteen years earlier.

**178 rent:** tear, hole.

**181 Mark:** notice.

**182–183 As rushing . . . or no:** Antony says Caesar's blood rushed out of that opening to find out if it really was Brutus who had made the wound.

185　Judge, O you gods, how dearly Caesar loved him!
　　This was the most unkindest cut of all;
　　For when the noble Caesar saw him stab,
　　Ingratitude, more strong than traitors' arms,
　　Quite vanquished him. Then burst his mighty heart;
190　And in his mantle muffling up his face,
　　Even at the base of Pompey's statue
　　(Which all the while ran blood) great Caesar fell.
　　O, what a fall was there, my countrymen!
　　Then I, and you, and all of us fell down,
195　Whilst bloody treason flourished over us.
　　O, now you weep, and I perceive you feel
　　The dint of pity. These are gracious drops.
　　Kind souls, what, weep you when you but behold
　　Our Caesar's vesture wounded? Look you here!
200　Here is himself, marred, as you see, with traitors.

[*Pulls the cloak off* Caesar's *body.*]

**First Citizen.** O piteous spectacle!

**Second Citizen.** O noble Caesar!

**Third Citizen.** O woeful day!

**Fourth Citizen.** O traitors, villains!

205　**First Citizen.** O most bloody sight!

**Second Citizen.** We will be revenged.

**All.** Revenge! About! Seek! Burn! Fire! Kill! Slay!
　　Let not a traitor live!

**Antony.** Stay, countrymen.

210　**First Citizen.** Peace there! Hear the noble Antony.

**Second Citizen.** We'll hear him, we'll follow him,
　　we'll die with him!

**Antony.** Good friends, sweet friends, let me not stir you up
　　To such a sudden flood of mutiny.
215　They that have done this deed are honorable.
　　What private griefs they have, alas, I know not,
　　That made them do it. They are wise and honorable,
　　And will no doubt with reasons answer you.
　　I come not, friends, to steal away your hearts.
220　I am no orator, as Brutus is,
　　But (as you know me all) a plain blunt man
　　That love my friend; and that they know full well
　　That gave me public leave to speak of him.
　　For I have neither wit, nor words, nor worth,

**189 vanquished:** defeated.

**197 dint:** force.

**198–200 weep you . . . traitors:** Do you cry when you look only at his wounded clothing **(vesture)?** Here, look at his body! (Antony pulls Caesar's toga aside and reveals the knife wounds.) The people find the sight repulsive, and it makes them angry.

**220–222 I am no . . . friend:** This is another speaker's trick. Antony has just shown himself to be a much better speaker **(orator)** than Brutus. Why, then, does he say he is "no orator"?

**224 wit:** intelligence.

Al Pacino (*center*) as Antony (New York Shakespeare Festival, 1988).
Photo by Martha Swope, copyright © Time Inc.

225    Action, nor utterance, nor the power of speech
        To stir men's blood. I only speak right on.
        I tell you that which you yourselves do know,
        Show you sweet Caesar's wounds, poor poor dumb
            mouths,
        And bid them speak for me. But were I Brutus,
230    And Brutus Antony, there were an Antony
        Would ruffle up your spirits, and put a tongue
        In every wound of Caesar that should move
        The stones of Rome to rise and mutiny.

    **All.** We'll mutiny.

    **First Citizen.**      We'll burn the house of Brutus.

235  **Third Citizen.** Away then! Come, seek the conspirators.

    **Antony.** Yet hear me, countrymen. Yet hear me speak.

    **All.** Peace, ho! Hear Antony, most noble Antony!

    **Antony.** Why, friends, you go to do you know not what.
        Wherein hath Caesar thus deserved your loves?
240    Alas, you know not! I must tell you then.

You have forgot the will I told you of.

**All.** Most true! The will! Let's stay and hear the will.

**Antony.** Here is the will, under Caesar's seal.
   To every Roman citizen he gives,
245   To every several man, seventy-five drachmas.

**Second Citizen.** Most noble Caesar! We'll revenge his
   death!

**Third Citizen.** O royal Caesar!

**Antony.** Hear me with patience.

**All.** Peace, ho!

250   **Antony.** Moreover, he hath left you all his walks,
   His private arbors, and new-planted orchards,
   On this side Tiber; he hath left them you,
   And to your heirs for ever—common pleasures,
   To walk abroad and recreate yourselves.
255   Here was a Caesar! When comes such another?

**245 drachmas:** silver coins, worth quite a bit to poor people such as those in the crowd.

**250–254** Reading from the will, Antony tells the crowd that Caesar has left all his private parks and gardens on this side of the Tiber River to be used by the public.

*"Here is the will, under
Caesar's seal."*

Al Pacino as Antony holds the will (New York Shakespeare Festival, 1988).
Photo copyright © George E. Joseph.

**First Citizen.** Never, never! Come, away, away!
 We'll burn his body in the holy place
 And with the brands the traitors' houses.
 Take up the body.

**258 brands:** pieces of burning wood.

260  **Second Citizen.** Go fetch fire!

**Third Citizen.** Pluck down benches!

**Fourth Citizen.** Pluck down forms, windows, anything!

[*Exeunt* Citizens *with the body.*]

**Antony.** Now let it work. Mischief, thou art afoot,
 Take thou what course thou wilt.

[*Enter a* Servant.]

        How now, fellow?

**263–264 Now let . . . wilt:** Alone, Antony gloats over what he has just accomplished. Let things take their course, he says. Whatever happens, happens.

265  **Servant.** Sir, Octavius is already come to Rome.

**Antony.** Where is he?

**Servant.** He and Lepidus are at Caesar's house.

**Antony.** And thither will I straight to visit him.
 He comes upon a wish. Fortune is merry,
270  And in this mood will give us anything.

**268 thither . . . him:** I will go right there to see him.

**269–270 He comes . . . anything:** Octavius has arrived just as Antony hoped; Antony believes that Fortune, the goddess of fate, is on his side.

**Servant.** I heard him say Brutus and Cassius
 Are rid like madmen through the gates of Rome.

**Antony.** Belike they had some notice of the people,
 How I had moved them. Bring me to Octavius.

[*Exeunt.*]

**272 Are rid:** have ridden.

**273 Belike:** probably.

# SCENE 3  A STREET IN ROME.

*This scene involves a famous Roman poet named Cinna. (He is not the same Cinna who took part in the assassination.) The angry Roman mob comes upon the poet, believing he is Cinna the conspirator. Soon, they realize this is the wrong man, yet they are so enraged that they slay him anyway. Then, they rush through the city after the true killers of Caesar.*

[*Enter* Cinna, *the poet, and after him the* Citizens, *armed with sticks, spears, and swords.*]

**Cinna.** I dreamt tonight that I did feast with Caesar,
 And things unluckily charge my fantasy.
 I have no will to wander forth of doors,
 Yet something leads me forth.

**2 things . . . fantasy:** Recent events have caused me to imagine awful things.

**5**  **First Citizen.** What is your name?

**Second Citizen.** Whither are you going?

**Third Citizen.** Where do you dwell?

**Fourth Citizen.** Are you a married man or a bachelor?

**Second Citizen.** Answer every man directly.

**10**  **First Citizen.** Ay, and briefly.

**Fourth Citizen.** Ay, and wisely.

**Third Citizen.** Ay, and truly, you were best.

**Cinna.** What is my name? Whither am I going? Where
do I dwell? Am I a married man or a bachelor?

**15**  Then, to answer every man directly and briefly,
wisely and truly: wisely I say, I am a bachelor.

**Second Citizen.** That's as much to say they are fools that
marry. You'll bear me a bang for that, I fear.
Proceed—directly.

**20**  **Cinna.** Directly I am going to Caesar's funeral.

**First Citizen.** As a friend or an enemy?

**Cinna.** As a friend.

**Second Citizen.** That matter is answered directly.

**Fourth Citizen.** For your dwelling—briefly.

**25**  **Cinna.** Briefly, I dwell by the Capitol.

**Third Citizen.** Your name, sir, truly.

**Cinna.** Truly, my name is Cinna.

**First Citizen.** Tear him to pieces! He's a conspirator.

**Cinna.** I am Cinna the poet! I am Cinna the poet!

**30**  **Fourth Citizen.** Tear him for his bad verses! Tear him
for his bad verses!

**Cinna.** I am not Cinna the conspirator.

**Fourth Citizen.** It is no matter; his name's Cinna!
Pluck but his name out of his heart, and turn him

**35**  going.

**Third Citizen.** Tear him, tear him!

[*They attack* Cinna.]

Come, brands, ho! To Brutus', to Cassius'! Burn all!
Some to Decius' house and some to Casca's; some to
Ligarius'! Away, go!

[*Exeunt all the* Citizens.]

---

**6 Whither:** where.

**17–18 That's . . . fear:** This
response shows that Cinna is in
danger. The citizen threatens to
beat him **(You'll bear me a bang)**,
even though Cinna's comment was
not meant to be insulting.

**34–35 Pluck . . . going:** Let's just
tear the name out of his heart and
send him away.

**36 The citizens murder Cinna the
poet.** Can you think of other
examples—from real life or
literature—of crowds that have
gotten out of control?

# Thinking *through the* LITERATURE

## Connect to the Literature

1. **What Do You Think?** What is your impression of Antony? Discuss it with your classmates.

> **Comprehension Check**
> - Where is Caesar assassinated?
> - As he is killed, what does Caesar say about Brutus?
> - What effect do Brutus' and Mark Antony's speeches have on the crowd?

## Think Critically

2. What do the conspirators believe they have accomplished by killing Caesar? Do you agree? Explain your answer.

3. **ACTIVE READING** | **READING SHAKESPEAREAN DRAMA** | For a better understanding of Brutus' and Mark Antony's famous funeral speeches, reread Scene 2, lines 13–63 and 75–255. Untangle any unusual word order, and use the sidenotes to decipher the meaning of unfamiliar terms. Then contrast the two speeches. Why is Antony's speech more effective at manipulating the crowd than Brutus' speech?

4. What might Shakespeare be suggesting through his portrayal of the crowd of Roman citizens in Act Three?

5. What is your response to the statement, "Brutus is an honorable man"?

 **THINK ABOUT**
- Caesar's final words to Brutus, and Antony's description of Brutus' act as "the most unkindest cut of all"
- Brutus' treatment of Antony after the assassination
- Brutus' explanation of why he killed Caesar
- other actions that might affect your view of Brutus

## Extend Interpretations

6. **What If?** What might have happened if Brutus had listened to Cassius and killed Antony? Support your answer.

7. **Comparing Texts** Compare and contrast the view of friendship presented in the play thus far with the view presented in other works in your text that explore this theme, such as "Two Friends" by Guy de Maupassant or "Cranes" by Hwang Sunwŏn.

8. **Connect to Life** Can public opinion today be as easily swayed as in Shakespeare's portrayal? Cite examples.

## Literary Analysis

**RHETORICAL DEVICES**

The funeral speeches by Brutus and Antony are famous examples of **rhetoric,** or persuasion. Both make use of the following **rhetorical devices** to persuade their audience:

- **Repetition** of words and sounds

*Believe me for mine honor, and have respect to mine honor, that you may believe.*

- **Parallelism,** or repeated grammatical structures

*As Caesar loved me, I weep for him; as he was fortunate, I rejoice at it; as he was valiant, I honor him; but —as he was ambitious, I slew him.*

- **Rhetorical questions,** or questions requiring no answer because the answer seems obvious

*Had you rather Caesar were living, and die all slaves, than that Caesar were dead, to live all freemen?*

**Cooperative Learning Activity**
Working in a small group, list examples of repetition, parallelism, and rhetorical questions in Mark Antony's famous funeral speech (Act Three, Scene 2, lines 75–255). Then take turns showing how you would give the speech to make its rhetorical devices seem as persuasive as possible.

**REVIEW** | **VERBAL IRONY**

In **verbal irony,** words that seem to say one thing actually mean the opposite. Where in Scene 2 do you think Mark Antony uses verbal irony?

# ACT FOUR

## SCENE 1

**AT A TABLE IN ANTONY'S HOUSE IN ROME.**

*Antony, Octavius, and Lepidus now rule Rome as a triumvirate—a committee of three. The scene opens on the triumvirate, meeting to draw up a list of their enemies who must be killed. They also discuss changing Caesar's will. As Lepidus goes to fetch the will, Antony expresses his low opinion of Lepidus as a leader. Then, Antony and Octavius begin to discuss how to defeat the armies of Brutus and Cassius.*

[*Enter* Antony, Octavius, *and* Lepidus.]

**Antony.** These many, then, shall die; their names are
    pricked.

**Octavius.** Your brother too must die. Consent you,
    Lepidus?

**Lepidus.** I do consent.

**Octavius.**                 Prick him down, Antony.

**Lepidus.** Upon condition Publius shall not live,
5    Who is your sister's son, Mark Antony.

**Antony.** He shall not live. Look, with a spot I damn him.
    But Lepidus, go you to Caesar's house.
    Fetch the will hither, and we shall determine
    How to cut off some charge in legacies.

10  **Lepidus.** What? shall I find you here?

**Octavius.** Or here or at the Capitol.

[*Exit* Lepidus.]

**Antony.** This is a slight unmeritable man,
    Meet to be sent on errands. Is it fit,
    The threefold world divided, he should stand
15    One of the three to share it?

**Octavius.**                 So you thought him,
    And took his voice who should be pricked to die

**6 with a spot . . . him:** I condemn him by marking him on this list.

**8–9 Fetch . . . legacies:** Bring Caesar's will here, so we can decide how to alter the amounts the people get. Does this statement change your opinion of Antony? Explain.

**12–27 This is . . . commons:** Now that Antony and Octavius are alone, Antony says what he really thinks of Lepidus. He does not believe Lepidus is worthy of being one of three men in control of Rome's lands in Europe, Asia, and Africa (**The threefold world**). Lepidus, he says, is fit (**Meet**) for running errands. Antony admits that they have accepted Lepidus' opinion about who should be put on the list of those who will die (**black sentence and proscription**), but they have done that only so he will take the blame for the many unpopular things (**divers sland'rous loads**) they plan to do.

In our black sentence and proscription.

**Antony.** Octavius, I have seen more days than you;
And though we lay these honors on this man
20 To ease ourselves of divers sland'rous loads,
He shall but bear them as the ass bears gold,
To groan and sweat under the business,
Either led or driven as we point the way;
And having brought our treasure where we will,
25 Then take we down his load, and turn him off
(Like to the empty ass) to shake his ears
And graze in commons.

**Octavius.**                    You may do your will;
But he's a tried and valiant soldier.

**Antony.** So is my horse, Octavius, and for that
30 I do appoint him store of provender.
It is a creature that I teach to fight,
To wind, to stop, to run directly on,
His corporal motion governed by my spirit.
And, in some taste is Lepidus but so.
35 He must be taught, and trained, and bid go forth:
A barren-spirited fellow; one that feeds
On objects, arts and imitations
Which, out of use and staled by other men,
Begin his fashion. Do not talk of him,
40 But as a property. And now, Octavius,
Listen great things. Brutus and Cassius
Are levying powers. We must straight make head.
Therefore let our alliance be combined,
Our best friends made, and our best means stretched
     out;
45 And let us presently go sit in council
How covert matters may be best disclosed
And open perils surest answered.

**Octavius.** Let us do so; for we are at the stake
And bayed about with many enemies;
50 And some that smile have in their hearts, I fear,
Millions of mischiefs.

[*Exeunt.*]

**29–40 So is my . . . property:**
Antony compares Lepidus to a
horse who is given food
**(provender)** and taught how to
behave. Antony also says that
Lepidus is interested in **(feeds / On)**
unimportant things **(objects, arts
and imitations)** that he learns of
from other people, and these
things attract his attention **(Begin
his fashion)** after others have lost
interest in them.

**41–42 Listen . . . head:** Listen to
important **(great)** matters. Brutus
and Cassius are raising an army
**(levying powers)**. We must move
fast **(straight make head)** to build
up our own army.

**45–47 let us . . . answered:** Let us
decide the best way to uncover
hidden **(covert)** dangers and to
deal with the threats we know
about.

**48–51 for we are . . . mischiefs:** We
are like a bear tied to a stake and
taunted by barking dogs. Some of
the people who smile at us may
have evil intentions **(mischiefs)** in
mind for us. What do these lines
tell you about Octavius' state of
mind?

# VIEW AND COMPARE

**What do each of the following images suggest about the character of Brutus? Which image comes closest to your own interpretation of his character?**

Orson Welles as Brutus in a street-dress production (Mercury Theater, 1937). Cropped image, copyright © Museum of the City of New York.

James Mason as Brutus (MGM film, 1953). S.S. Archives/Shooting Star.

Len Cariou as Brutus (Stratford Festival, 1982). Photo by Robert C. Ragsdale.

# SCENE 2

**A MILITARY CAMP NEAR SARDIS. IN FRONT OF BRUTUS' TENT.**

*Brutus seems displeased at the way events are developing, and he tells his servant about Cassius' new cold and distant attitude. Cassius arrives, and he and Brutus go into the tent to talk about their disagreements.*

[*Sound of drums. Enter* Brutus, Lucilius, Lucius, *and* Soldiers. Titinius *and* Pindarus, *from Cassius' army, meet them.*]

**Brutus.** Stand ho!

**Lucilius.** Give the word, ho! and stand!

**Brutus.** What now, Lucilius? Is Cassius near?

**Lucilius.** He is at hand, and Pindarus is come
5    To do you salutation from his master.

**Brutus.** He greets me well. Your master, Pindarus,
In his own change, or by ill officers,
Hath given me some worthy cause to wish
Things done undone; but if he be at hand,
10    I shall be satisfied.

**Pindarus.**            I do not doubt
But that my noble master will appear
Such as he is, full of regard and honor.

**Brutus.** He is not doubted. A word, Lucilius,
How he received you. Let me be resolved.

15 **Lucilius.** With courtesy and with respect enough,
But not with such familiar instances
Nor with such free and friendly conference
As he hath used of old.

**Brutus.**            Thou has described
A hot friend cooling. Ever note, Lucilius,
20    When love begins to sicken and decay
It useth an enforced ceremony.
There are no tricks in plain and simple faith;
But hollow men, like horses hot at hand,
Make gallant show and promise of their mettle;

[*Low march within.*]

25    But when they should endure the bloody spur,
They fall their crests, and like deceitful jades
Sink in the trial. Comes his army on?

**Lucilius.** They mean this night in Sardis to be quartered.

**5 do you salutation:** bring you greetings.

**6–10 He greets . . . satisfied:** Cassius sends a good man to greet me. Pindarus, your master has either had a change of heart or is surrounded by incompetent **(ill)** officers. Whatever the reason, he has made me wish that certain things had never happened **(Things done undone).** But if he is here **(at hand),** I will find out for myself **(be satisfied).**

**13–14 A word . . . resolved:** Brutus takes his officer aside and asks him privately how he was treated when he met Cassius. Why does Brutus want to know this?

**17 conference:** conversation.

**19–27 Ever note . . . trial:** Brutus tells Lucilius never to forget **(Ever note)** that when affection begins to cool, it turns into awkward politeness **(enforced ceremony).** Honest relationships, he says, do not involve tricks. Insincere **(hollow)** men, like eager horses, make a great show of courage **(mettle).** But when they get the signal **(spur)** to fight, they drop their heads **(fall their crests)** and fail, like worn-out horses **(jades).**

**28 They . . . quartered:** Cassius and his army intend to stay here (in Sardis) tonight.

I'll not endure it. You forget yourself
30    To hedge me in. I am a soldier, I,
Older in practice, abler than yourself
To make conditions.

**Brutus.**               Go to! You are not, Cassius.

**Cassius.** I am.

**Brutus.** I say you are not.

35 **Cassius.** Urge me no more! I shall forget myself.
Have mind upon your health, tempt me no farther.

**Brutus.** Away, slight man!

**Cassius.** Is't possible?

**Brutus.**           Hear me, for I will speak.
Must I give way and room to your rash choler?
40    Shall I be frighted when a madman stares?

**Cassius.** O ye gods, ye gods! Must I endure all this?

**Brutus.** All this? Ay, more! Fret till your proud heart
    break.
Go show your slaves how choleric you are
And make your bondmen tremble. Must I budge?
45    Must I observe you? Must I stand and crouch
Under your testy humor? By the gods,
You shall digest the venom of your spleen,
Though it do split you; for from this day forth
I'll use you for my mirth, yea, for my laughter,
50    When you are waspish.

**Cassius.**              Is it come to this?

**Brutus.** You say you are a better soldier;
Let it appear so. Make your vaunting true,
And it shall please me well. For mine own part,
I shall be glad to learn of noble men.

55 **Cassius.** You wrong me every way! You wrong me,
    Brutus!
I said an elder soldier, not a better.
Did I say "better"?

**Brutus.**         If you did, I care not.

**Cassius.** When Caesar lived he durst not thus have
    moved me.

**Brutus.** Peace, peace! You durst not so have tempted
    him.

60 **Cassius.** I durst not?

**28–32 bait not me . . . conditions:**
Do not try to provoke (**bait**) me
into fighting. I will not put up with
(**endure**) it. Since I am the more
experienced soldier, I should be the
one to make decisions (**conditions**).

**39–47 Must . . . spleen:** Brutus
refers to Cassius' quick temper
(**rash choler**), to the fact that he is
so angry (**choleric**), and to his
irritable mood (**testy humor**). You
can swallow the poison of your
own anger (**spleen**), he says.
(People once believed that the
spleen, an organ near the stomach,
was the source of certain
emotions, such as anger and spite.)

**50 waspish:** ill-tempered.

**52 vaunting:** bragging. What
challenge does Brutus make?

**55–56 You wrong . . . better:**
Cassius now controls his anger and
tries to soften some of the things
he said earlier. He will soon
become angry again, though, since
Brutus does not stop insulting him.

**58 he durst . . . me:** Even Caesar
would not have dared to provoke
me this way.

*"You wrong me every way!"*

Martin Sheen as Brutus and Edward Herrmann as Cassius (New York Shakespeare Festival, 1988). Photo by Martha Swope, copyright © Time Inc.

**Brutus.** No.

**Cassius.** What, durst not tempt him?

**Brutus.** For your life you durst not.

**Cassius.** Do not presume too much upon my love.
I may do that I shall be sorry for.

65 **Brutus.** You have done that you should be sorry for.
There is no terror, Cassius, in your threats;
For I am armed so strong in honesty
That they pass by me as the idle wind,
Which I respect not. I did send to you

70 For certain sums of gold, which you denied me,
For I can raise no money by vile means—
By heaven, I had rather coin my heart
And drop my blood for drachmas than to wring
From the hard hands of peasants their vile trash

75 By any indirection. I did send
To you for gold to pay my legions,

**71–75 For I can . . . indirection:** I cannot raise money by dishonest **(vile)** methods. I would rather make coins out of my heart and blood than steal money from peasants by lying **(indirection).**

**76 legions:** armies.

The enemy, marching along by them,
By them shall make a fuller number up,
Come on refreshed, new-added, and encouraged;
210 From which advantage we cut him off
If at Philippi we do face him there,
These people at our back.

**Cassius.**                              Hear me, good brother.

**Brutus.** Under your pardon. You must note beside
That we have tried the utmost of our friends,
215 Our legions are brimful, our cause is ripe.
The enemy increaseth every day;
We, at the height, are ready to decline.
There is a tide in the affairs of men
Which, taken at the flood, leads on to fortune;
220 Omitted, all the voyage of their life
Is bound in shallows and in miseries.
On such a full sea are we now afloat,
And we must take the current when it serves
Or lose our ventures.

**Cassius.**                    Then, with your will, go on.
225 We'll along ourselves and meet them at Philippi.

**Brutus.** The deep of night is crept upon our talk
And nature must obey necessity,
Which we will niggard with a little rest.
There is no more to say?

**Cassius.**                         No more. Good night.
230 Early tomorrow will we rise and hence.

**Brutus.** Lucius!
[*Reenter* Lucius.]

   My gown.

[*Exit* Lucius.]

   Farewell, good Messala.
Good night, Titinius. Noble, noble Cassius,
235 Good night and good repose!

**Cassius.**                         O my dear brother,
This was an ill beginning of the night!
Never come such division 'tween our souls!
Let it not, Brutus.

[*Reenter* Lucius, *with the gown.*]

**Brutus.**          Everything is well.

**Cassius.** Good night, my lord.

---

**213–217 Under . . . decline:** Brutus cuts Cassius off and insists on his own position. Their army, he says, is as good as it is ever going to get, while the enemy is getting stronger every day. Do you agree with Brutus or Cassius? Why?

**214 tried the utmost:** received all we can expect.

**218–224 There is . . . ventures:** Brutus compares life to a voyage on a ship. Following the high tide can lead to good fortune. Those who do not follow the tide might spend the rest of their lives in shallow water and misery. Our tide comes now, he insists, and we must act now.

**228 Which . . . rest:** We will reluctantly satisfy (**niggard**) nature by getting a little bit of rest.

**232 gown:** nightgown.

"*There is a tide in the affairs of men which, taken at the flood, leads on to fortune.*"

Martin Sheen as Brutus and Edward Herrmann as Cassius (New York Shakespeare Festival, 1988). Photo copyright © George E. Joseph.

**Brutus.**  Good night, good brother.

240 **Titinius and Messala.** Good night, Lord Brutus.

**Brutus.**  Farewell every one.

[*Exeunt all but* Brutus *and* Lucius.]

Give me the gown. Where is thy instrument?

**Lucius.** Here in the tent.

**Brutus.**  What, thou speak'st drowsily?
Poor knave, I blame thee not, thou art o'erwatched.
Call Claudius and some other of my men;
245 I'll have them sleep on cushions in my tent.

**Lucius.** Varro and Claudius!

[*Enter* Varro *and* Claudius.]

**Varro.** Calls my lord?

**Brutus.** I pray you, sirs, lie in my tent and sleep.
It may be I shall raise you by-and-by
250 On business to my brother Cassius.

**Varro.** So please you, we will stand and watch your
pleasure.

**Brutus.** I will not have it so. Lie down, good sirs.
It may be I shall otherwise bethink me.

[Varro *and* Claudius *lie down.*]

Look, Lucius, here's the book I sought for so;
255 I put it in the pocket of my gown.

**Lucius.** I was sure your lordship did not give it me.

**Brutus.** Bear with me, good boy, I am much forgetful.
Canst thou hold up by thy heavy eyes awhile,
And touch thy instrument a strain or two?

260 **Lucius.** Ay, my lord, an't please you.

**Brutus.**  It does, my boy.
I trouble thee too much, but thou art willing.

**Lucius.** It is my duty, sir.

**Brutus.** I should not urge thy duty past thy might.
I know young bloods look for a time of rest.

265 **Lucius.** I have slept, my lord, already.

**Brutus.** It was well done; and thou shalt sleep again;
I will not hold thee long. If I do live,
I will be good to thee.

[*Music, and a song.* Lucius *falls asleep as he sings.*]

**241 Where is thy instrument?:**
One of Lucius' duties as a personal servant is to play music that will help Brutus get to sleep.

**242–243 What . . . o'erwatched:** I see you're sleepy. It's no wonder, since you've been watching and waiting for so long.

**249–253 It may . . . bethink me:**
Brutus wants them to be handy in case he needs to send a message to Cassius. Varro offers to stand guard all night. Brutus insists the men sleep, not stand guard. He says he may change his mind (**otherwise bethink me**) about sending messages to Cassius.

This is a sleepy tune. O murd'rous slumber!
270 Layest thou thy leaden mace upon my boy,
That plays thee music? Gentle knave, good night.
I will not do thee so much wrong to wake thee.
If thou dost nod, thou break'st thy instrument;
I'll take it from thee; and, good boy, good night.
275 Let me see, let me see. Is not the leaf turned down
Where I left reading? Here it is, I think.

[*Sits.*]

[*Enter the* Ghost of Caesar.]

How ill this taper burns! Ha! Who comes here?
I think it is the weakness of mine eyes
That shapes this monstrous apparition.
280 It comes upon me. Art thou anything?
Art thou some god, some angel, or some devil,
That mak'st my blood cold and my hair to stare?
Speak to me what thou art.

**Ghost.** Thy evil spirit, Brutus.

**Brutus.**                         Why com'st thou?

285 **Ghost.** To tell thee thou shalt see me at Philippi.

**Brutus.** Well; then I shall see thee again?

**Ghost.** Ay, at Philippi.

**Brutus.** Why, I will see thee at Philippi then.

[*Exit* Ghost.]

Now I have taken heart thou vanishest.
290 Ill spirit, I would hold more talk with thee.
Boy! Lucius! Varro! Claudius! Sirs! Awake!
Claudius!

**Lucius.** The strings, my lord, are false.

**Brutus.** He thinks he still is at his instrument.
295    Lucius, awake!

**Lucius.** My lord?

**Brutus.** Didst thou dream, Lucius, that thou so criedst
out?

**Lucius.** My lord, I do not know that I did cry.

**Brutus.** Yes, that thou didst. Didst thou see anything?

300 **Lucius.** Nothing, my lord.

**Brutus.** Sleep again, Lucius. Sirrah Claudius!

[*To* Varro.]

Fellow thou, awake!

**270 mace:** a rod used as a symbol of authority. Brutus is addressing slumber as though it were an officer of the law who has arrested Lucius.

**277 How . . . burns:** How poorly this candle burns. Everyone in the tent is asleep, except Brutus. At first he thinks the thing he sees is only the result of poor eyesight. Then he realizes that something is really there.

**289 Now . . . vanishest:** Now that I have my courage back, you disappear. What might have been Shakespeare's purpose in adding a ghost to this play?

**293 false:** out of tune. Lucius, only half awake, thinks he is playing the instrument that Brutus took from him earlier. Why does Brutus accuse Lucius, Claudius, and Varro of crying out in their sleep?

*"Didst thou dream, Lucius, that thou so criedst out?"*

Wade Raley as Lucius and Martin Sheen as Brutus (New York Shakespeare Festival, 1988).
Photo copyright © George E. Joseph.

**Varro.** My lord?

**Claudius.** My lord?

305 **Brutus.** Why did you so cry out, sirs, in your sleep?

**Both.** Did we, my lord?

**Brutus.**                         Ay. Saw you anything?

**Varro.** No, my lord, I saw nothing.

**Claudius.**                         Nor I, my lord.

**Brutus.** Go and commend me to my brother Cassius.
   Bid him set on his pow'rs betimes before,
310   And we will follow.

**Both.**                         It shall be done, my lord.

[*Exeunt.*]

**308 commend me:** give my respects to.

**309 Bid . . . before:** Tell him to get his army (**pow'rs**) moving early in the morning.

# *Thinking* through the LITERATURE

## Connect to the Literature

1. **What Do You Think?** Were you surprised by the current state of the relationship between Brutus and Cassius? between Antony, Octavius, and Lepidus? Why or why not?

> **Comprehension Check**
> - Who are Rome's present rulers, and whom do they agree to kill?
> - What has strained the relationship between Brutus and Cassius?
> - Where does Caesar's ghost say he will see Brutus next time?

## Think Critically

2. How would you describe Mark Antony after reading Act Four, Scene 1? Do you think he has changed since Act Three? Cite details to explain your opinions.

3. Do the Romans seem better or worse off under their new rulers than they were under Julius Caesar?

> **THINK ABOUT**
> - the leadership of Julius Caesar
> - the behavior of Mark Antony in the opening scene of Act Four
> - Antony's plans regarding Julius Caesar's will
> - the looming warfare between the triumvirate and the conspirators

4. Would you say that Brutus himself has changed since the murder of Caesar? Cite evidence to support your opinion.

5. What new **ironies** do you see emerging in Act Four?

6. How would you describe the **mood** at the end of Act Four?

7. **ACTIVE READING** **READING SHAKESPEAREAN DRAMA** Using the sidenotes to help you, restate in contemporary English Brutus' speech to Cassius in Scene 3, lines 213–224. Compare your "translation" with that of another classmate.

## Extend Interpretations

8. **Critic's Corner** Many people think that Cassius becomes a more likable character than Brutus by Scene 3. Do you agree or disagree? Provide support with details from the scene.

9. **Connect to Life** Consider Brutus' often-quoted speech that begins "There is a tide in the affairs of men . . ." (Scene 3, lines 218–221). Share an incident from real life that either illustrates or refutes the opinion expressed in this speech.

## Literary Analysis

**DRAMATIC IRONY** Readers or audiences experience **irony** when they notice a contrast or discrepancy between appearance and reality, between the way things seem and the way they really are. In **dramatic irony,** the reader or audience knows something that one or more **characters** do not know, so that what appears true to the character or characters is not what the audience or reader knows to be true. For example, in the opening incident of Act Three, when Caesar confidently tells the Soothsayer that the ides of March are come, we recognize the irony of his confidence, since we know that he is to be assassinated that very day.

**Cooperative Learning Activity** Form a group of four and have each person go back through one of the four acts read thus far, looking for incidents that create dramatic irony. Each incident identified should then be included in a chart similar to the following:

| Act/Scene/Line Nos. | What Character(s) Thinks | What Reader/Audience Knows |
|---|---|---|
| | | |

Then come together again as a group and share your findings. Discuss the role that dramatic irony plays in your overall enjoyment of the play.

# ACT FIVE

## SCENE 1

**THE PLAINS OF PHILIPPI IN GREECE.**

*Antony and Octavius enter the battlefield with their army. Brutus and Cassius enter with their forces. The four leaders meet, but they only exchange insults and taunts. Antony and Octavius leave to prepare for battle. Cassius expresses his fears to Messala. Finally, Brutus and Cassius say their final farewells, in case they should die in battle.*

[*Enter* Octavius, Antony, *and their Army.*]

**Octavius.** Now Antony, our hopes are answered.
You said the enemy would not come down
But keep the hills and upper regions.
It proves not so, their battles are at hand.
5  They mean to warn us at Philippi here,
Answering before we do demand of them.

**Antony.** Tut! I am in their bosoms and I know
Wherefore they do it. They could be content
To visit other places, and come down
10  With fearful bravery, thinking by this face
To fasten in our thoughts that they have courage.
But 'tis not so.

[*Enter a* Messenger.]

**Messenger.**          Prepare you, generals,
The enemy comes on in gallant show;
Their bloody sign of battle is hung out,
15  And something to be done immediately.

**Antony.** Octavius, lead your battle softly on
Upon the left hand of the even field.

**Octavius.** Upon the right hand I. Keep thou the left.

**Antony.** Why do you cross me in this exigent?

20  **Octavius.** I do not cross you; but I will do so.

> **3 keep . . . regions:** stay in the higher areas (where they could defend themselves more easily).
>
> **5 warn:** challenge.
>
> **7–11 I am . . . courage:** I know their secrets (**am in their bosoms**) and why they have done this. They would rather be in other places, not here fighting us. They come down with a show of bravery, thinking they will convince us they have courage.
>
> **14 sign of battle:** a red flag symbolizing readiness for battle.
>
> **16–20** Antony and Octavius have a small argument about whose soldiers will fight on each side of the field. Who wins this argument?
>
> **19 exigent:** moment of crisis.

**What does each image suggest about Antony's attitude toward battle and his role as military leader? Which image comes closest to your own understanding of Antony?**

Charlton Heston as Antony (Commonwealth United film, 1970). S.S. Archives/Shooting Star.

Marlon Brando as Antony (MGM film, 1953). Photofest.

# SCENE 2

**THE BATTLEFIELD.**

*Brutus sends Messala with orders for the forces across the field.*

[*Alarum. Enter* Brutus *and* Messala.]

**Brutus.** Ride, ride, Messala, ride, and give these bills
    Unto the legions on the other side.

[*Loud alarum.*]

    Let them set on at once; for I perceive
    But cold demeanor in Octavius' wing,
5    And sudden push gives them the overthrow.
    Ride, ride, Messala! Let them all come down.

[*Exeunt.*]

**1–2 give . . . side:** Give these orders to our soldiers on that side of the field.

**4 cold demeanor:** lack of courage. How does Brutus feel about the battle at this point?

# SCENE 3

**ANOTHER PART OF THE BATTLEFIELD.**

*Cassius retreats, losing the battle to Antony's forces. He sends Titinius to see if nearby forces are friend or enemy. From a hill, Pindarus believes he sees Titinius killed. Completely discouraged, Cassius asks Pindarus to kill him. Titinius returns to find Cassius' body and kills himself. Brutus and others arrive, having defeated Octavius's army. Messala has brought them to see the body of Cassius. Now they see that Titinius is also dead. Brutus mourns the two, but also looks to a second battle with his enemies.*

[*Enter* Cassius *and* Titinius.]

**Cassius.** O, look, Titinius, look! The villains fly!
    Myself have to mine own turned enemy.
    This ensign here of mine was turning back;
    I slew the coward and did take it from him.

5  **Titinius.** O Cassius, Brutus gave the word too early,
    Who, having some advantage on Octavius,
    Took it too eagerly. His soldiers fell to spoil,
    Whilst we by Antony are all enclosed.

[*Enter* Pindarus.]

**Pindarus.** Fly further off, my lord! fly further off!
10    Mark Antony is in your tents, my lord.
    Fly, therefore, noble Cassius, fly far off!

**Cassius.** This hill is far enough. Look, look, Titinius!

**1–4 The villains . . . him:** Cassius is watching his men run away **(fly)** from the battle. He killed his own flag-bearer (the dead **ensign** lying on the ground near him) when he saw the man running away. How does Cassius seem to feel about the battle?

**7 His . . . spoil:** Brutus' soldiers began looting (instead of fighting the enemy).

Are those my tents where I perceive the fire?

**Titinius.** They are, my lord.

**Cassius.**                          Titinius, if thou lovest me,

15     Mount thou my horse and hide thy spurs in him
    Till he have brought thee up to yonder troops
    And here again, that I may rest assured
    Whether yond troops are friend or enemy.

**Titinius.** I will be here again even with a thought.

[*Exit.*]

20 **Cassius.** Go, Pindarus, get higher on that hill.
    My sight was ever thick. Regard Titinius,
    And tell me what thou not'st about the field.

[Pindarus *ascends the hill.*]

    This day I breathed first. Time is come round,
    And where I did begin, there shall I end.
25     My life is run his compass. Sirrah, what news?

**Pindarus.**

[*Above.*]

    O my lord!

**Cassius.** What news?

**Pindarus.**

[*Above.*]

    Titinius is enclosed round about
    With horsemen that make to him on the spur.
30     Yet he spurs on. Now they are almost on him.
    Now, Titinius!
    Now some light. O, he lights too! He's ta'en.

[*Shout.*]

    And hark!
    They shout for joy.

**Cassius.**                          Come down; behold no more.
35     O coward that I am to live so long
    To see my best friend ta'en before my face!

[*Enter* Pindarus *from above.*]

    Come hither, sirrah.
    In Parthia did I take thee prisoner,
    And then I swore thee, saving of thy life,
40     That whatsoever I did bid thee do,
    Thou shouldst attempt it. Come now, keep thine oath.

**15–18 Mount . . . enemy:** Ride my horse to those troops over there, and come back to tell me if they are friend or enemy.

**19 even with a thought:** as fast as you can think of it.

**25 is run his compass:** has come full circle (that is, my life is complete). What is Cassius planning to do?

**28–34** From a distance, Pindarus describes the capture of Titinius.

**32 ta'en:** taken (captured).

**38–46 In Parthia . . . the sword:** When I saved your life in Parthia (an ancient Asian land), you swore to do whatever I asked. Now keep your oath and become a free man. I'll cover my face as you stab me (**search this bosom**) with the same knife that killed Caesar. Don't argue (**Stand not to answer**). Why does Cassius finally decide to kill himself?

Brutus is not so convinced, however. He has no personal grudge against Caesar, and sees him as a man whose emotions never overrule his reason. Brutus wonders if Caesar might not change as he climbs the ladder of power, though, and think himself above all other men. Brutus compares him to a serpent's egg and is afraid of what will happen if the egg hatches and Caesar is crowned king. Cassius and the other conspirators convince Brutus that <u>if</u> Caesar were given such power, <u>then</u> he might turn against his friends and all the citizens of Rome. The best way to support Caesar, they conclude, is to kill him before he can become so evil and, as a result, save him from himself.

This was not an easy decision for Brutus to make, however, and his reasons for agreeing to the assassination are very different from Cassius'. He turns against Caesar not because he didn't love Caesar, but <u>because</u> he loves his country and its way of life more. He asks the Roman citizens, "Had you rather Caesar were living, and die all slaves, than that Caesar were dead, to live all freemen?"

Based on the evidence in the play *Julius Caesar*, there were two main causes of Caesar's assassination. One cause was the personal jealousy and self-interest of those who had once been his friends. These conspirators, led by Cassius, feared Caesar's popularity and worried about their own futures as he became more and more powerful. The other cause was not personal, but political. The spokesman for this point of view was Brutus. He loved Caesar and did not wish him harm. Cassius finally managed to convince Brutus that an all-powerful Caesar was a threat to the Roman republic and way of life, however. So these two causes—the personal and the political—together resulted in Caesar's death.

❹ Begins analysis of the second cause of the assassination

❺ Uses transitional words to show the cause-and-effect relationship

❻ Concludes by summarizing the effect and its causes

# Writing Your Cause-and-Effect Essay

*Happy the man who could search out the causes of things.*

**Virgil, Roman poet**

## ❶ Prewriting

Begin by exploring topics for your essay. What events puzzle you? What consequences would you like to examine before choosing a course of action? **Make a list** of ideas that occur to you. See the **Idea Bank** in the margin for more suggestions. Be sure to choose a topic that truly interests and inspires you. After you select a topic you would like to write about, follow the steps below.

### Planning Your Cause-and-Effect Essay

▶ **1. Think about the cause-and effect relationships.** Are the events really linked by cause and effect? An event that follows another in time isn't necessarily caused by it. Does a cause have one effect or many? Is an effect the result of a single cause, or of many causes?

▶ **2. Identify your audience.** What does your audience already know about your subject? What background information will you need to provide?

▶ **3. Gather supporting information.** What kind of information will you need to learn about your topic? Where can you find that information? Possibilities include personal observation and reflection, library research, or interviewing experts.

▶ **4. Sketch out your ideas.** How does the information you have collected fit together? You might create a table or chart to help you organize what you already know and discover what you still need to find out.

## ❷ Drafting

Use the drafting process to explore your topic and to think more about the cause-and-effect relationships you want to write about. Concentrate on just getting your ideas down on paper. You can revise them later. At some point be sure to clearly state the cause-and-effect relationship you're discussing. Then present **facts, statistics, examples, anecdotes,** or **quotations** to support your statements. You will also need to **organize** your ideas. You might show a single cause leading to multiple effects or multiple causes leading to a single effect.

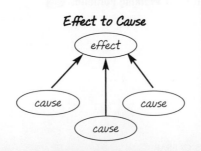

**IDEABank**

**1. Your Working Portfolio** 🗂
Look for ideas in the **Writing Option** you completed earlier in the unit:

<Selection 1>

**2. Crystal Ball**
Think of the decisions you might have to make about your life. Freewrite about the effects each choice might have on your future.

**3. Keys to Success**
With a group of classmates, list successful people you know. Brainstorm about the causes of their success.

**Have a question?**

See the **Writing Handbook** Cause and Effect, p. 1158–1159

### Ask Your Peer Reader

- How would you summarize the main cause-and-effect relationship that I wrote about?
- Where was the evidence most convincing? least convincing?
- What parts of the essay were confusing?
- What do you want to know more about?

Need revising help?

Review the **Rubric,**
p. 800

Consider **peer reader**
comments

Check **Revision
Guidelines,** p. 1145

## ❸ Revising

**TARGET SKILL ▶ EFFECTIVE TRANSITIONS** One way to be sure your cause-and-effect essay is clear is to use transitions that show the relationships between ideas. Words and phrases such as *therefore, because, as a result of, before,* and *if . . . then* signal causes and effects.

> ~~But~~ Cassius and the other conspirators ~~finally~~ convinced Brutus that
> *if Caesar were given such power, then he*
> ~~Caesar~~ might turn against his friends and all the citizens of Rome.
>
> The best way to support Caesar, they conclude, is to kill him before
> *, as a result,*
> he can become so evil and save him from himself.

**Mistified by
Modifiers?**

See the **Grammar
Handbook,**

**Misplaced Modifiers,**
p. 1190

**Phrases,** p. 1206

## ❹ Editing and Proofreading

**TARGET SKILL ▶ MISPLACED MODIFIERS** Misplaced modifiers can make your cause-and-effect writing confusing because they appear to modify something they cannot logically modify. Correct a misplaced modifier by moving it next to the word it actually modifies or by adding a word for it to modify.

> *Caesar has.*
> At the beginning of the play, ~~having~~ just returned from a long
>
> civil war after defeating Pompey, his rival for power, crowds
>
> *him*
> have lined the streets to glorify ~~Caesar~~ as a war hero and as the
>
> savior of Rome. In going against the orders of the Roman Senate
>
> in fighting Pompey, some people fear that Caesar wants to take
>
> control of Rome.

**Publishing
IDEAS**

• Present your essay
  orally to your class,
  using visual aids such
  as charts, photographs,
  or slides.

• Submit your essay to
  your school or local
  newspaper.

**More Online:
Publishing Options**
www.mcdougallittell.com

## ❺ Reflecting

**FOR YOUR WORKING PORTFOLIO** What did you learn about the cause-and-effect relationship you wrote about? What techniques did you learn that you can apply to other writing exercises? Attach your reflections to your finished cause-and-effect essay. Save your essay in your **Working Portfolio.**

Read this paragraph from the first draft of a cause-and-effect essay. The underlined sections may include the following kinds of errors:

- **run-on sentences**
- **misplaced modifiers**
- **lack of parallel structure**
- **lack of subject-verb agreement**

For each underlined section, choose the revision that most improves the writing.

---

Early in Shakespeare's play, Macbeth is drawn toward evil by three weird sisters. <u>They predict Macbeth will become king, as a result, he considers murdering</u> the current king. Lady Macbeth is <u>cunning, devious, and has a strong will</u>. Like her husband, she is anxious to seize the throne. She urges Macbeth to kill King Duncan. Macbeth and his wife <u>wants</u> the reward that the sisters have promised them. <u>Macbeth gives in to the corrupting power of evil his bloodthirsty reign soon begins.</u> <u>Innocent and helpless, Macbeth murders Macduff's family.</u> Macduff <u>feels</u> he is justified in killing Macbeth.

(1) ... (2) ... (3) ... (4) ... (5) ... (6)

---

**1. A.** They predict Macbeth will become king. As a result, he considers murdering the current king.

   **B.** They predict Macbeth will become king as a result, he considers murdering the current king.

   **C.** They predict Macbeth will become king as a result. He considers murdering the current king.

   **D.** Correct as is

**2. A.** cunning, devious, and a strong will

   **B.** cunning, devious, and having a strong will

   **C.** cunning, devious, and strong-willed

   **D.** Correct as is

**3. A.** wanting

   **B.** want

   **C.** has wanted

   **D.** Correct as is

**4. A.** Macbeth gives in to the corrupting power of evil, his bloodthirsty reign soon begins.

   **B.** Macbeth gives in to the corrupting power of evil, and his bloodthirsty reign soon begins.

   **C.** Macbeth gives in to the corrupting power of evil, his reign begins.

   **D.** Correct as is

**5. A.** Macduff's family is murdered by Macbeth, innocent and helpless.

   **B.** Macduff's family is murdered, innocent and helpless, by Macbeth.

   **C.** Macbeth murders Macduff's innocent and helpless family.

   **D.** Correct as is

**6. A.** feelings

   **B.** feel

   **C.** is feeling

   **D.** Correct as is

**Need extra help?**

See the **Grammar Handbook**

**Correcting Run-on Sentences**, p. 1199

**Modifiers**, p. 1190,

**Subject-Verb Agreement**, p. 1200–1202

# Lessons of History

How did the selections in this unit influence your
understanding of history and its effects upon people's lives?
What progress did you make in your reading and writing
skills? Explore these questions as you complete activities
in each of the following sections.

*Roman Forum, Rome, Italy.*
Copyright © Michael Yamashita.

## Reflecting on Theme

OPTION 1

**Comparing Foes**  Consider the enemies or opposing forces faced by the
protagonists in this unit. Choose the three that, in your judgment, are
the most threatening or powerful. Then, as you did in the activity on
page 542, consider what makes them so formidable and write a short
profile of each enemy or opposing force, explaining the reason for your
choice. Finally, choose one of the three and think about what you would
do if faced with such an opponent. Discuss your response with your
classmates.

OPTION 2

**Tests of Conviction**  Review the activity that you completed on
page 622. Based on your responses to this activity, what do you think
individuals have to gain from standing up for their convictions? With
a partner, look through the selections in this unit for characters who
stand up for their beliefs. Choose four that you think are particularly
courageous or admirable, and identify what they gained or lost as a
result of taking a stand. With your partner, explain your responses to
your class in a short oral presentation.

OPTION 3

**The Lessons of Power**  Consider different situations in which
people try to seize power, such as those you identified in the
activity on page 682. What types of people do you think are most
drawn to power? Working in a small group, create a two-column
chart. In the first column, list examples—drawn from the selections
and your own experience—of people who seek power for positive
reasons. In the second column, list examples of people who seek
power for negative reasons. Can you think of people who belong in
both columns? Discuss your chart with the rest of your classmates.

## Self ASSESSMENT

**READER'S NOTEBOOK**

Now that you have had a chance
to reflect on the lessons of history,
create a diagram centering on the
topic. The three categories should
be called "Human Nature,"
"Human Conflict," and "Human
Values." Under each category,
list your insights about that topic.
Put an X next to any entry that
represents an insight prompted
by a selection in this unit.

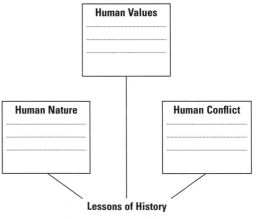

# Reviewing Literary Concepts

**Identifying Irony** Review the definition of irony on pages 543–544, and identify at least four selections in this unit that contain examples of irony. Then fill out a chart similar to the one shown. For each selection, list one or more examples of irony. Pair up with a classmate and compare charts.

| Selection | Situational Irony | Verbal Irony | Dramatic Irony |
|---|---|---|---|
| "Do not weep, maiden, for war is kind" | | Speaker says that war is kind but means that war is unkind. | |

**OPTION 2**

**Analyzing Point of View** The use of point of view in writing fiction may be compared to the use of a camera in making a movie. A close-up shot brings viewers very close to the subject, offering an intimate view. A wide-angle shot, on the other hand, presents a large scene. Which stories in this unit offer the most intimate view of their subjects? Are those stories told from a first-person or a third-person point of view? Review the definition of point of view on pages 623–624. Then discuss how point of view can affect a reader's sense of closeness to a character.

# Building Your Portfolio

- **Writing Options** Many of the Writing Options in this unit asked you to write letters for purposes ranging from political to personal. From your letters, choose two that most clearly and powerfully convey your concern for the subject matter. Write a cover note explaining the reason for your choices and attach it to the pieces. Then add the letters and the note to your **Presentation Portfolio.**

- **Writing Workshops** In this unit, you wrote a persuasive essay about an issue you feel strongly about. You also wrote an essay that explains the cause and effect of an event. Reread these pieces and assess the quality of your writing. In which of the pieces do you demonstrate a firmer grasp of your subject matter? Write a note explaining your choice and place it with the piece in your **Presentation Portfolio.**

- **Additional Activities** Think back to the assignments you completed under **Activities & Explorations** and **Inquiry & Research.** Keep a record in your portfolio of any assignments that you think are representative of your best work.

## Self ASSESSMENT

**READER'S NOTEBOOK**

Copy the following list of literary terms introduced or reviewed in this unit. Put a check next to terms that you believe you could easily define in your own words. Underline the terms that you feel are not easy to define. Then get together with a small group of classmates to discuss the meanings of the terms that seem difficult to define.

| | |
|---|---|
| situational irony | setting |
| protagonist | flashback |
| antagonist | blank verse |
| suspense | soliloquy |
| first-person | aside |
|  point of view | figurative |
| verbal irony |  language |
| sonnet structure | rhetorical |
| style |  devices |
| memoir | dramatic irony |
| tone | tragedy |
| diction | theme |
| third-person | |
|  point of view | |

## Self ASSESSMENT

**Presentation Portfolio**

Review the pieces in your portfolio. Which types of writing have proved troublesome? Have your strengths and weaknesses changed during the course of the year?

### Setting GOALS

The Reflect and Assess feature at the end of Unit One (pages 218-219) asked you to create a list of skills that you would like to work on. Review that list to judge your progress. Then create an updated list of skills, reflecting your current needs and interests, to work on during the rest of the year.

## LITERATURE CONNECTIONS
# Farewell to Manzanar

JEANNE WAKATSUKI HOUSTON AND JAMES D. HOUSTON

Here is the entire book from which the excerpt on pages 602–614 is taken, a true story of a Japanese-American family's confinement in the Manzanar internment camp in California during World War II. Jeanne Wakatsuki Houston was seven when Japan attacked Pearl Harbor and created the hysteria that forced almost 120,000 Japanese Americans from their homes. She remembers the stress of camp life. She also recalls what she took away from Manzanar after it closed—an odd sense of shame and a fierce determination to be accepted as American.

These thematically related readings are provided along with *Farewell to Manzanar*:

**from Legends from Camp**
LAWSON FUSAO INADA

**Sleep in the Mojave Desert**
SYLVIA PLATH

**I Remember Pearl Harbor**
CHARLES SHIRO INOUYE

**Wilshire Bus**
HISAYE YAMAMOTO

**Trains at Night**
ALBERTO ALVARO RÍOS

**Visiting Home**
KEVIN YOUNG

**from Unto the Sons**
GAY TALESE

**Lectures on How You Never Lived Back Home**
M. EVELINA GALANG

## And Even *More* . . .

## When Rain Clouds Gather

BESSIE HEAD

Fleeing the oppression of South Africa in the mid-1960s, Makhaya crosses the border into Botswana, arriving in a poor rural village. Makhaya becomes involved in political and cultural changes occurring in the village, which reflect those occurring in all of Botswana. This book is also part of the *Literature Connections* series published by McDougal Littell.

### Books
### Bronzeville Boys and Girls
GWENDOLYN BROOKS
Poems about the experiences of African-American children growing up in a big city.

### If Not Now, When?
PRIMO LEVI
This work tells of a personal war against the Nazis that ends with the affirmation of the human spirit.

### If I Die in a Combat Zone, Box Me Up and Ship Me Home
TIM O'BRIEN
A memoir of the author's tour of duty in Vietnam.

# The Underdogs

MARIANO AZUELA

First published in 1915, this novel offers a classic account of the Mexican Revolution of 1910. Demetrio Macías, the main character, has a ranch in the Juchipila River valley near the chaos and corruption of the revolutionary struggle. In an effort to save his family, the naive and peace-loving Indian joins in the revolution against dictator Porfirio Díaz. Macías becomes a general in the army of Pancho Villa. In the end, the peasant rebels become corrupted by the forces of lawlessness and greed unleashed during the revolution.

These thematically related readings are provided along with *The Underdogs*:

**Zapata** and *from* **Viva Zapata!**
JOHN STEINBECK

**The Festival of Bullets**
MARTIN LUIS GUZMÁN

**The Dictators**
PABLO NERUDA

**When Evil-Doing Comes Like Falling Rain**
BERTOLT BRECHT

**"It's Terrible" or "It's Fine"**
MAO ZEDONG

**Tienanmen Square: A Soldier's Story**
XIAO YE

**How Much Land Does a Man Need?**
LEO TOLSTOY

---

**All Quiet on the Western Front**
ERICH MARIA REMARQUE
Set in the trenches during World War I, this pacifistic novel tells the story of a young German soldier struggling against the hatred of war.

**Leaves of Grass**
WALT WHITMAN
The collected works of one of America's most influential poets. Whitman's poems celebrate America and the human spirit.

## Other Media

**Shakespeare: The Man and His Times**
Period paintings, prints, and woodcuts show major events of Shakespeare's life. Educational Audio Visual.
(VIDEOCASSETTE)

**Julius Caesar**
An adaptation of Shakespeare's play starring Charlton Heston, John Gielgud, and others. Republic Pictures.
(VIDEOCASSETTE)

**Rappin' with the Bard**
Familiar images are used to introduce Shakespearean language and stories. Beacon.
(VIDEOCASSETTE)

**Elie Wiesel: Witness to the Holocaust**
A portrait of the Nobel Peace Prize recipient. Sunburst Communication.
(VIDEOCASSETTE)

**Gwendolyn Brooks**
The Pulitzer Prize-winning poet reads her works. Amazon Books.
(AUDIOCASSETTE)

# Reading&Writing for Assessment

$W$hen you studied the test-taking strategies on pages 374–379, you learned and practiced techniques that you can apply in taking end-of-course examinations, standardized tests, and many other types of assessment.

The following pages will give you more practice using these strategies. Read the explanatory material that follows and then work through each of the models.

## PART 1  How to Read the Test Selection

Listed below are the basic reading strategies you studied earlier, along with several new ones geared to a different type of reading selection. Applying these strategies, taking notes, and highlighting or underscoring passages as you read can help you identify the information you will need to answer the test questions.

### STRATEGIES FOR READING A TEST SELECTION

▶ **Before you begin reading, skim the questions that follow the passage.** These can help focus your reading.

▶ **Think about the title.** What does it suggest about the overall message and tone of the passage?

▶ **Use active reading strategies such as analyzing, predicting, and questioning.** As you read, constantly ask yourself, "What does this mean, and what are its implications?" If the test directions allow you to mark on the test itself, make notes in the margin.

▶ **Look for main ideas.** These are often stated at the beginnings or ends of paragraphs. Sometimes they are implied, not stated. After reading each paragraph, summarize what it was about.

▶ **Note the literary elements and techniques used by the writer.** Consider the tone (writer's attitude toward the subject) and mood (the overall feeling or atmosphere the writer creates). What literary techniques, such as imagery and figurative language, contribute to those effects?

▶ **Examine the sequence of ideas.** Are the ideas developed in chronological order, presented in order of importance, or organized in some other way? Does the writer examine causes and effects, make comparisons and contrasts, or discuss problems and solutions?

▶ **Look for expert testimony.** What sources of information does the writer use? Why are these sources appropriate to the subject?

▶ **Think about the message and the writer's purpose.** What questions does the selection answer? What new questions does it raise? What generalizations can you make about the subject?

## Reading Selection

### Julius Caesar Takes Control

1 ❶ In 60 B.C., Julius Caesar joined forces with Crassus, a wealthy Roman, and Pompey, a popular general. With their help, Caesar was elected consul in 59 B.C. For the next ten years, these men dominated Rome as a triumvirate, a group of three rulers.

2 Caesar was a strong leader and a genius at military strategy. Abiding by tradition, he served only one year as consul. He then appointed himself governor of Gaul (now France). During 58–50 B.C., Caesar led his legions in a grueling but successful campaign to conquer all of Gaul. Because he shared fully in the hardships of war, he won his men's loyalty and devotion. Here he speaks of rallying his troops in battle:

3 ❷ I had no shield with me but I snatched one from a soldier in the rear ranks and went forward to the front line. Once there, I called to all the centurions by name and shouted encouragement to the rest of the men. . . . My arrival gave the troops fresh hope.

4 The reports of Caesar's successes in Gaul made him very popular with the people of Rome. Pompey, who had become his political rival, feared Caesar's ambitions. In 50 B.C., the senate, at Pompey's urgings, ordered Caesar to disband his legions and return home.

5 Caesar's next move led to civil war. He defied the senate's order. On the night of January 10, 49 B.C., he took his army ❸ across the Rubicon River in Italy, the southern limit of the area he commanded. He marched his army swiftly toward Rome, and Pompey fled. Caesar's troops defeated Pompey's armies in Greece, Asia, Spain, and Egypt. In 46 B.C., Caesar returned to Rome, where he had the support of the army and the masses. That same year, the senate appointed him dictator; in 44 B.C., he was named dictator for life.

6 ❹ **Caesar's Reforms** Caesar governed as an absolute ruler, one who has total power. He made sweeping changes, granting Roman citizenship to many people in the provinces. He expanded the senate, adding friends and supporters from Italy and the provinces. Caesar helped the poor by creating jobs, especially through the construction of new public buildings. He started colonies where the landless could own land and increased pay for soldiers.

7 Many nobles and senators were troubled by Caesar's growing power, success, and popularity. Some feared losing their influence; others considered him a tyrant. A number of important senators,

led by Marcus Brutus and Gaius Cassius, plotted his assassination. On March 15, 44 B.C., they stabbed him to death in the senate chamber.

8 **⑤ Beginning of the Empire** After Caesar's death, civil war broke out again and destroyed what was left of the Roman Republic. Three of Caesar's supporters banded together to crush the assassins. Caesar's 18-year-old grandnephew and adopted son, Octavian, joined with an experienced general named Mark Antony and a powerful politician named Lepidus. In 43 B.C., they took control of Rome and ruled for ten years as the Second Triumvirate. Among those killed in the Triumvirate's purge of Caesar's enemies was Cicero, a defender of the republic in the senate.

9　⑥ The Second Triumvirate ended in jealousy and violence. Octavian forced Lepidus to retire, and he and Mark Antony became rivals. While leading troops against Rome's enemies in Anatolia, Mark Antony met Queen Cleopatra of Egypt. He fell in love with her and followed her to Egypt. Octavian accused Antony of plotting to rule Rome from Egypt, and another civil war erupted. Octavian defeated the combined forces of Antony and Cleopatra at the naval battle of Actium in 31 B.C. Later, Antony and Cleopatra committed suicide.

10　Octavian claimed he would restore the republic and, in fact, did retain some of its forms and traditions. The senate, for example, continued to meet, and Octavian consulted it on important matters. However, Octavian became the unchallenged ruler of Rome. Eventually he accepted the title of Augustus, or "exalted one." He also kept the title Imperator, or supreme military commander, a term from which the word *emperor* is derived. Rome had become an empire ruled by one man.

**⑤ Look for main ideas.**

"This section must explain how the Roman Republic became the Roman Empire. The subhead mentions the empire, and, by skipping ahead, I see that the last sentence of paragraph 10 does, too."

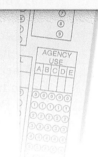

**⑥ Note the writer's tone.**

"The writer explains the motives for the various wars and rivalries but doesn't judge the people involved. The passage has a neutral, objective tone."

## PART 2

**How to Answer Multiple-Choice Questions**

Use the strategies in the box and notes in the side column to help you answer the questions below and on the following pages.

Based on the selection you have just read, choose the best answer for each of the following questions.

1. This selection describes Rome's transition from
   A. a time of peace to a time of war.
   B. a dictatorship to a democracy.
   C. an empire to a republic.
   D. a republic to an empire.

2. The ideas in this selection are presented in
   A. chronological order.
   B. order of importance.
   C. an order based on the geographic areas mentioned.
   D. none of the above

3. Judging from the selection, which of the following characteristics did a Roman citizen need MOST in order to become a ruler?
   A. relatives in government
   B. popularity with the people
   C. military expertise
   D. eloquence as a speaker

4. Which of the following passages from the selection has the LEAST objective tone?
   A. "Julius Caesar joined forces with Crassus. . . ."
   B. "He then appointed himself governor. . . ."
   C. "Pompey . . . feared Caesar's ambitions."
   D. "Caesar's troops defeated Pompey's armies. . . ."

5. Which of the following is the BEST example of cause and effect?
   A. Caesar was an absolute ruler, so the senators assassinated him.
   B. Caesar crossed the Rubicon to start a war.
   C. Antony went to Egypt, and Octavian defeated him at Actium.
   D. Octavian came to power and made himself emperor.

---

**STRATEGIES** FOR ANSWERING MULTIPLE-CHOICE QUESTIONS

▸ **Ask questions** that help you eliminate some of the choices.
▸ **Pay attention to choices such as "all of the above" or "none of the above."** To eliminate them, all you need to find is one answer that doesn't fit.
▸ **Skim your notes.** Details you noticed as you read may provide answers.

**STRATEGIES** IN ACTION

**Skim your notes.**

ONE STUDENT'S THOUGHTS

"The selection does not say that either Caesar or Octavian was particularly eloquent. *So I can eliminate choice D.*"

YOUR TURN

*What other answer choices were not mentioned in the selection?*

**Ask questions.** Was the event in the second part of each sentence a direct result of the event in the first part?

ONE STUDENT'S THOUGHTS

"Octavian didn't have to make himself emperor just because he came to power. *So I can eliminate choice D.*"

YOUR TURN

*Which of the events was definitely caused by the event that preceded it?*

## PART 3

**How To Respond in Writing**

You may also be asked to write answers to questions about a reading passage. **Short-answer questions** usually ask you to answer in a sentence or two. **Essay questions** require a fully developed piece of writing.

## Short-Answer Question

**STRATEGIES FOR RESPONDING TO SHORT-ANSWER QUESTIONS**

▶ **Identify the key words** in the writing prompt that tell you the ideas to discuss. Make sure you know what the key words mean.
▶ **State your response directly** and to the point.
▶ **Support your ideas** by using evidence from the selection.
▶ **Use correct grammar.**

> **Sample Question**
>
> Answer the following question in one or two sentences.
>
> Summarize the role Julius Caesar played in the decline of the republic and the rise of the Roman Empire.

**Identify the key words.**

**ONE STUDENT'S THOUGHTS**

"The key words are *summarize* and *role.* That means I have to briefly list Caesar's major contributions to Roman history."

**YOUR TURN**

*Which contributions will you include in your answer?*

## Essay Question

**STRATEGIES FOR ANSWERING ESSAY QUESTIONS**

▶ **Look for direction words** in the writing prompt, such as *essay, analyze, describe,* or *compare and contrast,* that tell you how to respond to the prompt.
▶ **List the points you want to make** before beginning to write.
▶ **Write an interesting introduction** that presents your main point.
▶ **Develop your ideas** by using evidence from the selection that supports the statements you make. Present the ideas in a logical order.
▶ **Write a conclusion** that summarizes your points.
▶ **Check your work** for correct grammar.

> **Sample Prompt**
>
> Caesar was named dictator of Rome for life. Later, Caesar's grandnephew and adopted son, Octavian, came to rule Rome as Augustus, "exalted one," and imperator, or supreme military commander. Compare and contrast the two leaders' rise to power and their military and social achievements.

**Look for direction words.**

"The important words are *compare and contrast.* This means that I'll have to show how Caesar and Octavian were alike and different."

**YOUR TURN**

*What evidence of similarities between the two rulers do you find in the selection?*

Here is a student's first draft in response to the writing prompt at the bottom of page 814. Read it and answer the multiple-choice questions that follow.

| | |
|---|---|
| 1 | Both Caesar and Octavian initially joined forces with other |
| 2 | leaders to rule Rome. As part of powerful triumvirates. The |
| 3 | members of both triumvirates eventually became political rivals. |
| 4 | Caesar and Octavian seized power. The writer says that Caesar |
| 5 | won the loyalty of his troops and he gives a quotation from him |
| 6 | to support this statement. There is no mention in the selection of |
| 7 | how Octavian's troops felt about him. They must have been loyal |
| 8 | to him, though, because he won many military battles. Both |
| 9 | Caesar and Octavian, who was then called Augustus, realized |
| 10 | how important the senate was and made it their ally. |

**STRATEGIES** FOR REVISING, EDITING, AND PROOFREADING

▶ **Read the passage carefully.**
▶ **Note the parts that are confusing or don't make sense.** What kinds of errors might cause that confusion?
▶ **Look for errors** in grammar, usage, spelling, and capitalization. Common errors include:
  • sentence fragments
  • lack of subject-verb agreement
  • unclear pronoun antecedents
  • lack of transition words

1. What is the BEST way to revise lines 1–2 ("Both Caesar . . . powerful triumvirates")?

   **A.** Both Caesar and Octavian initially joined forces with other leaders to rule Rome as part of powerful triumvirates.

   **B.** Both Caesar and Octavian initially joined forces, as part of powerful triumvirates, with other leaders to rule Rome.

   **C.** As part of powerful triumvirates, both Caesar and Octavian initially joined forces with other leaders to rule Rome.

   **D.** Make no change.

2. What is the BEST way to combine the sentences in lines 2–4 ("The members of both . . . seized power.")?

   **A.** The members of both triumvirates eventually became political rivals; Caesar and Octavian seized power.

   **B.** The members of both triumvirates eventually became political rivals, and therefore, Caesar and Octavian seized power.

   **C.** The members of both triumvirates eventually became political rivals, allowing Caesar and Octavian to seize power.

   **D.** Make no change.

3. What is the BEST change, if any, to the sentence in lines 4–6 ("The writer says . . . support this statement.")?

   **A.** The writer says that Caesar won the loyalty of his troops and the writer gives a quotation from him to support this statement.

   **B.** The writer says that Caesar won the loyalty of his troops and he gives a quotation from Caesar to support this statement.

   **C.** The writer says that Caesar won the loyalty of his troops and gives a quotation from Caesar to support this statement.

   **D.** Make no change.

# Discovering

# the TRUTH

*Sea Jewels* (1995), Paul Niemiec, Jr.
Watercolor, 18″ × 28″. Collection of
Mr. and Mrs. Stephen H. Palmer.

**T**ruth resides in
the human heart,
and one has to
search for it there.

**Mohandas Gandhi**

# Figurative Language: A Few Good Words

The difference between **literal** and **figurative language** is similar to the difference between the **denotation**, or the dictionary definition, of a word and its **connotation**, or mental associations. For example, think about the expression "caught between a rock and a hard place." Taken literally, the phrase doesn't mean much. It only makes sense as a way of expressing what it feels like to be stuck in a bad situation. Like symbols, **figures of speech** (another term for figurative language) say a lot with a few well-chosen words. Here are some common figures of speech:

- A **simile** makes a comparison between two unlike things using the word *like* or *as*. For example, R. K. Narayan's story "Like the Sun" (page 849) opens with a simile: "Truth, Sekhar reflected, is like the sun." The simile compares an abstract concept (truth) to a concrete one (sun), thus helping readers understand not only that truth is difficult to face but why.

- A **metaphor** is a comparison between two unlike things that have something in common. A metaphor does not use the word *like* or *as*. Carl Sandburg's poem "Moon Rondeau" (page 258) begins with a metaphor: "'Love is a door we shall open together.'" Sometimes a metaphor does not make a direct comparison but instead merely suggests one.

- A **personification** attributes human qualities to an object, animal, or idea. In "Tonight I Can Write" (page 352), Pablo Neruda personifies the wind in this line: "The night wind revolves in the sky and sings." This personification appears to make the wind a temporary companion to the poet in his sadness and in his solitary act of creating.

**YOUR TURN** Study the quotations at the right. Identify whether each is a simile, metaphor, or personification. Then analyze what the figure of speech communicates, and how.

---

**FIGURATIVE LANGUAGE**

I felt every fiber in my frame thrill as if I had touched the wire of a galvanic battery.

—Edgar Allan Poe, "The Pit and the Pendulum"

---

Sometime too hot the eye of heaven shines,

And often is his gold complexion dimmed;

—William Shakespeare, "Sonnet 18"

---

The noses of a great many Canadians resemble Porky Pig's. This comes from spending so much time pressing them against the longest undefended one-way mirror in the world.

—Margaret Atwood, "Through the One-Way Mirror"

---

Courage, I seemed to think, comes to us in finite quantities, like an inheritance, and by being frugal and stashing it away, and letting it earn interest, we steadily increase our moral capital in preparation for that day when the account must be drawn down.

—Tim O'Brien, "On the Rainy River"

---

You can't go through life without asking questions. Questions help guide your thinking in specific ways. Sometimes a good question is worth more than the answer because it directs you to think about important issues. The strategies on this page can help you ask questions about what you read.

# Questioning

Asking questions about a literary work focuses your concentration while you're reading and keeps you alert to important changes. You also feel more involved with what you read when you look for reasons behind events or motives for a character's feelings and actions. How did that happen? Why does the character make that choice? What does this word mean? How can the character possibly get out of this situation? These are the kinds of questions that you need to ask as you read.

## 1 Strategies for Asking Questions About a Literary Work

- Pay attention to all questions that naturally occur to you as you read. Trust your instincts.
- **Question** your own response to what you read: Why was I surprised by that? Why don't I like this character? Why am I confused here? Questions such as these can pinpoint key aspects of a work or help **clarify** what you may have missed.
- If you are confused, ask yourself what is confusing you. Is it the sequence of events, the character's motivation, the wording of a sentence? Then you can narrow your question to address the exact source of your confusion.
- Keep track of your questions as you read, and supply the answers when you find them. Sometimes the answers to one question can lead to a new, perhaps more important, question.

## 2 Strategies for Asking Questions About Symbols

- Look for references to concrete objects, and **question** whether they could be symbols.
- Notice objects or places that are emphasized by lengthy descriptions, repetition, or special placement in a work.
- **Question** whether a place, object, or minor character is essential to the theme of a literary work. If so, then chances are it is a symbol.

| "On the Rainy River" | |
|---|---|
| **Questions** | **Answers** |
| Why is the narrator so ashamed to tell this story? | because he thinks he's a coward for not running away to Canada |
| Why is he giving all these details about the meatpacking plant? | because it makes him (and me) think about killing and war |

## 3 Strategies for Asking Questions about Figurative Language

- Ask yourself what connotations you have for the words in the figure of speech. What feelings does the phrase evoke?
- **Question** why the author chose a particular comparison and not another.
- **Visualize** the image that the figurative phrase evokes. What does this picture tell you about the meaning of the phrase?

**Need More Help?**

Remember that active readers use the essential reading strategies explained on page 7: **visualize, predict, clarify, question, connect, evaluate, monitor.**

## The Mouse That ROARED

### by Richard Woodbury

*The Endangered Species Act restricts human activities that damage the habitat of any species in danger of becoming extinct. This law has often been a point of conflict between people who want to keep the environment unchanged and those who want economic development. As you read this article, focus on the opinions, or arguments, people put forth to support their particular viewpoints.*

Up and down the front range of the Rockies, one of the nation's hottest growth zones, a tiny, obscure rodent named the Preble's meadow jumping mouse is upsetting land planning, forcing developers to alter construction schedules, and snarling highway and utilities projects.

Not bad for a creature hardly anyone has seen.

All the fuss has come about not because the little mouse with the 5-inch tail is an officially endangered species—it isn't—but because it might soon be declared so. On that presumption, federal and local regulators are requiring developers to make elaborate surveys in wetland areas where the mouse allegedly thrives. ❶ Paul Banks, a bemused environmental consultant in Denver, says the elusive jumping mouse may be doing as much to curb Colorado's rampant development as all the slow-growth confabs and environmentalists' lawsuits put together.

If the U.S. Fish and Wildlife Service moves ahead and formally lists Preble's as endangered, as it's expected to do shortly, the obstacles to building will be stronger. And if the government fails to act, mouse advocates vow legal action to force listing. At issue as much as the rodent are the shrub-lined meadows and grassy marshes that abut the streams and creeks lacing the 170 miles from Cheyenne, Wyoming, to Colorado Springs. That stretch of land at the foothills of the Rockies is aswarm with housing and commercial development; three counties on the Front Range are among the Census Bureau's 10 fastest growing. ❷ "We're talking about critical habitat that's almost gone," says Jasper Carlton, director of the Biodiversity Legal Foundation. "We shouldn't be building in these areas anyway. Protecting the mouse saves the environment for all of us."

The little mouse is a reclusive character. Very few scientists have laid eyes on the buff-colored, black-striped mammal, which . . . measures barely 2 inches. Named for a Colorado naturalist . . . ,

---

## Reading for Information

Do we need more houses and malls and the jobs and profits that they create? Or do we need to preserve open space, wetlands, and wilderness? Controversial issues like this one can generate many different opinions.

### EVALUATING OPINIONS

This article presents opinions from individuals involved in an economy-versus-environment controversy. Readers need to be able to **evaluate** these **opinions** in order to form their own. Here are some questions to ask when evaluating an opinion:

• How might a person's profession impact his or her opinion?
• Does the person have sufficient education or experience that validates his or her opinion?
• Might the person have motives that could lead him or her to favor one side or the other?

**YOUR TURN** Use the questions and activities below to help you evaluate the different opinions in this article.

❶ Paul Banks is an environmental consultant—a person who helps developers and manufacturers comply with environmental laws. How might his job affect his opinion about the issue?

❷ Jasper Carlton works for a legal foundation that uses the law to support the case for biodiversity. How does knowing that information affect your reaction to his opinion?

the mouse hibernates for nine months. In summer it emerges only at night, when it commences to bound 4 feet at a leap through the tall grass, aided by . . . long hind legs and an outsize tail that helps stabilize it in flight. "There could be thousands out there, and there could be far fewer;

A researcher holds a Preble's meadow jumping mouse.

we just don't know," concedes Fish and Wildlife biologist Peter Plage, who has rarely seen the rodent in the wild.

**3** That's precisely the problem, says Linda Lacy, developer of an 18,000-acre project in Jefferson County, where wildlife agents set traps last summer seeking jumping mice. They caught no Preble's but did get 218 other mice and one rattlesnake. "It's ridiculous to protect the animal when no one can even seem to find it," says Lacy. . . .

With the certainty of greater disruption if the animal wins federal protection, Colorado officials have organized a 200-member coalition to draft the state's own protection plan, which may include finding the mice and relocating some of them into sanctuaries. "It's in the interest of both mouse and man to avoid drastic measures," says Congressman David Skaggs of Boulder, a Democrat who secured a $400,000 appropriation to fund the project. . . .

Environmentalist Carlton, whose lawsuit prodded the government to move on the mouse, says what the state may be scheming is "an end-run around the law to subvert restoring the ecosystem. You might have to move a golf course or road 100 feet or so, but protection isn't going to do in anybody. There's a lot of fearmongering going on." The Fish and Wildlife Service, apparently agreeing, contends that in 95% of cases only minimal disruption occurs when species are listed as endangered.

**4** In Washington, Colorado Senator Ben Nighthorse Campbell isn't waiting for studies. Denouncing the jumping mouse as a "killer" of jobs and economic growth, he says the federal government should be tossing animals and plants off the endangered list rather than putting them on. But the public feels otherwise. A *Denver Post* poll in March showed that 81% support protecting the little mouse that's seldom seen. "Their habitat is shrinking fast," warns Boulder mammalogist Carron Meaney. "We might find the mouse in 100 places now, but in 10 years 95 of those will be under concrete."

**3** What opinions are expressed up to this point? What are the backgrounds of the sources?

**4 Statistical Evidence** In these paragraphs, an opinion is followed by factual information that either supports it or contradicts it. Why do you think the reporter included this information? If it had not been included, how might your reaction to the opinions in these paragraphs be different?

**Constructing a Graphic** Review each opinion expressed in the article, using a chart like the one shown here. Compare your chart with that of a classmate, and discuss the opinion you've formed about the Preble's mouse and its future.

| Opinion | Background of Source | My Evaluation |
|---------|---------------------|---------------|
|         |                     |               |

**Inquiry & Research**

**Activity Link: "A White Heron," p. 834**

On the basis of this article, where do you stand on the conflict between protecting the environment and promoting economic progress? Take part in an informal debate on the topic.

*"So was I once myself a swinger of birches."*

# Birches

*Poetry by* ROBERT FROST

## Connect to Your Life

**Tree Climbers** Did you ever try to climb a tree? Perhaps, as a child, you hoisted yourself up to the lowest branches of a tree in your yard or a nearby park, or maybe you climbed up the trunk all the way to the top. Why do you think tree-climbing has such a strong appeal to children? Why do you think people generally lose interest in this type of activity as they grow older? Share your thoughts and experiences with classmates.

## Build Background

**Frost's Birches** In many of his poems, Robert Frost describes scenes from rural New England, where he lived as a child and later worked on his own farm. In "Birches," one of his most famous poems, Frost paints a vivid picture of the white birch trees that adorn much of the New England countryside. The white birch is a tall, delicate tree with a slender white trunk that can bend quite easily in a moderate wind or under the footsteps of a young tree climber.

## Focus Your Reading

**LITERARY ANALYSIS** **FIGURATIVE LANGUAGE** The poem "Birches" is rich in **figurative language,** which conveys ideas beyond the literal meanings of words. The general term *figurative language* includes specific **figures of speech,** such as **similes** and **metaphors,** which make comparisons between two unlike things that have at least one thing in common. Similes use the word *like* or *as,* while metaphors do not. In "Birches," the poet describes life with the following simile:

> *And life is too much like a pathless wood*

Look for other examples of figurative language throughout the poem.

**ACTIVE READING** **ANALYZING IMAGES** Frost uses **images** to create sensory experiences for the reader. The images in "Birches" convey in vivid detail two very different scenes, the birches after an ice storm and a boy swinging on the trees. The last third of the poem is more reflective but still contains powerful imagery.

**READER'S NOTEBOOK** As you read, try to see, hear, and feel what is described by the poem. Record your observations in a chart like the one shown.

| Birches | Images of Sight | Images of Sound or Touch |
|---------|-----------------|--------------------------|
| Line 1–20 | | |
| 21–40 | | |
| 41–59 | | |

# Birches

**Robert Frost**

When I see birches bend to left and right
Across the lines of straighter darker trees,
I like to think some boy's been swinging them.
But swinging doesn't bend them down to stay
5   As ice-storms do. Often you must have seen them
Loaded with ice a sunny winter morning
After a rain. They click upon themselves
As the breeze rises, and turn many-colored
As the stir cracks and crazes their enamel.
10  Soon the sun's warmth makes them shed crystal shells
Shattering and avalanching on the snow-crust—
Such heaps of broken glass to sweep away
You'd think the inner dome of heaven had fallen.
They are dragged to the withered bracken by the load,
15  And they seem not to break; though once they are bowed
So low for long, they never right themselves:
You may see their trunks arching in the woods
Years afterwards, trailing their leaves on the ground
Like girls on hands and knees that throw their hair
20  Before them over their heads to dry in the sun.
But I was going to say when Truth broke in
With all her matter-of-fact about the ice-storm
I should prefer to have some boy bend them
As he went out and in to fetch the cows—
25  Some boy too far from town to learn baseball,
Whose only play was what he found himself,
Summer or winter, and could play alone.
One by one he subdued his father's trees
By riding them down over and over again

30 Until he took the stiffness out of them,
And not one but hung limp, not one was left
For him to conquer. He learned all there was
To learn about not launching out too soon
And so not carrying the tree away
35 Clear to the ground. He always kept his poise
To the top branches, climbing carefully
With the same pains you use to fill a cup
Up to the brim, and even above the brim.
Then he flung outward, feet first, with a swish,
40 Kicking his way down through the air to the ground.
So was I once myself a swinger of birches.
And so I dream of going back to be.
It's when I'm weary of considerations,
And life is too much like a pathless wood
45 Where your face burns and tickles with the cobwebs
Broken across it, and one eye is weeping
From a twig's having lashed across it open.
I'd like to get away from earth awhile
And then come back to it and begin over.
50 May no fate willfully misunderstand me
And half grant what I wish and snatch me away
Not to return. Earth's the right place for love:
I don't know where it's likely to go better.
I'd like to go by climbing a birch tree,
55 And climb black branches up a snow-white trunk
*Toward* heaven, till the tree could bear no more,
But dipped its top and set me down again.
That would be good both going and coming back.
One could do worse than be a swinger of birches.

## Connect to the Literature

1. **What Do You Think?** What memories or thoughts did this poem trigger in your mind?

> **Comprehension Check**
> - What two explanations does the speaker give for the bent birches?
> - According to the speaker, which explanation is more likely?
> - How could birches help the speaker to "get away from earth awhile"?

## Think Critically

2. What kind of person do you imagine the speaker to be? Give details from the poem to support your answer.

3. What are the differences between the way branches bend from an ice storm and the way they bend from a boy swinging on them? Why are these differences so important to the speaker?

4. What do you think being a "swinger of birches" means to the speaker?

**THINK ABOUT**
- why swinging on birches is important to the boy in lines 25–40
- why the speaker "dreams" of again becoming a swinger of birches in lines 42–47
- why going up to heaven and coming back to earth are both considered

5. How do you think the statement "Earth's the right place for love: / I don't know where it's likely to go better" relates to the rest of the poem?

6. **ACTIVE READING  INTERPRETING IMAGES** Review the chart in your **READER'S NOTEBOOK**. What do you think is the most vivid or memorable **image** in each section of your chart? How do these images help you to imagine the scenes described by the **speaker?**

## Extend Interpretations

7. **Critic's Corner** One critic has said that Frost's "poems often sound . . . much like talk." Read some lines from "Birches" aloud. Do you think this poem resembles "talk"? Why or why not?

8. **Connect to Life** The speaker in this poem would like to leave the earth awhile but then return. One solution is to become a "swinger of birches." In what other ways do people temporarily retreat from the complications and worries of daily life?

## Literary Analysis

### FIGURATIVE LANGUAGE

Language that communicates ideas beyond the literal meaning of the words is called **figurative language.** Specific types of figurative language, called **figures of speech,** include **similes** and **metaphors.** A simile is a comparison between two things using the words *like* or *as.* Frost makes use of the following simile to compare the tree trunks to young girls:

> *You may see their trunks arching*
>   *in the woods . . .*
> *Like girls on hands and knees that*
>   *throw their hair*
> *Before them over their heads to*
>   *dry in the sun.*

A metaphor makes a comparison without using the words *like* or *as.* Frost uses a metaphor that compares the ice falling from trees to "heaps of broken glass."

**Paired Activity** Create a metaphor and a simile to add to Frost's description of the wintry scene. Compare your figures of speech with those of your classmates.

### ALLITERATION, ASSONANCE, AND CONSONANCE

**Alliteration** is the repetition of a consonant sound at the beginnings of words, as in "Soon the sun's warmth makes them shed crystal shells." **Assonance** is the repetition of vowel sounds within words, such as "When I see the birches bend to left and right." **Consonance** is the repetition of a consonant sound within and at the ends of words, as illustrated by "girls on hands and knees." Find two more examples each of alliteration, assonance, and consonance in this poem.

# *Choices & CHALLENGES*

## Writing Options

**1. Impressive Description** Think of a natural scene—a tree, a patch of flowers, a waterfall, or some other aspect of the natural world—that impresses you. Then, in one or two paragraphs, write a description of this scene, using figurative language to convey your impressions. You might begin by using a word web to explore your own reactions to

the scene you plan to describe.
**Writing Handbook**
See page 1153: Descriptive Writing.

**2. Interpretation of Poem** Write an essay interpreting the meaning of this poem and the speaker's attitude toward life. Defend your position with evidence from the poem. Place the essay in your **Working Portfolio.**

## Activities & Explorations

**1. Video Viewing** With classmates, watch the video of a dramatic reading of "Birches." Discuss how

the actor's reading affects your understanding of the poem. Decide whether you would read the poem in the same way.
**~ VIEWING AND REPRESENTING**

**VIDEO** Literature in Performance

**2. Leafy Scrapbook** Create a scrapbook of different tree pictures to illustrate why you think trees are so irresistible to young climbers. You could use photographs, magazine illustrations, your own drawings, or a combination of sources to capture various angles and types of trees. **~ ART**

---

## Robert Frost
### 1874–1963

**Other Works**
"The Road Not Taken"
"Mending Wall"
*North of Boston*
*New Hampshire*

**Unruly Years** Although Robert Frost was born in San Francisco, his ancestors were New Englanders. At age 11, shortly after his father's death, Frost moved with his mother and sister to Massachusetts. His mother was a teacher, but Frost was an undisciplined child who frequently skipped school. He did not become interested in books until high school. He then began studying, wrote poems for the school magazine, and was named co-valedictorian of his senior class, an honor he shared with his future wife.

**Farmer-Poet** Frost attended college briefly and then worked at a variety of jobs, including mill work and teaching. Between 1900 and 1909, he wrote many of his famous poems while living and working on a farm near Derry, New Hampshire. A

few were published in magazines, but Frost was almost 40 before his first book was published, in England. He had moved to England in 1912, and by the time he returned to the United States three years later, he was rapidly becoming a distinguished poet.

**Honors and Achievements** During his lifetime, Frost was awarded 44 honorary college degrees and was invited to teach at numerous colleges and universities, including Dartmouth and Harvard. Ironically, he had once attended and dropped out of both universities. Frost's other honors include four Pulitzer Prizes and a Congressional Gold Medal. He published his last book of poetry, *In the Clearing,* at age 88.

## Author Activity

**Presidential Inauguration** Frost was asked to read a poem at the inauguration of a United States president. He wrote a new poem for the occasion but, in the sun's glare, could not see to read it. Instead, he recited another poem from memory. Find out the name of the president and the name of the poem that Frost read.

# For the New Year, 1981

*Poetry by* DENISE LEVERTOV

# Pride

*Poetry by* DAHLIA RAVIKOVITCH
(dăl′yə rə-vē′kə-vĭch)

## Connect to Your Life

**Word Associations** What comes to mind when you hear the word *hope?* What about *pride?* For each of these terms, make a word web like the one shown. Write down whatever words or phrases you associate with hope and pride, and then share your webs with a classmate.

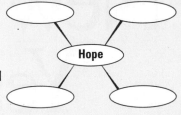

## Build Background

**Images of Nature** Hope and pride are the subjects of the next two poems, both of which were written by contemporary women poets. The speaker in Denise Levertov's "For the New Year, 1981" draws upon images from nature to convey her thoughts about hope. Toward the end of the poem, she makes a comparison to irises, popular perennial plants with orchidlike flowers. Like all perennials, irises can live and bloom for many years; however, they will do so only if they are dug up and divided when they get too crowded. Because the roots of irises are actually thick, gnarled underground stems called rhizomes, dividing the plants can be a difficult chore for a gardener.

The speaker in Dahlia Ravikovitch's "Pride" also uses images from the natural world—rocks at the edge of the sea. To the naked eye, rocks often appear changeless. Geologists tell us, however, that rocks, like all elements of the natural world, are subject to an aging process brought about by weathering and erosion.

## Focus Your Reading

**LITERARY ANALYSIS** **EXTENDED METAPHOR** As you know, a **metaphor** is a form of **figurative language** that makes comparisons between two things that have something in common. Unlike a **simile,** a metaphor does not use the words *like* or *as.* In an **extended metaphor,** two unlike things are compared in several ways. As you read the following poems, look for the extended metaphor in each one and consider how they make abstract concepts more concrete.

**ACTIVE READING** **MAKING INFERENCES** Although the **speakers** in the poems that follow do not directly state their ideas about hope and pride, readers can use clues in the texts to **make inferences,** or logical guesses, about the speakers' ideas. For example, consider what the following request in Levertov's poem reveals about the speaker's idea of hope:

*Please take*
*this grain of a grain of hope*
*so that mine won't shrink.*

**READER'S NOTEBOOK** As you read the poems, try to "read between the lines" and infer the speakers' ideas about their subjects. Note any words, phrases, or lines that contribute to your understanding of what the speakers mean by *hope* and *pride* respectively.

# For the New Year, 1981

Denise Levertov

I have a small grain of hope—
one small crystal that gleams
clear colors out of transparency.

I need more.

5   I break off a fragment
to send you.

Please take
this grain of a grain of hope
so that mine won't shrink.

10   Please share your fragment
so that yours will grow.

Only so, by division,
will hope increase,

like a clump of irises, which will cease to flower
15   unless you distribute
the clustered roots, unlikely source—
clumsy and earth-covered—
of grace.

## Thinking Through the Literature

1. **Comprehension Check** What does the **speaker** want to have happen?

2. **ACTIVE READING** **MAKING INFERENCES** Review what you wrote in your **READER'S NOTEBOOK.** What did you **infer** about the meaning of hope to the **speaker?**

   **THINK ABOUT**
   - the speaker's comparison of hope to a grain, "one small crystal that gleams / clear colors out of transparency" (lines 2–3)
   - the speaker's remark "I need more" (line 4)
   - the reason the speaker gives for sharing hope (lines 5–13)

3. Why do you think the speaker compares hope to irises?

4. What might be the relationship between the speaker and the person addressed?

*Tidal Flats, Deer Isle, Sunset* (1978),
A. Robert Birmelin. Acrylic on canvas,
50″ × 57½″, private collection.

# Pride

## Dahlia Ravikovitch

I tell you, even rocks crack,
and not because of age.
For years they lie on their backs
in the heat and the cold,
5   so many years,
it almost seems peaceful.
They don't move, so the cracks stay hidden.
A kind of pride.
Years pass over them, waiting there.
10   Whoever is going to shatter them
hasn't come yet.
And so the moss flourishes, the seaweed
whips around,
the sea pushes through and rolls back—
15   the rocks seem motionless.
Till a little seal comes to rub against them,
comes and goes away.
And suddenly the rock has an open wound.
I told you, when rocks break, it happens by surprise.
20   And people, too.

*Translated by Chana and Ariel Bloch*

## Connect to the Literature

**1. What Do You Think?**
What did you picture in your mind as you read "Pride"? Share your thoughts with a classmate.

## Think Critically

**2.** Why do you think the **speaker** compares people to rocks?

THINK
ABOUT

• what qualities you associate with rocks
• what aspects of human nature the speaker might be comparing to the cracks in a rock
• how the natural forces that act upon a rock might be compared to human experiences
• what an "open wound" might mean

**3.** **ACTIVE READING** **MAKING INFERENCES** Look back at the words, phrases, and lines you wrote down in your **READER'S NOTEBOOK**. Do you **infer** that the **speaker** of this poem views pride as positive or negative? Support your opinion with details from the poem.

**4.** Evaluate the **title** in terms of what it contributes to your understanding of the poem. Then, working with a classmate, brainstorm a list of alternative titles.

**5.** Compare the **tone** of "For the New Year, 1981" with that of "Pride."

## Extend Interpretations

**6. Comparing Texts** What fictional character or real person from the selections you have read might represent the type of hope that is described in "For the New Year, 1981"? Who might represent the type of pride described in "Pride"?

**7. Connect to Life** Review the word web for *pride* that you created for the Connect to Your Life activity on page 843. Then compare your notions of pride with the speaker's.

## Literary Analysis

**EXTENDED METAPHOR** An **extended metaphor** is a metaphor in which two unlike things are compared in more than one way. In "Pride," the rocks at the seaside are the basis for an extended metaphor that is carried out through the entire poem. The first comparison in "For the New Year, 1981," in which hope is called a "small grain," can also be considered an extended metaphor because it is continued across a number of stanzas.

**Activity** Analyze the extended metaphor in "For the New Year, 1981" by answering the following questions:

• What are the physical qualities of the small grain?
• What does the speaker do with the grain?
• Why does the speaker need to share the grain?
• Why do you think the speaker compares hope to a small grain?

Now compare the use of extended metaphors in both poems. Which extended metaphor do you think is more interesting?

**PERSONIFICATION** Another form of figurative language is **personification,** a figure of speech in which human qualities are attributed to something nonhuman, such as an object, an animal, or an idea. "The wind sighed" is an example of personification, since it suggests that a nonhuman force, the wind, can engage in the human act of sighing. With a partner, identify examples of personification in "Pride" and explain what human qualities are being personified.

## Writing Options

**1. Thesaurus Entries** Write thesaurus entries for the terms *pride* and *hope* on the basis of the views presented in the two poems. For each entry, include several synonyms and antonyms as well as a brief definition of the term.

**2. Abstract Poem** Write a poem about pride, hope, or another abstract human attitude or value that you associate with these ideas. The word webs you created for the Connect to Your Life activity on page 843 may help you get started. Try using images from nature to make the abstract attitude or value more concrete.

## Activities & Explorations

**Images from Nature** Choose other images from nature that could be used to communicate the same insights conveyed by the two poems. Find photographs, illustrations, or fine art—or create your own depictions—to suggest those insights. Present your findings to the class, and explain what is suggested by each image.
~ **VIEWING AND REPRESENTING**

## Denise Levertov
### 1923–1997

**Other Works**
*Collected Earlier Poems 1940–1960*
*New and Selected Essays*
*Candles in Babylon*
*Evening Train*

**A Poet's Destiny** Denise Levertov was born and raised in a suburb of London, England. She was educated by her parents at home and inherited her mother's love of nature. As a teenager, Levertov studied ballet and enjoyed painting; she loved traveling alone around London and spending time in the city's many museums and galleries. "Being a poet was, however, from my earliest childhood, what I never had any doubts about," Levertov said. "There is nothing I would ever for a moment prefer to have been." Indeed, Levertov published about two dozen volumes of poetry and received numerous honors and awards—including a Guggenheim Fellowship—for her work.

**Political Activist** Levertov moved to the United States in 1948 and became a U.S. citizen in 1955. After that time, she worked as the poetry editor of such magazines as *The Nation* and *Mother Jones* and taught at a number of colleges and universities. A pacifist, Levertov was active in antiwar and antinuclear movements over several decades; some of her poems reflect these political convictions.

## Dahlia Ravikovitch
### 1936–

**Other Works**
*A Dress of Fire*
*The Window: New and Selected Poems*

**Israeli Poet** Dahlia Ravikovitch is among the foremost poets writing in modern Hebrew, the language of Israel. She was born in a town called Ramat Gan, near Tel Aviv, and was raised on Kibbutz Geva, one of the country's many collective farms and settlements. After studying literature at Hebrew University in Jerusalem, she began publishing poetry in the noted journal *Orlogin*. From 1959 to 1963, she taught high school; then she left teaching to devote herself to writing. In addition to several volumes of verse, she has published short stories, children's books, and English-to-Hebrew translations of a number of works. Ravikovitch has also been active in the Israeli peace movement and in programs that teach adults to write poetry.

# Like the Sun

*Short Story by* R. K. NARAYAN (nə-rī′yən)

**Connect to Your Life**

**Tough Truths** Imagine that a friend has purchased a new outfit or has gotten a new haircut that you find unattractive. Your friend seems unsure about his or her appearance and looks to you for approval. Would you express your true feelings? Working in pairs, role-play the different conversations that you and your friend might have. Then discuss with your class whether it's always better to tell the absolute truth or whether truth needs to be tempered in order to spare people's feelings.

## Build Background

**School Life in India** Issues of truth are important to Sekhar, the main character in "Like the Sun." Sekhar is a teacher in India, where schools are modeled on the British educational system. Students begin upper primary school at age 11 and then secondary school at 14 or 15. For seven years they progress through forms, the equivalent of grades in the United States. Sekhar teaches the third form, or ninth grade; the principal of his school is called a headmaster. Sekhar is also a music critic in the small town in which he lives. In the story, he is asked to judge a performance of well-known traditional songs that reflect India's centuries-old musical heritage.

---

WORDS TO KNOW
**Vocabulary Preview**
essence
incessantly
shirk
stupefied
tempering

## Focus Your Reading

LITERARY ANALYSIS   HUMOR   The decision made by Sekhar at the beginning of the story sets the stage for the **humor** that will follow:

> *This day he set apart as a unique day—at least one day in the year we must give and take absolute Truth whatever may happen.*

As you read, note the sources of the story's humor. Does it arise from exaggerated situations, exaggerated **characters,** or humorous language?

ACTIVE READING   PREDICTING   During his day of absolute truth, Sekhar has a series of encounters with his wife, his colleagues, and his boss, the headmaster of the school where he works. Consider what humorous consequences may arise from Sekhar's decision. At the beginning of each encounter, try to **predict** what is going to happen.

READER'S NOTEBOOK
Record your predictions for each of Sekhar's encounters in a chart like the one shown. In the third column, note what actually happens.

| Event | Prediction | Outcome |
|-------|------------|---------|
| breakfast with his wife | | |

# Like the Sun

R. K. Narayan

Truth, Sekhar reflected, is like the sun. I suppose no human being can ever look it straight in the face without blinking or being dazed. He realized that, morning till night, the essence of human relationships consisted in tempering truth so that it might not shock. This day he set apart as a unique day—at least one day in the year we must give and take absolute Truth whatever may happen. Otherwise life is not worth living. The day ahead seemed to him full of possibilities. He told no one of his experiment. It was a quiet resolve, a secret pact between him and eternity.

The very first test came while his wife served him his morning meal. He showed hesitation over a titbit, which she had thought was her culinary[1] masterpiece. She asked, "Why, isn't it good?" At other times he would have said, considering her feelings in the matter, "I feel full up, that's all." But today he said, "It isn't good. I'm unable to swallow it." He saw her wince and said to himself, Can't be helped. Truth is like the sun.

His next trial was in the common room when one of his colleagues came up and said, "Did you hear of the death of so-and-so? Don't you think it a pity?"

"No," Sekhar answered. "He was such a fine man—" the other began. But Sekhar cut him short with: "Far from it. He always struck me as a mean and selfish brute."

During the last period when he was teaching geography for Third Form A, Sekhar received a note from the headmaster: "Please see me before you go home." Sekhar said to himself: It must be about these horrible test papers. A hundred papers in the boys' scrawls; he had shirked this work for weeks, feeling all the time as if a sword were hanging over his head.

The bell rang, and the boys burst out of the class.

Sekhar paused for a moment outside the headmaster's room to button up his coat; that was another subject the headmaster always sermonized about.

He stepped in with a very polite "Good evening, sir."

---

1. **culinary** (kyōō′lə-nĕr′ē): having to do with cooking or the kitchen.

WORDS TO KNOW

**essence** (ĕs′əns) *n.* the crucial element or basis
**tempering** (tĕm′pə-rĭng) *n.* modifying or adjusting  **temper** *v.*
**shirk** (shûrk) *v.* to neglect or avoid

**849**

The headmaster looked up at him in a very friendly manner and asked, "Are you free this evening?"

Sekhar replied, "Just some outing which I have promised the children at home—"

"Well, you can take them out another day. Come home with me now."

"Oh . . . yes, sir, certainly . . ." And then he added timidly, "Anything special, sir?"

"Yes," replied the headmaster, smiling to himself . . . "You didn't know my weakness for music?"

"Oh, yes, sir . . ."

"I've been learning and practicing secretly, and now I want you to hear me this evening. I've engaged a drummer and a violinist to accompany me—this is the first time I'm doing it full-dress,[2] and I want your opinion. I know it will be valuable."

Sekhar's taste in music was well-known. He was one of the most dreaded music critics in the town. But he never anticipated his musical inclinations would lead him to this trial. . . . "Rather a surprise for you, isn't it?" asked the headmaster. "I've spent a fortune on it behind closed doors. . . ." They started for the headmaster's house. "God hasn't given me a child, but at least let him not deny me the consolation of music," the headmaster said, pathetically, as they walked. He incessantly chattered about music: how he began one day out of sheer boredom; how his teacher at first laughed at him and then gave him hope; how his ambition in life was to forget himself in music.

At home the headmaster proved very ingratiating. He sat Sekhar on a red silk carpet, set before him several dishes of delicacies, and fussed over him as if he were a son-in-law of the house. He even said, "Well, you must listen with a free mind. Don't worry about these test papers." He added half humorously, "I will give you a week's time."

"Make it ten days, sir," Sekhar pleaded.

"All right, granted," the headmaster said generously. Sekhar felt really relieved now—he would attack them at the rate of ten a day and get rid of the nuisance.

The headmaster lighted incense sticks. "Just to create the right atmosphere," he explained. A drummer and a violinist, already seated on a Rangoon mat, were waiting for him. The headmaster sat down between them like a professional at a concert, cleared his throat, and began an alapana,[3] and paused to ask, "Isn't it good Kalyani?"[4] Sekhar pretended not to have heard the question. The headmaster went on to sing a full song composed by Thyagaraja[5] and followed it with two more. All the time the headmaster was singing, Sekhar went on commenting within himself, He croaks like a dozen frogs. He is bellowing like a buffalo. Now he sounds like loose window shutters in a storm.

The incense sticks burnt low. Sekhar's head throbbed with the medley of sounds that had assailed his eardrums for a couple of hours now. He felt half stupefied. The headmaster had gone nearly hoarse, when he paused to ask, "Shall I go on?" Sekhar replied, "Please don't, sir; I think this will do. . . ." The headmaster looked stunned. His face was beaded with perspiration. Sekhar felt the greatest pity for him. But he felt he could not help it. No judge delivering a sentence felt more pained and helpless. Sekhar noticed that the headmaster's wife peeped in from the kitchen, with eager curiosity. The drummer and the violinist put away their burdens with an air of relief. The headmaster removed his spectacles, mopped his brow, and

---

2. **full-dress:** complete in every respect.

3. **alapana:** improvisational Indian music in the classical style.

4. **Kalyani:** traditional Indian folk songs.

5. **Thyagaraja** (1767–1847): famous Indian composer.

Detail of *The Dance of Krishna* (about 1650, Mewar, Rajasthan, India). From a manuscript of the Sur-Sagar, opaque watercolor on paper, 11″ × 8⅝″, Collection Gopi Krishna Kanoria, Patna, India.

asked, "Now, come out with your opinion."

"Can't I give it tomorrow, sir?" Sekhar asked tentatively.

"No. I want it immediately—your frank opinion. Was it good?"

"No, sir . . ." Sekhar replied.

"Oh! . . . Is there any use continuing my lessons?"

"Absolutely none, sir . . ." Sekhar said with his voice trembling. He felt very unhappy that he could not speak more soothingly. Truth, he reflected, required as much strength to give as to receive.

All the way home he felt worried. He felt that his official life was not going to be smooth sailing hereafter. There were questions of increment and confirmation[6] and so on, all depending upon the headmaster's goodwill. All kinds of worries seemed to be in store for him. . . . Did not Harischandra[7] lose his throne,

---

6. **increment and confirmation:** salary increases and job security.

7. **Harischandra:** a legendary Hindu king and the subject of many Indian stories. His name has come to symbolize truth and integrity.

wife, child, because he would speak nothing less than the absolute Truth whatever happened?

At home his wife served him with a sullen face. He knew she was still angry with him for his remark of the morning. Two casualties for today, Sekhar said to himself. If I practice it for a week, I don't think I shall have a single friend left.

He received a call from the headmaster in his classroom next day. He went up apprehensively.

"Your suggestion was useful. I have paid off the music master. No one would tell me the truth about my music all these days. Why such antics at my age! Thank you. By the way, what about those test papers?"

"You gave me ten days, sir, for correcting them."

"Oh, I've reconsidered it. I must positively have them here tomorrow. . . ." A hundred papers in a day! That meant all night's sitting up! "Give me a couple of days, sir . . ."

"No. I must have them tomorrow morning. And remember, every paper must be thoroughly scrutinized."

"Yes, sir," Sekhar said, feeling that sitting up all night with a hundred test papers was a small price to pay for the luxury of practicing Truth. ❖

## LITERARY LINK

# *Tell all the Truth but tell it slant—*
### Emily Dickinson

Tell all the Truth but tell it slant—
Success in Circuit lies
Too bright for our infirm Delight
The Truth's superb surprise
5  As Lightning to the Children eased
With explanation kind
The Truth must dazzle gradually
Or every man be blind—

*June '70* (1970), Biren De. Oil on canvas, 72″ × 48″, National Gallery of Modern Art, New Delhi, India.

## Connect to the Literature

1. **What Do You Think?** Did you like the **character** Sekhar? Share what you think with your classmates.

> **Comprehension Check**
> - What does Sekhar decide to do for one day?
> - How do Sekhar's wife and the headmaster react to his behavior?
> - Why must Sekhar stay up all night?

## Think Critically

2. What kind of person is Sekhar? Use examples from the text to support your opinion.

**THINK ABOUT**
- his actions on the day of truth compared with those on other days
- his relationships with other people
- his attitude toward his work
- his reputation as a music critic

3. Why do you think that telling the absolute truth at least one day a year is so important to Sekhar?

4. **ACTIVE READING   PREDICTING** Review the **predictions** you made in your 📖 **READER'S NOTEBOOK.** How closely did your predictions match the events in the story? To what extent did your ability to predict events add to your enjoyment of the story? Explain your answer.

5. Is Sekhar's "experiment" one that you would like to repeat? Why or why not?

## Extend Interpretations

6. **Comparing Texts** Does the Literary Link poem "Tell all the Truth but tell it slant—" (page 852) help you to understand Sekhar's observations about truth? Explain your answer.

7. **Critic's Corner** According to critic Perry D. Westbrook, much of Narayan's work conveys this **theme:** "Human beings are human beings, not gods. Men and women can make flights toward godhood, but they always fall a bit short." How do you think this statement applies to "Like the Sun"?

8. **Connect to Life** Do you agree with Sekhar that truth generally requires "as much strength to give as to receive"? Why or why not?

## Literary Analysis

**HUMOR** In literature there are three basic types of **humor,** all of which may involve exaggeration or **irony.**

- **Humor of situation** is derived from the plot of a work. It usually involves exaggerated events or **situational irony,** which occurs when something happens that is different from what one expected.
- **Humor of character** is often based on exaggerated personalities or on characters who fail to recognize their own flaws, a form of **dramatic irony.**
- **Humor of language** may include **sarcasm,** exaggeration, **puns,** or **verbal irony,** which occurs when what is said is not what is meant.

**Activity** Do you think the humor in "Like the Sun" derives mainly from situation, character, or language? Cite details from the story to support your opinion.

**REVIEW**  **ALLITERATION, ASSONANCE, AND CONSONANCE**

Review the definitions of alliteration, assonance, and consonance on page 841. Work with a partner to decide which of these sound devices are employed by Emily Dickinson in "Tell all the Truth but tell it slant—"on page 852. Then practice reading the poem aloud to see if you can determine how such repetition contributes to the meaning and effect of the poem.

# Choices & CHALLENGES

## Writing Options

**1. Headmaster's Notes** As the headmaster of Sekhar's school, write two notes, one to your music master and one to Sekhar. Tell the music master why you are ending your lessons. Then tell Sekhar what you think of his honest evaluation of your performance.

**2. Theme Interpretation** Write a brief interpretation of the theme of the story. What do you think the author is trying to say about truth and personal relationships? Place the interpretation in your **Working Portfolio.**

**3. Scene Dialogue** If this day of "absolute truth" had been like any day of "tempered truth," how might Sekhar have responded to the questions asked by his colleague and by his boss? Rewrite Sekhar's two conversations. Temper the truth about what Sekhar really thinks so that he avoids hurting anyone's feelings.

## Activities & Explorations

**Truth Survey** Take a survey of at least six friends or classmates on the subject of truth. Create a series of questions based on situations from everyday life that are similar to those that Sekhar faced. For example, you might ask, "If a friend who lacked musical talent wanted your opinion about his or her performance, how truthful would you be?" Have participants rate their truthfulness on a scale of 1 to 5, with 1 being "not truthful at all" and 5 being "completely truthful." If you have a graphics program on your computer, use it to design your questionnaire.
**~ SPEAKING AND LISTENING**

## Inquiry & Research

**Legacy of Empire** As you know, the Indian school system described in the story is modeled on the British educational system. Find out more about the British colonization of India. In what other ways can the effects of the British Empire be felt in India? Share your findings with the class in an oral report.

**More Online: Research Starter**
www.mcdougallittell.com

The British game of cricket is still played in India.

## Vocabulary in Action

**EXERCISE: CONTEXT CLUES** On your paper, answer the questions that follow.

1. Are people who normally **shirk** their work likely to be lazy, efficient, or exhausted?

2. Is a person who can easily identify the **essence** of a problem someone with a sharp sense of smell, someone with an ability to see what's most important, or someone with a taste for the extraordinary?

3. Would a lecturer who spoke **incessantly** most likely find himself or herself applauded, arrested, or hoarse?

4. Does a person become **stupefied** by amusement, amazement, or annoyance?

5. Which of the following is the best synonym for *tempering: opposing, insisting,* or *moderating?*

**Building Vocabulary**

Several Words to Know in this lesson have interesting origins. For an in-depth study of word origins, see page 356.

# Grammar in Context: Adjective Clauses

In the following sentence, R. K. Narayan uses an adjective clause to help create a humorous description.

> **Sekhar's head throbbed with the medley of sounds that had assailed his eardrums for a couple of hours now.**

An **adjective clause** is a subordinate clause that functions as an adjective—that is, it modifies a noun or pronoun. In the example above, the adjective clause shown in blue modifies the noun phrase *medley of sounds.* The clause helps explain why the main character's head throbbed.

Most adjective clauses begin with relative pronouns, such as *that, which, who, whom,* and *whose. That* is usually used in an essential clause (a clause containing information that is part of the main idea of a sentence). *Which* is usually used in a nonessential clause (a clause adding information that is not part of a sentence's main idea). A nonessential clause is set off with commas; an essential clause is not.

*Who* is used when the relative pronoun functions as the subject of a verb in the clause. *Whom* is used when it functions as the object of a verb or preposition in the clause. *Who* and *whom* are used in both essential and nonessential clauses.

**WRITING EXERCISE** Rewrite each sentence, adding an adjective clause that modifies the underlined noun. Begin the adjective clause with the relative pronoun shown in parentheses.

**Example: *Original*** Sekhar makes a <u>decision</u>. (that)

***Rewritten*** Sekhar makes a <u>decision</u> <u>that he will be absolutely honest</u>.

1. Sekhar will tell the truth to <u>anyone</u>. *(who)*
2. Also, he will ignore the <u>test papers</u>. *(that)*
3. He complains about his morning <u>meal</u>. *(which)*
4. He hesitates before announcing his opinion of the <u>music</u>. *(which)*
5. The headmaster gives a difficult task to <u>Sekhar</u>. *(who)*

**Grammar Handbook** Clauses, p. 1197

# R. K. Narayan
1906–

**Other Works**
*The Guide*
*Malgudi Days*
*The English Teacher*
*My Days: A Memoir*
*Under the Banyan Tree*

**A Second Career** Born in Madras, India, R. K. Narayan is widely regarded as one of India's greatest authors. For his novel *The Guide* (1958), he won the National Prize of the Indian Literary Academy, his country's highest literary honor. Ironically, he turned to writing after he failed at teaching, having held two different jobs for a total of two days.

**Fictional Setting** Narayan sets most of his works in a fictional Indian town named Malgudi, a place that resembles both the city of his birth and the city of Mysore, where he has spent most of his life. He created Malgudi for his first novel, *Swami and Friends.* "As I sat in a room nibbling my pen and wondering what to write," he recalls, "Malgudi with its little railway station swam into view."

**English Narratives** Although Narayan knows the Indian language of Tamil, he always writes in English. Many of his stories were originally published in *Hindu,* one of India's English-language newspapers.

## Author Activity

**Epic Tradition** In addition to writing fiction, Narayan has translated into English certain Indian epics, including the *Ramayana.* Find out more about this great Indian epic, written by the poet Valmiki. Report your findings to your classmates.

## The Structure of Words

The English language has an amazingly rich vocabulary—a lexicon of hundreds of thousands of words. Moreover, the language is constantly growing. All the words in the language, though, have one thing in common. They are made up of various combinations of base words, roots, and **affixes,** or word parts. For example, in the passage on the right, consider the structure of the word *inexcusably*.

*Inexcusably* consists of the base word *excuse*, which means "to forgive," and two affixes. The affix *in-*, meaning "not," changes the meaning of the base word

> Nature had got **inexcusably** carried away on the summer question and let the whole thing get to be rather much. By duration alone, for instance, a summer's day seemed maddeningly excessive. . . .
>
> —Lorraine Hansberry, "On Summer"

to its opposite—"not to forgive." The affix *-ably* changes the part of speech of *excuse* from verb to adverb. Understanding how an affix can affect a word's meaning or its part of speech is an essential skill for building vocabulary.

## Strategies for Building Vocabulary

An affix may be either a **prefix,** which is attached to the beginning of a word, or a **suffix,** which is attached to the end of a word. Affixes may be added to base words and to roots. Learning the meanings of affixes can help you figure out unfamiliar words.

**❶ Learn Prefixes** When a prefix is added, it alters the meaning of a base word or root. For example, consider the word *imperfection*. When *im-* is added to *perfection*, it negates, or reverses, the meaning, making a word that means "flaw," or "not perfect." The chart below shows two categories of prefixes.

| Prefixes Expressing Size | Meaning | Examples |
|---|---|---|
| *micro-* | small | microcircuit, microscope |
| *mini-* | short, small | miniskirt, miniseries |

| Prefixes Expressing Time | Meaning | Examples |
|---|---|---|
| *ante-* | before | antebellum, antedate |
| *post-* | after | postdate, postscript |

**❷ Learn Suffixes** One or more suffixes can be added to the end of a base word or root to alter its meaning. There are two kinds of suffixes—derivational suffixes and inflectional suffixes.

| A Derivational Suffix . . . | |
|---|---|
| Changes the part of speech of a word | immigrate + -*ant* = immigrant |

| An Inflectional Suffix . . . | |
|---|---|
| Changes a word from singular to plural | birch + -*es* = birches |
| Changes the tense of a verb | walk + -*ed* = walked |
| Changes a word's degree of comparison | great + -*est* = greatest |

Knowing suffixes will help you analyze the parts of words and decipher meaning. Study the following chart to learn three types of derivational suffixes.

| Noun Suffixes | Meaning | Examples |
|---|---|---|
| -*ness* | state or quality of being | lawlessness, miserliness |
| -*ism* | system or theory; the condition of | capitalism, realism |

| Adjective Suffixes | Meaning | Examples |
|---|---|---|
| -*ate* | Characterized by | passionate |
| -*ive* | inclined to | excessive |

| Adverb Suffixes | Meaning | Examples |
|---|---|---|
| -*ly* | in such a manner | slowly |
| -*wise* | like | clockwise |

**EXERCISE** Break each word into its parts and give a definition of the word. If necessary, use a dictionary to help you find the meanings of the word parts. Then write a sentence using each word.

1. antemeridian
2. postoperative
3. affectionately
4. immobile
5. giantism

# On Summer

**Lorraine Hansberry**

Lorraine Hansberry was raised in Chicago, where summers can be hot and humid. When Hansberry was a child in the 1930s and 1940s, air conditioning was almost unheard of, so staying comfortable during the summers was nearly impossible. In this autobiographical selection, Hansberry tells about her experiences with the heat of the Chicago summer and why she finally came to "any measure of respect" for the season.

It has taken me a good number of years to come to any measure of respect for summer. I was, being May-born, literally an "infant of the spring" and, during the later childhood years, tended, for some reason or other, to rather worship the cold aloofness of winter. The adolescence, admittedly lingering still, brought the traditional passionate commitment to melancholy[1] autumn—and all that. For the longest kind of time I simply thought that *summer* was a mistake.

In fact, my earliest memory of anything at all is of waking up in a darkened room where I had been put to bed for a nap on a summer's afternoon, and feeling very, very hot. I acutely disliked the feeling then and retained the bias for years. It had originally been a matter of the heat but, over the years, I came actively to associate displeasure with most of the usually celebrated natural features and social by-products of the season: the too-grainy texture of sand; the too-cold coldness of the various waters we constantly try to escape into; and the icky-perspiry feeling of bathing caps.

It also seemed to me, esthetically[2] speaking, that nature had got inexcusably carried away on the summer question and let the whole thing get to be rather much. By duration alone, for instance, a summer's day seemed maddeningly excessive; an utter over-statement. Except for those few hours at either end of it, objects always appeared in too sharp a relief against back-grounds; shadows too pronounced and light too blinding. It always gave me the feeling of walking around in a motion picture which had been too artsily-craftsily exposed. Sound also had a way of coming to the ear without that

*Harlem Girl I* (about 1925), F. Winold Reiss. Graphite, charcoal, and pastels on illustration board, 55.5 cm. × 37.8 cm. Museum of Art and Archaeology, University of Missouri-Columbia. Gift of Mr. W. Tjark Reiss.

---

1. **melancholy** (mĕl´ən-kŏl´ē): sad.
2. **esthetically** (ĕs-thĕt´ĭk-lē): in a way that involves the level of good taste or artistic value.

*R*ealism as a general term refers to any effort to offer an accurate and detailed portrayal of actual life. The transforming heroes of comic books, the fiery explosions of action movies, the fantastic worlds of science fiction, and the menacing world of horror fiction are not realistic. Neither are Homer's *Odyssey* and the impressionistic stories of Edgar Allan Poe. But stories, novels, plays, and movies that dramatize ordinary human relationships or re-create actual historical events are considered realistic.

Realism is usually something you recognize when you see it. For instance, when you read a story such as Tim O'Brien's "On the Rainy River" (page 626), you immediately recognize the authenticity of time, place, and character. The narrator represents not only a real person but an ordinary one. He's no superhero, and that's the point.

*The Winnowers* (1855), Gustave Courbet. Oil on canvas, 131 cm × 167 cm. Musée des Beaux-Arts, Nantes, France/ Giraudon/Art Resource, New York.

## A Short History of Realism

Realism as an artistic movement and later an artistic method is a relatively new historical development. It started around the middle of the 19th century, when writers and artists decided to stop portraying ancient or idealized worlds and to start giving a truthful, objective depiction of the world they lived in. Thus, ordinary people—shopkeepers, workers, farmers—going about their daily affairs began to replace kings, nobles, heroes, and religious figures as the subjects of painting and literature. Some of the great realistic writers of the period include Leo Tolstoy in Russia, Honoré de Balzac in France, George Eliot in England, and Mark Twain in America.

By the end of the 19th century and into the 20th century, other artistic movements—such as naturalism, symbolism, surrealism, and modernism—sprang up to challenge the dominance of realism. But realism has remained very much alive as an artistic method, as you can see from most of the stories and art in this textbook.

**YOUR TURN** In your opinion, what is realistic about the passage at the right?

"I looked in that direction and between the ranks caught sight of something dreadful moving toward me. It was a man stripped to the waist, tied to the rifles of two soldiers, who led him. Next to him walked a tall officer in an overcoat and forage cap whose face seemed familiar to me. Resisting with his whole body, his feet splashing in the melting snow, the victim was lurching toward me under the blows falling on him from both sides; . . . And never leaving the victim's side, halting and advancing with a firm tread, was the tall officer. It was her father, with his rosy face and white mustache and sideburns."

—Leo Tolstoy, "After the Ball"

# Characteristics of Realistic Fiction

To some extent, realism has always been a significant element in literature. After all, epic heroes, such as Odysseus, do act in recognizably human ways. But the realism that developed in the mid-19th century marked a change in the nature and purpose of literature. Here are some characteristics that define the realist method.

**SUBJECT MATTER FROM ORDINARY LIFE** The rise of realism corresponded to the spread of revolution and democracy in Europe and North America, and so it is not surprising that realistic writers chose subject matter from the middle and lower classes. Details of setting became especially important to creating a convincing portrait of people's lives in a specific time and place. Dialect was increasingly used to characterize economic and regional differences.

**AN EMPHASIS ON CHARACTER** With democracy came a belief in the individual; with realism came the importance of character. For the realists, a character's destiny was no longer in the hands of fate but an outgrowth of his or her own actions. Thus, character rather than plot became the center of a realistic story. Think of the many stories you've read in which a character's choice drives the plot, as in "Initiation" and "On the Rainy River," for example. Think of other stories in which the plot is determined by a character's important discovery, such as in "The Prisoner Who Wore Glasses" and "After the Ball."

**CONCERN WITH ETHICAL ISSUES** Most literature addresses moral issues. For realistic writers, the situation from which an ethical issue arose had to be presented accurately and honestly. Otherwise, the morality of a story would have seemed too preachy or artificial. Thus, you have Sylvy in "A White Heron" (page 822) making the right decision only after long thought.

**YOUR TURN** Study the passages at the right, and identify what characteristics of realism are illustrated by each passage.

---

This day he set apart as a unique day—at least one day in the year we must give and take absolute Truth whatever may happen. Otherwise life is not worth living. The day ahead seemed to him full of possibilities. He told no one of his experiment. It was a quiet resolve, a secret pact between him and eternity.

—R. K. Narayan, "Like the Sun"

---

Still the young man looked at him in the same dazed, hopeless fashion. To Mr. Mayherne the case had seemed black enough, and the guilt of the prisoner assured. Now, for the first time, he felt a doubt.

"You think I'm guilty," said Leonard Vole, in a low voice. "But, by God, I swear I'm not! It looks pretty black against me; I know that. I'm like a man caught in a net—the meshes of it all round me, entangling me whichever way I turn. But I didn't do it, Mr. Mayherne; I didn't do it!"

—Agatha Christie, "The Witness for the Prosecution"

---

Then some went to the relief offices, and they came sadly back to their own people.

They's rules—you got to be here a year before you can git relief. They say the gov'-ment is gonna help. They don' know when.

And gradually the greatest terror of all come along.

They ain't gonna be no kinda work for three months.

In the barns, the people sat huddled together; and the terror came over them, and their faces were gray with terror. The children cried with hunger, and there was no food.

—John Steinbeck,
"The Flood" *from* The Grapes of Wrath

# *The* Active Reader: Skills and Strategies

Legend has it that the American mathematician and astronomer Benjamin Banneker once took a clock apart and put it back together again just to see how it worked. Although literature may not be as complicated as a clock, the same process Banneker used can help you understand how literature works. The strategies on this page can show you how.

## Analyzing

To **analyze** something is to separate it into parts for careful study. Analyzing is important to the study of literature because sometimes only by studying the parts of a literary work can you understand the whole. Use these general strategies to help you analyze different genres of literature.

### 1 Strategies for Analyzing Fiction

- Examine characters closely to identify their strengths and weaknesses. Use such character analysis to understand how and why a character changes, or what he or she has learned. Try using a chart like the one shown:

| Name of Character | |
|---|---|
| Strengths | Weaknesses |
| | |

How does he/she change?
(or what has he/she learned?)

- **Visualize** the setting. Look for clues in the detailed descriptions that might have an impact on the story. Consider whether the setting has a symbolic meaning.

- Study the sequence of events in the plot and identify conflict and the climax, or turning point. **Question** whether events could have turned out differently, and if so, how.

### 2 Strategies for Analyzing Nonfiction

- Determine whether the work is narrative (such as biography and autobiography), persuasive (such as a review or an essay), or expository (such as an essay or article).
- In a narrative, watch for bias in a writer's presentation and judgment.
- In a persuasive or expository piece, find the thesis and supporting points. **Evaluate** how well the supporting points prove the argument or clarify the explanation.

### 3 Strategies for Analyzing Poetry

- Read the whole poem through at least once, then study each stanza or grouping of lines separately to understand the impression or idea that they're building up to.
- Break down figures of speech into their component parts to **clarify** the comparison. What ideas or feelings does the figurative language convey?
- Look for objects, places, people, or actions that may have symbolic meaning.
- **Visualize** images and **evaluate** what purpose they serve.

**Need More Help?**

Remember that active readers use the essential reading strategies explained on page 7: **visualize, predict, clarify, question, connect, evaluate, monitor.**

# The Witness for the Prosecution

*Short Story by* AGATHA CHRISTIE

## Connect to Your Life

**Lie Detector** How do you decide whether someone is telling you the truth when all you have to go on is the speaker's word? Do you watch the expression on the speaker's face or listen to the tone of voice? With a classmate, talk about the kinds of clues you look for when you need to make a judgment about the truth of what someone tells you. Then share your ideas with the entire class.

## Build Background

**The Defender** In the selection you are about to read, a British lawyer seeks the truth about a murder case that is coming to trial. There are two kinds of lawyers in Britain: solicitors, who conduct legal work outside the court, and barristers, who actually try the cases in court. Defendants who are about to go on trial hire a solicitor to handle their case. The solicitor conducts most of the background work, such as researching evidence and interviewing witnesses. Then the solicitor hires a barrister to appear in court and question witnesses on the client's behalf. In the following mystery by British author Agatha Christie, a solicitor named Mr. Mayherne collects the evidence for his client and then turns it over to a barrister named Sir Charles.

| WORDS TO KNOW | **Vocabulary Preview** | |
| --- | --- | --- |
| amicable | churlish | infernal |
| animosity | cultivate | insolence |
| assiduously | dastardly | quell |
| averse | impotently | unfathomable |
| cajole | infatuated | vindicate |

## Focus Your Reading

**LITERARY ANALYSIS** **DIALOGUE** **Dialogue** is written conversation between two or more characters. Writers use dialogue to bring characters to life and to make their stories richer and more believable. As you read, consider how the dialogue contributes to your understanding of the characters and the plot.

**ACTIVE READING** **DRAWING CONCLUSIONS** Many people read mystery stories because they like to try to solve the mystery on their own, before the solution is revealed by the author. This process involves gathering clues and **drawing conclusions,** or making logical guesses based on those clues.

**READER'S NOTEBOOK** As you read "The Witness for the Prosecution," look for clues that point to the truth about the guilt or innocence of Mr. Mayherne's client. List the clues on a chart like the one shown, with clues indicating guilt on one side and those indicating innocence on the other. Then, just before the trial begins in the last section of the story, pause to weigh the clues and conclude what your verdict would be. Finish reading the story to see if you guessed right.

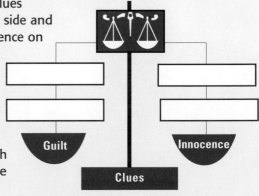

Guilt | Innocence

Clues

*Portrait of Count Fürstenberg-Herdringen* (1924), Tamara de Lempicka. Oil on canvas, 16⅛ ″ × 10¾ ″, courtesy of Barry Friedman Ltd., New York. Copyright © 1996 Artists Rights Society (ARS), New York/SPADEM, Paris.

# The Witness for the Prosecution

## Agatha Christie

**M**r. Mayherne adjusted his pince-nez[1] and cleared his throat with a little dry-as-dust cough that was wholly typical of him. Then he looked again at the man opposite him, the man charged with willful murder.[2]

Mr. Mayherne was a small man, precise in manner, neatly, not to say foppishly[3] dressed, with a pair of very shrewd and piercing gray eyes. By no means a fool. Indeed, as a solicitor, Mr. Mayherne's reputation stood very high. His voice, when he spoke to his client, was dry but not unsympathetic.

"I must impress upon you again that you are in very grave danger, and that the utmost frankness is necessary."

Leonard Vole, who had been staring in a dazed fashion at the blank wall in front of him, transferred his glance to the solicitor.

"I know," he said hopelessly. "You keep telling me so. But I can't seem to realize yet that I'm

---

1. **pince-nez** (păns′nā′): eyeglasses without side pieces, kept in place by a spring gripping the bridge of the nose.

2. **willful murder:** deliberate, not accidental, murder. In law, the term *willful* is used synonymously with *premeditated* (planned beforehand). Willful murder is a more serious crime than murder that is unplanned, accidental, or committed in self-defense.

3. **foppishly:** in the manner of a vain man who pays too much attention to his clothes and appearance.

charged with murder—*murder.* And such a dastardly crime too."

Mr. Mayherne was practical, not emotional. He coughed again, took off his pince-nez, polished them carefully, and replaced them on his nose. Then he said:

"Yes, yes, yes. Now, my dear Mr. Vole, we're going to make a determined effort to get you off—and we shall succeed—we shall succeed. But I must have all the facts. I must know just how damaging the case against you is likely to be. Then we can fix upon the best line of defense."

Still the young man looked at him in the same dazed, hopeless fashion. To Mr. Mayherne the case had seemed black enough, and the guilt of the prisoner assured. Now, for the first time, he felt a doubt.

"You think I'm guilty," said Leonard Vole, in a low voice. "But, by God, I swear I'm not! It looks pretty black against me; I know that. I'm like a man caught in a net—the meshes of it all round me, entangling me whichever way I turn. But I didn't do it, Mr. Mayherne; I didn't do it!"

In such a position a man was bound to protest his innocence. Mr. Mayherne knew that. Yet, in spite of himself, he was impressed. It might be, after all, that Leonard Vole was innocent.

"You are right, Mr. Vole," he said gravely. "The case does look very black against you. Nevertheless, I accept your assurance. Now, let us

# "I DIDN'T DO IT,

## MR. MAYHERNE;

# I DIDN'T DO IT!"

get to facts. I want you to tell me in your own words exactly how you came to make the acquaintance of Miss Emily French."

"It was one day in Oxford Street. I saw an elderly lady crossing the road. She was carrying a lot of parcels. In the middle of the street she dropped them, tried to recover them, found a bus was almost on top of her and just managed to reach the curb safely, dazed and bewildered by people having shouted at her. I recovered her parcels, wiped the mud off them as best I could, retied the string of one, and returned them to her."

"There was no question of your having saved her life?"

"Oh, dear me, no! All I did was to perform a common act of courtesy. She was extremely grateful, thanked me warmly, and said something about my manners not being those of most of the younger generation—I can't remember the exact words. Then I lifted my hat and went on. I never expected to see her again. But life is full of coincidences. That very evening I came across her at a party at a friend's house. She recognized me at once and asked that I should be introduced to her. I then found out that she was a Miss Emily French and that she lived at Cricklewood. I talked to her for some time. She was, I imagine, an old lady who took sudden and violent fancies to people. She took one to me on the strength of a perfectly simple action which anyone might have performed. On leaving, she shook me

WORDS TO KNOW

**dastardly** (dăs′tərd-lē) *adj.* mean and cowardly

warmly by the hand, and asked me to come and see her. I replied, of course, that I should be very pleased to do so, and she then urged me to name a day. I did not want particularly to go, but it would have seemed churlish to refuse, so I fixed on the following Saturday. After she had gone, I learned something about her from my friends. That she was rich, eccentric, lived alone with one maid and owned no less than eight cats."

"I see," said Mr. Mayherne. "The question of her being well off came up as early as that?"

"If you mean that I inquired—" began Leonard Vole hotly, but Mr. Mayherne stilled him with a gesture.

"I have to look at the case as it will be presented by the other side. An ordinary observer would not have supposed Miss French to be a lady of means. She lived poorly, almost humbly. Unless you had been told the contrary, you would in all probability have considered her to be in poor circumstances[4]—at any rate to begin with. Who was it exactly who told you that she was well off?"

"My friend, George Harvey, at whose house the party took place."

"Is he likely to remember having done so?"

"I really don't know. Of course it is some time ago now."

"Quite so, Mr. Vole. You see, the first aim of the prosecution will be to establish that you were in low water financially—that is true, is it not?"

Leonard Vole flushed.

"Yes," he said, in a low voice. "I'd been having a run of infernal bad luck just then."

"Quite so," said Mr. Mayherne again. "That being, as I say, in low water financially, you met this rich old lady and cultivated her acquaintance assiduously. Now if we are in a position to say that you had no idea she was well off, and that you visited her out of pure kindness of heart—"

"Which is the case."

"I daresay. I am not disputing the point. I am looking at it from the outside point of view. A great deal depends on the memory of Mr. Harvey. Is he likely to remember that conversation, or is he not? Could he be confused by counsel into believing that it took place later?"

Leonard Vole reflected for some minutes. Then he said steadily enough, but with a rather paler face:

"I do not think that that line would be successful, Mr. Mayherne. Several of those present heard his remark, and one or two of them chaffed[5] me about my conquest of a rich old lady."

The solicitor endeavored to hide his disappointment with a wave of the hand.

"Unfortunate," he said. "But I congratulate you upon your plain speaking, Mr. Vole. It is to you I look to guide me. Your judgment is quite right. To persist in the line I spoke of would have been disastrous. We must leave that point. You made the acquaintance of Miss French; you called upon her; the acquaintanceship progressed. We want a clear reason for all this. Why did you, a young man of thirty-three, good-looking, fond of sport, popular with your friends, devote so much of your time to an elderly woman with whom you could hardly have anything in common?"

Leonard Vole flung out his hands in a nervous gesture.

"I can't tell you—I really can't tell you. After the first visit, she pressed me to come again, spoke of being lonely and unhappy. She made it difficult for me to refuse. She showed so plainly her fondness and affection for me that I was placed in an awkward position. You see, Mr.

---

4. **circumstances:** financial condition.

5. **chaffed:** teased in a good-natured way.

Mayherne, I've got a weak nature—I drift—I'm one of those people who can't say 'No.' And believe me or not, as you like, after the third or fourth visit I paid her I found myself getting genuinely fond of the old thing. My mother died when I was young, an aunt brought me up, and she too died before I was fifteen. If I told you that I genuinely enjoyed being mothered and pampered, I daresay you'd only laugh."

Mr. Mayherne did not laugh. Instead he took off his pince-nez again and polished them, a sign with him that he was thinking deeply.

"I accept your explanation, Mr. Vole," he said at last. "I believe it to be psychologically probable. Whether a jury would take that view of it is another matter. Please continue your narrative. When was it that Miss French first asked you to look into her business affairs?"

"After my third or fourth visit to her. She understood very little of money matters and was worried about some investments."

Mr. Mayherne looked up sharply.

"Be careful, Mr. Vole. The maid, Janet Mackenzie, declares that her mistress was a good woman of business and transacted all her own affairs, and this is borne out by the testimony of her bankers."

**ACTIVE READING**

**EVALUATE** Do you think Leonard Vole is telling the truth?

"I can't help that," said Vole earnestly. "That's what she said to me."

Mr. Mayherne looked at him for a moment or two in silence. Though he had no intention of saying so, his belief in Leonard Vole's innocence was at that moment strengthened. He knew something of the mentality of elderly ladies. He saw Miss French, infatuated with the good-looking young man, hunting about for pretexts that would bring him to the house. What more likely than that she should plead ignorance of business and beg him to help her with her money affairs? She was enough of a woman of the world to realize that any man is slightly flattered by such an admission of his superiority. Leonard Vole had been flattered. Perhaps, too, she had not been averse to letting this young man know that she was wealthy. Emily French had been a strong-willed old woman, willing to pay her price for what she wanted. All this passed rapidly through Mr. Mayherne's mind, but he gave no indication of it and asked instead a further question.

"And you did handle her affairs for her at her request?"

"I did."

"Mr. Vole," said the solicitor, "I am going to ask you a very serious question, and one to which it is vital I should have a truthful answer. You were in low water financially. You had the handling of an old lady's affairs—an old lady who, according to her own statement, knew little or nothing of business. Did you at any time, or in any manner, convert to your own use the securities[6] which you handled? Did you engage in any transaction for your own pecuniary[7] advantage which will not bear the light of day?" He quelled the other's response. "Wait a minute before you answer. There are two courses open to us. Either we can make a feature of your probity[8] and honesty in conducting her affairs whilst pointing out how unlikely it is that you would commit murder to obtain money which you might have obtained by such infinitely easier means. If, on the other hand, there is anything in your dealings which the prosecution will get hold of—if, to put it baldly, it can be proved that you

---

6. **securities:** stock certificates or bonds.
7. **pecuniary** (pǐ-kyōō′nē-ĕr′ē): involving money; financial.
8. **probity** (prō′bǐ-tē): the holding of the highest principles and ideals; integrity.

---

WORDS TO KNOW

**infatuated** (ĭn-făch′ōō-ā′tĭd) *adj.* completely carried away by foolish or shallow love or attraction **infatuate** *v.*
**averse** (ə-vûrs′) *adj.* unwilling; deeply reluctant
**quell** (kwĕl) *v.* to crush; put an end to; quiet

swindled the old lady in any way—we must take the line that you had no motive for the murder, since she was already a profitable source of income to you. You perceive the distinction. Now, I beg of you, take your time before you reply."

But Leonard Vole took no time at all.

"My dealings with Miss French's affairs were all perfectly fair and aboveboard. I acted for her interests to the very best of my ability, as anyone will find who looks into the matter."

"Thank you," said Mr. Mayherne. "You relieve my mind very much. I pay you the compliment of believing that you are far too clever to lie to me over such an important matter."

"Surely," said Vole eagerly, "the strongest point in my favor is the lack of motive. Granted that I cultivated the acquaintanceship of a rich old lady in the hopes of getting money out of her—that, I gather, is the substance of what you have been saying—surely her death frustrates all my hopes?"

The solicitor looked at him steadily. Then, very deliberately, he repeated his unconscious trick with his pince-nez. It was not until they were firmly replaced on his nose that he spoke.

"Are you not aware, Mr. Vole, that Miss

# "MY DEALINGS WITH MISS FRENCH'S AFFAIRS WERE ALL PERFECTLY FAIR AND ABOVEBOARD."

French left a will under which you are the principal beneficiary?"[9]

"What?" The prisoner sprang to his feet. His dismay was obvious and unforced. "My God! What are you saying? She left her money to me?"

Mr. Mayherne nodded slowly. Vole sank down again, his head in his hands.

"You pretend you know nothing of this will?"

"Pretend? There's no pretense about it. I knew nothing about it."

"What would you say if I told you that the maid, Janet Mackenzie, swears that you *did* know? That her mistress told her distinctly that she had consulted you in the matter and told you of her intentions?"

"Say? That she's lying! No, I go too fast. Janet is an elderly woman. She was a faithful watchdog to her mistress, and she didn't like me. She was jealous and suspicious. I should say that Miss French confided her intentions to Janet, and that Janet either mistook something she said or else was convinced in her own mind that I had persuaded the old lady into doing it. I daresay that she herself believes now that Miss French actually told her so."

"You don't think she dislikes you enough to lie deliberately about the matter?"

Leonard Vole looked shocked and startled.

"No, indeed! Why should she?"

"I don't know," said Mr. Mayherne thoughtfully. "But she's very bitter against you."

The wretched young man groaned again.

"I'm beginning to see," he muttered. "It's

---

9. **beneficiary** (běn´ə-fǐsh´ē-ĕr´ē): person named in a will to receive money or goods.

The Voles lived in a small shabby house near Paddington Green. It was to this house that Mr. Mayherne went.

In answer to his ring, a big slatternly woman, obviously a charwoman, answered the door.

"Mrs. Vole? Has she returned yet?"

"Got back an hour ago. But I dunno if you can see her."

"If you will take my card to her," said Mr. Mayherne quietly, "I am quite sure that she will do so."

The woman looked at him doubtfully, wiped her hand on her apron and took the card. Then she closed the door in his face and left him on the step outside.

In a few minutes, however, she returned with a slightly altered manner.

"Come inside, please."

She ushered him into a tiny drawing room. Mr. Mayherne, examining a drawing on the wall, started up suddenly to face a tall, pale woman who had entered so quietly that he had not heard her.

"Mr. Mayherne? You are my husband's solicitor, are you not? You have come from him? Will you please sit down?"

Until she spoke, he had not realized that she was not English. Now, observing her more closely, he noticed the high cheekbones, the dense blue-black of the hair, and an occasional very slight movement of the hands that was distinctly foreign. A strange woman, very quiet. So quiet as to make one uneasy. From the very first Mr. Mayherne

was conscious that he was up against something that he did not understand.

"Now, my dear Mrs. Vole," he began, "you must not give way—"

He stopped. It was so very obvious that Romaine Vole had not the slightest intention of giving way. She was perfectly calm and composed.

"Will you please tell me about it?" she said. "I must know everything. Do not think to spare me. I want to know the worst." She hesitated, then repeated in a lower tone, with a curious emphasis which the lawyer did not understand: "I want to know the worst."

Mr. Mayherne went over his interview with Leonard Vole. She listened attentively, nodding her head now and then.

"I see," she said, when he had finished. "He wants me to say that he came in at twenty minutes past nine that night?"

"He did come in at that time?" said Mr. Mayherne sharply.

"That is not the point," she said coldly. "Will my saying so acquit him? Will they believe me?"

Mr. Mayherne was taken aback. She had gone so quickly to the core of the matter.

"That is what I want to know," she said. "Will it be enough? Is there anyone else who can support my evidence?"

There was a suppressed eagerness in her manner that made him vaguely uneasy.

> # "I MUST
> ### KNOW
> ### EVERYTHING.
> ## DO NOT
> ## THINK TO
> # SPARE
> # ME."

**ACTIVE READING**

**EVALUATE** What is your impression of Romaine Vole?

*Portrait de Madame M.*, Tamara de Lempicka (1898–1980). Oil on canvas, 99 cm × 65 cm, private collection, Paris. Copyright © 1996 Artists Rights Society (ARS), New York/ SPADEM, Paris.

scrawl, written on common paper and enclosed in a dirty envelope with the stamp stuck on crooked.

Mr. Mayherne read it through once or twice before he grasped its meaning.

> *"Dear Mister:*
>
> *"Youre the lawyer chap wot acts for the young feller. If you want that painted foreign hussy showd up for wot she is an her pack of lies you come to 16 Shaw's Rents Stepney to-night It ull cawst you 2 hundred quid[13] Arsk for Misses Mogson."*

The solicitor read and reread this strange epistle. It might, of course, be a hoax, but when he thought it over, he became increasingly convinced that it was genuine, and also convinced that it was the one hope for the prisoner. The evidence of Romaine Heilger damned him completely, and the line the defense meant to pursue, the line that the evidence of a woman who had admittedly lived an immoral life was not to be trusted, was at best a weak one.

Mr. Mayherne's mind was made up. It was his duty to save his client at all costs. He must go to Shaw's Rents.

He had some difficulty in finding the place, a ramshackle building in an evil-smelling slum, but at last he did so, and on inquiry for Mrs. Mogson was sent up to a room on the third floor. On this door he knocked and, getting no answer, knocked again.

At this second knock, he heard a shuffling sound inside, and presently the door was opened cautiously half an inch, and a bent figure peered out.

Suddenly the woman, for it was a woman, gave a chuckle and opened the door wider.

"So it's you, dearie," she said, in a wheezy voice. "Nobody with you, is there? No playing tricks? That's right. You can come in—you can come in."

With some reluctance the lawyer stepped across the threshold into the small dirty room, with its flickering gas jet.[14] There was an untidy unmade bed in a corner, a plain deal table[15] and two rickety chairs. For the first time Mr. Mayherne had a full view of the tenant of this unsavory apartment. She was a woman of middle age, bent in figure, with a mass of untidy gray hair and a scarf wound tightly round her face. She saw him looking at this and laughed again, the same curious, toneless chuckle.

"Wondering why I hide my beauty, dear? He, he, he. Afraid it may tempt you, eh? But you shall see—you shall see."

She drew aside the scarf, and the lawyer recoiled involuntarily before the almost formless blur of scarlet. She replaced the scarf again.

"So you're not wanting to kiss me, dearie? He, he, I don't wonder. And yet I was a pretty girl once—not so long ago as you'd think, either. Vitriol,[16] dearie, vitriol—that's what did that. Ah! but I'll be even with 'em—"

She burst into a hideous torrent of profanity which Mr. Mayherne tried vainly to quell. She fell silent at last, her hands clenching and unclenching themselves nervously.

"Enough of that," said the lawyer sternly. "I've come here because I have reason to believe you can give me information which will clear my client, Leonard Vole. Is that the case?"

Her eyes leered at him cunningly.

"What about the money, dearie?" she wheezed. "Two hundred quid, you remember."

"It is your duty to give evidence, and you can be called upon to do so."

---

13. **quid:** in England, slang for the basic monetary unit, the pound.
14. **gas jet:** natural gas flame used to light a room.
15. **deal table:** table made of fir or pine planks.
16. **vitriol:** a strong acid.

*Der Rote Turm in Halle II* [The red tower in Halle II] (1930), Lyonel Feininger. 100 cm × 85 cm, Kunstmuseum Mülheimander Ruhr sammlung ziegler.

# *Thinking* through the LITERATURE

## Connect to the Literature

**1. What Do You Think?**
Did you find the end of the story satisfying? Why or why not?

> **Comprehension Check**
> - With what crime is Leonard Vole charged?
> - How does Romaine try to discredit Vole?
> - What piece of evidence helps Leonard go free?

## Think Critically

**2.** **ACTIVE READING** **DRAWING CONCLUSIONS** Review the chart you made in your  **READER'S NOTEBOOK.** In drawing your own conclusion about Vole's guilt or innocence, what evidence did you think mattered the most? Compare your own conclusions about Vole with what you learn about him at the end of the story.

**3.** What is your opinion of Romaine Heilger?

**THINK ABOUT**
- her physical appearance and demeanor
- the details of her background
- her first interview with Mayherne
- her final revelations

**4.** Do you think Mr. Mayherne is good at his work? Why or why not?

**5.** Do you think the **plot** of the story is believable? Use evidence from the story to support your judgment.

## Extend Interpretations

**6. Critic's Corner** Commenting on Christie's popularity, H. R. F. Keating said, "She never tried to be clever in her writing, only ingenious in her plots." Do you think that "The Witness for the Prosecution" illustrates this distinction? Explain your view.

**7. Writer's Style** Many of Agatha Christie's mysteries have been adapted for dramatic presentation. Christie herself turned "The Witness for the Prosecution" into a stage play, which then became the basis of a popular 1957 movie; later, there was also a television production. Based on the style of this story, why do you think Christie's fiction lends itself to dramatic adaptation?

**8. Connect to Life** Based on this selection and on cases you may have seen in the news, how effective do you think courts are in finding out the truth?

## Literary Analysis

**DIALOGUE** Written conversation between two or more characters is called **dialogue.** Realistic, well-placed dialogue enlivens a narrative and often helps to advance the **plot.** Dialogue provides the reader with insights into **characters'** personalities and relationships with one another. Dialogue can also show something about the **setting** of a piece, reflecting the language and concerns of a particular place or time period. This lends richness and believability to a literary work.

**Cooperative Learning Activity** With a group, perform a dramatic reading of several scenes from this story. One member of the group can play the part of the narrator, reading all of the non-dialogue text. The other members can perform the parts of the story's characters, reading the dialogue as they would in a play. After you have performed the reading, discuss how details in the story influenced your oral performance. How does the dialogue contribute to your understanding of the plot, characters, and setting?

**REVIEW** **POINT OF VIEW**
Although the story is narrated from the **third-person point of view,** the reader can only see into the mind of Mr. Mayherne. How does this use of **third-person limited point of view** affect your sympathies or views toward the characters?

# *Choices* & CHALLENGES

## Writing Options

**1. Solicitor's Script** Write a script for the conversation Mr. Mayherne might have had with Leonard Vole after learning the truth from Romaine Heilger.

**2. Breaking News** Write a newspaper article that might have appeared just after the murder, just after the pretrial (police court) hearing, or the day after Vole was found not guilty.

**Writing Handbook**
See page 1155: Narrative Writing.

**3. Cast List** What current movie stars would you cast in the roles of the characters in a modern film version of "The Witness for the Prosecution"? Make a cast list of characters showing which star you would cast in each role. Briefly explain your reasons for each casting decision.

## Activities & Explorations

**1. Dramatic Role-Play** Working with a classmate, role-play the prosecution's examination or the defense's cross-examination of Romaine Heilger. To prepare, review this scene in the story for details that may be helpful for both the verbal and nonverbal aspects of your performance.
**~ PERFORMING**

**2. Courtroom Sketches** Draw sketches of the defendant, the lawyers, and the witnesses. **~ ART**

## Inquiry & Research

**Scientific Proof** What current scientific techniques for gathering evidence would make it harder for Vole to conceal his guilt today? Research these techniques, and record your findings in a written report.

 **More Online: Research Starter**
www.mcdougallittell.com

## Art Connection

**Portrait of the Witness** How well does the woman in the painting *Portrait de Madame M.* on page 881 match the way you pictured Romaine Heilger as you read the story?

## Vocabulary in Action

**EXERCISE A: SYNONYMS** For each phrase on the left, write the letter of the synonymous phrase on the right. The Words to Know are boldfaced.

1. **impotently** scream
2. notice **insolence**
3. **churlish** driver
4. **amicable** serf
5. sweet-talk the filly
6. **averse** to rehearsal
7. blushes from crushes
8. quiet the riot
9. intolerable officer
10. **cultivate** comrade

   a. **infernal** colonel
   b. **infatuated** rosiness
   c. observe nerve
   d. opposed to practice
   e. crabby cabbie
   f. **cajole** the foal
   g. pleasant peasant
   h. **quell** the crowd
   i. befriend Ben
   j. weakly shriek

**EXERCISE B: ASSESSMENT PRACTICE** For each group of words below, write the letter of the word that is the best antonym for the boldfaced word.

1. **dastardly** (a) admirable, (b) effective, (c) clever
2. **animosity** (a) jealousy, (b) sophistication, (c) friendliness
3. **vindicate** (a) accuse, (b) retrieve, (c) honor
4. **unfathomable** (a) encouraging, (b) likable, (c) clear
5. **assiduously** (a) respectfully, (b) lazily, (c) heavily

**Building Vocabulary**
For an in-depth lesson on context clues, focusing on synonym clues and antonym clues, see page 1000.

## Grammar in Context: Noun Clauses

In "The Witness for the Prosecution," the following two sentences contain noun clauses:

> "I want you to tell me in your own words exactly how you came to make the acquaintance of Miss Emily French."

> "Whether a jury would take that view of it is another matter."

A **noun clause** is a subordinate clause that functions as a noun—it can be a subject, an object, or a predicate nominative. In the first sentence above, the noun clause shown in blue is the direct object of the verb *tell*. In the second sentence, the noun clause is the subject of the sentence.

**Usage Tip:** Noun clauses can be introduced by a variety of words. Among these are *what, that, who, which, how, when,* and *where*.

**WRITING EXERCISE** Rewrite each sentence, adding a noun clause introduced by the underlined word.

**Example: *Original*** Mr. Mayherne tries to figure out <u>how</u>.

***Rewritten*** Mr. Mayherne tries to figure out <u>how he can prove</u> Leonard Vole's innocence.

1. Mr. Mayherne thinks about <u>who</u>.
2. He needs to know <u>when</u>.
3. He seems determined to learn <u>what</u>.
4. Romaine reveals <u>which</u>.

<u>Grammar Handbook</u>  Clauses, p. 1197

# Agatha Christie
## 1890–1976

**Other Works**
*Murder on the Orient Express
And Then There Were None
Three Blind Mice and Other Stories
Hickory, Dickory, Death*

**The Queen of British Mystery** Agatha Christie is one of the world's most popular writers of detective fiction. Her books have been translated into more than 100 languages, and probably more copies of her books have been sold than have those of any other writer in the 20th century. Christie's eccentric detective Hercule Poirot appeared on a Nicaraguan postage stamp. Several of her other detectives, including Miss Jane Marple, are still featured regularly in televised versions of her mysteries.

**The Path to Success** Christie grew up in Torquay, Devonshire, a small resort in the English countryside. Her father, an American, died when she was very young, and she was raised by her British mother. In 1914, after the outbreak of World War I, Christie was married. During the war, she worked as a hospital nurse and thereby gained, among other things, a knowledge of poisons. A challenge from her sister prompted Christie to write her first detective novel, *The Mysterious Affair at Styles,* which was published in 1920. In the next six years, she published six more books, including *The Murder of Roger Ackroyd* (1926), often hailed as her most ingenious mystery. Soon afterward came the famous mystery in Christie's own life: the celebrated author disappeared, and she was discovered, after a nationwide hunt, apparently suffering from amnesia. She subsequently divorced her first husband and married Max Mallowan, an archaeologist, with whom she later made frequent visits to the Middle East. These travels prompted several mysteries, including *Death on the Nile* (1937) and *Death Comes as the End* (1944).

## Author Activity

**From Page to Stage to Screen** Read the dramatic adaptation of this story or watch a video of the 1957 film version, which was based on the play. Then write a review in which you compare the short story with the play or the film version. Be sure to mention which you prefer and why.

# The Balek Scales

*Short Story by* HEINRICH BÖLL (hĭn'rĭk bœl)

## Connect to Your Life

**The Scales of Justice** What does the word *justice* mean to you? Explore the meaning of the word and its associations by creating a word web to answer the questions that are shown.

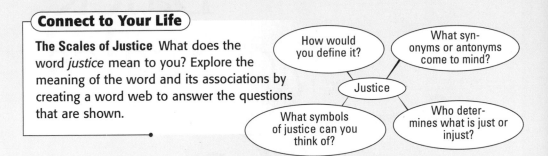

## Build Background

**European Social Order** This story takes place in central Europe around 1900. In that era, much of Europe was characterized by a strict social hierarchy in which a person's social position was largely determined by birth. At the top of the social ladder were such royal figures as kings or emperors, followed by counts and barons and other members of the aristocracy who passed their titles down to their children. Ranking below the aristocracy were wealthy landowners who had no titles but who often hoped to acquire them as a reward for service or influence. At the bottom of the social ladder were the common people.

In the story you are about to read, the Baleks, a wealthy family, have controlled the lives of the common people for five generations, even to the point of creating laws to control the system of justice. The Baleks live in an elegant chateau (shă-tō'), or country house, and own much of the land in the area.

WORDS TO KNOW
**Vocabulary Preview**
antiquated    meager
flout         preside
forlorn

## Focus Your Reading

**LITERARY ANALYSIS   TONE   Tone** is the attitude a writer or narrator takes toward a subject. A writer's use of language and details helps to create the tone, which might be serious, humorous, ironic, or detached, among other possibilities. As you read, pay attention to the story's tone and how it affects your reaction to the story.

**ACTIVE READING   ANALYZING RELEVANCE OF SETTING**   In "The Balek Scales," Böll opens the story by introducing its **setting**—the time and place in which the action occurs—and describing the work that the people do. This description also tells you something about the power of the Balek family and the hardships faced by the working people:

> *Where my grandfather came from, most of the people lived by working in the flax sheds. For five generations they had been breathing in the dust which rose from the crushed flax stalks, letting themselves be killed off by slow degrees.*

**READER'S NOTEBOOK** In order to **analyze** a story's setting, you must first break it down into parts. As you read this story, fill in a chart like the one started here. Identify key places in the setting, and give short descriptions of each place and what happens there.

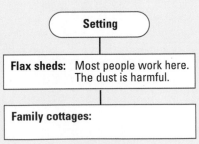

# The Balek Scales

**Heinrich Böll**

Where my grandfather came from, most of the people lived by working in the flax sheds. For five generations they had been breathing in the dust which rose from the crushed flax stalks, letting themselves be killed off by slow degrees, a race of long-suffering, cheerful people who ate goat cheese, potatoes, and now and then a rabbit; in the evening they would sit at home spinning and knitting; they sang, drank mint tea and were happy.

During the day they would carry the flax stalks to the <u>antiquated</u> machines, with no protection from the dust and at the mercy of the heat which came pouring out of the drying kilns.[1] Each cottage contained only one bed, standing against the wall like a closet and reserved for the parents, while the children slept all around the room on benches. In the morning the room would be filled with the odor of thin soup; on Sundays there was stew, and on feast days[2] the children's faces would light up with pleasure as they watched the black acorn coffee turning paler and paler from the milk their smiling mother poured into their coffee mugs.

The parents went off early to the flax sheds, the housework was left to the children: they would sweep the room, tidy up, wash the dishes and peel the potatoes, precious pale-yellow fruit whose thin peel had to be produced afterwards to dispel any suspicion of extravagance or carelessness.

As soon as the children were out of school, they had to go off into the woods and, depending on the season, gather mushrooms and herbs: woodruff and thyme, caraway, mint and foxglove, and in summer, when they had brought in the hay from their <u>meager</u> fields, they gathered hayflowers. A kilo[3] of hayflowers was worth one pfennig,[4] and they were sold by the apothecaries[5] in town for twenty pfennigs a kilo to highly strung ladies. The mushrooms were highly prized: they fetched twenty pfennigs a kilo and were sold in the shops in town for one mark twenty.[6] The

**ACTIVE READING**

**ANALYZE** How does this description of setting influence your understanding of the people in the village?

children would crawl deep into the green darkness of the forest during the autumn when dampness drove the mushrooms out of the soil, and almost every family had its own places where it gathered mushrooms, places which were handed down in whispers from generation to generation.

The woods belonged to the Baleks, as well as the flax sheds, and in my grandfather's village the Baleks had a chateau, and the wife of the head of the family had a little room next to the dairy where mushrooms, herbs and hayflowers were weighed and paid for. There on the table stood the great Balek scales, an old-fashioned, ornate bronze-gilt[7] contraption, which my grandfather's grandparents had already faced when they were children, their grubby hands holding their little baskets of mushrooms, their paper bags of hayflowers, breathlessly watching the number of weights Frau[8] Balek had to throw on the scale before the swinging pointer came to rest exactly over the black line, that thin line of justice which had to be redrawn every year. Then Frau Balek would take the big book covered in brown leather, write down the weight, and pay out the money, pfennigs or ten-pfennig pieces and very, very occasionally, a mark. And when my grandfather was a child,

---

1. **kilns** (kĭlnz): ovens, used here to dry the flax.
2. **feast days:** holidays, especially religious holidays honoring saints.
3. **kilo** (kē′lō): short for *kilogram,* a metric measure equal to 1,000 grams, or about 2.2 pounds.
4. **pfennig** (fĕn′ĭg): a coin equal to a hundredth of a mark, the basic unit of German currency. The word *pfennig* is related to the English *penny.*
5. **apothecaries** (ə-pŏth′ĭ-kĕr′ēz): pharmacists; druggists.
6. **one mark twenty:** one mark and twenty pfennigs.
7. **bronze-gilt:** covered with a thin layer of bronze.
8. **Frau** (frou): a German title indicating a married woman.

---

WORDS
TO
KNOW
**antiquated** (ăn′tĭ-kwā′tĭd) *adj.* old-fashioned; outmoded
**meager** (mē′gər) *adj.* lacking quantity, fullness, strength, or fertility; feeble; scanty

there was a big glass jar of lemon drops standing there, the kind that cost one mark a kilo, and when Frau Balek—whichever one happened to be presiding over the little room—was in a good mood, she would put her hand into this jar and give each child a lemon drop, and the children's faces would light up with pleasure, the way they used to when on feast days their mother poured milk into their coffee mugs, milk that made the coffee turn paler and paler until it was as pale as the flaxen pigtails of the little girls.

One of the laws imposed by the Baleks on the village was: no one was permitted to have any scales in the house. The law was so ancient that nobody gave a thought as to when and how it had arisen, and it had to be obeyed, for anyone who broke it was dismissed from the flax sheds, he could not sell his mushrooms or his thyme or his hayflowers, and the power of the Baleks was so far-reaching that no one in the neighboring villages would give him work either or buy his forest herbs. But since the days when my grandfather's parents had gone out as small children to gather mushrooms and sell them in order that they might season the meat of the rich people of Prague[9] or be baked into game pies, it had never occurred to anyone to break this law: flour could be measured in cups, eggs could be counted, what they had spun could be measured by the yard, and besides, the old-fashioned bronze-gilt, ornate Balek scales did not look as if there was anything wrong with them, and five generations had entrusted the swinging black pointer with what they had gone out as eager children to gather from the woods.

True, there were some among those quiet people who flouted the law, poachers bent on making more money in one night than they could earn in a whole month in the flax sheds, but even these people apparently never thought of buying scales or making their own. My grandfather was the first person bold enough to test the justice of the Baleks, the family who lived in the chateau and drove two carriages, who always maintained one boy from the village while he studied theology at the seminary[10] in Prague, the family with whom the priest played taroc[11] every Wednesday, on whom the local reeve,[12] in his carriage emblazoned with the Imperial coat of arms, made an annual New Year's Day call and on whom the Emperor conferred a title on the first day of the year 1900.

My grandfather was hard-working and smart: he crawled further into the woods than the children of his clan had crawled before him, he penetrated as far as the thicket where, according to legend, Bilgan the Giant was supposed to dwell, guarding a treasure. But my

---

9. **Prague** (präg): the capital of the present-day Czech (chĕk) Republic, which borders southeastern Germany. At the time of the story, Prague was ruled by German-speaking Austria and was home to many German merchants as well as native Czechs.

10. **studied theology at the seminary:** studied religious philosophy at the school for training members of the clergy.

11. **taroc** (tăr′ək): a European card game played with a 78-card pack; also spelled *tarok*.

12. **reeve** (rēv): a local authority, here representing the emperor's government.

WORDS TO KNOW
**preside** (prĭ-zīd′) *v.* to hold the chief position of authority or control
**flout** (flout) *v.* to show contempt for; to scorn

grandfather was not afraid of Bilgan: he worked his way deep into the thicket, even when he was quite little, and brought out great quantities of mushrooms; he even found truffles,[13] for which Frau Balek paid thirty pfennigs a pound. Everything my grandfather took to the Baleks he entered on the back of a torn-off calendar page: every pound of mushrooms, every gram of thyme, and on the right-hand side, in his childish handwriting, he entered the amount he received for each item; he scrawled in every pfennig, from the age of seven to the age of twelve, and by the time he was twelve the year 1900 had arrived, and because the Baleks had been raised to the aristocracy by the Emperor, they gave every family in the village a quarter of a pound of real coffee, the Brazilian kind; there was also free beer and tobacco for the men, and at the chateau there was a great banquet; many carriages stood in the avenue of poplars leading from the entrance gates to the chateau.

But the day before the banquet the coffee was distributed in the little room which had housed the Balek scales for almost a hundred years, and the Balek family was now called Balek von Bilgan because, according to legend, Bilgan the Giant used to have a great castle on the site of the present Balek estate.

My grandfather often used to tell me how he went there after school to fetch the coffee for four families: the Cechs, the Weidlers, the Vohlas[14] and his own, the Brüchers.[15] It was the afternoon of New Year's Eve: there were the front rooms to be decorated, the baking to be done, and the families did not want to spare four boys and have each of them go all the way to the chateau to bring back a quarter of a pound of coffee.

And so my grandfather sat on the narrow wooden bench in the little room while Gertrud the maid counted out the wrapped four-ounce packages of coffee, four of them, and he looked at the scales and saw that the pound weight was still lying on the left-hand scale; Frau Balek von Bilgan was busy with preparations for the banquet. And when Gertrud was about to put her hand into the jar with the lemon drops to give my grandfather one, she discovered it was empty: it was refilled once a year and held one kilo of the kind that cost a mark.

Gertrud laughed and said: "Wait here while I get the new lot," and my grandfather waited with the four four-ounce packages which had been wrapped and sealed in the factory, facing the scales on which someone had left the pound weight, and my grandfather took the four packages of coffee, put them on the empty scale, and his heart thudded as he watched the black finger of justice come to rest on the left of the black line: the scale with the pound weight stayed down, and the pound of coffee remained up in the air; his heart thudded more than if he had been lying behind a bush in the forest waiting for Bilgan the Giant, and he felt in his pocket for the pebbles he always carried with him so he could use his catapult[16] to shoot the sparrows which pecked away at his mother's cabbage plants—he had to put three, four, five pebbles beside the packages of coffee

---

13. **truffles** (trŭf´əlz): edible fungi that resemble mushrooms but are far rarer and are considered a great delicacy.

14. **the Cechs** (chĕks), **the Weidlers** (vīd´lərz), **the Vohlas** (vō´läz).

15. **Brüchers** (brü´KHərz): The name *Brücher* derives from the German words for "to break" and "to breach."

16. **catapult** (kăt´ə-pŭlt´): here, a slingshot.

before the scale with the pound weight rose and the pointer at last came to rest over the black line. My grandfather took the coffee from the scale, wrapped the five pebbles in his kerchief, and when Gertrud came back with the big kilo bag of lemon drops which had to last for another whole year in order to make the children's faces light up with pleasure, when Gertrud let the lemon drops rattle into the glass jar, the pale little fellow was still standing there, and nothing seemed to have changed. My grandfather only took three of the packages, then Gertrud looked in startled surprise at the white-faced child who threw the lemon drop onto the floor, ground it under his heel, and said: "I want to see Frau Balek."

"Balek von Bilgan, if you please," said Gertrud.

"All right, Frau Balek von Bilgan," but Gertrud only laughed at him, and he walked back to the village in the dark, took the Cechs, the Weidlers and the Vohlas their coffee, and said he had to go and see the priest.

**ACTIVE READING**

**CLARIFY** What has the grandfather discovered?

Instead he went out into the dark night with his five pebbles in his kerchief. He had to walk a long way before he found someone who had scales, who was permitted to have them; no one in the villages of Blaugau and Bernau[17] had any, he knew that, and he went straight through them till, after two hours' walking, he reached the little town of Dielheim[18] where Honig[19] the apothecary lived. From Honig's house came the smell of fresh pancakes, and Honig's breath, when he opened the door to the half-frozen boy, already smelled of punch, there was a moist cigar between his narrow lips, and he clasped the boy's cold hands firmly for a moment, saying: "What's the matter, has your father's lung got worse?"

"No, I haven't come for medicine, I wanted . . . " My grandfather undid his kerchief, took out the five pebbles, held them out to Honig and said: "I wanted to have these weighed." He glanced anxiously into Honig's face, but when Honig said nothing and did not get angry, or even ask him anything, my grandfather said: "It is the amount that is short of justice," and now, as he went into the warm room, my grandfather realized how wet his feet were. The snow had soaked through his cheap shoes, and in the forest the branches had showered him with snow which was now melting, and he was tired and hungry and suddenly began to cry because he thought of the quantities of mushrooms, the herbs, the flowers, which had been weighed on the scales which were short five pebbles' worth of justice. And when Honig, shaking his head and holding the five pebbles, called his wife, my grandfather thought of the generations of his parents, his grandparents, who had all had to have their mushrooms, their flowers, weighed on the scales, and he was overwhelmed by a great wave of injustice and began to sob louder than ever, and, without waiting to be asked, he sat down on a chair, ignoring the pancakes, the cup of hot coffee which nice plump Frau Honig put in front of him, and did not stop crying till Honig himself came out from the shop at the back and, rattling the pebbles in his hand, said in a low voice to his wife: "Fifty-five grams, exactly."

My grandfather walked the two hours home through the forest, got a beating at home, said nothing, not a single word, when he was asked about the coffee, spent the whole evening doing sums on the piece of paper on which he had written down everything he had sold to Frau Balek, and when midnight struck, and the cannon could be heard

---

17. **Blaugau** (blou′gou′) **and Bernau** (bĕr′nou).

18. **Dielheim** (dēl′hīm′).

19. **Honig** (hô′nYKH).

*Une Battue en Campine* [Beating the bushes in Campine] (about 1882–1885), Théodor Verstræte.
Oil on canvas, 41 ¼″ × 71″, collection of Crédit Communal, Brussels, Belgium.

from the chateau, and the whole village rang with shouting and laughter and the noise of rattles, when the family kissed and embraced all around, he said into the New Year silence: "The Baleks owe me eighteen marks and thirty-two pfennigs." And again he thought of all the children there were in the village, of his brother Fritz who had gathered so many mushrooms, of his sister Ludmilla; he thought of the many hundreds of children who had all gathered mushrooms for the Baleks, and herbs and flowers, and this time he did not cry but told his parents and brothers and sisters of his discovery.

When the Baleks von Bilgan went to High Mass on New Year's Day, their new coat of arms—a giant crouching under a fir tree—already emblazoned in blue and gold on their carriage, they saw the hard, pale faces of the people all staring at them. They had expected garlands in the village, a song in their honor, cheers and hurrahs, but the village was completely deserted as they drove through it, and in church the pale faces of the people were turned toward them, mute and hostile, and when the priest mounted the pulpit to deliver his New Year's sermon, he sensed the chill in those otherwise quiet and peaceful faces, and he stumbled painfully through his sermon and went back to the altar drenched in sweat. And as the Baleks von Bilgan left the church after Mass, they walked through a lane of mute, pale faces. But young Frau Balek von Bilgan stopped in front of the children's pews, sought out my grandfather's face, pale little Franz Brücher, and asked him, right there in the church: "Why didn't you take the coffee for your mother?" And my grandfather stood up and said: "Because you owe me as much money as five kilos of coffee would cost." And he pulled the five pebbles from his pocket, held them out to the young woman and said: "This much, fifty-five grams, is short in every pound of your justice"; and before the woman could say anything the men and women in the church lifted up their voices and sang: "The justice of this earth, O Lord, hath put Thee to death. . . ."

While the Baleks were at church, Wilhelm Vohla, the poacher, had broken into the little room, stolen the scales and the big fat leather-bound book in which had been entered every kilo of mushrooms, every kilo of hayflowers, everything bought by the Baleks in the village, and all afternoon of that New Year's Day the men of the village sat in my great-grandparents' front room and calculated, calculated one tenth of everything that had been bought—but when they had calculated many thousands of talers[20] and had still not come to an end, the reeve's gendarmes[21] arrived, made their way into my great-grandfather's front room, shooting and stabbing as they came, and removed the scales and the book by force. My grandfather's little sister Ludmilla lost her life, a few men were wounded, and one of the gendarmes was stabbed to death by Wilhelm Vohla the poacher.

Our village was not the only one to rebel: Blaugau and Bernau did too, and for almost a week no work was done in the flax sheds. But a great many gendarmes appeared, and the men and women were threatened with prison, and the Baleks forced the priest to display the scales publicly in the school and demonstrate that the finger of justice swung to and fro accurately. And the men and women went back to the flax sheds—but no one went to the school to watch the priest: he stood there all alone, helpless and <u>forlorn</u> with his weights, scales, and packages of coffee.

And the children went back to gathering mushrooms, to gathering thyme, flowers and foxglove, but every Sunday, as soon as the Baleks entered the church, the hymn was struck up: "The justice of this earth, O Lord, hath put Thee to death," until the reeve ordered it proclaimed in every village that the singing of this hymn was forbidden.

My grandfather's parents had to leave the village and the new grave of their little daughter; they became basket weavers but did not stay long anywhere because it pained them to see how everywhere the finger of justice swung falsely. They walked along behind their cart, which crept slowly over the country roads, taking their thin goat with them, and passers-by could sometimes hear a voice from the cart singing: "The justice of this earth, O Lord, hath put Thee to death." And those who wanted to listen could hear the tale of the Baleks von Bilgan, whose justice lacked a tenth part. But there were few who listened. ❖

*Translated by Leila Vennewitz*

**ACTIVE READING**

**EVALUATE** Why do you think the Baleks were able to return to business as usual?

---

20. **talers** (täʹlərz): silver coins used in central Europe until around 1900.
21. **gendarmes** (zhänʹdärmz´): police officers.

WORDS
TO
KNOW
**forlorn** (fər-lôrnʹ) *adj.* appearing sad or lonely because one has been left alone

900

## Connect to Literature

**1. What Do You Think?** What were your reactions to the final outcome of the villagers' protests?

**Comprehension Check**
- Who are the Baleks?
- What does the narrator's grandfather learn about the Baleks from their scale?
- What happens when the people rebel?

## Think Critically

**2.** How would you describe the **narrator's** grandfather as a boy? Support your answer with details from the story.

**3.** Consider the thoughts about justice that you explored in Connect to Your Life on page 893. In your opinion, what is the worst injustice in this story? Explain your position.

**4.** How would you explain the **theme** about justice that is communicated in this story?

> **THINK ABOUT**
> - what the Balek scales **symbolize**
> - why it took so long for the inaccuracy of the scales to be discovered
> - why the narrator's grandfather and his family found that "the finger of justice swung falsely" everywhere they went
> - the hymn sung by villagers when the Baleks enter church

**5.** | ACTIVE READING | ANALYZING RELEVANCE OF SETTING |
Look at the **setting** analysis you completed in your  **READER'S NOTEBOOK**. How does each element of the setting help you to understand the power of the Baleks? Could this same story take place in a different setting or in a different time period? Why or why not?

## Extend Interpretations

**6. Critic's Corner** Editor Ralph Ley described Böll as "the humane and incorruptible conscience of his country." What does this story reveal about Böll's conscience?

**7. Connect to Life** The Baleks seem to control nearly every aspect of life in the village, from the weighing of mushrooms to the activities of the police and clergy. Do you think wealthy people in the United States today exert a similar kind of power? Explain your reasoning.

## Literary Analysis

**TONE** **Tone** is the attitude a writer or narrator takes toward a subject. The language and details a writer chooses help to create the tone, which might be playful, serious, bitter, angry, or detached, among other possibilities. To identify the tone of a work, you might find it helpful to read the work aloud, as if giving a dramatic reading. The emotions that you convey in reading should give you hints as to the tone of the work.

In "The Balek Scales," Böll tells a tale of great injustice, with an unhappy and even violent ending. The story's tone, however, is surprisingly calm and detached. Böll's use of descriptive detail and long sentences and paragraphs create a sense of remoteness and an unhurried pace. The contrast between this remote slowness and the power of the story's tragic events lends an ominous quality to the narrative.

**Cooperative Learning Activity** With a small group of classmates, read aloud the opening and closing paragraphs of "The Balek Scales." Think of words or phrases that describe the tone of these paragraphs. Then analyze the language of the paragraphs to determine exactly how the author has created this tone. Compare your descriptions and analyses with those of other groups.

## Writing Options

**1. Sunday Sermon** Imagine that a new priest is assigned to the village and learns about the events related to the scales. Write a sermon in which the priest offers his moral judgment of these events.

**2. Aristocratic Editorial** Write a guest editorial that the Balek family might have placed in the local paper in which they attempt to win back the favor of the villagers.

**Writing Handbook**
See page 1161: Persuasive Writing.

**3. Autobiographical Tale** Think of a tale from your own youth that you might one day tell your grandchildren. Write the story, describing the events as you recall them. Place the story in your **Working Portfolio.**

## Vocabulary in Action

**EXERCISE: MEANING CLUES** On your paper, match each example below with the appropriate vocabulary word.

**1.** The machines used for drying the flax were so old that no one could remember when they had first been used.

**2.** Most of the people had very little to eat; even milk was considered a treat.

**3.** By refusing the coffee, the grandfather ridiculed the authority of the Baleks.

**4.** In the next generation, another Frau Balek would be in control of the room with the scales.

**5.** The grandfather and his family must have felt lonely as they moved from town to town.

**Building Vocabulary**
For an in-depth study of roots and base words, see page 183.

| WORDS TO KNOW | | | |
|---|---|---|---|
| antiquated | forlorn | preside | |
| flout | meager | | |

### Heinrich Böll
#### 1917–1985

**Other Works**
*Eighteen Stories*
*The Stories of Heinrich Böll*
*What's to Become of the Boy?*

**Soldier and Critic** Heinrich Böll grew up in Cologne (kə-lōn´), Germany, the descendant of English Catholics who centuries before had fled to the Continent to escape religious persecution. Raised in a tolerant household at a time when many Germans were practicing great intolerance, Böll watched in growing horror as the Nazis rose to power. During World War II, he was forced to join the German army; he was wounded four times and was captured and imprisoned by American forces. After the war, he began to publish novels and short stories. His early novels were harshly critical of warfare, which the Nazis had glorified. In *The Train Was on Time* (1949), he traced the despair of a sensitive young German soldier, not unlike himself. In *Adam, Where Art Thou?* (1951), he compared warfare to a contagious and deadly disease.

**Champion for Justice** With time, Böll broadened his themes, though he remained a social critic. The corruption of power, the victimization of the innocent by those in power, and the dehumanizing effects of modern life are often treated in his novels and short stories. Böll also championed the rights of oppressed fellow writers, providing lodgings for Russian author Aleksandr Solzhenitsyn (ăl´ĭk-săn´dər sōl´zhə-nēt´sĭn) when he was forced to leave his then-Communist homeland. Over the years, Böll produced nearly 40 books and was honored with a Nobel Prize in literature. "The Balek Scales," one of his most widely read stories, was first published in German in 1955.

# PREPARING to *Read*

## The Street / La Calle

*Poetry by* OCTAVIO PAZ
(ôk-tä′vē-ô päs)

## I Am Not I / Yo No Soy Yo

*Poetry by* JUAN RAMÓN JIMÉNEZ
(wän rä-môn′ hē-mě′něs)

### Connect to Your Life

**Who Are You?** If someone asked you to define your identity, how would you respond? Would you be one who looks inward, tapping the depths of the private self hidden from public view? Or would you look outward, defining yourself by your own unique place in the world? In writing, describe how you define your identity.

## Build Background

**Who Am I?** The mysteries of identity are key concerns of the two poems that follow. Both poems are by eminent Spanish-language poets whose achievements were honored with the Nobel Prize in literature. The poetry of Octavio Paz often contains elements of **surrealism,** in which dreamlike images from the unconscious mind are captured in writing. Juan Ramón Jiménez, who preceded Paz by a generation, is responsible in many respects for introducing modernism to Spanish poetry. "The Street" and "I Am Not I" both explore the hidden territories of the self and its relation to the rest of the world.

## Focus Your Reading

**LITERARY ANALYSIS  MODERN POETRY** Modern poets have often used their art to explore their own identity. These poets have had more freedom than their predecessors. Compared to poetry prior to the 20th century, **modern poetry** has few, if any, restraints on subject matter, form, or use of poetic language. As you read, think about how the following poems vary from more traditional poetry.

**ACTIVE READING  STRATEGIES FOR READING MODERN POETRY** **Modern poetry,** like other forms of modern art, can be difficult to understand. Readers encounter ambiguity, or unclear meaning, as well as **symbolism** that may be difficult to decipher. When reading such poetry, it is important to realize that you won't understand it all at once.

While the following strategies can be useful in getting the most out of any poem, they are especially helpful for modern poetry:

1. Read through the poem once to get a general idea of what it is about, using clues from the **title** to identify the topic.
2. Notice how **physical arrangement** and punctuation mark units of thought.
3. Consider the **literal meaning** of the situation described. What is going on, and who is involved?
4. Think about the associations that the words, **imagery,** and **figurative language** bring to mind. How do these associations influence understanding?
5. Identify the parts of the poem that puzzle you. Can you use the parts that are clear to you to help explain other parts that are less clear?
6. Consider different ways of interpreting the poem. Which interpretation explains the most?
7. Read the poem aloud, or read it so that you "hear" the poem in your head.

**READER'S NOTEBOOK** As you read the following poems, jot down observations or questions that come to mind.

# Octavio Paz The Street

## La Calle

A long and silent street.
I walk in blackness and I stumble and fall
and rise, and I walk blind, my feet
stepping on silent stones and dry leaves.
5 Someone behind me also stepping on stones,
    leaves:
if I slow down, he slows;
if I run, he runs. I turn: nobody.
Everything dark and doorless.
Turning and turning among these corners
10 which lead forever to the street
where nobody waits for, nobody follows me,
where I pursue a man who stumbles
and rises and says when he sees me: nobody.

*Translated by Muriel Rukeyser*

Es una calle larga y silenciosa.
Ando en tinieblas y tropiezo y caigo
y me levanto y piso con pies ciegos
las piedras mudas y las hojas secas
5 y alguien detrás de mí también las pisa:
si me detengo, se detiene;
si corro, corre. Vuelvo el rostro: nadie.
Todo está oscuro y sin salida,
y doy vueltas y vueltas en esquinas
10 que dan siempre a la calle
donde nadie me espera ni me sigue,
donde yo sigo a un hombre que tropieza
y se levanta y dice al verme: nadie.

## Thinking Through the Literature

1. What **images** came to your mind while you were reading "The Street"?

2. Do you think the **speaker** is describing a real or imagined event?

 **THINK ABOUT**
- details about the speaker's surroundings
- why the speaker feels that someone is following him
- what the speaker realizes when he turns and sees "nobody"
- who or what the speaker might be pursuing

3. How do you think the speaker views his own life?

**THINK ABOUT**
- how the speaker feels about the events he describes
- what the street might **symbolize**
- why the speaker keeps repeating the word "nobody"

# Juan Ramón Jiménez
# "I Am Not I"

I am not I.
           I am this one
walking beside me whom I do not see,
whom at times I manage to visit,
5    and whom at other times I forget;
who remains calm and silent while I talk,
and forgives, gently, when I hate,
who walks where I am not,
who will remain standing when I die.

*Translated by Robert Bly*

# Yo No Soy Yo

Yo no soy yo.
           Soy este
que va a mi lado sin yo verlo;
que, a veces, voy a ver,
5    y que, a veces, olvido.
El que calla, sereno, cuando hablo,
el que perdona, dulce, cuando odio,
el que pasea por donde no estoy,
el que quedará en pie cuando yo muera.

*La reproduction interdite (Portrait d'Edward James)* [Not to be reproduced (Portrait of Edward James)]
(1937), René Magritte. Oil on canvas, 81.3 cm × 65 cm, Museum Boymans–van Beuningen, Rotterdam, the
Netherlands, Giraudon/Art Resource, New York. Copyright © 1996 Artists Rights Society (ARS), New York.

# Connect to the Literature

1. **What Do You Think?** What went through your mind as you were reading "I Am Not I"? Describe your reaction.

# Think Critically

2. How would you describe the **speaker's** two different selves?

THINK ABOUT

- why the speaker visits his other self only some of the time
- the contrasts in lines 6–8
- your interpretation of the last line

3. How does the speaker seem to evaluate his two different selves?

4. **ACTIVE READING** **STRATEGIES FOR READING MODERN POETRY** Look back at the observations you recorded for "The Street" and "I Am Not I" in your **READER'S NOTEBOOK**. What questions, if any, do you still have about the two poems? Of the two poems, do you feel that you understand one better than the other? Explain.

# Extend Interpretations

5. **Comparing Texts** How do you think the speakers in "The Street" and "I Am Not I" see themselves in relation to the rest of the world?

6. **Connect to Life** Do you think that all people have an inner self that is different from the self they show the world? Explain your opinion.

# Literary Analysis

**MODERN POETRY** Compared to poetry prior to the 20th century, **modern poetry** is free of many traditional forms and conventions of subject matter and language. While many people find this liberating, some find it frustrating or confusing. To understand modern poetry, you should know about the following poetic techniques:

**Free Verse** Most modern poems are written in free verse, which has no meter and no fixed stanzas or fixed line lengths. Instead, the poet decides where the lines should break, based on where a pause is required or on how the poem will look on the page. The line breaks, punctuation, and spacing help convey the mood and the meaning of each poem.

**Literal and Symbolic Meanings** Modern poets often rely on situations drawn from everyday life, which are often charged with symbolic meaning to convey a message about life or human nature.

**Diction** In contrast to the poetry of long ago, notable for its formal language, modern poetry often makes use of informal language drawn from everyday speech.

**Imagery and Figurative Language** Like all poets, modern poets use imagery and figurative language to convey underlying ideas and emotions.

**Cooperative Learning Activity** Reread "The Street" and "I Am Not I," identifying the techniques of modern poetry described above. With a group of classmates, discuss how these techniques affect your understanding of both poems.

# *Choices* & CHALLENGES

## Writing Options

**Identity Poem** Write a poem about who you are. You may draw upon the Connect to Your Life questions on page 903.

## Activities & Explorations

**Dramatic Interpretation** With a classmate, prepare a dramatic scene of a situation in the life of the speaker of "I Am Not I." Decide on a situation to enact. Then, using clues from the poem, show how each "I" would react in that situation. ~ **SPEAKING AND LISTENING**

## Octavio Paz
### 1914–1998

**Other Works**
*Configurations*
*The Collected Poems of Octavio Paz, 1957–1987*

## Juan Ramón Jiménez
### 1881–1958

**Other Works**
*Three Hundred Poems: 1903–1953*

**A Precocious Youth** Octavio Paz, a poet, essayist, and literary scholar, is one of modern Mexico's best-known literary figures. Paz grew up outside Mexico City. He loved books and often devised games based on *Robinson Crusoe* and other popular adventure tales he read. At 17, Paz founded the first of many literary journals that he would establish; at 19, he published his first book of poetry, *Forest Moon* (1933). Like many young writers of the 1930s, he journeyed to Spain to support the Loyalists in the Spanish Civil War.

**Bard of Mexico** Paz's political convictions and his fascination with the interaction of native Indian and conquering Spanish elements in Mexican history are strong themes in his writing. His highly acclaimed prose work *The Labyrinth of Solitude* (1950) is a major study of Mexican culture. Mexico's early history also inspired his 1957 epic poem *Sun Stone,* whose title refers to the famous calendar stone of the Aztecs.

**Poet of the World** From 1945 until 1968, Paz served in the Mexican diplomatic corps. While stationed in Japan and India, he developed an interest in Asian arts and philosophy, which is reflected in some of his poems. After 1968, Paz continued to write, and he taught and lectured in Europe and the United States. His receipt of the 1990 Nobel Prize in literature was considered by many critics to be long overdue.

**A Literary Leader** Juan Ramón Jiménez's short and intensely personal poems were an inspiration to a generation of Spanish writers in the 1920s and 1930s. Born in Spain, Jiménez briefly studied law at the University of Seville, but he eventually quit to devote himself to writing. He published his first two volumes of verse in 1900.

**Spanish Classics** From 1912 until 1916, Jiménez lived in Madrid, where he wrote *Platero and I* (1914), prose poems about walks with a donkey. The book became a beloved Spanish classic. Also during this time, Jiménez met American-born Zenobia Camprubí Aymar, who was visiting in Spain. Jiménez's voyage to the United States to marry Camprubí inspired one of his most successful collections, *Diary of a Newlywed Poet* (1917).

**A Poet Abroad** After the couple returned to Spain, Jiménez continued to devote himself to poetry. At the outbreak of the Spanish Civil War in 1936, he was sent to the United States as a representative of Spain. Eventually, Jiménez took a position at the University of Puerto Rico. The couple were in San Juan when they received word that Jiménez had won the 1956 Nobel Prize in literature.

## On-the-Job Language

If you've ever watched a courtroom drama on television or in the movies, you may be familiar with language like this:

> **The police court proceedings were brief and dramatic. The principal witnesses for the prosecution were Janet Mackenzie, maid to the dead woman, and Romaine Heilger, Austrian subject.**
> —Agatha Christie, "The Witness for the Prosecution"

Words like *court proceedings, witnesses,* and *prosecution* belong to a specialized vocabulary used by members of the legal profession. Every trade or profession—for example, medicine, journalism, banking, or cinematography—has its specialized vocabulary, or **jargon.** This vocabulary consists of words and phrases that have special meanings to those on the inside but may sound like a foreign language to outsiders. To a cartoonist, for example, terms such as *thought balloons, idea balloons,* and *maladicta balloons* are part of his or her lingo on the job—easily understood by other cartoonists, but puzzling to those outside the field.

## Strategies for Building Vocabulary

When you come upon specialized terms in your reading, use these strategies to figure out their meanings.

❶ **Look at the Context** Sometimes you can find clues to the meaning of a term by examining its context, or surrounding words. For example, the passage below provides clues to the meaning of *prosecution* and *verdict.*

> **The prosecution endeavored to rally, but without great success . . . and the jury needed little time to consider their verdict.**
> **"We find the prisoner not guilty."**
> —Agatha Christie, "The Witness for the Prosecution"

You can infer that *prosecution* refers to those striving to convict the prisoner. The sentence "We find the prisoner not guilty" states the jury's final decision—its *verdict.*

❷ **Use a Glossary** A **glossary** is an alphabetical list of specialized terms that pertain to a particular subject. This list usually appears at the end of a book or an article. For example, at the back of this literature anthology, you will find a glossary that lists and defines such terms as *alliteration, protagonist, foil,* and *foreshadowing*—terms important to the study of literature. If you cannot find a specialized term in a dictionary, try looking it up in the glossary to a particular book about the subject.

---

**EXERCISE** Use the context to deduce the meaning of each underlined word. Then write another sentence using each word.

1. The lawyer tried to convince the jury that the victim's death was not accidental, but premeditated.
2. Dr. Morris was relieved to find that the patient's tumor was benign.
3. A witness who lies under oath commits perjury.
4. Because the child had the illness since birth as did some of his older relatives, the pathologist concluded that it was congenital.
5. The defendant felt relief when the jury acquitted him, setting him free.

In this short autobiographical selection, David Mamet tells a story involving his father and family expectations. His father was a lawyer who gave his son encouragement and support in pursuing his education as an actor and a playwright.

# THE WATCH

### David Mamet

■

The Chicago in which I wanted to participate was a workers' town. It was, and, in my memory, is, the various districts and the jobs that I did there: factories out in Cicero or down in Blue Island—the Inland Steel plant in East Chicago; Yellow Cab Unit Thirteen on Halsted.

I grew up on Dreiser and Frank Norris and Sherwood Anderson,[1] and I felt, following what I took to be their lead, that the bourgeoisie[2] was not the fit subject of literature.

---

1. **Dreiser . . . Anderson:** Theodore Dreiser, American novelist whose work exposed the seamier side of American life; Frank Norris, American author whose work attacked the greed and violence in American commerce; Sherwood Anderson, American author whose work described the frustrations of life in small Midwestern towns.

2. **bourgeoisie** (bōōr´zhwä-zē´): the middle class.

with the gift, his effort to understand me—*that* was the gift, the magnificent gift. Rather than insist that I be like him, he'd tried to make himself like me. And if my chums thought that the car was somewhat obvious, well, . . . I was not some kid in the schoolyard who could be embarrassed by his parents; I was a man, and the owner of a valuable possession. The car could take me to work, it could take me from one city to the next, and finally, my father'd given it to me.

As I walked close to it I saw the error of my momentary reluctance to appreciate its decoration. It was truly beautiful. That such a car would not have been my first choice spoke to the defects not of the car, but of my taste.

I remember the new car sticker on the window, and I remember thinking that my dad must have expected me to come into the building by the other door, or he wouldn't have left the gift out here so prominently. Or did he mean me to see it? That was my question, as I rode the elevator up.

He met me at the door. There was the table, laid out for a party in the living room beyond. Did he look wary? No. I wondered whether to say which route I had taken home, but, no, if he'd wanted to test me, he would ask. No. It was clear that I wasn't supposed to've seen the car.

But why would he have chanced my spotting it? Well, I thought, it's obvious. They'd delivered the car from the showroom, and he'd, carefully, as he did all things, instructed them on where it should be parked, and the car salesman had failed him. I saw that this could present a problem: if we came out of the building on the side opposite from where the car was parked—if we began what he would, doubtless, refer to as a simple walk, and could not *find* the car (which, after all, would not be parked where he'd directed it should be), would

it be my place to reveal I'd *seen* it?

No. For he'd be angry then, at the car salesman. It would be wiser to be ignorant, and not be part of that confluence[10] which spoiled his surprise. I could steer our progress back into the building by the other door. Aha. Yes. That is what I'd do.

There was another possibility: that we would leave the building by the door *near* the car, and that he'd come across it in the unexpected place, and be off-guard. But that need not be feared, as, if I stayed oblivious to his confusion for the scantest second, he would realize that my surprise would in no way be mitigated by the car's location. He would improvise, and say, "Look here!" That he'd surely have words with the car dealership later was not my responsibility.

We sat down to dinner. My father, my stepmother, my half-siblings, and several aunts. After the meal my father made a speech about my becoming a man. He told the table how he'd, in effect, demanded my return as he had something to give me. Then he reached in the lapel pocket of his jacket, draped over the back of his chair, and brought out a small case. Yes, I thought, this is as it should be. There's the key.

Some further words were said. I took the case, and fought down an impulse to confess that I knew what it contained, et cetera, thus finessing[11] the question of whether or not to feign[12] surprise. I thanked him and opened the case, inside of which there was a pocket watch.

I looked at the watch, and at the case beneath the watch, where the key would be found. There was no key. I understood that this gift would be in two parts, that *this* was the element of the trip that was the surprise. I'd

---

10. **confluence:** stream of events.

11. **finessing:** cleverly dealing with.

12. **feign** (fān): pretend.

underestimated my father. How could I have thought that he would let an opportunity for patriarchal[13] drama drift by unexploited.

No mention had been made of the car. It was possible, though unlikely, that he thought I'd forgotten that the car was owing to me; but in *any* case, and even if, as was most likely, I had returned to Chicago expecting the car, such hopes would indeed be dashed before they would be realized. He would make me the present of the watch, and, then, the party would go on, and at some point, he'd say, "Oh, by the way . . ." and draw my attention to the key, secreted in the lining of the watch case, or he'd suggest we go for a walk.

Once again, he would keep control. Well, that was as it should be, I thought. And a brand-new car— *any* car—was not the sort of present that should be given or accepted lightly, and if he chose to present the gift in his own way, it came not primarily from desire for control, but from a sense on his part of drama, which is to say, of what was fitting. I thought that that was fine.

That I had, accidentally, discovered the real present parked outside was to my advantage. It allowed me to feign, no, not to feign, to *feel* true gratitude for the watch he had given me. For, in truth, it was magnificent.

It was an Illinois pocket watch. In a gold Hunter case. The case was covered with scrollwork, and, in a small crest, it had my initials. The back of the case had a small diamond set in it. There was a quite heavy gold chain. In all, it was a superb and an obviously quite expensive present.

I thanked him for it. He explained that it was a railroad watch, that is, a watch made to the stringent standards called for by the railroads in the last century. The railroads, in the days before the radio, relied exclusively upon the accuracy of the railroaders' watches to ensure safety. Yes. I understood. I admired the watch at length, and tried it in various of my pockets, and said that, had I known, I would have worn a vest.

As the party wound down, I excused myself from the table, and took the watch and the case into a back room, where I pried up the lining of the case to find the key.

But there was no key, and there was, of course, no car; and, to one not emotionally involved, the presence of a convertible with a new-car sticker on the street is not worthy of note.

I pawned the watch many times; and once I sold it outright to the pawnbroker under the El[14] on Van Buren Street.

He was a man who knew my father, and, several years after I'd sold it, I ran into him and he asked if I'd like my watch back. I asked why such a fine watch had lain unsold in his store, and he said that he'd never put it out, he'd kept it for me, as he thought someday I'd like it back. So I redeemed it for what I had sold it for.

---

13. **patriarchal** (pā′trē-är′kəl): relating to a father or father figure.

14. **El:** elevated train, a form of public transportation that travels above street level.

I wore it now and then, over the years, with a tuxedo; but, most of the time, it stayed in a box in my desk. I had it appraised at one point, and found it was, as it looked, valuable. Over the years I thought of selling it, but never did.

I had another fantasy. I thought, or *felt,* perhaps, that the watch was in fact a token in code from my father, and that the token would be redeemed after his death.

I thought that, *after his death,* at the reading of his will, it would be shown that he'd never forgotten the convertible, and that the watch was merely a test; that if I would *present* the watch to his executors[15]—my continued possession of it a sign that I had never broken faith with him—I would receive a fitting legacy.[16]

My father died a year ago, may he rest in peace.

Like him I have turned, I'm afraid, into something of a patriarch, and something of a burgher.[17] Like him I am, I think, overfond of the few difficulties I enjoyed on my travels toward substantiality. Like him I will, doubtless, subject my children, in some degree, to my personality, and my affection for my youth.

I still have the watch, which I still don't like; and, several years ago I bought myself a convertible, which, I think, I never drive without enjoyment. ❖

---

15. **executors** (ĭg-zĕk′yə-tərz): people appointed to carry out the instructions of a will.

16. **legacy:** money or property bequeathed to someone by will.

17. **burgher** (bûr′gər): a solid, middle-class citizen.

## David Mamet
### 1947–

**Other Works**
*American Buffalo*
*Glengarry Glen Ross*
*Speed-the-Plow*
*The Untouchables*

**Language Playwright** David Mamet has been called a "language playwright" because of his skillful use of realistic dialogue and his ear for the sound and rhythm of language. He began early to develop these skills. He went to high school in Chicago, where he worked as a busboy at a comedy club and backstage at another theater. While on the job he absorbed the rhythms of stage dialogue and action. After high school, Mamet studied literature and drama at Goddard College in Vermont and took acting classes in New York. He briefly tried acting but then turned to writing and directing as a career.

**Mamet on Stage** Mamet's success was not immediate. While continuing to write, he earned a living as teacher, factory worker, taxi driver, and short-order cook. In the early 1970s, he made his breakthrough with two short plays. Since then, he has become one of America's most successful playwrights. He has received New York Drama Critics Circle Awards for *American Buffalo* and *Glengarry Glen Ross*. He was nominated for an Academy Award for the screenplay *The Verdict* and received a Pulitzer Prize for *Glengarry Glen Ross*.

## Inquiry & Research

Find out more about the reasons for the popularity of the Volkswagen in the 1960s and 1970s. How did the company establish its image?

**Real World Link**
Begin your research by reading the television ad on page 916.

# Volkswagen Television Ad

Created by Doyle Dane Bernbach, Inc.

*During the 1950s, the trend in American automobiles was toward big cars that consumed large amounts of gasoline. Designs would change every year to entice owners to trade in their old cars for the latest model. In the 1960s and 1970s, Volkswagen worked against that trend. Its advertisements boasted of a simple, reliable, and inexpensive car that changed only to improve performance, not to make earlier models look obsolete.*

**❶**

```
Open on funeral procession of limousines
each containing the benefactors of a will.

MVO [male voice-over]:
I, Maxwell E. Snavely, being of sound mind
and body do bequeath the following:
```

**❷**

```
To my wife Rose, who spent money like there was
no tomorrow, I leave $100 and a calendar . . .

To my sons Rodney and Victor, who spent every
dime I ever gave them on fancy cars and fast
women . . . . I leave $50 in dimes . . .
```

## Reading for Information

Have you ever taken the time to examine the advertisements you see on television? Many of them don't directly sell a product. Instead, they create an appealing image of the buyer, hoping the image will attract customers. Being able to analyze ads allows you to understand the persuasive techniques that manufacturers use to create a market for their products.

### EVALUATING ADVERTISING

These pages show a **storyboard**—a visual outline that presents the basic images and scripted dialogue—for a television ad for Volkswagen automobiles. When you read or view an **advertisement,** be aware of the commercial's basic message as well as the impression the advertiser is trying to create.

**YOUR TURN** Use the questions and activities that follow to help you evaluate this advertisement.

**❶ Setting the Scene** Considering the kind of product being advertised, what strikes you as unusual about the opening image and narration of the commercial?

**❷** In this frame, the ad begins to introduce humor. What effect does having a sad image paired with humorous narration have on the viewer? What do you think is important to the narrator?

By permission of Volkswagen of America, Inc., and Arnold Communications, Inc.

**③**

To my business partner, Jules, whose motto was "spend, spend, spend" I leave nothing, nothing, nothing.

And to my other friends and relatives who also never learned the value of a dollar, I leave . . . a dollar

**④**

Finally, to my nephew, Harold, who oft time said: "A penny saved is a penny earned." And who also oft time said "Gee, Uncle Max, it sure pays to own a Volkswagen."

I leave my entire fortune of one hundred billion dollars.

**③** Think about the narrator's attitude toward money as revealed in his will so far. What seems to be the narrator's values? What do you think the advertisers are trying to say about how consumers should choose to spend their money?

**④** Notice that this last frame is your first view of the product that's for sale. Why do you think the advertisers chose to delay the presentation of the image? Overall, what do you find humorous or surprising about this ad? Why do you think the ad was effective?

**Identifying Main Ideas** In an ad, the images and narration combine to convey an important message or **main idea.** What image of a Volkswagen owner do you think the advertisers have conveyed? What message was this ad communicating about Volkswagens?

## Inquiry & Research

**Activity Link: "The Watch," p. 915**
In "The Watch," David Mamet is moved by the appearance of the popular Volkswagen convertible. Do you think that Mamet and other young people of the time would have felt that this Volkswagen ad captured the appeal of the car?

*"The whole thing's nuts. There's work to do and people to do it, but them two can't get together. There's food to eat and people to eat it, and them two can't get together neither."*

*"She's awful pretty. An' she been to high school. She could help a man with figuring and stuff like that."*

# *Thinking* through the LITERATURE

## Connect to the Literature

**1. What Do You Think?**
Which photograph do you think best depicts the migrants' desperation? Explain.

**Comprehension Check**
- Why had the farmers of the photo essay migrated to California?
- What hardships did they find there?
- How is John Steinbeck associated with the *Life* magazine piece?

## Think Critically

**2.** How do you think *Life* magazine readers of the 1930s might have reacted to the photo essay?

**THINK ABOUT**

- the misconceptions many readers might have had about migrant workers
- the depictions of the flood's effects
- the people quoted in Steinbeck's captions

**3.** **ACTIVE READING** **AUTHOR'S PURPOSE** What purpose or purposes do you think the writer and photographer of the photo essay had in mind? To support your response, refer to the chart you made in your **READER'S NOTEBOOK**.

**4.** What personal qualities do you think are displayed by the migrants in both selections? List them in a web like this one.

**Personal Qualities**

**toughness**

## Extend Interpretations

**5. Critic's Corner** Literary critic Daniel Aaron, in his review of *The Grapes of Wrath,* said that the novel "unfolds cinematically almost as if Steinbeck had conceived of it as a documentary film." On the basis of the novel excerpt "The Flood" and Steinbeck's connection with *Life* photographer Horace Bristol, do you think Aaron's view is an accurate one? Why or why not?

**6. Different Perspectives** Consider how *Life* magazine chose to combine its photographs with captions written by a novelist. Take a more critical look at the essay, and choose an example of a paired photograph and caption that you think fit together especially well. Explain your choice.

**7. Connect to Life** Recall the ideas of the promised land that you discussed before exploring the selections. In your opinion, is a "promised land" more within the reach of today's poor people than it was for migrant workers in the 1930s? Discuss your views with other students.

## Literary Analysis

**SOCIAL CRITICISM** Writers of **social criticism** call people's attention to the conditions in society that require change. A writer may use **direct commentary,** by openly stating his or her views about a matter. Or the writer may use **indirect commentary,** which is more common in fiction, to show characters caught up in the issues of the larger world. In "The Flood," in passages such as this one, John Steinbeck draws attention to the unfair restrictions placed on newly arrived migrant workers through the workers' own words:

*They's rules—you got to be here a year before you can git relief. They say the gov'ment is gonna help. They don't know when.*

Throughout the selection, Steinbeck uses indirect commentary to give dramatic weight to experiences that reflect the hardships faced by real-life migrants in the 1930s.

**Cooperative Learning Activity**
Divide into two groups. One group should look for evidence of social criticism in "The Flood." The other group should examine the evidence of social criticism in the photo essay. Later, combine the groups and share your findings. Determine what elements of social criticism the selections have in common.

# Choices & CHALLENGES

## Writing Options

**Letter to the Editor** Imagine you were a subscriber to *Life* magazine in 1939. Write a letter to the editor about the conditions described in the photo essay.

## Activities & Explorations

**Monologue** Take the part of one of the persons pictured in "The Grapes of Wrath: Photo Essay." Deliver a monologue that begins with the caption and extends it. Refer to the captions and images to help you interpret the migrants' emotions—for example, the despair, weariness, or hopefulness. Rehearse by trying different interpretations until you discover the one that seems the most appropriate. Focus on those emotions as you perform your monologue. ~ **PERFORMING**

## Grammar in Context: Adverb Clauses That Express Conditions

In these two excerpts from "The Flood," John Steinbeck uses adverb clauses to show conditional relationships.

> Then the cars wouldn't start because the wires were shorted; and if the engines would run, deep mud engulfed the wheels.
>
> If they were shot at, they did not run, but splashed sullenly away; and if they were hit, they sank tiredly in the mud.

An **adverb clause** modifies a verb, an adjective, or another adverb, answering a question such as *how, when, where, why, to what extent,* or *under what circumstances.* In the excerpts above, the adverb clauses shown in blue express conditions, telling under what circumstances things happen. Steinbeck uses the adverb clauses to help him express the hopelessness of the workers' situation: no matter what they do during the flood, something unpleasant happens.

**WRITING EXERCISE** Combine each pair of sentences by changing one of them into an adverb clause that expresses a condition. Omit italicized words.

**Punctuation Tip:** A conditional clause at the start of a sentence should be followed by a comma. No comma is needed before one at the end of a sentence.

**Example:** *Original* The valley floods with water. *It does this whenever* it rains hard for more than two days.

*Rewritten* The valley floods with water <u>if it rains hard for more than two days.</u>

1. The fields *may* become flooded. *This would mean* the migrants will not have any work.

2. The sheriff will swear in more deputies. *He does this whenever* the desperate migrants begin stealing.

3. The migrants need help. *In such a situation,* the only person they can rely on is the coroner.

4. The migrants will have work in the spring. *But* they *will have to* find a way to survive until then.

**Grammar Handbook** Clauses, p. 1197

## Vocabulary in Action

**EXERCISE: MEANING CLUES** Read the book titles listed below. Then, on your paper, write the Word to Know suggested by each title.

1. *How to Hammer a Nail Properly*
2. *Working My Way Across America*
3. *Soaked to the Skin*
4. *Frenzy in the Emergency Room*
5. *The Consequences of Repressed Rage*

| WORDS TO KNOW | | | |
|---|---|---|---|
| frantic | penetrate | sodden | |
| migrant | smolder | | |

**Building Vocabulary**
Several Words to Know in this lesson have multiple meanings. For an in-depth lesson on words with multiple meanings, see page 678.

# *from* **Travels with Charley**

*Nonfiction by* JOHN STEINBECK

## Connect to Your Life

**Pet Personalities** We often attribute human qualities to our pets. Think of the pets you have known and how you would describe their behavior, or "personalities." Jot down your thoughts in a chart similar to the one shown.

| Pet Name | Type of Animal | General Behavior | Humanlike Traits |
|---|---|---|---|
| | | | |

## Build Background

**Charley Dog** In 1960, John Steinbeck decided to take an extended road trip across America, saying, "I'm going to learn about my own country. I've lost the flavor and taste and sound of it." His only companion was an "old French gentleman poodle" he and his wife called Charley Dog. Although bringing Charley was a last minute decision, it gave the travel journal that Steinbeck would write its focus. Charley served as a kind of ambassador for Steinbeck, reaching out to people along the way, providing a natural conversation starter for the author.

## Focus Your Reading

**LITERARY ANALYSIS** **COMIC IRONY** **Irony** is a technique that contrasts appearance and reality. **Comic irony** humorously contrasts what is expected to happen with what actually happens. In the excerpt from *Travels with Charley,* Steinbeck uses comic irony as he makes observations about his dog's behavior or about certain aspects of their trip. For example, when warned that Charley should be attached to a leash in a national park because of possible encounters with bears, Steinbeck replies:

> *I suggest that the greatest danger to your bears will be pique [anger] at being ignored by Charley.*

**ACTIVE READING** **WORD CHOICE** **Word choice,** or **diction,** involves a writer's selection of language. Through careful word choice, good writers, including Steinbeck, are able to capture on paper their own ideas, feelings, and experiences. Note the following sentence:

> *I must confess to a laxness in the matter of National Parks.*

The word *laxness* suggests both physical laziness and moral failing. Through this word choice, Steinbeck creates a humorous tone, suggesting that by not appreciating national parks he might be out of the ordinary, even unpatriotic.

**READER'S NOTEBOOK** Jot down any words that you think Steinbeck has specially chosen to communicate his thoughts about his experience.

# FROM TRAVELS WITH

I must confess to a laxness[1] in the matter of National Parks. I haven't visited many of them. Perhaps this is because they enclose the unique, the spectacular, the astounding—the greatest waterfall, the deepest canyon, the highest cliff, the most stupendous works of man or nature. And I would rather see a good Brady[2] photograph than Mount Rushmore. For it is my opinion that we enclose and celebrate the freaks of our nation and of our civilization. Yellowstone National Park is no more representative of America than is Disneyland.

This being my natural attitude, I don't know what made me turn sharply south and cross a state line to take a look at Yellowstone. Perhaps it was a fear of my neighbors. I could hear them say, "You mean you were that near to Yellowstone and didn't go? You must be crazy." Again it might have been the American tendency in travel. One goes, not so much to see but to tell afterward. Whatever my purpose in going to Yellowstone, I'm glad I went because I discovered something about Charley I might never have known.

# CHARLEY

## JOHN STEINBECK

A pleasant-looking National Park man checked me in and then he said, "How about that dog? They aren't permitted in except on leash."

"Why?" I asked.

"Because of the bears."

"Sir," I said, "this is an unique dog. He does not live by tooth or fang. He respects the right of cats to be cats although he doesn't admire them. He turns his steps rather than disturb an earnest caterpillar. His greatest fear is that someone will point out a rabbit and suggest that he chase it. This is a dog of peace and tranquility. I suggest that the greatest danger to your bears will be pique[3] at being ignored by Charley."

The young man laughed. "I wasn't so much worried about the bears," he said. "But our bears have developed an intolerance for dogs. One of them might demonstrate his prejudice with a clip on the chin, and then—no dog."

"I'll lock him in the back, sir. I promise you Charley will cause no ripple in the bear world, and as an old bear-looker, neither will I."

"I just have to warn you," he said. "I have no doubt your dog has the best of intentions. On the other hand, our bears have the worst. Don't leave food about. Not only do they steal but they are critical of anyone who tries to reform them. In a word, don't believe their sweet faces or you might get clobbered. And don't let the dog wander. Bears don't argue."

> LESS THAN A MILE FROM THE ENTRANCE I SAW A BEAR BESIDE THE ROAD, AND IT AMBLED OUT AS THOUGH TO FLAG ME DOWN.

We went on our way into the wonderland of nature gone nuts, and you will have to believe what happened. The only way I can prove it would be to get a bear.

Less than a mile from the entrance I saw a bear beside the road, and it ambled out as though to flag me down. Instantly a change came over Charley. He shrieked with rage. His lips flared, showing wicked teeth that have some trouble with a dog biscuit. He screeched insults at the bear, which hearing, the bear reared up and seemed to me to overtop Rocinante.[4] Frantically I rolled the windows shut and, swinging quickly to the left, grazed the animal, then scuttled on while Charley raved and ranted beside me, describing in detail what he would do to that bear if he could get at him. I was never so astonished in my life. To the best of my knowledge Charley had never seen a bear, and in his whole history had showed great tolerance for every living thing. Besides all this, Charley is a coward, so deep-seated a coward that he has developed a technique for concealing it. And yet he showed every evidence of wanting to get out

---

1. **laxness:** inattention to duty; slackness.
2. **Brady:** Mathew B. Brady, a famous Civil War photographer.
3. **pique** (pēk): a feeling of wounded pride; vexation.
4. **Rocinante** (rô-sē-nön´tĕ): the camper in which Steinbeck traveled, named for the broken-down horse ridden by Don Quixote in Miguel de Cervantes's satiric novel *Don Quixote*.

and murder a bear that outweighed him a thousand to one. I don't understand it.

A little farther along two bears showed up, and the effect was doubled. Charley became a maniac. He leaped all over me, he cursed and growled, snarled and screamed. I didn't know he had the ability to snarl. Where did he learn it? Bears were in good supply, and the road became a nightmare. For the first time in his life Charley resisted reason, even resisted a cuff on the ear. He became a primitive killer lusting for the blood of his enemy, and up to this moment he had had no enemies. In a bearless stretch, I opened the cab, took Charley by the collar, and locked him in the house. But that did no good. When we passed other bears he leaped on the table and scratched at the windows trying to get out at them. I could hear canned goods crashing as he struggled in his mania. Bears simply brought out the Hyde in my Jekyll-headed dog.[5] What could have caused it? Was it a pre-breed memory of a time when the wolf was in him? I know him well. Once in a while he tries a bluff, but it is a palpable lie.[6] I swear that this was no lie. I am certain that if he were released he would have charged every bear we passed and found victory or death.

It was too nerve-wracking, a shocking spectacle, like seeing an old, calm friend go insane. No amount of natural wonders, of rigid cliffs and belching waters, of smoking springs could even engage my attention while that pandemonium went on. After about the fifth encounter I gave up, turned Rocinante about, and retraced my way. If I had stopped the night and bears had gathered to my cooking, I dare not think what would have happened.

At the gate the park guard checked me out. "You didn't stay long. Where's the dog?"

"Locked up back there. And I owe you an apology. That dog has the heart and soul of a bear-killer and I didn't know it. Heretofore he has been a little tenderhearted toward an underdone steak."

"Yeah!" he said. "That happens sometimes. That's why I warned you. A bear dog would know his chances, but I've seen a Pomeranian[7] go up like a puff of smoke. You know, a well-favored bear can bat a dog like a tennis ball."

I moved fast, back the way I had come, and I was reluctant to camp for fear there might be some unofficial non-government bears about. That night I spent in a pretty auto court near Livingston. I had my dinner in a restaurant, and when I had settled in with a drink and a comfortable chair and my bathed bare feet on a carpet with red roses, I inspected Charley. He was dazed. His eyes held a faraway look and he was totally exhausted, emotionally no doubt. Mostly he reminded me of a man coming out of a long, hard drunk—worn out, depleted, collapsed. He couldn't eat his dinner, he refused the evening walk, and once we were in he collapsed on the floor and went to sleep. In the night I heard him whining and yapping, and when I turned on the light his feet were making running gestures and his body jerked and his eyes were wide open, but it was only a night bear. I awakened him and gave him some water. This time he went to sleep and didn't stir all night. In the morning he was still tired. I wonder why we think the thoughts and emotions of animals are simple. ❖

> ## BEARS SIMPLY BROUGHT OUT THE HYDE IN MY JEKYLL-HEADED DOG.

---

5. **brought out . . . dog:** brought out the viciousness in my mild-mannered dog. (In Robert Louis Stevenson's *The Strange Case of Dr. Jekyll and Mr. Hyde,* Dr. Jekyll (jĕ′kəl) develops a drug that releases the evil side of his personality, turning him into the murderous Mr. Hyde.)

6. **palpable** (păl′pə-bəl): obvious.

7. **Pomeranian** (pŏm′ə-rā′nē-ən): a small breed of dog with long, silky hair.

## Connect to the Literature

**1. What Do You Think?**
What is your explanation of Charley's behavior?

> **Comprehension Check**
> - Why has Steinbeck normally avoided national parks?
> - How does he assume Charley will react to bears?
> - How does Charley actually react?

## Think Critically

**2.** What are your impressions of John Steinbeck as the narrator of this selection?

**THINK ABOUT**
- his observations about national parks
- the concerns he expresses about Charley's reactions
- his conversations with the Yellowstone guard

**3.** **ACTIVE READING** **ANALYZING WORD CHOICE** Review the list of unusual words you jotted down in your **READER'S NOTEBOOK**. Point out to a partner a word or phrase that you found to be particularly effective in this humorous account.

**4.** At the start of his park visit, Steinbeck promises, "Charley will cause no ripple in the bear world." In your opinion, was Steinbeck more shaken by Charley's behavior or by his discovery that he hadn't really known his dog as well as he had thought? Support your opinion with evidence from the selection.

## Extend Interpretations

**5. The Writer's Style** The author and the National Park guard exchange pleasantries about the personalities of animals by referring to them as if they were humans: "He [Charley] respects the rights of cats to be cats," says Steinbeck. About bears, the guard warns, "Not only do they steal, but they are critical of anyone who tries to reform them." Find other examples of animals described in humanlike terms.

**6. Connect to Life** Think back to the chart of pet personality traits that you filled in earlier. In your opinion, do pets really have personalities, or do pet owners merely interpret pet behavior in familiar human terms? Give reasons for your opinion.

## Literary Analysis

**COMIC IRONY** **Comic irony** is a humorous contrast between appearance and reality. A writer usually creates this type of irony by stating one thing when he or she means another, commenting on a topic that is amusing or intriguing. One example of comic irony in the excerpt from *Travels with Charley* is the unexpected idea that a poodle, a breed of dog associated with very civilized behavior, could, in the right setting, behave as a wild animal. Steinbeck achieves comic irony through the use of two very different techniques.

- **Understatement** is the technique of deliberately saying less about a subject in order to emphasize it. For example, in the excerpt, the Yellowstone guard warns, "Bears don't argue," meaning in fact that bears can be ferociously deadly.

- **Hyperbole** is the technique of exaggerating the truth. Steinbeck uses hyperbole to describe Charley's reaction to the bear: ". . . he showed every evidence of wanting to get out and murder a bear that outweighed him a thousand to one."

**Activity** Review the selection to find two or three other examples of comic irony. Explain why each is ironic. Pay particular attention to the use of understatement and hyperbole.

## Writing Options

**1. Dog's-Eye Essay** In a short essay, relate the incident from the perspective of Charley. Exactly how does he view his master? the park guard? the bears?

**Writing Handbook**
See pages 1155–1156: Narrative Writing.

**2. Persuasive Essay** Near the beginning of the account of Charley's encounters, Steinbeck states, "Whatever my purpose in going to Yellowstone, I'm glad I went because I discovered something about Charley I might never have known." Do you think it's often possible to learn a life lesson through an experience with a pet? In a persuasive essay, express your opinions. Support your position with evidence from the excerpt or from your own life.

**3. Incident Report** Create the entry about Charley that the park guard might have recorded in a daily logbook.

## Activities & Explorations

**1. Brief Introduction** In the role of a television host, introduce the excerpt as if it had been adapted as an episode of a travel show.
**~ PERFORMING**

**2. Travel Comics** In small groups, share any humorous experiences you've had traveling. Then convey your experiences in the form of comic-strip drawings.

**~ SPEAKING AND LISTENING/ART**

*3:47 Camper John Steinbeck checked out early due to*

## Inquiry & Research

**Animal Defenses** Refer to Web sites, encyclopedias, and other reference sources to investigate the ways different animals protect themselves or to explore dog behavior. How closely does tame house dogs' behavior match that of their counterparts in the wild—wolves?

**More Online: Research Starter**
www.mcdougallittell.com

# Letter to Edith Mirrielees
## *from* Nobel Prize Acceptance Speech

*Nonfiction by* JOHN STEINBECK

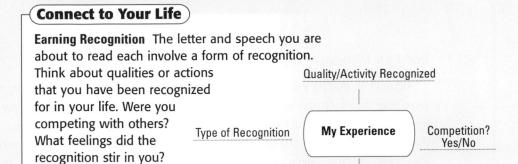

**Connect to Your Life**

**Earning Recognition** The letter and speech you are about to read each involve a form of recognition. Think about qualities or actions that you have been recognized for in your life. Were you competing with others? What feelings did the recognition stir in you? Record your experiences in a diagram like the one shown.

Quality/Activity Recognized

Type of Recognition

**My Experience**

Competition? Yes/No

Reaction

## Build Background

**Nobel Prize** In March of 1962, John Steinbeck wrote a letter to Edith Mirrielees, his short-story teacher at Stanford University, in recognition of the instruction he had received.

In October of the same year, Steinbeck was awarded the Nobel Prize for literature. Nobel laureates, or honorees, are generally regarded as among the most talented and worthy people of their generation. However, by the time Steinbeck had received the Nobel Prize, his work had fallen out of favor with some literary critics. One writer had declared, "Any critic knows it is no longer legal to praise John Steinbeck."

Nevertheless, when Steinbeck heard that a woman in Denmark had rowed eight miles to exchange two of her chickens for a copy of one of his books, he said: "That is what you write for. That is as good a prize as you can get."

## Focus Your Reading

**LITERARY ANALYSIS** **TONE AND AUDIENCE** **Tone** is the attitude a writer takes toward a subject. Writers adopt different tones for different audiences. For example, in this passage from his acceptance speech, Steinbeck uses a formal tone:

> *In my heart there may be doubt that I deserve the Nobel Award over other men of letters whom I hold in respect and reverence—but there is no question of my pleasure and pride in having it for myself.*

**ACTIVE READING** **MONITORING READING STRATEGIES** Understanding what you read involves being aware both of *what* you are reading and *how* you are reading. It's often necessary to **monitor** how you're reading in order to keep on track. Changing the pace of reading can be a particularly useful technique when reading nonfiction material. When unfamiliar information is conveyed, or when unfamiliar words or terms appear, slow down, as a bicyclist or driver would slow down over a difficult patch of road.

**READER'S NOTEBOOK** As you read Steinbeck's letter and speech, jot down references to passages that caused you to slow down and read more carefully.

# Letter to Edith Mirrielees

## John Steinbeck

Dear Edith Mirrielees:

Although it must be a thousand years ago that I sat in your class in story writing at Stanford, I remember the experience very clearly. I was bright-eyed and bushy-brained and prepared to absorb from you the secret formula for writing good short stories, even great short stories. You canceled this illusion very quickly. The only way to write a good short story, you said, is to write a good short story. Only after it is written can it be taken apart to see how it was done. It is a most difficult form, you told us, and the proof lies in how very few great short stories there are in the world.

The basic rule you gave us was simple and heartbreaking. A story to be effective had to convey something from writer to reader, and the power of its offering was the measure of its excellence. Outside of that, you said, there were no rules. A story could be about anything and could use any means and any technique at all—so long as it was effective. As a subhead[1] to this rule, you maintained that it seemed to be necessary for the writer to know what he wanted to say, in short, what he was talking about. As an exercise we were to try reducing the meat of a story to one sentence, for only then could we know it well enough to enlarge it to three or six or ten thousand words.

So there went the magic formula, the secret ingredient. With no more than that you set us on the desolate, lonely path of the writer. And we must have turned in some abysmally[2] bad stories. If I had expected to be discovered in a full bloom of excellence, the grades you gave my efforts quickly disillusioned me. And if I felt unjustly criticized, the judgments of editors for many years afterwards upheld your side, not mine. The low grades on my college stories were echoed in the rejection slips, in the hundreds of rejection slips.

It seemed unfair. I could read a fine story and could even know how it was done, thanks to your training. Why could I not then do it myself? Well, I couldn't, and maybe it's because no two stories dare be alike. Over the years I have written a great many stories and I still don't know how to go about it except to write it and take my chances.

If there is a magic in story writing, and I am convinced that there is, no one has ever been able to reduce it to a recipe that can be passed from one person to another. The formula seems to lie solely in the aching urge of the writer to convey something he feels important to the reader. If the writer has that urge, he may sometimes but by no means always find the way to do it. And if your

---

1. **subhead:** secondary idea.
2. **abysmally** (ə-bĭz′mə-lē): terribly.

book, Edith, does nothing more, it will teach many readers to perceive the excellence that makes a good story good or the errors that make a bad story. For a bad story is only an ineffective story.

It is not so very hard to judge a story after it is written, but, after many years, to start a story still scares me to death. I will go so far as to say that the writer who is not scared is happily unaware of the remote and tantalizing majesty of the medium.

I wonder whether you will remember one last piece of advice you gave me. It was during the exuberance of the rich and frantic 'twenties, and I was going out into that world to try to be a writer.

You said, "It's going to take a long time, and you haven't any money. Maybe it would be better if you could go to Europe."

"Why?" I asked.

"Because in Europe poverty is a misfortune, but in America it is shameful. I wonder whether or not you can stand the shame of being poor."

It wasn't too long afterward that the depression came down. Then everyone was poor and it was no shame any more. And so I will never know whether or not I could have stood it. But surely you were right about one thing, Edith. It took a long time—a very long time. And it is still going on, and it has never got easier. You told me it wouldn't.

*John Steinbeck*

John Steinbeck
March 8, 1962

> It is not so very hard to judge a story after it is written, but, after many years, to start a story still scares me to death.

## Thinking Through the Literature

1. After reading Steinbeck's letter, what two or three words would you use to describe him?

2. What do you think were Edith Mirrielees's thoughts after reading the letter?

3. What do you think motivated Steinbeck to write to his teacher so many years after his time at Stanford?

### John Steinbeck

I thank the Swedish Academy for finding my work worthy of this highest honor. In my heart there may be doubt that I deserve the Nobel Award over other men of letters whom I hold in respect and reverence—but there is no question of my pleasure and pride in having it for myself.

Steinbeck, receiving his award in Stockholm, Sweden.

It is customary for the recipient of this award to offer scholarly or personal comment on the nature and the direction of literature. However, I think it would be well at this particular time to consider the high duties and the responsibilities of the makers of literature.

Such is the prestige of the Nobel Award and of this place where I stand that I am impelled, not to squeak like a grateful and apologetic mouse, but to roar like a lion out of pride in my profession and in the great and good men who have practiced it through the ages.

Literature was not promulgated[1] by a pale and emasculated[2] critical priesthood singing their litanies[3] in empty churches—nor is it a game for the cloistered elect,[4] the tin-horn mendicants[5] of low-calorie despair.

Literature is as old as speech. It grew out of human need for it and it has not changed except to become more needed. The skalds, the bards,[6] the writers are not separate and exclusive. From the beginning, their functions, their duties, their responsibilities have been decreed by our species.

Humanity has been passing through a gray and desolate time of confusion. My great predecessor, William Faulkner,[7] speaking here, referred to it as a tragedy of universal physical fear, so long sustained that there were no longer problems of the spirit, so that only the human heart in conflict with itself seemed worth writing about. Faulkner, more than most men, was aware of human strength as well as of human weakness. He knew that the understanding and the resolution of fear are a large part of the writer's reason for being.

This is not new. The ancient commission of the writer has not changed. He is charged with exposing our many grievous faults and failures, with dredging up to the light our dark and dangerous dreams for the purpose of improvement.

Furthermore, the writer is delegated to declare and to celebrate man's proven capacity for greatness of heart and spirit—for gallantry in defeat, for courage, compassion and love. In the endless war against weakness and despair, these are the bright rally flags of hope and of emulation.[8] I hold that a writer who does not passionately believe in the perfectibility of man has no dedication nor any membership in literature.

1. **promulgated** (prŏm′əl-gā′tĭd): put into circulation.
2. **emasculated** (ĭ-măs′kyə-lā′tĭd): lacking manly strength.
3. **litanies** (lĭt′n-ēz): prayers.
4. **cloistered elect:** protected group of privileged people.
5. **tin-horn mendicants** (mĕn′dĭ-kənts): pretentious beggars.
6. **skalds . . . bards:** ancient Scandinavian and Celtic poets.
7. **William Faulkner:** a Nobel Prize-winning American novelist whose writings draw on the history, legends, and social problems of his native South.
8. **emulation** (ĕm′yə-lā′shən): a striving to imitate the accomplishments of others.

## Connect to the Literature

1. **What Do You Think?** Which of Steinbeck's statements about literature is most memorable to you?

**Comprehension Check**

- What does Steinbeck say is the customary thing to talk about in such a speech?
- Why does he praise William Faulkner?
- What kind of writers does Steinbeck scorn?

## Think Critically

2. **ACTIVE READING** **MONITORING READING STRATEGIES** Look back over any notes you may have recorded in your **READER'S NOTEBOOK** about difficult passages. What thought or statement expressed by Steinbeck did you understand better once you slowed down?

3. What do you think was Steinbeck's basic view of prizes and recognition?

**THINK ABOUT**
- his statement about receiving the prize
- his statements about the role of writers
- his thoughts about Faulkner and other writers

4. Both "Letter to Edith Mirrielees" and the "Nobel Prize Acceptance Speech" were written when Steinbeck was in the later stage of his writing career. On the basis of the views he expressed in both the letter and speech, what advice do you think he would have given to a beginning writer at that time?

## Extend Interpretations

5. **Critic's Corner** A biographer of Steinbeck's once said that whatever we read of his work "almost invariably strikes us as genuine." Think about the Steinbeck pieces you've encountered in this Author Study. Explain why you agree or disagree with that observation.

6. **Comparing Texts** Although Steinbeck's **tone** differs between the two selections, are his statements about the role of the writer consistent? Cite evidence from the selections to support your response.

7. **Connect to Life** Refer to the diagram in which you recorded details about an experience of earning recognition. Trophies, ribbons, medals, and certificates are common symbols of achievement. When do you think an award is most meaningful? Share your thoughts with others in your class.

## Literary Analysis

**TONE AND AUDIENCE** Writers convey different **tones**, or attitudes, towards their subjects, often depending on the audience and the form of the writing. In "Letter to Edith Mirrielees," for example, Steinbeck's basic tone is personal and conversational:

*I could read a fine story and could even know how it was done, thanks to your training.*

However, in the "Nobel Prize Acceptance Speech," he uses a formal, elevated tone:

*Such is the prestige of the Nobel Award . . . that I am impelled, not to squeak like a grateful and apologetic mouse, but to roar like a lion.*

Steinbeck also presents a more elevated tone in parts of the letter through rhythmic phrases that use **alliteration** to emphasize important words:

*the remote and tantalizing majesty of the medium . . .*

**Activity** Select other passages from both the letter and the speech, and identify what kind of tone Steinbeck has used. Be aware that there is a wider range of tone used in "Letter to Edith Mirrielees."

**REVIEW** **Author's Purpose** Authors write for one or more purposes: to inform, to express an opinion, to entertain, or to persuade. What would you identify as Steinbeck's purpose for writing both the letter and the speech? Cite details to support your response.

# The Author's Style
## Steinbeck's Stirring Descriptions

Although John Steinbeck was an experimenter, writing in different genres and expressing a range of moods, he was generally praised for his descriptive abilities.

### Key Aspects of Steinbeck's Style

- use of biblical rhythms and structures that add an air of significance to events ("For two days the earth drank the rain, until the earth was full.")
- repeated use of the word *and* to emphasize the building up of events and of characters' emotions
- use of figurative language ("The earth whispered under the beat of the rain.")
- use of humor through irony
- use of dialect reflecting the speech of ordinary people

## Analysis of Style

At the right are four excerpts from Steinbeck's work. Study the chart above, and then complete the following activities:

- Identify examples of different aspects of Steinbeck's style.
- Compare the style of Steinbeck's fiction with that of his nonfiction writings.
- Review the selections in this Author Study to find other examples of these key aspects of Steinbeck's style.

## Applications

**1. Speaking and Listening** With a partner, take turns reading aloud the passage from "The Flood" at the top right. One reader should place a stress on the content words; the other should read by placing stress only on the word *and*. After reading, compare the dramatic effects of these two interpretations.

**2. Changing Style** Discuss how differently a passage from the "Nobel Prize Acceptance Speech" might read if it had originally appeared as part of the "Letter to Edith Mirrielees." Rewrite a passage from the speech as if it were a passage in the letter.

**3. Imitating Style** In the style of "The Flood," write a page of description of a storm or any weather-related event you have witnessed. Use phrases that suggest the rhythmic flow of events.

### *from* "The Flood"

At last the mountains were full, and the hillsides spilled into the streams, built them to freshets, and sent them roaring down the canyons into the valleys.

### *from* Travels with Charley

We went on our way into the wonderland of nature gone nuts, and you will have to believe what happened. The only way I can prove it would be to get a bear.

### *from* "Letter to Edith Mirrielees"

Over the years I have written a great many stories and I still don't know how to go about it except to write it and take my chances.

### *from* "The Flood"

The sheriffs swore in new deputies and ordered new rifles; and the comfortable people in tight houses felt pity at first, and then distaste, and finally hatred for the migrant people.

## Writing Options

**1. Letter in Response** Put yourself in the place of Edith Mirrielees, having just received John Steinbeck's letter. Write back to him about any of the points he has made concerning literature. Assume that the timing of your response is after he has received the Nobel Prize for literature so that you can respond to his thoughts in that speech as well.

**2. Newspaper Article** Write an article for a literary newspaper reporting on Steinbeck's Nobel speech.

## Activities & Explorations

**1. Talk Show Skit** Using this Author Study as a resource, prepare a skit about "prepping" a talk show host who has never read Steinbeck but is about to interview a biographer of the author. Provide the host with a set of questions that would convince the author that the host is fascinated with Steinbeck's life and works. Also supply the host with the likely responses he or she will receive from the guest. ~ **PERFORMING**

**2. Making the Speech** Perform Steinbeck's acceptance speech in front of a group. Look for words or phrases within the speech that suggest what emotions to express and what ideas to emphasize. Choose the appropriate nonverbal gestures as well. How does the experience of reading it aloud, or listening to it, differ from reading the words silently? ~ **SPEAKING AND LISTENING**

## Inquiry & Research

**Nobel Lists** John Steinbeck was a much recognized writer, having won the Pulitzer Prize and the National Book Award as well as the Nobel Prize. Using this text and technical resources, find listings of the Nobel laureates, or honorees, for literature. Make your own list of laureates whose works you've read or would like to read.

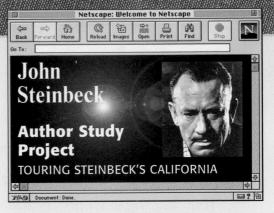

**John Steinbeck**

**Author Study Project**

TOURING STEINBECK'S CALIFORNIA

Much of Steinbeck's work centers around the 50 or so miles that surround his birthplace in California—its fertile farmland, rolling hills, and wondrous sea life. In small groups, investigate these lands Steinbeck loved, discovering what works these lands inspired and what themes the author used the settings to emphasize. Your guided tour might take the form of a travel brochure, a slide show, an oral interpretation of descriptions of Steinbeck settings, or some combination of these. To get started, research the following topics.

**Salinas Valley** Steinbeck was born and raised in this section of northern California. Locate photographic essays about this area (one example is the book *Steinbeck Country* by Steve Crouch). Skim the stories of Steinbeck's *The Red Pony* to find descriptions of settings. These stories also provide details about the nature of farm life in the region.

**Monterey Bay** Long before environmental writing became a popular literary form, Steinbeck wrote about the wonders of sea life. Using the book *Sea of Cortez* as one source, find out about his study of the sea, centering on the Great Tide Pool, an area on the tip of the Monterey Peninsula. Discover how Steinbeck's study of the sea helped to shape his philosophy of life and his views about the human condition. You might also skim a copy of *Travels with Charley* to find Steinbeck's comments about Monterey.

**More Online:** Research Starter
www.mcdougallittell.com

# *Writing* Workshop

## Describing a turning point. . .

**From Reading to Writing** In "A White Heron," Sylvia is unable to betray the location of the heron to a hunter: "She cannot tell the heron's secret and give its life away." Just as such a turning point can reveal character in a story, similar incidents can reveal some aspect of your own attitude or personality. Writers include such **autobiographical incidents** in their memoirs and essays.

### For Your Portfolio

**WRITING PROMPT** Write an essay describing a turning point or change in your life that was important to you.

**Purpose:** To share and explain
**Audience:** Family members and friends

---

## Basics in a Box

### Autobiographical Incident at a Glance

**Beginning**

Introduces the incident including the people involved and the setting

**Middle**

• Re-creates the incident using descriptive details
• Makes the significance clear

**End**

• Concludes by reflecting on the outcome and significance
• Presents the writer's feelings about the experience

---

### RUBRIC Standards for Writing

**A successful autobiographical incident should**

• focus on a well-defined incident or series of related incidents
• provide background information for the incident
• use elements such as plot, character, and setting as appropriate
• make the order of events clear
• use description or dialogue as appropriate
• include precise language and specific details
• show why the experience was significant
• maintain a consistent tone and point of view

# Analyzing a Student Model

**Bisco Hill**
**Southern Hills School**

**RUBRIC**
IN ACTION

### I Am Kwakkoli

A few months after my tenth birthday, my dad began to talk to me about receiving my Indian name. He said this had to be done in a ceremony by a medicine person or an elder in our tribe. My older sister, Megan, had received her Indian name, Maquegquay (Woman of the Woods), when she was only three. At that time my family lived on the Oneida Reservation just outside of Green Bay, Wisconsin.

My family moved from Wisconsin to Colorado three years before I was born. My grandfather died when I was only two and a half, and both of these major events delayed my Naming Ceremony. My dad talked about naming me for several years. Because of the sacred and traditional aspects of this, it is not like anyone can just call and order a Naming Ceremony, like ordering a pizza! As it happened, my Uncle Rick became the chairman of the tribe when I was ten, and he was able to talk to the right people and select the time. The right time was the summer solstice, near June 20, and it was also the time of the annual Strawberry Ceremony.

There are many traditions connected to the Naming Ceremony. For one thing, there are a limited number of names among the Oneida people. When a person dies, his or her name returns to the "pool" of available names and can be given to someone else. The medicine person decides whose energy fits which available name, or a person may ask for a certain name. In my case, I was named after my grandfather through my Anglo name, but I also wanted to take his Indian name. I felt that if I had both of his names, it made a full circle and I was wholly connected to him and to my family. The name that was his is "Kwakkoli," or "Whippoorwill" in English.

A few days before the ceremony in June of 1990, my parents and I flew to the Oneida Reservation. Oneida is very small and different from any other city I have known. My dad and his brother knew the names of everyone. They knew who was married to whom and who everyone's grandparents and parents were. They remembered all kinds of funny stories and laughed a lot. I thought it must be nice to live in a small town where everyone knows everyone for all those years. It is also a place where everyone is connected by common heritage, customs, and beliefs.

The night before the ceremony, I got very nervous. My stomach hurt as if I had the flu, but I think it was just butterflies. I finally fell asleep at about 3:30 in the morning. I don't know what I was afraid of—maybe just not knowing what was going to happen or what I would have to do.

**❶** This writer begins by giving the background for the incident.
**Other Options:**
• Start with dialogue.
• Begin with the incident itself.

**❷** Establishes the significance of the incident

**❸** Establishes the time and setting of the incident

**❹** Uses a transitional phrase to show the order of events

After getting about four hours of sleep, I woke up to the sound of a shower running. I quickly put on my ribbon shirt, a pair of black pants, and moccasins. The ceremony was set for 9:30 that morning, so we had to hurry.

On our short drive to the reservation, my stomach felt like it was going to explode! I had to at least get those butterflies flying in formation! I was pretty anxious but really excited about getting my Indian name. We arrived at the longhouse a little early, and I sat with my dad and one of his friends while other people finished setting up tables and chairs.

The ceremony finally began. The Faithkeeper called up the three clans of the Oneida Tribe: the Bear, the Turtle, and the Wolf. I am in the Turtle Clan, so I would be named in the second group. The Faithkeeper named all the children in the Bear Clan, then moved on to the Turtles. He named two people, then stepped in front of me. He spoke to me in Oneida. It is a language with unusual sounds like no other language I have ever heard. Most of the words were not understandable to me. He later translated them as, "You must try to learn the Oneida language and our ways. I would like you to come to some of the other ceremonies and events. You now have an Oneida name, 'Kwakkoli,' and the Creator will know you by that name." I was proud to have both of my grandfather's names because he was an important man in our tribe.

The Faithkeeper named the others, and we all sat down as the Chief said a few more prayers. After about an hour, we all danced to Indian songs and drum music.

Next, we ate and drank. One of the drinks was a kind of strawberry juice. It is sacred and is part of the ceremony because the Creator gave this gift of the strawberry to the Oneida people. The drink was very good.

When it was time to go, we thanked the Faithkeeper and the Chief and gave them gifts. The gift that I received, and will be mine for life, is a very special name that runs through my family and connects me to my grandfather, whom I barely knew. My name also reminds me of the many traditions and beliefs that are part of my heritage and about which I have a lot to learn and understand. I look forward to visiting my reservation as I grow up.

**❺** Maintains an excited, hopeful tone

**❻** This writer uses dialogue to illustrate the significance of the event.
**Another Option:**
· Describe actions that reveal significance.

**❼** Emphasizes why the experience was meaningful

# Writing Your Autobiographical Incident

## ❶ Prewriting

Begin by choosing the incident you will write about. You may choose to focus on something that happened to you, or you may decide to write about an event you witnessed but did not participate in.

You might make a list with three columns: *People, Places, Things.* Then list all the things that come to mind in each category that represent something important to you. You might also remember meaningful events in your past by using the phrase, "I remember when. . . ," then jotting down the thoughts that come to mind. See the **Idea Bank** in the margin for other suggestions. When you have chosen the event you want to write about, follow the steps below.

### Planning Your Autobiographical Incident

▶ **1. Test your topic.** Do you remember the incident well enough to write about it? Why is this memory important? Will you be comfortable sharing the memory? Will writing about it show what you learned from the event or what impact it had on you?

▶ **2. Think about your purpose and audience.** How can you show readers how and why the incident affected you?

▶ **3. Choose some of your building blocks.** What other people took part in the incident? Is the time or place important? What are some of the key events?

## ❷ Drafting

Get your memory down on paper. Don't worry about how it comes out. You can make improvements later. If you find yourself losing interest in the incident or have trouble telling it, choose another memory. As you draft, consider the following hints:

- Use some or all of the story elements—**plot, character,** and **setting.** Include any background information that the reader needs to know.

- Use **dialogue** when you can.

- Use language that appeals to the **senses.**

- **Organize** your incident. Usually **chronological order** is the clearest method of organization, but you might decide you can make a greater impact by starting in the middle of the incident. In that case, you can use a **flashback** to fill in all the missing parts.

After you finish your first draft, let it sit for a while. Then reread it. Ask your peer readers for reactions, too.

### IDEABank

**1. Your Working Portfolio**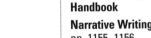
Build on the **Writing Option** you completed earlier in this unit:

- **Autobiographical Tale,** p. 902

**2. Life Map**
To jog your memory, make a road map of your life. Start with your birth, and draw figures or symbols for important events. Choose one event to write about.

**3. Special Days**
Try recalling memorable things that happened on birthdays, holidays, or vacations. Make short notes about the events. Then write about one of them.

**Need help with your autobiographical incident?**

See the **Writing Handbook**
**Narrative Writing,** pp. 1155–1156

### Ask Your Peer Reader

- Why do you think this experience was important to me?

- Which part of the incident is described most vividly?

- What parts are unnecessary or need more explanation?

Review the **Rubric**, p. 948

Consider **peer reader** comments

Check **Revision Guidelines**, p. 1145

**Puzzled by punctuating clauses?**

See the **Grammar Handbook**

**Independent and Subordinate Clauses** p. 1197

## Publishing
### IDEAS

- Gather a group of classmates and read your works aloud to each other.

- Read your work to your family. Ask whether they remember the events the same way as you wrote about them.

**More Online: Publishing Options** www.mcdougallittell.com

# ❸ Revising

*I can't write five words but that I change seven.*

**Dorothy Parker, writer and humorist**

**TARGET SKILL** ▶ **MAINTAINING CONSISTENCY OF TONE** Your autobiographical incident will have more impact if the tone is the same throughout. A humorous piece that unintentionally turns serious or a serious piece that suddenly becomes sarcastic will likely confuse the reader.

> The gift that I received, and ~~I'll have to live with forever~~ *will be mine for life,*
>
> ~~whether I want to or not, is (get this!)~~ Kwakkoli *is a very special* a name
>
> that my family ~~is stuck with. It's from~~ *runs through* *and connects me to* my grandfather,
>
> whom I barely knew.

# ❹ Editing and Proofreading

**TARGET SKILL** ▶ **PUNCTUATING CLAUSES** Your incident will have more impact if you vary the sentences you use to tell about it. To avoid too many short, choppy sentences, writers combine ideas into one sentence with two or more clauses. Using commas after introductory clauses and between independent clauses helps to make the meaning clear.

> As it happened, my uncle Rick became the chairmen of a
>
> the tribe when I was ten. *and* He was able to talk to the right
>
> people and select the time.

# ❺ Reflecting

**FOR YOUR WORKING PORTFOLIO** What did you remember about your life that you had forgotten? What details became clearer as you wrote? How important does this incident seem now? Attach your reflections to your finished essay. Save your autobiographical incident in your **Working Portfolio**.

Read this paragraph from the first draft of an autobiographical essay. The underlined sections may include the following kinds of errors:

- **double negatives**
- **comma errors**
- **run-on sentences**
- **incorrect verb tenses**

For each underlined section, choose the revision that most improves the writing.

When I was ten years old, my family and I were on a cruise ship that sank. Even at the start of our voyage, <u>there is trouble</u>. <u>As we set out to sea fuel oil</u> in
(1)                          (2)
the cargo hold caught fire. By the time we were miles from shore, <u>the lower</u>
(3)
<u>decks of the ship were burning no one could put the fire out</u>. We <u>couldn't hardly</u>
(4)
<u>believe</u> what was happening. The captain <u>radioed for help, and we all got into</u>
(5)
the lifeboats and rowed away from the burning ship. A few hours later, a Greek freighter rescued us. From the deck of the freighter, we <u>watch</u> our ship sink
(6)
into the ocean. What an experience that was!

1. **A.** there has been trouble
   **B.** there may be trouble
   **C.** there was trouble
   **D.** Correct as is

2. **A.** As we set out to sea fuel, oil
   **B.** As we set out to sea, fuel oil
   **C.** As we set out, to sea fuel oil
   **D.** Correct as is

3. **A.** the lower decks of the ship were burning. No one could put the fire out.
   **B.** the lower decks of the ship were burning and couldn't put the fire out.
   **C.** the lower decks of the ship were burning, which no one could put out.
   **D.** Correct as is

4. **A.** couldn't scarcely
   **B.** could hardly
   **C.** couldn't barely
   **D.** Correct as is

5. **A.** radioed for help and we all got into
   **B.** radioed for help: and we all got into
   **C.** radioed for help and we, all, got into
   **D.** Correct as is

6. **A.** are watching
   **B.** have watched
   **C.** watched
   **D.** Correct as is

**Need extra help?**

See the **Grammar Handbook**

**Correcting Run-on Sentences**, p. 1199

**Punctuation Chart**, pp. 1203–1204

**Subject-Verb Agreement**, p. 1200

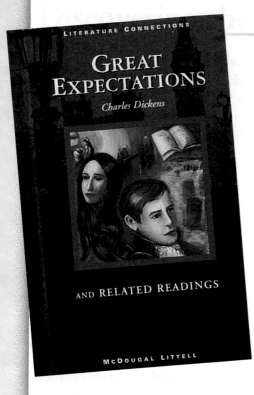

LITERATURE CONNECTIONS
# Great Expectations

### CHARLES DICKENS

Set in 19th-century England, this novel depicts the rags-to-riches story of the orphan Pip. After his contact with a wealthy eccentric, Pip dreams of becoming a gentleman. One day he learns that a secret patron has arranged for this to happen. Pip moves to London to fulfill his "great expectations," where he will learn eventually the true measures of nobility and love.

**These thematically related readings are provided along with *Great Expectations*:**

**The Duke's Children**
FRANK O'CONNOR

***from* Silent Dancing**
JUDITH ORTIZ COFER

**You Are a Part of Me**
FRANK YERBY

**Time Does Not Bring Relief**
EDNA ST. VINCENT MILLAY

**The Peasant Marey**
FYODOR DOSTOEVSKY

**The Spinster's Day/ Jornada de la Soltera**
ROSARIO CASTELLANOS
TRANSLATED BY MAGDA BOGIN

**The Jilting of Granny Weatherall**
KATHERINE ANNE PORTER

**The House on the Hill**
EDWARD ARLINGTON ROBINSON

## And Even *More* . . .

# The Chocolate War

### ROBERT CORMIER

Freshman Jerry Renault is trying to make his way at Trinity High. Jerry finds himself in a struggle between two leaders on an unlikely battlefield—the school's annual chocolate sale. When Jerry dares to disturb the order of things, the consequences are shocking. This book is also part of the *Literature Connections* series published by McDougal Littell.

## Books

### Siddhartha
HERMANN HESSE
A restless young man searches for a truth that will guide him through life.

### A Raisin in the Sun
LORRAINE HANSBERRY
An African-American family pursuing the American dream of their own home encounters racism and obstacles of their own making. This book is also part of the *Literature Connections* series published by McDougal Littell.

# A Place Where the Sea Remembers

SANDRA BENÍTEZ

This best-selling novel, published in 1993, is set in Santiago, Mexico, and consists of short interrelated narratives, each one focused on a single character. Benítez's work depicts the triumphs and tragedies of common people—a flower seller, a healer, a fisherman, a teacher, a midwife—whose lives are interwoven by fate and passion. The characters struggle to survive and prevail in a difficult and mysterious world, one that is edged by the rhythms, power, and beauty of the sea.

**These thematically related readings are provided along with *A Place Where the Sea Remembers*:**

**Night**
LOUISE BOGAN

**All day I hear the noise of waters**
JAMES JOYCE

**Talking to the Dead**
JUDITH ORTIZ COFER

**Paciencia**
JUDITH ORTIZ COFER

**Death of a Young Son by Drowning**
MARGARET ATWOOD

**Sophistication**
SHERWOOD ANDERSON

**An Astrologer's Day**
R. K. NARAYAN

## Other Media

**The Seekers**
DANIEL J. BOORSTIN
A famous historian offers a sweeping account of humanity's search for truth, ranging from prophets such as Moses to modern scientists such as Einstein.

**Of Mice and Men**
JOHN STEINBECK
The tragic story of two ranch hands, George and Lennie, who dream of one day owning a place of their own.

**The Grapes of Wrath**
John Ford's classic 1940 movie based on John Steinbeck's novel about the lives of migrant workers in the Depression. Filmic Archives.
(VIDEOCASSETTE)

**Of Mice and Men**
A 1992 film adaptation of Steinbeck's novel, starring John Malkovich and Gary Sinise. Filmic Archives.
(VIDEOCASSETTE)

**Robert Frost**
A biographical sketch of the famous poet, with a dramatic reading of "Mending Wall" by Leonard Nimoy. Part of the *Poetry by Americans* series. Filmic Archives.
(VIDEOCASSETTE)

**Emily Dickinson**
A look into the life and work of the mysterious and complex Emily Dickinson. Part of the *American Poets: Voices and Visions* series.
(VIDEOCASSETTE)

Detail of *Arming and Departure of the Knights* (1895–1896), Sir Edward Coley Burne-Jones.
From the *Holy Grail Tapestry Series*. Birmingham City Council Museums and Art Gallery, England.

# THE MAKING OF
# HEROES

THE HERO IN ONE
AGE WILL BE A HERO
IN ANOTHER.

CHARLOTTE LENNOX

A re you a strong person? In times of trial, can you find the strength to do what needs to be done—to overcome obstacles, to withstand opposition, even to face danger? Often, people never know what they are capable of doing until circumstances push them to the limit. In this part of Unit Six, you will encounter a number of ordinary people who must confront extraordinary challenges. As you will see, such challenges can produce unexpected heroes.

## ACTIVITY

List the names of three people whom you regard as heroes. These may be figures from history, people in the news, or personal acquaintances. Write a brief explanation of what makes each of these people heroic. Then compare your list with those of your classmates and discuss what you regard as the essential ingredients of heroism.

# LEARNING the Language of *Literature*

$\mathcal{S}$tyle, in general, is the particular way something is expressed. Almost everything has a style—from haircuts to shoes, architecture to music. People also express their individuality through their personal style of dressing, talking, and acting. Style as a literary term refers to the way a work is written. Just as your personal style expresses your individuality, a writer's literary style is a unique signature, expressing his or her personal way of writing.

## Style in Diction

An essential element of literary style is **diction**, or a writer's choice of words. When Agatha Christie described Mr. Mayherne's voice in "The Witness for the Prosecution" (page 871), she chose the word *dry* to characterize the reserved lawyer. Generally, Christie's diction is spare but telling. She gives readers just enough information to keep them guessing. Christie's reserved diction contrasts with Sarah Orne Jewett's more expressive diction in "A White Heron" (page 822). Jewett's purpose is quite different from Christie's, of course. She is not writing a mystery story but a story full of emotion and delicate beauty.

## Style in Sentence Structure

**Sentence structure** includes both sentence length and kind of sentence (simple, compound, complex, or compound-complex). Choices about sentence structure have a subtle influence on style. For example, Christie frequently used short, simple sentences, which are good vehicles for conveying details and giving a fast-paced rhythm to her story—key elements of a good mystery.

Sarah Orne Jewett, on the other hand, was more interested in the mystery of the human heart and the majesty of nature. She used long sentences in her story to express complicated feelings and to draw important connections between her characters and nature.

**YOUR TURN** Analyze the two passages at the right in terms of diction and sentence structure. Point to examples of differences between the two authors.

---

### DICTION AND SENTENCE STRUCTURE

Mr. Mayherne adjusted his pince-nez and cleared his throat with a little dry-as-dust cough that was wholly typical of him. Then he looked again at the man opposite him, the man charged with willful murder.

Mr. Mayherne was a small man, precise in manner, neatly, not to say foppishly dressed, with a pair of very shrewd and piercing gray eyes. By no means a fool. Indeed, as a solicitor, Mr. Mayherne's reputation stood very high. His voice, when he spoke to his client, was dry but not unsympathetic.

—Agatha Christie, "The Witness for the Prosecution"

---

The woods were already filled with shadows one June evening, just before eight o'clock, though a bright sunset still glimmered faintly among the trunks of the trees. A little girl was driving home her cow, a plodding, dilatory, provoking creature in her behavior. . . .

There was hardly a night the summer through when the old cow could be found waiting at the pasture bars; on the contrary, it was her greatest pleasure to hide herself away among the high huckleberry bushes, and though she wore a loud bell she had made the discovery that if one stood perfectly still it would not ring. So Sylvia had to hunt for her until she found her, and call Co'! Co'! with never an answering Moo, until her childish patience was quite spent.

—Sarah Orne Jewett, "A White Heron"

# Dialogue

Another important aspect of a writer's style is the use of **dialogue**, or the written conversation between two or more characters. Dialogue is a major feature of Christie's story: the facts of the case are primarily revealed through what the characters say. Characters also reveal and conceal aspects of themselves through their dialogue. Jewett relies less on dialogue and more on the comments of an omniscient narrator to express the rich inner life of her main character.

# Imagery

**Imagery**, or descriptive words and phrases that create sensory experiences for the reader, is perhaps the most recognizable aspect of a writer's style. In Christie's story, only a few telling images create a scene or distinguish a character, whereas Jewett's story is almost completely constructed with images. From the opening scene with the plodding cow to the climax of Sylvia at the top of the majestic pine tree, the reader is immersed in a lush woodland of fragrant pines and twittering birds. Images of light and dark help to evoke awe at nature's simple marvels and instill in the reader the sense of secrecy that Sylvia herself feels.

# Tone

**Tone**, the attitude a writer takes toward a subject, might be playful, serious, bitter, angry, or detached. Jewett's sympathetic tone in "A White Heron" comes mostly from the comments of the omniscient narrator. But the narrator's sympathy for Sylvia depends on the supporting imagery of nature to justify it. Mr. Mayherne's manner sets the tone in Christie's story, as he diligently searches dark corners for the truth.

**YOUR TURN** Analyze the imagery in the two passages at the right. Then identify the tone of each passage and explain how the imagery and tone are related.

## IMAGERY AND TONE

With some reluctance the lawyer stepped across the threshold into the small dirty room, with its flickering gas jet. There was an untidy unmade bed in a corner, a plain deal table and two rickety chairs. For the first time Mr. Mayherne had a full view of the tenant of this unsavory apartment. She was a woman of middle age, bent in figure, with a mass of untidy gray hair and a scarf wound tightly round her face. She saw him looking at this and laughed again, the same curious, toneless chuckle.

"Wondering why I hide my beauty, dear? He, he, he. Afraid it may tempt you, eh? But you shall see—you shall see."

She drew aside the scarf, and the lawyer recoiled involuntarily before the almost formless blur of scarlet. She replaced the scarf again.

—Agatha Christie, "The Witness for the Prosecution"

There was the huge tree asleep yet in the paling moonlight, and small and silly Sylvia began with utmost bravery to mount to the top of it, . . .

She crept out along the swaying oak limb at last, and took the daring step across into the old pine tree. The way was harder than she thought; she must reach far and hold fast, the sharp dry twigs caught and held her and scratched her like angry talons, the pitch made her thin little fingers clumsy and stiff as she went round and round the tree's great stem, higher and higher upward. The sparrows and robins in the woods below were beginning to wake and twitter to the dawn, yet it seemed much lighter there aloft in the pine tree, and the child knew she must hurry if her project were to be of any use.

—Sarah Orne Jewett, "A White Heron"

"What do you mean by that?" "Would you repeat the question?" "Let me see if I have this right: you're saying that . . ." These are expressions that you might use in your everyday life to clear up a confusion or a misunderstanding. The strategies on this page will help you apply this same skill to your reading.

# Clarifying

Clarifying can help you fully comprehend what you read. Basically, **clarifying** means stopping occasionally during your reading to review what you understand so far. Clarifying not only helps you find answers to questions you had before, but it can also signal when you're confused and need to reread a passage. Periodically clarifying your understanding helps you stay alert and follow the developments in a literary work—the twists and turns of a story, for instance, or the line of argument in an essay.

## 1 Strategies for Clarifying in Fiction

- **Question** the characters' feelings, attitudes, and behavior so that you can **clarify** their motivations. As you read, try to answer the five W's *(Who, What, When, Where,* and *Why)* about the characters and plot of the story.
- **Visualize** descriptions of character and setting. Is the setting real or imaginary? Think about the time and place of the story. Is the setting important to the plot? **Evaluate** how the setting might affect the characters. Are the two closely related?
- Use a chart like this to keep track of important events and details as you read.
- Stop periodically to review conflicts in a story and changes within a character.
- At the end, state the theme, or main idea.

| Setting: | |
|---|---|
| Characters: | |
| Conflict(s): | |
| Events: | |
| Resolution: | |

## 2 Strategies for Clarifying in Nonfiction

- Before you read, skim the selection: read the headline, the first and last paragraphs, the first sentence of other paragraphs, and any graphics, including maps, timelines, charts, and diagrams.
- **Clarify** your understanding by periodically summarizing main ideas as you read.
- Identify the writer's purpose. Is he or she entertaining, informing or explaining, persuading, or expressing ideas and feelings?
- Separate facts from opinions. Remember that a fact can be proved or disproved. An opinion expresses beliefs or attitudes about which people can disagree.

## 3 Strategies for Clarifying in Poetry

- **Visualize** all images and figurative language, and ask yourself why the poet chose those descriptions and comparisons.
- **Connect** personally with ideas, situations, and feelings in the poem.
- Read the poem at least three times, paraphrasing complex thoughts and feelings.

**Need More Help?**

Remember that active readers use the essential reading strategies explained on page 7: **visualize, predict, clarify, question, connect, evaluate, monitor.**

# A Chip of Glass Ruby

*Short Story by* NADINE GORDIMER

## Connect to Your Life

**Active Involvement** Think of a household where one parent is heavily involved in political or charitable activities outside the home. With a small group of classmates, discuss how the family might be affected by such activities. List the positive and negative effects that such involvement might have on the family.

## Build Background

**Life Under Apartheid** In this story, an Indian woman living in South Africa juggles the responsibilities of family life with her work as a political activist. The story takes place during the time of apartheid (ə-pärt′hīt′), a system of racial segregation. Under apartheid, every citizen was classified as either white, colored (mixed race), Asian (of East Indian ancestry), or Bantu (native black). Complex laws set limits on the lives of those who were not white. For example, the Group Areas Act, mentioned in this story, forced nonwhites to live in certain areas. Pass laws required that black South Africans carry passes identifying where they lived and what areas they could visit. While Asians did not have to carry passes, their movements also were restricted.

For decades, many South Africans struggled against apartheid, despite the threat of being jailed. Among the most influential groups was the African National Congress (ANC), called simply "Congress" in the story.

WORDS TO KNOW
**Vocabulary Preview**

| | |
|---|---|
| disarm | presumption |
| morose | sallow |
| patronize | |

## Focus Your Reading

**LITERARY ANALYSIS** **DIALOGUE** **Dialogue** is written conversation between two or more characters. Used in most fictional narratives, dialogue adds life to a story, moves the **plot** along, and provides the reader with insights into the **characters** and their relationships with one another.

As you read this story, pay attention to the dialogue and what it tells you about the characters.

**ACTIVE READING** **CLARIFYING** When you read, it is helpful to stop occasionally and review what you understand so far. "A Chip of Glass Ruby" is a story about a family, focusing primarily on the differences between a husband and wife. In order to understand the story, it will help you to stop and **clarify** the attitudes and behaviors of these two **characters.**

**READER'S NOTEBOOK** As you read the following story, stop at each major event. Pay attention to how Bamjee and Mrs. Bamjee, the husband and wife in the story, respond to that event. Record your observations in a chart like the one shown, noting their attitudes and behaviors. As you move through the story, be prepared for new ideas or perceptions. Be aware that your understanding may change as you read.

| Event | Attitude/Behavior | |
|---|---|---|
| | Bamjee | Mrs. Bamjee |
| Duplicating machine arrives | | |

# A Chip of Glass Ruby

## Nadine Gordimer

**W**hen the duplicating machine was brought into the house, Bamjee said, "Isn't it enough that you've got the Indians' troubles on your back?" Mrs. Bamjee said, with a smile that showed the gap of a missing tooth but was confident all the same, "What's the difference, Yusuf? We've all got the same troubles."

"Don't tell me that. We don't have to carry passes; let the natives protest against passes on their own; there are millions of them. Let them go ahead with it."

The nine Bamjee and Pahad children were present at this exchange as they were always; in the small house that held them all there was no room for privacy for the discussion of matters they were too young to hear, and so they had never been too young to hear anything. Only their sister and half-sister, Girlie, was missing; she was the eldest, and married. The children looked expectantly, unalarmed and interested, at Bamjee, who had neither left the room nor settled down again to the task of rolling his own cigarettes, which had been interrupted by the arrival of the duplicator. He had looked at the thing that had come hidden in a washbasket and conveyed in a black man's taxi, and the children turned on it too, their black eyes surrounded by thick lashes like those still, open flowers with hairy tentacles that close on whatever touches them.

"A fine thing to have on the table where we eat," was all he said at last. They smelled the machine among them; a smell of cold black grease. He went out, heavily on tiptoe, in his troubled way.

"It's going to go nicely on the sideboard!" Mrs. Bamjee was busy making a place by removing the two pink glass vases filled with plastic carnations and the hand-painted velvet runner with the picture of the Taj Mahal.[1]

After supper she began to run off leaflets on the machine. The family lived in that room—the three other rooms in the house were full of beds—and they were all there. The older children shared a bottle of ink while they did their homework, and the two little ones pushed a couple of empty milk bottles in and out the chair legs. The three-year-old fell asleep and was carted away by one of the girls. They all drifted off to bed eventually; Bamjee himself went before the older children—he was a fruit-and-vegetable hawker[2] and was up at half past four every morning to get to the market by five. "Not long now," said Mrs. Bamjee. The older children looked up and smiled at him. He

turned his back on her. She still wore the traditional clothing of a Moslem woman, and her body, which was scraggy and unimportant as a dress on a peg when it was not host to a child, was wrapped in the trailing rags of a cheap sari,[3] and her thin black plait[4] was greased. When she was a girl, in the Transvaal[5] town where they lived still, her mother fixed a chip of glass ruby in her nostril; but she had abandoned that adornment as too old-style, even for her, long ago.

She was up until long after midnight, turning out leaflets. She did it as if she might have been pounding chilies.

Bamjee did not have to ask what the leaflets were. He had read the papers. All the past week Africans had been destroying their passes and then presenting themselves for arrest. Their leaders were jailed on charges of incitement,[6] campaign offices were raided—someone must be helping the few minor leaders who were left to keep the campaign going without offices or equipment. What was it the leaflets would say—"Don't go to work tomorrow," "Day of Protest," "Burn Your Pass for Freedom"? He didn't want to see.

**ACTIVE READING**

**CLARIFY** Why doesn't Bamjee want to see the leaflets?

He was used to coming home and finding his wife sitting at the table deep in discussion with strangers or people whose names

---

1. **Taj Mahal** (täzh' mə-häl'): a beautiful white marble building in India, built in the seventeenth century by Shah Jahan as a tomb for his wife and himself.
2. **hawker:** a peddler who sells goods by calling out.
3. **sari** (sä'rē): a garment worn by East Indian women and girls, consisting of a long cloth wrapped around the body, with one end draped over the shoulder.
4. **plait** (plāt): a braid of hair.
5. **Transvaal** (trăns-väl'): a province in northeast South Africa.
6. **incitement** (ĭn-sīt'mənt): a rousing, stirring up, or calling to action.

*News from the Gulf* (about 1991), Robert A. Wade. Watercolor, 19″ × 29″, private collection.
Copyright © Robert A. Wade. From *Painting Your Vision in Watercolor*, North Light Books.

were familiar by repute.[7] Some were prominent Indians, like the lawyer, Dr. Abdul Mohammed Khan, or the big businessman, Mr. Moonsamy Patel, and he was flattered, in a suspicious way, to meet them in his house. As he came home from work next day, he met Dr. Khan coming out of the house, and Dr. Khan—a highly educated man—said to him, "A wonderful woman." But Bamjee had never caught his wife out in any <u>presumption</u>; she behaved properly, as any Moslem woman should, and once her business with such gentlemen was over would never, for instance, have sat down to eat with them. He found her now back in the kitchen, setting about the preparation of dinner and carrying on a conversation on several different wavelengths with the children. "It's really a shame if you're tired of lentils, Jimmy, because that's what you're getting—Amina, hurry up, get a pot of water going—don't worry, I'll mend that in a minute; just bring the yellow cotton, and there's a needle in the cigarette box on the sideboard."

"Was that Dr. Khan leaving?" said Bamjee.

"Yes, there's going to be a stay-at-home on Monday. Desai's ill, and he's got to get the word around by himself. Bob Jali was up all last night

---

7. **repute** (rĭ-py$\overline{oo}$t′): reputation; fame.

WORDS
TO
KNOW

**presumption** (prĭ-zŭmp′shən) *n.* behavior or language that is boldly arrogant or offensive

printing leaflets, but he's gone to have a tooth out." She had always treated Bamjee as if it were only a mannerism that made him appear uninterested in politics, the way some woman will persist in interpreting her husband's bad temper as an endearing gruffness hiding boundless goodwill, and she talked to him of these things just as she passed on to him neighbors' or family gossip.

"What for do you want to get mixed up with these killings and stonings and I don't know what? Congress should keep out of it. Isn't it enough with the Group Areas?"

She laughed. "Now, Yusuf, you know you don't believe that. Look how you said the same thing when the Group Areas started in Natal. You said we should begin to worry when we get moved out of our own houses here in the Transvaal. And then your own mother lost her house in Noorddorp,[8] and there you are; you saw that nobody's safe. Oh, Girlie was here this afternoon; she says Ismail's brother's engaged—that's nice, isn't it? His mother will be pleased; she was worried."

"Why was she worried?" asked Jimmy, who was fifteen, and old enough to patronize his mother.

"Well, she wanted to see him settled. There's a party on Sunday week at Ismail's place—you'd better give me your suit to give to the cleaners tomorrow, Yusuf."

One of the girls presented herself at once. "I'll have nothing to wear, Ma."

Mrs. Bamjee scratched her sallow face. "Perhaps Girlie will lend you her pink, eh? Run over to Girlie's place now and say I say will she lend it to you."

The sound of commonplaces often does service as security, and Bamjee, going to sit in the armchair with the shiny armrests that was wedged between the table and the sideboard, lapsed into an unthinking doze that, like all times of dreamlike ordinariness during those weeks, was filled with uneasy jerks and starts back into reality. The next morning, as soon as he got to market, he heard that Dr. Khan had been arrested. But that night Mrs. Bamjee sat up making a new dress for her daughter; the sight disarmed Bamjee, reassured him again, against his will, so that the resentment he had been making ready all day faded into a morose and accusing silence. Heaven knew, of course, who came and went in the house during the day. Twice in that week of riots, raids, and arrests, he found black women in the house when he came home; plain ordinary native women in doeks,[9] drinking tea. This was not a thing other Indian women would have in their homes, he thought bitterly; but then his wife was not like other

**This was not a thing other Indian women would have in their homes, he thought bitterly.**

**ACTIVE READING**

**CLARIFY** What seems to be Bamjee's attitude toward his wife?

---

8. **Natal** (nə-tăl′) . . . **Noorddorp** (nōrt′dôrp): provinces in South Africa.

9. **doeks** (düks): cloth head coverings.

WORDS
TO
KNOW

**patronize** (pā′trə-nīz) v. to behave in a manner that shows feelings of superiority
**sallow** (săl′ō) adj. of a sickly, yellowish color or complexion
**disarm** (dĭs-ärm′) v. to overcome or reduce the intensity of suspicion or hostility; to win the confidence of
**morose** (mə-rōs′) adj. gloomy; sullen

people, in a way he could not put his finger on, except to say what it was not: not scandalous, not punishable, not rebellious. It was, like the attraction that had led him to marry her, Pahad's widow with five children, something he could not see clearly.

**W**hen the Special Branch[10] knocked steadily on the door in the small hours of Thursday morning, he did not wake up, for his return to consciousness was always set in his mind to half past four, and that was more than an hour away. Mrs. Bamjee got up herself, struggled into Jimmy's raincoat which was hanging over a chair, and went to the front door. The clock on the wall—a wedding present when she married Pahad—showed three o'clock when she snapped on the light, and she knew at once who it was on the other side of the door. Although she was not surprised, her hands shook like a very old person's as she undid the locks and the complicated catch on the wire burglar-proofing. And then she opened the door and they were there—two colored policemen in plain clothes. "Zanip Bamjee?"

"Yes."

As they talked, Bamjee woke up in the sudden terror of having overslept. Then he became conscious of men's voices. He heaved himself out of bed in the dark and went to the window, which, like the front door, was covered with a heavy mesh of thick wire against intruders from the dingy lane it looked upon. Bewildered, he appeared in the room, where the policemen were searching through a soapbox of papers beside the duplicating machine. "Yusuf, it's for me," Mrs. Bamjee said.

At once, the snap of a trap, realization came. He stood there in an old shirt before the two policemen, and the woman was going off to prison because of the natives. "There you are!" he shouted, standing away from her. "That's what you've got for it. Didn't I tell you? Didn't I? That's the end of it now. That's the finish.

That's what it's come to." She listened with her head at the slightest tilt to one side, as if to ward off a blow, or in compassion.

Jimmy, Pahad's son, appeared at the door with a suitcase; two or three of the girls were behind him. "Here, Ma, you take my green jersey." "I've found your clean blouse." Bamjee had to keep moving out of their way as they helped their mother to make ready. It was like the preparation for one of the family festivals his wife made such a fuss over; wherever he put himself, they bumped into him. Even the two policemen mumbled, "Excuse me," and pushed past into the rest of the house to continue their search. They took with them a tome[11] that Nehru[12] had written in prison; it had been bought from a persevering traveling salesman and kept, for years, on the mantelpiece. "Oh, don't take that, please," Mrs. Bamjee said suddenly, clinging to the arm of the man who had picked it up.

The man held it away from her.

"What does it matter, Ma?"

It was true that no one in the house had ever read it; but she said, "It's for my children."

"Ma, leave it." Jimmy, who was squat and plump, looked like a merchant advising a client against a roll of silk she had set her heart on. She went into the bedroom and got dressed. When she came out in her old yellow sari with a brown coat over it, the faces of the children were behind her like faces on the platform at a railway station. They kissed her goodbye. The policemen did not hurry her, but she seemed to be in a hurry just the same.

"What am I going to do?" Bamjee accused them all.

The policemen looked away patiently.

"It'll be all right. Girlie will help. The big

---

10. **Special Branch:** the South African secret police.

11. **tome:** a book, especially a large or scholarly one.

12. **Nehru** (nā′rōō): Jawaharlal (jə-wä′hər-läl′) Nehru, nationalist leader in India's movement for self-governance and the first prime minister of independent India.

children can manage. And Yusuf—" The children crowded in around her; two of the younger ones had awakened and appeared, asking shrill questions.

"Come on," said the policemen.

"I want to speak to my husband." She broke away and came back to him, and the movement of her sari hid them from the rest of the room for a moment. His face hardened in suspicious anticipation against the request to give some message to the next fool who would take up her pamphleteering until he, too, was arrested. "On Sunday," she said. "Take them on Sunday." He did not know what she was talking about. "The engagement party," she whispered, low and urgent. "They shouldn't miss it. Ismail will be offended."

They listened to the car drive away. Jimmy bolted and barred the front door and then at once opened it again; he put on the raincoat that his mother had taken off. "Going to tell Girlie," he said. The children went back to bed. Their father did not say a word to any of them; their talk, the crying of the younger ones and the argumentative voices of the older, went on in the bedrooms. He found himself alone; he felt the night all around him. And then he happened to meet the clock face and saw with a terrible sense of unfamiliarity that this was not the secret night but an hour he should have recognized: the time he always got up. He pulled on his trousers and his dirty white hawker's coat and wound his grey muffler up to the stubble on his chin and went to work.

**T**he duplicating machine was gone from the sideboard. The policemen had taken it with them, along with the pamphlets and the conference reports and the stack of old newspapers that had collected on top of the wardrobe in the bedroom—not the thick dailies of the white men but the thin, impermanent-looking papers that spoke up, sometimes interrupted by suppression or lack of

money, for the rest. It was all gone. When he had married her and moved in with her and her five children, into what had been the Pahad and became the Bamjee house, he had not recognized the humble, harmless, and apparently useless routine tasks—the minutes of meetings being written up on the dining-room table at night, the government blue books that were read while the latest baby was suckled, the employment of the fingers of the older children in the fashioning of crinkle-paper Congress rosettes—as activity intended to move mountains. For years and years he had not noticed it, and now it was gone.

The house was quiet.

ACTIVE READING

EVALUATE Why do you think Bamjee hadn't paid attention to his wife's political activities?

The children kept to their lairs, crowded on the beds with the doors shut. He sat and looked at the sideboard, where the plastic carnations and the mat with the picture of the Taj Mahal were in place. For the first few weeks he never spoke of her. There was the feeling, in the house, that he had wept and raged at her, that boulders of reproach had thundered down upon her absence, and yet he had said not one word. He had not been to inquire where she was; Jimmy and Girlie had gone to Mohammed Ebrahim, the lawyer, and when he found out that their mother had been taken—when she was arrested, at least—to a prison in the next town, they had stood about outside the big prison door for hours while they waited to be told where she had been moved from there. At last they had discovered that she was fifty miles away, in Pretoria.[13] Jimmy asked Bamjee for five shillings to help Girlie pay the train fare to Pretoria, once she had been interviewed by the police and had been given a permit to visit her mother; he put three two-shilling pieces on the

---

13. **Pretoria** (prĭ-tôr′ē-ə): the administrative capital of South Africa.

*Light in the Souk,* (about 1991), Robert A. Wade. Watercolor, 19″ × 29″, private collection.
Copyright © Robert A. Wade. From *Painting Your Vision in Watercolor,* North Light Books.

table for Jimmy to pick up, and the boy, looking at him keenly, did not know whether the extra shilling meant anything, or whether it was merely that Bamjee had no change.

It was only when relations and neighbors came to the house that Bamjee would suddenly begin to talk. He had never been so expansive in his life as he was in the company of these visitors, many of them come on a polite call rather in the nature of a visit of condolence. "Ah, yes, yes, you can see how I am—you see what has been done to me. Nine children, and I am on the cart all day. I get home at seven or eight. What are you to do? What can people like us do?"

"Poor Mrs. Bamjee. Such a kind lady."

"Well, you see for yourself. They walk in here in the middle of the night and leave a houseful of children. I'm out on the cart all day; I've got a living to earn." Standing about in his shirt-sleeves, he became quite animated; he would call for the girls to bring fruit drinks for the visitors. When they were gone, it was as if he, who was orthodox[14] if not devout and never drank liquor, had been drunk and abruptly sobered up; he looked dazed and could not have gone over in his mind what he had been saying. And as he cooled, the lump of resentment and wronged-ness stopped his throat again.

---

14. **orthodox:** conforming to established religious rules or principles.

Bamjee found one of the little boys the center of a self-important group of championing brothers and sisters in the room one evening. "They've been cruel to Ahmed."

"What has he done?" said the father.

"Nothing! Nothing!" The little girl stood twisting her handkerchief excitedly.

An older one, thin as her mother, took over, silencing the others with a gesture of her skinny hand. "They did it at school today. They made an example of him."

"What is an example?" said Bamjee impatiently.

"The teacher made him come up and stand in front of the whole class, and he told them, 'You see this boy? His mother's in jail because she likes the natives so much. She wants the Indians to be the same as natives.' "

"It's terrible," he said. His hands fell to his sides. "Did she ever think of this?"

He had a sudden vision of her at the duplicating machine.

"That's why Ma's *there*," said Jimmy, putting aside his comic and emptying out his school-books upon the table. "That's all the kids need to know. Ma's there because things like this happen. Petersen's a colored teacher, and it's his black blood that's brought him trouble all his life, I suppose. He hates anyone who says everybody's the same because that takes away from him his bit of whiteness that's all he's got. What d'you expect? It's nothing to make too much fuss about."

"Of course, you are fifteen and you know everything," Bamjee mumbled at him.

"I don't say that. But I know Ma, anyway." The boy laughed.

There was a hunger strike among the political prisoners, and Bamjee could not bring himself to ask Girlie if her mother was starving herself too. He would not ask; and yet he saw in the young woman's face the gradual weakening of her mother. When the strike had gone on for nearly a week, one of the elder children burst into tears at the table and could not eat. Bamjee pushed his own plate away in rage.

Sometimes he spoke out loud to himself while he was driving the vegetable lorry.[15] "What for?" Again and again: "What for?" She was not a modern woman who cut her hair and wore short skirts. He had married a good plain Moslem woman who bore children and stamped her own chilies. He had a sudden vision of her at the duplicating machine, that night just before she was taken away, and he felt himself maddened, baffled, and hopeless. He had become the ghost of a victim, hanging about the scene of a crime whose motive he could not understand and had not had time to learn.

ACTIVE READING

CLARIFY How does Bamjee feel about his life?

---

15. **lorry:** a truck.

The hunger strike at the prison went into the second week. Alone in the rattling cab of his lorry, he said things that he heard as if spoken by someone else, and his heart burned in fierce agreement with them. "For a crowd of natives who'll smash our shops and kill us in our houses when their time comes." "She will starve herself to death there." "She will die there." "Devils who will burn and kill us." He fell into bed each night like a stone and dragged himself up in the mornings as a beast of burden is beaten to its feet.

One of these mornings, Girlie appeared very early, while he was wolfing bread and strong tea—alternate sensations of dry solidity and stinging heat—at the kitchen table. Her real name was Fatima, of course, but she had adopted the silly modern name along with the clothes of the young factory girls among whom she worked. She was expecting her first baby in a week or two, and her small face, her cut and curled hair, and the sooty arches drawn over her eyebrows did not seem to belong to her thrust-out body under a clean smock. She wore mauve lipstick and was smiling her cocky little white girl's smile, foolish and bold, not like an Indian girl's at all.

"What's the matter?" he said.

She smiled again. "Don't you know? I told Bobby he must get me up in time this morning. I wanted to be sure I wouldn't miss you today."

"I don't know what you're talking about."

She came over and put her arm up around his unwilling neck and kissed the grey bristles at the side of his mouth. "Many happy returns! Don't you know it's your birthday?"

"No," he said. "I didn't know, didn't think—" He broke the pause by swiftly picking up the bread and giving his attention desperately to eating and drinking. His mouth was busy, but his eyes looked at her, intensely black. She said nothing but stood there with him. She would not speak, and at last he said, swallowing a piece of bread that tore at his throat as it went down, "I don't remember these things."

The girl nodded, the Woolworth baubles in her ears swinging. "That's the first thing she told me when I saw her yesterday—don't forget it's Bajie's birthday tomorrow."

He shrugged over it. "It means a lot to children. But that's how she is. Whether it's one of the old cousins or the neighbor's grandmother, she always knows when the birthday is. What importance is my birthday, while she's sitting there in a prison? I don't understand how she can do the things she does when her mind is always full of woman's nonsense at the same time—that's what I don't understand with her."

"Oh, but don't you see?" the girl said. "It's because she doesn't want anybody to be left out. It's because she always remembers; remembers everything—people without somewhere to live, hungry kids, boys who can't get educated—remembers all the time. That's how Ma is."

"Nobody else is like that." It was half a complaint.

"No, nobody else," said his stepdaughter.

She sat herself down at the table, resting her belly. He put his head in his hands. "I'm getting old"—but he was overcome by something much more curious, by an answer. He knew why he had desired her, the ugly widow with five children; he knew what way it was in which she was not like the others; it was there, like the fact of the belly that lay between him and her daughter. ❖

## Connect to the Literature

1. **What Do You Think?** With which **character** did you sympathize more, Bamjee or Mrs. Bamjee? Share your response with a partner.

**Comprehension Check**
- What activities occupy Mrs. Bamjee's time and energy?
- How does Bamjee feel about his wife's activities?
- How does the government react to Mrs. Bamjee's activities?
- What message does Mrs. Bamjee send her husband from prison?

## Think Critically

2. Do you think that Mrs. Bamjee is a heroic character? Cite details from the story to support your opinion.

3. How would you describe the relationship between the husband and wife?

THINK ABOUT

- what Bamjee realizes at the story's conclusion about "why he had desired her"
- how he feels about his wife's political involvement
- how each of them handles the responsibilities of marriage and parenthood

4. In your judgment, what are the positive and negative effects of Mrs. Bamjee's political activities on her family?

5. **ACTIVE READING** **CLARIFYING** Refer to the observations in your 📖 **READER'S NOTEBOOK**. Did your understanding of Bamjee and Mrs. Bamjee change during the course of the story? Explain why or why not.

## Extend Interpretations

6. **The Writer's Style** Read aloud the description of Mrs. Bamjee's late-night arrest. After completing your oral reading, discuss Gordimer's **style.** Consider her **word choice,** her **tone,** her handling of **dialogue,** her use of **description,** and any other aspects of style that you notice.

7. **Critic's Corner** The critic Brigitte Weeks wrote that "Gordimer insists that her readers face South African life as she does: with affection and horror." How do you think this statement applies to "A Chip of Glass Ruby"?

8. **Connect to Life** In what ways might this story be relevant to people living in the United States?

## Literary Analysis

**DIALOGUE** **Dialogue** is written conversation between two or more characters. Dialogue is used in most forms of prose writing, especially in fiction. It enlivens **narrative** prose and often serves to move the **plot** along. Writers often use dialogue as a method of developing **characters** and revealing their relationships with one another.

**Paired Activity** Working with a partner, choose three characters from this story whom you would like to focus on. Then review the story to find examples of dialogue that reveal those characters' traits. Create three diagrams like the one shown to record your findings.

| Jimmy | |
|---|---|
| **Dialogue** | **Traits Revealed** |
| "Ma's there because things like this happen" | —respect for mother<br>—concern for social injustice |

# Choices & CHALLENGES

## Writing Options

**1. Interpretive Essay** A character in one of Gordimer's novels says, "The real definition of loneliness… is to live without social responsibility." Draft an essay explaining how Yusuf and Zanip Bamjee would respond to such a statement and how they would define their own responsibilities.

**2. Diary of a Daughter** Write the diary entry that Girlie might have written soon after Mrs. Bamjee's arrest.

**3. Title Analysis** Write a literary analysis in which you offer your own explanation of the significance of this story's title.

**Writing Handbook**
See page 1159: Analysis.

**4. Stage Scene** Rewrite an episode from the story as a dramatic scene with stage directions and dialogue.

## Activities & Explorations

**1. Interior Illustration** Create an illustration that shows an interior scene of the Bamjee household, based on details in the story. You may work in any medium that you like. Try to portray the household as you visualized it while reading. ~ **ART**

**2. Interview with an Activist** Conduct an interview with someone who is involved in political or charitable activities in your community. Determine why he or she is involved in this work and what—if anything—he or she has sacrificed to provide time for such a commitment.
~ **SPEAKING AND LISTENING**

## Inquiry & Research

**The Fight Against Apartheid** Find out more about antiapartheid protests led by the African National Congress or about earlier protests in South Africa led by India's Mohandas Gandhi. Use magazines, newspapers, and other print media, as well as the Internet. Share your findings with your class in an oral report.

 **More Online: Research Starter** www.mcdougallittell.com

Mohandas Gandhi (1869–1948), Indian leader famous for his philosophy of nonviolent protest.

## Vocabulary in Action

**EXERCISE: MEANING CLUES** Answer the following questions.

1. Would people be most likely to **patronize** someone they fear, look up to, or look down on?

2. Would a person with a **sallow** appearance be most likely to look as if he or she has spent a lot of time indoors, out in the sun, or at the gym lifting weights?

3. Does a **morose** person typically act conceited, depressed, or frightened?

4. Is a **presumption** an act that is usually seen as being humorous, bashful, or rude?

5. If you were trying to **disarm** someone, would you be most likely to behave in a friendly, bossy, or insulting manner?

**Building Vocabulary**
Several Words to Know in this lesson have multiple meanings. For an in-depth lesson on multiple meanings, see page 678.

| WORDS TO KNOW | disarm | patronize | sallow |
|---|---|---|---|
| | morose | presumption | |

## Grammar in Context: Compound-Complex Sentences

In "A Chip of Glass Ruby," a compound-complex sentence describes events involving Bamjee.

> **As he came home from work next day, he met Dr. Khan coming out of the house, and** Dr. Khan—a highly educated man—said to him, "A wonderful woman."

A **compound-complex sentence** consists of two or more independent clauses along with at least one subordinate clause. You may recall that an independent clause can stand alone as a sentence and a subordinate clause cannot. In the sentence above, the subordinate clause is shown in red type, and the two independent clauses are shown in blue and green type. Nadine Gordimer uses many long sentences to convey the complex relationships within South African society during apartheid.

**WRITING EXERCISE** Change each compound sentence into a compound-complex sentence by adding a subordinate clause in the place indicated by the caret. Begin the clause with the word in parentheses.

**Example: *Original*** ^ Mrs. Bamjee begins making leaflets, and Bamjee shows his displeasure. *(after)*

**Rewritten** <u>After the duplicating machine is brought into the house</u>, Mrs. Bamjee begins making leaflets, and Bamjee shows his displeasure.

1. ^ He sometimes sees important Indians coming out of his house, and this flatters him. *(when)*
2. One week there are riots, and native women twice arrive at the Bamjees' house ^. *(while)*
3. Early one morning the secret police knock at the Bamjees' door, and Mrs. Bamjee is taken away ^. *(because)*

<u>Grammar Handbook</u> The Structure of Sentences, p. 1198

# Nadine Gordimer
1923–

**Other Works**
*Selected Stories*
*Six Feet of the Country*
*My Son's Story*
*Jump and Other Stories*

**Upbringing and Discovery** Nadine Gordimer was born and raised in Springs, South Africa, a small mining town near Johannesburg, the country's largest city. She attended an all-white school and spent much of her free time reading at the local library. Gordimer realized early on that she had little in common with her peers, however, and she began questioning the racial attitudes of white South Africa. She discovered, in her words, that she "was not merely part of a suburban white life aping Europe" but "lived with and among a variety of colors and kinds of people."

**Success in Writing** Gordimer knew she would be a writer when, at the age of 15, she had her first short story published; her first story collection, *The Soft Voice of the Serpent,* appeared in 1952.

She was recognized almost immediately as a serious and talented artist, and she gained an American audience by publishing her stories in such magazines as *The New Yorker* and *Harper's*.

**Social Critic** Much of Gordimer's writing has focused on the theme of the destructive influence of apartheid on relationships among South Africans of all colors; as a result, several of her books were banned in her homeland for many years. Although she has said that she's not by nature a political person, she joined the African National Congress (ANC) and also helped found the Congress of South African Writers. "The real influence of politics on my writing is the influence of politics on people," she said. "Their lives, and I believe their very personalities, are changed by the extreme political circumstances one lives under in South Africa." On learning that she had won the 1991 Nobel Prize for literature, she called the event the second greatest thrill of recent years; the first, she said, was the release of ANC leader Nelson Mandela after 27 years as a political prisoner.

# The Man in the Water

*Essay by* ROGER ROSENBLATT

## Connect to Your Life

**Act Fast!** In a disaster—such as an earthquake, a flood, a tornado, or a plane crash—people react in many different ways. With your classmates, discuss how such disasters can bring out the best—or worst—in people. Draw upon your own knowledge for examples.

## Build Background

**The Crash of Flight 90** One of the most publicized disasters of its time occurred on January 13, 1982, when a passenger jet crashed in Washington, D.C., during the evening rush hour. The jet was taking off in freezing rain and failed to gain enough altitude. Crashing onto the 14th Street Bridge, which crosses the Potomac River, the plane broke in two and fell into the icy river. Seventy-eight people died in the disaster— some of them in the plane, some in their cars on the bridge, and some in the frigid waters of the Potomac.

Following the crash of Flight 90, news reports on television and in newspapers provided extensive details of the tragedy. This essay, which appeared in *Time* magazine shortly after the crash occurred, offers more than a news report. It presents the author's viewpoints on the meaning of the events that took place immediately following the crash. In particular, the author looks at how one passenger behaved in those confusing, terrifying moments and considers what his behavior says about all of us.

> WORDS TO KNOW
> **Vocabulary Preview**
> abiding    flail       chaotic
> anonymity  implacable

## Focus Your Reading

**LITERARY ANALYSIS    TONE**    **Tone** is the attitude a writer takes toward a subject. Through word choice and use of details, a writer can create a tone that is playful, angry, persuasive, or reverent, to name a few possibilities. In nonfiction a writer's tone is influenced by his or her purpose for writing, as well as the writing format. As you read "The Man in the Water," think about how you would describe the essay's tone.

**ACTIVE READING    SUMMARIZING**    When you **summarize** a text, you tell about it in your own words, leaving out all but the most important information. A summary is an objective recounting of information, identifying the text's main idea and supporting details. It does not include the opinions or ideas of the person writing the summary.

Summarizing can be helpful in that it requires you to understand and remember what you have read. It can also help you share what you have read with others. Sometimes it is desirable to summarize particular aspects of a text's contents for purposes of discussion.

**READER'S NOTEBOOK**    Create a two-column chart like the one shown. As you read, list in each column words and phrases (supporting details) from the essay that convey Rosenblatt's views about nature and human nature. Your notes will later help you to summarize his main points.

| Nature | Human Nature |
|--------|--------------|
|        |              |

# The Man in the Water

### Roger Rosenblatt

A paramedic pulls a woman from the Potomac River following the crash of Air Florida Flight 90. AP / Wide World Photos.

A woman holds on to a safety ring as she is pulled from the Potomac River. AP / Wide World Photos.

As disasters go, this one was terrible, but not unique, certainly not among the worst on the roster of U.S. air crashes. There was the unusual element of the bridge, of course, and the fact that the plane clipped it at a moment of high traffic, one routine thus intersecting another and disrupting both. Then, too, there was the location of the event. Washington, the city of form and regulations, turned <u>chaotic</u>, deregulated, by a blast of real winter and a single slap of metal on metal. The jets from Washington National Airport that normally swoop around the presidential monuments like famished gulls are, for the moment, emblemized by the one that fell; so there is that detail. And there was the aesthetic[1] clash as well—blue-and-green Air Florida, the name a flying garden, sunk down among gray chunks in a black river. All that was worth noticing, to be sure. Still, there was nothing very special in any of it, except death, which, while always special, does not necessarily bring millions to tears or to attention. Why, then, the shock here?

Perhaps because the nation saw in this disaster something more than a mechanical failure. Perhaps because people saw in it no

---

1. **aesthetic** (ĕs-thĕt′ĭk): relating to that which is beautiful or pleasing to the senses.

failure at all, but rather something successful about their makeup. Here, after all, were two forms of nature in collision: the elements and human character. Last Wednesday, the elements, indifferent as ever, brought down Flight 90. And on that same afternoon, human nature—groping and flailing in mysteries of its own—rose to the occasion.

Of the four acknowledged heroes of the event, three are able to account for their behavior. Donald Usher and Eugene Windsor, a park police helicopter team, risked their lives every time they dipped the skids into the water to pick up survivors. On television, side by side in bright blue jumpsuits, they described their courage as all in the line of duty. Lenny Skutnik, a twenty-eight-year-old employee of the Congressional Budget Office, said: "It's something I never thought I would do"—referring to his jumping into the water to drag an injured woman to shore. Skutnik added that "somebody had to go in the water," delivering every hero's line that is no less admirable for its repetitions. In fact, nobody had to go into the water. That somebody actually did so is part of the reason this particular tragedy sticks in the mind.

But the person most responsible for the emotional impact of the disaster is the one known at first simply as "the man in the water." (Balding, probably in his fifties, an extravagant mustache.) He was seen clinging with five other survivors to the tail section of the airplane. This man was described by Usher and Windsor as appearing alert and in control. Every time they lowered a lifeline and flotation ring to him, he passed it on to another of the passengers. "In a mass casualty, you'll find people like him," said Windsor. "But I've never seen one with that commitment." When the helicopter came back for him, the man had gone under. His selflessness was one reason the story held national attention; his anonymity another. The fact that he went unidentified invested him with a universal character. For a while he was Everyman, and thus proof (as if one needed it) that no man is ordinary.

Still, he could never have imagined such a capacity in himself. Only minutes before his character was tested, he was sitting in the ordinary plane among the ordinary passengers, dutifully listening to the stewardess telling him to fasten his seat belt and saying something about the "no smoking sign." So our man relaxed with the others, some of whom would owe their lives to him. Perhaps he started to read, or to doze, or to regret some harsh remark made in the office that morning. Then suddenly he knew that the trip would not be ordinary. Like every other person on that flight, he was desperate to live, which makes his final act so stunning.

For at some moment in the water he must have realized that he would not live if he continued to hand over the rope and ring to others. He *had* to know it, no matter how gradual the effect of the cold. In his judgment he had no choice. When the helicopter took off with what was to be the last survivor, he watched everything in the world move away from him, and he deliberately let it happen.

Yet there was something else about the man that kept our thoughts on him, and which

WORDS TO KNOW

**flail** (flāl) *v.* to wave or swing vigorously; thrash
**anonymity** (ăn′ə-nĭm′ĭ-tē) *n.* the state of being unknown or unidentified

on the other hand, was determined to snatch her from death. Someone brought him a tire, which he placed beneath her arms like a life buoy, and then laid a plank near the hole to hold his weight and allow him to stay closer to her. As it was impossible to remove the rubble blindly, he tried once or twice to dive toward her feet but emerged frustrated, covered with mud, and spitting gravel. He concluded that he would have to have a pump to drain the water, and radioed a request for one but received in return a message that there was no available transport and it could not be sent until the next morning.

"We can't wait that long!" Rolf Carlé shouted, but in the pandemonium no one stopped to commiserate. Many more hours would go by before he accepted that time had stagnated[11] and reality had been irreparably distorted.

A military doctor came to examine the girl and observed that her heart was functioning well and that if she did not get too cold she could survive the night.

"Hang on, Azucena, we'll have the pump tomorrow," Rolf Carlé tried to console her.

"Don't leave me alone," she begged.

"No, of course I won't leave you."

Someone brought him coffee, and he helped the girl drink it, sip by sip. The warm liquid revived her, and she began telling him about her small life, about her family and her school, about how things were in that little bit of world before the volcano erupted. She was thirteen, and she had never been outside her village. Rolf Carlé, buoyed by a premature optimism, was convinced that everything would end well: the pump would arrive, they would drain the water, move the rubble, and Azucena would be transported by helicopter to a hospital where she would recover rapidly and where he could visit her and bring her gifts. He thought, She's already too old for dolls, and I don't know what would please her; maybe a dress. I don't know much about women, he con-cluded, amused, reflecting that although he had known many women in his lifetime, none had taught him these details. To pass the hours he began to tell Azucena about his travels and adventures as a news hound, and when he exhausted his memory, he called upon imagination, inventing things he thought might entertain her. From time to time she dozed, but he kept talking in the darkness, to assure her that he was still there and to overcome the menace of uncertainty.

That was a long night.

Many miles away, I watched Rolf Carlé and the girl on a television screen. I could not bear the wait at home, so I went to National Television, where I often spent entire nights with Rolf editing programs. There, I was near his world, and I could at least get a feeling of what he lived through during those three decisive days. I called all the important people in the city, senators, commanders of the armed forces, the North American ambassador, and the president of National Petroleum, begging them for a pump to remove the silt, but obtained only vague promises. I began to ask for urgent help on radio and television, to see if there wasn't *someone* who could help us. Between calls I would run to the newsroom to monitor the satellite transmissions that periodically brought new details of the catastrophe. While reporters selected scenes with most impact for the news report, I searched for footage that featured Azucena's mud pit. The screen reduced the disaster to a single plane and accentuated the tremendous distance that separated me from Rolf Carlé; nonetheless, I was there with him. The child's every suffering hurt me as it did him; I felt his frustration, his

---

11. **stagnated:** stopped moving.

impotence.[12] Faced with the impossibility of communicating with him, the fantastic idea came to me that if I tried, I could reach him by force of mind and in that way give him encouragement. I concentrated until I was dizzy—a frenzied and futile activity. At times I would be overcome with compassion and burst out crying; at other times, I was so drained I felt as if I were staring through a telescope at the light of a star dead for a million years.

I watched that hell on the first morning broadcast, cadavers[13] of people and animals awash in the current of new rivers formed overnight from the melted snow. Above the mud rose the tops of trees and the bell towers of a church where several people had taken refuge and were patiently awaiting rescue teams. Hundreds of soldiers and volunteers from the civil defense were clawing through rubble searching for survivors, while long rows of ragged specters[14] awaited their turn for a cup of hot broth. Radio networks announced that their phones were jammed with calls from families offering shelter to orphaned children. Drinking water was in scarce supply, along with gasoline and food. Doctors, resigned to amputating arms and legs without anesthesia, pled that at least they be sent serum and painkillers and antibiotics; most of the roads, however, were impassable, and worse were the bureaucratic obstacles that stood in the way. To top it all, the clay contaminated by decomposing bodies threatened the living with an outbreak of epidemics.

Azucena was shivering inside the tire that held her above the surface. Immobility and tension had greatly weakened her, but she was conscious and could still be heard when a microphone was held out to her. Her tone was humble, as if apologizing for all the fuss. Rolf Carlé had a growth of beard, and dark circles beneath his eyes; he looked near exhaustion.

Even from that enormous distance I could sense the quality of his weariness, so different from the fatigue of other adventures. He had completely forgotten the camera; he could not look at the girl through a lens any longer. The pictures we were receiving were not his assistant's but those of other reporters who had appropriated Azucena, bestowing on her the pathetic responsibility of embodying the horror of what had happened in that place. With the first light Rolf tried again to dislodge the obstacles that held the girl in her tomb, but he had only his hands to work with; he did not dare use a tool for fear of injuring her. He fed Azucena a cup of the cornmeal mush and bananas the army was distributing, but she immediately vomited it up. A doctor stated that she had a fever but added that there was little he could do: antibiotics were being reserved for cases of gangrene.[15] A priest also passed by and blessed her, hanging a medal of the Virgin around her neck. By evening a gentle, persistent drizzle began to fall.

"The sky is weeping," Azucena murmured, and she, too, began to cry.

"Don't be afraid," Rolf begged. "You have to keep your strength up and be calm. Everything will be fine. I'm with you, and I'll get you out somehow."

Reporters returned to photograph Azucena and ask her the same questions, which she no longer tried to answer. In the meanwhile, more television and movie teams arrived with spools of cable, tapes, film, videos, precision lenses, recorders, sound consoles, lights, reflecting screens, auxiliary motors, cartons of supplies, electricians, sound

---

12. **impotence:** powerlessness.
13. **cadavers** (kə-dăv′ərz): dead bodies.
14. **specters:** ghosts or ghostlike visions.
15. **gangrene:** death and decay of body tissue, usually resulting from injury or disease.

technicians, and cameramen: Azucena's face was beamed to millions of screens around the world. And all the while Rolf Carlé kept pleading for a pump. The improved technical facilities bore results, and National Television began receiving sharper pictures and clearer sound, the distance seemed suddenly compressed, and I had the horrible sensation that Azucena and Rolf were by my side, separated from me by impenetrable glass. I was able to follow events hour by hour; I knew everything my love did to wrest the girl from her prison and help her endure her suffering; I overheard fragments of what they said to one another and could guess the rest; I was present when she taught Rolf to pray and when he distracted her with the stories I had told him in a thousand and one nights beneath the white mosquito netting of our bed.

When darkness came on the second day, Rolf tried to sing Azucena to sleep with old Austrian folk songs he had learned from his mother, but she was far beyond sleep. They spent most of the night talking, each in a stupor of exhaustion and hunger and shaking with cold. That night, imperceptibly, the unyielding floodgates that had contained Rolf Carlé's past for so many years began to open, and the torrent of all that had lain hidden in the deepest and most secret layers of memory poured out, leveling before it the obstacles that had blocked his consciousness for so long. He could not tell it all to Azucena; she perhaps did not know there was a world beyond the sea or time previous to her own; she was not capable of imagining Europe in the years of the war. So he could not tell her of defeat, nor of the afternoon the Russians had led them to the concentration camp to bury prisoners dead from starvation. Why should he describe to her how the naked bodies piled like a mountain of firewood resembled fragile china? How could he tell this dying child about ovens and gallows? Nor did he mention the night that he had seen his mother naked, shod in stiletto-heeled red boots, sobbing with humiliation. There was much he did not tell, but in those hours he relived for the first time all the things his mind had tried to erase. Azucena had surrendered her fear to him and so, without wishing it, had obliged Rolf to confront his own. There, beside that hellhole of mud, it was impossible for Rolf to flee from himself any longer, and the visceral terror he had lived as a boy suddenly invaded him. He reverted to the years when he was the age of Azucena and younger, and, like her, found himself trapped in a pit without escape, buried in life, his head barely above ground; he saw before his eyes the boots and legs of his father, who had removed his belt and was whipping it in the air with the never-forgotten hiss of a viper coiled to strike. Sorrow flooded through him, intact and precise, as if it had lain always in his mind, waiting. He was once again in the armoire[16] where his father locked him to punish him for imagined misbehavior, there where for eternal hours he had crouched with his eyes closed, not to see the darkness, with his hands over his ears to shut out the beating of his heart, trembling, huddled like a cornered animal. Wandering in the mist of his memories he found his sister, Katharina, a sweet, retarded child who spent her life hiding, with the hope that her father would forget the disgrace of her having been born. With Katharina, Rolf crawled beneath the dining room table, and with her hid there under the long white tablecloth, two children forever embraced, alert to footsteps and voices. Katharina's scent melded with his own sweat, with aromas of cooking, garlic, soup, freshly baked bread, and the unexpected odor of putrescent[17] clay. His sister's hand in his, her frightened breathing, her silk hair against his

---

16. **armoire** (ärm-wär′): a large, ornate wardrobe or cabinet.
17. **putrescent** (pyo͞o-trĕs′ənt): rotting and foul smelling.

WORDS TO KNOW

**stupor** (sto͞o′pər) *n.* a state of mental numbness, as from shock
**visceral** (vĭs′ər-əl) *adj.* instinctive or emotional rather than intellectual

Illustration by David Loew / ARTCO.

cheek, the candid gaze of her eyes. Katharina . . . Katharina materialized before him, floating on the air like a flag, clothed in the white tablecloth, now a winding sheet, and at last he could weep for her death and for the guilt of having abandoned her. He understood then that all his exploits as a reporter, the feats that had won him such recognition and fame, were merely an attempt to keep his most ancient fears at bay, a stratagem for taking refuge behind a lens to test whether reality was more tolerable from that perspective. He took excessive risks as an exercise of courage, training by day to conquer the monsters that tormented him by night. But he had to come face to face with the moment of truth; he could not continue to escape his past. He *was* Azucena; he was buried in the clayey mud; his terror was not the distant emotion of an almost forgotten childhood, it was a claw sunk in his throat. In the flush of his tears he saw his mother, dressed in black and clutching her imitation-crocodile pocketbook to her bosom, just as he had last seen her on the dock when she had come to put him on the boat to South America. She had not come to dry his tears, but to tell him to pick up a shovel: the war was over and now they must bury the dead.

"Don't cry. I don't hurt anymore. I'm fine," Azucena said when dawn came.

"I'm not crying for you," Rolf Carlé smiled. "I'm crying for myself. I hurt all over."

The third day in the valley of the cataclysm began with a pale light filtering through storm clouds. The president of the republic visited the area in his tailored safari jacket to confirm that this was the worst catastrophe of the century; the country was in mourning; sister nations had offered aid; he had ordered a state of siege; the armed forces would be merciless; anyone caught stealing or committing other offenses would be shot on sight. He added that it was impossible to remove all the corpses or count the thousands who had disappeared; the entire valley would be declared holy ground, and bishops would come to celebrate a solemn mass for the souls of the victims. He went to the army field tents to offer relief in the form of vague promises to crowds of the rescued, then to the improvised hospital to offer a word of encouragement to doctors and nurses worn down from so many hours of <u>tribulations</u>. Then he asked to be taken to see Azucena, the little girl the whole world had seen. He waved to her with a limp statesman's hand, and microphones recorded his emotional voice and paternal tone as he told her that her courage had served as an example to the nation. Rolf Carlé interrupted to ask for a pump, and the president assured him that he personally would attend to the matter. I caught a glimpse of Rolf for a few seconds kneeling beside the mud pit. On the evening news broadcast, he was still in the same position; and I, glued to the screen like a fortuneteller to her crystal ball, could tell that something fundamental had changed in him. I knew somehow that during the night his defenses had crumbled and he had given in to grief; finally he was <u>vulnerable</u>. The girl had touched a part of him that he himself had no access to, a part he had never shared with me. Rolf had wanted to console her, but it was Azucena who had given him consolation.

I recognized the precise moment at which Rolf gave up the fight and surrendered to the torture of watching the girl die. I was with them, three days and two nights, spying on them from the other side of life. I was there

WORDS TO KNOW

**tribulation** (trĭb′yə-lā′shən) *n.* great distress or suffering
**vulnerable** (vŭl′nər-ə-bəl) *adj.* unprotected and easily hurt; sensitive

when she told him that in all her thirteen years no boy had ever loved her and that it was a pity to leave this world without knowing love. Rolf assured her that he loved her more than he could ever love anyone, more than he loved his mother, more than his sister, more than all the women who had slept in his arms, more than he loved me, his life companion, who would have given anything to be trapped in that well in her place, who would have exchanged her life for Azucena's, and I watched as he leaned down to kiss her poor forehead, consumed by a sweet, sad emotion he could not name. I felt how in that instant both were saved from despair, how they were freed from the clay, how they rose above the vultures and helicopters, how together they flew above the vast swamp of corruption and laments. How, finally, they were able to accept death. Rolf Carlé prayed in silence that she would die quickly, because such pain cannot be borne.

By then I had obtained a pump and was in touch with a general who had agreed to ship it the next morning on a military cargo plane. But on the night of that third day, beneath the unblinking focus of quartz lamps and the lens of a hundred cameras, Azucena gave up, her eyes locked with those of the friend who had sustained her to the end. Rolf Carlé removed the life buoy, closed her eyelids, held her to his chest for a few moments, and then let her go. She sank slowly, a flower in the mud.

You are back with me, but you are not the same man. I often accompany you to the station, and we watch the videos of Azucena again; you study them intently, looking for something you could have done to save her, something you did not think of in time. Or maybe you study them to see yourself as if in a mirror, naked. Your cameras lie forgotten in a closet; you do not write or sing; you sit long hours before the window, staring at the mountains. Beside you, I wait for you to complete the voyage into yourself, for the old wounds to heal. I know that when you return from your nightmares, we shall again walk hand in hand, as before. ❖

*Translated by Margaret Sayers Peden*

# Nocturne    Nocturno

### Rosario Castellanos

Time is too long for life;
for knowledge not enough.

What have we come for, night, heart
  of night?

All we can do is dream, or die,
5  dream that we do not die
and, at times, for a moment, wake.

Para vivir es demasiado el tiempo;
para saber no es nada.

¿A qué vinimos, noche, corazón de la
  noche?

No es posible sino soñar, morir,
5  soñar que no morimos
y, a veces, un instante, despertar.

*Translated by Magda Bogin*

*Nocturnal Landscape* (1947),
Diego Rivera. Oil on canvas,
111 cm × 91 cm, courtesy of
Museo de Arte Moderno (INBA),
Mexico City. Photo Copyright © 1995,
Dirk Bakker/The Detroit Institute of Arts.

# Connect to the Literature

1. **What Do You Think?** How did you react to the outcome of the story? Jot down a few words and phrases that best describe your response.

**Comprehension Check**
- How is the narrator made aware of what Rolf is doing?
- What piece of equipment does Rolf need to rescue Azucena?
- What hidden memories does Rolf unlock during his time with Azucena?

# Think Critically

2. How would you describe the relationship that develops between Rolf and Azucena?

THINK ABOUT

- what they learn from each other
- the painful childhood memories he is able to recall
- why he tells Azucena that he loves her more than he could ever love anyone

3. **ACTIVE READING** **CLARIFYING** Look back at the notes you made in your **READER'S NOTEBOOK.** How did your understanding of Rolf change as you moved through the story? Cite details from the story to illustrate the changes in your understanding.

4. How do you think Rolf's experience with Azucena will affect him in the future?

5. According to the **narrator,** the name Azucena means "lily." Why do you think the author might have given her this name?

6. Describe the narrator's feelings about the events she relates and her relationship with Rolf.

# Extend Interpretations

7. **Comparing Texts** What connection do you see between the poem "Nocturne" on page 994 and Allende's story?

8. **Critic's Corner** After reading this story, student reviewer Quoleshna Elbert wrote, "The story got under my skin; that's what makes a good story." Do you feel the same way about this story? What makes a good story for you?

9. **Connect to Life** Azucena died partly because no one transported a pump to the disaster site. Could a similar situation happen in this country? Why or why not?

# Literary Analysis

**STYLE** **Style** refers to the way a piece of literature is written. It refers not to what is said but to how something is said. Elements such as **tone, imagery, sensory language, repetition, rhythm, syntax,** and **sentence length** all contribute to a writer's individual style. Allende's style is full of imagery and evocative description that appeal to the senses of sight, sound, and smell. She also writes long sentences and makes use of listing and repetition, as in the following passage:

*He smiled at her with **that** smile **that** crinkles his eyes and makes him look like a little boy; he told her **that** everything was fine, **that** he was here with her now, **that** soon they would have her out.*

**Cooperative Learning Activity** In a small group, choose one paragraph from the story that is typical of Allende's style and illustrates at least four of the elements described above. Designate one group member to read the paragraph aloud. In a group discussion, analyze how Allende's style influences each group member's response to the story.

**REVIEW** **DIALOGUE** With a partner, review the dialogue in Allende's story. How does the dialogue contribute to your understanding of the characters? Read aloud passages to support your opinion.

## Writing Options

**1. Television Commentary** Write the monologue that Rolf might give in a retrospective television broadcast one year after the tragic destruction of the town.

**2. Love Letter** Write a love letter that the narrator might write to Rolf in the months following the disaster.

*Dear Rolf,*

## Activities & Explorations

**1. Azucena's Eulogy** Assume the identity of Rolf or the narrator and deliver a eulogy for Azucena.
**~ SPEAKING AND LISTENING**

**2. Volcanic Poster** Read about the inner workings of a volcano and what happens when one erupts. Illustrate your findings on a poster to display for your class. **~ EARTH SCIENCE**

## Inquiry & Research

Find out more about what really happened to Omaira Sanchez, the girl this story was based on, when the Nevado del Ruiz volcano erupted.

**Real World Link** Begin your research by reading the newspaper article on page 998.

## Art Connection

**In Swirling Water** What is your interpretation of the illustration on page 991? Why do you think it was chosen to accompany this story?

## Vocabulary in Action

**EXERCISE A: ASSESSMENT PRACTICE** Identify each pair of words as synonyms or antonyms.

1. **visceral**–logical
2. **fortitude**–endurance
3. **tenacity**–doubt
4. **equanimity**–hysteria
5. **stupor**–daze
6. **pandemonium**–disturbance
7. **vulnerable**–immune
8. **tribulation**–blessing
9. **embody**–symbolize
10 **irreparable**–correctable

**EXERCISE B: WORD KNOWLEDGE** In a small group, tell a "round robin" story using the Words to Know. One person should begin a story and continue to speak until he or she has used one of the words in a sentence. Then the next person picks up the story where the first person left off, continuing until another of the words is used. Continue this process until all ten words are used and the story is brought to a conclusion.

**Building Vocabulary**

Most of the Words to Know in this lesson contain prefixes or suffixes. For an in-depth study of word parts, see page 856.

| WORDS TO KNOW | | | | | |
|---|---|---|---|---|---|
| | embody | fortitude | pandemonium | tenacity | visceral |
| | equanimity | irreparably | stupor | tribulation | vulnerable |

# Grammar in Context: Using Parallel Structures

In the following sentence, Isabel Allende uses parallel structures to describe how Rolf Carlé reassures Azucena.

> He smiled at her with that smile that crinkles his eyes and makes him look like a little boy; he told her that everything was fine, that he was here with her now, that soon they would have her out.

**Parallelism** is a repetition of similar grammatical structures within a sentence or paragraph. In the sentence above, the parallel elements shown in blue type are noun clauses. Notice how Allende's use of parallelism creates a nice rhythm and helps her convey Rolf's concern for the young woman.

**WRITING EXERCISE** Fill in each blank with a word, phrase, or clause that is parallel to the other items in the series.

**Example:** Rolf gets dressed, packs his bags, and _____.

Rolf gets dressed, packs his bags, and says goodbye.

1. The eruption looses a torrent of rocks, ash, and _____, which destroys the valley below.
2. The camera zooms in on the young girl, with _____, her large helpless eyes, and her tangled hair.
3. When Rolf is finally close enough to Azucena, he takes the rope, ties it around her, and _____.
4. Azucena's pulse weakens, her eyes lock with those of Rolf, and _____.

## Isabel Allende

1942–

**Other Works**
*Of Love and Shadows*
*Eva Luna*
*The Stories of Eva Luna*
*Paula*
*The Infinite Plan*

**Creative Childhood** Born in Lima, Peru, Isabel Allende moved with her mother to Santiago, Chile, when she was three years old and grew up in the home of her maternal grandparents. Her mother nurtured her creativity from the time she was very young, encouraging her to record her thoughts in a notebook and to draw anything she wanted on a bedroom wall. After graduating from high school, Allende worked for many years as a journalist and television interviewer. "My love for words induced me to work as a journalist since I was 17, but my vicious imagination was a great handicap," she said. "I could never be objective, I exaggerated and twisted reality, I would put myself in the middle of every feature."

**Forced Exile** Isabel Allende's uncle and godfather, Salvador Allende, became president of Chile in 1970 but was murdered when the military seized power in 1973. As a result, Isabel Allende and her family—along with many Chilean artists and intellectuals—went into exile, moving first to Venezuela and later to the United States. In her words, she felt "like a Christmas tree, cut off from all roots" after fleeing from her homeland, and for several years she was unable to write or to find work as a journalist.

**Writing to Remember** After receiving word in 1981 that her nearly 100-year-old grandfather was dying, however, she began writing a long letter to him. Her grandfather believed that people died only when you forgot them, and Allende says she wanted to prove to him that she had forgotten nothing, "that his spirit was going to live with us forever." Allende's letter became her first novel, *The House of the Spirits.* Written in the style of magical realism, the novel is based on her own family history and the political upheaval in modern Chile. The work became an international bestseller, hailed by critics as a powerful and original piece of historical fiction. Allende writes her novels and short stories in Spanish, then has her work translated.

# Girl Trapped in Water for 55 Hours Dies Despite Rescue Attempts

BY JULIA PRESTON

*In November 1985, a sudden volcanic eruption buried the town of Armero, Colombia, killing thousands of people. Isabel Allende drew on news reports of this disaster for her story, "And of Clay Are We Created." As you read the following news account, compare its facts with the details Allende uses in her story.*

**❶** **Armero, Colombia**—Omaira Sanchez, a 13-year-old girl trapped up to her neck for more than 55 hours in flood-water, died yesterday morning despite rescuers' frantic efforts to free her.

**❷** Omaira's legs were pinned in the ruins of what was once her home by a cement slab and by the body of an aunt who drowned in the avalanche of mud that rolled over Armero Wednesday night.

Trapped in the chilly water the little girl shivered violently and her hands turned a deathly white. Finally her blood pressure dropped so low she suffered a heart attack, according to Alejandro Jimenez, 23, a medical student volunteer at the disaster site who attended the child.

**❸** "You can imagine how I feel," said Jimenez, looking drawn and exhausted yesterday morning. "We stayed up all night trying to save her."

About a dozen rescuers from the Colombian Air Force, the Red Cross, and fire departments of towns near Armero radioed increasingly desperate pleas since Thursday for an electric pump to keep the fetid waters from rising above the girl's chin. They called for picks, shovels, and winches to clear away rubble trapping her.

## Reading for Information

Newspaper reporters generally write about real events, while fiction writers create their own plots. However, sometimes fiction writers draw inspiration from actual news accounts, as in the case of Allende and her story.

### COMPARING FACTUAL AND FICTIONAL VERSIONS

Comparing factual and fictional accounts of the same real-life event can provide readers with two kinds of insight. First, a **fictional** account of an event often enhances the drama of the event by revealing the personal details and emotional impact that a factual version might not offer. On the other hand, a **factual** account focuses on details that give readers a fuller understanding of the reality of an event.

**YOUR TURN** Use the following activities to help you explore how a news account differs from a story based on the same event.

**❶** A news account usually gives details that answer the questions *who, what, when, where,* and *why.* Which of these questions are answered in the first paragraph? What questions do you expect will be the focus of the paragraphs to follow?

**❷** **Comparing Texts** Recall how in the Allende story, the child is trapped by "the bodies of her brothers and sisters clinging to her legs." What is she trapped by in the article? Why do you think Allende might have made this change?

Rescue efforts to save Omaira Sanchez, the Colombian teenaged girl who inspired this story.

At 2 P.M. yesterday, four hours after Omaira died, a Colombian radio station announced that 18 pumps had just arrived in a town 45 miles from Armero. To the end, rescue workers dug with their bare hands at the cement slab leaning on Omaira's numb legs, and bailed the water with a tin can.

**④** Someone stretched a dirty blue-and-white checkered tablecloth over the scene of the tragedy, a scene that, displayed in news-papers around the world yesterday, came to represent the horror of the disaster.

Aftermath of disaster caused by Nevado del Ruiz eruption.

**③** The news account quotes a rescue worker named Alejandro Jimenez, who fills a role similar to that of Rolf Carlé in the story. Why do you think Allende gives this character so much more emphasis than Jimenez receives in the original news account?

**④** In what way are the details in the last paragraph of the news report similar to details you might find in a fictional account?

## Inquiry & Research

**Activity Link: "And of Clay Are We Created," p. 996**
Compare and contrast facts about the real event with those portrayed in the story. You may wish to present your findings in chart form.

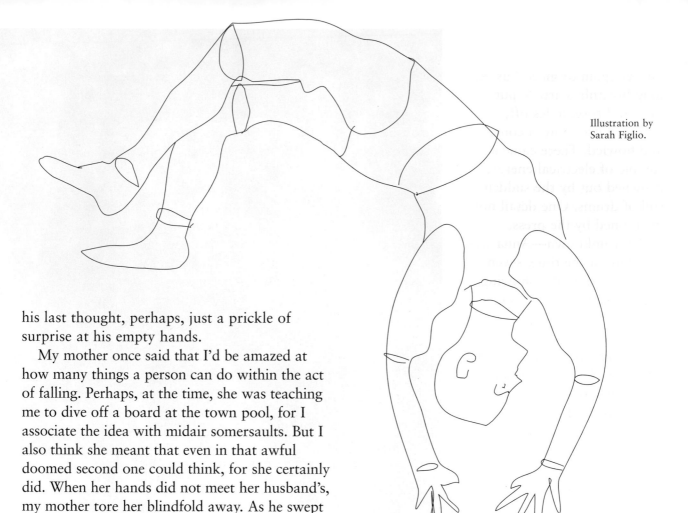

Illustration by
Sarah Figlio.

his last thought, perhaps, just a prickle of surprise at his empty hands.

My mother once said that I'd be amazed at how many things a person can do within the act of falling. Perhaps, at the time, she was teaching me to dive off a board at the town pool, for I associate the idea with midair somersaults. But I also think she meant that even in that awful doomed second one could think, for she certainly did. When her hands did not meet her husband's, my mother tore her blindfold away. As he swept past her on the wrong side, she could have grasped his ankle, the toe end of his tights, and gone down clutching him. Instead, she changed direction. Her body twisted toward a heavy wire, and she managed to hang on to the braided metal, still hot from the lightning strike. Her palms were burned so terribly that once healed they bore no lines, only the blank scar tissue of a quieter future. She was lowered, gently, to the sawdust ring just underneath the dome of the canvas roof, which did not entirely settle but was held up on one end and jabbed through, torn, and still on fire in places from the giant spark, though rain and men's jackets soon put that out.

Three people died, but except for her hands my mother was not seriously harmed until an overeager rescuer broke her arm in extricating her and also, in the process, collapsed a portion of the tent bearing a huge buckle that knocked her unconscious. She was taken to the town hospital, and there she must have hemorrhaged,[6] for they kept her, confined to her bed, a month and a half before her baby was born without life.

Harry Avalon had wanted to be buried in the circus cemetery next to the original Avalon, his uncle, so she sent him back with his brothers. The child, however, is buried around the corner, beyond this house and just down the highway. Sometimes I used to walk there just to sit. She was a girl, but I rarely thought of her as a sister or even as a separate person really. I suppose you could call it the egocentrism[7] of a child, of

---

6. **hemorrhaged** (hĕm′ər-ĭjd): bled heavily from a blood vessel.

7. **egocentrism:** self-centeredness; the belief that everything revolves around oneself.

all young children, but I considered her a less finished version of myself.

When the snow falls, throwing shadows among the stones, I can easily pick hers out from the road, for it is bigger than the others and in the shape of a lamb at rest, its legs curled beneath. The carved lamb looms larger as the years pass, though it is probably only my eyes, the vision shifting, as what is close to me blurs and distances sharpen. In odd moments, I think it is the edge drawing near, the edge of everything, the unseen horizon we do not really speak of in the eastern woods. And it also seems to me, although this is probably an idle fantasy, that the statue is growing more sharply etched, as if, instead of weathering itself into a porous mass, it is hardening on the hillside with each snowfall, perfecting itself.

It was during her confinement in the hospital that my mother met my father. He was called in to look at the set of her arm, which was complicated. He stayed, sitting at her bedside, for he was something of an armchair traveler and had spent his war quietly, at an air force training grounds, where he became a specialist in arms and legs broken during parachute training exercises. Anna Avalon had been to many of the places he longed to visit—Venice, Rome, Mexico, all through France and Spain. She had no family of her own and was taken in by the Avalons, trained to perform from a very young age. They toured Europe before the war, then based themselves in New York. She was illiterate.

It was in the hospital that she finally learned to read and write, as a way of overcoming the boredom and depression of those weeks, and it was my father who insisted on teaching her. In return for stories of her adventures, he graded her first exercises. He bought her her first book, and over her bold letters, which the pale guides of the penmanship pads could not contain, they fell in love.

I wonder if my father calculated the exchange he offered: one form of flight for another. For after that, and for as long as I can remember, my mother has never been without a book. Until now, that is, and it remains the greatest difficulty of her blindness. Since my father's recent death, there is no one to read to her, which is why I returned, in fact, from my failed life where the land is flat. I came home to read to my mother, to read out loud, to read long into the dark if I must, to read all night.

Once my father and mother married, they moved onto the old farm he had inherited but didn't care much for. Though he'd been thinking of moving to a larger city, he settled down and broadened his practice in this valley. It still seems odd to me, when they could have gone anywhere else, that they chose to stay in the town where the disaster had occurred, and which my father in the first place had found so constricting. It was my mother who insisted upon it, after her child did not survive. And then, too, she loved the sagging farmhouse with its scrap of what was left of a vast acreage of woods and hidden hay fields that stretched to the game park.

I owe my existence, the second time then, to the two of them and the hospital that brought them together. That is the debt we take for granted since none of us asks for life. It is only once we have it that we hang on so dearly.

I was seven the year the house caught fire, probably from standing ash. It can rekindle, and my father, forgetful around the house and perpetually exhausted from night hours on call, often emptied what he thought were ashes from cold stoves into wooden or cardboard containers. The fire could have started from a flaming box, or perhaps a buildup of creosote[8] inside the chimney was the culprit. It started

---

8. **creosote** (krē′ə-sōt′): an oily tar deposit from burned wood, which collects in a chimney.

**Need Revising help?**

Review the **Rubric**, p. 1008

Consider **peer reviewer** comments.

Check **Revision Guidelines**, p. 1145

## ❹ Refining Your Presentation

**TARGET SKILL ▶ VARYING YOUR MATERIAL** To maintain your audience's interest in your presentation, vary the types and structures of your sentences. For instance, asking a question can get your listeners' attention, but asking several questions may confuse or bore your audience.

> *How* ~~W~~ould you like to spend your summer outside in 90° weather~~?~~
>
> ~~Would you like to~~ mow*ing* lawns and paint*ing* porches? Doesn't sound
>
> like much fun, does it? ~~How do you think~~ *But it was for* 20 Kelley High
>
> School students ~~felt about it?~~

## ❺ Editing and Proofreading

**TARGET SKILL ▶ CONSISTENT FORM** Because visuals frequently present a great deal of information in a small space, it is important that they be clear and easy to read. Using correct and consistent capitalization can help you get your message across effectively.

> Repairs needed on Mrs. Wilson's House
>
> • ~~r~~Repair roof
>
> • replace windows ~~s and~~ screens
>
> • *fix* porch railing and ~~screens~~ *steps*
>
> • paint~~ing~~ house
>
> • clean up and mow lawn

## Publishing IDEAS

• Have someone videotape your presentation, and show it to other classes.

• Make your presentation to community members or other people interested in your hero.

**More Online: Publishing Options** www.mcdougallittell.com

## ❻ Reflecting

**FOR YOUR WORKING PORTFOLIO** What conclusions did you draw about your unsung hero? What did you learn about media while creating and presenting your multi-media presentation? Attach your reflections to your presentation script. Save your script in your **Working Portfolio.**

Read this paragraph from the first draft of a student essay. The underlined sections may include the following kinds of errors.

- **sentence fragments**
- **correctly written sentences that should be combined**
- **capitalization errors**
- **comma errors**

For each underlined section, choose the revision that most improves the writing.

---

<u>Mr. Wilkinson is the Hero of Grove street.</u> <u>He made it his responsibility. To</u>
(1)                                  (2)

<u>clean up Grove Street.</u> All year long, Mr. Wilkinson works to make the street

look nice. <u>He paints the rusty light poles. He also paints the benches. Finally, he</u>
          (3)

<u>picks up litter.</u> Other shop keepers have been inspired by Mr. Wilkinson's work.

<u>They have begun to take better care of the areas. Around their stores.</u> You will
(4)

see them <u>planting, sweeping, and painting</u> in front of their stores. <u>Jan Lewis our</u>
         (5)                                               (6)

<u>mayor recently</u> awarded Mr. Wilkinson the Clean Streets Award for the third

year in a row.

---

1. **A.** Mr. Wilkinson is the hero of Grove street.
   **B.** Mr. Wilkinson is the Hero of grove street.
   **C.** Mr. Wilkinson is the hero of Grove Street.
   **D.** Correct as is

2. **A.** He made it his responsibility, to clean up Grove Street.
   **B.** He made it his responsibility to clean up Grove Street.
   **C.** He made it his responsibility: to clean up Grove Street.
   **D.** Correct as is

3. **A.** He paints the rusty light poles and the benches and picks up litter.
   **B.** He paints the rusty light poles, the benches, and picks up litter.
   **C.** He paints the rusty light poles. Also the benches, and picks up litter.
   **D.** Correct as is

4. **A.** They have begun to take better care of the areas around their stores.
   **B.** They have begun to take better care of the areas, around their stores.
   **C.** They have begun to take better care of the areas and around their stores.
   **D.** Correct as is

5. **A.** planting sweeping, and painting
   **B.** planting sweeping and painting
   **C.** planting, sweeping, and, painting
   **D.** Correct as is

6. **A.** Jan Lewis, our mayor recently
   **B.** Jan Lewis our mayor, recently
   **C.** Jan Lewis, our mayor, recently
   **D.** Correct as is

**Need extra help?**

See the **Grammar Handbook**

**Capitalization Chart**, p. 1205

**Correcting Fragments**, p. 1199

**Punctuation Chart**, pp. 1203–1204

C an a hero exist without someone to tell his or her story? When you think about it, heroes and storytelling go hand in hand. From ancient times to the present, people have shared stories about great deeds, and each generation learns about the heroes of old. Often, these heroes represent qualities or character traits that are valued by the entire culture. As you will see in this part of Unit Six, stories of heroes can be kept alive for centuries.

**ACTIVITY**

Create a list of your own childhood heroes. Then describe one of those heroes to a small group of classmates, explaining what you found interesting about him or her. After every person in the group has described a hero, discuss how these heroes reflect qualities and character traits that are valued by cultures.

# *M*yths and legends are stories that have survived the

test of time. **Myths** are traditional stories, often concerning supernatural beings or events, that were told to explain natural processes or phenomena. For many ancient peoples, myths were both a kind of science and a religion, allowing humans to make sense of birth, death, and the origins of the universe. Classical mythology, the myths that have had the most influence on Western literature, took root in ancient Greece. Our earliest written example of Greek mythology is the *Iliad*, Homer's epic poem about gods and warriors that dates back approximately 3,000 years.

**Legends** are stories handed down from the past that are often believed to be based on actual historical events. Unlike myths, legends do not always incorporate supernatural events, although legendary heroes are often presented as "larger than life." The stories of Robin Hood and King Arthur are examples of legends.

## The Olympians: The Major Players

The ancient Greeks believed that powerful gods ruled the world from the top of Mount Olympus, the highest mountain in Greece. As Rome became an empire and conquered Greece, it adopted and adapted the gods of Greek mythology, often renaming them. Greek and Roman myths often portrayed the remarkable abilities of the gods and the brave deeds of heroes. The gods possessed both supernatural and humanlike qualities, as well as the very human weaknesses of stubbornness and jealousy. Yet despite their flaws, the gods controlled the destinies of mortals, including, for example, the heroes of Homer's *Iliad* (and later the *Odyssey*). At the right and below are a few of the most important Olympians.

**YOUR TURN** What myths and characters can you recall from Greek or Roman mythology? Which of these gods have you seen portrayed in movies or on TV? In your opinion, which gods have the most interesting roles?

**ZEUS**
**Roman Name**: Jupiter
**Role**: Ruler of the gods
**Controls Fate of**:
Hercules, Perseus

**HERA**
**Roman Name**: Juno
**Role**: Goddess of
marriage
**Controls Fate of**:
Paris, Echo, Orion

**ATHENA**
**Roman Name**: Minerva
**Role**: Goddess of
crafts, war, wisdom
**Controls Fate of**:
Odysseus, Arachne

**APOLLO**
**Roman Name**: Apollo
**Role**: God of light,
medicine, poetry
**Controls Fate of**:
Cassandra, Paris,
Achilles

# Greek Drama's Golden Age

One important literary source of classical mythology is ancient Greek drama. Writing 25 centuries ago, Sophocles and fellow dramatists drew from classical myths and legends to produce these dramas. For example, Sophocles' drama *Antigone* (page 1018) combines references to the gods with semi-historical legends of kings and queens. These myths and legends were familiar to the audience—and believed by many.

While the audience knew the story behind a play, the characters, of course, did not. This play device, known today as **dramatic irony**, has been used by playwrights across time. The lines at the right appear in the first scene from Sophocles' *Antigone*. The speaker is Creon, the new ruler of Thebes, who issues this command before other major characters are aware and are able to react.

> Polyneices, I say, is to have no burial: no man is to touch him or say the least prayer for him; he shall lie on the plain, unburied; and the birds and the scavenging dogs can do with him whatever they like.
>
> This is my command, and you can see the wisdom behind it.
>
> —Sophocles, *Antigone*

# Arthur Through the Ages

During the Middle Ages, traveling poets told long, glowing tales about legendary figures such as Arthur, a glorious king of medieval Britain. Some modern-day scholars suggest that the tales are based on a 6th-century high king. The legend of King Arthur and his knights of the Round Table has been told repeatedly through the ages. The term for Arthurian legends, **romance,** refers to any imaginative story concerned with noble heroes, codes of honor, passionate love, daring deeds, and supernatural events.

As with most oral literature, romances came to be written down, and probably the most famous version is Sir Thomas Malory's *Le Morte d'Arthur*. In this part of Unit 6, you will read two excerpts from Malory's work as well as excerpts from two modern retellings of the legend. Each retelling brings the tools of modern fiction to bear on the legend, exploring the motivations and personalities of characters.

**YOUR TURN** Read the excerpt at right from *Le Morte d'Arthur*. What elements do you think it contains that show the lasting appeal of Arthurian legends?

> "My good fellow, if you know the forest hereabouts, could you tell me in which direction I am most likely to meet with adventure?"
>
> "Sir, I can tell you: less than a mile from here stands a well-moated castle. On the left of the entrance you will find a ford where you can water your horse, and across from the ford a large tree from which hang the shields of many famous knights. Below the shields hangs a caldron, of copper and brass: strike it three times with your spear, and then surely you will meet with adventure—such, indeed, that if you survive it, you will prove yourself the foremost knight in these parts for many years."
>
> —Sir Thomas Malory, *from* Le Morte d'Arthur

Myths and legends still possess the power to captivate and inspire. Unlike listeners or readers of the distant past, you probably don't have complete knowledge of most myths and legends. The reading strategies explained here can help you to appreciate these classic retellings.

# Reading Myths and Legends

## Strategies for Using Your 📖 READER'S NOTEBOOK

As you read, take notes to

- **connect** your personal experiences to what you read about the heroes, their qualities, and their quests
- record any phrases, passages, or ideas you find particularly exciting
- write down questions you may have about the plot, character, setting, or theme of a myth or legend

## 1 Strategies for Understanding Myths and Legends

- **Consider** the source of what you're reading. Was a myth written at a time when the audience believed in the beings and events described? Is the myth a retelling from a later time?
- Do not read legends as history. Try to get a sense of the truth behind a legend but enjoy the adventurous elements.
- Suspend your disbelief. Myths and legends do not try to be as lifelike as modern "realistic" fiction.
- **Visualize** the wondrous characters and events.
- Don't be thrown by unfamiliar twists. There are numerous versions of many myths and legends.

## 2 Strategies for Exploring the Cultures Behind Myths and Legends

- Consider the purpose the tale may have had for those who created it. Was it meant to provide moral instruction? as an explanation of nature? Use a chart like this one to analyze cultural connections.

| Myth or Legend | Origin | Possible Purpose |
|---|---|---|
|  |  |  |

- **Evaluate** the source of a retold myth or legend. Look for what new perspectives and insights a modern reteller brings to a tale.

## 3 Strategies for Recognizing the Themes of Myths and Legends

- Fill in a diagram like the one at the right as you follow a hero's quest. It may be that a hero's actions or attitudes are connected to an important message. After reading, analyze the message.
- Try to separate what is universal—elements that deal with values common to all people—from elements specific to a particular time or culture.
- Ask yourself what views or beliefs of a different time or culture are evident in the tale. For example, do gods exist? Is magic possible?

Hero → Nature of Quest

Hero → Nature of Quest

Hero → Nature of Quest

Message About Life

**Need More Help?**

Remember that active readers use the essential reading strategies explained on page 7: **visualize, predict, clarify, question, connect, evaluate, monitor.**

# Antigone (ăn-tĭg′ə-nē)

*Drama by* SOPHOCLES (sŏf′ ə-klēz′)
*Translated by* DUDLEY FITTS *and* ROBERT FITZGERALD

**( Connect to Your Life )**

**A Matter of Principle** Consider the principles listed to the right, and rank them in the order of their importance to you. Discuss your ranking and your reasoning with the class. Which of the principles might you be willing to fight for—or willing to uphold if it meant making a sacrifice?

loyalty or obligation to family
obedience to civil law
observance of religious law
protection of personal dignity
freedom
protection of community or nation

# Build Background

**Basis in Legend** Sophocles was one of the great dramatists of ancient Greece, and his play *Antigone* is regarded as one of the finest examples of classical Greek tragedy. The main characters in this play come into conflict because they stand firmly behind their principles—principles that are contradictory.

Most Greek tragedies are based on legends or myths that the audience of ancient Greece was very familiar with. *Antigone* is based on the legend of the family of Oedipus (ĕd′ə-pəs), the doomed king of Thebes. As the play begins, Antigone and her sister, Ismene (ĭs-mē′nē), recall their dead father, Oedipus, who unknowingly killed his father and then married his own mother. Upon discovering the truth, Oedipus blinded himself and went into exile, where he was cared for by his two daughters until his death. After his death, his sons, Eteocles (ē-tē′ə-klēz′) and Polyneices (pŏl′ĭ-nī′sēz), agreed to share the kingship of Thebes, ruling in alternate years. However, when Eteocles had served his first term as king, he banished Polyneices from Thebes and refused to relinquish the throne to him, claiming that Polyneices was unfit to rule. Polyneices then enlisted an army from Argos, a powerful city-state and a long-standing enemy of Thebes, to fight his brother. In the course of battle, the brothers killed each other. Their uncle, Creon, has become king and faces the task of restoring order in Thebes. As the new king, he plans to honor one corpse and insult the other.

WORDS TO KNOW
**Vocabulary Preview**

| | |
|---|---|
| auspicious | lamentation |
| compulsive | lithe |
| defile | perverse |
| dirge | sated |
| edict | transgress |

# Focus Your Reading

**LITERARY ANALYSIS** **CLASSICAL DRAMA** **Classical drama** arose in Athens, Greece, from religious celebrations in honor of Dionysus (dī'ə-nī'səs), the god of wine and fertility. These celebrations included ritual chants and songs performed by a group called a chorus. Drama evolved from these celebrations during the sixth century B.C., when individual actors began entering into dialogue with the chorus to tell a story.

**The Theater** Greek drama was filled with the spectacle and pageantry of a religious festival. Attended by thousands, plays were performed during the day in an outdoor theater with seats built into a hillside. The action of each play was presented at the foot of the hill, often on a raised platform. A long building, called the **skene,** served as a backdrop for the action and as a dressing room. A spacious circular floor, the **orchestra,** was located between the skene and the audience.

**Actors and Chorus** The actors—all men—wore elegant robes, huge masks, and often elevated shoes, all of which added to the grandeur of the spectacle. Sophocles used three actors in his plays; between scenes, they changed costumes and masks when they needed to portray different characters. The **chorus**—a group of about 15—commented on the action, and the leader of the chorus, the **choragus** (kə-rā'gəs), participated in the dialogue. Between scenes, the chorus sang and danced to musical accompaniment in the orchestra, giving insights into the message of the play. The chorus is often considered a kind of ideal spectator, representing the response of ordinary citizens to the tragic events unfolding in the play.

**Tragedy and the Tragic Hero** During Sophocles' lifetime, three playwrights were chosen each year to enter a theatrical competition in the festival of Dionysus. Each playwright would produce three tragedies, along with a satyr (sā'tər) play, a short comic interlude. A **tragedy** is a drama that recounts the downfall of a dignified, superior character who is involved in historically or socially significant events.

The **protagonist,** or **tragic hero,** of the work is in conflict with an opposing character or force, the **antagonist.** The action builds from one event to the next and finally to a **catastrophe** that leads to a disastrous conclusion. Twists of fate play a key role in the hero's destruction.

---

### Aristotle's Theory of the Tragic Flaw

According to the Greek philosopher Aristotle, a tragic hero possesses a defect, or **tragic flaw,** that brings about or contributes to his or her downfall. This flaw may be poor judgment, pride, weakness, or an excess of an admirable quality. The tragic hero, noted Aristotle, recognizes his or her flaw and its consequences, but only after it is too late to change the course of events.

---

**ACTIVE READING** **STRATEGIES FOR READING CLASSICAL DRAMA** Use the following strategies to help you read classical drama.

- Imagine the spectacle of the play as staged, **visualizing** as you read.
- Try to understand the hero's **motivations** and the qualities that make him or her a noble figure.
- Pay close attention to the causes of the **conflict** between the hero and his or her antagonist.
- Determine the circumstances or flaws that lead to the hero's downfall.
- Consider how the words and actions of **minor characters** help you to understand the **main characters.**
- Notice how the comments of the chorus interpret the action and point to universal **themes.**
- Monitor your own reading strategies. Modify them when your understanding breaks down by rereading, using resources, and questioning.

**READER'S NOTEBOOK** As you read *Antigone,* record your answers to the questions printed in blue alongside the play. Apply the strategies listed above, and note any other thoughts, questions, and comments that you have.

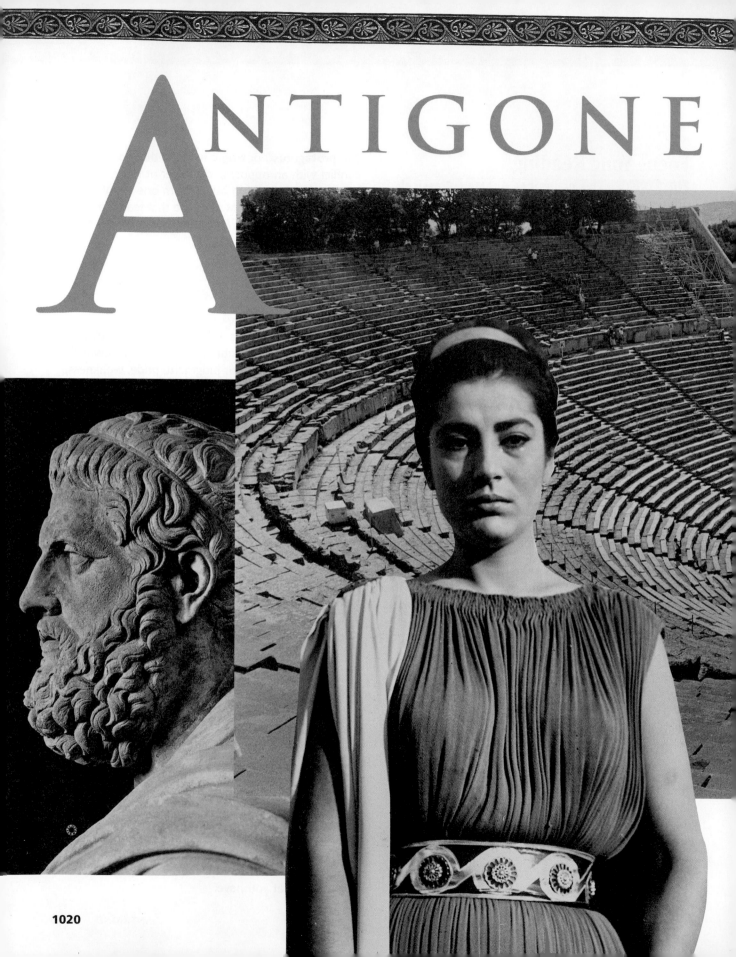

# ANTIGONE

## CAST OF CHARACTERS

**Antigone** ⎫ daughters of Oedipus, former king
**Ismene** ⎭ of Thebes

**Creon** (krē′ŏn′), king of Thebes, uncle of
  Antigone and Ismene

**Haemon** (hē′mŏn′), Creon's son, engaged to
  Antigone

**Eurydice** (yŏŏ-rĭd′ĭ-sē), wife of Creon

**Teiresias** (tī-rē′sē-əs), a blind prophet

**Chorus,** made up of about 15 elders of Thebes

**Choragus,** leader of the chorus

**a Sentry**

**a Messenger**

Bust of Sophocles. Museo
Lateranense, Vatican Museums,
Vatican City, Alinari / Art
Resource, New York.

Antigone contemplates her fate.
Culver Pictures.

Ruins of ancient theater
at Epidaurus, Greece.
Copyright © 1993
Barbara Ries / Photo
Researchers, Inc.

# SOPHOCLES

**Scene:** *Before the palace of Creon, king of Thebes. A central double door, and two doors at the side. A platform extends the length of the stage, and from this platform three steps lead down into the orchestra, or chorus ground.*

**Time:** *Dawn of the day after the repulse of the Argive army from the assault on Thebes*

## PROLOGUE

*(Antigone and Ismene enter from the central door of the palace.)*

**Antigone.** Ismene, dear sister,
    You would think that we had already suffered enough
    For the curse on Oedipus:
    I cannot imagine any grief
5    That you and I have not gone through. And now—
    Have they told you the new decree of our king Creon?

**Ismene.** I have heard nothing: I know
    That two sisters lost two brothers, a double death
    In a single hour; and I know that the Argive army
10    Fled in the night; but beyond this, nothing.

**9 Argive:** of Argos.

**Antigone.** I thought so. And that is why I wanted you
    To come out here with me. There is something we must do.

**Ismene.** Why do you speak so strangely?

**Antigone.** Listen, Ismene:
15    Creon buried our brother Eteocles
    With military honors, gave him a soldier's funeral,
    And it was right that he should; but Polyneices,
    Who fought as bravely and died as miserably—
    They say that Creon has sworn
20    No one shall bury him, no one mourn for him,
    But his body must lie in the fields, a sweet treasure
    For carrion birds to find as they search for food.
    That is what they say, and our good Creon is coming here
    To announce it publicly; and the penalty—
25    Stoning to death in the public square!
                      There it is,
    And now you can prove what you are:
    A true sister, or a traitor to your family.

**20–22** The obligation to bury the dead with appropriate burial rites was considered a sacred law among the ancient Greeks. They believed that the soul of someone left unburied would never find peace.

**Ismene.** Antigone, you are mad! What could I possibly do?

**Antigone.** You must decide whether you will help me or not.

30 **Ismene.** I do not understand you. Help you in what?

**Antigone.** Ismene, I am going to bury him. Will you come?

**28–35** What contrast between Antigone and Ismene is suggested by the conversation between them?

**Ismene.** Bury him! You have just said the new law forbids it.

**Antigone.** He is my brother. And he is your brother, too.

**Ismene.** But think of the danger! Think what Creon will do!

35 **Antigone.** Creon is not strong enough to stand in my way.

**Ismene.** Ah sister!
Oedipus died, everyone hating him
For what his own search brought to light, his eyes
Ripped out by his own hand; and Jocasta died,
40 His mother and wife at once: she twisted the cords
That strangled her life; and our two brothers died,
Each killed by the other's sword. And we are left:
But oh, Antigone,
Think how much more terrible than these
45 Our own death would be if we should go against Creon
And do what he has forbidden! We are only women;
We cannot fight with men, Antigone!
The law is strong, we must give in to the law
In this thing, and in worse. I beg the dead
50 To forgive me, but I am helpless: I must yield
To those in authority. And I think it is dangerous business
To be always meddling.

**Antigone.** If that is what you think,
I should not want you, even if you asked to come.
You have made your choice; you can be what you want to be.
55 But I will bury him; and if I must die,
I say that this crime is holy: I shall lie down
With him in death, and I shall be as dear
To him as he to me.
It is the dead,
Not the living, who make the longest demands:
60 We die forever. . . .
You may do as you like,
Since apparently the laws of the gods mean nothing to you.

**Ismene.** They mean a great deal to me; but I have no strength
To break laws that were made for the public good.

**Antigone.** That must be your excuse, I suppose. But as for me,
65 I will bury the brother I love.

**Ismene.** Antigone,
I am so afraid for you!

**Antigone.** You need not be:
You have yourself to consider, after all.

**39** Jocasta, the mother of Antigone and Ismene, hanged herself when she realized the truth about her relationship with Oedipus.

**55–61** What do these lines reveal about Antigone's feelings for her brother and the gods' laws?

**Choragus.** We are old men: let the younger ones carry it out.

**Creon.** I do not mean that: the sentries have been appointed.

**Choragus.** Then what is it that you would have us do?

**Creon.** You will give no support to whoever breaks this law.

55 **Choragus.** Only a crazy man is in love with death!

**Creon.** And death it is; yet money talks, and the wisest
Have sometimes been known to count a few coins too many.

(*Enter* Sentry.)

**Sentry.** I'll not say that I'm out of breath from running, King, because
every time I stopped to think about what I have to tell you, I felt
60 like going back. And all the time a voice kept saying, "You fool,
don't you know you're walking straight into trouble?"; and then
another voice: "Yes, but if you let somebody else get the news to
Creon first, it will be even worse than that for you!" But good sense
won out, at least I hope it was good sense, and here I am with a
65 story that makes no sense at all; but I'll tell it anyhow, because, as
they say, what's going to happen's going to happen, and—

**Creon.** Come to the point. What have you to say?

**Sentry.** I did not do it. I did not see who did it. You must not punish me for what someone else has done.

70 **Creon.** A comprehensive defense! More effective, perhaps,
If I knew its purpose. Come: what is it?

**Sentry.** A dreadful thing . . . I don't know how to put it—

**Creon.** Out with it!

**Sentry.**                    Well, then;
The dead man—
                    Polyneices—

(*Pause. The* Sentry *is overcome, fumbles for words.*
Creon *waits impassively.*)

                              out there—
                                        someone—
75 New dust on the slimy flesh!

(*Pause. No sign from* Creon.)

Someone has given it burial that way, and
Gone. . . .

(*Long pause.* Creon *finally speaks with deadly control.*)

**Creon.** And the man who dared do this?

**Sentry.**                                        I swear I
Do not know! You must believe me!

78 Note that Creon assumes it
is a man who has tried to bury
the body.

Listen:

80 The ground was dry, not a sign of digging, no,
Not a wheel track in the dust, no trace of anyone.
It was when they relieved us this morning: and one of them,
The corporal, pointed to it.

There it was,

The strangest—

Look:

85 The body, just mounded over with light dust: you see?
Not buried really, but as if they'd covered it
Just enough for the ghost's peace. And no sign
Of dogs or any wild animal that had been there.

And then what a scene there was! Every man of us
90 Accusing the other: we all proved the other man did it;
We all had proof that we could not have done it.
We were ready to take hot iron in our hands,
Walk through fire, swear by all the gods,
*It was not I!*

95 *I do not know who it was, but it was not I!*

(Creon's *rage has been mounting steadily, but the* Sentry *is too intent upon his story to notice it.*)

And then, when this came to nothing, someone said
A thing that silenced us and made us stare
Down at the ground: you had to be told the news,
And one of us had to do it! We threw the dice,
100 And the bad luck fell to me. So here I am,
No happier to be here than you are to have me:
Nobody likes the man who brings bad news.

**Choragus.** I have been wondering, King: can it be that the gods
have done this?

**Creon** (*furiously*). Stop!
105 Must you doddering wrecks
Go out of your heads entirely? "The gods!"
Intolerable!
The gods favor this corpse? Why? How had he served them?
Tried to loot their temples, burn their images,
110 Yes, and the whole state, and its laws with it!
Is it your senile opinion that the gods love to honor bad men?
A pious thought!—

No, from the very beginning
There have been those who have whispered together,
Stiff-necked anarchists, putting their heads together,

**85–88** Notice that the burial of Polyneices is symbolic and ritualistic rather than actual.

**104–109** Note how quickly Creon rejects a reasonable question posed by the choragus. Creon is convinced that he knows how the gods think.

**114 anarchists** (ăn′ər-kĭsts): persons favoring the overthrow of government.

Not even when we charged her with what she had done.
45  She denied nothing.

And this was a comfort to me,
And some uneasiness: for it is a good thing
To escape from death, but it is no great pleasure
To bring death to a friend.

Yet I always say
There is nothing so comfortable as your own safe skin!

50  **Creon** (*slowly, dangerously*). And you, Antigone,
You with your head hanging—do you confess this thing?

**Antigone.** I do. I deny nothing.

**Creon** (*to* Sentry).            You may go.

(*Exit* Sentry.)

(*to* Antigone) Tell me, tell me briefly:
Had you heard my proclamation touching this matter?

55  **Antigone.** It was public. Could I help hearing it?

**Creon.** And yet you dared defy the law.

**Antigone.**                          I dared.
It was not God's proclamation. That final Justice
That rules the world below makes no such laws.

Your edict, King, was strong,
60  But all your strength is weakness itself against
The immortal unrecorded laws of God.
They are not merely now: they were, and shall be,
Operative forever, beyond man utterly.

I knew I must die, even without your decree:
65  I am only mortal. And if I must die
Now, before it is my time to die,
Surely this is no hardship: can anyone
Living, as I live, with evil all about me,
Think Death less than a friend? This death of mine
70  Is of no importance; but if I had left my brother
Lying in death unburied, I should have suffered.
Now I do not.

**57–63** What law does Antigone recognize as the supreme one?

**64–70** What is Antigone's attitude toward death?

Film still from the 1960 movie *Antigone*. Antigone is about to be taken prisoner after sprinkling dust and wine over her brother's corpse. Culver Pictures.

You smile at me. Ah Creon,
Think me a fool, if you like; but it may well be
That a fool convicts me of folly.

75 **Choragus.** Like father, like daughter: both headstrong, deaf to
reason!
She has never learned to yield.

**Creon.**                                  She has much to learn.
The inflexible heart breaks first, the toughest iron
Cracks first, and the wildest horses bend their necks
At the pull of the smallest curb.

Pride? In a slave?

80 This girl is guilty of a double insolence,
Breaking the given laws and boasting of it.
Who is the man here,
She or I, if this crime goes unpunished?
Sister's child, or more than sister's child,
85 Or closer yet in blood—she and her sister
Win bitter death for this!

(*to servants*) Go, some of you,
Arrest Ismene. I accuse her equally.
Bring her: you will find her sniffling in the house there.

Her mind's a traitor: crimes kept in the dark
90 Cry for light, and the guardian brain shudders;
But how much worse than this
Is brazen boasting of barefaced anarchy!

**Antigone.** Creon, what more do you want than my death?

**Creon.**                                            Nothing.
That gives me everything.

**Antigone.**                     Then I beg you: kill me.
95 This talking is a great weariness: your words
Are distasteful to me, and I am sure that mine
Seem so to you. And yet they should not seem so:
I should have praise and honor for what I have done.
All these men here would praise me
100 Were their lips not frozen shut with fear of you.
(*bitterly*) Ah the good fortune of kings,
Licensed to say and do whatever they please!

**Creon.** You are alone here in that opinion.

**Antigone.** No, they are with me. But they keep their tongues in leash.

105 **Creon.** Maybe. But you are guilty, and they are not.

**Antigone.** There is no guilt in reverence for the dead.

82–83 Think about how Creon's perception of Antigone as a threat to his manhood heightens the conflict.

99–104 What does Antigone assume about the attitude of the chorus? Do you think she is right?

Confrontation between Antigone and Creon in the 1960 film. Photofest.

**Creon.** But Eteocles—was he not your brother too?

**Antigone.** My brother too.

**Creon.**                            And you insult his memory?

**Antigone** (*softly*). The dead man would not say that I insult it.

110 **Creon.** He would: for you honor a traitor as much as him.

**Antigone.** His own brother, traitor or not, and equal in blood.

**Creon.** He made war on his country. Eteocles defended it.

**Antigone.** Nevertheless, there are honors due all the dead.

**Creon.** But not the same for the wicked as for the just.

115 **Antigone.** Ah Creon, Creon,
    Which of us can say what the gods hold wicked?

**Creon.** An enemy is an enemy, even dead.

**Antigone.** It is my nature to join in love, not hate.

**Creon** (*finally losing patience*). Go join them, then; if you must have
    your love,
120 Find it in hell!

**Choragus.** But see, Ismene comes:

(*Enter* Ismene, *guarded.*)

    Those tears are sisterly; the cloud
    That shadows her eyes rains down gentle sorrow.

**Creon.** You too, Ismene,
125 Snake in my ordered house, sucking my blood
    Stealthily—and all the time I never knew
    That these two sisters were aiming at my throne!

                                        Ismene,
    Do you confess your share in this crime or deny it?
    Answer me.

130 **Ismene.** Yes, if she will let me say so. I am guilty.

**Antigone** (*coldly*). No, Ismene. You have no right to say so.
    You would not help me, and I will not have you help me.

**Ismene.** But now I know what you meant; and I am here
    To join you, to take my share of punishment.

135 **Antigone.** The dead man and the gods who rule the dead
    Know whose act this was. Words are not friends.

**Ismene.** Do you refuse me, Antigone? I want to die with you:
    I too have a duty that I must discharge to the dead.

**Antigone.** You shall not lessen my death by sharing it.

140 **Ismene.** What do I care for life when you are dead?

**Antigone.** Ask Creon. You're always hanging on his opinions.

**115–116** Unlike Creon, Antigone holds that humans cannot understand the thinking of the gods.

**131–143** What do you think of Antigone's treatment of her sister?

**Ismene.** You are laughing at me. Why, Antigone?

**Antigone.** It's a joyless laughter, Ismene.

**Ismene.**                                But can I do nothing?

**Antigone.** Yes. Save yourself. I shall not envy you.

145   There are those who will praise you; I shall have honor, too.

**Ismene.** But we are equally guilty!

**Antigone.**                                No, more, Ismene.
   You are alive, but I belong to Death.

**Creon** (*to the* Chorus). Gentlemen, I beg you to observe these girls:
   One has just now lost her mind; the other,
150   It seems, has never had a mind at all.

**Ismene.** Grief teaches the steadiest minds to waver, King.

**Creon.** Yours certainly did, when you assumed guilt with the guilty!

**Ismene.** But how could I go on living without her?

**Creon.**                                            You are.
   She is already dead.

**Ismene.**                     But your own son's bride!

155   **Creon.** There are places enough for him to push his plow.
   I want no wicked women for my sons!

**Ismene.** O dearest Haemon, how your father wrongs you!

**Creon.** I've had enough of your childish talk of marriage!

**Choragus.** Do you really intend to steal this girl from your son?

160   **Creon.** No; Death will do that for me.

**Choragus.**                                Then she must die?

**Creon.** You dazzle me.
                  —But enough of this talk!
   (*to guards*) You, there, take them away and guard them well:
   For they are but women, and even brave men run
   When they see Death coming.

(*Exeunt* Ismene, Antigone, *and guards.*)


# ODE 2

**Chorus.** Fortunate is the man who has never tasted God's vengeance!
   Where once the anger of heaven has struck, that house is shaken
   Forever: damnation rises behind each child
   Like a wave cresting out of the black northeast,
5   When the long darkness under sea roars up
   And bursts drumming death upon the wind-whipped sand.

**154** Ismene's line reveals a complication in the plot: Creon's son, Haemon, is engaged to Antigone. Creon's love for his immediate family is now an issue in his conflict with Antigone.

**155–156** How does Creon feel about the bond between Haemon and Antigone?

I have seen this gathering sorrow from time long past
Loom upon Oedipus' children: generation from generation
Takes the compulsive rage of the enemy god.
10 So lately this last flower of Oedipus' line
Drank the sunlight! but now a passionate word
And a handful of dust have closed up all its beauty.

What mortal arrogance
Transcends the wrath of Zeus?
15 Sleep cannot lull him, nor the effortless long months
Of the timeless gods: but he is young forever,
And his house is the shining day of high Olympus.
All that is and shall be,
And all the past, is his.
20 No pride on earth is free of the curse of heaven.

The straying dreams of men
May bring them ghosts of joy:
But as they drowse, the waking embers burn them;
Or they walk with fixed eyes, as blind men walk.
25 But the ancient wisdom speaks for our own time:
*Fate works most for woe*
*With Folly's fairest show.*
Man's little pleasure is the spring of sorrow.

**17 Olympus:** a mountain in northern Greece, home of the gods and goddesses.

**28** Do you think this line could apply to Creon?

WORDS
TO
KNOW
**compulsive** (kəm-pŭl′sĭv) *adj.* having the ability to compel or force

Painting on wine cup, showing the god Dionysus, the patron of theater, in his ship (540 B.C.), Exekias. Greek pottery often featured scenes from mythology. Antikensammlung, Munich, Germany. Photo Copyright © Erich Lessing / Art Resource, New York.

Theatrical masks on a fragment of a Greek bowl, about 410 B.C. The Granger Collection, New York.

# SCENE 3

**Choragus.** But here is Haemon, King, the last of all your sons.
Is it grief for Antigone that brings him here,
And bitterness at being robbed of his bride?

(*Enter* Haemon.)

**Creon.** We shall soon see, and no need of diviners.

—Son,

5    You have heard my final judgment on that girl:
Have you come here hating me, or have you come
With deference and with love, whatever I do?

**Haemon.** I am your son, Father. You are my guide.
You make things clear for me, and I obey you.

**4 diviners:** those who predict the future.

Lead me to my vigil, where I must have
Neither love nor <u>lamentation</u>; no song, but silence.

(Creon *interrupts impatiently*.)

**Creon.** If <u>dirges</u> and planned lamentations could put off death,
Men would be singing forever.
                    (*to the servants*) Take her, go!
55  You know your orders: take her to the vault
And leave her alone there. And if she lives or dies,
That's her affair, not ours: our hands are clean.

**Antigone.** O tomb, vaulted bride-bed in eternal rock,
Soon I shall be with my own again
60  Where Persephone welcomes the thin ghosts underground:
And I shall see my father again, and you, Mother,
And dearest Polyneices—
                    dearest indeed
To me, since it was my hand
That washed him clean and poured the ritual wine:
65  And my reward is death before my time!

And yet, as men's hearts know, I have done no wrong;
I have not sinned before God. Or if I have,
I shall know the truth in death. But if the guilt
Lies upon Creon who judged me, then, I pray,
70  May his punishment equal my own.

**Choragus.**                              O passionate heart,
Unyielding, tormented still by the same winds!

**Creon.** Her guards shall have good cause to regret their delaying.

**Antigone.** Ah! That voice is like the voice of death!

**Creon.** I can give you no reason to think you are mistaken.

75  **Antigone.** Thebes, and you my fathers' gods,
And rulers of Thebes, you see me now, the last
Unhappy daughter of a line of kings,
Your kings, led away to death. You will remember
What things I suffer, and at what men's hands,
80  Because I would not <u>transgress</u> the laws of heaven.
(*to the guards, simply*) Come: let us wait no longer.

(*Exit* Antigone, *left, guarded*.)

**60 Persephone** (pər-sĕf′ə-nē): wife
of Hades (hā′dēz) **and queen of the
underworld.**

**75–80** What do these lines suggest
about what Antigone values most?

# ODE 4

**Chorus.** All Danae's beauty was locked away
In a brazen cell where the sunlight could not come:
A small room, still as any grave, enclosed her.
Yet she was a princess too,
5    And Zeus in a rain of gold poured love upon her.
O child, child,
No power in wealth or war
Or tough sea-blackened ships
Can prevail against untiring Destiny!

10    And Dryas' son also, that furious king,
Bore the god's prisoning anger for his pride:
Sealed up by Dionysus in deaf stone,
His madness died among echoes.
So at the last he learned what dreadful power
15    His tongue had mocked:
For he had profaned the revels
And fired the wrath of the nine
Implacable sisters that love the sound of the flute.

And old men tell a half-remembered tale
20    Of horror done where a dark ledge splits the sea
And a double surf beats on the grey shores:
How a king's new woman, sick
With hatred for the queen he had imprisoned,
Ripped out his two sons' eyes with her bloody hands
25    While grinning Ares watched the shuttle plunge
Four times: four blind wounds crying for revenge,

Crying, tears and blood mingled. Piteously born,
Those sons whose mother was of heavenly birth!
Her father was the god of the north wind,
30    And she was cradled by gales;
She raced with young colts on the glittering hills
And walked untrammeled in the open light:
But in her marriage deathless Fate found means
To build a tomb like yours for all her joy.

**1–5** Danae (dăn′ə-ē′) was a princess who was imprisoned by her father because it had been predicted that her son would one day kill him. After Zeus visited Danae in the form of a shower of gold, she gave birth to his son Perseus, who eventually did kill his grandfather.

**10–18** King Lycurgus (lĭ-kûr′gəs), son of Dryas (drī′əs), was driven mad and imprisoned in stone for objecting to the worship of Dionysus. The nine implacable sisters are the Muses, the goddesses who presided over literature, the arts, and the sciences. Once offended, they were impossible to appease.

**19–34** These lines refer to the myth of King Phineus (fĭn′yōōs), who imprisoned his first wife, the daughter of the north wind, and allowed his new wife to blind his sons from his first marriage.

Two views of Sophocles, who was regarded by his Greek admirers as "the perfect man." *Left,* Museo Gregoriano Profano, Vatican Museums, Vatican State, Alinari / Art Resource, New York. *Right,* Museo Lateranense, Vatican Museums, Vatican City, Alinari / Art Resource, New York.

# SCENE 5

(*Enter blind* Teiresias, *led by a boy. The opening speeches of* Teiresias *should be in singsong contrast to the realistic lines of* Creon.)

**Teiresias.** This is the way the blind man comes, princes, princes,
   Lock step, two heads lit by the eyes of one.

**Creon.** What new thing have you to tell us, old Teiresias?

**Teiresias.** I have much to tell you: listen to the prophet, Creon.

5 **Creon.** I am not aware that I have ever failed to listen.

**Teiresias.** Then you have done wisely, King, and ruled well.

**Creon.** I admit my debt to you. But what have you to say?

**1–7** The blind Teiresias is physically blind but spiritually sighted. As a prophet, he is an agent of the gods in their dealings with humans. His revelation of the truth to Oedipus led Oedipus to leave Thebes, which indirectly helped Creon to become king.

**Teiresias.** This, Creon: you stand once more on the edge of fate.

**Creon.** What do you mean? Your words are a kind of dread.

10 **Teiresias.** Listen, Creon:
   I was sitting in my chair of augury, at the place
   Where the birds gather about me. They were all a-chatter,
   As is their habit, when suddenly I heard
   A strange note in their jangling, a scream, a
15 Whirring fury; I knew that they were fighting,
   Tearing each other, dying
   In a whirlwind of wings clashing. And I was afraid.
   I began the rites of burnt offering at the altar,
   But Hephaestus failed me: instead of bright flame,
20 There was only the sputtering slime of the fat thigh-flesh
   Melting: the entrails dissolved in grey smoke;
   The bare bone burst from the welter. And no blaze!

   This was a sign from heaven. My boy described it,
   Seeing for me as I see for others.

25 I tell you, Creon, you yourself have brought
   This new calamity upon us. Our hearths and altars
   Are stained with the corruption of dogs and carrion birds
   That glut themselves on the corpse of Oedipus' son.
   The gods are deaf when we pray to them; their fire
30 Recoils from our offering; their birds of omen
   Have no cry of comfort, for they are gorged
   With the thick blood of the dead.

                                    O my son,
   These are no trifles! Think: all men make mistakes,
   But a good man yields when he knows his course is wrong,
35 And repairs the evil. The only crime is pride.

   Give in to the dead man, then: do not fight with a corpse—
   What glory is it to kill a man who is dead?
   Think, I beg you:
   It is for your own good that I speak as I do.
40 You should be able to yield for your own good.

**Creon.** It seems that prophets have made me their especial province.
   All my life long
   I have been a kind of butt for the dull arrows
   Of doddering fortunetellers!

                              No, Teiresias:
45 If your birds—if the great eagles of God himself—
   Should carry him stinking bit by bit to heaven,
   I would not yield. I am not afraid of pollution:

**11–17** The chair of augury is the place where Teiresias sits to hear the birds, whose sounds reveal the future to him. The fighting among the birds suggests that the anarchy infecting Thebes has spread even to the world of nature.

**19 Hephaestus** (hĭ-fĕs′təs): god of fire.

**18–32** According to Teiresias, the birds and dogs that have eaten the corpse of Polyneices have become corrupt, causing the gods to reject the Thebans' offerings and prayers. What do these lines suggest about how the gods view Creon's refusal to allow Polyneices to be buried?

**44–48** What do these lines suggest about Creon's view of himself and the gods?

No man can <u>defile</u> the gods.

Do what you will;
Go into business, make money, speculate

50 In India gold or that synthetic gold from Sardis,
Get rich otherwise than by my consent to bury him.
Teiresias, it is a sorry thing when a wise man
Sells his wisdom, lets out his words for hire!

**Teiresias.** Ah Creon! Is there no man left in the world—

55 **Creon.** To do what? Come, let's have the aphorism!

**Teiresias.** No man who knows that wisdom outweighs any wealth?

**Creon.** As surely as bribes are baser than any baseness.

**Teiresias.** You are sick, Creon! You are deathly sick!

**Creon.** As you say: it is not my place to challenge a prophet.

60 **Teiresias.** Yet you have said my prophecy is for sale.

**Creon.** The generation of prophets has always loved gold.

**Teiresias.** The generation of kings has always loved brass.

**Creon.** You forget yourself! You are speaking to your king.

**Teiresias.** I know it. You are a king because of me.

65 **Creon.** You have a certain skill; but you have sold out.

**Teiresias.** King, you will drive me to words that—

**Creon.** Say them, say them!
Only remember: I will not pay you for them.

**Teiresias.** No, you will find them too costly.

**Creon.** No doubt. Speak:
Whatever you say, you will not change my will.

70 **Teiresias.** Then take this, and take it to heart!
The time is not far off when you shall pay back
Corpse for corpse, flesh of your own flesh.
You have thrust the child of this world into living night;
You have kept from the gods below the child that is theirs:

75 The one in a grave before her death, the other,
Dead, denied the grave. This is your crime:
And the Furies and the dark gods of hell
Are swift with terrible punishment for you.

Do you want to buy me now, Creon?

Not many days,

80 And your house will be full of men and women weeping,
And curses will be hurled at you from far

**49–53** What does Creon assume is the motive behind Teiresias' prophecies?

**50 Sardis** (sär'dĭs): the capital of ancient Lydia, where metal coins were first produced.

**77–78 Furies:** three goddesses who avenge crimes, especially those that violate family ties. How might this prophecy be fulfilled?

WORDS
TO
KNOW

**defile** (dĭ-fīl') *v.* to make foul, dirty, unclean, or impure

Cities grieving for sons unburied, left to rot before the walls of
   Thebes.

These are my arrows, Creon: they are all for you.

(*to boy*) But come, child: lead me home.

85   Let him waste his fine anger upon younger men.
Maybe he will learn at last
To control a wiser tongue in a better head.

(*Exit* Teiresias.)

**Choragus.** The old man has gone, King, but his words
Remain to plague us. I am old, too,
90   But I cannot remember that he was ever false.

**Creon.** That is true. . . . It troubles me.
Oh it is hard to give in! but it is worse
To risk everything for stubborn pride.

**Choragus.** Creon: take my advice.

**Creon.**                                      What shall I do?

95   **Choragus.** Go quickly: free Antigone from her vault
And build a tomb for the body of Polyneices.

**Creon.** You would have me do this?

**Choragus.**                                      Creon, yes!
And it must be done at once: God moves
Swiftly to cancel the folly of stubborn men.

100   **Creon.** It is hard to deny the heart! But I
Will do it: I will not fight with destiny.

**Choragus.** You must go yourself; you cannot leave it to others.

**Creon.** I will go.
                    —Bring axes, servants:
Come with me to the tomb. I buried her; I
105   Will set her free.
                    Oh quickly!
My mind misgives—
The laws of the gods are mighty, and a man must serve them
To the last day of his life!

(*Exit* Creon.)

# PAEAN

**Choragus.** God of many names

**Chorus.**                          O Iacchus
                                          son
of Cadmean Semele
                    O born of the thunder!
guardian of the West
                    regent
of Eleusis' plain
                    O prince of maenad Thebes
5      and the Dragon Field by rippling Ismenus:

**Choragus.** God of many names

**Chorus.**                          the flame of torches
    flares on our hills
                    the nymphs of Iacchus
    dance at the spring of Castalia:
    from the vine-close mountain
                                come ah come in ivy:
10    *Evohé evohé!* sings through the streets of Thebes

**Choragus.** God of many names

**Chorus.**                          Iacchus of Thebes
    heavenly child
                    of Semele bride of the Thunderer!
    The shadow of plague is upon us:
                                come
    with clement feet
                    oh come from Parnassus
15    down the long slopes
                    across the lamenting water

**Choragus.** Io Fire! Chorister of the throbbing stars!
    O purest among the voices of the night!
    Thou son of God, blaze for us!

**Chorus.** Come with choric rapture of circling Maenads
20    Who cry *Io Iacche!*
                    *God of many names!*

**PAEAN:** A paean (pē'ən) is a hymn appealing to the gods for assistance. In this paean, the chorus praises Dionysus, or Iacchus (yä'kəs), and calls on him to come to Thebes to show mercy and drive out evil.

**2** Cadmus was the legendary founder of Thebes. Dionysus was the son of Cadmus' daughter Semele (sə-mē'lē) and Zeus, who is referred to here as thunder.

**4–5** These lines name locations near Athens and Thebes. The maenads (mē'nădz') were priestesses of Dionysus.

**8–9** The spring of Castalia is on the sacred mountain Parnassus. Grape vines and ivy were symbols of Dionysus.

**10 evohé:** hallelujah.

## EXODOS

(*Enter* Messenger.)

**Messenger.** Men of the line of Cadmus, you who live
Near Amphion's citadel:
I cannot say
Of any condition of human life, "This is fixed,
This is clearly good, or bad." Fate raises up,
5  And Fate casts down the happy and unhappy alike:
No man can foretell his fate.
Take the case of Creon:
Creon was happy once, as I count happiness:
Victorious in battle, sole governor of the land,
Fortunate father of children nobly born.
10  And now it has all gone from him! Who can say
That a man is still alive when his life's joy fails?
He is a walking dead man. Grant him rich;
Let him live like a king in his great house:
If his pleasure is gone, I would not give
15  So much as the shadow of smoke for all he owns.

**Choragus.** Your words hint at sorrow: what is your news for us?

**Messenger.** They are dead. The living are guilty of their death.

**Choragus.** Who is guilty? Who is dead? Speak!

**Messenger.**                    Haemon.
Haemon is dead; and the hand that killed him
20  Is his own hand.

**Choragus.**         His father's? or his own?

**Messenger.** His own, driven mad by the murder his father had done.

**Choragus.** Teiresias, Teiresias, how clearly you saw it all!

**Messenger.** This is my news: you must draw what conclusions you
can from it.

**Choragus.** But look: Eurydice, our queen:
25  Has she overheard us?

(*Enter* Eurydice *from the palace, center.*)

**Eurydice.** I have heard something, friends:
As I was unlocking the gate of Pallas' shrine,
For I needed her help today, I heard a voice
Telling of some new sorrow. And I fainted
30  There at the temple with all my maidens about me.
But speak again: whatever it is, I can bear it:
Grief and I are no strangers.

**EXODOS:** The exodos is the last episode in the play. It is followed by a final speech made by the choragus and addressed directly to the audience.

**2 Amphion:** Niobe's husband, who built a wall around Thebes by charming the stones into place with music.

**15** How does the messenger compare with the sentry who appeared in Scenes 1 and 2?

**27 Pallas:** Athena, the goddess of wisdom.

**32 Megareus** (mə-găr′ē-əs), the older son of Eurydice and Creon, had died in the battle for Thebes.

**Messenger.** Dearest lady,
I will tell you plainly all that I have seen.
I shall not try to comfort you: what is the use,
35 Since comfort could lie only in what is not true?
The truth is always best.

                  I went with Creon
To the outer plain where Polyneices was lying,
No friend to pity him, his body shredded by dogs.
We made our prayers in that place to Hecate
40 And Pluto, that they would be merciful. And we bathed
The corpse with holy water, and we brought
Fresh-broken branches to burn what was left of it,
And upon the urn we heaped up a towering barrow
Of the earth of his own land.

                    When we were done, we ran
45 To the vault where Antigone lay on her couch of stone.
One of the servants had gone ahead,
And while he was yet far off he heard a voice
Grieving within the chamber, and he came back
And told Creon. And as the king went closer,
50 The air was full of wailing, the words lost,
And he begged us to make all haste. "Am I a prophet?"
He said, weeping. "And must I walk this road,
The saddest of all that I have gone before?
My son's voice calls me on. Oh quickly, quickly!
55 Look through the crevice there, and tell me
If it is Haemon, or some deception of the gods!"

We obeyed; and in the cavern's farthest corner
We saw her lying:
She had made a noose of her fine linen veil
60 And hanged herself. Haemon lay beside her,
His arms about her waist, lamenting her,
His love lost underground, crying out
That his father had stolen her away from him.
When Creon saw him, the tears rushed to his eyes,
65 And he called to him: "What have you done, child? Speak to me.
What are you thinking that makes your eyes so strange?
O my son, my son, I come to you on my knees!"
But Haemon spat in his face. He said not a word,
Staring—
                and suddenly drew his sword
70 And lunged. Creon shrank back; the blade missed, and the boy,
Desperate against himself, drove it half its length

**39–40 Hecate** (hĕk′ə-tē) **and Pluto:** other names for Persephone and Hades, the goddess and god of the underworld.

**43–44** Note the contrast between the barrow, or burial mound, erected by Creon and the handful of dirt used by Antigone to cover her brother.

**60** Note that this is the same way in which Jocasta, Antigone's mother, killed herself.

Into his own side and fell. And as he died,
He gathered Antigone close in his arms again,
Choking, his blood bright red on her white cheek.
75 And now he lies dead with the dead, and she is his
At last, his bride in the houses of the dead.

(*Exit* Eurydice *into the palace.*)

**Choragus.** She has left us without a word. What can this mean?

**Messenger.** It troubles me, too; yet she knows what is best;
Her grief is too great for public lamentation,
80 And doubtless she has gone to her chamber to weep
For her dead son, leading her maidens in his dirge.

**Choragus.** It may be so: but I fear this deep silence.

(*Pause*)

**Messenger.** I will see what she is doing. I will go in.

(*Exit* Messenger *into the palace. Enter* Creon *with attendants,
bearing* Haemon's *body.*)

**Choragus.** But here is the king himself: oh look at him,
85 Bearing his own damnation in his arms.

**Creon.** Nothing you say can touch me any more.
My own blind heart has brought me
From darkness to final darkness. Here you see
The father murdering, the murdered son—
90 And all my civic wisdom!
Haemon my son, so young, so young to die,
I was the fool, not you; and you died for me.

**Choragus.** That is the truth; but you were late in learning it.

**Creon.** This truth is hard to bear. Surely a god
95 Has crushed me beneath the hugest weight of heaven,
And driven me headlong a barbaric way
To trample out the thing I held most dear.

The pains that men will take to come to pain!

(*Enter* Messenger *from the palace.*)

**Messenger.** The burden you carry in your hands is heavy,
100 But it is not all: you will find more in your house.

**Creon.** What burden worse than this shall I find there?

**Messenger.** The queen is dead.

**Creon.** O port of death, deaf world,
Is there no pity for me? And you, angel of evil,
105 I was dead, and your words are death again.

Is it true, boy? Can it be true?
Is my wife dead? Has death bred death?

**Messenger.** You can see for yourself.

(*The doors are opened, and the body of* Eurydice *is disclosed within.*)

**Creon.** Oh pity!
110   All true, all true, and more than I can bear!
O my wife, my son!

**Messenger.** She stood before the altar, and her heart
Welcomed the knife her own hand guided,
And a great cry burst from her lips for Megareus dead,
115   And for Haemon dead, her sons; and her last breath
Was a curse for their father, the murderer of her sons.
And she fell, and the dark flowed in through her closing eyes.

**Creon.** O God, I am sick with fear.
Are there no swords here? Has no one a blow for me?

120   **Messenger.** Her curse is upon you for the deaths of both.

**Creon.** It is right that it should be. I alone am guilty.
I know it, and I say it. Lead me in,
Quickly, friends.
I have neither life nor substance. Lead me in.

125   **Choragus.** You are right, if there can be right in so much wrong.
The briefest way is best in a world of sorrow.

**Creon.** Let it come;
Let death come quickly and be kind to me.
I would not ever see the sun again.

130   **Choragus.** All that will come when it will; but we, meanwhile,
Have much to do. Leave the future to itself.

**Creon.** All my heart was in that prayer!

**Choragus.** Then do not pray any more: the sky is deaf.

**Creon.** Lead me away. I have been rash and foolish.
135   I have killed my son and my wife.
I look for comfort; my comfort lies here dead.
Whatever my hands have touched has come to nothing.
Fate has brought all my pride to a thought of dust.

(*As Creon* is being led into the house, the Choragus *advances and speaks directly to the audience.*)

**Choragus.** There is no happiness where there is no wisdom;
140   No wisdom but in submission to the gods.
Big words are always punished,
And proud men in old age learn to be wise.

## Connect to the Literature

1. **What Do You Think?** How did you react to what happens at the end of this play? Share your thoughts with a classmate.

   **Comprehension Check**
   • What does Antigone do against Creon's wishes?
   • How does Creon punish Antigone?
   • How does Antigone die?

## Think Critically

2. How much do you think Creon is to blame for the suicides of Antigone, Haemon, and Eurydice?

   **THINK ABOUT**
   • Creon's judgment of himself at the end
   • how Haemon and Eurydice feel about Creon at the moment of death
   • Creon's failed effort to rescue Antigone

3. What do you think is the main reason that Creon and Antigone cannot resolve their **conflict**?

   **THINK ABOUT**
   • the principles that motivate each character
   • the attitude of each character toward the gods
   • any flaws or defects exhibited by each character

4. How do the **minor characters**—such as Ismene, Teiresias, Haemon, and Eurydice—help you to understand and evaluate the actions of Antigone and Creon?

5. **ACTIVE READING** **STRATEGIES FOR READING CLASSICAL DRAMA** Compare the notes in your **READER'S NOTEBOOK** with those of a classmate. Discuss which of the strategies listed on page 1019 were most useful. How did you modify your reading strategies when your understanding broke down?

## Extend Interpretations

6. **The Writer's Style** Throughout *Antigone*, Sophocles makes **allusions** to myths that his original audience would have been familiar with. With a partner, research the full story of one of these myths. Then write an explanation of how the myth relates to the story of Antigone and why you think Sophocles included the allusion.

7. **Connect to Life** Which of the **themes**, or messages, conveyed by Sophocles do you think is most relevant today?

## Literary Analysis

**CLASSICAL DRAMA** Two aspects of **classical drama**, or the theater of ancient Greece, that are frequently still debated today are the role of the **chorus** and the concept of the **tragic hero.** Often, critics and scholars disagree with one another about how to interpret the comments of the chorus. Disagreement also arises about how to apply the concept of the tragic hero.

**Paired Activity** Review the information about classical drama on page 1019. Then discuss the following questions:
• Who do you think best fits the definition of a tragic hero, Antigone or Creon?
• How do the chorus and its leader, the **choragus,** influence your understanding of Antigone and Creon?
• How do the choral **odes** contribute to your understanding of the play's **themes?**
Use evidence from the text to support your answer.

**REVIEW** **DRAMATIC IRONY**
**Dramatic irony** occurs when readers or viewers are aware of information that a character is unaware of. For example, Creon tells Antigone, "That [her death] gives me everything." Once you know the outcome of the play, you realize that Antigone's death will take from Creon all that is meaningful in his life. This contrast between Creon's limited knowledge and your fuller understanding generates dramatic irony.

With a small group of classmates, find and explain other examples of dramatic irony in *Antigone.*

# Choices & CHALLENGES

## Writing Options

**1. Letter to a Character** Compare the way you ranked the principles listed in the Connect to Your Life activity on page 1018 with the way you think Antigone, Creon, or some other character in the play would rank them. Then write a letter to that character, either in support of or in opposition to his or her decisions and behavior.

**2. Diary Entry** Think about how one of the minor characters—such as Ismene, the sentry, or Teiresias—might have viewed what happened to Antigone. Write a diary entry expressing the thoughts and feelings of this character.

**3. Report on Athenian Women** At various times in *Antigone*, Creon's remarks show his attitude toward having his authority challenged by a woman. With a partner, research the typical role of noblewomen in Athens during the fifth century B.C. Working collaboratively, write a short report on this topic. Place the report in your **Working Portfolio.**

## Activities & Explorations

**1. Readers Theater** With a group of classmates, perform a Readers Theater production of a scene from this play. Sit in chairs at the front of the classroom and take turns reading the parts. Choose whether you want to present the scene in the formal manner of the ancient Greek theater or in a more contemporary style. ~ **PERFORMING**

**2. Tragedy Mask** Create a mask to be worn in a production of *Antigone.* You may research the masks worn in ancient Greek productions or create your own original version. ~ **ART**

**3. Antigone on Film** Watch the video clip of the opening scene of the play. How does the setting compare with the way you visualized the palace as you read? Do Antigone and Ismene play their roles as you imagined? Discuss your views with a small group of classmates. ~ **VIEWING AND REPRESENTING**

**VIDEO** **Side by Side: Literature in Performance**

## Inquiry & Research

**Comparing Translations** Locate one or two other translations of *Antigone.* Choose a passage from the play, and compare the different versions. With a small group of classmates, discuss which translation you find most effective and why.

## Vocabulary in Action

**EXERCISE: MEANING CLUES** Answer the questions that follow.

1. Is a **dirge** a piece of music that is sad, joyful, or complicated?
2. Are people who **transgress** a law those who make it, break it, or enforce it?
3. Would a person's appetite be **sated** by the smell of food, a light snack, or a large meal?
4. Is an **edict** a request, a command, or a question?
5. Would **lamentation** be most expected after a tragedy, a dinner party, or a graduation?
6. Does a person **defile** a lake by photographing it, polluting it, or stocking it with fish?
7. When is it most important to be **lithe**—while competing in a spelling bee, lifting weights, or performing gymnastics?
8. If people demonstrate **compulsive** behavior, is what they do rude, sympathetic, or beyond their control?
9. Is a person most likely to respond to **auspicious** events by feeling encouraged, frightened, or exhausted?
10. If a child was described to you as being **perverse,** would you expect the child to be angelic, disobedient, or shy?

**Building Vocabulary**

For an in-depth lesson on connotation and denotation, see page 494.

## Grammar in Context: Inverted Sentences

Notice where the translator of *Antigone* places the subject and its verb in each of these excerpts.

> **Chorus.** Numberless are the world's wonders, but none
> More wonderful than man; . . .

> **Chorus.** Fortunate is the man who has never tasted God's vengeance!

One way in which expert writers vary their sentences to make their writing more interesting is by changing the order of subjects and verbs. In most sentences subjects come before verbs, but in the sentences above, the verbs (in blue type) are placed before the subjects (in red type). Sentences like these are called **inverted sentences.** They can give a formal tone to writing and can be used to create poetic effects.

**WRITING EXERCISE** Rewrite each sentence, placing the main verb before the subject.

*Usage Tip:* When writing an inverted sentence, make sure the subject agrees in number with the verb.

**Example: *Original*** Creon is merciless in dealing with his dead nephew Polyneices.

***Rewritten*** Merciless <u>is Creon</u> in dealing with his dead nephew Polyneices.

1. Antigone pleads passionately with Ismene for help in burying their dead brother.
2. Creon, king of Thebes, is cruel.
3. The sentry who found Polyneices buried is frightened.
4. Antigone speaks eloquently when she is brought before Creon.

<u>**Grammar Handbook**</u>  Subject-Verb Agreement, p. 1200

## Sophocles
### 496?–406 B.C.

**Other Works**
*Ajax*
*Oedipus the King*
*Electra*
*Oedipus at Colonus*
*Trachinian Women*
*Philoctetes*

**Chorus Leader** Born near Athens in the village of Colonus, Sophocles was the son of a wealthy manu-facturer of armor. In his youth, he received a fine education and was said to be skilled in wrestling, dancing, and playing the lyre. These skills and a handsome appearance apparently led to his being chosen to lead a chorus in a celebration of the Greek victory over the Persians at the Battle of Salamis.

**Festival Winner** In 468 B.C., Sophocles defeated his teacher, the great playwright Aeschylus (ĕs′kə-ləs), in the Dionysian dramatic festival, an annual compe-tition. That first-place award was followed by as many as 23 other victories, more than any other Greek playwright. Sophocles also was active in the political life of Athens. He was elected several times

to the body of high executives commanding the mili-tary and was one of ten commissioners in charge of helping Athens recover after a severe military defeat in Sicily. In 406 B.C., the year of his death, he led a chorus of public mourners in honor of Euripides (yōō-rĭp′ĭ-dēz′), a younger playwright who had often been his rival at the annual drama festivals.

**Missing Work** Sophocles wrote more than 100 plays, although only 7 of them survive today. *Antigone,* which rivals *Oedipus the King* as his best-known play, was probably first performed in 442 or 441 B.C. *Oedipus at Colonus,* which shows the playwright's affection for his native village, was written when Sophocles was around 90.

## Author Activity

**Classical Age** Sophocles lived during a period often described as the pinnacle of ancient Athens. Research why this is the case, and find out what fate befell the city the year after Sophocles' death.

# PREPARING to *Read*

## *from* Le Morte d'Arthur
# The Crowning of Arthur
# Sir Launcelot du Lake

*Romance by* SIR THOMAS MALORY
*Retold by* KEITH BAINES

### ( Connect to Your Life )

**Round Table Discussion** In a small-group discussion, share what you know about the legend of King Arthur and his knights of the Round Table. What types of actions do you associate with Arthurian knights? What do you know about their ideals and motives? What personal qualities do they exhibit?

## Build Background

**Legendary King** According to legend, Arthur became king of England and established his court at Camelot. He then gathered the best knights of the realm to join with him in the fellowship of the Round Table. These knights lived according to a specific code of behavior—the chivalric code—which stressed, among other things, loyalty to the king, courage, personal honor, and defending those who could not defend themselves. The most famous model of chivalry was Sir Launcelot, Arthur's friend and the greatest knight of the Round Table.

The earliest tales of Arthur come from Welsh literature of the 6th through 12th centuries. Most English-speaking readers know of the Arthurian legend through Sir Thomas Malory's *Le Morte d'Arthur* ("The Death of Arthur"), completed about 1470, or one of its many adaptations. The excerpts you are about to read are from Keith Baines's modern retelling of *Le Morte d'Arthur.*

WORDS TO KNOW
**Vocabulary Preview**
adversary        prowess
champion        recompense
fidelity

## Focus Your Reading

**LITERARY ANALYSIS** **ROMANCE** In the Middle Ages in Europe, wandering storytellers would retell adventurous tales of knights and other noble heroes. Such tales were known as **romances,** and, by Malory's time, they had moved from the oral tradition into written versions. Like other medieval romances, *Le Morte d'Arthur* recounts the heroic deeds of noble knights and celebrates the chivalric code of honor.

**ACTIVE READING** **MAKING JUDGMENTS** The chivalric code is of great importance in the world Malory describes. For example, the code states that knights must be courteous to their opponents. This principle leads Sir Tarquine to pay the following compliment to his opponent in a joust:

*"That was a fine stroke; now let us try again."*

However, some characters live up to the ideals of the code better than others.

**READER'S NOTEBOOK** As you read, **make judgments** about the **main characters** on the basis of how well you think they follow the chivalric code of honor. Record your thoughts about each character in a chart like the one shown. Mark with a check whether you think the character lives up to, or falls short of, each aspect of the code listed.

| Chivalric Code | Character: Uther | |
| --- | --- | --- |
|  | Lives up to code | Falls short of code |
| Honorable |  |  |
| Chaste |  |  |
| Loyal |  |  |
| Courageous |  |  |
| Truthful |  |  |
| Courteous |  |  |

# The Crowning of Arthur

from **Le Morte d'Arthur**
**Sir Thomas Malory**

King Uther Pendragon,[1] ruler of all Britain, had been at war for many years with the Duke of Tintagil in Cornwall when he was told of the beauty of Lady Igraine,[2] the duke's wife. Thereupon he called a truce and invited the duke and Igraine to his court, where he prepared a feast for them, and where, as soon as they arrived, he was formally reconciled to the duke through the good offices[3] of his courtiers.

In the course of the feast, King Uther grew passionately desirous of Igraine and, when it was over, begged her to become his paramour.[4] Igraine, however, being as naturally loyal as she was beautiful, refused him.

---

1. **Uther Pendragon** (ōō'thər pĕn-drăg'ən): *Pendragon* was a title used in ancient Britain to refer to a supreme chief or leader.
2. **Igraine** (ē-grān').
3. **offices:** services.
4. **paramour** (păr'ə-mōōr'): lover or mistress.

The Granger Collection, New York.

"I suppose," said Igraine to her husband, the duke, when this had happened, "that the king arranged this truce only because he wanted to make me his mistress. I suggest that we leave at once, without warning, and ride overnight to our castle." The duke agreed with her, and they left the court secretly.

The king was enraged by Igraine's flight and summoned his privy council.[5] They advised him to command the fugitives' return under threat of renewing the war; but when this was done, the duke and Igraine defied his summons. He then warned them that they could expect to be dragged from their castle within six weeks.

The duke manned and provisioned[6] his two strongest castles: Tintagil for Igraine, and Terrabyl, which was useful for its many sally ports,[7] for himself. Soon King Uther arrived with a huge army and laid siege to Terrabyl; but despite the ferocity of the fighting, and the numerous casualties suffered by both sides, neither was able to gain a decisive victory.

Still enraged, and now despairing, King Uther fell sick. His friend Sir Ulfius came to him and asked what the trouble was. "Igraine has broken my heart," the king replied, "and unless I can win her, I shall never recover."

"Sire," said Sir Ulfius, "surely Merlin the Prophet could find some means to help you? I will go in search of him."

Sir Ulfius had not ridden far when he was accosted by a hideous beggar. "For whom are you searching?" asked the beggar; but Sir Ulfius ignored him.

"Very well," said the beggar, "I will tell you: you are searching for Merlin, and you need look no further, for I am he. Now go to King Uther and tell him that I will make Igraine his if he will reward me as I ask; and even that will be more to his benefit than to mine."

"I am sure," said Sir Ulfius, "that the king will refuse you nothing reasonable."

"Then go, and I shall follow you," said Merlin. Well pleased, Sir Ulfius galloped back to the king and delivered Merlin's message, which he had hardly completed when Merlin himself appeared at the entrance to the pavilion. The king bade him welcome.

"Sire," said Merlin, "I know that you are in love with Igraine; will you swear, as an anointed[8] king, to give into my care the child that she bears you, if I make her yours?"

The king swore on the gospel that he would do so, and Merlin continued: "Tonight you shall appear before Igraine at Tintagil in the likeness of her husband, the duke. Sir Ulfius and I will appear as two of the duke's knights: Sir Brastius and Sir Jordanus. Do not question either Igraine or her men, but say that you are sick and retire to bed. I will fetch you early in the morning, and do not rise until I come; fortunately Tintagil is only ten miles from here."

The plan succeeded: Igraine was completely deceived by the king's impersonation of the duke, and gave herself to him, and conceived Arthur. The king left her at dawn as soon as Merlin appeared, after giving her a farewell kiss. But the duke had seen King Uther ride out from the siege on the previous night and, in the course of making a surprise attack on the king's army, had been killed. When Igraine realized that the duke had died three hours before he had appeared to her, she was greatly disturbed in mind; however, she confided in no one.

Once it was known that the duke was dead, the king's nobles urged him to be reconciled to Igraine, and this task the king gladly entrusted to Sir Ulfius, by whose eloquence it was soon accomplished. "And now," said Sir Ulfius to his fellow nobles, "why should not the king marry the beautiful Igraine? Surely it would be as well for us all."

---

5. **privy** (prĭv′ē) **council:** a group of advisors who serve a ruler.

6. **provisioned:** supplied.

7. **sally ports:** gates or passages in the walls of fortifications, from which troops can make a sudden attack.

8. **anointed:** chosen as if by divine intervention.

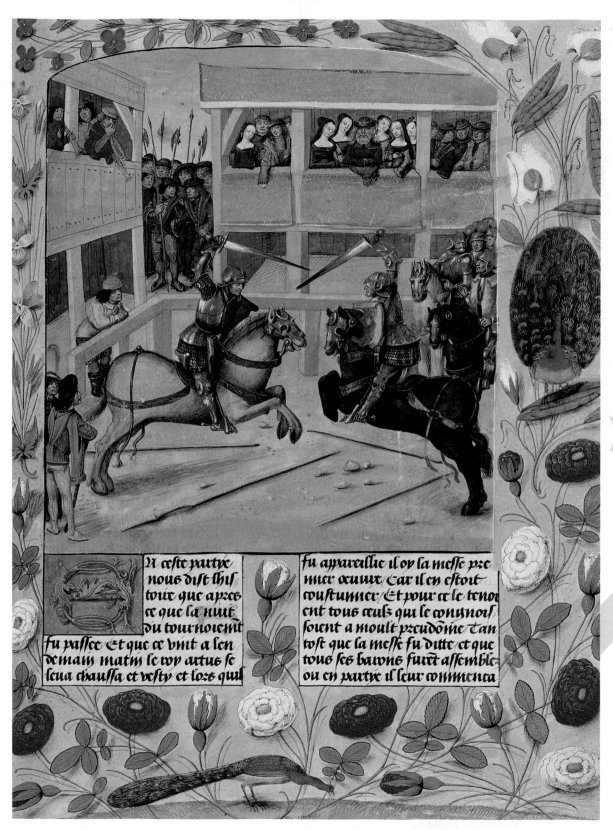

A ceste partie nous dist lh$\gamma$ tour que apres ce que la nuit du tournoiemt fu passee et que ce vint a len demam matm le roy artus se leua chaussa et vesty et lors quil fu appareillie il oy la messe pre mier ceuur car il en estoit coustumier Et pour ce le tenoi ent tous ceus qui le connois soient a moult preudome tan tost que la messe fu ditte et que tous ses barons furet assemble ou en partie il leur commenca

Tournament in King Arthur's court. MS Douce 383, fol. 16r. The Bodleian Library, Oxford, England.

# Sir Launcelot du Lake

from Le Morte d'Arthur
Sir Thomas Malory

When King Arthur returned from Rome, he settled his court at Camelot, and there gathered about him his knights of the Round Table, who diverted themselves with jousting and tournaments. Of all his knights one was supreme, both in prowess at arms and in nobility of bearing, and this was Sir Launcelot, who was also the favorite of Queen Gwynevere, to whom he had sworn oaths of fidelity.

One day Sir Launcelot, feeling weary of his life at the court, and of only playing at arms, decided to set forth in search of adventure. He asked his nephew Sir Lyonel to accompany him, and when both were suitably armed and mounted, they rode off together through the forest.

At noon they started across a plain, but the intensity of the sun made Sir Launcelot feel sleepy, so Sir Lyonel suggested that they should rest

WORDS TO KNOW

**prowess** (prou'ĭs) *n.* superior strength, courage, or daring, especially in battle
**fidelity** (fĭ-dĕl'ĭ-tē) *n.* faithfulness to duties and obligations; devotion; loyalty

and, coming upon a red silk pavilion, apparently unoccupied, decided to rest there overnight and continue his search in the morning.

He had not been asleep for more than an hour, however, when the knight who owned the pavilion returned and got straight into bed with him. Having made an assignation[6] with his paramour, the knight supposed at first that Sir Launcelot was she and, taking him into his arms, started kissing him. Sir Launcelot awoke with a start and, seizing his sword, leaped out of bed and out of the pavilion, pursued closely by the other knight. Once in the open they set to with their swords, and before long Sir Launcelot had wounded his unknown adversary so seriously that he was obliged to yield.

The knight, whose name was Sir Belleus, now asked Sir Launcelot how he came to be sleeping in his bed and then explained how he had an assignation with his lover, adding:

"But now I am so sorely wounded that I shall consider myself fortunate to escape with my life."

"Sir, please forgive me for wounding you; but lately I escaped from an enchantment, and I was afraid that once more I had been betrayed. Let us go into the pavilion, and I will staunch your wound."

Sir Launcelot had just finished binding the wound when the young noblewoman who was Sir Belleus's paramour arrived and, seeing the wound, at once rounded in fury on Sir Launcelot.

"Peace, my love," said Sir Belleus. "This is a noble knight, and as soon as I yielded to him, he treated my wound with the greatest care." Sir Belleus then described the events which had led up to the duel.

"Sir, pray tell me your name, and whose knight you are," the young noblewoman asked Sir Launcelot.

"My lady, I am called Sir Launcelot du Lake."

"As I guessed, both from your appearance and from your speech; and indeed I know you

Lancelot rescuing Guinevere by crossing the sword bridge (about 1300). From *Le Roman de Lancelot du Lac*, M. 806, f. 166, The Pierpont Morgan Library, New York/Art Resource, New York.

better than you realize. But I ask you, in recompense for the injury you have done my lord, and out of the courtesy for which you are famous, to recommend Sir Belleus to King Arthur, and suggest that he be made one of the knights of the Round Table. I can assure you that my lord deserves it, being only less than yourself as a man-at-arms, and sovereign of many of the Outer Isles."

"My lady, let Sir Belleus come to Arthur's court at the next Pentecost. Make sure that you come

---

6. **assignation** (ăs′ĭg-nā′shən): an appointment for a meeting between lovers.

| WORDS TO KNOW | **adversary** (ăd′vər-sĕr′ē) *n.* an opponent; enemy<br>**recompense** (rĕk′əm-pĕns′) *n.* amends made, as for damage or loss; payment in return for something, such as a service |
| --- | --- |

with him, and I promise I will do what I can for him; and if he is as good a man-at-arms as you say he is, I am sure Arthur will accept him."

As soon as it was daylight, Sir Launcelot armed, mounted, and rode away in search of the abbey, which he found in less than two hours. King Bagdemagus's daughter was waiting for him and, as soon as she heard his horse's footsteps in the yard, ran to the window and, seeing that it was Sir Launcelot, herself ordered the servants to stable his horse. She then led him to her chamber, disarmed him, and gave him a long gown to wear, welcoming him warmly as she did so.

King Bagdemagus's castle was twelve miles away, and his daughter sent for him as soon as she had settled Sir Launcelot. The king arrived with his retinue[7] and embraced Sir Launcelot, who then described his recent enchantment, and the great obligation he was under to his daughter for releasing him.

"Sir, you will fight for me on Tuesday next?"

"Sire, I shall not fail you; but please tell me the names of the three Round Table knights whom I shall be fighting."

"Sir Modred, Sir Madore de la Porte, and Sir Gahalantyne. I must admit that last Tuesday they defeated me and my knights completely."

"Sire, I hear that the tournament is to be fought within three miles of the abbey. Could you send me three of your most trustworthy knights, clad in plain armor, and with no device,[8] and a fourth suit of armor which I

7. **retinue** (rĕt′n-ōō): attendants.

8. **device**: a design, often a motto, on a coat of arms.

## Grammar in Context: Creating Subject-Verb Splits

In this sentence from *Le Morte d'Arthur,* a descriptive element appears between the subject and the verb.

**subject**
One day Sir Launcelot, feeling weary of his life at the court, and of only playing at arms, decided to **verb** set forth in search of adventure.

Expert writers sometimes make their writing more interesting by adding descriptive details to the beginning, middle, or end of simple sentences. When a descriptive element is inserted between the subject and the verb of a sentence, the sentence is said to contain a **subject-verb split.** In the example above, the subject and verb are separated by a participial phrase (shown in blue) that indicates why Sir Launcelot went off in search of adventure. Participial phrases are not, however, the only grammatical structures that can come between subjects and verbs;

others include appositive phrases, adjective clauses, and adverb clauses.

***Punctuation Tip:*** In a sentence containing a subject-verb split, the element that comes between the subject and the verb is usually set off with commas.

**WRITING EXERCISE** Rewrite each sentence, creating a subject-verb split by correctly inserting the words in parentheses between the subject and the verb.

**Example:** *Original* King Uther Pendragon has been at war for many years. (ruler of all Britain)

***Rewritten*** King Uther Pendragon, ruler of all Britain, has been at war for many years.

1. Lady Igraine's beauty is brought to the attention of King Uther. (which many people admire)
2. Merlin makes the king look like the Duke of Tintagil. (after he gets Uther to pledge him a child)
3. Young Arthur is declared to be the rightful heir to the throne. (having removed the sword from the stone)

**Grammar Handbook** Punctuation, p. 1203

## Sir Thomas Malory
1405?–1471

**A Knight Himself** The man who wrote *Le Morte d'Arthur* called himself "Syr Thomas Maleore, knyght." He also indicated that he completed this work in the ninth year of Edward IV's reign (1469 or 1470), and he added a prayer that he be safely delivered from prison. Although his precise identity remains uncertain, most scholars feel that he is Sir Thomas Malory (1405?–1471), a knight from the English county of Warwickshire who led a life of adventure at the end of the Middle Ages.

**Behind Bars** As a youth, Malory served bravely in battle under the Earl of Warwick, fighting for England during the final years of the Hundred Years' War with France. He inherited his father's

estates in 1433 or 1434 and about a decade later represented Warwickshire in Parliament. In 1451, however, he was arrested and jailed for violently entering and robbing an abbey. Malory was imprisoned several more times in the next decade, accused of crimes such as cattle theft, highway robbery, and attempted murder, though the charges may have been politically motivated. Twice he escaped from prison but was recaptured. In 1462 he joined rebels opposing King Edward IV in the civil war known as the Wars of the Roses. Imprisoned for treason in 1468, he was specifically excluded from the pardons Edward granted to many of the other rebels. He spent the remainder of his life in London's Newgate Prison, where he apparently occupied his time by writing *Le Morte d'Arthur.* The work was published in 1485, 14 years after his death.

# from The Mists of Avalon

*Romance by* MARION ZIMMER BRADLEY

## Connect to Your Life

**New Arrivals** What effect can the arrival of a baby brother or sister have on an older sibling? Imagine how you would react if such a circumstance occurred. If you actually have a younger brother or sister, recall how you reacted when he or she was born. Share your thoughts with a classmate.

## Build Background

**Morgan le Fay** The character Morgaine in Bradley's novel *The Mists of Avalon* is based on Morgan le Fay, one of the more mysterious figures in the Arthurian legends. Her name comes from the Irish word *morrigain,* which means "great queen," and the French words *le fée,* which mean "the fairy." She probably originated in several myths about pagan goddesses. Some legends portray Morgan as a benevolent healer, but others portray her as a sorceress who plots against King Arthur and his wife. In the tradition that Bradley follows, she is Arthur's half-sister. Their mother, Igraine, (ē-grān'), married Arthur's father, Uther Pendragon (o͞o' thər pĕn-drăg' ən), after the death of her first husband, Gorlois (gôr-loiz' ).

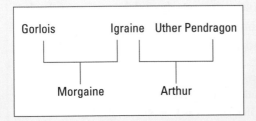

## Focus Your Reading

**LITERARY ANALYSIS** **FIRST-PERSON POINT OF VIEW** When a character who participates in a story also narrates the action, the writer is using the **first-person point of view.** The events in this excerpt are told by the character Morgaine:

> *I think that my first real memory is of my mother's wedding to Uther Pendragon. I remember my father only a little.*

A first-person **narrator** is able to give the reader an eyewitness account of the events in a story. As you read this selection, notice how Morgaine expresses her feelings about each of the characters.

**ACTIVE READING** **ANALYZING CHARACTERS** Bradley's modern retelling of Arthurian legend involves revision of traditional versions of the story, presenting views of Arthurian characters that are quite different from those in previous versions. As you read, be aware of what you learn about each character, including the narrator. Remember that since Morgaine narrates this selection, all of our information is colored by her judgment.

**READER'S NOTEBOOK** Create a word web, like the one shown, for each of these characters: Uther, Arthur, Igraine, and the narrator. Use the web to analyze what you learn about each character and Morgaine's feelings about him or her. In the case of Morgaine herself, include information about how she views herself.

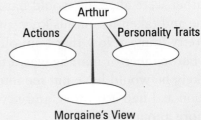

*from*

# THE MISTS OF AVALON

## MARION ZIMMER BRADLEY

*Morgan Le Fay*, Aubrey Beardsley.
Courtesy of the Newberry Library,
Chicago.

### Morgaine speaks . . .

I think that my first real memory is of my mother's wedding to Uther Pendragon. I remember my father only a little. When I was unhappy as a little girl, I seemed to remember him, a heavyset man with a dark beard and dark hair; I remember playing with a chain he wore about his neck. I remember that as a little maiden when I was unhappy, when I was chidden[1] by my mother or my teachers, or when Uther—rarely—noticed me to disapprove of me, I used to comfort myself by thinking that if my own father were alive, he would have been fond of me and taken me on his knee and brought me pretty things. Now that I am older and know what manner of man he was, I think it more likely he would have put me into a nunnery as soon as I had a brother, and never thought more about me.

Not that Uther was ever unkind to me; it was simply that he had no particular interest in a girl child. My mother was always at the center of his heart, and he at hers, and so I resented that—that I had lost my mother to this great fair-haired, boorish[2] man. When Uther was away in battle—and there was battle a good deal of the time when I was a maiden—my mother Igraine cherished me and petted me, and taught me to spin with her own hands and to weave in colors. But when Uther's men were sighted, then I went back into my rooms and was forgotten until he went away again. Is it any wonder I hated him and resented, with all my heart, the sight of the dragon banner on any horsemen approaching Tintagel?[3]

And when my brother was born it was worse. For there was this crying thing, all pink and white, at my mother's breast; and it was worse that she expected me to care as much for him as she did. "This is your little brother," she said, "take good care of him, Morgaine, and love him." Love him? I hated him with all my heart, for now when I came near her she would pull away and tell me that I was a big girl, too big to be sitting in her lap, too big to bring my ribbons to her for tying, too big to come and lay my head on her knees for comfort. I would have pinched him, except that she would have hated me for it. I sometimes thought she hated me anyhow. And Uther made much of my brother. But I think he always hoped for another son. I was never told, but somehow I knew—maybe I heard the women talking, maybe I was gifted even then with more of the Sight[4] than I realized—that

---

1. **chidden:** scolded.
2. **boorish:** rude; ill-mannered.
3. **Tintagel** (tĭn-tăj′əl): a castle in Wales—the legendary birthplace of King Arthur.
4. **the Sight:** a supernatural ability to see future, past, or faraway events.

he had first lain with my mother when she was still wedded to Gorlois, and there were still those who believed that this son was not Uther's but the son of the Duke of Cornwall.

How they could believe that, I could not then understand, for Gorlois, they said, was dark and aquiline,[5] and my brother was like Uther, fair-haired, with grey eyes.

Even during the lifetime of my brother, who was crowned king as Arthur, I heard all kinds of tales about how he came by his name. Even the tale that it was from Arth-Uther, Uther's bear; but it was not so. When he was a babe, he was called Gwydion[6]—bright one—because of his shining hair; the same name his son bore later—but that is another story. The facts are simple: when Gwydion was six years old he was sent to be fostered by Ectorius, one of Uther's vassals[7] in the North country near Eboracum,[8] and Uther would have it that my brother should be baptized as a Christian. And so he was given the name of Arthur.

But from his birth until he was six years old, he was forever at my heels; as soon as he was weaned, my mother, Igraine, handed him over to me and said, "This is your little brother and you must love him and care for him." And I would have killed the crying thing and thrown him over the cliffs, and run after my mother begging that she should be all mine again, except that my mother cared what happened to him.

Once, when Uther came and she decked herself in her best gown, as she always did, with her amber and moonstone necklaces, and looked down on me with a careless kiss for me and one for my little brother, ready to run down to Uther, I looked at her glowing cheeks—heightened with color, her breathing quickened with delight that her man had come—and hated both Uther and my brother. And while I stood weeping at the top of the stairs, waiting for our nurse to come and take us away, he began to toddle down after her, crying out, "Mother,

Mother"—he could hardly talk, then—and fell and cut his chin on the stair. I screamed for my mother, but she was on her way to the King, and she called back angrily, "Morgaine, I told you, look after the baby," and hurried on.

I picked him up, bawling, and wiped his chin with my veil. He had cut his lip on his tooth—I think he had only eight or ten, then—and he kept on wailing and calling out for my mother, but when she did not come, I sat down on the step with him in my lap, and he put up his little arms around my neck and buried his face in my tunic[9] and after a time he sobbed himself to sleep there. He was heavy on my lap, and his hair felt soft and damp; he was damp elsewhere, too, but I found I did not mind much, and in the way he clung to me I realized that in his sleep he had forgotten he was not in his mother's arms. I thought, *Igraine has forgotten both of us, abandoned him as she abandoned me. Now I must be his mother, I suppose.*

And so I shook him a little, and when he woke, he put up his little arms around my neck to be carried, and I slung him across my hip as I had seen my nurse do.

"Don't cry," I said, "I'll take you to nurse."

"Mother," he whimpered.

"Mother's gone, she's with the King," I said, "but I'll take care of you, brother." And with his chubby hand in mine I knew what Igraine meant; I was too big a girl to cry or whimper for my mother, because I had a little one to look after now.

I think I was all of seven years old. ❖

---

5. **aquiline** (ăk′wə-līn′): having a prominent nose, like an eagle's beak.

6. **Gwydion** (gwĭd′ē-ən).

7. **vassals** (văs′əlz): nobles subject to a king or lord.

8. **Eboracum** (ĭ-bôr′ə-kəm): the ancient Roman name for the city of York in England.

9. **tunic**: a loose-fitting garment, with or without sleeves, that extends to the knees.

## Connect to the Literature

1. **What Do You Think?** Which **character** do you find most sympathetic? Give reasons for your choice.

**Comprehension Check**
- How is Morgaine related to Uther and Arthur?
- What changes occur in Morgaine's life after Arthur is born?
- What does Morgaine feel she has in common with Arthur?

## Think Critically

2. **ACTIVE READING**  **ANALYZING CHARACTERS**  Based on the information provided by Morgaine, what opinions did you form of Arthur, Uther, Igraine, and the narrator herself? Use the character webs in your  **READER'S NOTEBOOK** to support your **analysis** of each **character.** Consider how your opinion was influenced by Morgaine's judgment.

3. Do you consider Morgaine a **static** or **dynamic character?** Explain your answer.

   THINK ABOUT
   - her behavior toward Arthur
   - her thoughts about herself
   - her relationship with her mother

4. Why do you think that Igraine begins to pull away whenever Morgaine approaches her?

5. What do you think of the way Igraine and Uther treat their children? Explain your answer.

## Extend Interpretations

6. **Comparing Texts**  This selection describes many of the events recounted in "The Crowning of Arthur." What differences do you see between the two selections?

7. **Critic's Corner**  Critic Charlotte Spivack maintains that *The Mists of Avalon* is "probably the most ambitious retelling of the Arthurian legend in the 20th century." Why do you think so many modern writers return to Arthurian legend for their stories?

8. **Connect to Life**  Based on your reading of this selection, what modern concerns do you think Bradley has in mind in her retelling of the Arthurian legend?

## Literary Analysis

**FIRST-PERSON POINT OF VIEW**
In the **first-person point of view,** a character within the story relates the action as a participant. Because of this, the **narrator** cannot describe with certainty the thoughts and feelings of other characters. In this selection, Morgaine often expresses confusion about her mother's feelings, as in the following example:

*I would have pinched him [Arthur], except that she would have hated me for it. I sometimes thought she hated me anyhow.*

Readers sometimes have to be skeptical about a first-person narrator's remarks because he or she may lack objectivity or understanding.

**Paired Activity**  With a partner, write down a list of incidents that the narrator describes. Discuss whether the narrator is objective about each of the incidents and whether she has a good understanding of the events. Use elements from the text to defend your response.

**ACTIVE READING  COMPARING AND CONTRASTING**

When the same character appears in two different versions of a story, we can often gain insight into the writers' views by **comparing** and **contrasting** how that character is portrayed in each work. With a partner, discuss the similarities and differences between the portrayals of Uther Pendragon in *Le Morte d'Arthur* and *The Mists of Avalon.* To guide your discussion, go back over each selection and consider the following:
- the character's traits
- the character's actions
- the narrator's attitude

## Writing Options

**Another View** Using Igraine, Uther, or Arthur as the narrator, retell one of the incidents described by Morgaine. Before you begin, consider your narrator's personality traits and how he or she feels about the other characters.

## Activities & Explorations

**1. Igraine's Monologue** Think about how Morgaine's mother might explain her actions and her relationship with her daughter. Review the selection, paying attention to how Igraine might interpret the events portrayed. Then perform a monologue in which you give her side of the story. After your performance, ask for audience feedback on the verbal and nonverbal aspects of your monologue.
**~ PERFORMING**

**2. Comic Strip** Create a four-panel comic strip about Morgaine's experiences growing up in Uther's household. Your comic strip may refer to incidents described in the selection or to incidents you have imagined.
**~ VIEWING AND REPRESENTING**

## Inquiry & Research

**Mysterious Wizard** Every retelling of Arthurian legend includes Merlin, but the ways in which the wizard is portrayed vary greatly. Find out more about this legendary character and the different ways he has been characterized.

 **Real World Link** Start your research by reading the magazine article by Bradley on page 1088.

---

## Marion Zimmer Bradley

1930–

**Other Works**
*The Shattered Chain*
*The Firebrand*
*Lady of Avalon*

**From Fan to Writer** Marion Zimmer Bradley grew up on a farm in upstate New York. Her mother, a historian, encouraged her love for reading. Bradley wrote science fiction and fantasy stories as a teenager. In 1949 she married a fellow science-fiction fan named Robert Bradley. Soon afterward she started writing professionally to help support her family.

**Exploring Other Worlds** Bradley has published over 50 books in the science fiction and fantasy genres. Her career took off in the early 1960s with a series of novels set on "Darkover," a harsh, cold planet settled by colonists from Earth. The Darkover books are so popular that they have inspired story collections in which other writers set their tales on Bradley's fictional planet. In addition to writing fiction, Bradley has edited anthologies and magazines.

**Arthurian Legends** *The Mists of Avalon* was Bradley's first mainstream bestseller. Her fascination with the Arthurian legends goes back to her childhood, when she was introduced to them in a comic book series called Prince Valiant. She says that "the legends were a lot more interesting than the farming community where we lived." Bradley has written other books focusing on the Arthurian female characters.

# THE ONCE AND FUTURE
## *Merlin*

by Marion Zimmer Bradley

*When the miniseries* Merlin *brought the Arthurian legend to television, Marion Zimmer Bradley wrote this background article for* TV Guide. *The article describes Merlin as a split character—both good and not so good—who has a role outside of literature in the popular culture.*

❶ Of all the characters in the Arthurian saga, only Arthur and Merlin are immortal in any sense other than the literary. Arthur, of course, is the warrior, the king who was and who will be, who lies in enchanted slumber until Britain has need of him again. Merlin is something else entirely, something much more mysterious.

❷ Over the centuries the story has been told and retold and told again, often with a widely varying cast of characters. Knights, priests and priestesses, kings and queens, and various users of magic come and go, but always there is Arthur, the sun around which all else revolves: his faithless wife (Guinevere), his equally faithless best friend (Lancelot), the illegitimate son (Mordred) who becomes his bane[1]—and Merlin. Whatever his role, Merlin is always there, and it is always clear that Arthur could not have existed, survived, or become king without him. But Merlin's role is mostly in the background. He's visible, but no one is quite certain exactly what he has done or is doing. If Arthur is the sun, perhaps Merlin is gravity, keeping the dance of the spheres in place and at tempo, or trying to do so and occasionally failing in spots—after all, it's such a great task.

❸ When the story starts, Arthur is the new character, the simple, straightforward young boy, young man, warrior and king. All of his roles are well defined. He is the light and the Christian, the champion of the New Religion. . . . Merlin is the old one—even as a young man—the magic, the enigma. . . . Merlin works by dark and in secret; even when you see him, you never know what he's up to. He's a wizard, and trickery is part of his job. He may have been created to save the Old Religion, but if he saved any of it, it was only a small part hidden away somewhere—in an oak tree, perhaps? One is never sure of Merlin's goals, let alone his actions or beliefs.

---

1. **bane:** a cause of death or destruction.

## Reading for Information

This article falls into an unusual category of written work: it is a nonfiction piece about a famous fictional literary figure. When reading any nonfictional material that is complex or for which you have a limited background, it is helpful to stop at times to put what you are reading into your own words.

### SUMMARIZING

A **summary,** a shortened version of a text put into the reader's own words, helps you to better understand the content, because you only restate the most important points.

**YOUR TURN** Use the questions that follow to help you summarize the writer's ideas.

❶ **Identifying the Main Idea** In the first paragraph, Bradley introduces the topic of her article. Identify the **main idea** of the paragraph.

❷ **Paraphrasing** In summarizing nonfiction, you zero in on major points and leave out unimportant ones. Bradley uses details in this paragraph to support the main idea. Paraphrase the most important point she makes about Merlin here.

❸ In this section, Bradley contrasts her view of Merlin with the accepted views of Arthur. She states that "Merlin is the old one—even as a young man—the magic, the enigma [mystery]." Identify other specific details that support the main idea.

Merlin was the man (assuming he was a man) who came from a place no one knew, whose parentage was unknown, who had no kin in a society in which kinship was very important. . . .

So many things come from Merlin's decisions and actions; he is the point at which the paths diverge. Merlin is a set of contradictions, and each person who tells the story must find a way to deal with him (one writer even did it by having him live backward!).

When I started to write *The Mists of Avalon*, my version of the Matter of Britain, I had been incubating the work in my head for almost 40 years. Some characters were easy. . . . But when I came to Merlin and tried to create or envision a character who could do all the things he did in the story, I couldn't do it. His actions were not only mysterious; they were so inconsistent and contradictory that I could not reconcile them in a single person.

So my solution was to make "The Merlin" a title, a sort of arch-druid,[2] and use two different characters. The "old Merlin" (Taliesin) was responsible for Arthur's existence and ascension to the throne, while the "young Merlin" (Kevin) was the one who betrayed Avalon. . . . One Merlin built up Arthur and Camelot, the other helped bring them down. . . .

❹ The story always ends with Arthur dead or otherwise out of action (in his enchanted slumber), the New Religion superseding[3] the Old and Merlin somewhere out of sight.

But like Arthur, although in a different way, Merlin is immortal. Even in my version, where Kevin is killed, there would be a new Merlin to follow him. Even separate from the world, Avalon and its magic live on. And in many other versions, Merlin is shut up in a tree, which can hardly be expected to hold him forever. . . .

Perhaps Merlin has been free and wandering about, quietly working his magic behind the scenes for centuries (that was quite a storm the Spanish Armada ran into in 1588, wasn't it?), or perhaps he is still drowsing in a tree somewhere, waiting until we really need him, for whatever it is we need him for. It's clear we need him for something, but I'm still not certain just quite what it is. And I don't think we'll be comfortable with it if we get it; the comfort of the people around him was never part of Merlin's job.

---

2. **arch-druid:** a chief or principal priest of ancient Ireland or England who appears in literature as a prophet with magical abilities.

3. **superseding:** taking the place of or replacing.

❹ Paraphrase Bradley's comments about the role of Merlin in her retelling.

**Summarizing** With a partner, compare your paraphrasings of the article. If necessary, revise any paraphrase that now seems incomplete. Then summarize the entire article.

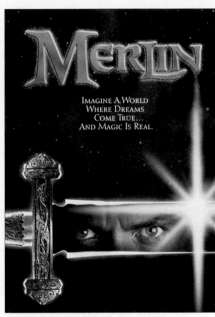

Advertisement for the television miniseries on Merlin.

## Inquiry & Research

**Activity Link:** *from* **The Mists of Avalon, p. 1087**
Use the information in this article as well as any additional materials you've encountered about Merlin to contribute to a class chart of Merlin portrayals.

# *from* The Acts of King Arthur and His Noble Knights

### *Romance by* JOHN STEINBECK

## Connect to Your Life

**Fame for a Day** Think of a famous person you admire. Make notes on what it would be like to live the life of this person for one day, including both positive and negative aspects. Then discuss your ideas with classmates, comparing your views of fame with theirs.

## Build Background

**Steinbeck and Arthur** In this selection, modern novelist John Steinbeck portrays what it might be like to be Lancelot (also spelled *Launcelot*), the most famous knight of the Round Table. From childhood, Steinbeck was fascinated by the Arthurian legend, and as an adult he attempted to set down a retelling that his own sons could enjoy. He researched the legend in England and Italy, studying rare manuscripts, and wrote in a room he named Joyous Garde, after Lancelot's castle. Unfortunately, Steinbeck never completed his version of the legend; in 1976, several years after his death, his unfinished work was published as *The Acts of King Arthur and His Noble Knights.* The excerpt you are about to read offers a new perspective on some of the events from Malory's tale of Sir Launcelot.

WORDS TO KNOW
**Vocabulary Preview**

| | |
|---|---|
| carriage | haggard |
| decorous | intemperate |
| disparagement | penitence |
| exalt | reprisal |
| fallible | vagrant |

## Focus Your Reading

**LITERARY ANALYSIS** **STYLE** In his introduction to *The Acts of King Arthur and His Noble Knights,* Steinbeck states his aim to set down the story of Arthur in "plain present-day speech," avoiding the archaic language of Malory's version. As you read the excerpt, notice the distinctive aspects of the author's **style.** Consider how Steinbeck's style adds to his retelling of Arthurian legend.

**ACTIVE READING** **MAKING INFERENCES** **Inferences** are logical guesses based on information in the text, common sense, and your own experience. To get the most out of this story, which presents a day in the life of the famed Lancelot, you will need to make **inferences,** or logical guesses, about Lancelot's feelings and behavior. For example, when Queen Guinevere (also spelled *Gwynevere*) asks Lancelot whether he has really encountered fair queen enchantresses, he looks away nervously and does not answer her directly. The reader can infer that he did meet such women and that he does not want to tell Guinevere about his encounters. As you read, look for other clues to help you understand Lancelot.

**READER'S NOTEBOOK** Keep track of your inferences by making a chart like the one shown. Consider both the evidence in the text and your own experience when making your inferences.

| Inferences About Lancelot | | |
|---|---|---|
| | **Clues** | **Inferences** |
| His Attitude Toward His Fame | | |
| His Feelings About Guinevere | | |
| Other Aspects of His Life | | |

# from THE ACTS of KING ARTHUR and HIS NOBLE KNIGHTS

## JOHN STEINBECK

King Arthur held Whitsun[1] court at Winchester, that ancient royal town favored by God and His clergy as well as the seat and tomb of many kings. The roads were clogged with eager people, knights returning to stamp in court the record of their deeds, of bishops, clergy, monks, of the defeated fettered to their paroles,[2] the prisoners of honor. And on Itchen water, pathway from Solent[3] and the sea, the little ships brought succulents, lampreys, eels and oysters, plaice and sea trout, while barges loaded with casks of whale oil and casks of wine came tide borne. Bellowing oxen walked to the spits on their own four hooves, while geese and swans, sheep and swine, waited their turn in hurdle pens. Every householder with a strip of colored cloth, a ribbon, any textile gaiety, hung it from a window to flap its small festival, and those in lack tied boughs of pine and laurel over their doors.

In the great hall of the castle on the hill the king sat high, and next below the fair elite company of the Round Table, noble and <u>decorous</u> as kings themselves, while at the long trestle boards the people were as fitted as toes in a tight shoe.

Then while the glistening meat dripped down the tables, it was the custom for the defeated to celebrate the deeds of those who had overcome them, while the victor dipped his head in <u>disparagement</u> of his greatness and fended off the compliments with small defensive gestures of his hands. And as at public <u>penitence</u> sins are given stature they do not deserve, little sins grow up and baby sins are born, so those knights who lately claimed mercy perchance might raise the exploits of the brave and merciful beyond reasonable gratitude for their lives and in anticipation of some small notice of value.

This no one said of Lancelot, sitting with bowed head in his golden-lettered seat at the Round Table. Some said he nodded and perhaps dozed, for the testimony to his greatness was long and the monotony of his victories continued for many hours. Lancelot's immaculate fame had grown so great that men took pride in being unhorsed by him—even this notice was an honor. And since he had won many victories, it is possible that knights he had never seen claimed to have been overthrown by him. It was a way to claim attention for a moment. And as he dozed and wished to be otherwise, he heard his deeds <u>exalted</u> beyond his recognition, and some mighty exploits once attributed to other men were brought bright-painted out and laid on the shining pile of his achievements. There is a seat of worth beyond the reach of envy whose occupant ceases to be a man and becomes the receptacle of the wishful longings of the world, a seat most often reserved for the dead, from whom neither <u>reprisal</u> nor reward may be expected, but at this time Sir Lancelot was its unchallenged tenant. And he vaguely heard his strength favorably compared with elephants, his ferocity with lions, his agility with deer, his cleverness with foxes, his beauty with the stars, his justice with Solon,[4] his stern probity[5] with St. Michael, his humility with newborn lambs; his military

---

1. **Whitsun:** another name for Pentecost, a Christian festival celebrated on the seventh Sunday after Easter.
2. **fettered to their paroles:** bound by their word of honor to lay down arms.
3. **Itchen . . . Solent:** waterways in southern England.
4. **Solon:** Athenian statesman and lawgiver who lived in the sixth century B.C.
5. **probity:** uprightness; honesty.

WORDS
TO
KNOW

**decorous** (dĕk′ər-əs) *adj.* behaving in a manner appropriate to the occasion; proper
**disparagement** (dĭ-spăr′ĭj-mənt) *n.* belittlement
**penitence** (pĕn′ĭ-təns) *n.* expression of regret for sins or wrongdoing
**exalt** (ĭg-zôlt′) *v.* to glorify, praise, or honor
**reprisal** (rĭ-prī′zəl) *n.* retaliation in the form of harm or injury similar to that received; revenge

*Study for Lancelot* (1893), Sir Edward Burne-Jones. From *Drawings of Sir Edward Burne-Jones*, published by Charles Scribner's Sons, New York. Photo by Hollyer.

# Reading Different Genres

*Reading an autobiography and reading a poem require different skills. Here are some tips to help you get the most out of the different genres, or types, of literature you read. The graphic organizers shown are just suggestions—use the note-taking method that works best for you.*

## Reading a Short Story

### Strategies for Reading
- Keep track of events as they happen. Creating a chart like this one may help you.

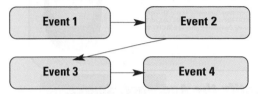

- From the details the writer provides, **visualize** the characters. **Predict** what they might do next.
- Look for specific adjectives that help you visualize the **setting**—the time and place in which events occur.

## Reading a Poem

### Strategies for Reading
- Notice the **form** of the poem, or the number of its lines and their shape on the page.
- Read the poem aloud a few times. Listen for **rhymes** and **rhythms.**
- **Visualize** the images and comparisons.
- **Connect** with the poem by asking yourself what message the poet is trying to send.
- Create a word web or other **graphic organizer** to record your reactions and questions.

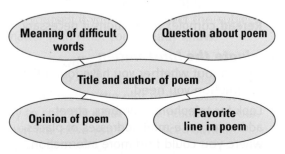

## Reading a Play

### Strategies for Reading
- Read the stage directions to help you **visualize** the setting and characters.
- **Question** what the title means and why the playwright chose it.
- Identify the main conflict (struggle or problem) in the play. To **clarify** the conflict, make a chart that shows what the conflict is and how it is resolved.
- **Evaluate** the characters. What do they want? How do they change during the play? You may want to make a chart that lists each character's name, appearance, mannerisms, and other information.

## Reading Nonfiction

### Strategies for Reading
- If you are reading a biography or autobiography, keep track of the people who are mentioned. You may want to sketch a family tree or a word web.
- When reading an essay, **evaluate** the writer's ideas and reasoning. Does the writer support opinions with facts?
- When reading an article or interview, **skim** it first to learn what its subject is. Look at any **headings** or **captions.** Then read slowly, looking for the **main idea.** Use a chart like this one to help you.

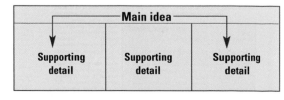

# Reading Different Formats

*These strategies will help you when you need to do research, learn about current events, or just find out more about a topic that interests you.*

## Reading Online Text

### Strategies for Reading

- Notice the page's **Web address,** sometimes called a URL. You may want to make a note of it if you will need to return to that page. Most Web addresses begin with the coding http://www.
- Read the **title** of the page to get a general idea of what topics the page covers.
- Notice **links** to related pages. Links are often "buttons" or underlined words. Clicking on a link will take you to a different page—one that may or may not have been created by the same person or organization.
- Look for a **menu bar** along the top, bottom, or side of the page. This gives you links to other parts of the Web site.
- Notice any **source citations.** Some sites tell you where their information is from, enabling you to judge its reliability.
- Write down **important ideas** and **details.** Try to restate the text in your own words. Then decide whether you need to check other sources.

## Reading a Newspaper or Magazine Article

### Strategies for Reading

- Read the **headline** and any **subheads** to learn what the article is about and how it is organized.
- Notice any photographs, charts, graphs, or other **visuals.** Read their **captions.** Be sure you understand how the visuals and the main text are related.
- Notice any **quotations.** Think about whether the people who are quoted are likely to be reliable authorities on the topic.

## Reading an Encyclopedia Article

### Strategies for Reading

- Read the **headline** and any **subheads** to make sure that the article covers the topic of interest to you.
- Look at **visuals** and read their **captions.** Some online or CD-ROM encyclopedias also include sound files, animated maps, and short movies.
- Pay attention to how the article is organized. You may want to **skim** the article, or read it quickly, as you look for **key words** related to your topic. Once you find the information you need, read slowly and carefully.
- Watch for a **"see also"** or **"related articles"** section or—if the encyclopedia is online—for highlighted links. These features direct you to additional articles that may include information on your subject.

# Enriching Your Vocabulary

## Context Clues

One way to figure out the meaning of a word you don't know is by using context clues. The context of a word consists of the punctuation marks, other words, sentences, and paragraphs that surround the word.

**General Context** Sometimes you need to read all the information in the sentence or paragraph in order to infer the meaning of an unfamiliar word.

> When Mike felt the paint and found it was still **tacky,** he looked at the directions to see <u>how long it should take to dry.</u>

> The <u>gray, gloomy day</u> made Ann feel <u>weepy</u> and **melancholy.**

**Definition Clues** Often a difficult word will be followed by its definition. Commas, dashes, or other punctuation marks may signal a definition.

> **Permafrost**—<u>a layer of permanently frozen ground</u>—is underneath about one-fifth of Earth's land surfaces.

**Restatement Clues** Sometimes a writer restates a word or term in easier language. Commas, dashes, or other punctuation as well as expressions such as *that is, in other words,* and *or,* may signal restatement clues.

> The film critic complained that *My Only Love* was too **sentimental;** <u>in other words, it was mushy and overly emotional.</u>

**Example Clues** Sometimes writers suggest the meanings of words with one or two examples.

> The hero of the novel faced many **imperilments,** including <u>poisonous snakes, hungry tigers, and huge deserts.</u>

**Comparison Clues** Sometimes a word's meaning is suggested by a comparison to something similar. *Like* and *as* are words that signal comparison clues.

> At night our house is as **frigid** <u>as the North Pole.</u>

**Contrast Clues** Sometimes writers point out differences between things or ideas. Contrast clues are often signaled by words and phrases such as *although, but, however, unlike,* and *in contrast to.*

> The swimmer was **agile** in the water <u>but</u> clumsy on dry land.

**Idioms and Slang** An idiom is an expression whose overall meaning is different from the meaning of the individual words. Slang is informal language that comprises both made-up words and ordinary words that carry different meanings than in formal English. Use context clues to figure out the meaning of idioms and slang.

> None of us finished our homework, so we are **all in the same boat.** (idiom)

> Stop **bugging out!** We'll make it to the concert on time. (slang)

**TIP** One way to clarify your understanding of a word is to write a sentence using that word. Even better, use one of the context-clue strategies in your sentence. For example, include a restatement or definition clue.

*For more about context clues, see pages 56, 908, and 1000; for more about idioms and slang, see page 419.*

## Word Parts

If you know base words, roots, and affixes—that is, prefixes and suffixes—you can figure out the meanings of many new words.

*Base Words* A **base word** is a word that can stand alone. Other words or word parts can be added to base words to form new words.

*Roots* Many English words contain roots that come from older languages, such as Greek, Latin, and Old English. A **root** is a word part that contains the core meaning of the word. Knowing the meaning of a word's root or roots can help you figure out the word's meaning.

| Root | Meaning | Examples |
|---|---|---|
| *dynam* (Greek) | power, force | dynamic, dynamo |
| *paleo* (Greek) | ancient, early, prehistoric | paleobiology, paleolithic |
| *cent* (Latin) | one hundred | century, percent |
| *gress* (Latin) | step | progress, regressive |
| *port* (Latin) | carry | portable, transport |
| *lor(e)n* (Old English) | lost | forlorn, lovelorn |
| *mer(e)* (Old English) | sea, pool | mermaid, merman |

*Prefixes* A **prefix** is a word part that appears at the beginning of a base word or another word part. Attaching a prefix to an existing word usually changes the meaning of that word. Familiarizing yourself with the meanings of common prefixes can help you be prepared to figure out the meanings of unfamiliar words.

| Prefix | Meaning | Examples |
|---|---|---|
| *hyper-* | over, excessive | hyperactive, hypersensitive |
| *inter-* | among, between | interactive, Internet |
| *re-* | again | renew, replace, refinish |
| *tele-* | distant | television, telescope |
| *un-* | not | uncomfortable, unlike |

*Suffixes* A **suffix** is a word part attached to the end of a base word or another word part. Attaching a suffix to an existing word may alter the word's meaning. However, a suffix does not change a word's meaning when it is added as follows:

- to a noun to change the number
- to a verb to change the tense
- to an adjective to change the degree of comparison
- to an adverb to show how

| Suffix | Purpose | Examples |
|---|---|---|
| *-s, -es* | to change the number of a noun | sock + *s*, socks |
| *-ed, -ing* | to change verb tense | jump + *ed*, jumped jump + *ing*, jumping |
| *-er, -est* | to change the degree of comparison in modifiers | young + *er*, younger young + *est*, youngest |
| *-ly* | to show how | wild + *ly*, wildly |

Other suffixes are added to a base word or root to change the word's meaning. These suffixes can also be used to change the word's part of speech.

| Suffix | Meaning | Examples |
|---|---|---|
| *-ist* | one who is or does | artist, florist, terrorist |
| *-ish* | of, relating to, being | boyish, selfish |
| *-ize* | to make | energize, dramatize |

To infer the meaning of an unfamiliar word from its parts, follow these steps.

- Divide the word into parts. Think of other words you know that share the same root(s) or base word.
- Ask, Do these other words all have the same or similar meanings?
- Consider the meanings of any prefixes or suffixes in the word.
- From the meanings of the unfamiliar word's parts, predict what the word means.
- Check the context and consult a dictionary or glossary to find out whether your prediction is correct.

*For more about roots, prefixes, and suffixes, see pages 183 and 356.*

# Word Origins

When you study a word's history and origin, you find out when, where, and how the word came to be. A complete dictionary entry includes each word's history.

**dra•ma** (drä′mə) *n.* **1.** A work that is meant to be performed by actors. **2.** Theatrical works of a certain type or period in history. [Late Latin *drāma*, *drāmat-*, from Greek *drān*, to do or perform.]

This entry shows you that the earliest form of the word *drama* was the Greek word *drān*.

**Word Families** Words that have the same root have related meanings. Such words make up a word family. The charts below show common Greek and Latin roots. Notice how the meanings of the English words are related to the meanings of their roots.

| Greek Root: | **soph,** wise |
| --- | --- |
| **English:** | **sophomore** "wise fool"; a student in the second year of high school or college |
| | **sophisticated** worldly, refined, or complex |
| | **philosophy** "love of wisdom"; the study of logic and basic truths |

| Latin Root: | **circum,** around or about |
| --- | --- |
| **English:** | **circumference** the boundary line of a circle |
| | **circumnavigation** the act of moving completely around |
| | **circumstance** a condition or fact surrounding an event |

| Latin Root: | **fin,** to end |
| --- | --- |
| **English:** | **final** forming or occurring at the end |
| | **finish** to bring to an end |
| | **finite** having bounds; limited |

| Latin Root: | **struct,** to build |
| --- | --- |
| **English:** | **construct** to build |
| | **destructive** causing the ruin or elimination of something |
| | **structure** a building |

**TIP** Once you recognize a root in one English word, you will notice the same root in other words—members of the same word family. Because these words developed from the same root, they are similar in meaning.

**Foreign Words** Some words that enter the English language keep their original form.

| Dutch | French | Italian | Japanese |
| --- | --- | --- | --- |
| aloof | boutique | graffiti | judo |
| cookie | chauffeur | paparazzi | kimono |
| gruesome | espionage | soprano | origami |
| knack | mirage | spaghetti | samurai |
| maelstrom | sabotage | staccato | tsunami |
| sloop | vague | virtuoso | soy |

*For more about word families, see pages 183 and 356; for more about foreign words, see page 584.*

# Synonyms and Antonyms

When you read, pay attention to the precise words a writer uses.

**Synonyms** A **synonym** is a word that has the same or almost the same meaning as another word. Read each set of synonyms listed below.

happen/occur

plagiarize/cheat

woods/forest

lukewarm/mild

pact/agreement

considerate/thoughtful

rarely/seldom

gently/lightly

**TIP** You can find synonyms in a thesaurus or dictionary. In a dictionary, synonyms are often given following the definition of a word.

**Antonyms** An **antonym** is a word with a meaning opposite of that of another word. Read each set of antonyms listed below:

idle/busy

early/late

generous/stingy

comfort/irritate

hard/soft

hurry/dawdle

before/after

rough/smooth

Some antonyms are formed by adding one of the negative prefixes *anti-, in-,* and *un-* to a word, as in the chart below.

| Word | Prefix | Antonym |
|------|--------|---------|
| bacterial | *anti-* | antibacterial |
| thesis | *anti-* | antithesis |
| accurate | *in-* | inaccurate |
| consistent | *in-* | inconsistent |
| true | *un-* | untrue |
| usual | *un-* | unusual |

**TIP** You can find antonyms in dictionaries of synonyms and antonyms, as well as in some thesauruses.

**TIP** Some dictionaries contain notes that discuss synonyms and antonyms. These notes often include sentences that illustrate the relationships among the words.

*For more about synonyms and antonyms, see page 1000.*

# Denotative and Connotative Meaning

Good writers choose just the right word to communicate a specific meaning.

**Denotative Meaning** A word's dictionary meaning is called its **denotation.** The denotation of the word *thin*, for example, is "having little flesh; spare; lean."

**Connotative Meaning** The images or feelings you connect to a word are called **connotations.** Connotative meaning stretches beyond a word's dictionary definition. Writers rely on connotations of words to communicate shades of meaning, as well as positive or negative feelings. For example, which of these sentences gives you a positive mental picture, and which gives you a negative mental picture?

A season on the track team left Xavier looking **lean** and **slender.**

A season on the track team left Xavier looking **skinny** and **scrawny.**

Examples of similar words with different connotations are listed below.

| Positive Connotations | Negative Connotations |
|-----------------------|------------------------|
| aroma | stench |
| assertive | bossy |
| bold | reckless |
| casual | sloppy |
| caution | cowardice |
| gaze | glare |
| inquisitive | nosy |
| popular | commonplace |
| slender | scrawny |

**TIP** Some dictionaries contain notes that discuss connotative meanings of the entry word and other related words.

*For more information about denotative and connotative meanings, see page 494.*

## Homonyms, Multiple-Meaning Words, and Homophones

Homonyms, multiple-meaning words, and homophones can be confusing to readers and can plague writers.

***Homonyms*** Words that have the same spelling and pronunciation but different meanings and, in most cases, different origins are called **homonyms**. Consider this example:

> The city's oldest **bank** was on the **bank** of the Charles River.

*Bank* can mean "a place or organization where money is kept, loaned, or invested," but it can also mean "the land alongside a river, creek, or pond."

***Words with Multiple Meanings*** Multiple-meaning words are those that have over time acquired additional meanings based on the original meaning. Consider these examples:

> I hurt my **back** and neck last Friday.

> We were playing stickball in **back** of the convenience store.

*Back* clearly has multiple meanings, but all of the additional meanings have developed from the same original meaning. You will find all the meanings for *back* under one entry in the dictionary.

***Homophones*** Words that sound alike but have different meanings and spellings are called homophones. Consider these examples:

> The birds **soar** gracefully in the air.

> Kristin's legs were **sore** after she ran a marathon.

Many common words with Anglo-Saxon origins have homophones *(there, their; write, right).* Check your writing to make sure you have used the right word and not its homophone.

*For more about homonyms and multiple-meaning words, see page 678.*

# Analogies

***Analogy*** An **analogy** is a comparison between two things that are similar in some way. Analogies often appear on tests, usually in a format like this:

> BRANCH : TREE :: A) floral : pattern
> B) toe : foot
> C) autumn : season
> D) limb : arm
> E) tree : limb

To choose the correct answer, follow these steps:

- Read the part in capital letters as "*Branch* is to *tree* as . . . "
- Read the answer choices as "*floral* is to *pattern,*" "*toe* is to *foot,*" "*autumn* is to *season,*" and so on.
- Ask yourself how the first two words, *branch* and *tree,* are related. (A branch is a part of a tree. So *branch* and *tree* have a part-to-whole relationship.)
- Then look for the answer that best shows the same relationship. (Of these possible answers, only item B shows the relationship of a part to a whole. The trickiest answer is E, because it shows a whole-to-part relationship, which is close to, but not exactly, the same relationship.)

***Types of Analogies*** Here are some common relationships that are often expressed in analogies:

| Relationship | Example |
|---|---|
| Part to whole | BRANCH : TREE |
| Synonyms | EASY : SIMPLE |
| Antonyms | BOILING : FREEZING |
| Degree of intensity | HAPPY : ECSTATIC |
| Characteristics to object | SMOOTHNESS : SILK |
| Item to category | TRACTOR : VEHICLE |

*For more about analogies, see page 263.*

## Specialized Vocabulary

Professionals who work in fields such as law, science, or sports use their own technical or specialized vocabulary.

> The high court **reversed** and **remanded** the case, ordering the lower-court judge to reexamine her faulty reasoning.

Use these strategies to help you figure out the meanings of specialized vocabulary.

***Use Context Clues*** Often the surrounding text gives clues that help you infer the meaning of an unfamiliar term.

> The computer-generated **special effects** in the movie are incredibly realistic.

***Use Reference Tools*** Textbooks often define a special term when it is first introduced. Look for definitions or restatement clues in parentheses. Also you can try to find definitions in footnotes, a glossary, or a dictionary. If you need more information, refer to a specialized reference, such as one of the following:

- an encyclopedia
- a field guide
- an atlas
- a user's manual
- a technical dictionary

## Decoding Multisyllabic Words

Many words that are familiar to you when you speak or hear them may be unfamiliar to you when you see them in print. When you come across a word unfamiliar in print, first try to pronounce it to see if you recognize it. The following syllabication generalizations can help you figure out a word's pronunciation:

### Generalization 1: VCCV
When there are two consonants between two vowels, divide between the two consonants, unless they are a blend or a digraph.

> lum/ber  shat/ter  broth/er

### Generalization 2: VCCCV
When there are three consonants between two vowels, divide between the blend or the digraph and the other consonant.

> an/gler  mer/chant  tum/bler

### Generalization 3: VCCV
When there are two consonants between two vowels, divide between the consonants, unless they are a blend or a digraph, the first syllable is a closed syllable, and the vowel is short.

> traf/fic  ush/er  sum/mer

### Generalization 4: Common Vowel Clusters
Do not split common vowel clusters, such as long vowel digraphs, *r*-controlled vowels, and vowel diphthongs.

> gar/den  pain/ful  gar/age

### Generalization 5: VCV
When you see a VCV pattern in the middle of a word, divide the word either before or after the consonant. If you divide the word after the consonant, pronounce the first vowel sound as short. If you divide the word before the consonant, pronounce the first vowel sound as long.

> lev/er  o/boe  spi/der

### Generalization 6: Compound Words
Divide compound words between the individual words.

> bath/tub  some/one

### Generalization 7: Affixes
When a word includes an affix, divide between the base word and the affix.

> like/ness  uni/form

# Reading for Information

*Reading informational materials—such as textbooks, magazines, newspapers, and Web pages—requires the use of special strategies. For example, you need to study text organizers, such as headings and special type, to learn the main ideas, facts, terms, and names that are of importance. You also need to identify patterns of organization in the text. Using such strategies will help you to read informational materials with ease and quickly gain a clear understanding of their contents.*

## Reading a Textbook

Look for headings, large or dark type, pictures, and drawings that signal the most important information on the page. These special features, called **text organizers,** help you understand and remember what you read.

### Strategies for Reading

**A** First, look at the **title** and any **subheads.** These will tell you the main ideas.

**B** Many textbooks include a list of **objectives** or **key terms** at the start of each lesson. Keep these in mind as you read. They will help you focus on the most important facts and details.

**C** **Key terms** are often boldfaced or underlined where they first appear in the text. Be sure that you understand what they mean.

**D** Notice any **special features,** such as sidebar articles or extended quotations. These provide important details and can help you visualize the information.

**E** Look at the **visuals**—charts, maps, time lines, photographs, illustrations—and read any **captions** or **questions** that accompany them. Visuals often present information that is not in the main text.

---

**B**

TERMS & NAM
• Napoleon Bon
• coup d'état
• plebiscite
• lycée
• concordat
• Napoleonic Co
• Battle of Trafa

**3** ## Napoleon Forges an Empire **A**

| MAIN IDEA | WHY IT MATTERS NOW |
|---|---|
| A military genius, Napoleon Bonaparte, seized power in France and made himself emperor. | In times of political turmoil, military dictators often seize control of nations, as in Haiti in 1991. |

**SETTING THE STAGE** Napoleon was a short man (five feet three inches tall) who cast a long shadow over the history of modern times. He would come to be recognized as one of the world's greatest military geniuses, along with Alexander the Great of Macedonia, Hannibal of Carthage, and Julius Caesar of Rome. In only four years (1795–1799), Napoleon rose from relative obscurity to become master of France.

**A** ### Napoleon Grasps the Power

**Napoleon Bonaparte** was born in 1769 on the Mediterranean island of Corsica. When he was nine years old, his parents sent him to a military school in northern France. In 1785, at the age of 16, he finished school and became a lieutenant in the artillery. When the Revolution broke out, Napoleon joined the army of the new government.

**D** **HISTORY MAKERS**

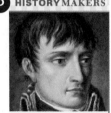

**Napoleon Bonaparte
1769–1821**

Napoleon Bonaparte had a magnetism that attracted the admiration of his men. His speeches were designed to inspire his troops to valorous feats. In one speech, he told soldiers, "If the victory is for a moment uncertain, you shall see your Emperor place himself on the front line."

Bonaparte was generous in his rewards to the troops. Many received the Legion of Honor—a medal for bravery. Sometimes Napoleon would take the medal from his own chest to present it to a soldier. (He kept a few spares in his pocket for these occasions.) A cavalry commander, Auguste de Colbert, wrote, "He awakened in my soul the desire for glory."

**Hero of the Hour** In October 1795, fate handed the young officer a chance for glory. When royalist rebels marched on the National Convention, a government official told Napoleon to defend the delegates. Napoleon and his gunners greeted the thousands of royalists with a cannonade. Within minutes, the attackers fled in panic and confusion. Napoleon Bonaparte became the hero of the hour and was hailed throughout Paris as the savior of the French republic.

In 1796, the Directory appointed Napoleon to lead a French army against the forces of Austria and the Kingdom of Sardinia. Crossing the Alps, the young general swept into Italy and won a series of remarkable victories, which crushed the Austrian troops' threat to France. Next, in an attempt to protect French trade interests and to disrupt British trade with India, Napoleon led an expedition to Egypt. Unfortunately, his luck did not hold. His army was pinned down in Egypt, and his naval forces were defeated by the British admiral Horatio Nelson. However, he managed to keep the reports of his defeat out of the press, so that by 1799 the words "the general" could mean only one man to the French—Napoleon.

**Vocabulary**
cannonade:
bardment wi
artillery fire.

**Coup d'État** By 1799, the Directory had lost control of the political situation and the confidence of the French people. Only the directors' control of the army kept them in power. Upon Napoleon's return from Egypt, the Abbé Sieyès urged him to seize political power. Napoleon and Josephine, his lovely socialite wife, set a plan in motion. Napoleon met with influential persons to discuss his role in the Directory, while Josephine used her connections with the wealthy directors to influence their decisions. The action began on November 9, 1799, when Napoleon was put in charge of the military. It ended the next day when his troops drove out the members of one chamber of the

**584** Chapter 23

## More Strategies for Reading Textbooks

- Before you begin the text, read any **questions** that appear at the end of the lesson or chapter. These will help you focus your reading.

- Read slowly and carefully. If you see an unfamiliar word and can't find a definition in the text or in a marginal note, check the **glossary** or a dictionary. Look for **pronunciation guides** as you read.

- Take **notes** as you read. These will help you understand new ideas and terms. Review your notes before a test to jog your memory.

- You may want to take notes in the form of a **graphic organizer,** such as a cause-and-effect chart, or a comparison-and-contrast chart.

---

THINK THROUGH HISTORY

**Analyzing Causes** For what reasons was Napoleon able to become a dictator?

national legislature. The legislature voted to dissolve the Directory. In its place, the legislature established a group of three consuls, one of whom was Napoleon. Napoleon quickly assumed dictatorial powers as the first consul of the French republic. A sudden seizure of power like Napoleon's is known as a coup—from the French phrase **coup d'état** (KOO day-TAH), or "blow of state."

**C**

At the time of Napoleon's coup, France was still at war. In 1799, British diplomats assembled the Second Coalition of anti-French powers—Britain, Austria, and Russia—with the goal of driving Napoleon from power. Once again, Napoleon rode from Paris at the head of his troops. Eventually, as a result of war and diplomacy, all three nations signed peace agreements with France. By 1802, Europe was at peace for the first time in ten years. Napoleon was free to focus his energies on restoring order in France.

### Napoleon Rules France

At first, Napoleon pretended to be the constitutionally chosen leader of a free republic. In 1800, a **plebiscite** (PLEHB-ih-SYT), or vote of the people, was held to approve a new constitution, the fourth in eight years. Desperate for strong leadership, the people voted overwhelmingly in favor of the constitution, which gave all real power to Napoleon as first consul.

**Restoring Order at Home** Under Napoleon, France would have order and stability. He did not try to return the nation to the days of Louis XVI; instead, he kept many of the changes that had come with the Revolution. He supported laws that would both strengthen the central government and achieve some of the goals of the Revolution, such as a stable economy and more equality in taxation.

The first order of business was to get the economy on a solid footing. Napoleon set up an efficient tax-collection system and established a national bank. In addition to assuring the government a steady supply of tax money, these actions promoted sound financial management and better control of the economy.

Napoleon also needed to reduce government corruption and improve the delivery of government services. He dismissed corrupt officials and, in order to provide his government with trained officials, set up **lycées,** or government-run public schools. The students at the lycées included children of ordinary citizens as well as children of

**E**

#### Napoleon Brings Order After the Revolution

| | The Economy | Government & Society | Religion |
|---|---|---|---|
| **Goals of the Revolution** | • Equal taxation<br>• Lower inflation | • Less government corruption<br>• Equal opportunity in government | • Less powerful Catholic Church<br>• Religious tolerance |
| **Napoleon's Actions** | • Set up fairer tax code<br>• Set up national bank<br>• Stabilized currency<br>• Gave state loans to businesses | • Appointed officials by merit<br>• Fired corrupt officials<br>• Created lycées<br>• Created code of laws | • Recognized Catholicism as "faith of Frenchmen"<br>• Signed concordat with pope<br>• Retained seized church lands |
| **Results** | • Equal taxation<br>• Stable economy | • Honest, competent officials<br>• Equal opportunity in government<br>• Public education | • Religious tolerance<br>• Government control of church lands<br>• Government recognition of church influence |

**SKILLBUILDER: Interpreting Charts**
Napoleon's changes brought France closer to achieving the Revolution's goals.
1. Which goals of the Revolution did Napoleon achieve?
2. If you had been a member of the bourgeoisie in Napoleon's France, would you have been satisfied with the results of Napoleon's actions? Why or why not?

*The French Revolution and Napoleon* **585**

---

### More Examples

To examine the structural features of other kinds of informational materials, see the pages listed below.

For an example of a **newspaper article,** see page 998.

For examples of **magazine articles,** see pages 181, 276, 482, 590, 662, 836, 1088, and 1132.

## Reading a Magazine Article

### Strategies for Reading

**A** Read the **title** and any other **headings** to get an idea of what the article is about and how it is organized.

**B** As you read the main text, notice any **quotations.** Who is quoted? Is the person a reliable authority on the subject?

**C** Notice text that is set off in some way, such as a passage in a **different typeface.** A quotation or statistic that sums up the article is sometimes presented in this way. A **sidebar article** can present more information.

**D** Study **visuals,** such as photographs, graphs, charts, and maps. Read their captions and make sure you know how they relate to the main text.

# Is "youth sports rage" on the rise?

### Parents become violent and abusive during kids' games

by Belinda Liu

The news stories are frightening. In Virginia, the mother of a soccer player assaults a 14-year-old referee and is fined. In Pennsylvania, a "midget league" football game results in a brawl involving about 100 players and spectators. Accounts of "youth sports rage" are reported in Britain, Canada, Australia, and New Zealand.

Are spectators at youth sports becoming more violent? Some observers believe they are.

"There have always been problem parents in kids' sports," explains soccer coach Larry Fiore. "But the vast majority of parents, coaches, and athletes act appropriately."

However, some factors are making the problem worse, believes sports psychologist Theresa Mathelier. "Sports are getting more expensive for parents in terms of equipment, traveling, and coaching," she explains. "The tendency now is to start kids in organized sports earlier and to get them to specialize in one sport."

As a result, Mathelier says, "a few parents get unrealistic ideas about col-

*"Parents should be role models."*

lege scholarships and professional careers in sports. They start to live through their kids, and if something goes wrong, they blow up."

Fiore and Mathelier both say that it is rarely the athletes who cause the problems. Serena Terell, a 15-year-old soccer player, agrees. "It's so embarrassing when the parents yell and curse," Serena explains, adding that her parents always behave themselves. "Their kids just want them to stop. After all, it's only a game, and parents should be role models."

### Stopping sports rage

Here are steps that some groups have taken to prevent youth sports rage.

- The National Youth Sports Safety Foundation has created a Sport Parent Code of Conduct. Penalties range from a verbal warning to a season suspension for parents.
- Some soccer leagues designate one day as "Silent Sunday." Spectators are not allowed to cheer or even talk until the game is over.
- Some coaches choose one parent to be in charge of crowd control. This parent patrols the bleachers or sidelines, making sure that fans of his or her team behave.

## Reading a Web Page

### Strategies for Reading

**A** Look for the page's **Web address,** sometimes called a URL. You may want to write down the Web address if you think you will need to return to the page.

**B** Read the **title** of the page to find out what topics the page covers.

**C** Look for a **menu bar** along the top, bottom, or side of the page. This tells you about other parts of the site.

**D** Notice any **links** to related pages. Links are often "buttons" or underlined words.

**E** Some sites have **interactive areas** where you can communicate with experts or with other users of the site. This site allows users to participate in a forum with other users.

# Functional Reading

*Functional reading is reading to discover such information as instruction in how to do something. When you read a map, a technical manual, a job application, or a recipe, you are engaged in functional reading. These guidelines show how you can improve your functional-reading skills.*

## Technical Directions

### Strategies for Reading

**A** Read the **title** to learn what material the page covers. This page is from the manual for a graphing calculator.

**B** Notice any **introductory text** to find general information.

**C** Look for **numbered steps** or a **bulleted list** to learn how to perform a particular task. Some manuals present the steps of a process in paragraph form, with signal words such as *first, next, then,* and *finally.*

**D** Examine **pictures** or other **graphics** that illustrate the steps. If you are having trouble completing the process, pictures can help you pinpoint where you are going wrong.

### PRACTICE AND APPLY

Reread the page from the manual and then answer the following questions:

1. What does this page explain how to do?
2. According to the instructions, how do you select a menu item?
3. What key should you press to zoom in?
4. What key should you press to display the new window settings?

---

**A** Zooming on the Graph

**B** You can magnify the viewing **WINDOW** around a specific location using the **ZOOM** instructions to help identify maximums, minimums, roots, and intersections of functions.

**C** 1. Press ZOOM to display the ZOOM menu.

   This menu is typical of TI-82 menus. To select an item, you may either press the number to the left of the item, or you may press ▼ until the item number is highlighted and then press ENTER.

```
ZOOM  MEMORY
1:ZBox
2:Zoom In
3:Zoom Out
4:ZDecimal
5:ZSquare
6:ZStandard
7↓ZTrig
```

2. To zoom in, press **2**. The graph is displayed again. The cursor has changed to indicate that you are using a ZOOM instruction.

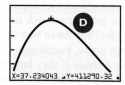

X=37.234043   Y=411290.32

3. Use ◄, ▲, ►, and ▼ to position the cursor near the maximum value on the function and press ENTER.

   The new viewing **WINDOW** is displayed. It has been adjusted in both the **X** and **Y** directions by factors of 4, the values for ZOOM factors.

X=37.234043   Y=411290.32

4. Press WINDOW to display the new **WINDOW** settings.

```
WINDOW  FORMAT
Xmin=24.734042...
Xmax=49.734042...
Xscl=10
Ymin=348790.32...
Ymax=473790.32...
Yscl=100000
```

## Recipe

### Strategies for Reading

**A** Read the entire recipe at least once before beginning. Look at the **list of ingredients** to make sure that you have everything you need. Some recipes also include a list of kitchen equipment.

**B** Watch for notations of **preparation time** and **cooking time.** Does this recipe need to be made hours or days before it is served? Do you have enough time to prepare it?

**C** Notice the **number of servings** the recipe makes. You may need to double or halve the recipe to feed the right number of people.

**D** Read the **cooking directions** carefully. Follow the steps in the order they are given. Some recipes are not written in complete sentences.

**E** If you don't understand certain **terms** in the recipe, check a dictionary. Some cookbooks include a **glossary** of difficult words at the back of the book.

### PRACTICE AND APPLY

Reread the recipe and answer the questions:

1. What does this recipe tell you how to make?
2. How much cheese does the recipe require?
3. About how much time should you set aside to prepare and cook this dish?
4. If you needed to feed six people, would you double or halve the recipe?
5. What does "sauté" mean? (Use context clues, a dictionary, or a cookbook glossary to figure this out.)

## Vegetable Pizza Supreme

**A** You will need:

1 loaf of French bread (about 1 pound)

1/4 cup red bell pepper, chopped

1/4 cup mushrooms, cleaned and sliced

1/4 cup whole black olives (optional)

1/4 cup white or red onion, peeled and chopped

Cooking spray or 1 tablespoon olive oil

1/2 cup of your favorite bottled spaghetti sauce or pizza sauce

1 cup mozzarella cheese, shredded

a sprinkle of ground black pepper (for seasoning)

102

**B** Preparation time: about 20 minutes
Cooking time: about 18 minutes
Serves: 2 to 3 **C**

**D**
1. Preheat the oven to 450 degrees.
2. Slice the bread lengthwise. Scoop out the soft bread center from the bottom half. Set aside the top half—you won't need it for this recipe.
3. Line a cookie sheet with aluminum foil. Place the bottom half of the bread on it and bake for 3 to 5 minutes. Remove from oven, turn over, and bake for 3 to 5 minutes on the other side.
4. As the bread is browning, heat the oil or cooking spray in the frying pan. Sauté **E** the chopped onions and peppers for about 5 minutes, until they begin to soften.
5. Take bread out of oven. Spread cut side with sauce. Sprinkle with cheese and top with onions, peppers, mushrooms, and olives.
6. Return to oven and bake 6 to 8 minutes or until cheese is bubbly.
7. Remove from oven. To slice, press a large, sharp knife into the pizza at about three-inch intervals. Do not use a sawing motion, as this will remove the cheese.
8. Top with black pepper and serve!

103

# ❷ Building Blocks of Good Writing

*Whatever your purpose in writing, you need to capture your readers' interest, organize your ideas well, and present your thoughts clearly. Giving special attention to some particular parts of a story or an essay can make your writing more enjoyable and more effective.*

## 2.1 Introductions

When you flip through a magazine trying to decide which articles to read, the opening paragraph is often critical. If it does not grab your attention, you are likely to turn the page.

### Kinds of Introductions

Here are some introduction techniques that can capture a reader's interest.

- Make a surprising statement
- Provide a description
- Pose a question
- Relate an anecdote
- Address the reader directly
- Begin with a thesis statement

**Make a Surprising Statement** Beginning with a startling statement or an interesting fact can capture your reader's curiosity about the subject, as in the model below.

> MODEL
> September should be the seventh month, and October should be the eighth. Any Latin student knows that the root *septem* is "seven" and *octo* is "eight." Where did the calendar makers go wrong? The truth is that when the months acquired their names, during Roman times, the year started in March.

**Provide a Description** A vivid description sets a mood and brings a scene to life for your reader. Here, details about a lion observing possible prey set the tone for an essay on survival in the wild.

> MODEL
> Cool and cunning eyes followed the impala herd from a sturdy low-slung tree branch. The young female lion watched hungrily to see whether any of the impalas might be sickly or slower than the others. She kept every muscle quiet, though tense and ready to spring if an opportunity arose.

**Pose a Question** Beginning with a question can make your reader want to read on to find the answer. The following introduction asks questions about the incredible persistence of racial segregation.

> MODEL
> How is it possible that as late as the mid-twentieth century in the United States of America, "the land of the free," riders on public buses were segregated by race? How is it possible that even today there are segregated social events, schools, and towns, no longer segregated by law but with effects just as real and damaging?

**Relate an Anecdote** Beginning with a brief anecdote, or story, can hook readers and help you make a point in a dramatic way. The anecdote below introduces an essay about the downside of self-closing shoe straps.

> MODEL
> My five-year old nephew, Ali, has never tied a shoelace. All his shoes have self-closing straps. Little boys already suffer because they are encouraged to develop large muscles by throwing and climbing, while little girls gain dexterity by dressing dolls and coloring in coloring books. Ali's younger sister, who has learned to tie bows on her doll clothes, may well have to stick around to tie the bows on Ali's gift packages and tie his bow tie for his tuxedo.

**Address the Reader Directly** Speaking directly to readers establishes a friendly, informal tone and involves them in your topic.

> MODEL
>
> **If you've ever wondered how to avoid using pesticides in your garden, you can find answers from Natural Gardens, Inc. It's easy to protect the environment and have pest-free plants.**

**Begin with a Thesis Statement** A thesis statement expressing a paper's main idea may be woven into both the beginning and the end of nonfiction writing. The following is a thesis statement that introduces an essay on the relationship of caring for pets and children.

> MODEL
>
> **Pet owners who are casual about their pet's health and safety are likely to be the same ones who are casual about the health and safety of their children.**

**WRITING TIP** In order to write the best introduction for your paper, you may want to try more than one of the methods and then decide which is the most effective for your purpose and audience.

## 2.2 Paragraphs

A paragraph is made up of sentences that work together to develop an idea or accomplish a purpose. Whether or not it contains a topic sentence stating the main idea, a good paragraph must have unity and coherence.

### Unity

A paragraph has unity when all the sentences support and develop one stated or implied idea. Use the following techniques to create unity in your paragraphs.

**Write a Topic Sentence** A topic sentence states the main ideas of the paragraph; all other sentences in the paragraph provide supporting details. A topic sentence is often the first sentence in a paragraph. However, it may also appear later in the paragraph or at the end, to summarize or reinforce the main idea, as shown in the model that follows.

> MODEL
>
> **Plastic that does not rust, rot, or shatter is useful, of course, but does add to the ever-increasing problems of waste disposal. It is possible to add chemicals to plastic that make it dissolvable by other chemicals. There are plastics that slowly disintegrate in sunlight. Biodegradable plastic is available and should be preferred over non-biodegradable plastic.**

**Relate All Sentences to an Implied Main Idea** A paragraph can be unified without a topic sentence as long as every sentence supports the implied, or unstated, main idea. In the example below, all the sentences work together to create a unified impression of a swim meet.

> MODEL
>
> **The swimmers were lined up along the edge of the pool. Toes curled over the edge, arms swung back in the ready position, and bodies leaned forward. The swimmers' eyes looked straight ahead. Their ears were alert for the starting signal.**

### Coherence

A paragraph is coherent when all its sentences are related to one another and flow logically from one to the next. The following techniques will help you achieve coherence in paragraphs.

- Present your ideas in the most logical order.
- Use pronouns, synonyms, and repeated words to connect ideas.
- Use transitional devices to show the relationships among ideas.

In the model below, the writer used some of these techniques to create a unified paragraph.

> MODEL
>
> **As we experience day and night repeatedly, it is hard to imagine the enormous significance of that change. We have day and night because our planet rotates on its axis. We have seasons because Earth revolves around our solar system's star, the sun. Our solar system, along with many others, rotates with the Milky Way Galaxy. The universe is a gigantic structure of which our daily experiences of day and night, summer and winter are tiny parts.**

## 2.3 Transitions

Transitions are words and phrases that show the connections between details. Clear transitions help show how your ideas relate to each other.

### Kinds of Transitions

Transitions can help readers understand several kinds of relationships:

• Time or sequence

• Spatial relationships

• Degree of importance

• Compare and contrast

• Cause and effect

**Time or Sequence** Some transitions help to clarify the sequence of events over time. When you are telling a story or describing a process, you can connect ideas with such transitional words as *first, second, always, then, next, later, soon, before, finally, after, earlier, afterward,* and *tomorrow.*

MODEL
**Teaching a puppy to come when called takes patience from the owner and the puppy. First tie a lightweight rope to the dog's collar and go to a large play area. Play with the pup a while and then call to it. At the same time pull gently on the rope. Always praise the puppy for coming when called. Next allow the puppy to play again. Carry out this exercise several times a day.**

**Spatial Relationships** Transitional words and phrases such as *in front, behind, next to, along, nearest, lowest, above, below, underneath, on the left,* and *in the middle* can help readers visualize a scene.

MODEL
**On the porch, wicker chairs stand in casual disorder along the red wall of the house. Next to the red-and-white porch railing, orange day lilies nod in the breeze. Overhead, a flycatcher perches on a bare branch, alert for her next meal. Beyond the lawn, a small stream flows from beneath an arched stone bridge.**

**Degree of Importance** Transitional words such as *mainly, strongest, weakest, first, second, most important, least important, worst,* and *best* may be used to rank ideas or to show degree of importance, complexity, or familiarity.

MODEL
**The Repertory Theater performed six plays last year. All the plays were exciting, but the most outstanding one was *Master Class*.**

**Compare and Contrast** Words and phrases such as *similarly, likewise, also, like, as, neither . . . nor,* and *either . . . or* show similarity between details. *However, by contrast, yet, but, unlike, instead, whereas,* and *while* show difference. Note the use of both types of transitions in the model below.

MODEL
**Dr. Herriot was a successful veterinarian. Mrs. Donovan also took care of sick animals. He cured his patients with medical treatments and laboratory medications. Mrs. Donovan, by contrast, used home remedies and constant affection.**

**WRITING TIP** Both *but* and *however* may be used to join two independent clauses. When *but* is used as a coordinating conjunction, it is preceded by a comma. When *however* is used as a conjunctive adverb, it is preceded by a semicolon and followed by a comma.

**Cause and Effect** When you are writing about a cause-and-effect relationship, use transitional words and phrases such as *since, because, thus, therefore, so, due to, for this reason,* and *as a result* to help clarify that relationship and to make your writing coherent.

MODEL
**Because we never feed our dog from the table, she doesn't beg for food while we are eating. We are happy to take credit for her one good habit.**

**Conclusions**

A conclusion should leave readers with a strong final impression. Try any of these approaches.

### Kinds of Conclusions

Here are some effective methods for bringing your writing to a conclusion:

- Restate your thesis
- Ask a question
- Make a recommendation
- Make a prediction
- Summarize your information

**Restate Your Thesis** A good way to conclude an essay is by restating your thesis, or main idea, in different words. The conclusion below restates the thesis introduced on page 1149.

> MODEL
>
> Although each pet has a personality of its own just as each child does, there are many ways of encouraging the best behavior in each. Love, persistence, patience, and consistency make all the difference in training pets as well as in raising children.

**Ask a Question** Try asking a question that sums up what you have said and gives readers something new to think about. The question below concludes an appeal to support a local politician.

> MODEL
>
> Have you noticed that the roads are in better repair and that there are more safe playgrounds and parks since Mayor Ballwin has been in office?

**Make a Recommendation** When you are persuading your audience to take a position on an issue, you can conclude by recommending a specific course of action.

> MODEL
>
> Today's youth are at risk of damaging their hearing by listening to very loud music. Consider turning down the bass and turning down the volume on your headphones.

**Make a Prediction** Readers are concerned about matters that may affect them and therefore are moved by a conclusion that predicts the future.

> MODEL
>
> If the government continues to spend money from Social Security taxes for current operations, we will create a disastrous burden of debt for future generations.

**Summarize Your Information** Summarizing reinforces the writer's main ideas, leaving a strong, lasting impression. The model below concludes with a statement that summarizes a film review.

> MODEL
>
> The movie *The Postman* shows the tremendous influence of the Chilean poet Pablo Neruda on a young Italian man—not only in his love life but also in his acquired self-confidence and his dedication to a cause.

 **Elaboration**

Elaboration is the process of developing a writing idea by providing specific supporting details that are relevant and appropriate to the purpose and form of your writing.

- **Facts and Statistics** A fact is a statement that can be verified, while a statistic is a fact stated in numbers. Make sure the facts and statistics you supply are from a reliable, up-to-date source. As in the model below, the facts and statistics you use should strongly support the statements you make.

> MODEL
>
> Our entire solar system speeds through the Milky Way Galaxy at a speed of 180 miles a second. One could worry about the ability of any of us to stay in place with our feet on the ground. Or one could marvel at the magnificence of a universe that keeps everything whirling with such constancy.

• **Sensory Details** Details that show how something looks, sounds, tastes, smells, or feels can enliven a description, making readers feel they are actually experiencing what you are describing. Which senses does the writer appeal to in this paragraph?

MODEL

The campers lay as quiet as mice inside their tent as they considered the power of the massive beast they'd glimpsed through the tent flap. Snuffling and crackling brought news that the black bear had found something delectable inside the garbage can, probably leftover corncobs and pork-chop bones. The campfire smoke lingered, and the campers fervently hoped that the odors of grease and butter wouldn't bring the animal even closer to the tent.

• **Incidents** From our earliest years, we are interested in hearing "stories." One way to illustrate a point powerfully is to relate an incident or tell a story, as shown in the example below.

MODEL

January 24, 1848, began one of the most colorful periods of United States history. On that day James Marshall found gold at Sutter's Mill in California. That discovery brought on massive immigration of European Americans to the West. It also brought many new images and words—*gold rush*, *gold miners*, and *forty-niners*, to name a few.

• **Examples** An example can help make an abstract or a complex idea concrete or can provide evidence to clarify a point for readers.

MODEL

The mere mention of the names of some writers causes distinct reactions, even from those who have not read the writers' works. For example, the mention of William Shakespeare causes many people to take in a sharp breath of admiration and others to think of something long and tedious. On the other hand, the name Edgar Allan Poe brings an involuntary shiver to almost everyone.

• **Quotations** Choose quotations that clearly support your points, and be sure that you copy each quotation word for word. Remember always to credit the source.

MODEL

In her book *How to Talk to Your Cat*, Patricia Moyes replies to certain authorities who claim that cats cannot smile: "I can only presume that these people have never owned a cat in the true sense of the word." She goes on to describe the cat's smile as a "relaxed upward tilting of the corners of the mouth" that occurs when the cat is feeling peaceful or pleased, perhaps while being stroked or while having happy dreams.

## 2.6 Using Language Effectively

Effective use of language can help readers to recognize the significance of an issue, to visualize a scene, or to understand a character. The specific words and phrases that you use have everything to do with how effectively you communicate meaning. This is true of all kinds of writing, from novels to office memos. Keep these particular points in mind.

• **Specific Nouns** Nouns are specific when they refer to individual or particular things. If you refer to a *city*, you are being general. If you refer to *London*, you are being specific. Specific nouns help readers identify the *who*, *what*, and *where* of your message.

• **Specific Verbs** Verbs are the most powerful words in sentences. They convey the action, the movement, and sometimes the drama of thoughts and observations. Verbs such as *trudged, skipped,* and *sauntered* provide a more vivid picture of the action than the verb *walked*.

• **Specific Modifiers** Use modifiers sparingly, but when you use them, make them count. Is the building *big* or *towering*? Are your poodle's paws *small* or *petite*? Once again, it is the more specific word that carries the greater impact.

# ③ Descriptive Writing

*Descriptive writing allows you to paint word pictures about anything and everything in the world, from events of global importance to the most personal feelings. It is an essential part of almost every piece of writing, including essays, poems, letters, field notes, newspaper reports, and videos.*

---

**RUBRIC** **Standards for Writing**

**A successful description should**

- have a clear focus and sense of purpose.
- use sensory details and precise words to create a vivid image, establish a mood, or express emotion.
- present details in a logical order.

---

## ③.1 Key Techniques

**Consider Your Goals** What do you want to accomplish in writing your description? Do you want to show why something is important to you? Do you want to make a person or scene more memorable? Do you want to explain an event?

**Identify Your Audience** Who will read your description? How familiar are they with your subject? What background information will they need? Which details will they find most interesting?

**Think Figuratively** What figures of speech might help make your description vivid and interesting? What simile or metaphor comes to mind? What imaginative comparisons can you make? What living thing does an inanimate object remind you of?

> MODEL
>
> After the 10-mile hike, we pounced on the buffet table like starving lions. Some of us stuffed pieces of bread and morsels of roast beef into our mouths before we'd even finished filling our plates. By the time we flopped into chairs, we looked even more like scavenging carnivores, with our dripping hands and greasy mouths. But the predatory look in our eyes had abated somewhat.

**Gather Sensory Details** Which sights, smells, tastes, sounds, and textures make your subject come alive? Which details stick in your mind when you observe or recall your subject? Which senses does it most strongly affect?

> MODEL
>
> Light snowflakes brushed her cheek as she poised at the top of the mountain. After an admiring glance at the spots of bright color on the slope, she lifted both ski poles and crouched in preparation for the leap forward to start her fifth run through the powdery snow.

You might want to use a chart like the one shown here to collect sensory details about your subject.

| Sights | Sounds | Textures | Smells | Tastes |
|--------|--------|----------|--------|--------|
|        |        |          |        |        |

**Create a Mood** What feelings do you want to evoke in your readers? Do you want to soothe them with comforting images? Do you want to build tension with ominous details? Do you want to evoke sadness or joy?

> MODEL
>
> It was always difficult to see the dangerous rocks just below the surface of the lake, but in the dark and without the light it was impossible. If only Guy had remembered the backup batteries. Although he had only been on this lake twice before, he had been confident he could run this fishing trip without incident. Now, as gray clouds gathered to cover even the faint light of the new moon, Guy worried not just about his summer job but also about the safety of his first paying customers.

## 3.2 Options for Organization

**Spatial Order** Choose one of these options to show the spatial order of a scene.

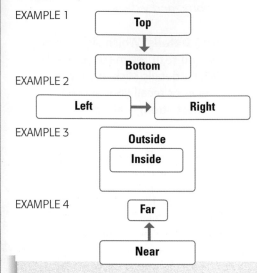

EXAMPLE 1

Top → Bottom

EXAMPLE 2

Left → Right

EXAMPLE 3

Outside / Inside

EXAMPLE 4

Far ← Near

MODEL

Thunder's nostrils quivered as he was led into the barn. How would this be as a place to spend nights from now on? In the stall to the left, the straw smelled fresh. Beyond that stall a saddle hung from rough boards. To the right of his stall was another, from which a mare looked at him curiously. So far, so good. From the far right, beyond two empty stalls, strode the barn cat.

**WRITING TIP** Use transitions that help the reader picture the relationship among the objects you describe. Some useful transitions for showing spatial relationships are *behind, below, here, in the distance, on the left, over,* and *on top.*

**Order of Impression** Order of impression is how you notice details.

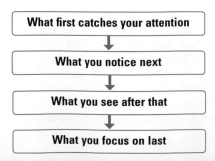

What first catches your attention

↓

What you notice next

↓

What you see after that

↓

What you focus on last

MODEL

As her foot slipped on the pebbles, her first thought was of whether she would sprain an ankle sliding into the surf. Her heart began a dangerous thumping, but soon the soft sand provided a comfortable seat so that her body responded by calming down. She realized that the water was shallow and warm. Her hat would shade her eyes and prevent sunburn. By the time she remembered she had on dry-clean-only shorts, she'd decided that sitting in the surf while her friends gathered shells was a perfectly fine way to enjoy the beach.

**WRITING TIP** Use transitions that help readers understand the order of the impressions you are describing. Some useful transitions are *after, next, during, first, before, finally,* and *then.*

**Order of Importance** You might want to use order of importance as the organizing structure for your description.

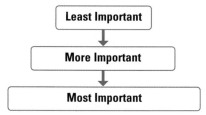

Least Important

↓

More Important

↓

Most Important

MODEL

Annaliese tried to imprint on her memory everything about the accident. She remembered unimportant details, like the song that was playing on her radio before the truck loomed up ahead. She remembered her panic as she steered into the guard rail. Gradually she recalled more important information—her conservative speed, the fact that the truck was on the wrong side of the road coming toward her, the driver's long beard. Finally, when she closed her eyes and really concentrated, she could remember the license plate number at eye level as the truck zoomed on by.

**WRITING TIP** Use transitions that help the reader understand the order of importance that you attach to the elements of your description. Some useful transitions are *first, second, mainly, more important, less important,* and *least important.*

# 4 Narrative Writing

*Narrative writing tells a story. If you write a story from your imagination, it is a fictional narrative. A true story about actual events is a nonfictional narrative. Narrative writing can be found in short stories, novels, news articles, and biographies.*

## RUBRIC   Standards for Writing

**A successful narrative should**

- include descriptive details and dialogue to develop the characters, setting, and plot.
- have a clear beginning, middle, and end.
- have a logical organization, with clues and transitions to help the reader understand the order of events.
- maintain a consistent tone and point of view.
- use language that is appropriate for the audience.
- demonstrate the significance of events or ideas.

## 4.1  Key Techniques

**Identify the Main Events** What are the most important events in your narrative? Is each event part of the chain of events needed to tell the story? In a fictional narrative, this series of events is the story's plot.

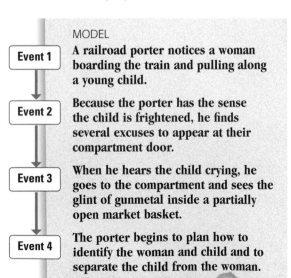

MODEL

**Event 1** A railroad porter notices a woman boarding the train and pulling along a young child.

**Event 2** Because the porter has the sense the child is frightened, he finds several excuses to appear at their compartment door.

**Event 3** When he hears the child crying, he goes to the compartment and sees the glint of gunmetal inside a partially open market basket.

**Event 4** The porter begins to plan how to identify the woman and child and to separate the child from the woman.

**Describe the Setting** When do the events occur? Where do they take place? How can you use setting to create mood and to set the stage for the characters and their actions?

MODEL

Bright spring sunshine highlighted the auburn hair of the child being pulled along by the matronly woman carrying a market basket. Joshua helped her up the steps onto the train. He stooped to lift the little girl at the same moment the woman jerked the small arm, so that the child stumbled up the stairs on her own.

**Depict Characters Vividly** What do your characters look like? What do they think and say? How do they act? What vivid details can show readers what the characters are like?

MODEL

Joshua hardly noticed the other passengers as his eyes followed the woman and child. His instincts warned him that something was wrong here.

**WRITING TIP** Dialogue is an effective way of developing characters in a narrative. As you write dialogue, choose words that express your characters' personalities and show how the characters feel about one another and about the events in the plot.

MODEL

"Hello, ma'am. I'm Joshua, and I'll be in soon to get your compartment ready for the night."

The woman's whisper sent chills down Joshua's spine. "Yeah, OK."

"Are you having a nice ride?" he asked the thin little girl.

"She likes the train," answered the woman.

## 4.2 Options for Organization

**Option 1: Chronological Order** One way to organize a piece of narrative writing is to arrange the events in chronological order, as shown below.

**MODEL**

**Introduction** *characters and setting*

It is the middle of March, the beginning of the year in Rome, and the first time in a while that young Marius has been able to go into the center of the city near the senate house and capitol.

**Event 1**

A crowd gathers to watch the senators arrive. There is a rumor that the emperor will also come. Marius hurries toward the front of the crowd.

**Event 2**

The crowd thickens, and Marius can barely make out the laurel-wreath head-covering indicating that indeed the emperor has arrived. There is great commotion, with shouts and screams.

**End** *perhaps show the significance of the events*

Marius witnesses the assassination of Julius Caesar and hears the speeches condemning Caesar. He then goes home with the sad news of the murder and a premonition that there are bad times ahead for Rome.

**Option 2: Flashback** It is also possible in narrative writing to arrange the order of events by starting with an event that happened before the beginning of the story.

**Flashback**
Begin with a key event that happened before the time in which the story takes place.

↓

Introduce characters and setting.

↓

Describe the events leading up to the conflict.

**Option 3: Focus on Conflict** When the telling of a fictional narrative focuses on a central conflict, the story's plot may follow the model shown below.

**MODEL**

**Describe the main characters and setting.**

The brothers arrive at the school gym long before the rest of the basketball team. Although the twins are physically identical, their personalities couldn't be more different. Mark is outgoing and impulsive, while Matt is thoughtful and shy.

**Present the conflict.**

Matt realizes his brother is missing shots on purpose and believes they will lose the championship.

**Relate the events that make the conflict complex and cause the characters to change.**

- Matt has a chance at a basketball scholarship if they win the championship.

- Mark needs money to buy a car.

- Matt and Mark have stood by each other no matter what.

**Present the resolution or outcome of the conflict.**

Matt retells a family story in which their grandfather chose honor and integrity over easy money. Mark plays to win.

# ⑤ Explanatory Writing

*Explanatory writing informs and explains. For example, you can use it to evaluate the effects of a new law, to compare two movies, to analyze a piece of literature, or to examine the problem of greenhouse gases in the atmosphere.*

## 5.1 Types of Explanatory Writing

There are many types of explanatory writing. Think about your topic and select the type that presents the information most clearly.

**Compare and Contrast** How are two or more subjects alike? How are they different?

> MODEL
> As Isaac Asimov points out, both dial and digital clocks show the time, but only dial clocks show at a glance the relationship of the hours to one another.

**Cause and Effect** How does one event cause something else to happen? Why do certain conditions exist? What are the results of an action or a condition?

> MODEL
> Because Charley did not want his brother to appear "country" carrying a brown paper bag through a fancy hotel lobby, he pretended he was taking the sweet potato pie home with him.

**Analysis** How does something work? How can it be defined? What are its parts?

> MODEL
> Some contributions of dial clocks that Asimov fears will be lost if the clocks disappear are concepts of clockwise and counterclockwise and of establishing location by referring to position, such as pointing out an object "at the two o'clock position."

**Problem-Solution** How can you identify and state a problem? How would you analyze the problem and its causes? How can it be solved?

> MODEL
> The narrator, Shanshan, in "Love Must Not Be Forgotten" has some questions about marrying her fiancé; she decides that it will be better to be single than to marry without love.

## 5.2 Compare and Contrast

Compare-and-contrast writing examines the similarities and differences between two or more subjects. You might, for example, compare and contrast two short stories, the main characters in a novel, or two movies.

> **RUBRIC** **Standards for Writing**
>
> **Successful compare-and-contrast writing should**
> - clearly identify the subjects that are being compared and contrasted.
> - include specific, relevant details.
> - follow a clear plan of organization, dealing with the same features of both subjects under discussion.
> - use language and details appropriate to the audience.
> - use transitional words and phrases to clarify similarities and differences.

### Options for Organization

Compare-and-contrast writing can be organized in different ways. The examples that follow demonstrate feature-by-feature organization and subject-by-subject organization.

## **6.2** Options for Organization

In a two-sided persuasive essay, you want to show the weaknesses of other opinions as you explain the strengths of your own.

The example below demonstrates one method of organizing your persuasive essay to convince your audience.

### Option 1: Reasons for Your Opinion

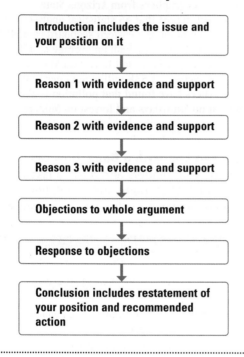

Introduction includes the issue and your position on it

↓

Reason 1 with evidence and support

↓

Reason 2 with evidence and support

↓

Reason 3 with evidence and support

↓

Objections to whole argument

↓

Response to objections

↓

Conclusion includes restatement of your position and recommended action

### Option 2: Point-by-Point Basis

In the organization that follows, each reason and its objections are examined on a point-by-point basis.

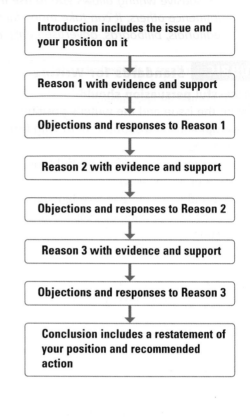

Introduction includes the issue and your position on it

↓

Reason 1 with evidence and support

↓

Objections and responses to Reason 1

↓

Reason 2 with evidence and support

↓

Objections and responses to Reason 2

↓

Reason 3 with evidence and support

↓

Objections and responses to Reason 3

↓

Conclusion includes a restatement of your position and recommended action

**Beware of Illogical Arguments** Be careful about using illogical arguments. Opponents can easily attack your argument if you present illogical material.

**Circular reasoning**—trying to prove a statement by just repeating it in different words

> Precipitation is heavier on weekends because of higher rainfall then.

**Overgeneralization**—making a statement that is too broad to prove

> Nobody is doing anything to reduce air pollution.

**Either-or fallacy**—stating that there are only two alternatives when there are many

> Either we cut weekday car travel by fifty percent or pollution will make our city unlivable.

**Cause-and-effect fallacy**—falsely assuming that because one event follows another, the first event caused the second

> The growing population of our region has caused the increase in air pollution.

# ❼ Research Report Writing

*A research report explores a topic in depth, incorporating information from a variety of sources.*

---

**RUBRIC  Standards for Writing**

**An effective research report should**

- clearly state the purpose of the report in a thesis statement.
- use evidence and details from a variety of sources to support the thesis.
- contain only accurate and relevant information.
- document sources correctly.
- develop the topic logically and include appropriate transitions.
- include a properly formatted Works Cited list.

---

## ⁊⒈ Key Techniques

**Develop Relevant, Interesting, and Researchable Questions** Asking thoughtful questions is an ongoing part of research. Begin with a list of basic questions that are relevant to your topic. Focus on getting basic facts that answer the *who, what, where, when,* and *why* of your topic. If you were researching the civil rights movement you might develop a set of questions like these.

MODEL

**What wrongs did the civil rights movement hope to correct?**

**How did African Americans live when they were denied the right to vote?**

As you become more familiar with your topic, think of questions that might provide an interesting perspective that makes readers think.

MODEL

**What groups of people have been denied equal rights in the United States?**

Check that your questions are researchable. Ask questions that will uncover facts, statistics, case studies, and other documentable evidence.

**Clarify Your Thesis** A thesis statement is one or two sentences clearly stating the main idea that you will develop in your report. A thesis may also indicate the organizational pattern you will follow and reflect your tone and point of view.

MODEL

**The struggle for civil rights in the United States has been a series of peaks and valleys for those struggling for their rights.**

**Document Your Sources** You need to document, or credit, the sources where you find your evidence. In the example below, the writer uses and documents a quotation from an essay.

MODEL

**In a 1967 essay, "The Civil Rights Movement: What Good Was It?" Alice Walker states that the civil rights movement "is dead for the white man because it no longer interests him" (121).**

**Support Your Ideas** You should support your ideas with relevant evidence—facts, anecdotes, and statistics—from reliable sources. In the example below the writer includes a fact about racial discrimination in the armed forces.

MODEL

**By executive order issued July 30, 1948, President Truman banned segregation and racial discrimination in the United States armed forces (Morris and Morris 498).**

## 7.2 Gathering Information: Sources

You will use a range of sources to collect the information you need to develop your research paper. These will include both print and electronic resources.

**General Reference Works** To clarify your thesis and begin your research, consult reference works that give quick, general overviews on a subject. General reference works include encyclopedias, almanacs and yearbooks, atlases, and dictionaries.

**Specialized Reference Works** Once you have a good idea of your specific topic, you are ready to look for detailed information in specialized reference works. In the library's reference section, specialized dictionaries and encyclopedias can be found for almost any field. For example, in the field of literature, you will find specialized reference sources such as *Contemporary Authors* and *Twentieth-Century Literary Criticism.*

**Periodicals** Journals and periodicals are a good source for detailed, up-to-date information. Periodical indexes, found in print and on-line catalogs in the library, will help you find articles on a topic. The *Readers' Guide to Periodical Literature* indexes many popular magazines. More specialized indexes include the *Humanities Index* and the *Social Sciences Index.*

**Electronic Resources  Commercial information services** offer access to reference works such as dictionaries and encyclopedias, databases, and periodicals.

The **Internet** is a vast network of computer networks. News services, libraries, universities, researchers, organizations, and government agencies use the Internet to communicate and to distribute information. The Internet gives you access to the World Wide Web, which provides information on particular topics and links you to related topics and resources.

A **CD-ROM** is a research aid that stores information on a compact disk. Reference works on CD-ROMs may include text, sound, images, and video.

**Databases** are large collections of related information stored electronically. You can scan the information or search for specific facts.

**RESEARCH TIP** To find books on a specific topic, check the library's on-line catalog. Be sure to copy the correct call numbers of books that sound promising. Also look at books shelved nearby. They may relate to your topic.

## 7.3 Gathering Information: Validity of Sources

When you find source material, you must determine whether it is useful and accurate.

**Credibility of Authorship** Check whether an author has written several books or articles on the subject and has published in a well-respected newspaper or journal.

**Objectivity** Decide whether the information is fact, opinion, or propaganda. Reputable sources credit other sources of information.

**Currency** Check the publication date of the source to see whether the information is current.

**Credibility of Publisher** Seek information from a respected newspaper or journal, not from a tabloid newspaper or popular-interest magazine.

**WEB TIP** Be especially skeptical of information you locate on the Internet since virtually anyone can post anything there. Read the URL, or Internet address. Sites sponsored by a government agency (*.gov*) or an educational institution (*.edu*) are generally more reliable.

## 7.4 Taking Notes

As you find useful information, record the bibliographic information of each source on a separate index card. Then you are ready to take notes on your sources. You will probably use these three methods of note-taking.

**Paraphrase,** or restate in your own words, the main ideas and supporting details of the passage.

**Summarize,** or rephrase in fewer words, the original materials, trying to capture the key ideas.

**Quote,** or copy word for word, the original text, if you think the author's own words best clarify a particular point. Use quotation marks to signal the beginning and the end of the quotation.

For more details on making source cards and taking notes, see the Research Report Workshop on pages 1105–1112.

## 7.5 Options for Organization

Begin by reading over your note cards and sorting them into groups. The main-idea headings may help you find connections among the notes. Then arrange the groups of related note cards so that the ideas flow logically from one group to the next.

Like other forms of writing, research reports can be organized in several different ways. Some subjects may fit in chronological order. For other subjects, you may want to compare and contrast two topics. Other possibilities are a cause-and-effect organization or least-important to most-important evidence. If your material does not lend itself to any of the above organizations, try a general-to-specific approach.

Whatever your organizational pattern, making an outline can help guide the drafting process. The subtopics that you located in sorting your note cards will be the major topics of your outline, preceded by Roman numerals. Make sure that items of the same importance are parallel in form. For example, in the Option 1 Topic Outline below, topics I and II are both phrases. So are subtopics A and B.

A second kind of outline, shown below in Option 2, uses complete sentences instead of phrases for topics and subtopics.

### Option 1: Topic Outline

The Ups and Downs of Civil Rights
**Introduction** In the United States many groups have had to struggle for equal rights.

I. Early Years
    A. Bill of Rights
    B. African Americans
    C. Women
    D. Native Americans

II. Post-Civil War Years

### Option 2: Sentence Outline

The Ups and Downs of Civil Rights
**Introduction** In the United States many groups have had to struggle for equal rights.

I. The early years of the nation saw the most egregious violations of civil rights in the way slaves, Native Americans, and women were treated.
    A. The Bill of Rights Amendments to the Constitution reflect early concerns about individual freedoms.
    B. Slavery of African Americans was the most pervasive denial of civil rights.
    C. Women could not vote or hold office.
    D. Native Americans were not considered citizens of the United States.

II. The Civil War ended slavery, but many groups, including African Americans, were still denied certain civil rights.

Writing Handbook

## 7.6 Documenting Sources

When you quote, paraphrase, or summarize information from a source, you need to credit that source. Parenthetical documentation is the accepted method for crediting sources. You may choose to name the author in parentheses following the information, along with the page number on which the information is found.

> MODEL
>
> **Slaves had fought with the Continental Army for American independence, and when they were denied basic human rights by the new nation, many were ready to take up arms to overthrow slavery (McKissack and McKissack 6).**

In parenthetical documentation, you may also use the author's name in the sentence, along with the information. If so, enclose, in parentheses after the sentence, only the page number on which the information is found.

> MODEL
>
> **As Eve Merriam points out, "English law had discriminated severely against women; the colonies carried on that tradition" (9).**

In either case, your reader can find out more about the source by turning to your Works Cited page, which lists complete bibliographical information for each source.

PUNCTUATION TIP When only the author and page number appear in parentheses, there is no punctuation between the two items. Also notice that the parenthetical citation comes after the closing quotation marks of a quotation, if there is one, and before the end punctuation of the sentence.

The examples above show citations for books with one author. The list that follows shows the correct way to write parenthetical citations for several kinds of sources.

### Guidelines for Parenthetical Documentation

**Work by One Author**

Put the author's last name and the page reference in parentheses: (Walker 120).

If you mention the author's name in the sentence, put only the page reference in parentheses: (120).

**Work by Two or Three Authors**

Put the authors' last names and the page reference in parentheses: (McKissack and McKissack 6).

**Work by More Than Three Authors**

Give the first author's last name followed by *et al.* and the page reference: (Armento et al. 127).

**Work with No Author Given**

Give the title or a shortened version and (if appropriate) the page reference: ("The Factory Girl" 305).

**One of Two or More Works by Same Author**

Give the author's last name, the title or a shortened version, and the page reference: (Walker, Living 41).

**Selection from a Book of Collected Essays**

Give the name of the author of the essay and the page reference: (Irwin 33).

**Dictionary Definition**

Give the entry title in quotation marks: ("feminist").

**Unsigned Article in an Encyclopedia**

Give the article title in quotation marks, followed by a shortened source title: ("Uncle Tom," Encyclopedia of Word and Phrase Origins).

WRITING TIP Presenting someone else's writing or ideas as your own is plagiarism. To avoid plagiarism, you need to credit sources. However, if a piece of information is common knowledge—information available in several sources—you do not need to credit a source.

**1166**   WRITING HANDBOOK

## 7.7 Following MLA Manuscript Guidelines

The final copy of your report should follow the Modern Language Association (MLA) guidelines for manuscript preparation.

- The heading in the upper left-hand corner of the first page should include your name, your teacher's name, the course name, and the date, each on a separate line.

- Below the heading, center the title on the page.

- Number all the pages consecutively in the upper right-hand corner, one-half inch from the top. On the second and suceeding pages, include your last name before the page number.

- Double-space the entire paper.

- Except for the margins above the page numbers, leave one-inch margins on all sides of every page.

The Works Cited page at the end of your report is an alphabetized list of the sources you have used and documented. In each entry all lines after the first are indented an additional one-half inch.

**WRITING TIP** When your report includes a quotation that is longer than four lines, set it off from the rest of the text by indenting the entire quotation one inch from the left margin. In this case, you should not use quotation marks.

---

**Works Cited**

Models for Works Cited entries

**Works Cited**

Armento, Beverly J., et al. A More Perfect Union. Boston: Houghton, 1991.

❶ Book with more than three authors; note that publishers' names are shortened.

Irwin, Inez Haynes. "Why I Earn My Own Living." These Modern Women: Autobiographical Essays from the Twenties. Ed. Elaine Showalter. Old Westbury: Feminist, 1978.

❷ Selection from a book of collected essays

McKissack, Patricia, and Fredrick McKissack. Rebels Against Slavery: American Slave Revolts. New York: Scholastic, 1996.

❸ Book with two authors

---. The Civil Rights Movement in America from 1865 to the Present. Chicago: Childrens, 1987.

❹ Second work by same author

Merriam, Eve, ed. Growing Up Female in America: Ten Lives. Garden City: Doubleday, 1971.

❺ Book with editor but no single author

Mitchell, Michael Dan. "Acculturation Problems Among the Plains Indians." The Chronicles of Oklahoma 3 (1966): 281-289.

❻ Article in scholarly journal

Walker, Alice. In Search of Our Mother's Gardens. Orlando: Harcourt, 1983.

❼ Book with one author

## 7.8 MLA Documentation: Electronic Sources

As with print sources, information from electronic sources such as CD-ROMs or the Internet must be documented on your Works Cited page. You may find a reference to a source on the Internet and then use the print version of the article. If so, document it as you do other printed works. However, if you read or print out an article directly off the Internet, document it as shown below for an electronic source. Although electronic sources are shown separately below, they should be included on the Works Cited page with print sources.

**Internet Sources** Works Cited entries for Internet sources include the same kind of information as that for print sources. They also include the date you accessed the information and the electronic address of the source. Some of the information about the source may be unavailable. Include as much as you can. For more information on how to write Works Cited entries for Internet sources, see the MLA guidelines posted on the Internet or access this document through the McDougal Littell Website.

 **More Online: Style Guidelines**
www.mcdougallittell.com

**CD-ROMs** Entries for CD-ROMs include the publication medium (CD-ROM), the distributor, and the date of publication. Some of the information shown may not always be available. Include as much as you can.

---

**Works Cited**

Models for Works Cited entries for electronic sources

### Works Cited

"Civil Rights." <u>Grolier Multimedia Encyclopedia</u>. 1998 ed. CD-ROM. Danbury: Grolier Interactive.

❶ Encyclopedia article from CD-ROM version

Lien, Pei-te. "An Examination of Policy Opinions Among Asian Americans." <u>Asian American Policy Review</u> 7 (1997). Abstract. 10 Sept. 1998 <http://www.ksg.harvard.edu/ ~aapr/Volume7.html#Lien>.

❷ Abstract of an article in a scholarly journal, available on the Internet; includes access date

Park, Maud Wood. <u>Lucy Stone: A Chronicle Play</u>. Boston: Baker, 1938. <u>Votes for Women: Selections from the National American Woman Suffrage Association Collection, 1848–1921</u>. 17 Aug. 1998 <http://lcweb2.loc.gov/cgi-bin/query/r?ammem/naw: @field(FLD001+38008512+):@@@$REF$>.

❸ Complete text of a play, available on the Internet; includes access date

"Reconstruction." <u>Britannica Online</u>. Vers. 98.2. Apr. 1998. Encyclopaedia Britannica. 24 Sept. 1998 <http://www.eb.com.180>.

❹ Encyclopaedia entry from online version

<u>U.S. Department of Justice Home Page</u>. 10 Sept. 1998 <http://www.usdoj.gov>.

❺ Home page; shows date you accessed it

# 8 Business Writing

*The ability to write clearly and succinctly is an essential skill in the business world. As you prepare to enter the job market, you will need to know how to create letters, memos, and résumés.*

## RUBRIC
### Standards for Writing

**Successful business writing should**

- have a tone and language geared to the appropriate audience.
- state the purpose clearly in the opening sentences or paragraph.
- use precise words and avoid jargon.
- present only essential information.
- present details in a logical order.
- conclude with a summary of important points.

## 8.1 Key Techniques

**Think About Your Purpose** Why are you doing this writing? Do you want to "sell" yourself to a college admissions committee or a job interviewer? Do you want to order or complain about a product? Do you want to set up a meeting or respond to someone's ideas?

**Identify Your Audience** Who will read your writing? What background information will they need? What questions might they have? What tone or language is appropriate?

**Support Your Points** What specific details clarify your ideas? What reasons do you have for your statements? What points most strongly support them?

**Finish Strongly** How can you best sum up your statements? What is your main point? What action do you want others to take?

## 8.2 Options

### Model 1: Letter

**Heading** *Where the letter comes from and when*

#1 Andover Lane
Sunnydale, CA 93933
July 16, ____

**Inside Address** *To whom the letter is being sent*

Customer Service Representative
Bionic Bikes, Inc.
12558 Industrial Drive
Schaumburg, IL 60193

**Salutation** *Greeting*

Dear Customer Service Representative:

**Body** *Text of the message*

I was really pleased to get a Bionic Bike for my birthday in March. I've ridden it every day—to school, to the rec center, and everywhere.

The bike is great, but the handlebars are not comfortable. I think you should raise the angle of the hand grips about two inches so that riders can hold them comfortably while looking straight ahead.

Thank you for considering my suggestion.

Sincerely yours,
*Marisa LaPorta*

**Closing**

## Model 2: Memo

**Heading** *Whom the memo is to and from, what it's about, and when it's being sent*

To: Jeff Kniffen
From: LaDonna Ford
Re: customer letter
Date: 8/15/__

**Body**

Jeff, please send a brief note to this customer thanking her for her suggestion. Enclose a brochure explaining the structure of the handlebars.

Also, please forward the suggestion to the engineers.

Thanks.

**Model 3: Résumé** A well-written résumé is invaluable when you apply for a part-time or full-time job or to college. It should highlight your skills, accomplishments, and experience. Proofread your résumé carefully to make sure it is clear and accurate and free of errors in grammar and spelling. It is a good idea to save a copy of your résumé on your computer or on a disk so that you can easily update it.

**State your purpose.** *This résumé is for a job application. A modified style can be used for a college application.*

**List your previous employment experience** *in reverse chronological order.*

**Extracurricular activities and hobbies** *can give a fuller picture of you and point out special job-related skills.*

**JENNIFER RUDY**
P.O. Box 2211
White Horse, TX 79801

*Objective*  Part-time position at veterinary clinic

*Qualifications*  Love of animals
Owner of three dogs and one cat
Serious, hard worker

*Work Experience*  1998—Junior counselor at Camp Wanabe, White Horse, TX
1997–Present—Partner in pet-sitting service

*Education*  Currently a sophomore at White Horse High School

*Extracurricular Activities*  Science Club, varsity cheerleader, Honor Society

*Hobbies*  Pet-sitting, reading, swimming

*References*  Available upon request

# ❶ Inquiry and Research

*In this age of seemingly unlimited information, the ability to locate and evaluate resources efficiently can spell the difference between success and failure—in both the academic and the business worlds. Make use of print and nonprint information sources.*

## ⟨1.1⟩ Finding Sources

Good research involves using the wealth of resources available to answer your questions and raise new questions. Knowing where to go and how to access information can lead you to interesting and valuable sources.

### Reference Works
Reference works are print and nonprint sources of information that provide quick access to both general overviews and specific facts about a subject. These include

**Dictionaries**—word definitions, pronunciations, and origins

**Thesauruses**—lists of synonyms and antonyms for each entry

**Glossaries**—collections of specialized terms, such as those pertaining to literature, with definitions

**Encyclopedias**—detailed information on nearly every subject, arranged alphabetically (*Encyclopaedia Britannica*). Specialized encyclopedias deal with specific subjects, such as music, economics, and science (*Encyclopedia of Economics*).

**Almanacs and Yearbooks**—current facts and statistics (*World Almanac, Statistical Abstract of the United States*)

**Atlases**—maps and information about weather, agricultural and industrial production, and other geographical topics (*National Geographic Atlas of the World*)

**Specialized Reference Works**—biographical data (*Who's Who, Current Biography*), literary information (*Contemporary Authors, Book Review Digest, Cyclopedia of Literary Characters, The Oxford Companion to English Literature*), and quotations (*Bartlett's Familiar Quotations*)

**Electronic Sources**—Many of these reference works and databases are available on CD-ROMs, which may include text, sound, photographs, and video. CD-ROMs can be used on a home or library computer. You can subscribe to services that offer access to these sources on-line.

### Periodicals and Indexes
One kind of specialized reference is a periodical.

- Some periodicals, such as *Atlantic Monthly* and *Psychology Today,* are intended for a general audience. They are indexed in the *Readers' Guide to Periodical Literature.*

- Many other periodicals, or journals, are intended for specialized or academic audiences. These include titles and subject matter as diverse as *American Psychologist* and *Studies in Short Fiction.* These are indexed in the *Humanities Index* and the *Social Sciences Index.* In addition, most fields have their own indexes. For example, articles on literature are indexed in the *MLA International Bibliography.*

- Many indexes are available in print, CD-ROM, and on-line forms.

### Internet
The Internet is a vast network of computers. News services, libraries, universities, researchers, organizations, and government agencies use the Internet to distribute information and to communicate. The Internet can provide links to library catalogs, newspapers, government sources, and many of the reference sources described above. The Internet includes two key features:

**World Wide Web**—source of information on specific subjects and links to related topics

**Electronic mail (e-mail)**—communications link to other e-mail users worldwide

### Other Resources

In addition to reference works found in the library and over the Internet, you can get information from the following sources: corporate publications, lectures, correspondence, and media such as films, television programs, and recordings. You can also observe directly, conduct your own interviews, and collect data from polls or questionnaires that you create yourself.

##  Evaluating Sources

Not all information is equal. You need to be a discriminating consumer of information and evaluate the credibility of the source, the reliability of the specific information included, and its value in answering your research needs.

### Credibility of Sources

You must determine the credibility and appropriateness of each source in order to write an effective report or speech. Ask yourself the following questions:

**Is the writer an authority?** A writer who has written several books on a subject or whose name is included in many bibliographies may be considered an authoritative source.

**Is the source reliable and unbiased?** What is the author's motivation? For example, a defense of an industry in which the author has a financial interest may be biased. A profile of a writer or scientist written by a close relative may also be biased.

WEB TIP Be especially skeptical of information you locate on the Internet, since virtually anyone can post anything there. Read the URL, or Internet address. Sites sponsored by a government agency (*.gov*) or an educational institution (*.edu*) are generally more reliable.

**Is the source up-to-date?** It is important to consult the most recent material, especially in fields such as medicine and technology that undergo constant research and development. Some authoritative sources have withstood the test of time, however, and should not be overlooked.

**Is the source appropriate?** What audience is the material written for? In general, look for information directed at the educated reader. Material geared to experts or to popular audiences may be too technical or too simplified and therefore not appropriate for most research projects.

### Distinguishing Fact from Opinion

As you gather information, it is important to recognize facts and opinions. A **fact** can be proven to be true or false. You could verify the statement "Congress rejected the bill" by checking newspapers, magazines, or the *Congressional Record.* An **opinion** is a judgment based on facts. The statement "Congress should not have rejected the bill" is an opinion. To evaluate an opinion, check for evidence presented logically and validly to support it.

### Recognizing Bias

A writer may have a particular bias. This does not automatically make his or her point of view unreliable. However, recognizing an author's bias can help you evaluate a source. Recognizing that the author of an article about immigration is a Chinese immigrant will help you understand that author's bias. In addition, an author may have a hidden agenda that makes him or her less than objective about a topic. To avoid relying on information that may be biased, check an author's background and gather a variety of viewpoints.

##  Collecting Information

People use a variety of techniques to collect information during the research process. Try out several of those suggested below and decide which ones work best for you.

### Paraphrasing and Summarizing

You can adapt material from other sources by quoting it directly or by paraphrasing or summarizing it. A paraphrase involves restating the information in your own words. It is often a simpler version but not necessarily a shorter version. A summary involves extracting the main ideas and supporting details and writing a shorter version of the information.

Remember to credit the source when you paraphrase or summarize. See the Writing Handbook—Research Report, pp. 1163–1168.

### Strategies for Paraphrasing

1. Select the portion of the article you want to record.

2. Read it carefully and think about those ideas you find most interesting and useful to your research. Often these will be the main ideas.

3. Retell the information in your own words.

### Strategies for Summarizing

1. Read the article carefully. Determine the main ideas.

2. In your own words, write a shortened version of these main ideas.

## *Avoiding Plagiarism*

Plagiarism is copying someone else's ideas or words and using them as if they were your own. This can happen inadvertently if you are sloppy about collecting information and documenting your sources. Plagiarism is intellectual stealing and can have serious consequences.

### How to Avoid Plagiarism

1. When you paraphrase or summarize, be sure to change entirely the wording of the original by using your own words.

2. Both in notes and on your final report, enclose in quotation marks any material copied directly from other sources.

3. Indicate in your final report the sources of any ideas that are not general knowledge—including those in the visuals—that you have paraphrased or summarized.

4. Include a list of Works Cited with your finished report. See the Writing Handbook—Research Report, pp. 1163–1168.

# ② Study Skills and Strategies

*As you read an assignment for the first time, review material for a test, or search for information for a research report, you use different methods of reading and studying.*

## **2.1** Skimming

When you run your eyes quickly over a text, paying attention to overviews, headings, topic sentences, highlighted words, and graphic features, you are skimming.

Skimming is a good technique for previewing material in a textbook or other source that you must read for an assignment. It is also useful when you are researching a self-selected topic. Skimming a source helps you determine whether it has pertinent information. For example, suppose you are writing a research report on Mark Twain. Skimming an essay on the literature of the frontier can help you quickly determine whether any part of it deals with your topic.

## **2.2** Scanning

To find a specific piece of information in a text, use scanning. To scan, place a card under the first line of a page and move it down slowly. Look for key words and phrases that signal the information you are looking for.

Scanning is useful in reviewing for a test or in finding a specific piece of information for a paper. Suppose you are looking for a discussion of Twain's relationship with his family for your research report. You can scan a book chapter or an essay, looking for the key names *Olivia, Susy, Clara,* and *Jean Clemens.*

## 2.3 In-Depth Reading

When you must thoroughly understand the material in a text, you use in-depth reading.

In-depth reading involves asking questions, taking notes, looking for main ideas, and drawing conclusions as you read slowly and carefully. For example, in researching your report on Twain, you may find an essay on how Twain's point of view changed in his later literature. Since this is closely related to your topic, you will read it in depth and take notes. You also should use in-depth reading for reading textbooks and literary works.

## 2.4 Outlining

Outlining is an efficient way of organizing ideas and is useful in taking notes.

Outlining helps you retain information as you read in depth. For example, you might outline a chapter in a history textbook, listing the main subtopics and the ideas or details that support them. An outline can also be useful for taking notes for a research report or in reading a piece of literature. The following is an example of a topic outline that summarizes, in short phrases, part of a chapter.

MAIN IDEA: **Mark Twain as a mirror of American culture.**
I. **Early Years**
   A. **Humorous newspaper accounts**
   B. **Successful lecture tour**
II. **Hartford Years**
   A. **Successful humorous books**
   B. **Satiric criticisms of some American behavior**
III. **Later Years**
   A. **Personal tragedy, business problems**
   B. **Works emphasize gloomy view of human selfishness**
IV. **Evaluations of Twain**
   A. **Distinctly American voice**
   B. **Outstanding humorist**
   C. **More than a humorist**

## 2.5 Identifying Main Ideas

To understand and remember any material you read, identify its main idea.

In informative material, the main idea is often stated. The thesis statement of an essay or article and the topic sentence of each paragraph often state the main idea. In other material, especially literary works, the main idea is implied. After reading the piece carefully, analyze the important parts, such as characters and plot. Then try to sum up in one sentence the general point that the story makes.

## 2.6 Taking Notes

As you listen or read in depth, take notes to help you understand the material. Look and listen for key words that point to main ideas.

One way to help you summarize the main idea and supporting details is to take notes in modified outline form. In using a modified outline form, you do not need to use numerals and letters. Unlike a formal outline, a modified outline does not require two or more points under each heading, and headings do not need to be parallel grammatically. Yet, like a formal outline, a modified outline organizes a text's main ideas and related details. The following modified outline describes methods of communication:

**Preliterate Methods**
- **storytelling**
- **messengers**
- **smoke signals**
- **drums**

**Literate Methods**
- **writing**
- **printing press**

**Electronic Methods**
- **telegram**
- **telephone**
- **movies**
- **television**
- **Internet**

Use abbreviations and symbols to make note taking more efficient. Following are some commonly used abbreviations for note taking.

| w/ | with | re | regarding |
|----|------|-----|-----------|
| w/o | without | = | is, equals |
| # | number | * | important |
| &, + | and | def | definition |
| > | more than | Amer | America |
| < | less than | tho | although |

# ❸ Critical Thinking

*Critical thinking includes the ability to analyze, evaluate, and synthesize ideas and information. Critical thinking goes beyond simply understanding something. It involves making informed judgments based on sound reasoning skills.*

## 3.1 Avoiding Faulty Reasoning

When you write or speak for a persuasive purpose, you must make sure your logic is valid. Avoid these mistakes in reasoning, called **logical fallacies.**

### Overgeneralization
Conclusions reached on the basis of too little evidence result in the fallacy called overgeneralization. A person who saw three cyclists riding bicycles without helmets might conclude, "Nobody wears bicycle helmets." That conclusion would be an overgeneralization.

### Circular Reasoning
When you support an opinion by simply repeating it in different terms, you are using circular reasoning. For example, "Sport utility vehicles are popular because more people buy them than any other category of new cars." This is an illogical statement because the second part of the sentence simply uses different words to restate the first part of the sentence.

### Either-Or Fallacy
Assuming that a complex question has only two possible answers is called the either-or fallacy. "Either we raise the legal driving age or accidents caused by teenage drivers will continue to increase" is an example of the either-or fallacy. The statement ignores other ways of decreasing the automobile accident rate of teenagers.

### Cause-and-Effect Fallacy
The cause-and-effect fallacy occurs when you say that event B was caused by event A just because event B occurred after event A.

A person might conclude that because a city's air quality worsened two months after a new factory began operation, the new factory caused the air pollution. However, this cause-and-effect relationship would have to be supported by more specific evidence.

## 3.2 Identifying Modes of Persuasion

Understanding persuasive techniques can help you evaluate information, make informed decisions, and avoid persuasive techniques intended to deceive you. Some modes of persuasion appeal to your various emotions.

### Loaded Language
Loaded language is words or phrases chosen to appeal to the emotions. It is often used in place of facts to shape opinion or to evoke a positive or negative reaction. For example, you might feel positive about a politician who has a *plan.* You might, however, feel negative about a politician who has a *scheme.*

### Bandwagon
Bandwagon taps into the human desire to belong. This technique suggests that "everybody" is doing it, or buying it, or believing it. Phrases such as "Don't be the only one . . ." and "Everybody is . . . " signal the bandwagon appeal.

### Testimonials
Testimonials present well-known people or satisfied customers who promote and endorse a product or idea. This technique taps into the appeal of celebrities or into people's need to identify with others just like themselves.

## ③③ Logical Thinking

Persuasive writing and speaking require good reasoning skills. Two ways of creating logical arguments are deductive reasoning and inductive reasoning.

### Deductive Arguments

A deductive argument begins with a generalization, or premise, and then advances with facts and evidence that lead to a conclusion. The conclusion is the logical outcome of the premise. A false premise leads to a false conclusion; a valid premise leads to a valid conclusion provided that the specific facts are correct and the reasoning is correct.

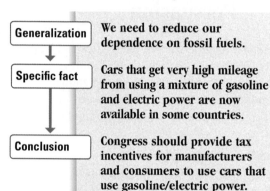

| Generalization | We need to reduce our dependence on fossil fuels. |
| Specific fact | Cars that get very high mileage from using a mixture of gasoline and electric power are now available in some countries. |
| Conclusion | Congress should provide tax incentives for manufacturers and consumers to use cars that use gasoline/electric power. |

You may use deductive reasoning when writing a persuasive paper or speech. Your conclusion is the thesis of your paper. Facts in your paper supporting your premise should lead logically to that conclusion.

### Inductive Arguments

An inductive argument begins with specific evidence that leads to a general conclusion.

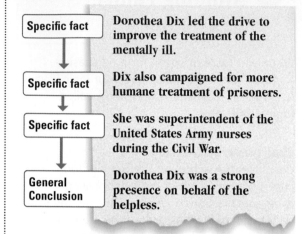

| Specific fact | Dorothea Dix led the drive to improve the treatment of the mentally ill. |
| Specific fact | Dix also campaigned for more humane treatment of prisoners. |
| Specific fact | She was superintendent of the United States Army nurses during the Civil War. |
| General Conclusion | Dorothea Dix was a strong presence on behalf of the helpless. |

The conclusion of an inductive argument often includes a qualifying term such as *some, often,* or *most.* This usage helps to avoid the fallacy of overgeneralization.

# ④ Speaking and Listening

*Good speakers and listeners do more than just talk and hear. They use specific techniques to present their ideas effectively, and they are attentive and critical listeners.*

## ④① Giving a Speech

In school, in business, and in community life, giving a speech is one of the most effective ways of communicating. Whether to persuade, to inform, or to entertain, you may often speak before an audience.

### Analyzing Audience and Purpose

In order to speak effectively, you need to know to whom you are speaking and why you are speaking. When preparing a speech, think about how much knowledge and interest your audience has in your subject. A speech has one of two main purposes: to inform or to persuade. A third purpose, to entertain, is often considered closely related to these two purposes.

A speech **to inform** gives the audience new information, provides a better understanding of information, or enables people to use information in a new way. An informative speech is presented in an objective way.

In a speech **to persuade,** a speaker tries to change the actions or beliefs of an audience.

### Preparing and Delivering a Speech

There are four main methods of preparing and delivering a speech:

**Manuscript** When you speak from **manuscript,** you prepare a complete script of your speech in advance and use it to deliver your speech.

**Memory** When you speak from **memory,** you prepare a written text in advance and then memorize it so you can deliver it word for word.

**Impromptu** When you speak **impromptu,** you speak on the spur of the moment without any special preparation.

**Extemporaneous** When you give an **extemporaneous** speech, you research and prepare your speech and then deliver it with the help of notes.

---

**Points for Effective Speech Delivery**

- Avoid speaking either too fast or too slow. Vary your **speaking rate** depending on your material. Slow down for difficult concepts. Speed up to convince your audience that you are knowledgeable about your subject.

- Speak loud enough to be heard clearly, but not so loud that your voice is overwhelming.

- Use a **conversational tone.**

- Use a change of **pitch,** or inflection, to help make your tone and meaning clear.

- Let your **facial expression** reflect your message.

- Make **eye contact** with as many audience members as possible.

- Use **gestures** to emphasize your words. Don't make your gestures too small to be seen. On the other hand, don't gesture too frequently or wildly.

- Use **good posture**—not too relaxed and not too rigid. Avoid nervous mannerisms.

---

## 4.2 Analyzing, Evaluating and Critiquing a Speech

Evaluating speeches helps you make informed judgments about the ideas presented in a speech. It also helps you learn what makes an effective speech and delivery. Use these criteria to help you analyze, evaluate, and critique speeches.

---

**CRITERIA** **How to Evaluate a Persuasive Speech**

- Did the speaker have a clear goal or argument?
- Did the speaker take the audience's biases into account?
- Did the speaker support the argument with convincing facts?
- Did the speaker use sound logic in developing the argument?
- Did the speaker use voice, facial expression, gestures, and posture effectively?
- Did the speaker hold the audience's interest?

---

**CRITERIA** **How to Evaluate an Informative Speech**

- Did the speaker have a specific, clearly focused topic?
- Did the speaker take the audience's previous knowledge into consideration?
- Did the speaker cite sources for the information?
- Did the speaker communicate the information objectively?
- Did the speaker present the information in an organized manner?
- Did the speaker use visual aids effectively?
- Did the speaker use voice, facial expression, gestures, and posture effectively?

## 4.3 Using Active Listening Strategies

Listeners play an active part in the communication process. A listener has a responsibility just as a speaker does. Listening, unlike hearing, is a learned skill.

As you listen to a public speaker, use the following active listening strategies:

- Determine the **speaker's purpose.**
- Listen for the **main idea** of the message and not simply the individual details.
- **Anticipate the points** that will be made based on the speaker's purpose and main idea.
- Listen with an open mind, but **identify faulty logic, unsupported facts,** and **emotional appeals.**

## 4.4 Conducting Interviews

Conducting a personal interview can be an effective way to get information.

### Preparing for the Interview

- Read any articles by or about the person you will interview. This background information will help you get to the point during the interview.
- Prepare a list of questions. Think of more questions than you will need. Include some yes/no questions and some open-ended questions. Order your questions from most important to least important.

### Participating in the Interview

- Listen interactively. Be prepared to follow up on a response you find interesting.
- Avoid arguments. Be tactful and polite.

### Following Up on the Interview

- Summarize your notes while they are still fresh in your mind.
- Send a thank-you note to the interviewee.

# 5 Viewing and Representing

*In our media-saturated world, we are immersed in visual messages that convey ideas, information, and attitudes. To understand and use visual representations effectively, you need to be aware of the techniques and the range of visuals that are commonly used.*

## 5.1 Understanding Visual Messages

Information is communicated not only with words but with graphic devices. A **graphic device** is a visual representation of data and ideas and the relations among them.

### Reading Charts and Graphs

A chart organizes information by arranging it in rows and columns. It is helpful in showing complex information clearly. When interpreting a chart, first read the title. Then analyze how the information is presented. Charts can take many different forms. The following chart shows

comparison and contrast in Ray Bradbury's description of a Tyrannosaurus Rex in "A Sound of Thunder."

| Comparison and Contrast in a Description of a Dinosaur ||
|---|---|
| **Massive** | **Delicate** |
| thirty feet above trees | delicate watchmaker's claws |
| each thigh a ton of meat | two delicate arms |
| head a ton of sculptured stone | gliding ballet step |

There are several different types of **graphs,** visual aids that are often used to display numerical information.

- A **circle graph** shows proportions of the whole.
- A **line graph** shows the change in data over a period of time. The following line graph shows the change in the area of the United States during the 19th century.

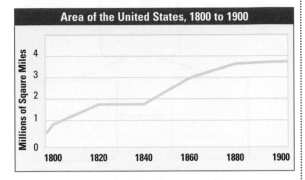

**Area of the United States, 1800 to 1900**

- A **bar graph** compares amounts. The following bar graph shows how many books Twain wrote in each period of his writing career.

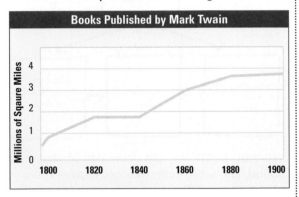

**Books Published by Mark Twain**

## Interpreting Images

Speakers and writers often use visual aids to inform or persuade their audiences. These aids can be invaluable in helping you understand the information being communicated. However, you must interpret visual aids critically, as you do written material.

- **Examine photographs critically.** Does the camera angle or the background in the photo intentionally evoke a positive or negative response? Has the image been altered or manipulated?

- **Evaluate carefully the data presented in charts and graphs.** Some charts and graphs may exaggerate the facts. For example, a circle graph representing a sample of only ten people may be misleading if the speaker suggests that this data represents a trend.

## 5.2 Evaluating Visual Messages

When you view images, whether they are cartoons, advertising art, photographs, or paintings, there are certain elements to look for.

### CRITERIA    How to Analyze Images

- Is color used realistically? Is it used to emphasize certain objects? to evoke a specific response?
- What tone is created by color and by light and dark in the picture?
- Do the background images intentionally evoke a positive or negative response?
- What is noticeable about the picture's composition, that is, the arrangement of lines, colors, and forms? Does the composition emphasize certain objects or elements in the picture?
- For graphs and charts, does the visual accurately represent the data?

## 5.3 Using Visual Representations

Tables, graphs, diagrams, pictures, and animations often communicate information more effectively than words alone do.

Use visuals with written reports to illustrate complex concepts and processes or to make a page look more interesting. Computer programs, CD-ROMs, and on-line services can help you generate

- **graphs** that present numerical information
- **charts** and **tables** that allow easy comparison of information
- **logos** and **graphic devices** that highlight important information
- **borders** and **tints** that signal different kinds of information
- **clip art** that adds useful pictures
- **interactive animations** that illustrate difficult concepts

You might want to explore ways of displaying data in more than one visual format before deciding which will work best for you.

## 5.4 Making Multimedia Presentations

A multimedia presentation is an electronically prepared combination of text, sound, and visuals such as photographs, videos, and animation. Your audience reads, hears, and sees your presentation at a computer, following different "paths" you create to lead the user through the information you have gathered.

### Planning Presentations

To create a multimedia presentation, first choose your topic and decide what you want to include. Then plan how you want your user to move through your presentation. For a multimedia presentation on the role of the setting in literature, you might include the following items:

- text defining setting and discussing elements of settings
- taped reading from "The Son from America" describing the hut and village accompanied by photo of a painting of a simple place
- taped reading from "A White Heron" accompanied by a sequence of slides showing scenes similar to those described
- chart comparing two descriptions of a family farm setting, one positive, one negative
- video interview with an author on the role of the setting in his or her work
- video of Mississippi River as seen from a river pilot's seat, voice-over discussing Twain's *Life on the Mississippi*
- series of short film clips showing spooky settings from horror movies

You can choose one of the following ways to organize your presentation:

**step by step,** with only one path, or order, in which the user can see and hear the information

**a branching path** that allows users to make some choices about what they will see and hear, and in what order

A flow chart can help you figure out the paths a user can take through your presentation. Each box in the flow chart that follows represents something about setting for the user to read, see, or hear. The arrows on the flow chart show the possible paths the user can follow.

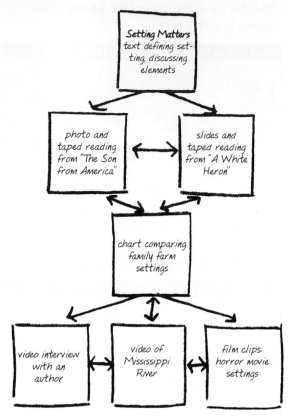

**TECHNOLOGY TIP** You can download photos, sound, and video from Internet sources onto your computer. This process lets you add to your presentation elements that would usually require complex editing equipment.

### Guiding Your User

Your user will need directions to follow the path you have planned for your multimedia presentation.

Most multimedia authoring programs allow you to create screens that include text or audio directions that guide the user from one part of your presentation to the next.

If you need help creating your multimedia presentation, ask your school's technology adviser. You may also be able to get help from your classmates or your software manual.

# Grammar Handbook

## ① Quick Reference: Parts of Speech

| Part of Speech | Definition | Examples |
|---|---|---|
| **Noun** | Names a person, place, thing, idea, quality, or action. | Margaret, Texas, knuckles, nature, beauty, beginning |
| **Pronoun** | Takes the place of a noun or another pronoun. | |
| Personal | Refers to the one speaking, spoken to, or spoken about. | I, me, my, mine, we, us, our, ours, you, your, yours, she, he, it, her, him, hers, his, its, they, them, their, theirs |
| Reflexive | Follows a verb or preposition and refers to a preceding noun or pronoun. | myself, yourself, herself, himself, itself, ourselves, yourselves, themselves |
| Intensive | Emphasizes a noun or another pronoun. | (Same as reflexives) |
| Demonstrative | Points to specific persons or things. | this, that, these, those |
| Interrogative | Signals questions. | who, whom, whose, which, what |
| Indefinite | Refers to person(s) or thing(s) not specifically mentioned. | both, all, most, many, anyone, everybody, several, none, some |
| Relative | Introduces subordinate clauses and relates them to words in the main clause. | who, whom, whose, which, that |
| **Verb** | Expresses action, condition, or state of being. | |
| Action | Tells what the subject does or did, physically or mentally. | run, reaches, listened, consider, decides, dreamt |
| Linking | Connects subjects to that which identifies or describes them. | am, is, are, was, were, sound, taste, appear, feel, become, remain, seem |
| Auxiliary | Precedes and introduces main verbs. | be, have, do, can, could, will, would, may, might |
| **Adjective** | Modifies nouns or pronouns. | **strong** women, **two** epics, **enough** time |
| **Adverb** | Modifies verbs, adjectives, or other adverbs. | walked **out**, **really** funny, **far** away |
| **Preposition** | Relates one word to another (following) word. | at, by, for, from, in, of, on, to, with |
| **Conjunction** | Joins words or word groups. | |
| Coordinating | Joins words or word groups used the same way. | and, but, or, for, so, yet, nor |
| Correlative | Join words or word groups used the same way and are used in pairs. | both . . . and, either . . . or, neither . . . nor |
| Subordinating | Joins word groups not used the same way. | although, after, as, before, because, when, if, unless |
| **Interjection** | Expresses emotion. | wow, ouch, hurrah |

## 2 Nouns

*A noun is a word used to name a person, place, thing, idea, quality, or action. Nouns can be classified in several ways. All nouns can be placed in at least two classifications. They are either common or proper. All are also either abstract or concrete. Some nouns can be classified as compound, collective, and possessive as well.*

**2.1 Common Nouns** are general names, common to an entire group.
> EXAMPLES: *motor, tree, time, children*

**2.2 Proper Nouns** name specific, one-of-a-kind things. (See Capitalization, page 1205.)
> EXAMPLES: *Bradbury, Eastern Standard Time, Maine*

**2.3 Concrete Nouns** name things that can be perceived by the senses.
> EXAMPLES: *stadium, jacket, St. Louis, Wrigley Field*

**2.4 Abstract Nouns** name things that cannot be observed by the senses.
> EXAMPLES: *intelligence, fear, joy, loneliness*

|          | Common | Proper              |
|----------|--------|---------------------|
| **Abstract** | beauty | Age of Enlightenment |
| **Concrete** | planet | Mars                |

**2.5 Compound Nouns** are formed from two or more words but express a single idea. They are written as single words, as separate words, or with hyphens. Use a dictionary to check the correct spelling of a compound noun.
> EXAMPLES: *sunshine, call waiting, job-sharing*

**2.6 Collective Nouns** are singular nouns that refer to groups of people or things. (See Collective Nouns as Subjects, page 1202.)
> EXAMPLES: *army, flock, class, species*

**2.7 Possessive Nouns** show who or what owns something. Consult the chart below for the proper use of the possessive apostrophe.

| Category | Possessive Nouns Rule | Examples |
|----------|-----------------------|----------|
| All singular nouns | Add apostrophe plus -s | Lily's, bass's, pitcher's, daughter-in-law's |
| Plural nouns not ending in -s | Add apostrophe plus -s | children's women's people's |
| Plural nouns ending in -s | Add apostrophe only | witnesses' churches' males' Johnsons' |

### GRAMMAR PRACTICE

**A.** For each underlined noun, first tell whether it is common or proper. Then tell whether it is concrete or abstract.

1. <u>Atwood</u> says many <u>Canadians</u> seem to be looking through a one-way mirror.
2. Canadian <u>society</u> has been accused of having an identity <u>crisis</u>.
3. Sometimes Canadians think it is their <u>job</u> to explain the <u>Yanks</u> to the rest of the world.
4. There are some disputes about minor issues such as <u>fish</u>.
5. She thinks both <u>superpowers</u> suffer from <u>arrogance</u>.
6. Pat Mora misses the language sounds of <u>El Paso</u> and the <u>Southwest</u> where she grew up.
7. She misses the <u>pleasure</u> of weaving in and out of Spanish and English.
8. Sounds burst forth from the radio <u>broadcast</u> like <u>confetti</u>.
9. She reads <u>poetry</u> in <u>Spanish</u>.
10. The sky fills her with energy and reveals the glare of <u>truth</u>.

**B. 11–15.** From the sentences above, write three compound nouns and two collective nouns.

**C.** Write the possessive form of the following nouns.

16. Margaret Atwood
17. Pat Mora
18. fish
19. thorns
20. culture
21. Southwest
22. humans
23. hearts
24. crisis
25. businessmen

##  3  Pronouns

*A pronoun is a word that is used in place of a noun or another pronoun. The word or word group to which the pronoun refers is called its antecedent.*

**3.1** *Personal Pronouns* are pronouns that change their form to express person, number, gender, and case. The forms of these pronouns are shown in the chart that follows.

| | Nominative | Objective | Possessive |
|---|---|---|---|
| **Singular** | | | |
| First Person | I | me | my, mine |
| Second Person | you | you | your, yours |
| Third Person | she, he, it | her, him, it | her, hers, his, its |
| **Plural** | | | |
| First Person | we | us | our, ours |
| Second Person | you | you | your, yours |
| Third Person | they | them | their, theirs |

**3.2** *Pronoun Agreement* Pronouns should agree with their antecedents in number and person. Singular pronouns are used to replace singular nouns. Plural pronouns are used to replace plural nouns. Pronouns must also match the gender (masculine, feminine, or neuter) of the nouns they replace.

**3.3** *Pronoun Case* Personal pronouns change form to show how they function in a sentence. This change of form is called *case*. The three cases are **nominative, objective,** and **possessive.**

**A nominative pronoun** is used as the subject or the predicate nominative of a sentence.

**An objective pronoun** is used as the direct or indirect object of a sentence or as the object of a preposition.

SUBJECT     OBJECT

*He will lead them to us.*

OBJECT OF PREPOSITION

**A possessive pronoun** shows ownership. The pronouns *mine, yours, hers, his, its, ours*, and *theirs* can be used in place of nouns.

   EXAMPLE: *This horse is mine.*

The pronouns *my, your, her, his, its, our*, and *their* are used before nouns.

   EXAMPLE: *This is my horse.*

USAGE TIP To decide which pronoun to use in a comparison, such as *He tells better tales than (I or me),* fill in the missing words: *He tells better tales than I tell.*

WATCH OUT! Many spelling errors can be avoided if you watch out for *its* and *their*. Don't confuse the possessive pronoun *its* with the contraction *it's*, meaning *it is* or *it has*. The homonyms *they're* (contraction for *they are*) and *there* (a place or an expletive) are often mistakenly used for *their*.

**3.4** *Reflexive and Intensive Pronouns* These pronouns are formed by adding *-self* or *-selves* to certain personal pronouns. Their forms are the same, and they differ only in how they are used.

**Reflexive pronouns** follow verbs or prepositions and reflect back on an earlier noun or pronoun.

   EXAMPLES: *He likes himself too much. She is now herself again.*

**Intensive pronouns** intensify or emphasize the nouns or pronouns to which they refer.

   EXAMPLES: *They themselves will educate their children. You did it yourselves.*

| Singular | |
|---|---|
| First Person | myself |
| Second Person | yourself |
| Third Person | herself, himself, itself |

| Plural | |
|---|---|
| First Person | ourselves |
| Second Person | yourselves |
| Third Person | themselves |

**WATCH OUT!** Avoid using *hisself* or *theirselves.* Standard English does not include these forms.

> **NONSTANDARD:** *The children sang theirselves to sleep.*
> **STANDARD:** *The children sang themselves to sleep.*

**USAGE TIP** Reflexive and intensive pronouns should never be used without antecedents.

> **INCORRECT:** *Read a tale to my brother and myself.*
> **CORRECT:** *Read a tale to my brother and me.*

**3.5** *Demonstrative Pronouns* point out things and persons near and far.

| | Singular | Plural |
|---|---|---|
| **Near** | this | these |
| **Far** | that | those |

**WATCH OUT!** Avoid using the objective pronoun *them* in place of the demonstrative *those.*

> **INCORRECT:** *Let's dramatize one of them tales.*
> **CORRECT:** *Let's dramatize one of those tales.*

**3.6** *Indefinite Pronouns* do not refer to specific persons or things and usually have no antecedents. The chart shows some commonly used indefinite pronouns:

| Singular | Plural | Singular or Plural | |
|---|---|---|---|
| each | both | all | half |
| either | few | any | plenty |
| neither | many | more | none |
| another | several | most | some |

Here is another set of indefinite pronouns, all of which are singular. Notice that, with one exception, they are spelled as one word:

| | | | |
|---|---|---|---|
| anyone | everyone | no one | someone |
| anybody | everybody | nobody | somebody |
| anything | everything | nothing | something |

**USAGE TIP** Since all these are singular, pronouns referring to them should be singular.

> **INCORRECT:** *Did everybody play their part well?*
> **CORRECT:** *Did everybody play his or her part well?*

If the antecedent of the pronoun is both male and female, *his or her* may be used as an alternative, or the sentence may be recast:

> **EXAMPLES:** *Did everybody play his or her part well?*
> *Did all the students play their parts well?*

## GRAMMAR PRACTICE

Write the correct form of all incorrect pronouns in the sentences below.

1. In "By the Waters of Babylon," him who touches the metal in the Dead Places must be a priest or son of a priest.
2. The narrator's father hisself questioned him.
3. He feared that the swift current would carry the raft and he out into the Bitter Water.
4. When John saw a heap of broken stones, he cautiously approached them stones.
5. Each of the god roads John saw were in constant motion.

**3.7** *Interrogative Pronouns* tell a reader or listener that a question is coming. The interrogative pronouns are *who, whom, whose, which,* and *what.*

> **EXAMPLES:** *Who is going to rehearse with you? From whom did you receive the script?*

**USAGE TIP** *Who* is used for subjects, *whom* for objects. To find out which pronoun you need to use in a question, change the question to a statement:

> **QUESTION:** *(Who/Whom?) did you meet there?*
> **STATEMENT:** *You met ( ? ) there.*

Since the verb has a subject *(you)*, the needed word must be the object form, *whom.*

> **EXAMPLE:** *Whom did you meet there?*

**WATCH OUT!** A special problem arises when you use an interrupter such as *do you think* within a sentence:

> **EXAMPLE:** *(Who/Whom) do you think will win?*

If you eliminate the interrupter, it is clear that the word you need is *who*.

**3.8** *Relative Pronouns* relate, or connect, clauses to the words they modify in sentences. The noun or pronoun that the clause modifies is the antecedent of the relative pronoun. Here are the relative pronouns and their uses:

| Replacing: | Subject | Object | Possessive |
|---|---|---|---|
| **Persons** | who | whom | whose |
| **Things** | which | which | whose |
| **Things/Persons*** | that | that | whose |

*\* That generally will not replace specific names, such as Nikki Giovanni.*

Often short sentences with related ideas can be combined using relative pronouns to create a more effective sentence.

> **SHORT SENTENCE:** *Amy Tan won a writing contest at the age of eight.*
> **RELATED SENTENCE:** *Amy Tan did not plan to have a literary career.*
> **COMBINED SENTENCE:** *Amy Tan, who won a writing contest at the age of eight, did not plan to have a literary career.*

### GRAMMAR PRACTICE

Choose the appropriate interrogative or relative pronoun from the words in parentheses.

1. The narrator thinks people gossip and say, "(Who/Whom) does she think she is, to be so choosy?"

2. Qiao Lin, (who/whom) she is considering marrying, is athletic and handsome.

3. She thinks it would be sad to marry a man (who/whom) she doesn't love.

4. Law and morality are factors (that/who) bind a married couple.

5. Her nurse, (who/whom) is shrewd but uneducated, is critical of the narrator's reluctance to marry.

6. Her mother had told her about her father, (who/whom) was a fine handsome fellow.

7. The narrator wonders whether her mother was miserable, being deprived of a man to (who/whom) she was devoted.

 **Verbs**

*A verb is a word that expresses an action, a condition, or a state of being. There are two main kinds of verbs: action and linking. Other verbs, called auxiliary verbs, are sometimes used with action verbs and linking verbs.*

**4.1** *Action Verbs* tell what action someone or something is performing, physically or mentally.

> **PHYSICAL ACTION:** *You hit the target.*
> **MENTAL ACTION:** *She dreamed of me.*

**4.2** *Linking Verbs* do not express action. Linking verbs link subjects to complements that identify or describe them. Linking verbs may be divided into two groups:

> **FORMS OF** *TO BE*: *She is our queen.*
> **VERBS THAT EXPRESS CONDITION:** *The writer looked thoughtful.*

**4.3** *Auxiliary Verbs,* sometimes called helping verbs, precede action or linking verbs and modify their meanings in special ways. The most commonly used auxiliary verbs are parts of the verbs *be, have,* and *do.*

> **Be:** *am, is, are, was, were, be, being, been*
> **Have:** *have, has, had*
> **Do:** *do, does, did*

Other common auxiliary verbs are *can, could, will, would, shall, should, may, might,* and *must.*

> **EXAMPLES:** *I always have admired her.*
> *You must listen to me.*

**4.4** *Transitive and Intransitive Verbs*
Action verbs can be either transitive or intransitive. A transitive verb directs the action towards someone or something. The transitive verb has an object. An intransitive verb does not direct the action towards someone or something. It does not have an object. Since linking verbs convey no action, they are always intransitive.

> **Transitive:** *The storm sank the ship.*
> **Intransitive:** *The ship sank.*

**4.5** *Principal Parts* Action and linking verbs typically have four principal parts, which are used to form verb tenses. The principal parts are the *present*, the *present participle*, the *past*, and the *past participle*.

If the verb is a regular verb, the past and past participle are formed by adding the ending *-d* or *-ed* to the present part. Here is a chart showing four regular verbs:

| Present | Present Participle | Past | Past Participle |
|---------|--------------------|------|-----------------|
| risk | (is) risking | risked | (have) risked |
| solve | (is) solving | solved | (have) solved |
| drop | (is) dropping | dropped | (have) dropped |
| carry | (is) carrying | carried | (have) carried |

Note that the present participle and past participle forms are preceded by a form of *be* or *have*. These forms cannot be used alone as main verbs and always need an auxiliary verb.

**EXAMPLES:** *She once thought her mother was wasting her time.*

*Now she has stopped trying to be like everyone else.*

The past and past participle of irregular verbs are not formed by adding *-d* or *-ed* to the present; they are formed in irregular ways.

| Present | Present Participle | Past | Past Participle |
|---------|--------------------|------|-----------------|
| begin | (is) beginning | began | (have) begun |
| break | (is) breaking | broke | (have) broken |
| bring | (is) bringing | brought | (have) brought |
| choose | (is) choosing | chose | (have) chosen |
| go | (is) going | went | (have) gone |
| lose | (is) losing | lost | (have) lost |
| see | (is) seeing | saw | (have) seen |
| swim | (is) swimming | swam | (have) swum |
| write | (is) writing | wrote | (have) written |

**4.6** *Verb Tense* The tense of a verb tells the time of the action or the state of being. An action or state of being can occur in the present, the past, or the future. There are six tenses, each expressing a different range of time.

**Present tense** expresses an action that is happening at the present time, occurs regularly, or is constant or generally true. Use the present part.

**EXAMPLES**
**NOW:** *This soup tastes delicious.*
**REGULAR:** *I make vegetable soup often.*
**GENERAL:** *Crops require sun, rain, and rich soil.*

**Past tense** expresses an action that began and ended in the past. Use the past part.

**EXAMPLE:** *The storyteller finished his tale.*

**Future tense** expresses an action (or state of being) that will occur. Use *shall* or *will* with the present part.

**EXAMPLE:** *They will attend the next festival.*

**Present perfect tense** expresses action (1) that was completed at an indefinite time in the past or (2) that began in the past and continues into the present. Use *have* or *has* with the past participle.

**EXAMPLE:** *Poetry has inspired readers throughout the ages.*

**Past perfect tense** shows an action in the past that came before another action in the past. Use *had* before the past participle.

**EXAMPLE:** *Before we left, we had asked him to find a place to stay.*

**Future perfect tense** shows an action in the future that will be completed before another action in the future. Use *shall have* or *will have* before the past participle.

**EXAMPLE:** *They will have finished the novel before seeing the movie version of the tale.*

**4.7** *Progressive Forms* The progressive forms of the six tenses show ongoing action. Use a form of *be* with the present participle of a verb.

**PRESENT PROGRESSIVE:** *She is rehearsing her lines.*
**PAST PROGRESSIVE:** *She was rehearsing her lines.*
**FUTURE PROGRESSIVE:** *She will be rehearsing her lines.*

**PRESENT PERFECT PROGRESSIVE**: *She has been rehearsing her lines.*
**PAST PERFECT PROGRESSIVE**: *She had been rehearsing her lines.*
**FUTURE PERFECT PROGRESSIVE**: *She will have been rehearsing her lines.*

**WATCH OUT!** Do not shift tense needlessly. Watch out for these special cases.

• In most compound sentences and in sentences with compound predicates, keep the tenses the same.

> **INCORRECT**: *I keyed in the password, but I get an error message.*
> **CORRECT**: *I keyed in the password, but I got an error message.*

• If one past action happens before another, do shift tenses—from the past to the past perfect:

> **INCORRECT**: *They wished they started earlier.*
> **CORRECT**: *They wished they had started earlier.*

### GRAMMAR PRACTICE

Identify the tense of the verb(s) in each of the following sentences. If you find an unnecessary tense shift, correct it.

**1.** Plath's story "Initiation" is about a high school sorority initiation.

**2.** No one who joined the sorority fails to get through initiation.

**3.** Millicent tells Tracy they still will be best friends after the initiation.

**4.** She thought, "This is getting serious."

**5.** When Millicent made her decision, she remembers the reply of the man on the bus.

**4.8** ***Active and Passive Voice*** The voice of a verb tells whether the subject of a sentence performs or receives the action expressed by the verb. When the subject performs the action, the verb is in the active voice. When the subject is the receiver of the action, the verb is in the passive voice.

Compare these two sentences:

> **ACTIVE**: *Her sunglasses hid most of her face.*
> **PASSIVE**: *Most of her face was hidden by her sunglasses.*

To form the passive voice use a form of *be* with the past participle of the main verb.

**WATCH OUT!** Use the passive voice sparingly. It tends to make writing less forceful and less direct. It can also make the writing awkward.

> **AWKWARD**: *She was given the handmade quilts by her mother.*
> **CORRECT**: *Her mother gave her the handmade quilts.*

There are occasions when you will choose to use the passive voice because

• you want to emphasize the receiver: *The king was shot.*

• the doer is unknown: *My books were stolen.*

• the doer is unimportant: *French is spoken here.*

**4.9** ***Mood*** The mood identifies the manner in which the verb expresses an idea. There are three moods.

**The indicative mood** states a fact or asks a question. You use this mood most often.

> **EXAMPLE**: *His trust was shattered by the betrayal.*

**The imperative mood** is used to give a command or make a request.

> **EXAMPLE**: *Be there by eight o'clock sharp.*

**The subjunctive mood** is used to express a wish or a condition that is contrary to fact.

> **EXAMPLE**: *If I were you, I wouldn't get my hopes up.*

### GRAMMAR PRACTICE

For the first five items below, identify the boldfaced verbs as active or passive.

**1.** In her stories, Alice Walker **has shown** the dignity of people who are her subjects.

**2.** The story "Everyday Use" **was written** by Alice Walker.

**3.** The mother in the story **knows** both her daughters very well.

**4.** The yard in front of the house **was swept** clean as a floor.

**5.** Their other house **had been burned** down.

For the following items, identify the boldfaced verbs as indicative or subjunctive in mood.

6. The story **shows** how the mother respects the everyday use of the quilts.

7. If Dee **were** more like Maggie, she would understand the value of the quilts in a different way.

8. Dee **wanted** to hang the quilts on the wall because of their beauty and their history.

9. Maggie and her mother **were planning** to use the quilts as bedcovers.

10. If Walker **were** not such a good writer, she might have made the story seem commonplace.

---

## ⑤ Modifiers

*Modifiers are words or groups of words that change or limit the meanings of other words. The two kinds of modifiers are adjectives and adverbs.*

**5.1** *Adjectives* An adjective is a word that modifies a noun or pronoun by telling *which one, what kind, how many,* or *how much.*

**WHICH ONE:** *this, that, these, those*
**EXAMPLE:** *These tomatoes have grown quickly.*

**WHAT KIND:** *tiny, impressive, bold, rotten*
**EXAMPLE:** *The bold officer stood in front of the crowd.*

**HOW MANY:** *some, few, thirty, none, both, each*
**EXAMPLE:** *Some of us had three helpings of sweet potatoes.*

**HOW MUCH:** *more, less, enough, scarce*
**EXAMPLE:** *There was enough chicken to serve everyone.*

The **articles** *a, an,* and *the* are usually classified as adjectives. These are the most common adjectives that you will use.

**EXAMPLES:** *The bridge was burned before the attack.*
*A group of peasants led the procession in the town.*

**5.2** *Predicate Adjectives* Most adjectives come before the nouns they modify, as in the examples above. Predicate adjectives, however, follow linking verbs and describe the subject.

**EXAMPLE:** *My friends are very intelligent.*

Be especially careful to use adjectives (not adverbs) after such linking verbs as *look, feel, grow, taste,* and *smell.*

**EXAMPLE:** *The weather grows cold.*

**5.3** *Adverbs* modify verbs, adjectives, or other adverbs by telling *where, when, how,* or *to what extent.*

**WHERE:** *The children played outside.*
**WHEN:** *The author spoke yesterday.*
**HOW:** *We walked slowly behind the leader.*
**TO WHAT EXTENT:** *He worked very hard.*

Unlike adjectives, adverbs tend to be mobile words; they may occur in many places in sentences.

**EXAMPLES:** *Suddenly the wind shifted. The wind suddenly shifted. The wind shifted suddenly.*

Changing the position of adverbs within sentences can vary the rhythm in your writing.

**5.4** *Adjective or Adverb* Many adverbs are formed by adding *-ly* to adjectives.

**EXAMPLES:** *sweet, sweetly; gentle, gently*

However, *-ly* added to a noun will usually yield an adjective.

**EXAMPLES:** *friend, friendly; woman, womanly*

**5.5** *Comparison of Modifiers* The form of an adjective or adverb indicates the degree of comparison that the modifier expresses. Both adjectives and adverbs have three forms, or degrees: the positive, comparative, and superlative.

**The positive form** is used to describe individual things, groups, or actions.

**EXAMPLES:** *The emperor's chariots are fast. Cassius's speech was effective.*

**The comparative form** is used to compare two things, groups, or actions.

**EXAMPLES:** *The emperor's chariots are faster than the senators' chariots.*
*Brutus's speech was more effective than Cassius's speech.*

**The superlative form** is used to compare more than two things, groups, or actions.

> **EXAMPLES**: *The emperor's chariots are the fastest in the empire.*
> *Antony's speech was the most effective of all.*

**5.6** ***Regular Comparisons*** One-syllable and some two-syllable adjectives and adverbs form their comparative and superlative forms by adding -*er* or -*est*. All three-syllable and most two-syllable modifiers form their comparative and superlative by using *more* or *most*.

| Positive | Comparative | Superlative |
|----------|-------------|-------------|
| small | smaller | smallest |
| thin | thinner | thinnest |
| sleepy | sleepier | sleepiest |
| useless | more useless | most useless |
| precisely | more precisely | most precisely |

**WATCH OUT!** Note that spelling changes must sometimes be made to form the comparative and superlative of modifiers.

> **EXAMPLES**: *friendly, friendlier* (change *y* to *i* and add the ending)
> *sad, sadder* (double the final consonant and add the ending)

**5.7** ***Irregular Comparisons*** Some commonly used modifiers have irregular comparative and superlative forms. You may wish to memorize them.

| Positive | Comparative | Superlative |
|----------|-------------|-------------|
| good | better | best |
| bad | worse | worst |
| far | farther or further | farthest or furthest |
| little | less or lesser | least |
| many | more | most |
| well | better | best |
| much | more | most |

**5.8** ***Using Modifiers Correctly*** Study the tips that follow to avoid common mistakes.

***Farther* and *Further*** *Farther* is used for distances; use *further* for everything else.

**Avoiding double comparisons** You make a comparison by using -*er*/-*est* or by using *more*/*most*. Using -*er* with *more* or using -*est* with *most* is incorrect.

> **INCORRECT**: *I like her more better than she likes me.*
> **CORRECT**: *I like her better than she likes me.*

**Avoiding illogical comparisons** An illogical or confusing comparison results if two unrelated things are compared or if something is compared with itself. The word *other* or the word *else* should be used in a comparison of an individual member with the rest of the group.

> **ILLOGICAL**: *Shakespeare's plays are more popular than those of any Elizabethan writer.* (Was Shakespeare an Elizabethan writer?)
> **LOGICAL**: *Shakespeare's plays are more popular than those of any other Elizabethan writer.*

***Bad* vs. *Badly*** *Bad,* always an adjective, is used before nouns or after linking verbs to describe the subject. *Badly,* always an adverb, never modifies a noun. Be sure to use the right form after a linking verb.

> **INCORRECT**: *Ed felt badly after his team lost.*
> **CORRECT**: *Ed felt bad after his team lost.*

***Good* vs. *Well*** *Good* is always an adjective. It is used before nouns or after a linking verb to modify the subject. *Well* is often an adverb meaning "expertly" or "properly." *Well* can also be used as an adjective after a linking verb, when it means "in good health."

> **INCORRECT**: *Helen writes very good.*
> **CORRECT**: *Helen writes very well.*
> **CORRECT**: *Yesterday I felt bad; today I feel well.*

**Double negatives** If you add a negative word to a sentence that is already negative, the result will be an error known as a double negative. When using *not* or *-n't* with a verb, use "*any-*" words, such as *anybody* or *anything,* rather than "*no-*" words, such as *nobody* or *nothing,* later in the sentence.

> **INCORRECT:** *I don't have no money.*
> **CORRECT:** *I don't have any money.*
>
> **INCORRECT:** *We haven't seen nobody.*
> **CORRECT:** *We haven't seen anybody.*

Using *hardly, barely,* or *scarcely* after a negative word is also incorrect.

> **INCORRECT:** *They couldn't barely see two feet ahead.*
> **CORRECT:** *They could barely see two feet ahead.*

**Misplaced modifiers** A misplaced modifier is one placed so far away from the word it modifies that the intended meaning of the sentence is unclear. Place modifiers as close as possible to the words they modify.

> **MISPLACED:** *We found the child in the park who was missing.* (The child was missing, not the park.)
>
> **CLEARER:** *We found the child who was missing in the park.*

### GRAMMAR PRACTICE

Choose the correct word from each pair in parentheses.

1. Shakespeare's plays are (popularer/more popular) than those of any other playwright.
2. The play *Julius Caesar* is about the death of the (powerfulest, most powerful) emperor of Roman times.
3. The emperor didn't pay (no/any) attention to the soothsayer who warned him about the ides of March.
4. Caesar (could/couldn't) hardly know what lay in store for him.
5. He thought Brutus loved him (well/good).
6. He didn't have (any/no) fear of his friends.
7. Some Romans thought that Caesar was the (most good/best) leader they would ever have.
8. Between Antony and Brutus, Brutus was supposed to be the (better/best) public speaker.

9. In this scene, we learn that Mark Antony felt (bad/badly) that Caesar was killed.
10. Antony didn't want (anyone/no one) to know his plans.

## 6 Prepositions, Conjunctions, and Interjections

**6.1** *Prepositions* A preposition is a word used to show the relationship between a noun or a pronoun and another word in the sentence.

| Commonly Used Prepositions | | | |
|---|---|---|---|
| above | down | near | through |
| at | for | of | to |
| before | from | on | up |
| below | in | out | with |
| by | into | over | without |

The preposition is always followed by a word or group of words that serve as its object. The preposition, its object, and modifiers of the object are called the **prepositional phrase.** In each example below, the prepositional phrase is underlined and the object of the preposition is in boldface type.

> **EXAMPLES**
> *The future <u>of the entire **kingdom**</u> is uncertain.*
> *We searched <u>through the deepest **woods.**</u>*

Prepositional phrases may be used as adjectives or as adverbs. The phrase in the first example is used as an adjective modifying the noun *future.* In the second example, the phrase is used as an adverb modifying the verb *searched.*

**WATCH OUT!** Prepositional phrases must be as close as possible to the word they modify.

> **MISPLACED:** *We have clothes for leisure wear of many colors.*
> **CLEARER:** *We have clothes of many colors for leisure wear.*

**6.2** *Conjunctions* A conjunction is a word used to connect words, phrases, or sentences. There are three kinds of conjunctions: **coordinating conjunctions, correlative conjunctions,** and **subordinating conjunctions.**

**Coordinating conjunctions** connect words or word groups that have the same function in a sentence. These include *and, but, or, for, so, yet,* and *nor.*

Coordinating conjunctions can join nouns, pronouns, verbs, adjectives, adverbs, prepositional phrases, and clauses in a sentence.

These examples show coordinating conjunctions joining words of the same function:

**EXAMPLES**

*I have many friends <u>but</u> few enemies.* (two noun objects)

*We ran out the door <u>and</u> into the street.* (two prepositional phrases)

*They are pleasant <u>yet</u> seem aloof.* (two predicates)

*We have to go now, <u>or</u> we will be late.* (two clauses)

**Correlative conjunctions** are similar to coordinating conjunctions. However, correlative conjunctions are always used in pairs.

| Correlative Conjunctions | | |
|---|---|---|
| both . . . and | neither . . . nor | whether . . . or |
| either . . . or | not only . . . but also | |

**Subordinating conjunctions** introduce subordinate clauses—clauses that cannot stand by themselves as complete sentences. The subordinating conjunction shows how the subordinate clause relates to the rest of the sentence. The relationships include time, manner, place, cause, comparison, condition, and purpose.

| SUBORDINATING CONJUNCTIONS | |
|---|---|
| TIME | *after, as, as long as, as soon as, before, since, until, when, whenever, while* |
| MANNER | *as, as if* |
| PLACE | *where, wherever* |
| CAUSE | *because, since* |
| COMPARISON | *as, as much as, than* |
| CONDITION | *although, as long as, even if, even though, if, provided that, though, unless, while* |
| PURPOSE | *in order that, so that, that* |

In the example below, the boldface word is the conjunction, and the underlined words are called a subordinate clause:

**EXAMPLE:** *We sing **<u>because</u>** we are happy.*

*We sing* is an independent clause because it can stand alone as a complete sentence. *Because we are happy* cannot stand alone as a complete sentence; it is a subordinate clause.

**Conjunctive adverbs** are used to connect clauses that can stand by themselves as sentences. Conjunctive adverbs include *also, besides, finally, however, moreover, nevertheless, otherwise,* and *then.*

**EXAMPLE:** *She loved the fall; <u>however</u>, she also enjoyed winter.*

**6.3** *Interjections* are words used to show strong emotion, such as *wow* and *cool*. Often followed by an exclamation point, they have no grammatical relationship to the rest of a sentence.

**EXAMPLE:** *You've written a poem? Great!*

**GRAMMAR PRACTICE**

Label each of the boldfaced words as a preposition, conjunction, or interjection.

1. Carl Sandburg was a writer **and** lecturer.

2. He is well-known **for** his poetry, **but** he also won prizes **for** his biographies.

3. **In** Sandburg's poem "Moon Rondeau," the lovers feel that they own the moon. **Wonderful!**

4. They felt this way **because** they were in love.

5. They thought the moon looked like a silver button **as well as** a plaque of gold.

6. They looked at the moon one evening **when** they could smell leaves and roses.

7. The lovers talk together of love, **yet** they notice the way things look and smell.

8. They looked long **at** the moon and talked about it as if it were special just for them. **Terrific!**

9. Is it spring **because** there is the smell of "the beginnings of roses **and** potatoes"?

10. They sat together until late **in** the evening.

# 7 Quick Reference: The Sentence and Its Parts

*The diagrams that follow will give you a brief review of the essentials of the sentence—subjects and predicates—and of some of its parts.*

**The writer's pen hit the floor.**

The **complete subject** includes all the words that identify the person, place, thing, or idea that the sentence is about.

The **complete predicate** includes all the words that tell or ask something about the subject.

**pen**

**hit**

The **simple subject** tells exactly whom or what the sentence is about. It may be one word or a group of words, but it does not include modifiers.

The **simple predicate**, or **verb**, tells what the subject does or is. It may be one word or several, but it does not include modifiers.

**For his graduation, the family had given the young Buddy money.**

A **prepositional phrase** consists of a preposition, its object, and any modifiers of the object. In this phrase, *for* is the preposition and *graduation* is its object.

**subject**

An **indirect object** is a word or a group of words that tells *to whom* or *for whom* or *to what* or *for what* about the verb. A sentence can have an indirect object only if it has a direct object. The indirect object always comes before the direct object in a sentence.

Verbs often have more than one part. They may be made up of a **main verb**, like *given*, and one or more **auxiliary**, or **helping**, **verbs**, like *had*.

A **direct object** is a word or group of words that tells who or what receives the action of the verb in the sentence.

# 8 The Sentence and Its Parts

*A sentence is a group of words used to express a complete thought. A complete sentence has a subject and predicate.*

## 8.1 Kinds of Sentences

Sentences make statements, ask questions, give commands, and show feelings. There are four basic types of sentences.

| Type | Definition | Example |
|------|-----------|---------|
| Declarative | states a fact, wish, intent, or feeling | I read White's essay last night. |
| Interrogative | asks a question | Did you like the essay? |
| Imperative | gives a command, direction | Read this paragraph aloud. |
| Exclamatory | expresses strong feeling or excitement | I wish I had thought of that! |

**WRITING TIP** One way to vary your writing is to employ a variety of different types of sentences. In the first example below, each sentence is declarative. Notice how much more interesting the revised paragraph is.

**SAMPLE PARAGRAPH:** *You have to see Niagara Falls in person. You can truly appreciate their awesome power in no other way. You should visit them on your next vacation. They are a spectacular sight.*

**REVISED PARAGRAPH:** *Have you ever seen Niagara Falls in person? You can truly appreciate their awesome power in no other way. Visit them on your next vacation. What a spectacular sight they are!*

**WATCH OUT!** Conversation frequently includes parts of sentences, or **fragments.** In formal writing, however, you need to be sure that every sentence is a complete thought and includes a subject and predicate. (See Correcting Fragments, page 1199.)

## 8.2 Complete Subjects and Predicates

A sentence has two parts: a subject and a predicate. The complete subject includes all the words that identify the person, place, thing, or idea that the sentence is about. The complete predicate includes all the words that tell what the subject did or what happened to the subject.

| Complete Subject | Complete Predicate |
|------------------|--------------------|
| The poets of the time | wrote about nature. |
| This new approach | was extraordinary. |

## 8.3 Simple Subjects and Predicates

The simple subject is the key word in the complete subject. The simple predicate is the key word in the complete predicate. In the examples that follow they are underlined.

| Simple Subject | Simple Predicate |
|----------------|------------------|
| The <u>poets</u> of the time | <u>wrote</u> about nature. |
| This new <u>approach</u> | <u>was</u> extraordinary. |

## 8.4 Compound Subjects and Predicates

A compound subject consists of two or more subjects that share the same verb. They are typically joined by the coordinating conjunction *and* or *or.*

**EXAMPLE:** <u>*Lawrence and Hayden*</u> *write about families.*

A compound predicate consists of two or more predicates that share the same subject. They, too, are usually joined by the coordinating conjunction *and, but,* or *or.*

**EXAMPLE:** *The father in "Those Winter Sundays"* <u>*got up early and dressed in the dark.*</u>

## 8.5 Subjects and Predicates in Questions

In many interrogative sentences, the subject may appear after the verb or between parts of a verb phrase.

**INTERROGATIVE:** *Did <u>Father</u> get up early?*

**INTERROGATIVE:** *Why has that <u>book</u> sold so well?*

**8.6** **Subjects and Predicates in Imperative Sentences** Imperative sentences give commands, requests, or directions. The subject of an imperative sentence is the person spoken to, or *you*. While it is not stated, it is understood to be *you*.

> **EXAMPLE:** *(You) Please tell me what you're thinking.*

**8.7** **Subjects in Sentences That Begin with There and Here** When a sentence begins with *there* or *here*, the subject usually follows the verb. Remember that *there* and *here* are never the subjects of a sentence. The simple subjects in the example sentences are underlined.

> **EXAMPLES**
>
> *Here is the <u>solution</u> to the mystery.*
> *There is no <u>time</u> to waste now.*
> *There were too many <u>passengers</u> on the boat.*

### GRAMMAR PRACTICE

Copy each of the following sentences. Then draw one line under the complete subject and two lines under the complete predicate.

1. Eugenia Collier wrote the short story "Sweet Potato Pie."
2. The narrator recounts events from his childhood and from that afternoon.
3. There are two flashbacks in the story.
4. Lil and Charley took care of the younger children in the family.
5. Now Charley drives a cab in New York City.
6. In the afternoon, Buddy left his meeting and headed uptown.
7. Bea gave Buddy fried fish and cornbread for dinner.
8. All evening they talked and remembered their past lives.
9. Why didn't Charley want Buddy to take the sweet potato pie?
10. None of the people in the lobby carried a paper bag.

**8.8** **Complements** A complement is a word or group of words that completes the meaning of the sentence. Some sentences contain only a subject and a verb. Most sentences, however, require additional words placed after the verb to complete the meaning of the sentence. There are three kinds of complements: **direct objects, indirect objects,** and **subject complements.**

**Direct objects** are words or word groups that receive the action of action verbs. A direct object answers the question *what?* or *whom?* In the examples that follow the direct objects are underlined.

> **EXAMPLES**
>
> *The students asked many <u>questions</u>.*
> (asked what?)
>
> *The teacher quickly answered <u>them</u>.*
> (answered what?)
>
> *The school accepted <u>girls and boys</u>.*
> (accepted whom?)

**Indirect objects** tell *to* or *for whom* or *what* the action of the verb is performed. Indirect objects come before direct objects. In the examples that follow the indirect objects are underlined.

> **EXAMPLES**
>
> *My sister usually gave <u>her friends</u> good advice.* (gave to whom?)
>
> *Her brother sent the <u>post office</u> a heavy package.* (sent to what?)
>
> *His kind grandfather mailed <u>him</u> a new tie.* (mailed to whom?)

**Subject complements** come after linking verbs and identify or describe the subject. Subject complements that name or identify the subject of the sentence are called **predicate nominatives.** These include **predicate nouns** and **predicate pronouns.** In the examples that follow the subject complements are underlined.

> **EXAMPLES**
>
> *My friends are very hard <u>workers.</u>*
> *The best writer in the class is <u>she.</u>*

Other subject complements describe the subject of the sentence. These are called **predicate adjectives**.

**EXAMPLE:** *The pianist appeared very <u>energetic</u>.*

### GRAMMAR PRACTICE

Write all of the complements in the following sentences and label them as direct objects, indirect objects, predicate nouns, predicate pronouns, or predicate adjectives.

1. The playwright Sophocles was famous in ancient Greece.
2. He gave the world many important dramas.
3. *Antigone* is a respected example of Greek tragedy.
4. Two of the main characters in the play are Antigone and Ismene.
5. Without the king's consent, Antigone buries her brother.
6. Polyneices had attacked Thebes during the war.
7. Creon condemns Antigone and Ismene.
8. The Greek chorus represents the ordinary citizens.
9. The final victim of Creon's pride is he himself.
10. Fate dealt Creon great misfortune.

## ⑨ Phrases

*A phrase is a group of related words that does not have a subject and predicate and functions in a sentence as a single part of speech.*

**9.1 *Prepositional Phrases*** A prepositional phrase is a phrase that consists of a preposition, its object, and any modifiers of the object. Prepositional phrases that modify nouns or pronouns are called **adjective phrases**. Prepositional phrases that modify a verb, an adjective, or another adverb are **adverb phrases**.

**ADJECTIVE PHRASE:** *The central character <u>of the story</u> is a wicked villain.*
**ADVERB PHRASE:** *He reveals his nature <u>in the first scene</u>.*

**9.2 *Appositives and Appositive Phrases*** An appositive is a noun or pronoun that usually comes directly after another noun or pronoun and identifies or provides further information about that word. An appositive phrase includes the appositive and all its modifiers. In the following examples, the appositive phrases are underlined.

**EXAMPLES**

*This poem was written by Walt Whitman, <u>a great poet</u>.*

*He wrote this poem, <u>a sad remembrance of war</u>, about an artilleryman.*

Occasionally, an appositive phrase may precede the noun it tells about.

**EXAMPLE:** *<u>A great poet</u>, Walt Whitman wrote many of the poems we are studying.*

## ⑩ Verbals and Verbal Phrases

*A verbal is a verb form that is used as a noun, an adjective, or an adverb. A verbal phrase consists of a verbal, all its modifiers, and all its complements. There are three kinds of verbals: infinitives, participles, and gerunds.*

**10.1 *Infinitives and Infinitive Phrases*** An infinitive is a verb form that usually begins with *to* and functions as a noun, adjective, or adverb. The infinitive and its modifiers constitute an infinitive phrase. The examples that follow show several uses of infinitives and infinitive phrases. Each infinitive phrase is underlined.

**NOUN:** *<u>To know her</u> is my only desire.* (subject)

*She wrote <u>to voice her opinions</u>.* (direct object)

*Her goal was <u>to promote women's rights</u>.* (predicate nominative)

**ADJECTIVE:** *We saw his need <u>to be loved</u>.* (adjective modifying *need*)

**ADVERB:** *I'm planning <u>to walk with you</u>.* (adverb modifying *wrote*)

Like verbs themselves, infinitives can take objects (*her* in the first noun example), be made passive (*to be loved* in the adjective example), and take modifiers (*with you* in the adverb example).

Because *to*, the sign of the infinitive, precedes infinitives, it is usually easy to recognize them. However, sometimes *to* may be omitted.

> **EXAMPLE:** *Let no one dare [to] <u>enter this shrine</u>.*

### 10.2 Participles and Participial Phrases

A participle is a verb form that functions as an adjective. Like adjectives, participles modify nouns and pronouns. Most participles use the present participle form, ending in *-ing*, or the past participle form, ending in *-ed* or *-en*. In the examples below the participles are underlined.

> **MODIFYING A NOUN:** *The <u>dying</u> man had a smile on his face.*
> **MODIFYING A PRONOUN:** *<u>Frustrated</u>, everyone abandoned the cause.*

**Participial phrases** are participles with all their modifiers and complements.

> **MODIFYING A NOUN:** *The dogs <u>searching for survivors</u> are well trained.*
> **MODIFYING A PRONOUN:** *<u>Having approved your proposal</u>, we are ready to act.*

### 10.3 Dangling and Misplaced Participles

A participle or participial phrase should be placed as close as possible to the word that it modifies. Otherwise the meaning of the sentence may not be clear.

> **MISPLACED:** *The boys were looking for squirrels <u>searching the trees</u>.*
> **CLEARER:** *The boys <u>searching the trees</u> were looking for squirrels.*

A participle or participial phrase that does not clearly modify anything in a sentence is called a **dangling participle.** A dangling participle causes confusion because it appears to modify a word that it cannot sensibly modify.

Correct a dangling participle by providing a word for the participle to modify.

> **CONFUSING:** *Running like the wind, my hat fell off.* (The hat wasn't running.)
> **CLEARER:** *Running like the wind, I lost my hat.*

### 10.4 Gerunds and Gerund Phrases

A gerund is a verb form ending in *-ing* that functions as a noun. Gerunds may perform any function nouns perform.

> **SUBJECT:** *<u>Running</u> is my favorite pastime.*
> **DIRECT OBJECT:** *I truly love <u>running</u>.*
> **SUBJECT COMPLEMENT:** *My deepest passion is <u>running</u>.*
> **OBJECT OF PREPOSITION:** *Her love of <u>running</u> keeps her strong.*

**Gerund phrases** are gerunds with all their modifiers and complements. The gerund phrases are underlined in the following examples.

> **SUBJECT:** *<u>Wishing on a star</u> never got me far.*
> **OBJECT OF PREPOSITION:** *I will finish before <u>leaving the office</u>.*
> **APPOSITIVE:** *Her avocation, <u>flying airplanes</u>, finally led to full-time employment.*

### GRAMMAR PRACTICE

Identify the underlined phrases as appositive phrases, infinitive phrases, participial phrases, or gerund phrases.

1. <u>Born into an aristocratic family</u>, Tolstoy was orphaned by the age of nine.
2. *War and Peace,* <u>Tolstoy's longest novel</u>, was published in 1869.
3. His attempt <u>to get rid of his property</u> brought about disagreements with his wife.
4. <u>Dancing with Varenka</u> made Ivan indescribably happy.
5. Ivan gradually lost interest in Varenka, <u>his former sweetheart</u>.

# ⑪ Clauses

*A clause is a group of words that contains a subject and a verb. There are two kinds of clauses: independent clauses and subordinate clauses.*

## ⑪.1 Independent and Subordinate Clauses

An independent clause can stand alone as a sentence, as the word *independent* suggests.

> **INDEPENDENT CLAUSE:** *Emily Dickinson did not wish her poems to be published.*

A sentence may contain more than one independent clause.

> **EXAMPLE:** *Emily Dickinson did not wish her poems to be published, but seven were published during her lifetime.*

In the example above the coordinating conjunction *but* joins the two independent clauses.

A subordinate clause cannot stand alone as a sentence. It is subordinate to, or dependent on, the main clause.

> **EXAMPLE:** *Emily Dickinson did not wish her poems to be published, although she shared them with friends.*

*Although she shared them with friends* cannot stand by itself.

## ⑪.2 Adjective Clauses

An adjective clause is a subordinate clause used as an adjective. It usually follows the noun or pronoun it modifies.

> **EXAMPLE:** *Robert Frost wrote about birch tree branches that boys swing on.*

Adjective clauses are typically introduced by the relative pronouns *who, whom, whose, which,* and *that* (see Relative Pronouns, page 1185). In the examples that follow, the adjective clauses are underlined.

> **EXAMPLES**
> *One song that we like became our theme song.*
>
> *Emily Dickinson, whose poems have touched many, lived a very quiet life.*

*The candidate whom we selected promised to serve us well.*

**WATCH OUT!** The relative pronouns *whom, which,* and *that* may sometimes be omitted when they are objects of their own clauses.

> **EXAMPLE:** *Robert Frost is a poet [whom/that] many have read.*

## ⑪.3 Adverb Clauses

An adverb clause is a subordinate clause that is used as an adverb to modify a verb, an adjective, or another adverb. It is introduced by a subordinating conjunction (see Subordinating Conjunctions, page 1191).

Adverb clauses typically occur at the beginning or end of sentences. The clauses are underlined in these examples.

> **MODIFYING A VERB:** *When we need you, we will call.*
> **MODIFYING AN ADVERB:** *I'll stay here where there is shelter from the rain.*
> **MODIFYING AN ADJECTIVE:** *Roman felt good when he finished his essay.*

## ⑪.4 Noun Clauses

A noun clause is a subordinate clause that is used in a sentence as a noun. A noun clause may be used as a subject, a direct object, an indirect object, a predicate nominative, or an object of a preposition. Noun clauses are often introduced by pronouns such as *that, what, who, whoever, which,* and *whose,* and by subordinating conjunctions, such as *how, when, where, why,* and *whether.* (See Subordinating Conjunctions, page 1191.)

**USAGE TIP** Because the same words may introduce adjective and noun clauses, you need to consider how the clause functions within its sentence.

To determine if a clause is a noun clause, try substituting *something* or *someone* for the clause. If you can do it, it is probably a noun clause.

> **EXAMPLES:** *I know whose woods these are.* ("I know *something*." The clause is a noun clause, direct object of the verb *know*.)
>
> *Give a copy to whoever wants one.* ("Give a copy to *someone*." The clause is a noun clause, object of the preposition *to*.)

Identify each underlined clause as an adjective clause, an adverb clause, or a noun clause.

1. R.K. Narayan, <u>who is regarded as one of India's greatest writers</u>, was a teacher very briefly.

2. The teacher in Narayan's "Like the Sun" thought <u>that telling the absolute truth was important</u>.

3. <u>When he told his wife the meal wasn't very good</u>, he made her angry.

4. He seemed not to question <u>whether he really should tell exactly what he thought</u>.

5. His decision, <u>which would last one day</u>, might have cost him his job.

## ⑫ The Structure of Sentences

*When classified by their structure, there are four kinds of sentences: simple, compound, complex, and compound-complex.*

### 12.1 *Simple Sentences*

A simple sentence is a sentence that has one independent clause and no subordinate clauses. The fact that such sentences are called "simple" does not mean that they are uncomplicated. Various parts of simple sentences may be compound, and they may contain grammatical structures such as appositives and verbals.

EXAMPLES

*Mark Twain, an unsuccessful gold miner, wrote many successful satires and tall tales.* (appositive and compound direct object)

*Pablo Neruda, drawn to writing poetry at an early age, won celebrity at age 20.* (participial and gerund phrases)

### 12.2 *Compound Sentences*

A compound sentence has two or more independent clauses. The clauses are joined together with a comma and a coordinating conjunction (*and, but, or, nor, yet, for, so*), a semicolon, or a conjunctive adverb with a semicolon. Like simple sentences, compound sentences do not contain any dependent clauses.

EXAMPLES

*The main character in "Lalla" happily goes to London, but she eventually returns to rural Cornwall.*

*Amy Lowell's poem "The Taxi" has powerful images; however, it does not use the word* taxi *anywhere in it.*

**WATCH OUT!** Do not confuse compound sentences with simple sentences that have compound parts.

**EXAMPLE:** *A subcommittee drafted a document and immediately presented it to the entire group.* (here *and* signals a compound predicate, not a compound sentence)

### 12.3 *Complex Sentences*

A complex sentence has one independent clause and one or more subordinate clauses. Each subordinate clause can be used as a noun or as a modifier. If it is used as a modifier, a subordinate clause usually modifies a word in the main clause and the main clause can stand alone. However, when a subordinate clause is a noun clause, it is a part of the independent clause; the two cannot be separated.

**MODIFIER:** *One should not complain, <u>unless she or he has a better solution.</u>*

**NOUN CLAUSE:** *We sketched pictures of <u>whomever we wished.</u>* (noun clause is the object of the preposition *of* and cannot be separated from the rest of the sentence)

### 12.4 *Compound-Complex Sentences*

A compound-complex sentence has two or more independent clauses and one or more subordinate clauses. Compound-complex sentences are, simply, both compound and complex. If you start with a compound sentence, all you need to do to form a compound-complex sentence is add a subordinate clause.

**COMPOUND:** *All the students knew the answer, yet they were too shy to volunteer.*

**COMPOUND-COMPLEX:** *All the students knew the answer that their teacher expected, yet they were too shy to volunteer.*

## GRAMMAR PRACTICE

Tell whether each sentence is a simple sentence, a compound sentence, a complex sentence, or a compound-complex sentence.

1. Born in Massachusetts, Mary Lavin has spent most of her life in Ireland.

2. Owen wants Brigid to live close by, but his wife wants to send Brigid to a care home.

3. Owen's wife thinks that her daughters cannot be happy with Brigid nearby.

4. After Owen died, his wife felt that she had failed him.

5. The neighbors thought that she would send Brigid away, but Owen's wife invited Brigid to live with her.

# ⓭ Writing Complete Sentences

*A sentence is a group of words that expresses a complete thought. In writing that you wish to share with a reader, try to avoid both sentence fragments and run-on sentences.*

**⓭.1** **Correcting Fragments** A sentence fragment is a group of words that is only part of a sentence. It does not express a complete thought and may be confusing to the reader or the listener. A sentence fragment may be lacking a subject, a predicate, or both.

**FRAGMENT:** *waited for the boat to arrive* (no subject)
**CORRECTED:** *We waited for the boat to arrive.*
**FRAGMENT:** *people of various races, ages, and creeds* (no predicate)
**CORRECTED:** *People of various races, ages, and creeds gathered together.*
**FRAGMENT:** *near the old cottage* (neither subject nor predicate)
**CORRECTED:** *The burial ground is near the old cottage.*

In your own writing, fragments are usually the result of haste or incorrect punctuation. Sometimes fixing a fragment will be a matter of attaching it to a preceding or following sentence.

**FRAGMENT:** *We saw the two girls. Waiting for the bus to arrive.*
**CORRECTED:** *We saw the two girls waiting for the bus to arrive.*
**FRAGMENT:** *Newspapers appeal to a wide audience. Including people of various races, ages, and creeds.*
**CORRECTED:** *Newspapers appeal to a wide audience, including people of various races, ages, and creeds.*

**⓭.2** **Correcting Run-on Sentences**
A run-on sentence is made up of two or more sentences written as though they were one. Some run-ons have no punctuation within them. Others may use only a comma where a conjunction or stronger punctuation is necessary. Use your judgment in correcting run-on sentences, as you have choices. You can make two sentences if the thoughts are not closely connected. If the thoughts are closely related, you can keep the run-on as one sentence by adding a semicolon or a conjunction.

**RUN-ON:** *We found a place by a small pond for the picnic it is three miles from the village.*
**MAKE TWO SENTENCES:** *We found a place by a small pond for the picnic. It is three miles from the village.*
**RUN-ON:** *We found a place by a small pond for the picnic it was perfect.*
**USE A SEMICOLON:** *We found a place by a small pond for the picnic; it was perfect.*
**ADD A CONJUNCTION:** *We found a place by a small pond for the picnic, and it was perfect.*

**WATCH OUT!** When you add a conjunction, make sure you use appropriate punctuation before it: a comma for a coordinating conjunction, a semicolon for a conjunctive adverb. (See Conjunctions, page 1191.) A very common mistake is to use a comma instead of a conjunction or an end mark. This error is called a **comma splice**.

**INCORRECT:** *He finished the apprenticeship, then he left the village.*
**CORRECT:** *He finished the apprenticeship, and then he left the village.*

**GRAMMAR PRACTICE**

Rewrite the following paragraph, correcting all fragments and run-ons.

Anton Chekhov was born in the south of Russia. To a poor family. To support his family, he began writing comical sketches he sold them to newspapers and journals. Chekhov had a medical degree he practiced medicine only occasionally. *The Seagull* received very poor reviews for the first production this discouraged Chekhov so much he almost quit writing. Now, however, known as one of Russia's greatest authors. Best remembered for *Uncle Vanya, The Three Sisters,* and *The Cherry Orchard.*

---

## 14 Subject-Verb Agreement

*The subject and verb of a sentence must agree in number. Agreement means that when the subject is singular, the verb must be singular; when the subject is plural, the verb must be plural.*

---

**14.1 Basic Agreement** Fortunately, agreement between subject and verb in English is simple. Most verbs show the difference between singular and plural only in the third person present tense. The present tense of the third person singular ends in *-s.*

| Present Tense Verb Forms | |
|---|---|
| **Singular** | **Plural** |
| I sleep | we sleep |
| you sleep | you sleep |
| she, he, it sleeps | they sleep |

**14.2 Agreement with Be** The verb *be* presents special problems in agreement because this verb does not follow the usual verb patterns.

| Forms of *Be* | | | |
|---|---|---|---|
| **Present Tense** | | **Past Tense** | |
| **Singular** | **Plural** | **Singular** | **Plural** |
| I am | we are | I was | we were |
| you are | you are | you were | you were |
| she, he, it is | they are | she, he, it was | they were |

**14.3 Words Between Subject and Verb** A verb agrees only with its subject. When words come between a subject and its verb, ignore them when considering proper agreement. Identify the subject and make sure the verb agrees with it.

> **EXAMPLES**
> *A story in the newspapers tells about the 1890s.*
>
> *Dad as well as Mom reads the paper daily.*

**14.4 Agreement with Compound Subjects** Use a plural verb with most compound subjects joined by the word *and.*

> **EXAMPLE:** *My father and his friends (they) read the paper daily.*

You could substitute the plural pronoun *they* for *my father and his friends.* This shows that you need a plural verb.

If the compound subject is thought of as a unit, you use the singular verb. Test this by substituting the singular pronoun *it.*

> **EXAMPLE:** *Peanut butter and jelly [it] is my brother's favorite sandwich.*

Use a singular verb with a compound subject that is preceded by *each, every,* or *many a.*

> **EXAMPLE:** *Each novel and short story seems grounded in personal experience.*

With *or, nor,* and the correlative conjunctions *either . . . or* and *neither . . . nor,* make the verb agree with the noun or pronoun nearest the verb.

> **EXAMPLES**
> *Cookies or <u>ice cream is</u> my favorite dessert.*
>
> *Either Cheryl or <u>her friends are</u> being invited.*
>
> *Neither ice storms nor <u>snow is</u> predicted today.*

**14.5 Personal Pronouns as Subjects** When using a personal pronoun as a subject, make sure to match it with the correct form of the verb *be.* (See the chart in 14.2.) Note especially that the pronoun *you* takes the verbs *are* and *were,* regardless of whether it is referring to the singular *you* or to the plural *you.*

**WATCH OUT!** *You is* and *you was* are nonstandard forms and should be avoided in writing and speaking. *We was* and *they was* are also forms to be avoided.

> **INCORRECT:** *You was helping me. They was hoping for this.*
>
> **CORRECT:** *You were helping me. They were hoping for this.*

### 14.6 Indefinite Pronouns as Subjects

Some indefinite pronouns are always singular; some are always plural. Others may be either singular or plural.

| Singular Indefinite Pronouns | | | |
|---|---|---|---|
| another | either | neither | other |
| anybody | everybody | nobody | somebody |
| anyone | everyone | no one | someone |
| anything | everything | nothing | something |
| each | much | one | |

> **EXAMPLES**
> *Each of the writers was given an award.*
> *Somebody in the room upstairs is sleeping.*

The indefinite pronouns that are always plural include *both, few, many,* and *several.* These take plural verbs.

> **EXAMPLES**
> *Many of the books in our library are not in circulation.*
>
> *Few have been returned recently.*

Still other indefinite pronouns may be either singular or plural.

| Singular or Plural Indefinite Pronouns | | | |
|---|---|---|---|
| all | enough | most | plenty |
| any | more | none | some |

The number of the indefinite pronouns *any* and *none* depends on the intended meaning.

> **EXAMPLES**
> *Any of these topics has potential for a good article.* (any one topic)
>
> *Any of these topics have potential for a good article.* (all of the many topics)

The indefinite pronouns *all, some, more, most,* and *none* are singular when they refer to a quantity or part of something. They are plural when they refer to a number of individual things. Context will usually give a clue.

> **EXAMPLES**
> *All of the flour is gone.* (referring to a quantity)
>
> *All of the flowers are gone.* (referring to individual items)

### 14.7 Inverted Sentences

**Inverted Sentences** Problems in agreement often occur in inverted sentences beginning with *here* or *there;* in questions beginning with *why, where,* and *what;* and in inverted sentences beginning with a phrase. Identify the subject—wherever it is—before deciding on the verb.

> **EXAMPLES**
> *There clearly are far too many cooks in this kitchen.*
>
> *What is the correct ingredient for this stew?*
>
> *Far from the embroiled cooks stands the master chef.*

#### GRAMMAR PRACTICE

Locate the subject of each sentence. Then choose the correct verb.

1. Most scholars (think/thinks) the author of *Le Morte d'Arthur* is Sir Thomas Malory.
2. (Is/Are) the author "Syr Thomas Maleore, knyght," the same as "Sir Thomas Malory"?
3. Sir Thomas himself, who lived during the Middle Ages, (was/were) a knight.
4. There (is/are) many knights and ladies in the tales of King Arthur.
5. One of the greatest prose works in the English language, *Le Morte d'Arthur* (was/were) based on French versions that were told earlier.
6. Many legends of King Arthur (was/were) also preserved in Wales.
7. Nearly everyone reading these tales (enjoy/ enjoys) the adventures of the knights and ladies.
8. Several times Malory (was/were) put in prison.
9. He spent the last three years of his life in prison; he wrote *Le Morte d'Arthur* while he (was/were) there.
10. These tales featuring King Arthur (was/were) published after Malory's death.

**14.8 Sentences with Predicate Nominatives** When a predicate nominative serves as a complement in a sentence, use a verb that agrees with the subject, not the complement.

**EXAMPLES**

*The tales of King Arthur are a great work of literature.* (*Tales* is the subject—not *King Arthur*—and it takes the plural verb *are.*)

*A great work of literature is the tales of King Arthur.* (The subject is the singular noun *work.*)

**14.9 Don't and Doesn't as Auxiliary Verbs** The auxiliary verb *doesn't* is used with singular subjects and with the personal pronouns *she, he,* and *it.* The auxiliary verb *don't* is used with plural subjects and with the personal pronouns *I, we, you,* and *they.*

**SINGULAR**

*She doesn't want to be without her cane.*
*Doesn't the school provide help?*

**PLURAL**

*They don't know what it's like to be hungry.*
*Bees don't like these flowers by the door.*

**14.10 Collective Nouns as Subjects**

Collective nouns are singular nouns that name a group of persons or things. *Team,* for example, is the collective name of a group of individuals. A collective noun takes a singular verb when the group acts as a single unit. It takes a plural verb when the members of the group act separately.

**EXAMPLES**

*Our team usually wins.* (the team as a whole wins)

*Our team vote differently on most issues.* (the individual members vote)

**14.11 Relative Pronouns as Subjects**

When a relative pronoun is used as a subject of its clause—*who, which,* and *that* can serve as subjects—the verb of the clause must agree in number with the antecedent of the pronoun.

**SINGULAR**: *Have you selected one of the poems that is meaningful to you?*

The antecedent of the relative pronoun *that* is the singular *one;* therefore, *that* is singular and must take the singular verb *is.*

**PLURAL**: *The younger redwoods, which grow in a circle around an older tree, are also very tall.*

The antecedent of the relative pronoun *which* is the plural *redwoods.* Therefore, *which* is plural, and it takes the plural verb *grow.*

**GRAMMAR PRACTICE**

Choose the correct verb for each of the following sentences.

1. "A Sound of Thunder" (involves/involve) time travel.

2. A group of travelers (go/goes) on a safari into the past.

3. In the travel office there (was/were) lots of colors and sounds.

4. The destination of the safari, 60 million years in the past, (was/were) in the time of dinosaurs.

5. The leader explains that the government (doesn't/don't) approve of the trip.

6. He also reminds the group that none of the famous leaders of later times (exists/exist) at the time of the safari.

7. A huge dinosaur, its flesh glittering like thousands of coins, (rises/rise) up in front of the hunters.

8. One of the characters (do/does) not obey orders to stay on the path.

9. This character who changed the future by his actions (finds/find) things very much different back in the present.

10. What do you think Bradbury (is/are) saying through this story?

# Quick Reference: Punctuation

| Punctuation | Function | Examples |
|---|---|---|
| **End Marks** <br> period, <br> question mark, <br> exclamation point | to end sentences | The games begin today. <br> Who is your favorite contestant? <br> What a play Jamie made! |
| | initials and other abbreviations | Prof. Ted Bakerman, D. H. Lawrence, <br> Houghton Mifflin Co., P.M., A.D., oz., ft., Blvd., St. |
| | items in outlines | I. Volcanoes <br>     A. Central-vent <br>         1. Shield |
| | **exception:** P.O. states | NE (Nebraska), NV (Nevada) |
| **Commas** | before conjunction in compound sentence | I have never disliked poetry, but now I really love it. |
| | items in a series | She is brave, loyal, and kind. <br> The slow, easy route is best. |
| | words of address | Oh wind, if winter comes. . . . <br> Come to the front, children. |
| | parenthetical expressions | Well, just suppose that we can't? <br> Hard workers, as you know, don't quit. <br> I'm not a quitter, believe me. |
| | introductory phrases and clauses | In the beginning of the day, I feel fresh. <br> While she was out, I was here. <br> Having finished my chores, I went out. |
| | nonessential phrases and clauses | Ed Pawn, captain of the chess team, won. <br> Ed Pawn, who is the captain, won. <br> The two leading runners, sprinting toward the finish line, ended in a tie. |
| | in dates and addresses | August 18, 1999. Send it by August 18, 1999, to Cherry Jubilee, Inc., 21 Vernona St., Oakland, Minnesota. |
| | in letter parts | Dear Jim,  Sincerely yours, |
| | for clarity, or to avoid confusion | By noon, time had run out. <br> What the minister does, does matter. <br> While cooking, Jim burned his hand. |
| **Semicolons** | in compound sentences that are not joined by coordinators *and,* etc. | The last shall be first; the first shall be last. I read the Bible; however, I have not memorized it. |
| | with items in series that contain commas | We invited my sister, Jan; her friend, Don; my uncle Jack; and Mary Dodd. |
| | in compound sentences that contain commas | After I ran out of money, I called my parents; but only my sister was home, unfortunately. |

| Punctuation | Function | Examples |
|---|---|---|
| **Colons** | to introduce lists | **Correct:** Those we wrote were the following: Dana, John, and Will.<br>**Incorrect:** Those we wrote were: Dana, John, and Will. |
| | before a long quotation | Susan B. Anthony said: "Woman must not depend upon the protection of man. . . ." |
| | after the salutation of a business letter | To Whom It May Concern:<br>Dear Ms. Costa: |
| | with certain numbers | 1:28 P.M., Genesis: 2:5 |
| **Dashes** | to indicate an abrupt break in thought | I was thinking of my mother—who is arriving tomorrow—just as you walked in. |
| **Parentheses** | to enclose less important material | Throughout her life (though some might think otherwise), she worked hard.<br>The temperature on this July day (Would you believe it?) is 65 degrees! |
| **Hyphens** | with a compound adjective before nouns | She lives in a first-floor apartment. |
| | in compounds with *all-, ex-, self-, -elect* | The president-elect is a well-respected woman. |
| | in compound numbers (to *ninety-nine*) | Today, I turn twenty-one. |
| | in fractions used as adjectives | My cup is one-third full. |
| | between prefixes and words beginning with capital letters | Is this a pre-Bronze Age artifact?<br>Caesar had a bad day in mid-March. |
| | when dividing words at the end of a line | Finding the right title has been a challenge for the committee. |
| **Apostrophes** | to form possessives of nouns and indefinite pronouns | my friend's book, my friends' book, anyone's guess, somebody else's problem |
| | for omitted letters in contractions or numbers in dates | don't (omitted **o**); he'd (omitted **woul**)<br>the class of '99 (omitted **19**) |
| | to form plurals of letters and numbers | I had two A's and no 2's on my report card. |
| **Quotation Marks** | to set off a speaker's exact words | Sara said, "I'm finally ready." "I'm ready," Sara said, "finally." Did Sara say, "I'm ready"? Sara said, "I'm ready!" |
| | for titles of stories, short poems, essays, songs, book chapters | We read Hansberry's "On Summer" and Alvarez's "Exile."<br>My eyes watered when I heard "The Star-Spangled Banner." |
| **Ellipses** | for material omitted from a quotation | "Neither slavery nor involuntary servitude . . . shall exist within the United States . . . ." |
| **Italics** | for titles of books, plays, magazines, long poems, operas, films, TV series, recordings | *The Mists of Avalon, Julius Caesar, Newsweek, Paradise Lost, La Bohème, ET, The Cosby Show, The Three Tenors in Concert* |

# Quick Reference: Capitalization

| Category/Rule | Examples |
|---|---|
| **People and Titles** | |
| Names and initials of people | **A**lice **W**alker, **E. B. W**hite |
| Titles used with or in place of names | **P**rofessor **H**olmes, **S**enator **L**ong, The **P**resident has arrived. |
| Deities and members of religious groups | **J**esus, **A**llah, the **B**uddha, **Z**eus, **B**aptists, **R**oman **C**atholics |
| Names of ethnic and national groups | **H**ispanics, **J**ews, **A**frican **A**mericans |
| **Geographical Names** | |
| Cities, states, countries, continents | **C**harleston, **N**evada, **F**rance, **A**sia |
| Regions, bodies of water, mountains | the **M**idwest, **L**ake **M**ichigan, **M**ount **M**cKinley |
| Geographic features, parks | **C**ontinental **D**ivide, **E**verglades, **Y**ellowstone |
| Streets and roads, planets | 361 **S**outh **T**wenty-third **S**treet, **M**iller **A**venue, **J**upiter, **S**aturn |
| **Organizations and Events** | |
| Companies, organizations, teams | **M**onsanto, the **E**lks, **C**hicago **B**ulls |
| Buildings, bridges, monuments | the **A**lamo, **G**olden **G**ate **B**ridge, **L**incoln **M**emorial |
| Documents, awards | the **C**onstitution, **W**orld **C**up |
| Special named events | **S**uper **B**owl, **W**orld **S**eries |
| Governmental bodies, historical periods and events | the **S**upreme **C**ourt, **C**ongress, the **M**iddle **A**ges, **B**oston **T**ea **P**arty |
| Days and months, holidays | **T**uesday, **O**ctober, **T**hanksgiving, **V**alentine's **D**ay |
| Specific cars, boats, trains, planes | **C**adillac, *Titanic*, *Orient Express* |
| **Proper Adjectives** | |
| Adjectives formed from proper nouns | **D**oppler effect, **M**exican music, **E**lizabethan age, **G**ulf coast |
| **First Words and the Pronoun *I*** | |
| The first word in a sentence or quote | **T**his is it. **H**e said, "**L**et's go." |
| Complete sentence in parentheses | (**C**onsult the previous chapter.) |
| Salutation and closing of letters | **D**ear **M**adam, **V**ery truly yours, |
| First lines of most poetry <br> The personal pronoun *I* | **T**hen am **I** <br> **A** happy fly <br> If **I** live <br> **O**r if **I** die. |
| First, last, and all important words in titles | *A **T**ale of **T**wo **C**ities*, "**T**he **W**orld **I**s **T**oo **M**uch with **U**s" |

# Little Rules That Make A Big Difference

## Sentences

### Avoid sentence fragments. Make sure all your sentences express complete thoughts.

A sentence fragment is a group of words that does not express a grammatically complete thought. It may lack a subject, a predicate, or both. Fragments may be corrected by adding the missing element(s) or by changing the punctuation to make the fragment part of another sentence.

> **FRAGMENT:** *One of my heroes is Barbara Jordan. A Texas senator who had an impressive record and great dedication to justice.*

> **COMPLETE:** *One of my heroes is Barbara Jordan. She was a Texas senator who had an impressive record and great dedication to justice.* (adding a subject and a predicate)

> **COMPLETE:** *One of my heroes is Barbara Jordan, a Texas senator who had an impressive record and great dedication to justice.* (changing the punctuation)

### Avoid run-on sentences. Make sure all clauses in a sentence have the proper punctuation and/or conjunctions between them.

A run-on sentence consists of two or more sentences written as though they were one or separated only by a comma. Correct run-ons by making two separate sentences, using a semicolon, adding a conjunction, or rewriting the sentence.

> **RUN-ON:** *James Galway is a great musician, he plays the flute.*

> **CORRECT:** *James Galway is a great musician. He plays the flute.*

> **CORRECT:** *James Galway is a great musician; he plays the flute.*

> **CORRECT:** *James Galway, who plays the flute, is a great musician.*

### Use end marks correctly. Use a period, not a question mark, at the end of an indirect question.

An indirect question is a question that does not use the exact words of the original speaker. Note the difference between the following sentences, and observe that the second sentence ends in a period, not a question mark.

> **DIRECT:** *Lou asked, "What is that?"*

> **INDIRECT:** *Lou asked what it was.*

### Do not use quotation marks with indirect quotations within a sentence.

A direct quotation uses the speaker's exact words. An indirect quotation puts the speaker's words in other words. Compare these sentences:

> **DIRECT:** *Jean said, "I'm going to be up all night writing my essay."* (quotation marks appropriate)

> **INDIRECT:** *Jean said that she was going to be up all night writing her essay.* (no quotation marks)

## Phrases

### Place participial and prepositional phrases as close as possible to the words they modify.
Participial and prepositional phrases are modifiers; that is, they tell about some other word in a sentence. To avoid confusion, they should be placed as close as possible to the word that they modify.

> **INCORRECT:** *Tiny microphones are planted by agents called bugs.*

> **CORRECT:** *Tiny microphones called bugs are planted by agents.*

### Avoid dangling participles. Make sure a participial phrase does modify a word in the sentence.

> **INCORRECT:** *Disappointed in love, a hermit's life seemed attractive.* (Who was disappointed?)

> **CORRECT:** *Disappointed in love, the man became a hermit.*

## Clauses

### Use commas to set off nonessential adjective clauses.

Do you need the clause in order to indicate precisely who or what is meant? If not, it is nonessential and should be set off by commas.

**USE COMMAS:** *Jim's dogs, who had barked from morning until night, were suddenly quiet.*

**NO COMMAS:** *The dogs who had barked from morning until night were suddenly quiet.*

## Verbs

### Don't use past tense forms with an auxiliary verb or past participle forms without an auxiliary verb. (See Auxiliary Verbs, page 1185.)

**INCORRECT:** *I have saw her somewhere before.* (*saw* is past tense and shouldn't be used with *have*)

**CORRECT:** *I have seen her somewhere before.*

**INCORRECT:** *I seen her somewhere before.* (*seen* is a past participle and shouldn't be used without an auxiliary)

### Shift tense only when necessary.

Usually, when you are writing in present tense, you should stay in present tense; when you are writing in past tense, you should stay in past tense.

**INCORRECT:** *When Cosby spoke at the fair, we all pay attention.*

**CORRECT:** *When Cosby spoke at the fair, we all paid attention.*

Sometimes a shift in tense is necessary to show a logical sequence of actions or the relationship of one action to another.

**CORRECT:** *After he had told his story, everybody went to sleep.*

## Subject-Verb Agreement

### Make sure subjects and verbs agree in number.

**INCORRECT:** *Several plays of Sophocles is based on the legend of Oedipus.*

**CORRECT:** *Several plays of Sophocles are based on the legend of Oedipus.*

**INCORRECT:** *Antigone as well as others in the play are in the family.*

**CORRECT:** *Antigone as well as others in the play is in the family.*

**INCORRECT:** *Antigone and Ismene was daughters of Oedipus.*

**CORRECT:** *Antigone and Ismene were daughters of Oedipus.*

### Use a singular verb with nouns that look plural but have singular meaning.

Some nouns that end in *-s* are singular, even though they look plural. Examples are *measles, news, Wales,* and the names ending in *-ics* when they refer to a school subject, science, or general practice.

**EXAMPLES:** *Has headquarters heard from you yet?*
*Physics is available to everyone who qualifies to take it.*

### Use a singular verb with titles.

**EXAMPLE:** The Mists of Avalon *is on my summer reading list.*
*"The Interlopers" was written by Saki.*

### Use a singular verb with words of weight, time, and measure.

**EXAMPLES:** *Forty pounds is what my niece weighs now.*
*One hundred dollars is the price of the new equipment.*

## Pronouns

### Use personal pronouns correctly in compounds.

Don't be confused about case when *and* joins a noun and a personal pronoun; the case of the pronoun still depends upon its function.

**INCORRECT:** *Marlene and her will conduct the interview.*

**CORRECT:** *Marlene and she will conduct the interview.*

**INCORRECT:** *She asked Sunny and I to wait for her.*

**CORRECT:** *She asked Sunny and me to wait for her.*

**INCORRECT:** *Show Anne and they how to work the video recorder.*

**CORRECT:** *Show Anne and them how to work the video recorder.*

Usually, if you remove the noun and *and,* the correct pronoun will be obvious.

### Use *we* and *us* correctly with nouns.

When a noun directly follows *we* or *us,* the case of the pronoun depends upon its function.

**INCORRECT:** *Us cheerleaders have many new cheers.*

**CORRECT:** *We cheerleaders have many new cheers.* (*we* is the subject)

**INCORRECT:** *It makes a big difference to we players.*

**CORRECT:** *It makes a big difference to us players.* (*us* is the object of *to*)

### Avoid unclear pronoun reference.

The reference of a pronoun is ambiguous when the reader cannot tell which of two preceding nouns is its antecedent. The reference is indefinite when the idea to which the pronoun refers is only weakly or vaguely expressed.

**AMBIGUOUS:** *Mary Oliver, not Adrienne Rich, wrote "The Sun," and she* [who?] *also wrote "Wild Geese."*

**CLEARER:** *Mary Oliver, not Adrienne Rich, wrote "The Sun," and Oliver also wrote "Wild Geese."*

**INDEFINITE:** *Oliver won a National Book Award in 1992, which is a prestigious award for writers.*

**CLEARER:** *In 1992, Oliver won a National Book Award, which is a prestigious award for writers.*

### Avoid change of person.

If you are writing in third person—using pronouns such as *she, he, it, they, them, his, her, its*—do not shift to second person—*you.*

**INCORRECT:** *The feudal laborer had to obey his lord, and you needed to obey the king as well.*

**CORRECT:** *The feudal laborer had to obey his lord, and he needed to obey the king as well.*

### Use correct pronouns in elliptical comparisons.

An elliptical comparison is a comparison from which words have been omitted. In order to choose the proper pronoun, fill in the missing words. Note the difference below:

**EXAMPLES:** *I like Carlos better than* (I like) *her. I like Carlos better than she* (likes Carlos).

### Don't confuse pronouns and contractions.

Personal pronouns are made possessive without the use of an apostrophe, as is the relative pronoun *whose.* Whenever you are unsure whether to write *it's* or *its, who's* or *whose,* ask if you mean *it is/has* or *who is/has.* If you do, write the contraction. Do the same for *you're* and *your, they're* and *their,* except that the contraction in this case is for the verb *are.*

### Modifiers

### Avoid double comparisons.

A double comparison is a comparison made twice. In general, if you use *-er* or *-est* on the end of a modifier, you would not also use *more* or *most* in front of it.

**INCORRECT:** *Juan cooks more better since he's taken the chef's course.*

**CORRECT:** *Juan cooks better since he's taken the chef's course.*

**INCORRECT:** *Now he's the most greatest cook in the class.*

**CORRECT:** *Now he's the greatest cook in the class.*

## Avoid illogical comparisons.

Can you tell what is wrong with the following sentence?

*Plays are more entertaining than any kind of performance art.*

This sentence is difficult to understand. To avoid such illogical comparisons, use *other* when comparing an individual member with the rest of the group.

*Plays are more entertaining than any other kind of performance art.*

To avoid another kind of illogical comparison, use *than* or *as* after the first member in a compound comparison.

**ILLOGICAL:** *Sophocles wrote as many great plays if not more than Aeschylus.* (Did he write as many plays or as many great plays?)

**CLEARER:** *Sophocles wrote as many great plays as Aeschylus, if not more.*

## Avoid misplacing modifiers.

Modifiers of all kinds must be placed as close as possible to the words they modify. If you place them elsewhere, you risk being misunderstood.

**MISPLACED:** *Flying from the hemlock tree, Sylvia sees the white heron.*

**CLEARER:** *Sylvia sees the white heron flying from the hemlock tree.*

Sylvia isn't flying—the heron is.

---

### Words Not to Capitalize

---

## Do not capitalize *north, south, east,* and *west* when they are used to tell direction.

**EXAMPLE:** *London is east of New York City. Charleston is the capital of West Virginia.* (Here *West* is part of a proper name.)

## Do not capitalize *sun* and *moon,* and capitalize *earth* only when it is used with the names of other planets.

**EXAMPLES:** *The sun and the moon are heavenly bodies in a solar system that includes Mars, Jupiter, and the Earth.*

*We now live on the earth, not in heaven.*

## Do not capitalize the names of seasons.

**EXAMPLE:** *The winter snows have nearly disappeared.*

## Do not capitalize the names of most school subjects.

School subjects are capitalized only when they name a specific course, such as World History I. Otherwise, they are not capitalized.

**EXAMPLE:** *I'm taking physics, social studies, and a foreign language this year.*

Note: English and the names of other languages are always capitalized.

**EXAMPLE:** *Everybody takes English and either Spanish or French.*

---

### GRAMMAR PRACTICE

Rewrite each sentence correctly.

1. Mrs. Kulpinsky asked Trish and I to help with the decorations.
2. Let's keep this information between we girls.
3. An award-winning collection of poems, Mary Oliver wrote *Dream Work.*
4. Babe Ruth who played for the New York Yankees hit 60 home runs in one season.
5. *The Producers,* starring Zero Mostel and Gene Wilder, are a funny movie.
6. We wanted to know what the speaker means.
7. In Harrison Bergeron's time everyone was equal, and you had to wear clumsy weights if you were graceful.
8. I like Frank O'Connor more better than Nicholas Gage.
9. Preserving nature, a major concern of most citizens.
10. Stumbling forward at the finish line, the race was barely won by the shortest runner.

# Commonly Confused Words

| | | |
|---|---|---|
| **accept/except** | The verb *accept* means "to receive or believe"; *except* is usually a preposition meaning "excluding." | The teams accept everyone except those who don't have at least a C average. |
| **advice/advise** | *Advise* is a verb; *advice* is a noun naming that which an *adviser* gives. | How did the soothsayer advise Julius Caesar? Was Caesar given good advice? |
| **affect/effect** | As a verb, *affect* means "to influence." *Effect* as a verb means "to cause." If you want a noun, you will almost always want *effect*. | How did Antony's speech affect the crowd? Did it effect a change in their attitude? The effect was dramatic. |
| **all ready/already** | *All ready* is an adjective meaning "fully ready." *Already* is an adverb meaning "before or by this time." | Before Antony's speech, they were all ready to praise Brutus. One citizen had already talked of crowning Brutus. |
| **allusion/illusion** | An *allusion* is an indirect reference to something. An *illusion* is a false picture or idea. | Modern literature has many allusions to the works of Shakespeare. The world's apparent flatness is an illusion. |
| **among/between** | *Between* is used when you are speaking of only two things. *Among* is used for three or more. | There is respect between Dove and Angelou. "Birches" is among my favorite Frost poems. |
| **bring/take** | *Bring* is used to denote motion toward a speaker or place. *Take* is used to denote motion away from such a person or place. | Bring the books over here, and I will take them to the library. |
| **fewer/less** | *Fewer* refers to the number of separate, countable units. *Less* refers to bulk quantity. | We have less literature and fewer selections in this year's curriculum. |
| **leave/let** | *Leave* means "to allow something to remain behind." *Let* means "to permit." | The librarian will leave some books on display but will not let us borrow any. |
| **lie/lay** | To *lie* is "to rest or recline." It does not take an object. *Lay* always takes an object. | Dogs love to lie in the sun. We always lay some bones next to him. |
| **loose/lose** | *Loose* (lo͞os) means "free, not restrained"; *lose* (lo͞oz) means "to misplace or fail to find." | Who turned the horses loose? I hope we won't lose any of them. |
| **precede/proceed** | *Precede* means "to go or come before." Use *proceed* for other meanings. | The drum major preceded the other band members. The band director proceeded to direct the national anthem. |
| **than/then** | Use *than* in making comparisons; use *then* on all other occasions. | I like Asimov better than Bradbury. We read one, then the other. |
| **two/too/to** | *Two* is the number. *Too* is an adverb meaning "also" or "very." Use *to* before a verb or as a preposition. | Meg had to go to town, too. We had too much reading to do. Two chapters is too much. |

# Grammar Glossary

*This glossary contains various terms you need to understand when you use the Grammar Handbook. Used as a reference source, this glossary will help you explore grammar concepts and the ways they relate to one another.*

**Abbreviation** An abbreviation is a shortened form of a word or word group; it is often made up of initials. (B.C., A.M., *Maj.*)

**Active voice.** *See* **Voice.**

**Adjective** An adjective modifies, or describes, a noun or pronoun. (*happy* camper, she is *small*)

A *predicate adjective* follows a linking verb and describes the subject. (The day seemed *long.*)

A *proper adjective* is formed from a proper noun. (*Jewish* temple, *Alaskan* husky)

The *comparative* form of an adjective compares two things. (*more alert, thicker*)

The *superlative* form of an adjective compares more than two things. (*most abundant, weakest*)

| What Adjectives Tell | Examples |
| --- | --- |
| How many | *some* writers *much* joy |
| What kind | *grand* plans *wider* streets |
| Which one(s) | *these* flowers *that* star |

**Adjective phrase.** *See* **Phrase.**

**Adverb** An adverb modifies a verb, an adjective, or another adverb. (Clare sang *loudly.*)

The *comparative* form of an adverb compares two actions. (*more generously, faster*)

The *superlative* form of an adverb compares more than two actions. (*most sharply, closest*)

| What Adverbs Tell | Examples |
| --- | --- |
| How | climb *carefully* chuckle *merrily* |
| When | arrived *late* left *early* |
| Where | climbed *up* moved *away* |
| To what extent | *extremely* upset *hardly* visible |

**Adverb, conjunctive.** *See* **Conjunctive adverb.**

**Adverb phrase.** *See* **Phrase.**

**Agreement** Sentence parts that correspond with one another are said to be in agreement.

In *pronoun-antecedent agreement,* a pronoun and the word it refers to are the same in number, gender, and person. (*Bill* mailed *his* application. The *students* ate *their* lunches.)

In *subject-verb agreement,* the subject and verb in a sentence are the same in number. (*A child cries* for help. *They cry* aloud.)

**Ambiguous reference** An ambiguous reference occurs when a pronoun may refer to more than one word. (Bud asked his brother if *he* had any mail.)

**Antecedent** An antecedent is the noun or pronoun to which a pronoun refers. (If *Adam* forgets *his* raincoat, *he* will be late for school. *She* learned *her* lesson.)

**Appositive** An appositive is a noun or phrase that explains one or more words in a sentence. (Cary Grant, *an Englishman,* spent most of his adult life in America.)

An *essential appositive* is needed to make the sense of a sentence complete. (A comic strip inspired the musical *Annie.*)

A *nonessential appositive* is one that adds information to a sentence but is not necessary to its sense. (O. Henry, *a short-story writer,* spent time in prison.)

**Article** Articles are the special adjectives *a, an,* and *the.* (*the* day, *a* fly)

The *definite article* (the word *the*) is one that refers to a particular thing. (*the* cabin)

An *indefinite article* is used with a noun that is not unique but refers to one of many of its kind. (*a* dish, *an* otter)

**Auxiliary verb.** *See* **Verb.**

**Clause** A clause is a group of words that contains a verb and its subject. (*they slept*)

An *adjective clause* is a subordinate clause that modifies a noun or pronoun. (Hugh bought the sweater *that he had admired.*)

An *adverb clause* is a subordinate clause used to modify a verb, an adjective, or an adverb. (Ring the bell *when it is time for class to begin.*)

A **noun clause** is a subordinate clause that is used as a noun. (*Whatever you say* interests me.)

An **elliptical clause** is a clause from which a word or words have been omitted. (We are not as lucky as *they*.)

A **main (independent) clause** can stand by itself as a sentence. (*the flashlight flickered*)

A **subordinate (dependent) clause** does not express a complete thought and cannot stand by itself. (*while the nation watched*)

| Clause | Example |
|---|---|
| **Main** (independent) | The hurricane struck |
| **Subordinate** (dependent) | while we were preparing to leave. |

**Collective noun.** *See* **Noun.**

**Comma splice** A comma splice is an error caused when two sentences are separated with a comma instead of a correct end mark. (*The band played a medley of show tunes, everyone enjoyed the show.*)

**Common noun.** *See* **Noun.**

**Comparative.** *See* **Adjective; Adverb.**

**Complement** A complement is a word or group of words that completes the meaning of a verb. (The kitten finished the *milk*.) *See also* **Direct object; Indirect object.**

An **objective complement** is a word or a group of words that follows a direct object and renames or describes that object. (The parents of the rescued child declared Gus a *hero*.)

A **subject complement** follows a linking verb and renames or describes the subject. (The coach seemed *anxious*.) *See also* **Noun (predicate noun); Adjective, (predicate adjective).**

**Complete predicate** The complete predicate of a sentence consists of the main verb plus any words that modify or complete the verb's meaning. (The student *produces work of high caliber*.)

**Complete subject** The complete subject of a sentence consists of the simple subject plus any words that modify or describe the simple subject. (*Students of history* believe that wars can be avoided.)

| Sentence Part | Example |
|---|---|
| Complete subject | The man in the ten-gallon hat |
| Complete predicate | wore a pair of silver spurs. |

**Compound sentence part** A sentence element that consists of two or more subjects, verbs, objects, or other parts is compound. (*Lou* and *Jay* helped. Laura *makes* and *models* scarves. Jill sings *opera* and *popular music*.)

**Conjunction** A conjunction is a word that links other words or groups of words.

A **coordinating conjunction** connects related words, groups of words, or sentences. (*and, but, or*)

A **correlative conjunction** is one of a pair of conjunctions that work together to connect sentence parts. (*either . . . or, neither . . . nor, not only . . . but also, whether . . . or, both . . . and*)

A **subordinating conjunction** introduces a subordinate clause. (*after, although, as, as if, as long as, as though, because, before, if, in order that, since, so that, than, though, till, unless, until, whatever, when, where, while*)

**Conjunctive adverb** A conjunctive adverb joins the clauses of a compound sentence. (*however, therefore, yet*)

**Contraction** A contraction is formed by joining two words and substituting an apostrophe for a letter or letters left out of one of the words. (*didn't, we've*)

**Coordinating conjunction.** *See* **Conjunction.**

**Correlative conjunction.** *See* **Conjunction.**

 **D**

**Dangling modifier** A dangling modifier is one that does not clearly modify any word in the sentence. (*Dashing for the train, the barriers got in the way*.)

**Demonstrative pronoun.** *See* **Pronoun.**

**Dependent clause.** *See* **Clause.**

**Direct object** A direct object receives the action of a verb. Direct objects follow transitive verbs. (Jude planned the *party*.)

**Direct quotation.** *See* **Quotation.**

**Divided quotation.** *See* **Quotation.**

**Double negative** A double negative is the incorrect use of two negative words when only one is needed. (*Nobody didn't care.*)

 **E**

**End mark** An end mark is one of several punctuation marks that can end a sentence. See the punctuation chart on page 1203.

**F**

**Fragment.** *See* **Sentence fragment.**

**Future tense.** *See* **Verb tense.**

 **G**

**Gender** The gender of a personal pronoun indicates whether the person or thing referred to is male, female, or neuter. (My cousin plays the tuba; *he* often performs in school concerts.)

**Gerund** A gerund is a verbal that ends in *-ing* and functions as a noun. (*Making* pottery takes patience.)

 **H**

**Helping verb.** *See* **Verb (auxiliary verb).**

 **I**

**Illogical comparison** An illogical comparison is a comparison that does not make sense because words are missing or illogical. (My computer is *newer than Kay.*)

**Indefinite pronoun.** *See* **Pronoun.**

**Indefinite reference** Indefinite reference occurs when a pronoun is used without a clear antecedent. (My aunt hugged me in front of my friends, and *it* was embarrassing.)

**Independent clause.** *See* **Clause.**

**Indirect object** An indirect object tells to whom or for whom (sometimes to what or for what) something is done. (Arthur wrote *Kerry* a letter.)

**Indirect question** An indirect question tells what someone asked without using the person's exact words. (*My friend asked me if I could go with her to the dentist.*)

**Indirect quotation.** *See* **Quotation.**

**Infinitive** An infinitive is a verbal beginning with *to* that functions as a noun, an adjective, or an adverb. (He wanted *to go* to the play.)

**Intensive pronoun.** *See* **Pronoun.**

**Interjection** An interjection is a word or phrase used to express strong feeling. (*Wow! Good grief!*)

**Interrogative pronoun.** *See* **Pronoun.**

**Intransitive verb.** *See* **Verb.**

**Inverted sentence** An inverted sentence is one in which the subject comes after the verb. (*How was the movie? Here come the clowns.*)

**Irregular verb.** *See* **Verb.**

 **L**

**Linking verb.** *See* **Verb.**

 **M**

**Main clause.** *See* **Clause.**

**Main verb.** *See* **Verb.**

**Modifier** A modifier makes another word more precise. Modifiers most often are adjectives or adverbs; they may also be phrases, verbals, or clauses that function as adjectives or adverbs. (*small* box, smiled *broadly,* house *by the sea,* dog *barking loudly*)

An *essential modifier* is one that is necessary to the meaning of a sentence. (Everybody *who has a free pass* should enter now. None *of the passengers* got on the train.)

A *nonessential modifier* is one that merely adds more information to a sentence that is clear without the addition. (We will use the new dishes, *which are stored in the closet.*)

 **N**

**Noun** A noun names a person, a place, a thing, or an idea. (*auditor, shelf, book, goodness*)

An *abstract noun* names an idea, a quality, or a feeling. (*joy*)

A *collective noun* names a group of things. (*bevy*)

A *common noun* is a general name of a person, a place, a thing, or an idea. (*valet, hill, bread, amazement*)

A *compound noun* contains two or more words. (*hometown, pay-as-you-go, screen test*)

A *noun of direct address* is the name of a person being directly spoken to. (*Lee,* do you have the package? No, *Suki,* your letter did not arrive.)

A *possessive noun* shows who or what owns or is associated with something. (*Lil's* ring, a *day's* pay)

A *predicate noun* follows a linking verb and renames the subject. (Karen is a *writer.*)

A *proper noun* names a particular person, place, or thing. (*John Smith, Ohio, Sears Tower, Congress*)

**Number** A word is **singular** in number if it refers to just one person, place, thing, idea, or action, and **plural** in number if it refers to more than one person, place, thing, idea, or action. (The words *he, waiter,* and *is* are singular. The words *they, waiters,* and *are* are plural.)

 **O**

**Object of a preposition** The object of a preposition is the noun or pronoun that follows a preposition. (The athletes cycled along the *route.* Jane baked a cake for *her.*)

**Object of a verb** The object of a verb receives the action of the verb. (Sid told *stories.*)

**Participle** A participle is often used as part of a verb phrase. (had *written*) It can also be used as a verbal that functions as an adjective. (the *leaping* deer, the medicine *taken* for a fever)

The **present participle** is formed by adding *-ing* to the present form of a verb. (*Walking* rapidly, we reached the general store.)

The **past participle** of a regular verb is formed by adding *-d* or *-ed* to the present form. The past participles of irregular verbs do not follow this pattern. (*Startled,* they ran from the house. *Spun* glass is delicate. A *broken* cup lay there.)

**Passive voice.** *See* **Voice.**

**Past tense.** *See* **Verb tense.**

**Perfect tenses.** *See* **Verb tense.**

**Person** Person is a means of classifying pronouns.

A **first-person** pronoun refers to the person speaking. (*We* came.)

A **second-person** pronoun refers to the person spoken to. (*You* ask.)

A **third-person** pronoun refers to some other person(s) or thing(s) being spoken of. (*They* played.)

**Personal pronoun.** *See* **Pronoun.**

**Phrase** A phrase is a group of related words that does not contain a verb and its subject. (*noticing everything, under a chair*)

An **adjective phrase** modifies a noun or a pronoun. (The label *on the bottle* has faded.)

An **adverb phrase** modifies a verb, an adjective, or an adverb. (Come *to the fair.*)

An **appositive phrase** explains one or more words in a sentence. (Mary, *a champion gymnast,* won gold medals at the Olympics.)

A **gerund phrase** consists of a gerund and its modifiers and complements. (*Fixing the leak* will take only a few minutes.)

An **infinitive phrase** consists of an infinitive, its modifiers, and its complements. (*To prepare for a test,* study in a quiet place.)

A **participial phrase** consists of a participle and its modifiers and complements. (*Straggling to the finish line,* the last runners arrived.)

A **prepositional phrase** consists of a preposition, its object, and the object's modifiers. (The Saint Bernard does rescue work *in the Swiss Alps.*)

A **verb phrase** consists of a main verb and one or more helping verbs. (*might have ordered*)

**Possessive** A noun or pronoun that is possessive shows ownership or relationship. (*Dan's* story, *my* doctor)

**Possessive noun.** *See* **Noun.**

**Possessive pronoun.** *See* **Pronoun.**

**Predicate** The predicate of a sentence tells what the subject is or does. (The van *runs well even in winter.* The job *seems too complicated.*) *See also* **Complete predicate; Simple predicate.**

**Predicate adjective.** *See* **Adjective.**

**Predicate nominative** A predicate nominative is a noun or pronoun that follows a linking verb and renames or explains the subject. (Joan is a computer *operator.* The winner of the prize was *he.*)

**Predicate pronoun.** *See* **Pronoun.**

**Preposition** A preposition is a word that relates its object to another part of the sentence or to the sentence as a whole. (Alfredo leaped *onto* the stage.)

**Prepositional phrase.** *See* **Phrase.**

**Present tense.** *See* **Verb tense.**

**Pronoun** A pronoun replaces a noun or another pronoun. Some pronouns allow a writer or speaker to avoid repeating a proper noun. Other pronouns let a writer refer to an unknown or unidentified person or thing.

A **demonstrative pronoun** singles out one or more persons or things. (*This* is the letter.)

An **indefinite pronoun** refers to an unidentified person or thing. (*Everyone* stayed home. Will you hire *anybody?*)

An **intensive pronoun** emphasizes a noun or pronoun. (The teacher *himself* sold tickets.)

An **interrogative pronoun** asks a question. (*What* happened to you?)

A **personal pronoun** shows a distinction of person. (*I* came. *You* see. *He* knows.)

A **possessive pronoun** shows ownership. (*My* spaghetti is always good. Are *your* parents coming to the play?)

A *predicate pronoun* follows a linking verb and renames the subject. (The owners of the store were *they*.)

A *reflexive pronoun* reflects an action back on the subject of the sentence. (Joe helped *himself*.)

A *relative pronoun* relates a subordinate clause to the word it modifies. (The draperies, *which* had been made by hand, were ruined in the fire.)

**Pronoun-antecedent agreement.** *See* **Agreement.**

**Pronoun forms**

The *subject form* of a pronoun is used when the pronoun is the subject of a sentence or follows a linking verb as a predicate pronoun. (*She* fell. The star was *she*.)

The *object form* of a pronoun is used when the pronoun is the direct or indirect object of a verb or verbal or the object of a preposition. (We sent *him* the bill. We ordered food for *them*.)

**Proper adjective.** *See* **Adjective.**

**Proper noun.** *See* **Noun.**

**Punctuation** Punctuation clarifies the structure of sentences. See the punctuation chart below.

**Quotation** A quotation consists of words from another speaker or writer.

A *direct quotation* is the exact words of a speaker or writer. (Martin said, *"The homecoming game has been postponed."*)

A *divided quotation* is a quotation separated by words that identify the speaker. (*"The homecoming game,"* said Martin, *"has been postponed."*)

An *indirect quotation* reports what a person said without giving the exact words. (*Martin said that the homecoming game had been postponed.*)

**Reflexive pronoun.** *See* **Pronoun.**

**Regular verb.** *See* **Verb.**

**Relative pronoun.** *See* **Pronoun.**

**Run-on sentence** A run-on sentence consists of two or more sentences written incorrectly as one. (*The sunset was beautiful its brilliant colors lasted only a short time.*)

**Sentence** A sentence expresses a complete thought. The chart at the top of the next page shows the four kinds of sentences.

A *complex sentence* contains one main clause and one or

| Punctuation | Uses | Examples |
|---|---|---|
| Apostrophe (') | Shows possession | Lou's garage      Alva's script |
| | Indicates a contraction | I'll help you.      The baby's tired. |
| Colon (:) | Introduces a list or quotation | three colors: red, green, and yellow |
| | Divides some compound sentences | This was the problem: we had to find our own way home. |
| Comma (,) | Separates ideas | The glass broke, and the juice spilled all over. |
| | Separates modifiers | The lively, talented cheerleaders energized the team. |
| | Separates items in series | We visited London, Rome, and Paris. |
| Exclamation point (!) | Ends an exclamatory sentence | Have a wonderful time! |
| Hyphen (-) | Joins parts of some compound words | daughter-in-law, great-grandson |
| Period (.) | Ends a declarative sentence | Swallows return to Capistrano in spring. |
| | Indicates most abbreviations | min.    qt.    Blvd.    Gen.    Jan. |
| Question mark (?) | Ends an interrogative sentence | Where are you going? |
| Semicolon (;) | Divides some compound sentences | Marie is an expert dancer; she teaches a class in tap. |
| | Separates items in series that contain commas | Jerry visited Syracuse, New York; Athens, Georgia; and Tampa, Florida. |

more subordinate clauses. (*Open the windows before you go to bed. If she falls, I'll help her up.*)

A *compound sentence* is made up of two or more independent clauses joined by a conjunction, a colon, or a semicolon. (*The ship finally docked, and the passengers quickly left.*)

| Kind of Sentence | Example |
|---|---|
| **Declarative** (statement) | Our team won. |
| **Exclamatory** (strong feeling) | I had a great time! |
| **Imperative** (request, command) | Take the next exit. |
| **Interrogative** (question) | Who owns the car? |

A *simple sentence* consists of only one main clause. (*My friend volunteers at a nursing home.*)

**Sentence fragment** A sentence fragment is a group of words that is only part of a sentence. (*When he arrived. Merrily yodeling.*)

**Simple predicate** A simple predicate is the verb in the predicate. (John *collects* foreign stamps.)

**Simple subject** A simple subject is the key noun or pronoun in the subject. (The new *house* is empty.)

**Split infinitive** A split infinitive occurs when a modifier is placed between the word *to* and the verb in an infinitive. (*to quickly speak*)

**Subject** The subject is the part of a sentence that tells whom or what the sentence is about. (*Lou* swam.) *See* **Complete subject; Simple subject.**

**Subject-verb agreement.** *See* **Agreement.**

**Subordinate clause.** *See* **Clause.**

**Subordinating conjunction.** *See* **Conjunction.**

**Superlative.** *See* **Adjective; Adverb.**

**Transitive verb.** *See* **Verb.**

**Unidentified reference** An unidentified reference usually occurs when the word *it, they, this, which,* or *that* is used. (In California *they* have good weather most of the time.)

**Verb** A verb expresses an action, a condition, or a state of being.

An *action verb* tells what the subject does, has done, or will do. The action may be physical or mental. (Susan *trains* guide dogs.)

An *auxiliary verb* is added to a main verb to express tense, add emphasis, or otherwise affect the meaning of the verb. Together the auxiliary and main verb make up a verb phrase. (*will* intend, *could have* gone)

A *linking verb* expresses a state of being or connects the subject with a word or words that describe the subject. (The ice *feels* cold.) Linking verbs include *appear, be (am, are, is, was, were, been, being), become, feel, grow, look, remain, seem, smell, sound,* and *taste.*

A *main verb* expresses action or state of being; it appears with one or more auxiliary verbs. (will be *staying*)

The *progressive form* of a verb shows continuing action. (She *is* knitting.)

The past tense and past participle of a *regular verb* are formed by adding -*d* or -*ed.* (*open, opened*) An *irregular verb* does not follow this pattern. (*throw, threw, thrown; shrink, shrank, shrunk*)

The action of a *transitive verb* is directed toward someone or something, called the object of the verb. (Leo *washed* the windows.) An *intransitive verb* has no object. (The leaves *scattered.*)

**Verb phrase.** *See* **Phrase.**

**Verb tense** Verb tense shows the time of an action or the time of a state of being.

The *present tense* places an action or condition in the present. (Jan *takes* piano lessons.)

The *past tense* places an action or condition in the past. (We *came* to the party.)

The *future tense* places an action or condition in the future. (You *will understand.*)

The *present perfect tense* describes an action in an indefinite past time or an action that began in the past and continues in the present. (*has called, have known*)

The *past perfect tense* describes one action that happened before another action in the past. (*had scattered, had mentioned*)

The *future perfect tense* describes an event that will be finished before another future action begins. (*will have taught, shall have appeared*)

**Verbal** A verbal is formed from a verb and acts as another part of speech, such as a noun, an adjective, or an adverb.

| Verbal | Example |
|---|---|
| **Gerund** (used as a noun) | Lamont enjoys *swimming.* |
| **Infinitive** (used as an adjective, an adverb, or a noun) | Everyone wants *to help.* |
| **Participle** (used as an adjective) | The leaves *covering the drive* made it slippery. |

**Voice** The voice of a verb depends on whether the subject performs or receives the action of the verb.

In the ***active voice*** the subject of the sentence performs the verb's action. (We *knew* the answer.)

In the ***passive voice*** the subject of the sentence receives the action of the verb. (The team *has been eliminated.*)

# Analyzing Text Features

## Reading a Magazine Article

A **magazine article** is designed to catch and hold your interest. Learning how to recognize the items on a magazine page will help you read even the most complicated articles. Look at the sample magazine article as you read each strategy below.

### *Strategies for Reading*

**A** Read the **title** and other **headings** to get an idea of what the article is about. Frequently, the title presents the article's main topic. Smaller headings may introduce subtopics related to the main topic.

**B** Note introductory text that is set off in some way, such as an **indented paragraph** or a passage in a **different typeface.** This text often summarizes the article.

**C** Pay attention to terms in **quotation marks, italics,** or **boldface.** Look for definitions or explanations before or after these terms.

**D** Study **visuals**—photos, pictures, or maps. Visuals help bring the topic to life and enrich the text.

**E** Look for **special features,** such as charts, tables, or boxed text, that provide more detailed information on the topic or on a subtopic.

### PRACTICE AND APPLY

Use the sample magazine page at right and the tips above to help you answer the following questions.

1. What is the article's main topic?
2. What does the quote under the photo tell you about how some parents might behave at youth sports games?
3. What does the term "Silent Sunday" mean?
4. How do the visuals help you understand the article?
5. What information appears in the box?

# Is "youth sports rage" on the rise?

## Parents become violent and abusive during kids' games

by Belinda Liu

The news stories are frightening. In Virginia, the mother of a soccer player assaults a 14-year-old referee and is fined. In Pennsylvania, a "midget league" football game results in a brawl involving about 100 players and spectators. Accounts of "youth sports rage" are reported in Britain, Canada, Australia, and New Zealand.

Are spectators at youth sports becoming more violent? Some observers believe they are.

"There have always been problem parents in kids' sports," explains soccer coach Larry Fiore. "But the vast majority of parents, coaches, and athletes act appropriately."

However, some factors are making the problem worse, believes sports psychologist Theresa Mathelier. "Sports are getting more expensive for parents in terms of equipment, traveling, and coaching," she explains. "The tendency now is to start kids in organized sports earlier and to get them to specialize in one

*"Parents should be role models."*

sport."

As a result, Mathelier says, "a few parents get unrealistic ideas about college scholarships and professional careers in sports. They start to live through their kids, and if something goes wrong, they blow up."

Fiore and Mathelier both say that it is rarely the athletes who cause the problems. Serena Terell, a 15-year-old soccer player, agrees. "It's so embarrassing when the parents yell and curse," Serena explains, adding that her parents always behave themselves. "Their kids just want them to stop. After all, it's only a game, and parents should be role models."

## Stopping sports rage

Here are steps that some groups have taken to prevent youth sports rage.

- The National Youth Sports Safety Foundation has created a Sport Parent Code of Conduct. Penalties range from a verbal warning to a season suspension for parents.
- Some soccer leagues designate one day as "Silent Sunday." Spectators are not allowed to cheer or even talk until the game is over.
- Some coaches choose one parent to be in charge of crowd control. This parent patrols the bleachers or sidelines, making sure that fans of his or her team behave.

## Reading a Textbook

The first page of a **textbook** lesson introduces you to a particular topic. The page also provides important information that will guide you through the rest of the lesson. Look at the sample textbook page as you read each strategy below.

### Strategies for Reading

**A** Preview the **title** and other **headings** to find out the lesson's main topic and related subtopics.

**B** Look for a list of terms or **vocabulary words.** These words will be identified and defined throughout the lesson.

**C** Read the **main idea, objectives,** or **focus.** These items summarize the lesson and establish a purpose for your reading.

**D** Find words set in special type, such as **italics** or **boldface.** Also look for material in **parentheses.** Boldface is often used to identify the vocabulary terms in the lesson.

**E** Notice text on the page that is set off in some way. For example, text placed in a tinted, or colored, box may be from a **primary source** or a **quotation** that gives firsthand knowledge or historical perspective on a topic.

**F** Examine **visuals,** such as photos and drawings, and their captions. Visuals can help the topic come alive.

**PRACTICE AND APPLY**

Use the sample textbook page and the tips above to help you answer the following questions.

1. What is the subject of the lesson?
2. List the vocabulary terms that will be defined in the lesson.
3. What is the lesson's main idea?
4. What does the sidebar tell you about Napoleon's personality?
5. How did Napoleon become a hero?

Understanding Visuals

Reading a Graph

## 3 Napoleon Forges an Empire

**TERMS & NAMES**
- **Napoleon Bonaparte**
- **coup d'état**
- **plebiscite**
- **lycée**
- **concordat**
- **Napoleonic Code**
- **Battle of Trafalgar**

| MAIN IDEA | WHY IT MATTERS NOW |
|---|---|
| A military genius, Napoleon Bonaparte, seized power in France and made himself emperor. | In times of political turmoil, military dictators often seize control of nations, as in Haiti in 1991. |

**SETTING THE STAGE** Napoleon was a short man (five feet three inches tall) who cast a long shadow over the history of modern times. He would come to be recognized as one of the world's greatest military geniuses, along with Alexander the Great of Macedonia, Hannibal of Carthage, and Julius Caesar of Rome. In only four years (1795–1799), Napoleon rose from relative obscurity to become master of France.

### Napoleon Grasps the Power

**Napoleon Bonaparte** was born in 1769 on the Mediterranean island of Corsica. When he was nine years old, his parents sent him to a military school in northern France. In 1785, at the age of 16, he finished school and became a lieutenant in the artillery. When the Revolution broke out, Napoleon joined the army of the new government.

**Hero of the Hour** In October 1795, fate handed the young officer a chance for glory. When royalist rebels marched on the National Convention, a government official told Napoleon to defend the delegates. Napoleon and his gunners greeted the thousands of royalists with a cannonade. Within minutes, the attackers fled in panic and confusion. Napoleon Bonaparte became the hero of the hour and was hailed throughout Paris as the savior of the French republic.

In 1796, the Directory appointed Napoleon to lead a French army against the forces of Austria and the Kingdom of Sardinia. Crossing the Alps, the young general swept into Italy and won a series of remarkable victories, which crushed the Austrian troops' threat to France. Next, in an attempt to protect French trade interests and to disrupt British trade with India, Napoleon led an expedition to Egypt. Unfortunately, his luck did not hold. His army was pinned down in Egypt, and his naval forces were defeated by the British admiral Horatio Nelson. However, he managed to keep the reports of his defeat out of the press, so that by 1799 the words "the general" could mean only one man to the French—Napoleon.

**Coup d'État** By 1799, the Directory had lost control of the political situation and the confidence of the French people. Only the directors' control of the army kept them in power. Upon Napoleon's return from Egypt, the Abbé Sieyès urged him to seize political power. Napoleon and Josephine, his lovely socialite wife, set a plan in motion. Napoleon met with influential persons to discuss his role in the Directory, while Josephine used her connections with the wealthy directors to influence their decisions. The action began on November 9, 1799, when Napoleon was put in charge of the military. It ended the next day when his troops drove out the members of one chamber of the

**D**

**Vocabulary**
cannonade: a bombardment with heavy artillery fire.

HISTORY MAKERS

**E** **Napoleon Bonaparte**
**1769–1821**

Napoleon Bonaparte had a magnetism that attracted the admiration of his men. His speeches were designed to inspire his troops to valorous feats. In one speech, he told soldiers, "If the victory is for a moment uncertain, you shall see your Emperor place himself on the front line."

Bonaparte was generous in his rewards to the troops. Many received the Legion of Honor—a medal for bravery. Sometimes Napoleon would take the medal from his own chest to present it to a soldier. (He kept a few spares in his pocket for these occasions.) A cavalry commander, Auguste de Colbert, wrote, "He awakened in my soul the desire for glory."

# Reading a Diagram

**Diagrams** combine pictures with a few words to provide a lot of information. Look at the example on the opposite page as you read each of the following strategies.

## *Strategies for Reading*

**A** Look at the **title** to get a quick idea of what the diagram is about.

**B** Study the **images** closely to understand each part of the diagram.

**C** Look at the **captions** and the **labels** for more information.

**PRACTICE AND APPLY**

Study the diagram, then answer the following questions using the strategies above.

**1.** What is the diagram about?

**2.** What are the three forms of liquid water?

**3.** What happens if water vapor condenses?

**4.** How does ice become water vapor?

## States of Water

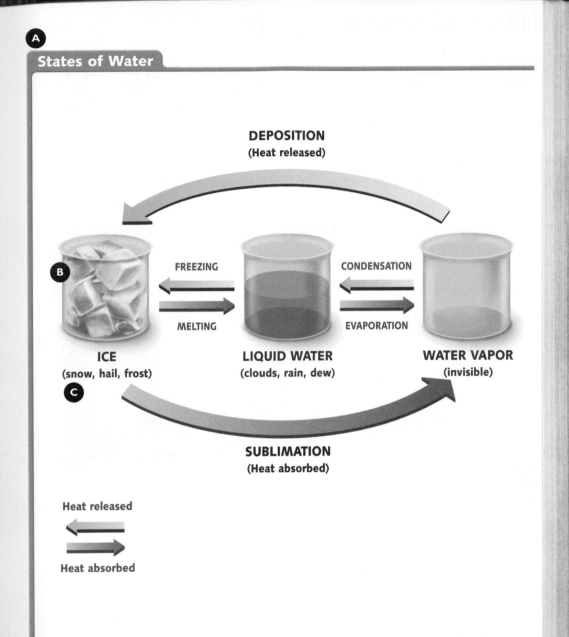

**DEPOSITION**
(Heat released)

FREEZING

CONDENSATION

MELTING

EVAPORATION

**ICE**
(snow, hail, frost)

**LIQUID WATER**
(clouds, rain, dew)

**WATER VAPOR**
(invisible)

**SUBLIMATION**
(Heat absorbed)

Heat released

Heat absorbed

# Recognizing Text Structures

## Main Idea and Supporting Details

The **main idea** in a paragraph is its most important point. **Details** in the paragraph support the main idea. Identifying the main idea will help you focus on the main message the writer wants to communicate. Use the following strategies to help you identify a paragraph's main idea and supporting details.

### Strategies for Reading

- Look for the **main idea,** which is often the first sentence in a paragraph.
- Use the main idea to help you **summarize** the point of the paragraph.
- Identify specific **details,** including facts and examples, that **support** the main idea.

### Queen Elizabeth I and the Church of England

**Main Idea** — Under Queen Elizabeth I, who ruled from 1558 to 1603, the Protestant faith again became England's official religion. In 1559, Parliament passed the Act of Supremacy. The Act made the queen the sole head of the Church of England. Also, English replaced **Details** Latin as the main language of the church, and clergy were allowed to marry. Elizabeth further strengthened the Church of England by personally appointing all but one of the bishops.

### PRACTICE AND APPLY

Read the following paragraph. Write down the main idea and list three supporting details.

When Elizabeth I inherited the English throne in 1558, she quickly began making changes within the country. Elizabeth reduced the size of the Privy Council to make it more efficient as an advisory body. She also reorganized the large royal household and assembled a group of experienced advisers. Furthermore, England was soon restored to the Protestantism it had known under Henry VIII, Elizabeth's father.

## Problem and Solution

Does the proposed **solution** to **a problem** make sense? In order to decide, you need to look at each part of the text. Use the following strategies to read the text below.

### Strategies for Reading

- Look at the beginning or middle of a paragraph to find the **statement of the problem.**
- Find **details** that explain the problem and tell why it is important.
- Look for the **proposed solution.**
- Identify the **supporting details** for the proposed solution.
- Think about whether the **solution** is a good one.

## Too Much Noise *by Joan Matson*

It's midnight, and you're trying to sleep. A car alarm goes off outside your window. A street sweeper drives by. Then a neighbor turns on a stereo. If you have ever found yourself in this situation, **Statement of problem** you are a victim of one of today's most common problems: noise pollution.

**Explanation of problem** According to hearing experts, noise in excess of 85 decibels can cause hearing loss if exposure is long enough. Hair dryers and lawn mowers commonly reach levels of 90 decibels. Noise pollution is not just an annoyance—it can actually be dangerous.

Forming a community antinoise group can be useful in the battle for peace and quiet. Ask neighbors if they share your concerns about noise. Then invite interested people to a meeting. Your group can fight noise by

- researching your community's laws about noise levels.
- printing fliers and making presentations about noise pollution.
- setting a good example instead of adding to the volume.

### PRACTICE AND APPLY

Read the text above. Then answer these questions.

**1.** What is the proposed solution?

**2.** Give at least one detail that supports the need for a solution.

**3.** Do you think the solution is a good one? Explain why or why not.

## Sequence

It's important to understand the **sequence,** or order of events, in what you read. It helps you know what happens and why. Read the tips below to make sure a sequence is clear to you. Then look at the example on the opposite page.

### Strategies for Reading

- Read through the passage and think about what its **main steps,** or stages, are.
- Look for **words and phrases that signal time:** *in a year, three hours earlier, 202 B.C.,* or *later.*
- Look for **words and phrases that signal order:** *first, second, now, after that,* or *finally.*

**PRACTICE AND APPLY**

Read the article on the next page, which describes the main events of Napoleon Bonaparte's career. Use the information from the article and the tips above to answer the questions.

**1.** List any words or phrases that signal time.

**2.** List the phrases in the article that signal order.

**3.** A timeline can help you understand a sequence of events. Use the information from the article to copy and complete this timeline.

### Life of Napoleon Bonaparte

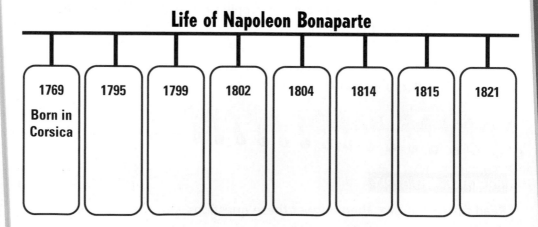

| 1769 Born in Corsica | 1795 | 1799 | 1802 | 1804 | 1814 | 1815 | 1821 |
|---|---|---|---|---|---|---|---|

# Napoleon's Accomplishments

Napoleon Bonaparte was born in 1769 on the Mediterranean island of Corsica. As a boy, he was sent to boarding school in France. At 16, he joined the French army and began his military career.

After becoming a soldier, Napoleon was gradually assigned more important duties, including the defense of a revolutionary convention in 1795 against royalist rebels. After many military successes, Napoleon was given control of the military on November 9, 1799. The next day, he drove out members of the legislature and seized power. By 1802, after failing to defeat Napoleon, Britain, Austria, and Russia signed a peace agreement with France. For the first time in 10 years, Europe was at peace.

Next, Napoleon began to restore order to France. He set up an efficient tax collecting system, established a national bank, introduced a code of law, and reduced government corruption. In 1804, he crowned himself emperor.

Napoleon controlled the largest European empire since the time of the Romans. However, unlike the Roman Empire, Napoleon's empire lasted only 10 years. His failed attempt to invade Russia in 1812 weakened the French military. His enemies were quick to take advantage of this weakness. By March 1814, the Russian czar and the Prussian king were leading their troops through Paris.

In April 1814, Napoleon gave up his throne and was exiled to the island of Elba. After an escape from Elba and a brief return to power in 1815, he was defeated at the Battle of Waterloo on June 15, 1815. Napoleon was again banished, this time to the island of St. Helena, in the South Atlantic. He died in 1821.

Historians recognize Napoleon as a military genius. However, his most lasting accomplishments were his law code and other reforms.

## Cause and Effect

A **cause** is an event that brings about another event. An **effect** is something that happens as a result of the first event. Identifying causes and effects helps you understand how events are related. The tips below can help you find causes and effects in any reading.

### Strategies for Reading

- Look for an action or event that answers the question "What happened?" This is the **effect.**

- Look for an action or event that answers the question "Why did it happen?" This is the **cause.**

- Identify words or phrases that **signal** causes and effects, such as *because, as a result, therefore, thus, consequently, since,* and *led to.*

### PRACTICE AND APPLY

Read the cause-and-effect passage on the next page. Then answer the following questions. Notice that the first cause and effect in the passage are highlighted.

**1.** List any words in the passage that signal causes and effects. The first one is highlighted for you.

**2.** Why do wood storks prefer somewhat dry weather?

**3.** Sometimes an effect has more than one cause. Use information from the article to copy and complete the following diagram.

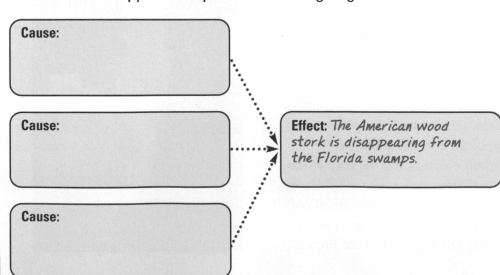

**Cause:**

**Cause:**

**Cause:**

**Effect:** *The American wood stork is disappearing from the Florida swamps.*

# Why Are Wood Storks Leaving Florida?

**Effect**

The endangered American wood stork is disappearing from its native Florida swamps, changing the delicate ecological balance in southern Florida wildlife sanctuaries. Researchers have found that the storks have been migrating north to Georgia and South Carolina during mating season. Commercial development of swamplands, changes in weather conditions, and varying water levels have all contributed to the storks' migration.

Since 1900, Florida swamplands have been drained to make room for homes, farms, golf courses, and roads. As a result, the wood storks and other wildlife that lived in the swamps have had to find other places to feed.

**Cause**

**Signal word**

Drought is also a cause of the wood storks' migration. Wood storks prefer somewhat dry weather because fish become concentrated in small pools of water and are easy to find. Too much drought, however, brings water down to a level where even wood storks have to fly elsewhere for food. Dry spells also often force the U.S. Army Corps of Engineers to drain swamps to provide running water for Floridians.

This process continues the destruction of swamps, including protected areas such as the Everglades.

Unusually wet weather can also be a reason for wood stork migration. Water is pumped into the Everglades during wet years to keep cities and farms safe and dry. High water levels cause fish and other food sources to spread out. Consequently, birds must fly long distances for food.

Flying north is not a perfect solution for the wood stork because it puts storks and their young in danger of cold spells. Luckily, plans to restore the Florida swamps and better manage swamp water are being developed. If these plans succeed, the wood stork might return to nest in Florida. John Ogden, a biologist from the South Florida water management district, has this message for northern states: "We're going to get those South Carolina and Georgia wood storks back!"

# Comparison and Contrast

**Comparing** two things means showing how they are the same. **Contrasting** two things means showing how they are different. Comparisons and contrasts are often used in science and history books to make a subject clearer. Use these tips to help you understand comparison and contrast in reading assignments, such as the article on the opposite page.

## *Strategies for Reading*

- Look for **direct statements** of comparison and contrast: "These things are similar because . . ." or "One major difference is. . . ."
- Pay attention to **words and phrases that signal comparisons,** such as *also, both, is the same as,* and *in the same way.*
- Notice **words and phrases that signal contrasts.** Some of these are *however, still, but,* and *on the other hand.*

**PRACTICE AND APPLY**

Read the essay on the opposite page. Then use the information from the article and the tips above to answer the questions.

**1.** List any words and phrases that signal comparisons. A sample has been highlighted for you.

**2.** List any words and phrases that signal contrasts. A sample has been highlighted for you.

**3.** A Venn diagram shows how two subjects are similar and how they are different. Copy this diagram, which uses information from the essay to compare and contrast ancient pyramids in Egypt and the Americas. Add at least one similarity to the middle part of the diagram. Add at least one difference in each outer circle.

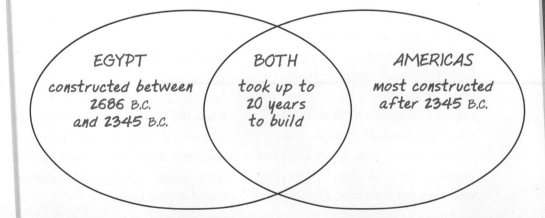

EGYPT

constructed between
2686 B.C.
and 2345 B.C.

BOTH

took up to
20 years
to build

AMERICAS

most constructed
after 2345 B.C.

# Pyramids in Egypt and the Americas

The pyramid is perhaps the most well-known accomplishment of ancient peoples. When most people think of these amazing structures, they think of Egypt.

**Contrast** However, Egypt was not the only place where pyramids were built. Pyramids were also constructed in the Americas, mainly in Central and South America.

Most pyramid construction in Egypt took place between 2686 and 2345 B.C. In contrast, most Central and South American pyramids were built much later. So far, only one pyramid of the Americas has been

**Comparison** found to be similar in age to those in Egypt. A pyramid in Caral, Peru, has been dated to 2627 B.C.

Both the Pyramid of the Sun at Teotihuacán, Mexico, and the Great Pyramid at Giza, Egypt, measure nearly the same at their base. Egyptian pyramids are taller, however. The Great Pyramid originally reached a height of 481 feet, while the tallest pyramid in the Americas is 216 feet high. Even the pyramid at Caral is only one-eighth the height of the Great Pyramid.

Pyramids in Egypt and the Americas have major structural differences as

The Pyramid of Kukulkán in Mexico

well. Pyramids in the Americas have receding steps that resemble the layers of a cake. Egyptian pyramids, on the other hand, have smooth sides that connect in a point at the top.

Egyptian pyramids were always part of a larger collection of buildings, including temples and houses. Similarly, American pyramids were built in the middle of cities. However, pyramids in the Americas typically served as temples and were the sites of human and animal sacrifices. In contrast, all Egyptian pyramids were built to be royal burial chambers.

Modern scientists are still amazed at the size and durability of these structures. Many pyramids took as long as 20 years to build, using millions of stone blocks and thousands of laborers. Pyramids in Egypt and in the Americas were both outstanding accomplishments for the civilizations that created them.

## Argument

An **argument** is an opinion backed up with reasons and facts. Examining an opinion and the reasons and facts that back it up will help you decide if the opinion makes sense. Look at the argument on the right as you read each of these tips.

### Strategies for Reading

- Look for words that **signal an opinion:** *I believe; I think; in my view; they claim, argue,* or *disagree.*
- Look for reasons, facts, or expert opinions that **support** the argument.
- Ask yourself if the argument and reasons **make sense.**
- Look for overgeneralizations or other **errors in reasoning** that may affect the argument.

### PRACTICE AND APPLY

Read the argument on the next page, and then answer the questions below.

**1.** List any words that signal an opinion.

**2.** Write down the words or phrases that give the writer's opinion.

**3.** The writer presents both sides of the argument. Copy and complete the chart below to show the two sides. One example is shown.

| Benefits of Working Part-Time | Disadvantages of Working Part-Time |
|---|---|
| 1. Students are able to be responsible for expenses. | |

# Should Students Work? *by David Azarian*

Americans tend to assume that working is good for students. In the United States, nearly two-thirds of all high school students hold part-time jobs. But in countries like Sweden and Switzerland, only 10 percent of students work as much as a typical American teen. Evidence is mounting that part-time jobs can hurt students' academic performance.

Students who work up to 15 hours a week usually benefit from having a job. Their paychecks allow them to be responsible for expenses such as clothes and car insurance. They build good work habits by following a work schedule and meeting an employer's expectations. Those who find work related to a field they're interested in can learn whether that industry would be a good fit for them.

However, students who work more than 20 hours a week often find that school is just one more thing competing for their attention. If they work late, they come to school tired and may even fall asleep in class. Working longer hours also limits their participation in extra-curricular activities.

Other costs of working long hours are less obvious. In 1991, researcher David Stern found that students' grade point averages dropped if they worked more than 15 to 20 hours a week. Those who worked the most were also the most likely to drop out of school. Compared with their classmates, they were 33 percent more likely to use drugs and alcohol. Other studies have confirmed the link between working longer hours and lowered achievement.

Does that mean high school students should stick to their books? I've learned a lot from my part-time jobs, so I think that that position ignores the benefits of work experience. But the experts have a point—high school students should work no more than 20 hours a week.

# Reading in the Content Areas

## Social Studies

**Social studies** class becomes easier when you understand how your textbook's words, pictures, and maps work together to give you information. Following these tips can make you a better reader of social studies lessons. As you read the tips, look at the sample lesson on the right-hand page.

### Strategies for Reading

**A** First look at any **headlines** or **subheads** on the page. These give you an idea of what each section covers.

**B** Make sure you know the meaning of any boldfaced or underlined **vocabulary terms.** These terms often appear on tests.

**C** Carefully read the text and think about **ways the information is organized.** Social studies books are full of sequence, comparison and contrast, and organization by geographic location.

**D** Look closely at **graphics,** such as **maps, charts,** and **illustrations.** Think about how the graphic and the text are related.

**E** Read any **study tips** in the margins or at the bottom of the page. These let you check your understanding as you read.

### PRACTICE AND APPLY

Carefully read the textbook page at right. Use the information from the page and from the tips above to answer these questions.

1. What is the main idea covered on this page?
2. List some important terms covered on this page.
3. Give three examples of languages descended from the original Indo-European language.
4. What can historians learn by studying how languages spread?
5. What is the definition of Slavic-speakers?

# **1** Indo-European Migrations

**TERMS & NAMES**
- Indo-Europeans
- steppes
- migration
- Hittites
- Anatolia
- Aryans
- *Vedas*
- Brahmin
- caste
- *Mahabharata*

| MAIN IDEA | WHY IT MATTERS NOW |
|---|---|
| Indo-European peoples migrated into Europe, India, and Southwest Asia and interacted with peoples living there. | Half the people living today speak languages that stem from the original Indo-European languages. |

**SETTING THE STAGE** In India and in Mesopotamia, civilizations first developed along lush river valleys. Even as large cities such as Mohenjo-Daro and Harappa declined, agriculture and small urban communities flourished. These wealthy river valleys attracted seminomadic tribes. These peoples may have left their own homelands because of politics or changes in the environment.

## Indo-Europeans Migrate

**Background**
This steppe area included parts of present-day Romania, Moldova, Ukraine, southern Russia, and Kazakhstan.

The **Indo-Europeans** were a group of seminomadic peoples who came from the **steppes**—dry grasslands that stretched north of the Caucasus (KAW·kuh·suhs). The Caucasus are the mountains between the Black and Caspian seas. (See the map on pages 54–55.) These primarily pastoral people herded cattle, sheep, and goats. The Indo-Europeans also tamed horses and rode into battle in light, two-wheeled chariots. They lived in tribes that spoke forms of a language that we call Indo-European.

**The Indo-European Language Family** The languages of the Indo-Europeans were the ancestors of many of the modern languages of Europe, Southwest Asia, and South Asia. English, Spanish, Persian, and Hindi all trace their origins back to different forms of the original Indo-European language.

**Vocabulary**
Slavic-speakers: speakers of a language that developed into most of today's eastern European languages.

Historians can actually tell where different Indo-European tribes settled by the languages they spoke. Some Slavic-speakers moved north and west. Others, who spoke early Celtic, Germanic, and Italic languages, moved west through Europe. Still others, Greek- and Persian-speakers, went south. The Aryans (AIR·ee·uhnz), who spoke an early form of Sanskrit, penetrated the mountain passes of the Hindu Kush and entered India.

Notice the similarities of words within the Indo-European family of languages.

### Language Family Resemblances

| English | mother | father | daughter | new | six |
|---|---|---|---|---|---|
| Sanskrit | mātár | pitár | duhitá | návas | sát |
| Persian | muhdáhr | puhdáhr | dukhtáhr | now | shahsh |
| Spanish | madre | padre | hija | nuevo | seis |
| German | Mutter | Vater | Tochter | neu | sechs |

**An Unexplained Migration** No one is quite sure why these people left their homelands in the steppes. The lands where their animals grazed may have dried up. Their human or animal population may have grown too large to feed. They may also have tried to escape from invaders, or from an outbreak of disease.

Whatever the reason, Indo-European nomads began to migrate outward in all directions between 1700 and 1200 B.C. These **migrations,** movements of a people from one region to another, did not happen all at once, but in waves over a long period of time.

## Science

Reading a **science** textbook becomes easier when you understand how the explanations, drawings, and special terms work together. Use the strategies below to help you better understand your science textbook. Look at the examples on the opposite page as you read each strategy in this list.

### Strategies for Reading

**A** Preview the **title** and **headings** on the page to see what scientific concepts will be covered.

**B** Read the **key idea, objectives,** or **focus.** These items summarize the lesson and establish a purpose for your reading.

**C** Look for **boldfaced** and **italicized** words that appear in the text. Look for **definitions** of those words.

**D** Carefully examine any **pictures** or **diagrams.** Read the **captions** and evaluate how the graphics help to illustrate and explain the text.

**E** Many science textbooks discuss **scientific concepts** in terms of **everyday events** or **experiences.** Look for these places and consider how they improve your understanding.

### PRACTICE AND APPLY

Use the sample science page and the tips above to help you answer the following questions.

1. What main idea will be covered in this lesson? Where on the page did you find this information?
2. What is the definition of the term *phytoplankton?*
3. What are three factors that affect the survival of phytoplankton?
4. What is one fact given in the photograph and caption?

**A**

# Ocean Life

The diversity of life found in the oceans is extraordinary. Scientists estimate that the oceans harbor as many as 10 million species. The life forms range from microscopic organisms to the largest known animal, the blue whale.

## Photosynthesis in the Oceans

Sunlight is vital to ocean life. Like land plants, most sea plants need sunlight to grow. However, as you learned in Section 22.3, sunlight penetration decreases rapidly with depth. Only within the mixed layer is there enough sunlight for most plants to carry out photosynthesis.

While many types of plants live in the ocean's mixed layer, one of the most important groups is the microscopic phytoplankton. **Phytoplankton** are typically single-celled plants that float freely in the ocean's surface waters. One of the most abundant kind of phytoplankton is the **diatom,** a one-celled plant with a delicate, thin shell made of silica. Phytoplankton, including diatoms, make up the base of the ocean's food chain and are the primary energy source for the marine ecosystem.

When large numbers of phytoplankton concentrate in one area, they can change the color of the water. Such formations are called *blooms*. Large blooms are visible from space and can help scientists predict where to find groups of life forms.

The survival of phytoplankton populations depends on factors like ocean currents, temperature, and the amount of nutrients available. Areas with large phytoplankton populations can support large numbers of microscopic marine animals, which eat the phytoplankton. During photosynthesis, the phytoplankton consume the animals' carbon dioxide waste and then give off oxygen, which the animals then use to survive.

When diatoms die, their shells settle to the sea bottom and become part of the sediment. Marine geologists can use shells preserved in this way to trace changes in diatom populations, to determine the age of the sediment, and even to hypothesize the water temperature at the time the diatoms lived.

# 22.4

**B KEY IDEAS**

Marine organisms are an important part of the ocean and provide clues to the ocean's history.

**E** While most marine life needs many of the same nutrients that land plants and animals do, some have adapted to use other resources.

**KEY VOCABULARY**

- phytoplankton
**C**
- diatom
- zooplankton
- coral
- nekton

**VISUALIZATIONS**
CLASSZONE.COM

Discover areas of highest photosynthetic productivity in the ocean.
*Keycode:* ES2203

**D**

**DIATOMS** This microscope photograph shows that one-celled diatoms are remarkably diverse. (Magnification is approximately 150X.)

## Mathematics

Reading in **mathematics** is different from reading in history, literature, or science. Use the strategies below to help you better understand your mathematics textbook. Look at the example on the opposite page as you read each strategy in the list.

### Strategies for Reading

**A** Preview the **title** and **headings** on the page to see what math concepts will be covered.

**B** Find and read the **goals** or **objectives** for the lesson. These will tell you the most important points to know.

**C** Read **explanations** carefully. Sometimes a concept is explained in more than one way to make sure you understand it.

**D** Look for **special features**, such as vocabulary tips or real-life problems. They provide more help or information.

**E** Study any **worked-out solutions** to sample problems. These are the key to understanding how to do the homework assignment.

### PRACTICE AND APPLY

Use the sample mathematics page and the strategies above to help you answer the following questions.

1. What is the title of the lesson?
2. What are the learning goals for this lesson?
3. Give an explanation of the distributive property.
4. What does the worked-out solution show you how to do?

## 2.6

Reading Beyond the Classroom

### (A) The Distributive Property

**What you should learn**

(B) **GOAL 1** Use the distributive property.

**GOAL 2** Simplify expressions by combining like terms.

**Why you should learn it**

(D) ▼ To solve **real-life** problems such as finding how much you can spend on jeans in **Exs. 70 and 71.**

**GOAL 1** USING THE DISTRIBUTIVE PROPERTY

To multiply 3(68) mentally, you could think of 3(68) as

$$3(60 + 8) = 3(60) + 3(8) = 180 + 24 = 204.$$

This is an example of the *distributive property*.

The distributive property is a very important algebraic property. Before discussing (C) the property, study an example that suggests why the property is true.

**EXAMPLE 1** *Using an Area Model*

Find the area of a rectangle whose width is 3 and whose length is $x + 2$.

**SOLUTION** (E)

You can find the area in two ways.

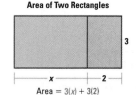

**Area of One Rectangle**

3

$x + 2$

Area = $3(x + 2)$

**Area of Two Rectangles**

3

$x$     2

Area = $3(x) + 3(2)$

▶ Because both ways produce the same area, the following statement is true.

$$3(x + 2) = 3(x) + 3(2)$$

(C) Example 1 suggests the **distributive property.** In the equation above, the factor 3 is *distributed* to each term of the sum $(x + 2)$. There are four versions of the distributive property, as follows.

---

**THE DISTRIBUTIVE PROPERTY**

The product of $a$ and $(b + c)$:

$a(b + c) = ab + ac$      **Example:** $5(x + 2) = 5x + 10$

$(b + c)a = ba + ca$      **Example:** $(x + 4)8 = 8x + 32$

The product of $a$ and $(b - c)$:

$a(b - c) = ab - ac$      **Example:** $4(x - 7) = 4x - 28$

$(b - c)a = ba - ca$      **Example:** $(x - 5)9 = 9x - 45$

---

# Reading Beyond the Classroom

## Reading an Application

Reading and understanding an **application** will help you fill it out correctly and avoid mistakes. Use the following strategies to help you understand any application. Look at the example on the next page as you read each strategy.

### *Strategies for Reading*

**A** **Begin at the top.** Scan the application to understand the different sections.

**B** Look for special **instructions for filling out** the application.

**C** Note any **request for materials** that must be attached to the application.

**D** Watch for **sections you don't have to fill in** or **questions you don't have to answer.**

**E** Look for difficult or confusing words or abbreviations. Look them up in a dictionary or ask someone what they mean.

**PRACTICE AND APPLY**

Imagine that you are applying for a job at Fruit Junction. Read the application on the next page. Then answer the following questions.

**1.** If you are under 18, what document will you need to supply?

**2.** In what order should you list your present and past employers?

**3.** What should you do if there isn't enough room to list all of your employers?

**4.** How many references do you need to provide?

## Ⓐ Fruit Junction

**APPLICATION FOR EMPLOYMENT**

**PERSONAL INFORMATION**

Name (Last, First, Middle) _____

Current Address _____

Phone #   Daytime ( ) _____   Evening ( )_____

E-mail address _____

**Are you over 16 years of age? (circle one)   Y / N** (If you are under 18, you will need to have a work permit.)

Ⓒ **Are you a U.S. citizen? (circle one)   Y / N**
(If not, you will need to provide proof of your identity and of your legal right to work in the United States.)

**Have you ever been convicted of a criminal offense? (circle one)  Y / N** (Minor traffic offenses are not considered "criminal.")

**If you have any physical limitations that require accommodation to do the job for which you are applying, please explain accommodation requirements.** _____

**EDUCATION**

| Name of School | Location | Years Completed | Did You Graduate? |
|---|---|---|---|
| | | 1 2 3 4 | Y / N |
| | | 1 2 3 4 | Y / N |
| | | 1 2 3 4 | Y / N |

Ⓑ Please provide an accurate and complete full-time and part-time employment record.
List employers chronologically, starting with your present or most recent employer. Attach additional pages, if needed.

**EMPLOYMENT HISTORY**

| Employer | Job(s) Held | Time Worked | Reason for Leaving |
|---|---|---|---|
| **Name** _____<br>**Address** _____<br>**Supervisor** _____<br>**Phone #** _____ | | Start date<br><br>End date* | _____<br>*If you are currently employed, may we contact your present employer? (Y / N) |
| **Name** _____<br>**Address** _____<br>**Supervisor** _____<br>**Phone #** _____ | | Start date<br><br>End date* | |

**REFERENCES:** Please provide at least one business (B) and one personal (P) reference we can contact.

| B / P | Name | Phone # | Relationship | Years Known |
|---|---|---|---|---|
| | | | | |
| | | | | |

**ADDITIONAL INFORMATION:** Please fill in the hours you are available to work each week.

| | Mon. | Tues. | Wed. | Thurs. | Fri. | Sat. | Sun. |
|---|---|---|---|---|---|---|---|
| **Starting at** | | | | | | | |
| **Ending at** | | | | | | | |

Ⓓ **Optional: What else should we know about you that might be pertinent to considering you for this job?**_____
_____

**APPLICANT'S STATEMENT**  I certify that the information provided in this employment application (and accompanying documentation, if any) is true, valid, and complete to the best of my knowledge. I understand that if I am employed, any falsified statements or documents or misleading information given in my application or interview may be considered sufficient grounds for termination. I also Ⓔ agree by my signature to allow the company to verify the information I provide and to release from legal liability any person, school, current employer, past employer, or organization named in this application for statements given with regard to my qualifications.

**Applicant's Signature** _____   **Date** _____

## Reading a Public Notice

**Public notices** can tell you about events in your community and give you valuable information about safety. When you read a public notice, follow these tips. Each tip relates to a specific part of the notice on the opposite page.

### Strategies for Reading

**A** Read the notice's **title,** if it has one. The title often gives the main idea or purpose of the notice.

**B** See if there is a logo, credit, or other way of telling **who created the notice.**

**C** Ask yourself, **"Who should read this notice?"** If the information in it might be important to you or someone you know, then you should pay attention to it.

**D** Look for **instructions**—things the notice is asking or telling you to do.

**E** See if there are details that tell you how you can **find out more** about the topic.

**PRACTICE AND APPLY**

The notice on the opposite page is from a city government department. Read it carefully and answer the questions below.

**1.** Who is the notice from?

**2.** Who is the notice for?

**3.** What is the purpose of the notice?

**4.** What does the City want residents to do during construction?

**5.** According to the notice, how will the city try to minimize the length of the construction period?

# PUBLIC NOTICE

## THE DEPARTMENT OF PUBLIC WORKS

**Ⓐ** *TEMPORARY ROAD CLOSURES AND DETOURS*

Jack Witthaus
Senior Transportation Planner
(888) 555-1234

Dan Rich
Assistant to the City Manager
(888) 555-1234

**FOR IMMEDIATE RELEASE**

**Ⓑ** Sunnyvale, CA (3/26/02)—The City of Sunnyvale announces two temporary road closures in Sunnyvale for roadway improve-
**Ⓓ** ment. Railroad crossings at Mary Avenue and Sunnyvale Avenue will be closed for up to four full days to allow replacement of pavement. Mary Avenue at the Caltrain tracks will be closed from 8:00 P.M. on Friday, April 6, to 5:00 P.M. on Monday, April 9. Sunnyvale Avenue at the Caltrain tracks will be closed from 8:00 A.M. on Friday, April 13, to 5:00 P.M. on Monday, April 16.

**Ⓒ** The City is alerting the public that detours will be in effect, and construction noise and lighting may be noticeable. In order to minimize the length of the construction period and accommodate the Caltrain commute schedule, work will occur continuously during the road closures.

**Ⓔ** We appreciate your patience while we work toward improved pavement conditions at these locations. Please contact the Sunnyvale Department of Public Works at (888) 555-1234 with any questions or comments. Site maps of the road closure locations and detailed maps are available on the City's Web site at www.ci.sunnyvale.ca.us/news-releases/0103281a.htm.

# Reading a Web Page

If you need information for a report, project, or hobby, the World Wide Web can probably help you. The tips below will help you understand the **Web pages** you read. As you look at the tips, notice where they match up to the sample Web page on the right.

## Strategies for Reading

**A** Notice the page's **Web address**, or URL. You may want to write it down in case you need to access the same page at another time.

**B** Look for **menu bars** along the top, bottom, or side of the page. These guide you to other parts of the site that may be useful.

**C** Look for **links** to other parts of the site or to related pages. Links are often shown as underlined words.

**D** Use a **search** feature to quickly find out whether information about a specific topic can be found anywhere on the site.

### PRACTICE AND APPLY

Read the Web page on the next page. Then use the information from the page and the tips above to answer the questions.

**1.** What is the Web address?

**2.** What link would you click on to view actual video segments of a storm?

**3.** Read the description of the link "Lt. Governor." What would you expect to find if you clicked on this link?

**4.** What link would help you find newspaper articles about tornadoes in Kansas?

**5.** What is this site designed to give information about?

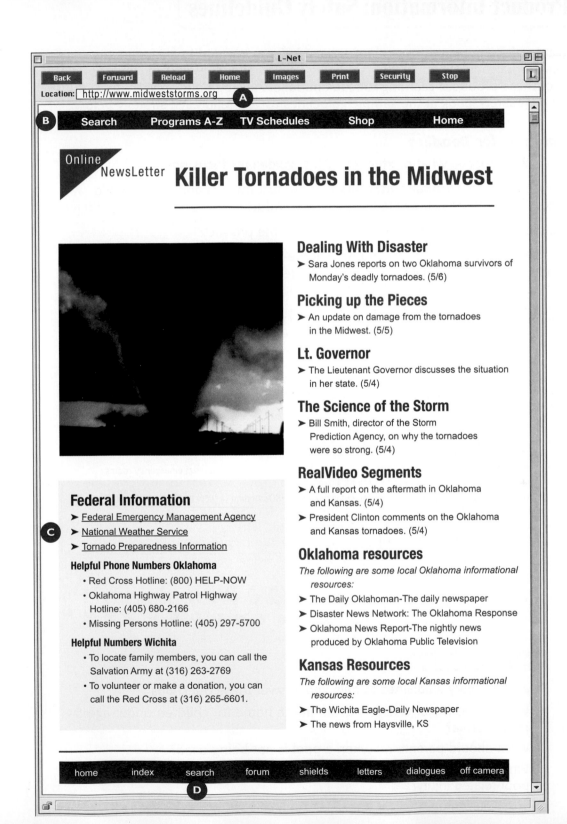

**L–Net**

Back | Forward | Reload | Home | Images | Print | Security | Stop

Location: http://www.midweststorms.org — **A**

**B** — Search · Programs A-Z · TV Schedules · Shop · Home

Online NewsLetter

# Killer Tornadoes in the Midwest

## Dealing With Disaster
➤ Sara Jones reports on two Oklahoma survivors of Monday's deadly tornadoes. (5/6)

## Picking up the Pieces
➤ An update on damage from the tornadoes in the Midwest. (5/5)

## Lt. Governor
➤ The Lieutenant Governor discusses the situation in her state. (5/4)

## The Science of the Storm
➤ Bill Smith, director of the Storm Prediction Agency, on why the tornadoes were so strong. (5/4)

## RealVideo Segments
➤ A full report on the aftermath in Oklahoma and Kansas. (5/4)
➤ President Clinton comments on the Oklahoma and Kansas tornadoes. (5/4)

## Oklahoma resources
*The following are some local Oklahoma informational resources:*
➤ The Daily Oklahoman-The daily newspaper
➤ Disaster News Network: The Oklahoma Response
➤ Oklahoma News Report-The nightly news produced by Oklahoma Public Television

## Kansas Resources
*The following are some local Kansas informational resources:*
➤ The Wichita Eagle-Daily Newspaper
➤ The news from Haysville, KS

## Federal Information

**C**
➤ Federal Emergency Management Agency
➤ National Weather Service
➤ Tornado Preparedness Information

**Helpful Phone Numbers Oklahoma**
• Red Cross Hotline: (800) HELP-NOW
• Oklahoma Highway Patrol Highway Hotline: (405) 680-2166
• Missing Persons Hotline: (405) 297-5700

**Helpful Numbers Wichita**
• To locate family members, you can call the Salvation Army at (316) 263-2769
• To volunteer or make a donation, you can call the Red Cross at (316) 265-6601.

home · index · search · forum · shields · letters · dialogues · off camera

**D**

## Product Information: Safety Guidelines

**Safety guidelines** are facts and recommendations provided by government agencies or product manufacturers offering instructions and warnings about safe use of these products. Learning to read and follow such guidelines is important for your own safety. Look at the sample guidelines as you read each strategy below.

### Strategies for Reading

**A** The **title** identifies what product the safety guidelines focus on.

**B** This section lists **recommendations** that product owners and users should follow in order to ensure safe usage of the product.

**C** This section lists the **hazards** associated with the product.

**D** This section includes a phone number and e-mail address where dangerous products or product-related injuries can be reported.

**A**
### Pool Safety Information

The U.S. Consumer Product Safety Commission (CPSC) recommends that parents install the following safety devices to prevent access and give parents time to locate a child before tragedy strikes:

**B**
• A fence or barrier at least 4 feet high with no footholds or handholds should surround the entire pool.

• If a wall of the house serves as a side of the barrier, alarms should be installed on the house doors.

• In addition to the barriers, a power safety cover should protect the pool when it is not in use.

**C** CPSC warns about these **hazards** related to pools:

**Drownings**—For children under 5, drowning is the leading cause of accidental death in the home in states such as California, Arizona, Texas, and Florida. A child can drown in less than 5 minutes.

**Submersion Injuries**—Each year more than 2,000 young children are treated in hospital emergency rooms nationwide for submersion injuries, such as brain damage.

**D** To report a dangerous product or a product-related injury, call CPSC's hotline at (800) 638-2772 or report product hazards to info@cpsc.gov.

SOURCE: press release from Consumer Product Safety Commission:
http://www.kidsource.com/CPSC/pool.safety.html

### PRACTICE AND APPLY

Read the safety guidelines to help you answer these questions.

1. What is the major cause of death in the home for children under age 5 in California?

2. What should parents do when a pool is not being used?

3. What e-mail address can you use to report a dangerous product or a pool-related injury?

4. Where are these safety guidelines from?

## Reading a Museum Schedule

Knowing how to read a **museum schedule** accurately will help you figure out how to plan your visit. Look at the example as you read each strategy on this list.

### Strategies for Reading

**A** Scan the **title** to know what the schedule covers.

**B** Look for **labels** that show **dates** or **days of the week** to help you understand how the weekly or daily schedule works.

**C** Look for **expressions of time** to know what hours or minutes are listed on the schedule.

**D** Study the **labels** identifying the different events on the schedule.

**E** Look for **changes** or **exceptions** to the regular schedule.

| **A** National Museum of Natural History Summer Schedule | | |
|---|---|---|
| **Extended Summer Hours** <br> *Through September 2. Regular museum hours resume September 3. Note: The museum will be closed on July 4.* | **B** **Days of the Week** <br> Tuesday–Sunday | **C** **Times** <br> 10 A.M. to 8 P.M. *(except when preempted by a special event)* |
| **Exhibits and Activities** | | |
| **IMAX Theater** | The Johnson IMAX® Theater will show late movies at the following times: 5:45 P.M., 6:45 P.M., and 7:45 P.M. On Fridays and Saturdays, there will be an extra show at 8:45 P.M. | |
| **Visitors' Favorites** | | |
| **D** **O. Orkin Insect Zoo** | The O. Orkin Insect Zoo on the museum's second floor is an exhibition of living insects and their relatives. | |
| **Butterfly Habitat Garden** | Tours of the garden meet at garden entrance, Madison Dr. and 9th St. Tour Schedule: Thursdays at 2:00 P.M. through September. **E** | |
| **Tarantula Exhibit** | Tarantula feeding schedule: Tuesday–Friday at the following times: 10:30 A.M., 11:30 A.M., and 1:30 P.M. | |

### PRACTICE AND APPLY

Answer the following questions using the museum schedule and the strategies on this page.

**1.** What are the most popular exhibits?

**2.** List the museum's regular hours.

**3.** On what days can you watch the tarantula feedings?

**4.** On what holiday is the museum closed?

# Glossary of Literary Terms

**Act** An act is a major unit of action in a play. Acts are sometimes divided into scenes; each scene is limited to a single time and place.

**Examples:** Shakespeare's plays, such as *Julius Caesar,* all have five acts. Contemporary plays usually have two or three acts, although some only have one act. Anton Chekhov's *The Bear* is an example of a one-act play.

**Alliteration** Alliteration is the repetition of initial consonant sounds. Alliteration occurs in everyday speech and in all forms of literature. Poets, in particular, use alliteration to emphasize certain words, to create mood, to underscore meaning, and to enhance rhythm. Notice the repeated *h* and *s* sounds in the following lines:

> Mother whose <u>h</u>eart <u>h</u>ung <u>h</u>umble as a button
> On the bright <u>s</u>plendid <u>sh</u>roud of your <u>s</u>on,
>
> —Stephen Crane,
> from "Do not weep, maiden, for war is kind"

*See pages 225, 841, 853.*
*See also* **Assonance; Consonance.**

**Allusion** An allusion is an indirect reference to a historical or literary person, place, thing, or event with which the reader is assumed to be familiar.

**Example:** The title of Stephen Vincent Benét's "By the Waters of Babylon" is an allusion to the beginning of Psalm 137 in the Bible: "By the rivers of Babylon, there we sat down, yea, we wept, when we remembered Zion."

**Analogy** An analogy is a point-by-point comparison between two things that are alike in some respect. Often, analogies are used in nonfiction, when an unfamiliar subject or idea is explained in terms of a familiar one. In the following analogy, the border between the United States and Canada is compared to a one-way mirror:

> The noses of a great many Canadians resemble Porky Pig's. This comes from spending so much time pressing them against the longest undefended one-way mirror in the world. The Canadians looking through this mirror behave the way people on the hidden side of such mirrors usually do: they observe, analyze, ponder, snoop and wonder what all the activity on the other side means. . . .
>
> —Margaret Atwood,
> from "Through the One-Way Mirror"

*See also* **Extended Metaphor; Metaphor; Simile.**

**Antagonist** The antagonist in a work of literature is the character or force against which the main character, or protagonist, is pitted. The antagonist may be another character, something in nature or society, or even an internal force within the protagonist.

**Examples:** In Guy de Maupassant's "Two Friends," the German officer who encounters the fishermen is the main antagonist. In Isabel Allende's "And of Clay Are We Created," the destructive force unleashed by the volcano may be considered an antagonist.

*See page 556.*
*See also* **Conflict; Protagonist.**

**Aside** In drama, an aside is a remark spoken in an undertone by one character either to the audience or to another character, which the remaining characters supposedly do not hear. The aside is a traditional dramatic convention, a device that the audience accepts even though it is obviously unrealistic. The aside can be used to express a character's feelings, opinions, and reactions, and thus functions as a method of characterization. In the following example, the aside reveals Trebonius' murderous intentions after Caesar has asked him to stand near him in the Forum:

> Trebonius. Caesar, I will. [*Aside*] And so near
> will I be
> That your best friends shall wish I had been
> further.
>
> —William Shakespeare, from *Julius Caesar*

*See page 735.*

**Assonance** Assonance is the repetition of a vowel sound within nonrhyming words. *Helter-skelter, sweet dreams,* and *high and mighty* are examples of assonance. Writers of both poetry and prose use assonance to give their work a musical quality and unify stanzas and passages. Robert Frost uses assonance in this line from "Birches": "With the same pains you use to fill a cup. . . ." Notice also the long *a* assonance in the following lines:

> then with cracked hands that ached
> from labor in the weekday weather made
> banked fires blaze. . . .
>
> —Robert Hayden,
> from "Those Winter Sundays"

*See pages 225, 841, 853.*
*See also* **Alliteration; Consonance.**

**Atmosphere.** *See* **Mood.**

**Audience** The audience for a piece of writing is the person or persons intended to read it. Every writer has an audience in mind when he or she is writing. The intended audience of a work influences a writer's choice of form, style, tone, and the details included.

*Example:* Nicholas Gage wrote his essay "The Teacher Who Changed My Life" for a general magazine audience, choosing information and details that would make his story clear to that audience. For a different audience—for instance, a group of young children—he may have presented different details and written in a simpler style.

*See pages 491, 945.*

**Author's Perspective** An author's perspective is the set of beliefs, feelings, and attitudes that he or she brings to a piece of writing. Sometimes an author's perspective is recognizable through the tone of a piece, or the attitude the writer displays toward the subject matter.

An author's perspective is more likely to be visible in nonfiction than in fiction. Often a writer will conceal personal attitudes and beliefs when creating fictional characters.

*Example:* Alice Walker, who is both a feminist and a civil-rights advocate, seems to be guided by her feminist perspective in *In Search of Our Mothers' Gardens.*

*See pages 452–453, 460.*
*See also* **Tone.**

**Author's Purpose** Authors write for one or more of the following purposes: to inform, to express an opinion, to entertain, or to persuade. For instance, the purpose of a news report is to inform; the purpose of an editorial is to persuade the readers or audience to do or believe something.

*Example:* Elie Wiesel wrote *Night* to inform readers about the horrors of concentration camps and to persuade them to resist evil that made these horrors possible.

*See page 945.*

**Autobiography** An autobiography is a writer's account of his or her own life and is, in almost every case, told from the first-person point of view. Generally, an autobiography focuses on the most significant events and people in the writer's life over a period of time and on the ways in which those events and people affected the writer. Shorter autobiographical narratives include such private writings as **journals, diaries,** and **letters.** An autobiographical essay, another type of short autobiographical work, focuses on a single person or event in the writer's life, as illustrated by Lorraine Hansberry's "On Summer" and David Mamet's "The Watch." A **memoir** is a form of autobiography that may also deal with historical events affecting the writer. In "Montgomery Boycott," Coretta Scott King shares her recollections of how the boycott led to her husband's becoming a leader of the protest movement. The excerpt from *Farewell to Manzanar* recounts Jeanne Wakatsuki Houston's memories of life in a World War II internment camp.

*See pages 104, 121, 613.*

**Ballad** A ballad is a narrative poem that was originally meant to be sung. Ballads usually begin abruptly, focus on a single tragic incident, contain dialogue and repetition, and imply more than they actually tell. Traditional ballads are written in four-line stanzas with regular rhythm and rhyme. The rhythm often alternates between four-stress and three-stress lines, and the rhyme scheme usually is *abcb* or *aabb*.

Folk ballads were composed orally and handed down by word of mouth. These ballads usually tell about ordinary people who have had unusual adventures or have performed daring deeds. The literary ballad is a poem written by a poet who imitates the form and content of the folk ballad.

The following anonymous ballad was popular during the Civil War. Each line has four stresses, and the rhyme scheme is *abcb.*

> "Mother, is the battle over?
>     Thousands have been slain, they say.
> Is my father come? and tell me,
>     Has the army gained the day?
> "Is he well, or is he wounded?
>     Mother, do you think he's slain?
> If he is, pray will you tell me.
>     Will my father come again?
> "Mother, I see you always sighing
>     Since that paper last you read;
> Tell me why you are crying:
>     Is my dearest father dead?"
> "Yes, my boy, your noble father
>     Is one numbered with the slain;
> Though he loves me very dearly,
>     Ne'er on earth we'll meet again."

*See also* **Meter; Narrative Poem; Rhyme.**

**Biography** A biography is an account of a person's life written by another person. The writer of a biography, or biographer, often researches his or her subject in order to present accurate information. A biographer may also draw upon personal knowledge of his or her subject. Although a biographer—by necessity and by inclination—presents a subject from a certain point of view, a skilled biographer strives for a balanced treatment, highlighting weaknesses as well as strengths, failures as well as achievements.

*Example:* André Brink's biographical essay "Nelson Mandela" gives a brief account of the South African leader's life and the hardships that he had to overcome.

*See pages 104, 121.*

**Blank Verse** Blank verse is unrhymed poetry written in iambic pentameter. Each line has five metrical feet, and each foot has an unstressed syllable followed by a stressed syllable.

Much of *Julius Caesar* is written in blank verse. The following lines, spoken by the conspirator Casca, describe one of the wonders Casca observed during the storm on the night before Caesar was assassinated. Note the iambic pentameter and the lack of end rhyme:

> A common slave—you know him well by
>     sight—
> Held up his left hand, which did flame and
>     burn
> Like twenty torches joined; and yet his hand,
> Not sensible of fire, remained unscorched.
>     —William Shakespeare, from *Julius Caesar*

*See page 713.*
*See also* **Meter; Rhythm.**

**Character** Characters are the individuals who participate in the action of a literary work. The most important characters are called **main characters.** Less prominent characters are known as **minor characters.** In Joan Aiken's "Searching for Summer," Tom and Lily are main characters; William Hatching is a minor character.

Whereas some characters are two-dimensional, with only one or two dominant traits, a fully developed character possesses many traits, mirroring the psychological complexity of a real person. In longer works of fiction, main characters often undergo change as the plot unfolds. Such characters are called **dynamic characters,** as opposed to **static characters,** who remain the same. In Doris Lessing's "No Witchcraft for Sale," Gideon is a dynamic character because his attitude about his duty to the Farquars changes; on the other hand, the Farquars are static characters.

*See pages 17, 39, 101, 156, 284.*
*See also* **Antagonist; Characterization; Foil; Protagonist.**

***Characterization*** Characterization refers to the techniques writers use to develop characters. There are four basic methods of characterization:

1. The writer may use physical description. In "Sweet Potato Pie," author Eugenia Collier presents a picture of "Charley's slender, dark hands whittling a toy from a chunk of wood, his face thin and intense, brown as the loaves Lil baked when there was flour."

2. The character's own speech, thoughts, feelings, or actions may be presented. In Collier's story, Charley's opinion of himself is revealed when he says, ""I didn't want your students to know your brother wasn't nothing but a cab driver.'"

3. The speech, thoughts, feelings, or actions of other characters provide another means of developing a character. In the scene in Charley's apartment, it is clear that his wife and children have an easy, loving relationship with him.

4. The narrator's own direct comments also serve to develop a character. The narrator says that "Charley never had any childhood at all," that within the family Charley was "somehow the protector of them all."

*See pages 252, 326, 479.*
*See also* **Character; Narrator; Point of View.**

***Chorus*** In the theater of ancient Greece, the chorus was a group of actors who commented on the action of the play. Between scenes the chorus sang and danced to musical accompaniment in the orchestra—the circular floor between the stage and the audience—giving insights into the message of the play. The chorus is often considered a kind of ideal spectator, representing the response of ordinary citizens to the tragic events unfolding in the play. In Sophocles' *Antigone,* the chorus represents the leading citizens of Thebes.

*See page 1019.*
*See also* **Drama.**

***Climax*** In dramatic or narrative literature, the climax is the moment when the interest and emotional intensity reach their highest point. This moment is also called the **turning point,** since it usually determines how the conflict of the story will be resolved.

***Example:*** In Stephen Vincent Benét's "By the Waters of Babylon," John's discovery of the dead "god" can be considered the climax of the story. As a result of his discovery, John realizes the truth about the past and the destruction of a way of life.

*See pages 384, 394, 407.*
*See also* **Falling Action; Plot; Rising Action.**

***Comedy*** A comedy is a dramatic work that is light and often humorous in tone, usually ending happily with a peaceful resolution of the main conflict. A comedy differs from farce by having a more believable plot, more realistic characters, and less boisterous behavior.

*See also* **Drama; Farce.**

***Comic Relief*** Comic relief is a humorous scene, incident, or speech that is included in a serious drama to break the tension and allow the audience to prepare emotionally for events to come. In many of Shakespeare's plays, comic relief is provided by a fool or through scenes with servants or common folk.

***Conflict*** Conflict is the struggle between opposing forces and is the basis of plot in dramatic and narrative literature. **External conflict** occurs when a character is pitted against an outside force, such as another character, a physical obstacle, or an aspect of nature or society. **Internal conflict** occurs when the struggle takes place within a character.

***Examples:*** In Mary Lavin's "Brigid," Owen's wife experiences internal conflict when she struggles with her feelings of guilt over letting Owen down. The main source of the external conflict between Owen and his wife is Brigid herself. In some stories, as in Chinua Achebe's "Marriage Is a Private Affair," the source of the conflict is cultural; that is, it arises from differences in beliefs and values.

*See pages 194, 326, 407.*
*See* **Antagonist; Plot; Rising Action.**

**Connotation** Connotation is the emotional response evoked by a word, in contrast to its **denotation,** which is its literal or dictionary meaning. *Kitten,* for example, is defined as a "young cat." However, the word also suggests, or connotes, images of softness, warmth, and playfulness.

***Example:*** In W. P. Kinsella's "The Thrill of the Grass," the narrator describes baseball players who "recall sprawling in the lush outfields of childhood." The word *sprawling* connotes the joy and ease of childhood.

**Consonance** Consonance is the repetition of consonant sounds within and at the ends of words. "Last but not least" and a "stroke of luck" contain examples of consonance. Consonance, assonance, alliteration, and rhyme give writing a musical quality and contribute to the **melodies of literary language.** Such devices may be used to unify poems and passages of prose writing. Notice the repetition of internal and final consonant *s* sounds in the following lines:

> But in another wilderness,
> the possibilities,
> the loneliness,
> can strangulate like jungle vines.
>
> —Cathy Song, from "Lost Sister"

*See pages 225, 841, 853.*
*See also* **Alliteration; Assonance.**

**Couplet**  *See* **Sonnet.**

**Denotation**  *See* **Connotation.**

**Dénouement**  *See* **Falling Action.**

**Description** Description is writing that appeals to the senses. Good descriptive writing helps the reader to see, hear, smell, taste, or feel the subject that is described and usually relies on precise adjectives, adverbs, nouns, and verbs, as well as on vivid, original phrases. Figurative language, such as simile, metaphor, and personification, is also an important tool in description. The following passage illustrates the use of vivid descriptive language:

> He came to a cloverleaf intersection which stood silent where two main highways crossed the town. During the day it was a thunderous surge of cars, the gas stations open, a great insect rustling and a ceaseless jockeying for position as the scarab-beetles, a faint incense puttering from their exhausts, skimmed homeward to the far directions. But now these highways, too, were like streams in a dry season, all stone and bed and moon radiance.
>
> —Ray Bradbury, from "The Pedestrian"

*See page 101.*
*See also* **Connotation; Imagery; Style.**

**Dialect** A dialect is the particular variety of a language spoken in a definite place by a distinct group of people. Dialects vary in pronunciation, vocabulary, colloquial expressions, sentence structure, and grammatical constructions. Writers use dialect to establish setting, to provide local color, and to develop characters.

***Example:*** In Eugenia Collier's "Sweet Potato Pie," all the characters in the narrator's family speak in an African-American dialect. Here is Charley speaking to his brother: "Buddy, you ain pressed out them pants right. . . . Can't you git a better shine on them shoes? . . . Lord, you done messed up that tie!"

*See page 252.*

**Dialogue** Dialogue is written conversation between two or more characters. Dialogue is used in most forms of prose writing and also in narrative poetry. In drama the dialogue carries the story line. Realistic, well-placed dialogue enlivens narrative, descriptive, and expository prose and provides the reader with insights into characters' personalities and relationships with one another. The dialogue can also reflect the time and place in which the action takes place, giving a richness and believability to the literary work.

*See pages 284, 300, 890, 962, 974, 995.*
*See also* **Characterization; Drama.**

**Diary** A diary is a writer's personal day-to-day account of his or her experiences and impressions. Most diaries are private and not intended to be shared. Some, however, have been published because they are well written and provide useful perspectives on historical events or on the everyday life of particular eras. Anne Frank's *The Diary of a Young Girl* is an example of a famous diary. Though Elie Wiesel's *Night* is actually a memoir, its day-to-day retellings of what happened in the concentration camp make it sound like a diary.

*See also* **Autobiography.**

**Diction** Diction is a writer's choice of words. Diction encompasses both vocabulary (individual words) and syntax (the order or arrangement of words). Diction can be described in terms such as formal or informal, technical or common, abstract or concrete, literal or figurative.

The writer of a scientific essay on thunderstorms, for example, would use formal, technical, and abstract words with precise denotative meanings. In the following essay, however, a more informal language is used, relying on words that are common and concrete, as shown by this figurative description of a thunderstorm at a lake:

Then the kettledrum, then the snare, then the bass drum and cymbals, then crackling light against the dark, and the gods grinning and licking their chops in the hills. Afterward the calm, the rain steadily rustling in the calm lake. . . .
—E. B. White, from "Once More to the Lake"

*See pages 600, 649, 906, 961.*

**Drama** Drama is literature that develops plot and character through dialogue and action; in other words, drama is literature in play form. Dramas are meant to be performed by actors and actresses who appear on a stage, before radio microphones, or in front of television or movie cameras.

Unlike other forms of literature, such as fiction and poetry, a work of drama requires the collaboration of many people in order to come to life. In an important sense, a drama in printed form is an incomplete work of art. It is a skeleton that must be fleshed out by a director, actors, set designers, and others who interpret the work and stage a performance. When an audience becomes caught up in a drama and forgets to a degree the artificiality of a play, the process is called the "suspension of disbelief."

Most plays are divided into acts, with each act having an emotional peak, or climax, of its own. The acts sometimes are divided into scenes; each scene is limited to a single time and place. Shakespeare's plays, such as *Julius Caesar*, all have five acts. Contemporary plays usually have two or three acts, although some have only one act. Anton Chekhov's *The Bear* is an example of a one-act play.

*See pages 284–285, 300, 1019.*
*See also* **Act; Chorus; Dialogue; Props; Scene; Stage Directions.**

**Dramatic Irony** *See* **Irony.**

**Dramatic Monologue** A dramatic monologue is a lyric poem in which a speaker addresses a silent or absent listener in a moment of high intensity or deep emotion, as if engaged in private conversation. To increase the dramatic impact of the poem, the poet often reveals the motivations as well as the feelings, personality, and circumstances of the speaker. "Exile" by Julia Alvarez is a dramatic monologue.

**Epic** An epic is a long narrative poem on a serious subject, presented in an elevated or formal style. In most epics, the hero is a figure of high social status and often of great historical or legendary importance. Homer's *Iliad* and *Odyssey* are famous epics in the Western tradition. The *Ramayana* is a great epic of India.

**Essay** An essay is a brief nonfiction composition on a single subject, usually presenting the personal views of the writer. An essay may seek to persuade, as does E. M. Forster's "Tolerance." An essay may offer a personal reflection on an episode in the writer's life, in the manner of E. B. White's "Once More to the Lake." Other essays, such as Roger Rosenblatt's "The Man in the Water," are reflections on current events. Essays may also be expository, explaining topics as well as providing writers' opinions about them, as illustrated by Isaac Asimov's "Dial Versus Digital."

Some essays are formal and impersonal, and the major argument is developed systematically. Other essays are informal, personal, and less rigidly organized. The informal essay often includes anecdotes and humor.

*See pages 105, 110, 121.*

**Exposition** Exposition is the part of a literary work that provides the background information necessary to understand characters and their actions. Exposition typically occurs at the beginning of a work and introduces the characters, describes the setting, and summarizes significant events that took place before the action begins.

**Examples:** In Stephen Vincent Benét's "By the Waters of Babylon," the exposition introduces the narrator and his priest-father and establishes the primitive setting. The exposition in Joan Aiken's "Searching for Summer" introduces the main characters Lily and Tom on their wedding day, tells about the bombs that permanently darkened the sky, and announces the newlyweds' intention to find the sun.

*See pages 383, 394.*
*See also* **Plot; Rising Action.**

**Extended Metaphor** In an extended metaphor two unlike things are compared in several ways. Sometimes the comparison is carried throughout a paragraph, a stanza, or an entire selection. The whole text of Dahlia Ravikovitch's "Pride" is an extended metaphor comparing people and their pride with rocks. Shakespeare makes a comparison between ambition and a ladder in this extended metaphor:

> That lowliness is young ambition's ladder,
> Whereto the climber-upward turns his face;
> But when he once attains the upmost round,
> He then unto the ladder turns his back,
> Looks in the clouds, scorning the base degrees
> By which he did ascend.
>
> —William Shakespeare, from *Julius Caesar*

*See page 846.*
*See also* **Analogy; Figurative Language; Metaphor; Simile.**

**External Conflict** *See* **Conflict.**

**Falling Action** In a dramatic or narrative work, the falling action occurs after the climax, or high point of intensity or interest. The falling action shows the results of the major events and resolves loose ends in the plot. The final resolution or clarification of the plot is sometimes called the **dénouement.**

**Example:** In Stephen Vincent Benét's "By the Waters of Babylon," the falling action occurs after the main character, John, has discovered the dead "god." During the falling action, John realizes the truth about the past and the destruction of a way of life.

*See pages 384, 394.*
*See also* **Climax; Plot; Rising Action.**

**Fantasy** The term *fantasy* is applied to a work of fiction characterized by extravagant imagination and disregard for the restraints of reality. The aim of a fantasy may be purely to delight or may be to make a serious comment on reality. One type of fantasy is represented by *Alice's Adventures in Wonderland,* in which Lewis Carroll creates a nonexistent, unreal, imaginary world. A less extreme form of fantasy, such as Joan Aiken's "Searching for Summer," portrays realistic characters within a world that marginally oversteps the bounds of reality. Finally, science fiction is a form of fantasy, for it extends scientific principles to new realms of time or place. An example is Ray Bradbury's "A Sound of Thunder," which is set in both the distant future and the distant past.

*See page 39.*
*See also* **Science Fiction.**

**Farce** A farce is a play that prompts laughter through ridiculous situations, exaggerated behavior and language, and physical comedy. Characters are often stereotypes; that is, they conform to a fixed pattern or are defined by a single trait. In Anton Chekhov's *The Bear,* for example, Luke might be seen as a stereotype of a loyal but critical servant who tells the lady of the house more than she wants to hear.

*See pages 287, 300.*
*See also* **Comedy; Stereotype.**

**Fiction** A work of fiction is a narrative that springs from the imagination of the writer, though it may be based on actual events and real people. The writer shapes his or her narrative to capture the reader's interest and to achieve desired effects. The two major types of fiction are novels and short stories. The basic elements of fiction are character, setting, plot, and theme.

*See pages 17–18.*
*See also* **Novel; Short Story.**

**Figure of Speech.** *See* **Figurative Language; Hyperbole; Metaphor; Personification; Simile; Understatement.**

**Figurative Language** Figurative language is language that communicates ideas beyond the literal meanings of the words. Although what is said is not literally true, it stimulates vivid pictures or concepts in the mind of the reader. Figurative language appears in poetry and prose as well as in spoken language. The general term *figurative language* includes specific figures of speech, such as simile, metaphor, personification, and hyperbole.

*Example:* The narrator in Alice Walker's "Everyday Use" says of Dee's hair, "It stands straight up like the wool on a sheep. It is black as night and around the edges are two long pigtails that rope around like small lizards disappearing behind her ears." Obviously, Dee's pigtails do not literally move like lizards, but the passage vividly suggests the look of Dee's hair.

*See pages 226, 260, 349, 354, 735, 841.*
*See also* **Hyperbole; Metaphor; Personification; Simile; Understatement.**

**First-Person Point of View** *See* **Point of View.**

**Flashback** A flashback is an account of a conversation, an episode, or an event that happened before the beginning of a story. Often a flashback interrupts the chronological flow of a story to give information that can help readers to understand a character's present situation.

*Examples:* Tolstoy's "After the Ball" is a story told almost entirely in flashback. The events that happened to the main character, Ivan, as a young man help readers to understand his present situation and beliefs. Similarly, flashbacks play a vital role in Louise Erdrich's "The Leap," in which the narrator recounts her memories of her mother.

*See page 675.*

**Foil** A foil is a character who provides a striking contrast to another character. By using a foil, a writer calls attention to certain traits possessed by a main character or simply enhances a character by contrast. In Anton Chekhov's *The Bear,* for example, Luke, the dutiful servant, is a foil for Smirnov, the loud, rude, and quarrelsome visitor.

**Foreshadowing** Foreshadowing is a writer's use of hints or clues to indicate events that will occur later in a narrative. This technique often creates suspense and prepares the reader for what is to come.

*Examples:* Ray Bradbury's "A Sound of Thunder" and Mark Twain's "The Californian's Tale" both contain elements of foreshadowing. In Bradbury's story, the discussion of Deutscher as a leader who would create the "worst kind of dictatorship" and the constant warnings about staying on the path both foreshadow what will happen at the end of the story.

*See pages 82, 311.*

**Form**  At its simplest, the word *form* refers to the physical arrangement of words in a poem—the length and placement of the lines and the grouping of lines into stanzas. The term can also be used to refer to other types of patterning in poetry, anything from rhythm and other sound patterns to the design of a traditional poetic type, such as a sonnet or dramatic monologue. Finally, *form* can be used as a synonym for genre, which refers to literary categories ranging from the broad (short story, novel) to the narrowly defined (sonnet, dramatic monologue). William Shakespeare's "Sonnet 18" and Edna St. Vincent Millay's "Sonnet 30" illustrate the use of sonnet form. "Exile" by Julia Alvarez is an example of a dramatic monologue.

*See pages 225, 233, 236.*

**Frame Story**  A frame story exists when a story is told within a narrative setting or frame—hence, there is a story within a story. This storytelling technique has been used for over one thousand years and was employed in famous works such as *One Thousand and One Arabian Nights* and Geoffrey Chaucer's *The Canterbury Tales.*

**Free Verse**  Free verse is poetry that does not contain regular patterns of rhyme and meter. The lines in free verse often flow more naturally than do rhymed, metrical lines and thus achieve a rhythm more like everyday human speech. Much of the poetry written in the 20th century is free verse. Notice the natural flow of these free-verse lines:

> What did we say to each other
> that now we are as the deer
> who walk in single file
> with heads high . . .
>
> —N. Scott Momaday, from "Simile"

*See pages 260, 906.*

**Hero**  The word *hero* has come to mean the main character in a literary work. A traditional hero possesses good qualities that enable him or her to triumph over an antagonist who is evil or bad in some way.

The term **tragic hero,** first used by the Greek philosopher Aristotle, refers to a central character in a drama who is dignified or noble. According to Aristotle, a tragic hero possesses a defect, or **tragic flaw,** that brings about or contributes to his or her downfall. This flaw may be poor judgment, pride, weakness, or an excess of an admirable quality. The tragic hero, noted Aristotle, recognizes his or her own flaw and its consequences, but only after it is too late to change the course of events. Brutus is often considered the tragic hero of *Julius Caesar.*

The term **cultural hero** refers to a hero who represents the values of his or her culture. King Arthur, for example, represents the physical courage, moral leadership, and loyalty that were valued in Anglo-Saxon society. Antigone can also be considered a cultural hero because her sense of duty to family and the gods, as well as her courage, reflects the values of ancient Greece.

*See pages 794, 1019, 1061.*
*See also* **Tragedy.**

**Humor**  In literature there are three basic types of humor, all of which may involve exaggeration or irony. **Humor of situation** is derived from the plot of a work. It usually involves exaggerated events or situational irony, which occurs when something happens that is different from what is expected. **Humor of character** is often based on exaggerated personalities or on characters who fail to recognize their own flaws, a form of dramatic irony. **Humor of language** may include sarcasm, exaggeration, puns, or verbal irony, which occurs when what is said is not what is meant. R. K. Narayan's "Like the Sun" contains, to varying degrees, all three types of humor. So does Anton Chekhov's *The Bear.*

*See page 853.*

**Hyperbole** Hyperbole is a figure of speech in which the truth is exaggerated for emphasis or for humorous effect. The expression "I'm so hungry I could eat a horse" is an example of hyperbole. The following lines describing the meekness of John Steinbeck's dog illustrate hyperbole:

> He turns his steps rather than disturb an earnest caterpillar. His greatest fear is that someone will point out a rabbit and suggest that he chase it.
>
> —John Steinbeck, from *Travels with Charley*

**Iambic Pentameter** *See* **Meter.**

**Imagery** Imagery describes words and phrases that re-create vivid sensory experiences for the reader. Because sight is the most highly developed sense, the majority of images are visual. Imagery may also appeal to the senses of smell, hearing, taste, and touch. Effective writers of both prose and poetry frequently use imagery that appeals to more than one sense simultaneously.

**Examples:** In D. H. Lawrence's "Piano," the phrase "the boom of the tingling strings" appeals to the senses of hearing and touch. The expression "with eyes the color of caterpillar," from Sandra Cisneros's "Salvador Late or Early," appeals to the sense of sight.

*See pages 231, 466, 906, 962.*

**Internal Conflict** *See* **Conflict.**

**Irony** Irony is a contrast between what is expected and what actually exists or happens. There are three basic types of irony.

**Situational irony** occurs when a character or the reader expects one thing to happen but something entirely different occurs. In Guy de Maupassant's "Two Friends," the reader expects the Frenchmen to eat the fish they have caught. However, it is the German officer who eats the fish, after he executes the men. In John Steinbeck's *Travels with Charley,* the narrator expects his dog to behave meekly when he encounters bears. In actuality, however, bears cause Charley to become aggressive. This second example shows how situational irony can have comic results.

**Verbal irony** occurs when someone says one thing but means another. The speaker in Stephen Crane's poem continually repeats that "war is kind" while presenting images that suggest just the opposite. The father who "tumbled in the yellow trenches. . . gulped and died" and the "bright splendid shroud" of a dead soldier communicate the horror of war.

**Dramatic irony** refers to the contrast between what a character knows and what the reader or audience knows. For example, Julius Caesar goes to the Senate on the Ides of March in the belief that he may receive a crown. The audience knows, however, that the conspirators are planning his assassination.

*See pages 543–544, 556, 581, 777, 853, 939.*
*See also* **Hyperbole; Understatement.**

**Legend** A legend is a story handed down from the past, especially one that is popularly believed to be based on historical events. The story of the rise and fall of King Arthur is a famous example of a legend. Though legends often incorporate supernatural elements and magical deeds, they claim to be the story of a real human being and are often set in a particular time and place. These characteristics separate a legend from a myth.

*See page 1015–1016.*
*See also* **Myth.**

**Lyric Poem** In ancient Greece, the lyre was a musical instrument, and the lyric became the name for a song accompanied by music. In ordinary speech, the words of songs are still called lyrics. In literature, a lyric poem is any short poem that presents a single speaker who expresses his or her innermost thoughts and feelings. In a love lyric, such as Amy Lowell's "The Taxi" or Carl Sandburg's "Moon Rondeau," the speaker expresses romantic love. In other lyrics, a speaker may meditate on nature or explore personal issues, such as those addressed by Juan Ramón Jiménez's "I Am Not I" and José Martí's *Simple Poetry.*

**Magical Realism** Magical realism refers to a style of writing that often includes exaggeration, unusual humor, magical and bizarre events, dreams that come true, and superstitions that prove warranted. Magical realism differs from pure fantasy in combining fantastic elements with realistic elements such as recognizable characters, believable dialogue, a true-to-life setting, a matter-of-fact tone, and a plot that sometimes contains historic events. A famous example of magical realism is Gabriel García Márquez's novel, *One Hundred Years of Solitude.*

**Melodies of Literary Language** *See* **Alliteration; Assonance; Consonance; Meter; Rhythm.**

**Memoir** *See* **Autobiography.**

**Metaphor** A metaphor is a form of figurative language that makes a comparison between two things that have something in common. Unlike a simile, a metaphor does not use the word *like* or *as.* The first line of Carl Sandburg's "Moon Rondeau" is a metaphor: "Love is a door we shall open together."

The comparison in a metaphor is often suggested rather than directly expressed. In the following lines, the loved one is indirectly compared to a bird in flight:

> Suddenly I've felt you flying through my soul
> in quick, lofty flight,
>
> —Luis Lloréns Torres,
> from "Love Without Love"

See pages 226, 260, 349, 354.
*See also* **Extended Metaphor; Figurative Language; Simile.**

**Meter** Meter is the repetition of a regular rhythmic unit in a line of poetry. The meter of a poem is like the beat of a song; it establishes a predictable means of emphasis.

Each unit of meter is known as a **foot,** with each foot having one stressed and one or two unstressed syllables. The four basic types of metrical feet are the **iamb,** an unstressed syllable followed by a stressed syllable ($\breve{}$ $\acute{}$); the **trochee,** a stressed syllable followed by an unstressed syllable ($\acute{}$ $\breve{}$); the **anapest,** two unstressed syllables followed by a stressed syllable ($\breve{}$ $\breve{}$ $\acute{}$); and the **dactyl,** a stressed syllable followed by two unstressed syllables ($\acute{}$$\breve{}$$\breve{}$).

A line of poetry is named not only for the type of meter but also for the number of feet in the line. The most common metrical names are **trimeter,** a three-foot line; **tetrameter,** a four-foot line; **pentameter,** a five-foot line; and **hexameter,** a six-foot line. These lines illustrate iambic pentameter, the most common form of meter in the English language:

> Nŏr yĕt ă flóatĭng spár tŏ mén thăt sínk
>
> Ănd rísĕ ănd sínk ănd rísĕ ănd sínk ăgáin;
>
> —Edna St. Vincent Millay, from "Sonnet 30"

See pages 226, 236, 713.

**Minor Characters** *See* **Character.**

**Monologue** *See* **Soliloquy.**

**Mood** Mood is the feeling, or atmosphere, that a writer creates for the reader. The writer's use of connotation, imagery, and figurative language, as well as sound and rhythm, can all help to develop mood. Notice how the author makes use of all of these techniques to create a tense mood in the following passage, where the narrator's grandfather begins to realize that he has been cheated:

> . . . my grandfather took the four packages of coffee, put them on the empty scale, and his heart thudded as he watched the black finger of justice come to rest on the left of the black line: the scale with the pound weight stayed down, and the pound of coffee remained up in the air; his heart thudded more than if he had been lying behind a bush in the forest waiting for Bilgan the Giant. . . .
>
> —Heinrich Böll, from "The Balek Scales"

*See also* **Connotation; Diction; Figurative Language; Imagery; Style.**

**Myth** A myth is a traditional story, usually concerning some supernatural being or unlikely event. Frequently, myths attempt to explain natural phenomena, such as solar and lunar eclipses and the cycle of the seasons. For some peoples, myths were both a kind of science and a religion. In addition, myths served as literature and entertainment, just as they do for modern-day audiences.

Some of the most famous myths in the Western tradition, such as the stories of Theseus and Hercules, originated among the ancient Greeks and Romans. Norse mythology, consisting of myths from Scandinavia and Germany, is also important classical literature. Native Americans have produced fascinating myths of various kinds, as have the peoples of Africa, Asia, and Latin America.

Many Greek dramas were based on myths that would have been familiar to the audience. The origins of *Antigone,* for example, can be traced to myths about the family of King Oedipus.

*See pages 1015–1016.*
*See also* **Legend.**

**Narrative** A narrative is any type of writing that is primarily concerned with relating an event or a series of events. A narrative can be imaginary, as is a short story or novel, or it can be factual, as is a newspaper account or a work of history. Maya Angelou's "Getting a Job" is an example of narrative nonfiction.

*See pages 384, 417.*
*See also* **Fiction; Nonfiction; Novel; Plot; Short Story.**

**Narrative Poem** A narrative poem tells a story. Like a short story, a narrative poem has characters, a setting, a plot, and a point of view, all of which combine to develop a theme.

**Examples:** Epics, such as Homer's *Iliad* and Virgil's *Aeneid,* are narrative poems, as are ballads. "Exile," by Julia Alvarez, is an example of a contemporary narrative poem; it tells the story of her family's move from the Dominican Republic to the United States.

*See page 437.*

**Narrator** The narrator is the character or voice from whose point of view events are told. In "The Leap" by Louise Erdrich, the narrator is the daughter of the main character in the story. In James Herriot's nonfictional "A Case of Cruelty," the narrator is the author himself.

*See page 343.*
*See also* **Point of View; Speaker.**

**Nonfiction** Nonfiction is prose writing that is about real people, places, and events. Unlike fiction, nonfiction is largely concerned with factual information, although the writer shapes the information according to his or her purpose and viewpoint. Nonfiction includes an amazingly diverse range of writing; newspaper articles, cookbooks, letters, movie reviews, editorials, speeches, true-life adventure stories—all are considered nonfiction. E. B. White's "Once More to the Lake," Margaret Atwood's "Through the One-Way Mirror," Maya Angelou's "Getting a Job" and Elie Wiesel's "Nobel Prize Acceptance Speech" are some examples of nonfiction.

*See pages 104, 178.*
*See also* **Autobiography; Biography; Diary; Essay; Fiction.**

**Novel** The novel is an extended work of fiction. Like a short story, a novel is essentially the product of a writer's imagination. The most obvious difference between a novel and a short story is length. Because the novel is considerably longer, a novelist can develop a wider range of characters and a more complex plot. George Orwell's *Animal Farm* is an example of a novel.

**Onomatopoeia** The word *onomatopoeia* literally means "name-making." It is the process of creating or using words that imitate sounds. The *buzz* of the bee, the *honk* of the car horn, the *peep* of the chick are onomatopoetic, or echoic, words. Onomatopoeia as a literary technique goes beyond the use of simple echoic words. Writers, particularly poets, choose words whose sounds suggest their denotative and connotative meanings: for example, *whisper, kick, gargle, gnash,* and *clatter.* In D. H. Lawrence's poem "Piano," examples of onomatopoeia include "the boom" of the strings and "the tinkling piano."

*See page 225.*

**Paradox** A paradox is a seemingly contradictory or absurd statement that may nonetheless suggest an important truth.

**Examples:** Shakespeare employed a paradox in these lines from *Julius Caesar:* "Cowards die many times before their deaths; / The valiant never taste of death but once." The statement suggests the fearful and constant anticipation of death is worse than death itself. Juan Ramón Jiménez's poem "I Am Not I" reflects upon the paradox expressed in the title, which suggests that the speaker feels separated from himself.

**Parallelism** Parallelism is the use of similar grammatical constructions to express ideas that are related or equal in importance. The parallel elements may be words, phrases, sentences, or paragraphs. Parallelism occurs in the following lines:

> So long as men can breathe, or eyes can see,
> So long lives this, and this gives life to thee.
> —William Shakespeare from "Sonnet 18"

**Parody** A parody imitates or mocks another serious work or type of literature. Like caricature in art, parody in literature mimics a subject or a style. The purpose of a parody may be to ridicule through broad humor. On the other hand, a parody may broaden understanding or add insight to the original work. Some parodies are even written in tribute to a work of literature. Mark Twain's book *A Connecticut Yankee in King Arthur's Court,* in which a time traveler from Twain's era tries to make sense of what he encounters in the Arthurian Age, parodies the legend of King Arthur.

**Personification** Personification is a figure of speech in which human qualities are attributed to an object, animal, or idea. Writers use personification to make images and feelings concrete for the reader.

**Examples:** In Pablo Neruda's "Tonight I Can Write . . . ," human physical attributes are given to stars in the phrase "the blue stars shiver." In

Dahlia Ravikovitch's "Pride," rocks "lie on their backs" and "the rock has an open wound."

*See pages 226, 354, 466, 846.*
*See also* **Figurative Language; Imagery; Metaphor; Simile.**

**Persuasion** Persuasion is a technique used by speakers or writers to convince an audience to adopt an opinion, perform an action, or both. Effective persuasion appeals to both the emotions and the intellect. Persuasion is often used in essays; essayists try to convince readers to accept their views. E. M. Forster's "Tolerance" is an example.

**Plot** The word *plot* refers to the chain of related events that take place in a story. The plot is the writer's blueprint for what happens, when it happens, and to whom it happens. Usually, the events of a plot progress because of a **conflict,** or struggle between opposing forces. Although there are many types of plots, most include the following stages:

1. **Exposition** The exposition lays the groundwork for the plot and provides the reader with essential background information. Characters are introduced, the setting is described, and the plot begins to unfold. Although the exposition generally appears at the opening of a story, it may also occur later in the narrative. In Stephen Vincent Benét's "By the Waters of Babylon," the exposition introduces the narrator and his priest-father and establishes the primitive setting, particularly the characters' fear of the Place of the Gods.

2. **Rising Action** As the story progresses, complications usually arise, causing difficulties for the main characters and making the conflict more difficult to resolve. As the characters struggle to find solutions to the conflict, suspense builds. In "By the Waters of Babylon" the rising action begins as the narrator sets off on his journey.

3. **Climax** The climax is the turning point of the action, the moment when interest and intensity reach their peak. The climax of a story usually involves an important event, decision, or discovery that affects the final outcome. In

"By the Waters of Babylon" the climax comes when John goes to the Place of the Gods and discovers the dead "god"—a man.

4. **Falling Action** The falling action consists of the events that occur after the climax. Often, the conflict is resolved, and the intensity of the action subsides. Sometimes this phase of the plot is called the **dénouement** (dā′nōō-mäɴ′), from a French word that means "untying." In the dénouement, also known as the **resolution,** the tangles of the plot are untied and mysteries are solved. In "By the Waters of Babylon" the falling action comes as John realizes the truth about the past and what it means to his own people.

*See pages 17, 53, 167, 285, 383, 394.*
*See also* **Climax; Conflict; Falling Action; Rising Action.**

**Poetry** Poetry is language arranged in lines. Like other forms of literature, poetry attempts to re-create emotions and experiences. Poetry, however, is usually more condensed and suggestive than prose. Because poetry frequently does not include the kind of detail and explanation found in prose, poetry tends to leave more to the reader's imagination. Poetry also may require more work on the reader's part to unlock meaning.

Poems often are divided into stanzas, or groups of lines. The stanzas in a poem may contain the same number of lines or they may vary in length. Some poems have definite patterns of meter and rhyme. Others rely more on the sounds of words and less on fixed rhythms and rhyme schemes. The use of figurative language is also common in poetry.

*See also* **Figurative Language; Form; Free Verse; Meter; Repetition; Rhyme; Rhythm.**

**Point of View** Point of view refers to the narrative method used in a short story, novel, or nonfiction selection. The two basic points of view are first-person and third-person.

When a character within a selection describes the action as a participant, in his or her own words, the writer is using the **first-person point of view.** A first-person narrator tends to involve the reader in the story and to communicate a sense of immediacy and personal concern. Tim O'Brien's "On the Rainy River" and Rosamund Pilcher's "Lalla" are examples of the first-person point of view. The excerpt from Marion Zimmer Bradley's *The Mists of Avalon* shows how the use of first-person narration can bring a legendary character to life.

**Third-person point of view** occurs when a narrator outside the action describes events and characters. In **third-person omniscient point of view,** the narrator is omniscient, or all-knowing, and can see into the minds of more than one character. The use of a third-person narrator gives the writer tremendous flexibility and provides the reader with access to all the characters and to events that may be occurring simultaneously. Sarah Orne Jewett's "A White Heron" is told from a third-person omniscient point of view. In this story, the reader has access to the thoughts and feelings not only of Sylvia, but also to some extent of the grandmother and the stranger. We learn, for example, about the stranger's thoughts upon awakening, which are occurring at approximately the same time as which Sylvia is out spotting the heron.

In the **third-person limited point of view** events are related through the eyes of one character. The narrator describes only that character's feelings and the events that he or she witnesses. Bessie Head's "The Prisoner Who Wore Glasses" is an example of the third-person limited point of view. In this story, we know only the thoughts of Brille, and everything is filtered through the perspective of this character.

*See pages 18, 53, 93, 343, 575, 623–624, 642, 660, 833, 890, 1086.*

**Props** The word *prop,* an abbreviation of *property,* refers to the physical objects that are used in a stage production. In Anton Chekhov's *The Bear,* the props include a snapshot of Mrs. Popov's late husband and the pistols to be used in her duel with Smirnov. Props help to establish the setting for a play.

*See also* **Drama.**

**Protagonist** The central character in a story or play is called the protagonist. The protagonist is always involved in the central conflict of the plot and often changes during the course of the work. Sometimes more than one character can be the protagonist of a story.

**Examples:** The protagonist in R. K. Narayan's "Like the Sun" is the character Sekhar, who encounters problems while seeking to tell the truth. The protagonist in Doris Lessing's "No Witchcraft for Sale" is Gideon, the servant who displays his knowledge of medicinal herbs.

*See page 556.*
*See also* **Antagonist.**

**Quatrain** A quatrain is a four-line stanza, or unit of poetry. The most common stanza in English poetry, the quatrain can display a variety of meters and rhyme schemes. Quatrains are often used in sonnets, as in these lines from William Shakespeare's "Sonnet 18." The rhyme scheme in this quatrain is *abab.*

> Shall I compare thee to a summer's day?  *a*
> Thou art more lovely and more temperate:  *b*
> Rough winds do shake the darling buds
>   of May,  *a*
> And summer's lease hath all too short
>   a date:  *b*
> —William Shakespeare, from "Sonnet 18"

*See also* **Meter; Poetry; Rhyme; Sonnet; Stanza.**

**Realism** In literature, realism has both a general meaning and a special meaning. As a general term, *realism* refers to any effort to offer an accurate and detailed portrayal of actual life. Thus, critics talk about Shakespeare's realistic portrayals of his characters and praise the medieval poet Chaucer for his realistic descriptions of people from different social classes.

More specifically, realism refers to a literary method developed in the 19th century. The realists based their writing on careful observations of their contemporary life, often focusing on the middle or lower classes. They attempted to present life objectively and honestly, without the sentimentality or idealism that had characterized earlier literature. Typically, realists developed their settings in great detail in an effort to re-create a specific time and place for the reader. Guy de Maupassant, Leo

Tolstoy, Mark Twain, and Sarah Orne Jewett are all considered realists.

**Repetition** Repetition is a literary technique in which a sound, word, phrase, or line is repeated for emphasis. Note the use of repetition in the following lines:

> Love is not all: it is not meat nor drink
> Nor slumber nor a roof against the rain;
> Nor yet a floating spar to men that sink
> And rise and sink and rise and sink again;
> —Edna St. Vincent Millay, from "Sonnet 30"

*See pages 225, 354, 759.*

**Resolution** *See* **Falling Action.**

**Rhyme** Words rhyme when the sound of their accented vowels and all succeeding sounds are identical, as in *tether* and *together.* For **true rhyme,** the consonants that precede the vowels must be different, as in Shakespeare's rhyming of *day* and *May* in "Sonnet 18." Rhyme that occurs at the ends of lines of poetry is called **end rhyme.** End rhyme that is not exact but approximate is called **off rhyme,** as in *other* and *bother.* Rhyme that occurs within a single line, as in the following example, is called **internal rhyme:**

> Once upon a midnight <u>dreary</u>, while I pondered
>   weak and <u>weary</u>,
> Over many a quaint and curious volume of
>   forgotten lore—
> While I nodded, nearly <u>napping</u>, suddenly there
>   came a <u>tapping</u>,
> As of someone gently <u>rapping</u>, <u>rapping</u> at my
>   chamber door.
> —Edgar Allan Poe, from "The Raven"

*See pages 225, 233.*

**Rhyme Scheme** A rhyme scheme is the pattern of end rhyme in a poem. The pattern is charted by assigning a letter of the alphabet, beginning with the letter *a,* to each line. Lines that rhyme are given the same letter. The following example has an *abab* rhyme scheme:

> But thy eternal summer shall not fade,    *a*
> Nor lose possession of that fair thou owest;    *b*
> Nor shall Death brag thou wander'st in
>    his shade,    *a*
> When in eternal lines to time thou growest:    *b*
>      —William Shakespeare, from "Sonnet 18"

*See pages 225, 233.*

**Rhythm**   Rhythm refers to the pattern or beat of stressed and unstressed syllables in a line of poetry. Poets use rhythm to bring out the musical quality of language, to emphasize ideas, to create mood, and to reinforce subject matter.

*See pages 226, 236.*
*See also* **Meter.**

**Rising Action**   Rising action refers to the part of the plot in which complications develop and the conflict intensifies, building to the climax, or highest point of interest and intensity in the plot. The rising action in Anton Chekhov's *The Bear* describes the growing conflict between Smirnov and Mrs. Popov.

*See pages 384, 394.*
*See also* **Climax; Falling Action; Plot.**

**Romance**   A romance refers to any imaginative story concerned with noble heroes, chivalric codes of honor, passionate love, daring deeds, and supernatural events. Writers of romances tend to idealize their heroes as well as the eras in which the heroes live. Medieval romances, such as Malory's *Le Morte d'Arthur*, are stories of kings, knights, and ladies who are motivated by love, religious faith, or simply a desire for adventure. Such romances are comparatively lighthearted in tone and loose in structure, containing many episodes. Usually the main character has a series of adventures while on a quest to accomplish some goal.

*See page 1080.*

**Satire**   Satire is a literary technique in which ideas, customs, behaviors, or institutions are ridiculed for the purpose of improving society. Satire may be gently witty, mildly abrasive, or

bitterly critical, and it often uses exaggeration to force readers to see something in a more critical light.

*Example:* Kurt Vonnegut Jr.'s "Harrison Bergeron" is a satire that criticizes those who pursue an ideal at the expense of common sense. Vonnegut depicts a future society that has gone to ridiculous lengths to ensure complete equality among its citizens, rewarding mediocrity and penalizing individual talent.

**Scene**   A scene is a subdivision of an act in drama. Each scene usually establishes a different time or place. In Shakespeare's *Julius Caesar,* for example, the first scene of Act One takes place at a public celebration on a street in Rome. The last scene in Act Five takes place on a battlefield.

**Science Fiction**   Science fiction is prose writing that presents the possibilities of the future, using known scientific data and theories as well as the creative imagination of the writer. Most science fiction comments on present-day society through the writer's fictional conception of a future society.

*Examples:* Ray Bradbury's "A Sound of Thunder" presents a vision of the future in order to show how all aspects of nature are interrelated and that human interference with the ecological cycle can lead to disaster. Bradbury's "The Pedestrian" portrays a future in which human beings are rendered completely passive by television.

*See pages 27, 82.*

**Setting**   Setting is the time and place of the action of a short story, novel, play, narrative poem, or narrative nonfiction work. In addition to place and time, however, setting may include the larger historical and cultural contexts that form the background for a narrative. Setting is one of the main elements in fiction and often plays an important role in what happens and why.

*Examples:* In Ray Bradbury's "There Will Come Soft Rains," the house setting is essential to what happens in the story; it functions almost as a character. The desolate frontier setting of

Mark Twain's "The Californian's Tale" provides a historical context that helps to explain Henry's actions. The setting of Zhang Jie's "Love Must Not Be Forgotten" includes information about the cultural environment that enables the reader to understand the actions of the characters.

*See pages 18, 93, 209, 311, 660.*

**Shakespearean Sonnet** *See* **Sonnet.**

**Short Story** A short story is a work of fiction that can be read in one sitting. Generally, a short story develops one major conflict. The four basic elements of a short story are setting, character, plot, and theme.

A short story must be unified; all the elements must work together to produce a total effect. This unity of effect is reinforced through an appropriate title and through the use of literary devices, such as symbolism and irony.

*See also* **Character; Conflict; Plot; Setting; Theme.**

**Simile** A simile is a stated comparison between two things that are actually unlike but that have something in common. Like metaphors, similes are figures of speech, but whereas a metaphor implies a comparison, a simile expresses the comparison clearly by the use of the word *like* or *as.*

**Example:** In W. P. Kinsella's "The Thrill of the Grass," the narrator describes his shadow as being "black as an umbrella." This simile links the shadow and the umbrella by their common color.

*See pages 226, 260, 349, 354.*
*See also* **Figurative Language; Metaphor.**

**Situational Irony** *See* **Irony.**

**Soliloquy** In a dramatic work, a soliloquy is a speech in which a character speaks his or her private thoughts aloud. The character is usually on stage alone and generally appears to be unaware of the presence of an audience. Soliloquies are characteristic of Shakespeare's plays; *Julius Caesar* has several soliloquies. Casca begins plotting how to win over Brutus in a soliloquy that begins with these lines:

> Well, Brutus, thou art noble; yet I see
> Thy honorable mettle may be wrought
> From that it is disposed.
>
> —William Shakespeare, from *Julius Caesar*

*See page 735.*

**Sonnet** A sonnet is a lyric poem of 14 lines, commonly written in iambic pentameter. For centuries the sonnet has been a popular form, for it is long enough to permit development of a complex idea yet short and structured enough to challenge any poet's artistic skills.

The **Shakespearean,** or **English, sonnet** is sometimes also called the **Elizabethan sonnet.** It consists of three quatrains, or four-line units, and a final **couplet,** or two-line unit, which reflect the logical organization of the poem. The typical rhyme scheme is *abab cdcd efef gg.* In the English sonnet, the rhymed couplet at the end of the sonnet provides a final commentary on the subject developed in the preceding three quatrains. The poems by William Shakespeare and Edna St. Vincent Millay included in this text are sonnets.

Some poets have written a series of related sonnets that have the same subject. These are called **sonnet sequences,** or **sonnet cycles.** Toward the end of the 16th century, writing sonnets became fashionable, with a common subject being love for a beautiful but unattainable woman. Shakespeare's sonnets are the most famous of all sonnet sequences.

*See pages 233, 236, 581.*
*See also* **Meter; Poetry; Quatrain; Rhyme; Rhythm.**

**Sound Devices** *See* **Alliteration; Assonance; Consonance; Onomatopoeia; Meter; Repetition; Rhyme.**

**Speaker** The speaker in a poem is the voice that "talks" to the reader, similar to the narrator in fiction. Speaker and poet are not necessarily synonymous. Often a poet creates a speaker with a distinct identity in order to achieve a particular effect.

**Example:** In Stephen Crane's "Do not weep, maiden, for war is kind," the speaker is an ironic observer of war's tragedy.

*See page 231.*

**Stage Directions**  The stage directions in a dramatic script serve as a kind of instructional manual for the director, actors, and stage crew as well as for the general reader. Often the stage directions are printed in italic type, and they may be enclosed in parentheses or brackets.

Stage directions serve a number of important functions. They may describe the scenery, or setting, as well as lighting, costumes, props, music, sound effects, or, in the case of film productions, camera angles and shots. Most important, the stage directions usually provide hints to the performers on how the characters look, move, and speak.

**Example:** In Chekhov's *The Bear,* the stage directions give information about the actions and expressions of the characters, as well details about the props and Mrs. Popov's drawing room, where the action takes place.

*See page 285, 300.*
*See also* **Props.**

**Stanza**  A stanza is a group of lines that form a unit of poetry. The stanza is roughly comparable to the paragraph in prose. In traditional poems, the stanzas usually have the same number of lines and often have the same rhyme scheme and meter as well. In the 20th century, poets have experimented more freely with stanza form than did earlier poets, sometimes writing poems that have no stanza breaks at all.

**Stereotype**  In literature, simplified or stock characters who conform to a fixed pattern or are defined by a single trait are called stereotypes. Such characters do not usually demonstrate the complexities of real people.

**Examples:** Familiar stereotypes in popular literature include the absent-minded professor, the dumb athlete, and the busybody. In Chekhov's *The Bear,* the servant Luke might be seen as a stereotype of a loyal but critical servant who tells the lady of the house more than she wants to hear.

*See page 300.*
*See also* **Farce.**

**Structure**  Structure is the way in which the parts of a work of literature are put together. In poetry, structure refers to the arrangement of words and lines to produce a desired effect. A common structural unit in poetry is the stanza, of which there are numerous types. In prose, structure is the arrangement of larger units or parts of a selection. Paragraphs, for example, are a basic unit in prose, as are chapters in novels and acts in plays. The structure of a poem, short story, novel, play, or nonfiction selection usually emphasizes certain important aspects of content.

*See pages 233, 236.*
*See also* **Act; Stanza.**

**Style**  Style is the way in which a piece of literature is written. Style refers not to what is said but to how it is said. Elements such as word choice, sentence length, tone, imagery, figurative language, use of dialogue, and point of view contribute to a writer's personal style.

**Examples:** Sarah Orne Jewett's style in "A White Heron" might be described as a blend of the poetic and realistic. Through her use of sensory details, regional dialect, and a sensitive narrator, she creates both an accurate and an admiring picture of the main character and her world. Frank O'Connor's style in "The Study of History" might be described as matter-of-fact and humorously understated, reflecting the engaging personality of its youthful narrator.

*See pages 460, 600, 995, 1099.*

**Surprise Ending**  A surprise ending is an unexpected twist in plot at the conclusion of a story. The conclusion of Guy de Maupassant's "Two Friends" surprises the reader because earlier events in the story had suggested a different outcome.

**Suspense**  Suspense is the tension or excitement felt by the reader as he or she becomes involved in a story and eager to know the outcome of the conflict. Suspense is created when a writer purposely leaves readers uncertain or apprehensive about what will happen.

**Example:** In Edgar Allan Poe's "The Pit and the

Pendulum," the reader wants to know if the narrator can possibly escape from his situation. The tension is maintained as the narrator finds a way to cope with each threat that he encounters, only to be faced with a new and even greater threat.

*See page 575.*

**Symbol** A symbol is a person, place, or object that represents something beyond itself. For instance, a star on a door represents fame; a star pinned to the shirt of a sheriff stands for authority and power. Symbols can succinctly communicate complicated, emotionally rich ideas. A flag, for example, can symbolize patriotism and a national heritage.

**Examples:** The cranes in Hwang Sunwŏn's story of the same name symbolize the childhood friendship of the two main characters, as well as peace and tranquillity. The medicinal plant in Doris Lessing's "No Witchcraft for Sale" symbolizes native African culture.

*See pages 407, 833, 906.*

**Tall Tale** A tall tale is a humorously exaggerated story about impossible events, often relating the supernatural abilities of the main character. The tales about folk heroes such as Paul Bunyan and Davy Crockett are typical tall tales.

**Theme** The theme is the central idea or message in a work of literature. Theme should not be confused with subject, or what the work is about. Rather, theme is a perception about life or human nature shared with the reader. Sometimes the theme is directly stated within a work; at other times it is implied, and the reader must infer the theme. For example, Kurt Vonnegut, Jr., in "Harrison Bergeron" never directly states his criticism of the society and government. The reader needs to put details and events together to identify his theme about the damage that can be done when people go to extremes in service of equality.

One way to discover the theme of a work of literature is to think about what happens to the central characters. The importance of those events, stated in terms that apply to all human

beings, is often the theme. For example, in Doris Lessing's "No Witchcraft for Sale," the misunderstanding and distrust between Gideon and Mrs. Farquar suggests the more general theme that lack of understanding between races and cultures can create tension. Several other selections in this book have themes that involve the need for people to accept one another by dealing with differences in their culture.

*See pages 18, 27, 156, 167, 178, 794.*

**Third-Person Narration** *See* **Point of View.**

**Title** The title of a literary work introduces the readers to the piece and usually reveals something about its subject or theme. Some titles are deliberately straightforward, stating exactly what the reader can expect to discover in the work. Others suggest possibilities, perhaps hinting at the subject and forcing the reader to search for interpretations.

**Example:** The title of Nadine Gordimer's "A Chip of Glass Ruby" refers to a traditional Indian adornment. When Mrs. Bamjee was a girl, her mother had fixed a glass ruby in her daughter's nostril, "but she [Mrs. Bamjee] had abandoned that adornment . . . long ago." On one hand, the title suggests her rejection of a narrowly defined traditional role. On the other hand, the title suggests the husband's frustrated desire for a wife solely focused on traditional duties.

**Tone** Tone is the attitude a writer takes toward a subject. The language and details a writer chooses help to create the tone, which might be playful, serious, bitter, angry, or detached, among other possibilities. To identify the tone of a work of literature, you might find it helpful to read the work aloud, as if giving a dramatic reading before an audience. The emotions that you convey in reading should give you hints as to the tone of the work.

Unlike mood, which refers to the emotional response of the reader to a work, tone reflects the feelings of the writer.

**Examples:** Rudolfo A. Anaya uses an admiring, respectful tone to describe his grandfather in "A Celebration of Grandfathers." Roger Rosenblatt's "The Man in the Water" exhibits a philosophic, somber tone, reflecting the author's efforts to draw a lesson from a tragic yet heroic event.

*See pages 452, 460, 649, 901, 945, 962, 981.*
*See also* **Connotation; Diction; Mood; Style.**

**Tragedy** In broad terms, tragedy is literature, especially drama, in which actions and events turn out disastrously for the main character or characters. In tragedy the main characters, and sometimes other involved characters and innocent bystanders as well, are destroyed. Usually the destruction is death, as in Shakespeare's *Julius Caesar* or Sophocles' *Antigone.* In some tragedies, however, the main characters are alive at the end but are devastated. Tragic heroes evoke both pity and fear in readers or viewers—pity because they feel sorry for the characters and fear because they realize that the problems and struggles faced by the characters are perhaps a necessary part of human life. At the end of a tragedy, a reader or viewer generally feels a sense of waste, because humans who were in some way superior have been destroyed.

*See pages 794, 1019, 1061.*
*See also* **Hero.**

**Tragic Flaw** *See* **Hero.**

**Tragic Hero** *See* **Hero.**

**Turning Point** *See* **Climax.**

**Understatement** Understatement is the technique of creating emphasis by saying less than is actually or literally true. As such, it is the opposite of exaggeration, or hyperbole. The statement made by the park guide in John Steinbeck's *Travels with Charley,* "Bears don't argue," is an example of understatement. It suggests that even though bears don't talk, they know of more aggressive ways to express their wants. Understatement can be a biting form of sarcasm or verbal irony. Jonathan Swift, the 18th-century English writer best known for *Gulliver's Travels,* often used understatement as a satiric weapon. For example, Swift wrote, "Last week I saw a woman flayed [skinned alive], and you will hardly believe how much it altered her appearance for the worse."

*See page 939.*
*See also* **Hyperbole; Irony.**

**Verbal Irony** *See* **Irony.**

**Voice** The term *voice* refers to a writer's unique use of language that allows a reader to "hear" a human personality in his or her writing. The elements of style that determine a writer's voice include sentence structure, diction, and tone. For example, some writers are noted for their reliance on short, simple sentences, while others make use of long, complicated ones. Certain writers use concrete words, such as *lake* or *cold,* which name things that you can see, hear, feel, taste, or smell. Others prefer abstract terms like *memory,* which name things that cannot be perceived with the senses. A writer's tone also leaves its imprint on his or her personal voice.

The term can also be applied to the narrator of a selection. In Alice Walker's "Everyday Use," the narrator establishes her personality through her manner of narration. She emerges as a strong, down-to-earth character with a gift for descriptive language.

**Word Choice** *See* **Diction.**

# Glossary of Words to Know
## In English and Spanish

## A

**abdicate** (ăb′dĭ-kāt′) *v.* to give up an office or position
**abdicar** *v.* renunciar a un cargo

**abiding** (ə-bī′dĭng) *adj.* lasting or enduring
**abide** *v.*
**duradero** *adj.* perdurable; resistente  **durar** *v.*

**acquaint** (ə-kwānt′) *v.* to inform; familiarize
**conocer** *v.* informar; familiarizarse

**acquiescence** (ăk′wē-ĕs′əns) *n.* passive agreement; agreement without protest
**consentimiento** *s.* aceptación pasiva; aceptación sin protestar

**acute** (ə-kyōōt′) *adj.* very sharp or severe
**agudo** *adj.* grave o severo

**adamant** (ăd′ə-mənt) *adj.* remaining firm despite the pleas or reasoning of others; stubbornly unyielding
**obstinado** *adj.* que permanece firme a pesar de ruegos o razonamientos; testarudo; inflexible

**adversary** (ăd′vər-sĕr′ē) *n.* an opponent; enemy
**adversario** *s.* opositor; enemigo

**amicable** (ăm′ĭ-kə-bəl) *adj.* having or showing a friendly attitude
**amigable** *adj.* que tiene una actitud amistosa

**analyze** (ăn′ə-līz′) *v.* to study carefully by separating into parts
**analizar** *v.* estudiar cuidadosamente, separando en partes

**anecdote** (ăn′ĭk-dōt′) *n.* a short account of an interesting or humorous incident
**anécdota** *s.* narración breve de un incidente interesante o chistoso

**animosity** (ăn′ə-mŏs′ĭ-tē) *n.* active dislike; hatred
**animosidad** *s.* desagrado fuerte; odio

**annihilate** (ə-nī′ə-lāt′) *v.* to destroy completely; wipe out
**aniquilar** *v.* destruir completamente; desbaratar; eliminar

**annul** (ə-nŭl′) *v.* to do away with or make invalid; cancel
**anular** *v.* abolir; invalidar; cancelar

**anonymity** (ăn′ə-nĭm′ĭ-tē) *n.* the state of being unknown or unidentified
**anonimato** *s.* estado en que no se es reconocido o identificado

**antiquated** (ăn′tĭ-kwā′tĭd) *adj.* old-fashioned; outmoded
**anticuado** *adj.* a la antigua; pasado de moda

**ardent** (är′dnt) *adj.* displaying great warmth of feeling; passionate
**ardiente** *adj.* de sentimientos muy cálidos; apasionado

**ascend** (ə-sĕnd′) *v.* to rise; climb
**ascender** *v.* subir; trepar

**assiduously** (ə-sĭj′ōō-əs-lē) *adv.* in a way that shows steady and careful attention
**asiduamente** *adv.* con constancia y perseverancia

**astutely** (ə-stōōt′lē) *adv.* with keen perceptiveness; wisely
**astutamente** *adv.* con perspicacia; inteligentemente

**atonement** (ə-tōn′mənt) *n.* the act of making up for a serious error, sin, or wrong
**expiación** *s.* acto de reparar un error, un pecado o un mal

**atrocity** (ə-trŏs′ĭ-tē) *n.* a very cruel or brutal act
**atrocidad** *s.* acto muy cruel o brutal

**auspicious** (ô-spĭsh′əs) *adj.* promising success; favorable
**propicio** *adj.* que promete éxito; favorable

**authoritarian** (ə-thôr′ĭ-târ′ē-ən´) *adj.* expecting or demanding absolute obedience
**autoritario** *adj.* que espera o demanda obediencia absoluta

**averse** (ə-vûrs′) *adj.* unwilling; deeply reluctant
**adverso** *adj.* opuesto; muy reacio

**aversion** (ə-vûr′zhən) *n.* a strong, definite dislike
**aversión** *s.* antipatía clara y fuerte

## B

**balmy** (bä′mē) *adj.* soothingly fragrant; mild and pleasant
**suave** *adj.* de fragancia tranquilizante; delicado y placentero

**bedlam** (bĕd′ləm) *n.* a place or situation of great noise and confusion
**jaleo** *s.* situación de mucho ruido y confusión

**benediction** (bĕn′ĭ-dĭk′shən) *n.* a blessing
**bendición** *s.* acto de bendecir; don o favor

**benign** (bĭ-nīn′) *adj.* mild; gentle
**benigno** *adj.* suave; benévolo

**bereft** (bĭ-rĕft′) *adj.* suffering the death of a loved one; deprived of someone or something important
**privado (de)** *adj.* desolado; que sufre por la muerte de un ser querido; que ha perdido alguien o algo importante

**biased** (bī′əst) *adj.* marked by an unfair preference; prejudiced
**tendencioso** *adj.* caracterizado por una preferencia injusta; prejuiciado

**boding** (bō′dĭng) *n.* a warning or omen about the future, especially of evil **bode** *v.*
**presagio** *s.* pronóstico o advertencia acerca del futuro, especialmente de algo malo **presagiar** *v.*

**boisterous** (boi′stər-əs) *adj.* loud, noisy, and unrestrained
**escandaloso** *adj.* alborotado, ruidoso y sin control

**brooding** (brōōd′ĭng) *adj.* having a moody or depressed disposition **brood** *v.*
**decaído** *adj.* que tiene una disposición melancólica o deprimida **decaer** *v.*

## C

**cajole** (kə-jōl′) *v.* to persuade by pleasant words, flattery, or false promises
**engatusar** *v.* persuadir con bellas palabras; convencer con halagos o falsas promesas

**calculating** (kăl′kyə-lā′tĭng) *adj.* crafty; cunning
**calculador** *adj.* mañoso; hábil

**calibrated** (kăl′ə-brā′tĭd) *adj.* marked with measurements **calibrate** *v.*
**calibrado** *adj.* marcado con medidas **calibrar** *v.*

**callousness** (kăl′əs-nĭs) *n.* emotional hardness; lack of feeling
**insensibilidad** *s.* dureza emocional; indiferencia

**carriage** (kăr′ĭj) *n.* manner of moving one's body
**porte** *s.* modo de andar

**catalyst** (kăt′l-ĭ) *n.* something that causes change or action
**catalizador** *s.* algo que causa un cambio o acción

**censure** (sĕn′shər) *v.* to criticize severely; to blame
**censurar** *v.* criticar severamente; culpar

**chagrin** (shə-grĭn′) *n.* a feeling of humiliation or embarrassment
**disgusto** *s.* sentimiento de humillación o vergüenza

**champion** (chăm′pē-ən) *v.* to fight for; defend
**abogar** *v.* defender una causa o persona; apoyar

**chaos** (kā′ŏs′) *n.* total disorder
**caos** *s.* desorden total

**chaotic** (kā-ŏt'ĭk) *adj.* extremely confused or disordered
**caótico** *adj.* extremadamente confuso o desordenado

**charade** (shə-rād') *n.* an ill-disguised pretense
**charada** *s.* farsa o payasada; acertijo

**churlish** (chûr'lĭsh) *adj.* rude or ill-tempered
**grosero** *adj.* rudo o insolente

**coercion** (kō-ûr'zhən) *n.* the use of power or threats to force someone to do something
**coerción** *s.* uso de poder o amenazas para obligar a actuar

**coherently** (kō-hîr'ənt-lē) *adv.* in a manner that shows clear thinking and makes sense
**coherentemente** *adv.* con claridad, constancia y sensatez

**commiserate** (kə-mĭz'ə-rāt') *v.* to express sorrow or pity for another's trouble
**conmiserarse** *v.* expresar dolor o piedad por los problemas de otro

**commodity** (kə-mŏd'ĭ-tē) *n.* an item—especially a farming or mining product—that can be turned to commercial use or that can provide another advantage
**mercancía** *s.* producto —especialmente agrícola o minero— que puede tener uso comercial u otras ventajas

**complacently** (kəm-plā'sənt-lē) *adv.* in a contented, unconcerned manner
**complacientemente** *adv.* en forma bonachona o tolerante

**comprehend** (kŏm'prĭ-hĕnd') *v.* to understand
**comprender** *v.* entender

**compulsive** (kəm-pŭl'sĭv) *adj.* having the ability to compel or force
**compulsivo** *adj.* que obliga o fuerza

**comradeship** (kŏm'răd-shĭp') *n.* companionship
**camaradería** *s.* compañerismo

**conclusively** (kən-kloo'sĭv-lē) *adv.* unquestionably; decisively
**concluyentemente** *adv.* de modo terminante; incuestionablemente

**consensus** (kən-sĕn'səs) *n.* general agreement by a group
**consenso** *s.* acuerdo general de grupo

**consternation** (kŏn'stər-nā'shən) *n.* a confused amazement or fear
**consternación** *s.* aflicción y temor; pesadumbre

**construe** (kən-stroo') *v.* to interpret
**interpretar** *v.* explicar

**contemptuously** (kən-tĕmp'choo-əs-lē) *adv.* in a way that shows one's low opinion of someone or something; scornfully
**desdeñosamente** *adv.* con desprecio; burlonamente

**contour** (kŏn'toor') *n.* an outline of a shape
**contorno** *s.* borde de una figura

**convalescence** (kŏn'və-lĕs'əns) *n.* the gradual return to health and strength after an illness or an injury
**convalecencia** *s.* retorno gradual de la salud y la fuerza después de una enfermedad o herida

**conviction** (kən-vĭk'shən) *n.* certainty; a strong belief
**convicción** *s.* seguridad; creencia firme

**coquettishly** (kō-kĕt'ĭsh-lē) *adv.* in a flirtatious manner
**coquetamente** *adv.* de forma seductora

**cosmopolitan** (kŏz'mə-pŏl'ĭ-tn) *adj.* worldly; sophisticated
**cosmopolita** *adj.* mundano; sofisticado

**cower** (kou'ər) *v.* to cringe in fear
**agazaparse** *v.* esconderse u ocultarse con miedo

**coyness** (coi'nĭs) *n.* the pretense of being more modest and innocent than one really is
**gazmoñería** *s.* apariencia de modestia o inocencia

**cultivate** (kŭl'tə-vāt') *v.* to seek to become familiar with
**cultivar** *v.* hacer lo necesario para mejorar un conocimiento o una relación

# D

**dastardly** (dăs′tərd-lē) *adj.* mean and cowardly
**vil** *adj.* cruel y cobarde

**decipher** (dĭ-sī′fər) *v.* to read or interpret something unclear; to figure out
**descifrar** *v.* leer o interpretar algo que no está claro; explicar

**decorous** (děk′ər-əs) *adj.* behaving in a manner appropriate to the occasion; proper
**decoroso** *adj.* que se comporta de manera apropiada a la ocasión; correcto

**deference** (děf′ər-əns) *n.* courteous regard or respect
**deferencia** *s.* atención o respeto cortés

**defile** (dĭ-fīl′) *v.* to make foul, dirty, unclean, or impure
**profanar** *v.* ensuciar o deshonrar; quitarle su pureza

**degrading** (dĭ-grā′dĭng) *adj.* tending to lower one's dignity; insulting **degrade** *v.*
**degradante** *adj.* que quita dignidad; insultante **degradar** *v.*

**deliberately** (dĭ-lĭb′ər-ĭt-lē) *adv.* as a result of careful thought
**deliberadamente** *adv.* con cuidadoy premeditación

**desolation** (děs′ə-lā′shən) *n.* the state of being empty, deserted, or forlorn; barrenness; loneliness
**desolación** *s.* sensación de vacío, abandono o aislamiento; aridez; soledad

**detestable** (dĭ-těs′tə-bəl) *adj.* worthy of scorn; hateful
**detestable** *adj.* despreciable y abominable; odioso

**devoid** (dĭ-void′) *adj.* completely lacking; empty
**desprovisto** *adj.* despojado; vacío

**dexterous** (děk′stər-əs) *adj.* skillful; clever
**diestro** *adj.* hábil; ingenioso

**diametrically** (dī′ə-mět′rĭ-klē) *adv.* in complete opposition
**diametralmente** *adv.* en completa oposición

**din** (dĭn) *n.* a jumble of loud noises
**estruendo** *s.* mezcla de ruidos fuertes

**dirge** (dûrj) *n.* a slow, mournful piece of music; a funeral hymn
**canto fúnebre** *s.* pieza musical lenta y dolida

**disarm** (dĭs-ärm′) *v.* to overcome or reduce the intensity of suspicion or hostility; to win the confidence of
**desarmar** *v.* vencer o reducir sospecha u hostilidad; ganarse la confianza

**discordant** (dĭ-skôr′dnt) *adj.* marked by a harsh mixture of sounds
**discordante** *adj.* caracterizado por una mezcla desagradable de sonidos

**discreetly** (dĭ-skrēt′lē) *adv.* in a manner showing good judgment; cautiously
**discretamente** *adv.* con buen juicio; cautelosamente

**disinherited** (dĭs′ĭn-hěr′ĭ-tĭd) *adj.* deprived of a rightful inheritance **disinherit** *v.*
**desheredado** *adj.* privado de su herencia **desheredar** *v.*

**disparagement** (dĭ-spăr′ĭj-mənt) *n.* belittlement
**desprecio** *s.* menosprecio

**disreputable** (dĭs-rěp′yə-tə-bəl) *adj.* having a bad reputation; not respectable
**desprestigiado** *adj.* que tiene mala reputación; que no es respetable

**dissuasion** (dĭ-swā′zhən) *n.* the persuading of someone not to perform an action
**disuasión** *s.* acto de persuadir o convencer de no hacer algo

**distasteful** (dĭs-tāst′fəl) *adj.* unpleasant; disagreeable
**desagradable** *adj.* fastidioso; de mal gusto

**doctrine** (dŏk′trĭn) *n.* a principle or rule taught by a religious, political or philosophic group
**doctrina** *s.* principio o regla de un grupo religioso, político o filosófico

# E

**edict** (ē′dĭkt′) *n.* an order put out by a person in authority
**edicto** *s.* orden de una persona de autoridad

**edifice** (ěd′ə-fĭs) *n.* building; structure
**edificio** *s.* construcción; estructura

**efficacy** (ĕf'ĭ-kə-sē) *n.* the power to produce a desired effect; effectiveness
**eficacia** *s.* capacidad para producir un efecto deseado; habilidad

**eloquent** (ĕl'ə-kwənt) *adj.* vividly expressive
**elocuente** *adj.* que se expresa de modo eficaz

**elusive** (ĭ-lōō'sĭv) *adj.* hard to catch or discover
**elusivo** *adj.* difícil de descubrir o de interpretar

**emaciated** (ĭ-mā'shē-ā-tĭd) *adj.* extremely thin, especially as a result of starvation **emaciate** *v.*
**emaciado** *adj.* en los huesos; muydelgado por pasar hambre **emaciarse** *v.*

**emancipation** (ĭ-măn'sə-pā'shən) *n.* a setting free from restraint or controls
**emancipación** *s.* liberación; independencia

**embody** (ĕm-bŏd'ē) *v.* to give a concrete shape to; personify or represent
**encarnar** *v.* dar forma concreta; personificar o representar

**emphatically** (ĕm-făt'ĭ-klē) *adv.* forcefully; strongly
**enfáticamente** *adv.* con énfasis; con fuerza

**encompass** (ĕn-kŭm'pəs) *v.* to surround; enclose
**abarcar** *v.* rodear; encerrar

**encumber** (ĕn-kŭm'bər) *v.* to burden
**estorbar** *v.* recargar; molestar

**enmity** (ĕn'mĭ-tē) *n.* the hatred between enemies; antagonism; hostility
**enemistad** *s.* odio entre enemigos; antagonismo; hostilidad

**entity** (ĕn'tĭ-tē) *n.* a being
**entidad** *s.* ente; ser

**equanimity** (ē'kwə-nĭm'ĭ-tē) *n.* the quality of being calm and even-tempered; composure
**ecuanimidad** *s.* capacidad de mantener la calma sin cambios de ánimo;compostura

**essence** (ĕs'əns) *n.* the crucial element or basis
**esencia** *s.* elemento crucial o básico

**ethereal** (ĭ-thîr'ē-əl) *adj.* not earthly; heavenly
**etéreo** *adj.* irreal; celestial

**exalt** (ĭg-zôlt') *v.* to glorify, praise, or honor
**exaltar** *v.* glorificar, alabar u honrar

**exaltation** (ĕg'zôl-tā'shən) *n.* the act of glorifying, praising, or honoring
**exaltación** *s.* acto de glorificar, alabar u honrar

**exasperated** (ĭg-zăs'pə-rā'tĭd) *adj.* made impatient or angry; annoyed **exasperate** *v.*
**exasperado** *adj.* impaciente o enojado; irritado **exasperar** *v.*

**exclusive** (ĭk-sklōō'sĭv) *adj.* tending to exclude others; select
**exclusivo** *adj.* que excluye a otros; selecto

**expendable** (ĭk-spĕn'də-bəl) *adj.* dispensable; unnecessary
**dispensable** *adj.* que sale sobrando; innecesario

**expenditure** (ĭk-spĕn'də-chər) *n.* an act of spending
**gasto** *s.* acto de gastar

**exposé** (ĕk'spō-zā') *n.* an account that reveals something negative to the public
**exposé** *s.* relato que revela algo negativo al público

# F

**fallible** (făl'ə-bəl) *adj.* capable of being wrong or mistaken
**falible** *adj.* capaz de equivocarse o de cometer errores

**fanatical** (fə-năt'ĭ-kəl) *adj.* extremely enthusiastic
**fanático** *adj.* extremadamente entusiasta

**fanfare** (făn'fâr') *n.* showy display or celebration
**fanfarria** *s.* demostración deslumbrante o celebración

**fathom** (făth'əm) *v.* to penetrate the meaning or understand the nature of
**descifrar** *v.* penetrar en el significado o entender la naturaleza de algo

**fidelity** (fĭ-dĕl'ĭ-tē) *n.* faithfulness to duties and obligations; devotion; loyalty
**fidelidad** *s.* responsabilidad hacia tareas y obligaciones; dedicación; lealtad

**flail** (flāl) *v.* to wave or swing vigorously; thrash
**sacudir** *v.* mover vigorosamente; zarandear

**flax** (flăks) *n.* a plant that is the source of the fibers used to make linen
**lino** *s.* planta que produce las fibras con que se fabrica la tela de lino

**flout** (flout) *v.* to show contempt for; to scorn
**mofarse** *v.* mostrar desprecio; humillar

**forlorn** (fər-lôrn′) *adj.* appearing sad or lonely because one has been left alone
**abandonado** *adj.* con aspecto triste o desolado por la soledad

**formidable** (fôr′mĭ-də-bəl) *adj.* inspiring awe, fear, or wonder
**formidable** *adj.* que inspira admiración, miedo o asombro

**forsaken** (fôr-sā′kən) *adj.* abandoned
**forsake** *v.*
**desamparado** *adj.* abandonado **desamparar** *v.*

**fortitude** (fôr′tĭ-tōōd′) *n.* strength of mind to endure misfortune or pain with courage
**fortaleza** *s.* fuerza emocional para soportar desgracias o dolor con valentía

**frantic** (frăn′tĭk) *adj.* emotionally out of control
**frenético** *adj.* sin control emocional

**furtive** (fûr′tĭv) *adj.* shifty; having a hidden motive or purpose
**furtivo** *adj.* solapado; que tiene un motivo o propósito oculto

**futile** (fyōōt′l) *adj.* serving no useful purpose
**fútil** *adj.* inútil; de poca importancia

# G

**gaunt** (gônt) *adj.* thin and bony
**flaco** *adj.* delgado y huesudo

**genially** (jēn′yə-lē) *adv.* in a friendly manner
**cordialmente** *adv.* de manera amable

**gnome** (nōm) *n.* an imaginary dwarflike creature that lives underground
**gnomo** *s.* enano imaginario que vive bajo la tierra

**grizzled** (grĭz′əld) *adj.* streaked with or partly gray
**grisáceo** *adj.* con tintes grises o parcialmente gris

# H

**haggard** (hăg′ərd) *adj.* appearing worn and exhausted
**ojeroso** *adj.* de aspecto cansado y exhausto

**haphazardly** (hăp-hăz′ərd-lē) *adv.* in an aimless or random manner
**fortuitamente** *adv.* de cualquier modo; al azar

**haughty** (hô′tē) *adj.* proud; arrogant
**altivo** *adj.* orgulloso; arrogante

**haunt** (hônt) *n.* a place visited frequently
**lugar predilecto** *s.* lugar visitado con frecuencia

**heretic** (hĕr′ĭ-tĭk) *n.* a person who holds controversial opinions that do not conform to the prevailing opinions of a society, religion, or group
**hereje** *s.* persona de opiniones polémicas que no están de acuerdo con las opiniones generales de una sociedad, religión o grupo

**hindrance** (hĭn′drəns) *n.* something that interferes with an activity; obstacle
**impedimento** *s.* algo que interfiere con una actividad; obstáculo

**hinterland** (hĭn′tər-lănd′) *n.* a region far from large cities
**interior** *s.* región alejada de las grandes ciudades

**homily** (hŏm′ə-lē) *n.* a tedious, moralizing lecture; sermon
**homilía** *s.* sermón aburrido

**hone** (hōn) *v.* to sharpen
**afilar** *v.* afinar

**hypocrisy** (hĭ-pŏk′rĭ-sē) *n.* a pretense of being what one is not; falsehood
**hipocresía** *s.* apariencia distinta de lo que se es; falsedad

# I

**illegible** (ĭ-lĕj′ə-bəl) *adj.* unreadable
**ilegible** *adj.* que no puede leerse

**impassive** (ĭm-păs′ĭv) *adj.* revealing no emotion; expressionless
**impasible** *adj.* que no muestra emociones; inexpresivo

**impatient** (ĭm-pā′shənt) *adj.* unable to tolerate irritation
**impaciente** *adj.* incapaz de tolerar algo irritante

**impeccably** (ĭm-pĕk′ə-blē) *adv.* flawlessly; perfectly
**impecablemente** *adv.* sin falla; perfectamente

**impenetrable** (ĭm-pĕn′ĭ-trə-bəl) *adj.* impossible to understand; incapable of being pierced
**impenetrable** *adj.* imposible de entender; que no puede ser perforado

**imperative** (ĭm-pĕr′ə-tĭv) *n.* urgent necessity or duty
**imperativo** *s.* necesidad u obligación urgente

**imperceptible** (ĭm′pər-sĕp′tə-bəl) *adj.* impossible to perceive; unnoticeable
**imperceptible** *adj.* que no se puede percibir; inadvertido

**impersonal** (ĭm-pûr′sə-nəl) *adj.* showing no emotion or signs of personality
**impersonal** *adj.* que no muestra emoción o indicios de personalidad

**impertinent** (ĭm-pûr′tn-ənt) *adj.* rude; insolent
**impertinente** *adj.* rudo; insolente

**implacable** (ĭm-plăk′ə-bəl) *adj.* impossible to appease or satisfy; relentless
**implacable** *adj.* imposible de apaciguar o satisfacer; despiadado

**imploring** (ĭm-plôr′ĭng) *adj.* begging; making an urgent appeal **implore** *v.*
**implorante** *adj.* suplicante; que hace un ruego urgente **implorar** *v.*

**imposing** (ĭm-pō′zĭng) *adj.* impressive
**imponente** *adj.* impresionante

**impotently** (ĭm′pə-tənt-lē) *adv.* helplessly; powerlessly
**impotentemente** *adv.* inútilmente; sin poder

**impudent** (ĭm′pyə-dənt) *adj.* bold and shameless
**impúdico** *adj.* atrevido y desvergonzado

**incessantly** (ĭn-sĕs′ənt-lē) *adv.* endlessly; constantly
**incesantemente** *adv.* sin final; constantemente

**incredulously** (ĭn-krĕj′ə-ləs-lē) *adv.* in a manner expressing skepticism or disbelief
**incrédulamente** *adv.* con escepticismo o desconfianza

**indelible** (ĭn-dĕl′ə-bəl) *adj.* impossible to remove or eliminate; permanent
**indeleble** *adj.* imposible de quitar o eliminar; permanente

**indifferently** (ĭn-dĭf′ər-ənt-lē) *adv.* in a way showing no particular interest or concern
**indiferentemente** *adv.* sin interés o preocupación

**indignation** (ĭn′dĭg-nā′shən) *n.* anger aroused by something unjust, mean, or unworthy
**indignación** *s.* ira causada por injusticia o crueldad

**indomitable** (ĭn-dŏm′ĭ-tə-bəl) *adj.* not easily discouraged, defeated, or subdued
**indomable** *adj.* que no es fácilmente desalentado, derrotado o sometido

**infatuated** (ĭn-făch′ōō-ā′tĭd) *adj.* completely carried away by foolish or shallow love or attraction **infatuate** *v.*
**encaprichado** *adj.* enamorado tonta o superficialmente **encapricharse** *v.*

**infernal** (ĭn-fûr′nəl) *adj.* fit to have come from hell; outrageous
**infernal** *adj.* como salido del infierno; escandaloso

**infinitesimally** (ĭn′fĭn-ĭ-tĕs′ə-mə-lē) *adv.* in steps so small as to be immeasurable or incalculable
**infinitesimalmente** *adv.* en tramos o pasos tan pequeños que no puede ser medido; incalculable

**ingenious** (ĭn-jēn′yəs) *adj.* creatively clever
**ingenioso** *adj.* ocurrente; de inteligencia creativa

**insolence** (ĭn′sə-ləns) *n.* bold rudeness; insulting behavior
**insolencia** *s.* rudeza descarada; conducta ofensiva

**insuperable** (ĭn-sōō'pər-ə-bəl) *adj.* impossible to overcome
**insuperable** *adj.* imposible de vencer

**intemperate** (ĭn-těm'pər-ĭt) *adj.* extreme
**inmoderado** *adj.* extremado; desmedido

**interminable** (ĭn-tûr'mə-nə-bəl) *adj.* endless or seemingly endless
**interminable** *adj.* que no tiene final o parece no tener fin

**irate** (ī-rāt') *adj.* extremely angry; enraged
**iracundo** *adj.* muy enojado; furioso

**irrelevant** (ĭ-rěl'ə-vənt) *adj.* not related to the matter at hand
**irrelevante** *adj.* que no tiene relación con el tema o la situación

**irreparably** (ĭ-rěp'ər-ə-blē) *adv.* in a way that is impossible to repair or correct
**irreparablemente** *adv.* de forma que es imposible de reparar o corregir

# L

**lamentation** (lăm'ən-tā'shən) *n.* an expression of grief
**lamentación** *s.* expresión de dolor

**languidly** (lăng'gwĭd-lē) *adv.* without vigor or energy; listlessly
**lánguidamente** *adv.* sin vigor o energía; débilmente

**languish** (lăng'gwĭsh) *v.* to suffer with longing
**languidecer** *v.* sufrir abatimiento o debilidad

**lethargy** (lěth'ər-jē) *n.* sluggishness; unconsciousness
**letargo** *s.* sopor; inconsciencia

**liberty** (lĭb'ər-tē) *n.* an action that is too bold or forward
**libertades** *s.* manera de tratar demasiado atrevida

**lithe** (līth) *adj.* limber; physically flexible
**ágil** *adj.* ligero; flexible

**lucid** (lōō'sĭd) *adj.* clear
**lúcido** *adj.* claro

**ludicrous** (lōō'dĭ-krəs) *adj.* laughably absurd; ridiculous
**risible** *adj.* tan absurdo que causa risa; ridículo

**luminous** (lōō'mə-nəs) *adj.* bright; brilliant
**luminoso** *adj.* resplandesciente; brillante

# M

**majestic** (mə-jěs'tĭk) *adj.* showing lofty dignity or nobility; stately
**majestuoso** *adj.* que muestra dignidad o nobleza; señorial

**maliciously** (mə-lĭsh'əs-lē) *adv.* with ill will; spitefully
**maliciosamente** *adv.* con mala voluntad; perversamente

**meager** (mē'gər) *adj.* lacking quantity, fullness, strength, or fertility; feeble; scanty
**magro** *adj.* de poca cantidad, fuerza o fertilidad; débil; escaso

**medium** (mē'dē-əm) *n.* a specific type of artistic technique or means of expression
**medio** *s.* tipo específico de técnica artística o de expresión

**mentor** (měn'tôr') *n.* a wise and trusted teacher
**mentor** *s.* maestro sabio y de confianza

**migrant** (mī'grənt) *adj.* moving from one area to settle in another
**migrante** *adj.* que se muda de un lugar para vivir en otro

**militant** (mĭl'ĭ-tənt) *adj.* showing a fighting spirit; aggressive
**militante** *adj.* de espíritu de lucha; agresivo

**morose** (mə-rōs') *adj.* gloomy; sullen
**moroso** *adj.* lento; triste

**mortify** (môr'tə-fī') *v.* to cause to feel shame or humiliation
**mortificar** *v.* causar vergüenza o humillación

**muse** (myōōz) *n.* guiding spirit or source of inspiration
**musa** *s.* espíritu que guía; fuente de inspiración

**myopia** (mī-ō′pē-ə) *n.* nearsightedness
**miopía** *s.* cortedad de vista

**mystic** (mĭs′tĭk) *adj.* showing supernatural powers; spiritual; inspiring mystery or wonder
**místico** *adj.* que muestra poderes sobrenaturales; espiritual; que inspira misterio o asombro

# N

**naiveté** (nä′ēv-tā′) *n.* lack of sophistication; childlike innocence
**ingenuidad** *s.* falta de sofisticación; inocencia infantil

**notorious** (nō-tôr′ē-əs) *adj.* having a widely known, usually very bad reputation; infamous
**notorio** *adj.* de mala reputación; tristemente célebre

**nuance** (nōō′äns′) *n.* subtle or slight variation
**matiz** *s.* variación sutil o ligera

# O

**omen** (ō′mən) *n.* a thing or event supposed to foretell good or evil; a sign
**presagio** *s.* cosa o suceso que supuestamente anuncia algo bueno o malo; señal

**oppress** (ə-prĕs′) *v.* to keep down by the cruel or unjust use of power or authority
**oprimir** *v.* someter mediante poder o autoridad cruel o injusta

**oppression** (ə-prĕsh′ən) *n.* unjust or cruel exercise of power or authority
**opresión** *s.* ejercicio injusto o cruel del poder o de la autoridad

**ordained** (ôr-dānd′) *adj.* established by authority or fate  **ordain** *v.*
**ordenado** *adj.* establecido por la autoridad o el destino  **ordenar** *v.*

**ostensibly** (ŏ-stĕn′sə-blē) *adv.* apparently; supposedly
**ostensiblemente** *adv.* visiblemente; aparentemente; supuestamente

# P

**pandemonium** (păn′də-mō′nē-əm) *n.* a wild uproar or noise
**pandemonio** *s.* alboroto o escándalo incontrolable

**panorama** (păn′ə-răm′ə) *n.* an unobstructed view of a wide area
**panorama** *s.* vista amplia de un lugar; vista sin obstáculos

**parry** (păr′ē) *v.* to turn aside or avoid (a question) with a clever reply
**esquivar** *v.* hacerse a un lado; evitar una pregunta con una respuesta ingeniosa

**patronize** (pā′trə-nīz) *v.* to behave in a manner that shows feelings of superiority
**condescender** *v.* actuar con superioridad

**pendant** (pĕn′dənt) *n.* a piece of jewelry made to hang from a necklace or bracelet
**dije** *s.* pieza de joyería hecha para colgar de un collar o pulsera

**penetrate** (pĕn′ĭ-trāt′) *v.* to enter, especially by forcing a way in
**penetrar** *v.* entrar, especialmente por medio de la fuerza

**penitence** (pĕn′ĭ-təns) *n.* expression of regret for sins or wrongdoing
**penitencia** *s.* expresión de arrepentimiento por pecados o males

**pensive** (pĕn′sĭv) *adj.* thoughtful in a wistful or sad way
**pensativo** *adj.* meditabundo; triste o preocupado

**perfunctorily** (pər-fŭngk′tə-rĭ-lē) *adv.* in a careless, uninterested way
**superficialmente** *adv.* de manera descuidada; sin interés

**perpetrate** (pûr′pĭ-trāt′) *v.* to commit
**perpetrar** *v.* cometer

**perpetuation** (pər-pĕch′ōō-ā′shən) *n.* a long-lasting continuation
**perpetuación** *s.* continuación a largo plazo

**persevere** (pûr´sə-vîr´) *v.* to persist in the face of difficulties
**perseverar** *v.* persistir; seguir adelante a pesar de dificultades

**perspicacity** (pûr´spĭ-kăs´ĭ-tē) *n.* keen perception or understanding
**perspicacia** *s.* percepción o comprensión aguda o acertada

**pertinacity** (pûr´tn-ăs´ĭ-tē) *n.* a persistent stubbornness
**pertinacia** *s.* terquedad; persistencia

**perverse** (pər-vûrs´) *adj.* willfully determined to go against what is expected or desired
**perverso** *adj.* que actúa con mala intención y se divierte haciendo daño

**petulant** (pĕch´ə-lənt) *adj.* showing unreasonable annoyance over little things
**petulante** *adj.* que se molesta en exceso por cosas pequeñas

**placidly** (plăs´ĭd-lē) *adv.* in an undisturbed manner; quietly; calmly
**plácidamente** *adv.* de manera tranquila; serenamente; apaciblemente

**platitude** (plăt´ĭ-tōōd´) *n.* a trite or unoriginal statement, especially one expressed as if it were original or significant; a cliché
**trivialidad** *s.* declaración superficial o poco original, especialmente cuando se expresa como si fuera original o importante; lugar común

**ponderous** (pŏn´dər-əs) *adj.* very heavy; bulky
**pesado** *adj.* corpulento; abultado

**potent** (pōt´nt) *adj.* powerful
**potente** *adj.* poderoso

**precariousness** (prĭ-kâr´ē-əs-nĭs) *n.* insecurity; uncertainty
**precariedad** *s.* inseguridad; incertidumbre

**predecessor** (prĕd´ĭ-sĕs´ər) *n.* someone who came before and has been succeeded or replaced by another
**predecesor** *s.* persona anterior o que ocupó un cargo y fue sucedida o reemplazada por otra

**preoccupied** (prē-ŏk´yə-pīd´) *adj.* absorbed in one's thoughts; distracted **preoccupy** *v.*
**preocupado** *adj.* absorto en sus pensamientos; distraído **preocupar** *v.*

**preside** (prĭ-zīd´) *v.* hold the chief position of authority or control
**presidir** *v.* ocupar la principal posición de autoridad o control

**prestige** (prĕ-stēzh´) *n.* high status; esteem
**prestigio** *s.* fama; reconocimiento

**presumption** (prĭ-zŭmp´shən) *n.* behavior or language that is boldly arrogant or offensive
**presunción** *s.* conducta o lenguaje arrogante u ofensivo

**pretense** (prē´tĕns´) *n.* a false outward appearance
**pretensión** *s.* fingimiento; apariencia falsa

**prevalent** (prĕv´ə-lənt) *adj.* widespread; common
**predominante** *adj.* ampliamente extendido; frecuente; común

**primeval** (prī-mē´vəl) *adj.* belonging to the earliest times or ages
**primitivo** *adj.* que pertenece a las épocas o edades más antiguas

**profusely** (prə-fyōōs´lē) *adv.* in great abundance
**profusamente** *adv.* con mucha abundancia

**prowess** (prou´ĭs) *n.* superior strength, courage, or daring, especially in battle
**valor** *s.* gran fuerza, valentía y arrojo, especialmente en la batalla

**proximity** (prŏk-sĭm´ĭ-tē) *n.* closeness
**proximidad** *s.* cercanía

**prudent** (prōōd´nt) *adj.* caracterized by good judgment
**prudente** *adj.* caracterizado por el buen juicio

**pummel** (pŭm´əl) *v.* to hit repeatedly; beat
**aporrear** *v.* golpear repetidamente; dar puñetazos

# Q

**quell** (kwĕl) *v.* to crush; put an end to; quiet
**sofocar** *v.* aplastar; poner fin; aquietar

# R

**radiant** (rā′dē-ənt) *adj.* bright; glowing
**radiante** *adj.* brillante; resplandeciente

**rank** (răngk) *adj.* growing abundantly or excessively
**frondoso** *adj.* que crece abundante o excesivamente

**raspingly** (răs′pĭng-lē) *adv.* in a harsh manner; gratingly
**ásperamente** *adv.* con tono áspero o irritante

**raucous** (rô′kəs) *adj.* loud and disorderly; boisterous
**estridente** *adj.* chillón y desordenado; escandaloso

**recite** (rĭ-sīt′) *v.* to say out loud something memorized
**recitar** *v.* decir en voz alta algo que ha sido memorizado

**recompense** (rĕk′əm-pĕns′) *n.* amends made, as for damage or loss; payment in return for something, such as a service
**recompensa** *s.* pago como premio o a cambio de un servicio

**rejuvenated** (rĭ-jōō′və-nā′tĭd) *adj.* made new or young again  **rejuvenate** *v*
**rejuvenecido** *adj.* que ha recuperado la juventud  **rejuvenecer** *v.*

**relapse** (rĭ-lăps′) *v.* to fall back into a former state
**recaer** *v.* regresar a un estado anterior

**reminiscence** (rĕm′ə-nĭs′əns) *n.* pleasant memory or recollection
**reminiscencia** *s.* recuerdo o evocación placentera

**remorse** (rĭ-môrs′) *n.* a deep sense of guilt over a wrong one has done
**remordimiento** *s.* profundo sentimiento de culpa por un mal cometido

**renounce** (rĭ-nouns′) *v.* to give up, especially as a matter of principle
**renunciar** *v.* dejar, especialmente cuando se hace por principios

**reprisal** (rĭ-prī′zəl) *n.* retaliation in the form of harm or injury similar to that received; revenge
**revancha** *s.* represalia con daños o heridas similares a los recibidos; venganza

**resignation** (rĕz′ĭg-nā′shən) *n.* the act of giving up; submission
**renuncia** *s.* acto de dejar; sumisión

**resilient** (rĭ-zĭl′yənt) *adj.* capable of bouncing or springing back to an original shape after being stretched, bent, or compressed
**elástico** *adj.* capaz de regresar a su estado o forma original después de haber sido estirado, doblado o comprimido

**resolution** (rĕz′ə-lōō′shən) *n.* determination
**resolución** *s.* determinación

**respite** (rĕs′pĭt) *n.* a temporary stop; a brief period of rest or relief from activity
**respiro** *s.* tregua; alto temporal; período breve de descanso o alivio

**reticence** (rĕt′ĭ-səns) *n.* the state or quality of being reserved and keeping one's thoughts to oneself
**reticencia** *s.* reserva; prudencia y discreción

**reverently** (rĕv′ər-ənt-lē) *adv.* with great respect
**reverentemente** *adv.* con gran respeto

**revoke** (rĭ-vōk′) *v.* to cancel or withdraw
**revocar** *v.* cancelar o retirar

**ruefully** (rōō′fə-lē) *adv.* with regret
**tristemente** *adv.* con pena o dolor

# S

**sallow** (săl′ō) *adj.* of a sickly, yellowish color or complexion
**cetrino** *adj.* amarillento y enfermizo

**sated** (sā′tĭd) *adj.* satisfied fully  **sate** *v.*
**saciado** *adj.* satisfecho por completo  **satisfacer** *v.*

**saucy** (sô′sē) *adj.* disrespectful in a bold or high-spirited way; pert
**fresco** *adj.* descarado; desfachatado; impertinente

**sedate** (sǐ-dāt') *adj.* serenely deliberate, composed, and dignified
**sereno** *adj.* deliberadamente tranquilo, compuesto y digno

**sever** (sěv'ər) *v.* to cut or break off
**cortar** *v.* separar o dividir; romper

**sheathed** (shēthd) *adj.* enclosed in a protective covering **sheathe** *v.*
**enfundado** *adj.* envuelto en una cubierta protectora **enfundar** *v.*

**shirk** (shûrk) *v.* to neglect or avoid
**rehuir** *v.* ignorar o evitar

**sidle** (sīd'l) *v.* to move sideways, especially in a shy or sneaky way
**escurrirse** *v.* moverse de lado con sigilo

**smolder** (smōl'dər) *v.* to burn without flame; to exist in a concealed form, ready to break out
**arder en rescoldo** *v.* arder sin llama; estar latente o a la espera

**sniveling** (snǐv'əl-ǐng) *adj.* whining
**llorón** *adj.* que lloriquea o gimotea

**sodden** (sŏd'n) *adj.* thoroughly wet; soaked
**empapado** *adj.* totalmente mojado; bañado

**spontaneous** (spŏn-tā'nē-əs) *adj.* occurring or acting without a plan; impulsive
**espontáneo** *adj.* que ocurre o actúa sin un plan; impulsivo

**squalor** (skwŏl'ər) *n.* a filthy and wretched condition
**escualidez** *s.* miseria y suciedad

**stature** (stăch'ər) *n.* a person's height
**estatura** *s.* altura de una persona

**stealthily** (stěl'thǐ-lē) *adv.* in a quiet, secretive way
**furtivamente** *adv.* de manera callada y secreta

**stipulate** (stǐp'yə-lāt') *v.* to state as a condition; specify
**estipular** *v.* poner como condición; especificar

**stupefied** (stōō'pə-fīd') *adj.* dazed; stunned
**estupefacto** *adj.* asombrado; atónito

**stupor** (stōō'pər) *n.* a state of mental numbness, as from shock
**estupor** *s.* pasmo; profundo asombro

**subliminal** (sŭb-lǐm'ə-nəl) *adj.* below the threshold of conscious perception; subconscious
**subliminal** *adj.* por debajo del umbral de la percepción consciente; subconsciente

**sultry** (sŭl'trē) *adj.* warm and humid
**bochornoso** *adj.* caliente y húmedo

**supplicating** (sŭp'lǐ-kāt'ǐng) *adj.* humbly or sincerely asking, begging, or praying **supplicate** *v.*
**suplicante** *adj.* que pide, ruega o reza con humildad y sinceridad **suplicar** *v.*

**supposition** (sŭp'ə-zǐsh'ən) *n.* an opinion or assumption
**suposición** *s.* opinión o creencia

**symmetry** (sǐm'ǐ-trē) *n.* a similarity between the two sides of something; balance
**simetría** *s.* similitud entre los dos lados de algo; equilibrio

**synchronizing** (sǐng'krə-nī'zǐng) *n.* matching the timing of **synchronize** *v.*
**sincronización** *s.* operación que se realiza para que dos cosas ocurran al mismo tiempo **sincronizar** *v.*

# T

**tact** (tăkt) *n.* the sensitivity to say and do what is appropriate when dealing with other people
**tacto** *s.* sensibilidad para tratar a otras personas con delicadeza

**taint** (tānt) *n.* a trace of something that harms, spoils, or corrupts
**mancha** *s.* huella de algo que daña, arruina o corrompe

**tempering** (těm'pə-rǐng) *n.* modifying or adjusting **temper** *v.*
**modificación** *s.* ajuste **modificar** *v.*

**tenacity** (tə-năs'ǐ-tē) *n.* the state or quality of holding persistently to something; firm determination
**tenacidad** *s.* tesón y constancia; obstinación

**tentatively** (těn'tə-tǐv-lē) *adv.* hesitantly; uncertainly
**tentativamente** *adv.* dudosamente; inciertamente

**terse** (tûrs) *adj.* brief; concise
**seco** *adj.* cortante; breve; conciso

**thatched** (thăcht) *adj.* covered with plant stalks or leaves **thatch** *v.*
**techado de paja** *adj.* cubierto con ramas u hojas **techar con paja** *v.*

**theological** (thē'ə-lŏj'ĭ-kəl) *adj.* having to do with the study of God and religion
**teológico** *adj.* relacionado con el estudio de Dios y la religión

**tirade** (tī'rād') *n.* a long, angry speech
**perorata** *s.* discurso largo y con ira

**transcend** (trăn-sĕnd') *v.* to move above and beyond; to be greater than expected or desired
**trascender** *v.* rebasar; ser mejor de lo esperado o deseado

**transgress** (trăns-grĕs') *v.* to violate or break a law, command, or moral code
**transgredir** *v.* violar una ley, una orden o un código moral

**traverse** (trə-vûrs') *v.* to travel or pass across, over, or through
**atravesar** *v.* viajar de un lado a otro de un lugar o de una cosa

**treacherous** (trĕch'ər-əs) *adj.* dangerous
**peligroso** *adj.* inseguro; traicionero

**trepidation** (trĕp'ĭ-dā'shən) *n.* a state of alarm or dread; apprehension; anxiety
**trepidación** *s.* estado de alarma o miedo; aprensión; ansiedad

**tribulation** (trĭb'yə-lā'shən) *n.* great distress or suffering
**tribulación** *s.* gran sufrimiento o preocupación

# U

**unassuming** (ŭn'ə-sōō'mĭng) *adj.* not pretentious; modest
**modesto** *adj.* sin pretensiones; humilde

**unavailing** (ŭn'ə-vā'lĭng) *adj.* useless; ineffective
**inservible** *adj.* inútil; ineficaz

**uncanny** (ŭn-kăn'ē) *adj.* strange; eerie; weird
**extraordinario** *adj.* extraño; misterioso; raro

**undulate** (ŭn'jə-lāt') *v.* to move in waves or in a smooth, wavelike motion
**ondular** *v.* mover en forma de ondas; mover suavemente como las olas

**unfathomable** (ŭn-făth'ə-mə-bəl) *adj.* too mysterious to be understood
**insondable** *adj.* inexplicable; misterioso

**unnervingly** (ŭn-nûrv'ĭng-lē) *adv.* in a way that causes someone to become nervous or upset; disturbingly
**desconcertantemente** *adv.* de manera que causa nerviosismo o alteración; inquietantemente

# V

**vacillating** (văs'ə-lāt'ĭng) *adj.* swinging indecisively from one course of action or opinion to another **vacillate** *v.*
**vacilante** *adj.* indeciso; que cambia de parecer **vacilar** *v.*

**vagrant** (vā'grənt) *adj.* wandering
**vagabundo** *adj.* que va de un lado al otro sin rumbo fijo

**vague** (vāg) *adj.* unclear; hazy
**vago** *adj.* confuso; impreciso

**venerable** (vĕn'ər-ə-bəl) *adj.* worthy of respect by virtue of age or dignity
**venerable** *adj.* que merece respeto por su edad o dignidad

**versatility** (vûr'sə-tĭl'ĭ-tē) *n.* an ability to do many things well
**versatilidad** *s.* capacidad para hacer muchas cosas bien

**vibrant** (vī'brənt) *adj.* full of energy and activity
**vibrante** *adj.* lleno de energía y actividad

**vigil** (vĭj'əl) *n.* a watch kept by a person, especially during normal sleeping hours or to show devotion
**vigilia** *s.* vela; desvelo; acción de mantenerse despierto de noche o como señal de devoción

**vigilance** (vĭj'ə-ləns) *n.* alert attention; watchfulness
**vigilancia** *s.* atención alerta; cuidado

**vindicate** (vĭn′dĭ-kāt′) *v.* to clear of blame or suspicion
**vindicar** *v.* justificar; retirar culpa o sospecha

**visceral** (vĭs′ər-əl) *adj.* instinctive or emotional rather than intellectual
**visceral** *adj.* instintivo; más emocional que intelectual

**vivacious** (vĭ-vā′shəs) *adj.* lively; spirited
**vivaz** *adj.* animado; vital; lleno de vida

**void** (void) *n.* a feeling of loss; emptiness
**desolación** *s.* sentimiento de pérdida; vacío

**voluble** (vŏl′yə-bəl) *adj.* in or with a long flow of words; talkative
**locuaz** *adj.* hablador; charlatán

**voracity** (vô-răs′ĭ-tē) *n.* greed for food; ravenousness
**voracidad** *s.* apetito ansioso; hambre intensa

**vulnerable** (vŭl′nər-ə-bəl) a*dj.* unprotected and easily hurt; sensitive
**vulnerable** *adj.* desprotegido y fácil de lastimar; delicado

# W

**wince** (wĭns) *v.* to shrink or flinch involuntarily, especially in pain
**estremecerse** *v.* encogerse o contraerse involuntariamente por dolor

**wistful** (wĭst′fəl) *adj.* full of wishful longing; sad
**melancólico** *adj.* lleno de nostalgia; triste

**withered** (wĭth′ərd) *adj.* shriveled or shrunken, as if from lack of water or food
**marchito** *adj.* seco encogido por falta de agua o de comida

## Pronunciation Key

| Symbol | Examples | Symbol | Examples | Symbol | Examples |
|---|---|---|---|---|---|
| ă | at, gas | m | man, seem | v | van, save |
| ā | ape, day | n | night, mitten | w | web, twice |
| ä | father, barn | ng | sing, anger | y | yard, lawyer |
| âr | fair, dare | ŏ | odd, not | z | zoo, reason |
| b | bell, table | ō | open, road, grow | zh | treasure, garage |
| ch | chin, lunch | ô | awful, bought, horse | ə | awake, even, pencil, pilot, focus |
| d | dig, bored | oi | coin, boy | | |
| ĕ | egg, ten | ŏŏ | look, full | ər | perform, letter |
| ē | evil, see, meal | ōō | root, glue, through | | |
| f | fall, laugh, phrase | ou | out, cow | | **Sounds in Foreign Words** |
| g | gold, big | p | pig, cap | KH | *German* ich, auch; *Scottish* loch |
| h | hit, inhale | r | rose, star | | |
| hw | white, everywhere | s | sit, face | N | *French* entre, bon, fin |
| ĭ | inch, fit | sh | she, mash | œ | *French* feu, cœur; *German* schön |
| ī | idle, my, tried | t | tap, hopped | | |
| îr | dear, here | th | thing, with | ü | *French* utile, rue; *German* grün |
| j | jar, gem, badge | th | then, other | | |
| k | keep, cat, luck | ŭ | up, nut | | |
| l | load, rattle | ûr | fur, earn, bird, worm | | |

**Stress Marks**

′ This mark indicates that the preceding syllable receives the primary stress. For example, in the word *language,* the first syllable is stressed: lăng′gwĭj.

′ This mark is used only in words in which more than one syllable is stressed. It indicates that the preceding syllable is stressed, but somewhat more weakly than the syllable receiving the primary stress. In the word *literature,* for example, the first syllable receives the primary stress, and the last syllable receives a weaker stress: lĭt′ər-ə-chŏŏr′.

Adapted from *The American Heritage Dictionary of the English Language, Third Edition;* Copyright © 1992 by Houghton Mifflin Company. Used with the permission of Houghton Mifflin Company.

# Index of Fine Art

# Index of Skills

## Literary Concepts

Act, 285, 1218
Alliteration, 225, 841, 853, 1218
Allusion, 1061, 1218
Analogy, 1218. *See also* Metaphor.
Antagonist, 556, 794, 1019, 1218
Aphorism, 417
Aside, 284, 687, 735, 1218
Assonance, 225, 841, 853, 1219
Audience, 484, 491, 941, 945, 1219
Author's perspective, 452–453, 455, 460, 522, 527, 552, 1219. *See also* Author's perspective *in* Reading and Critical Thinking Skills.
    in fiction, 453
    in nonfiction, 452, 527
Author's purpose, 455, 945, 1219
Autobiographical essay, 104, 112, 121, 170, 357, 455, 522
Autobiography, 104, 112, 121, 133, 613, 1219
    diaries, 104
    essay, 104, 112, 121, 357, 455, 522
    journals, 104
    letters, 104, 120, 410, 941
Ballad, 1220
Bias, 453, 455, 522, 799. *See also* Author's perspective *and* Credibility *in* Reading and Critical Thinking Skills.
Biography, 104, 133, 1220
Blank verse, 686, 689, 713, 1220
Catastrophe, 794, 1019
Character, 17, 30, 39, 82, 101, 145, 148, 156, 1220. *See also* Characterization.
    in drama, 284, 300
    dynamic, 17, 30, 39, 284, 1221
    evaluating, 148, 156
    in fiction, 17, 30, 39, 82, 101, 145, 148, 156
    flat, 284
    main, 17, 284, 664, 1220
    minor, 17, 284, 1220
    round, 284
    static, 17, 30, 39, 284, 1221
Characterization, 17, 39, 239, 252, 326, 468, 479, 664, 983, 1221. *See also* Character.
Choragus, 1019, 1061
Chorus, 1019, 1061, 1221
Classical drama, 1019, 1061
Climax, 17, 53, 384, 386, 394, 1221, 1230. *See also* Plot.
Comedy, 287, 300, 1221
Comic relief, 1221
Conflict, 17, 42, 167, 188, 285, 316, 326, 394, 503, 513, 1221. *See also* Plot.
    cultural, 188, 194
    external, 285, 316, 326
    internal, 285, 316, 326, 397, 407
    understanding, 42, 167
Connotation and denotation, 494, 516, 520, 1222
Consonance, 225, 841, 853, 1222
Couplet, 233. *See also* Sonnet.
Cultural context, 452, 453

Cultural hero, 1226
Denouement, 17, 384. *See also* Falling action.
Description, 95, 101, 417, 1099, 1222
Dialect, 252, 1222
Dialogue, 284, 300, 460, 871, 890, 962, 964, 974, 995, 1223
Diary, 104, 1223
Diction, 462, 491, 516, 520, 645, 649, 906, 935, 961, 1099, 1223
Drama, 284, 300, 686, 1019, 1223
    act, 285, 1218
    antagonist in, 284
    asides in, 284, 687, 735, 1218
    catastrophe in, 794
    characters in, 284, 300
    chorus in, 1019, 1221
    classical, 1019, 1061
    conflict in, 17, 42, 167, 188, 285, 316, 326, 394, 503, 513
    dialogue in, 284, 300
    farce, 287, 300
    monologue in, 284
    plot in, 285
    props, 285, 1231
    protagonist in, 284, 1231
    scenes in, 285, 1233
    setting and, 285
    Shakespearean, 686
    soliloquy, 284, 687, 1234
    stage directions in, 285, 300
    tragedy, 686, 794, 1019
    tragic flaw and, 686, 1019
    tragic hero in, 686, 1019
Dramatic monologue, 1223
Dynamic character, 17, 30, 39, 284, 1221
Epic, 1224
Essay, 105, 107, 110, 112, 121, 170, 484, 522, 857, 977, 1224
    expository, 107, 110, 170
    personal, 105, 112, 121, 170, 484, 522, 857, 977
Exposition, 17, 53, 383, 386, 394, 1230
Expository essay, 107, 110
Falling action, 17, 53, 384, 386, 394, 503, 1224, 1230. *See also* Plot.
Fantasy, 39, 1224
Farce, 287, 300, 1225
Fiction, 17, 453, 1225
Figurative language, 226, 255, 260, 346, 349, 351, 354, 419, 735, 819, 820, 838, 841, 906, 1225
Figures of speech, 260, 351, 820, 838, 841
    metaphor, 226, 260, 346, 349, 820, 838, 841, 1228
    personification, 351, 820, 1230
    simile, 226, 260, 346, 349, 820, 838, 841, 1234
Flashback, 239, 397, 664, 675, 1225
Foil, 1225
Foreshadowing, 71, 82, 311, 1225
Foot, 236. *See also* Meter.
Form, 225, 432, 433, 1226. *See also* Poetry.

Point of view, 18, 53, 93, 329, 343, 623, 626, 652, 660, 833, 890, 1231
   first-person, 18, 53, 343, 468, 575, 623, 626, 660, 1083, 1086, 1231
   limited, 18, 623, 624, 660, 890, 1231
   naive narrator, 329
   omniscient, 18, 623, 624, 660, 833, 1231
   third-person, 18, 93, 623, 624, 652, 660, 833, 890, 1231
   unreliable narrator, 623
Props, 285, 1231
Protagonist, 556, 794, 1019, 1231
Quatrain, 233, 1232
Realism, 868–869, 1232
Repetition, 137, 351, 354, 687, 759, 995, 1232
   in poetry, 351, 354
Resolution, 503, 513. *See also* Falling action.
Rhetorical devices, 687, 759. *See also* Parallelism, Repetition, *and* Rhetorical questions.
   Rhetorical questions, 687, 759
Rhyme scheme, 225, 233, 1232
Rhythm, 236, 1233
Rising action, 17, 53, 384, 386, 394, 1233. *See also* Plot.
Romance, 1016, 1064, 1080, 1233
Sarcasm, 543. *See also* Irony.
Satire, 1233
Scene, 285, 1233
Scenery, 285
Science fiction, 27, 39, 82, 1233
Sentence length and structure, 460, 961, 995
Setting, 18, 86, 93, 145, 196, 209, 285, 303, 311, 417, 660, 1233
   cultural, 196, 209, 329, 439, 442
   in drama, 285, 300
   historical, 311
Shakespearean drama, 686–687
   aside, 687, 735
   blank verse, 686, 689
   dramatic irony, 687, 777
   rhetorical devices, 687, 759
   soliloquy, 687, 735, 1234
   tragedy and tragic hero, 686
Short story, 1234
Simile, 226, 260, 346, 349, 354, 796, 820, 838, 841, 1234
Skene, 1019
Social criticism, 922, 933
   direct commentary, 933
   indirect commentary, 933
Soliloquy, 284, 687, 735, 1234
Sonnet, 233, 236, 1234
   Shakespearean, 233, 1234
   sonnet sequences, 1234
Sound devices in poetry, 225. See also Alliteration; Assonance; Consonance; Onomatopoeia; Rhyme.
Speaker, in poetry, 231, 645, 1234
Stage directions, 285, 1235
Stanzas, 225, 433, 1235
Static character, 17, 30, 39, 284, 1221. *See also* Character.
Stereotypes, 287, 300, 1235
Structure, 233, 236, 581, 1235. *See also* Form.

Style, 102, 460, 528, 600, 946, 961–962, 983, 995, 1090, 1099, 1235. *See also* Dialogue; Diction; Figurative language; Imagery; Sentence length and structure; Syntax; Tone.
Surprise ending, 1235
Surrealism, 903
Suspense, 311, 384, 559, 575, 1235
Symbols, 439, 442, 819, 822, 833, 1236
   cultural, 439, 442, 819
   literary, 439, 442, 819
Synonyms, 494
Syntax, 462, 516, 645, 649, 995
Tall tale, 1236
Theme, 18, 20, 145–146, 148, 156, 159, 167, 170, 178, 794, 954, 1236
Title, 1236
Tone, 452, 455, 460, 645, 649, 893, 901, 941, 945, 962, 977, 981, 1099, 1236
Tragedy, 686, 794, 1019, 1237
Tragic flaw, 686, 1019, 1226
Tragic hero, 686, 794, 1019, 1061, 1226
Understatement, 939, 1237
Voice, 515, 1237
Word choice. *See* Diction.

# Reading and Critical Thinking Skills

Advertising, evaluating, 916–917
Analogies. *See also* Analogies *under* Vocabulary Skills.
   formulating, 263
   reading and understanding, 263, 1128
Analyzing, 107, 124, 209, 262, 311, 316, 410, 798–799, 838, 841, 870, 893, 901, 1083, 1086
Arguments, evaluating, 590, 1176
Author's attitude. *See* Tone, recognizing.
Author's perspective, 452–453, 455, 460, 522, 527, 1219
Author's purpose (motivation),
   evaluating, 454, 460
   identifying, 454, 455, 460, 922, 933, 945, 1121
Author's style. *See* Style, analyzing.
Bias, identifying, 522, 798–799, 836
Brainstorming, 351, 542, 682
Cause and effect, 107, 124, 133, 385, 386, 392, 394, 411, 417, 1134, 1138
Characterization, 17, 39, 239, 252, 468, 479, 664, 983, 1221
Characters, 19
   analyzing, 19, 1083, 1086
   classifying, 39, 1083, 1086
   evaluating, 664, 675
   identifying motive, 30, 39, 407
Chronological order, 42, 53, 239, 252, 314–315, 385, 397, 407, 662, 1134, 1136
Clarifying, 7–13, 106, 119, 200, 204, 392, 870, 898, 963, 964, 966, 968, 972, 974, 983, 995, 1120, 1122
Classifying and categorizing
   chart, 20, 39, 42, 71, 82, 86, 95, 107, 121, 133, 148, 159, 167, 170, 188, 209, 231, 252, 255, 286, 300, 316, 346, 351, 386, 484, 503, 513, 516, 537, 600, 626, 664, 689, 735, 777, 806, 837, 838, 871, 893, 922, 935, 964, 977, 983, 1017, 1064, 1090, 1099
   graph, 182, 451, 575, 822, 1131

## Inquiry and Research

## Speaking and Listening

## Viewing and Representing

906, 933, 995, 1080

Creative reader response
    cartoon strip, 395, 1087
    comic book, 103
    dance, 582
    demonstration, 1100
    diorama, 94
    fashion design, 408
    historical exhibit, 134
    illustrations, 40, 83, 179, 576, 650, 940, 975, 1081
    images of nature, 847
    journey map, 54
    map, 179
    mask, 1062
    painting, 312, 327
    portrait, 168, 467
    poster, 344
    scrapbook, 168, 842
    set building, 253
    set design, 301
    sketch, 350, 891
    story quilt, 514, 529
    storyboard, 103, 438, 480, 557
    three-dimensional art, 514, 582, 643, 795
    travel advertisement, 122

Evaluating visual messages, 1179

Images, interpreting, 1178–1180

LaserLinks, 30, 54, 70, 83, 124, 148, 157, 159, 188, 195, 196, 238, 273, 287, 311, 329, 433, 468, 484, 502, 503, 546, 589, 593, 644, 652, 664, 677, 822, 848, 893, 907, 921, 964, 976, 977, 983, 1018, 1063, 1082, 1090, 1101, 1108

Multimedia presentations, 461, 529, 1010–1012, 1180

Technology. *See also* Electronic resources *under* Inquiry and Research.
    CD-ROMs, 1164, 1168, 1171
    creating visuals with, 111, 157, 461, 514, 982, 1008–1012, 1100
    e-mail, 1168, 1171
    Internet, 40, 83, 103, 142, 179, 216, 253, 281, 301, 344, 368, 410, 418, 449, 461, 492, 502, 529, 534, 582, 620, 804, 854, 865, 891, 921, 940, 947, 952, 975, 1012, 1081, 1112
    multimedia programs, 461, 529, 1010–1012
    World Wide Web, 940, 1168, 1172. *See also* Internet.

Videos, 54, 66, 363, 493, 601, 681, 860, 892, 1081
    literature in performance, 28, 83, 614, 795, 842, 1062

View and Compare
    Antony as a military leader, 779
    Antony's response to Caesar's death, 752
    Brutus and the conspirators, 719
    Brutus, 762
    Julius Caesar, 712
    Portia and Brutus, 734

Visual literacy, 1178–1179

Visuals, using, 1178–1179

# Assessment

Assessment Practice
    grammar, 143, 217, 282, 369, 450, 535, 621, 805, 866, 953, 1013, 1113
    revising and editing, 143, 217, 282, 369, 450, 535, 621, 805, 866, 953, 1013, 1113
    vocabulary, 83, 134, 168, 195, 210, 253, 312, 480, 492, 676, 891, 996, 1081

Criteria, using to analyze, evaluate, and critique, 1172–1173, 1175–1176
    explanatory writing, 1155, 1157–1160
    images, 1153, 1178–1179
    informative message, 1163–1170
    literary performance, 232, 284, 355, 395, 492, 661, 676, 687, 795, 834, 907, 934, 947, 1087
    oral presentation, 1176, 1178
    persuasive message, 1161–1162

Goals, setting, 219, 371, 537, 807, 955, 1115

Literary concepts, identifying and analyzing
    author's perspective, 452–453, 460, 537, 1219
    character development, 17, 39, 145, 148, 252, 468, 479, 1220–1221
    dialogue, 284, 300, 460, 871, 890, 962, 964, 974, 995, 1223
    figurative language, 371
    imagery, 955, 1178, 1180
    irony, 807
    meter, 236, 686, 1228
    mood, 82, 311, 1228
    myth and legend, 1015–1016, 1115
    plot, 17, 42, 53, 159, 167, 285, 383–384, 537, 1230
    poetry, 255, 955, 1231
        sonnet, 371
    point of view, 18, 53, 93, 329, 343, 623, 626, 652, 660, 807, 833, 890, 1231
    rhyme, 236, 1233
    style, 102, 460, 528, 600, 946, 961–962, 1090, 1115, 1235
    theme, 18, 20, 145–146, 156, 170, 178, 219, 794
    tone, 452, 455, 460, 645, 893, 901, 941, 1099, 1236

Portfolio, 219, 371, 537, 807, 955, 1115

Reading and writing strategies for assessment
    answering essay questions, 814
    answering multiple-choice questions, 813
    reading a test selection, 810–812
    responding to short-answer questions, 814
    revising, editing, and proofreading, 815

Reflecting and assessing
    connecting to history, 124, 578, 593, 600, 602, 613, 622
    insight into human nature, 370, 536, 806, 955, 1114
    literary terms, understanding of, 219, 371, 536, 807, 955, 1115
    responses to literature, 370

# Index of Titles and Authors

Page numbers that appear in italics refer to biographical information.

# Acknowledgments *(continued)*

**Unit One**

**Don Congdon Associates:** "A Sound of Thunder" by Ray Bradbury. First published in *Collier's,* 28 June 1952. Copyright © 1952 by Crowell-Collier Publishing, renewed 1980 by Ray Bradbury. Reprinted by permission of Don Congdon Associates, Inc.

Excerpt from "An Interview with Ray Bradbury" by Frank Filosa, from *On Being a Writer* (Cincinnati: Writer's Digest Books, 1989). Copyright © 1989 by Writer's Digest Books. Reprinted by permission of Don Congdon Associates, Inc.

"There Will Come Soft Rains" by Ray Bradbury. First Published in *Collier's,* 6 May 1950. Copyright © 1950 by Crowell-Collier Publishing, renewed 1977 by Ray Bradbury. Reprinted by permission of Don Congdon Associates, Inc.

"The Pedestrian" by Ray Bradbury. First published in *The Reporter,* 7 August 1951. Copyright © 1951 by The Fortnightly Publishing Company, renewed 1979 by Ray Bradbury. Reprinted by permission of Don Congdon Associates, Inc.

**Ralph M. Vicinanza, Ltd.:** "Dial Versus Digital," from *The Dangers of Intelligence and Other Scientific Essays* by Isaac Asimov. Copyright © 1986 by Isaac Asimov. Published by permission of the Estate of Isaac Asimov, c/o Ralph M. Vicinanza, Ltd.

**Tilbury House:** "Once More to the Lake," from *One Man's Meat* by E. B. White. Text copyright © 1941 by E. B. White, renewed 1998 by Joel White. Reprinted by permission of Tilbury House, Publishers, Gardiner, Maine.

**E. B. White Estate:** Excerpt from "A Letter from E. B. White" by E. B. White (*The Norton Sampler,* 1985). Reprinted by permission of Allene M. White on behalf of the E. B. White Estate.

**Henry Holt & Company:** "Montgomery Boycott," from *My Life with Martin Luther King, Jr.* (rev. ed.) by Coretta Scott King. Copyright © 1969, 1993 by Coretta Scott King. Reprinted by permission of Henry Holt & Company, Inc.

**University of Georgia Press:** "Sit-Ins," from *This Is My Century: New and Collected Poems* by Margaret Walker Alexander. Copyright © 1989 by Margaret Walker Alexander. Reprinted by permission of the University of Georgia Press.

**Simon & Schuster and Jonathan Clowes Ltd.:** "No Witchcraft for Sale," from *African Stories* by Doris Lessing. Copyright © 1951, 1953, 1954, 1957, 1958, 1962, 1963, 1964, 1965, 1972, 1981 by Doris Lessing. Reprinted with the permission of Simon & Schuster and Jonathan Clowes Ltd., London, on behalf of Doris Lessing.

**Farrar, Straus & Giroux:** "The Son from America," from *A Crown of Feathers and Other Stories* by Isaac Bashevis Singer. Copyright © 1973 by Isaac Bashevis Singer. Reprinted by permission of Farrar, Straus & Giroux, Inc.

**W. W. Norton & Company:** "Grudnow," from *The Imperfect Paradise* by Linda Pastan. Copyright © 1988 by Linda Pastan. Reprinted by permission of W. W. Norton & Company, Inc.

**Phoebe Larmore Literary Agency:** "Through the One-Way Mirror" by Margaret Atwood, *The Nation,* 22 March 1986. Reprinted by permission of Phoebe Larmore Literary Agency on behalf of the author.

**University of New Mexico Press:** "The Border: A Glare of Truth," from *Nepantla: Essays from the Land in the Middle* by Pat Mora. Copyright © 1993 by University of New Mexico Press. Reprinted by permission of the University of New Mexico Press.

**U.S. News & World Report:** Excerpt from "To Make a Nation: How Immigrants Are Changing America" by Penny Loeb, Dorian Friedman, and Mary C. Lord, with Dan

McGraw and Kukula Glastris, *U.S. News & World Report,* 4 October 1993. Copyright © October 4, 1993, U.S. News & World Report. Reprinted by permission.

**Sandra Dijkstra Literary Agency:** "Fish Cheeks" by Amy Tan. First appeared in the *Seventeen Magazine.* Copyright © 1987 by Amy Tan. Reprinted by permission of Amy Tan and the Sandra Dijkstra Literary Agency.

**Doubleday and Harold Ober Associates:** "Marriage Is a Private Affair," from *Girls at War and Other Stories* by Chinua Achebe. Copyright © 1972, 1973 by Chinua Achebe. Used by permission of Doubleday, a division of Bantam Doubleday Dell Publishing Group, Inc., and Harold Ober Associates Incorporated.

**Chinese Literature Press:** "Love Must Not Be Forgotten" by Zhang Jie, from *Seven Contemporary Chinese Women Writers* (Panda Books, 1982). Published by Chinese Literature Press, Beijing, China. Copyright © 1983 by Chinese Literature Press. Reprinted by permission of Chinese Literature Press.

**Katie Eskra:** Adaptation of "A Momentary Sadness" by Katie Eskra. Copyright © 1995 by Katie Eskra. Reprinted by permission of the author.

**Unit Two**

**Viking Penguin:** "Piano" by D. H. Lawrence, from *The Complete Poems of D. H. Lawrence,* edited by V. de Sola Pinto and F. W. Roberts. Copyright © 1964, 1971 by Angelo Ravagli and C. M. Weekley, Executors of the Estate of Frieda Lawrence Ravagli. Used by permission of Viking Penguin, a division of Penguin Putnam Inc.

**Liveright Publishing Corporation:** "Those Winter Sundays," from *Angle of Ascent: New and Selected Poems* by Robert Hayden. Copyright © 1966 by Robert Hayden. Reprinted by permission of Liveright Publishing Corporation.

**Elizabeth Barnett, Literary Executor:** Sonnet XXX of *Fatal Interview,* from *Collected Poems* by Edna St. Vincent Millay (HarperCollins). Copyright © 1931, 1958 by Edna St. Vincent Millay and Norma Millay Ellis. All rights reserved. Reprinted by permission of Elizabeth Barnett, Literary Executor.

**Eugenia Collier:** "Sweet Potato Pie" by Eugenia Collier, from *Black World* magazine, 1969. Copyright © 1969 by Eugenia W. Collier. Reprinted by permission of the author.

**Susan Bergholz Literary Services:** "Salvador Late or Early," from *Woman Hollering Creek and Other Stories* by Sandra Cisneros. Copyright © 1991 by Sandra Cisneros. Published by Vintage Books, a division of Random House, Inc., and originally in hardcover by Random House, Inc. Reprinted by permission of Susan Bergholz Literary Services, New York. All rights reserved.

**N. Scott Momaday:** "Simile," from *Angle of Geese and Other Poems* by N. Scott Momaday. Copyright © 1974 by N. Scott Momaday. Reprinted by permission of the author.

**Harcourt Brace & Company:** "Moon Rondeau," from *Honey and Salt* by Carl Sandburg. Copyright © 1958 by Carl Sandburg and renewed 1986 by Margaret Sandburg, Helga Sandburg Crile, and Janet Sandburg. Reprinted by permission of Harcourt Brace & Company.

**William Morrow & Company:** "Woman," from *Cotton Candy on a Rainy Day* by Nikki Giovanni. Copyright © 1978 by Nikki Giovanni. Reprinted by permission of William Morrow & Company, Inc.

**St. Martin's Press and Harold Ober Associates:** "A Case of Cruelty," from *All Things Bright and Beautiful* by James Herriot. Copyright © 1973, 1974 by James Herriot. Reprinted by permission of St. Martin's Press, Incorporated and Harold Ober Associates Incorporated.

**Joan Daves Agency:** "Ocho Perritos"/"Eight Puppies" by Gabriela Mistral, from *Selected Poems of Gabriela Mistral,* translated by Doris Dana. Copyright © 1971 by

Doris Dana. Reprinted by arrangement with Doris Dana, c/o Joan Daves Agency as agent for the proprietor.

**Time Inc.:** "An Angry Public Backs Champ," *People Weekly,* 21 May 1990. Copyright © 1990 Time Inc. Reprinted by permission.

**Sheila Schmitt:** "Through Whispers in the Wind" by Sheila Schmitt. Copyright © 1997 by Sheila Schmitt. Reprinted by permission of the author.

**The Apprentice Writer:** "Perspective" by Nathan Fellman, *The Apprentice Writer* 14 (1997). Reprinted by permission of *The Apprentice Writer,* Susquehanna University, Selinsgrove, Pennsylvania.

**Hanging Loose Press:** "In the Steel City" by Mara Noëlle Scanlon, from *Bullseye: Stories and Poems by Outstanding High School Writers,* edited by Mark Pawlak and Dick Lourie. Copyright © 1995 by Hanging Loose Press. Reprinted by permission.

**Sterling Lord Literistic:** *The Bear* by Anton Chekhov, translated by Ronald Hingley. Copyright © 1968 by Ronald Hingley. Reprinted by permission of Sterling Lord Literistic, Inc.

**American Heritage Magazine:** "Gold Is Found and a Nation Goes Wild," from *The American Heritage Book of the Pioneer Spirit.* Copyright © Forbes, Inc. Reprinted by permission of American Heritage Magazine, a division of Forbes, Inc.

**Elizabeth Walsh Peavoy, Literary Executor:** "Brigid," from *Collected Stories* by Mary Lavin (Boston: Houghton Mifflin, 1971). Copyright © 1971 by Mary Lavin. Reprinted by permission of Elizabeth Walsh Peavoy, Literary Executor.

**Felicity Bryan:** "Lalla," from *Love Stories* by Rosamunde Pilcher. Copyright © Rosamunde Pilcher. Reprinted by permission of Felicity Bryan, Oxford, England.

**Editorial Cordillera:** "Love Without Love" ("Amor sin amor") by Luis Lloréns Torres. Copyright © 1967 by Editorial Cordillera. Reprinted by permission of Editorial Cordillera, San Juan, Puerto Rico.

**Random House UK:** "Puedo Escribir Los Versos"/"Tonight I Can Write . . . ," from *Selected Poems* by Pablo Neruda, translated by W. S. Merwin. Originally published by Jonathan Cape Ltd. Reprinted by permission of Random House UK Ltd.

**Doubleday:** Excerpt from *Love & Marriage* by Bill Cosby. Copyright © 1989 by Bill Cosby. Used by permission of Doubleday, a division of Bantam Doubleday Dell Publishing Group, Inc.

**Unit Three**

**HarperCollins Publishers:** "Initiation," from *Johnny Panic and the Bible of Dreams* by Sylvia Plath. Copyright © 1952, 1953, 1954, 1955, 1956, 1957, 1960, 1961, 1962, 1963 by Sylvia Plath. Copyright © 1977, 1979 by Ted Hughes. Reprinted by permission of HarperCollins Publishers, Inc.

**Letter,** October 6, 1952, by Sylvia Plath, from *Letters Home by Sylvia Plath: Correspondence, 1950–1963* by Aurelia Schober Plath. Copyright © 1975 by Aurelia Schober Plath. Reprinted by permission of HarperCollins Publishers, Inc.

**Random House:** Excerpt from *I Know Why the Caged Bird Sings* by Maya Angelou. Copyright © 1969 and renewed 1997 by Maya Angelou. Reprinted by permission of Random House, Inc.

**Academy Chicago Publishers:** "The Opportunity" by John Cheever, from *Thirteen Uncollected Stories by John Cheever,* edited by Franklin H. Dennis. Copyright © 1994 by Academy Chicago Publishers. Reprinted by arrangement with Academy Chicago Publishers, Ltd..

**Susan Bergholz Literary Services:** "Exile," from *The Other Side/El Otro Lado* by Julia Alvarez, published by Dutton, a division of Penguin USA. Copyright © 1995 by Julia

Alvarez. Reprinted by permission of Susan Bergholz Literary Services, New York. All rights reserved.

Excerpt from "A Celebration of Grandfathers" by Rudolfo Anaya. First published in *New Mexico Magazine,* March 1983. Copyright © 1983 by Rudolfo Anaya. Reprinted by permission of Susan Bergholz Literary Services, New York. All rights reserved.

**Yale University Press:** "Lost Sister," from *Picture Bride* by Cathy Song. Copyright © 1983 by Cathy Song. Reprinted by permission of Yale University Press.

**W. W. Norton & Company:** "Fifth Grade Autobiography," from *Grace Notes* by Rita Dove. Copyright © 1989 by Rita Dove. Reprinted by permission of the author and W. W. Norton & Company, Inc.

**Naomi Shihab Nye:** "Remembered," from *Words Under the Words: Selected Poems* by Naomi Shihab Nye. Copyright © 1980, 1982, 1986, 1995 by Naomi Shihab Nye. Reprinted by permission of the author.

**Alfred A. Knopf and Joan Daves Agency:** "The Study of History," from *Collected Stories* by Frank O'Connor. Originally appeared in *The New Yorker.* Copyright © 1957 by Frank O'Connor. Copyright © 1981 by Harriet O'Donovan Sheehy, Executrix of the Estate of Frank O'Connor. Reprinted by permission of Alfred A. Knopf, Inc., and by arrangement with Harriet O'Donovan Sheehy, Executrix of the Estate of Frank O'Connor, c/o Joan Daves Agency as agent for the proprietor.

**Time Inc.:** Excerpt from "Were You Born That Way?" by George Howe Colt, *Life,* April 1998. Copyright © 1998 Time Inc. Reprinted by permission.

**Nicholas Gage:** "The Teacher Who Changed My Life" by Nicholas Gage, *Parade,* 17 December 1989. Copyright © 1989 by Nicholas Gage. Reprinted by permission of the author.

**Alfred A. Knopf:** "Afro-American Fragment," from *Collected Poems* by Langston Hughes. Copyright © 1994 by the Estate of Langston Hughes. Reprinted by permission of Alfred A. Knopf, Inc.

**Carcanet Press:** "Bora Ring," from *Collected Poems, 1942–1985* by Judith Wright. Copyright © 1994 Judith Wright. Reprinted by permission of Carcanet Press Limited.

**Harcourt Brace & Company:** "Everyday Use," from *In Love & Trouble: Stories of Black Women* by Alice Walker. Copyright © 1973 by Alice Walker. Reprinted by permission of Harcourt Brace & Company.

"Women," from *Revolutionary Petunias & Other Poems* by Alice Walker. Copyright © 1970 by Alice Walker. Reprinted by permission of Harcourt Brace & Company.

"Poem at Thirty-Nine," from *Horses Make a Landscape Look More Beautiful* by Alice Walker. Copyright © 1983 by Alice Walker. Reprinted by permission of Harcourt Brace & Company.

Excerpt from "In Search of Our Mothers' Gardens," from *In Search of Our Mothers' Gardens: Womanist Prose* by Alice Walker. Copyright © 1974 by Alice Walker. Reprinted by permission of Harcourt Brace & Company.

**Wendy Weil Agency:** "On Writing Poetry" by Alice Walker, excerpt from *Interviews with Black Writers* by John O'Brien. Copyright © 1973 by Alice Walker. Reprinted by permission of the Wendy Weil Agency on behalf of Alice Walker.

**Jack Clark:** Excerpt from "West Side Stories" by Mary Jo Clark as told to Jack Clark, *Reader* [Chicago], 26 June 1998. Copyright © 1998 by Jack Clark and Mary Jo Clark. Reprinted by permission of Jack Clark.

## Unit Four

**Carroll & Graf Publishers:** "Two Friends" by Guy de Maupassant, from *The Dark Side of Guy de Maupassant,* translated by Arnold Kellett. Copyright © 1972, 1976, 1989 by Arnold Kellett. Reprinted by permission of Carroll & Graf Publishers Inc.

**Holmes & Meier Publishers:** Poem XXIII of *Versos Sencillos/Simple Poetry* by José Martí, from *José Martí: Major Poems, a Bilingual Edition,* translated by Elinor Randall and edited by Philip S. Foner (New York: Holmes & Meier, 1982). Copyright © 1982 by Holmes & Meier Publishers, Inc. Reproduced with the permission of the publisher.

**Gwendolyn Brooks:** "The Sonnet-Ballad," from *Blacks* by Gwendolyn Brooks (Chicago: Third World Press, 1991). Copyright © 1991 by Gwendolyn Brooks. Reprinted by permission of the author.

**Peter H. Lee:** "Cranes" by Hwang Sunwŏn, translated by Peter H. Lee, from *Flowers of Fire: Twentieth-Century Korean Stories,* edited by Peter H. Lee. Reprinted by permission of Peter H. Lee.

**Newsweek:** Excerpt from "The Remembered War: A Korean War Vet Offers a History Lesson" by Angus Deming, *Newsweek,* 7 August 1995. Copyright © 1995 Newsweek, Inc. All rights reserved. Reprinted by permission.

**Hill and Wang:** Excerpt from *Night* by Elie Wiesel. Copyright © 1960 by MacGibbon & Kee. Copyright renewed © 1988 by The Collins Publishing Group. Reprinted by permission of Hill and Wang, a division of Farrar, Straus & Giroux, Inc.

**Nobel Foundation:** Excerpt from Nobel Prize acceptance speech by Elie Wiesel. Copyright © 1962 The Nobel Foundation. Reprinted by permission of The Nobel Foundation.

**Houghton Mifflin Company:** Excerpt from *Farewell to Manzanar* by James D. Houston and Jeanne Wakatsuki Houston. Copyright © 1973 by James D. Houston. Reprinted by permission of Houghton Mifflin Company. All rights reserved.

**Houghton Mifflin Company/Seymour Lawrence:** "On the Rainy River," from *The Things They Carried* by Tim O'Brien. Copyright © 1990 by Tim O'Brien. Reprinted by permission of Houghton Mifflin Company/Seymour Lawrence. All rights reserved.

**W. W. Norton & Company:** "Ghost of a Chance," from *Collected Early Poems, 1950–1970* by Adrienne Rich. Copyright © 1993, 1967, 1963 by Adrienne Rich. Reprinted by permission of the author and W. W. Norton & Company, Inc.

**Liveright Publishing Corporation:** "look at this)," from *Complete Poems, 1904–1962* by E. E. Cummings, edited by George J. Firmage. Copyright 1926, 1954, © 1991 by the Trustees for the E. E. Cummings Trust. Copyright © 1985 by George J. Firmage. Reprinted by permission of Liveright Publishing Corporation.

**John Johnson Ltd.:** "The Prisoner Who Wore Glasses," from *Tales of Tenderness and Power* by Bessie Head, published by Heinemann International in the African Writers Series. Copyright © 1989 The Estate of Bessie Head. Reprinted by permission of John Johnson Ltd. on behalf of the Estate of Bessie Head.

**Georges Borchardt, Inc.:** Excerpt from "Nelson Mandela" by André Brink, *Time,* 13 April 1998. Copyright © 1998 Time Inc. Reprinted by permission.

**Harcourt Brace & Company; the Provost and Scholars of King's College, Cambridge; and The Society of Authors:** Excerpt from "Tolerance," from *Two Cheers for Democracy* by E. M. Forster. Copyright © 1951 by E. M. Forster and renewed 1979 by Donald Parry. Reprinted by permission of Harcourt Brace & Company; the Provost and Scholars of King's College, Cambridge; and The Society of Authors as literary representatives of the E. M. Forster Estate.

**The Nation:** Excerpt from "Julius Caesar" by Thomas M. Disch. Reprinted with permission from the April 23, 1988, issue of *The Nation.*

**The New Yorker:** "Hail, Caesar!" by Edith Oliver. Originally published in *The New Yorker,* 28 March 1988. Copyright © 1988 Edith Oliver. Reprinted by permission. All rights reserved.

**Unit Five**

**Time Inc.:** "The Mouse That Roared" by Richard Woodbury, *Time,* 4 May 1998. Copyright © 1998 Time Inc. Reprinted by permission.

"The Grapes of Wrath: Photo Essay," *Life,* 5 June 1939. Copyright 1939 Time Inc. Reprinted with permission.

**Henry Holt & Company:** "Birches" by Robert Frost, from *The Poetry of Robert Frost,* edited by Edward Connery Lathem. Copyright © 1944 by Robert Frost. Copyright 1916, © 1969 by Henry Holt & Company. Reprinted by permission of Henry Holt and Company, Inc.

**New Directions Publishing Corporation:** "For the New Year, 1981," from *Candles in Babylon* by Denise Levertov. Copyright © 1982 by Denise Levertov. Reprinted by permission of New Directions Publishing Corp.

"La calle"/"The Street" by Octavio Paz, from *Early Poems of Octavio Paz,* translated by Muriel Rukeyser. Copyright © 1973 by Octavio Paz and Muriel Rukeyser. Reprinted by permission of New Directions Publishing Corp.

**Chana Bloch:** "Pride," from *The Window: New and Selected Poems* by Dahlia Ravikovitch, translated and edited by Chana Bloch and Ariel Bloch. Copyright © 1989 by Chana Bloch and Ariel Bloch. Reprinted by permission of Chana Bloch.

**Viking Penguin:** "Like the Sun," from *Under the Banyan Tree* by R. K. Narayan. Copyright © 1985 by R. K. Narayan. Used by permission of Viking Penguin, a division of Penguin Putnam Inc.

"The Flood," from *The Grapes of Wrath* by John Steinbeck. Copyright 1939, renewed © 1967 by John Steinbeck. Used by permission of Viking Penguin, a division of Penguin Putnam Inc.

Excerpts from *The Grapes of Wrath* by John Steinbeck. Copyright 1939, renewed © 1967 by John Steinbeck. Used by permission of Viking Penguin, a division of Penguin Putnam Inc.

Excerpt from *Travels with Charley* by John Steinbeck. Copyright © 1961, 1962 by The Curtis Publishing Co., © 1962 by John Steinbeck, renewed © 1990 by Elaine Steinbeck, Thom Steinbeck, and John Steinbeck IV. Used by permission of Viking Penguin, a division of Penguin Putnam Inc.

"Nobel Prize Acceptance Speech," from *The Portable Steinbeck* by John Steinbeck, introduction by Pascal Covici. Copyright 1943, renewed © 1971 by The Viking Press, introduction. Used by permission of Viking Penguin, a division of Penguin Putnam Inc.

**Estate of Robert Nemiroff:** "On Summer" by Lorraine Hansberry. Copyright © 1960 by Robert Nemiroff as Executor of the Estate of Lorraine Hansberry, © 1988 Robert Nemiroff. All rights reserved. Used by permission of the Estate of Robert Nemiroff.

**Putnam Berkley and Harold Ober Associates:** "The Witness for the Prosecution," from *Witness for the Prosecution and Other Stories* by Agatha Christie. Copyright 1924 by Agatha Christie, renewed. Used by permission of Putnam Berkley, a division of Penguin Putnam Inc., and Harold Ober Associates Incorporated.

**Joan Daves Agency and Leila Vennewitz:** "The Balek Scales," from *Eighteen Stories* by Heinrich Böll, translated by Leila Vennewitz. Copyright © 1966 by Heinrich Böll. Reprinted by permission of Verlag Kiepenheuer & Witsch, c/o the Joan Daves Agency as agent for the proprietor, and Leila Vennewitz.

**Robert Bly:** "I Am Not I" by Juan Ramón Jiménez, from *Lorca and Jiménez: Selected Poems,* translated by Robert Bly (Boston: Beacon Press, 1973, 1997). Copyright © 1973, 1997 by Robert Bly. Reprinted by permission of Robert Bly.

**Carmen Hernández-Pinzón:** "Yo No Soy Yo" by Juan Ramón Jiménez, from *Lorca and Jiménez: Selected Poems,* chosen and translated by Robert Bly (Boston: Beacon Press, 1973, 1997). Copyright © 1973, Herederos de Juan Ramón Jiménez, Madrid, España. Reprinted by permission of Carmen Hernández-Pinzón on behalf of the Estate of Juan Ramón Jiménez.

**Random House:** "The Watch," from *The Cabin* by David Mamet. Copyright © 1992 by David Mamet. Reprinted by permission of Random House, Inc.

**McIntosh & Otis:** "Letter to Edith Mirrielees" by John Steinbeck, from *John Steinbeck: A Study of the Short Fiction,* edited by R. S. Hughes (Boston: Twayne Publishers, 1989). Copyright © 1989 by John Steinbeck. Reprinted by permission of McIntosh & Otis, Inc.

**Merlyn's Pen Publishing:** "I Am Kwakkoli" by Bisco Hill. First appeared in *Merlyn's Pen* magazine. Copyright © Merlyn's Pen, Inc. All rights reserved. Reprinted by permission of Merlyn's Pen Publishing.

## Unit Six

**Viking Penguin:** "A Chip of Glass Ruby," from *Selected Stories* by Nadine Gordimer. Copyright © 1961 by Nadine Gordimer. Used by permission of Viking Penguin, a division of Penguin Putnam Inc.

**Time Inc.:** "The Man in the Water" by Roger Rosenblatt, *Time,* 25 January 1982. Copyright © 1982 Time Inc. Reprinted by permission.

**Scribner:** "And of Clay Are We Created," from *The Stories of Eva Luna* by Isabel Allende, translated from the Spanish by Margaret Sayers Peden. Copyright © 1989 by Isabel Allende. English translation copyright © 1991 by Macmillan Publishing Company. Reprinted with the permission of Scribner, a division of Simon & Schuster.

**Magda Bogin:** "Nocturne" by Rosario Castellanos, from *The Selected Poems of Rosario Castellanos,* translated by Magda Bogin. Translation copyright © 1988 by Magda Bogin. Reprinted by permission of Magda Bogin.

**Fondo de Cultura Económica:** "Nocturno" by Rosario Castellanos, from *The Selected Poems of Rosario Castellanos,* edited by Cecilia Vicuña and Magda Bogin. Copyright © 1988 by the Estate of Rosario Castellanos. Reprinted by permission of Fondo de Cultura Económica.

**Boston Globe:** "Girl Trapped in Water for 55 Hours Dies Despite Rescue Attempts" by Julia Preston, *The Boston Globe,* 16 November 1985. Reprinted courtesy of The Boston Globe.

**Harper's Magazine:** "The Leap" by Louise Erdrich, *Harper's Magazine,* March 1990. Copyright © 1990 by Harper's Magazine. All rights reserved. Reproduced from the March 1990 issue by special permission.

**Harcourt Brace & Company:** *Antigone,* from *Sophocles: The Oedipus Cycle, An English Version* by Dudley Fitts and Robert Fitzgerald. Copyright 1939 by Harcourt Brace & Company and renewed © 1967 by Dudley Fitts and Robert Fitzgerald. Reprinted by permission of the publisher. CAUTION: All rights, including professional, amateur, motion picture, recitation, lecturing, performance, public reading, radio broadcasting, and television, are strictly reserved. Inquiries on all rights should be addressed to Harcourt Brace & Company, Permissions Department, Orlando, FL 32887-6777.

**Clarkson N. Potter:** Excerpts from *Le Morte D'Arthur* by Sir Thomas Malory, translated by Keith Baines. Copyright © 1967 by Keith Baines. Reprinted by permission of Clarkson N. Potter, Inc., a division of Crown Publishers, Inc.

**Scovil Chichak Galen Literary Agency:** Excerpt from *The Mists of Avalon* by Marion Zimmer Bradley. Copyright © 1982 by Marion Zimmer Bradley. Reprinted by permission of the author and the author's agents, Scovil Chichak Galen Literary Agency, Inc.

Excerpt from "The Once and Future Merlin" by Marion Zimmer Bradley, *TV Guide,* 25 April 1998. Reprinted by permission of the author and the author's agents, Scovil Chichak Galen Literary Agency, Inc.

**Farrar, Straus & Giroux:** Excerpt from *The Acts of King Arthur and His Noble Knights* by John Steinbeck. Copyright © 1976 by Elaine Steinbeck. Reprinted by permission of Farrar, Straus & Giroux, Inc.

**W. W. Norton & Company:** "The Knight," from *Collected Early Poems, 1950–1970* by Adrienne Rich. Copyright © 1993, 1967, 1963 by Adrienne Rich. Reprinted by permission of the author and W. W. Norton & Company, Inc.

The editors have made every effort to trace the ownership of all copyrighted material found in this book and to make full acknowledgment for its use. Omissions brought to our attention will be corrected in a subsequent edition.

**Reading Handbook**

**Texas Instruments:** Excerpt from *TI-82 Guidebook*. Copyright © 1993, 2000, 2001 Texas Instruments. Reproduced by permission.

# Art Credits

**Cover, Frontispiece**

Illustration copyright © 1998 Lee Christiansen.

**Front Matter**

**x** *left, The Spirit of Our Time* (about 1921), Raoul Hausmann. Assemblage with wigmaker's dummy head, 12¾″ high. Collections Musée National d'Art Moderne, Centre Georges Pompidou, Paris; *right, Chicago Tribune* photo by Heather Stone. Copyright © 1998 Chicago Tribune. World rights reserved; **xi** *top* AP/Wide World Photos; *bottom, Girl with Tear III* (1977), Roy Lichtenstein. Oil and magna on canvas, 46″ × 40″. Copyright © Estate of Roy Lichtenstein/Leo Castelli Gallery, New York; **xii** *Red Peonies* (1929), Ch'i Pai-Shih. Ink and colors on paper, 53½″ × 12⅞″. Courtesy of the Arthur M. Sackler Museum, Harvard University Art Museums, loan from the family of F. Y. Chang (321.1985). Copyright © President and Fellows, Harvard College, Harvard University Art Museums; **xiii** *The Lovers (Somali Friends)* (1950), Lois Mailou Jones. Casein on canvas. The Evans-Tibbs Collection, Washington, D.C.; **xv** *Allées Piétonnières* [Pedestrian walkways] (1995), Jean-Pierre Stora. Oil on canvas, 61″× 50″. The Grand Design, Leeds, England/SuperStock; **xvi** *left* Copyright © Ilene Perlman/Impact Visuals/PNI; *right* Haitian drum (1940s), unknown artist. Wood and goat skin, 43″ × 24″ × 24″. Collection of Virgil Young; **xvii** Copyright © Michael Yamashita; **xviii** *bottom, Hombre y su sombra* [Man and his shadow] (1971), Rufino Tamayo. Oil on canvas, 50 cm × 40 cm. Collection of INBA–Museo de Arte Moderno, Mexico City; **xix** Martha Swope. Copyright © Time Inc.; **xx** *Sea Jewels* (1995), Paul Niemiec, Jr. Watercolor, 18″ × 28″. Collection of Mr. and Mrs. Stephen H. Palmer; **xxi** Copyright © Archive Photos/PNI; **xxii** *right* Musée de Picardie, Amiens, France/Giraudon/Art Resource, New York; **xxiii** Antikensammlung, Munich, Germany/Erich Lessing/Art Resource, New York; **2** *right* Photofest; **3** *left* Copyright © Hallmark Entertainment/Shooting Star. All rights reserved; *right* Illustration by Arthur Rackham. Christie's Images, New York; **6–7** Copyright © 1993 Jay Ullah/Stern/Black Star.

**Unit One**

**29** AP/Wide World Photos; **40** Copyright © Sovfoto/Eastfoto/PNI; **42** *Toto* (1988), Jimmy Lee Sudduth. Paint with mud on wood, 31¾″ × 24″. From *American Self-Taught* by Frank Maresca and Roger Ricco, published by Knopf, 1993; **55** National Archives; **57** *background* Copyright © Michael W. Thomas/Stock South/PNI; **60, 64, 65** Copyright © 1997 PhotoDisc; **66** Canapress Photo Service; **67–71** *border* Photo by Sharon Hoogstraten; **67** *portrait* AP/Wide World Photos; *frame* Photo by Sharon Hoogstraten; **68** *top* Courtesy of Bantam Doubleday Books; *bottom* Sovfoto/Eastfoto; **69** NASA; **70** *top, center left* Photofest; *center right* Copyright © 1988 PhotoDisc; *bottom right* Copyright © 1990

Chicago Sun-Times. Reprinted with permission; **71** Copyright © 1996 Glenn Dean; **72–73, 74, 79** *ferns* Photo by Sharon Hoogstraten; **72, 74, 76–77, 78, 79** *patterned background* Copyright © 1995 PhotoDisc; **81, 82–83** *border,* **83** Photos by Sharon Hoogstraten; **84, 85** Copyright © 1986 Jay Kay Klein; **86** *Girl with Tear III* (1977), Roy Lichtenstein. Oil and magna on canvas, 46"× 40". Copyright © Estate of Roy Lichtenstein/Leo Castelli Gallery, New York; **93–95** *border* Photo by Sharon Hoogstraten; **95** *Flying Man with Briefcase No. 2816932* (1983), Jonathan Borofsky. Painted Gatorfoam, 94½" × 24½" × 1". Copyright © 1983 Jonathan Borofsky/Gemini G.E.L., Los Angeles, California; **101–103** *border* Photo by Sharon Hoogstraten; **102, 103** *portraits* Copyright © 1986 Jay Kay Klein; **111** AP/Wide World Photos; **112** *Morning of Life* (1907), David Ericson. Oil on canvas, 27" × 22¼". Collection of Tweed Museum of Art, University of Minnesota, Duluth, gift of Mrs. E. L. Tuohy; **113, 118** *backgrounds* Illustration by Gary Head; **122** Photo courtesy of Maria Mariottini; **123** The Granger Collection, New York; **134** Copyright © 1965 Bob Adelman/Magnum Photos; **135** Globe Photos; **136** UPI/Corbis-Bettmann; **138–142** Photos by Sharon Hoogstraten; **148** Detail of *The Ukimwi Road* (1994), John Harris; **157** H. Armstrong Roberts; **158** Globe Photos; **159, 163, 165** Photos by Sharon Hoogstraten; **168** Copyright © Bill Aron/PhotoEdit; **169** AP/Wide World Photos; **171** *left, right* Copyright © 1997 PhotoDisc; *center* Copyright © Warner Brothers/Shooting Star; **173** Photofest; **174–175** R. Krubner/H. Armstrong Roberts; **176, 177** *top* Photos by Sharon Hoogstraten; **177** *bottom* Corbis; **180** *left* Photo by Anthony Loew; *right* Arte Público Press; **186** *portrait* AP/Wide World Photos; **187** Corbis; **188** *Wooing* (1984), Varnette Honeywood. Collage. Copyright © 1984 Varnette P. Honeywood; **195** The Schomburg Center for Research in Black Culture, The New York Public Library, Astor, Lenox and Tilden Foundations; **197** *Red Peonies* (1929), Ch'i Pai-Shih. Ink and colors on paper, 53 ½" × 12⅞". Courtesy of the Arthur M. Sackler Museum, Harvard University Art Museums, loan from the family of F. Y. Chang (321.1985). Copyright © President and Fellows, Harvard College, Harvard University Art Museums; **210** *top, New Look of a Village* (about 1970), Niutung People's Commune Spare-Time Art Group; *bottom* Copyright © Dennis Cox/China Stock; **212–216** Photos by Sharon Hoogstraten.

**Unit Two**
**228** Detail of *Sunday Morning Breakfast* (1943), Horace Pippin. Private collection, courtesy Galerie St. Etienne, New York; **232** *left* The Granger Collection, New York; **233, 234** Copyright © Eiji Vanagi/Photonica; **238** *left* North Wind Picture Archive; *right* The Bettmann Archive; **239, 240** *top left,* **242, 244, 246, 247** J. Graham/H. Armstrong Roberts; **250** Detail of *Street Corner Shop,* Colin Middleton. Christie's Images, New York; **253** *Spring Planting* (1988), Jonathan Green. Oil on masonite, 24" × 32". Collection of Shigeki Masui. Photograph by Tim Stamm; **256** Details of *Corn Maiden* (1982) David Dawangyumptewa. Photo copyright © 1987 by Jerry Jacka; **261** *left* AP/Wide World Photos; *right, White Breeze* (1995), Jonathan Green. Oil on canvas, 48" × 60". Collection of Gilbert and Elizabeth Ney. Photograph by Tim Stamm; **262** *left* The Granger Collection, New York; *right* Copyright © Nancy Crampton; **264–265** Copyright © Masakazu Kure/Photonica; **273** AP/Wide World Photos; **277–281** Photos by Sharon Hoogstraten; **283** Copyright © Uniphoto; **285** Mander & Mitchenson, Kent, England; **287, 288** Photo by Sharon Hoogstraten; **301, 302** Sovfoto; **303** Photo courtesy of Carmine Fantasia; **304, 305** *backgrounds* Courtesy of the Economics and Public Affairs Division, The New York Public Library, Astor, Lenox and Tilden Foundations; **306** Photo courtesy of Carmine Fantasia; *frame* Photo by Sharon Hoogstraten; **307** *background* Courtesy of the Economics and Public Affairs Division, The New York Public Library, Astor, Lenox and Tilden Foundations; **312, 314** Corbis-Bettmann; **327** Sean Sexton Collection/Corbis; **328** Drawing by Sean O'Sullivan; **329** *top* Illustration by

Robbin Gourley; **335, 341** *backgrounds* Photo by Sharon Hoogstraten; **344** Leo de Wys, Inc./ de Wys/D & J Heaton; **346, 347** *foreground* Copyright © Uniphoto; **347** *background* Copyright © David Rigg/Tony Stone Images; **350** By permission of the Houghton Library, Harvard University; **352–353** Illustration by Sarah Figlio; **355** *left* Globe Photos; **355** *right,* **359** Photos by Sharon Hoogstraten; **361** Copyright © SuperStock; **362** Photo from European Picture Service/FPG International; **363** AP/Wide World Photos; **364–368** Photos by Sharon Hoogstraten; **370** Detail of *The Lovers (Somali Friends)* (1950), Lois Mailou Jones. Casein on canvas. The Evans-Tibbs Collection, Washington, D.C.; **374–376** Photos by Sharon Hoogstraten.

## Unit Three

**386** Courtesy Cluett, Peabody & Co., Inc.; **395** The Granger Collection, New York; **396** Stock Montage; **397** Illustration by Emma Baron. Copyright © Stock Illustration Source; **409** Courtesy the Lilly Library, Indiana University, Bloomington, Indiana; **410** Photo first appeared in *Letters Home.* Copyright © 1975. Reprinted with permission from Aurelia Schober Plath. All rights reserved; **414–415** Corbis; **418** Corbis-Bettmann; **431** Globe Photos; **432** Copyright © Culver Pictures; **433** Illustration by Meredith Nemirov; **438** Copyright © 1995 Bill Eichner; **439** *Portrait of Miss Jen Sun-ch'ang* (1934), William McGregor Paxton. Pastel on dark tan paper, 18″ × 14″. Courtesy of Robert Douglas Hunter; **443** *top* Photo by Sharon Hoogstraten; *bottom* Lynette Tom; **445–449** Photos by Sharon Hoogstraten; **455** *Campesino* [Farmer] (1976), Daniel DeSiga. Oil on canvas, 50½″ x 58½″. Collection of Alfredo Aragón, courtesy UCLA at the Armand Hammer Museum of Art and Cultural Center, Los Angeles, California; **467** *left* Photo by Fred Viebahn; *right* Photo by Michael Nye; **468** *Jimmy O'D* (about 1925), Robert Henri. Oil on canvas, 24″ × 20″. Collection of the Montclair (New Jersey) Art Museum, museum purchase, Picture Buying Fund (26.1); **480** AP/Wide World Photos; **481** Copyright © G. Paul Bishop; **482** Corbis; **485** *background,* Photo by Sharon Hoogstraten; **492** *right* Corbis; **493** AP/Wide World Photos; **496–497, 498** *photographic backgrounds* Copyright © H. Franca/SuperStock; **498** *left* The Granger Collection, New York; *right* Coward of Canberra; **499–503** *border* Photo by Sharon Hoogstraten; **499** *top* Copyright © Ilene Perlman/Impact Visuals/PNI; *frame* Photo by Sharon Hoogstraten; *bottom* Carl Iwasaki/*Life* magazine. Copyright © 1953 Time, Inc.; **500** *left* UPI/Corbis-Bettmann; *right* Courtesy of Spelman College, Atlanta, Georgia; **501** *bottom left* Copyright © 1990 TIB/West/J .P. Pieuchot; *top right (three images)* Photofest; **502** *top* Copyright © 1963 Bob Adelman/Magnum Photos; *television* Copyright © PhotoDisc; *bottom* Copyright © James Keyser/Contact Press Images/PNI; **503, 506** Photo by Sharon Hoogstraten; **507, 509** Details of *Nia: Purpose* (1991), Varnette Honeywood. Monoprint. Collection of Karen Kennedy. Copyright © 1991 Varnette P. Honeywood; **510–511, 512** Photos by Sharon Hoogstraten; **513–516** *border* Photo by Sharon Hoogstraten; **514** *Working Woman* (1947), Elizabeth Catlett. Oil on canvas. Courtesy of the Barnett-Aden Collection, Museum of African American Art, Tampa, Florida; **519** From *Always My Dad* by Sharon Dennis, illustrated by Raul Colon. Illustrations copyright © 1994 Raul Colon. Reprinted by permission of Alfred A. Knopf, Inc.; **520** *border* Photo by Sharon Hoogstraten; **521** Copyright © Anthony Barboza/Shooting Star; **522, 527–529** *border* Photo by Sharon Hoogstraten; **528** Copyright © Ilene Perlman/Impact Visuals/PNI; **529** Copyright © Frank Capri/Saga/Archive Photos/PNI; **530–534** Photos by Sharon Hoogstraten.

## Unit Four

**546** *Portrait of André Derain* (1905), Henri Matisse. Tate Gallery, London/Art Resource, New York. Copyright © 1995 Succession H. Matisse, Paris/Artists Rights Society (ARS), New York; **557** *Green Fish* (about 1928), Selden Gile. Oil on board. Bedford Gallery, Dean Lesher Regional Center for the Arts, Walnut Creek, California; **558** The Granger Collection,

New York; **559, 561, 565, 571** Illustrations from *Tales of Edgar Allan Poe,* illustrated by Barry Moser, one of the Books of Wonder Series. Illustrations copyright © 1991 Pennyroyal Press. By permission of Morrow Junior Books, a division of William Morrow & Company, Inc.; **576** *Detail of Auto de Fe in the Plaza Mayor, Madrid, 30 June 1680,* Francisco Rizi. Museo del Prado, Madrid, Spain/Art Resource, New York; **577** From the collections of the Library of Congress; **582** Imperial War Museum, London; **583** *left* The Granger Collection, New York; *right* Howard Simmons; **585** Illustration by Lee Steadman; **590** Peter Finger/Corbis; **592** National Archives; **593** The Bettmann Archive; **594–599** *barbed wire* Photo by Sharon Hoogstraten; **599** The Bettmann Archive; **601** Erich Hartmann/Magnum Photos; **602** The Bettmann Archive; **603** From the collections of the Library of Congress; **614** Howard Ikemoto; **616–620** Photos by Sharon Hoogstraten; **644** Copyright © Jerry Bauer; **645** Copyright © 1998 Medford Taylor/Black Star; **647** From the collections of the Library of Congress; **648** Copyright © 1998 Medford Taylor/Black Star; **650** Michael Rougier/*Life* magazine. Copyright © Time, Inc.; **651** *left* National Archives; *right* By permission of the Houghton Library, Harvard University; **661** Globe Photos; **662** AP/Wide World Photos; **664** Detail of *The Monument to Peter I on Senate Square in Petersburg* (1870), Vasilii Ivanovich Surikov.The State Russian Museum, St. Petersburg, Russia; **665, 666–667** *background* Photo by Sharon Hoogstraten; **676** *Self-Portrait* (about 1865), James Tissot. The Fine Arts Museums of San Francisco, Mildred Anna Williams Collection (1961.16); **677** Itar-Tass/Sovfoto; **681** Culver Pictures; **682** Photofest; **683** *portrait* The Granger Collection, New York; *frame* Image Farm; **684** *top* The Granger Collection, New York; *bottom left* Drawing by C. Walter Hodges; *bottom right* Photo by Chantal Schütz, courtesy of Shakespeare's Globe, London; **685** The Granger Collection, New York; **686** Museo Pio Clementino, Vatican Museums, Vatican State/Scala/Art Resource, New York; **690–691** Copyright © Antonio Attini/White Star; **692** *reconstruction of Forum* Soprintendenza alle Antichità, Rome/Scala/Art Resource, New York; *inset* Map by Bill Graham/Koralik Associates; **762** *top center* Museum of the City of New York Theatre Collection, gift of Mrs. Barry Sommers (53.215.45); **797** North Wind Picture Archive; **798, 800–804, 810–812** Photos by Sharon Hoogstraten.

**Unit Five**

**834** Amos Nachoum/Corbis; **835** The Granger Collection, New York; **837** Photo by Marcia Booth Murdock, courtesy of Rocky Flats Photography Department; **842** National Archives; **847** *left* The Luce Studio; *center* Copyright © Jan Kanter; *right* Copyright © Layle Silbert; **849** Detail of Jain ceremonial scroll *(Surya Pragnapti)*. Spencer Collection, The New York Public Library, Astor, Lenox and Tilden Foundations (Indian MS 69); **854** Catherine Karnow/Corbis; **855** Globe Photos; **860** AP/Wide World Photos; **861–865** Photos by Sharon Hoogstraten; **871** *Portrait of Count Fürstenberg-Herdringen* (1924), Tamara de Lempicka. Oil on canvas, 16⅛″ × 10¾″. Courtesy of Barry Friedman Ltd., New York. Copyright © 1996 Artists Rights Society (ARS), New York/SPADEM, Paris; **891** *Portrait de Madame M.,* Tamara de Lempicka. Oil on canvas, 99 cm × 65 cm. Private collection, Paris. Copyright © 1996 Artists Rights Society (ARS), New York/SPADEM, Paris; **892** The Granger Collection, New York; **893, 894** *Scales* (about 1968–1977), Mitsumasa Anno. From *The Unique World of Mitsumasa Anno,* published by Kodansha Ltd., Tokyo; **896, 897** Illustrations by Rebecca McClellan; **902** German Information Service; **903** *La reproduction interdite (Portrait d'Edward James)* [Not to be reproduced (Portrait of Edward James)] (1937), René Magritte. Oil on canvas, 81.3 cm × 65 cm. Museum Boymans–van Beuningen, Rotterdam, Netherlands/Giraudon/Art Resource, New York. Copyright © 1996 Artists Rights Society (ARS), New York; **907** *left* Neil Libbert/Camera Press/Globe Photos; *right* UPI/Bettmann; **909, 911** Photo by Sharon Hoogstraten; **913** Copyright © 1990 Ron Kimball; **914** Photo by Sharon

Hoogstraten; **915** AP/Wide World Photos; **918–922** *border* Photo by Sharon Hoogstraten;
**918** *signature* The Granger Collection, New York; *top right* Copyright © Archive
Photos/PNI; *bottom left* Copyright © Myrleen Ferguson/PhotoEdit; *bottom right* Courtesy of
The Steinbeck House, Salinas, California; **920** *right* Courtesy of The Steinbeck House,
Salinas, California; **921** *counterclockwise from left* Photofest; Photofest; Photo by Michael
Brosilow, courtesy of Steppenwolf Theater, Chicago; Photofest; S.S. Archives/Shooting Star
International; **926, 928** *bottom* Horace Bristol/Corbis; **928** *top*, **929, 930, 931** Copyright ©
Horace Bristol; **932** t*op, bottom* Horace Bristol/Corbis; **933–935** *border* Photo by Sharon
Hoogstraten; **935, 936** UPI/Corbis-Bettmann; **939–941** *border* Photo by Sharon
Hoogstraten; **940** D. Robert Franz/Corbis; **943** *signature* The Granger Collection, New
York; **944** AP/Wide World Photos; **945–947** *border* Photo by Sharon Hoogstraten; **946**
UPI/Corbis-Bettmann; **947** Copyright © Archive Photos/PNI; **948–952** Photos by Sharon
Hoogstraten.

**Unit Six**
**964** Detail of *News from the Gulf* (about 1991), Robert A. Wade. Watercolor,
19″ × 29″. Private collection. Copyright © Robert A. Wade. From *Painting Your Vision in
Watercolor* (North Light Books); **965, 967** *background,* **968, 971** *background,* **972** Photos
by Sharon Hoogstraten; **975** Corbis-Bettmann; **976** Reuters/Bettmann; **977** AP/Wide World
Photos; **996** Illustration by David Loew/ARTCO; **997** AP/Wide World Photos; **999** *top*
Carraro/Rex USA Ltd.; *bottom* Reuters/Bettmann; **1001** *left* Copyright © 1989 Michelle
Barnes/The Image Bank; **1007** Michael Dorris; **1008** Photo by Sharon Hoogstraten; **1009**
*top* Copyright © Mary Kate Denny/PhotoEdit; *bottom* Copyright © Monkmeyer
Press/Shackman; **1012** Photo by Sharon Hoogstraten; **1018** Copyright © 1992 Michal
Daniel; **1032** *theater diagram* From *The History of the Greek and Roman Theater* by
Margarete Bieber, published by Princeton University Press, 1939; **1063** The Granger
Collection, New York; **1064** Detail of illumination showing Lancelot rescuing Guinevere by
crossing the sword bridge (about 1300), from a manuscript of *Le Roman de Lancelot du
Lac* (M. 806, fol. 166). The Pierpont Morgan Library, New York/Art Resource, New York;
**1081** The Granger Collection, New York; **1087** *left* Copyright © 1978 Jay Kay Klein; *right*
Stock Montage; **1089** Copyright © Hallmark Entertainment/Shooting Star. All rights
reserved; **1101** AP/Wide World Photos; **1104** *top* Detail of millefleurs tapestry with horse-
man and arms of Jean de Daillon (late 1400s), unknown Flemish artist. National Trust
Photographic Library; *bottom* Annie F. Valva; **1105–1112** Photos by Sharon Hoogstraten.

**Reading Handbook**
**1120** *bottom inset left* Copyright © Paul Simcock/Brand X Pictures/PictureQuest; *bottom
inset center* Copyright © PhotoDisc/Getty Images; *bottom inset right* Copyright © Paul
Simcock/Brand X Pictures/PictureQuest; **1132** *left* Copyright © Paul Simcock/Brand X
Pictures/PictureQuest; *center* Copyright © PhotoDisc/Getty Images; *right* Copyright © Paul
Simcock/Brand X Pictures/PictureQuest; **1141** Copyright © PhotoDisc/Getty Images. **1219** ©
PhotoDisc/Getty; **1221** © Soalhat/Sipa Press, New York; **1223** © Mapquest.com; **1226**
© Nicholas Hilliard/The Bridgeman Art Library/Getty Images; **1229** © Getty Images;
**1231** © Joel Sartore/National Geographic/Getty Images; **1233** © PhotoDisc/Getty
Images; **1235** © Foodpix/Getty Images; **1239** Jan Hinsch/SPL/Photo Researchers; **1241**
© Carl J. Single/The Image Works; **1247** NOAA.

## Multicultural Advisory Board *(continued)*

*Liz Sawyer-Cunningham,* Los Angeles Senior High School, Los Angeles, California

*Michelle Dixon Thompson,* Seabreeze High School, Daytona Beach, Florida

## Teacher Review Panels *(continued)*

### FLORIDA *(continued)*

*Eileen Jones,* English Department Chairperson, Spanish River High School, Palm Beach County School District

*Jan McClure,* Winter Park High School, Orange County School District

*Wanza Murray,* English Department Chairperson (retired), Vero Beach Senior High School, Indian River City School District

*Shirley Nichols,* Language Arts Curriculum Specialist Supervisor, Marion County School District

*Debbie Nostro,* Ocoee Middle School, Orange County School District

*Barbara Quinaz,* Assistant Principal, Horace Mann Middle School, Dade County School District

### CALIFORNIA

*Steve Bass,* 8th Grade Team Leader, Meadowbook Middle School, Ponway Unified School District

*Cynthia Brickey,* 8th Grade Academic Block Teacher, Kastner Intermediate School, Clovis Unified School District

*Karen Buxton,* English Department Chairperson, Winston Churchill Middle School, San Juan School District

*Bonnie Garrett,* Davis Middle School, Compton School District

*Sally Jackson,* Madrona Middle School, Torrance Unified School District

*Sharon Kerson,* Los Angeles Center for Enriched Studies, Los Angeles Unified School District

*Gail Kidd,* Center Middle School, Azusa School District

*Corey Lay,* ESL Department Chairperson, Chester Nimitz Middle School, Los Angeles Unified School District

*Myra LeBendig,* Forshay Learning Center, Los Angeles Unified School District

*Dan Manske,* Elmhurst Middle School, Oakland Unified School District

*Joe Olague,* Language Arts Department Chairperson, Alder Middle School, Fontana School District

*Pat Salo,* 6th Grade Village Leader, Hidden Valley Middle School, Escondido Elementary School District

### OHIO

*Glyndon Butler,* English Department Chairperson, Glenville High School, Cleveland City School District

*Ellen Geisler,* English/Language Arts Department Chairperson, Mentor Senior High School, Mentor School District

*Dr. Paulette Goll,* English Department Chairperson, Lincoln West High School, Cleveland City School District

*Loraine Hammack,* Executive Teacher of the English Department, Beachwood High School, Beachwood City School District

*Marguerite Joyce,* English Department Chairperson, Woodridge High School, Woodridge Local School District

*Sue Nelson,* Shaw High School, East Cleveland School District

*Dee Phillips,* Hudson High School, Hudson Local School District

*Carol Steiner,* English Department Chairperson, Buchtel High School, Akron City School District

*Nancy Strauch,* English Department Chairperson, Nordonia High School, Nordonia Hills City School Dictrict

*Ruth Vukovich,* Hubbard High School, Hubbard Exempted Village School District

## TEXAS

*Dana Davis,* English Department Chairperson, Irving High School, Irving Independent School District

*Susan Fratcher,* Cypress Creek High School, Cypress Fairbanks School District

*Yolanda Garcia,* Abilene High School, Abilene Independent School District

*Patricia Helm,* Lee Freshman High School, Midland Independent School District

*Joanna Huckabee,* Moody High School, Corpus Christi Independent School District

*Josie Kinard,* English Department Chairperson, Del Valle High School, Ysleta Independent School District

*Mary McFarland,* Amarillo High School, Amarillo Independent School District

*Gwen Rutledge,* English Department Chairperson, Scarborough High School, Houston Independent School District

*Bunny Schmaltz,* Assistant Principal, Ozen High School, Beaumont Independent School District

*Michael Urick,* A. N. McCallum High School, Austin Independent School District

## Manuscript Reviewers *(continued)*

*Kathleen M. Anderson-Knight,* United Township High School, East Moline, Illinois

*Anita Arnold,* Thomas Jefferson High School, San Antonio, Texas

*Cassandra L. Asberry,* Dean of Instruction, Carter High School, Dallas, Texas

*Jolene Auderer,* Pine Tree High School, Longview, Texas

*Don Baker,* English Department Chairperson, Peoria High School, Peoria, Illinois

*Beverly Ann Barge,* Wasilla High School, Wasilla, Alaska

*Louann Bohman,* Wilbur Cross High School, New Haven, Connecticut

*Rose Mary Bolden,* J. F. Kimball High School, Dallas, Texas

*Lydia C. Bowden,* Boca Ciega High School, St. Petersburg, Florida

*Angela Boyd,* Andrews High School, Andrews, Texas

*Judith H. Briant,* Armwood High School, Seffner, Florida

*Hugh Delle Broadway,* McCullough High School, The Woodlands, Texas

*Stephan P. Clarke,* Spencerport High School, Spencerport, New York

*Kathleen D. Crapo,* South Fremont High School, St. Anthony, Idaho

*Dr. Shawn Eric DeNight,* Miami Edison High School, Miami, Florida

*JoAnna R. Exacoustas,* La Serna High School, Whittier, California

*Linda Ferguson,* English Department Head, Tyee High School, Seattle, Washington

*Ellen Geisler,* Mentor Senior High School, Mentor, Ohio

*Ricardo Godoy,* English Department Chairman, Moody High School, Corpus Christi, Texas

*Meredith Gunn,* Secondary Language Arts Instructional Specialist, Katy, Texas

*Judy Hammack,* English Department Chairperson, Milton High School, Alpharetta, Georgia

*Robert Henderson,* West Muskingum High School, Zanesville, Ohio

*Martha Watt Hosenfeld,* English Department Chairperson, Churchville-Chili High School, Churchville, New York

*Janice M. Johnson,* Assistant Principal, Union High School, Grand Rapids, Michigan

*Eileen S. Jones,* English Department Chair, Spanish River Community High School, Boca Raton, Florida

*Paula S. L'Homme,* West Orange High School, Winter Garden, Florida

*Bonnie J. Mansell,* Downey Adult School, Downey, California

*Linda Maxwell,* MacArthur High School, Houston, Texas

*Ruth McClain,* Paint Valley High School, Bainbridge, Ohio

*Rebecca Miller,* Taft High School, San Antonio, Texas

*Deborah Lynn Moeller,* Western High School, Fort Lauderdale, Florida

*Bobbi Darrell Montgomery,* Batavia High School, Batavia, Ohio

*Bettie Moody,* Leesburg High School, Leesburg, Florida

*Margaret L. Mortenson,* English Department Chairperson, Timpanogos High School, Orem, Utah

*Marjorie M. Nolan,* Language Arts Department Head, William M. Raines Sr. High School, Jacksonville, Florida

*Julia Pferdehirt,* freelance writer, former Special Education teacher, Middleton, Wisconsin

*Cindy Rogers,* MacArthur High School, Houston, Texas

*Pauline Sahakian,* English Department Chairperson, San Marcos High School, San Marcos, Texas

*Jacqueline Y. Schmidt,* Department Chairperson and Coordinator of English, San Marcos High School, San Marcos, Texas

*David D. Schultz,* East Aurora High School, East Aurora, New York

*Milinda Schwab,* Judson High School, Converse, Texas

*John Sferro,* Butler High School, Vandalia, Ohio

*Brad R. Smedley,* English Department Chairperson, Hudtloff Middle School, Lakewood, Washington

*Faye S. Spangler,* Versailles High School, Versailles, Ohio

*Rita Stecich,* Evergreen Park Community High School, Evergreen Park, Illinois

*GayleAnn Turnage,* Abiline High School, Abiline, Texas

*Ruth Vukovich,* Hubbard High School, Hubbard, Ohio

*Kevin J. Walsh,* Dondero High School, Royal Oak, Michigan

*Charlotte Washington,* Westwood Middle School, Grand Rapids, Michigan

*Tom Watson,* Westbridge Academy, Grand Rapids, Michigan

*Linda Weatherby,* Deerfield High School, Deerfield, Illinois